THE CONSENSUS BUILDING HANDBOOK

THE
CONSENSUS
BUILDING
HANDBOOK

A Comprehensive Guide to Reaching Agreement

Editors
Lawrence Susskind
Sarah McKearnan
Jennifer Thomas-Larmer

The Consensus Building Institute

SAGE Publications
International Educational and Professional Publisher
Thousand Oaks   London   New Delhi

For information:

SAGE Publications, Inc.
2455 Teller Road
Thousand Oaks, California 91320
E-mail: order@sagepub.com

SAGE Publications Ltd.
6 Bonhill Street
London EC2A 4PU
United Kingdom

SAGE Publications India Pvt. Ltd.
M-32 Market
Greater Kailash I
New Delhi 110 048 India

Printed in the United States of America

Library of Congress Cataloging-in-Publication Data

Main entry under title:

The consensus building handbook: A comprehensive guide to reaching agreement / edited by Lawrence Susskind, Sarah McKearnan, and Jennifer Thomas-Larmer.
    p.   cm.
  Includes bibliographical references and index.
  ISBN 0-7619-0844-7 (cloth: acid-free paper)
  1. Group decision-making—Handbook, manuals, etc. 2. Consensus (Social sciences) Handbooks, manuals, etc. 3. Consensus (Social sciences) Case studies. 4. Conflict management handbooks, manuals, etc. I. Susskind, Lawrence. II. McKearnan, Sarah.
III. Thomas-Larmer, Jennifer.
  HM746.C66 1999
  302.3—dc22   99-6318

99 00 01 02 03 10 9 8 7 6 5 4 3 2 1

Acquiring Editor:	Marquita Flemming
Editorial Assistant:	MaryAnn Vail
Production Editor:	Diana E. Axelsen
Editorial Assistant:	Karen Wiley
Typesetter/Designer:	Janelle LeMaster
Indexer:	Virgil Diodato
Cover Designer:	Ravi Balasuriya

CONTENTS

Preface   xiii

Introduction   xvii
  Areas of Application   xviii
  Common Misperceptions   xx
  About This Book   xxii

PART 1: A SHORT GUIDE TO CONSENSUS BUILDING

**An Alternative to Robert's Rules of Order for Groups,
Organizations, and Ad Hoc Assemblies That Want to
Operate by Consensus**   **3**
  Lawrence Susskind

  What's Wrong with Robert's Rules?   5
  Definitions   5
  A Complete Matrix   13
  Section I: Helping an Ad Hoc Assembly Reach Agreement   20
  Section II: Helping a Permanent Group or Organization Reach
    Agreement   35
  Section III: Dealing with the Barriers to Consensus Building   55

PART 2: HOW TO BUILD CONSENSUS

Chapter 1. Choosing Appropriate Consensus Building Techniques and Strategies   **61**
Susan Carpenter

Who Initiates and Who Designs a Process   62

Determining Whether Consensus Building Is Appropriate   66

Additional Issues to Consider Before Developing a Specific
Consensus Strategy   70

Structuring a Specific Consensus Process   76

Summary   97

Chapter 2. Conducting a Conflict Assessment   **99**
Lawrence Susskind and Jennifer Thomas-Larmer

The Practice of Confict Assessment   101

How to Conduct a Conflict Assessment   107

Identify the Parties to Be Interviewed   108

Dilemmas and Debates in the Practice of Conflict Assessment   130

Conclusion   135

Chapter 3. Designing a Consensus Building Process Using a Graphic Road Map   **137**
David A. Straus

The Process Design Phase   138

The Process Design Committee   140

The Graphic Road Map   148

Typical Agenda Flow for a Process Design Committee   152

Building Support for the Proposed Process Design   166

Conclusion   167

Chapter 4. Convening   **169**
Chris Carlson

Roles   170

The Importance of Convening: Two Examples   171

Step 1: Assess the Situation   174

Step 2: Identify and Engage Participants   185

Step 3: Locate the Necessary Resources   190

Step 4: Plan and Organize the Process   195

Special Challenges to Convening for Government Agencies   195

Conclusion   197

Chapter 5. The Role of Facilitators, Mediators, and Other Consensus Building Practitioners   199
Michael L. Poirier Elliott

Use of Convening, Facilitation, Mediation, and Dispute Systems Design in Consensus Building   201

Core Tasks of Consensus Building Practitioners   218

Selecting a Consensus Building Practitioner   230

Conclusion   238

Chapter 6. Representation of Stakeholding Interests   241
David Laws

Practice Problems   245

Conclusion: The Problem of Ratification   272

Chapter 7. Managing Meetings to Build Consensus   287
David A. Straus

The Value of Face-to-Face Meetings   289

Before a Meeting: Setting Up for Success   292

During the Meeting: Attitudes, Behaviors, and Tools   305

After the Meeting   321

Conclusion   322

Chapter 8. Producing Consensus   325
Sarah McKearnan and David Fairman

Prologue: The Task Force Meeting   325

Producing Consensus: An Analytic Framework   327

Applying the Strategies to Produce Consensus   337

Conclusion   371

Chapter 9. Joint Fact-Finding and the Use of Technical Experts   375
John R. Ehrmann and Barbara L. Stinson

Advantages of Joint Fact-Finding   377

When to Use Joint Fact-Finding Procedures   380

Who Does the Fact-Finding?   386

Building Lasting Agreements: Steps in a Joint Fact-Finding Process   391

Obstacles to Effective Joint Fact-Finding   397

Conclusion   398

Chapter 10. Making the Best Use of Technology   401
Connie P. Ozawa

Dissemination of and Access to Written Documents   403

Discussion, Debate, and Deliberation   410

Analysis   417

Computer-Based Decision-Making Technologies   423

Drafting Written Documents   425

Conclusion   428

Chapter 11. Dealing with the Press   435
James E. Kunde

Case Examples: The Extremes of Media Coverage   437

Conducting a Media Assessment   439

Dealing with the Press during and after a Process   454

Conclusion   459

Chapter 12. Dealing with Deep Value Differences   463
John Forester

Value Differences and Consensus Building: Mediation Snake Oil?   465

Setting Priorities for HIV/AIDS Prevention in Colorado:
A Case Example   479

Practical Implications: Consensus Building in the Face of Value
Differences   489

Chapter 13. Legal Issues in Consensus Building 495
Dwight Golann and Eric E. Van Loon

Relationship to Government Agencies and the Courts 497
Procedural Requirements Imposed by Laws and Regulations 502
Substantive Restrictions on the Power of Government Representatives 505
Disclosure Requirements and Confidentiality Protections 510
Liability Issues 515
Implementation and Enforcement Considerations 517
Conclusion 522

Chapter 14. Implementing Consensus-Based Agreements 527
William R. Potapchuk and Jarle Crocker

The Challenge of Implementation 528
Before the Party Starts: Getting to the Table 532
A Menu for Success: At the Table 541
When the Music's Over: Closing the Deal 548
After the Party's Over: Moving Forward 551
Conclusion 553

Chapter 15. Visioning 557
Carl M. Moore, Gianni Longo, and Patsy Palmer

The Benefits and Pitfalls of Visioning 560
The Preconditions for Community-Wide Visioning 561
The Phases of Community-Wide Visioning 562
Variations in Visioning: Beyond the Community-Wide Approach 581
Lessons and Principles for Community-Wide Visioning 588

Chapter 16. Collaborative Problem Solving within Organizations 591
Christopher W. Moore and Peter J. Woodrow

Consensus-Based Decision Making in Organizations 594
Consensus Building and Dispute Resolution Systems Design 603
Roles of Leaders and Managers in Consensus Building 619
Conclusion 628

Chapter 17. Evaluating Consensus Building   631
    Judith E. Innes

    What Consensus Building Can Accomplish   634
    Existing Evaluations of Consensus Building   636
    The Challenge of Evaluating Consensus Building   638
    Complexity Science as the Basis for a New Evaluation Framework   642
    Criteria for Evaluating Consensus Building   647
    Evaluation Options   654
    Gathering and Analyzing Data   662
    Who Should Conduct an Evaluation   670
    Concluding Comments   671

PART 3: CASES AND COMMENTARIES

Introduction to the Cases and Commentaries   679
    Michèle Ferenz

Case 1. **Activating a Policy Network:**
        The Case of Mainport Schiphol   685
        Peter Driessen
        COMMENTATORS: Mark Kishlansky, Howard Raiffa,
                    and Charles F. Sabel

Case 2. **The Northern Oxford County Coalition:**
        Four Maine Towns Tackle a Public Health Mystery   711
        Sarah McKearnan and Patrick Field
        COMMENTATORS: Max H. Bazerman and Charles F. Sabel

Case 3. **The Chelsea Charter Consensus Process**   743
        Susan L. Podziba
        COMMENTATORS: Mark Kishlansky, Jane Mansbridge,
                    and Carrie J. Menkel-Meadow

Case 4. **Affordable Housing Mediation: Building Consensus**
        for Regional Agreements in the Hartford Area   773
        Lawrence Susskind and Susan L. Podziba
        COMMENTATORS: Sally Engle Merry and Charles F. Sabel

Case 5. San Francisco Estuary Project   801
      Judith E. Innes and Sarah Connick
      COMMENTATOR: Carrie J. Menkel-Meadow

Case 6. Resolving Science-Intensive Public Policy Disputes:
      Reflections on the New York Bight Initiative   829
      Scott McCreary
      COMMENTATOR: William Moomaw

Case 7. Negotiating Superfund Cleanup at the
      Massachusetts Military Reservation   859
      Edward Scher
      COMMENTATORS: Carrie J. Menkel-Meadow, William Moomaw,
      and Howard Raiffa

Case 8. RuleNet: An Experiment in Online Consensus Building   879
      Michèle Ferenz and Colin Rule
      COMMENTATOR: William Moomaw

Case 9. Regulatory Negotiations:
      The Native American Experience   901
      Jan Jung-Min Sunoo and Juliette A. Falkner
      COMMENTATOR: Carrie J. Menkel-Meadow

Case 10. Cross-Cultural Community-Based Planning:
      Negotiating the Future of Haida Gwaii (British Columbia)   923
      Norman Dale
      COMMENTATORS: Max H. Bazerman and Sally Engle Merry

Case 11. The Chattanooga Process: A City's Vision Is Realized   951
      John Parr
      COMMENTATORS: Mark Kishlansky and Sally Engle Merry

Case 12. From City Hall to the Streets:
      A Community Plan Meets the Real World   969
      Kate Connolly
      COMMENTATOR: Jane Mansbridge

Case 13. The Catron County Citizens Group:
A Case Study in Community Collaboration   985
Melinda Smith
COMMENTATOR: Max H. Bazerman

Case 14. Facilitating Statewide HIV/AIDS Policies and
Priorities in Colorado   1011
Michael A. Hughes with John Forester and Irene Weiser
COMMENTATOR: Daniel Markovits

Case 15. Finding Common Ground on Abortion   1031
Michelle LeBaron and Nike Carstarphen
COMMENTATOR: Carrie J. Menkel-Meadow

Case 16. Organizational Trauma Recovery: The "God's Fellowship
Community Church" Reconciliation Process   1051
David Brubaker
COMMENTATOR: Sally Engle Merry

Case 17. Building Consensus for Change within a Major
Corporation: The Case of Levi Strauss & Co.   1065
Judy Mares-Dixon, Julie A. McKay, and Scott Peppet
COMMENTATOR: Sally Engle Merry

Selected Bibliography   1087

Index   1091

About the Editors   1125

About the Contributors   1127

PREFACE

The Consensus Building Institute (CBI) is a nonprofit organization that provides dispute resolution services to public agencies, nongovernmental groups, and corporations around the world. When we opened our doors in 1993, one of the things we set out to do was to document *best practices* in the consensus building field. In particular, we wanted to make this material accessible and useful—in book form—to anyone who has to solve problems or make decisions in a group setting. It was a daunting task. To accomplish it, we enlisted the help of 21 of the foremost thinkers in the dispute resolution field. The result of their efforts are the 17 chapters that make up Part 2 of this volume.

At the same time, we wanted to assess the effectiveness of the many consensus-based approaches to helping groups reach agreement. Susan Carpenter, a member of CBI's Board of Directors and a very skilled mediator, suggested that we ask the global network of dispute resolution professionals to chronicle instances in which they had succeeded or failed in noteworthy ways. This idea led to the collection of the 17 case studies in Part 3, which were authored by 24 experienced facilitators, mediators, and scholars.

Other members of our board then challenged us to look closely at the cases and chapters that were submitted, as well as at existing theoretical literature in the field, to see if we could summarize the most salient guidance on how to build consensus in groups. As we pursued this suggestion, it became clear that there were substantial differences of opinion worth exploring. So we convened a cross section of consensus building professionals and initiated a dialogue among them. The results of this effort became Part 1, "A Short Guide to Consensus Building."

Finally, we felt it was important to look beyond the dispute resolution field for insight into the practice of consensus building. We thus sought out nine experts in related fields, ranging from law to environmental science to anthropology, to provide commentary on the cases. These commentaries accompany the case studies in Part 3.

The *Handbook* that emerged from these disparate sources makes what we think is a very important distinction between consensus building in temporary groups and permanent organizations. The former includes ad hoc assemblies, particularly in the public arena, established to take on short-term dispute resolution assignments of one kind or another. These collections of individuals and organizations face special obstacles as they try to reach agreement. Everyone involved has split loyalties—first and foremost to the organization or group that sent them and then to the processes they have agreed to join. Also, participants in ad hoc assemblies may have no shared culture of decision making, no history of working together, and no guarantee that the people participating will be there when implementation problems arise later.

Permanent organizations face many of the difficulties experienced by ad hoc assemblies, but they usually have a shared history, commitments, and even loyalty to the well-being of a common entity and, often, a hierarchical leadership that can make things happen and ensure that long-term institutional promises are honored. Presumably, group learning and institutional memory help permanent organizations get better over time at certain consensus building tasks. Of course, permanent organizations sometimes find it hard to reach agreement because relationships within an organization have soured or because there is so much resistance to change.

Our strategy, especially in preparing the "Short Guide," was to look first at ad hoc assemblies and then to highlight important differences between the process of consensus building in these situations and the process in permanent organizations. Since one of our key objectives is to offer a replacement for *Robert's Rules of Order,* and that volume focuses exclusively on how to get agreement in ad hoc or representative assemblies, it seemed appropriate that we start at that end of the spectrum.

While this *Handbook* draws from a broad range of disciplines relating to consensus building, we had to set boundaries somewhere. For example, only some of the extensive guidance on how to run effective meetings has been incorporated into the *Handbook.* Much of that material is aimed in a different direction from our work—our interest is only in meetings that are part of a larger consensus building process. Also, there is an enormous literature on organizational development that we have not tried to incorporate, even by reference. While these dynamics are crucial to improving the long-term capacity of permanent entities to build consensus, they are not relevant to the kind of short-term problem solving and dispute resolution that command our attention. After all, every time a group is assembled and given a consensus building task, it is too late to initiate the most desirable program of organizational development. There are undoubtedly other issues or themes that we should have addressed. If so, the three editors absolve the rest of the CBI staff and all of our colleagues from any responsibility for these omissions.

The three of us played complementary roles in the development of this *Handbook.* Larry Susskind, who initiated and conceptualized the project, also facilitated the dialogue among the authors, coauthored one of the chapters, and prepared the "Short Guide." Sarah McKearnan served as project director, and as such was involved in both the editorial process and the business details of the effort. In addition, she coauthored one of the chapters and one of the cases. Jennifer Thomas-Larmer served as editor in chief, assisting the chapter contributors as they moved from preliminary outlines through successive drafts. She also coauthored a chapter.

Fundamentally, however, this *Handbook* is the result of the cumulative effort of many dedicated friends and colleagues. We would like to acknowledge, first and foremost, the 52 contributing authors, without whose wisdom and effort there would be no book. We also want to thank the members of CBI's Board of Directors, who provided support, guidance, and good critical thinking at various points throughout this process. They include Max Bazerman, Susan Carpenter, Michael Lewis, John Marks, Robert Mnookin, William Moomaw, Howard Raiffa, Kilaparti

Ramakrishna, Frank Sander, Linda Singer, Leslie Tuttle, Lauren Walters, and Michael Wheeler. Many of these individuals, along with Bob Barrett and Jack Wofford, provided comments on the "Short Guide."

Our many thanks also go to Michèle Ferenz, who took the lead in gathering and editing the case studies and working with the case authors and commentators—while pursuing her doctoral studies full time. We would also like to acknowledge Rebecca Carman and Heather Davis, who assisted with the copyediting, and Sid Straley, Polly O'Brien, and John Mitchell at CBI, who helped to prepare the final version of the manuscript. Finally, a thank-you to Marquita Flemming at Sage Publications for enabling us to imagine the final product and for providing us with encouragement and guidance at crucial moments along the way.

We have learned a great deal from this supportive and exciting group of colleagues, and we are pleased to have had the opportunity to work with them.

LAWRENCE SUSSKIND
SARAH MCKEARNAN
JENNIFER THOMAS-LARMER

INTRODUCTION

Every day, people are faced with the need to work with others in group settings to make decisions and solve problems. Whether they are part of a corporate team that is seeking to set strategic goals for the year or members of an ad hoc community task force tackling a complex public issue such as urban sprawl, most group members would probably rather make decisions and solve problems in a way that meets their own needs and satisfies everyone else around the table. Many people are convinced, however, that consensus—especially within large groups—is not a reasonable objective. They believe that most people are selfish and will pursue their own goals rather than search for solutions that satisfy everyone. They also assume that whenever hard choices have to be made, some people will win and some will have to lose.

From our standpoint, these assumptions are simply not true. Through a new approach to problem solving—called *consensus building*—groups *can* forge agreements that satisfy everyone's primary interests and concerns. Using consensus-based approaches, groups can jointly develop solutions and make decisions that are more creative and more widely supported than those made using traditional decision-making methods (such as top-down decision making or even parliamentary procedure). In the process, group participants gain a mutual respect for and an understanding of each other's viewpoints, enabling them to work together more effectively in the long term. Agreements made by consensus are often more readily implemented than decisions made in other ways, because people are more likely to support an agreement that they had a hand in shaping. The benefits of consensus building have been proven true by hundreds of groups around the United States and elsewhere.

By looking closely at the experiences of a wide range of such groups, we have determined that consensus building works best when four preconditions are met. First, group participants must tap the right kind of facilitation or mediation assistance. In the same way that groups have relied in the past on parliamentarians or experienced moderators, consensus building depends on facilitators and mediators to help manage the *process,* so that participants can bring all their energies to bear on the *substance.* Second, groups need to formalize their commitment to consensus building by adopting written ground rules or bylaws. Those who participate in consensus-based discussions are more productive and more comfortable operating within agreed-on behavioral and procedural guidelines. Third, groups that want to operate by consensus must allow themselves sufficient time to build their capacity to work in this way. Members must learn how to think about not only what meets their needs but also what might satisfy the interests of others. This may feel awkward at first, but over time, their patience and commitment will be rewarded. Finally, and perhaps most important, participants need a clear map outlining how to build consensus. This *Handbook* seeks to provide that map.

■ *Areas of Application*

Consensus building knows no topical boundaries. The examples in this *Handbook* deal with topics as diverse as corporate employment practices, the public health effects of air pollution, and the rights of indigenous peoples. Consensus building processes can be organized around public issues of concern at the neighborhood scale, the city level, and the state level, as well as the national or even international level. Such discussions typically involve people who represent a diverse range of interests and opinions. So, for example, a consensus-based negotiation regarding a community's air pollution problem might include doctors and public health experts, representatives of environmental groups, residents affected by the pollution, local industries that emit regulated substances, other local business interests, and officials from the state agency responsible for regulating air quality. Consensus building techniques and strategies are also productively employed, of course, to address issues that concern only a few people, such as a corporate team, a board of directors, or a church committee.

Ad Hoc versus Permanent Groups

In developing this book, we discovered that the advice we had to offer was best directed to two categories of groups: temporary (or ad hoc) groups and permanent groups. While the distinction between ad hoc and permanent groups is not entirely satisfying or clear, it leads to important insights regarding the practice of consensus building.

In trying to articulate the distinction, we have focused on where group participants' loyalties lie. So, while a work team drawn from different parts of a corporation and given a short-term assignment is technically ad hoc, that team is best understood as part of an ongoing corporate entity. The participants on the team probably think of themselves as long-term members of the corporation. Likewise, a coalition of community organizations created to take on a new problem might continue its efforts for several months or even years, but because the members share no history or long-term responsibility to each other, the coalition is best understood as a temporary entity. The members of that coalition will (if they do their jobs well) stay focused on their long-term obligations to the organizations that sent them. The members of a body, such as a board of directors or a city council, may turn over very quickly, but while members of such a body, they would do well to take account of the history of that group and their obligations to the entity's long-term well-being. Thus, we consider groups such as these to be "permanent."

People who are members of ad hoc groups focus on their obligations and responsibilities to the organizations or groups they have been asked to represent. By contrast, people who serve as members of permanent organizations, even for a short time, typically pay special attention to the long-term well-being of that entity. The implications for the design and implementation of consensus building processes are quite important. For example, the participants in a consensus building process at a permanent organization should probably invest considerable time evaluating how they are doing and what they have learned. Such an investment would not make sense in a temporary group. Ad hoc assemblies must always spend a great deal of time getting organized. In the absence of institutionalized relationships and prior understandings, every aspect of process design and communication is "up for grabs." While permanent organizations may want to change how they have done things in the past, they still have a history to build on. Moreover, the participants share at least their commitment to the organization of which they are all a part. The full significance of the distinction between ad hoc assemblies and permanent organizations and its impact on consensus building will become clear as the *Handbook* unfolds.

■ *Common Misperceptions*

People who have never been part of a consensus building process often make a number of wrong assumptions about what is involved. We want to dispel five common misperceptions.

I Will Have to Give Up Authority

Elected or appointed officials, in the case of ad hoc dialogues in the public arena, and senior managers in a corporate context, often react negatively to the idea of consensus building. They assume that the only way agreement can be reached is if they give up some or all of their authority. In practice, this is not true. In a consensus building process, any player can walk away at any time. Unless the most important stakeholders "buy into" an agreement, there won't be one. If the process produces an agreement that meets each party's needs, all key stakeholders will concur. If it doesn't, they will walk away and return to whatever form of decision making they used before attempting to operate by consensus.

I Will Be Pressured to Betray My Constituents

Inexperienced participants sometimes assume that the way consensus is reached is through compromise—by everyone giving up some of what they want for the sake of agreement. Experienced negotiators, however, know that this is not the case. They understand that consensus must represent an outcome that is better for each stakeholder than his or her next-best option (if agreement is not reached). No one should ever give up what is important to them just so a group can reach agreement.

I Will Lose Face

Even some experienced negotiators assume that the way to get what they want is to "look tough" and to "give the other side a hard time." Consensus building, they assume, is for "weaklings." As it turns out, the negotiators with the best reputations are the ones who almost always get a good deal for the person across the table as well. The pressure they feel is to generate an agreement that meets everyone's interests. They are not concerned with looking tough. They stay focused on the outcomes they want to achieve. If consensus building produces good outcomes (and leaves relationships intact so that future negotiations are easier), then they know they will get credit for their success.

I Will Have to Help My "Enemies"

Experienced negotiators, agents, and representatives usually concentrate on meeting their own interests very well, while meeting other groups' interests tolerably. While they don't seek to help their "enemies" at their own expense, they aren't out to hurt them either. For participants in controversies who are as concerned about hurting their adversaries as they are about meeting their own interests, consensus building may not be a good way to proceed. The goal of consensus building is to do well for yourself or your "side," not to hurt your enemies.

I Will Be Forced to Abandon My Principles

No participants in a consensus building process need ever assume that they must abandon their principles for the sake of agreement. Even when participants cannot explain why they feel that something is wrong or why they can't go along with it, they are entitled to stay out of an emerging agreement. Every participant in a consensus building process is free to disagree with whatever is proposed, *for any reason whatsoever,* and it should be the mediator's (or facilitator's) job to protect the person from harsh group reactions if he or she is the only holdout. While it helps a problem-solving process if everyone gives reasons for their opposition to particular ideas or suggestions, even that is not required. Consensus building does not assume that principles should be traded or abandoned for the sake of agreement. No agreement is always a legitimate outcome!

■ *About This Book*

The Consensus Building Handbook is meant as a reference, like an encyclopedia. We don't expect that very many people will read it from cover to cover. We do expect, however, that it will be useful to a wide range of audiences—essentially anyone who is contemplating convening or participating in a consensus building process. While we also believe dispute resolution professionals will be interested in the book, and may find the "best practices" described within it useful, it is written for a much broader audience. The *Handbook* stresses the advantages of informal, commonsense approaches to working together. It describes how any group can put these approaches into practice, and it relates numerous examples of situations in which such approaches have been applied.

The *Handbook* has three interrelated parts. Part 1 is called "A Short Guide to Consensus Building." It offers a summary of the prescriptive advice contained in the rest of the *Handbook*. The "Short Guide" is written as an alternative to the most well-known method of group decision making: the parliamentary procedures spelled out in *Robert's Rules of Order* (Robert, 1990). *Robert's Rules* assumes that the majority should get what it wants, even if the minority is left with little or nothing. All that is necessary to "win" is a larger coalition with more votes. The losers must wait until they can attract more supporters and try again. Parliamentary procedure relies on elaborate rules specifying when and how motions (i.e., proposals) can be made, how discussions should be managed (by a moderator), and how voting should be handled. The "Short Guide to Consensus Building" spells out procedural alternatives to *Robert's Rules* for groups that want to operate by consensus. These procedures can be referenced by any group or organization trying to write bylaws or draft guidelines to govern how they will make decisions and conduct their business. The

"Short Guide" also provides helpful definitions for the most commonly used (and confused!) terms relating to consensus building.

A summary matrix in the "Short Guide" lists the most important topics and techniques covered in the *Handbook*. For readers interested in how to sort and modify ground rules, for example, the matrix indicates the relevant prescriptions in the "Short Guide" as well as the relevant chapters that discuss the underlying theory.

Part 2 is made up of 17 chapters that describe the various phases, facets, and forms of consensus building. These chapters capture the wisdom of America's most experienced dispute resolution professionals; each is written by a mediator, facilitator, or scholar with specific expertise in the chapter's subject matter. Chapter 1, "Choosing Appropriate Consensus Building Techniques and Strategies," serves as an introduction to the chapters and cases; it describes the many factors that need to be considered in organizing a consensus-based effort and, in the process, touches on points made in all the other chapters and cases in the *Handbook*. Of the remaining chapters, some focus on a step or phase in a typical consensus building process (such as convening or implementing agreements); some describe activities that are typically undertaken in any attempt to build consensus (such as managing meetings or using facilitators or mediators); others explain how to deal with specific issues (such as press coverage or deep value differences among participants); and still others describe how to use consensus-based procedures in specific settings (such as within a single organization). All of the chapters provide practical advice for both organizers of and participants in consensus building processes on how to successfully seek agreement in and among diverse groups.

Part 3 of the *Handbook* contains 17 case studies that illustrate the many applications of and variations on consensus building. The cases, which are cross-referenced in the chapters, describe consensus-based efforts that have taken place in both the public and private sectors, in ad hoc and permanent groups, from the local level up to the national level, on a wide range of substantive topics. Some of the cases were written by independent evaluators or researchers; others describe the firsthand experiences of those involved. The cases can be read independently of the chapters, but readers should be aware that many of the cases illustrate only selected aspects of consensus building. The "Introduction to the Cases and Commentaries" summarizes each case.

The cases are accompanied by commentaries, written by experts in nine different fields (law, anthropology, political philosophy, environmental science, decision science, ethics, political economics, history, and social psychology). In the commentaries, these experts provide insight into and questions about the consensus processes described in the cases, from their particular disciplinary or professional perspective. None of the commentators' voices is heard in more than five of the cases.

At the back of the book readers will find a selected bibliography, a list of contributors, and a comprehensive index. If you are not sure where to begin, you could look in the index for a topic or case study that intrests you.

■ Reference

Robert, H. M. (1990). *Robert's rules of order: Newly revised* (9th ed.). New York: Scott, Foresman.

PART 1

A SHORT GUIDE TO CONSENSUS BUILDING

AN ALTERNATIVE TO ROBERT'S RULES OF ORDER FOR GROUPS, ORGANIZATIONS, AND AD HOC ASSEMBLIES THAT WANT TO OPERATE BY CONSENSUS

■ *Lawrence Susskind*

Let's compare what this "Short Guide" has to say with what *Robert's Rules of Order* requires. Assume that a few dozen people have gotten together, on their own, at a community center because they are upset with a new policy or program recently announced by their local officials. After several impassioned speeches, someone suggests that the group appoint a moderator to "keep order" and ensure that the conversation proceeds effectively. Someone else wants to know how the group will decide what to recommend after they are done debating. "Will we vote?" this person wants to know. At this point, everyone turns to Joe, who has had experience as a moderator. Joe moves to the front of the room and explains that he will follow *Robert's Rules of Order*. From that moment on, the conversation takes on a very formal tone.

Instead of just saying what's on their mind, everyone is forced to frame suggestions in the cumbersome form of *motions*. These have to be *seconded*. Efforts to *move the question* are proceeded by an explanation from Joe about what is and isn't an acceptable way of doing this. Proposals to *table* various items are considered, even though everyone hasn't had a chance to speak. Ultimately, all-or-nothing votes are the only way the group seems able to make a decision.

As the hour passes, fewer and fewer of those in attendance feel capable of expressing their views. They don't know the rules, and they are intimidated. Every once in a while, someone makes an effort to restate the problem or make a suggestion, but the person is shouted down ("You're not following *Robert's Rules*!"). No one takes responsibility for ensuring that the concerns of everyone in the room are met, especially the needs of those individuals who are least able to present their views effectively. After an hour or so, many people have left. A final proposal is approved by a vote of 55 percent to 45 percent of those remaining.

If the group had followed the procedures spelled out in this "Short Guide to Consensus Building," the meeting would have been run differently and the result would probably have been a lot more to everyone's liking. The person at the front of the room would have been a trained facilitator or mediator—a person adept at helping groups build consensus—not a moderator with specialized knowledge about how motions should be made or votes should be taken. His or her job would have been to get agreement at the outset on how the group wanted to proceed. Then, the facilitator would have focused on producing an agreement that could meet the underlying concerns of everyone in the room: no motions, no arcane rituals, and no vote at the end. Instead, the facilitator might have pushed the group to brainstorm (e.g., "Can anyone propose a way of proceeding that meets all the interests we have heard expressed thus far?"). After as thorough a consideration of options as time permitted, the facilitator would ask, "Is there anyone who can't live with the last version of what has been proposed? If so, what improvement or modification can you suggest that will make it more acceptable to you, while continuing to meet the interests of everyone else with a stake in the issue?" The group would have likely developed a proposal that everyone—or nearly everyone—in the room could support. And participants would leave satisfied that their opinions and needs had been heard, understood, and taken into account.

■ *What's Wrong with Robert's Rules?*

Robert's Rules of Order was first published in 1870. It was based on the rules and practices of Congress, and presumed that parliamentary procedures (and majority rule) offered the most appropriate model for any and all groups. The author presumed that the *Rules of Order* would "assist an assembly in accomplishing the work for which it was designed" by "restraining the individual" so that the interests of the group could be met.

In the more than 125 years since *Robert's Rules* was first published, many other approaches to group work and organizational activity have emerged. The goal of this "Short Guide" and the full *Handbook* is to codify the best possible advice to groups and organizations that prefer to operate with broad support, by consensus, rather than simply by majority rule. We believe that something greater than a bare majority achieved through voting is almost always more desirable than majority rule. Moreover, the formalism of parliamentary procedure is particularly unsatisfying and often counterproductive, getting in the way of commonsense solutions. It relies on insider knowledge of obscure rules of the game. It does not tap the full range of facilitative skills of group leaders. And it typically leaves many stakeholders (often something just short of a majority) angry and disappointed, with little or nothing to show for their efforts.

Even with these weaknesses, many social groups and organizations, especially in community settings, adhere to *Robert's Rules* (by referencing them in their by-laws or articles of incorporation) because they have no other option. "A Short Guide to Consensus Building" offers an alternative that builds on several decades of experience with effective consensus building techniques and strategies. No longer must groups and organizations settle for *Robert's Rules* when they would be better off with an alternative that puts the emphasis on cooperation and consensus.

■ *Definitions*

To explain what has been learned about consensus building over the past several decades, certain terms are important. Indeed, they are central to the presentation in this "Short Guide." They are not part of everyday language and, thus, require some explanation. The key terms we will define are *interests, consensus building, facilitation, mediation, recording, convening, conflict assessment, single-text procedure, creating and claiming value,* and *circles of stakeholder involvement.* These definitions have been developed over the past two decades. There is still not complete agreement among dispute resolution professionals about how they should be defined; so, where important disagreements remain, we will point them out.

Interests (participants' underlying values and needs)

Interests are what each participant in a group process seeks to achieve. Interests are not the same as positions or demands. Demands and positions are what people say they must have, but interests are the underlying reasons, needs, or values that explain why they take the positions they do. Interests can change in light of new information or a deeper understanding of a problem. They often reflect deeply held beliefs.

Consensus Building (an agreement-seeking process)

Consensus building is a process of seeking unanimous agreement. It involves a good-faith effort to meet the interests of all stakeholders. Consensus has been reached when everyone agrees they can live with whatever is proposed after every effort has been made to meet the interests of all stakeholding parties. Thus, consensus building requires that someone frame a proposal after listening carefully to everyone's concerns. Participants in a consensus building process have both the right to expect that no one will ask them to undermine their interests and the responsibility to propose solutions that will meet everyone else's interests as well as their own.

Most consensus building efforts set out to achieve unanimity. Along the way, however, there are sometimes *holdouts:* people who believe that their interests are better served by remaining outside the emerging agreement. Should the rest of the group throw in the towel? No, this would invite blackmail (i.e., outrageous demands by the holdouts that have nothing to do with the issues under discussion). Most dispute resolution professionals believe that groups or assemblies should seek unanimity, but settle for overwhelming agreement that goes as far as possible toward meeting the interests of all stakeholders. This effort to meet the interests of all stakeholders should be understood to include an affirmative responsibility to ensure that those who are excluded really are holdouts and are rejecting the proposal on reasonable grounds that would seem compelling to anyone who found themselves in the holdouts' shoes. It is absolutely crucial that the definition of success be clear at the outset of any consensus building process.

Facilitation (a way of helping groups work together in meetings)

Facilitation is a meeting management skill. When people are face-to-face, they need to talk and to listen. When there are several people involved, especially if they don't know each other or they disagree sharply, getting the talking-listening-deciding sequence right is hard. Often, it is helpful to have someone who has no stake in the outcome assist in managing the conversation. Of course, a skilled group member can, with the concurrence of the participants, play this role, too. As the parties try to collect information, formulate proposals, defend their views, and take account of what others are saying, a facilitator reminds them of the ground rules they have adopted and, much like a referee, intervenes when someone violates the ground rules. The facilitator is supposed to be nonpartisan or neutral.

There is some disagreement in various professional circles about the extent to which an effective facilitator needs to be someone from outside the group. Certainly in a corporate context, work teams have traditionally relied on the person "in charge" to play a facilitative role. The concept of facilitative leadership is growing in popularity. Even work teams in the private sector, however, are turning more and more to skilled outsiders to provide facilitation services. In the final analysis, there is reason to worry that a stakeholder might use facilitative authority to advance his or her own interests at the expense of the others.

*Mediation (a way of helping parties
deal with strong disagreement)*

Mediation is a means of helping parties resolve a dispute. While facilitators do most of their work "at the table" when the parties are face-to-face, mediators are often called on to work with the parties before, during, and after their face-to-face meetings. While most mediators are skilled facilitators, not all facilitators have been trained to mediate. The classic image of the mediator comes from the labor relations field where an outside *neutral* often shuttles back and forth between representatives of labor and management, each of whom has retreated to a separate room as the strike deadline looms. These days, mediators work in an extraordinarily wide range of conflict situations. Mediation is both a role and a group management skill. A manager or team leader may have mediation skills and may be able to broker agreement by putting those skills to use. But, again, when the search for innovative solutions rests in the hands of one of the stakeholders, it is often hard for the others to believe that the leader/mediator isn't trying to advance his or her own interests at their expense.

The big debate in professional circles is whether any mediator really can (or should) be neutral. The referee in a sporting match must be nonpartisan; he or she can't secretly be working for one team. The referee tries to uphold the rules of the game to which everyone has agreed. This is what is commonly meant by neutrality—nonpartisanship and an absence of bias with respect to the parties. However, some people have argued that a mediator should not be indifferent to blatant unfairness. They believe that a mediator should not turn a blind eye to potentially unfair or unimplementable agreements, even if the "rules of the game" have not been violated. Yet if a mediator intervenes on behalf of a party that may be about to "give away the store," why should the others accept that mediator's help? The answer probably depends on the level of confidence the parties have in the mediator and the terms of the mediator's contract with the group.

Before the parties in a consensus building process come together, mediators (or facilitators) can play an important part in helping to identify the right participants, assist them in setting an agenda and clarifying the ground rules by which they will operate, and even in "selling" recalcitrant parties on the value of participating. Once the process has begun, mediators (and facilitators) try to assist the parties in their efforts to generate creative resolution of differences. During these discussions or negotiations, a mediator may accompany a representative back to a meeting with his or her constituents to explain what has been happening. The mediator might serve as a spokesperson for the process if the media are following the story. A mediator might (with the parties' concurrence) push them to accept an accord (because they need someone to blame for forcing them to back off some of the demands they made at the outset). Finally, the mediator may be called on to monitor implementation of an agreement and reassemble the parties to review progress or deal with perceived violations or a failure to live up to commitments.

Facilitation and *mediation* are often used interchangeably. We think the key distinction is that facilitators work mostly with parties once they are at the table, while mediators do that as well as handle the prenegotiation and postnegotiation tasks described above. Also, mediators tend to be called on in particularly conflictual situations. In addition, some facilitators do not necessarily strive for agreement as mediators always do, but rather seek to ensure productive deliberation. Some professionals have both sets of skills; many do not. Neither form of consensus building assistance requires stakeholders to give up their authority or their power to decide what is best for them.

Recording (creating a visual record of what a group has discussed and decided)

Recording involves creating a visual record that captures the key points of agreement and disagreement during a dialogue. Some facilitators (and mediators) work in tandem with a recorder. Recording can be done on large sheets of paper, often called flip charts, tacked up in front of a room. With the introduction of new computer and multimedia technologies, this can be done electronically as well. The important thing is to have an ongoing visual representation of what the group has discussed and agreed. Unlike formal minutes of a meeting, this "group memory" may use drawings, illustrations, maps, or other icons to help people recall what they have discussed. Visual records prepared by a recorder ultimately need to be turned into written meeting summaries. Like minutes, these summaries must be reviewed in draft by all participants to ensure that everyone agrees with the review of what happened.

Convening (bringing parties together)

Convening, or the gathering together of parties for a meeting or a series of meetings, is not a skill that depends on training. An agency or organization that has decided to host a consensus building process (and wants to encourage others to participate) can play an important convening role. In a private firm, for example, a senior official might be the convenor. In the public arena, a regulatory agency might want to convene a public involvement process. There is some disagreement about whether or not the convenor or the convening organization is obliged to stay at the table as the conversation proceeds. In general, convening organizations want to be part of the dialogue, but we do not feel they must commit to ongoing participation in a consensus building process.

Someone has to finance a consensus building process. When it takes place inside an existing organization, financial arrangements are reasonably straightforward. When consensus building involves a wide range of groups in an ad hoc assembly, it is much less obvious who can and will provide the financial support. If costs are not shared equally by the parties, for example, and if they are covered by the convening organization, special steps must be taken to ensure that the facilitator or mediator has a contract with the entire group, and not just the convenor, and that the organization(s) providing the financing do not use that sponsorship to dictate the outcome.

Conflict Assessment (an essential convening step)

A conflict assessment is a document that spells out what the issues are, who the stakeholding interests are, where they disagree, and where they might find common ground. It is usually prepared by a neutral outsider based on confidential interviews with key stakeholders. There is some disagreement over whether the same neutral who prepared the conflict assessment should then be the one to facilitate or mediate, if the process goes

forward. Typically, after interviewing a wide range of stakeholders, a neutral party will suggest whether or not it makes sense to
go forward with a consensus building process and, if so, how the
process ought to be structured.

Such an assessment can be presented orally to the convenor,
but it is probably better that it be written and distributed in draft
to everyone interviewed, before it is finalized. The recommendations resulting from a conflict assessment are not the final word.
Only the stakeholders themselves can decide whether or not they
want to proceed and, if so, how they want to organize their
efforts.

Single-Text Procedure
(a way to generate agreement)

Roger Fisher, Bill Ury, and Bruce Patton, in their well-known
book *Getting to Yes* (1991), first suggested the concept of "single
text" negotiation. Rather than having each party propose its own
version of an ideal agreement, a neutral party carries a single
version of a possible agreement from party to party seeking
"improvements" that will make it acceptable to all people on the
list. (No one needs to know who suggested which modifications
along the way.) It is also possible to work together in a meeting
to collectively revise a single text, although in that setting it is
more likely that some parties will find it harder to accept a
proposed improvement because they know who suggested it.

Creating and Claiming Value
(a way to maximize joint gains)

Our colleagues Howard Raiffa, in his book *The Art and
Science of Negotiation* (1982), and David Lax and Jim Sebenius,
in their book *The Manager as Negotiator* (1986), have helped to
popularize the idea of "creating value." Most people think of
negotiation or problem solving as a "zero sum" game in which a
fixed amount is allocated among competing parties. An efficient
agreement, therefore, is presumed to be one in which all the gains
available have been allocated among the parties. This tends to
overlook the fact that there are numerous ways to "make the pie
larger" in most situations. Thus, an efficient agreement is really

one in which the parties have done all they can to create value as well as allocated all the value they have created.

Lax and Sebenius describe what they call "the negotiator's dilemma" as the key problem facing everyone in a consensus building or dispute resolution process: How should those parties manage the tension between creating and claiming value? This tension results from the fact that creating value requires cooperative behaviors while claiming value revolves almost entirely around competition. Given that everyone in a group process has "mixed motives" (i.e., they want the pie to be as large as possible, but they also want as much for themselves or their side as they can get), they've got to figure out how much to cooperate and how hard to compete.

There is some disagreement among experienced practitioners about how likely it is that value can be created in every situation. On the one hand, those who are generally optimistic assume that value can almost always be created by trading across issues that parties value differently (e.g., "I'll give you this—which is not that important to me—if you'll give me that—which you don't seem to care that much about."). Even in a situation in which there appears to be just one issue—price—under discussion, there are ways to "fractionate" the issue (i.e., break it into parts that can be traded) or to link that issue to future considerations. Those who are generally pessimistic assume that there are severe restrictions on the possibility of creating value in many situations, either because there's nothing to trade or because asymmetries in power allow one side to demand what it wants.

We want to differentiate the idea of maximizing joint gain from the simplistic language of "win-win" negotiating. We are interested in helping parties do better than what no agreement probably holds in store for them. Doing better than one's BATNA (best alternative to a negotiated agreement) is the way to measure success in consensus building. There are few, if any, situations where everyone can get everything they want (which is what "winning" sounds like to us).

Circles of Stakeholder Involvement (a strategy for identifying representative stakeholders)

Stakeholders are persons or groups likely to be affected by (or who think they will be affected by) a decision—whether it is their decision to make or not. When we talk about "circles of stakeholders," we are talking about individuals or groups that want or ought to be involved in decision making, but at different levels of intensity. Some stakeholders may be involved in a core negotiating team, others may have their interests represented on that team, and still others may choose to observe the process from the sidelines.

Some stakeholders are very hard to represent in an organized way. Think about "future generations," for example. Who can represent them in a dialogue about sustainable development? In the law, various strategies have evolved so that surrogates or stand-ins can represent hard-to-represent groups (such as the members of a class of consumers who have been hurt by a certain product or children who have no capacity to speak for themselves in a court proceeding).

Sometimes, it is necessary to caucus all the groups or individuals who think they represent a certain set of stakeholders for the purposes of selecting a representative for a particular dialogue or problem-solving purpose. Such meetings typically need to be facilitated by an outside party. Finally, there are various statutes that govern who may and who must be invited to participate in various public and private dialogues. Ad hoc consensus building processes must take these laws into account.

■ *A Complete Matrix*

The matrix that follows provides an overview of the elements and shows where those topics are discussed in detail in the chapters and cases contained in the remaining three sections of the "Short Guide." Section I contains a set of procedures that should be used when a group will be meeting for a short period of time or when a temporary or ad hoc assembly of stakeholders is organized for a single purpose. The procedures in the first section are organized under five steps. While these are presented in more or less chronological fashion, they do not necessarily need to be applied sequentially.

Section II of the guide focuses on the interaction of participants involved in a permanent group or organization. The suggestions in Section II build on (and are presented in contrast to) what we have suggested for temporary or ad hoc assemblies. Section II deals with consensus building in situations where the

(text continues on p. 20)

SECTION I

Helping an Ad Hoc Assembly Reach Agreement

CHAPTER	1: Techniques and Strategies	2: Conflict Assessment	3: Process Design	4: Convening	5: Use of Facilitators and Mediators	6: Representation	7: Managing Meetings	8: Producing Consensus
Step 1: Convening								
1.1 Determine Whether to Have a Consensus Building Dialogue	X	X	X	X	X		X	
1.2 Prepare a Written Conflict Assessment	X	X		X	X			
1.3 Identify Appropriate Representatives	X	X	X	X	X	X	X	
1.4 Locate Necessary Funding		X			X			
Step 2: Clarifying Responsibilities								
2.1 Clarify the Roles of Facilitators, Mediators, and Recorders	X			X	X		X	
2.2 Set Rules Regarding the Participation of Observers	X		X	X				
2.3 Set an Agenda and Ground Rules	X	X	X		X		X	
2.4 Assess Computer-Based Communication Options	X							
2.5 Establish a Mailing List								
Step 3: Deliberating								
3.1 Pursue Deliberations in a Constructive Fashion	X				X	X	X	
3.2 Separate Inventing From Committing	X				X			
3.3 Create Subcommittees and Seek Expert Advice	X				X	X		
3.4 Use a Single-Text Procedure	X							
3.5 Modify the Agenda and Ground Rules (if necessary)								
3.6 Complete the Deliberations	X				X			
Step 4: Deciding								
4.1 Try to Maximize Joint Gains	X				X			
4.2 Keep a Record	X						X	
Step 5: Implementing Agreements								
5.1 Seek Ratification by Constituencies	X				X	X		

Topic	9: Joint Fact-Finding	10: Use of Technology	11: Dealing With the Press	12: Handling Value Differences	13: Legal Issues	14: Implementing Agreements	15: Visioning	16: Intraorganizational Processes	17: Evaluating Consensus Building	CASE	1: Schiphol Airport Expansion	2: Northern Oxford County Coalition	3: Chelsea Charter Process	4: Affordable Housing Mediation	5: San Francisco Estuary Project	6: New York Bight Initiative	7: Massachusetts Military Reservation	8: RuleNet: Online Mediation	9: Native American Reg-Neg	10: Planning on Haida Gwaii	11: Chattanooga Visioning Process	12: Community-Based Planning	13: Catron County Citizens' Group	14: HIV/AIDS Policies in Colorado	15: Common Ground on Abortion	16: Organizational Trauma Recovery	17: Levi Strauss & Company
		x					x				x						x			x	x	x	x				
			x		x							x					x										
		x			x	x					x	x							x	x			x	x	x		
				x			x										x							x	x		
		x		x			x				x	x		x	x	x	x	x		x	x			x	x		
		x	x			x	x				x			x													
			x				x				x	x	x						x					x	x	x	
	x															x	x		x								
	x										x																
		x		x		x	x					x					x	x		x		x		x	x	x	
	x						x				x			x											x		
	x	x					x				x	x		x	x	x	x					x			x		
		x					x				x	x	x	x			x			x	x	x			x		
							x				x	x												x	x		
	x					x	x				x	x													x		
			x		x	x	x					x	x	x											x	x	
	x					x	x												x								
		x	x			x	x				x		x	x		x					x		x				

SECTION II

This section includes the same items as the previous section, but with a focus on permanent groups and organizations. The items below in italics are unique to this section.

Helping a Permanent Group or Organization Reach Agreement

CHAPTER	1: Techniques and Strategies	2: Conflict Assessment	3: Process Design	4: Convening	5: Use of Facilitators and Mediators	6: Representation	7: Managing Meetings	8: Producing Consensus
Step 1: Convening								
1.1 Determine Whether to Have a Consensus Building Dialogue	x	x	x	x	x		x	
1.2 Prepare a Written Conflict Assessment	x	x		x	x			
1.3 Identify Appropriate Representatives	x	x	x	x	x	x	x	
1.4 Locate Necessary Funding		x		x				
1.5 *Expect Greater Understanding of Prevailing Ground Rules*				x				
Step 2: Clarifying Responsibilities								
2.1 Clarify the Roles of Facilitators, Mediators, and Recorders	x			x	x		x	
2.2 Set Rules Regarding the Participation of Observers	x		x					
2.3 Set an Agenda and Ground Rules	x	x		x		x		
2.4 Assess Computer-Based Communication Options	x							
2.5 Establish a Mailing List								
2.6 *Expect Greater Acceptance of Legitimacy of Participants*	x							
2.7 *Expect Fewer Problems Clarifying & Allocating Responsibilities*			x					
Step 3: Deliberating								
3.1 Pursue Deliberations in a Constructive Fashion	x				x	x	x	
3.2 Separate Inventing From Committing	x				x			
3.3 Create Subcommittees and Seek Expert Advice	x				x	x		
3.4 Use a Single-Text Procedure	x							
3.5 Modify the Agenda and Ground Rules (if necessary)								
3.6 Complete the Deliberations	x				x			
3.7 *Build on Prior Relationships*	x							
Step 4: Deciding								
4.1 Try to Maximize Joint Gains	x				x			
4.2 Keep a Record	x						x	
4.3 *Expect Commitments to be Taken More Seriously*								
Step 5: Implementing Agreements								
5.1 Seek Ratification by Constituencies	x				x	x		
5.2 *Focus on Long-Term Relationships*					x	x		
Step 6: Organizational Learning and Development								
6.1 *Invest in Organizational Learning*					x		x	
6.2 *Invest in Organizational Development*					x		x	

9: Joint Fact-Finding	10: Use of Technology	11: Dealing With the Press	12: Handling Value Differences	13: Legal Issues	14: Implementing Agreements	15: Visioning	16: Intraorganizational Processes	17: Evaluating Consensus Building	CASE — 1: Schiphol Airport Expansion	2: Northern Oxford County Coalition	3: Chelsea Charter Process	4: Affordable Housing Mediation	5: San Francisco Estuary Project	6: New York Bight Initiative	7: Massachusetts Military Reservation	8: RuleNet: Online Mediation	9: Native American Reg-Neg	10: Planning on Haida Gwaii	11: Chattanooga Visioning Process	12: Community-Based Planning	13: Catron County Citizens' Group	14: HIV/AIDS Policies in Colorado	15: Common Ground on Abortion	16: Organizational Trauma Recovery	17: Levi Strauss & Company
	X					X	X																	X	X
		X				X	X	X																	X
	X					X	X	X																X	X
																									X
							X																	X	
	X			X		X	X																		
	X	X				X	X																		
		X				X	X																	X	X
	X																								
	X																								
						X	X																	X	
						X	X																		X
	X			X		X	X	X																X	
X						X																			
X	X					X																			
	X					X																			
						X																			
	X					X																			
						X	X																	X	
		X				X	X	X																	
	X					X	X																		
						X	X																		
	X	X				X	X	X																	X
		X				X																		X	
						X	X	X																X	X
						X	X	X																X	X

SECTION III

Dealing with the Barriers to Consensus Building

	CHAPTER	1: Techniques and Strategies	2: Conflict Assessment	3: Process Design	4: Convening	5: Use of Facilitators and Mediators	6: Representation	7: Managing Meetings	8: Producing Consensus
Step 1: Convening									
7.0 Respond to Disruptive Behavior							x		
8.0 Accept an Advisory Role If That Is All That Is Allowed		x	x						
9.0 Clarify the Presumed Liability of the Participants									
10.0 Clarify Confidentiality Arrangements									
11.0 Clarify Legal Obligations, If the Participants Are Simultaneously Involved in Pending Litigation									

9: Joint Fact-Finding	10: Use of Technology	11: Dealing With the Press	12: Handling Value Differences	13: Legal Issues	14: Implementing Agreements	15: Visioning	16: Intraorganizational Processes	17: Evaluating Consensus Building	CASE	1: Schiphol Airport Expansion	2: Northern Oxford County Coalition	3: Chelsea Charter Process	4: Affordable Housing Mediation	5: San Francisco Estuary Project	6: New York Bight Initiative	7: Massachusetts Military Reservation	8: RuleNet: Online Mediation	9: Native American Reg-Neg	10: Planning on Haida Gwaii	11: Chattanooga Visioning Process	12: Community-Based Planning	13: Catron County Citizens' Group	14: HIV/AIDS Policies in Colorado	15: Common Ground on Abortion	16: Organizational Trauma Recovery	17: Levi Strauss & Company
				x	x					x					x		x						x			
					x			x										x								
				x																						
					x																		x			
					x											x										

parties or their organizations expect to interact indefinitely, such as the board of directors of a company or the members of a city council. Even if the participants change (and they surely will over time), everyone knows that whether they personally stay involved or not, others who come after them will have to live with the impact of what occurred and will be asked to take responsibility for the long-term interest of the organization.

Section II covers the same five steps as Section I but highlights several important differences between ad hoc and permanent situations. Also, a sixth step is added, when groups are ongoing, to take account of the need to capture whatever has been learned so that the organization can continue to improve.

Section III of the guide anticipates several serious obstacles to consensus building and suggests procedures for handling them, regardless of whether the participants are involved in an ad hoc or a permanent interaction.

■ Section I: Helping an Ad Hoc Assembly Reach Agreement

We have identified five steps in the consensus building process: convening, clarifying responsibilities, deliberating, deciding, and implementing agreements. The key problems for ad hoc assemblies (as opposed to permanent entities) are organizational. Selecting the relevant stakeholders, finding individuals who can represent those interests effectively, getting agreement on ground rules and an agenda, and securing funding are particularly difficult when the participants have no shared history and may have few, if any, interests in common.

Step 1: Convening

1.1 Initiate a Discussion about Whether to Have a Consensus Building Dialogue.

Every consensus building effort needs to be initiated by someone or some group in a position to bring the key stakeholders together.

1.2 *Prepare a Written Conflict Assessment.*

1.2.1 Assign responsibility for preparing the conflict assessment. Responsibility for preparing a written conflict assessment should be assigned to a neutral party. A contract for this work should be made between the convening entity and a neutral assessor, typically someone with facilitation or mediation expertise. The convenor should consult informally with other key parties in making the selection of a qualified conflict assessor.

1.2.2 Identify a first circle of essential participants. The convenor and the conflict assessor should identify the obvious categories of stakeholders with an interest in the issue or dispute, as well as individuals or organizations who can represent those views. These are the individuals who should be interviewed, preferably in person, at the outset of a conflict assessment. Interviewees should receive a promise that nothing they say will be attributed to them or their organizations, orally or in writing.

1.2.3 Identify a second circle of suggested participants. The first set of interviewees in a conflict assessment process should be asked to help identify a second round of individuals or organizations who might be able to contribute to or in some way block a consensus building effort. These individuals and organizations should be interviewed in the same manner as the first circle of participants.

1.2.4 Complete initial interviews. After individuals are interviewed as part of a conflict assessment, they ought to be given an opportunity to review a written summary of what the assessor thinks they have said.

1.2.5 Prepare a draft conflict assessment. A draft conflict assessment ought to include a clear categorization of all the relevant stakeholders, a summary of the interests and concerns of each category (without attribution to any individual or organization), and—given the results of the interviews—a proposal as to whether the assessor thinks it is worth going forward with a consensus building process. If the assessor believes such a process should be organized, he or she also ought to recommend a possible agenda, timetable, and budget for the process.

1.2.6 **Prepare a final conflict assessment.** Every interviewee ought to receive a copy of the draft conflict assessment and be given adequate time to offer comments and suggestions. The assessor ought to use this period as an occasion to modify the conflict assessment in a way that will allow all the key stakeholders to agree to attend at least an organizational meeting, if a recommendation to go forward is accepted by the convening entity. If key stakeholding groups refuse to participate, the process should probably not go forward. The final conflict assessment ought to include an appendix listing the name of every individual and organization interviewed. In appropriate instances, especially those involving public agencies, the final conflict assessment ought to become a public document.

1.2.7 **Convene an organizational meeting to consider the recommendations of the conflict assessment.** Interviewees should be invited to attend the organizational meeting. If this would make the meeting too large, each category of stakeholders ought to be asked to identify spokespeople to represent their views.

1.3 If a Decision Is Made to Proceed, Identify Appropriate Representatives.

To be credible, a consensus building group must include participants representing the full range of interests and views relating to the issue or dispute. Stakeholder groups and organizations should be invited to identify their own spokespeople to take part in the consensus building process.

1.3.1 **Identify missing actors likely to affect the credibility of the process.** If a decision to proceed is made at the organizational meeting, everyone in attendance ought to review the makeup of the group and try to identify missing actors whose absence would likely affect the credibility of a consensus building process. Those in attendance (in response to invitations from the convening entity) should work together to find ways of identifying appropriate individuals to add to the group.

1.3.2 **Use facilitated caucusing, if necessary.** If the members of a stakeholder category are quite diffuse, or if representation (i.e., selection of a spokesperson) of one category of stakeholders is challenged by another, a process of facilitated caucuses should be initiated. At such sessions—either by invitation (from the convenor) or on an open basis—individuals or groups willing to represent a category of stakeholders can be selected by the relevant stakeholders. They should use supermajority voting (e.g., 65 percent) or select a representative by unanimous acclaim. It is often helpful to have a neutral facilitator or mediator organize and manage such caucusing sessions. Facilitated caucusing is the best way for a category of stakeholders to answer a charge made by others that their selection of a representative was flawed.

1.3.3 Use proxies to represent hard-to-represent groups. If the participants in a consensus building process decide that it is important to find a way to represent a hard-to-represent or diffuse group, they may decide to invite proxy individuals or organizations to represent those interests. Representation by proxy must be agreed on by all the other groups and individuals who agreed to participate, as must the selection of specific individuals or organizations who agree to accept such an assignment. Proxy representatives must agree to do their best to speak for a hard-to-represent category of stakeholders.

1.3.4 Identify possible alternate representatives. If a consensus building process is likely to extend over several months or years, participants may decide to appoint alternates to stand in for them on occasion. The role and responsibility of alternates should be carefully defined in writing. Alternates who attend on a regular basis, when their regular representative is also present, may be asked to play a less active role or to accept other restrictions on their involvement. Participants are responsible for keeping their alternates apprised of the substantive discussion and the practices of the deliberative body.

1.4 Locate the Necessary Funding.

There are almost always costs associated with convening, preparing a conflict assessment, and implementing a consensus building process, if that is what the stakeholders decide to do. Sometimes these costs can be subsumed within the existing budgets of the convenor and the participating stakeholders. Other times, funds have to be raised specifically to underwrite a consensus building effort.

Step 2: Clarifying Responsibilities

2.1 Clarify the Roles of Facilitators, Mediators, and Recorders.

2.1.1 Select and specify responsibilities of a facilitator or a mediator. If a trained facilitator or mediator is going to be asked to assist the parties in a consensus building effort, it is important to select an appropriate individual who is acceptable to all the key stakeholders. It is also important to clarify, in writing, the facilitator's or mediator's responsibilities to the group. Consensus building services can be provided by an individual or a team.

2.1.2 Select and specify the responsibilities of a recorder. A qualified recorder, if one is to be hired, must work in tandem with a facilitator or a mediator. A recorder also needs a written indication of his or her obligations to the group. Usually, the recorder captures a group discussion on flip charts and works with any other neutrals involved to produce draft meeting summaries. In general, written summaries of all group decisions, as well as highlights of the dialogue (i.e., points of agreement and disagreement), should be circulated after each meeting for group approval.

2.1.3 Form an executive committee. If there are more than two categories of stakeholders involved in a consensus building effort (e.g., environmentalists, business interests, and unions), it is useful to appoint an executive committee or steering committee. Such a committee should be composed of one person selected by each major category of stakeholders and should be responsible for making decisions between meetings, approving the allocation of funds to support the effort, and being available to the facilitator or the mediator if logistical decisions must be made between meetings.

2.1.4 Consider appointing a chair. Even if a facilitator or a mediator is involved, it is helpful to appoint a chair (either of the executive committee or of the full assembly). This position can rotate if the dialogue goes on for an extended period. The primary responsibility of the chair is to represent the process to the world at large. It is also appropriate to assign this function to the mediator or the facilitator and to forgo the appointment of a chair.

2.2 *Set Rules Regarding the Participation of Observers.*

Some consensus building processes will proceed on a confidential basis, depending on the content of the discussions. Many will proceed in a very public way. If sessions are open to the public, the rights and obligations of observers should be spelled out in writing as part of the ground rules endorsed by the participants. It is not inappropriate to allow observers a brief comment period at the end of some or all formal sessions. In some instances, uninvited observers may even be offered a larger role. It is crucial that rules governing the participation of observers be posted prior to any and all meetings and that they be enforced consistently by the facilitator, mediator, or chair. It is also important to take account of legal requirements regarding the use of closed meetings when public officials are involved.

2.3 *Set an Agenda and Ground Rules.*

2.3.1 **Get agreement on the range of issues to be discussed.** If the agenda for a consensus building process is drawn too narrowly, some potential participants may have a good reason not to come to the table. If it is drawn too broadly, other participants will become discouraged, and may drop out, because the task facing the group seems overwhelming. While it is possible to add issues along the way (in response to new developments in the dialogue) and with the agreement of the full group, it is important to get concurrence on a sufficiently rich but manageable agenda at the outset. The completion of a conflict assessment, based on confidential interviews, is the best way to pinpoint the most important items to include on a consensus building agenda.

2.3.2 **Specify a timetable.** It is important to be realistic about the amount of time it will take for a group that is not used to working together to reach agreement on the items to include on a complex work agenda. At the outset, a great deal of a group's time is usually spent clarifying procedural matters. Under such circumstances, it is often necessary to "go slow to go fast." That is, it is not a good idea to rush through early procedural matters to get to the most difficult issues on the agenda. Early exchanges on peripheral issues may offer a good opportunity to begin building relationships and establishing trust. Success along these lines will provide a foundation on which the group can build. It is important for the full group to participate in setting a realistic timetable. In some instances, a group might be forced to set a target date for completion, and then build a work plan that fits that timetable.

2.3.3 **Finalize procedural ground rules.** The final version of the conflict assessment should contain a set of suggested ground rules. These should address procedural concerns raised in the interviews undertaken by the assessor. The suggested ground rules should be reviewed and ratified at the opening organizational meeting. Most ground rules for consensus building cover a range of topics including (a) the rights and responsibilities of participants, (b) behavioral guidelines that participants will be expected to follow, (c) rules governing interaction with the media, (d) decision-making procedures, and (e) strategies for handling disagreement and ensuring implementation of an agreement if one is reached.

2.3.4 **Require all participants to sign the ground rules.** At the outset of any consensus building process, every participant should be expected to sign the ground rules agreed to by the group. Copies of these ground rules should be sent directly to every organization, group, or department that has designated a representative to participate in the process. Observers should be asked to sign the ground rules before they are allowed to attend meetings—even those open to the public.

2.3.5 **Clarify the extent to which precedents are or are not being set.** One of the reasons people engage in consensus building efforts is to formulate tailored solutions to whatever problem, issue, or dispute they face. It is important that the participants in these processes feel free to generate plans or solutions that fit their unique circumstances. If everyone agrees that no precedent will be set, it is usually easier to convince reluctant groups or organizations to participate. Moreover, this allows future consensus building processes to proceed unimpeded.

2.4 *Assess Computer-Based Communication Options.*

Participants must determine how computer technologies will be used during deliberations and create e-mail mailing lists, Web-based conferencing capabilities, and listservs as needed. Assess participant access to computers and Internet connections and respond appropriately to any disparities in technological capacity that exist among stakeholders.

2.5 *Establish a Mailing List.*

Once a consensus building process is under way, some groups or individuals eligible to participate may decide not to attend on a regular basis, or not to participate at all. These individuals, as well as any other interested but nonparticipating stakeholders, should be added to a mailing list so that they can receive either periodic progress reports or regular meeting summaries.

Step 3: Deliberating

3.1 *Pursue Deliberations in a Constructive Fashion.*

3.1.1 **Express concerns in an unconditionally constructive manner.** It is important to maintain a problem-solving orientation, even in the face of strong differences and personal antagonism. It is in every participant's best interest to behave in a fashion he or she would like others to follow. Concerns or disagreement should be expressed in an unconditionally constructive manner. That is, there should be a premium on reason-giving and explanation. Those who disagree with the direction in which the discussion is headed should always explain the basis for their disagreement.

3.1.2 **Never trade interests for relationships.** No one in a consensus building process should be pressed to give up the pursuit of his or her best interests in response to the "feelings" or the "best interests" of the group. Thus, no one should be asked to give up his or her own interests to ensure harmony or the success of the process.

3.1.3 Engage in active listening. Participants in every consensus building process should be encouraged (indeed, instructed, if necessary) to engage in what is known as active listening: the process of checking to be sure that communications are being heard as intended.

3.1.4 Disagree without being disagreeable. Participants in every consensus building process should be instructed to "disagree without being disagreeable." They should also avoid attacking the motives and character of others. Guidelines of this sort should probably be included in the group's written ground rules.

3.1.5 Strive for the greatest degree of transparency possible. To the greatest extent possible, consensus building processes should be transparent. That is, the group's mandate, its agenda and ground rules, the list of participants and the groups or interests they are representing, the proposals they are considering, the decision rules they have adopted, their finances, and their final report should, at an appropriate time, be open to scrutiny by anyone affected by the group's recommendations.

3.2 *Separate Inventing from Committing.*

3.2.1 Strive to invent options for mutual gain. The goals of a consensus building process ought to be to create as much value as possible and to ensure that whatever value is created be divided in ways that take account of all relevant considerations. The key to creating value is to invent options for mutual gain. This is best done by separating inventing from committing—engaging in cooperative behaviors that "make the pie larger" before giving in to competitive pressures "to get the most for one's self."

3.2.2 Emphasize packaging. The best way to create value is by packaging multiple issues and subissues. If parties "trade" items or options that they value differently and bundle them together properly, they ought to be able to help most, if not all, stakeholders exceed the value of their most likely "walk away" option. If that is not possible, then no agreement is likely; indeed, agreement may well be inappropriate.

3.2.3 **Test options by playing the game of "what if?"** The most important technique for creating value is the exploration of options and packages using "what if?" questions. Sometimes these are best asked by a neutral party (and sometimes they may need to be asked confidentially) before stakeholders will feel comfortable answering them.

3.3 *Create Subcommittees and Seek Expert Advice.*

3.3.1 **Formulate joint fact-finding procedures.** If left to their own devices, participants in a consensus building process will produce their own versions of the relevant facts (or technical data) consistent with their definition of the problem and their sense of how the problem or issue should be handled. This often leads to what is called *adversary science.* It is better if all participants can agree on the information that ought to be used to answer unanswered or contested questions. An agreement on joint fact-finding should specify (a) what information is sought, (b) how it should be generated (i.e., by whom and using which methods), and (c) how gaps or disagreements among technical sources will be handled. It is perfectly reasonable for there to be agreement on facts while substantial disagreement on how to interpret such facts remains.

3.3.2 **Identify expert advisers.** It is often helpful to supplement ad hoc consensus building discussions with input from expert advisers. Such individuals should be selected with the concurrence of the participants and in response to the needs of the group. Typically, neutral parties assisting the process should be in touch with expert advisers before, during, and after their involvement to ensure that they understand the objectives of the consensus building effort and that they offer their advice in a form that will be most helpful to the group.

3.3.3 **Organize drafting or joint fact-finding subcommittees.** Joint fact-finding should be handled by a subcommittee or a working group appointed by the full set of participants in a consensus building process. Fact-finding should be viewed as an opportunity to learn more about the issues under discussion; thus, not only the most technically sophisticated participants should be assigned to these subcommittees or working groups. Subcommittees should have a clear mandate. They should not be decision-making bodies; instead, they should bring information and alternative policy choices back to the full group.

3.3.4 Incorporate the work of subcommittees or expert advisers. The findings of subcommittees or expert advisers should be viewed as only one input into a consensus building process. Differences in interpretation as well as conflicting interests among the participants often mean that the work of subcommittees or expert advisers will not lead to agreement. It is important, nevertheless, to tap the best available sources of technical assistance.

3.4 Use a Single-Text Procedure.

3.4.1 Draft preliminary proposals. Often, the best way to focus a consensus building dialogue is to provide a set of preliminary proposals to focus the conversation. Each set of proposals should deal with an item on the agenda and present the widest possible range of ideas or options. Preliminary proposals can be prepared by the facilitator or the mediator. They can also be prepared by a proposal-drafting subcommittee that includes members of each key category of stakeholders. Preliminary proposals are meant to focus conversation, not end it.

3.4.2 Brainstorm. Brainstorming is an important step in a consensus building process. Whether undertaken by a subcommittee or the full group, brainstorming should seek to expand the range of proposals considered with regard to each agenda item. Brainstorming techniques should also be used to generate packages that incorporate trade-offs among agenda items.

3.4.3 Withhold criticism. The best way to encourage brainstorming is to adopt a formal ground rule that urges participants to withhold criticism when new options are suggested. The withholding of criticism should not be viewed as an indication of support or agreement; it is, however, the best way to encourage creative thinking.

3.4.4 Avoid attribution and individual authorship. Consensus building is best viewed as a group enterprise. When individuals or a single group insists on claiming authorship of a particular proposal (i.e., in an effort to enhance its standing with its own constituents), they are likely to provoke criticism or counterproposals. Consensus is much more likely to emerge if participants avoid attributing or claiming authorship of specific ideas or packages.

3.4.5 Consolidate improvements in the text. As the dialogue proceeds, participants should focus on "improving" a consolidated single text prepared by a drafting subcommittee or a neutral party. Avoid competing texts that seek to maximize the interests of one or just a few parties. When changes to a text are made, do not indicate where they originated. All revisions to the single text need to be acceptable to the group as a whole.

3.4.6 Search for contingent options. As the discussion proceeds, participants should search for ways of bridging differences by suggesting contingent agreements. Using an "if . . . then" format is likely to be helpful. That is, if a set of participants is opposed to the prevailing draft of a recommendation or a consolidated agreement, then the set of participants should suggest the changes necessary for it to accept that proposal.

3.5 Modify the Agenda and Ground Rules (if necessary).

3.5.1 Reconsider the responsibilities, obligations, and powers of sponsoring agencies and organizations. During the course of a consensus building process, it is not inappropriate to revisit the assignment of responsibilities and obligations of sponsoring agencies and organizations set by the participants at the outset. Changes should be made only if consensus can be reached on suggested revisions.

3.5.2 Consider the obligations and powers of late arrivals. During the course of a consensus building process, as unanticipated issues or concerns arise, it may be desirable to add new participants. With the concurrence of the group, representatives of new stakeholding groups—attracted or recruited because of the emerging agreement or shifts in the agenda—can be added. The obligations and powers of latecomers (especially with regard to requesting that issues already covered be reconsidered) should be considered by the full group upon the arrival of new participants. Changes in the agenda or the ground rules should be made only with the concurrence of all parties.

3.6 Complete the Deliberations.

Step 4: Deciding

4.1 Try to Maximize Joint Gains.

4.1.1 Test the scope and depth of any agreement. The results of every effort to maximize joint gains should be continuously assessed. This is best accomplished by having a neutral party ask whether the participants can think of any "improvements" to the proposed agreement. In addition, it is important to ask whether each representative is prepared to "sell" the proposal to his or her constituents and whether each can "live with" the group's recommendation.

4.1.2 Use straw polls. Even groups that agree to operate by consensus may find nonbinding straw polls helpful for testing the scope of agreement along the way. Each time such polling devices are employed, it is important to explain that the results are intended to explore the scope of agreement that has or has not been reached, and not to seek commitments.

4.1.3 Seek unanimity. It is appropriate to seek unanimous agreement within the time frame set by a consensus building group.

4.1.4 Settle for an overwhelming level of support. It is appropriate to settle for an overwhelming level of support for final recommendations or decisions, if unanimity cannot be achieved within the agreed-on time frame. While it is not possible to specify an exact percentage of support that would constitute an overwhelming endorsement, it would be hard to make a claim for consensus having been reached if fewer than 80 percent of the participants in a group were not in agreement.

4.1.5 Make every effort to satisfy the concerns of holdouts. Prior to making its final recommendations or decisions, a consensus building group should make one final attempt to satisfy the concerns of any remaining holdout(s). This can be done by asking those who can't live with the final recommendations or decisions to suggest modifications to the package or tentative agreement that would make it acceptable to them without making it less attractive to anyone who has already expressed support for it.

4.2 Keep a Record.

4.2.1 Maintain a visual summary of key points of agreement and disagreement. It is important for a recorder to keep a written record of a consensus building dialogue. This is best done in a form that is visually accessible to all participants throughout the process. It is not necessary to keep traditional minutes of all discussions as long as key points of agreement and disagreement are captured in writing.

4.2.2 Review written versions of all decisions before they are finalized. A written draft of the final report of a consensus building process should be circulated to all participants before they are asked to indicate support or opposition. Initial drafting responsibility may be allocated to the neutral, but ultimately all parties must take responsibility for a final report if one is produced.

4.2.3 Maintain a written summary of every discussion for review by all participants. A written summary of every formal group discussion should be kept, even after a final report is produced by a consensus building group. Such an archive can be important to the credibility of the group's recommendation and can help to clarify the group's intent should problems of interpretation arise later.

Step 5: Implementing Agreements

5.1 Seek Ratification by Constituencies.

5.1.1 Hold representatives responsible for canvassing constituent responses to a penultimate draft. The participants in a consensus building process should be asked to canvass the response of their constituents to the penultimate draft of the group's final report. Copies of the draft should be circulated with sufficient time for the members of the group or organization to let their representatives know how the report might be improved.

5.1.2 Hold representatives responsible for signing and committing to a final agreement in their own name. At the conclusion of a consensus building process, the participants should be asked to endorse the final report (if there is one). Representatives should be responsible for endorsing the proposal in their own names even if their organization or group is not able to commit collectively. A signature should be interpreted as a commitment to do everything possible to assist with implementation, if an agreement was reached.

5.1.3 Include the necessary steps to ensure that informal agreements are incorporated or adopted by whatever formal mechanisms are appropriate. Often, the results of a consensus building process are advisory. Sometimes they must be ratified by a set of elected or appointed officials. Any agreement resulting from a consensus building process should contain within it a clear statement of the steps that will be taken (and who they will be taken by) to ensure that the informal agreement will be incorporated or adopted by whatever formal means are appropriate. For example, informally negotiated agreements can be stipulated as additional conditions when a permit is granted by a government agency or the head of an organization. This must be done according to the rules of the permitting agency or the organization.

5.1.4 Incorporate appropriate monitoring procedures. Negotiated agreements must often be monitored to ensure effective implementation. Responsibilities and methods for overseeing implementation should be specified in the written report of any consensus building group.

5.1.5 Include reopener and dispute resolution procedures. Any agreement reached by a consensus building group should include within it a mechanism by which the participants can be reassembled if a change in circumstances or a failure on the part of one or more participants to live up to their commitments suggests that another meeting is necessary. Appropriate dispute resolution procedures (and ways of activating them) should be described in the agreement or report.

5.1.6 Evaluate. Even in an ad hoc situation, it is important for each participant to learn all that he or she can—both procedurally and substantively—about what was attempted and what was accomplished. Each participating individual and organization should be encouraged to reflect on what ought to be handled differently "next time."

■ *Section II: Helping a Permanent Group or Organization Reach Agreement*

The same five consensus building steps apply when dealing with permanent groups, although there is a sixth step—organizational learning—that needs to be emphasized. Permanent groups and organizations are likely to have well-established decision-making procedures. This can be an advantage in that less time should be needed to reach agreement on how the group should operate. At the same time, resistance to change may be a new source of difficulty. An organization that has historically operated in a top-down management style may have a hard time adapting to a consensus building approach. A shared commitment to the long-term well-being of the organization, however, can provide common ground on which to build.

This section is essentially a repeat of Section I, except that new guidance relevant to permanent groups and organizations has been added. This new text, *which appears in italics,* highlights the differences between building consensus in permanent organizations and in ad hoc assemblies.

Step 1: Convening

1.1 Initiate a Discussion about Whether to Have a Consensus Building Dialogue.

Every consensus building effort needs to be initiated by someone or some group in a position to bring the key stakeholders together. *In a single, permanent organization, there is likely to be less of a need to convince stakeholders to participate in a consensus building process, or, at the very least, less work involved in doing so. Especially in organizations with a top-down management style, an invitation to participate will be taken seriously by almost everyone invited. There is also likely to be less of a need to establish the convenor's legitimacy.*

1.2 Prepare a Written Conflict Assessment.

In a single, permanent organization, there will be less of a need to undertake a full-fledged conflict assessment. It may be possible, in fact, for an inside convenor to preempt the need for a formal conflict assessment and to rely instead on preliminary conversations with key stakeholders as a basis for proceeding. In permanent organizations that are alliances or partnerships involving numerous separate organizations, however, consensus building efforts probably require a conflict assessment similar to those used by ad hoc assemblies and described below.

1.2.1 Assign responsibility for preparing the conflict assessment. Responsibility for preparing a written conflict assessment should be assigned to a neutral party. A contract for this work should be made between the convening entity and a neutral assessor, typically someone with facilitation or mediation expertise. The convenor should consult informally with other key parties in making the selection of a qualified conflict assessor.

1.2.2 Identify a first circle of essential participants. The convenor and the conflict assessor should identify the obvious categories of stakeholders with an interest in the issue or dispute, as well as individuals or organizations who can represent those views. These are the individuals who should be interviewed, preferably in person, at the outset of a conflict assessment. Interviewees should receive a promise that nothing they say will be attributed to them or their organizations, orally or in writing.

1.2.3 Identify a second circle of suggested participants. The first set of interviewees in a conflict assessment process should be asked to help identify a second round of individuals or organizations who might be able to contribute to or in some way block a consensus building effort. These individuals and organizations should be interviewed in the same manner as the first circle of participants.

1.2.4 Complete initial interviews. After individuals are interviewed as part of a conflict assessment, they ought to be given an opportunity to review a written summary of what the assessor thinks they have said.

1.2.5 Prepare a draft conflict assessment. A draft conflict assessment ought to include a clear categorization of all the relevant stakeholders, a summary of the interests and concerns of each category (without attribution to any individual or organization), and—given the results of the interviews—a proposal as to whether or not the assessor thinks it is worth going forward with a consensus building process. If the assessor believes such a process should be organized, he or she also ought to recommend a possible agenda, timetable, and budget for the process.

1.2.6 Prepare a final conflict assessment. Every interviewee ought to receive a copy of the draft conflict assessment and be given adequate time to offer comments and suggestions. The assessor ought to use this period as an occasion to modify the conflict assessment in a way that will allow all the key stakeholders to agree to attend at least an organizational meeting, if a recommendation to go forward with consensus building is accepted by the convening entity. If key stakeholders refuse to participate, the process should probably not go forward. The final conflict assessment ought to include an appendix listing the name of every individual and organization interviewed. In appropriate instances, especially those involving public agencies, the final conflict assessment ought to become a public document.

1.2.7 Convene an organizational meeting to consider the recommendations of the conflict assessment. Interviewees should be invited to attend the organizational meeting. If this would make the meeting too large, each category of stakeholders ought to be asked to identify spokespeople to represent their views.

1.3 If a Decision Is Made to Proceed, Identify Appropriate Representatives.

To be credible, a consensus building group must include participants representing the full range of interests and views relating to the issue or dispute. Stakeholder groups and organizations should be invited to identify their own spokespeople to take part in the consensus building process. *In permanent organizations, it ought to be more obvious who the stakeholders are and who can represent them. With greater clarity about who ought to participate, it ought to take much less time to initiate a consensus building process.*

1.3.1 Identify missing actors likely to affect the credibility of the process. If a decision to proceed is made at the organizational meeting, everyone in attendance ought to review the makeup of the group and try to identify missing actors whose absence would be likely to affect the credibility of a consensus building process. Those in attendance (in response to invitations from the convenor) should work together to identify ways of identifying appropriate individuals to add to the group.

1.3.2 Use facilitated caucusing, if necessary. If the members of a stakeholder category are quite diffuse, or if representation (i.e., selection of a spokesperson) of one category of stakeholders is challenged by another, a process of facilitated caucuses should be initiated. At such sessions—either by invitation (from the convenor) or on an open basis—individuals or groups willing to represent a category of stakeholders can be selected by the relevant stakeholders. They should use supermajority voting (e.g., 65 percent) or select a representative by unanimous acclaim. It is often helpful to have a neutral facilitator or mediator organize and manage such caucusing sessions. Facilitated caucusing is the best way for a category of stakeholders to answer a charge made by others that their selection of a representative was flawed.

1.3.3 **Use proxies to represent hard-to-represent groups.** If the participants in a consensus building process decide that it is important to find a way to represent a hard-to-represent or diffuse group, they may decide to invite proxy individuals or organizations to represent those interests. Representation by proxy must be agreed on by all the other groups and individuals who agreed to participate, as must the selection of specific individuals or organizations who agree to accept such an assignment. Proxy representatives must agree to do their best to "speak for" a hard-to-represent category of stakeholders.

1.3.4 **Identify possible alternate representatives.** If a consensus building process is likely to extend over several months or years, participants may decide to appoint alternates to stand in for them on occasion. The role and responsibility of alternates should be carefully defined in writing. Alternates who attend on a regular basis, when their regular representative is also present, may be asked to play a less active role or to accept other restrictions on their involvement. Participants are responsible for keeping their alternates apprised of the substantive discussion and the practices of the deliberative body.

1.4 *Locate the Necessary Funding.*

There are almost always costs associated with convening, preparing a conflict assessment, and implementing a consensus building process, if that is what the stakeholders decide to do. Sometimes these costs can be subsumed within the existing budgets of the convenor and the participating stakeholders. Other times, funds have to be raised specifically to underwrite a consensus building effort.

1.5 *Expect Greater Understanding of Prevailing Ground Rules.*

In permanent organizations, the parties ought to be familiar with the ways in which decisions are made within the group. If consensus building represents a shift in the style of decision making, it should nevertheless be easier to define and implement new consensus building ground rules.

Step 2: Clarifying Responsibilities

2.1 Clarify the Roles of Facilitators, Mediators, and Recorders.

In permanent organizations (both those that involve a single organization and those that are assemblies or partnerships), there is likely to be less interest in using the services of external professional neutrals, although this is changing. While all the benefits that neutrals can provide (enumerated below) are equally applicable, the participants in permanent organizations usually feel as if they know each other well enough that they can handle the process of consensus building on their own. When relationships have eroded, however, the use of neutral assistance should be seriously considered. It may be that permanent organizations are in even greater need of such help than ad hoc assemblies because the parties know each other too well.

2.1.1 Select and specify responsibilities of a facilitator or a mediator. If a trained facilitator or mediator is going to be asked to assist the parties in a consensus building effort, it is important to select an appropriate individual who is acceptable to all the key stakeholders. It is also important to clarify, in writing, the facilitator's or mediator's responsibilities to the group. Consensus building services can be provided by an individual or a team.

2.1.2 Select and specify the responsibilities of a recorder. A qualified recorder, if one is to be hired, must work in tandem with a facilitator or a mediator. A recorder also needs a written indication of his or her obligations to the group. Usually, the recorder captures a group discussion on flip charts and works with any other neutrals involved to produce draft meeting summaries. In general, written summaries of all group decisions, as well as highlights of the dialogue (i.e., points of agreement and disagreement), should be circulated after each meeting for group approval.

2.1.3 Form an executive committee. If there are more than two categories of stakeholders involved in a consensus building effort (e.g., environmentalists, business interests, and unions), it is useful to appoint an executive committee or steering committee. Such a committee should be composed of one person selected by each major category of stakeholders and should be responsible for making decisions between meetings, approving the allocation of funds to support the effort, and being available to the facilitator or the mediator if logistical decisions must be made between meetings.

2.1.4 **Consider appointing a chair.** Even if a facilitator or a mediator is involved, it is helpful to appoint a chair (either of the executive committee or of the full assembly). This position can rotate if the dialogue goes on for an extended period. The primary responsibility of the chair is to represent the process to the world at large. It is also appropriate to assign this function to the mediator or the facilitator and to forgo the appointment of a chair.

2.2 Set Rules Regarding the Participation of Observers.

Some consensus building processes will proceed on a confidential basis, depending on the content of the discussions. Many will proceed in a very public way. If sessions are open to the public, the rights and obligations of observers should be spelled out in writing as part of the ground rules endorsed by the participants. It is not inappropriate to allow observers a brief comment period at the end of some or all formal sessions. In some instances, uninvited observers may even be offered a larger role. It is crucial that rules governing the participation of observers be posted prior to any and all meetings and that they be enforced consistently by the facilitator, mediator, or chair. It is also important to take account of legal requirements regarding the use of closed meetings when public officials are involved.

2.3 Set an Agenda and Ground Rules.

2.3.1 **Get agreement on the range of issues to be discussed.** If the agenda for a consensus building process is drawn too narrowly, some potential participants may have a good reason not to come to the table. If it is drawn too broadly, other participants will become discouraged, and may drop out, because the task facing the group seems overwhelming. While it is possible to add issues along the way (in response to new developments in the dialogue) and with the agreement of the full group, it is important to get concurrence on a sufficiently rich but manageable agenda at the outset. The completion of a conflict assessment, based on confidential interviews, is the best way to pinpoint the most important items to include on a consensus building agenda.

2.3.2 **Specify a timetable.** It is important to be realistic about the amount of time it will take for a group that is not used to working together to reach agreement on the items to include on a complex work agenda. At the outset, a great deal of a group's time is usually spent clarifying procedural matters. Under such circumstances it is often necessary to "go slow to go fast." That is, it is not a good idea to rush through early procedural matters to get to the most difficult issues on the agenda. *This is as true for permanent groups that are used to consensus building approaches as it is for ad hoc groups.* Early exchanges on peripheral issues may offer a good opportunity to begin building relationships and establishing trust. Success along these lines will provide a foundation on which the group can build. It is important for the full group to participate in setting a realistic timetable. In some instances, a group might be forced to set a target date for completion, and then build a work plan that fits that timetable.

2.3.3 **Finalize procedural ground rules.** The final version of the conflict assessment should contain a set of suggested ground rules. These should address procedural concerns raised in the interviews undertaken by the assessor. The suggested ground rules should be reviewed and ratified at the opening organizational meeting. Most ground rules for consensus building cover a range of topics including (a) the rights and responsibilities of participants, (b) behavioral guidelines that participants will be expected to follow, (c) rules governing interaction with the media, (d) decision-making procedures, and (e) strategies for handling disagreement and ensuring implementation of an agreement if one is reached.

2.3.4 **Require all participants to sign the ground rules.** At the outset of any consensus building process, every participant should be expected to sign the ground rules agreed to by the group. Copies of these ground rules should be sent directly to every organization, group, or department that has designated a representative to participate in the process. Observers should be asked to sign the ground rules before they are allowed to attend meetings—even those open to the public.

2.3.5 Clarify the extent to which precedents are or are not being set. One of the reasons people engage in consensus building efforts is to formulate tailored solutions to whatever problem, issue, or dispute they face. It is important that the participants in these processes feel free to generate plans or solutions that fit their unique circumstances. If everyone agrees that no precedent will be set, it is usually easier to convince reluctant groups or organizations to participate. Moreover, this allows future consensus building processes to proceed unimpeded.

2.4 *Assess Computer-Based Communication Options.*

Participants must determine how computer technologies will be used during deliberations and create e-mail mailing lists, Web-based conferencing capabilities, and listservs as needed. Assess participant access to computers and Internet connections and respond appropriately to any disparities in technological capacity that exist among stakeholders.

2.5 *Establish a Mailing List.*

Once a consensus building process is under way, some groups or individuals eligible to participate may decide not to attend on a regular basis, or not to participate at all. These individuals, as well as any other interested but nonparticipating stakeholders, should be added to a mailing list so that they can receive either periodic progress reports or regular meeting summaries.

2.6 *Expect Greater Acceptance of the Legitimacy of Other Participants.*

In permanent organizations, there is likely to be greater acceptance of the right of other participants to be part of a consensus building process. The fact that stakeholders have been invited or designated by the leadership of an organization to participate in a problem-solving group is usually sufficient to establish their bona fides.

2.7 *Expect Less of a Problem Clarifying and Allocating Responsibilities.*

If there is confusion in a permanent organization about the assignment of responsibilities within a consensus building process (as in Steps 2.1.1–2.1.4) or the operating methods the group will use (as in Steps 2.3.1–2.3.5), these are relatively easy for the leadership of the organization to settle by exercising the prerogatives of management.

Step 3: Deliberating

3.1 Pursue Deliberations in a Constructive Fashion.

3.1.1 Express concerns in an unconditionally constructive manner. It is important to maintain a problem-solving orientation, even in the face of strong differences and personal antagonism. It is in every participant's best interest to behave in a fashion he or she would like others to follow. Concerns or disagreement should be expressed in an unconditionally constructive manner. That is, there should be a premium on reason-giving and explanation. Those who disagree with the direction in which the discussion is headed should always explain the basis for their disagreement.

3.1.2 Never trade interests for relationships. No one in a consensus building process should be pressed to give up the pursuit of his or her best interests in response to the "feelings" or the "best interests" of the group. Thus, no one should be asked to give up his or her own interests to ensure harmony or the success of the process.

3.1.3 Engage in active listening. Participants in every consensus building process should be encouraged (indeed, instructed, if necessary) to engage in what is known as active listening: the process of checking to be sure that communications are being heard as intended.

3.1.4 Disagree without being disagreeable. Participants in every consensus building process should be instructed to "disagree without being disagreeable." They should also avoid attacking the motives and character of others. Guidelines of this sort should probably be included in the group's written ground rules.

3.1.5 Strive for the greatest degree of transparency possible. To the greatest extent possible, consensus building processes should be transparent. That is, the group's mandate, its agenda and ground rules, the list of participants and the groups or interests they are representing, the proposals they are considering, the decision rules they have adopted, their finances, and their final report should, at an appropriate time, be open to scrutiny by anyone affected by the group's recommendations.

3.2 *Separate Inventing from Committing.*

3.2.1 Strive to invent options for mutual gain. The goals of a consensus building process ought to be to create as much value as possible and to ensure that whatever value is created be divided in ways that take account of all relevant considerations. The key to creating value is to invent options for mutual gain. This is best done by separating inventing from committing—engaging in cooperative behaviors that "make the pie larger" before giving in to competitive pressures "to get the most for one's self."

3.2.2 Emphasize packaging. The best way to create value is by packaging multiple issues and sub-issues. If parties "trade" items or options that they value differently and bundle them together properly, they ought to be able to help most, if not all, stakeholders exceed the value of their most likely "walk away" option. If that is not possible, then no agreement is likely; indeed, agreement may well be inappropriate.

3.2.3 Test options by playing the game of "what if?" The most important technique for creating value is the exploration of options and packages using "what if?" questions. Sometimes these are best asked by a neutral party (and sometimes they may need to be asked confidentially) before stakeholders will feel comfortable answering them.

3.3 Create Subcommittees and Seek Expert Advice.

3.3.1 Formulate joint fact-finding procedures. If left to their own devices, participants in a consensus building process will produce their own versions of the relevant facts (or technical data) consistent with their definition of the problem and their sense of how the problem or issue should be handled. This often leads to what is called *adversary science.* It is better if all participants can agree on the information that ought to be used to answer unanswered or contested questions. An agreement on joint fact-finding should specify (a) what information is sought, (b) how it should be generated (i.e., by whom and using which methods), and (c) how gaps or disagreements among technical sources will be handled. It is perfectly reasonable for there to be agreement on facts while substantial disagreement on how to interpret such facts remains.

3.3.2 Identify expert advisers. It is often helpful to supplement ad hoc consensus building discussions with input from expert advisers. Such individuals should be selected with the concurrence of the participants and in response to the needs of the group. Typically, neutral parties assisting the process should be in touch with expert advisers before, during, and after their involvement to ensure that they understand the objectives of the consensus building effort and that they offer their advice in a form that will be most helpful to the group.

3.3.3 Organize drafting or joint fact-finding subcommittees. Joint fact-finding should be handled by a subcommittee or a working group appointed by the full set of participants in a consensus building process. Fact-finding should be viewed as an opportunity to learn more about the issues under discussion; thus, not only the most technically sophisticated participants should be assigned to these subcommittees or working groups. Subcommittees should have a clear mandate. They should not be decision-making bodies; instead, they should bring information and alternative policy choices back to the full group.

3.3.4 Incorporate the work of subcommittees or expert advisers. The findings of subcommittees or expert advisers should be viewed as only one input into a consensus building process.

Differences in interpretation as well as conflicting interests among the participants often mean that the work of subcommittees or expert advisers will not lead to agreement. It is important, nevertheless, to tap the best available sources of technical assistance.

3.4 Use a Single-Text Procedure.

3.4.1 Draft preliminary proposals. Often, the best way to focus a consensus building dialogue is to provide a set of preliminary proposals to focus the conversation. Each set of proposals should deal with an item on the agenda and present the widest possible range of ideas or options. Preliminary proposals can be prepared by the facilitator or the mediator. They can also be prepared by a proposal drafting subcommittee that includes members of each key category of stakeholders. Preliminary proposals are meant to focus conversation, not end it.

3.4.2 Brainstorm. Brainstorming is an important step in a consensus building process. Whether undertaken by a subcommittee or the full group, brainstorming should seek to expand the range of proposals considered with regard to each agenda item. Brainstorming techniques should also be used to generate packages that incorporate trade-offs among agenda items.

3.4.3 Withhold criticism. The best way to encourage brainstorming is to adopt a formal ground rule that urges participants to withhold criticism when new options are suggested. The withholding of criticism should not be viewed as an indication of support or agreement; it is, however, the best way to encourage creative thinking.

3.4.4 Avoid attribution and individual authorship. Consensus building is best viewed as a group enterprise. When individuals or a single group insists on claiming authorship of a particular proposal (i.e., in an effort to enhance its standing with its own constituents), they are likely to provoke criticism or counterproposals. Consensus is much more likely to emerge if participants avoid attributing or claiming authorship of specific ideas or packages.

3.4.5 **Consolidate improvements in the text.** As the dialogue proceeds, participants should focus on "improving" a consolidated single text prepared by a drafting subcommittee or a neutral party. Avoid competing texts that seek to maximize the interests of one or just a few parties. When changes to a text are made, do not indicate where they originated. All revisions to the single text need to be acceptable to the group as a whole.

3.4.6 **Search for contingent options.** As the discussion proceeds, participants should search for ways of bridging differences by suggesting contingent agreements. Using an "if . . . then" format is likely to be helpful. That is, if a set of participants is opposed to the prevailing draft of a recommendation or a consolidated agreement, then the set of participants should suggest the changes necessary for it to accept that proposal.

3.5 Modify the Agenda and Ground Rules (if necessary).

3.5.1 **Reconsider the responsibilities, obligations, and powers of sponsoring agencies and organizations.** During the course of a consensus building process, it is not inappropriate to revisit the assignment of responsibilities and obligations of sponsoring agencies and organizations set by the participants at the outset. Changes should be made only if consensus can be reached on suggested revisions.

3.5.2 **Consider the obligations and powers of late arrivals.** During the course of a consensus building process, as unanticipated issues or concerns arise, it may be desirable to add new participants. With the concurrence of the group, representatives of new stakeholding groups—attracted or recruited because of the emerging agreement or shifts in the agenda—can be added. The obligations and powers of latecomers (especially with regard to requesting that issues already covered be reconsidered) should be considered by the full group upon the arrival of new participants. Changes in the agenda or the ground rules should be made only with the concurrence of all parties.

3.6 Complete the Deliberations.

3.7 Build on Prior Relationships.

3.7.1 *Discussions may be more effective because of prior relationships. It may be easier for participants in permanent organizations (of any kind) than those involved in ad hoc assemblies to adapt to the mutual-gains approach to negotiation. By appealing to shared interests (or obligations) and to the well-being of the larger organization of which they are all a part, a convenor or a facilitator can often help the participants inside a single organization proceed in a manner that enhances joint problem solving. Of course, there are dysfunctional relationships inside many single organizations that may make constructive deliberations difficult.*

3.7.2 *Experience with consensus building techniques ought to build up more quickly. In a permanent organization of any kind, experience with consensus building techniques ought to be more readily institutionalized than in ad hoc assemblies. Even if membership inside a single organization turns over rapidly, the "institutional memory" and the integration of new ways of working into the culture of the organization ought to occur more readily than in ad hoc assemblies.*

3.7.3 *The need to maintain long-term relationships will be clear. In permanent organizations, the parties ought to be more aware of the negative consequences of undercutting or destroying long-term relationships. Thus, it should be easier (at least in theory) to encourage adherence to the "rules" of constructive dialogue than in an ad hoc assembly.*

Step 4: Deciding

4.1 Try to Maximize Joint Gains.

4.1.1 **Test the scope and depth of any agreement.** The results of every effort to maximize joint gains should be continuously assessed. This is best accomplished by having a neutral party ask whether the participants can think of any "improvements" to the proposed agreement. In addition, it is important to ask whether each representative is prepared to "sell" the proposal to his or her constituents and whether each can "live with" the group's recommendation.

4.1.2 **Use straw polls.** Even groups that agree to operate by consensus may find nonbinding straw polls helpful for testing the scope of agreement along the way. Each time such polling devices are employed, it is important to explain that the results are intended to explore the scope of agreement that has or has not been reached, and not to seek commitments.

4.1.3 **Seek unanimity.** It is appropriate to seek unanimous agreement within the time frame set by a consensus building group.

4.1.4 **Settle for an overwhelming level of support.** It is appropriate to settle for an overwhelming level of support for final recommendations or decisions, if unanimity cannot be achieved within the agreed-on time frame. While it is not possible to specify an exact percentage of support that would constitute an overwhelming endorsement, it would be hard to make a claim for consensus having been reached if fewer than 80 percent of the participants in a group were not in agreement.

4.1.5 **Make every effort to satisfy the concerns of holdouts.** Prior to making its final recommendations or decisions, a consensus building group should make one final attempt to satisfy the concerns of any remaining holdout(s). This can be done by asking those who can't live with the final recommendations or decisions to suggest modifications to the package or tentative agreement that would make it acceptable to them without making it less attractive to anyone who has already expressed support for it.

4.2 *Keep a Record.*

4.2.1 **Maintain a visual summary of key points of agreement and disagreement.** It is important for a recorder to keep a written record of a consensus building dialogue. This is best done in a form that is visually accessible to all participants throughout the process. It is not necessary to keep traditional minutes of all discussions as long as key points of agreement and disagreement are captured in writing.

4.2.2 Review written versions of all decisions before they are finalized. A written draft of the final report of a consensus building process should be circulated to all participants before they are asked to indicate support or opposition. Initial drafting responsibility may be allocated to the neutral, but ultimately all parties must take responsibility for a final report if one is produced.

4.2.3 Maintain a written summary of every discussion for review by all participants. A written summary of every formal group discussion should be kept, even after a final report is produced by a consensus building group. Such an archive can be important to the credibility of the group's recommendation and can help to clarify the group's intent should problems of interpretation arise later.

4.3 Commitments Are More Likely to Be Taken Seriously.

In permanent organizations of any kind, commitments made by the parties are likely to be viewed with less skepticism than in ad hoc assemblies because long-term relationships are involved. There is also likely to be a sense, particularly in hierarchically run organizations, that top management will hold participants to their promises. While neither of these assumptions is true in all permanent organizations, it ought to be easier, in general, for parties to assume that commitments will be honored in this context. This, in turn, should make it easier to reach agreement.

4.3.1 Decision making should be easier. For a variety of reasons, it should be easier to reach consensus in a permanent organization than in an ad hoc or temporary assembly. Appealing to shared interests in the well-being of the organization should encourage holdouts and outliers to accept an emerging agreement. Presumably, participants who are part of the same organization are more likely to hold a set of common values than the total strangers who often find themselves having to work together in ad hoc assemblies. Thus, it should be easier to find reasons and arguments that carry weight. Pressure from top management to reach an agreement (often within a stipulated time frame) is also likely to push the parties toward agreement. In the context of a permanent organization, each participant must consider the possibility that he or she could be the "odd person out" the next time. The mere fact that there is likely to be a next time can create pressure to be part of whatever consensus emerges.

4.3.2 Informally negotiated agreements are likely to set a precedent. In permanent organizations, whether the parties desire it or not, informally negotiated agreements are more likely to set a precedent than in ad hoc assemblies. Even unwritten agreements are likely to "take on a life of their own" in a permanent organization and become part of the institutional memory. Thus, there may be less opportunity to craft unique responses in each situation when consensus building is initiated in a permanent organization.

Step 5: Implementing Agreements

5.1 Seek Ratification by Constituencies.

5.1.1 Hold representatives responsible for canvassing constituent responses to a penultimate draft. The participants in a consensus building process should be asked to canvass the response of their constituents to the penultimate draft of the group's final report. Copies of the draft should be circulated with sufficient time for the members of the group or organization to let their representatives know how the report might be improved.

5.1.2 Hold representatives responsible for signing and committing to a final agreement in their own name. At the conclusion of a consensus building process, the participants should be asked to endorse the final report (if there is one). Representatives should be responsible for endorsing the proposal in their own names even if their organization or group is not able to commit collectively. A signature should be interpreted as a commitment to do everything possible to assist with implementation, if an agreement was reached.

5.1.3 **Include the necessary steps to ensure that informal agreements are incorporated or adopted by whatever formal mechanisms are appropriate.** Often, the results of a consensus building process are advisory. Sometimes they must be ratified by a set of elected or appointed officials. Any agreement resulting from a consensus building process should contain within it a clear statement of the steps that will be taken (and who they will be taken by) to ensure that the informal agreement will be incorporated or adopted by whatever formal means are appropriate. For example, informally negotiated agreements can be stipulated as additional conditions when a permit is granted by a government agency or the head of an organization. This must be done according to the rules of the permitting agency or the organization.

5.1.4 **Incorporate appropriate monitoring procedures.** Negotiated agreements must often be monitored to ensure effective implementation. Responsibilities and methods for overseeing implementation should be specified in the written report of any consensus building group.

5.1.5 **Include reopener and dispute resolution procedures.** Any agreement reached by a consensus building group should include within it a mechanism by which the participants can be reassembled if a change in circumstances or a failure on the part of one or more participants to live up to their commitments suggests that another meeting is necessary. Appropriate dispute resolution procedures (and ways of activating them) should be described in the agreement or report.

5.1.6 **Evaluate.** Even in an ad hoc situation, it is important for each participant to learn all that he or she can—both procedurally and substantively—about what was attempted and what was accomplished. Each participating individual and organization should be encouraged to reflect on what ought to be handled differently "next time."

5.2 *Focus on Long-Term Relationships.*

5.2.1 *Long-term relationships increase the focus on implementation. In permanent organizations of all kinds, the likelihood that long-term relationships will be maintained increases the confidence of the parties that agreements will be implemented. While this may not be true in certain circumstances (e.g., when leadership has changed or the mission of an organization has been radically altered), there ought to be more willingness to rely on existing organizational "machinery" to achieve implementation of consensus agreements than in ad hoc assemblies where such arrangements often have to be constructed anew.*

5.2.2 Resistance to change may make implementation more difficult. *In permanent organizations of all kinds, entrenched ways of doing things may make it difficult to implement innovative consensus agreements. Internal incentives and controls may have to be altered as part of a negotiated agreement to increase the chances of effective implementation. This is especially true when new patterns of cooperation among departments or elements of an existing organization are required.*

5.2.3 Participants can use existing dispute resolution systems. *In permanent organizations of all kinds, consensus building agreements can and should build on and incorporate existing dispute resolutions systems.*

Step 6: Organizational Learning and Development

6.1 Invest in Organizational Learning.

For groups that will continue to work together, it is important to reflect collectively on what can be learned from each episode in the group's history. Time should be set aside, periodically, to determine which features of the group's activities have worked well and which have not. Organizational learning can be assisted by qualified neutral parties.

6.2 Invest in Organizational Development.

The lessons of organizational learning will not lead automatically to increased group capacity or improved decision making. Training and other organizational development efforts must be made. These will require the time and attention of all participants to be effective. Organizational development can be assisted by qualified outside consultants. It may also be necessary to identify or add a person inside a permanent organization who will take responsibility for ensuring proper attention to organizational learning and development.

■ *Section III: Dealing with the*
  Barriers to Consensus Building

Both ad hoc and permanent groups and organizations are likely to encounter certain predictable obstacles to consensus building. It is important that participants handle these obstacles with great care.

7.0 *Respond to Disruptive Behavior.*

If a participant or an observer of a consensus building process acts in a disruptive manner, the facilitator, mediator, or chair—whoever is managing the meeting—should remind that individual of the procedural ground rules he or she signed. If that does not result in the desired change in behavior, other participants with the closest ties to the disruptive party should be asked to intercede on behalf of the group. If that, too, fails to deter the disruptive individual, it may be advisable to adjourn the meeting temporarily and allow the group as a whole to convince the disruptive person to either alter his or her behavior or leave. If that fails as well, participants should not be afraid to contact the relevant civil authorities and ask for assistance in removing the individual involved.

8.0 *Accept an Advisory Role If That Is All That Is Allowed.*

In many instances, both in the public arena and in private organizations, consensus building groups are often granted only advisory and not decision-making authority. Formal decision making may still reside with elected or appointed officials or officers. This need not diminish the contribution that a consensus building effort can make. From the standpoint of a decision maker, it is always helpful to know which options or packages are likely to have the full support of all the relevant stakeholders. Moreover, if those with decision-making authority are involved in a consensus building effort—or, at least, kept apprised of its progress—they may feel sufficiently comfortable with the result to endorse it.

9.0 *Clarify the Presumed Liability of the Participants.*

If the participants in a consensus building process are dealing with confidential or proprietary information that could create legal liability, the scope of this liability should be stated in the invitation to participate extended by the convenor, and be explained in the ground rules governing the group's operations.

10.0 *Clarify Confidentiality Arrangements.*

There are legitimate reasons for consensus building processes, however public they may be, to adopt confidentiality arrangements. Both the arrangements and the rationale for adopting them should be spelled out in the group's ground rules. These arrangements must take account of open-meeting and sunshine laws if public officials are involved.

11.0 *Clarify Legal Obligations If the Participants Are Simultaneously Involved in Pending Litigation.*

If a consensus building effort is meant to resolve issues that are simultaneously the subject of litigation, the participants in the informal dialogue should be apprised (by counsel) of their legal rights and the impact that informal consensus building conversations might have on the legal proceedings, and vice versa. They should also approach the judge or adjudication body to talk about the best way of coordinating the two processes.

■ *References*

Fisher, R., Ury, W., & Patton, B. (1991). *Getting to yes: Negotiating agreement without giving in* (2nd ed.). New York: Penguin.

Lax, D. A., & Sebenius, J. K. (1986). *The manager as negotiator: Bargaining for cooperative and competitive gain.* New York: Free Press.

Raiffa, H. (1982). *The art and science of negotiation.* Cambridge, MA: Harvard University Press.

Robert, H. M. (1990). *Robert's rules of order: Newly revised* (9th ed.). New York: Scott, Foresman.

PART 2

HOW TO BUILD
CONSENSUS

1

CHOOSING APPROPRIATE CONSENSUS BUILDING TECHNIQUES AND STRATEGIES

───────────────────────────

■ *Susan Carpenter*

C onsensus building can be used to solve problems and make decisions in a wide variety of circumstances and settings. A consensus process can be organized around virtually any substantive topic and can involve a handful of people or several hundred. It can take place among representatives of multiple organizations, or among individuals within a single organization. In the public policy arena, consensus building can be used at any level of government, from the local up to the international level. Consensus-based approaches can be applied, for example, by project team members at a high-tech firm who must devise a plan for the rollout of their next product; board members at a non-profit organization seeking to set strategic goals for the next five years; a diverse set of stakeholders in a community who want to jointly establish guidelines for the preservation of historic buildings; or federal officials working with a multiplicity of interested parties to develop a new regulation for protecting air quality.

Because consensus-based approaches can be applied in so many different contexts and can involve such a diversity of issues and people, these approaches must be tailored to fit the unique circumstances of each situation. There is no single consensus building strategy that will work in all cases. Every process should be guided by general principles, such as inclusive participation and decisions made without voting, but they will differ with regard to the ground rules used, the use of facilitators or technical experts, the procedures by which parties educate each other and work toward agreements, the length of time involved, and so forth.

The purpose of this chapter is to help readers determine whether a consensus-based process is appropriate in a given situation, and then to think through the many choices that must be made when designing a consensus building effort to fit particular circumstances. The chapter begins with a discussion of *who* undertakes these tasks—who typically initiates a process and who designs it. The second section describes the various factors that need to be considered in determining whether consensus building is an appropriate method for solving a particular problem or making a specific decision. The third section looks at key contextual issues that must be assessed before designing a process (e.g., political dynamics, legal issues). The fourth and final section describes the steps that must be taken to structure a specific consensus-based process. Because this chapter introduces many topics relating to consensus building, it touches on issues that are discussed in more depth in the chapters and cases that follow. Cross-references are thus provided where appropriate.

■ *Who Initiates and Who Designs a Process*

"A basic tenet is that those involved in discussions must have a sense of ownership of the process."

Before describing the decisions that must be made in assessing a situation and designing a consensus process, we must first address the question of who makes these decisions. A basic tenet of consensus building is that those involved in discussions must have a sense of ownership of the process. At a minimum, therefore, stakeholders need to be consulted early, understand why a process is structured in a particular way, and feel that it is fair. Ideally, participants will work together to design a process. This section looks at the types of individuals who typically initiate a consensus-based effort and the ways that process design can be undertaken.

Who Can Initiate a Consensus Process

People initiate a consensus process when they contact stakeholders or contract with a mediator or facilitator to determine parties' willingness to work together to solve a problem. Process initiators are frequently people in positions of leadership, either from one of the groups directly affected by a problem or from an organization or person that holds a general interest in the issue. Occasionally, a neutral party may initiate a process by approaching stakeholders to introduce the idea of consensus building and explain how it might work. In Catron County, New Mexico, a consensus process to discuss divisive natural resource issues was initiated by a local physician, because he was concerned about the stress-related effects the controversies were having on his patients (see Case 13). By contrast, a community-based planning process on the Haida Gwaii islands in British Columbia was initiated by the Planning and Coordination Committee, a group of federal and provincial officials (see Case 10).

In general, the person or organization that initiates a process should be seen by all stakeholders as credible. If the initial suggestion comes from an individual or organization that is not trusted, the proposal will be suspect. (For more on this topic, see Chapter 4, on convening.)

Who Should Design a Consensus Process

The design of a consensus building process is typically undertaken by a neutral party, an organization or agency, a group of stakeholders or other interested parties, or a neutral party together with representatives of all stakeholders. These four options—any of which can work effectively—are described in this section.

A Neutral Party Is Engaged to Develop a Process

In many cases, and particularly those involving serious conflict, an outside neutral party will be invited to conduct an assessment of a problem and propose a process for resolving it. The use of a neutral may be suggested by one of the parties, a small set of stakeholders, or an interested but not directly involved group, such as a town council. An appropriate neutral party has training as a mediator or a facilitator and will be familiar with a wide variety of process design options.

An assessment will include interviews with stakeholders to determine their perceptions of the problem and to seek advice regarding whether and how to move forward. In the interviews, the facilitator will gather information regarding stakeholders' willingness to negotiate, the substantive issues involved, the political and historical context, and so forth. The facilitator will then recommend a process for the parties to consider. The recommendations should be circulated to all interviewees for review and comment, and revised as needed. The proposed process design should be reviewed yet again at a first meeting of a negotiating group, if one is formed.

In the Northern Oxford County Coalition (NOCC) case—a community-based effort in Maine to address residents' concerns about a perceived link between air pollution from a nearby paper mill and local cancer rates—a team of mediators prepared the first draft of a work plan and invited parties to react to it (Case 2). The draft drew on information gained from 48 interviews conducted with stakeholders, initial group meetings of the NOCC, and consultations with experts. The proposed plan was adjusted by group members at the outset and then continued to evolve. (See Chapter 2, on conducting a conflict assessment, for more on how a neutral party can design a process.)

An Interested Organization or Agency Proposes a Way to Proceed

A company or nonprofit organization that has either a stake in an issue or a general interest in it may design a consensus building process and propose it to all stakeholders. A government agency that has regulatory or enforcement responsibilities for a problem might do the same. For example, a local planning commission or a federal agency may be involved in a problem that promises to become a protracted dispute if an alternative procedure is not introduced. A senior executive at a company or the president of a nonprofit group may suggest a specific consensus building process to deal with a difficult issue. Processes designed by an individual or organization can work as long as individuals representing the full range of interests are asked to

review and comment on the proposed process. Potential participants may be convened as a group to discuss the merits of a
proposal, or reviewers may respond individually with their reactions and suggestions. In the Haida Gwaii case, the Planning and
Coordinating Committee that initiated the process also proposed
a procedure for carrying it out. (See Chapter 4, on convening,
for more about how an organization can conduct or support
process design activities.)

A Group of Interested Parties
Gathers to Suggest a Process

A third way to proceed is for a group of individuals concerned
about an issue to work together to design a process. These people
generally represent different interests concerned about an issue
and are all motivated to do something about it. They may have a
direct stake in the outcome or they may be serving in leadership
roles and want to help facilitate a resolution. This approach
works well when the participating individuals are comfortable
working with each other, knowledgeable about the issue, and
familiar with consensus building techniques. Many local water-
shed-planning processes use this approach. In these cases, local
landowners, ranchers, timber company representatives, environmentalists, and recreation users work together to determine what
can be done jointly to maintain or improve the health of a
watershed. Together they initiate a process, design an overall
structure, and select representatives to participate in the development of a watershed management plan.

All Parties Are Convened to Design a Process

A broad cross section of stakeholders can be convened by an
organization, agency, or leadership group to reach agreement on
whether and how to proceed with and structure a consensus
process. These process design meetings are generally facilitated
by a neutral party. The stakeholders determine how to define the
issues, what the goal or outcome of a process should be, what
sequence of steps should be followed to reach consensus, what
ground rules are needed, how long a process is likely to take,
when and where the meetings should be conducted, who should

participate, and so forth. This approach has the advantage of building trust among parties and fostering participants' sense of ownership of a process. The use of a neutral party with process expertise helps to ensure that critical questions are raised, considered, and decided. (See Chapter 3 for more on this method of designing a process.)

These four process design methods can be combined. For example, a group of community leaders can propose a process, work with a few of the parties to refine the proposal, and then convene representatives of all the stakeholder groups to critique, modify, and adopt the proposed process design.

■ Determining Whether Consensus Building Is Appropriate

No matter who is seeking to initiate a consensus building effort, the first question to ask is, "Should we be using a consensus process?" To answer this question, several factors need to be taken into account, including the nature of the issues, the types of relationships that exist among parties, and any procedural constraints that may exist. Sometimes these factors are considered by a mediator or facilitator during a conflict assessment; other times they are discussed by participants during a process design meeting.

Considering the Nature of the Issues

Not all issues are appropriate for consensus. Some problems have a clear definition and a clear solution. If an employee discovers broken windows in her office building, she should either call the building manager to report the damage or contact a window repair company to get the windows fixed. She does not need to gather a representative group of tenants to seek consensus on how to proceed. Consensus decisions are appropriate when the solution to a problem is not immediately clear to all affected parties or when people disagree on the best solution or decision.

Consensus building is also typically not an appropriate way to deal with violations of the law. If a company is flagrantly violating environmental standards, for example, concerned parties will be better off seeking judicial or administrative intervention. Disputes based on deeply held values do not lend themselves to consensus decision making unless they can be reframed in a productive way. For example, parties on opposite sides of the abortion debate probably should not try to build agreement on whether or not abortions should be legal—they would make little progress. But the opposing parties may be able to find agreement on some topics, such as strategies to avoid unwanted pregnancies. (See Case 15 for an example of pro-life and pro-choice advocates who have done just that, and see Chapter 12 and Case 14 for more on dealing with deep value differences.)

For consensus building to work, parties need to agree on a definition of the problem, at least in a broad sense, and have some belief that solutions exist or can be developed. They need not agree on the causes of the problem, however. For example, participants in a watershed management-planning process might agree that the problem is "declining ecological health of the watershed," but they may hold differing opinions on the causes of that problem or the best solutions. If a problem involves numerous sub-issues, parties will need to categorize those issues in a meaningful way or consider dropping some to make the process manageable.

Determining Parties' Willingness to Negotiate

In some cases, an issue may be suited to resolution using a consensus-based process, but one or more key stakeholders may refuse to participate. These stakeholders may believe that another strategy, such as a lawsuit or an administrative appeal, will better meet their interests. In this situation, a mediator or facilitator can help parties explore their options by explaining how consensus building works and asking questions that encourage them to weigh their options carefully. After some thought, parties may change their minds and decide to participate, or they may not.

Stakeholders may also decide they don't want to come to the table because they distrust or dislike other participants. When relationships among stakeholders are strained, facilitators can organize *dialogues* or *workshops* to bring parties together to build better relationships. If these activities are successful, stakeholders may then choose to negotiate.

Dialogues are conversations held among small groups of diverse individuals for the purpose of improving understanding. Generally moderated by a facilitator, they provide a safe environment in which parties can discuss stressful and divisive topics. They offer opportunities for stakeholders to learn why individuals hold particular points of view and to develop respect for those who are different. They have been used successfully to work on value-based controversies, such as abortion, as well as general discussions about problems in a community and about controversial public policy issues. Like dialogues, workshops gather people together to identify and discuss issues, and they can also be used to develop options or recommendations. Workshops can accommodate larger numbers of people than dialogues. Dialogues and workshops are generally perceived to be less threatening activities than consensus building processes because they engage parties without the expectation of reaching agreements. (Note that some dispute resolution practitioners do use the term *dialogue* to refer to a consensus building effort.)

The consensus-based planning group in Catron County, New Mexico evolved from a series of dialogue sessions. The dialogue approach was effective in this case because the issues were so polarized and parties were deeply suspicious of one another. In that case, U.S. Forest Service employees, local officials, ranchers, loggers, and environmentalists were locked in a bitter battle over the management of federal lands in the area. Preliminary discussions among these parties led to tangible, mutually agreed-on activities, including a tree-removal project and the transfer of some public lands to the county to create a business park.

In addition to (or in lieu of) convening dialogues and workshops, mediators and facilitators can take certain steps to ensure that parties who do not trust each other can feel comfortable taking part in a consensus-based effort. They can suggest, for example, that a group adopt ground rules that define how individuals will be expected to behave toward each other; define accountability measures that describe the consequences of not producing what is promised; and include opportunities for informal interaction among parties to build better relationships. Common behavioral ground rules include statements such as "Parties will treat each other with respect," "Parties will not impugn the motives of others," and "Parties will refrain from using stereotypic language." Ground rules that are used to hold parties accountable include "Information is not to be withheld for tactical advantage," "Parties agree to refrain from making public statements that characterize the position of any of the other parties," accompanied by, "Failure to observe these ground rules may be used as the basis for termination of the negotiations."

Parties may also be reluctant to participate because they lack familiarity with consensus building. A mediator, facilitator, or convenor can provide information about the process in general and describe cases in which consensus has been successfully used on similar problems.

If every effort has been made to secure full participation, and stakeholders representing the complete range of interests on a topic still do not agree to come to the table, a process probably should not go forward. A process that lacks inclusive participation will not likely develop solutions that address all interests, and nonparticipating stakeholders may try to thwart the deliberations or the implementation of agreements. (See Chapter 6 for more on representation issues, and Case 8, on the RuleNet effort, for an example of the challenges that can arise when a process proceeds without inclusive participation.)

Assessing the Procedural Feasibility

Even when an issue may be appropriate for consensus building and parties want to engage in negotiations, procedural barriers may make it impossible. One common barrier is timing. If either formal requirements or informal pressures demand a quick resolution, then an alternative tool such as a public workshop or an advisory meeting may be more desirable. Public workshops and advisory meetings enable agencies or organizations to bring parties together to discuss an issue and to seek advice regarding a desirable solution. While no effort is made to reach agreement, an agency may gain a clearer understanding of the issues at stake, the viewpoints and interests of affected groups, and options that may be acceptable. Such a process may be used, for example, by a mayor who promised a quick solution to a community's homeless problem if elected. Rather than risk being perceived as reneging on an election promise by initiating a lengthy consensus building effort, the mayor may decide to invite a national expert to quickly produce a set of recommendations. Community members can then be brought together in a public meeting to react to the ideas.

In other cases, procedural constraints may influence the scope of authority a consensus-based group can have. For example, an agency that is mandated to make a decision may not want or be able to relinquish that responsibility. A diverse group of stakeholders may convene to develop a joint recommendation to the agency, but the agency cannot guarantee that it will adopt the recommendation. In this case the stakeholders can follow consensus-based procedures to develop their proposals, but their suggestions will not be implemented without the agency's final approval. (See Chapter 13 for more on procedural issues that can arise in consensus building.)

■ Additional Issues to Consider Before Developing a Specific Consensus Strategy

After deciding to proceed with consensus building, individuals responsible for convening, designing, and running a process need to consider the context in which the process will operate. Facilitators who are asked to work with parties and issues not familiar to them, for example, must spend time educating themselves about the context, the central issues, and the views of the parties involved. To do this, facilitators may interview stakeholders and other knowledgeable people, observe relevant activities or sites, and read background material. They also seek to uncover external pressures and influences that may affect a negotiation. "One size fits all" consensus processes that do not identify and adapt to these influences are unlikely to succeed. Being knowledgeable and responsive to the context helps facilitators avoid unnecessary mistakes and enhances participants' chances of reaching agreement. These contextual influences include social and cultural factors, legal issues, political dynamics, economic factors, and the history of the situation.

Social and Cultural Factors

In designing a process, it is important to understand the organizational culture of each stakeholder group. For example, if a consensus process is occurring within a single organization, it is helpful to know whether the culture is strongly hierarchical or more egalitarian. In a hierarchical system, only a few people will generally need to "buy off" on a proposed decision. While buy-off from a few may take less time to achieve than efforts to gain the support of many, those without a say in a decision may be unhappy and uncooperative during implementation. (See Chapter 16, on collaborative problem solving within organizations, and Case 17, on Levi Strauss & Company's experience with consensus building, for more on adapting consensus-based processes to fit an organization's culture.)

When multiple organizations are involved and their respective organizational cultures differ, it is important to acknowledge the specific needs of each group before misunderstandings arise. One organization, for example, may not be able to sign a final agreement without the approval of multiple levels of managers, while another may need the acceptance of an entire constituency. Both of these organizations will take more time to reach internal decisions than a participant who needs approval only from a single individual.

Organizational culture also influences the degree of formality required. If a consensus building effort is to occur within an organization that functions primarily by consensus, the process may need fewer formal ground rules and explanatory protocols. If an organization is not accustomed to operating by consensus, more process guidelines will be needed. In multistakeholder public processes, in which participants come from many different types of organizations, considerable time may be needed to develop ground rules and procedures acceptable to all participants.

It is also important to consider whether participants come from different ethnic, racial, religious, or economic backgrounds. The more diverse participants are, the greater the risks for misunderstandings among them. Facilitators and mediators need to be familiar with cultural differences so they can avoid inadvertently offending individuals in their personal interactions with them, help participants do the same among themselves, and design consensus building processes to honor and reflect different cultural expectations and problem-solving styles.

If facilitators are not familiar with the implications of cultural differences, they need to learn more about each cultural group involved and ask representatives for advice about how a consensus process should be structured to respect the different cultures. Some groups may want each session to begin and end with a moment of silence, other groups may request ample time for personal interactions or want meals to be included as part of an agenda, while other people may stress the importance of efficiency and staying focused on the substantive topic.

In one federal-level consensus process, representatives from 48 Native American tribes and more than 10 federal agencies and offices worked out detailed regulations to guide tribes, tribal organizations, and federal contractors in framing service contracts (Case 9). Before convening the parties, the lead mediator interviewed representatives of the parties and read relevant background material to learn, among other things, more about the cultural norms of the Native American participants. Negotiation sessions opened with a prayer, sometimes in English, sometimes in a tribal language, and the final day of each negotiation session ended with a prayer.

Language can also be a factor to consider when different cultural groups are represented. In cases in which only one or two people do not speak the language of other participants, or when multiple languages are spoken, arrangements can be made for interpreters to sit next to participants and interpret as others speak. Sometimes parties may prefer to have comments interpreted sequentially.

The Legal Framework

The legal context is another key factor to consider when designing a consensus building process. Government agencies, for example, are subject to rules and regulations governing how they make decisions and interact with the public. So, for instance, local or state "open-meeting laws" may require that all meetings be open to the public if a quorum of any elected or appointed public body is present. The federal government has its own set of administrative procedure rules, including the Federal Advisory Committee Act (FACA), which must be observed when a federal agency chooses to participate.

Many consensus-based processes also address topics that involve legal issues or relate to existing laws. Facilitators should make sure that all participants are fully aware of relevant legislation. Participants in the Northern Oxford County Coalition in

Maine had to learn about federal and state air quality regulations to move forward with their discussions.

A facilitator should also determine whether any pending legal actions will affect discussions. If a relevant, precedent-setting legal decision or administrative ruling is on the verge of being decided, the timing of a consensus-based effort may be affected. Parties may choose to wait until a ruling is made before they proceed with negotiations.

Participants should also be aware of whether any stakeholder is currently engaged in or considering litigation against another stakeholder and, if so, whether such legal action will conflict with or hinder consensus building. A group may need to coordinate closely with a court to ensure that the two processes do not conflict, for example, or they may decide to take up only those topics that are unrelated to the legal case. Alternatively, the opposing parties may decide to postpone a case while consensus building is under way. (See Chapter 13, on legal issues in consensus building, for more information on these topics.)

The Political Dynamics

"Issues taken up during a consensus-based effort seldom stand in isolation."

Problems and issues taken up during a consensus-based effort seldom stand in isolation; related decision-making activities will inevitably be going on during a group's deliberations. If a consensus process is part of a larger decision-making effort, parties will need to pay attention to the scheduling of other activities so that decisions are delivered in a timely fashion. If the process is related, but not formally connected, to other decision-making efforts, parties will need to clarify how the outcomes of the two processes can best complement each other. A consensus process mandated by a town council to develop a youth policy for a community, for example, may be part of a broader strategic-planning effort. It would thus need to fit within the time frame established for that broader effort. Also, because the town council will likely have to formally adopt the policy before it can be implemented, participants may want to periodically hold briefings for town council members to keep them apprised of the group's process. A lobbying effort may also need to be organized after the policy is drafted to encourage council members to ratify and implement it.

It is also important, in organizing a consensus process, to know how receptive key leaders are toward that process. If a process is endorsed by key figures in the public or private sector, stakeholders may be more willing to participate in it. Conversely, when leaders are skeptical or even hostile toward a consensus effort, stakeholders may be reluctant to participate, and any agreement reached may be difficult to implement. When leadership figures are not supportive, a mediator, facilitator, or trusted stakeholder can help educate them about the use of consensus building in general and the risks and benefits of engaging in a particular process. If an influential person is still opposed to a process and his or her support is essential to the implementation of any agreement, then the process probably should not move forward. If a leader does not want to endorse a process but is not actively opposed to it either, group members can offer to consult with the person periodically during the process to receive input.

A consensus building process in Chelsea, Massachusetts took place in an unusual and rather volatile political climate (Case 3). The process was initiated in response to a crisis in local governance in the city. Widespread graft and corruption had led to the deterioration of basic municipal services. The political climate had become so dysfunctional that the state legislature intervened, suspending Chelsea's local government and placing the city under receivership. Many Chelseans had lost faith in the city's ability to govern itself. In an effort to restore a healthy democracy, a consensus building process was established to create a new city charter—a new structure of government for the city. All the community leaders and people who formerly held elective office had a stake in what the new government would look like. In an effort to be sure the new charter would meet the interests of all residents, the facilitation team made a great effort to reach out to and involve the entire community in developing the charter.

Economic Factors

The overall economic climate may affect parties' willingness to participate in discussions. If the economy is robust, the pressure to resolve an issue may not be as strong as in harder times. A sand and gravel company, for example, that finds a steady demand for its products because of an expanding market may not be as anxious to engage in a consensus process that may affect its operations. But the opposite may also be true. Good economic times may provide the incentive for parties to take part, because they feel more generous and accommodating.

In addition to thinking about the effect of the overall economy, facilitators and convenors should consider participants' individual financial situations. A key party, for example, may be reluctant to participate due to the costs of traveling to meetings. Also, organizations that operate on small budgets may find it difficult to justify releasing a staff person to participate. Some negotiating groups work out methods for compensating individuals who need financial assistance. They may reimburse members of nonprofit advocacy groups, for example, for the out-of-pocket expenses they incur while participating. The budget for a consensus building effort might, therefore, have to include resources for travel and lodging.

Historic Factors

If parties have previously tried to address an issue collaboratively and were unsuccessful, it is important to know why the effort failed. Was the process inappropriate? For example, were some key parties not invited, were the real issues not addressed, or was the timing of meetings unrealistic? Were parties not committed to the process? Past failures can reveal specific barriers that may need to be overcome if parties are to agree to participate in a new consensus-based initiative. If a previous effort was characterized by "poorly run meetings that were a waste of time," a facilitator should explain to prospective participants how meetings will be run with carefully planned agendas and agreed-on ground rules. If parties complained that one side seemed to dominate the discussions in a past attempt, ground rules can be developed to ensure that all parties' voices will be heard.

It is also important to consider whether any changes have recently occurred in the social, political, or economic climate surrounding an issue. If the leadership of one or more of the stakeholder groups changes and is more favorably disposed toward a consensus process, or is willing to take a more active role advocating a consensus solution, the chances for a successful process increase.

■ *Structuring a Specific Consensus Process*

Having determined that consensus building is an appropriate approach to solving a particular problem or making a certain decision, and having reviewed the contextual factors that will influence the negotiations, parties are ready to tailor a process to fit their unique issues and circumstances. To structure an appropriate consensus-based process, parties must

> define the problem,
> determine a feasible goal or outcome,
> select a general approach to reaching agreement,
> identify process steps,
> consider other process components and activities,
> identify participants,
> clarify additional roles, and
> agree on logistics.

Defining the Problem

The first step in creating a consensus-based process is to define, to the satisfaction of all stakeholders, the problem or issue to be addressed. Sometimes the definition comes easily. "Identify our work priorities for the next year" might be an obvious mission for a departmentwide planning session inside a company. But often it's more difficult. A community that is wrestling over whether to build affordable housing on its last undeveloped parcel of wooded land might find itself caught between factions that want to focus on the question "How can we best provide low-income housing for our community?" and those that would prefer to ask, "How can the community preserve its remaining open space?" In this case, community members will need to come to an agreement regarding the most appropriate focus before they can proceed further. They may choose one question or the other, or they may try to integrate the two (e.g., "What is the best use of this land?").

Determining the Goal or Outcome

The goal of consensus building is to reach an agreement that all parties can live with. This agreement may take the form of a signed statement, a final report, a newsletter for the public, or some other document.

Parties who engage in a consensus building process need to understand whether their efforts will result in an implementable agreement or whether that agreement will need to be forwarded to another entity or entities for approval. Consensus building, after all, can be used to develop recommendations for a separate decision-making authority, such as a body of elected officials, a government agency, or a senior executive in a company. For example, an agency may ask stakeholders to develop recommendations on a policy issue for its review and approval. In a negotiation over affordable housing issues in Connecticut (Case 4), representatives from 32 political entities came together to craft a "compact" that specified the number of affordable housing units each community would supply over a five-year period. The compact, according to state law, could not become binding until all the local governing bodies formally ratified it.

Selecting a General Approach to Building Consensus

Parties must choose a general approach to achieving consensus. The most commonly used method is a conventional problem-solving approach, but the single-text method and visioning are also sometimes employed. In fact, participants may choose to use a combination of these methods. Simple issues involving just a few stakeholders may be resolved using one of these approaches in just a few hours, while more complex issues with multiple parties may take months or years.

Using a Conventional Problem-Solving Approach

Most consensus processes follow a conventional approach to problem solving. Using this approach, participants first work together to clarify and agree on a definition of the problem they are to address. Then they discuss and build agreement on the procedures by which they will conduct their deliberations. Next comes the education phase, during which participants share information about the context of the problem, explain their respective issues and interests, and offer appropriate technical information from their own expertise or draw on outside experts for help. During this phase, participants are exposed to the problem from different perspectives. The next step is to develop options. In this phase, parties work together to generate potential solutions to the problem. Parties establish and apply criteria to evaluate the options they have developed. They then seek agreement on a "package" that all parties can support.

Working with a Single-Text Document

The single-text approach involves introducing a working draft of an agreement early in a process for parties to discuss and revise. The single-text method provides a clear structure for discussions and a focal point for identifying areas of agreement and disagreement. The single text itself is usually developed either by a mediator, who conducts interviews with all the parties to gather enough information to draft a document, or by a technical resource person, who is knowledgeable about the issues and familiar with participants' views on those issues. A subgroup of stakeholders may also be asked to work together to draft a single-text document. Single texts work well when technical, regulatory, or statutory language is required and in situations in which a large number of parties are involved.

Taking a Visioning Approach

A third approach is to focus participants' attention toward the future in the course of identifying options and seeking agreements. Most visioning approaches ask the basic questions "What do we have?" "What do we want?" and "How do we get there?" The first question, "What do we have?" provides an opportunity for participants to assess the strengths and weaknesses of their current situation. The second question, "What do we want?" asks people to think normatively and describe an ideal outcome that will meet the interests (not positions) of the different parties. Parties in conflict frequently find it easier to think about solutions in the future than in the present. It frees them up to be more creative. Once participants agree on what they want, they move to the question "How do we get there?" They then offer implementation strategies, which can become part of a consensus agreement.

Visioning can be applied to most issues. It is particularly helpful in situations in which parties hold entrenched positions, because the exercise of thinking about the future can produce more common ground than discussions that remain focused on the present.

Community-wide visioning processes have taken place in numerous cities and counties, including Catron County, New Mexico; Chattanooga, Tennessee; and "Middletown" (see Cases 13, 11, and 12, respectively). In Chattanooga's broad-based public visioning process, citizens were invited to identify their goals, hopes, and dreams for the city. The results of that process included a reengaged citizenry and numerous new projects and programs that have revitalized the once-declining city. (See Chapter 15, on visioning, for more on this topic.)

Identifying an Appropriate Sequence of Process Steps

No matter which general approach to consensus building is employed, the process of working toward agreement will typically involve the same fundamental components. The cases included in Part 3 of this volume provide an excellent illustration of the diverse methods people have used to structure consensus processes. Closer examination of these cases, however, reveals that each initiative includes the same basic components. Each established some form of ground rules; invested time to understand the context, key issues, and the concerns of the respective participants; and developed and assessed options before attempting to reach agreements. Ground rules describe the structure, procedures, and behaviors all participants are expected to follow. They clarify activities of the group and decision-making roles of the participants. Education gives participants an opportunity to tell their story, hear how others view a problem, and learn how the issues affect others. It also provides the foundation for generating options. The options phase is separated from reaching agreements so that parties do not rush prematurely to closure before they have developed and explored multiple ways to satisfy the needs of the various stakeholders. After thorough deliberation and negotiation, participants can then package the options that best meet all of their interests. When drafting agreements, parties also address issues of how their proposed agreements will be implemented—this enhances the likelihood that agreements actually will be implemented.

These general process steps, which provide a road map for parties to follow, should be discussed and agreed on by participants prior to engaging in a process. The specifics of how to accomplish each step must be determined by the parties and may change as the process evolves.

Developing and Agreeing on
Ground Rules and Protocols

"Parties must agree to abide by a common set of ground rules, which will govern their activities."

Parties must agree to abide by a common set of ground rules, which will govern their activities during a consensus process. Ground rules can cover *behavioral* expectations, such as how parties should treat each other; *substantive* issues, such as an agreed-on description of the issues that will be negotiated; and *procedural* issues, such as how decisions will be made and how information will be shared.

Parties may also choose to prepare more detailed *protocols,* which cover additional topics such as the mandate of a group, a list of participants and their affiliations, a description of roles and who will fill them, and expectations regarding implementation. Explicit ground rules and detailed protocols are most needed when parties are less familiar with consensus building and the issues are complex. In a consensus process created to address the controversies over expansion plans for Amsterdam's Schiphol Airport, the parties drew up a joint "statement of intent," which, among other things, clarified the purpose of the process, the organizational structure, and the financing, and provided a rationale for cooperation (Case 1). The parties in that case included several federal government agencies, provincial and local government representatives, the airport authority, and representatives from KLM, the major Dutch airline. The negotiators were seeking agreement on how to balance the economic benefits and environmental impacts of airport expansion. The detailed ground rules in the statement of intent helped the diverse parties deal effectively with these complex issues.

Educating the Parties

The education phase gives parties an opportunity to learn more about the history and context of a problem and to describe to each other their respective interests and concerns. During this phase, parties may gather and share data relevant to the topic and, in some situations, decide to conduct new research. In cases that involve detailed legal or technical questions, a good deal of background information may need to be collected and distributed so that all parties can participate effectively. After agreeing on a purpose and process, the participants in the Schiphol Airport case began to exchange information on relevant issues. During this education phase, they split into three groups: A project group explored and documented the participants' diverse viewpoints on key topics, a research group initiated 13 research projects, and a scenario group developed three projections of airport traffic, each based on different assumptions.

Developing Options

After exploring a problem and identifying the issues and interests that need to be addressed, parties begin to develop options. This step precedes efforts to reach agreement. Depending on the number of participants and the range of issues being discussed, parties may consider one or more of the following methods to generate options: (1) A whole group works together to brainstorm options, (2) task groups develop recommendations for the full group, (3) comprehensive proposals or single-text documents are prepared, (4) outside experts provide assistance, and (5) interest or caucus groups develop proposals for the whole group.

Whole-group work is appropriate when smaller numbers of people are involved in a consensus process or when the issue being addressed is of particular interest to all stakeholders. Brainstorming is a common way to develop options in a full-group setting. In brainstorming, people develop a generous list of potential solutions by verbalizing every possible option they can think of, taking care not to criticize the ideas at this point. Task groups (also called work groups or subcommittees) can be an efficient way to organize a large group of stakeholders who are dealing with multiple, complex issues. Task groups are commonly used when technical or scientific issues require specialized expertise. If a process has relied on task groups to organize and conduct work during the education phase, parties may want each task group to produce options related to its focus. If the issues are complex, but task groups have not been used during the educational phase, a full group may decide to create smaller subcommittees for the purpose of generating options.

Options may also be included in a comprehensive, single-text proposal. Single texts, which provide a focal point for negotiations, may be crafted with information gathered from individual interviews with stakeholders or from large-group discussions. Outside experts can also be used to jump-start the identification of options by describing solutions to problems that have proven useful in other places and that are known to be technically feasible. Alternatively, interest or caucus groups may be asked to offer proposals to address specific issues that they think will meet their needs and the needs of the other parties. When caucus groups are challenged to develop their own proposals, they are forced to adopt a problem-solving mode rather than simply criticizing the ideas of others. The various caucus proposals must be reviewed and blended into a final set of agreements. (See Chapter 8, on producing consensus, for more on developing options.)

During the options-generating phase in the Schiphol Airport case, parties reviewed, refined, and organized the problems and issues that had been identified during their education phase. Project group members were asked to suggest mutually agreeable solutions to the diverging viewpoints they had identified and present these solutions to a steering committee for review and comment. Some were accepted, while others were sent back to the project group for further refinement.

Reaching Agreements

After identifying options, participants move to the next phase, reaching agreements. To begin this phase, they may want to review their respective interests and generate a list of criteria that they would like to see met by any agreement. Generating criteria gives parties an objective tool by which to assess options.

Strategies for reaching agreements include reaching "agreements in principle" first and then working from there to specific agreements, working for closure issue by issue, and developing and negotiating comprehensive proposals that address all of the issues in one document. If parties choose to seek agreement on one issue at a time, the result is a collection of separate agreements that are bundled together for a final package. Some groups prefer to develop and negotiate around one or more comprehensive proposals. It may be easier to reach an agreement on a comprehensive package of proposals than on issues one at a time, because the former allows for "trading" across differences in priorities (e.g., "I'll give you a little more of X, if you'll give me a little more of Y."). In consensus processes that tackle a large number of topics, the issues may be clustered into broad categories for all parties to handle or delegated to task groups to develop draft agreements for the whole group to approve. (See Chapter 8, on producing consensus, for more detail on this topic.) A group has completed its task when all participants, or at least an overwhelming majority, have reached agreement.

In the Schiphol Airport case, the possible solutions that were developed by the project group and refined by the steering committee became the basis for a draft plan for airport expansion. Each government entity involved in the process went to the public with the proposed plan and collected comments and concerns about it. Additional organizations were brought into the process for advice. Frequent bilateral discussions occurred between key stakeholders. The proposed agreement was repeatedly rewritten in response to the comments steering committee members received from their constituents. Once the plan was deemed acceptable, parties developed a covenant summarizing their main agreements.

Implementing Agreements

The organizers of a consensus process must think about what will be needed to implement an agreement, such as the ratification of components by an elected or an administrative body, to determine who should be at the table and who needs to be kept informed as the discussions progress. To the greatest degree possible, implementation considerations should be folded into an agreement. The clearer a group can be about what is to be done, by whom, and by when, the easier it will be to monitor progress and make appropriate adjustments. (See Chapter 14, on implementation, for more on this topic.)

In the Schiphol case, the final agreement laid out a long-term development plan that clarified the main direction for the future expansion of the airfield. The negotiators had built a united front of diverse organizations—what they called a *policy network*. This newly activated policy network became the vehicle for the ongoing negotiations needed to implement the agreement.

Determining Other Process Components and Activities

The steps described in the previous section provide the basic foundation for a consensus building process. Depending on the particulars of a problem and its context, other activities may be desirable, if not essential. Some of these activities will be identified and integrated during the planning phase. Others may be suggested after a process has begun and stakeholders identify a specific need. Additional components and activities may include

preparing individuals to participate,
building working relationships,
going on field trips and site visits,
organizing task groups,
identifying research needs,
keeping records,
involving constituents,
engaging other interested individuals and organizations,
handling the press, and
evaluating the process.

Preparing Individuals to Participate

Thoughtful preparation will help individuals participate more productively in discussions. Because stakeholders may not have the same basic information about the issues at hand, reports, articles, and project proposals can provide them with useful information about the context, history, and nature of a problem. Parties do not need to be overwhelmed with information, but some well-prepared overviews can provide all participants with a place to start. These overviews must be carefully crafted by a facilitator or mediator, often with the help of participants, so as not to further polarize a situation. In addition to substantive materials, many groups have found it helpful to provide information about consensus building in general, in some cases offering training in interest-based negotiation or consensus decision making. Four leadership-development workshops, for example, preceded the negotiations in the Haida Gwaii community-planning case. The workshops were offered to stakeholders for the purpose of developing collaborative skills and enhancing their understanding of specific topics, such as cross-cultural relations, negotiations, planning processes, and tourism development.

Building and Maintaining Working Relationships

The better the relationships among participants, the more they can focus their attention on substantive questions. If relationships are poor entering the discussions, activities designed to build better relationships can be integrated into a consensus building process. These activities cover such things as proposing ground rules that protect individuals from verbal attacks and encourage positive behavior, organizing an agenda to include small-group discussion, including meals and other opportunities for informal conversations, asking people to share stories about how a topic affects them personally, and organizing field trips. These strategies are useful for maintaining productive relationships as well as building them.

For example, a church congregation in Oklahoma embarked on a reconciliation process after its pastor was charged with misconduct and resigned, leaving behind a deeply polarized congregation (Case 16). Members needed to rebuild their relationships and regain each other's trust before any consensus process could be initiated about the future of the church. They decided to go through carefully structured and facilitated sessions designed to "neutralize the history" and "let go" of the past. Once their relationships improved, they could talk more productively about how to move forward.

Going on Field Trips or Site Visits

Consensus processes that address issues involving a program, facility, or a particular site should consider scheduling a field trip to view the place under discussion. Generally, a trip occurs during the educational phase of a process. Site visits allow participants to get a clear visual image of a place and enable them to ask questions and gain a more realistic understanding of it. Parties may also schedule visits during the options phase if they want to explore how a particular program works or compare different facilities. A side benefit of such a trip is the rapport that can develop among the participants. Participants in the consensus building process in Catron County, New Mexico organized two tours of local riparian areas to educate parties about riparian conditions and practices and to get input from participants regarding standards and guidelines for a forest management plan.

Organizing Subgroups or Task Forces

"Task groups offer an efficient way to divide the work."

If an overall problem is complex and includes many sub-issues, task groups offer an efficient way to divide the work. By using task groups, participants do not have to learn all of the details of every issue. Similarly, if some issues are highly technical in nature, individuals who have expertise in those areas can be asked to focus on them, eliminating the need for others to spend time getting up to speed. Task groups should be representative of the diversity of views in a full group.

Task groups also provide a mechanism for expanding the number of people who can participate in a process. Task groups may be made up of people who are core members of a negotiating group and other individuals who are invited due to their expertise or interest in a topic. In San Francisco, for example, a consensus building group was organized to produce an agreement on a Comprehensive Conservation and Management Plan for the San Francisco Estuary (Case 5). Because of the technical nature of the case and the number and diversity of parties involved, the organizers of the project established a management committee, a Technical Advisory Committee (TAC), and six issue-focused committees. The TAC, composed of relevant scientists and engineers, was set up to advise the management committee on technical matters, among other tasks. The issue committees provided a way to divide work into six substantive areas: aquatic resources, land use, wetlands, wildlife, pollutants, and dredging. Each committee was composed of TAC members along with other stakeholders who did not have technical expertise.

Identifying Research Needs

To determine whether a group needs to conduct research or gather information, parties should ask themselves several questions: How much information will participants need to be able to discuss the issues, develop options, and reach agreements? What is the nature of this information—technical, scientific, or personal? Does the necessary information exist and need to be assembled and distributed to all parties, or does new information have to be generated? If it must be generated, who will be responsible for producing it? If a group determines that additional research is needed, it may need to organize a joint fact-finding effort. This may involve setting up a task group to gather and analyze information or hiring technical experts to do the research. The information that is gathered can then be incorporated back into the main negotiations and used to help the group reach agreement.

One of the most valuable contributions of the San Francisco Estuary Project was the mutual learning among scientists and between the scientists and laypeople that occurred over the production of a technical "status and trends report." Participants also developed an index to assess water quality that became accepted among most of the stakeholders, including the U.S. Environmental Protection Agency, as the appropriate measure for monitoring the estuary's health.

(Chapter 9 discusses joint fact-finding at length. Also, Case 6, on the New York Bight Initiative, and Case 7, about a Superfund cleanup process in Massachusetts, provide excellent examples of participants engaging in collaborative research efforts.)

Keeping Records

In a consensus process with no facilitator and only few participants, parties may choose to keep their own notes for personal reference. As processes become larger and more formal, participants need to decide what type of recordkeeping will best serve their needs. Many groups designate a recorder who takes notes on a flip chart in front of a room to capture issues and ideas that are discussed and agreements that are reached. This is sometimes called creating a *group memory.* These flip chart notes may also become the basis for meeting records, either transcribed verbatim or used to create a meeting summary. Alternatively, a group may designate a person to take notes on notebook-sized paper or a laptop computer, which can then be turned into a meeting summary or meeting minutes. Either way, a draft summary should be circulated to all participants for their comments. The revised summary is then adopted at the next meeting of the group.

Occasionally, a group will want to tape sessions to help a recorder produce more accurate and detailed minutes or give to individuals who were unable to attend. While helpful under some circumstances, tape recording can also inhibit the candor and creativity of a group. A group must be asked permission before tape recording is used.

Involving Constituents

Members of a negotiating group who participate on behalf of an interest group or organization need to be clear about how they will communicate with their constituents throughout a process. Ground rules or protocols should lay out expectations for individuals at the table and suggest ways these expectations can be met. A ground rule can be stated as follows, for example: "Participants are responsible for communicating with their respective constituencies between each meeting of the negotiating group. The purpose of this communication is to share information covered at the session with constituency members and to gather ideas to bring back to the negotiating group." Groups can develop other ways to keep constituents informed. They could encourage constituents to attend full-group meetings as observers, for example, or invite them to caucus meetings. Whatever the means, every consensus building process should include explicit guidelines for how individual representatives should communicate with their constituents.

Engaging Other Interested Individuals and Organizations

Some consensus building groups will receive requests for information from individuals and organizations that may not hold a direct stake in an issue, but are interested in the topic or the outcome of the discussions. It may be appropriate to send summaries of meeting notes or informational memos to these individuals or organizations to periodically update them on the progress of the talks.

In cases in which the outcome of a negotiation will affect the public, some form of public outreach (e.g., meetings, workshops) should be planned in conjunction with formal discussions. These public sessions can be used to help identify the full range of issues and interests that need to be addressed during negotiations and to help brainstorm additional options.

The charter development process in Chelsea, Massachusetts used community meetings, public forums, ward meetings, a survey, newsletters, cable TV, and a charter hot line as vehicles to engage citizens. Through these avenues, negotiating group members elicited information about citizens' concerns, educated residents about options, clarified the issues, and ultimately achieved support from city residents for the newly created city charter.

Handling the Press

During the convening of a group, the facilitator or mediator ought to consider whether the press is likely to be interested in the negotiation. Have there been articles in the newspapers or on the radio or television about the issues to be discussed? Is the media likely to be interested in a story if parties do come together to try to work out their differences? Would press attention be useful to a negotiating group, to help educate the public about the issues and build support for a consensus outcome? If the answer to any of these questions is yes, then it is important to establish ground rules that address the role of the press in the consensus building process. These ground rules should cover how the facilitator and participants will interact with the media and what types of information the media can expect to receive from the group. (See Chapter 11, on dealing with the press, for a thorough discussion of this topic.)

Evaluating the Process

Evaluations of consensus building processes are becoming more and more commonplace. Evaluations can be conducted midway into a process, to determine if any changes in procedure or focus need to be made; right after a process concludes, to assess the quality of an agreement and how participants' relationships improved over the course of the effort; or a year or more after a process ends, to determine how well the agreement was implemented and to look for any second- and third-order effects of the process. All these types of evaluations help to develop *best practices* in the consensus building field, and can build support for consensus building among those who are skeptical of its effectiveness.

The outset of a process is the best time for facilitators, convenors, sponsors, and participants to determine whether they want to contract a professional evaluator to conduct an evaluation. Early consideration, even if an end-of-process evaluation is to be done, enables the evaluator to gather additional firsthand information during the deliberations. An evaluator may come from a university, a consulting firm, or a government agency. (These ideas were drawn from Chapter 17, on evaluation, where they are discussed in detail.)

Identifying Participants

"A key activity in designing a process is selecting stakeholders to participate."

A key activity in designing a process is selecting appropriate stakeholders to participate. This task involves determining an appropriate form of participation, identifying key interests, determining an optimal number of participants, and selecting individuals to take part.

Deciding on a Form of Participation

Some consensus processes lend themselves to an open form of participation and others are better served using representative participation.

Open participation. Open participation means that all individuals who are affected by a problem are invited to participate. Open participation works best when the number of people involved is manageable, interest in the issue is high, and any agreement will require broad-based support for implementation. The reconciliation workshops offered by the church in Oklahoma, for example, were open to the entire congregation. Likewise, a company of 20 employees might invite all of its staff to make a decision about new office equipment. A developer may invite all adjacent neighbors to participate in design decisions for a new housing and park project. In these instances, those who have a stake in an issue will not feel left out or compelled to complain that a process was not inclusive. Open participation enhances ownership of an agreement among all affected people.

Representative participation. In a process with representative participation, individuals who represent different interests and concerns are designated to participate on behalf of other individuals who share the same concerns. In many circumstances, it is not practical to involve all affected individuals, either because the number of people affected is too large or the time required for full participation is too extensive. In a representative process, it is the job of the representative to maintain ongoing communication with his or her constituents—those individuals who share his or her concerns and are not at the table. Processes involving public issues frequently use a representative form of participation, but allow nonparticipants to attend meetings as observers. For example, an 11-member advisory committee may be charged with developing an open-space plan for a county using a consensus building process. Committee members may be chosen to represent different interests within the county, but meetings may also be open to all interested citizens. (After all, the committee does not want to develop recommendations that will affect the entire county behind closed doors.) Each meeting may also include a period of time for observers to offer comments to the committee.

Identifying Key Interests

To help determine which individuals should participate in a representative process, care needs to be taken to identify the categories of concerns people have regarding the central issue, to ensure that each area of concern will be represented. For example, a proposed youth center in a community may be welcomed by neighbors with teenagers but opposed by neighbors who fear increased noise and traffic. In a consensus building process to discuss the proposed center, a category of interests labeled *neighbors* would be too broad to cover both concerns. Each interest merits its own category and representative. Categories should include individuals or groups who will be directly affected by the outcome or otherwise have a stake in it. Categories may also include individuals and organizations who can make positive contributions to a solution, such as financial resources or legislative support, as well as people who have reservations about an issue and are in a position to undermine implementation.

Determining an Appropriate Number of Participants

The third step in selecting participants is to determine how many people should participate in a consensus process. This decision will be influenced by the nature of the issue, the number of interest categories involved, and the level of interest in participating. Generally, it is not wise to include more than 25 people, to keep meetings productive and give everyone a chance to participate. In large, complex cases, however, there may be as many as 40 participants, and some consensus processes have involved more than 100.

The same number of people do not need to represent each interest category. In larger cases, interest groups may have one, two, or three representatives, depending on the size of their constituency and the degree to which they will be affected by the outcome. In cases that involve only three interest categories, on the other hand, participants may decide to have six people at the table, two from each group. Because voting is not used as a means of making decisions, equal representation is not essential.

Selecting Representatives

Finally, after identifying the generic interests that need to be included and determining the number of people who should represent each interest category, individual representatives must be selected. Those selected should be knowledgeable about the issues at hand, able to work productively with others, supported by their constituency, interested in participating, and available for periodic meetings during the expected duration of the project. It is usually desirable to invite people who have the same status within their respective organizations. If the president or other high-level decision maker of one organization has agreed to participate, discussions are generally more productive if that person's counterparts from the other interest categories also participate. On technical matters, resource specialists might be the best people at the table. (See Chapter 4, on convening, for more about choosing representatives.)

Clarifying Roles in the Process

In addition to participants, consensus building processes may also involve a convenor, sponsor, mediator or facilitator, chairperson, recorder, resource or technical adviser, and observers. While designing a process, parties should review these roles to determine whether they would be useful, and if so, who should be asked to fill them. (See also Chapter 7, on managing meetings, for more detail on these roles.)

Convenor. A convenor is generally a person of stature who is respected by all stakeholders. The primary task of a convenor is to invite stakeholders or their representatives to participate. A good convenor adds an air of legitimacy to the process and motivation to participate. Convenors may be people who hold formal offices, such as a mayor or a governor, or who are widely known and respected, such as a religious leader or a highly regarded businessperson. A convenor may also be an agency or organization. In the Northern Oxford County Coalition case, the director of the Department of Environmental Protection's Bureau of Air Quality in Maine decided to organize a consensus process, hired a facilitator, and convened the first multistakeholder meetings. (See Chapter 4, on convening, for more about the convenor's role.)

Sponsor. Some consensus building processes have sponsors: individuals or organizations willing to support and endorse the use of consensus-based approaches to address a particular issue. Sponsors can offer legitimacy to an effort and can provide financial assistance to help cover the associated costs. Sometimes a sponsor may be an interested party who is not directly involved in a negotiation, such as a town council or a county's board of commissioners. In other cases, a negotiating group may have multiple sponsors that represent a full spectrum of interests. In fact, if a stakeholder group that is clearly aligned with one "side" in a debate offers to be a sponsor, participants may find it useful to seek additional sponsors representing the other major points of view.

Mediator or facilitator. Most consensus processes engage a mediator or facilitator to assist parties with the design and management of a process. A mediator is trained to help parties negotiate productively. Some mediators have additional training in working with large groups. Facilitators are trained to help groups hold productive meetings. The larger the number of participants in a consensus process and the more complex the issues, the more desirable it is to have a person with both sets of skills. (See Chapter 5 for more on the role of mediators and facilitators.)

Chair. In addition to a mediator or facilitator, parties may wish to designate a chair. A chair is a figure respected by all sides who brings legitimacy to a process by his or her presence. A chair may do as little as open and close each session, or may take a more active role in representing the full group to the public or the press. A chair may also take part in overseeing the agenda of the meetings, but generally defers the management of the process to a mediator or facilitator. Chairs usually have some familiarity with the substance of the issues at hand. Sometimes the convenor serves as the chair.

Recorder. The role of recorder is important in any consensus process. The recorder may be someone from the mediation team or a person from an agency or organization familiar with the subject matter and has been approved for this role by all the parties. Recorders may capture key ideas on flip charts or take more detailed meeting "minutes" on a computer, as discussed previously. The more formal and complex the process, the more detailed notes parties may want. If both meeting minutes and group memory tools are to be used, separate individuals should be assigned to perform each task.

Resource or technical adviser. When technical issues are central to a debate, parties may find it helpful to invite resource people or technical advisers to participate. These individuals, who possess in-depth knowledge of a topic relevant to the deliberation, may or may not be affiliated with a party in the process, depending on how controversial the technical information is. Parties may want an agency scientist present, even when that agency is a party at the table. Whoever is designated as a resource person should be acceptable to all participants. Usually, people serving as technical resources for a process are expected to be present at all general sessions of a consensus group to answer questions that might arise, and they are often asked to participate in task group meetings related to their areas of expertise as well. Resource people may be knowledgeable about legal matters, economic factors, or scientific issues. Parties can also invite additional resource people to participate as the need arises.

Observers. When participation in a consensus process is limited to designated representatives, members of a constituency group or individuals who have an interest in the issues but no stake in the outcome may want to follow the discussions closely. One option that allows access to discussions (without over-whelming a process with additional participants) is to invite these individuals to observe the deliberations. Public policy consensus building processes may be subject to open-meeting laws that require discussions be open to the public. In other cases, the observer role helps to minimize charges of decisions being made behind closed doors. Individuals can be formally appointed as observers or may assume that role by simply attending sessions. Observers are typically asked to follow the ground rules adopted by the participants. Ground rules that include provisions for observers may identify the conditions under which an observer can speak in a session. For example: "Any designated participant at the table may suggest that the group hear from an observer. The observer may speak if all designated participants grant permission."

Making Logistical Choices

One of the first questions parties will ask when invited to participate in a consensus process is, "How much time will it take?" Parties need specific information about the time they will be expected to commit to a consensus effort and other logistical matters.

Determining How Long a Process Will Take

Individuals invited to take part in a process will want to know how long it will last, how many meetings they will be expected to attend, how frequently the group will meet, how long the meetings will last, and so forth. The answers to these questions are driven by substantive and logistical factors. Substantive factors include how complex the problem is, how many issues will need to be addressed, how up to speed all the parties are on key issues, how many options currently exist, and how polarized the issues are. On the logistical side, it is important to consider how frequently parties are able to meet, how much time they need between meetings to ensure that they are able to communicate with their constituencies, and how capable they are of communicating with each other at the table. Access to computer tools, such as e-mail and Web-based discussion forums, is another logistical factor; if all participants have and are comfortable using on-line capabilities, they may choose to continue their deliberations between face-to-face meetings and can quickly transfer draft documents. (See Chapter 10 for more on how to use computer technologies in consensus building.)

Parties should agree on a time frame at the beginning of a process, with the understanding that it can be modified as they deem appropriate. Parties generally underestimate the amount of time a process will take. The cases described in Part 3 of this volume range in duration from a few days to five years.

Deciding Where to Hold the Meetings

Consideration also needs to be given to the location of meetings. Factors to consider include determining whether parties want to meet in a retreat location away from their normal business and community setting or whether they prefer a convenient local site. Any selected site should be large enough to accommodate the expected numbers of people and comfortable such that discussions are not impeded by poor light or inadequate ventilation or heating. A site should also be checked for specific meeting needs such as the ability to hang newsprint on the walls. Attractive historic buildings may offer a wonderful ambiance, but they can be awkward places to conduct meetings if the walls cannot be papered with newsprint and food and beverages are not permitted. Parties should understand the reason for selecting a particular location and feel comfortable with the choice.

■ *Summary*

This chapter is intended to be a guide for persons who are interested in using consensus as a means for making a decision or solving a problem, whether it be a simple decision about office hours or a complex controversy about international trade policy. We encourage readers to recognize that a consensus process will be structured differently depending on the nature of the problem and the parties affected by it. While adhering to general principles of consensus building, each problem has its own context, history, and specific characteristics that need to be reflected in the design of a process.

Even when care has been taken to develop an appropriate process, the dynamics and circumstances might require the group to modify its approach along the way. Being prepared to tailor a process at the outset, and then adapt it as needed, enhances the chances that a consensus building process will succeed.

2

CONDUCTING A
CONFLICT ASSESSMENT

■ *Lawrence Susskind*
■ *Jennifer Thomas-Larmer*

O rganizing and launching a consensus building process can be a daunting task, especially when there are a great many parties involved. The person convening the process must first determine whether there is a reasonable chance of succeeding. And because each conflict is different, and there are no hard-and-fast rules about when consensus building is likely to work, it is difficult to make this determination before the fact. If a consensus building effort seems likely to succeed, the convenor must ascertain who the stakeholders are and whether or not they will agree to participate. Decisions must also be made about how to frame the issues to be negotiated, how many meetings to hold, how to share the costs of the process, and so on. All of these determinations must be made carefully, because the ultimate success of every consensus building process depends on these early "design" decisions.

The authors wish to thank Howard Bellman, David Fairman, Patrick Field, Philip J. Harter, Fredie D. Kay, Sarah McKearnan, Susan Podziba, and Charles Pou, Jr. for sharing their thoughts about conflict assessment.

The convenor's best bet for sorting through these decisions is to hire a professional neutral (an *assessor*) to conduct a *conflict assessment* (sometimes called an *issues assessment*). A conflict assessment is an information-gathering exercise that produces recommendations regarding

- who has a stake in a conflict or proposed consensus building effort;
- what issues are important to those stakeholders;
- whether or not it makes sense to proceed, given the institutional, financial, and other constraints; and
- if so, under what circumstances the key parties will agree to participate.

An assessment prepared as part of an effort to resolve a state-level regulatory dispute in Delaware provides a good example of how this tool can be used. The Department of Natural Resources and Environmental Control (DNREC) is the Delaware state agency responsible for enforcing the Coastal Zone Act (CZA), a powerful environmental and zoning law prohibiting heavy industry from locating new facilities in the state's coastal region. Although the CZA had been on the books in Delaware for 25 years, regulations implementing it had never been successfully promulgated. (The law had been enforced by DNREC on a case-by-case basis rather than under the guidance of overarching rules.) As a result, industry and environmental groups battled for years over the implementation of the law. At one point, DNREC convened a group of stakeholders to try to develop regulations, but the effort failed. In fact, that failure only heightened the distrust and acrimony among the parties. In December 1995, DNREC decided, once again, that regulations had to be drafted and that a consensus building effort should be convened. Given the long history of conflict among the parties, however, DNREC officials weren't sure that a consensus building process would be feasible. If it did go ahead, the agency wanted to make sure the process had a good chance of succeeding. So DNREC hired a team of neutral assessors to conduct a conflict assessment.

The assessors conducted one-on-one, in-person, confidential interviews with 53 stakeholders, including representatives of industry, environmental organizations, and government. The list of interviewees was constructed by first noting everyone who had taken a public position on the issue, and then asking those people to name others who should be involved. Based on the interviews, the assessors determined that a consensus building process would only be feasible if a limited agenda of issues was discussed and certain preconditions were met. Their report suggested a six-month work plan. The consultation process enabled the assessors—who went on to mediate the process—to become fully aware of the issues at stake and to build a rapport with the parties involved.

DNREC, as the convenor, accepted the assessors' recommendations and, in October 1996, convened the first meeting of the consensus building group. By early 1998, the group had successfully completed its mission, allowing DNREC to formally enact CZA regulations without any objection. In retrospect, it is clear that the conflict assessment was instrumental in ensuring the group's success.

This chapter describes exactly what is involved in conflict assessment. The first section discusses assessments in general: how the concept developed, variations on its use, why it is essential, and who is best prepared to produce a credible assessment report. The second section provides prescriptive advice for those conducting conflict assessments. It explains how to identify stakeholders, arrange and conduct interviews, design a work plan, write a summary report, and use the report as a springboard to convening a consensus building process. The third section addresses some of the debates surrounding the practice of conflict assessment, including its educative potential, conflict-of-interest questions, problematic relationships between assessor and convenor, the need to deal with the media, and the costs involved. The fourth and final section looks at the likely future of conflict assessment in the dispute resolution field.

■ *The Practice of Conflict Assessment*

Conflict assessment, as practiced today, probably derived from the custom in two-party mediations in which a neutral party meets with each "side" separately before meeting with them together. Consensus building, however—particularly when a situation has not reach loggerheads—requires a more elaborate premeeting process, since it is often unclear who should participate and what set of questions should be discussed.

Assessments have been used in public dispute resolution since the field's inception in the early 1970s (H. Bellman, personal communication, April 27, 1998). Gerald Cormick (1976) describes undertaking an assessment-like process in 1973 before mediating a dispute over a proposed dam on the Snoqualmie River in Washington—a dispute that he says was perhaps "the first formal effort to apply the mediation process to an environmental conflict" (p. 219).

In the early 1980s, the assessment idea was formalized in the context of prospective negotiated rulemaking. A 1982 article in the *Georgetown Law Journal* outlined a conflict assessment procedure for such cases (Harter, 1982, pp. 72-75), and in 1990, the Administrative Conference of the United States formally recommended that assessments be conducted for all prospective negotiated rulemakings (Pritzker & Dalton, 1990, pp. 98-103).

In the late 1980s, Moore (1986) and Carpenter and Kennedy (1988) suggested that neutrals conduct assessments in a broad range of dispute resolution settings. And in 1997, the Society for Professionals in Dispute Resolution, a professional association of mediators and consensus builders, adopted a set of *best practices* for government agencies that included guidelines for conducting conflict assessments ("Best Practices," 1997, p. 5). Conflict assessments are now common practice for many types of consensus building and dispute resolution processes.

Groups and organizations that meet and work together permanently—for example, school committees and teams within corporations—do not usually use outside assessors to conduct formal assessments such as those described in this chapter. However, conflict assessments can be very useful (and have been used) in cases in which established groups want to design a new process for dealing with a particularly difficult problem or need help untangling a messy internal dispute. Thus, the approach to conflict assessment described in this chapter applies equally well to permanent organizations and groups, although they are not likely to go through all the steps most of the time.

Differing Approaches to Conflict Assessment

Although most dispute resolution practitioners agree that some sort of assessment should be conducted at the outset of a convening effort, they differ on exactly what needs to be done and what to call the process. Although it's true that some approaches may be more appropriate than others in certain situations, the overall objective is always the same: to identify stakeholders and key issues, analyze the feasibility of moving forward, and design a work plan for proceeding.

Most practitioners agree that an assessment should be carried out by a neutral party who will protect stakeholder confidentiality. Some, however, advocate for convening a small group of key stakeholders, assisted by a process consultant, to do much of the work of identifying participants and designing the process. (See Chapter 3 for details on this approach.)

Many practitioners prefer the term *conflict assessment* to describe the process. Others use the terms *issues assessment, situation assessment, convening assessment, conflict analysis,* or *stakeholder analysis* (McKearnan, 1997, p. 9). Some call the product of the conversations a *conflict assessment report,* as we do. Others refer to it as a *convening report* (S. Podziba, personal communication, December 18, 1997; C. Pou, personal communication, December 11, 1997).

It is the word *conflict* that creates the disagreement. Some practitioners feel the term should not be used because stakeholders may not see themselves as in conflict or because the use of the word may inflame the situation (P. J. Harter, personal communication, April 22, 1998). We have—in cases in which parties were clearly not (yet) in conflict or that were particularly sensitive—substituted the term *issues assessment.*[1]

Practitioners also disagree on how formal or thorough these before-the-fact conversations need to be. Some practitioners prefer a "quick and dirty" approach, in which they speak to a few influential stakeholders on the phone to get a general sense of things. Others prefer to conduct in-depth, in-person interviews with all stakeholders, if possible. Some assessors prefer to make a brief oral report to the convenor when they are finished. Others write a detailed document that is distributed in draft to the convenor and all stakeholders for review (McKearnan, 1997, p. 9). Later in this chapter we discuss the pros and cons of each approach and describe the method we think is most effective.

Why Conflict Assessments Are Essential

"A conflict
assessment
enables the
assessor—and
thereby the
convenor—to
identify the
relevant
stakeholders."

A conflict assessment enables the assessor—and thereby the convenor—to identify the relevant stakeholders, map their substantive interests, and begin to scope areas of agreement and disagreement among them. It also allows the assessor to explore the parties' incentives and willingness to negotiate in good faith. All of this information is crucial to deciding whether a consensus building effort should proceed and, if it does, how it should be structured (what issues should be on the agenda, how many meetings should be held over what time period, what technical assistance will be required, what the final product should be, etc.).

A conflict assessment also creates an opportunity for the assessor to educate the stakeholders about what it takes to bring a consensus process to a successful conclusion. The assessor can answer questions and address concerns in private, so that each potential participant can make an informed decision about whether or not to participate.

Relationship building is another important side benefit of these before-the-fact conversations. The individual who conducts them often goes on to mediate the group conversation, if it goes forward. One-on-one, confidential interviews allow the assessor to get to know each stakeholder individually. The stakeholders can also "assess the assessor" and gauge whether that person is likely to be impartial and effective as a mediator.

Finally, the conflict assessment report, with its detailed analysis of the issues, provides the parties with an impartial map of the underlying conflicts that will need to be addressed. Seeing their own interests described in print often helps each party feel heard and understood. Reading about other parties' interests provides everyone with an accurate portrait of opposing views and the prospects for agreement. The report can also be used to explain to the community at large what the consensus building process is setting out to do and add legitimacy to the procedures by which participants are selected.

The Pitfalls of Proceeding without a Conflict Assessment

Some convenors argue that a conflict assessment is unnecessary or that they have no time "to waste" on such preliminaries. They may think that before-the-fact interviews are too expensive or believe that the key issues and stakeholders are self-evident. Convenors often forget that everyone does not share their perspective. A neutral party can canvass the views of all stakeholders, smoke out difficulties and reluctant participants, and help set credible ground rules.

The greatest danger of proceeding without a conflict assessment is leaving out a key stakeholder. Just one party, inadvertently overlooked, may later undermine the legitimacy of the effort by publicly criticizing it as noninclusive. A conflict assessment conducted for a community consensus building process in Maine (addressing concerns about pollution-related cancer risks), for example, turned up an important organization that had not been involved in previous attempts to address the matter: the Maine Bureau of Health (BOH). Representatives from BOH proved to be crucial to the agreement that was reached; they provided all of the public health data that allowed the group to come to grips with the problem they were facing. (See Case 2.)

Another danger of proceeding without a conflict assessment is that an assessor may design a consensus building process that does not address the right issues. If key issues are left off the agenda, the credibility of the effort could be challenged. Or the group could try to address the question in a way that is too difficult to handle. A conflict assessment offers an opportunity for all important topics and perspectives to be considered.

The Delaware assessment revealed one issue that the assessors decided should not be included in the ensuing consensus building process. The issue involved whether local power-generating plants should be classified as "heavy industry" or "manufacturing." (Only heavy industry would be covered by the new regulations.) The conflict assessment report stated that "this issue . . . threatens to consume a great deal of any group's energies without a great likelihood of reaching consensus." The assessors recommended that the topic be handled separately (Consensus Building Institute, 1996, p. 46).

Finally, a conflict assessment can reveal that a consensus building effort should not be initiated at all. A key stakeholder may admit during a confidential interview that he or she is unwilling to accept consensus as a goal, or has an attractive alternative to agreement that makes the process entirely unattractive. The assessor might also discover that a stakeholder has reason to actively undermine any agreement reached. A process that is sure to fail is not worth starting.

The Delaware assessment uncovered several possible pitfalls and recommended moving forward only if they could be addressed. For example, a number of interviewees said their interests might best be met by lobbying the legislature or the executive branch. So the report recommended that a group be convened only if leaders in the state's executive and legislative branches publicly endorsed the effort. The assessors believed that the right endorsements would "signal to all the interested parties that an 'end run' around the negotiation process would not be fruitful" (Consensus Building Institute, 1996, p. 39). Ultimately, these endorsements were received, and the process was successful.

Who Should Conduct a Conflict Assessment

Most assessments are conducted by dispute resolution professionals (i.e., mediators) who expect to facilitate the consensus process that follows. They may come from private or nonprofit organizations or from state offices of dispute resolution. Not all conflict assessments, however, are carried out by mediators. A court-appointed special master or an ombudsman could play this role, as could an individual with special standing in a community (but no special training), such as a member of the clergy or a tribal elder.

A conflict assessment must be conducted by someone who will be perceived by all stakeholders as impartial. An assessor should not have a stake in the conflict nor can he or she be perceived as partisan in the debate. An assessor must also have some knowledge of the issues at stake, although extensive experience in the given field is not required. Experience in the practice of consensus building is preferred, because educating stakeholders about consensus building is easier if the proponent has firsthand experience. The assessor must also be an effective interviewer. He or she must know how to elicit direct answers, ask for elaboration, request clarification, summarize comments, and read facial expressions and body language (Moore, 1986, pp. 90-95). Finally, an assessor must be able to "connect" with the stakeholders. The more comfortable an interviewee feels, the better the interview. Age, gender, race, education, and professional status can contribute to the connection between interviewee and interviewer, and thus, how much information is elicited (Carpenter & Kennedy, 1998, p. 78; Moore, 1986, p. 82). For example, a recent college graduate would probably not be the best choice to assess a conflict over a proposed senior citizens center. Sometimes, conflict assessment teams are most appropriate.

In addition to the requisite knowledge, skill, and background, an assessor should have a mandate from a convenor to conduct a conflict assessment. The assessor's mandate should be contained in a contract signed by the assessor and the convenor. The assessor-convenor relationship gives the assessor the authority to go forward. Without a mandate, an assessor is essentially engaged in marketing—trying to drum up business by meeting with people and trying to convince them to undertake a consensus building effort. The conflict assessment process described in this chapter is not meant to be a marketing tool.

■ How to Conduct a Conflict Assessment

So where does the assessor begin? Who should be interviewed? What should they be asked? How should the answers be interpreted? Each assessment will vary, of course, but most include (1) introductions, (2) information gathering, (3) analysis, (4) process design (if appropriate), (5) report writing, and (6) report distribution. This section offers advice on how to handle each phase of the process.

Phase 1: Introductions

An assessor must get a clear mandate from a convenor and then gather preliminary information about the conflict or situation. The remainder of the introductory phase involves preparing to interview stakeholders. The assessor must work with the convenor to draft a letter of introduction to potential interviewees, identify the parties to be interviewed, schedule the interviews, and prepare an interview protocol (i.e., a list of questions).

Preliminary Work

The assessor should begin by clarifying his or her mandate. To do this, the assessor and the convenor should prepare a contract (or "letter of agreement") outlining the terms of the relationship, the product to be delivered, the expected cost, and the deadline for delivery. (See the section "The Cost of a Typical Conflict Assessment" later in this chapter for a discussion of reasonable costs.) The contract should ensure that the assessor operates autonomously; that is, he or she should make recommendations based only on his or her best judgment. The assessor must be allowed to keep confidential statements confidential, even from the convenor. Also, the convenor should not try to influence the assessor's recommendation. The contract should make it clear, too, that the assessor's role will change if he or she becomes the mediator later on. The assessor usually works for the convenor or a group of key parties identified by the convenor. During an actual consensus building process, however, the mediator works for all the stakeholders.

Next, the assessor should collect background information. The convenor should be able to provide a preliminary list of likely stakeholders, as well as documentation regarding the relationships among the parties, the history of the conflict, the issues at stake, and the language stakeholders tend to use to characterize their views. The convenor should also provide relevant reports, letters, press releases, and the like. The assessor should search the Internet and the local library for news reports about the issues under discussion.

The assessor should work with the convenor to draft a letter of introduction to all stakeholders that introduces the assessor, describes the assessment process, promises confidentiality, and requests each recipient's participation. These letters should be sent on the convenor's letterhead to all potential interviewees. (Figure 2.1 is the letter of invitation used in the DNREC case.)

Identify the Parties to Be Interviewed

"We think of the process of identifying stakeholders to interview as 'moving outward in concentric circles.'"

The assessor must decide whom to interview. The stakeholders on the preliminary list provided by the convenor should be contacted first. Each should be asked (when arranging an interview) to suggest others who might have a stake in the conflict. The individuals named, if they aren't already on the preliminary list, can be thought of as a "second circle" of stakeholders. The first circle might number 40 or so, and the second circle 20 more, in a typical community-based situation. We think of the process of identifying stakeholders to interview as "moving outward in concentric circles." This ensures that all possible interests are included.

Dear _____ :

I am writing to encourage your participation in an important initiative. The Governor's Office and the Department of Natural Resources and Environmental Control are eager to move ahead with the preparation of revised regulations that will enable us to implement the Delaware Coastal Zone Act. We have asked a team from the Consensus Building Institute (CBI), a nonprofit organization in Cambridge, Massachusetts, to design, with your help, a consensus building process to prepare these regulations. The CBI team of facilitators will include [*names listed here*].

The first step is for the CBI team to conduct a series of confidential interviews with all affected stakeholders. Because we want to be sure your viewpoint is included, we invite you to talk with the CBI facilitators during this "assessment" process.

From the results of the interviews, CBI will

- Identify all relevant stakeholders and their concerns;
- Highlight points of agreement and disagreement;
- Identify the key sections of the draft regulations (approved and adopted in 1993 by the Coastal Zone Industrial Control Board) that need to be renegotiated;
- Assess the willingness of key stakeholders to work collaboratively, despite their differences, to achieve a consensus;
- Suggest ground rules for consensus building;
- Identify any joint fact-finding procedures we ought to follow; and
- Propose a work plan for proceeding with a consensus building process.

The Governor and I believe that this conflict assessment procedure will help us design an informal consensus building plan that will work. We hope you will take time out of your schedule to discuss this important matter with the CBI team. You will be contacted soon to arrange an interview.

Sincerely,

Christophe A. G. Tulou, Secretary
Department of Natural Resources
and Environmental Control

Figure 2.1. Letter of Invitation Sent to Prospective Interviewees in the DNREC-Convened Consensus Building Process (modified)

Often, a stakeholder will urge the assessor to contact a particular organization, but the stakeholder may not know who the appropriate individual is within that group. In such instances, it's best to approach someone at or near the top of the organization and let him or her to decide who should be interviewed.

The assessor may also find that some groups with a stake in a conflict may not be aware of what's going on, or may not be organized in a way that makes it easy to identify an appropriate spokesperson. For example, residents living near a farm may not know that the farmland was recently purchased by a developer, that the developer has asked the municipality to rezone, or that the town might be considering a consensus building process to formulate new land use guidelines for the area. In such cases, the assessor may need to take a number of extra steps to find appropriate interviewees. For example, the convenor and the assessor might decide to organize a public meeting to explain the situation and assist residents in choosing representatives to be interviewed. (See Chapter 6 for more on "unorganized" stakeholders.)

The total number of people to be interviewed will vary widely depending on the conflict. Not everyone needs to be interviewed. Those who hold positions of authority in relevant organizations or who are seen as leading players in the debate because of their special knowledge of or history of involvement in the conflict are all good candidates. The assessor should talk with people from the full range of interests, including everyone on the preliminary list and as many as possible from the second circle. Another rule of thumb is that the assessor should interview everyone whose name is mentioned by two or more people.

In the Delaware case, the facilitators interviewed 53 individuals from three categories of stakeholders: business and industry, environmental organizations, and government. Recall that the conflict concerned the preparation of guidelines to protect the state's coastal area. The breakdown of people interviewed is shown in Table 2.1. This breakdown is fairly typical for a public sector conflict that concerns environmental and economic trade-offs, although it should not be viewed as a precise formula for what should be done in other, similar situations.

Call the Interviewees

Once the convenor has sent the letters of introduction, the assessor should call each person to schedule an interview. In this first call, the assessor should explain once again why the assessment is being done, who is sponsoring it, and why it is important for all stakeholders' views to be heard.

**TABLE 2.1 Breakdown of Interviewees for the Delaware
Conflict Assessment**

Interest Represented	No. of People Interviewed
Business and industry	
Business	16
Power generators	5
Ports	1
Labor	2
Environmental interests	
Organizational	5
Individual	10
Government	
Natural resource agencies	7
Economic development agencies	2
Legislature	4
Local government	1
Total	53

A promise of confidentiality should also be offered. Confidentiality in this case means that comments made by the interviewee will not be attributed to that person by name, title, or organization in either discussions with others or in the report that is prepared. A list of all interviewees will be made public, however, and comments will be grouped by stakeholder category and paraphrased in the report.

Prospective interviewees should be assured that being interviewed does not oblige them to participate in a subsequent consensus building process. They may be invited to participate—and, indeed, they may be asked during the interview to attend a first meeting—but the assessment is fundamentally separate from any dialogue that may follow.

Stakeholders are generally amenable to providing their views on issues they feel are important. Occasionally, however, stakeholders will be reluctant to be interviewed. They may not trust the convenor or may feel their true concerns will somehow work against them. The assessor may need to offer a sample conflict assessment report so that it is clear how comments will be summarized without attribution. If an oral promise of confidentiality is not enough, a written agreement can be drafted and signed by the assessor and the interviewee.

Assessors will need to accommodate the schedules of others, perhaps offering to talk on the phone during evening hours. A prospective interviewee may insist that he or she is not sufficiently involved or knowledgeable to have anything to offer. If this is the case, the assessor should explain that mere perceptions are important. If the interviewee is still reluctant, it may be best to find another person with similar interests. If the reluctant party is a key player, pointing out that the "opposition" will control the way the "story" unfolds is usually enough to elicit an interview.

Prepare the Interview Protocol

The assessor should draft an interview protocol—a list of questions to be asked—before proceeding. The protocol should be available in written form prior to the interviews.

The questions will depend on the conflict and the information needed to design a consensus building process. All interviews, however, should include some variation on the following questions.

- What is the history of the conflict?[2]
- What issues relating to the situation are important to you, and why?
- What other individuals or organizations have a stake in the situation?
- What are the interests and concerns of those individuals or organizations, as you see them?
- Would you be willing to engage in a consensus building effort designed to address this situation?

Note that all but the last question are open-ended; that is, they are designed to encourage interviewees to talk at some length about whatever they feel is important. Open-ended questions "allow interviewees to share their perception of reality . . . without the imposition of an alien framework of analysis" (Moore, 1986, p. 93). Most questions should be open-ended to elicit detailed responses unaffected by the assessor's perspective, knowledge, or bias.

Closed-ended questions—those designed to elicit a short, specific response—can be used as well. Indeed, the last question above is a closed-ended question. An assessor may use questions of this sort to clarify a point, probe a topic, or raise an idea the interviewee hadn't mentioned.[3]

Protocols should be designed so that interviews can be completed in 30 minutes or less, and they should be pretested before they are used.

Phase 2: Information Gathering

Dispute resolution practitioners use a variety of interview formats and techniques. Those that we have found to be most useful are described in this section.

Arrange the Interviews

Stakeholders should be interviewed in person, individually. The eye-to-eye contact possible in an in-person interview (as opposed to a telephone interview) is important for both gathering accurate information and building rapport. In-person interviews allow the assessor to observe each interviewee's facial expressions and mannerisms, revealing the depth of emotion and, sometimes, a clearer sense of the person's status within his or her organization. In-person interviews also allow assessors to communicate understanding and empathy, thereby fostering trust.

Individual interviews are preferable to group interviews because they encourage more candor. Group interviews do save time and money, and if such interviews must be conducted, only groups of stakeholders with very similar interests should be interviewed together (e.g., a group of labor union representatives).

In general, interviews should not last much more than 30 minutes each, and all interviews should be scheduled within a two- to three-day period. This minimizes costs when the assessor has to travel to the area. It will only work, of course, when stakeholders live within a relatively well-defined region and can come to a central location to be interviewed. For statewide or regional conflicts, interview sessions may need to be scheduled in more than one location (e.g., one day of interviews in a state capitol and another day in another large city). For national-level dialogues, in which stakeholders are spread over a large geographic area, phone interviews are probably the only option.

Key stakeholders—those central to the dispute or most senior in their organizations—should be interviewed during the second half of the interviewing period. This enables the assessor to adjust the protocol, if necessary, based on ideas that emerge early on. It also gives the assessor time to become more comfortable conducting the interviews (Moore, 1986, pp. 84-85).

Interviews should be conducted in a neutral location in private meeting rooms, thereby creating a "safe" atmosphere, encouraging candid conversations, and enabling the assessor to project the most "neutral" image possible. Meeting in the convenor's office, for example, may give the impression that the assessor is biased in favor of the convenor.

Some dispute resolution practitioners advocate meeting in each interviewee's office, so that the assessor can get a better idea of the person's status within his or her organization (McKearnan, 1997, p. 9). While useful information can be gained this way, it is more time-consuming and expensive.

During each interview, two assessors should be present: one to ask questions and one to take notes (in writing or on a computer). The lead assessor can concentrate on what the interviewee is saying—following up on the answers, watching facial expressions, and so on—and not worry about writing down what is said. Costs can be minimized by having the note-taker be an intern or lower-level staff person.

If an assessor must work solo, he or she should concentrate more on interacting with the interviewee than on taking notes, and should write (or type) more detailed information from memory immediately after each interview is completed. An assessor who takes elaborate notes while a person is speaking gives the impression of not listening.

We do not recommend tape-recording interviews. Taping often makes interviewees uneasy, and it can be complicated by technical problems: Tapes run out, batteries wear down, and so on. In addition, tape transcription takes much longer than the interview itself. If a tape recorder is used, it should be as a backup only, and permission should be obtained beforehand.

Conduct the Interviews

During the interviews, the protocol should be followed, but not too strictly. The assessor must strike a balance between adhering to the protocol and allowing the conversation to take its own course, which may reveal important and unanticipated information. In general, it is important to ask each interviewee the main set of questions, but assessors should feel free to request clarification and ask follow-up questions as well. How far afield an interview goes is up to the assessor and may be a function of the time available.

Interview protocols usually need to be edited and supplemented with new questions as interviews proceed. The earliest interviews will often reveal information that was not anticipated. When this happens, the assessor begins to formulate an idea about how the consensus building process might be designed. Later interviewees should be given a chance to react to these ideas.

At the end of each interview, the interviewee should be asked if there is anything more he or she would like to add. The assessor should also thank everyone for their time and participation. A written summary of the highlights of the interview should be sent to each participant, to be certain that nothing has been misunderstood.

The note-taker should aim to capture the main points, in the interviewee's own language when possible. Complete, verbatim quotes, however, are not needed. It is important to record the answers to the main questions (e.g., What are your main concerns? Who are the other key players?) as well as additional, related information, such as

> the interviewee's exact involvement in the conflict,
> what the interviewee thinks of the other parties,
> what the interviewee doesn't think is important,
> the names and organizational affiliations of people mentioned by the interviewee,
> whether the interviewee thinks the media are interested in the issues,
> acronyms explained,
> concerns expressed about the convenor or the assessment process,
> the person's status within his or her organization, and
> information about nonwork affiliations.

Other information that should be written down can be gained by observation alone: level of comfort with the interview process, nonverbal cues, and so on (Carpenter & Kennedy, 1988, pp. 82-83).

Phase 3: Analysis

By the time the interviews are complete, the assessor should have a good idea of who the central players are, what concerns them, and whether or not a consensus building process is likely to succeed. It's important that the assessor sort through the accumulated information in a methodical way, to confirm these impressions and to generate a complete report. In the analysis phase, the assessor must (1) summarize the findings, (2) map the areas of agreement and disagreement, and (3) assess the feasibility of moving forward.

Summarize the Findings

The first step in analyzing the results is to read through the interview notes and draft a summary of the concerns and interests of everyone involved. These "findings" will be included in the written assessment. They should be organized by stakeholder category (e.g., business/industry, state government, environmental advocates). Each type of stakeholder forms a heading, and the key concerns form the subheadings, under which the primary opinions of those stakeholders should be summarized. In the Delaware conflict assessment, for example, under the heading "Business and Industry" there was a subheading "What Is at Stake in the Debate." Under that subheading was this item, summarizing the thoughts of a number of the business leaders interviewed: "The future of continued heavy industry in Delaware is at stake. Plants must be allowed to expand and change in order to stay competitive and adjust to a rapidly changing marketplace" (Consensus Building Institute, 1996, p. 6).

When the findings are organized by stakeholder categories, it is easy to preserve confidentiality. No attribution is needed; the opinions and ideas are simply reported. Even if the findings are organized differently, it's important that the summary not attribute ideas or opinions to specific individuals or organizations. The summary should never include statements such as "Jane Johnson of ABC Chemicals is concerned that . . . " or even "A representative from ABC Chemicals believes that . . . ." At most, the assessor could say, "Industry representatives expressed concern that . . . ." This makes for inelegant writing, but it preserves confidentiality.

It is also important not to indicate which ideas or opinions represent a majority view. The purpose of the assessment is simply to set forth the range of ideas, not to polarize the debate by gauging whose views are dominant.

Map Areas of Agreement and Disagreement

Once the findings have been summarized, the assessor should make note of issues on which there is disagreement. One way to do this is with a matrix. On one axis are listed the issues in contention; on the other are the stakeholder groups. The assessor can place either Xs (indicating that the issue is a primary concern for a stakeholder group) or numbers from 1 to 5 (indicating the relative importance of the issue to the group). Matrixes are helpful to the assessor and can be included in the written assessment. Stakeholders may not agree with the priorities indicated in the matrix because not all stakeholders within a stakeholder group agree with each other. (See Figure 2.2 for a sample matrix showing the key concerns of interest groups in a hypothetical landfill-siting case.)

The assessor should also make note of potential opportunities for *mutual gain,* were the parties to enter negotiations. The concept of mutual gains is described in detail in Chapter 8, but the basic premise is this: Because stakeholders generally differ regarding which issues are of greatest importance to them, they can "trade" across those issues to create gains for each other in the negotiated agreement. In the Delaware case, for example, it may appear that there was no room for agreement because the industry groups and the environmental groups held such sharply differing opinions on almost every issue. But they did, in fact, have different priorities. Industry was most concerned that any CZA regulations provide them with the flexibility to make changes, as needed, in their manufacturing processes and products. The environmental groups, on the other hand, were most concerned that there be continuous improvement in the environmental health of the coastal zone. The final agreement gave industry the flexibility to make changes as needed, while requiring them to offset any environmental impacts from new projects

	Groundwater Contamination	Aesthetics (incl. odor)	Remediation (after closure)	Gas Leaks	Truck Traffic	Property Values	Economic Development	Tipping Fees	Profitability	Transportation Costs
State environmental regulators	X		X	X	X					
County officials	X		X			X	X			
Host town officials	X		X		X	X	X	X		
Nearby town officials	X							X		
Abutting residents	X	X	X	X	X	X				
Other county residents	X	X			X			X		
Local environmental group	X		X	X						
County businesses							X	X		
Landfill developer	X							X	X	X
Waste-hauling company	X							X	X	X

Figure 2.2. Sample Matrix of Issues of Significant Concern to Stakeholders Regarding the Siting of a New Landfill: A Hypothetical Case

with environmental improvements, either at their facility or elsewhere in the coastal zone. (The improvements had to be "worth more" than the impacts, as measured by agreed-on environmental indicators.) Each side got what it felt was most important, while giving away something of lesser importance. By mapping stakeholder interests with a matrix, the assessor may be able to spot potential trades such as this.

The assessor should also note potential obstacles to reaching agreement. These might include issues on which mutual gain does not seem possible (i.e., strongly held, mutually exclusive opinions on the same high-priority issue), deeply entrenched positions leading to illogical stubbornness, insufficient incentive to come to agreement, lack of financial support for a consensus process, and so on.

Assess the Feasibility of a Consensus Building Process

An analysis of disagreements can help to determine whether or not a consensus building process should proceed. In general, consensus building efforts are *not* likely to succeed if any of the following conditions hold.

- There are few if any areas of potential agreement among stakeholders and no obvious opportunities to trade across issues valued differently.
- One or more key stakeholders refuses to participate or has good reasons not to negotiate.
- An unrealistic deadline for reaching consensus has been imposed on the parties.
- There is a better option available (i.e., stakeholders can count on meeting their interests through other channels).
- The convenor is incapable of granting the neutral facilitator the autonomy he or she requires (or wants to control the process and the outcome solely for its own gain).
- Huge power imbalances exist among the stakeholders.
- There is no way to fund the consensus building effort.
- There is no pressure to form a consensus building process (i.e., there is no deadline, no political mandate, and no interest on the part of key stakeholders).

If just one of these conditions exists, it can usually be overcome, and a qualified recommendation to proceed may still be appropriate. For example, if a key stakeholder refuses to participate, the assessor can recommend going forward *only if* that stakeholder or someone with similar views can be convinced to take part.

"Stakeholders' skepticism regarding the potential success of an effort is not a reason to recommend against proceeding."

Stakeholders' skepticism regarding the potential success of a consensus building effort is not a reason to recommend against proceeding. Most people have not been involved in consensus building efforts before and have difficulty judging whether or not such an effort is likely to be successful. Nor is the lack of a legislative or regulatory mandate sufficient reason to call a halt; most consensus building processes can operate without one.

If an assessor determines that a consensus building process is likely to be productive, the next step is to suggest the best way to proceed (Phase 4, below). If it doesn't make sense to move forward, the assessor should write a report that explains why (Phase 5).

Phase 4: Process Design

If the assessor believes a consensus process is feasible, the next step is to produce a preliminary process design. This should take the form of a *recommendation* to be included in the conflict assessment report. The recommendation may be modified based on suggestions from interviewees after they review the draft conflict assessment. Also, the elements of a proposed process should be discussed and modified (as necessary) at the first meeting of the full group. Ultimately, a consensus building group must take "ownership" of the process in which it is involved. The inclusion of a proposed process design in the assessment report provides a starting point for discussion.

There is no analytical process that can produce the "proper" design of a consensus building effort. It is not difficult, however, to describe the elements of a typical process design and list the primary questions that need to be answered. In general, recommendations should be made regarding (1) the goals of the consensus building effort, (2) the agenda of issues to be discussed, (3) procedures for selecting the appropriate stakeholder representatives, (4) the time frame and schedule for meetings, (5) ground rules, (6) the relationship of the process to other decision-making efforts, and (7) funding.

Goals

The assessor should suggest an appropriate mission for the consensus building effort (e.g., formulate policy recommendations, design a cleanup plan, determine a fair allocation of funds). The convenor probably has such an objective in mind, so the assessor should decide whether that objective is feasible. The assessor should suggest a modification if those goals are not appropriate given the results of the assessment. In other cases—particularly those in which a group has already begun to meet and is unclear about its purpose—it is important that the assessor recommend clear, reachable goals.

Issues to Be Discussed

The richer the array of issues on the table, the greater the possibility of negotiating mutually advantageous "packages." This principle, of course, has its limits. Some issues may be too complex to handle in a single forum. A discussion about the quality of elementary education, for example, probably wouldn't be appropriate in a collaborative effort aimed at cleaning up a toxic waste site next to an elementary school. In other circumstances, an issue may be too contentious to make much progress. For a policy dialogue on endangered species protection, for example, the assessors determined that it would be more productive to discuss the narrow issue of "incentives for private landowners to protect endangered species" than to take on other, highly contentious issues related to the Endangered Species Act (Keystone Center, 1995). The assessor should suggest an agenda that will allow for simplicity of discussion, and present it in the report.

Participation

In recommending who should participate, the assessor should think about inclusion and balance. All categories of stakeholders should be identified, and an approximately equal number of representatives from each major category should be determined. Ideally, the resulting mix should not be skewed toward one interest or another (i.e., a group should not include 12 industry representatives and 1 environmentalist). The assessor's recommendations about who should be included must build on the suggestions of the interviewees as well as the assessor's judgment about the issues likely to be covered. (A newly formed consensus building group should also review representation at its first meeting and be sure that all appropriate interests are adequately represented at the table.)

Dispute resolution practitioners hold varying opinions about how large a consensus building group can be and still be productive. We will not add to the debate by suggesting an optimal group size, because we have seen groups of widely varying sizes (ranging from 5 to 100) successfully forge consensus agreements.

Time Frame and Schedule of Meetings

The assessor will be expected to make a recommendation regarding how many meetings are likely to be needed to cover the items on the agenda, when they should be held, and the order in which issues should be addressed. Meetings should be spaced at regular intervals, with adequate time between each to draft or review documents, undertake joint fact-finding, or complete other tasks. The total amount of time needed to complete a consensus building process will vary widely, depending on (among other factors)

- outside pressures constraining or driving the timeline (e.g., a statutory deadline);
- whether the situation is acute or chronic (e.g., an imminent public health threat that must be addressed or an abandoned junkyard that could be cleaned up);
- the level of interest, initiative, and energy shown by the participants;
- whether the situation is contained within a small geographic area in which people live near each other and can meet often, or a regional or national issue for which people will have to travel to meetings; and
- the level of joint fact-finding or original research needed to generate answers to the group's questions.

For a conflict that involves an acute situation, contained in a single community, for which there is a high level of interest, three or four 4-hour meetings, spaced at weekly intervals, may be sufficient. For a conflict that involves a chronic problem, at a national level, requiring a great deal of joint fact-finding, a series of 10 or more daylong sessions over a two-year period may be required.

Ground Rules

The assessor should make preliminary recommendations regarding the ground rules that should govern the dialogue. In general, ground rules should address the following.

- How group decisions will be made (i.e., how consensus is defined).
- The roles and responsibilities of participants, the mediator(s), the convenor, and the public.
- How participants should interact with each other.
- How media inquiries will be handled.
- How working groups or subcommittees will be used and their work integrated into the efforts of the plenary.
- How draft documents will be circulated and reviewed.
- Confidentiality (if the process is not public).

In addition, ground rules should address other issues about which stakeholders might be concerned. For example, a multistakeholder group in Connecticut had been meeting for several months, without making much progress, when a dispute resolution practitioner was hired to conduct a conflict assessment. The assessment revealed that many stakeholders were angry that an important meeting had been canceled and rescheduled with only one day's notice. Many stakeholders missed the meeting, at which several key decisions were made. The assessor thus recommended that the group adopt a ground rule outlining a better procedure for rescheduling meetings (S. McKearnan, personal communication, May 28, 1998). (See Figure 2.3 for the ground rules used in the DNREC-convened process in Delaware.)

(text continues on page 127)

I. Purpose

The purpose of the Coastal Zone consensus-based negotiation process is to build agreement among all the stakeholding groups regarding regulations for implementing the Coastal Zone Act, 70 Delaware Code, Chapter 7. The process shall provide the Secretary of the Department of Natural Resources and Environmental Control (DNREC) clear and detailed guidance to assist the Secretary in proposing effective and long-lasting regulations to the Coastal Zone Industrial Control Board consistent with DNREC's policy goals and the Coastal Zone Act. While the process will be advisory, it is the stated intent of the Secretary to adhere to the intent of the guidance in proposing regulations if consensus is reached.

II. Representation

A. *Selection*

Members and alternates of the Coastal Zone Act Regulatory Advisory Committee are appointed by the Governor. The membership is as follows. [*Members listed here*]. Upon convening of the first full meeting of this Committee, the members will consider whether essential stakeholders are missing and if so, may nominate additional members to the Governor.

B. *Role of Members*

Members are expected to fully participate in all meetings of the Committee and to articulate their views and the views of their constituencies. They are also expected to keep constituencies informed about the deliberations and to actively seek their input. To this end, members should make an effort to stay in contact with all relevant individuals and groups with regard to the subject and the results of each meeting.

C. *Role of Alternates*

If a member is unable to attend a Committee meeting, then the member's designated alternate will sit at the table and participate in the discussion. To the extent that time permits, alternates may address the group on a particular issue under discussion. If working groups are formed, alternates may participate fully in the discussions. Alternates will be on the mailing lists and will receive copies of all meeting summaries, reports, handouts, and other documents necessary to keep informed of the process so that they will be ready at any time to participate. They are encouraged to attend all meetings in order to keep informed about the progress of the consensus group's deliberations.

D. *Role of Advisers*

Members and alternates may actively seek out the support and input of advisers who can aid them in expressing their concerns and interests and provide members the information necessary to make decisions. Advisers will not be allowed to speak for members or alternates at the table. However, they may confer with members by speaking to them away from the table during negotiations, at breaks, or when members call for caucuses with their advisers and/or constituents during the deliberations.

E. *Role of Other Members of the Public*

Meetings are open to the public, and interested citizens are invited and encouraged to attend for the purpose of observing the proceedings. Observers will be seated separately from the members, away from the negotiating table. They will not be permitted to interrupt the discussion taking place at the table. At designated times during meetings, members of the public will be invited to address the Committee.

III. Primary Responsibilities of Members and Alternates

Members and alternates agree to

1. Attend all of the regularly scheduled meetings.
2. Arrive at each meeting fully prepared to discuss the issues on the agenda. Preparation will include reviewing meeting summaries, technical information, and drafts of single-text documents distributed in advance of each meeting.
3. Present their own views and the views of the members of their constituencies on the issues being discussed and be willing to engage in respectful, constructive dialogue with other members of the group.
4. Strive throughout the process to bridge gaps in understanding, to seek creative resolution of differences, and to commit to the goal of achieving consensus.

IV. Decision Making

The purpose of the process is to share information, discuss concerns and viewpoints, and build consensus. The group will operate by consensus, and every effort will be made to meet the interests of all the participating stakeholder groups.

A. *Definition of Consensus*

Consensus means that there is no dissent by any member. There will be no formal votes taken during deliberations. No one member can be outvoted. Members should not block or withhold consensus unless they have serious reservations with the approach or solution that is proposed for consensus. If members disagree with the approach or solution selected by the rest of the group, they should make every effort to offer an alternative satisfactory to all stakeholders. Members should remain at the table during deliberations to hear the full discussions in order to make informed judgments when decision making occurs. Willful absence will be equivalent to not dissenting. Any consensus achieved on a specific issue will be tentative pending an agreement on all the issues being considered by the group.

B. *Interaction with the Secretary of DNREC*

The goal of the process is to develop written guidelines to inform the Secretary, who must promulgate a set of regulations under the Coastal Zone Act. Upon receipt of a consensus set of guidelines, the Secretary will draft the regulations. The draft regulations will be circulated to Committee members for a review for consistency with the guidance.

C. *Dispute Resolution Mechanism*

If any member, after conferring with his or her constituency, believes that any portion of the regulations has not met the intent of the consensus guidelines, the member shall contact the facilitators. Subsequently, the facilitators will assist the Secretary and the Committee members in an effort to resolve whatever differences have emerged. If a satisfactory solution cannot be achieved through informal discussion, then members may call for the reconvening of the process. As needed, the facilitators will reconvene a single meeting of the consensus-based advisory group within six weeks of the issuance of the draft regulations. All members will work with the Secretary at this meeting to resolve any and all outstanding issues. Upon acceptance of the draft regulations, or upon completion of this dispute resolution meeting (if necessary), the Secretary will forward the draft regulations to the Coastal Zone Industrial Control Board to initiate the formal promulgation process as required by law.

D. *Support for the Consensual Agreement*

If the process generates a consensus on the guidelines, members agree to support and advocate for the agreement within their own organizations and stakeholder groups as well as with the public. If consensus is reached, members agree to refrain from commenting negatively on the agreement. To the extent that the process does not reach a final consensus on some or all issues, members shall retain the right to comment negatively on those aspects of the agreement that are not based on a final consensus.

V. Communication

Participation in discussions will be restricted to the members seated at the table, unless the facilitator sets aside time on the agenda for others to speak. In order to facilitate an open and collaborative discussion, all those seated at the table will seek to abide by the following rules.

1. Only one person will speak at a time and no one will interrupt when another person is speaking.
2. Each person will express his or her own views rather than speaking for others at the table.
3. No one will make personal attacks or issue statements blaming others for specific actions or outcomes.
4. Each person will make every effort to stay on track with the agenda and avoid grandstanding and digressions in order to move the deliberations forward.
5. Each person will strive to maintain a sense of humor, listen well, and be open minded.

Members are expected to communicate concerns, interests, and ideas openly and to make the reasons for their disagreements clear. In the event that a member is unable to speak about a concern directly to another member, he or she can contact the facilitators by phone (or in person). The facilitators will serve as a channel for such concerns. Upon request, all information or views shared during conversations with the facilitators will be kept confidential.

VI. Role of Facilitators

Facilitation will be provided by the Consensus Building Institute. The members of the facilitation team will

1. Formulate the agenda for all meetings and facilitate these proceedings;
2. Conduct or coordinate any joint fact-finding required;
3. Identify and synthesize points of agreement and disagreement and communicate these in the form of written meeting summaries (see below for further detail);
4. Prepare single-text drafts of proposals between meetings to serve as a basis for deliberations;
5. Assist in building consensus among members;
6. Ensure compliance with all the ground rules;
7. Serve as a confidential communication channel for members, alternates, and observers who wish to express views but do not feel comfortable addressing the full group;
8. Advocate for a fair, effective, and credible process, but remain utterly nonpartisan with respect to the outcome of the deliberations;
9. Communicate the results of the process to the Governor and the Secretary of the Department of Natural Resources and Environmental Control; and

10. Facilitate discussions between members and the Secretary, and/or the full group, if necessary, to resolve disagreements over the Secretary's draft of the regulations.

The facilitation team will prepare a summary of each meeting. The summary will include the key points of discussion as well as items of agreement and disagreement described without attribution. A draft version will be sent to members and alternates after each meeting. Approval of the summary will occur at the following meeting, after the facilitators take note of any proposed additions, corrections, or clarifications. If substantial changes are made, a revised version will be sent to members and alternates, as well as any observers who wish to receive it. Attendance will be kept at each meeting, and a roster of those in attendance will be mailed out with each meeting summary.

VII. Working Groups

Working groups may be established to undertake more in-depth discussion or carry out discrete tasks. These working groups will meet between meetings of the full group and will report back on the results of their discussions when asked to do so. The representation, roles, and responsibilities of the members of working groups will be determined by the full membership.

VIII. Media

All meetings will be open to the public and the media. Press conferences will not be held in conjunction with these meetings. However, the facilitators may, at the request of the Committee, periodically produce press releases, for approval by the members, to keep the media informed of the deliberations.

DNREC will be responsible for ensuring compliance with the Delaware Freedom of Information Act, and will notify the public and media of Advisory Committee meetings.

Members and alternates are free to make statements to the press regarding their own opinions, but agree to not attribute statements to others involved in the process. No member or alternate should presuppose to speak for the group as a whole. In order to facilitate productive deliberations, members and alternates will make every effort to abide by the ground rules under the section "Communication" listed above while interacting with the media. If an article or report appears that misquotes or inaccurately represents an individual, that individual should inform the group of that occurrence as soon as possible.

Figure 2.3. Ground Rules for Delaware's Coastal Zone Act Regulatory Advisory Committee

Relationship to Other Efforts

Interlocking activities relating to the issues addressed in the consensus building process will undoubtedly take place before, during, and after the process. Town meetings, public hearings, elections, court cases, the promulgation of administrative rules, academic research, and even other consensus-based processes may overlap. The assessor must determine, to the extent possible, how the consensus building process might interact with these activities. Agreement may be needed by a certain date, for example, to meet a separate but linked deadline. It may be best not to begin a consensus process until after an election, so the political landscape is clear. Or a faculty member at a local university may have a research project under way that could influence the dialogue.

Budget and Funding Mechanism

The assessor should determine and make recommendations regarding the likely cost of the process, if it goes forward. The estimate will probably be a "best guess." It should take into account the expected costs of professional services, staff travel, meeting room rental, catering, and other administrative needs. A more precise, itemized budget can be drawn up later if the process goes ahead.

The assessor may also want to recommend to the convenor that, once a process is under way, the group appoint an executive committee to oversee whatever funds are contributed by the convenor or other parties. Money may come solely from the convening organization or from a great many sources. Either way, the funding committee should determine how the money should be spent. The group must have autonomy so that the funding is not contingent on achieving a certain result.

Phase 5: Report Writing

The analysis of the interview results and the proposed process design should be presented to the convenor and the interviewees in summary form. Some dispute resolution practitioners prefer to present their findings in an oral report. This may take less time and therefore cost less, leaving whatever funds are available for the consensus building effort itself. An oral report may also give the assessor more freedom to be candid with the convenor, although confidentiality must still be protected (McKearnan, 1997, p. 9). Oral presentations may be particularly useful in those instances in which the number of parties interviewed is so small that it might not be possible to write a detailed analysis of the results without revealing who said what. An assessor could also present his or her findings to one or more focus groups. These can be composed of stakeholders with similar interests who are in a position to give the assessor feedback on the results. This method is suggested for use in intraorganizational disputes (Costantino & Merchant, 1996, pp. 107-108). In general, however, we recommend a written report.

What to Include in a Written Report

A written conflict assessment report should include the following.

Introduction. This section should review the initiation of the assessment, naming the convenor, the assessor, the purpose of the assessment, how the assessment was conducted, the number of people interviewed, and, perhaps, a short summary of the points of agreement and disagreement among the interviewees.

Findings. As discussed previously, this section should summarize the interests and concerns of the interviewees, using language that protects confidentiality.

Analysis. This section should include the assessor's analysis of the findings, including a matrix. It should point out where stakeholders' interests overlap and where they diverge, and identify potential barriers to agreement.

Recommendations. This section should include, first, a recommendation regarding whether or not the assessor thinks a consensus building process should proceed. Second, if the assessor recommends that such an effort go forward, this section should sketch a possible process design—the work plan for proceeding. It should cover (1) the goals of the consensus building process, (2) issues to be discussed, (3) who should participate, (4) time frame and schedule of meetings, (5) ground rules, (6) relationship to other decision-making efforts under way, and (7) the budget and funding mechanism.

Phase 6: Report Distribution

Report distribution can be used to help launch a consensus building effort, serving as a "springboard" to convening. The first step in distribution is to circulate the report—with the word *draft* stamped on every page—to all interviewees and the convenor. Comments should be sought on both the description of stakeholder interests and on the proposed work plan. This will enable the assessor to ensure that he or she has accurately portrayed each stakeholder's interests and test the parties' readiness to proceed. Once the deadline for comment has passed, the assessor should revise the draft and issue a final report.

This document can then be circulated to a wider audience, if appropriate. If a process hinges on public support, for example, the final document should be distributed to all relevant media outlets as well as the public and elected officials. A report that makes a case for a consensus building process will help strengthen public support.

If a consensus building effort is recommended, the convenor should move ahead with the selection of a mediator, a first meeting of stakeholders (to ratify the work plan, budget, and mediator selection), and the securing of adequate funds. If the assessment was conducted according to the guidelines set forth in this chapter, all the pieces should be in place to proceed.

■ *Dilemmas and Debates in the Practice of Conflict Assessment*

This section discusses the tensions that often arise during the preparation of a conflict assessment and some suggestions that experienced practitioners have to offer about how to handle them. Included are a review of how to handle perceived conflicts of interest, how to structure a relationship between the assessor and the convenor, how media contact should be handled, and what conflict assessments typically cost.

Conflict Assessment as an Educative Process

We believe that a conflict assessment is, willy-nilly, an educative process. Stakeholder interviews should always touch on what consensus building is and what it takes to make a process work. Although consensus building is more common these days, stakeholders are still relatively unfamiliar with the concept. In addition, many groups are represented by inexperienced negotiators. Those in positions of leadership are likely to be familiar with the traditional adversarial approach to dealing with differences, but not with the mutual gains approach outlined in Chapter 8. Because this is true, we consider it to be a responsibility of the assessor to help those with less knowledge and experience think about creating the right conditions for effective participation. Some may need negotiation training. Some may require financial support to cover travel expenses. The assessor can help by offering all parties "off-line" training (or finding another qualified professional to provide this help) or by working with the parties to identify financial support.

An assessor must be careful not to jeopardize his or her neutrality. It is not appropriate, for example, for the assessor to give "extra" information, advice, or training to one stakeholder or group but not to the others. All should be treated equally, even though they may have different needs and levels of ability. The assessor should offer negotiation training to all stakeholders, for example, not just those who need it most.

Assessors should not offer strategic advice to one "side" during an assessment process either (e.g., "Push hard on Issue X but not on Issue Y to achieve your goals"). In our view, this is a clear ethical violation. The assessor should ask questions that force each stakeholder group to think hard about its options (e.g., "What is your best alternative to a negotiated agreement? What makes you think that? What do you think the most important issues are for other stakeholders?"). But questions like these should be asked of all parties, to ensure fairness.

Dealing with Perceived Conflicts of Interest

Part of an assessor's job is to make a recommendation about whether or not to proceed with consensus building. Yet most assessors are experienced mediators who hope to be selected to facilitate the process if it goes forward. It would appear, therefore, that the assessor has an inherent incentive to recommend that a group be convened.

There is a simple—though problematic—way to avoid this possible conflict of interest: The assessor can be prohibited from competing for the consensus building contract. Such a prohibition, however, would undermine one of the primary purposes of a conflict assessment, which is to build relationships. In the course of an assessment, the assessor works to build the trust of the stakeholders. This trust is essential for mediating successfully. Any new mediator would have to start from scratch (which is practically impossible once the process has begun).

But a general recommendation about whether or not to proceed is not the primary purpose of a conflict assessment. (It may be clear, for example, that some sort of consensus building process is desirable.) In these instances, the primary purposes are to build relationships, secure stakeholder participation, and develop a work plan. There is no conflict of interest, therefore, if the outcome is more or less predetermined and everyone expects the assessor to mediate the process that follows.

In situations in which the feasibility recommendation is, indeed, the primary focus, it is not uncommon for the assessor to recommend *not* proceeding (C. Pou, personal communication, December 11, 1997). In fact, one study revealed that, of 81 environmental disputes in which mediators sought to intervene, 57 were found during the assessment phase to be inappropriate for mediation. Another 16 never got past a first organizational meeting. Mediation was pursued in only 11 percent of the cases that were fully assessed (Buckle & Thomas-Buckle, 1986, p. 61). It is also common for conflict assessments—as in the Delaware case—to recommend going forward only if certain conditions can be met. Assessors, too, have an interest in ensuring that a process that does continue has a good chance of succeeding.

"Assessors only make recommendations; they do not have decision-making authority." It should be remembered, as well, that assessors only make recommendations; they do not have decision-making authority and cannot force the parties to proceed. Also, if a written report is submitted, the assessor's findings and analysis will be thoroughly reviewed by the convenor and the stakeholders. There has to be a basis, on the merits, for going forward. This is the best safeguard against potential conflict of interest.

The Relationship with the Convenor

The assessment and the final report should be used to help the convenor survey the complexities of the conflict at hand. We do not assume that a convenor is knowledgeable about mediation or consensus building. Indeed, the concept of neutrality, the principles of mutual gains negotiation, and the definition of consensus will probably all need to be explained. Furthermore, the convenor and the assessor usually need to discuss what the convenor's role actually is. The assessor's insights are extremely useful to the convenor.

The contract between the convenor and the assessor should specify that a conflict assessment involves an independent analysis based on the professional judgment of the assessor. This means that it is the assessor's call as to who should be interviewed, what should be asked, and how the findings should be interpreted.

Even with a signed contract, the relationship between the assessor and the convenor can be tricky, and occasionally it turns sour. For example, a convenor may want to rewrite the assessment report so that the recommendations reflect his or her own conclusions. Or the convenor may insist, after a draft is completed, that the assessor interview additional stakeholders or present the concerns of a certain group in a different way. Most will say no to such requests.

The best solution to problems of this sort is prevention. Through open communication before and during the assessment process, these difficulties can usually be avoided. But if a conflict does emerge, the assessor should negotiate with the convenor, using the mutual gains approach outlined in Chapter 8 (and, perhaps, with the assistance of another mediator). The assessor may have to take a hard line and opt out. If an assessor is forced to abandon the process, he or she should let the interviewees know what has happened (in general terms), being careful to leave the door open for a return if the convenor has a change of heart.

Dealing with the Media

Media attention can complicate a conflict assessment, in part, because it can undermine a promise of confidentiality. Therefore, there is rarely a reason for an assessor to seek media attention—at least not until an assessment has been completed.

The media are interested in "news," and conflict assessments are not really newsworthy until a decision has been made to go forward. If the subject of a conflict assessment is highly controversial, however, the media may take an interest. If a reporter does call during an assessment process, the assessor should focus on the purpose of the assessment, including its timing, the types of stakeholders being interviewed, and the qualifications of the convenor. The assessor should definitely not characterize the concerns of the stakeholders, name the interviewees, or offer a preview of his or her recommendations. Interviewees, of course, are entitled to speak with the media about their own views, but they should be advised not to talk about their attitudes toward others being interviewed. Once a written conflict assessment has been prepared, the assessor and the convenor may wish to release it to the media, as discussed in the previous section, "Report Distribution."

If media coverage does follow and this escalates interviewees' concerns, those fears can be assuaged. The assessor should encourage stakeholders to talk to others involved in previous conflict assessments and to review completed assessments. They will quickly realize that even if word does get out about the recommendations contained in a conflict assessment, the parties retain the sole authority to decide whether to go ahead or not and to set the terms for the conversation.

The Cost of a Typical Conflict Assessment

Costs depend on the fees of the assessor and the number of interviewees. Convenors often prefer a fixed-price contract to an open-ended one based on hourly rates. The cost of a fixed-price contract is generally determined by multiplying the daily or hourly fee of the assessors by the amount of time required to arrange and conduct interviews, analyze the results, write the report, and revise it in light of comments received. The costs of travel, long-distance calls and faxes, and related administrative overhead must also be factored in. It is customary for all costs to be covered by the convening organization.

Assessors' fees vary. An informal survey done in 1998 found that dispute resolution practitioners' fees depend on their level of experience and their clients' ability to pay. Fees for senior-level mediators averaged between $130 and $190 per hour. Average hourly rates for midlevel mediators were $75 to $110, and fees for entry-level practitioners ranged from approximately $50 to $70 per hour (Thomas-Larmer, 1998, p. 5).

In making a rough forecast of costs, it's best to figure about six hours per interviewee (including the time needed to arrange the interviews through revision of the completed document). So an assessment that includes interviews with 25 people will require roughly 150 hours to complete. At an average cost of $100 per hour, the assessment would cost $15,000 plus expenses.

The assessment in the Delaware case, in which 53 people were interviewed, cost just under $30,000. The high cost was due in part to the fact that the assessment was conducted by a four-person team led by a senior-level consultant who charged about $200 per hour. At the other end of the spectrum, we recently conducted a conflict assessment for a multistakeholder negotiating group in Connecticut that required interviewing 25 people, and it cost $9,800. Not only were there fewer interviews, but we used lower-level staff, charged lower daily fees, and minimized expenses in a variety of ways. The typical cost of a conflict assessment in a public policy dispute is somewhere between these two extremes—about $15,000.

■ Conclusion

As consensus building becomes more widespread, convenors, stakeholders, and even mediators may assume that conflict assessments are unnecessary. They may think they know from experience how to spot the likely stakeholders and how every process should be structured. This would be a serious mistake. Each potential effort must be designed anew. In fact, conflict assessments may become even more important as the public learns more about consensus building and becomes more comfortable with it. We hope they will become more discriminating, rejecting processes that are likely to be inefficient and demanding appropriately tailored processes in each case. Conflict assessments should ensure that every consensus building effort gets off to a good start. Every dispute resolution practitioner should be skilled in conducting conflict assessments, since assessments are, and will continue to be, crucial to the success of all consensus building efforts.

■ Notes

1. It should be noted that the term *issues assessment* has a different meaning in the realm of international treaty negotiations. In that setting, it means an effort by a neutral to gather the best available information on a given set of issues, without reference to the interests or concerns of the parties. It is

used, in particular, in highly technical matters in which stakeholders have very unequal levels of scientific knowledge and capabilities.

2. In inquiring about the history of a situation or conflict, the assessor should ask interviewees whether or not the press has covered the issue in the past or is likely to if a consensus process moves forward. Chapter 11 describes in detail how a mediator, during a conflict assessment process, should consider issues relating to the potential coverage of a consensus building effort by the media.

3. Moore (1986, pp. 90-94) includes a thorough and very useful discussion of the types of questions that can be used in these interviews.

■ *References*

Best practices for government agencies: Guidelines for using collaborative agreement-seeking processes. (1997, April). *Consensus, 34,* 5-7.

Buckle, L. G., & Thomas-Buckle, S. R. (1986). Placing environmental mediation in context: Lessons from "failed" mediations. *Environmental Impact Review, 6,* 55-70.

Carpenter, S. L., & Kennedy, W. J. D. (1988). *Managing public disputes.* San Francisco: Jossey-Bass.

Consensus Building Institute. (1996). *Conflict assessment: The prospects for building consensus on new regulations pursuant to Delaware's Coastal Zone Act.* Cambridge, MA: Author.

Cormick, G. W. (1976). Mediating environmental controversies: Perspectives and first experience. *Earth Law Journal, 2,* 215-224.

Costantino, C. A., & Merchant, C. S. (1996). *Designing conflict management systems: A guide to creating productive and healthy organizations.* San Francisco: Jossey-Bass.

Harter, P. J. (1982). Negotiating regulations: A cure for malaise. *Georgetown Law Journal, 71*(1), 1-113.

Keystone Center. (1995). *Final report of the Keystone dialogue on incentives for private landowners to protect endangered species.* Washington, DC: Author.

McKearnan, S. (1997, April). Preliminary step that enhances chance of success. *Consensus, 34,* 3, 9, 12.

Moore, C. W. (1986). *The mediation process: Practical strategies for resolving conflict.* San Francisco: Jossey-Bass.

Pritzker, D. M., & Dalton, D. S. (1990). *Negotiated rulemaking sourcebook.* Washington, DC: Government Printing Office.

Thomas-Larmer, J. (1998, April). Survey finds wide range in mediators' fees. *Consensus, 38,* 5, 7, 8.

3

DESIGNING A CONSENSUS BUILDING PROCESS USING A GRAPHIC ROAD MAP

■ *David A. Straus*

Imagine how a corporate executive or government official would react if approached by a consultant with the following proposition: "I'm organizing a consensus-based process to build agreement on an issue I know you care a lot about. We're not really sure who will be involved in the process, how much time it will take, or how we're going to get to agreement, but we're ready to dive in and get the discussions started. Can we have your commitment to participate fully?"

Any reasonable person would refuse to become involved in such an ill-defined and poorly planned process.

But the opposite case is also problematic. If detailed, step-by-step procedures for reaching agreement are designed in advance by a consultant, potential participants may feel that a cookie-cutter method is being imposed on them, and as before, they may refuse to take part.

Stakeholders need a way to jointly plan a consensus building process that is appropriate to their situation, so that they "own" the process and feel comfortable participating in it. They need to work together to figure out where they are going and how they are going to get there. They need a map.

This chapter is about the power of a *graphic road map* (or *process map*) as a tool for designing a consensus process. It is also about the value of having a subset of stakeholders form a process design committee (PDC) to develop such a map.[1] It is written as a guide for the process design phase of a consensus building effort. The first section describes the process design phase and introduces the case example used throughout the chapter. The second section discusses the concept of a PDC—its benefits, its purpose, the role of a process consultant, guidance on who should participate, and so forth. The third section introduces graphic road maps and describes their benefits. The remainder of the chapter outlines the steps a PDC should follow to design a consensus-based process using a graphic road map.

■ *The Process Design Phase*

Consensus building and collaborative planning processes typically have four major phases (see Figure 3.1).

The *start-up phase* begins when one or more leaders within a community or organization (1) acknowledges that a problem exists beyond the power of a single individual to solve and (2) decides to explore the possibility of bringing together people with diverging views of the problem to try to solve it. The end result of this phase is often a decision to hire a consultant to assist with the next phase.

The *process design phase* involves determining whether or not a consensus-based process will succeed, who should be involved, and how to proceed. These tasks may be taken up by a consultant, who conducts a *conflict assessment* and brings recommendations for a proposed process design (including, perhaps, a process map) back to a larger group of stakeholders (see Chapter 2). We recommend, however, that the work of conflict assessment and process design be performed by a subgroup of stakeholders—a PDC—with the support of a consultant or facilitator.

In the *consensus building phase,* stakeholders convene in a series of meetings to build consensus step-by-step, from creating a common understanding of a problem to coming to agreement on a solution. In an organizational setting, this phase is typically called *planning,* because participants are trying to reach consen-

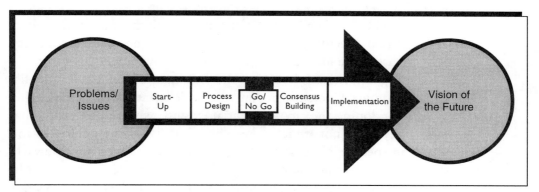

Figure 3.1. Phases of Consensus Building

sus on a course of action—a strategic plan, a downsizing plan, or a budgetary plan, for example.

In the *implementation phase,* the agreements reached in the consensus building phase are put into action. A representative group of stakeholders may need to monitor implementation to ensure that an agreement is faithfully and effectively carried out. Implementation is often performed by a single organization, public agency, or corporate department.

The phases of consensus building in Figure 3.1 become increasingly concrete and operational from left to right. This progression can be described as follows: The start-up phase involves initiating an approach to process design, or "planning to plan to plan"; the process design phase involves determining how to conduct a consensus-based process, or "planning to plan"; the consensus building phase involves reaching agreement on actions to take, or "planning to do"; and the implementation phase involves taking action, or "doing."

To illustrate how a process design phase can be completed using a design committee and a graphic road map, this chapter refers periodically to a large-scale consensus building effort called the Newark Collaboration Process. This effort was convened in 1984 to conduct a comprehensive planning process for Newark, New Jersey, a city that had been torn apart by race riots in the 1970s and was often used as a dramatic example of urban decay. The city was plagued by high crime rates, poverty, continuing racial tensions, and poor-quality schools, among many other problems. In addition, community leaders were often at odds. Those in the nonprofit, social service fields felt that business leaders were not doing enough to invest in the community and provide jobs, while business executives felt that nonprofit leaders were ineffective and unable to deliver on their vision for the city. Trust in the local government was also low.

Newark was home to the headquarters of the Prudential Insurance Company of America, which was actively considering abandoning the city. Prudential executives were concerned that they could not attract or keep high-quality talent; employees and prospective hires simply did not want to live in or near Newark. Before making the relocation decision, however, company officials decided they should work harder to reverse Newark's downward spiral. Alex Plinio, then vice president for community affairs, was tapped to lead Prudential's efforts to help the city. Plinio began by talking one-on-one with a number of leaders in Newark's business, government, and nonprofit sectors and inviting them to a meeting to discuss what might be done to save their city. Many expressed an interest in attending.

Plinio realized, however, that he could not both convene and facilitate the meeting without appearing to control the process. Through an intermediary, he contacted my organization, Interaction Associates, and contracted with us to facilitate the meeting. We also agreed to serve as process consultants through at least the process design phase, if local leaders agreed to proceed in that direction.

Approximately 60 leaders, including the mayor of Newark, attended the meeting. They discussed the many critical problems facing the city, noted that the adversity among community leaders was hindering attempts to resolve the problems, and agreed, at a minimum, to explore how a more collaborative, consensus-based planning process might help. They selected a PDC from among the stakeholders present. The committee agreed to meet several times and return to the large group with a proposal for a consensus building process.[2] This chapter will explore in some detail the ways in which this process design phase unfolded.

■ *The Process Design Committee*

A PDC like that used in Newark has numerous benefits that spill over into an ensuing consensus building process. A PDC must be set up and run properly, however, to be most effective.

Benefits of a Process Design Committee

"We believe
strongly that
a consensus
building effort
should not be
designed by an
outside party."

We believe strongly that a consensus building effort should not be designed by an outside party. It is imperative that stakeholders themselves plan it, with the assistance of a process consultant, if necessary. The benefits of a PDC far outweigh the additional time this endeavor may take.

First, the use of a PDC ensures that the principles guiding a consensus-based effort are consistent from the beginning. When diverse stakeholders work together to outline their own consensus process, collaboration is being modeled from the start. Group members learn, before committing to seek a consensus agreement, the skills and behaviors they need to reach such an agreement. Stakeholders are more likely to buy into the concept of consensus building if they have seen how it works than if it is described to them by an outside party.

If Interaction Associates had presented a completed process design proposal to the group of 60 leaders in Newark, we would surely have met with strong resistance. The participants had not previously participated in a consensus building effort, did not trust one another, and probably would not have trusted us—the outsiders—as process experts. Even if they had accepted our proposal, they would have had little ownership of the ensuing effort and therefore may not have been committed to seeing it through to completion. In a planning effort in Denver, for example, in which the process design was driven by the staff of a downtown business association and outside consultants, participants resisted implementing the design for six months. Ultimately, they redesigned the process themselves.

A second benefit of collaborative design is that a core group of stakeholders—the design committee members—learns about the various methods of planning and resolving conflict. This enables them to choose an approach that is appropriate to their situation and the culture of their constituencies. The members of a PDC can also help to educate their constituents about consensus building.

Members of the Newark PDC became strong advocates for the principles of consensus building, and in many ways they were more effective in educating their fellow stakeholders than we, as consultants, could have been. Committee members also came up with innovative ways to build credibility for the consensus building effort. For example, they recommended holding large community meetings—an important feature of the final design—in different parts of the city. Each meeting was hosted by a different community organization, thereby encouraging a wide diversity of residents to attend and enabling participants to learn about neighborhoods other than their own.

A PDC also helps to create a sense of ownership in an ensuing consensus building process. Members of a PDC feel responsible for the success of a process because they designed it themselves. Those in the larger community or organization are likely to accept as legitimate a process that has been recommended by their peers.

In Newark, members of the PDC crafted an elegant and compelling proposal for a consensus building process. They presented it to the group of 60 with so much enthusiasm that it was accepted with little debate. The PDC created such a groundswell of support, in fact, that business leaders tried to outdo each other in providing funding for the process, and they worked together to seek additional contributions from local foundations.

Finally, the process design phase is a test of the viability of consensus building itself, especially in high-conflict situations. If a group can reach consensus on the design of a process, members may begin to believe they will reach consensus on a solution to the problem itself. During PDC meetings, stakeholders constantly test each other and the collaborative process: "Do I trust your intentions and commitment?" "Will we ever be able to agree on anything?" "Is this facilitator skillful enough to handle our group?" "Can consensus building work here?" As a PDC moves toward consensus on a recommended process, members become confident that consensus may be possible on the tougher issues that lie ahead.

In Newark, these tests began during the first PDC meeting. The trust level among participants was so low that the community groups refused to begin work on the process design until the business sector demonstrated its commitment to the city. After a lot of heated exchanges and hard work, the PDC agreed on three short-term projects that would demonstrate the willingness of all sectors to commit resources to the city and work collaboratively. These projects included a summer employment program for youth, progress on a low-income housing project that had been stalled, and the cleanup of a main street that connected the city to the airport. The projects were presented to the group of 60 for its approval, and then undertaken immediately. The fact that PDC participants could negotiate with each other, make agreements by consensus, and produce results fueled their belief in the power of collaborative action.

It should be noted that the Newark case presents an extreme example of distrust and antagonism within a PDC. Usually, the experience of working through conflicting ideas about the elements of a process design (e.g., how long an effort should last, who should be involved) is enough to demonstrate to PDC participants that they may be able to reach agreement on larger issues. Short-term demonstration projects are generally not required!

The Role of the Process Consultant

Ideally, a PDC should operate with the assistance of a *process consultant*. This term probably warrants some explanation. In our consulting practice, we make clear distinctions among levels of competency, from the most basic skills in meeting facilitation to the highest-level skills of process consultation. A process consultant must be able to coach senior executives and community leaders in facilitative leadership; design complex, multilevel intervention processes; and lead a team of consultants and trainers to support an intervention.

In a PDC, for example, a process consultant must play the roles of facilitator, recorder, educator, process design expert, and advocate. Because norms are being set in a PDC for how meetings will be conducted throughout the rest of the intervention, the often-contentious PDC sessions must model the best practices of effective, facilitated meetings. If a process consultant is working alone, he or she must function as a recorder and capture participants' comments on flip charts or butcher paper. Because PDC members are not typically knowledgeable about alternative planning or consensus building approaches, a consultant must also serve as educator, by presenting the basic principles of consensus building as guidelines for a design session, and as an expert, by laying out the advantages and disadvantages of different approaches. The consultant must also lead the committee through the step-by-step construction of a process map. Finally, if members of a PDC get discouraged about the likelihood of completing a consensus building process, a consultant may need to serve as an advocate and cheerleader for the power of collaborative action, by describing how others have tackled equally difficult problems. (It should be noted that many senior-level dispute resolution practitioners who call themselves *facilitators* or *mediators* do have all of these skills. We simply believe *process consultant* is a more accurate label.)

Given the multiple roles a process consultant must play, we recommend, if possible, that at least two consultants work as a team: One person can serve as the facilitator and recorder and the other as the process expert and educator. If a consulting team is not possible, then it is helpful for the consultant to be very clear about when he or she is playing which role. For example, a consultant might say, "OK, now that you have agreed on the components of the final report, let me step out of my facilitator role to talk about how other process design committees have approached the task of designing a process road map. . . . Now I am moving back into my facilitator role. How would you like to proceed?" This conscious demarcation of changing roles will prevent committee members from becoming confused and will teach them about the importance of separating process from content.

The Charter of a Process Design Committee

The purpose of a PDC is to recommend the steps that the larger community, group, or organization might take to build consensus on the issue or problem at hand. Specifically, a PDC is expected to answer the following questions.

1. What are the key decision points in the consensus building process?
2. What are different tasks and types of activity that should occur?
3. What might a graphic road map of the process look like?
4. Who is going to be involved and how?
5. How will the overall process be managed (e.g., by a steering committee; with the help of designated, internal staff)?
6. Who will serve as internal staff (i.e., to do logistical and administrative work, coordinate work group meetings)?

7. How will final decisions be made?
8. How will information be gathered, stored, and disseminated?
9. What kind of process consulting and facilitation services are needed, and how will they be acquired?
10. What kinds of technical experts will be needed, and how will those services be acquired?
11. What kinds of training do participants need?
12. What communication tools and opportunities will be needed to update the larger community on the effort? What kinds of tools will be needed to support communication among participants and between participants and their constituencies?
13. How much will the effort cost, and how will the necessary resources be obtained?

In our experience, a PDC can answer these questions in three to four 3-hour meetings. Sometimes additional subgroup meetings are needed to interview prospective staff or to conduct fund-raising activities.

Who Should Take Part in a Process Design Committee?

The question of who should participate in a PDC—who should be chosen to represent the broader set of stakeholders—is less critical than the issue of representation in a consensus building phase. After all, the focus of the PDC is process, not content—the committee is formed to plan a road map, not to resolve a problem. Also, a PDC only makes recommendations; the complete set of stakeholders (or the senior executive[s], in an organizational situation) must review, modify if necessary, and approve the recommendations. Nonetheless, it is important to form a PDC that is credible to all stakeholder groups. Therefore, what is needed is a group of people who are broadly representative of the competing interests and, more important, are willing to work collaboratively to design a process that will include a much larger set of stakeholders. We like to think of representatives as those people who represent *points of view* and *interests,* not specific *organizations* or *numbers of people.* Therefore, if several groups generally have the same interests or points of view, one person may be able to represent all of them on a PDC.

We suggest that a PDC include 7 to 15 members, because that is generally considered the most efficient size for a problem-solving group. If stakeholders distrust each other and are wary of the concept of consensus building, however, many more may insist on being involved. In the Newark Collaboration Process, about 40 people volunteered and insisted on participating in the PDC, including the mayor. In cases like this, it is advisable to go with a larger group rather than forcing volunteers to drop off. While facilitation may be more challenging and subgroups may need to be formed, allowing for a large PDC proves to stakeholders that the process is in their hands, and it enables more people to become educated about and experienced in consensus building.

Forming a Process Design Committee

PDCs can be formed in a variety of ways. If the setting is a single, hierarchical organization, the senior management team typically serves as the PDC during the process design phase—sometimes called the engagement phase by management consultants. If the senior managers are too busy or cannot meet frequently enough, they may appoint midlevel managers or other employees to a PDC. (Serving on a PDC is a wonderful development opportunity for promising middle managers and up-and-coming leadership talent.) This group may be asked to serve as a steering committee during the consensus building phase as well. A PDC's legitimacy in this situation results from the "blessing" of senior management and a conscious effort to include representatives of all the major divisions or functions of the organization.

In the public sector, building legitimacy for a PDC is more difficult. In our experience, a consensus building process is usually initiated by the leader of a government agency or private sector organization who begins to explore with leaders of other organizations whether there is interest in working collaboratively to resolve a specific issue. This exploration gathers momentum during the start-up phase until there is a critical mass of interest, at which point several questions arise: Who should be involved in the effort? How should it work? Who should facilitate it? Who should pay for it? A PDC, assisted by a process consultant, is often suggested as a way to help answer these questions.

There are several ways to organize and gain broad-based support for a PDC in a public sector context. One approach is to have the leaders involved in the start-up phase convene a large meeting of all the interested parties. (A group of up to 300 people is workable.) In Newark, Alex Plinio from Prudential, with the support of the mayor, served as the convenor and invited other stakeholders to take part in this organizational meeting. In other cases, a letter of invitation may go out with the signatures of several leaders representing different sectors and interests. The meeting should be as widely publicized as possible and open to anyone who wants to attend. After all, the power of a collaborative effort comes from inclusion, not exclusion. The point of this meeting is to create as large a group of stakeholders and concerned citizens as possible to test consensus and build legitimacy—first for the formation of a PDC, second for the PDC's recommendations, third for the recommendations of any consensus building group that is formed, and, ultimately, for a final agreement.

During the first meeting, participants may identify a key stakeholder group that the convenors neglected to invite. It is important that the convenors not get defensive in this situation. They should, rather, apologize and keep asking who else should be involved. After the first session, the convenor can invite representatives from the missing groups to attend the second meeting.

The first two- to three-hour session should be designed as a task-oriented conference. If there are more than 30 or so participants, the problem-solving work should be done in small subgroups of 10 to 20 people. Community members can be trained to facilitate these breakout sessions. Participants in the small groups should be asked to brainstorm the key issues they believe a consensus building process could take up. When each subgroup reports its ideas back to the full plenary group, common themes should begin to emerge, around which a general consensus on key issues can be built. The consultant should then ask participants whether or not there is support for at least exploring how a consensus building process could work. For example, the facilitator can ask, "Are there any objections to working together to investigate how a consensus building process might be used to resolve these issues?" If an overwhelming number of participants respond affirmatively (and they almost always do), then the convenors or facilitator can talk to the group about the role of a PDC. They can, for instance, present a draft charter of a PDC; emphasize that the group is to work on process, not content; and explain how a PDC makes a recommendation back to the full plenary group for approval. The facilitator can also suggest an optimal size for the PDC, make a list of the major categories of stakeholders on a flip chart (emphasizing the need for broad representation), and then ask for volunteers. Finally, he or she can ask the group to review the proposed membership, check for completeness, and give the newly formed PDC its blessing.

Another approach to the formation of a PDC is the "snowball" technique. Using this method, the initiating group from the start-up phase keeps adding membership until it feels it has enough credibility to begin the task of process design. The self-selected PDC then convenes a larger group representing all possible interests to seek approval of its design and to launch the consensus building phase.

One final method for forming a PDC is for a convenor to contact key stakeholder groups individually and ask them to appoint a member to a PDC. This approach can work if there are a limited number of legitimate, organized parties in a dispute or situation. It may not be the best choice, however, if there are scores of groups who may want to be involved or will feel left out if not given a chance to volunteer.

■ The Graphic Road Map

"A graphic road map is a visual representation of the flow of face-to-face meetings and other activities."

A primary responsibility of a PDC is to develop a graphic road map: a visual representation of the flow of face-to-face meetings and other activities that take place in a consensus building process. In such a map, meetings are indicated by symbols (usually circles) and the flow of information is represented by connecting lines. Time, by convention, flows from left to right. For example, a conference that starts with a plenary session, then breaks into three subgroups, and then reconvenes as a large group is shown in Figure 3.2. Times or dates can be written above the circles, agenda items below (see Figure 3.3).

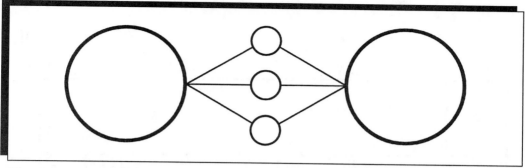

Figure 3.2. Basic Graphic Road Map

NOTE: This figure shows a plenary session, then subgroups, then another plenary session.

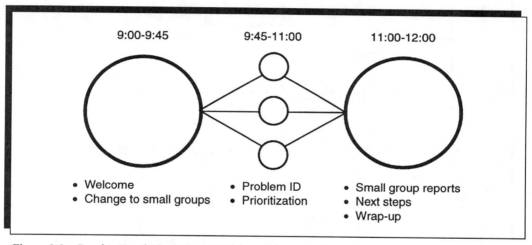

Figure 3.3. Graphic Road Map, Times and Agenda Items Added

A more complex process road map is constructed like a game board. (See Figure 3.4, a road map for a hypothetical planning effort in a hierarchical organization.) The major phases of the project are laid out across the top of the graphic from left to right. Phases are the steps that need to be taken or agreements that need to be built as the process moves toward consensus. In the example shown in Figure 3.4, the phases include *educating* the participants about the problem, developing a *vision* of what the organization might look like if the problem is resolved, assessing the organization's *needs,* and so forth. There are many possible pathways or sequences of phases for any problem-solving effort. The results

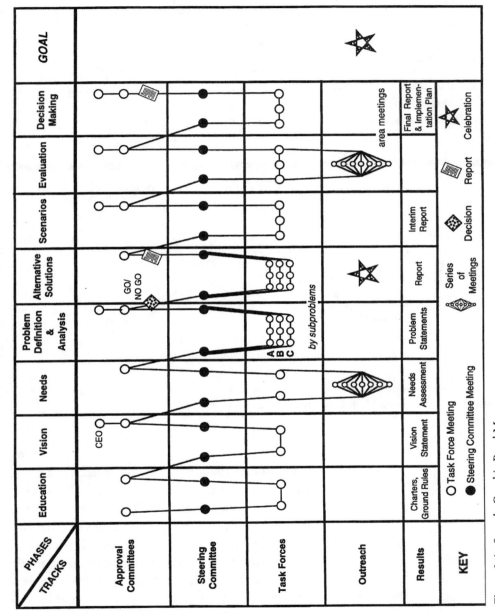

Figure 3.4. Sample Graphic Road Map

or deliverables of each phase can be presented along the bottom of the map.

The major *tracks of activity* (or levels of involvement) are presented in horizontal bands. In our example, there is an *approval track,* because the senior management committee and the CEO must approve the final decisions. There is also a *steering committee* to manage the effort. Much of the work is going to be done in *task forces,* with an *outreach* effort that will include meetings with the full range of stakeholders during the needs assessment and evaluation phases.

Symbols for meetings and other activities are placed on the "game board" with connecting lines showing their interdependencies. Other symbols can be used to indicate the release of a report, a celebration, or one-on-one interviews. In this graphic road map, the key to the symbols lies at the very bottom.

Why Use a Graphic Road Map?

The power of visual representation and imagery as a collaborative communication medium and learning tool is often underestimated. Our own experience and numerous studies in the field of cognitive psychology confirm the ancient adage "A picture is worth a thousand words" (Arnheim, 1969; McKim, 1980). Facilitators, for example, can present a detailed verbal or textual approximation of the process map, but many individuals will be perplexed by the number of tracks and phases, meetings, and other activities necessary to obtain consensus. It is difficult to follow and retain such a huge amount of interrelated information. A map provides a clear way to present this information. It can be used to demonstrate the flow of sessions in a single event (such as a conference); a series of meetings over time (as in a task force project); or a complex, multitrack process (such as a large-scale consensus building effort or organizational intervention).

The process map is a wonderful design tool, much like an architect's drawing for a building. It helps people visualize a process, identify potential problems, and gain a sense of assurance that the consensus building phase will be managed in an organized, methodical manner. In addition, a graphic road map

- educates key stakeholders and constituent groups about consensus processes;
- builds support for an effort by demonstrating commitment to thoughtful planning and collaboration;
- illustrates visually how different sets of stakeholders will be included in a process (i.e., via the various tracks);
- illustrates for key decision makers and resource providers, in a single graphic, the entire flow of a project from start to finish, including the phases, when and how people will be involved, what meetings will be organized, and so forth;
- enables latecomers to quickly understand the flow of a process;
- schedules critical meetings on a common calendar and provides a focal point for resolving complicated issues of sequence and timing;
- reminds individuals of what needs to be done by a certain time;
- orients people toward the broader context and purpose of a meeting or activity;
- facilitates the management of multiple tracks of concurrent activities;
- serves as a "working hypothesis" from which a group may consciously choose to deviate;
- provides an overview, to help a steering committee contemplate the many process issues involved in a collaborative effort;
- acts as a scaffold on which to hang and move new and changing ideas; and
- documents what occurs in a project, thereby serving as a historical record.

■ *Typical Agenda Flow for a Process Design Committee*

The work of most PDCs follows a fairly predictable flow. Figure 3.5—itself a type of process map—displays a typical PDC agenda, which may be implemented over one or more meetings. The following sections describe each major task within this sequence

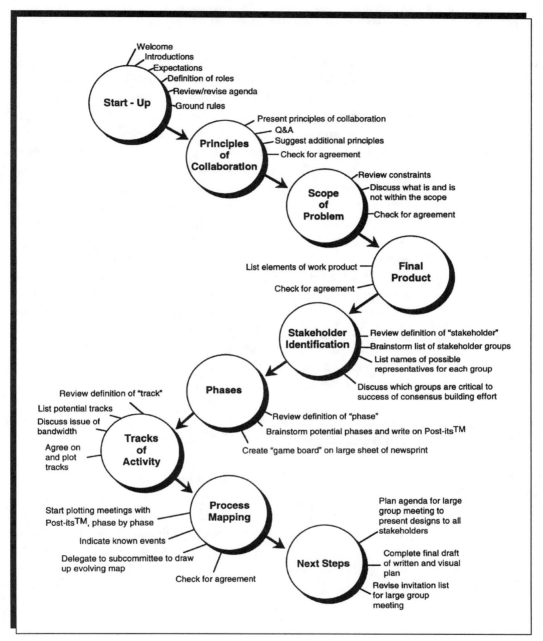

Figure 3.5. Agenda Flow for a Process Design Committee

of agenda items. We will skip over the typical start-up activities, which include welcoming the participants, introductions, reviewing roles, discussing expectations, reviewing and revising the agenda, and establishing ground rules.

Agreement on Principles of Collaboration

Consensus building comes in myriad forms. Each process consultant, depending on his or her training, background, and area of expertise, takes a somewhat different approach to consensus building and operates with a unique set of underlying values, assumptions, and principles. We have found that when we work as process consultants with a PDC, it is helpful to present our own assumptions and principles at the beginning of a process design activity (see Figure 3.6 for our preferred set). We then ask participants to review and revise them as needed. This presentation, and the discussion that follows, helps participants to externalize their own implicit ideas about consensus building and enables them to build agreement on a set of principles appropriate to their situation. For example, they may agree to most of the principles in Figure 3.6 but also want to add one that says that the consensus process must be completed before the next election. Early agreement on principles helps to boost people's confidence that they *can* work together, and the principles themselves serve as design specifications for building an effective process road map.

Agreement on the Scope of the Problem

Members of a PDC need to decide what the general scope of their discussions will be. It is important that they not get bogged down in an argument over different interpretations of "the problem," but rather strive to think in broad terms. A PDC may agree, for example, to focus on "the downtown area, not the whole city" or "elementary education, not high school education." The task is to agree on a general statement of the issue or conflict to be resolved.

Agreement on the Form of the Final Product

It is also important for a PDC to agree on what kind of product it expects a consensus building group to develop. Obviously, the members should not try to solve the whole problem at once, but they *can* develop a common understanding of the

1. A collaborative problem-solving process must include, from the beginning, all the individuals or groups who are responsible for final decisions, are affected by the decisions, have relevant information or expertise, and have the power to block decisions.
2. The key decision maker(s) must agree to participate in the collaborative process and consider it as an integral part of their "real" decision-making process.
3. The power of a collaborative process comes from inclusion, not exclusion. The process itself has no formal authority. Power results from the fact that members are people with power and authority in formal organizations in business, government, and the community.
4. Participants in a collaborative process represent points of view and interests, not numbers of people.
5. People may be involved in a collaborative process at various levels (i.e., through a steering committee, task forces, public hearings). People must be able to increase their level of involvement in a process.
6. Participants in a collaborative process must own the process. They must be involved in designing the process.
7. The commitment of the key decision-making organizations must be evidenced by a commitment of resources (e.g., dollars, in-kind support services, personnel).
8. A participative process takes time and money and staff support. Often, you must go slow to go fast.
9. In general, collaborative problem solving should proceed phase by phase, with a checkpoint for consensus at the end of each phase.
10. The process of collaboration must be educational. The process of educating participants about the issues is one of the important benefits of a collaborative process.
11. A collaborative effort must produce some immediate successes or spin-offs in order to demonstrate its legitimacy and effectiveness.
12. If participants don't agree on the problem, they'll never agree on the solution.
13. The key to effective collaboration is how the meetings are run. The role of a neutral facilitator is critical.
14. A collaborative process must be open and visible. The public must be aware of it as it happens. Media and outreach are important tools.

Figure 3.6. Sample Principles of Collaboration and Consensus Building

probable form of the final product. For example, they should be able to decide whether a consensus building group should strive for a one-page settlement agreement, a detailed final report with recommendations for a decision-making body, an oral presentation to the board of directors, a newsletter to send to the public, or some other outcome. If the final product is to be a major report or presentation, a PDC can also try to specify its major sections. The more specific it can be in describing what success will look like, the easier it will be to design a process to get there.

Agreement on Key Stakeholders

The PDC must also identify all the key stakeholders critical to the success of a consensus effort. One way to do this is to first review a definition of *stakeholder*[3] and then brainstorm all the possible categories of people or viewpoints that should be represented. A PDC should be encouraged to look at potential stakeholders through a variety of lenses: power to block, power to make final decisions, vitally affected, relevant expertise, and so forth. The members should also ensure that the list of stakeholders that emerges includes the full range of possible viewpoints and appropriate geographic, racial, and gender representation. The categories of stakeholders (e.g., local elected leaders, state agency officials, small business representatives) can then be displayed visually as large circles on a flip chart. After all relevant categories have been listed, clarified, and agreed on, members can brainstorm the names of people who might be good representatives of each category; they can write the names within the appropriate circles on the flip chart.

Ultimately, the groups and people named in each category must determine what their level of involvement in a consensus process needs to be. For example, in a strategic-planning process in a hierarchical organization, the president may have fall-back decision-making power (in the event a group fails to reach consensus), the executive committee may be charged with reaching consensus, the division leaders might give their input to the executive committee, and everyone in the organization may simply need to be aware of the process. In an public, multiparty consensus building effort, the levels of involvement may not be so clear-cut, but there are probably certain individuals and groups whose active participation or support is critical. In an educational reform process in Newark, for example (a follow-on to the Newark Collaboration Process), the superintendent and the school board were critical decision makers; the support and involvement of the teachers union, the Parent-Teacher Association, and the mayor were essential for a meaningful consensus; and many other groups and individuals had a vital interest in being involved. Most consensus building efforts have several levels of involvement or "tracks of activity," in recognition of the fact that different stakeholders have different incentives and constraints governing their involvement.

Agreement on Phases

Once potential participants have been identified, it is time to begin building a graphic road map. The first step in building a map is to define the key phases of a proposed collaborative process. Consensus building does not occur at the end of a process; rather, it is reached by building on a series of agreements along the way. These agreements, in fact, can be said to define the individual phases of problem solving. Thus, the naming and plotting of specific phases is not an exercise in "wordsmithing," but a major component of designing a process. The objectives of this part of the design are to define the phases and clarify the basic agreements that should emerge from each phase.

It is important at this stage to emphasize that there is no single, "right" way for a consensus effort to proceed. PDC members should develop a logical sequence of events and activities that is appropriate to their situation.

The phases may follow the traditional "steps" of problem solving, which include sharing perceptions, defining and analyzing the problem, generating alternative solutions, evaluating the solutions based on an explicit set of criteria, and decision making. Or the members may choose some variation on this concept. A group could begin by exploring a common vision of the future, for example. A PDC must decide which pathway and what sequence of phases is best suited to its specific issue and context.

At this point, it is helpful to lay out what we call the game board—the horizontal and vertical axes on which the map is plotted. As we saw in the sample process map (Figure 3.4), the horizontal axis contains the sequence of phases. In that case, after an "education" phase, the PDC chose to build agreement on a "vision" before looking at "needs" and then "problems." The game board can be plotted on a long stretch of butcher paper that has been taped to a wall. A border should be drawn across the top and down the left-hand side, several inches from the edge of the paper, on which the phases and tracks can be labeled (see the heavy line in the sample process map). Rather than writing directly on the chart at first, it is often easier to write the proposed phases on large Post-it® notes, which can be changed around until the PDC has come to some agreement and has determined how much room is needed on the paper to plot the meetings.

In the Newark Collaboration Process, the PDC chose to have a task force organize all the issues generated in the large community meetings and propose a limited number of issue-focused task forces (see Figure 3.7). The next phases involved convening the task forces, which proceeded to define and analyze their problem areas and generate alternative strategies. At the end of each phase, each task force reported its findings to the large community group of stakeholders. The final phases involved organizing the work of the task forces into coherent alternative plans or scenarios, evaluating these alternatives, and then building consensus on one comprehensive plan.

Agreement on Tracks of Activity

Tracks of activity are parallel work processes focused on different objectives and often demanding different levels of involvement on the part of participants. Each track represents a "container" for a sequence of meetings related to one aspect of a consensus process and serves as a locus of problem solving or dispute resolution. For example, in our sample process map in Figure 3.4, the four tracks are labeled on the left-hand side: approval committees, steering committee, task forces, and outreach. Each track is made up of a series of meetings of a different group (or groups) with a specific role and task.

In the Newark Collaboration Process (Figure 3.7), the tracks are also indicated in the left margin: the longest, the Newark Collaboration Group track, included the activities of the Steering Committee (which became the Executive Committee) and the periodic large community meetings. The communications track was created to house all the publicity work that was required to make the effort visible to the public; the specific programs track was created to manage the short-term projects that spun out of the effort; the comprehensive planning track included all the activities of the task forces (in which the actual planning took place); and the public participation track included the outreach and local neighborhood meetings.

To determine what tracks are needed, a PDC needs to answer questions such as the following.

- Should there be a steering committee responsible for managing the consensus building process, and, if so, how should its members be selected?

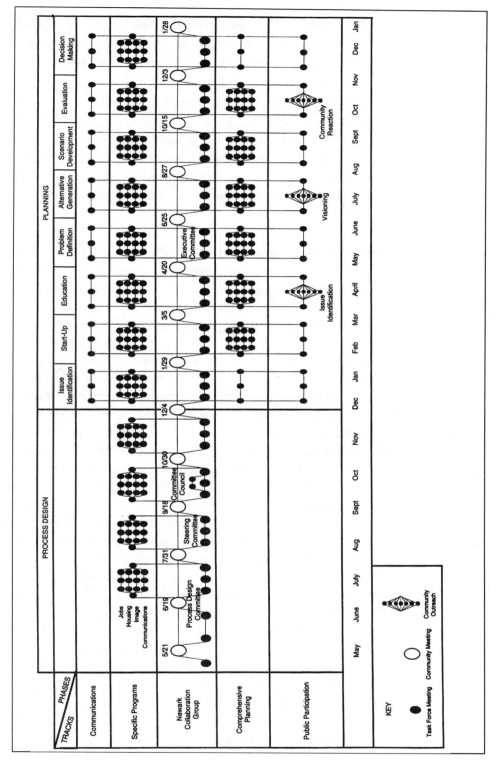

Figure 3.7. Newark Collaboration Process

- Who will need to ratify or implement the recommendations of a consensus building group? How many times should these decision makers be involved along the way?
- Who will do the actual work? Will task forces need to be created? If so, how many should be organized?
- How many other tracks of activity are required? Will there need to be an outreach track (local neighborhood or organizational unit meetings), a fact-finding track, a track to handle short-term issues and to produce immediate results, or a communications track to work with the media and the public?

Bandwidth is a term used to describe the number of tracks required to implement a consensus building project. Ideally, the bandwidth should be narrow enough to make the process manageable and efficient, but wide enough to ensure that opportunities exist for key stakeholders and constituents to be involved in meaningful ways. It is a great challenge to assess how much complexity a particular community or organization can support. In some situations, time constraints or the nature of the community or organization will dictate a comparatively simple process with a narrow bandwidth. For example, a rapid change in the market environment or an offer to be acquired might force an executive committee or board to meet several times behind closed doors to reach a consensus decision. In cases such as these, speed and confidentiality are essential, so the bandwidth is very narrow (and the process is probably designed by the executive committee itself, not a separate PDC). On the other hand, a citywide visioning process, if it is to be meaningful, may require the broadest possible participation with many tracks of activity.

There are trade-offs involved in either case. It is true that a small number of stakeholders can accomplish a great deal and move quickly if they do not have to keep checking in with others. But too few tracks may lessen the possibility of building broad-based consensus, because the larger community feels left out. On the other hand, while a wide bandwidth may help to ensure buy-in, we have seen consensus building efforts collapse under the weight of their own bureaucratic structure—they become too elaborate to manage with limited staff resources. In general, the number of tracks should be limited to keep efforts from becoming too diffuse and complex.

The following is a discussion of some of the most common tracks in consensus building efforts.

Management Track

Consensus building processes are often quite complex and require some kind of management or steering function. A steering committee acts as a sort of process management group; it coordinates the activities of various tracks, monitors their progress, makes corrections as needed, and organizes the reports of subcommittees for presentation to decision makers or the larger community. This committee ought to include, at a minimum, the chairs of any task forces or subcommittees and, at least informally, the subcommittee facilitators. The process consultant should advise and facilitate the steering committee. A PDC may evolve into a steering group, although sometimes its membership needs to be expanded for this purpose.

Due to the amount of staff work that may be required to support a consensus process, it is often necessary to appoint or hire someone to be a *process manager*: a person who provides staffing support and logistical coordination throughout a project's life. The process manager, who may first be appointed to help the PDC and then go on to work for any consensus building group that forms, is responsible for all the coordination, scheduling, subcontracting, logistics, and communication necessary to keep the tracks of activity moving forward in alignment. Process managers are also useful for coordinating the activities of the process consultants and facilitators. They typically report to a steering committee.

The person who is chosen to be the process manager ought to have the respect of all stakeholders and be knowledgeable or able to quickly learn about both consensus building and how the organization or group functions. In intraorganizational consensus building, the process manager is typically an up-and-coming leader who is, most important, knowledgeable about the organization. As a result of serving in this role, such individuals often receive valuable training, are more quickly promoted, and gain exposure and access to many people and parts of the organizational structure. In a public sector or multiparty effort, a process manager is often hired to serve as an *executive director* of the project on a time-limited contract. In some cases, a consulting or nonprofit firm may agree to assume the process management as well as the facilitation role. In these situations, however, the process management function is usually handled by someone other than the facilitators. If a process is supported and run entirely by outside consultants and facilitators, it is less empowering for the participants and can become quite expensive.

Decision-Making Track

In some consensus building situations, all the key stakeholders, including those with the power to make final decisions, can be assembled in a room for a facilitated problem-solving session. If consensus can be reached, the decision makers have the authority to make commitments on the spot. A good example of this scenario is a meeting of a manager and all her direct reports working collaboratively on a departmental issue. If the group (including the manager) reaches consensus, then the manager can implement the decision knowing she has the full support of her people.

In many consensus building efforts, however, the final decision makers cannot all assemble in a room at the same time. Any consensus reached must be approved by them, and they generally reserve the right to agree or disagree with it. Check-in and ratification procedures will differ for each consensus process, and PDC members must determine what is appropriate for their situation and indicate it on the graphic road map.

In hierarchical organizations, consensus decisions typically must be approved by a senior executive, management committee, or board of directors. These decision makers generally authorize the formation of a consensus process and charge the group with returning to them with a recommendation, although they retain final authority on the matter. In these cases, meetings should be held in each phase of a process with the executive committee or the CEO, to get their approval for the work that has gone on so far and to enable them to preview the work still to come. The approval committees track in our sample process map (Figure 3.4) shows this kind of check-in and approval process; task forces complete each phase of their work and their recommendations pass through the steering committee and on to the executive committee and CEO for approval and final decisions.

In a public sector effort, final decisions usually need to be ratified by elected bodies or government agency officials. Their "proxy" can rarely be delegated to a representative. Decisions made by a consensus building group must be passed back to the agency or legislative body for approval and implementation. Sometimes an ad hoc group with an officially appointed and limited membership is charged with seeking consensus; for example, a government entity may form an advisory body or task force to build consensus on a specific set of issues. But in many visioning processes or community-planning projects, consensus is built in large, often open, public meetings that are not officially sanctioned or organized by a particular government entity. In this case, stakeholders carry forward any plan or proposal approved by the "vast majority" of participants to the relevant public and private sector entities and lobby for its implementation. In the Newark Collaboration Process, consensus was tested in bimonthly meetings of all the stakeholders and interested individuals; at times up to 300 people were in attendance. In a hierarchical organization, consensus decisions flow up to the top for approval, while in these types of public sector processes consensus is built and approval sought by flowing "out" to as wide a group of participants as possible. The broad-based support that results helps to ensure agreements will be approved and implemented by relevant government bodies and other groups.

The decision-making track of a graphic road map also indicates, implicitly, the "fallback" decision mechanism: the person or group that will make the decision if a consensus building group fails to reach agreement. In hierarchical organizations, the fallback is always up the chain of authority. If the manager and her direct reports don't reach consensus, the fallback is to the manager. In a horizontal organization, such as a board of directors, the fallback is often to a majority vote. In a public consensus building process, the fallback is typically to a government entity (as in the case of a regulatory negotiation) or to the status quo (as in a community-planning process, in which no specific action is taken if a group does not reach agreement). In any consensus building process, it is critical to identify the fallback decision-making process, if any exists, so participants are clear about what will happen if they cannot reach consensus.

Spin-Out Track

Consensus building can take months, even years. Few groups are able to sustain a long-term effort without some tangible evidence that what they are doing makes a difference. It is also hard to maintain the confidence of the larger community or organization without some interim results. Sometimes partial solutions come up in a process that lend themselves to immediate action. Although these are only "quick fixes," not substitutes for the long-term goal, they can have an energizing effect on participants and provide external observers with evidence that an effort will, indeed, have an impact. Subcommittees and working groups should make recommendations about interim activities as the ideas arise. In response, "quick-fix task forces" can spin off on an ad hoc basis to refine and implement the ideas.

One example of a successful quick fix took place in a planning process for a school system in California. Early in the process, the lack of doors on the stalls in the boys' bathrooms was identified and agreed on as a problem. The solution was obvious, the principal acted, and doors were installed. A small success, a large impact. It offered evidence that community involvement could produce real results.

The Newark Collaboration Process provides another example. As mentioned previously, the PDC was not willing to proceed with process design until some short-term projects were negotiated and initiated. Thus, the spin-out track (labeled *specific programs* on Figure 3.7) began even before the comprehensive planning track was launched.

Task Force or Planning Track

In most complex consensus building processes, the work of defining and analyzing issues and generating solutions is delegated to task forces (also called subcommittees or work groups). These groups, which are made up of stakeholders representing diverse points of view, are given access to staff and technical resources and are charged with bringing back consensus-based recommendations to the steering committee or plenary group. The challenge for a PDC is to decide how many task forces will be required, how to divide up the issues, and how to support and coordinate the activities of the task forces so that their work is complementary. Examples of a task force track can be seen in the Newark Collaboration Process map (Figure 3.7) and the sample process map (Figure 3.4).

Outreach Track

The more people who feel included in a process and who can support its outcome, the more powerful and effective it will be. In most cases, however, many people with an interest in a process cannot participate actively, either because they do not have the time or inclination or because the process cannot accommodate everyone. Therefore, it is important to create a track of activity that offers nonparticipants some alternative, less intensive way of being involved or kept informed. We call this the outreach track. It can include meetings in a specific region or neighborhood, meetings of a single category of stakeholders, community-wide presentations, briefings, surveys, media events, and one-on-one interviews. The challenge for a PDC is to decide what kinds of outreach will be most effective for the situation at hand, and at what points these activities will be most effective.

Drafting and Agreeing on a Detailed Process Map

Once a PDC has agreed on phases and tracks and has written them on the horizontal and vertical axes of the game board, it is time to plot the meetings and other activities. To do this, the PDC must estimate the number of meetings that will be required to accomplish each phase on each track, make sure the flow of work is logical, and plot any events and meeting dates that are fixed or given. The challenge is to design a process that will accomplish all the tasks in a limited amount of time, without overloading the system.

Initially, meetings can be indicated on a map with Post-it notes. It is often helpful for a group to work phase by phase, estimating the number of meetings that will be required and debating how frequently certain groups will be able to get together. Ultimately, they will need to either redraw the completed map neatly by hand on standard size paper or plot it on a computer graphics program (e.g., ClarisImpact, ClarisDraw, MacDraw Pro, Aldus Freehand). It is helpful to use a computer program that can construct a map in "layers," keeping the core grid of phases and tracks, the symbols representing meetings and other activities, and the text all on separate "levels."

As a PDC plots the meetings, members are forced to become realistic about how often certain groups can meet, how they will work around holidays and vacations, and how they are going to meet deadlines. Sometimes, to accommodate time and resource limits, a road map may have to be shortened or simplified. The ensuing debates over this balancing act (efficiency vs. comprehensiveness) are healthy and educational.

In all likelihood, a PDC will focus on the first phase, looking one or two months out, and the rest of the map will be rather sketchy. This is normal. Any management or steering committee that is subsequently formed must continually revise the road map as the process proceeds. To complete the process design phase, it is necessary to create a road map that looks "doable," clearly includes the appropriate stakeholders, and seems to flow logically, phase by phase. Once approved by the larger community or management group, specific work plans, agendas, and dates will need to be developed for each meeting and activity and continually revised as needed.

Other Agreements for the Process Design Committee

Once a process road map has been sketched out and agreed to in principle, the PDC, to complete its charter, must develop recommendations about staffing, process and technical consultants, funding, and publicity. Most of these issues are discussed at length in other chapters (see, in particular, Chapter 5 on facilitation, Chapter 9 on the use of technical experts, and Chapter 11 on dealing with the media). We only want to point out here that one (or more) of these issues may be challenging enough that the PDC may need to set up a subcommittee to address it. The final report of the PDC must cover how all of these issues will be addressed.

■ Building Support for the Proposed Process Design

At the end of the process design phase, PDC members should prepare a written report summarizing their proposed design and including a copy of the graphic road map. Their final task, then, is to invite all key stakeholders to a meeting, at which a decision will be made about whether or not to undertake a consensus building effort. Ideally, this broader set of interests will support the process design and commit publicly to participate in the consensus process.

At the meeting, PDC members should distribute the report and present the process map, the proposed process design, and the assumptions and reasoning that went into both. We believe it is important for PDC members themselves to present their work, assisted by a consultant if necessary. This allows a PDC to own and understand the process design more fully, and the resulting presentation is usually more credible and convincing than one given by any consultant.

When the PDC makes its presentation, it is important not to overwhelm the audience. For those who haven't participated in the process of building the road map, the final graphic—with all its circles and lines—can be daunting. Sometimes it is advisable to reveal the design gradually, presenting the phases first, then the tracks, and finally the meetings. The computer graphics programs can produce drawings that incrementally reveal the building blocks of the road map, layer by layer. The use of highlighting and color can also help to make the road map readable.

■ *Conclusion*

Over many years of designing and facilitating consensus building efforts, we at Interaction Associates have come to rely on a carefully planned process design as the key to a successful consensus building effort. The Newark Collaborative Process is a case in point—it was successful in part due to the well-designed process developed by the PDC. That process produced many positive results, both directly and indirectly. Investments in excess of $2 billion were made in Newark to develop its commercial and industrial base. More than 7,000 units were added to the city's housing inventory. A nationally recognized recycling program was developed. The Newark Education Council and Newark Literacy Campaign were created to improve education. For its outstanding work, Newark received the National Civic League's prestigious All-American City Award in 1991.

As the Newark case illustrates, graphic road maps are an invaluable tool for managing large complex efforts and for orienting people in a multilevel process. They render the conceptual and procedural complexity inherent in large consensus building efforts less daunting. A PDC's careful planning of the graphic road map communicates a hopefulness and a "can-do" spirit that is contagious; it often shapes the attitudes of those who participate in the ensuing consensus building process and sets a group on the right course.

■ Notes

1. It should be noted that process mapping is a useful design tool, whether used by an individual or a group.

2. For further information on the Newark Collaboration Process, see David Chrislip's book on collaborative leadership (Chrislip & Larson, 1994).

3. We define stakeholders as all those people or groups affected by an issue or conflict, with the power to make the decision or block the decision, or with relevant expertise.

■ References

Arnheim, R. (1969). *Visual thinking.* Berkeley: University of California Press.

Chrislip, D., & Larson, C. E. (1994). *Collaborative leadership: How citizens and civic leaders can make a difference.* San Francisco: Jossey-Bass.

McKim, R. H. (1980). *Experiences in visual thinking.* Monterey, CA: Brooks/Cole.

4

CONVENING

■ *Chris Carlson*

When someone *convenes* a meeting, he or she typically finds appropriate meeting space, invites people to attend, and perhaps drafts an agenda. In a consensus building process, however, which may involve multiple meetings over the course of weeks, months, or years, convening is a more complex task. In this context, convening typically involves

1. assessing a situation to determine whether or not a consensus-based approach is feasible;
2. identifying and inviting participants to ensure that all key interests (i.e., stakeholders) are represented;
3. locating the necessary resources to help convene, conduct, and support the process; and
4. planning and organizing the process with participants, or working with a facilitator or mediator to do so.

It may be helpful to think of convening as Phase 1 in a consensus building process, which is followed by Phase 2, the actual negotiating or consensus building phase. Phase 2 begins only after the

Members of the Critical Issues Committee of the SPIDR Environment/Public Disputes Sector provided the framework for this chapter based on their work describing convening and their many insights into how to carry it out. They also produced the report *Best Practices for Government Agencies: Guidelines for Using Collaborative Agreement-Seeking Processes*, which is described herein. Thank you to the Udall Center for the Fellowship that enabled me to begin work on this chapter. Thanks also go to Jim Arthur and Lee Moore for reading drafts, contributing material, and straightening out my thinking.

convening stage is completed, when a decision is made to proceed.[1]

This chapter describes how to convene a consensus building process. It begins by describing the people and organizations typically involved in convening and the roles each one plays. The second section provides two examples of convening: one in which the convening phase was handled appropriately, and one in which it was not. The next four sections describe and provide guidelines for carrying out the four steps involved in convening: assessing a situation, identifying and inviting participants, locating the necessary resources, and planning and organizing the process. The final section describes special challenges that arise when government agencies serve as convenors.

■ Roles

A number of different actors are involved in the convening stage, including sponsors, convenors, neutrals, stakeholders, and participants.

Sponsors are individuals or organizations that endorse and support a consensus building process, often by providing financial assistance.

The *convenor* is the person or organization that initiates a consensus building process and that carries out the convening steps (or oversees how they are carried out). Often, because of the complexity or contentiousness of a situation, or due to lack of trust or credibility, a convenor may decide to use a professional neutral to carry out the convening steps.

The *neutral* is the facilitator or mediator who works with the convenor and other participants during the convening stage. Often, but not always, the neutral who assists with convening goes on to facilitate the consensus building process. A facilitator is a person who has experience leading large group meetings, including planning and using a variety of processes to assist groups in joint decision making. A mediator is skilled at handling conflicts and disputes and assisting people who are in conflict to reach resolution. Some people have both facilitation and mediation experience; however, they may identify themselves by one term or the other. For simplicity's sake, this chapter will refer to them both as neutrals.

The *stakeholders* are the key individuals, groups, and organizations that have an interest in the issue at hand. They may be responsible for seeing a problem resolved or a decision made, they may be affected by a problem or decision, or they may have the power to thwart a solution or decision. Stakeholders need to be consulted as part of a conflict assessment and engaged in selecting participants.

Participants are stakeholders who take part in consensus-based negotiations. Often, particularly in processes involving public issues, participants represent other individuals with similar interests and concerns. They are thus sometimes called *representatives.*

■ The Importance of Convening: Two Examples

"The parties who serve as convenors need to be viewed as credible and fair-minded."

How the convening steps are carried out, and who carries them out, can have an impact on whether or not a consensus process will be successful. The parties who serve as convenors, whether they are government agencies, private corporations, nonprofit organizations, or individuals, need to be viewed as credible and fair-minded, especially in those cases in which issues are contentious or parties are distrustful of each other. At the community level, consensus processes are often sponsored and convened by a local leader, an organization, or a steering committee made up of representatives of different groups. At the state and federal levels, government agencies or officials often serve as sponsors, and sometimes as convenors. Let us look at two examples illustrating the importance of effective convening—one convened by an individual, the other by a federal agency.

A Community Collaboration Gets Off on the Right Foot

In the first example, a divisive conflict over logging practices and their impact on endangered species was under way in a rural community in southern Oregon. By the early 1990s, there had been numerous skirmishes between environmental interests and timber industry supporters over logging in the Applegate Valley. In 1992, the listing of the northern spotted owl on the federal endangered species list led to an injunction prohibiting logging on federal lands. There were bitter and sometimes violent protests. Yet, in the midst of the crisis, some representatives of industry and environmental groups were able to negotiate land exchanges and timber sales. These agreements seemed to signal the possibility that a consensus building approach might be useful for developing a longer-range plan for the watershed.

A local environmentalist who had been one of the architects of the earlier cooperative effort served as the sponsor and convenor. He put together a proposal to use a consensus building approach to develop a comprehensive ecosystem management plan. He distributed his proposal to all the involved and affected stakeholders. He then shuttled back and forth among them, discussing and revising the proposal, and got their agreement to start meeting. The participants included most of the major interests: government agency staff, environmentalists, timber industry representatives, farmers and ranchers, and a variety of other local residents.

The convenor decided that rather than begin with a formal meeting, complete with flip charts and facilitators, he would host a potluck at his home. The first meeting was spent reaching agreement about how the process would be organized and developing ground rules. The partnership rapidly took shape, and after several months of meetings, the group arrived at an agreement on basic objectives.

After a promising beginning, the Applegate Partnership got swept up in the national politics surrounding the spotted owl issue in Oregon. All the outside attention and publicity caused the partnership to founder, but it managed to survive because participants continued to see a need for building consensus on plans and actions to serve the community's interests. The partnership has been able to develop consensus on projects to restore watersheds, improve agricultural irrigation practices, and initiate economic development projects in the community. By almost any assessment, this convening led to successful outcomes (KenCairn, 1997).

A Federal Agency Convenes a Similar Process That Fails

Our second example came about as a result of the Applegate experience. Word spread quickly about the success of the Applegate Partnership. Federal officials caught wind of Applegate's success, and Interior Secretary Bruce Babbitt dropped in on one of the partnership meetings. What he saw fit nicely into the administration's plans for resolving the spotted owl issue: Getting communities involved in working out how federal policies could be implemented locally. The federal government decided that there were 10 communities in which it wanted to stimulate similar partnership efforts.

However, when the federal agency tried to convene local groups and get them to form partnerships, it failed. In each case, stakeholders attended one or two meetings, but were not willing to commit to a longer-term, consensus building process. One probable reason for the failure was that the agency's attempts were made unilaterally, without consulting local stakeholders about what should be discussed and what it would take to make the discussions "safe" for participants, among other things. When the federal government organized meetings, stakeholders came, but they participated only grudgingly. They felt compelled to be there to protect their interests.

When asked, the participants revealed a variety of concerns about how the process had been planned and convened by the federal government. They were concerned, for example, about the federal government's motives, the balance of power at the table, and the availability of resources to enable all groups to participate on an equal footing (KenCairn, 1997). Because these questions were not addressed during the convening stage, the groups were ultimately unable and unwilling to form partnerships to work toward consensus on watershed management. Genuine partnerships result from people agreeing to come together voluntarily, not because they feel coerced into participating by a government agency.

What made the difference in these two cases? The difference was not in *who* carried out the convening role. Federal agencies can convene processes just as successfully as individual community members. The difference in this case lay in how the convening role was handled. Some of the problems in the second case might have been avoided if the federal agency had followed the appropriate convening steps, including conducting a conflict assessment to learn how to plan the process so that all stakeholders would be willing to participate. By using a neutral to assist, the federal agency might have learned of the parties' concerns about power imbalances and identified ways of addressing them.

Successful convening requires, among other things, a determination of whether the right conditions and incentives are present for the parties to want to participate.

We will now look closely at the four steps involved in successful convening.

■ Step 1: Assess the Situation

The convenor should begin by determining if it makes sense to initiate a consensus building process. There are two parts to this assessment. The first is an *initial screening*, and the second is an *external assessment* made in consultation with other stakeholders. This chapter focuses on the initial screening, which is conducted internally by the convening organization to determine whether there is enough support and commitment within the organization to move forward with an external assessment and the other convening steps. (External assessments are described in detail in Chapter 2, on conflict assessment.)

In the initial screening, the convenor needs to identify what he or she wants to accomplish, clarify and frame the issues to address, examine the context, and determine the kind of mandate or authority he or she has to convene a decision-making process. This requires considering, from the outset, how any consensus agreement will be formally adopted and implemented. The convenor needs to identify who must be consulted to ensure legitimacy and to ensure the necessary linkages to formal decision making. The convenor also needs to identify the resources that will be needed, as well as the obstacles that must be overcome to convene a successful consensus building process.

An external assessment helps to determine how other stakeholders view the issues and ensures that joint negotiations are feasible. It also provides an opportunity to educate stakeholders about the nature of the process. Based on interviews with key parties, the convenor learns whether or not the stakeholders are willing to participate or if they have better alternatives.

In the Applegate example, the convenor was a local environmentalist who had already established his credibility in the community. His initial screening, based on firsthand experience, was that the time was right to propose a consensus building approach to develop a watershed plan. He conducted the external assessment by taking his proposal to stakeholders, discussing it, and securing their agreement to meet. In the second example, the federal agency served as the convenor. The agency made an initial screening and decided it had a mandate from the administration to foster local partnerships as a part of the president's forest plan for the Pacific Northwest. Unfortunately, the agency failed to conduct an external assessment, a consultation with the other stakeholders, to see if the key players were willing to participate.

It is perfectly reasonable for a convenor to carry out the convening steps, including making the external assessment, without outside, professional assistance, as in the Applegate example. This is most likely to be effective if the convenor is known, trusted, and credible in the eyes of all the stakeholders, and it is more likely to work at the local or community level. The convenor may need assistance from a neutral when the convenor is not known or trusted by other stakeholders, or there is a past history or power imbalance between the convenor and other stakeholders. If a convenor is not trusted or seen as credible in the eyes of stakeholders, stakeholders will not likely provide candid answers to the questions that must be asked as part of the external assessment. Had the federal agency in the second example used a neutral to assist it with the external assessment, it probably would have gotten the answers needed to determine whether or not to proceed.

The remainder of this section provides detailed guidance on how to carry out an initial screening, including how to secure the assistance of a professional neutral to conduct an external assessment and how to reconfirm the convenor's commitment before proceeding.

Guidelines for Carrying Out the Initial Screening

The initial screening helps the convenor to determine at the outset whether it is appropriate to undertake the other convening steps, or whether some other process would be more appropriate given the issues and situation at hand. The convenor begins an initial screening by determining what he or she wants to accomplish, and then by exploring the issues, context, stakeholders, obstacles, and resource needs that must be addressed to determine whether or not to propose the use of a consensus building process. When the convenor is an agency or organization, a staff member gathers the information and discusses it with the leadership to determine whether or not to proceed. Sometimes the initial screening can be done more effectively with some guidance from an experienced neutral. The following are the major items to examine as part of an initial screening.

Determine What the Convenor Wants to Accomplish

One of the central reasons for conducting an initial screening is to clarify the convenor's goals and objectives. To do this, convenors must ask themselves a number of questions about why they might want to gather diverse stakeholders together. Do they simply want to solicit information from stakeholders? Are they seeking to provide stakeholders with information about a decision that has already been made, to win support for it? Is the motive to de-escalate a conflict, consult with others, or seek advice? Do the leadership and staff of the convening organization have doubts about using a consensus building approach? Do they believe that taking part in a joint decision-making process will mean forfeiting their authority and responsibility? Are they likely to resist, stall, or prevent implementation of any agreement that is reached? Can the convenor make a unilateral decision that will likely be supported by all and easily implemented? If the answer to any of these questions is yes, the convenor probably should not convene a consensus building process. Consensus building takes time and financial resources and should not be undertaken unless the convenor is legitimately seeking and comfortable with supporting a broad-based agreement.

Consensus building can satisfy many kinds of objectives. It can be used to develop sound decisions that have the support of a wide range of stakeholders. It can be used to solve problems that affect multiple organizations and individuals—problems that no single person or organization could solve alone. It can build effective working relationships, which are necessary to ensure the implementation of a decision. It can also be used to develop recommendations for a government agency or legislative body to consider implementing, although it is best if that agency or legislative body supports the process from the beginning and indicates that it will implement any agreement reached. If those at the convening organization are willing to share control over how a decision is made or an issue is resolved, and their objectives are compatible with a consensus-based approach, it may be appropriate for them to initiate a consensus building process.

Identify the Issues

At the outset, convenors need to identify and define the issues that need to be addressed. During the external assessment, they must then test whether or not stakeholders are willing to come to the table to discuss those issues. The entire consensus building process can be significantly expedited if the issues are framed in a way that makes sense to all parties and gives them an incentive to reach agreement.

The convenor must determine how complex the issues are, whether they are linked to other issues, and whether they are well-enough defined. If the issues are not clear and well developed, it may take considerable time to clarify them.

The convenor must also consider the following questions: Is information about the issues known and readily available to the stakeholders? Will the convenor benefit by gaining additional insights into the issues and potential ways of approaching them from other stakeholders? Will negotiations over the issues be likely to produce better, more durable outcomes than can be achieved through other means?

Are the issues controversial? This is often the chief factor that propels a convenor toward the use of a joint decision-making approach. The convenor must determine what is at the root of the controversy. If the convening agency is the source of the controversy, it may be best for a neutral to carry out the convening phase.

Are the issues ripe for decision? In other words, is there a shared perception that something needs to happen? Consensus building is more likely to succeed if there is general dissatisfaction with the existing situation than if some stakeholders are benefiting from the status quo.

Is the timing favorable? Can a reasonable timetable be set? Are there deadlines that will help or hinder the process? It takes time to exchange information, identify issues, develop proposals, and build agreement, especially when there are multiple parties involved. As part of the assessment, the convenor and all other potential participants must be realistic about the amount of time needed to accomplish the goals of the consensus building process.

The initial screening is just the first step toward issue framing. Throughout the convening phase, especially during the external assessment, other stakeholders will have an opportunity to express their views about how the issues should be framed. The convenor needs to be receptive to how other stakeholders view the issues. Stakeholders will have ideas about how the issues should be framed, whether other issues need to be addressed, and which issues they think should or should not be included for discussion. Stakeholders may have very different ways of viewing the issues. What looks like an endangered species issue to one party, for example, may look like an economic survival issue to another. Part of the convenor's task is to determine whether the issues can be framed so that parties can agree to work collaboratively.

If the convening organization attempts to control the issues placed on the table, it risks the possibility that other stakeholders may not take part in the process because their concerns will not be addressed. In one convening process in which I was involved in Ohio, a government agency was very interested in reaching an agreement with stakeholders, but was unwilling to consider the issues a key stakeholder group wanted to address. Stakeholder group members told the neutral that they were more likely to achieve their goals by going to the legislature than by negotiating with the agency. Members said they would be obliged to attend the meetings to protect their interests, but they would try to block any agreement. The agency decided not to go forward with a consensus building process and, in so doing, saved itself from what promised to be an unproductive expenditure of time and resources.

Examine the Context

In an initial screening, the convenor must also examine the context in which a potential consensus building process would take place. Will the process occur within an organization, a community, or a government? What is the convenor's mandate to engage other stakeholders and to implement the results? Is there someone who has to give "permission" for the convenor to proceed with a consensus building process? Who is responsible for formalizing and implementing the agreement reached through the process, and do they support the use of this approach? If a legislature or government agency must ratify an agreement, for example, it may be important to seek its support for or participation in the consensus building process.

In the example above, the stakeholders believed they were likely to be more successful with the legislature than they would be in dealing with the administrative agency. The convenor could have consulted with legislators to learn whether or not they would support the use of a consensus building approach. If they were supportive, the reluctant stakeholders might have felt compelled to take part in the process.

Identify Other Stakeholders

Who is involved and affected by the issues? Who will need to implement any agreement that is reached? Who could potentially block implementation of an agreement? The convenor must identify the key groups and individuals who meet these descriptions. Once the key parties are identified, they will need to be interviewed during the external assessment.

Does the convenor already know that certain stakeholders are unwilling to participate? If it is known with certainty at the outset that a key stakeholder will likely refuse to take part in joint discussions, then the convenor should consider using another approach to reaching a decision.

What is the past history of relationships among the convening agency and the other stakeholders? What is the balance of power among the parties? What implications do the power dynamics have for whom, or how, the convening is carried out, or the process is facilitated? How will these factors influence what needs to happen in the convening phase to get people to the table? What will need to be done to establish the credibility and impartiality of the process in the eyes of other stakeholders? Convenors must consider each of these questions carefully during the initial screening.

Identify the Potential Resource Needs

A convenor should do a cursory assessment to determine whether or not resources are available to support a process. Key resource needs will likely include information, process expertise or facilitation assistance, and staff support, as well as funding to cover the associated costs. Resource needs can be significant, and a convenor must anticipate as many of them as possible and make a realistic appraisal of whether and how they can be met. The convenor is responsible for finding ways to meet these needs. If it appears from the outset that they cannot be met, then the convenor should not convene a process. Alternatively, the convenor can consult other stakeholders during the external assessment to find out about their resource needs and gather ideas about how to meet them all.

Identify the Obstacles

By now, the people doing the initial screening should have a good sense of the nature of the obstacles that must be overcome before convening a consensus-based process. If significant obstacles have been identified and the convenor has real doubts about whether they can be overcome, it is better not to move forward with the other convening steps. When the convenor is an agency, organization, or committee, its leaders need to be informed about the results of the initial screening and consulted about whether or not to proceed.

When internal support for a process is weak, and yet a decision is made to move forward, a host of negative consequences may follow. The process may begin, only to be abandoned when things don't proceed as planned. Stakeholders may come initially to protect their interests, but later leave, causing the process to be fatally weakened or terminated. The process may produce an agreement, only to have the convening agency fail to implement it. These kinds of results produce skepticism about consensus building processes and reduce the chances of success for future efforts. When convenors can decide, based on the initial screening, that it does not make sense to use consensus decision making, they save themselves the frustration and negative side effects of investing their time and energy in a process that is doomed.

Guidelines for Determining Who Should Carry Out the Convening Steps

Before proceeding with an external assessment (i.e., consulting other stakeholders about how they view the situation), the convening organization should determine whether it can effectively carry out the remaining convening tasks, or whether these should be handled by a neutral party. If the convenor expects to hire a neutral to facilitate any consensus-based process that goes forward, it is useful to get the neutral involved at this stage. By conducting an external assessment, a neutral can gather the information needed to design a process and can begin to establish credibility with potential participants. This section discusses the conditions under which a neutral is needed to ensure impartiality or to provide process expertise, how stakeholders should be involved in selecting a neutral, and how to find and select a neutral.

When a Professional Neutral May Be Helpful

When the issues are complex or contentious, when many parties are involved, when there is a history of distrust between the convenor and other parties, when this is a first effort to use consensus building, or when past efforts to resolve differences have failed, it may be problematic for the convenor to carry out all of the convening steps.

The convenor's goal is to use the external assessment as a means of understanding the situation from the perspective of each of the stakeholders. Typically, stakeholders will give more candid assessments to an impartial, disinterested person than they will to an interested party. Often, to learn about the stakeholders' underlying interests and concerns, the convenor must keep the discussions confidential. Stakeholders need to believe a convenor's assertion that he or she can maintain confidentiality. In considering using an internal staff person to conduct a conflict assessment, the convenor needs to ask, "Is it likely that participants will regard this person as unbiased and capable of keeping confidences?" If the answer is no, then the convenor needs to consider using an outside neutral.

When a situation is particularly contentious or parties are not experienced negotiators, a neutral may be needed to describe the process in sufficient detail to make them comfortable enough to participate. Let's turn to an example of how a neutral was selected to help establish credibility for the proposed use of a consensus building process. Chelsea, Massachusetts is a city of 28,000 people, located just north of Boston, and made up of very diverse immigrant groups. Chelsea was $10 million in debt and had been placed in receivership as a result of financial mismanagement and corruption among municipal officials. The city was required to develop a new city charter, and after one failed attempt, the legislatively appointed receiver decided he needed help. Because of the complexity of the issues, the number of parties, and the past history, he wanted a neutral to assist with the convening stage. The neutral was asked to determine whether a consensus process could be used to develop a proposal for a new city charter that would be put before the public for a vote.

The receiver involved some members of the city council in selecting a neutral. They solicited proposals from prospective neutrals and selected one after interviewing the candidates.

After the neutral was selected, she interviewed community leaders to learn how they viewed the situation in Chelsea. She not only gained the information she needed to convene the consensus building process, she also established relationships with people who were suspicious of outsiders. These interviews helped establish her credibility and enabled her, as an outsider, to facilitate both the convening stage and the process itself. The convening stage was effectively carried out and laid the groundwork for a successful process. (See Case 3.)

Now let us contrast Chelsea's approach to use of a neutral with what happened in Catron County, New Mexico. Catron County has gained national notoriety as the leader in the "county rights movement." It is the largest county in New Mexico, more than 2,700 square miles, 80 percent of which are federal lands. Ranchers and loggers in the region have been dependent on public land for their livelihoods for three generations. Like many rural western communities, Catron County faced dramatic changes during the past decade because of environmental pressure to restrict logging and grazing. Conflict was steadily escalating among environmental groups, the Forest Service, county government, ranchers, and timber industries. Lumber mills had closed. Lawsuits and countersuits were filed. Tensions were running high, and fears of violence lurked just below the surface.

Out of concern for the physical and emotional health of the community, the only physician in the county decided something needed to be done. He was seeing increasing numbers of patients with symptoms of anxiety, depression, and drug and alcohol abuse, and a rise in family violence. He asked the New Mexico

Center for Dispute Resolution for assistance. The center recommended that he sponsor a process to bring people together to begin discussing the issues that divided them. The center further recommended that the doctor play the convening role, because local residents would be very suspicious of outsiders trying to play that role. The center did provide assistance to the convenor in the convening stage and trained facilitators to conduct the process. (See Case 13.)

Involving Stakeholders in Selecting a Neutral

A neutral who is chosen to play a convening role should ideally be chosen by all stakeholders. In practice, if the neutral is needed at the front end of the process to assist with the convening steps, it is not feasible to involve all stakeholders in the selection since they have not yet been identified.

Convenors have developed a variety of ways to address this problem. In some cases, a convenor has formed a selection committee made up of a group of people highly respected by stakeholders and the public. In other circumstances, the convenor has involved a small group representative of diverse stakeholders in the selection. When a selection committee is not feasible, convenors often contract with a neutral for Phase 1 (the convening phase) and then allow the negotiating group that forms to choose its own neutral for Phase 2 (the consensus building phase). Other convenors have turned to public policy dispute resolution centers for advice. These centers provide rosters of or references to qualified neutrals and can help in the selection of a neutral whose experience matches the convenor's needs. In all these examples, the convenors' actions help ensure participants that the neutral assisting with the convening steps is impartial, independent, and accountable.

How to Find and Select a Neutral

To make a determination about a practitioner's competence, it is important to gather information about the neutral's background, training, and past experience. The level of experience, sometimes referred to as "flying time," is the most important factor in determining competence. Experience should be relevant to the context in which the convening will occur. Has the person done work in similar situations? With similar parties and issues? What have been the results? What do the people who were involved in those processes say about his or her competence?

There are a number of ways to go about selecting a neutral whose background and experience are suitable. There are several sources to turn to for assistance in finding qualified neutrals with experience in assessing, planning, and facilitating consensus building processes. Several states have offices or centers for conflict resolution that keep rosters or resource lists of approved professionals. They can be asked for advice about how to go about finding a neutral. The Society of Professionals in Dispute Resolution (SPIDR) and the International Association for Public Participation (IAP2) also maintain lists of neutrals.

In addition to seeking information about competent neutrals from these sources, a convenor or selection committee can send out a request for proposals (RFP) describing the situation and soliciting proposals and references from neutrals. Then, the selection committee can review these materials to determine which individuals seem most promising. Another approach is for a selection committee to identify criteria for choosing a neutral, identify possible candidates, review résumés and references, interview the most promising candidates, and make a selection based on the criteria. Other suggestions are contained in Chapter 5 on the use of facilitators, mediators, and other professional neutrals.

Reconfirm the Convenor's Commitment before Proceeding

Once an initial screening has been done and a conflict assessment has been completed, the information gathered is used by the convenor, in consultation with the neutral, to make a "go" or "no go" decision.

At this stage, it is important to reconfirm that the convenor is still committed to using the process. These commitments need to be reconfirmed because, after the assessment, the issues may be reframed, the potential participants will be known, and resource needs and other requirements will be more fully understood.

If the decision is to go forward with a consensus building process, other stakeholders should be informed. This can be done as part of the effort to select participants and secure their commitment to participate. Based on the assessment, before approaching potential participants, a proposed plan should be developed for the process including an initial description of the issues to be addressed, a time line, and a "map" of how the process will unfold. This should be shared with potential participants so they can decide whether or not to participate.

■ Step 2: Identify and Engage Participants

"A bedrock principle is that everyone with a stake in the decision should be represented at the table."

The legitimacy of consensus building processes, which are often used as adjuncts to more traditional democratic forums, depends on whether they are viewed by stakeholders and the public at large as representative of all interests and points of view. A bedrock principle of consensus-based processes, therefore, is that everyone with a stake in the decision should be represented at the table. This principle helps to ensure that any consensus agreement reached will be seen as legitimate by all relevant parties and have broad support when implemented.

The convenor must determine how to achieve representative and inclusive participation. However, stakeholders themselves should be involved in deciding who should be at the table. The convenor should not assume that he or she is in a position to name the participants.

In the Applegate example, the people invited to the organizing meeting named 18 representatives of the various interest groups as participants. In the second example, the federal agency apparently made a unilateral decision about who would be invited to participate. When convenors make that kind of decision they take a big risk. Others will not likely agree with their selection of representatives.

This section describes detailed guidelines for ensuring appropriate and complete participation in a consensus building process.

All Interests Must Be Adequately Represented

Because consensus decision-making processes have such potential power, they should be used only when people representing key interests can be identified, want to participate, and have the resources to participate effectively. Determinations about representation are easiest when stakeholders are obvious and they are prepared to participate. Reaching agreement during negotiations may be difficult, but at least there is no question about the legitimacy of the forum and the process.

Recent subjects for negotiated rulemakings in Washington State met the "inclusiveness" test by being limited in scope. One negotiation involved the liability of construction contractors for the actions of their subcontractors. The parties were clearly defined business interests and a state agency. Another negotiation addressed the level of expertise needed to design small sewerage and water systems. In addition to septic system installers and licensed engineers, representatives of state and local health departments and the state engineering board were at the table. A third case involved storage of pesticides on farms (Jim Arthur, personal communication, September 1996). It could be argued that these three negotiations left out homeowners, clients of contractors, and consumers of apples and wheat, but these parties were considered to be represented by the public interest mandates of the convening agencies.

Representation becomes more problematic when the issues affect a large segment of the population and not just a subset of identifiable interests. If some interests are obvious but others are not so clear, or if the interests are clear but some are disorganized or lack sufficient power, time, or money to participate, there are real dilemmas to be confronted about whether it is appropriate to convene a collaborative process.

A convening agency may be tempted to invite someone whose views it expects will be representative of diffused interests—a "generic farmer," for example. But that approach may not work when the goal is to develop agreements that can be implemented. Being "representative of" is not the same as "representing." The structural linkages essential for the generic farmer to speak for and be advised by the farming community may be missing.

Nor, as a general rule, is it part of the neutral's role to help establish these linkages, to help "organize the farmers." In some circumstances that may be appropriate, but only with the approval of the other interests and the convenor. Neutrals performed this function during negotiations between the oil industry and commercial fishermen operating in the Santa Barbara Channel in California. The oil industry and participating state and federal agencies approved of the neutrals undertaking this task because they wanted to negotiate an agreement with the fishermen. The fishermen agreed to organize and negotiate because they knew that if they did not come to the table, they had little hope of preventing oil operations from being conducted in sensitive fishing grounds (Jim Arthur, personal communication, September 1996).

Sometimes the task of organizing an interest group can be assigned to an actor in the process, someone who is neither the convenor nor the neutral. In Seattle, for example, numerous communities were concerned about noise at the Seattle Airport. Most were municipalities, but as an "interest" they were not organized. Furthermore, they were in a sense competitors because they each wanted to avoid being in the flight path to the airport. As part of a mediated negotiation to reduce noise, the convenor arranged for someone to help these communities negotiate among themselves and then prepare for the dialogue with other interests (Jim Arthur, personal communication, September 1996).

The burden of ensuring that key parties have the ability to participate effectively falls most heavily on the convenor. One option is to provide training in how the process works. The convenor may need to establish support systems—expertise, information resources, or financial support—to enable participants to get to meetings or to communicate with their constituencies.

On the other hand, some parties may be wary of negotiating, even if assistance is provided. They may fear co-optation, or the potential for co-optation, if pressed to participate. Sitting down to negotiate with government agencies, interests with far greater resources, or with a group that is primarily representative of the dominant culture can be formidable. Environmental and other public resource issues increasingly intersect with issues of social and political justice. When these factors are combined with cultural differences, there are some very real challenges to designing and managing a consensus building process.

Involving Stakeholders in Identifying and Selecting Participants

The external assessment provides an opportunity to identify the stakeholding interests that need to participate. Representatives should include those who can implement an agreement, or block it, as well as those who are affected by it. As part of the conflict assessment, stakeholders are asked for their opinions about who should be at the table. They can also be asked about the criteria that should be used to select participants.

The process of selecting participants can be handled in a number of ways. These suggestions are listed from the least to the most inclusive. (In all cases, participants should have the opportunity to review, add to, and ratify the makeup of the negotiating group during the first meeting of any consensus building process.)

First, based on the external assessment (in which all stakeholders are asked for their thoughts on who should participate) the convenor can draw up a list of potential participants and submit it to stakeholders for their review and consent. Participants should be selected by the convenor in consultation with their respective interest groups or organizations.

The convenor should ask if those who have been selected are willing to participate. If a stakeholder has serious reservations about participating, sometimes the convenor can find ways to overcome those reservations. If a key stakeholder group is not willing to participate, the convenor should explore with the other parties whether another group representing the same interests would be an acceptable substitute. If this is not acceptable, the convenor should ask the sponsor and other parties to decide whether they want to proceed in the absence of a key stakeholder. If key stakeholders are not willing to participate, that is a signal that a consensus process may not be appropriate, at least at that point in time (Thomas-Larmer, 1998).

In Catron County, New Mexico, the sponsor invited an initial group of 20 people to an organizational meeting. The group was chosen to include ranchers, Forest Service representatives, environmentalists, representatives of county government, church and community leaders, and the mayor. At the meeting, those present suggested others who needed to be included. With these additions and changes, the participants continue to serve as the nucleus of the Catron County Citizens Group. They are working together to build understanding and manage the conflicts in their community.

Second, a small, representative group of stakeholders can develop criteria and name the interests or individuals who need to be represented in the process. This was the procedure used to select participants in Chelsea, Massachusetts. At the conclusion of the conflict assessment interviews, there was a list of 70 potential participants. The convenor and neutral decided the list needed to be reduced to about 20. Three of the most highly regarded people in the community were selected to help make the choices. This selection committee identified criteria for membership on the charter preparation group, and then chose 20 members. Their criteria for making the choices were as follows: Individuals must have the ability and willingness to operate by consensus and be able to take a long-term view of the city rather than focus on a narrow agenda, participants should be ethnically diverse, and participants should be people respected throughout the community.

The selection committee had to make tough decisions about how to involve politicians and how to represent the ethnic diversity of the community. When the committee completed its work, the list was published in the local paper and the public was asked to call if an important point of view was missing. There were no calls.

Finally, a convenor can bring together all stakeholders and assist them in choosing participants through a process of criteria development and self-selection. A consensus building effort in South Carolina in which I was involved illustrates how a large number of stakeholder groups can be helped to select their representatives. In Charleston County, a group was convened to decide on a plan for building parks and recreation centers. The city of Charleston formed a community "team" to represent their interests in the countywide discussions. A neutral helped the city to identify 250 organizations to invite to a meeting to determine who should represent the stakeholding interests in the community. The meeting was also widely publicized through the media. At the meeting, attended by over 100 people, the convenor described the purpose of the process. Then the audience was asked to suggest criteria to use in determining who should be at the table. The audience suggested geographic representation, gender and racial balance, knowledge of community affairs, communication skills, and ability to marshal other citizens.

After they had agreed to the criteria, they were divided into small groups representing different stakeholding interests—environment, sports, tax reduction, and so on—and each was asked to nominate people for consideration who would meet the criteria. After the nominations were made and the names listed on poster paper around the room, those present were asked to briefly describe their qualifications and interest in serving, while others were asked to speak for nominees who were not present. The convenor asked whether the nominees adequately represented the range of interests in the community. No dissension was expressed. Each attendee was given five colored "dots" and asked to vote for five candidates of his or her choice. The seven persons who received the most votes were selected as members of the community team.

A word about the role of a convening agency or organization as a participant: Convenors need to ensure that they are appropriately represented at the table and are prepared to support their representative(s) and to speak with one voice throughout the process.

■ Step 3: Locate the Necessary Resources

"A convenor must identify the kinds of assistance needed and ensure that those resources are available."

A convenor's third step is to identify the kinds of assistance (and resources) needed to carry out a process and to ensure that those resources are available.

One of those resource needs may be assistance with convening and facilitation. As discussed previously, a neutral will need to be chosen and funds found to pay for neutral services.

The convenor is responsible for seeing to it that resource needs can be met before undertaking Phase 2. In addition to assistance with convening and facilitation, resource needs may include gathering and preparing information, finding and consulting with experts, preparing or assisting some or all of the parties to cover the costs of their participation, and providing staff assistance to help manage logistics. If these needs exist, funds must be raised to cover them. And participants will need to be comfortable with whatever strategy is adopted to meet the needs.

Guidelines for Ensuring That Resource Needs Can Be Met and That the Group Is Consulted about How to Meet Them

Convenors need to ensure that sufficient resources are available to support the process from its initiation through the implementation of an agreement. Convenors need to determine what allowances they will need to make to meet evolving resource needs as they emerge.

In the course of the convening process, the following kinds of resource needs may be identified: the training and preparation of participants, information needs, mechanisms for public outreach, the costs of conducting and participating in the process, and staff and logistical support.

Participant Preparation

Even when participants agree to come to the table, they may only have experience with traditional ways of negotiating and making decisions. People tend to slip back easily into familiar patterns of behavior. Joint training or at least an orientation session has proven very beneficial, especially when participants have never before been part of a consensus building process. An interest-based approach to negotiation and the use of consensus decision making are new concepts for many people. Learning how these approaches work will help participants function more effectively and shorten the time it takes to achieve results.

For example, in Hampton, Virginia, participants were about to begin a consensus process to resolve a dispute over the location of a highway. A training session introduced them to the principles of collaborative problem solving. A videotape depicting an actual process was used to illustrate how they might proceed. Simulations were used to engage participants in trying out these new concepts. Based on two days of training, the group was able to move forward and resolve the controversy (Plotz, 1991).

Another approach to preparing participants is to rely on peers who have participated in similar processes. For example, in helping a state agency representative to prepare for a dialogue on a contentious health care issue, another agency staff member who had been extremely effective in that same role (on another issue) met with his colleague to describe his experience.

Orientation and training can be carried out as part of an initial organizing meeting. The orientation or training can be done by the neutral, the convenor, or experienced participants from other consensus building efforts. Information about training is available from the same resources identified above as sources of information about how to locate neutrals.

Providing Information to Participants

Sometimes the technical nature of issues requires the convenor to work with the group, prior to holding any meetings, to gather and exchange information so that all participants have what they need to prepare themselves for the discussions. The convenor(s) may be able to supply the necessary information. However, participants may need additional technical help beyond what the convenor can provide. If a key party lacks sufficient staff or other resources, it may be important to provide them with organizational or technical assistance.

Convening may mean finding additional resources, or finding help to finance everything from information collection to expert advice. Members of the group need to agree on how these resources will be provided and how costs will be covered.

Creating Mechanisms for Outreach to Constituencies and the Public

Convening a consensus building process may require ways of communicating with a wider public beyond those who can be directly involved to make sure that an agreement will be supported by the constituencies of those around the table. It may mean building partnerships with the media or others to achieve broad dissemination of information and to solicit the views of the public. Sometimes, as in the Chelsea case, the media can be an important resource for reaching the wider public to establish the credibility of the process. In Catron County, the Citizens Committee relied on its partnership with a weekly newspaper to distribute its mission statement to every mailbox in the county. (See Chapter 11 for more on working with the media.)

Convening may also mean assisting some stakeholder groups in determining how to communicate with their constituencies. Especially in situations where groups are diffuse or unorganized, they may not have a regular means of communication. This can be problematic since they all need feedback from their constituents. A convenor can provide assistance in helping stakeholder groups think through these kinds of issues and develop plans to address them. Sometimes newsletters can be helpful. Sometimes special briefings can trigger the necessary feedback.

Costs of Conducting the Process
and Enabling Participation

In addition to contracting with the neutral, gathering information, and communicating with the public and various constituencies, there may be other costs associated with initiating a process, for example, support for the preparation of materials, agendas, meeting notices and summaries, as well as logistical arrangements for meeting space and meals. Some participants may need financial support to travel to and attend meetings, including help with child care. Some groups with representatives at the table may need money to support their efforts to communicate with their constituents.

Finding Ways to Fund
Consensus Building Processes

Most consensus building processes are funded by one or more of the following sources: foundation grants, government contracts, or contributions from individuals, charitable groups, or corporations. The convenor needs to be thinking about potential sources of funding as well as other ways of meeting resource needs (such as acquiring in-kind contributions of services).

When the convenor is a government agency or private corporation, it is often prepared to provide the necessary resources. When the convenor is a community steering committee or a nonprofit group, it may be able to attract foundation support or contributions from other charitable groups. When the convenors are both public and private entities, funds may come from all these sources, including in-kind contributions. Whatever the case, participants should understand how the costs will be met and agree to the mechanisms by which decisions about the use of money will be made.

Even when a convenor can pay for everything, there may be difficulties. For example, there may be a perception that the group providing the funding controls the process. If this is the case, steps must be taken to overcome this perception. A steering committee can be created to approve and manage all contributed funds. Sometimes participants can work out cost-sharing agreements, or they may decide that some will contribute in-kind support while others contribute money.

Ultimately, the convenor must find a way to meet the relevant resource needs as part of the convening effort. If the convenor does not have access to the necessary resources, he or she must develop a funding strategy. This involves, first, identifying the resource needs. Second, the convenor should identify potential sources of funding. The context, the issues, and the potential participants are key factors to examine as the convenor searches for likely sources of support. Some sources of support are available only in particular geographic contexts, communities, states, or regions. Others are only available depending on the issue under discussion.

Let us examine some ways to go about identifying potential funding. At the local level, the United Way, chambers of commerce, or a community foundation may be able to help support a consensus building effort. At the state or national level, the Council on Foundations provides a number of ways to readily access their information about foundations and the issues and groups they are interested in supporting. Federal and state agencies may have suggestions as well; state and community centers for dispute resolution may also be able to offer funding advice.

The next step in formulating a funding strategy is to make a list of potential supporters and identify who among the convenors and stakeholders can assist in contacting those individuals and organizations. It may be that different sources can be approached about funding different segments of the process. An agency might be able to support the training, for instance, or a foundation may be able to provide funds for a public information effort. A newspaper might be willing to carry information about the process, and some of the participants (or the convenor) may be able to offer in-kind staff or logistical support.

Once a funding strategy is developed, it should be shared with all stakeholders. Usually, stakeholder groups will be knowledgeable about possible funding sources. They also need to agree to how the funds will be managed once they are secured. As described above, steering committees, selected to be broadly representative of the group, can be formed to oversee the expenditure of funds. Where convenors are themselves representative of the diversity of the group, the group may agree that the convenors can play this kind of role.

■ *Step 4: Plan and Organize the Process*

Once a decision is reached to move forward, the final step is to organize the process. When the assessment is completed, participants selected, and resource needs identified, the convenor will have the information necessary to plan the process. If the decision has been made to employ a neutral to carry out the convening stage, the neutral will lead the planning and organizing activities. Once participants are identified, the convenor will be able to involve other participants.

One of the key reasons convenors decide to initiate a process is to ensure implementation. Steps must also be taken to link the informal or ad hoc collaborative process with the formal mechanisms of decision making. Those who will be responsible for implementing the agreement must be part of the process. At the very least, they must be kept informed, or else support for whatever agreement is reached may not be forthcoming. Planning should include ways to ensure ongoing communication with those who are key to implementation.

The other activities involved in planning and organizing a process are discussed at length in Chapter 1, on choosing appropriate consensus building techniques and strategies; Chapter 2, on conducting a conflict assessment; and Chapter 3, on designing a consensus building process using a graphic road map.

■ *Special Challenges to Convening for Government Agencies*

"Government convenors face some special challenges and barriers."

Government convenors face some special challenges and barriers in introducing new ways of reaching agreement. Because public mistrust in government is high, processes convened and facilitated by government are sometimes viewed by the public as a form of co-optation, especially when the issues have already been framed by government, and the participants and neutral are selected by a government agency. Government officials need to deal with these perceptions during the convening stage. The following suggestions point out some ways government agencies can demonstrate their intent to ensure that a consensus-seeking process is open and impartial.

Government agencies can begin by clarifying their objectives in convening the process and stating their commitment to implement the outcomes. The authorized decision maker, either the administration or the legislature, should be prepared at the outset to endorse the consensus-seeking process. An endorsement should be preceded by careful consideration of whether the agency or legislature is really committed to using a consensus-seeking approach, including its willingness to share control over the process.

To undertake a consensus building process, policy makers need to believe the issue is of high-enough priority for them to give their time and attention to creating a useful and implementable outcome. If leaders are aware of obstacles that could stand in the way of implementing a negotiated agreement, they must address those obstacles and offer incentives that make it worthwhile for all the appropriate stakeholders to participate.

When leaders show visible support, including consistent involvement in meetings and substantive discussions, participants will be reassured that their investment of time and resources is worthwhile. If leaders do not provide such support, caution should be exercised in initiating a consensus building process. Without the support of the key convening groups, the likelihood of success is greatly diminished.

To live within their statutory responsibilities, government policy makers need to identify the form an agreement should take to make it easy to implement. For example, in Chelsea, the city government was clear that if the group reached consensus on the elements of a new charter, the city would adopt that language and put it on the ballot.

How can government convenors overcome participants' lack of trust or fears of being co-opted? When agencies act openly and transparently, clearly stating the purposes for convening a consensus-seeking process and involving other stakeholders every step of the way, their actions will go a long way toward establishing the credibility of the process. When they abide by the ground rules adopted by all the parties, they demonstrate that they are willing to level the playing field. And finally, when they demonstrate their commitment by implementing the outcomes of the agreement, the congruence between their talk and their action will establish their credibility and overcome concerns about co-optation (SPIDR, 1997).

■ Conclusion

All in all, careful convening is critical to the success of a consensus building process. It takes more than checking off the convening steps. It is how well the steps are carried out that enables the convenor to lay the groundwork for an effective, legitimate, and credible process. A thorough and impartial convening paves the way to success.

■ Note

1. Note that Chapter 3, on designing a consensus process, uses the terms *start-up phase* and *process design phase*. The term *convening*, as used in this chapter, comprises both the start-up and process design phases as defined in Chapter 3.

■ References

KenCairn, B. (1997). The partnership phenomenon. *Chronicle of Community, 3,* 37-41.

Plotz, D. A. (1991). *Community problem solving case summaries* (Vol. 3). Washington, DC: Program for Community Problem Solving.

Society of Professionals in Dispute Resolution. (1997). *Best practices for government agencies: Guidelines for using collaborative agreement-seeking processes.* Washington, DC: Author.

Thomas-Larmer, J. (1998, July). Getting reluctant stakeholders to the table. *Consensus, 39,* 5-6.

5

THE ROLE OF FACILITATORS, MEDIATORS, AND OTHER CONSENSUS BUILDING PRACTITIONERS

■ *Michael L. Poirier Elliott*

Conflicts grow out of diverse values, perceptions, and interests that exist within a community or organization. Examples abound. In Chelsea, Massachusetts, a long-submerged conflict over corrupt local politics erupted when the city government was put into receivership. In Atlanta, Georgia, historic preservationists repeatedly battled developers, disrupting redevelopment but failing to preserve historic properties. On the Haida Gwaii islands in British Columbia, a native people struggled with the provincial government over the future of their community. And in Hartford, Connecticut, affordable housing advocates clashed with local communities over the distribution and availability of lower-cost housing throughout the region.

In each of these communities, existing institutions were incapable of resolving the conflicts. Also, the disputants lacked the productive working relationships necessary for constructive decision making and problem solving. Impasse resulted. Despite this impasse, however, all four communities successfully resolved their disputes. Moreover, the residents of Chelsea and Haida

Gwaii forged substantially stronger communities out of their efforts to build consensus.

The communities and the disputes in these cases differ a great deal; each story is unique. Yet the cases share two important elements. In each, the disputants chose (sometimes after much coaxing) to seek consensus solutions. Equally important, all four communities sought help from mediators.

Practitioners skilled in mediation and consensus building are frequently found at the center of visioning, decision making, and dispute resolution processes within communities and within organizations. Resolving conflict requires skill, communication, and trust. Experienced practitioners help stakeholders to build consensus by identifying existing barriers to effective negotiation and communication, assessing the structure and extent of a dispute, designing and implementing dispute resolution processes, and helping parties to develop options and reach consensus. In addition, practitioners help to build working relationships among diverse stakeholders, thereby encouraging communication across lines that traditionally divide disputants.

Consensus building requires its practitioners to promote dialogue under conditions of conflict, where communication and trust are weak. Consensus processes are therefore usually designed and implemented by trained individuals who bring experience and ability to the task at hand and seek to protect the impartiality and credibility of the process in the eyes of all parties. As can be seen in Chelsea, Atlanta, and Hartford, these individuals are most frequently professional mediators, facilitators, or dispute systems designers, affiliated with organizations that have no direct stake in the conflict or its resolution.

Yet, given the variety of conflict, occasions exist when an involved party, even one with a vested interest in the outcome, may serve effectively as a mediator. In Haida Gwaii, the consensus process was promoted and implicitly mediated by a planning consultant hired by federal and provincial agencies to act as their community liaison. The agencies, as the legitimate authorities designated to implement the program under dispute, designed a traditional planning process. They were to hand down decisions after receiving community input. These agencies did not envision convening a consensus building process when they appointed the community liaison, although he was a trained mediator. The liaison, therefore, was doubly suspect. To the local communities, he represented the interests of the "outside" agencies. To the agencies, he was potentially undermining their planning authority by promoting consensus building. Nonetheless, he worked effectively to bring parties to agreement and, in the process, transformed their views of each other.

In this chapter, we explore the use of facilitation, mediation, and dispute systems design in building consensual agreements. We focus on the involvement of experienced practitioners in this process, examining the core activities conducted by these practitioners, the conditions under which professional practitioners are needed, and how best to select such individuals when the need exists. Three of the four cases we use to illustrate these points— Chelsea, Hartford, and Haida Gwaii—are more fully described in Cases 3, 4, and 10, respectively. The Atlanta case is described in detail in an article in the *Journal of Architectural and Planning Research* (Elliott, 1999). Because these cases all involve the use of consensus building practitioners in public settings, the chapter necessarily focuses more on public sector than private sector conflicts. The wisdom and guidance it contains, however, are certainly applicable to the use of practitioners in intraorganizational and other private settings. (The use of dispute resolution practitioners in intraorganizational settings is also discussed in Chapter 16.)

■ Use of Convening, Facilitation, Mediation, and Dispute Systems Design in Consensus Building

This section explores the functions that convening, facilitation, mediation, and dispute systems design play in a consensus building process. It begins with a discussion of how consensus building efforts typically get started and the barriers to reaching agreement that can arise in the process. Next, the section describes in general terms the activities involved in convening, facilitation, mediation, and dispute systems design, and how these activities help disputing parties overcome the barriers to reaching agreement. Finally, the section sets forth a model of consensus building that is used in the following section to help us understand the specific tasks of consensus building practitioners.

Entry into Consensus Processes

In consensus building processes, participants seek to reach decisions through discussion and negotiation for the purpose of arriving at a mutually acceptable agreement. Consensus processes gain legitimacy by involving those directly affected by a decision in the process of developing the decision, by conducting their dialogues in an open and inclusive manner, and by searching for agreements that speak to all the interests involved. In most cases, the negotiations are conducted face-to-face, in groups that represent the range of interests involved.

While some communities and organizations incorporate consensus building into their everyday decision making, most do not. Rather, they enter into consensus processes—and seek the help of consensus building practitioners—when current conditions become unacceptable or when members develop a greater desire for participatory control over decision making. Motivations to enter into a consensus process and seek trained assistance vary, as can be seen by our four examples.

Chelsea. With its corrupt local government in state receivership, Chelsea residents were cynical, apathetic, and deeply frustrated with the status quo. Citizens distrusted existing government institutions (local and state) and had little experience in working with each other. The issues were complex and difficult to discuss. The consensus process, initiated from outside the community, offered a seed of hope that was nurtured and grew.

Atlanta. In Atlanta, historic preservation disputes were long-standing and recurring. Disputes about both preservation policy and the fate of specific buildings repeatedly escalated. Conflicts pitted the Urban Design Commission, the city council, and the mayor's office against each other. A particularly difficult deadlock involving preservationists, developers, and political leaders led disputants to seek an alternative. The consensus building process was initiated through direct negotiations between developers, historic preservationists, and city administrators.

Haida Gwaii. On Haida Gwaii, 150 years of antagonism between the native Haida people and the descendants of European settlers kept these communities apart. Despite a common island home, the communities were sharply divided and knew little about each other's culture. When faced with a federal and provincial initiative to invest $38 million Canadian in local economic development, however, the shared interests of these residents evolved into a mediated dialogue. The process leading up to the dialogue required considerable trust building among the various communities, and between the communities and the federal and provincial agencies.

Hartford. Local governments throughout the Hartford metropolis grappled with a lack of affordable housing. State legislation enabled regional compacts, through which communities would commit to supply a specified number of affordable housing units over a five-year period, but only if all communities within the region consented to the agreement. With each local government retaining autonomy over the issue, a regional compact could only emerge from a consensus process. With state support, the communities hired a team of mediators to manage the process.

What do these stories tell us? Communities often enter into consensus processes indirectly, only after trying more conventional approaches to resolving conflicts. Stakeholders may be skeptical that consensus is even possible, because relationships among them are often strained and the issues are typically complex. Yet frustration with the status quo, combined with the costs of ongoing conflict, provide powerful incentives to participate in consensus processes. For stakeholders who are actively involved in a dispute, consensus processes offer a particularly useful forum for focusing on and resolving the issues. In some communities, a tradition of collaborative decision making and a desire to promote civic engagement further motivate disputants to seek consensus.

Barriers to Consensus Building

These stories also suggest reasons why consensus building may prove difficult. In each case, barriers to consensus building exist. We can summarize these barriers as follows.

- *Institutions.* Existing institutions are unable to resolve the conflict, either because the institution is itself a participant in the dispute (in Chelsea it was the source of the dispute) or because traditional institutions do not provide a forum for the resolution of nontraditional conflicts.

- *Deadlock.* The positions of disputants have become inflexible, and disputants have little experience working with each other and lack the trust needed to proceed.

- *Escalation and positional bargaining.* Hostility, distrust, bias, concealment, or unwillingness to communicate preclude negotiations or dialogues. Also, behaviors that contribute to positional bargaining, threats, accusations, or unreal expectations sidetrack dialogues after they are initiated.

- *Communication.* The lack of clear communication channels among conflicting stakeholders contributes to misperception and divergence.

- *Complexity.* The number of issues or parties to a dispute prevents participants from effectively addressing their concerns. Also, the dialogue process may become inefficient or inequitable, leading to frustration and disengagement.

- *Ambiguity.* The rights and responsibilities of the various participants remain undefined or disputed, contributing to confusion over how best to proceed with consensus building.

Thus, consensus building requires that participants overcome a number of barriers. To work together effectively, the parties must organize their efforts and repair their relationships. They must at least *convene* a process of participation and *facilitate* meetings. In almost all cases of community consensus building, *mediation* between the parties over goal setting, fact-finding, options, communications, and relationships must also take place. If the conflict is structural and recurring, parties may also become involved in *dispute systems design.*

Consensus Building Activities

"Consensus building practitioners typically fulfill four fundamental functions: convening, facilitation, mediation, and dispute systems design."

Consensus building practitioners, then, typically fulfill four fundamental functions in a collaborative process: convening, facilitation, mediation, and dispute systems design. These activities may be conducted by a single person or team, so that the person who performs the convening tasks also facilitates the meetings, mediates the disputes, and, if needed, designs systems for resolving future disputes. Or different individuals may perform each function.

It should be noted that professionals in the consensus building field hold differing opinions and preferences about what the practitioners who perform these various functions should be called. People who have expertise in both facilitation and mediation, for example, may refer to themselves as either facilitators or mediators or both. Also, as discussed in Chapter 4, the term *convenor* is typically used to describe the organization or person who initiates a consensus building process—often a government agency or another stakeholder. But the tasks involved in convening are often carried out by a dispute resolution practitioner, who may thus also be referred to as a convenor. To minimize that confusion, we avoid using the word *convenor* to mean a consensus building practitioner in this chapter. We do use the terms *mediator, facilitator,* and *dispute systems designer* when speaking of someone with the specific expertise or performing the specific functions suggested by those terms. And we use the term *practitioner* generically, to mean someone with any or all of these skills who performs any or all of these roles.

Convening

Convening is the initiation and design of an appropriate consensus building process in a particular context. During the convening phase, practitioners typically help disputants assess the sources and characteristics of the conflict, the relationship between the parties, the barriers to resolution, and the issues that need to be resolved. (See Chapter 2 for more on these conflict assessment activities.) They may also work with disputants to identify parties with a stake, design an appropriate decision-making process (including ground rules of conduct, a timetable, and an overall agenda), ensure appropriate representation of the stakeholders, build the capacity of parties to engage in meaningful negotiations, facilitate more effective communication, and initiate the process. Through these activities, the practitioner helps build the capacity of the participants to solve problems and resolve differences effectively.

The convening phase, while generally essential to a well-functioning consensus process, varies in its implementation. It often takes considerably more work than disputants first envision. In Atlanta and Hartford, the disputants sought to implement a consensus process, were willing to work with other parties, and organized themselves sufficiently to hire mediators to assist them in their efforts. In convening the process, the mediators interviewed a wide spectrum of stakeholders and designed a consensus process that was intended to comprehensively describe the activities and ground rules to which the participants were committing themselves. The mediators worked with disputants to select participants, set ground rules, and establish a work plan. The mediators put considerable emphasis on working with participants both to ensure participant commitment to the process and build patterns of cooperation before bringing the parties together for face-to-face dialogue and negotiations. Hence, even though conditions were already ripe for initiating a consensus process, the convenings each took about two months and constituted about 20 percent of the total work conducted by the mediation teams.

In many ways, Haida Gwaii represents an extreme example of convening. The community liaison spent eight months brokering the start of an unofficial negotiation between the Haida people and the local townships. The federal and provincial agencies knew little of these exchanges and initially did not support a consensus-based process. The community liaison worked within a mediation model, but without ever being hired to mediate the dispute. Convening consisted of a series of relationship-building activities, including sharing personal stories and hopes for the future. Each activity was designed to increase the understanding of parties separated by a wide cultural divide. Over time, a level of trust grew out of these discussions, paving the way for more focused dialogue over the management of the economic development funds.

Faced with widespread skepticism, the Chelsea mediation team also engaged in an elaborate convening process. Like Haida Gwaii, the mediators designed the convening to build community support for consensus building. In this case, issues of cross-cultural understanding were less important than building the capacity for civic engagement. Forty-five community meetings, newsletters, a survey questionnaire, a telephone hot line, and television programming were all tools for increasing community awareness of and interest in the process. The mediators even developed a process for selecting the 18 participants in the Charter Preparation Team that was specifically designed to support the legitimacy of the team members selected.

Facilitation

Facilitation is the impartial management of meetings designed to enable participants to focus on substantive issues and goals. Facilitators develop an agenda for each meeting, enforce ground rules of conduct, promote interaction and communication during meetings, and bring issues to closure. A facilitator remains neutral concerning the content of the group's work and typically has no decision-making authority within the group (Doyle & Straus, 1982; Schwarz, 1994).

Consider a group of individuals who must work collaboratively together, either for a single meeting or over a period of time. What conditions tend to increase the effectiveness of such a group? Successful teams typically have the following characteristics.

- Members are committed to a clear goal.
- The team is organized to achieve specific results, within a collaborative climate.
- Team members are technically competent, capable of collaborating effectively, and motivated to contribute.
- Members of the group take on leadership responsibilities that are consistent with the objectives of the group and the desires of group members.
- The group receives external support and recognition from the organizations and communities within which they function. (Larson & LaFasto, 1989)

Examining the four cases for conformance to these elements, not a single one of the negotiating groups can be characterized as "likely to succeed" at the start of their consensus processes. Chelsea was perhaps furthest from the ideal. The community lacked the capacity to self-organize. Its leadership was dysfunctional, and its participants were disempowered. The mediator developed specific strategies to promote the capacity of the community to govern itself, to engage its citizenry in productive team settings. The mediator trained local residents to facilitate public forums. These residents would not have known how to convene a process and would have been lost in efforts to mediate a dispute. Nor could they have facilitated complex meetings, such as those held by the Charter Preparation Team (the core consensus building group). But they successfully ran the 45 community meetings and in the process gained skills that would help them participate effectively in the overall process.

At the same time, in each of the four cases cited, the negotiating groups substantially improved in their functioning over time. They improved in part because effective facilitation tends to breed effective teams. Participants who feel empowered to contribute ideas and influence the outcome of a process, and who perceive a facilitator to be evenhanded and neutral, generally become more committed to the collaborative effort, developing leadership within the group and a respect for their fellow negotiators.

Mediation

Mediation is the intervention by an impartial party into a negotiation or dispute. It is designed to help the disputing parties resolve their differences in a voluntary and mutually acceptable manner. Mediations are structured negotiations, in which a mediator assists participants in negotiating more effectively. Mediators use various forms of interaction—including plenary sessions of all participants, caucuses, work groups, and one-on-one discussions—to clarify interests, improve communication and cooperation, strengthen relationships, and help parties generate options and reach consensus.

Like a facilitator, a mediator must remain neutral concerning the content of a group's work and has little or no decision-making authority within a group (Carpenter & Kennedy, 1988; Gray, 1989; Moore, 1996). However, because mediation seeks to enhance negotiations, a mediator works explicitly to manage not just the interactions that occur within meetings but also the dynamics that occur outside meetings. As a consequence of this deeper involvement in negotiations among disputing parties, the effectiveness of a mediator depends even more on legitimacy and trust than does the effectiveness of a facilitator. A mediator works across conflicting perspectives and interests and shapes both process and group identity. As a consequence, mediator selection is itself often conflictual.

All four case studies involve mediation. Yet they focus on different activities because the needs of the communities differed. In Hartford and Atlanta, mediation supported explicitly interest-based bargaining. The techniques and tools used by the mediators were primarily designed to explore interests systematically and in depth, encourage joint fact-finding, generate and explore options, and bring closure to the negotiations. In both cases, because the issues were particularly complex, mediators used a single negotiating text to help focus the discussions. The text documented all agreements and disagreements and was repeatedly revised to reflect new thinking. Technical experts perceived by both sides to be neutral helped the parties develop common understandings and conduct analyses.

In Haida Gwaii, mediation supported an explicit relationship-building process, in which interest-based bargaining was secondary. The techniques and tools used by the mediators in this case were designed to explore cultures and stories, share identities, and construct a forum for interaction and community building. The motivation behind this process grew from an interest in the $38 million development fund, but for the Haida at least, an interest-based process would have led nowhere under the conditions of mistrust and alienation that characterized the relationships at the start of the process.

Dispute Systems Design

Dispute systems design is a process for devising institutions, organizations, and dispute management procedures that promote consensus building across a wide range of recurring issues. Practitioners adept at dispute systems design diagnose systems to determine causes of recurring conflict, design systematic interventions to promote conflict prevention or dispute management, implement and test these interventions, and make readjustments based on feedback from implemented programs.

Dispute systems designers carefully examine the effectiveness by which an entire class of conflicts is managed and work to improve the effectiveness of the dispute resolution systems at resolving differences. Dispute systems design views the management of conflict as a core function of any organization or social system. Typical responses to conflict—that of fight or flight—tend to accentuate problems over time and reduce the capacity of social systems to resolve differences productively. Dispute systems designers seek to reconfigure the set of procedures, incentives, resources, and skills available within the social system, such that particular classes of disputes will be more effectively resolved. The design can focus on improving dispute management within a single organization (such as the procedures used by a university system to resolve disputes within each of its colleges) or across a range of institutions working to resolve a specific class of disputes (such as efforts to improve management of land tenure disputes in Nicaragua) (Costantino & Merchant, 1996; Ury, Brett, & Goldberg, 1993).

Consider two examples of dispute systems design.[1] In 1996, the Board of Regents of the University System of Georgia passed a dispute resolution initiative. The board had become increasingly concerned about the escalation of conflicts between faculty, staff, administrators, and students in the 34 colleges and universities under its management. It was particularly disturbed that such conflicts were not being resolved within the units, but rather were being appealed for review to the board or to the courts. As a result, the board required all units to review and revise their dispute management procedures and made changes at the system-wide level to support more effective dispute management.

In Nicaragua, the dispute system that needed to be revised was not based within a single organization, but rather in a series of interconnected policies, laws, and institutions. Multiple owners claimed 20 percent of all land in the country, each with a legal basis to the claims. The problem emerged both in the Somozan regime, during which ownership of land was concentrated into the hands of the ruling elite, and during the 1980s, when the

Sandanistas sought through land reform to reallocate land among the poor. Because of the way the various laws were written, legal claims to much of the land could be made by both the original owners and the new owners. Given the scale of the problem, litigation to clarify landownership claims would have absorbed Nicaragua's entire court system for 10 years. Moreover, until land title was clarified, banks would not lend money for development, thereby blocking economic activity in a significant portion of the country. The work of the dispute systems designer, then, was to identify disputes that were amenable to more streamlined resolution and to develop procedures for resolving these disputes more efficiently. The dispute system that was developed is now in the process of being implemented.

Dispute systems designers seek to alter existing procedures and patterns of relationships, such that these procedures and relationships

- promote the legitimate interests of disputants,
- maximize the potential joint gains between disputants while protecting the public or communal interests,
- resolve conflicting interests fairly by including the full range of legitimate interest groups and informing and empowering those groups to make wise decisions,
- produce agreements that protect outside interests and set good precedent for future decision making,
- function effectively within the context of existing legislative or administrative authority and responsibility,
- generate agreements that are durable and implementable,
- reach agreements efficiently when agreement is possible, and
- stabilize or improve relationships between the parties to the dispute.

The dispute systems designer works with specific clients but in ways that intricately involve multiple parties. The implementability of a resulting design will greatly depend on its acceptability to the various parties. As such, the designer combines the skills of a mediator with that of an organizational development specialist and systems analyst.

Substance, Relationships, Processes: A Model for Understanding the Role of Practitioners

As we have seen, dispute resolution practitioners can play a variety of roles in the construction of consensus. The complexity of the issues, the diversity of participants, and the duration of the process all influence which roles are important in a particular consensus building effort. Yet all of these roles involve managing three core elements that underpin all consensus building efforts: concerns about substance (*what* underlies the conflict?) and relationships (*who* is in conflict?) in the context of a dispute resolution process (*how* will stakeholders work out their differences?).

"The use of consensus building practitioners is inextricably linked to the choice of the dispute resolution process."

This section provides an overview of the interactions between the substance of a dispute, the relationships between disputants, and the process choices available. The use of consensus building practitioners is, after all, inextricably linked to the choice of the dispute resolution process. By gaining a better grasp of these three core elements of consensus building, we can better understand the specific tasks practitioners must undertake.

Substance

Substantive issues are the core of almost all complex, multi-party conflicts. Stakeholders are typically concerned with the outcomes of a decision-making process, and how those outcomes will affect either the stakeholders themselves or some other group of concern. What historic structures will be protected in Atlanta? How will affordable housing be provided across the Hartford region? What form of government will Chelsea adopt?

In any particular context, each stakeholder "frames" the dispute by developing a working theory about the substantive issues of importance and their value. The stakeholders are engaged in a process of sense-making whereby they each seek to order a potentially confusing array of characteristics, perceptions, interests, and values. Each participant then uses this frame to interpret the events and characteristics of the dispute (*interpretive frames*) and to value potential outcomes (*goal frames*).

The frames used by disputants can differ overtly. Compare the Haida conception of the living environment, for example, with the European conception of utilitarian property. In Chelsea, "good government" was an oxymoron to many disillusioned residents. Actions taken by the state to promote good government were first interpreted by residents as efforts to undermine local autonomy and oppress the less powerful.

In other cases, these frames differ subtly. All participants in the Atlanta process declared themselves in favor of protecting historically significant properties, but they differed in their conception of "historically significant." Likewise, all participants shared a belief that historic buildings must provide a "reasonable rate of return" to their owners, but differed in what this meant and in their sense of how often developers faced a problem in this regard. In a development dispute, one disputant may focus on community and change, another on environmental integrity and aesthetics, and yet a third on private property rights and the value of growth. The consensus building practitioner does not seek to change the values and interests held by the participants, but rather to clarify them and to assist participants in reexamining how their values and interests might be best met.

The give-and-take of consensus building is built on the capacity of the participants to work together to design a jointly created agreement in the face of perceived or actual competition over the content of the dispute, complicating perceptions about that content, and distinct interests and values. Progress is usually not built on efforts to conform all participants to a single, shared sense of the nature of the dispute and its characteristics, but rather by building options that meet each participant's interests and values. While stakeholders will differ in their interpretation of substantive issues, and on the value afforded them, an effective resolution depends in part on the capacity of stakeholders to work within a compatible, general framework of understanding. By focusing on interests and the development of integrative options based on objective criteria, a practitioner helps parties to identify the characteristics of importance and the range of possible solutions. While perceptual differences may not be easily resolvable, they can be understood and communicated as a basis for consensus building. To reveal core perceptions, practitioners use techniques such as joint fact-finding, structured data queries that help expose differences in assumptions and perceptions, and storytelling.

Relationship

Relationships and social dynamics are central to consensus building (Kramer & Messick, 1995). Consensus building can help members of a community, group, or team construct a better sense of how they can best resolve differences, make decisions, and work together to enhance their basic interests and values. When most successful, consensus building promotes social learning, whereby a community not only resolves an immediate conflict but also learns how to better manage disputes in the future.

Problems associated with relationships can be divided into two types: interpersonal and structural. *Interpersonal problems* emerge from distorted communications, stereotyping, strong emotions, and destructive behaviors. These patterns may be unintentional or they may be the result of strategic choices. In either case, they distort the ability of stakeholders to understand each other and to act with a clear understanding of the values, interests, or perceptions held by other disputants.

Consensus building is fundamentally a communicative act, and consensus is frequently built on efforts to improve communications. Mediation and facilitation practitioners work with participants to establish ground rules that promote constructive dialogue. In Chelsea, mediators and participants agreed to assign three individuals the responsibility of acting as spokespersons for the process. Such a ground rule, developed jointly by participants within the process, helped to foreclose negotiating through the media in favor of direct negotiations. Facilitators also structure communication within a meeting, by encouraging brainstorming when ideas need to be generated but not when negotiating the final details of an agreement. Practitioners can also use caucuses and interviews to create safe havens for exploring issues.

Structural problems emerge from the social configuration of power, rights, and identity. Power, built on unequal control over resources, authority, expertise, or position, can fundamentally alter the capacity of disputants to work together. Power-based disputes involve the use of force, explicit or implied, to gain acquiescence by opposing groups, against the will of those groups (Kritek, 1994). Until the state took the city of Chelsea into receivership, disputes were based on power.

Rights involve the use of independent standards to resolve differences. These standards may be legal or contractual, or they may emerge from accepted norms of behavior. Conceptions of justice may go beyond socially defined rights. Conceptions of justice may involve claims to rights that are not widely accepted. Rights-based disputes involve an appeal to higher authority, and frequently inhibit communication because they are often associated with highly emotional differences over principles and values. In Hartford, initial opposition to an affordable housing accord was linked to the right to self-autonomy shared by all jurisdictions in the region.

Identity (Rothman, 1997) involves the interpretive dynamics of culture, history, values, and beliefs. These dynamics are fundamentally psychological and social, growing from our sense of who we are, who constitutes our communities, and what this implies concerning our relationship to people both within our communities and outside. Identity-based disputes involve our construction of community, our fundamental conceptions of relationships. In Haida Gwaii, identity formed the core barrier to consensus building between the Haida and local communities, and between all residents of Haida Gwaii and the federal and provincial officials with authority over the development fund.

Structural impediments to communication are more difficult for practitioners to help groups overcome than interpersonal impediments, largely because consensus building rarely seeks to explicitly alter the structural configuration of power, rights, and identity. The status quo almost invariably works to the advantage of some groups over others, and in the absence of a painful stalemate, the dominant groups have little incentive to promote fundamental change. Yet in our cases, we also see examples in which mediators help parties to overcome structural impediments. In Chelsea and Haida Gwaii, in fact, the consensus building process transformed the relationships themselves, promoting not just satisfaction and settlement but also empowerment and recognition (see Bush & Folger, 1994).

Process

Issues of substance and relationships are brought together within the context of a specific consensus building process. Practitioners may design and manage a participatory or conflict resolution process in very different ways, depending on the foci

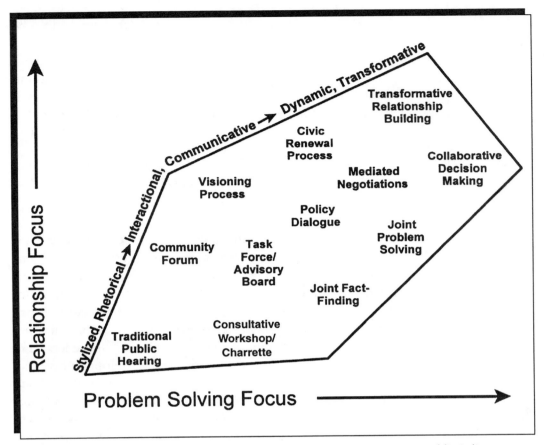

Figure 5.1. The Variety of Participatory and Consensus Building Processes in Public Policy
NOTE: A *charrette* is a short and intensive visioning process. Stakeholders convene in a series of meetings (lasting from one day to several weeks) to develop a plan for a major facet of community life, such as the downtown, recreation, or transportation.

of the process. Processes can adopt a problem-solving focus, a relationship-building focus, both, or neither. As shown in Figure 5.1, process design varies considerably by objectives. These objectives can include information sharing, knowledge acquisition, problem solving, visioning, agreement seeking, and community building. More broadly, these objectives lead to processes that are stylized and rhetorical, interactional and communicative, or dynamic and transformative.

Stylized, rhetorical. Many forms of public participation are not designed to build consensus. In a traditional public hearing, for example, the objective is information sharing. Communication is one-way: first as public officials present findings (one way from officials to the audience), and second as attendees present their comments (one way from participants to either the officials or, more likely, to the media). In many ways, these interactions are highly scripted, meaning that they are patterned forms of inter-action, in which little effort is made to enter into meaningful dialogue. As such, the communication is stylized and rhetorical. In Haida Gwaii, the federal and provincial officials originally designed a public participation process that was top-down, with little opportunity for dialogue.

Interactional, communicative. Teams, organizations, and com-munities frequently seek to develop processes that allow not only for the sharing of knowledge and experience but also for the social creation of new ideas and understandings. In processes such as these, participants focus on acquiring knowledge, solving problems, making decisions, or visioning a desired future. At their most interactional, these processes develop consensus around the resolution of particular issues or the management of particular relationships. The process of interaction between the participants is thus more complex than in a stylized process as described above. Participants in interactional, communicative processes enter into a dialogue over concerns, interests, and options, seeking to improve both problem solving and relationship build-ing. These processes require considerably more management than do simpler processes. The Atlanta and Hartford cases are exam-ples of higher-order interactional, communicative processes, be-cause while the processes resolved particular substantive prob-lems through consensus, they did not seek to fundamentally alter the manner in which power, rights, or identity affected commu-nity relationships or problem solving in the future.

Dynamic, transformative. Groups may also come together not only to seek agreement on an immediate problem but also to build community out of conflictual relationships and solve the under-lying causes of conflict. These groups are involved in the funda-mental work of relationship building and community problem solving. Processes such as these require clear articulation and communication, and even more effective listening. Processes must be structured to overcome deep-rooted barriers that grow out of power, rights, and identity or that are embedded in the characteristics of the dispute itself. These processes almost always require systematic analysis of the causes of the dispute and barriers to effective resolution of the dispute. The issues are complex, and they require time and multiple meetings to create an environment in which dynamic exchange is possible. At their best, such processes transform the relationships and problem-solving abilities of the participants, such that they are better able to resolve future differences in a productive manner. The Chelsea and Haida Gwaii cases are examples of dynamic, transformative processes.

■ Core Tasks of Consensus Building Practitioners

What are we to make of this plethora of possible participatory and consensus building processes? First, whatever the scale of intervention, consensus building activities are built around the triple demands of substance, relationship, and process. Second, consensus building practitioners must carry out a number of specific tasks relating to each of these three demands if consensus building processes are to be successful. This section discusses some of the core tasks in detail.

"Two key principles underlie all these tasks: neutrality and accountability." It is important to note first, however, two key principles that underlie all these tasks: neutrality and accountability. Only a practitioner who is perceived as neutral will be able to gain the trust and confidence of all participants. Trust and confidence are essential, because effective intervention frequently requires the confidential exchange of information and ideas, and because a practitioner must often probe, test, and challenge parties in their efforts to make sense of a conflict and its resolution. A participant who believes that a practitioner is seeking to promote a certain viewpoint will be less forthcoming than one who perceives him or her as substantively neutral. Similarly, practitioners must be accountable to stakeholders, convenors, and resource providers. Accountability implies standards of professional practice, standards that the parties accept and to which the practitioner is willing to commit.

Yet pure neutrality is in fact difficult to achieve and impossible to verify. Practitioners may, rather, promote the legitimacy of a process (Society of Professionals in Dispute Resolution [SPIDR], 1997) by taking specific steps to

- ensure the representation and effective participation of key stakeholders,
- refrain from advocating for any particular perspective on substantive issues,
- protect the confidentiality of all private communications with participants,
- develop and enforce ground rules that are acceptable to the participants,
- clarify how decisions will be made and by whom within the process, and
- structure and implement a process that is accountable and fair.

So what are the specific tasks mediators and facilitators need to undertake to promote the legitimacy of a process in this way and help a group reach consensus? How can practitioners help "create the organization" by linking disparate stakeholders into a functioning consensus building team? We will now examine in more detail the work conducted by consensus building practitioners to address issues of substance, relationship, and process (Susskind & Cruikshank, 1987).

Substance

Map Stakeholder Interests

To be effective, a practitioner must understand the concerns and interests of stakeholders. The design of a consensus-based process therefore begins with an assessment of the nature of the conflict. Practitioners conduct conflict assessments by interviewing key stakeholders and collecting other forms of data. The interviews should identify stakeholder groups, possible representatives who may take part in a process, and the relationships that exist between the parties. With this knowledge, a practitioner can determine how best to promote negotiations and collaborative problem solving, as well as identify strategies for helping stakeholders explore their own interests, understandings, and perspectives.

Establish a Work Plan or Agenda

Consensus building, whether developed within a single meeting or in a complex, collaborative problem-solving process, requires a significant commitment on the part of participants. In addition, the issues associated with a complex dispute may not be clearly demarcated. Practitioners develop work plans (or agendas, in a single-meeting situation) to delineate the length of time a process or meeting will take, the level of commitment required of participants, the issues that are open for negotiation, and the activities needed to resolve the dispute. A practitioner must ensure that the issues presented for discussion deal effectively with the interests and goals of the participants. Early in a process, participants must discuss and come to agreement on the issues that will be up for negotiation.

In formulating a work plan, a facilitator or mediator often must prioritize the activities that are needed to resolve the dispute. If the future impacts of options being considered are highly uncertain, then joint fact-finding may be necessary. If different stakeholders have radically differing concerns, then detailed exploration of interests becomes essential. At the same time, a practitioner should ensure that a work plan can be altered as new information, issues, or tasks are identified.

Create a Climate for Joint Fact-Finding

Any consensus building process, short or long, involves a process of opening up issues, exploring them, and then resolving them. These phases are not distinct, but they are sequential. Issues cannot be resolved until they are clearly delineated. While the natural inclination of most participants is to spend little time on problem definition, it is absolutely essential that they clearly understand the dimensions, characteristics, and perspectives that give shape to a problem before seeking to develop solutions.

Facilitators and mediators typically devote initial meetings in a consensus process to identifying and creating a common understanding of the issues and reviewing the context of the dispute. Practitioners use these meetings to open up direct communications among the participants and to probe deeply into both individual and group interests. Facilitators lead discussions that help participants clarify areas of agreement and sources of disagreement, with the ultimate purpose of empowering them to seek creative solutions to the problems they share. These activities build cohesiveness among negotiators and point the way toward possible agreements.

Problem definition is particularly difficult in complex disputes. Frequently, the issues under dispute are technically complex, the impact of options is highly uncertain, and participants frame the issues in significantly different ways. Interpretation of data can also be strategic, with disputants seeking to interpret the information in ways that support their positions. In these cases, a facilitator or mediator will work to manage the conflicts over data. They may coordinate the joint development and sharing of information, for example. They may also promote more extensive efforts to conduct joint research studies, based on agreements among participants on the types of data to collect, the assumptions underlying a study, the experts who will conduct the study, and the criteria for assessing data. (See Chapter 9 for more on joint fact-finding.)

Create a Climate for Problem Solving

Many conflicts bind stakeholders in a cycle of escalation that inhibits creativity in seeking new solutions. Participants become wedded to their positions. A participant may support an idea simply because he or she has invested time and energy into promoting it. Before progress can be made, therefore, new potential solutions will need to be generated. Facilitators and mediators should design processes for generating options, and separate these processes from the task of evaluating the resulting alternatives. Brainstorming, in which ideas are generated in rapid succession but not immediately evaluated, provides a useful way to develop new options. Participants can then assess the strengths and weaknesses of each option. If participants generate separate options for each major aspect of the issues under discussion, mediators can then help participants experimentally combine these options into packages.

Before evaluating alternative packages, a mediator helps participants develop criteria for evaluation. Criteria that link jointly shared goals (such as fair-share distribution of affordable housing in Hartford) with objective standards (such as the increase in affordable housing as a percentage of households created within a community) work most effectively. Criteria promote openness by making options more concrete. Specific criteria help participants identify packages that best meet the underlying interests of the various stakeholders, and to openly discuss trade-offs among the options.

Jointly Assess the Impacts of Alternatives

Once participants eliminate clearly unacceptable options, they can further analyze the most promising options. In this stage, mediators help to organize task groups or identify independent experts to assist the participants in evaluating the likely consequences of proposed alternatives. This evaluation is iterative. A mediator uses the results of these assessments to challenge participants to redesign proposed options or to design entirely new options to better meet their collective needs. New designs, in turn, may need to be assessed for their potential impacts. A mediator must manage this process closely, ensuring that experts present their findings to participants in a timely and easy-to-understand manner. To do this, a mediator needs sufficient understanding of the issues under dispute to reasonably assess the analyses.

Reach Agreements in Principle

As participants refine their assessments of how proposed options affect their own interests, mediators and facilitators must help them to alter the options. Participants thereby seek to increase benefits to multiple stakeholders by identifying opportunities for joint gain, or seek to redistribute the costs and benefits among the stakeholders. Because issues within a dispute are often highly interconnected, the negotiators must merge specific alternatives into a comprehensive package. A mediator may then help participants organize this package by creating a *single negotiating text:* a document that describes the key issues and associated options for resolution, with areas of agreement clearly defined and areas of disagreement presented for further discussion.

Mediators construct a single negotiating text in several iterations. Early in a consensus building process, the text may consist of general statements of principles with which participants agree, as well as areas of disagreement that participants identify as important and in need of resolution. Mediators draw these statements primarily from the *group memory:* the notes taken during meetings on a flip chart by a member of the facilitation team. This allows participants to confirm the accuracy of the record. A mediator may also incorporate into the single text any ideas or possible agreements that he or she believes to be possible based on private conversations with participants.

Each participant (or, more efficiently, each team of like-minded participants) then reviews the document for clarification and refinement. To deal with particularly difficult issues, a mediator may organize task groups, hold caucuses among negotiators with similar interests, or discuss issues with participants in private. A mediator incorporates all new agreements and refinements into the single text, which is then reviewed by all participants.

The document thus becomes increasingly specific. The level of detail in a single negotiating text may vary. While some issues may be resolved in final form, other agreements may not be fully developed. If a consensus process is successful, the negotiators eventually develop a comprehensive package for resolving the dispute as a whole. By organizing the process around a single text, mediators improve participants' understanding of the issues and increase the efficiency of a negotiation.

Promote Implementable Agreements

Too often, participants consider their work complete after they resolve the substantive issues under negotiation. Many agreements unravel after they are reached, however, because participants give insufficient attention to how agreements will be implemented. A mediator helps to ensure that participants create a workable implementation plan.

Most agreements that resolve complex disputes require some legal, procedural, or administrative action to be implemented: Perhaps legislation must be enacted, new policy guidelines instituted, staff reallocated, or additional financial resources provided. A mediator should help participants identify these actions and develop ways of ensuring that they are carried out.

Participants must also identify the individuals who will carry out the implementation tasks. A mediator can help a group to develop a time line charting when certain tasks must be accomplished and by whom. If implementation will require significant coordination of tasks and individuals, a mediator will help participants establish an organizational structure for overseeing implementation. A small *implementation advisory group,* with representatives from each of the major interest groups, can be an effective way of ensuring that the tasks are accomplished. A mediator may be retained to help this group resolve future difficulties, though often this is not necessary.

Participants also need mechanisms for monitoring progress during implementation. These mechanisms should identify deadlines that are missed or slippage that occurs in an implementation schedule before it is too late to rectify the situation. An advisory group can use this information to help its members shepherd the implementation of an agreement through to completion. A comprehensive implementation plan will also specify criteria for measuring compliance with the terms of the agreement. These criteria, when coupled with a monitoring plan and procedures for resolving unexpected problems with or violations of the settlement agreement, greatly enhance the likelihood of successful implementation.

Evaluate Outcomes

Ideally, an implementation plan will also identify a method for evaluating the outcomes of an implemented agreement. An evaluation will help to determine if the intent and objectives of the original agreement were met. If an agreement was provisional or contained contingencies, an evaluation may alter the policies to be implemented. An evaluation may also prompt a renegotiation of specific provisions in the agreement.

Relationship

Facilitate Effective Communication

From the outset of a consensus building process, a practitioner will seek to promote more effective communication among disputants. Parties to disputes, particularly those involving complex issues and multiple parties, typically engage in strategic or emotional discourse. This discourse is rarely intended to provide a meaningful exchange of information about perspectives, goals, and interests. Rather, it is intended to shape perceptions and alter power. The presence of an intractable dispute, however, indicates that such discourse has not achieved its purpose and that participants need to communicate more openly and directly.

The transition to a more open pattern of communication is frequently difficult. Patterns of concealment breed distrust, which in turn build expectations of further concealment and deception. Yet, if a conflict is to be resolved in a manner satisfactory to all parties, a more thorough understanding of facts, analyses, perspectives, and interests is essential.

A mediator promotes improved communication during the convening phase both through personal conversations and the management of relationships between stakeholders. A mediator builds a personal rapport with participants during convening interviews. These interviews, which are designed to assess the conflict and existing relationships, provide a vehicle for opening dialogue between the mediator and each party.

During a negotiation, issues of personality, precedent, positions, power, and pride can have profound effects. A mediator who understands these potential interrelationships will be better prepared to design processes that compensate for these difficulties and to respond more proactively to the dynamics of a negotiation process.

Ensure Appropriate Representation of Stakeholders

The power of negotiation to fashion wise and sustainable solutions grows out of its ability to bring divergent interests and perspectives into commonality. One of the first tasks of a process convenor is therefore to identify the individuals and groups whose interests are at stake or whose agreement may be necessary to resolve the dispute.

Practitioners conducting convening tasks must identify and interview major stakeholders to assess the structure of a conflict. Stakeholders include groups and individuals who may be affected by the outcome of the process, who can scuttle an agreement whether or not they participate, or who can block implementation of an agreement. Interviews with stakeholders allow a practitioner, in conjunction with the interested parties, to more thoroughly determine who should be represented at the table.

The task of selecting representatives to engage in direct negotiations is difficult but extremely important. For meetings involving more than 20 people, facilitators must use structured procedures for maintaining order. These procedures may significantly inhibit communication, flexibility, and creativity. Facilitators often, therefore, try to limit direct negotiations to 20 or fewer individuals. Thus, many more individual stakeholders exist than can effectively participate around the negotiating table.

To cope with this problem, facilitators and mediators often establish negotiation teams—groups with shared interests—and help them to jointly select representatives. The practitioner may also design a process to include broader participation, in which individuals not actively engaged in negotiations may nonetheless participate in a process. This can be accomplished by incorporating workshops, resource groups, and education programs into consensus processes. Practitioners also work to ensure that representatives are open to scrutiny by those individuals and groups that they represent and are capable of obtaining the assent of those groups if necessary.

In selecting participants for a public process, a practitioner should give special care to creating opportunities for the involvement of elected and appointed officials and members of community groups. Officials (e.g., mayors, city council members, and legislators) have a dual role in public dispute resolution processes. On the one hand, they are stakeholders, with clear interests in the negotiation. On the other hand, they represent the citizenry and cannot abdicate their legislative or executive responsibilities. Ultimately, most public policy decisions that emerge from a dispute resolution process will require their approval. Practitioners must therefore help government representatives examine and clarify their roles before engaging in a collaborative decision-making process.

Selection of community group representatives may also be problematic. Community groups (including public interest groups, neighborhood associations, and nonprofit business associations) are usually self-organized and represent a particular perspective within the community. As voluntary organizations, however, they typically have no mechanism for holding their members accountable. Moreover, they may claim to speak for a wider group of residents or interests than they in fact do. During development-related disputes, in particular, it is not uncommon for splinter groups to form out of previously cohesive community groups. Practitioners therefore seek to identify the full range of interests and viewpoints that exist in a community or organization and ensure that appropriate groups represent those interests.

Manage Face-to-Face Negotiations

While the convening phase includes many aspects of negotiation, these discussions generally occur one-on-one with a practitioner or in small groups. By bringing together all representatives for face-to-face discussions, mediators and facilitators formalize a process and obtain participants' commitment to negotiate.

In a first meeting, a mediator or facilitator typically introduces participants to each other, provides an overview of their interests, reviews what has already been accomplished, and finalizes both the work plan (or agenda) and the details of the negotiation process. A practitioner also uses the first meeting to formalize the ground rules of a process. While the mediator frequently proposes a set of ground rules, these rules will effectively guide a group's conduct only if members of the group find them acceptable. All participants must therefore review the ground rules, to ensure that they enter into negotiations with shared expectations concerning the "rules of the game" and the process of negotiations.

Typically, ground rules cover three facets of the negotiation: the *process* (e.g., decision-making procedures, communication with the press, attendance at meetings), the *agenda* (e.g., range of issues to be addressed, the introduction and use of data, the time line), and *behavior* (e.g., prohibition on personal attacks, rules for governing information exchange). In particular, ground rules will likely clarify the following.

The roles of and relationships among participants. Many complex negotiations involve a core group of decision makers (often called a steering committee) as well as other groups of interested parties who may play subsidiary roles (such as technical work groups or citizens advisory groups). A support staff, either voluntary or paid, might also be available. Community and interest groups not directly involved in the negotiations may also have some role to play. The relationships among all of these types of stakeholders must be clearly understood and set forth in the ground rules.

The latitude and authority afforded to a mediator or facilitator. Typically, facilitators and mediators help groups of participants make substantive decisions and do not actively engage in these decisions. On issues of process, however, a neutral party's role may vary widely. While some processes provide a mediator with considerable discretion (such as control of a fact-finding budget), other processes restrict the mediator in terms of budget, staff, and involvement. The mediator's or facilitator's roles and responsibilities should be set forth in the ground rules.

The openness of the process to outside scrutiny. In public processes, a coherent policy for communicating with the press is necessary. Furthermore, sunshine laws in many states specify the degree to which policy negotiations must be open to the public. When participants are negotiating issues of public policy or community interest, the process must be accountable and open to scrutiny. An excessively "public" negotiation, however, can reduce creativity by increasing the reticence of participants to present new ideas and openly discuss alternatives. Hence, such openness tends to promote positional bargaining at the expense of joint problem solving. Sometimes, this tension can be managed by holding both public forums and private meetings. Ground rules should include guidance regarding participants' dealings with the public and the press. (See Chapter 11 for more on dealing with the media.)

Options for enhancing meetings and communications. Steering committee meetings, while essential, are often not sufficient for resolving disputes. Typically, groups of stakeholders with similar interests (e.g., the neighborhood conservation interests or the development interests) may wish to meet to discuss joint concerns. Work groups may need to be established to examine particularly difficult issues. The mediator may promote *shuttle diplomacy,* in which he or she transmits information between groups. A single negotiating text may be used to focus debate.

Discussion of these and other options, while they need not be developed before the negotiations begin, will nonetheless provide participants with a fuller sense of how negotiations might proceed.

The existence of reasonable deadlines. Deadlines create an incentive to negotiate seriously and efficiently. If no fixed deadline exists, deadlines can usually be created based on the legislative agenda or other circumstances. Deadlines that do not provide for sufficient time are to be avoided, however, since they reduce both the legitimacy of the process and the creativity used in problem solving. The ground rules should specify the expected length of time of a process and note any fixed deadlines.

Build the Capacity of the Parties to Engage in Meaningful Negotiation

In complex, multiparty disputes, in particular, participants may have little negotiating experience, few resources to engage in technical analysis, or little power to bind other individuals whom they represent in an agreement. If the negotiations are to be meaningful, a mediator may need to build parties' capacity to negotiate. In particular, technical assistance is frequently provided to encourage more realistic expectations and to set the framework for negotiations. A mediator may also help parties to engage in *vertical team bargaining,* in which stakeholders with similar interests (and their representatives) negotiate among themselves to develop a clearer vision about the options that are acceptable and why.

Process

The process emerges from the context. Practitioners focus on concerns of substance and relationship to help define how a process should be structured, what issues should be dealt with and when, and what interventions are likely to be of greatest import. In working with participants, practitioners seek to model behaviors that will be useful once a consensus building process is initiated. Disputants can often develop agreements on process before they are able to make progress on substance or relationships. In addition, practitioners seek to build shared commitment to the process, to prepare the participants for the cycle of opening up, dealing with, and resolving their differences. Finally, a practitioner seeks to match resources (time, money, and political will) to the design of a process. (See Chapters 1-4 for more information on various aspects of process design.)

■ Selecting a Consensus Building Practitioner

Consensus building and conflict resolution are normal social activities. In the process of social discourse and interaction, disputants regularly employ the skills and behaviors necessary to manage conflict. Under some circumstances, however, this normal process of social decision making breaks down. We are neither able to make a decision on our own nor able to effectively reach a joint decision with others whose support or acquiescence we need. Under these conditions, we may seek help from someone with consensus building expertise.

Consensus building practitioners are not licensed or certified. Hence, anyone can offer his or her services as a facilitator, mediator, or dispute systems designer. For those seeking consensus building assistance, this section provides guidance regarding the places such expertise can be found and the skills and experience that are desirable.

Internal versus External Assistance

Stakeholders involved in a dispute may look for assistance either within one of their own organizations or from an outside organization. For example, if officials at the U.S. Environmental Protection Agency (EPA) were involved in a dispute with other parties, they could seek mediation expertise from trained mediators either within the EPA itself, within an allied organization or institution (e.g., the Department of Interior or the Council on Environmental Quality), or from an independent organization (e.g., a nonprofit or for-profit dispute resolution organization).

In any particular situation, then, where is the best place to look for a consensus building practitioner? Let us look at the advantages and disadvantages of selecting consensus builders from each of these three sources (internal to a stakeholder organization, from an allied organization, from an independent organization). For facilitators and process designers, there are three major characteristics along which we can examine these relative advantages: ability to understand the context, ability to design and manage the process, and impartiality. For mediators and those involved in convening, we can add a fourth: ability to handle sensitive information. Table 5.1 presents these observations.

What can we conclude from this table? In general, an organization seeking to resolve a dispute through consensus building must make a trade-off between expense and ease of access, on the one hand, and impartiality, capacity to deal with sensitive information, and possibly skills and objectivity, on the other. As issues of confidentiality and impartiality increase, the need to go outside a stakeholding organization also increases.

"In most situations, mediators should come from outside a stakeholding organization."

In most situations, then, mediators and those assisting with convening tasks should come from outside a stakeholding organization. Facilitators may more often be drawn from within an organization. This is particularly true when disputes spring from within a single organization, the issues are relatively clear and demarcated, the facilitator has no interest in the outcome of a decision, and the roles and responsibilities of the facilitator are clear and well understood by participants (Schwarz, 1994, p. 238).

Practitioners who come from outside a stakeholding organization can be either community based or professionally based. Community-based practitioners build on a social network that lends legitimacy to a mediation effort. Such consensus builders can emerge from ongoing relationships (a neighborhood elder), local leadership positions (a local political leader or planner), or structured institutions (a neighborhood dispute resolution center). Often, they work as volunteers or are paid to conduct work other than mediation.

Professional neutrals, on the other hand, build on expertise and adherence to a professional code of practice. They serve at the pleasure of the parties, place a high value on both neutrality and impartiality, and work to help parties fashion a consensus solution to their own problem. They are almost always paid to work in this role.

TABLE 5.1 Advantages and Disadvantages of Neutrals Selected from Varying Organizations

	Consensus Building Practitioner Selected From		
Criteria	Inside the Organization	An Allied Organization	An Independent Organization
Ability to understand the context	High accessibility to organization's values, history, and dynamics; insider's perspective; potential biases from internal perspective	Presumed shared values; general understanding of history and dynamics; potential unwillingness to test assumptions	Greater likelihood to test assumptions held by people from within organizations; more objective perspective; outsider's perspective; can work more effectively across organizations
Ability to design and manage the process	Least expensive; potential acceptance by stakeholders from within the organization; access to groups early in the process; larger group demands on consensus builder; greater likelihood of rejection by stakeholders from outside the organization	Less expensive; ease of initiating; reasonable distance from group; competing demands on consensus builder's time for other projects; possibility of distrust growing out of organizational competition	Most expensive; usually initiated after problem becomes more serious; clearest delineation of the role of the consensus builder; possibly more fully developed consensus building skills
Impartiality	Potentially high within the organization, presuming consensus builder has no substantive interest in the outcome; potentially subject to authority within the organization; likely to be perceived as partial by stakeholders outside the organization	Mixed, depending on how participant organizations perceive the hosting organization	Highest, particularly if consensus builder is selected by participants in the process
Ability to handle sensitive information	Potentially the least likely to reveal information to parties outside the organization, but most likely to reveal information to others within the organization	Potential organizational pressure to use sensitive information strategically to the advantage of the host organization	Highest incentive to maintain confidentiality, and least organizational pressure to reveal information

In community- or ethnically based conflicts, in particular, a trusted local elder or leader may be the best choice. But this model is inherently limited to communities that share common leaders who are widely trusted. Institutionally based voluntary mediators and facilitators may be able to work across community lines, but time, experience, and other resources often limit their applicability.

The greater the complexity of substantive issues, relationships, or process, the more pronounced the need for an independent, professional facilitator, mediator, or process designer. In any given situation, the complexity of the substantive issues increases as the number of issues, the technical complexity of issues, and the number of diverging perspectives and interests increases. The complexity of relationships is affected by the number of parties, the history of antagonistic relationships, and weak patterns of communication. The complexity of a process is increased by the need to protect confidentiality, neutrality, legitimacy, trust, and accountability; by the need for a long-term process with multiple meetings; and by the degree of integration between negotiating issues and the larger policy-making processes.

These conditions, in and of themselves, may not require an independent, professional practitioner. However, they frequently lead to conditions in which parties have difficulty communicating and negotiations either cannot commence or become deadlocked. Particularly in complex organizational or public policy issues, professional facilitators and mediators are often able to identify existing barriers to negotiation and effective communication and to develop processes that enable a dispute to be resolved.

During a process, a practitioner frequently intervenes to keep discussions on track. These interventions, while decisive to the resolution of conflicts, can be seen by parties as potentially serving the strategic interests of other parties. Participants' trust in a mediator therefore will likely be tested during a process. To maintain legitimacy, mediators must work to keep a process (and what they are doing in the process) transparent and accessible to participants. Equally important, practitioners are usually selected or approved by the participants in the mediation process and serve at the pleasure of the parties as a group.

How to Find Qualified, Professional Practitioners

When a professional neutral is needed, then, how can one best be selected? The most common system for identifying professional practitioners for consideration is the use of rosters run by various state offices of dispute resolution, or by other state or federal agencies. These offices and agencies rarely certify the qualifications of the mediators on the roster. Rather, they serve as information services, promoting more informed choice among disputants. Rosters thus work best when supported by an informed staff capable of helping disputants understand their core needs, develop criteria for selecting a good neutral, and identify individuals on the roster who meet those criteria.

While drawing from a roster creates the opportunity for parties to a dispute to mutually select a mediator, the process poses several challenges. In real-life conflicts, disputants are frequently pressured by time, budget, and resource constraints. The selection of a practitioner from a roster may itself require building consensus among disputants, which can be time-consuming and contentious. It may require considerable guidance by a convenor.

Practitioners may also be identified and secured via special contracts at federal or state agencies. Under "sole source, indefinite deliverable contracts," as they are called, an agency makes an agreement with a prime contractor who develops and manages a long list of qualified subcontractors. Such contracts help to ensure that mediation and facilitation services can be obtained quickly and reliably. The prime contractor frequently works with the agency on each project to clarify process goals and identify an appropriate neutral. While this facilitates the process of neutral selection, it usually does not extensively involve all stakeholders in the selection process. Moreover, the practitioner is often paid exclusively by the lead agency, thereby potentially confusing the relationship between the practitioner and the convenor and raising questions of neutrality with other stakeholders.

Professional practitioners can also be identified through a request for proposals (RFP). RFPs can provide selection teams with a great deal of flexibility in their search. Traditional RFPs, however, which request a proposal for a process design and an estimate of total costs and then award the contract to the lowest qualified bidder, are inappropriate. A dispute resolution process must be designed based on the context of the dispute, which can be determined only through extensive discussions with stakeholders and cannot be adequately discerned from a description of a conflict in an RFP. Likewise, total cost estimates for a process are impossible to determine before conducting a conflict assessment and process design. A practitioner's rate structure will provide a more meaningful indicator of potential cost. Generally, an RFP should request information on the experience, knowledge, and style of intervention typically used by the practitioner, as well as references from parties involved in previous interventions.

Other resources for finding mediation and facilitation candidates include professional organizations, the Internet, and publications. SPIDR and the International Association of Public Participation (IAP2) are two particularly active organizations, with SPIDR focusing on convening, mediation, and dispute systems design services and IAP2 focusing on convening and facilitation services. Membership in both organizations is subdivided by area of practice specialization. On the Internet, the Mediation Information and Resource Center (at http://mediate.com) provides extensive information on mediation and lists mediators who pay to register with the center. The newsletter *Consensus*, published by the MIT-Harvard Public Disputes Project, not only provides extensive information on consensus building and conflict management practice but also contains practitioners' advertisements, listed by geographic region.

Specific Characteristics to Look for in Selecting a Facilitator or Mediator

Someone seeking the services of a professional consensus building practitioner should look for a person with the following characteristics.

Experience in managing complex organizational or public policy issues is the best predictor of a practitioner's skill. Look at a practitioner's history as a professional neutral and his or her experience working on similar issues. Ask for, and call, references. Ask a practitioner to explain his or her general experience, as well as experience with situations similar to yours. Have the practitioner describe his or her involvement in these processes, how the process was managed, and the outcomes.

Look for evidence of the process skills needed to manage complex organizational or public policy consensus building. Key skills include interviewing, process design and management, meeting management, handling confidential information, and bringing processes to a close. In an interview, ask practitioners to describe the processes they usually use in situations similar to yours, why they use those approaches, and what they would recommend in your situation. Ask them to share advice on how best to proceed in your situation. Look to see whether they ask good questions and grasp the situation quickly.

A capacity to understand and communicate clearly on the substantive issues in dispute will assist a practitioner in resolving that dispute. What is needed is the capacity to analyze complex problems, a general understanding of the issues under dispute and the language used to describe those issues, and (if applicable) the ability to deal with complex facts and technical analysis. Ask practitioners to describe their substantive background and their experience with the issues under dispute. If the practitioner lacks the knowledge needed to understand the dispute, ask the practitioner to describe how he or she intends to gain this knowledge.

The capacity to work with a broad array of stakeholder groups is extremely important, but difficult to evaluate. Look for the use of neutral and impartial language, sensitivity to participants' values, and effective listening skills. Ask practitioners to relate stories about working with participants from other processes. If cultural differences will be important, ask for experience in cross-cultural dialogues. Look for practitioners who appear to be patient and flexible. Look for dispute management styles that are consistent with the expectations of the participants.

Training in dispute resolution techniques is useful, but is no substitute for experience. Increasingly, young mediators and other practitioners receive graduate education in dispute resolution. Look for programs that effectively incorporate internships and other forms of practice-based experience.

The acceptability of a practitioner to all stakeholders is an important determinant of success. Look at practitioners' previous work experience and institutional affiliations. Are there any conflicts of interest? Will they be perceived as favoring one set of interests over another? Ask them to describe any code of ethics or conduct to which they subscribe.

Finally, consider the cost of services, the availability of practitioners within the time frame needed, and the capacity of practitioners to manage the logistics of a process. Ask practitioners how they charge for services, and what you can do to reduce costs. Have them describe the logistical arrangements that they think are important in your situation, and how they will manage those arrangements.

Organizing the Selection Process

Ideally, the participants in a process will select their own mediator. Such a selection process is rare, however, because participants are typically chosen only after a practitioner conducts a conflict assessment, and in most cases the practitioner is hired to both convene and mediate or facilitate the process. While some convenors hire a practitioner to initiate the process and then select a separate mediator to conduct the process, this arrangement has drawbacks. The practitioner who carries out the conflict assessment builds a rapport with participants and becomes well educated on the issues in dispute and the interests of the various stakeholders. A mediator brought on only to mediate the process will have to quickly get up to speed on these important items.

Sometimes, a small but diverse cross section of stakeholders will jointly design a selection process. While not all participants are involved in the selection, representatives of their interests are. This process has clear advantages. The practitioner is subject to the direct scrutiny of key parties, thereby enhancing his or her legitimacy in the eyes of other stakeholders. Practitioners can be interviewed by a group, which provides a more realistic setting within which to evaluate their skills and sensitivities. The committee generally selects the practitioner based on a consensus decision of the group, thereby building up a pattern of agreement between the disputing parties.

In many situations, a practitioner is selected by one of the parties involved in the dispute. Typically, this is the convenor or the public agency responsible for making the decision. While this offers considerable flexibility and efficiency in initiating a process, it has inherent drawbacks. Participants may question the legitimacy and neutrality of the practitioner. Following the convening process, then, participants should be afforded an opportunity to raise questions and concerns they may have about the practitioner, and to change practitioners if appropriate.

■ Conclusion

Techniques used by consensus building practitioners allow for an understanding of the issues at conflict, a clear identification of the underlying interests, improved communication, and an accommodation of the public good. Yet the use and availability of facilitators, mediators, process designers, and other practitioners remains context specific. By describing conditions that affect the use and appropriateness of various types of consensus building neutrals, this chapter seeks to equip organizational and community leaders with the skills necessary to initiate these nonadversarial approaches to decision making. While there are no guarantees of success, organizational and public policy disputes are increasingly resolved through mediation and consensus building. As the trend toward participatory management and policy development continues to grow, these techniques are likely to become even more integral to decision making.

■ Note

1. The author was involved in both of these cases as a dispute systems designer or evaluator.

■ References

Bush, R. A. B., & Folger, J. P. (1994). *The promise of mediation*. San Francisco: Jossey-Bass.

Carpenter, S. L., & Kennedy, W. J. D. (1988). *Managing public disputes*. San Francisco: Jossey-Bass.

Costantino, C. A., & Merchant, C. S. (1996). *Designing conflict management systems*. San Francisco: Jossey-Bass.

Doyle, M., & Straus, D. (1982). *How to make meetings work*. New York: Jove.

Elliott, M. (1999). Reconceiving historic preservation in the modern city: Conflict and consensus building in Atlanta. *Journal of Architectural and Planning Research, 16*(2), 149.

Gray, B. (1989). *Collaborating: Finding common ground for multiparty problems.* San Francisco: Jossey-Bass.

Kramer, R. M., & Messick, D. M. (Eds.). (1995). *Negotiation as a social process.* Thousand Oaks, CA: Sage.

Kritek, P. B. (1994). *Negotiating at an uneven table.* San Francisco: Jossey-Bass.

Larson, C., & LaFasto, F. (1989). *Teamwork: What must go right, what can go wrong.* Newbury Park, CA: Sage.

Moore, C. W. (1996). *The mediation process: Practical strategies for resolving conflict* (2nd ed.). San Francisco: Jossey-Bass.

Rothman, J. (1997). *Resolving identity-based conflict.* San Francisco: Jossey-Bass.

Schwarz, R. M. (1994). *The skilled facilitator.* San Francisco: Jossey-Bass.

SPIDR Environment/Public Disputes Sector Critical Issues Committee. (1997, January). *Best practices for government agencies: Guidelines for using collaborative agreement-seeking processes.* Symposium conducted at the meeting of the Board of the Society for Professionals in Dispute Resolution, Washington, DC.

Susskind, L. E., & Cruikshank, J. (1987). *Breaking the impasse: Consensual approaches to resolving public disputes.* New York: Basic Books.

Ury, W. L., Brett, J. M., & Goldberg, S. B. (1993). *Getting disputes resolved: Designing systems to cut the cost of conflict.* Cambridge, MA: Program on Negotiation Books.

6

REPRESENTATION OF STAKEHOLDING INTERESTS

■ *David Laws*

The path to becoming a representative in a consensus building process can start with something as simple as glancing at the Sunday paper over a cup of coffee. The Metro section, page 12, lower left. A small article catches your eye. Something about the photograph looks familiar. The headline confirms it: "Mixed use development proposed for hospital grounds."

The land looks familiar because it's two blocks away, a short walk through the woods that border your neighborhood. It's a place you walk your dog and take the children sledding. You scan the article for more detail. The scope of the proposal brings you up short: 111 luxury townhouses with a private club, 606 units of luxury senior housing with associated care facilities, a restaurant, and a 200,000-square-foot office park. Can all this possibly fit on that site? Will the zoning allow it? How will they protect the wetlands and the stream that runs through the land?

The kicker is the parking: 2,800 spaces, more than the nearby subway garage. What happens when all those cars empty out into streets that are already congested? The previous week, a different article highlighted the increase in accidents and traffic delays in town. Moreover, all the children from the neighborhood have to cross the street near the proposed site to get to school and home again. What will this mean for their safety?

Conversations with neighbors reveal similar concerns. The common sentiment is, "We should speak up, do something." A potluck dinner becomes a meeting, and soon you're asked to present the concerns of the newly formed neighborhood alliance at the next planning board meeting. Shared interests create solidarity and confirm everyone's sense that your demands are legitimate. "Make sure they know we won't take this lying down. We'll fight this thing to the bitter end."

The planning board meeting is more crowded than anyone expected. The proposal is the last item of business. You're one of a dozen people who want to speak. Realizing your opportunity is limited, you present your group's concerns as vigorously as you can. It sounds like you are making demands, but anything else would be drowned out by the din of the meeting. Discussion is tabled and your comments hang in the air. You had so much more to say.

You are surprised when a letter comes from the planning board inviting you to represent the neighborhood alliance in a conversation about the proposed development. The hospital and the developer have agreed to participate, and the other stakeholding groups are being invited to send representatives. You're somewhat taken aback. When you bring the invitation to the next meeting with your neighbors, they all agree that it's better to be at the table than to be excluded. They want you to continue as their representative. "Continue?" you think, "I agreed to go to one meeting." You consent on the condition that everyone is able to reach agreement on what they want you to say.

This is more of a challenge than anyone anticipated. Agreement among group members begins to dissolve as people spell out their concerns and desires more specifically. There is disagreement over the facts. There is disagreement over what is possible. There is disagreement over whether anything short of blocking the project is acceptable. Still, strong common interests exist. Everyone agrees, or seems to agree, on a reasonably clear list of concerns and demands.

Armed with this list, you attend the first meeting. It's not what you expected. You anticipated a struggle: people using rules and resources to jockey for position; coalitions forming between like-minded groups to either support or challenge proposals; the outcome determined by resources, tactics, and skill.

Instead, everyone is given an opportunity to speak. Ground rules are set that give each representative a chance to express what's on his or her mind and encourage others to listen and try to understand. Sometimes people say things you don't want to hear. Sometimes you just disagree. Sometimes it takes hard work just to understand what others are trying to say.

With great effort you're able to grasp most of what the others have to say. You begin to appreciate how the problem and the issues look to *them*. The effort this takes seems worthwhile when others treat you the same way. As you begin to understand what they are saying, some of it begins to make sense. Even when you disagree, it is often difficult to portray them as unreasonable. The hospital is trying to stay in business. The advocate for downtown businesses believes the project will help keep the local economy vital. As your understanding of others develops, you also find out much more than you ever wanted to know about the economics of real estate development, traffic forecasting and management, wetlands regulations, and site planning.

Some of this learning reflects back on the way you understand your own position. Some of your aspirations now seem overly optimistic. The way you framed the issues looks a little short-sighted and naive. Not that this makes you less committed to the concerns you share with your neighbors. Yet, even as you confirm the legitimacy of your concerns, you are forced to acknowledge the legitimacy of others'. You begin to see the problem in more complex terms. The fact that others have listened to you and taken your concerns seriously makes it doubly hard to portray them as unreasonable when they disagree.

As these discussions turn into negotiations, you find yourself engaged in a collective effort to meet the concerns and address the interests of everyone. New information and ideas come forward. The site planners are responsive to the concerns that you and others have expressed. They present some intriguing plans that protect the existing wetlands while providing accessible public space.

You find you've changed your mind about some aspects of the situation and are excited by new opportunities that have emerged. You're inclined to support the scaled-back and redesigned proposal on the table. It makes sense, given your expanded understanding of all the interests at stake. It makes sense when you think about the future of the community. Many of your concerns have been addressed. This is about as much as you can expect given the need to respond to the concerns of everyone else at the table.

Now you have a new problem. The other members of your neighborhood group are going to be surprised by the position you are taking. They may even question your judgment and loyalty. They sent you to block the proposal, and now you're siding with the enemy. You've tried to keep them abreast of what's been happening, but you doubt they're ready to hear you come out in favor of the proposal.

So what do you do? If you remain faithful to your original mandate, you will violate the commitment to reason constructively that you've made and upheld in your negotiations with the other representatives. After months of work, you have a lot invested. To adhere strictly to the mandate also will mean going against your better judgment. You don't think you've been manipulated or coerced into changing your mind. You understand the grounds on which changes have taken place.

On the other hand, you're not certain the neighborhood alliance is ready to go along. They have not had the experience you've had. For them, this will appear like a big leap rather than a series of small steps. Some may feel you have violated the trust they placed in you. You find yourself in the position of being as much a spokesperson for the negotiating group as for the alliance. You feel caught between the demands of the negotiating table and the demands of your "constituents."

* * *

This chapter is about the tension that representatives experience at just this moment. I will discuss how this tension arises, why it makes sense, and what representatives can do about it. It is produced by conflict between the imperatives of the internal negotiation (i.e., the discussions taking place at the negotiating table) and those of the external interactions with constituents. The demands of negotiating with other representatives will almost always create a tension with the mandate with which representatives enter a consensus building process.

In the first section, I discuss a series of practice problems that raise this tension for representatives. I begin with the challenge that they face in simply trying to talk to each other and examine the effects this can have on their understanding of the substantive issues and their own situation. This problem is particularly acute when the representatives come from diverse backgrounds or when a sharp disagreement disrupts a prior consensus. Next, the section examines how the demands of managing technical complexity contribute to this tension—how the addition of information and development of understanding complicate the problem. A third concern arises when representatives see that the issues at hand have implications for parties who are absent, because they could not or would not participate. Future generations are a particularly challenging example of hard-to-represent constituencies. Finally, I discuss how concerns about the common good are likely to come up and complicate a representative's task.

In the conclusion, I look at the problem of ratification. When representatives bring a tentative agreement back to their constituents, all the contributing factors outlined above converge and the resulting tension must be addressed in practical terms. I close by reviewing a series of questions that representatives or organizations asked to designate representatives need to address.

■ *Practice Problems*

This account of representation is organized around a set of exemplars: problems that illustrate the character of practice. Understanding these exemplars and the way they interact to produce tensions is a practical necessity for representatives. Without a sense of how these interactions shape their experience, representatives will find themselves confused by demands that pull in different directions and unsure how to respond to conflicting responsibilities.

By understanding the dynamics that characterize the experience of representatives, and consensus building more generally, participants can also gain a broader perspective on their practice. They may come to see, for instance, that the lack of formal authority and inability to commit that characterize representation can be seen as strengths rather than weaknesses of ad hoc consensus building processes. These limitations enforce a requirement on representatives not to substitute authority for common sense, creativity, or the need to provide grounds on which choices can be justified. Participants may also recognize the parallels between the demands of the ratification process—characterized by the need to justify decisions to those who will be affected by them—and contemporary arguments about what is at the core of a commitment to democracy.

The account of representation that emerges from this examination may seem theoretical. Its origins are practical, however. Participants need the kind of perspective that "theory" provides to keep pace with a consensus building process that is fluid, unpredictable, and characterized by tensions. The particular mix of problems that any group of representatives faces will be shaped by the history and context of its particular situation. To maintain a sense of where they are and respond intelligently and effectively to the exigencies of their situation, representatives will be pushed by practical demands to develop a theory of their own practice. Without such a theoretical perspective, they will have difficulty comprehending the challenges they face and may find themselves lost in a mire of details and contradictions.

The practice problems that are described below should be understood as contributing to such a perspective. The tensions that are described characterize the process of consensus building broadly. Representatives are likely to experience them at a personal level, however, as the outcome of flawed choices or outright mistakes, rather than as indicative of their engagement with central dynamics of consensus building.

Talking to Diverse Counterparts

If the convenors have been successful, one of the first things that representatives will confront in a consensus building process is their own diversity. They will likely find themselves sitting around a table together precisely because some problem or question has brought out differences that are not easily resolved. In many cases, these divisions will correlate with deep and persistent social cleavages such as race, ethnicity, sexual orientation, and religious or ideological commitments. In such circumstances, one of the ways this diversity manifests itself is in communication difficulties. The very act of having a conversation can become problematic. To put it another way, the difficulties that always characterize conversation can become so prominent that participants will be forced to confront them explicitly.

These difficulties are especially problematic because they are often not discernible ahead of time. Moreover, the circumstances in which tacit difficulties surface are likely to be heated and may strain representatives' capabilities. The good news is that participants *can* respond to communication challenges, and they can emerge with a deeper and more complex understanding of each other and their common situation.

Consider, for example, Norman Dale's description in Case 10 in this volume of several pivotal events. These events unfolded in an effort to build consensus over an investment strategy for economic development on Haida Gwaii (the Queen Charlotte Islands) in British Columbia. The stakeholders included representatives of First Nations (the Canadian term for Native Americans), non-Native residents, and the provincial and federal governments. The effort to initiate a conversation between the stakeholders revealed "deep needs for change in the way that the parties saw each other and the place they now shared as home."

As significant as these needs were, they were not prominent. They were revealed only in a series of small events and brief moments of recognition. The first occurred during a discussion of how to increase local control over decision making about the use of public funds available for redevelopment. The conversation began as a search for ways to be more inclusive, but took a turn that led to an unexpected conclusion.

As Dale was facilitating the meeting, he began to notice "nonverbal cues of discomfort" from Gitsga, the sole representative of the First Nations (the Haida, specifically), even as the parties carried on "an ardent dialogue about planning" for the islands. When Dale asked Gitsga to share his views, the group suddenly confronted one of the "most dramatic moments" in the process.

> Gitsga spoke briefly but with visible anger about how, once again, as had been the case for more than a century, white people were ready to surge ahead without considering the Haida's views or interests. After asking rhetorically whether [the Resident's Planning Advisory Committee (RPAC)] had heard anything at [a recent] cross-cultural workshop, Gitsga ended by saying: "You want to create a system for deciding what to do with this land. But there is a system here already. It works." With those words, he stood, said that he could no longer be part of RPAC, and left. (p. 930 in Case 10, this volume)

The effect on the group was immediate and dramatic. The "bubbly enthusiasm over grassroots planning" was gone. Dale returned from attempting to speak to Gitsga to a "stunned and somber group." The question on everyone's mind was, "What the heck was that all about?" Dale tried to translate the event into terms the others could grasp.

> Having just spent three years employed by First Nations, I had some thoughts about Gitsga's outburst, and I shared them with the group. Basically, I linked the personal powerlessness felt by so many Natives to the continuing scant recognition of their political system. As I found out later, my observations offended the Parks Canada superintendent. . . . This . . . had ramifications for me and for the secretariat, but at least some RPAC members were better able to make sense of Gitsga's behavior. (p. 931 in Case 10, this volume)

The key to what followed was Dale's choice to treat this incident as an "opportunity to undermine any complacency within RPAC" and help the parties develop the capacity to translate such events for themselves.

A second incident, as unpredictable as the first, highlighted the difficulties the group was discovering were involved in simply trying to talk to each other. While waiting for a meeting to start, some participants became involved in an animated discussion of an incident that had provoked a local controversy. An anonymous sculptor had adorned a large rock in the ocean with a five-foot-tall metal sculpture of a mariner. Someone had removed the sculpture, only to have it replaced with a second figure. Some residents liked the sculpture. Others criticized it because they felt it bothered the eagles that perched on the rock.

Gitsga, who had rejoined the group, joined the conversation and related the Haida view of the matter. "The Haida don't like it, but not because of the eagles. The rock is sacred. It is the Wasco."[1] He described his frustration with people who went ahead and did what they liked with the landscape, treating it as a "blank sheet" of paper. When a representative inquired whether this meant nothing could be touched on the islands, Gitsga replied that not everything was storied or sacred. When another asked how non-Haida were supposed to know what was and wasn't sacred, Gitsga responded, "Just ask." The beginning of the meeting was then postponed as Gitsga told the story of the Wasco.

This immediate encounter with the story of the Wasco forced the non-Haida participants to confront something that stood "outside [their] ken" and illustrated the limits of their own understanding. Like the surprising outburst at the previous meeting, they needed help to comprehend it. This experience drove home how little interpersonal discussion had taken place between Haida and non-Haida people about values and places, despite years of living in close vicinity. It underscored the "time and care" that would be necessary to sustain a conversation. One member captured the effect on the group: "I guess we're going to have to move real slow in everything from now on if we're going to have any hope of understanding." As the group moved ahead, the story of the Wasco became part of a larger story about "how hard it was to fathom each other's frame of reference."

Consider for a moment how disorienting this experience must have been for the representatives. We take our ability to converse for granted. This series of events first surfaced, then quickly disrupted the representatives' tacit reliance on this ability. They found themselves in the position of the tourist in an old comic sketch who suddenly discovers that random words in her phrase book have been mistranslated. The book is not entirely worthless, and it is all she has. But she can't rely on it. Shared meaning cannot be assumed, but must be reconfirmed. The actors in the Haida Gwaii case faced a similar challenge. Latent ambiguities could erupt at any moment, disrupting their sense that they understood each other or the problem they were talking about.

As the participants in this story discovered, acknowledging these difficulties does not resolve them. The strain representatives feel is likely to persist. In Dale's story, the non-Haida continually had to work to grasp how the Haida's historical experience shaped their beliefs and actions. With effort they came to understand that the Haida's reluctance to negotiate was tied to their identity as an independent nation. The Haida had to work to be able to see acts and offers by non-Haida as evidence that those outside the tribe could, with effort, grasp and respect the Haida perspective.

The persistence of these difficulties was illustrated in an incident that followed the group's success in reaching agreement on an investment strategy. As part of their lobbying effort with the federal government, a group of representatives went to a national conference to tell the story of their success. The need to agree on an account of their shared experience revealed that even this common ground was underpinned by differences and disagreements. As they discussed their common history, the group "discovered strikingly different versions of the group's shared history." The common experience did not transcend differences, but did provide sufficient common ground and confidence for representatives to confront the disharmony and probe hitherto unexamined assumptions about the shared context. It underwrote their commitment to "process" these different versions of history and "coauthor" an integrated account of their efforts.

A central theme in Dale's story is the challenge raised by cultural differences. I have tried to highlight how these differences affected participants' efforts to talk with each other. Their ability to make progress hinged on their capacity to *translate* across these differences. The problems are not limited to instances where the cleavages are so clear and well defined, however. The other cases in this volume illustrate how ubiquitous these challenges are.

Consider, for instance, Mike Hughes's account of the policy dialogue on HIV and AIDS prevention in Colorado (Case 14). The convenors' success in recruiting a diverse set of stakeholders raised similar challenges for these participants. Representatives from Colorado for Family Values found themselves sitting across the table from prostitutes who had contracted AIDS. Hughes describes the effect this had on the group:

> We had a member of the Latino community and a Native American. We had gay people, straight people, bi-people. We had people who were HIV-positive but didn't have full-blown AIDS. We had people who did have AIDS. We tried to cover all the bases; one guy stood up and said, "I think I'm supposed to represent white straight people," and he got a huge laugh. . . . From the beginning his message was about people's differences. He stated that acknowledging these differences— in life experiences, in political perspectives, and in socio-economic backgrounds—would be crucial to the success of this project. (p. 1015 in Case 14, this volume)

In this case, race, gender, and ethnic diversity created distinct perspectives that participants had to work to understand in devising proposals.

A central feature of each of these accounts is the significance of representatives' status as participants in a conversation. Their ability to make progress on substantive issues is tied to their ability to carry on a conversation in light of (rather than in spite of) their differences. The account in Case 7 of the effort to design a cleanup plan for the Massachusetts Military Reservation suggests how deep this current runs. The Technical Review and Evaluation Team (TRET) that is the central locus of action in that story brought together hydrologists, geologists, ecologists, civil engineers, and risk assessors. Despite the prominence of technical issues, the case author turns to conversational metaphors to describe the challenge the technical team faced and identify the factors that affected its performance. The TRET's success was tied to characteristics that enabled these specialists to carry on a conversation across disciplinary boundaries.

> These daily meetings were successful in spite of the heterogeneity of [the] experts' views, because a "workshop" atmosphere predominated in which different *members tried to understand each other's perspectives and carried on a continuous dialogue.* For instance, for the first time ecologists were explaining to hydrologists why the maintenance of groundwater and pond levels was crucial to ecological health. The hydrologists' heightened understanding of ecological concepts, and vice versa, was a direct result of the double role each member played as both teacher and student. (p. 875 in Case 7, this volume, emphasis added)

The significance of conversation in these accounts of practice underscores the role representatives play as interlocutors and the demands this places on them to extend their perspective. This is captured in the HIV case in the mediator's comments on a particularly difficult conversation about racial issues.

> For some, the discussion about race was too much. They believed that the acrimony drove a wedge in the group. I think it simply named the wedge that was already there and gave

them a chance to talk it out. At the next meeting, people stood up and said, "I hated that. I thought that was painful and awful." Then other people stood up and said, "Yes, it was painful. Yes, it was awful, but I needed to do what I did in that meeting and I needed to have that conversation, and it was time well spent." (p. 1026 in Case 14, this volume)

These stories illustrate the demands that conversation makes on representatives. They must find ways to translate across the idiosyncratic experiences and diverse commitments they each bring to the table. They must be opportunists, ready to take advantage of moments that open up unexpectedly and make these differences accessible. Astute facilitators and representatives will try to prepare for these opportunities by using formal and informal discussions to create a common base of experience that representatives can turn to when communication is disrupted. They will also try to set and uphold ground rules that encourage candor and, at the same time, set norms that prevent candor from polarizing a conversation unnecessarily.

"As we understand others, it often becomes difficult to demonize them or treat their claims as illegitimate."

These practical steps all work, in one way or another, by enhancing the ability of representatives to "enlarge their thinking" and grasp the intuitions and experiences that motivate others.[2] The implications for representatives are serious and practical. If shared meaning is not trivial and translation is necessary, then representatives (as participants in a conversation) will be drawn to consider the problem they face from different perspectives. This demand is placed on them by the need to communicate. The purpose of this communication is to make decisions collectively, not to change minds.[3] In practice, however, the "enlargement" this entails will often reshape individual representatives' views. We may want to understand others to avoid attributing motives and desires that aren't there and to prevent the accumulation of small misunderstandings (Mnookin, Peppet, & Tulumello, 1996). Yet, as we understand others, it often becomes difficult to demonize them or treat their claims as illegitimate. In the process, we may come to see the "other" as a "self" and to see our self through someone else's eyes as an "other."[4] With this new perspective, some of the demands we have been making may begin to seem less compelling, and some of our claims may sound strident.

The persistent demand on representatives to make sense of a diverse and uncertain world fuels an imperative to continually reassess language, meaning, and positions. For representatives, these revisions will appear as learning, instigated by encounters with the limits of their understanding and driven by persistent demands to make sense of what others are saying. Constituents lack this context and immediate experience and may have difficulty keeping pace with the changes and developments that consensus building entails. This mismatch is likely to surface as tensions in representatives' relationships with their constituents. These tensions will be more intense when this relationship is based on a strict agenda or inflexible commitments that bind representatives to particular views of a problem or other groups. In responding to the practical demands of conversation, representatives should not lose sight of the fact that they are also bound by these external relationships and have obligation to justify reassessments of the problem and reinterpretations of their mandate.

Managing Technical Complexity

Representatives will also be challenged when the problem they face involves technical issues. A common, reasonable reaction to such circumstances is to seek the guidance of experts. While the assistance of technical consultants will often be invaluable, representatives will also commonly find themselves facing a situation in which experts disagree with each other, or in which an analysis involves judgments that experts are not in a privileged position to make. There may not be a single "correct" way to pose questions, interpret evidence, or conduct analysis. Representatives will find that they must take responsibility for framing the questions they want experts to address and for playing an active role in interpreting the implications of technical information for the decisions that must be made.

Consider the following case, in which representatives in a consensus building process interpreted their position in just these terms. In the summer of 1989, after previous efforts to review potential sites for a low-level radioactive waste disposal facility had failed, the Maine Low-Level Radioactive Waste Authority brought together a large group of citizens and administrative staff from state agencies. The Authority asked these representatives to try to build consensus on the kinds of issues it should consider, and how it should bring these concerns into play, in making choices about how to site and manage a waste facility.

The individuals who made up this citizens advisory group (CAG) "represented" antinuclear groups, groups concerned with the preservation of forest and marine habitats, major civic institutions such as hospitals and universities, and the building trades, as well as all the state agencies with relevant regulatory oversight. Some opposed the stated goal of siting a facility, but participated because they believed it was an important contribution to democratic governance. Others retained an open mind, but were willing to endorse a process and a decision only if it could be demonstrated that an appropriate site could be found and that the wastes could be managed safely. Very few were there for their technical knowledge.

Despite their lack of technical expertise, the members of the CAG were reluctant to limit their role to expressing preferences on issues raised in the siting process. The broader sense of responsibility they sought is reflected in the way they reframed their mandate. Representatives were originally invited to participate in the CAG to "advise the Authority on key decisions that will have to be made in the siting process."[5] They were asked to speak for the "widest possible interests of the people of Maine."[6] After much discussion, CAG members revised and extended this mandate. They adopted goals that would allow them to respond to the Authority's problem and acknowledge the commitments and concerns they shared with their constituents. This reframing shaped their role in the following terms. The CAG agreed to (1) provide advice and make recommendations that "would result in the safest possible management of Maine's radioactive waste in the State of Maine," (2) assist the Authority "in evaluating siting policies," and (3) share information and illuminate viewpoints and differences "to help the Authority and the people of Maine reach the wisest and fairest decisions for the people of Maine."

Adopting these goals immediately raised a problem for representatives. The broader mandate meant that they would have to try to understand the technical problems that were clearly involved in making choices about siting criteria and safe waste management practices. They could not responsibly give advice without examining these problems. The facilitator summarized the effect on the CAG's agenda.

> I'm listening to what people are saying, and [I'm] feeling very strongly that if we were to say, "Thank you for listing all those concerns and now we will go along with the process of talking about siting," that it would be utterly inappropriate. So the only way I know to take on the broader issues that have been raised is to [re]structure the agenda, stretch it, divide it, and, if we're going to talk about it in a way that answers questions, we're going to have to get people in who can answer questions.

The representatives concurred on the need for technical assistance, but also recognized that they were interested in precisely those questions about which experts could be expected to disagree. This made their problem difficult. The representatives were clear, however, about the way they wanted to approach technical consultation in such disputed terrain. One participant explained it as follows.

> [I] don't have any technical knowledge and background. [So] when we have outside speakers who are going to come in and present this to the CAG, [I would appreciate it if] in those cases where there is more than one legitimate point of view that both points of view, or if there are more than two, that a number of points of view, be presented so that the CAG can be fully apprised of various alternatives and various perspectives. I would appreciate, as one member of the group, a commitment to do that throughout the process.

The representatives who made up the CAG saw that technical consultants could extend the group's understanding of technical issues from core findings to include the debates and disagreements that characterize the field. They did not want someone to tell them what to believe or do, but someone to help them understand technical questions in their complexity. They were aware that this would require them to confront questions about which experts disagreed. A CAG member framed the goal of technical consultation in the following terms.

The goal was not to get someone to say what the truth was. The goal was to get someone to array the debate and say, "This group over here thinks this because of that, but these people have these studies over here and they think this because of that. . . . And it isn't going to be a simple presentation. But the hope is that it [won't be] a partisan presentation.

This goal proved, in practice, to be more elusive than the CAG members anticipated. A number of factors contributed to the trials they experienced. It was difficult in a contentious area like nuclear waste to even find someone who was both knowledgeable and regarded as sufficiently objective to make an evenhanded presentation. When the group finally found someone who they thought could play this role, they were unable to transfer the responsibility for developing the view they desired. The speaker had his own views about how a process of consultation should work, which were tied to different norms and expectations.

The differences in their expectations became clear as the speaker began his presentation. His interpretation of his mandate diverged, almost immediately, from the expectations the CAG had articulated. He began: "I regard it as a privilege to be here to tell you what I think is the consensus opinion about the effects of radiation, not only in the U.S., but internationally."

The divergence grew as the speaker moved on to present this international consensus. He associated it with the findings of standard-setting committees he had served on. When pressed about whether there had been disagreement within these committees, his comments revealed a view of the relationship between disagreement and consensus that was quite different from the norms that the CAG had established for its own deliberations.

There was a dispute. Of course there was. Dr. Radford wrote a minority report of one, one out of 16. And Dr. Rossi wrote a counter-balancing minority report which said that not only was it not linear, but that there's no effect at all down there at low doses. And they sort of canceled each other out and the other 14 people agreed. So we had a consensus and we have a report.[7]

By presenting the summary opinion of the committee, the speaker covered over differences that had been winnowed out by the effort to reach consensus. The relationships between core and peripheral views, which were obscured, were precisely what the CAG members wanted to understand. They wanted the speaker's help in approaching the debate in the same way these committees had internally. The representatives wanted to make their own decisions about what to make of these differences. Instead, they got a summary opinion. The CAG's sense of the disparity between what they wanted (and expected) and what they got is clear in the reaction of one member to the presentation on health effects:

> Frankly, through the past month what I had been expecting from your presentation was a rather factual explanation of what the different positions were. In other words, this is the majority position; this is the minority position on one side; this the minority position on the other side. I didn't hear a single word on the[se] minority position[s].

The representatives were unsuccessful in their effort to transfer the responsibility for developing the complex view of the health effects that they sought to an outside consultant. They did, however, manage to achieve something of the kind of understanding they wanted. Their success was tied to their ability to interact with the speaker, to challenge him and ask questions. One member asked, for example, why the speaker had neglected studies that suggested the effects of low doses of radiation might be much higher than predicted by conventional models (i.e., "supralinear").

> I didn't hear a single word on the minority position of supralinearity, which is an increased effect at low doses over other doses. So far [our speaker] has been portraying the linear dose response as entirely the most conservative, but I can read a little bit from an EPA [Environmental Protection Agency] document that I have.

The CAG member went on to read from the EPA's document, which highlighted studies that suggested that low, "fractionated" doses (the kind that might be associated with a disposal facility) could have more dramatic effects than were predicted by linear dose-response models. When confronted with the disparity between these studies and the findings he had presented, the speaker was able to comment on the apparent disagreement.

> Yes, that's different. If I could respond to that, since you've triggered something right away. That's a different kind of radiation from the ones that I was considering. That's known as high "LET" radiation. . . . And you're indeed correct. There's a reverse dose-rate effect.

This exchange opened other questions. Representatives inquired about the sources of these other kinds of radiation and what is known about their health effects. As the divergence between the kind of review they had requested and the kind of summary they were getting became more explicit, the CAG members sought to clarify how choices were being made about what to include and what to leave out. The following exchange between the facilitator and the speaker gives some idea of the character of this interaction:

Facilitator: But the point Bob's generally making is, are you leaving it out because you don't agree with it?
Speaker: No, I agree with [it]. I left it out because I was talking mostly about low "LET" radiation. I can give you another hour on high "LET" if you like.

This led a CAG member to press for the kind of summary the group desired.

> The question is, what are some of the other—if there are other—views about low doses, or low levels of doses of various kinds of radiation that you may not have touched on that would lead people to different conclusions perhaps?

The speaker's response demonstrated that he was acting on the basis of a complex amalgam of norms derived from his participation in standard-setting committees and scientific research. He was reluctant to volunteer information on studies that expert committees had concluded were at the margins of accepted belief. When pressed to do so, he provided (quite appropriately) a sense of why he thought these studies are marginal.

> There are various minorities, some of them are very small minorities I might add, but there's John Goffman, for example, . . . who believes there's a supralinear effect. He's put some material out on it, . . . but there's no mechanism and the data that in fact he uses is hotly contested. He uses Japanese data and people say he uses it in the wrong way.

His comments also illustrate a reluctance to discuss work he has not done or verified personally.

> Now I can't speak to the negative personally because I haven't done that work. I haven't tried to reproduce his graphs. But that's a fairly consensual opinion. Dr. Goffman is almost unique in the world of American science.

At the same time he portrayed these views as marginal, the speaker also confirmed the CAG's sense that understanding the disagreements was essential to understanding the "consensus" view. He noted, for instance, the effect some of these views had on the terms in which health effects are understood and the standards by which they are assessed.

> And some of [Goffman's] predictions as a matter of fact have come true, or seem to be coming true. But not by any means the whole hog, so to speak. His estimates of radiation risk were about 50 times higher than the risks that the [Biological Effects of Ionizing Radiation] committee came up with in 1980. I think we've gone part of the way to meeting his factor . . . by having . . . an increase by a factor of 3. That's a long way short of 50. And people have adopted his idea that the future cancer risk depends on the underlying level of cancer in a population.

In the end, the CAG members came away with something like the complex understanding of contemporary views about health effects they set out to achieve. They understood many of the major disputes and how the interplay between these views was affecting the development of standards over time. This outcome should be understood, however, as the result of the active role they took, rather than as a result of the way they set the goals for the process of consultation or framed the speaker's mandate.

"Representatives will often be driven to take an active role in shaping or interpreting technical analysis."

Representatives will often be driven to take this kind of active role in shaping or interpreting technical analysis. They should be aware, however, how it can complicate the challenges they face in their effort to build consensus. If their commitment to taking on this role is incomplete (or if representatives fail to appreciate the tension it can raise with the goal of advancing interests), their negotiations can be crippled. If the commitment to help shape a technical inquiry is complete, then this new role will, almost inevitably, raise tensions in representatives' relationships with their constituents.

Consider first the case of incomplete commitment. When they extend their mandate as the CAG did, representatives embark on a process of inquiry that implies correlative commitments to some kind of standards of discussion and reasonable belief. They agree, for instance, to ground rules that require them to discuss their beliefs publicly and to give reasons that support their interpretation of the evidence. They must be ready to change their minds under some circumstances. Without such commitments, the broader commitment to inquiry and learning is empty. Representatives must make these commitments before they can forecast how new evidence will affect the assumptions that have shaped their views or the arguments they have used to advance their interests.

Some representatives may find that the analysis of a technical issue is not turning out as they anticipated. If they are unwilling to change their minds, or unable to because they are bound by a strict mandate, *and* they are unable to offer some kind of reasonable justification for their intransigence, they will appear to others to be unreasonable.[8] By clinging tenaciously to their initial beliefs, and discarding or discounting any evidence that might lead them to question or revise these beliefs, these representatives will confound the standards of discussion and belief that were implied by taking up these technical questions.[9] This will raise a tension in their relationship with other representatives and threaten the norms of conversation and commitment to constructive negotiation that characterize this relationship.

Something very much like this happened in the Maine CAG. The health effects question eventually became divisive for just these reasons. A minority of representatives were bound, by ties to the groups they represented, to views on the health effects issue that others did not feel were sustainable in light of the evidence and opinions the group had reviewed. The former's "tenacious" loyalty to their initial assessments was experienced by other members as a form of intransigence that crippled the conversation and the commitment to reaching informed consensus.

A related problem may occur when it comes time to assess the significance of the accumulated technical evidence. Representatives who agree on the implications of evidence for a technical question may disagree about its significance for taking action. Representatives might, for instance, agree about the number of additional cancers that will be associated with a given exposure to radiation, but disagree about the kind of monitoring program that should be required. This divergence will heighten the practical challenges that representatives face in trying to craft an agreement. If there is a reasonable basis for it, however, the effects on internal relationships will be much less severe than in the preceding case, since the behavior does not violate the norms of inquiry. The parties can see themselves as disagreeing on reasonable grounds.

If representatives are free to change their minds as they learn, they have a different set of problems. They are likely to face tensions in their ties to their constituents, rather than in their relationship with other representatives. These tensions arise because the path by which they reach an understanding of technical issues is unlikely to be straightforward. For the same reasons they feel compelled to take an active role in technical analysis (e.g., disagreement among experts), representatives will be unable to justify their choices by pointing to unanimity in the scientific or technical community. They will be forced to make choices about how to interpret evidence and weigh different opinions, and the sum of these choices may surprise their constituents. Representatives cannot (and should not) expect their constituents to accept such developments on faith or at face value. The price they pay for having the freedom to learn and change their minds is the responsibility to explain and justify the terms in which they understand technical issues and assess their implications for the problems at hand.

When problems merge technical and nontechnical questions and *nonobjective judgments* figure prominently in analysis, representatives will also be pushed to take an active role in the debate about technical questions (Susskind & Dunlop, 1981). The tensions they experience will be similar to the second case described above. In the story of environmental cleanup on the Massachusetts Military Reservation, the representatives who made up the TRET faced this sort of problem. The members of the TRET sought to promote public health and ecological preservation. Because pursuing the goal of public health aggressively meant pumping and treating groundwater at a rate that would draw down kettle ponds and threaten the local ecology, the group had to find a way to balance these goals. Each issue could be stated in technical terms. The appropriate balance between public health risks and ecological health risks, however, could not be stated or resolved on purely technical grounds. Instead, it required a judgment that had to be debated and justified publicly.

Nonobjective judgments often play a pivotal role when technical discussions are tied to forecasts based on computer modeling. Forecasts often prove useful in consensus building and may be the best grounds available for making decisions. Representatives should be careful to avoid treating these forecasts as facts, however. They invariably involve estimates or use the results of prior forecasts in ways that merit public scrutiny.

The case of extending a subway line in Cambridge, Massachusetts suggests how forecasts can trigger an active role for representatives in the debate over technical issues. A major piece of the plan was the construction of a parking garage at the last stop on the subway line. The design for the garage was based on estimates of the demand for parking that the extension would generate. These estimates were based, in turn, on a travel-demand forecast that had been made years earlier. Some of the nonobjective judgments about the rate and pattern of urban expansion that consultants had used at that time no longer seemed appropriate, and eventually they were revised in a conversation between representatives and consultants.

This conversation did not happen automatically, however. As is often the case, the representatives had difficulty in opening technical issues up for discussion. Initially, all they had access to was a design for a parking garage that seemed unacceptably large. To surface and confront the judgments that had produced and legitimated this design, the representatives had to take an active role and unpack (with the reluctant cooperation of the technical consultants) the numbers that went into the demand forecast. Only then could they challenge the design goals and open the door to constructive negotiations (Forester, 1994).

Nonobjective judgments may also play a determinative role when analysis demands selection from among a set of competing theories, or even among standard software packages. The need for representatives to take an active role is underscored by the fact that these forecasting models may be compared with other models but are seldom tested against the kind of "experimental, field, or historical evidence, which would normally form the basis for scientific theories" (Funtowicz & Ravetz, 1991).

Representatives can take an active role in debating and offering advice on these nonobjective judgments as they come into play in analysis and modeling. In addition to looking out for the interests of their constituents, representatives can also play a valuable public role as part of the "extended peer community" that performs essential "quality assurance" on technical analysis that is used in public decisions.[10] Finally, they can offer valuable local knowledge that can ground, enrich, and extend more conventional expertise.

As this discussion suggests, it will be the rare case where representatives can be merely consumers of information or analysis. They are likely to be drawn into framing analysis, interpreting findings, and ensuring that questions and forecasts proceed on grounds that make sense. They should expect to play a role in shaping the terms of the discussion as well as the terms of agreement. This role can raise tensions in the relationships with each other and with their constituents. Representatives can anticipate the former and be ready to respond to the latter by explaining interim conclusions and justifying the grounds on which analysis has proceeded. These tensions will be especially prominent when participating in analysis leads representatives to learn and to look at problems in a fresh way.

Considering the Views of Absent Parties

Consensus building usually involves affirmative efforts to be inclusive. Convenors search for groups and individuals who they feel should or would want to participate. They work hard to get them to commit to the process. Convenors often assume their responsibilities extend to identifying and helping to coalesce groups of stakeholders who are not organized in any formal way. It is also common to enlist representatives who have agreed to participate to help identify groups that should be represented, but aren't. These efforts derive both from a normative commitment to be inclusive and from a practical knowledge of the delegitimizing force that charges of exclusion have when they carry the slightest shred of credibility.

Even an exhaustive effort to bring everyone to the table, however, is likely to leave participants to contemplate on "who's missing?" Some groups may be unable to participate. Others might be affected only by a specific part of the agenda and, thus, be unable or unwilling to commit the resources to participate. Other groups may choose not to participate, hoping to be able to undermine the legitimacy of the proceedings or improve their bargaining position later on. Finally, there may be groups whose welfare is clearly at stake but who, nonetheless, are unable to participate. The classic cases of this last category are children and future generations.

Given representatives' commitment to try to reach consensus, and the affirmative efforts they often undertake to be broadly inclusive, it is natural for representatives to think about the groups that are not at the table. They may try to bring the concerns, interests, or questions they associate with these groups into play in the conversation. In doing so, they take another step in enlarging the terms in which they see problems and in which they understand their own responsibilities. This enlarged perspective can be difficult to square with a model of representation based on strict mandates and fixed interests or positions.

It is possible to illustrate the problem with a simple thought experiment. Imagine you are a representative in a consensus building process that has been going on for long enough for the parties to get to know one another. At one meeting, a prominent member of the group ("Nancy") is absent. The habits of the group may even be developed to the point that her chair sits empty. At some point in the discussion, a point is raised that everyone knows Nancy would have a strong view about. Some people may find themselves involuntarily turning toward her empty chair, imagining what she would say.

How the other representatives respond to this situation is telling. Before looking at some of the ways other representatives might respond, imagine two kinds of comments Nancy might make. On one hand, she might comment on the acceptability of the proposal and say something like, "My group could never live with that." On the other, Nancy might question whether the proposal makes sense: "Does the group accept the assumptions it proceeds from, or the implications it has for other cases?" "Does it seem fair when considered from the position of those who will be affected?"

The representatives present could respond to these immanent comments in several ways. They could ignore them. "If she chooses not to come and doesn't send an alternate, she will have to live with the outcome." If her comment is of the first kind, this choice may depend on their strategic assessment of Nancy's group's ability to derail the agreement or block implementation. Depending on how this assessment goes, other representatives may be drawn into an effort to imagine what Nancy and her group would be willing to accept. It may be a waste of time to go forward without testing whether Nancy and her constituents could live with what is on the table.

The analysis is different in the other case. If what Nancy would say is important because it makes sense, rather than because it describes a willingness to accept terms, the argument for ignoring her likely comments is much less compelling. To the extent that the parties at the table ignore Nancy's views, they proceed on grounds that are compromised.

As an alternative, a member of the group may try to speak for Nancy. This stand-in may (or may not) claim special knowledge that allows him to act as her advocate. He might try to remind the group what is important to Nancy and her constituents. He might also seek to show how the proposal is unfair to Nancy and her constituents, animating how it looks from their perspective. "Imagine how you would feel if someone did this to you," he might ask. Finally, he might raise the kinds of questions that Nancy usually asks, inquiring about whether the proposal makes sense, whether the assumptions it proceeds from are plausible and acceptable.

The other representatives may accept their colleague's rendering of Nancy's interests or perspective. It is unlikely, however, that they will accept it because of his claim to authority or specialized knowledge. He will need to convince them that he understands Nancy's perspective. His claims will need to make sense in light of representatives' experience and other information they have about her situation. It follows that other members of the group may reject the way the stand-in has animated

Nancy's perspective. They may offer competing renderings of her perspective on her interests, on fairness, or on making sense. Since this is an imaginary discussion, we can let it run for a while, as everyone gets into the act, offering their insight on what Nancy wants and needs and how she might look at the problem the group is grappling with. In the extreme, Nancy might, by being absent, exert more influence on the discussion than she ever did in person.

What I want to call attention to with this experiment is that the choice of whether to try to understand Nancy's interests, or how concerns about fairness would look from her perspective, is a question of volition, not capacity. If they choose to, the representatives present can explore these concerns in Nancy's absence. The capabilities they need to draw on are similar to the ability to take another's perspective, which was shown in a preceding section to be central to the ability to have a conversation.

In this process, no single representative can claim unique access to Nancy's interests and thoughts. While advocacy may be a common strategy that people will turn to in the case of absent parties, it should be understood that it is the rare case where an advocate will be in the position to speak authoritatively about an absent party's interests or concerns. Advocates may be useful, but their role should be thought of as initiating or elaborating a conversation, rather than having the definitive word. The opportunity to explore Nancy's perspective is, and should be, open to everyone. The ability to do so is not tied to specialized knowledge, but to representatives' abilities to animate her perspective on the issues before them in a convincing manner.

Once "perspective-taking" has begun, it may be difficult to terminate the process. There may be other groups whose perspective the representatives around the table want to consider, either because those groups have the ability to influence the fate of agreements or because they may be able to make claims that will undermine the legitimacy of an agreement. Or those at the table may just want to try to understand what is fair by looking at a proposal from the perspective of each affected party. They may want to consider how the reasons that justify the proposal would sound to someone in each of these perspectives, and whether some party might have reasonable grounds for rejecting the proposal.[11]

In each of these cases, representatives can go a long way toward understanding how issues and proposals might look to groups who will be affected by decisions but are not around the table because they are not able to participate or have refused to participate. How much representatives choose to adjust proposals in light of the insights they derive from taking these perspectives may vary depending on the nature of the issues and the circumstances of the absent party. The effort to understand how proposals, or even questions, look from missing perspectives is limited, however, only by the imagination of the participants.

The desire to understand and act on concerns about absent parties is plausible. Representatives, like most people, can be motivated by concerns about children and about future generations. People often have a vivid sense of what they think will be important to their children. They want to know how decisions they make today will influence their children's welfare and the kinds of opportunities that will be open to them. The following comment by a participant in a consensus building process in Maine on the health risks posed by paper manufacturing is typical of the kinds of concerns representatives might have.

> The older people like myself . . . aren't going to benefit too much. If we made it this far, we've made it. It's the grandchildren coming up and their children. And industry should be able to get along with the improvements that have to be met in order to keep the community healthy. . . . And I am doing whatever I can for my grandchildren, because at my age there isn't too much more they can do for me. (Cluck, 1997, p. 29; see also Case 2)

The ties that bind people in the present to the more distant future are less personal and immediate. When decisions have clear, if uncertain, implications for the future and representatives are acting in some capacity (e.g., as citizens) that they can see themselves sharing with future generations, the demand to consider the implications for the more distant future can be compelling. We want to understand what our actions will mean for posterity. The comment below, drawn from the Maine radioactive waste case, is an example of the kinds of concerns that motivate people.

We have to talk about the equitability of risk and benefits between our and future generations. We're the only ones getting electricity from the generation of waste, yet we're sitting here talking about a 100-year institutional control period. We're talking about a 500-year range of dangers, according to [the Nuclear Regulatory Commission], and there are those who think that the time of danger could last much longer. I don't want to do anything that is going to put future generations in jeopardy or give them difficulty in dealing with this waste.

The difficulties that absent parties create for participants underscore the importance of exhausting every possible means of cultivating broad participation. As problematic as representation is, the alternatives are even more problematic. To encourage participation, convenors and facilitators can provide the kind of technical and financial support that parties need to participate in a meaningful way. They should also be available to address concerns that parties have about the nature of a process, or what participation means, and to provide sufficient assistance for parties to at least agree to try to participate. It may be desirable to leave the door open for parties to join a process in progress. Arrangements that allow for intermediate status may also help. These could either permit potential participants to test the water as observers or to join a process as individuals rather than as official representatives who bear the responsibilities and burdens that go along with speaking for a group.

The argument for making an active effort to try to understand the perspective of absent parties is underscored by historical experience. One of the ways disadvantaged groups have made progress is by finding ways to get their claims heard in the political conversation. Because the barriers to entry may not look as prominent from inside this conversation as they do from outside, and because we know it can be difficult to anticipate the views of others, the obligation to understand must be shared by those who participate in a conversation.

The refrain to the problem of absent parties should begin to sound familiar. If representatives pursue concerns about children, future generations, or other absent parties, they will alter the perspective with which they entered the consensus building process. By acknowledging these ties, representatives also acknowledge some responsibility for responding to them in a substantive manner. The kind of broadening of perspectives that is likely to result from considering absent parties will imply limits on what is acceptable or place positive requirements on proposals. In either case, it will influence the kind of proposals representatives will make and be willing to support and, thus, may compromise their pursuit of sectarian interests. Even if their constituents see the interests of children or future generations as a central issue, their interpretation of the demands this places on decision making is unlikely to be identical to the negotiating group's. In the effort to make sense of the situation, representatives will be drawn to consider absent parties. In doing so, however, they contribute to the tension that characterizes their situation.

Common Interests: Common Ground

The problems and challenges outlined in the preceding three sections have two important implications for representatives. First, they broaden the negotiating group's agenda. Representatives are likely to see their participation as shaped by some sense of broader responsibilities that entail understanding each other, shaping and interpreting technical analysis, and considering how interests and considerations of fairness will look to actors not represented at the table. In the words of a representative in the consensus building process over the health effects of paper manufacturing:

> This is an issue that has been here and been talked about quietly for a couple of generations. And nobody has really confronted it—for a number of factors. [I'm a] reluctant member. I don't really relish the idea of getting out in controversial issues and being out front. . . . *But it was important enough I felt someone has to do the job.* (Cluck, 1997, p. 29, emphasis added)

This sense of responsibility may affect the way representatives approach each other and the quality of their conversation. They will feel pressure not just to advance a set of interests but to understand the issues and "get the choices right" (Kymlicka, 1989). As Michael Wheeler (1993) has written:

Representatives who come grudgingly to the bargaining table expecting at the most to make horse trades with other interest groups, instead get caught up in group learning and civic discovery that may fundamentally alter their expectations, goals, and even language. (p. 143)

In this section, I want to suggest an explanation for why the shift apparent in this description makes sense.

The problems outlined in the preceding sections suggest that representatives in a consensus building process will come to see themselves as participants in a conversation. They may recognize that to understand a problem, they need to grasp how it looks to others from the inside. They may feel a responsibility to make decisions on a basis that makes sense to them, and thus be drawn into an effort to understand the facts of the case. Even when experts are involved, they will still need to shape or construct the terms in which they understand the problem and assess its significance. Finally, representatives may come to see the problem as having implications that are broader and more enduring than may be captured by the groups represented around the table. This may lead them to try to assess what their choices will mean for absent parties, for children, and for future generations. The effort to "get the choices right" will involve them in acts of "regulated imagination," mutual consultation, and reflection on their own position.[12]

"Representatives will discover that they cannot define their role solely as the agent for a set of fixed interests." As they come to see a problem as demanding a kind of attention that is other-regarding, fact-regarding, and future-regarding, representatives will discover that they cannot define their role solely as the agent for a set of fixed interests.[13] This shift is substantial. As seamless as it may appear to a representative caught up in the process, it may be jarring to those outside the process who suddenly confront their agents talking about each other and the problem in new terms. Representatives had better be able to explain themselves if they are to have any hope of getting their constituents to approve.

The nature of the issues involved offers a partial explanation of why this happens. This is not meant to suggest that consensus building is, or should be, limited to the kind of issues identified below. Consensus building is particularly appropriate to these issues, however, and the kind of sea change that is palpable to representatives makes sense in this context. To the extent that issues such as economic development, public health, affordable housing, and environmental protection have motivational force, it is because they are regarded as issues in which individuals and groups, who may have aims and values that are otherwise diverse, have an interest in common.[14] These common commitments reveal our interdependence and the need for collective action. The effort to develop an AIDS policy in Colorado required, for example, not only that representatives understand each other but also recognition that the problem demanded this kind of common commitment. In the words of the facilitator:

> People were sure of one thing: If this group was going to be able to work together, its members were going to have to embrace the group's larger mission. In developing a plan, they would have to go beyond their own personal agendas. . . . We hoped to help people see that what they needed to accomplish for the state of Colorado was bigger than their own goals and, hopefully, inclusive of their unique priorities. (p. 1015 in Case 14, this volume)

This presents two rationales for the shift referred to above. First, the substantive nature of the issue may, in and of itself, provide a rationale. In the affordable housing negotiation in Connecticut (Case 4), for instance, suburban representatives began to see the housing issue not simply as "one of homeless people on urban streets" but as encompassing "the need to provide their own municipal workers with a place to live" (Wheeler, 1993, p. 143). In the Maine radioactive waste case, the problem that representatives saw themselves as facing was not how to prevent the facility from being sited in their community, but how to "make recommendations . . . which would result in the safest possible management of radioactive waste in the State of Maine for the people of the State of Maine."[15]

Representatives may also see themselves as having a shared interest in there being standards for public health, for environmental protection, or more generally for fairness (Pitkin, 1981). In this sense, representatives may see themselves as contributing to a different kind of substantive good. In addition to contributing to the resolution of a particular problem, representatives, through their actions and interactions, create legitimacy for a set of institutions that are available for solving other problems.[16]

Thus participants may acknowledge responsibility for shaping political institutions and adding to the common ground that is available for carrying out political discourse (Cohen, 1993). As with the sections above, acknowledging these ties to broader concerns can raise tensions in representatives' relationships with their constituents. The need to address these tensions becomes most explicit when representatives bring an agreement to their constituents for ratification. This problem is the subject of the concluding section.

■ *Conclusion: The Problem of Ratification*

In consensus building, we have, I believe, experience with a process we only partly understand. We know some important things about how to do it. We have a clear sense that it works in cases where other approaches fail. Moreover, there is something about the way consensus building works that is important. It builds or contributes to a set of background conditions that increases the likelihood that such efforts will continue to work in the future. Finally, it works in a way that participants find acceptable and consistent with the conditions of diversity, complexity, and uncertainty that characterize their lives. Consensus does not always emerge, but by encouraging and supporting constructive acts through which participants come to understand each other and acknowledge their interdependence and common problems, it is achieved often enough to be worth noting.

I have suggested that the consensus building process is one in which participants may begin from beliefs they acknowledge, but they come to reason in ways they may not have anticipated. Indeed, one way to understand consensus building is that it supports representatives' efforts to create an experience that will, at some point, challenge their expectations and the grounds on which they initiated the process. It should create a situation in which they have no choice but to try to understand, to reason, and to interact creatively in pursuit of their common and diverse interests and commitments.

I want to close by looking at problems that arise when representatives have reached agreement and must seek ratification from their "constituents." The terms in which this problem is often understood are misleading. Representatives may think that they need to "sell" an agreement by showing how it meets, as well as possible and better than the alternatives, a preexisting set of interests.

The problem with this approach is that, as we have seen, representatives' understanding is likely to shift as they interact with other representatives and participate in framing and interpreting the results of technical analysis. Constituents may be surprised by these changes, and feel cheated or betrayed when their representative backs an agreement that is at odds with their initial position. A representative sent to block a development project is now saying that, given certain conditions, it should be allowed to go forward. The representative who was sent to ensure that AIDS education reflects proper moral values is endorsing a campaign that will use sexually graphic materials in some contexts. Moreover, he is sitting around the table talking sympathetically with the "enemy."

"Ratification is a process of justification, as well as a process of selling the agreement."

In this light, representatives should understand that ratification is a process of justification, as well as a process of selling the agreement. Representatives should, and often do, direct their efforts at developing an agreement that they not only can live with but are willing to stand behind. This means they should expect to provide good reasons why the agreement is desirable.

Rather than undercutting the importance of meeting interests, this emphasis underscores it. Meeting interests does double duty. It provides an instrumental rationale for accepting an agreement. It gives constituents more of what they want. It also is a grounded and tangible way of expressing understanding of others at the negotiating table. A convincing way to demonstrate that I have comprehended your needs and concerns is to craft a proposal that responds to them.

Representatives should also be prepared to provide their constituents with more explicit justification for the way they have approached problems and the terms in which they have framed a proposed agreement. They should be ready to say why the need for affordable housing is a problem that should be solved, or why siting a disposal facility in Maine may be the safest and most responsible way to manage the state's low-level radioactive waste. The ability to provide adequate reasons should not be taken for granted.

Representatives who anticipate the need to justify agreements will use what resources and time are available to engage in discussions with the people they represent, and try to justify agreement incrementally, as it develops, rather than only at the conclusion of the process. Representatives can also take steps as a group that will ease the burden of justification. Meeting summaries should not be written solely for participants, but also for the people they represent. These accounts should enable all constituents to follow the developing sense of the negotiations and the grounds on which decisions are being made. Other outreach programs can be approached on similar grounds.

The process used by the TRET in devising a cleanup plan for the Massachusetts Military Reservation is exemplary in this regard. The members of the TRET knew from the beginning that they had no authority, formal or informal, to commit to an agreement. The legitimacy and acceptability of any proposal they made hinged on their ability to justify it. This "weakness" influenced the way they talked to each other and led them to set up regular consultations with the broader public that were both substantive and interactive. These aspects of the process became its greatest strengths. The steps outlined in this case provide a good model for consensus building practice.

This account of consensus building I have developed should not be seen as undercutting the importance of creative bargaining. Representatives must see their job in two dimensions. As noted above, attention to interests plays both an instrumental and a justificatory role in generating support for agreements. This interaction is mirrored in the internal negotiation among representatives. In productive negotiations, interest-based bargaining and reason-giving interlock. Negotiators make progress by "bootstrapping." They extend their understanding and then craft practical arrangements that make this understanding tangible (i.e., that "create value"). Success depends both on negotiators' abilities to animate and understand each other's complex interests, fears, and values and to revise assessments of oneself and others in light of ongoing communication, and their ability as bargainers to make these developments manifest by giving them practical shape.

Representatives and organizations asked to designate representatives can be expected to encounter a series of questions as they become involved in a consensus building process. The following comments are meant to offer some guidance on common questions.

Advice to Representatives in a Consensus Building Process

1. *What do I do if the interests of my organization are not clear?*

This significant and common problem is compounded by the tensions that characterize representation. It is clear that to craft proposals that have some hope of being ratified, you must understand the interests of your constituents. At the same time, you don't want to harden group members' conception of their interests too early, or you will lose the flexibility necessary to negotiate with other representatives and respond to your emerging understanding of the problem.

The trick is to initiate a discussion within your group about how members understand their interests and commitments to values such as fairness and equity. You should try to keep this discussion open, so that you can bring new ideas and concerns back from the negotiating table. Ideally, you want the within-group discussion to follow the conversation you're having with other representatives. You want to involve your constituents in the developments that occur in fact-finding and negotiation. You also want a forum in which you can test your emerging understanding against the questions and concerns your constituents have. Your obligations to your constituents to listen and respond to reasonable concerns are as strict as those you uphold at the negotiating table.

You should try to sustain the discussion of interests with your constituents throughout the negotiations. You will need to make the language of this analysis increasingly explicit and issue oriented as negotiations move forward. By the time different packages are on the table, you will have to work with your constituents to develop guidelines you can follow in assessing trade-offs between issues.

2. *What if my group does not have the technical background to address the issues involved in the problem?*

Don't confuse expertise with the ability to contribute. Focus on your ability to learn and contribute by asking thoughtful questions. Good, insightful questions can play a pivotal role in shaping appropriate analysis. For any recommendation a consultant makes, you may want to ask if there are other studies that reach different conclusions and what prompts the disagreement.

You may also want to inquire about the data on which the findings are based, and examine the fit between the context in which the data were collected and the situation in which you're interested.

If forecasting or modeling is involved, you may want to ask about where the "facts" came from that are being used as the baseline. Do they continue to make sense and fit the situation? In a similar vein, you may want to ask about the models that will be used for extrapolation. What assumptions are they based on and do these make sense for your situation?

Getting at these assumptions is likely to be a challenge and will require an active effort on your part. The first step is often to take responsibility for setting the ground rules for consultation with experts. Appropriate ground rules will give you the authority to ask questions about the basis and shape of an analysis, as well as about findings. In the Cambridge, Massachusetts subway case discussed above, the transportation-demand forecast was controversial, but it was embedded in the design for the parking garage. It only surfaced and was subjected to scrutiny because representatives demanded answers to a series of questions.

This kind of public scrutiny is particularly important where forecasts figure prominently in analysis and decision making. You should see yourself not only as a watchdog for your group's interests but also as filling a significant public role. Finally, you and other members of your organization will often have valuable local knowledge that can sharpen and enrich the discussion of technical issues. You should be ready, for instance, to test whether the "facts" and assumptions being used fit with your understanding of local history and conditions. Your understanding of the local context will often be valuable in ways that are difficult to anticipate.

3. What if my understanding of the problem is different from my group's, or my mandate is not specific?

Most of this chapter is devoted to describing common, predictable, and even desirable ways in which your understanding of the problem is likely to diverge from your group's. Tension between the kind of understanding you begin consensus building with and the learning and creativity that drive negotiation in consensus building is unavoidable. As a representative, you are likely to experience this tension firsthand. Your role is to help manage the tension rather than avoid it.

Consensus building is not simply a matter of compromise. It works precisely because you don't know what is possible until you try. The learning and creativity that goes on around the table are crucial to making progress and may lead you to see problems and opportunities in new ways. While it may not be possible to re-create this experience for members of your group, it is important to explain how your understanding has changed and to provide reasons for why you see things differently. You should also be ready to respond to questions and comments that your constituents have, even if this requires further revisions in your own understanding. If you want to sustain trust in your judgment, you should not ask for blind trust, but cultivate an informed trust that can acknowledge disagreements and minimize misunderstandings.

The more specific your mandate is, the sharper the tension between your view and your constituents' is likely to be. If you go to the table with specific demands and limits on what you can agree to, you will either have a hard time negotiating with other representatives or quickly find yourself at odds with your own mandate. You should expect and even favor a mandate that requires interpretation. At the same time, you should treat interpretation as a process of renegotiating your mandate with your group. You should strive to inform this developing mandate with new knowledge about technical issues and your developing sense of how other groups will be affected. You should use this process to help your constituents develop informed views of their interests and priorities.

4. *What if my own interests diverge from those of my group?*

It is important to distinguish this case from the one discussed immediately above. The premise in that case was that there were good reasons why your view of your group's interests, or how these interests will be best served, diverges from the group at large. New information, changes in the way you view other groups, and an increased assessment of the importance of fairness or legitimacy all might cause you to diverge on grounds that are reasonable and can be explained.

This case, in which your particular interests will be served by different terms than serve your constituents', is sharply different. In this case, the choice is clear. As a representative, you are bound to pursue some defensible version of the group's interests rather than your own distinct, private interests.

This problem raises two practical issues, however. First, it may not be easy to detect whether you are pursuing your own interests or those of the group. It is likely to be all too easy to come to understand the interests of your group in terms that are favorable to you. You need to build in checks and safeguards to try to control this kind of unintentional divergence. The best way to accomplish this may be to meet regularly with the group so that you can confirm your understanding of how they see things and clarify for them how your sense of the problem is changing. If you find that your own stake in the outcome is significantly different from your group's—either because of the way your interests will be affected or because your understanding has shifted in ways that you just cannot get your group to agree with—you may have to ask whether you can continue to represent your group. If, on the other hand, you find that others share your views, you face a different challenge. The question becomes, "Can you find a way to respond to the diverse interests of your group or to build agreement on a set of core interests?"

5. How should I handle disagreements in my group?

Consensus building works in light of, rather than in spite of, disagreements and differences. This is as true for differences within groups as it is for differences among groups. If internal differences persist, however, your job will be difficult. How will you portray the interests of your group to other representatives? How will you behave in negotiations if the balance within your group shifts back and forth? How will you hope to be able to deliver an agreement that meets the interests of your group, if the members remain divided?

This may mean that you have to take (or provide) a facilitative role in building an internal consensus on your constituents' sense of their interests, priorities, and vision of the future. All the practical strategies laid out in this volume can be used within as well as among groups. If your views on the substantive issues make it difficult for you to be accepted as nonpartisan, you should find someone in the group who can play this role or seek the assistance of a trained facilitator. Even if you can't facilitate this internal consensus building process, you may be able to act as the convenor. If there are persistent internal disagreements between small factions, you may want to consider using mediation to try to help them work out their differences. The HIV/AIDS case includes a discussion of a similar use of mediation.

6. Should I set up formal procedures for consultation with the people I represent?

In the end, the answer to this question will turn on your judgment. Consensus building is likely to put significant demands on the resources you have available. When you have frequent informal contacts with the people you represent, it may be more efficient to rely on these interactions to keep members of your group apprised of developments. A formal approach may seem inappropriate and too much of a drain on everyone's resources in cases where neighbors see each other regularly or where members of a group work together and see each other on a daily basis.

Even in such cases, however, there are risks of which you should be aware. If you see your constituents regularly, you will still need to create opportunities to talk in a focused way. Informal conversations are unlikely to be focused enough to bring out ambiguities and misunderstandings. You may feel you have communicated developments clearly, only to find out that some members of your group have understood something differently from what you intended to say. You may communicate clearly with individuals, but they may each take a slightly different understanding away from your conversations and find that they disagree with each other about the facts of the case.

Given these risks, it may help to supplement informal procedures with some kind of formal mechanism. This may be as simple as annotating and distributing meeting summaries prepared by the facilitator, or formalizing the lines of communication in your informal network. It could mean distributing a newsletter that tracks the developing sense of the group and can serve as an internal version of a single negotiation text. The important thing to remember is that the meaning, significance, and even facts of the problem are likely to be renegotiated several times during the course of consensus building. Whatever system you use will need to be up to these demands. In the end, you are likely to have to justify the recommendations you make. This will be much easier if you have brought your group along with you. Whenever the negotiations with other representatives take a major turn, you should consider holding a meeting with your full constituent group or with an executive committee that can interact with the broader membership. In the end, you want to craft not only an agreement that makes sense but also a climate of understanding in which ratification and implementation are possible.

Advice for Organizations Asked to Designate Representatives

1. What qualities are important for a representative?

The qualities of a good representative are different in consensus building than in advocacy processes. You want to select someone who can contribute to a consensus building group's negotiations. This means finding a representative who can communicate the concerns of your group clearly and provide a convincing rationale. It also means finding someone who is not only able to reason convincingly but is "open to reason." Your representative should be someone who can listen to what others have to say, even if others' views seem misguided or irrational initially. Even if a negotiating group never reaches agreement, your organization will be in a better position if your representative can understand the views of other participants. If your representative's commitment to your group's goals is too single-minded, it is likely to interfere with his or her ability to understand and communicate back what others have to say.

You also want someone who is open to learning about the problem, capable of playing an active role in the process (which is different from having expertise), and willing and able to revise his or her assessment of the problem. Finally, you want someone whose judgment you trust and who is capable of sustaining this trust through regular consultation with other members of the group, either formally or informally.

2. How should we frame our mandate to our representative?

You want the mandate to reflect your group's best understanding of your interests and of the problem. What you are likely to know the most about initially is your interests—the things about which you care most. Even if you are unsure how they will be affected, the list of things that are important to your group is likely to have a core that will be fairly stable over time. You may augment the list, but these core interests will remain relevant. Be careful that you don't frame these interests in terms that are so specific that they lock your representative into a position or a particular view of the problem and what is possible. You want to keep an open mind, and your mandate should reflect this.

Over the course of the consensus building process, you should expect to renegotiate this mandate and make sure that there are opportunities to do so. You may need to take account of new information about the problem or about other groups. These discussions will also allow your representative to clarify interests and priorities that no one anticipated would be affected by the negotiations. Unexpected opportunities and unforeseen options may also arise, and you don't want to tie your representative's hands so that he or she can't take advantage of attractive options.

Finally, you will have to negotiate the mandate in more specific terms as negotiations proceed. You will want to not only (re)specify your interests but also give your representative as vivid a sense as possible of the group's priorities and how members would prefer to make trade-offs between issues that are important to them. The final mandate may look quite different from the one with which you began.

3. What kind of internal demands should we anticipate?

This process of renegotiating your mandate will create internal demands. Your group will have to try to keep an open mind. In some ways, the burdens on your group's members will be greater than those on your representative. They will have to be ready to learn and revise their understanding of the problem and assessment of other groups without the benefit of the kind of immediate experience and interaction that your representative is involved in.

In the end, you will face a choice about a proposal that may vary significantly from what you anticipated when the consensus building process began. You have to be ready to evaluate proposals with an open mind. You should be ready to consider not only how well your interests are met but also how sensible the justification is that your representative and other representatives provide.

4. *What kinds of internal processes should we put in place?*

The most significant internal demand will be for communication. Your group should have a process in place that ensures adequate communication with your representative and with each other. This responsibility should not be left to the representative, whose time and energy will already be taxed. The internal process should be sufficient to resolve disagreements that arise as new information is revealed and as other groups change their positions. It should be adequate to support a renegotiation of your group's sense of its interests and commitments and your mandate to your representative. Finally, the process will have to be up to the challenge of discussing any proposed agreement that your representative brings back.

There are no strict rules about how formal or informal a process should be to accomplish this. You will have to work with the relationships, resources, and traditions that exist. You should test this system early and regularly and not wait until a significant disagreement arises or you must make a decision about a proposed agreement that has caught everyone by surprise and prompted internal disagreement.

■ Notes

1. According to the case, the Wascos were "giant sea dogs that were large enough to catch killer whales. These amazing creatures had kept Haida villages well fed until a jealous sorcerer conjured up a sea storm. The rough seas exhausted the Wascos, and they turned into the great rocks along the shore."

2. The notion of "enlarged thinking" is Hannah Arendt's. Its implication for the kind of civic conversation I'm referring to here is discussed at length by Seyla Benhabib in *Situating the Self* (1992).

3. The distinction between changing minds and collective decision making is taken from numerous personal communications with Joshua Cohen from 1993 to 1996.

4. For an insightful discussion of the broader implications of this dynamic, see Charles Sabel's "Studied Trust: Building New Forms of Cooperation in a Volatile Economy" (1992).

5. Letter to potential representatives from the Maine Low-Level Radioactive Waste Authority, dated May 8, 1989.

6. This quotation and those that follow are from transcriptions made by the author from audio- and videotapes of the proceedings made by the Maine Low-Level Radioactive Waste Authority, the sponsoring agency in the case.

7. The dispute was over whether there was a linear relationship between exposure to radiation and health effects. The dissenting views on one side hold that there is a threshold below which no effects can be attributed. On the other, there is the view that small chronic doses may have a greater effect.

8. Note that if a reasonable justification can be supplied, then the problem is like the problem of judgment that follows. For instance, we may disagree about the assessment of a health risk because we disagree about how likely accidents are to occur. If we each have more or less equally reasonable grounds for our assessments, then we have a reasonable disagreement.

9. The difficulties involved in participating in an inquiry that might have implications for deeply held beliefs and commitments should not be underestimated. The psychological literature is full of documented effects that suggest individuals will have a hard time acknowledging or assessing evidence that goes against such beliefs and that we should expect that some will be more willing to change their assessment of facts rather than their beliefs. See, for instance, any of Leon Festinger's (1962; Festinger, Riecken, & Schachter, 1956) writings on cognitive dissonance. For a discussion of the interplay between inquiry and belief see Charles Peirce's "The Fixation of Belief" (1992).

10. The argument for this role for representatives is put crisply by Funtowicz and Ravetz (1991): "The democratization of political life is now commonplace; its hazards are accepted as a small price to pay. Now it becomes possible to achieve a parallel democratization of knowledge, not merely in mass education but in enhanced participation in decision making for common problems. The democratization of science in this respect is therefore not a matter of benevolence by the established groups. Rather it is (as in the sphere of politics) the creation of a system which in spite of its inefficiencies is the most effective means for avoiding the disasters that in our environmental affairs, as much as in society, result from the prolonged stifling of criticism. *Let us be quite clear on this: we are not calling for the democratization of science out of some generalized wish for the greatest possible extension of democracy into society.* The epistemological analysis of post-normal science, rooted in the practical tasks of quality assurance, shows that *such an extension of peer communities, with the corresponding extension of facts, is necessary for the effectiveness of this new sort of science in meeting the challenges of global environmental issues* (p. 151, emphasis added).

11. This understanding of justification is posed by Thomas Scanlon (1982).

12. The phrase is Sheldon White's (personal communication, May 1995).

13. Claus Offe (n.d.) has summarized the demands that deliberation puts on citizens in these terms in an unpublished paper.

14. The consensus may, as John Rawls (1993) has described it, be overlapping.

15. From the CAG ground rules.

16. "For me it was an experiment about whether a community could be empowered to meaningfully address environmental issues within a community. . . . I think the concept was more than does this work? I think that it was a good thing to do if the model worked, it was a model that we might [want] to perpetuate" (Cluck, 1997, p. 39).

■ *References*

Benhabib, S. (1992). *Situating the self.* New York: Routledge.

Cluck, V. (1997). *The Northern Oxford County Coalition: An analysis of representation and communication.* Unpublished master's thesis, Massachusetts Institute of Technology, Cambridge.

Cohen, J. (1993). Moral pluralism and political consensus. In D. Copp, J. Hampton, & J. E. Roemer (Eds.), *The idea of democracy.* Cambridge, UK: Cambridge University Press.

Festinger, L. (1962). *A theory of cognitive dissonance.* Stanford, CA: Stanford University Press.

Festinger, L., Riecken, H. W., & Schachter, S. (1956). *When prophecy fails.* Minneapolis: University of Minnesota Press.

Forester, J. (1994). Lawrence Susskind: Activist mediation and public disputes. In D. Kolb (Ed.), *When talk works: Profiles of mediators.* San Francisco: Jossey-Bass.

Funtowicz, S., & Ravetz, J. (1991). A new scientific methodology for global environmental issues. In R. Costanza (Ed.), *Ecological economics: The science and management of sustainability.* New York: Columbia University Press.

Kymlicka, W. (1989). *Liberalism, community and culture.* Oxford, UK: Clarendon.

Mnookin, R., Peppet, S., & Tulumello, A. (1996). The tension between empathy and assertiveness. *Negotiation Journal, 12,* 217-229.

Offe, C. (n.d.). *What makes for the competence of citizens?* Unpublished manuscript.

Peirce, C. (1992). The fixation of belief. In N. Houser & C. Kloesel (Eds.), *The essential Peirce* (Vol. 1). Bloomington: Indiana University Press.

Pitkin, H. (1981). Justice: On relating public and private. *Political Theory, 9,* 327-347.

Rawls, J. (1993). *Political liberalism.* New York: Columbia University Press.

Sabel, C. (1992). Studied trust: Building new forms of cooperation in a volatile economy. In F. Pyke & W. Sengenberger (Eds.), *Industrial districts and local economic generation.* Geneva, Switzerland: Institute for Labor Studies.

Scanlon, T. (1982). Contractualism and utilitarianism. In A. Sen & B. Williams (Eds.), *Utilitarianism and beyond.* Cambridge, UK: Cambridge University Press.

Susskind, L., & Dunlop, L. (1981). The importance of non-objective judgments in environmental impact assessments. *Environmental Impact Assessment Review, 2*(4), 335-366.

Wheeler, M. (1993). Regional consensus on affordable housing: Yes in my backyard? *Journal of Planning Education and Research, 12*(2), 143.

7

MANAGING MEETINGS TO BUILD CONSENSUS

■ *David A. Straus*

F‾ace-to-face meetings are the building blocks of consensus-based processes. Such meetings must be well planned and well facilitated, however, to be productive—to enable participants to make steady progress toward reaching agreement. Poorly run meetings leave participants frustrated, angry, and (rightly) feeling that they have wasted their time. Let's look at a hypothetical case.

Maria sees a flyer posted in the window of the local coffee shop about a public meeting to take place next Tuesday at 7:00 p.m. at the community center. The purpose of the meeting, according to the flyer, is to discuss the possibility of building a new elementary school in town. Maria has two young children, so this piques her interest. The flyer isn't specific about who is hosting the meeting or what exactly will occur. Maria arrives at the community center at 7:00 p.m. on Tuesday to discover that the door is locked. A handful of people are sitting in their cars, waiting for someone to open the door and trying to keep warm in the winter cold. Maria does the same. At 7:15, a maintenance person shows up and lets everyone in, but much to Maria's chagrin, the community center is freezing; no one came early to turn on the heat. At 7:25, the president of the PTA arrives and mumbles an apology for her tardiness. By this time, about 30 people have arrived, scattered throughout a room set up for 100. The school superintendent is not present, nor is anybody from the school board. Before the meeting even starts, Maria is irritated. "Why did they keep us waiting in the cold so long?" she wonders. "Why is this room set up so poorly? Why aren't the school board members here? Why did I bother to come!"

The PTA president rises to chair the meeting. She begins with a long-winded statement about how the town's population is growing and how nearby towns are building beautiful new schools for their children. She says the purpose of the meeting is to develop recommendations for the school board regarding whether a new school should be built and, if so, where, and how it should be paid for. She then turns to a consultant who has apparently been hired by the school district. He sets off on a confusing, statistics-filled speech that first seems to be about the district's budget constraints, but then veers off into a discussion of the national trend toward smaller class size. After this presentation, people begin asking questions and sharing their opinions on a wide variety of topics relating to education in their town. Maria is, at this point, completely confused about what is going on. "Why don't we have an agenda?" she wonders. "What will we focus on first? How are we even supposed to know if a new school is needed? Are the existing elementary schools overcrowded? And are the right people here to represent the community and make meaningful recommendations to the school board?" Others are apparently as confused as Maria. The discussion becomes a free-for-all. People continue to make statements and ask questions on a wide variety of topics; the conversation has no focus. People interrupt each other, repeat the same points, and sometimes become quite rude. The PTA president apparently has no idea how to help the group work together productively; she is sitting back watching people argue. Maria, frustrated with what seems to be a pointless, meandering, and ever-escalating argument, quietly slips out of the meeting room. "What a waste of time!" she thinks.

"A consensus building process may collapse if face-to-face encounters are not run well."

If consensus building meetings are managed poorly, as in Maria's case, participants will become so frustrated with and distracted by the logistical and process problems that they will not be able to focus on reaching mutually agreeable solutions. High-quality, consensus-based agreements are, in large part, the cumulative effect of the discussions, activities, and learning that take place among diverse participants in well-run meetings. Indeed, a process may collapse if face-to-face encounters are not organized and run well.

This chapter describes how to plan for and run a successful meeting during a consensus building effort. It is based on a facilitated approach to meeting management called the *Inter-action Method*.[1] The chapter begins with a discussion of the importance of well-run, face-to-face meetings. The next three sections describe (1) what to do before a meeting (i.e., how to set up for success), (2) what to do during a meeting (i.e., how to structure and facilitate a meeting and handle problems that arise), and (3) what to do after a meeting (i.e., what kinds of follow-up activities may be needed). Facilitators, convenors, and consensus building participants alike should find the guidance in this chapter useful, but much of the chapter is aimed primarily at those who facilitate meetings. Also, although the chapter focuses on face-to-face meetings, many of the suggestions and skills described in it can also be applied to meetings that involve telephone, video, or computer conferencing.

■ The Value of Face-to-Face Meetings

Some models of mediation call for keeping opposing parties separate, minimizing their interactions, and engaging in *shuttle diplomacy*. In consensus building, on the other hand, most of the work of building agreements is accomplished in face-to-face, facilitated meetings. In these meetings, participants' interests are articulated and acknowledged so they can be discussed, understood, and used as the basis for seeking mutually agreeable solutions. The commitments that parties make to each other in meetings are built on a wide base of shared effort and learning—a base that brokered agreements developed through shuttle diplomacy often lack.

Participants sometimes find that effective meetings, in which opposing parties begin with strongly entrenched, opposing positions and then build consensus step-by-step, can actually be a transforming experience. They learn constructive ways of working together and communicating. They become empowered by the experience of being understood by, and understanding, their adversaries. They are often surprised at what they all have in common, and this realization can help them to see ways to meet everyone's needs. Indeed, in well-facilitated meetings, participants can develop agreements that they can enthusiastically support and help implement, for which they have not compromised their basic values, and that they can present to their constituents (those they represent) as worthy of support. Even when consensus is not achieved, the process of respectful, face-to-face exploration helps people to better understand each other's points of view and makes future attempts at consensus building more likely to succeed.

The Importance of Well-Run Meetings

As Maria's experience illustrates, it is not enough to simply bring people together. For a meeting to be effective, it must be well planned and well run. Meetings can be evaluated in terms of three dimensions of success.

- *The results achieved.* Was the meeting productive? Did the group reach its goals? Did the participants produce a high-quality product?
- *The process used.* Were participants satisfied with the way the meeting was run? Did they feel in control of the meeting and not manipulated in any way? Did the facilitator employ effective and efficient consensus building techniques?
- *The relationships built.* Are participants able to communicate with each other more constructively as a result of the meeting? Do they feel that their viewpoints and concerns were acknowledged and understood by their fellow participants?

Effective meetings achieve positive results in all three dimensions. They are conducted according to proven principles of collaboration,[2] include clear roles and responsibilities for participants and organizers, and offer carefully managed opportunities for discussion and decision making. In effective meetings, facilitators and participants are well prepared.[3] Facilitators use effective problem-solving skills and tools, plan workable agendas, and model appropriate conflict resolution behaviors. They clearly delineate between content (*what* is to be discussed) and process (*how* to proceed with discussions). Participants recognize that the meeting's success depends on their positive, productive input; they do not rely on a facilitator to do it all for them. The atmosphere is safe and stimulating. Time is used well. There is little repetitious arguing, "speechifying," or personal gossip or attacks. Often, agreements are reached. People leave such meetings energized to implement decisions and, in fact, are eager to meet again to report on their efforts and take up new assignments.

Poorly run meetings—those that do not rate highly on the three criteria above—are an altogether different experience. As we saw in Maria's case, poorly run meetings are those that do not have a clearly defined purpose, agenda, or roles for organizers and participants. In poorly run meetings, participants do not distinguish between process and content. Logistical details, such as appropriate seating configurations and lighting, are disregarded as unimportant. A few outspoken people may be allowed to dominate, while those who are less assertive, articulate, or powerful are simply shut out of discussions. Participants may insult each other or make accusatory statements. Discussions may wander aimlessly, so that they are hard to sum up, and their results are not easily communicated to those who did not attend. In such meetings, little actual progress is made, and desired outcomes are not met. Consensus building meetings that include these kinds of problems tend to

- decrease participants' motivation to commit themselves to a consensus-based process,
- increase the possibility of unproductive dissension in every phase of a process's life span,
- waste valuable and limited resources (e.g., time and money),
- damage the credibility of project sponsors and facilitators, and
- contribute to "lowest common denominator" thinking by limiting the ways in which people perceive problems and their solutions.

Facilitators must attend to all three dimensions of success. It is not desirable for a group to achieve its goals in a meeting but have members leave saying, "We never really had a chance to talk to each other," or "I felt steamrollered by the process." Neither is it good if people walk away saying, "It was a good discussion, but we didn't really accomplish much." The following sections provide guidance on how to plan for, run, and follow up on effective meetings.

■ *Before a Meeting: Setting Up for Success*

Effective meetings do not just happen; they require considerable preparation and planning. To set up a meeting to succeed, the meeting planner(s) must consider and make conscious choices about every factor that could influence the outcome of the meeting. In particular, they must think through and make decisions about

> the purpose of the meeting,
> who should be involved and how,
> the desired outcomes,
> the agenda,
> the roles and responsibilities of participants and
> organizers,
> what ground rules will guide discussions,
> how group decisions will be made, and
> where the meeting will be held.

This section is addressed toward those taking part in a premeeting planning session. Typically, this would include a facilitator and a convenor. (The convenor is the person organizing the meeting and inviting people to take part. See Chapter 4 for more on the convenor's role.) Sometimes the convenor must plan the meeting alone. Sometimes a planning group, made up of key stakeholders, is charged with the task. Other times, meeting participants design the agenda at the beginning of a meeting. In some situations, particularly those involving highly charged, public conflicts, the facilitator may also serve as convenor and, with input from stakeholders, plan the agenda alone. Regardless of the situation, the meeting planner(s) must consider the following issues in advance, always keeping in mind that the proposed plan for a meeting should be reviewed and revised, as needed, by all participants at the beginning of the meeting.

Although the suggestions in this section are directed toward those responsible for meeting planning, anyone taking part in a meeting can display the "facilitative behaviors" described here as well. Participants can be very helpful in premeeting planning, for example, and by offering process suggestions during a session. One of the beneficial side effects of productive meetings is that everyone taking part learns facilitative skills, which are then disseminated throughout the community or organization.

Determining the Purpose of the Meeting

Early in a meeting design process, it is important to clarify the purpose of the proposed meeting. The first step is to make sure the meeting *has* a purpose. The facilitator should talk with the chairperson or convenor to determine whether a meeting is truly necessary. Would telephone calls, e-mail exchanges, or one-on-one sessions accomplish the same end? Do limitations in time, resources, or information present obstacles for the group that cannot be overcome? Is the purpose too trivial or, conversely, too overwhelming to warrant bringing people together? Does so much hostility or anger exist among individuals or groups that too much energy or time will be required to get down to work? Is there confidential information that affects the group's discussions, but to which only a few have access? Is the meeting simply window dressing to divert attention from the real, behind-the-scenes negotiations taking place? If the answer to any of these questions is yes, it may be best not to hold a meeting at all.

If it is clear that a meeting should be held, the purpose of that session must be articulated. Is the meeting primarily informational? That is, will data or information be gathered or shared? Or is the meeting being held to plan an activity or event, solve a problem, or make a decision? Perhaps its purpose, as with many meetings, is a combination of both information sharing and decision making.

Deciding Who Should Attend

The power of a consensus-based decision is directly proportional to the inclusiveness of the process used to make that decision. In other words, the full range of stakeholders must be involved in consensus building. *Stakeholders* are those people or organizations who are responsible for a decision or problem, will be affected by the outcome of an agreement, have the power to block it, or have information or expertise relevant to the discussions. Often, when there are many stakeholders, *representatives* must be chosen from among them to keep the negotiating group to a manageable size.

In a multimeeting consensus building process, the task of identifying stakeholders to participate takes place during the process design phase (also called the convening phase). In this *stakeholder analysis,* a process design committee made up of a cross section of stakeholders identifies the various viewpoints that must be represented in a process and develops recommendations for who should participate (see Chapter 3). A stakeholder analysis can also be done by a facilitator during a conflict assessment; in this case, the facilitator interviews stakeholders to gather their views on who should take part in a process (see Chapter 2). In planning a single, stand-alone meeting, a similar but much briefer analysis is necessary. (See also Chapter 4 for more on choosing appropriate participants.)

In meetings held within single organizations, participants are too often invited based on their position or job title, rather than on whether they truly have an interest or stake in the issues to be discussed. For example, instead of holding a departmentwide meeting to discuss a difficult or complex topic, a manager should consider bringing together people who are truly affected by the issue but who may come from multiple departments.

Determining Desired Outcomes

Meeting planners must also decide what they want a group to achieve in a meeting: what lists, plans, agreements, or information they want individuals to have in hand when they leave the room and what actions they want participants to commit to carry out. A desired outcome for a department's planning meeting might be the following: "A prioritized list of tasks to be completed in the next month." Of course, the content of any such lists, plans, or agreements cannot be predetermined. We are only talking about proposing the form of such products. Any proposed outcomes suggested by a facilitator or convenor should be discussed, revised as needed, and agreed to by all participants at the outset of a meeting. Participants must feel that they are working toward a useful and reasonable goal if a meeting is to be productive.

Meeting objectives that are articulated in clear, concise statements, written from the perspective of participants, give a group a way to measure its performance—a way to chart its progress. Clear goals also help to keep meetings on track. When a discussion begins to stray from the main topic, the facilitator can remind participants of the desired outcomes and the importance of keeping conversations focused on meeting them. Also, once desired outcomes are articulated, it is much easier to devise an appropriate agenda for the meeting.

Drafting an Agenda

"Thoughtful agenda planning is an essential element of an effective meeting."

Thoughtful agenda planning is an essential element of an effective meeting—an element that is too often taken for granted. An agenda serves as a map that represents what participants collectively agree they want to accomplish during a meeting. It is an important facilitation aid. A facilitator can focus a group on the agenda during a meeting to help get a discussion back on track (e.g., "Remember, we'll be talking about possible solutions later; let's stick with learning more about the problem right now"). Also, when a group seems tired or frustrated, a facilitator can direct participants' attention to the agenda so that they can see how much progress they have made. (See Table 7.1 for a sample agenda. Figure 3.5 in Chapter 3 is another example of an agenda.)

Ideally, a draft agenda should be distributed in advance of every meeting. This allows meeting participants to know what they can expect and what is expected of them; it also gives them an opportunity to think about any alterations to the agenda they would like to suggest. The draft agenda should be displayed on a flip chart at the beginning of (and during) the meeting. One of the first steps in any meeting is to build agreement on the agenda by reviewing and revising the draft.

To create a draft agenda, a facilitator or convenor must think carefully about how the desired outcomes can be achieved. To do this, he or she must identify the "what, how, who, and when" of a meeting.

- The *what* are the topics or issues that must be addressed to reach the desired outcomes. These topics become the primary

TABLE 7.1 Sample Agenda: Visioning Meeting for "Healthy Boston" (a nonprofit organization)

What	How	Who	Time
Orientation			7:45-8:45
Briefing and room setup	Rearrange seating	Facilitators, recorders, Healthy Boston staff	
	Prepare breakout areas with paper and markers		
Large-group session			8:45-9:15
Welcome, introduce facilitators		Ted	5 min
Define roles, introductions, review and revise agenda	Everyone introduces him- or herself	David (lead facilitator)	10 min
History/progress report Existing vision of Healthy Boston		Ted	10 min
Charge to breakout groups for both the exchange and visioning session	Groups form around membership and outreach, organization structure, action plan and special projects	David	5 min
Small-group exchange			9:15-10:00
Sharing of information, strategies, experiences	Introductions	Facilitators	45 min
	Brainstorm list of issues or questions within topic		
	Prioritize		
	Exchange ideas, resources		
Small-group visioning and feedback			10:00-11:30
Vision of a Healthy Boston 10 years from now	Brainstorm images, pictures, and words, then discuss (don't try for consensus)		45 min
Vision of how all the stakeholders would be working together	Brainstorm as above		30 min
Feedback about Healthy City project so far	What's working, what needs to be improved		15 min
Large group			11:30-12:30
Small-group reports	5 minutes per group	Spokespeople	30 min
Whole-group discussion of issues raised by small groups	Facilitated discussion and response by staff	David	20 min
Next steps		David	5 min
Closing remarks		Ted	5 min

agenda items. For example, if the desired outcome at a meeting of a nonprofit group is to build consensus on a plan for using next year's crop of interns, the agenda items might include "Intern selection process," "Projects to assign to interns," "Managing interns," "Intern orientation session," and "Stipends."

• The *how* are the processes, methods, and techniques that can be used to deal with an agenda item. These might include presentations, discussions, "round-robin" sharing, brainstorming, and so forth. At the nonprofit group's meeting, for example, the "Projects to assign to interns" agenda item may begin with presentations by each program manager, describing the tasks he or she could have an intern complete. The ideas raised in the presentations may be listed on a flip chart, at which point all participants may discuss which are most crucial to the organization and which would provide the best learning experience for the interns.

• The *who* describes the person(s) who will take responsibility for the agenda item, for example, the person to start a discussion or give a presentation. Often, this will simply be the facilitator or chair. At the nonprofit group, the program officers will be responsible for the "Projects" section, while the financial officer may initiate the "Stipends" discussion.

• The *when* is the order and amount of time to be devoted to each item, whether it be 10 minutes or two hours. The facilitator of the nonprofit group's meeting may estimate, for example, that the group set aside an hour for the "Projects" discussion and 15 minutes for the "Stipends" conversation.

We find it helpful to think of an agenda as a "sandwich." The first layer (the "bread") involves introducing group members (if necessary), reviewing and agreeing on the purpose of the meeting, identifying who will fulfill the various meeting roles, agreeing on ground rules for participation and decision making, and reviewing the agenda itself. The middle layer (the "meat" of the meeting) includes working through the agenda items, consistent with the desired outcomes, and arriving at action steps that people commit to taking. The third layer (more "bread") includes summarizing what has been accomplished, clarifying action steps and responsibilities, discussing deadlines for the completion of action steps, and making a decision about whether and when a next meeting is to take place. This third layer should also include a review of the meeting process: what worked, what didn't, and what needs to take place for the next meeting to be even more successful. A facilitator typically manages and leads the group through all of the process-related tasks in the first and third layers, in addition to facilitating the substantive discussions in the middle layer.

Assigning Meeting Roles and Responsibilities

The framework for face-to-face meetings that we call the Interaction Method involves a set of four roles and functions:

> facilitator,
> recorder,
> leader (i.e., the chair or manager), and
> group members.

The activities performed by people in these roles are based on explicit "contracts" agreed to by all participants at the outset of a meeting, that is, verbal agreements about the proper responsibilities of those in each role. These contracts create a self-correcting system, in which each member of the group shares responsibility for making sure everyone else stays in role. We have found that this system of checks and balances works so well that after only a little training, group members can learn to stay in role and perform their roles well by giving each other constructive feedback.

All four functions need to be served in any meeting, even if one person has to play several roles simultaneously. In small groups, for example, a leader might have to facilitate, record, and participate. If a leader and facilitator are present, the facilitator may both facilitate and record.

The Role of the Facilitator

The role of a facilitator is to be a neutral, nonevaluative, noncontributing *process guide*. Facilitators may offer process suggestions at any moment in a discussion—suggestions such as "Shall we agree not to evaluate options until we get them all on the table?" and "How about we talk about Topic X first and then get into Topic Y. OK?" But facilitators do not, while in role, offer or evaluate any substantive suggestions, including ideas or proposed solutions or decisions. Facilitators focus on the process so that group members can focus on the substance. In this way, facilitators help a group achieve the tasks it must achieve and ensure that all can participate safe from abuses of power or personal attack. The bottom-line contract a facilitator has with a group is to maintain neutrality and to serve the group. In return, group members must speak up if they feel that a facilitator is "pushing" or "manipulating" the group in a direction that participants do not wish to go.

From time to time, a facilitator may step out of role to offer expertise or an idea from past experience in dealing with a specific substantive issue. This should be done, however, only with the explicit permission of the group, while clearly identifying that a role change is being proposed for a limited time and purpose. A facilitator may say, for example, "I would like to step out of my facilitator role for a moment to share with you my experience with the problem you are currently addressing. Is that OK with you? . . . Now, I am out of role and here are my thoughts. . . . I am now returning to my facilitator role. Where do you want to go from here?" We have witnessed many occasions in which a person stepped out of the facilitator role with the permission of the group, argued strongly and persuasively for a particular position, and resumed acting in a neutral and unbiased manner once back in role.

The facilitator role can be filled in one of three ways. For day-to-day meetings in an organization, the facilitation function can be handled by rotating the role among group members or having the leader facilitate the discussions. As group size gets larger or the stakes get higher, it may be wise to ask someone from outside the group to facilitate. Some organizations have designated certain individuals to serve as facilitators for critical meetings. Finally, for very important organizational meetings or multistakeholder consensus building efforts in the public sector, it is advisable to hire a professional facilitator with process expertise. (See Chapter 5 for more on the role of facilitators and mediators.)

The Role of the Recorder

The recorder also functions in an impartial, nonevaluative manner. He or she is responsible for capturing the ideas of group members, in their own words, on large sheets of newsprint in front of the group. In return, participants are responsible for correcting the record if the group's ideas are not adequately captured.

Recording is a very powerful tool that helps groups make their way through complex consensus building and problem-solving activities. It allows group members to focus on the discussions, assured that their contributions are being preserved and can be recalled at any time. Because the recorder captures the essence of spoken ideas as the meeting proceeds, the act of recording does not slow down the meeting, but may in fact make it possible to move along more quickly. People seem to have less need to repeat themselves when they know they have not only been heard, but their ideas have been recorded on paper. The recording process enables people to engage effectively in mul-tistep problem-solving processes such as brainstorming, listing, and clarifying. When brainstorming is going well, for example, group members may offer a cascade of different ideas in quick succession. Recording captures these ideas before they evaporate. It also enables the group to return to the list and clarify any ideas that are not completely clear to everyone. Also, recording "de-personalizes" ideas in a constructive way. Ideas are recorded without personal attribution and, therefore, the question of who raised the idea is less important than how good it is.

As a result of this process, a graphic record—what we call the *group memory*—is created. A group memory documents what is said, so that there is an agreed-on record of the conversation rather than just a collection of individual, postmeeting interpretations. In fact, the sheets of newsprint can be transcribed or reproduced and then distributed to the group as a meeting summary. This record can be added to as each new meeting takes place.

To perform the role well, recorders should keep the following guidelines in mind. First, spelling is not important; capturing the key ideas is. When recorders stop to think about spelling, they lose the "rhythm" of the recording and sometimes fall behind the discussion. Second, using markers of different colors to highlight separate ideas helps to maintain visual interest. Third, sometimes a brief diagram or sketch can capture an idea more succinctly and clearly than the words originally used to express it, and partici-pants often become quite involved in and excited about seeing their thoughts in graphic form.[4] Finally, a recorder can invite participants to draw or write their ideas on the group memory themselves during a meeting, to enhance participation or capture a point more accurately. The facilitator may also intervene on behalf of a participant or the group if he or she thinks that an idea was missed or not well captured.

In high-conflict situations, it is best to separate the roles of facilitator and recorder. A facilitator needs to be able to focus on the participant's interactions, and he or she may slow a meeting down by constantly turning away from the group to record comments. A person who is recording must move into a special, "acoustic" space, letting the ideas flow through the marker to the flip chart paper, capturing one idea while listening to the next. Even stopping to think about the ideas can be enough to break a recorder's rhythm. A good facilitating and recording team perform a graceful, coordinated dance. The facilitator constantly watches out for the recorder, making sure there are fresh sheets of paper available, slowing down the flow of ideas enough to allow the recorder to capture them, and clarifying, repeating, and condensing ideas when necessary. The recorder anticipates the facilitator's interventions and sometimes quietly gives the facilitator process suggestions, but in general, is not addressing the group directly.

Financial or other constraints, however, may require the facilitator or a group member to take on the recorder role. If a participant is serving as recorder, he or she can ask to step out of the recording role to contribute ideas. The process of having participants rotate in and out of the recording role is actually an excellent team-building activity.

The Role of the Leader

In a meeting within a hierarchical organization, the person who functions as the group leader is usually the senior manager in attendance. In a nonhierarchical group like a board of directors or an ad hoc, public group like a community task force, the chair or convenor of the group plays the leader role. A leader typically has organizational roles and decision-making responsibilities beyond those of other members.

The role of the leader is to help keep a group focused on its task. Because of his or her seniority, leaders are sometimes looked to for guidance in a meeting when a group is unsure of how to proceed or how a potential solution would be perceived by others in positions of authority. Leaders also may be helpful in reminding a group of its objectives and the importance of meeting them. In public consensus building processes, a leader may also serve as a spokesperson, representing the group to the public and the press. A leader does not run meetings, but participates and contributes to the process of building consensus like any other group member.

The Role of Group Members

The role of group members involves contributing ideas, listening to one another's ideas with an open mind, stating concerns clearly, and making commitments to follow through on agreements and action steps. Participants must work to meet their own interests and those of their constituents, while making a good faith effort to reach agreement. (The tension that arises in trying to fulfill these dual functions is discussed in Chapter 6.) Group members are free to focus on the task at hand and advocate for their ideas knowing that someone else is worrying about the meeting process. Participants should also make process suggestions as appropriate and ensure that the facilitator and recorder honor the boundaries of their roles.

Other Roles

Sometimes people will attend meetings in the role of consultant. A consultant may be an expert in process or the content of the subject being addressed. Such a person is there to serve the group and is generally not included in a formal check for consensus. Another role is that of the designated observer. Observers may include staff people who are there to assist participants, constituents or other interested parties, or professional process evaluators. It is helpful, in all but large public meetings, for all persons in a room to introduce themselves and identify what role they are playing at a meeting. Participants feel more comfortable speaking when they know who is listening.

Drafting Proposed Ground Rules

Meeting planners must develop a list of proposed ground rules. Ground rules, in a single-meeting setting, typically set forth behavioral norms that participants are expected to follow. In multimeeting consensus building processes, by contrast, ground rules are often quite detailed. They may describe, for example, the issues to be discussed in the process, the range of interests represented, the decision rule to be used, the goals of the process, and so forth. Chapters 1 and 2 describe these kinds of ground rules in more detail.

For ground rules governing a single meeting, we suggest guidelines such as the following.

- One person speaks at a time.
- No side conversations.
- No personal attacks (i.e., criticize ideas, not people).
- Listen as an ally.
- Respect agreements about time (e.g., return from breaks promptly).
- Turn off beepers and cell phones.

Draft ground rules should be presented to a group at the outset of a meeting and revised according to participants' suggestions. When process problems arise during a meeting that are not covered by the ground rules, participants should be asked to suggest additional ground rules to prevent the problems from recurring.

Determining the Decision Rule

Meeting planners must be prepared to suggest a decision rule for the meeting, that is, to recommend *how* a group will make decisions (e.g., by consensus, by majority vote). Their recommendation should be discussed with group members at the beginning of the meeting. When people have had a role in determining how decisions are to be made, they are more likely to support the outcomes of a process. When consensus building is the prevailing method of decision making, a group must agree on a definition of *consensus*. Participants in one meeting may want it to mean that everyone in the group must actively support a decision, for example. Those in another meeting might agree to move forward with an agreement even if there are one or two holdouts. (See Chapter 8 for more on decision rules.)

Meeting planners and participants should also clarify what will happen if consensus can't be reached, that is, who the fallback decision makers will be. In a hierarchical organization, the fallback is usually an individual; in a horizontal organization, a majority vote; and in public sector consensus building efforts, the fallback is often a formal decision-making body (such as a public agency or a court). It is often the threat of having to rely on the fallback method of decision making that keeps participants engaged in the search for mutually agreeable solutions.

Arranging the Meeting Space

The physical environment in which a group meets can contribute a great deal to a meeting's success or failure. Facilitators and convenors ought to choose a location and room arrangement that serve the purpose of the meeting. If major conflicts or acute differences are likely to erupt among participants, for example, the location of the meeting ought to be in a place perceived by all as "neutral territory." Uncomfortable seating and inadequate lighting interfere with the ability of people to concentrate on the tasks at hand. Lots of wall space is generally needed to display the group memory.

The meeting room should be set up in a way that suggests a flexible, problem-solving orientation. Ideally, seats should be arranged in a semicircle or "horseshoe," facing a blank wall where the group memory can be hung. Tables should be avoided (unless participants will be required to review printed materials), as they force a semicircle to be larger and create a more formal atmosphere. A semicircle, especially one without tables, permits people to see each other without having to turn around. It also decreases the possibility that one individual will dominate the meeting space by being the only person to face the group, as in a traditional lecture setting. If participants insist on tables, try to locate long, narrow ones and arrange them in a "U" shape, allowing room for the facilitator to get inside the "U" and physically "control" the space.

Some people prefer seats that are arranged in a circle or rectangle. While this setup encourages eye contact, it also increases the risk that participants will be drawn into arguments or get "stuck" on fixed positions. This can occur because people in a circle become focused on each other—on each person's words and personality—rather than on the group memory, where ideas are captured in a depersonalized way so that people can focus on the task at hand. Rows of seats set up "theater style" do not allow for eye contact and therefore discourage collaborative interaction altogether. Likewise, a room filled with numerous small, round tables does not allow for full-group interaction and encourages people with similar viewpoints and interests to cluster together.

■ *During the Meeting: Attitudes, Behaviors, and Tools*

Once a meeting has been appropriately planned, the facilitator can focus on what to do during the meeting. Many other books provide extensive detail on "how to facilitate" (see, e.g., Doyle & Straus, 1982; Kaner, 1996; Schwarz, 1994). Also, numerous organizations offer multiday training programs that teach facilitation skills. This one section cannot describe in great depth all the skills and techniques facilitators use to help a group build consensus during a meeting. We have chosen, therefore, to focus on the attitudes, behaviors, and skills we believe are most important in facilitating consensus building meetings. Attitudes and behaviors are crucial because a facilitator's mind-set can have a major impact on a group's ability to reach agreement. The first part of this section describes some of the most essential. The second part of the section describes the tools we believe are important. These are organized into preventions and interventions. The section also describes some common facilitation challenges and how to avoid or handle them.

Attitudes and Behaviors

Facilitators' mental models about how conflicts can be resolved and consensus can be reached have as much influence on outcomes as the techniques they use. This section describes some of the most useful, perhaps even essential, mind-sets required for successful face-to-face consensus building.

Believe in the Possibility of Consensus

A facilitator who is convinced of the ability of groups to reach consensus decisions and solve problems creatively can have a substantial and positive impact on a group. An effective facilitator knows that a consensus building process can end in a mutually agreeable solution, with relationships among participants strengthened. This attitude helps a group to maintain confidence when a process looks as if it is headed toward collapse. A facilitator who enters a meeting with the belief that consensus will be very difficult to achieve may inadvertently convey those fears to the group, which, in turn, may bring those concerns to fruition.

Value Diversity and Conflict

An effective facilitator knows that diversity of opinion and conflict are useful in working toward consensus. When multiple stakeholders come together in a dialogue, describe their own points of view, and listen to others do the same, they often become better able to articulate their interests, rather than remaining locked into their initial positions. Ultimately, they may find mutually beneficial solutions that meet all of their interests. But the process of moving toward these kinds of breakthroughs is not always harmonious. Differences in viewpoint inevitably come out into the open, arguments may erupt, people may get upset. A facilitator must recognize these conflicts as simply part of the process.

A consensus building process in Colorado provides an excellent example of a case in which the facilitators, as well as participants, had to learn to value and deal constructively with serious conflict (see Case 14). The purpose of the process was to build agreement on policies and funding priorities for preventing the spread of HIV and AIDS in Colorado. It brought together representatives of the state health department, health professionals, gay rights organizations, conservative "family values" groups, African American and Hispanic communities, and others—more than 100 people altogether. The issues being discussed were literally of life-and-death importance, and participants' views on these issues were extremely polarized. The potential for conflict erupting during the meetings was very high. Anticipating this, the facilitators taught participants early in the process how to raise difficult issues and deal productively with the conflict that resulted. They gave participants 10 ideas for how to handle conflict. Among them were "Be clear with yourself about your real concerns," "Use 'I' messages. Avoid blaming, finger-pointing, etc.," and "Everyone has a right to the way they feel. Work to accept other people's strong feelings as well as your own." By sharing these facilitative behaviors with participants, the facilitators showed that they valued conflict and diversity and that participants could work through conflict effectively.

Listen as an Ally

A facilitator has an opportunity to model the good listening skills that participants ought to use in interacting with each other. A facilitator should listen attentively to all participants and express empathy with their viewpoints, taking care not to appear to favor the ideas of some people over others. It is also important that a facilitator be open-minded to new ideas, no matter how outlandish or inflammatory, and look for the value in each contribution. By demonstrating this behavior, facilitators often find that individuals who come to a process with a reputation as "problem people" are those who are most passionate or even knowledgeable about an issue, but have not yet found a constructive way to make a contribution. A sensitive and creative facilitator often discovers that these individuals ultimately become some of the most committed supporters of a process, because it offers them an opportunity to be heard and understood.

Let the Group Do Its Work

"Remember that the job of reaching consensus belongs to the group, not to the facilitator."

An effective facilitator always remembers that the job of reaching consensus belongs to the group, not to the facilitator. Members of a group must take responsibility for developing good solutions. If a facilitator presses too hard toward agreement, a group may wrongly place the burden of consensus building on the shoulders of the facilitator. A facilitator might then become overly invested in advancing a particular solution and forget that his or her job is to manage the process. It is sometimes difficult for facilitators to "back off," because they may feel they are not doing their job well if a group does not reach consensus. But there is no 1:1 correlation between a good process and a consensus result, and it is the group members' responsibility to achieve consensus, not the facilitator's.

In the HIV/AIDS prevention case in Colorado, the facilitators came up with a unique and effective way to put the responsibility for the process onto the group. The first few meetings involved full-group discussion in which a facilitator called on people to speak. The group was so large, however (more than 100 people), and participants were so eager to talk, that many became frustrated and felt that the facilitator was not calling on them quickly enough. The facilitators decided that they needed to put group members more directly in control of the process. At the next meeting, they arranged the chairs in concentric circles, with a small table and four chairs at the center of the circles. They made aisles in the concentric circles, so people could move down to the small table easily. The facilitators explained the new process to the participants: "If you've got something to say, come sit in a chair. There are four chairs, and four of you can talk with one another—loudly, so we all can hear it. When you're done, get out of the chair. If you see somebody waiting . . . make room for them. You don't have to be called on. You don't have to raise your hand." This system put the responsibility for the meeting directly on the group. People had to take the initiative to walk up to the table to speak. Those at the table were responsible for watching to see if anyone was waiting and give up their seat at the appropriate time. A facilitator sat at the small table, too, to make sure the discussion stayed on track, but the responsibility for running the discussion was no longer his alone. This technique might not work for all groups, but in this circumstance it proved to be just what the group needed.[5]

Do Not Be Defensive

Group members may sometimes criticize a facilitator's actions or words. Because a facilitator's job is to serve the group and not his or her own ego, he or she needs to accept and legitimize such comments and resist becoming defensive. Rather than pushing back against such criticisms, in fact, a facilitator can use the energy of the group and redirect it, in a manner similar to that used in the martial arts, such as judo or tai chi. For example, if a group wants to pursue a direction that a facilitator thinks will be unhelpful, he or she can first offer a view on where such a path might lead. But if a group insists on proceeding, the facilitator should simply "go with the flow." If the group's direction proves to be faulty, the facilitator's credibility is strengthened. If the group is proven right, the facilitator's respectful and sincere acknowledgment of that fact enhances his or her credibility as neutral and impartial.

In the HIV/AIDS prevention case, the lead facilitator had to be careful not to take offense when people were unhappy with the way early meetings were proceeding (before they implemented the "four chairs" idea). The participants were clearly directing their anger at him. "Suddenly it was all my fault," he recalled. But he did not react. Instead, he agreed with them and affirmed their right to criticize him. He said, "Yeah, we've got to fix this process, and you've got to fix me and make sure that I'm doing this well." This enabled the group to move forward in a more productive manner.

Teach about Problem Solving and Conflict Resolution

One of the most positive side effects of face-to-face consensus building is that participants learn constructive problem-solving and conflict resolution techniques and behaviors. To make sure this learning takes place, facilitators should always explain the rationale behind any interventions they make and elaborate on problem-solving concepts as appropriate. This demystifies the consensus building process for group members and allows them to internalize many useful mind-sets, tools, and techniques.

A group may learn, for example, that there is no single, "best" way to resolve problems. Through an attitude of openness and willingness to tolerate lengthy and complex discussions, a facilitator demonstrates a heuristic, rather than algorithmic, approach to problem solving. The former is flexible and problem focused. The latter is more systematic, but less responsive to changing circumstances or local contexts. These two approaches can be illustrated through an example of finding a lost contact lens. An algorithmic approach to finding the lens might involve breaking the room into 1-foot-by-1-foot squares and searching up and down each row until the lens was or was not found. A heuristic orientation would involve using a variety of intuitive approaches, such as thinking about where one was last aware of the lens, asking each person to search the floor right where he or she stands, turning off the lights and beaming a flashlight across the floor to see what glints, and so on. No single strategy will guarantee success, but each may produce immediate results. For most problems, there is no "right" solution and no "right" problem-solving method. Most consensus building efforts must be approached heuristically, and the facilitator must assist the group in being the "light on its feet" by addressing a problem using an number of heuristic strategies, one at a time.

Be Sensitive to Strategic Moments

A strategic moment is a point in a meeting where whatever has been happening has been completed or is not working. It is a time when something different must begin. Part of the art of facilitation is recognizing these strategic moments and knowing when to let go of a preplanned agenda and make a spontaneous suggestion. The more experienced the facilitator, the larger the repertoire of tools he or she will have from which to draw. A facilitator should be open and sensitive to the mood and flow of the meeting and, when strategic moments arise, suggest or ask for suggestions about how to move forward.

Remain Committed to a Mutually Agreeable Solution

As a group moves toward consensus, it is common for one or more people to harbor significant doubts about the emerging agreement. It is particularly important at this point that the facilitator resist the efforts of other participants to steamroll over the objections. Indeed, the facilitator's own wish for resolution may create a temptation to push too hard at this stage. The facilitator needs to be empathetic, focus intently on understanding the concerns of the objectors, and work with the group to find ways to successfully address those concerns. While group members may at first see such extra effort as only a frustrating delay, they are often able to forge better agreements in the end by patiently working through such difficulties.

Facilitative Tools: Preventions and Interventions

The most useful set of tools a facilitator possesses is what we call *preventions* and *interventions*. Preventions are the actions a facilitator takes before and during meetings to head off potential obstacles to success. Interventions are actions a facilitator can take to help a group get back on track during a meeting, after difficulties have occurred. The most skillful facilitators rely primarily on preventions; in a way, this makes their facilitation "invisible." After a meeting in which a facilitator was very skillful, participants will often leave saying, "That was a great meeting. I'm not sure we needed a facilitator." When a facilitator does not prepare well or makes mistakes, and then uses interventions to get back on track, participants are more aware of the role of facilitation and may compliment the facilitator on a job well done. Thus, a facilitator's best work may go unrecognized.

Preventions

The preventions described below include reaching key agreements with participants at the outset of a meeting, making process suggestions, and checking for agreement.

Up-front agreements. Facilitators have no formal power to control a group. It is only by building agreements among participants on various process decisions and then holding them to those agreements (at least until they choose to change them) that facilitators develop a measure of control—and even then always as a servant to the group. So, at the outset of a meeting, a facilitator must seek agreement on

> who is playing which roles in the meeting,
> the basic "contract" between the group and the facilitator and recorder,
> the desired outcomes for the meeting,
> the agenda (i.e., the flow or sequence of agenda items),
> the decision-making rule to be used, and
> the ground rules to govern the meeting.

A facilitator should come to a meeting with proposed ground rules, an agenda, desired outcomes, and so forth. (These proposals should be drafted before the meeting with the input of the convenor or leader and perhaps a few key participants.) The proposals should be posted on flip charts, and each should be discussed and revised, as needed, by participants at the beginning of the meeting. Armed with the group's approval of each item, the facilitator can proceed with confidence and authority. If discussions veer off on tangential topics, for example, a facilitator simply has to remind participants of the agenda they agreed to or the desired outcomes they are seeking, to bring them back on track. A group may need to spend a bit of time clarifying and revising these up-front agreements, but they can then move more quickly through the rest of the meeting. Up-front agreements are an example of the consensus building principle called "Go slow to go fast."

Suggest a process. An agenda typically sets forth the flow of a meeting in fairly broad brush strokes. It may describe what will be discussed and how (i.e., the basic process to be used), but in general terms. Many times during a meeting a facilitator will need to make suggestions about exactly what process to use to move forward. So, for example, an agenda may indicate the group should brainstorm potential solutions. During a meeting, then, the facilitator will need to suggest a way for the group to do this. Should participants just call out ideas for the recorder to capture? Should they use a round-robin format, in which each person proposes an idea in turn? Should the facilitator post multiple sheets of newsprint on the wall and have participants write their ideas on the paper themselves, all at once? To be effective, facilitators must acquire a large repertoire of facilitative interventions and consensus building tools and learn when to advise a group to employ each one. A good process suggestion can steer a group in a constructive direction and avoid polarization. A facilitator should not proceed with a particular process, however, until he or she has the consent of the group.

Checking for agreement. To determine if a group has reached consensus on a significant issue of substance, a facilitator should generally take the time to ask each participant for his or her approval. Often, facilitators check for agreement on major issues by phrasing the question as "Is this decision acceptable to you?" or "Can you live with this solution?"

On minor issues—little process agreements, for example—it's often best for a facilitator to ask for objections: "Any objections to moving on to the next issue? (Pause) OK. Let's move on." By framing these questions in the negative, silence is taken as approval, and the meeting can proceed quickly.

Facilitators may devise other creative ways to determine whether a group has reached agreement. In the HIV/AIDS pre-

vention case, the facilitators initiated a "thu
down, thumbs sideways" procedure. Whenever th
needed to check for consensus, on large or small issues, they a
to "see people's thumbs." Thumbs up meant the person was in
agreement. Thumbs sideways meant the person was not sure,
wanted to ask a question, or needed more information before
deciding. Thumbs down meant the person did not agree and did
not want the process to move forward until his or her concerns
were addressed. The group used this procedure hundreds of times
in the course of the eight-month process.

Interventions

The interventions described in this section include reflecting
questions back to a group, refocusing a group, using body language, employing escalating levels of intervention, and allowing
a group to "ebb and flow."

Reflect questions back to the group. One of the most useful
interventions a facilitator can employ is the *boomerang,* the
technique of reflecting a group's questions back to itself. A
facilitator can use the boomerang technique when he or she is
asked to offer an answer to a specific question or problem,
particularly those relating to the overall direction of the group
(i.e., "When are we going to be meeting again?" or even "Isn't
Option *A* really the only feasible way to go?"). Rather than
directly responding to the group's query, an effective facilitator
will "boomerang" the question back to the group: "I can't answer
that question for you; what do *you* think?" or "Who might have
an idea about that?" This technique keeps group members focused on the fact that they are responsible for the meeting, rather
than thinking of the facilitator as an expert.

Refocus the group. A second common intervention is to refocus
a discussion that has gone astray. For example, a facilitator may
need to refocus a group if too many side conversations are taking
place at one time. Simply saying, "Just a moment, one person at
a time" or "Let's hear Janet before Joe" sets the norm of holding
a single conversation among group members during a meeting. A
facilitator may also need to intervene to enforce any process
agreements that have been made, such as time limits on presentations or staying focused on one substantive issue at a time. Also,

comments about a group's general "demeanor" can help a group clarify difficulties, refocus, and move on. A facilitator might say, for example, "It's very quiet right now, what's going on?" And humor, of course—though never at anyone's expense—enables group members to relax and get back on track.

Use body language consciously. The conscious use of body language is a powerful intervention. When a facilitator goes from sitting to standing up, or from standing in front of a group to walking into the semicircle, group members suddenly become more aware of him or her and, consciously or not, begin to pay more attention to their own behavior. If a facilitator believes someone has spoken too long or too often, for example, a move toward the person often makes him or her aware of the situation and more likely to stop. Taking a few steps toward the group memory sheets encourages participants to reorient themselves to the task at hand.

"As a rule, facilitators should choose less confrontational interventions first, and escalate them as needed."

Escalate the levels of intervention. As a rule, facilitators should choose less confrontational interventions first, and escalate them as needed. For example, if an individual is dominating the discussion or intimidating others, a facilitator can first try to make eye contact with the person—a brief glare or a slightly raised eyebrow might be enough. If it isn't, the facilitator could stand up, which is usually sufficient to get someone's attention, or even walk partway toward the area where that individual is seated. If necessary, the facilitator could walk right up to the individual. If there is still no response, the facilitator could gently invite the person to stop (e.g., "Could you hold back for a moment while somebody else speaks?") At the highest levels of intervention, the facilitator could give the person feedback at a break, and, as a last resort, confront the issue directly and firmly in front of the group.

Allow a group to ebb and flow. One of the most important skills a facilitator can hone is to be sensitive to a group's ebb and flow. If a facilitator intervenes too frequently or holds the process reins too tightly, the group may arrive at a successful solution quite efficiently, but the level of participation and satisfaction with the process may be quite low. Members of a group may resent a facilitator who is too task oriented and may resist attempts to make them focus. Also, if a facilitator drives a group too hard through an agenda, the group will lack a sense of ownership in the result of their work.

Every group needs to go ramble a bit and then get back on track. Sometimes an active intervention can help, but sometimes the best "intervention" is to do nothing. A group often finds its own way back if a facilitator is able to keep quiet during silence, allow others to make suggestions rather than feeling obliged to rescue a process, ask open-ended questions, physically move away from the center or front of the group, and even move to its periphery and sit down.

Typical Meeting Problems

As a way of demonstrating how these interventions and preventions can be used in specific situations, this section describes some typical meeting problems and suggests how you, in the role of facilitator, might intervene.

Problem: One or several participants dominate the conversation, while others are silent.

Suggested interventions:
Ask questions of the silent participants, to get them involved. For example: "Do you have any comments on this subject, John?"

Make direct eye contact with or perhaps move a bit closer to the silent participant, as nonverbal ways of encouraging him or her to participate.

Suggest a process that will naturally get quiet participants to take part: "Let's go around the room and have each of you comment on this idea," or "Take a few minutes to talk to the person sitting next to you about your ideas as preparation for a group brainstorming session."

Make a general observation and then ask for a process suggestion: "I have noticed that a number of people have not been speaking up. Any suggestions about how we could encourage more balanced participation?"

Problem: Two or more participants have a disagreement. It escalates to the point where they are angry and abusive toward each other.

Suggested interventions:

Use your physical presence to de-escalate the situation. Move into the space between the two participants, getting them to focus on you rather than each other. Then move back to the group memory with a process suggestion that refocuses the participants' attention on the issues. For example, "It's clear that there are several different points of view here. Let's capture them on the flip chart before deciding how to proceed."

Remind participants about the ground rules. "Please remember our agreements about abstaining from personal attacks and listening as an ally before criticizing an idea."

Suggest a structured process that legitimizes and encourages both positive and negative comments. "Let's try to understand both sides of this issue. I suggest we first list all the 'positives' about this idea and then list all the 'concerns.' "

Problem: A participant becomes angry or verbally abusive toward you as facilitator.

Suggested interventions:

Do not be defensive. You are there to serve the group. Be responsive by listening actively and calmly to the concerns. Respond thoughtfully: "I'm sorry if I have offended you in any way. When I failed to see your attempts to get into the conversation you felt angry and manipulated. I apologize."

Use a sequence of interventions we call "accept, legitimize, deal with, or defer." First *accept* and acknowledge the criticism. "I hear that you have some concerns about how I am facilitating." Then *legitimize* the concerns. "I asked you all to let me know if you ever had any problems with how I was playing my role, so thank you for the feedback." Then you face a strategic moment in which you can either *defer* the concern or *deal with* it directly. Try to defer first. "Now that I understand your concern, I will try to change my behavior so as not to repeat the mistake. Are you willing to continue and see how it goes for the next hour or so?" If the response is no, then you have to deal with the issue directly. In this case, you might want to move to the next suggested intervention.

Check with the group. Just because one person is angry with the facilitation doesn't mean everyone is. Often, other group members will come to your defense if given the opportunity. "I understand that Terrell has some concerns. How do the rest of you feel about how this meeting is going?"

Finally, remember that it is more important for the group to do its work than for you to remain as facilitator. If the group seems to agree with Terrell, offer to step aside and let someone else facilitate. Just the offer may be enough to demonstrate a desire to serve the group and no need to remain in the driver's seat.

Problem: Two participants with a long history of animosity toward each other cannot seem to get past an old disagreement, and that dynamic affects the whole group.

Suggested interventions:

Try coaching the participants individually at a break or between meetings. Point out how certain behaviors heighten conflict, and suggest more constructive ways of participating. "Jonathan, when you bring up that old issue, it only sets Yvonne off. Can you try to stick to the current problem?"

Intervene quickly when positional language is used and ask for the underlying interest. "Yvonne, can you explain what your concern is? What criteria would a solution have to meet in order to be acceptable to you?"

Discuss with the group the problem of adversarial inter-actions, and ask for suggested ground rules to guide constructive discourse. "There is a lot of history of conflict in this room. Can you think of any process agreements we could make to try to prevent the group from getting mired in old disagreements?"

Point out how the two participants are "pushing each other's buttons" and, if appropriate, use humor to gently remind them to work constructively. "Wait a moment, Yvonne. Don't go in that direction. You know where it will lead. Try to make your point without criticizing Jonathan's."

Problem: Technical experts begin a presentation that is far too complicated for most participants to understand.

Suggested preventions and interventions:

As a prevention, talk with all presenters before a meeting to explain who will be at the meeting and what their level of expertise on the subject is. Clarify what participants hope to learn from the presentation, and ask what exactly the presenter plans to say. Try to reach agreement on how long the talk will be, how much time will be set aside for questions and answers, and what role the presenter will play during the discussion after the talk (e.g., will he or she facilitate or simply stand ready to answer questions?). Review all presentations in advance, if possible.

If you haven't spoken in depth with the presenter in advance, have a quick conversation just before the meeting starts to discuss these points. It may be possible to head off any serious problems. Also check to see if the presenter will take clarifying questions during the talk, especially if participants are not following what is being presented.

During the meeting, if it is obvious that the expert is losing the audience, offer to record or diagram the main points. This permits you as facilitator to ask the "dumb" questions about what the presenter is saying rather than relying on the participants to do it.

At the end of the presentation, solicit questions and record them all on flip charts before letting the expert respond. This can keep the expert from getting defensive about each question and also allows him or her to hear the full range of topics that need to be covered.

Problem: Participants become frustrated because they feel progress is not being made and they will never reach agreement.

Suggested interventions:

Be positive and upbeat. Remember that the facilitator's attitude has an important impact on the group. Legitimize the frustration. "This is a challenging problem, and I know this is hard work." But remind participants about their progress and encourage them to stay the course. "Hang on and we'll get through this."

Boomerang the concerns back to the group by asking for process suggestions. "I hear that some of you are frustrated by the rate at which we are proceeding. Any suggestions about how we could speed things up?"

Give the group a mini-lesson in consensus building. "As we discussed at the beginning of this consensus building effort, it's important to 'go slow to go fast.' If you don't agree on the issues, it will be hard to agree on the solutions. The final consensus will be built on the backs of many small agreements. So recognize that we are making progress, and we need to keep plugging along."

Problem: The meeting lacks energy, participants seem bored, and some are even dozing off.

Suggested interventions:

Counter the lack of energy in the group by being a more energetic facilitator. Stand up, move around, and be more animated.

Comment on the situation and ask the group what is going on. "The group's energy level seems really low right now. What's going on? Do we need to take a break?"

Sometimes large groups don't offer enough opportunity for participation, so participants get bored. Suggest breaking into smaller groups to work on specific issues. Small groups give each participant more of an opportunity and a responsibility to contribute.

If it seems appropriate, suggest an "energizer," such as taking a walk around the block or conducting a team-building exercise. Just a minute or two of doing something physical can reenergize a group.

Problem: Participants come late or begin slipping out of the room before the meeting is over.

Suggested preventions and interventions:

At the beginning of a meeting, ask, "Does anyone have to leave early?" Those who don't speak up are then committed to stay; those who do speak up feel obliged to give an explanation to the group.

Begin the meeting on time, and promise participants it will end on time as well. They may be less likely to slip out early if they know the facilitator is conscious of the clock and will end the meeting promptly.

In a multimeeting process, propose and seek agreement on a ground rule that participants will arrive on time and stay until the end of each meeting. Explain that for the process to work, it is critical that everyone be in the room at the same time. If participants disregard the ground rule, comment on what is going on and ask for process suggestions from the group. "I've been noticing that some of you have been coming late and leaving early. It's going to be hard to build consensus without all the stakeholders in the room. Any suggestions about how we can make this process work more effectively?"

Problem: In a meeting that is part of a larger consensus building process, a participant (Bill) storms out of the room, announcing his intention to quit the process as the door slams shut.

Suggested interventions:

If possible, ask Bill to state his concerns before leaving. "Before you go, can you let us know why you are leaving? What's not working for you?"

If the door slams without a response, ask the group for suggestions about how to repair the damage. "Does anyone know why Bill is so upset? Any thoughts about how we can get him back in the process? Who would be willing to talk to him after this meeting?"

Try to set up a one-on-one conversation with Bill before the next meeting. Don't be defensive. Listen to his concerns and try to get him to suggest ways to modify the consensus building process to meet his needs. Bill's issues may be legitimate and his process ideas constructive.

If Bill cannot be convinced to return to the process, and his interests are represented by others at the table, it may be best to simply let him leave and go on with the process. If he is a key stakeholder, however, and his departure tips the balance of interests at the table, the facilitator should speak with the convenor or group leader and assess whether or not the process should continue without him.

Problem: Two or more participants in a consensus building process have a very different understanding of what happened at the previous meeting. Conflict erupts, as one participant accuses the other of backtracking.

Suggested interventions:

Try to shift the focus from the two participants to the whole group. Ask other group members for their understanding of the previous agreements. "There seems to be some disagreement about what agreements we made during the last meeting. Who has a clear recollection of what we decided?"

If possible, consult the flip charts or the meeting summary from the last meeting to remind the participants of the actual words used. This is one of the most powerful uses of the group memory.

Do not spend too much time dwelling on the past. Rather, try to rebuild agreement in the present. If a stakeholder cannot live with an agreement made at a previous meeting, the problem would have emerged sooner or later. It is best to stop now, listen to the concerns, and try to forge a new agreement.

■ After the Meeting

Most consensus building processes involve a sequence of meetings, in which each meeting builds on the work of the previous one. For a group to avoid backsliding and spending excessive time reviewing what happened before, meeting organizers should provide participants with a record of each meeting. We have found the most useful documentation to be the group memory itself. The handwritten sheets of newsprint contain "memory hooks" to remind meeting attendees of what was said at each point in the meeting. The diagrams, the placement of comments on the page, and even the misspellings all carry clues that jog participants' memories. Because the group memory was created in front of all the participants, it is hard to dispute its accuracy.

It can therefore be helpful to provide participants with a copy of the group memory as soon as possible after a meeting. Fortunately, there are several new technologies that make it easy to copy sheets of newsprint onto 8½-by-11-inch pieces of paper. Several types of flatbed scanners are now sold, for example, that can scan a flip-chart page and produce a good-quality reduction. Also available are high-quality, digital cameras that can take photos of flip-chart pages. These photos are captured in digital form on a computer disk and can easily be cropped, enlarged, and printed on a computer printer. If these technologies are not available, a typed version of the group memory is acceptable.

As an alternative, old-fashioned meeting minutes can be drafted. These can be especially helpful for people who did not attend the meeting. When writing minutes, a reporter typically uses the group memory as a basis, but puts the ideas into complete sentences and fills in details as necessary. He or she should avoid paraphrasing and should try to capture the flow of the discussion as well as the ultimate agreements.

In addition to the group memory or meeting minutes, it is often useful to organize the "data" produced during one meeting to assist with problem solving in the next. For example, a facilitator might sort all the agreements that have been made previously, or organize and restate all of the definitions of the problem. This information can be charted and presented at the beginning of the following meeting for review and revision, serving as a strong foundation for the next steps in the consensus building process.

It is also helpful, after a meeting is over, for the facilitator to call the convenor, group leader, and several key participants to get their thoughts on how the meeting went. Were they satisfied with what was accomplished? What did they think went well? What did not go well? What would they like to see done differently next time? Feedback on these kinds of questions can help a facilitator continually improve his or her craft.

■ *Conclusion*

High-quality, consensus-based agreements do not just spring to life. They are the cumulative result of a series of conscious choices made by groups of people—choices about the procedures and ground rules under which to discuss key issues, choices about how best to meet everyone's interests, and choices about ways to implement and monitor those agreements. People make these choices in meetings. By following the guidance in this chapter, and through lots of trial and error, facilitators and group members will be able to plan and run *effective* meetings—meetings that enable group members to focus on the substance of a problem and steadily work toward consensus.

■ *Notes*

1. The Interaction Method is described in detail in *How to Make Meetings Work* by Michael Doyle and David Straus (1982). Interaction Associates has employed and taught this method in a wide range of community and organizational settings since 1969.

2. See Figure 3.6 in Chapter 3 for a sample list of principles of collaboration.

3. We have found that it usually takes the same amount of time to prepare for a meeting as the length of the meeting itself.

4. Indeed, the concept of *graphic recording*, in which recorders use huge sheets of butcher paper and capture ideas using sketches and symbols more than words, is gaining popularity (Ball, 1998).

5. This technique is called the *Samoan circle*. It was popularized by facilitator Larry Aggens.

■ *References*

Ball, G. (1998, April). Graphic facilitation focuses a group's thoughts. *Consensus,* p. 2.

Doyle, M., & Straus, D. (1982). *How to make meetings work.* New York: Jove.

Kaner, S. (1996). *Facilitator's guide to participatory decision-making.* Philadelphia: New Society.

Schwarz, R. M. (1994). *The skilled facilitator: Practical wisdom for developing effective groups.* San Francisco: Jossey-Bass.

8

PRODUCING CONSENSUS

■ *Sarah McKearnan*
■ *David Fairman*

For consensus building groups, it is often true that "90 percent of the work gets done in the last 10 percent of the time." Whether the issue is siting a local landfill or negotiating a global treaty, consensus building processes often become far more challenging as they enter their final stages. In this chapter, we present a basic framework for building consensus in groups. Then we explore the obstacles that emerge as groups try to produce consensus, and we offer techniques and strategies for overcoming them. Throughout the chapter, we use the story of a consensus building group that is nearing the end of its work to illustrate both the obstacles and strategies for dealing with them. We begin by joining a meeting of the Regional Health and Human Services Task Force (a composite of several consensus building groups with whom we have worked).

■ Prologue: The Task Force Meeting

There were raised eyebrows, frowns, and a few groans around the table as the members of the Regional Health and Human Services Task Force listened to the comments of three of their colleagues. The task force was meeting to review its final draft strategic plan, the product of 11 months' hard work. After an extensive review of the region's current health and human services programs, the group had identified overlaps and gaps in program coverage and proposed several new initiatives, including a new regional health care facility. Under the state legislation that created the task force, the strategic plan was due in three weeks, at the opening of the legislative session.

The task force facilitator, Jan Philips, had asked task force members to begin by reporting back to the group on the way their constituencies had responded to the final draft.

The first comment was from Bob Salva, first selectman of the town of Harrington. In Bob's usual terse style, he said, "Folks, the selectmen agreed with me last night that we can't live with the Wilton site for the health clinic. It's just got to go in Harrington."

The second comment was from Barry Dinsmore, advocacy director for the Provider Council, a group of the region's major human service agencies with an interest in closer coordination of health and human service delivery. Barry was one of the less active task force members. "I know this is going to cause some problems, but I finally got to talk to my executive committee at the end of last week, and our chairman is not happy with the direction things have been going. I've tried to keep him in the loop, but this was pretty much his first review in nine months. I think we're going to have to take a second look at a few things."

The third comment was from Wilma Carter, executive vice president of Guardian Health Associates. Guardian was the region's leading health maintenance organization (HMO) and the most likely investor in a new clinic. "I still don't know what we're going to do if enrollment at the new clinic falls below what we've projected. We ran the numbers a few more times in the last couple of days, and the clinic siting team is a little nervous."

The task force faces three problems that often bedevil efforts to produce consensus. These three participants are saying:

1. I can't live with the package agreement that most other members in the group are ready to accept.
2. I have to backtrack on what I said before. The current package won't meet my constituency's needs.
3. I can't commit unless I have more assurance about what will happen in the future.

These problems are especially challenging because the group is nearly out of time and resources for deliberation. Many participants want to submit their recommendations soon, even if not everyone agrees to them. These circumstances raise an additional challenge that crosscuts all the others: Group members are going to have trouble controlling the strong emotions they feel as they come to the end of a long, intensive negotiation.

The challenges that the Regional Health and Human Services Task Force faces are typical ones for consensus building groups nearing the end of their deliberations. To manage them successfully, both participants and facilitators need a deeper understanding of why it is hard to move from inventing options and generating potential "package" agreements (i.e., agreements that cover all the issues of concern) to reaching consensus on a particular package. They also need practical advice on strategies and techniques they can use to produce consensus in this final stage.

This chapter begins by presenting a framework for understanding the stages in building consensus, and the obstacles that confront groups in the final stages of the process.

■ Producing Consensus: An Analytic Framework

In this section, we define consensus, present the stages of consensus building (preparing, creating value, and producing consensus), and highlight the particular obstacles that groups face as they seek to produce consensus. We also outline three strategies we recommend for overcoming these obstacles:

- Creating additional joint gains by trading across issues
- Using fair standards to distribute joint gains
- Using dispute resolution procedures to handle impasse and the strong emotions that come with it

A Definition of Consensus

"We strongly recommend that groups *seek* consensus, but do not *require* it to reach closure."

Before discussing the process of producing consensus, we should be clear about what we mean by the term *consensus*. We define consensus as "agreement among all participating stakeholders." A consensus agreement is one that all stakeholders participating in a consensus building process can accept. We strongly recommend that consensus building groups *seek* consensus, but do not *require* it to reach closure on the group's recommendations or decisions. Groups that require unanimous agreement risk being held hostage to their most demanding member(s). Groups that seek consensus but do not achieve it should acknowledge dissent, without forfeiting the opportunity to move forward with recommendations or actions that a very large majority of members do support.

Although we argue that consensus should not be a requirement, much of our advice in this chapter is aimed at ensuring that consensus building groups "go the extra mile" to meet the concerns and interests of all participating stakeholders. Before a group gives up on the goal of consensus, its members should make full use of the strategies that we discuss in this chapter.[1]

The Challenge of Producing Consensus

Why is it often so difficult for groups to produce consensus in the final stage of their work? One easy explanation is that the participants have been inattentive during the early stages. Sometimes participants only begin to "take the process seriously" at the end, when it becomes clear they are nearly out of time and they still want to reach agreement. Another possibility is that participants have used a "hard bargaining" approach to their deliberations—staking out extreme opening positions, withholding information, making little effort to learn the interests of others, and trading small concessions. If so, they may reach the end of the process with little more in the way of information and ideas than they had at the start, and far less trust in each other's good faith.

The participants in these situations are in trouble because they have not prepared effectively and because they have not used their deliberations to create joint gains. As a result, they have an enormous amount of work to do in a very short time if they want to produce consensus.

We think that the failure to prepare well and the failure to deliberate effectively are, indeed, serious problems. They are not, however, our primary concern in this chapter. Instead, we want to examine a set of obstacles that even the best-prepared and most creative groups face when they seek to produce consensus. These problems arise when there are real and only partially resolvable conflicts of interest among stakeholders.

To understand the problems that confront even the "best" groups, we will review how a well-managed group proceeds through the three main stages of consensus building negotiations: preparing to seek consensus, creating joint gains, and producing consensus. For each stage, we present a *best practice* approach to consensus building, using *mutual gains* principles and strategies.[2]

Preparing to Seek Consensus

A consensus building process begins when a group of individuals comes together to seek consensus on a set of issues of common concern. Most (but not necessarily all) of the individuals who participate in consensus building processes represent a constituency. Some representatives will come to the table with the authority to commit their constituencies, others will not. (See Chapter 6, on representation, for more on this topic.)

For convenience, we will refer to all the individuals and constituencies whose interests are represented in a consensus building process as *stakeholders*. We will call the individuals and representatives who are actively involved in deliberations and negotiations the *participants* in the process.

To be well prepared, participants should, before the group's first meeting,

- Learn something about the issues and develop a set of questions about issues that they do not fully understand;
- Develop an initial sense of their interests on each issue and try to learn something about the interests of other stakeholders;
- Begin thinking about options (things that the group could do to address an issue) that might meet their own interests and those of other stakeholders;
- Make a preliminary assessment of their best alternative to a negotiated agreement (BATNA): the best outcome they could reasonably expect if the consensus building group is unable to reach an agreement; and
- Based on their assessment of their BATNA,[3] make a preliminary attempt to define their minimum requirements for agreement.

Participants who formally represent constituencies need to do this preparation in consultation with those who have the authority to define the constituency's interests: the leaders and/or members of the constituent group. Representatives and their constituencies also need to define a representative's decision-making authority and fashion procedures by which representatives will keep their constituencies informed during the negotiations.

As a process continues, participants may need to revisit each of these preparation tasks. As they learn more about the issues and the interests of other stakeholders and begin to explore options, they may need to rethink their own interests, BATNAs, and minimum requirements for agreement. By starting prepared and staying prepared, participants can dramatically increase a group's effectiveness.

Creating Joint Gains

When participants are well prepared, they can engage in the most exciting and expansive stage of the consensus building process: creating joint gains. Stakeholders create joint gains by developing options and packages that meet their own interests as well as the interests of other stakeholders.

To maximize joint gains, participants need to go through several steps. These may happen sequentially or simultaneously, and participants may go through them once or many times.

Exploring interests. Participants express their concerns and goals and learn the concerns and goals of others with regard to each of the issues that is the focus of the group's work. The goal of exploration is to understand not only each other's *positions* (answers to the question "what do you want?") but also each other's *interests* (answers to the question "why do you want that?").

By asking and explaining why, participants may discover that their initial positions may not be the only or the best way to meet their underlying interests. For example, a mayor may state his position as "the health clinic has to go in my town." If other participants ask why, it may turn out that the mayor's underlying interest is for the clinic to be easily accessible to the large number of elderly residents in the town. Knowing this, the group can consider other ways of meeting the mayor's interest, for example, by providing low-cost transportation from the town to the clinic or providing a mobile health van that visits the neighborhoods where elderly persons are concentrated.

Joint fact-finding. Participants identify questions of fact that they need to answer to understand an issue better or to understand how a proposal made by someone else might affect them. They seek agreement on the methods and people that will be needed to answer these questions. When the fact-finding process has produced new information, participants review and interpret it together. The advantage of a joint fact-finding approach is that it helps separate the process of generating information from the process of advocating interests. (See Chapter 9 for more on joint fact-finding.)

Inventing options without committing. Participants brainstorm specific proposals on each of the issues, with the understanding that no one is being asked to agree to anything at this stage. In responding to each other's ideas, they weed out proposals that are "nonstarters" and refine potentially viable proposals into options that could meet the interests of all or most stakeholders.

For example, the HMO may propose that it should own and operate the health clinic, with an advisory board of local elected officials, regional health and human services providers and service users, and state regulatory agencies. This might be the best way to meet the HMO's underlying interest on the issue of how the clinic should be managed, but it might not meet the interests of some other stakeholders.

If the HMO representative were a joint-gains negotiator, however, she wouldn't present this proposal as a bottom-line demand *at this stage in the process.* Instead, she would present it as an option: "What if we took responsibility for all management decisions, with regular input from some kind of regional advisory body? That would meet our interest in integrating this clinic into our management structure. Would it meet your interest in having some continuing input into the clinic's operations?" Other participants could respond to this option by saying, "That might work for us, if . . ." or "That's probably no good for us, unless. . . ."

Inventing options without committing liberates participants to "think outside the box." By stating their ideas as "what ifs" and their responses as "maybe, if . . . ," participants create and maintain a spirit of creativity and joint problem solving. By avoiding premature commitments, they can continue generating new information and ideas. Sometimes (surprisingly often, in our experience) they develop options that meet their interests better than their own initial proposals!

Creating packages. Once they have developed options that could meet the interests of all or most stakeholders on each issue, participants need to put together one or more *packages*. A package is set of proposals that addresses most or all of the issues that are the focus of the group's work. For example, if the issues were the location, design, staffing, and budget of a new health clinic, the group could create one or two packages that address all of these issues.

In creating packages, stakeholders may be able to resolve some disagreements by making trade-offs across issues. For example, the HMO and the Provider Council may disagree about the location and the staffing of the clinic. If the HMO cares more about location and the Provider Council cares more about staffing, however, they may both be able to meet their *most important interests* by agreeing on a package that includes the HMO's preferred option on location and the Provider Council's preferred option on staffing. The stakeholders could not have resolved this disagreement by focusing on either of the two issues in isolation. It is only by trading across issues that they are able to reach agreement.

To summarize, when participants are well prepared, they have the potential to deliberate efficiently and effectively. When they use the joint-gains approach in their deliberations—by exploring interests, engaging in joint fact-finding, inventing options without committing, and developing packages across issues—they can create packages that have the potential to meet the interests of all stakeholders.

At this point, let us assume that participants have "done it right" by using the mutual-gains approach in the first two stages of the consensus building process. We now explore why the last stage of our framework—producing consensus—is so difficult, even for well-prepared groups that have already created joint gains and put together a package that has the support of almost everyone involved.

Producing Consensus

Even when a group has developed a package that seems promising because it meets or exceeds the minimum requirements of almost all stakeholders on all issues, it will often face at least one of the three situations that were troubling the task force at the beginning of the chapter:

1. A stakeholder can't live with the package deal that most other members in the group are ready to accept. In the case of the task force, we will show that the underlying problem is *unmet interests.*
2. A representative has to backtrack on an earlier statement that the proposed package meets his or her constituency's needs. In the case of the task force, we will show that the problem is *unrealistic aspirations.* We are also going to assume that poor communication between the representative and the constituency has contributed to the problem.
3. A stakeholder can't commit unless he or she has more assurance about what will happen in the future. Here, we will show that the underlying problem is the need for a *contingent agreement* to protect the stakeholder against a specific kind of risk.

Faced with one or more of these problems, what can the participants do? There are three strategies worth pursuing:

- Create more joint gains.
- Use fair standards to divide joint gains.
- Use dispute resolution procedures to handle impasse and the strong emotions that come with it.

Group members will need to use all three of these strategies to resolve each of the problems identified above. We reiterate: There is *not* a one-to-one match between the three problems (unmet interests, unrealistic aspirations, and the need for contingent agreements) and the three strategies. On the contrary, it is often necessary to use more than one of the strategies to deal with *each* problem.

The remainder of this chapter explores the three strategies in depth, with the aim of helping stakeholders and facilitators produce consensus. Immediately below, we present an overview of the strategies. In the sections that follow, we use the case of the Regional Health and Human Services Task Force to show how these strategies can be applied to deal with the problems of unmet interests, unrealistic aspirations, and the need for contingent agreements. We will also identify several ways for dealing with strong emotions, a problem that cuts across all of the others.

Create more joint gains. By the time a group is ready to seek agreement on a particular package, participants may feel that they have done all they can to meet each other's interests. No matter how effective they were during the "inventing without committing" stage of the dialogue, however, some participants may report that the package does not meet their interests on one or more key issues. The fact that unmet needs become apparent close to the end of the negotiation is not surprising; participants have, up until that point, rightly been concentrating on "enlarging the pie" rather than dividing it up. Only when it is time to consolidate agreement will some participants realize that there is not enough in what is being proposed to satisfy their constituencies' most important interests.

At this point, frustration and impatience may well appear. It may be tempting for the majority who can live with the current package to gloss over the concerns of the minority who can't, for fear that any dissension will lead to an erosion of majority support. Alternatively, a group may be tempted to start over, reopening the negotiation from "ground zero."

A more effective strategy for producing consensus is to work on improving what the group has already developed, by focusing on remaining areas of disagreement and searching for additional joint gains to resolve those sticking points.

Joint gains can be sought in one of two places: (1) within the package, on issues on which some participants may be willing to make trade-offs to bring others into the agreement; and (2) beyond the package, on issues the group as a whole has not yet considered. Participants can also trade across differences in their assessment of future risks, by making contingent agreements. Finally, participants can reduce the cost of the commitments stakeholders are being asked to make by formulating their package as a "first round" agreement—one that can be fully reopened at a later date. We will discuss each of these strategies in more detail.

Use fair standards to divide joint gains. After a group has searched as hard as possible for joint gains, it may develop a package that meets the interests of all the stakeholders. In fact, it may develop more than one package that meets the interests of the stakeholders. For example, a site-selection process may produce two sites that are acceptable to all.

Although the availability of more than one potentially acceptable package is certainly good news, it may also create serious difficulties for the group. Each stakeholder is likely to prefer one of the possible packages. Some stakeholders may decide that it is in their interest to state that they "must have" the package that is closest to their aspirations, even if *either* package would meet their interests better than not having a site at all. Much of the hard work that a group has done to create potentially acceptable packages can be undone at a rapid pace if participants fight over which one to select.

There is no easy way to choose among multiple, potentially acceptable packages. Voting is one option, but it is likely to leave the minority feeling frustrated that they have lost the opportunity to secure the best possible deal for their constituents.

Another strategy—using objective standards and criteria—is more likely to help a group produce consensus. Participants should refer back to overarching goals, standards, or criteria that they agreed to at the outset of the process, or try to define them in the context of specific issues, as a way to decide among competing proposals.

For example, in trying to decide between three sites for a new health clinic, of which all seem like good options to most stakeholders, a group may decide that the cost of renovation, the suitability of the building for its new use, and its proximity to major transport corridors are the three most important criteria to use in selecting among the three. It can then rule out sites that are inferior on all three criteria. If there is still more than one site remaining, the group will have to decide which criterion should carry the most weight in the final siting decision.

This approach cannot resolve all conflicts, but it can help stakeholders clarify the underlying goals or criteria that drive their preferences. By focusing on objective criteria, the group can shift the focus from a competition among stakeholders to a search for balance among several legitimate goals.

Use dispute resolution procedures to resolve impasse. No matter how hard a group tries to craft a package that meets the interests of all stakeholders, it may find that one or a few continue to insist that their interests are not being met well enough. In situations in which one or a few stakeholders cannot live with the package that is favored by a large majority, a group needs to have some procedures and tools for dealing with strong emotions and for resolving the underlying impasse.

In situations like this, a facilitator can play a critical role both as an advocate for good communication and as a problem solver. First, a facilitator can periodically help the group refocus on the goal with which they began: seeking an agreement that maximizes joint gains and has the support of all stakeholders. A facilitator can also reinforce a group's commitment to respectful and constructive communication, not only by calling attention to violations of the group's ground rules but also by consciously modeling behaviors that suggest how participants should talk and listen to each other. Finally, when there are intense conflicts between two or more stakeholders, a facilitator can step in to resolve disputes.

The group as a whole should always work as hard as possible to address the concerns of those stakeholders who are not yet satisfied with the proposed package. Stakeholders who are not yet satisfied have an equal responsibility to make constructive proposals that could meet not only their interests but also the interests of all other stakeholders on the unresolved issue(s).

Despite the best efforts of all participants, there may come a time when a group has gone as far as it can toward meeting the interests of "holdouts" and still finds that some stakeholders can't live with the result. When no one can suggest a further improvement to break an impasse, participants should (1) use a non-unanimity decision rule to reach closure, and (2) think carefully about how to present dissenting views on the final agreement without damaging relationships or undermining support for the agreement.

■ *Applying the Strategies to Produce Consensus*

The following sections show how these strategies can be applied to deal with the problems we identified earlier. Each section begins by dramatizing one or more problems through the experience of the Health and Human Services Task Force. It then discusses ways that the strategies might help to address the problems. Finally, each section returns to the task force to show how the strategies might be implemented to help the group produce consensus.

Dealing with Strong Emotions and Unmet Interests

In this section, we show how the strategy of seeking additional joint gains can be applied to deal with the problem of unmet interests and strong emotions. First, we return to the task force meeting to see how these problems unfold.

The Task Force Meeting Continues

After other Regional Health and Human Services Task Force members made their initial comments, Jenny Collins, first selectman of the town of Wilton, turned to face First Selectman Bob Salva of Harrington. Bob had said that his town could not live with the choice of Wilton over Harrington as the clinic site. Jenny spoke strongly, her voice tight, a finger jabbing in Bob's direction. "Bob, this is *outrageous*! You know full well that we all agreed on what we were going to do to select a site. You agreed to those criteria. We got the data, and the data showed that far more people will use the clinic if it's in Wilton."

Bob responded harshly: "Jenny, stop playing games. The deal we made was to look at the data and see what came back. I never committed to anything, and I'm telling the group that the town of Harrington is not going to sign an agreement that doesn't meet our needs. Period."

"Bob, you can pack up and go home, if that's what you need to do. But don't try to torpedo the whole agreement just because you didn't get the clinic in your town," Jenny said. Jan, the facilitator, spoke up: "Bob and Jenny, could we take a step back and let the group look at each of the major issues in the draft plan, now that we've heard from everyone? It's clear that we have more work to do. Can we take the issues one by one?"

Bob replied, "I'm only interested in talking about one issue: the clinic. And I've got one interest: the health of the people in my town. Is the group going to meet Harrington's needs, or not?" He looked angrily around the table. Before Jan could speak, Jenny said, "Bob, that's just blackmail. You can't undo the whole plan just because you can't live with what it says on one issue." Some other members of the group nodded in agreement. Bob began to gather his papers; it was obvious that he was planning to walk out.

Bob, Jenny, Jan, and the other members of the group are dealing with a challenging problem: Bob and his Harrington constituents have a very strong interest in one issue; what they want conflicts with the interests of most members of the group, and it is not obvious what can be done to meet that interest without unraveling much of what the group has accomplished.

In this situation, the participants and the facilitator need to start by dealing with the strong emotions being expressed, so that the group can stay focused. Then, they need to see whether it is possible to meet Bob's interest on the siting issue in some way that does not jeopardize the whole strategic plan. To do so, the group needs to return to the process of seeking joint gains. Unlike earlier attempts, this attempt must be constrained by the fact that most stakeholders are already satisfied with the key elements of the package. Therefore, the group needs to focus on

- exploring the interests that underlie Bob's demand for the Harrington site;
- inventing options that might meet those interests without leaving other stakeholders worse off; and
- in the event that no new options can be developed to meet Harrington's interests on this issue, seeking to meet other interests of Harrington stakeholders in exchange for Harrington's agreement to live with the Wilton site.

Dealing with Strong Emotions

In the final stage of a consensus building process, emotions are likely to run high. Participants who are seen as holdouts may be sharply criticized by other group members, and participants who cannot accept a package may feel that the group as a whole has betrayed them and their constituents.

Use ground rules. When a small minority of stakeholders says that it can't accept the current package, some in the majority may be inclined to push for a group decision, even if it excludes the minority. Conversely, some in the minority may demand that the group keep working until it meets their interests, even if the group is nearly out of time or resources.

In these charged situations, it is essential for all participants to observe ground rules about respecting each other's views and interests, maintaining a constructive approach, and avoiding personal attacks. The facilitator can play a very important role by enforcing these ground rules, both in meetings of the full group and in conversations with individual participants.

The facilitator can also help the group consider its options at this juncture, given its ground rules about consensus decision making. For example, if the facilitator thinks that consensus may indeed still be possible, he or she may want to remind group members of their collective commitment to give their best effort at developing an agreement that meets the interests and concerns of *all* participating stakeholders. Group members could decide to spend a limited additional period of time seeking the best possible agreement—where *best* is defined as coming as close as possible to meeting all stakeholder interests, and *possible* means within the resources available. The group may want to start this endeavor by asking those whose interests have not yet been met to suggest one or more proposals that (a) meet their interests and (b) leave no stakeholder worse off than if the group had accepted the current package. The group may also want to designate a subset of its members to develop some possible ways of bridging the gap for full group consideration.

Show empathy. Group members and the facilitator can also deal with strong emotions by maintaining empathy toward individual participants, even while disagreeing with their views. Empathy (showing understanding and respect for someone else's views, values, and emotions) is not a substitute for meeting interests, but it makes it much more likely that participants will be able to maintain good working relationships even if they cannot reach agreement.

The facilitator has a special responsibility to maintain empathy with participants at moments of impasse. Participants may have difficulty being empathetic in these moments, and the facilitator can remind the group by his or her actions that all participants deserve each other's respect and consideration.

Creating More Joint Gains to Satisfy Unmet Interests

"Ask the holdouts why they can't live with particular elements of the package and seek to invent options that bridge the gap."

If emotions can be contained sufficiently for dialogue to continue, a group can try to satisfy the interests of holdouts without sacrificing the interests of others. Just as they did when they were fully engaged in seeking joint gains, participants need to ask the holdouts why they can't live with particular elements of the package and seek to invent options that bridge whatever gaps exist.

With limited time and resources, and broad agreement on most elements of the package, it will be hard for the group to develop radically new options. Instead, the group should try to find more cross-issue trades, and use issue linkage to compensate stakeholders whose interests cannot be fully met by the package.

Trade across issues. The goal in cross-issue trades is to use differences in the *priority* that participants place on particular issues as a way to reconcile conflicts of interest. The basic strategy is simple. Participants need to ask those who cannot live with the proposed agreement on a particular issue whether there is another issue that they care more about. If so, the next question is, "What could we give you on the issue you care more about that would allow you to live with the proposed agreement on the issue you care less about?"

For example, a group that designed the layout of a new day care center and playground in the middle of a large university housing complex had been able to resolve most concerns about loss of open space, noise, and safety. Nevertheless, residents and the center staff were still at odds over whether and how children enrolled in the center and unenrolled children of residents would share the new playground. The center could not take responsibility for the unenrolled children, and the residents were unwilling to give up their outdoor play area.[4]

To resolve the impasse, the center offered to reduce the amount of space its playground occupied and to provide additional play equipment for the open space outside the playground. The residents then agreed to give up their demand to use the playground. Each stakeholder gave up something in this trade, but it also enabled both stakeholders to satisfy their most important interests. Both ended up with more than they would have gotten if no agreement had been reached.

Link issues. If more trades across issues aren't possible, participants may have to look elsewhere for joint gains. Often, participants become so focused on the details of their agreement that they lose sight of opportunities for issue linkage. Issue linkage occurs when one stakeholder offers to do something for another on an issue that is *not* the focus of the group's work.

For example, a regional economic development planning group decided to support a job-training voucher program to give workers greater choice in acquiring training. The regional community college—a member of the planning group—was initially reluctant to support a program that might reduce its enrollment. Other members of the group came up with the idea that the state department of education could offer to give the community college additional funds for buying computers. Funding for computers was tangential to the group's work on economic development, but it did give the community college some compensation for the potential decline in enrollment and made it possible for the college to support the economic development package as a whole.[5]

The following section illustrates ways that the Health and Human Services Task Force might deal with strong emotions, and ways it might seek to produce consensus through cross-issue trades and issue linkage.

The Task Force Seeks More Joint Gains

Seeing that Bob is on the verge of walking out, Jan asks him if he would be willing to speak with her outside. She knows that he is very angry and that he will probably not be able to recover his composure in front of the full group. Bob hesitates, but agrees. Jan then asks the group to take a short break while she speaks with Bob.

Outside, the following exchange takes place:

Jan: Bob, I think it's fair to say that the whole group respects your work on behalf of Harrington. You've made a very compelling case that the town has serious health needs. Right now, though, it seems that the group is struggling to meet those needs while still sticking with its site-selection process.

Bob: Well, I think there are a few people in that room who don't give a damn about Harrington. They're only interested in getting a few million dollars in state and private money for their towns, for facilities they don't need nearly as much as we do. And I'm sick of their posturing.

Jan: I really understand your frustration. I'm wondering whether you'd be willing to think about other options for meeting Harrington's health needs if the clinic does go somewhere else. If you were, I'd be glad to ask the group to consider them.

Bob: I'm very, very doubtful that that's worth my time right now.

Jan: I'd be willing to ask the group to schedule another meeting, but I'm worried about running up against the deadline. What if we were to discuss some other issues first, and then come back to the siting issue later in this meeting?

Bob: I'll use the time to think about what else we could do if Harrington can't get the clinic. But if I hear another insulting comment from Jenny Collins, I promise you I'm walking out.

Jan: I'll do my best to keep everyone focused on constructive problem solving. Why don't I go and check with the group about putting this topic on the agenda for later today? I'll come back out and confirm. You can take some more time to think, then come back in and rejoin the group.

What is Jan doing? She is trying to let Bob know that she and the members of the group have heard his concerns and recognize that they are legitimate. She is also trying to let Bob know that it's going to be very tough to change the site of the clinic. She is putting the emphasis on the group's site-selection process, not the specific reasons why the other site is preferable. She is also trying to get Bob to think about what is in his community's best interest *at this stage,* given that the group is just about out of time.

She encourages him to think of some options that could meet Harrington's interests without changing the siting decision.

Let's assume that Jan goes back into the meeting room and reconvenes the group. She explains that Bob is thinking about other ways that the strategic plan could meet his community's health needs, and she asks whether the group is willing to put Harrington's concerns on the agenda later in the meeting. Looking directly at Jenny Collins, she emphasizes that the group is not being asked to reopen the siting decision. Several members of the group nod their assent. Jan looks again at Jenny, who shrugs and says, "Fine." Jan then steps out into the hall for a moment to let Bob know that the group will revisit Harrington's health needs later in the meeting.

Searching for smart trades. Let's fast-forward to later in the meeting. Bob has spent some time cooling off and thinking hard about how to meet Harrington's needs. After he rejoins the group, Jan turns to him and asks whether he has some new ideas for the group to consider.

Harrington is the poorest town in the region, and it has a high proportion of children and elderly people—two groups with substantial health care needs and limited transport options. Despite Harrington's significant needs, other siting criteria weighed more heavily in the final decision. Wilton is far more centrally located—the region's major north-south and east-west roads run through it. In addition, though Wilton is one of the wealthier towns in the region, it has a much larger population than Harrington. When the Department of Health and the HMO developed their demand projections for different sites, they found that Wilton's easier access and higher population density would generate significantly higher demand for the clinic's services than if it were sited in Harrington.

Having thought extensively about Harrington's problems and about solutions that might be acceptable to the group, Bob has several options to propose:

- Build a second, smaller clinic in Harrington.
- Offer incentives for other public and private health care providers to locate facilities in Harrington.
- Provide free transportation to Wilton for Harrington residents and subsidize their cost of care at the Wilton clinic.

The group listens to Bob's proposals. There are several responses. First, it is clear that the group does not think there are sufficient resources to pay for a second clinic. The HMO is strongly opposed, because a second clinic could siphon off demand from the Wilton clinic.

The second option, giving incentives to other public and private health providers to locate in Harrington, sparks quite a bit of discussion. Selectmen from several other towns are uneasy about whether their own providers might move to Harrington, so they propose that incentives be targeted at the whole region. The Department of Health representative says the state probably can't justify a regionwide incentive program. After some heated back-and-forth between Bob and other selectmen, the Department of Health representative proposes a way to compensate Harrington through issue linkage: Harrington could move to the top of the state's list of communities eligible for state-subsidized elderly housing. These housing developments include on-site nursing services.

The last option, subsidizing the cost of transport and care for Harrington residents who use the Wilton facility, also leads to an intense discussion. The major question here is who would underwrite the subsidies. The HMO is reluctant to do so, because it has already committed to reduce annual premiums for lower-income residents who are not eligible for Medicaid or Medicare. The state health agency is also loathe to offer any additional funds, because it does not want to set a precedent.

Bob digs in his heels, saying, "A 'maybe' on an elderly housing complex isn't going to cut it. We need to know that our people are going to get to use the Wilton facility, or we're going to raise hell in the legislature." Jan asks the group whether there is any way to solve this problem. The regional transit agency representative says that his agency cannot put up new money, but would be willing to realign existing transit routes in the region so that Harrington residents will have easier access to the Wilton clinic. Bob asks Jenny Collins whether Wilton would be willing to subsidize fares on the Harrington-Wilton route, using some of the additional tax revenue they will generate by hosting the clinic. Jenny reluctantly agrees. Bob says he thinks he can sell this agreement to the Harrington Board of Selectmen. He promises to come to the next task force meeting (scheduled in two weeks) prepared to report their reactions.

In this scenario, Bob and the other members of the task force have looked for smart trades: resources that stakeholders can provide at relatively low cost to themselves, which have substantial value to those whose interests have not yet been met. As noted above, inventing substantial new options may not be possible, but issue linkage and cross-issue trades are other forms of invention that can help meet interests without unraveling the package.

Dealing with Imperfect Representation and Unrealistic Aspirations

After working hard to create additional joint gains, and to allocate those gains in a fair way, the Regional Health and Human Services Task Force might finally be able to meet the interests of Bob Salva's constituency and persuade Harrington's other selectmen to support the task force's draft strategic plan. Still, the task force can't rest easy. It has quite a challenging problem to work through with Barry Dinsmore, the advocacy director for the Provider Council.

In this section, we look at the problem of unrealistically high aspirations. We show how the group can search for additional joint gains and try to apply fair standards to help the Provider Council meet its interests while also recognizing the constraints on other stakeholders. We also look at ways to handle the communication breakdown between representative and constituency that has contributed to the aspirations problem. To begin, we return to the task force, where Barry Dinsmore is explaining the Provider Council's concerns.

The Task Force Meeting Continues

Barry has announced that the Provider Council's chairman is not happy with the task force's draft agreement. Unfortunately, the Provider Council's executive committee is not meeting for another month, long after the task force was scheduled to have completed its work. When Barry makes this announcement to the group, other stakeholders express dismay and frustration. Michelle Robinson, a representative of the region's organized human service users (primarily elderly, disabled, and low-income groups) is the first to speak, followed by Wilma Carter of Guardian Health Associates:

Michelle: Barry, what are you saying? I thought you told us at our last meeting that the draft strategic plan met your organization's main interests, and you thought they would support it! You even said the Wilton site was a perfect spot for the new clinic.

Barry: Well, I know I said that, and I'm sorry. I'm in a bind here. There's nothing I can do if our chairman doesn't like it—I take my marching orders from him.

Wilma: But Barry, why is this coming up now? What were you doing all those months when we were developing the provisions of this plan? Our ground rules say it's *your* responsibility to check with your higher-ups.

Barry: Look, I know this looks like I haven't been doing my job, but the fact is, I have sent the committee every single meeting summary. I just haven't been able to get on their agenda, and I didn't know this was brewing.

Wilma: Hey Barry, that's not our problem. We've been keeping our organizations in the loop! What do you expect us to do now?

As the conversation gets more heated and Barry finds himself confronted by other participants who are frustrated by his 11th-hour opposition to the plan, the prospects for any agreement appear to hang in the balance. Barry is defensive. He explains that he *did* talk with his leadership early on, and he did his best to bring their views and concerns to the table. That just hasn't been possible lately. He insists that he's done his best, given the circumstances. But other participants are angry. They point out that Barry's inability to keep his constituency well-informed has put the task force in a difficult position.

The Problem of Imperfect Representation

Barry's situation highlights a constituency representation problem that can appear at any stage in a consensus building process, but is especially dangerous when it happens during the stage when the group is seeking to produce consensus. Barry and his constituency have not been in close contact during the deliberations, and as a result, Barry has not been able to fully represent their views.

"The facilitator should peiodically ask representatives to check in with their constituents."

The origins of this problem may lie with the ground rules, the representative, the constituency, or all three. Sometimes representatives lack a clear understanding of their responsibilities. A group's ground rules should always clearly spell out representatives' responsibilities for keeping their constituencies informed and testing the acceptability of the group's proposals. Moreover, the facilitator or mediator should periodically ask representatives to check in with their constituencies during their deliberations, so that they don't lose sight of the importance of regular contact with those they represent.

Sometimes, though, groups encounter this problem even when there are clear ground rules in place. For example, representatives of a more diffuse constituency (such as the residents of a neighborhood where a new waste facility has been proposed) may have no easily identifiable channel for communicating with their constituencies.

A lack of communication between a representative and his or her constituents is problematic because it obscures not just the fact that a particular package may be unacceptable to a stakeholder group but also *why* this is so. It may be that the package does not meet a key interest of the constituency, or it may be that the constituency has unrealistically high aspirations and has failed to realize that its aspirations cannot be met given the interests of the other stakeholders.

The question is, what should a consensus building group do when it finds itself in this situation? First, the participants and the facilitator need to open up communication with the constituency. Then, they need to figure out whether the constituency's interests can be met through modifications to the agreement. The specific sequence of steps might be as follows:

- Arrange to meet.
- Review the consensus building process with the constituency.
- Seek additional joint gains by exploring the constituency's interests and brainstorming options that might meet those interests.

- If it appears that the problem is in fact one of unrealistic aspirations, use the goal of consensus and the standards of procedural fairness to argue for acceptance of the package, but avoid thin-ice agreements.

Arrange to meet. Face-to-face communication is a core element of any consensus building process. The value of face-to-face communication is not limited to interactions among stakeholder representatives at the table. When a consensus building group is having difficulty winning support for its proposals from a key constituency, arranging a face-to-face meeting between those constituents and their representative is an essential first step.

It may also be a good idea for the facilitator or other group members to come to the meeting. The facilitator may be especially helpful in explaining the group's process, and also in keeping the discussion on track if anger or other emotions begin to get in the way. Other group members may be able to support the representative's reports about what the group has done, explain the tentative agreement, shed light on the views of other stakeholders, and engage in brainstorming to see how the constituency's interests might best be met. Whether the representative should bring the facilitator or the other members of the group to the meeting is a decision that must be made on a case-by-case basis.

One caution should be mentioned. It is always unwise to leave a representative out of a meeting with his or her own constituents, even when a consensus building group fears that the representative has done a poor job of communicating what has occurred. The representative is the agent of the stakeholding group. Going over the representative's head usurps his or her authority and risks alienating both the representative and his or her constituents. A much better strategy is to talk openly with the representative about how best to involve his or her constituency in the deliberations.

Review the process. What should be accomplished during the face-to-face meeting with constituents? In a sense, the goal should be to conduct a mini-consensus building process by identifying the issues at stake, exploring the stakeholder group's concerns on those issues, developing options that might meet those interests and the interests of other stakeholders, and then seeking consensus. The goal, then, is to treat the constituents as if they were direct participants at the negotiating table.

To begin the discussion, the representative (or perhaps the facilitator) should give a brief, informal report on how the consensus building group has operated. Constituents have not had the benefit of participating in the ongoing negotiations. As a result, they may have only a partial understanding of how and why the current package emerged. They may also lack an appreciation of how hard the group has worked to achieve consensus (i.e., they may not realize that all participants have been asked to make trade-offs to produce an agreement that all stakeholders can live with). They may also be unaware that other representatives have been actively communicating with their constituencies.

While the review of the process should be geared toward helping the constituents understand how far the group has come, the constituency should not be criticized for raising its concerns so late in the process. The simple reason for this is that it may be hard to determine who is at fault. The best strategy is to avoid trying to determine who failed to fulfill their responsibilities, and instead seek to solve the present problem.

Seek additional joint gains. The next step is to explore ways that the current package could be modified to meet the interests of this constituency while still retaining the support of other stakeholder groups. The representative and whoever else is present should aim to marshal the same careful listening skills and the same determination to search for joint gains that they have relied on in the past. However, it is important to begin this conversation with a caveat: Any proposed change to the agreement must be accepted by all stakeholders.

At first, constituents may make very positional statements, emphasizing their general dislike of the tentative agreement. The representative, the facilitator, and other group members should ask the question "Why?" to uncover real interests. "Why are you concerned about the provisions of this agreement? Can you help me understand what is really at stake?"

While it is always worth exploring ways to modify a proposed agreement to meet a stakeholder's interests, the real problem may not be that the group couldn't live with the proposed agreement.

Rather, it may be that some constituents of a stakeholder group want to see if they can get more from other stakeholder groups.

Key stakeholders may have set their aspirations very high and may not have adjusted those aspirations in light of new information about other parties' interests, resources, and BATNAs. In general, it is a good idea to set a high aspiration. On the other hand, sticking to it regardless of what happens in the dialogue can be a big mistake. In the worst case, a stakeholder group may turn down an agreement that meets most of its core interests and is significantly better than its BATNA because it refuses to let go of its initial aspiration. In effect, these groups "make the perfect the enemy of the good."

When it appears that a stakeholder's opposition to an agreement is driven by a poor estimate of its BATNA or unrealistically high aspirations, an open and frank discussion with the neutral may turn things around. The facilitator can act as the "agent of reality," gently prodding the group to compare its BATNA with the current package. Rejecting the agreement may still make sense if a stakeholder needs to take a principled stand against it. If, however, the stakeholder's primary concern is meeting a set of interests rather than upholding a set of principles, then it needs to consider whether an imperfect agreement is better than none at all.

After exploring interests, the representative and others at the meeting should see if there is any way to modify the provisions of the agreement to better meet the constituency's interests. This conversation should be closely modeled on the brainstorming sessions the consensus building group has conducted. The most potent strategy for pinpointing modifications that might work is to ask: "What if?" Throughout this conversation, it is important for everyone at the meeting to remind the constituency that inventing should remain separate from committing. The goal should be to discover as many means as possible of making the agreement acceptable to the constituents, with the recognition that there can be no commitment to these changes until they are brought back to the full group.

Use fair standards to help constituents let go of unrealistic aspirations. Even the most careful exploration of interests and the most determined search for viable options may not lead to a new package that satisfies the aspirations of the constituency. On the other hand, careful exploration of interests should help the constituency, other group members, and the facilitator determine whether the constituency's BATNA truly does meet its interests better than the proposed package.

If the constituency's BATNA does not appear to meet its interests as well as the proposed package, then it should be clear that the challenge is to help the constituency let go of aspirations that simply could not be met by the group. The best way to do so is by making well-reasoned arguments to the constituency, using objective criteria and standards.

One line of argument should focus on the procedural fairness of the consensus building process itself. Here, the challenge is to demonstrate to the reluctant constituency that its interests received equal weight in the process and that other constituencies also accepted a package that did not meet all of their aspirations. At this stage, it may be useful to invite some other stakeholder representatives who are on good terms with the constituency to confirm that the process was fair and that the outcome required shared sacrifice.

A second line of argument should focus on the criteria the group used to develop the proposed package. If the group has used objective criteria to select options for inclusion in the package, then the group needs to review these criteria with the constituency, and explain how and why it made trade-offs among competing criteria to arrive at the proposed package.

Avoid thin-ice agreements. If these arguments on the merits do not satisfy the constituency that it was treated fairly and that the outcome meets mutually accepted goals, then the constituency still has the option to dissent from the agreement. Although it is easy to say that any stakeholder has the right to dissent, it is remarkable how much pressure other stakeholders can bring to bear when they want to achieve unanimity. In the worst case, the group as a whole may become quite coercive with the remaining holdouts. Both the facilitator and the members of a consensus building group have a special responsibility to respect any participant's right to reject an agreement that does not meet his or her constituency's minimum requirements.

Returning to the Regional Health
and Human Services Task Force

We left the task force in a quandary about Barry's constituency. Barry says he doesn't know what to do: His executive committee's members say they don't like the agreement, and they're not meeting again for a month. Other negotiators in the group are angry and frustrated. They feel that Barry hasn't fulfilled his responsibilities as a representative.

Before the dialogue degenerates further into angry accusations and equally angry defenses, Barry and the group need to talk about what they can do together to solve the problem. Both Jan (the facilitator) and the participants should ask, "How can we help you present the group's proposed plan to your constituency?"

To begin, they should ask Barry to request a special meeting of his executive committee or, at a minimum, a one-on-one meeting with the chair himself. Barry should emphasize that the group is nearly out of time and resources and would appreciate an opportunity to discuss the proposed agreement again with the aim of seeing whether there is a way the Provider Council's concerns can be addressed. Barry may or may not want to bring Jan or other members of the group to this meeting; the decision should be left to him, because he is in the best position to judge how the chair and other members of the executive committee will respond to outsiders.

The meeting. Let's assume Barry asks for Jan's help, and together they contact the chair, who agrees to call a special meeting of the executive committee. At the meeting, Jan and Barry jointly present a brief history of the task force. They list the stakeholders represented on the task force, describe how it was convened, and review its goals. They also talk briefly about the ground rules the group has employed, including the ground rule that representatives are at the table to articulate the concerns of their constituencies. Finally, they review the key provisions of the draft strategic plan.

After this brief report, Jan and Barry ask the members of the executive committee if they can explain the nature of their concerns about the strategic plan, but the chair interrupts:

Chair: Barry, you know I told you that we needed certain
           guarantees about staffing in order to be able to
           support this plan. We want a contract with this HMO
           that gives providers responsibility for handling intake
           for the clinic's health insurance program for the
           working poor. It makes *no* sense that this is not a
           feature of this agreement!

At this point, Jan and Barry know they need to focus on
exploring the interests behind the chair's position. Before they
get to their own questions, however, they need to confirm for the
chair that the group had thoroughly and thoughtfully discussed
the possibility of having providers take the lead in handling
intake. Jan and Barry recap the task force discussion of intake
options. Jan reports that the group brainstormed two ways of
handling intake. One was for human service providers who
worked with the region's lower-income residents to review their
eligibility for the new health insurance program and administer
their intake into the program; providers would offer this service
under contract to Guardian Health Associates. The other option
was to have the HMO handle intake for this program directly, as
it would for all of its other patients.

Jan explained that the task force had considered several
criteria for choosing between these options, including ease of
access for the user, cost-effectiveness, and precedent. The group
decided that the high administrative costs of a provider intake
system outweighed the access benefits that a provider intake
system could provide to low-income health service users.

Once the members of the executive committee have been
brought up to speed on *how* the task force had deliberated about
staffing, Jan and Barry are ready to explore in more depth what
the interests of the Provider Council are, and how they might be
met. Jan probes to learn more about why the chair and the other
members of the executive committee care so deeply about the
intake contract. She asks, "Can you help me understand what
interest of yours an intake contract would meet?"

The chair and the other members of the Provider Council
insist that providers deserve compensation for work they are
going to have to do anyway: referring patients to the new clinic
program. The chair says forcefully, "The bottom line is, we need

this contract or we're not going to be able to support the strategic plan. It would be pointless to discuss other options."

Jan and Barry now realize they may be confronting an unrealistically high aspiration. They know that it will be just about impossible to persuade the task force to change its views on intake. They have also heard nothing from the executive committee to suggest that the members of the Provider Council would be substantially better off if they refused to help implement the low-income health insurance program.

Jan now seeks to help the executive committee understand that the group cannot meet its interest, by reminding them of the task force's commitment to an objective decision-making process. She notes that virtually all of the task force members—not just Guardian Health Associates—are reluctant to reopen the intake staffing issue. She emphasizes that this does not stem from a lack of willingness to try to meet the Provider Council's most important concerns. Rather, task force participants feel they can't give on this particular issue because their initial decision to support internal intake at Guardian was the result of a process of evaluating each option against jointly developed criteria.

She also points out that every member of the task force, including Barry, has deliberated in good faith. Members have all made trade-offs to reach agreement on a new site for the health clinic and a basic program design. She acknowledges the strength of the Provider Council's desire to have a contract for intake: "I know that securing this role is very important for providers, and I think I can say that in principle, task force members would like to find a way to respond. Having the support of providers is very important. Unfortunately, though, I don't think there is much room for negotiation on this issue."

She also encourages the executive committee to think again both about its BATNA and the BATNAs of other stakeholder groups. "Have you given any thought to what might happen if providers do reject the agreement on a new regional health clinic?" she asks. "How might the Department of Health react? And what would you do next?"

The members of the executive committee respond to Jan's words with a stony silence. Realizing that she is making little progress, she decides they may need some time to talk privately about what they want to do. So she proposes adjourning the meeting, but is careful to leave them with a clear charge: "If the

Provider Council comes to our next meeting with the same proposal for an intake contract, I don't think the task force will be able to accommodate you," she explains. "But if the Provider Council can develop another proposal—one that squeezes additional gain out of this agreement for providers but also anticipates the interests of other stakeholders—then we might be able to break this impasse," she says, mustering as much optimism as she can.

"We'll think it over," replies the chair. "But I'm not optimistic."

Dealing with Impasse Created by Uncertainty

The Regional Health and Human Services Task Force has now confronted two challenging problems: Bob Salva's opposition to the site for the regional health clinic and the Provider Council's insistence on a contract for staffing intake. But a third problem remains: dealing with a stakeholder's concern about a future risk that may or may not materialize.

The Task Force Meeting Continues

At the beginning of the meeting, Wilma Carter, the executive vice president of Guardian Health Associates (the most likely investor in a new regional health clinic), reported that her clinic-siting team was nervous. Assuming that the task force would ultimately choose the Wilton site, they did additional research to assess the probable demand for services at that site. When they integrated the new projections into their financial analysis, they didn't like what the numbers said. As we rejoin the task force, other stakeholders have questions for Wilma.

Business rep:	Wilma, I thought you said the Wilton site is the best site for Guardian, because it's smack in the middle of your prime market area!
Wilma:	Well, that's still true. Wilton is the best site of the ones we've looked at. But we're doing a finer-scale analysis now, using some new estimates of demand under the best- and worst-case scenarios. Right now, the worst-case scenario would guarantee bankruptcy—we can't go forward as long as that's a significant possibility.

Users' rep: The way you say that makes it sound very reasonable, but the fact is this is a hell of a time to be telling us that the clinic might not be financially viable!

Wilma: Look, I know this is frustrating, but we're very confident that our analysis is sound. Our new demand projections are based on a round of interviews with providers in the region who may join our network. When we integrate those estimates with our analysis of the cost of providing services and the fees we can charge, it's very clear that our risk is *much* greater than we originally thought.

Users' rep: I still don't get it. What about the Department of Health's data? They've assured us that a clinic at the Wilton site would have the highest demand of any of the sites!

As Elaine Cahill, the representative from the Department of Health, listens to this conversation, she can feel her anger rising. Elaine's agency has supplied much of the demand data that Guardian has been using to estimate profitability. From the beginning of the site-selection discussions, Elaine has urged Guardian to conduct its analysis in the open, in collaboration with other stakeholders. Specifically, she proposed that she, Wilma, and several other stakeholder representatives form a small subcommittee to integrate her agency's demand projections with Guardian's projections of costs and fees, and jointly determine the clinic's potential profitability at each candidate site on the task force's short list.

Wilma declined this offer. She maintained that Guardian had its own proprietary method for estimating profitability (including its own methods for projecting demand), and she said she couldn't share it with other task force members because of its close ties with company marketing strategy. She told the task force that the best she could do would be to have Guardian's clinic-siting team do an independent assessment of each site, and then report back to the group about which sites were best suited to ensuring the clinic's financial viability.

The discussion at that meeting was rocky. Task force members told Guardian that they were uncomfortable with the HMO conducting its analysis behind closed doors, but ultimately they accepted the company's claims that its financial analysis was proprietary. Now, Elaine is surprised and frustrated by Guardian's last-minute announcement, and she initiates the following exchange with Wilma.

Elaine:	Wilma, help me understand something here. When we first began reviewing possible sites for the new clinic, the Department of Health did its best to assess how a clinic would do at the Wilton site, given the limited information we had from you. And you agreed with our judgment that Wilton was the best site. Now we're hearing a whole new story!
Wilma:	Look, I said it before and I'll say it again. The Wilton site still appears to be the best one. But we've done a more careful analysis using some new demand estimates, and our lowest projection shows that we could be at risk of losing our shirts, even at the preferred site. What more do I need to say?
Elaine:	Hey, don't act surprised that it's hard for people to accept this analysis; you took an awfully long time to come out with it!
Wilma:	Look, Elaine, you know as well as I do that there is a very good reason for that. Doing a full-scale analysis just didn't make sense until we were sure the task force was really interested in the Wilton site. We needed to bring in more sophisticated approaches to estimating profitability than your agency could supply, but we waited until it made sense to invest in those approaches.
Elaine:	Our agency's methods for projecting demand are perfectly good! Regardless, you won't even share your methods with us, so how can you expect us to believe that your demand projections come out lower than ours?
Wilma:	Are you questioning my company's motives?

The escalating confrontation has taken over the whole meeting. Wilma is angry that others are questioning Guardian's integrity, and she wants to get Elaine and other task force members focused on the problem at hand: finding a way to make sure Guardian is protected if these conditions are realized. Old resentments about the company's need to keep its methods proprietary are surfacing again.

Meanwhile, Elaine is upset that Wilma is suggesting that the Department of Health's demand projections might not be on target. Furthermore, she's worried that the whole agreement could fall through, and if it does, the Department of Health and Guardian might be singled out as those responsible.

As this interaction unfolds, two problems emerge for the task force. The first is one of communication. Wilma and Elaine are not communicating in a constructive way. Their mutual accusations threaten to unravel the trust that has been built up over the past 11 months. Moreover, there is a risk that the discord could spill over into the interactions between other task force members and reverse the group's forward progress. Something needs to be done to diffuse emotions and get the group back on track.

The second problem goes to the substance of the agreement itself. As the most likely investor in the regional health clinic, Guardian is the linchpin of the whole strategic plan. The company now appears concerned that there is too much uncertainty about the clinic's future financial viability. Wilma signaled that Guardian can't live with this degree of uncertainty in the final strategic plan.

These two problems are both tough to handle. Yet how the task force members handle them will determine whether or not they are able to reach a consensus on a new health services system. What should they do?

The first step should be to address the immediate conflict between Elaine and Wilma in a session that does not involve the full task force. Once anger has been smoothed over, Elaine and Wilma should work jointly on behalf of the task force to

- see if the uncertainty surrounding future demand for the clinic can be resolved through joint fact-finding;
- explore whether building contingencies into the strategic plan would make the agreement workable for Guardian and other stakeholders; and
- in the event that neither joint fact-finding nor contingent agreements adequately address Guardian's concern about its future downside risk, explore whether a shorter-term agreement might close the gap.

Seek to Resolve Uncertainty through Joint Fact-Finding

Uncertainty poses a challenge to decision making of all kinds, and consensus building is no exception. Usually, consensus building groups aim to reach agreement on a set of commitments that participating stakeholder groups or other organizations and individuals will make. But spelling out the exact terms of these commitments can be made vastly more complicated by the impossibility of predicting the future.

When participants have different and conflicting views about what the future is likely to bring, they may have difficulty reaching agreement. Some participants may say they can commit to take action under some future conditions, but not under others. Wilma Carter, for example, is telling other members of the task force that her HMO can only afford the financial investment in a new regional health clinic if demand for clinic services stays above the lower range of the company's projections. The Department of Health has concluded, based on its own projections, that demand will be high enough to ensure a financially viable clinic.

When uncertainty about the future becomes a stumbling block on the way to agreement, what can a group do? An essential first step is to see whether uncertainty can be eliminated or reduced quickly, through a joint fact-finding process. Joint fact-finding is most often used at the stage when a group is seeking a better understanding of the issues on its agenda, or is evaluating different options identified during brainstorming sessions. However, joint fact-finding can also be useful later in the process, when a group has reached an impasse because of uncertainty. Participants may be able to identify one or multiple sources of information that could improve the group's understanding of which future events or trends are most likely.

Develop Contingent Agreements

If joint fact-finding can't eliminate uncertainty, and one stakeholder group fears that potential future circumstances may make the agreement unworkable for them, the next step is to search for a contingent agreement.

"Under contingent agreements, stakeholders follow through on commitments only if certain future conditions are realized."

Contingent agreements transform the fact that stakeholders view the future differently into an opportunity. They allow stakeholders to follow through on particular commitments only if certain future conditions are realized. For example, the task force members might agree that a subsidized bus service would help low-income people gain access to the clinic, but disagree over who should pay for it. The HMO and the Department of Health could be confident that advocates for low-income residents could secure funding from a regional foundation, while the advocates themselves doubt that they can secure a grant. To resolve this problem, the Department of Health and the HMO could commit to jointly subsidize the bus service if and only if users are unable to secure a grant. This provision takes advantage of different views about the future to resolve disagreement.[6]

First-Round Agreements

When neither joint fact-finding nor a contingent agreement can break an impasse that springs from uncertainty, the next step may be to shorten the time horizon of the agreement itself. Stakeholders need only agree to follow through on their commitments for a limited period of time—a first round—after which the entire agreement must be reopened. Pilot programs are prime examples. Stakeholders essentially agree to "test-drive" their commitments, and then reconsider them depending on what they learn. First-round agreements may be the only way to reach consensus when some stakeholders are more concerned about the future viability of the whole package than about any one issue.

Returning to the Regional Health and Human Services Task Force

When we left the task force, Wilma Carter of Guardian Associates and Elaine Cahill of the Department of Health were exchanging angry barbs. As Wilma and Elaine begin to make more and more charged comments, Jan and the task force must decide what to do. They must address the immediate issue at hand: friction between two stakeholders who are central to the plan for a new regional health network. But beyond that, they must consider how to ensure Guardian's support for the agreement given the HMO's new concern about future demand. The strategies outlined above should help.

Let's assume that Jan intervenes just at the point when the conversation between Wilma and Elaine takes a hostile turn. She sees clearly that these two could quickly undermine the good working relationship they have developed over the past few months if they continue to level public accusations and criticisms.

"Let me interrupt for a moment," she says. "It seems like it would be beneficial for you two to get together after this meeting for a one-on-one conversation with plenty of time to figure out what ought to be done. I would be happy to offer what assistance I can. What do you think?" Jan avoids labeling this session as *mediation*, even though that's what she has in mind, because she doesn't want to further inflame bruised egos and short tempers by highlighting the need for a formal intervention.

Elaine and Wilma agree to defer their conversation until after the meeting. When they get together as a threesome a few days later, Jan's first step is to remind them about the ground rules task force members agreed to abide by. In particular, she emphasizes the importance of the ground rule that "no one will make personal attacks or issue statements blaming others for specific actions or outcomes."

At the beginning of the mediation session, there is substantial tension in the air. Both Wilma and Elaine bristle, and launch jabs about the other's behavior at the last task force meeting. After giving them some time to vent their emotions, Jan makes a proposal. She asks if they could agree to examine their organizations' projections together, under the condition that the conversation be kept completely confidential. Jan is banking that the process of jointly reviewing Guardian's integrated demand and financial analysis might help Elaine and Wilma reach agreement on the legitimacy of Guardian's claim that its downside risk is too large.

Once Elaine agrees to keep the conversation confidential, Wilma agrees to share Guardian's analysis. The joint review turns out to be very helpful. Elaine is persuaded that Guardian has gone through a careful and well-thought-out process for determining the clinic's potential profitability. The clinic team has analyzed several scenarios with different assumptions about demand, the cost of providing care, and the fees that the clinic will be able to charge. Elaine recognizes that Guardian's financial risk is substantial: At the lower end of potential demand, the clinic would not be able to operate in the black.

Now Jan poses a question: "What can be done to ensure that Guardian's financial risk is reduced?" She suggests that Elaine and Wilma brainstorm some contingencies that could be built into the final agreement to give Guardian some insurance. During the conversation that follows, two options are identified.

1. If patient visits fall below an agreed-on level in the first three years of the clinic's operations, the Department of Health could make a payment to Guardian to cover most of the difference between actual and projected clinic revenue. This option would protect Guardian against most but not all downside risk. Guardian could still make a substantial profit if demand is higher than expected.

2. The Department of Health could make a fixed payment to the clinic for the first three years, independent of demand. This option would eliminate the downside risk for Guardian, but would also limit its upside profit potential.

Elaine favors the first option. It would provide financial assistance to Guardian on a contingent basis: If demand for the clinic's health services turned out to be at the lower end of the HMO's projections, the company would receive an infusion of money from a special state fund. Elaine is candid about the fact that she likes this option in part because she still thinks it's unlikely that Guardian's worst-case scenario will ever become a reality.

Wilma prefers the second option. It would provide Guardian with guaranteed financial assistance for a set period of time. The agency and Guardian would meet after the three-year period to discuss the clinic's financial viability. If demand in the first three years turned out to be low, the agency would not be obligated to continue subsidizing the clinic's operations beyond the three-year mark. If demand were high, Guardian could stop accepting the fixed fee and switch to a service-based payment system. Wilma argues that one merit of this option is that it would allow the HMO to begin operations with a staffing level appropriate for meeting demand at the upper range of Guardian's estimates, without risking financial disaster if demand bottomed out. Guaranteed funding would give the company a short-term cushion while it adjusted its services and staffing levels to fit the regional market.

By the end of the session, both Elaine and Wilma are pleased with their progress, but they can't quite reach agreement on which option to recommend to the task force. Each prefers the one she proposed. Elaine also points out that her superiors at the Department of Health may find Wilma's option unacceptable. "I just won't be able to sell a guaranteed funding stream to my agency unless the other members of the task force are behind it," Elaine insists. Jan suggests that Wilma and Elaine present both options at next week's task force meeting and seek the group's help in deciding between them.

Dealing with Less Than Unanimous Agreement

"The challenge is to reach closure when not all stake-holders can live with a proposed agreement."

Perhaps the hardest challenge a consensus building group ever faces is reaching closure when not all stakeholders can live with a proposed agreement, and nothing more can be done to meet their interests. In this situation, it is essential for the group to have a clear decision rule that allows the group to reach closure. It is equally important for the group to acknowledge dissent in any final statement of its decisions or recommendations. We rejoin the task force at its final meeting, as it confronts these thorny problems.

The Task Force Seeks Closure

As task force members make their way to their chairs in anticipation of their last scheduled meeting, there is none of the usual chatter. Everyone is expectant. Just two weeks earlier, participants were frustrated when Bob Salva, Wilma Carter, and Barry Dinsmore raised objections to what everyone thought was a final agreement. Since then, some members of the task force have been hard at work to bridge remaining differences, and everyone is eager to hear the results.

Opening comments reveal that task force members are worried about the prospects for unanimous agreement. A representative of health service users appeals to the group, "It would be such a shame if what we've worked so hard for disappeared into thin air because one or two members couldn't get it together." A local elected official concurs, but says, "As much as we all want to reach closure, let's not rush it. Let's make sure we've done all we can to meet everyone's interests first."

Jan previews the agenda, then asks participants who raised concerns at the last meeting to report on their progress in resolving outstanding issues. First, Wilma and Elaine present the two options they have developed for reducing the downside risk to Guardian. The discussion is brief—other members accept their joint recommendation that Guardian needs some insurance. They think both options have merit, but they clearly prefer the idea of a first-round agreement. Providers, in particular, are vocal supporters of a guaranteed stream of revenue for the first three years—they see it as a way to ensure that the HMO doesn't skimp on staffing when it opens its doors. In the end, the task force agrees to add this guarantee to the strategic plan, and Guardian agrees to support the plan.

Next is Bob Salva. Once again, the report and subsequent discussion are brief. "This time, I'm bringing good news," Bob begins. "Last night the Harrington Board of Selectmen got together again, and the vote was unanimous. If the task force is committed to adding the three points we discussed at the last meeting—that is, moving Harrington to the top of the state's list of communities eligible for state-subsidized elderly housing developments, rerouting bus routes so our low-income residents can get to the clinic, and having some subsidy for their bus fare—then you can count on our support."

Next, Jan turns to Barry Dinsmore, the Provider Council's representative. Barry clears his throat and adjusts his tie nervously. "Well, folks, Jan and I met with the executive committee of the Provider Council, and I met with them separately, and here's where we're at: The council just isn't willing to budge on having a contract for referral and intake services. I don't think we can shift much from there."

Jan probes more deeply: "Barry, my recollection is that when we met with the council's executive committee, we concluded the meeting by asking the committee to suggest a way to improve the strategic plan for providers without making it worse for the other stakeholder groups. We encouraged them to steer away from the idea of an intake contract, because my conversations with task force members suggested that wasn't going to work for others.

Has the Provider Council been able to develop a new proposal on any other issues?"

"From the perspective of my constituency," Barry answers, "this strategic plan really *must* include an intake contract for providers. This is a make-or-break issue for us." He goes on to say that the executive committee has agreed to modify its original proposal somewhat: The intake contract could be funded by some other stakeholder group rather than Guardian. "Providers just want to be in charge of intake, we don't really care who funds us to do it," he concludes.

It doesn't take the task force long to reject this slightly modified version of the Provider Council's initial proposal. Many task force members voice their opposition. Wilma Carter feels strongly that intake should be done within the clinic; she emphasizes the extra cost and administrative hassle involved in a provider-managed intake system. Other participants are put off by the way that the Provider Council has presented its position. They feel that the council hasn't made a good argument—an argument on the merits—for altering a decision based on a careful comparison of all the staffing options against a set of jointly developed criteria.

At this point, the task force has arrived at one of the hardest moments in a consensus building process. The vast majority can now live with the draft strategic plan, but a key group is holding out, and there is no apparent way to overcome the impasse. Jan steps in in an effort to help the task force assess its progress: "The question I think the task force needs to consider now is: Is there anything more the group can do to reach consensus, or is it time to talk about how to bring closure to the task force's work?" Her question sparks a heated exchange between Jenny Collins of Wilton, Wilma Carter, and Barry Dinsmore.

Barry: Jan, talking about closure may be jumping the gun. Maybe if the executive committee had more time it could come back with a more specific proposal about who could fund this thing.

Jenny: You know, Barry, I have to disagree. We can't satisfy the Provider Council and still keep everyone else on board, so let's say we did the best we can, submit the plan as is, and go home.

Barry: What about our goal of achieving a unanimous agreement? You're going to give up on our whole purpose just like that? I think we need more time to deliberate, or we risk steamrolling my constituency.

Wilma: Barry, we've asked the Provider Council to help us find another way of meeting their interests, and they haven't really tried. They're not working with us on this.

Barry: Look, I'm the first to agree that the executive committee spoke up pretty late about their strong desire for this contract, but I can't believe you would contemplate leaving the providers out of this agreement after we all worked so hard!

This is a tough moment. Back at the beginning of the process, the task force set a ground rule about how it would reach an ultimate decision. That ground rule said they would *seek* a unanimous agreement, but it also said that the group would accept "overwhelming" support as an outcome if unanimity was not possible.

Using Decision Rules to Reach Closure

This moment in the work of the task force shows how important it is for consensus building groups to make some provision for reaching closure even if they have not achieved full consensus. Groups that adopt a *unanimity* rule risk being held hostage to their most demanding and inflexible member(s). Sometimes a group will not be able to find a way of responding to those demands without making the package worse for other stakeholders. In fact, there could well be a case in which one stakeholder simply judges that its BATNA is better than what is being proposed for agreement, and thus has little incentive to work with the group on improving the package in a way that is consistent with the others' interests. For example, a community that has been participating in a consensus building process to select a site for a waste treatment facility and ends up being selected as the site may dissent from the decision, even if it agrees with all of the criteria that drove the decision.

For these reasons, we believe that groups should strive for full (unanimous) consensus, but be willing to accept overwhelming agreement, meaning agreement of all but a very few participating stakeholders. If a consensus building group must make decisions that are binding on participating stakeholders, it may be necessary to define *overwhelming agreement* explicitly (e.g., four out of five stakeholder teams, or three-fourths of all participants). If the group is advisory, however, it may not be necessary to define a non-unanimity decision rule. Advisory groups can always summarize points of agreement and disagreement if they are unable to reach a full consensus. This summary can be submitted to those who have asked for the group's recommendations.

Having a non-unanimity decision rule does not, however, make reaching closure easy. First, as the dialogue above illustrates, participants in a consensus building group may not agree on whether they have worked hard enough to justify suspending the quest for *every* stakeholder's support. In fact, for obvious reasons, the few who cannot live with the proposed package may strongly resist the view of the majority that this moment has been reached. Moreover, shifting from the goal of unanimous agreement to overwhelming agreement can be a disappointing and painful process. And even after that decision has been made, the group must still work through difficult decisions about how to finalize its results: Will dissenters have any voice in the final agreement? What will the group say to the public and the press about the degree of its success? Will there be any room for renegotiation?

The task force should go through a two-step process to navigate through these difficult waters:

1. Use the non-unanimity rule only as a last resort, and
2. Find ways of acknowledging dissent.

Use the Non-Unanimity Rule Only as a Last Resort

While we strongly support decision rules that allow the group to ratify a package that has won agreement from almost all stakeholders, we think it is equally critical that consensus building groups be wary of abandoning the goal of full consensus too early.

As the story of the Regional Health and Human Services Task Force illustrates, obstacles to producing consensus often surface as a group is nearing the end of its deliberations. Even though a group may feel it has done all it can to create the best possible package, there may still be stakeholders who feel they can't sign on until changes are made. At this point, those who are emotionally invested in the package they helped to create may be impatient with the suggestion that the group continue working to meet the interests of the holdouts. They may also put unfair pressure on those whose interests have not yet been fully met to abandon their resistance. As discussed earlier, consensus building groups must be very careful to avoid thin-ice agreements at moments like these.

Avoiding thin-ice agreements requires using a non-unanimity decision rule only as the very last resort. In our experience, groups with the strongest commitment to consensus are the most creative and successful in developing options and packages to meet the interests of all stakeholders. In contrast, groups that have established majority or supermajority decision rules are less likely to put their creative energy to work to satisfy all stakeholders.[7]

Before applying a non-unanimity decision rule, group members need to determine whether they have done everything they can to meet the interests of those stakeholders who say they cannot live with the proposed agreement. Specifically, a group needs to ask:

1. Have we looked as hard as we can for additional joint gains?
2. Have we used fair standards to allocate joint gains?
3. Have we given all stakeholders who can't live with this agreement an opportunity to propose another option or package that (a) better meets their interests and (b) leaves no other stakeholder worse off than if the group accepted the current package?

The facilitator has an important role to play at this moment. When some group members begin advocating acceptance of overwhelming agreement, the facilitator can put these questions before group members and remind them that a final result that meets these three tests will be far more durable. If the group's efforts do stand up to those three tests, then group members ought to feel good about what they have been able to accomplish, even if the ultimate goal of unanimity was not realized.

Acknowledge Dissent

If, after careful deliberation, a consensus building group decides that it cannot meet the demands of one or several stakeholders and that accepting overwhelming agreement (however it was defined in the group's ground rules) appears to be the best option for bringing the group's work to a close, then members should engage in a frank conversation about how the results of the group's work will be presented.

Consistent with the core principles of consensus building, we recommend that groups in this position decide on a way of presenting their agreement that not only acknowledges the fact that there are dissenters but also allows their views to be heard. This communicates the group's respect for the interests of the stakeholder group(s) that withheld support. It also supports the group's commitment to pursue open and honest dialogue and to avoid glossing over differences of opinion at any stage in the process.

Assuming that the group creates a written record of its agreement, there are several specific options for acknowledging dissent. If an opposing stakeholder is having trouble with one element of the agreement but can support the other elements, then the group may want to consider including a statement of this dissent within the section of the written agreement that addresses this element. The task force might, for example, offer the Provider Council an opportunity to add some language describing why it disagrees with the task force's decision on how to handle intake for the low-income health insurance program. This language could be inserted into the section describing the task force's recommendation on intake staffing. (In some cases, an offer to include a description of the range of views on a particular provision might be enough to tip the opposing stakeholder toward a decision to "live with" the agreement after all.)

If the opposing member is unhappy not with one particular recommendation but rather with the agreement as a whole, then a better option may be to ask if the member would like to attach a "dissenting opinion" to the final written document, in the form of a letter or formal statement.

One final option is to acknowledge dissent on a final signature page of the document. Consensus building groups often include such a page indicating that each stakeholder supports the agreement and is committed to supporting its implementation. In cases where unanimous consent has not been possible, the signature page can also include a column for the signatures of those who are withholding their support. It might also include a column for abstainers: participants who cannot fully commit to supporting the agreement but who do not feel the need to express active opposition. Acknowledging dissent on a signature page gives a snapshot of where a group stands, but it does not explain *why* one or more groups are not fully satisfied with the outcome.

Which option for acknowledging dissent makes the most sense will depend on the group's particular circumstances. In every case, though, a group should develop a way of acknowledging dissent that will help clarify for group members and the public at large what the extent of support for the agreement actually is, and why.

Finally, what a group says publicly about the nature of the agreement it has reached can be as important as the actual words on the page. When a group decides it has achieved closure on an agreement that has overwhelming but not unanimous support, it is essential for participants to discuss what will be said in the world beyond the negotiating room about the outcome. The one or few stakeholders who are unable to lend their support to the agreement may be especially anxious about this; they may want some assurance that a group won't gloss over the fact that the agreement has deficiencies from their perspective. (See Chapter 11 for more on sharing the results of a process with the media.)

The Task Force Reaches Closure

The task force has now heard the Provider Council's final proposal on the staffing issue, and the exchange between Barry and Jenny about whether the task force has done as much as it can to seek consensus. At this point, facilitator Jan Philips polls the group on whether members want to continue deliberating on the Provider Council's proposal. All of the task force members except Barry say that they believe the time has come for the group to ratify the current package, staying with the recommendation for the HMO, not human service providers, to handle intake for the subsidized health insurance program. Barry notes that the Provider Council cannot support the strategic plan and would like the plan to include a letter from the Provider Council explaining why not.

Jan asks the group for responses to the Provider Council's request. Most members say that they are willing to include a letter from the Provider Council. Speaking for the HMO, Wilma Carter says that her organization would like to review the letter before agreeing to attach it to the plan. Several other members also say that they would like to review the letter. Barry responds, with some bitterness, that the group has nothing to fear from the Provider Council. "The council won't sabotage this agreement, but we will keep on advocating for the region's low-income residents, because we don't think the plan does enough to meet their interests." The meeting closes with an agreement that Barry will provide a draft letter from the Provider Council to Jan, who will circulate it to all members of the task force for review.

■ *Conclusion*

In this chapter, we have reviewed several key challenges that groups face as they seek to produce consensus. We noted that these challenges are not necessarily the result of inadequate preparation, deliberation, or negotiation. They may arise even in groups whose participants have prepared well and created substantial joint gains. They often reflect underlying conflicts of interest that simply cannot be resolved with the time and resources available to the group. We also pointed out that strong emotions are a crosscutting challenge during the "end game" of a consensus building process.

We suggested three basic strategies for meeting these challenges, and for achieving the best possible agreement even when the group cannot produce full consensus. Through the saga of the Health and Human Services Task Force and other examples from our consensus building work, we saw how these strategies can be applied in difficult situations.

In conclusion, we want to underscore the need for all consensus building groups to take a few key procedural steps that maximize the opportunities for producing consensus.

1. At the beginning of a process, clearly define the group's goals and decision rules. Be sure that *seeking* consensus (meaning agreement of all stakeholders) is a core goal and that the ground rules include some provision for reaching

closure in the event that not all stakeholders can live with a proposed agreement.

2. When the group has created one or more packages that almost all stakeholders can support, offer those whose interests are still not satisfied the opportunity to propose alternatives that they could live with and that leave no other member of the group worse off.

3. If it is necessary to reach closure without unanimity, offer those who cannot live with the final agreement the opportunity to express their dissent, and recognize all participants' efforts to seek consensus.

Churchill once said of democracy that it may be "the worst system ever invented, except for all the others." As a form of democratic politics, consensus building certainly has its share of maddening moments and procedural limitations. Still, despite the challenges and frustrations, groups that seek consensus usually produce better agreements than those that do not try.

■ *Notes*

1. See also the procedural tests proposed in Lawrence Susskind's "A Short Guide to Consensus Building," Part 1 of this volume.

2. Our view of best practice has been shaped by Doyle and Straus (1982), Fisher, Ury, and Patton (1991), Schwarz (1994), Susskind and Cruikshank (1987), and Moore (1996); by our practice; and by our conversations with other facilitators and students of group work.

3. The better a stakeholder's alternative to any agreement that the consensus building group might reach, the higher the stakeholder's minimum requirements for agreement can be.

4. This example is loosely based on a case mediated by the authors in 1998.

5. This example is loosely based on the work of a group facilitated by the authors in 1998.

6. Contingent agreements can appeal to risk takers as well as to those seeking to minimize risk. Imagine two venture capitalists, Karen and Carlos, are negotiating how much each will contribute to a new investment. Karen is confident that the investment will do extremely well, whereas Carlos is skeptical. Carlos might propose to Karen that (1) she puts up 60 percent of the investment money, and he puts up 40 percent; (2) they split the first $1 million in profits 50-50; and (3) if the investment yields more than $1 million Karen takes 75 percent of everything above that level.

7. We are indebted to Patrick Field, Matt McKinney, Susan Podziba, Ric Richardson, Greg Sobel, Ralph Steinglass, Larry Susskind, and other Consensus Building Institute staff and colleagues for their comments on the use of non-unanimity decision rules at an informal meeting held October 29, 1998 in Cambridge, Massachusetts.

■ References

Doyle, M., & Straus, D. (1982). *How to make meetings work.* New York: Jove.

Fisher, R., Ury, W., & Patton, B. (1991). *Getting to yes: Negotiating agreement without giving in* (2nd ed.). New York: Penguin.

Moore, C. W. (1996). *The mediation process: Practical strategies for resolving conflict* (2nd ed.). San Francisco: Jossey-Bass.

Schwarz, R. (1994). *The skilled facilitator: Practical wisdom for developing effective groups.* San Francisco: Jossey-Bass.

Susskind, L. E., & Cruikshank, J. (1987). *Breaking the impasse: Consensual approaches to resolving public disputes.* New York: Basic Books.

9

JOINT FACT-FINDING AND THE USE OF TECHNICAL EXPERTS

- *John R. Ehrmann*
- *Barbara L. Stinson*

Picture yourself in a controversial dispute that puts you at odds with your friends and neighbors. Local developers in your town have proposed to build a 25,000-square-foot office building on the edge of your subdivision, an area zoned for commercial use (but left vacant) for the past 25 years. You are concerned that the development will create traffic and noise problems and will encourage more businesses to move into the area. You also think that, for aesthetic and environmental reasons, the land should remain open. Some of your neighbors, however, argue that a new office building will generate tax dollars, provide local businesses with more customers, and increase property values. Ever since you learned about the project two years ago, you have complained to the city council and the planning board, but they seem unconcerned about possible impacts on the community. The developers have received nearly all the permits they need; barring any delays, they will begin construction in four months.

You recently learned, though, that a rare songbird nests in the area and will soon be listed as a "threatened species" by the U.S. Fish and Wildlife Service. You and your like-minded neighbors have raised money to study the nesting area on the chance that this rare bird will be disturbed if the development proceeds. Your consultant's findings are conclusive; they support reexamining the construction permits that have already been granted.

As the consultant prepares to present his findings at a city council meeting, you are horrified to learn that an equally prominent biologist has also studied the area and drawn the opposite conclusion. She sees no threat to the habitat. You have been told that, through administrative hearings, public meetings, and even courtroom confrontations, the "dueling experts" might still be able to delay things, but eventually local leaders will make a decision about who "wins." You groan, thinking, "There must be a better way!"

Fortunately, there is. *Joint fact-finding* offers an alternative to the process of *adversary science* when important technical or science-intensive issues are at stake. Joint fact-finding is a central component of many consensus building processes; it extends the interest-based, cooperative efforts of parties engaged in consensus building into the realm of information gathering and scientific analysis. In joint fact-finding, stakeholders with differing viewpoints and interests work together to develop data and information, analyze facts and forecasts, develop common assumptions and informed opinion, and, finally, use the information they have developed to reach decisions together.[1]

Information gaps and scientific uncertainty are inherent in policy disputes in our society. Many disputes, after all, grow out of disagreements over economic, environmental, and social priorities. The "fuel" for these disputes is often data about the likely impact—on a particular group of citizens, on someone's financial investment, or on the environment—of a decision.

Parties with differing interests, therefore, will quite naturally look to scientific experts to influence the outcome of a dispute. This is particularly true when parties are engaged in litigation, in which a judge or jury makes the decision, or when parties are seeking to influence the policy decision of a government agency or body of elected officials. In these traditional decision-making arenas, proponents and opponents of a project might each hire technical experts to provide analyses, forecasts, and impact assessments to support or undermine a proposed project, as in the example above. This creates difficulties for both sides. They both must go to great expense to "buy" technical expertise so that they can participate effectively. And, it seems, there are always experts available to provide the answers that support each side's point of view. Does this make technical expertise less valuable? No, but it suggests that the manner in which technical or scientific information is gathered may be as relevant as the information itself.

"Joint fact-finding assumes that parties with conflicting interests will interpret material differently."

Consensus-based processes invest decision-making responsibility in a group of stakeholders with diverse interests, not just in an elected or appointed decision maker. Joint fact-finding in a consensus process assumes that parties with conflicting interests will interpret technical material differently but that they ought to gather and develop facts and forecasts together. Specifically, stakeholders should jointly determine the issues of concern that require technical analysis, the questions that the experts ought to ask (and who those experts should be), the best process for gathering information and answering questions, the limitations of the various analytical methods that will be used, and the best way of proceeding once a scientific or technical analysis is completed.

In an effort to describe how these tasks should be completed, the rest of this chapter is organized as follows. It begins by describing the advantages of joint fact-finding, and then it outlines the circumstances under which fact-finding should and should not be used. Next, it looks at the roles participants and technical experts can play in joint fact-finding and offers a process for selecting the appropriate experts. Finally, the chapter describes the five key steps in a typical joint fact-finding effort and the obstacles to effective joint fact-finding.

■ *Advantages of Joint Fact-Finding*

Joint fact-finding offers a unique opportunity for participants in a consensus building process to address information gaps and scientific uncertainty. Participants involved in joint fact-finding often learn a great deal about the scientific underpinnings of various arguments—something they would not otherwise have an opportunity to do. In addition, consensus processes that include a joint fact-finding step will likely produce agreements that are more credible, more creative, and more durable than they would be otherwise. Joint fact-finding also enables parties to build strong relationships, as they gain a better understanding of each other's interests. These benefits are explored below.

Gaining Knowledge and Understanding

If stakeholders are to forge agreements that address complex, technical issues, they need to develop a common understanding of those issues. Joint fact-finding enables parties to explore difficult topics together, so that they can develop a common knowledge base. It also allows those stakeholders with less knowledge, education, or expertise to learn more about the technical issues involved so that they can negotiate on a more equal footing.

The Northern Oxford County Coalition (NOCC, Case 2) is an excellent example of a situation in which stakeholders gained knowledge and expertise together through joint fact-finding. In this case, some residents of the Androscoggin River valley in northern Oxford County, Maine became increasingly concerned that they faced higher than average risks of cancer due to air pollution from a local paper mill. The media, in fact, dubbed the region "Cancer Valley." Other residents were equally concerned that any action against the mill would cause it to close, costing hundreds of people their jobs and severely damaging the local economy. The mill, which was in compliance with all environmental regulations, disputed the charges made against it, and almost no scientific data existed to support or disprove the various viewpoints.

In response to growing fears, the Maine Department of Environmental Protection convened the NOCC—a diverse group of local residents that included concerned citizens, business owners, public health officials, and representatives of the mill—to study and analyze cancer incidence and air pollution levels in the valley. NOCC ultimately formed two subcommittees (one on public health and one on air quality) and commissioned a study by a jointly selected independent consultant. Most NOCC members did not have any previous technical expertise on these issues and were not scientists, but through a long process of jointly analyzing and synthesizing data and learning from the consultant about basic scientific methods and limitations, group members gained enough of a technical background to feel comfortable presenting their findings in a clear and concise way to the public. Although much of the data they gathered were inconclusive, stakeholders were able to understand why that was the case.

Crafting Better Agreements

When participants in a collaborative process conduct statistical analyses, risk assessments, surveys, or other types of joint research (or work with a technical expert to do so), they have a better chance of identifying the most accurate information possible. The New York Bight Initiative (Case 6) provides a good example of how a sound agreement was based on jointly developed technical data. In that consensus building process, 22 parties met in more than 10 plenary meetings over a three-year period to analyze PCB contamination in the New York Bight and explore Bight management and restoration options. In the end, 18 parties ratified an agreement resulting from the negotiations. Almost all the parties felt that the document was "a good synthesis" of the technical information available about PCB sources, fates, and effects. Clearly, the participants believed that the recommendations for action included in the document were based on the best available scientific information.

Joint fact-finding can also help parties construct agreements that are not just more credible but also more creative. When diverse stakeholders work together to gather and interpret data, they draw on each other's experience, knowledge, and ideas. They can look for innovative ways to develop and use technical information to find an agreement that no single individual could have generated alone.

More durable decisions can also result from joint fact-finding. If all parties who must support an agreement are involved in gathering and assessing the information on which that agreement is based, they are more likely to stand by the agreement that is ultimately reached.

Finally, collaborative processes incorporating joint fact-finding are more likely to reach consensus than might otherwise be the case. In negotiations in which adversary science prevails, coalitions form behind technical experts or interpretations. Each side seeks to discredit the data offered by others. Often, this convinces the public and the press that the technical aspects of the debate are either hopelessly irresolvable or irrelevant. Parties working together, however, investing their ideas, time, and resources into jointly seeking good information, become devoted to reaching a mutually agreeable outcome and explaining that outcome to their constituencies and the public.

Improved Relationships

Joint fact-finding enables individuals with differing interests to work together toward a shared goal. This process fosters trust, enhances communication, and builds understanding—all of which make for a more productive consensus building process.

In the NOCC case, participants came to know and respect one another better in the joint fact-finding process than they had when verbally sparring in public meetings or through the press. Relationships were so significantly improved, in fact, that the diverse stakeholders agreed to work together after the NOCC process was completed on a Healthy Communities effort, a collaborative endeavor that focuses broadly on improving environmental quality, public health, public safety, and economic health in the area.

■ When to Use Joint Fact-Finding Procedures

Joint fact-finding is useful in many situations. Cases involving highly technical, science-intensive decision making often benefit from joint fact-finding procedures. Disputes that hinge on a lack of critical information, or where charges of inaccuracy have been made publicly, should have a fact-finding component. Parties who have a long history of disagreement and poor relationships can benefit from undertaking collaborative research. Joint fact-finding can also be used to assist participants in breaking a deadlock.

To assess in more detail when joint fact-finding should be used, we will look closely at two situations in which it was very helpful. The first case—that of the Massachusetts Military Reservation (MMR, Case 7)—involves a science-intensive dispute; that is, technical and scientific data, and the interpretation of those data, were central to every aspect of the negotiations. The second case—that of a federal regulatory negotiation involving architectural and industrial maintenance (AIM) paints and coatings (the

"AIM negotiated rulemaking")—is a situation in which the information necessary to make decisions was lacking and had to be compiled in a central database.

The MMR is a 22,000-acre active military facility on Cape Cod that was declared a Superfund site due to soil and groundwater contamination. At MMR, local residents, environmentalists, state and federal agency officials, and the military disagreed about the method that should be used to clean up groundwater contamination plumes and what level of remediation was necessary. There was a great deal of scientific uncertainty and disagreement regarding which cleanup methods would be most effective. To address this uncertainty, stakeholders created a multidisciplinary team of technical experts, called the Technical Review and Evaluation Team (TRET), to develop recommendations regarding treatment options. TRET members included representatives of the U.S. Environmental Protection Agency (EPA), the Massachusetts Department of Environmental Protection, the National Guard, the U.S. Geological Survey, and the Cape Cod Commission (a regional planning body). The TRET devised a process for jointly gathering information, analyzing it, and developing recommendations. Using a joint fact-finding approach that involved risk assessments and hydrogeological modeling, TRET members devised consensus recommendations within less than two months.

In the MMR case, joint fact-finding made sense for three reasons. First, uncertainty about the likely effectiveness of alternative cleanup technologies was at the heart of the dispute. It made more sense to bring technical experts together to take a first cut at this issue than to ask elected or appointed officials to wrestle with what was a daunting technical task. Second, a great many technical specialties needed to be tapped. It was better to have them working together, drawing on a common database, than working at cross-purposes. Third, joint fact-finding made it easier for the public to understand the scope of the technical uncertainty involved. Because all the technical matter was discussed in a single setting, the decision-making process was very transparent and therefore publicly accountable.

The AIM negotiated rulemaking began in 1993, when the EPA convened a multiparty group to help set federal standards regarding acceptable levels of volatile organic compounds (VOCs)[2] in paints and other coatings. (The authors facilitated the group's negotiations.) The EPA agreed that if a balanced group of diverse stakeholders could agree on VOC limits for paints and coatings, the draft EPA rule aimed at controlling these emissions would be based on their agreement. Not all the stakeholders who came to the table believed that VOCs were harmful to humans or the environment, but given that the EPA was required by law to regulate this class of products, they decided it was better to take part than to remain on the sidelines.

At the outset, participants agreed that existing information on the VOC content of paints and coatings was inadequate. In particular, the EPA did not know the volume of paints and coatings being manufactured or the current VOC content of each. This information was necessary to negotiate appropriate future levels of VOCs. Participants jointly developed a protocol (i.e., a common set of questions and methods for data collection) regarding the type of information that needed to be collected, how it should be collected, and how it should be analyzed. They decided to undertake a detailed, industrywide survey of paint manufacturers of all types. An independent consulting firm that was acceptable to all parties was selected to conduct the analysis. The firm collected detailed information from 900 companies on more than 9,000 products. Each company reported the volume of paints and coatings it produced and the VOC content of each product. The result of this data-gathering and analysis effort was a list of 22 categories of products with data on the volume produced, volume sold, and VOC content of each category.

The National Paint and Coatings Association (NPCA), an industry group, offered to pay for the consultant, because its members believed that it was in their interest to have the regulation based on the best available information. The other parties readily agreed to have NPCA pay. They were not concerned about NPCA influencing the outcome of the analysis, because all parties helped to design the scope of work and chose the technical consultant. They also interacted directly with the consultant during ongoing discussions.

The results of the survey served as the factual basis for the negotiations that followed. The data compiled were used to assess potential reductions in emissions that might be achieved, as well as to determine the paints that required higher levels of VOCs to perform as designed. The information-gathering process proved useful in two ways. First, it provided a valuable database of industrywide information; second, it enabled parties to learn more about paint and coating properties and functions and industry trends regarding the use of different products.

The parties worked for three years to develop a negotiated rule. In the final stage of the negotiation, some parties could not support the proposed emissions limits. However, the proposed agreement and the data generated during the joint fact-finding phase served as the basis for the EPA's final regulation.

We will now look at what these two cases reveal about when joint fact-finding can and should be used.

Disagreements about Information

Joint fact-finding is particularly useful in disputes in which parties interpret data and information differently, or where there is a great deal of scientific uncertainty, as in the MMR case. In these situations, some information may be available, but parties differ in their assessment of the quality of the information, the reliability of the methodology used to develop it, what additional data are needed, how they should be used, and so forth. Participants can always argue that more information might lead to a better decision, which they may be inclined to do if they are not happy with the direction in which a negotiation is headed.

In other cases, such as the AIM negotiated rulemaking, adequate information simply is not available in a useful form and must be developed. A carefully constructed process of joint fact-finding can enable stakeholders to obtain additional information, gain agreement on how it should be used, and agree on methods to check whatever analysis is done. Similarly, joint fact-finding can assist parties when information or data are available but some people believe them to be inaccurate or flawed.

Low Levels of Trust among Participants

In complex public disputes, participants often say they want to rely on "good science." Many factors influence their determination of what good science is and what it is not. One important factor is the strength of the parties' relationships and the level of trust among them. Parties that do not trust or respect each other are more likely to criticize each other's interpretations of scientific findings.

In cases in which trust is low and the dueling-experts problem seems likely to emerge, joint fact-finding can be useful. As in the AIM case, collaborative information gathering can enable participants to work together to develop a common base of knowledge from which to negotiate. A successful joint fact-finding endeavor can help improve the dynamics of a group, giving participants confidence that they may be able to reach consensus.

One joint fact-finding process, initiated by a regional transportation agency, began as an effort to confirm that a decision made by state and federal agencies to extend an urban mass transit system into a sensitive environmental area in the surrounding suburbs was reasonable. Through a multiyear joint study of impacts and options, a 45-member task force was able to generate an entirely new transit system design and assist the agencies involved in modifying their plans for highway changes and related land uses. By the end of the process, the participants had worked together long enough to be able to transform their concerns into detailed, jointly agreed-on alternative plans (Forester, 1994).

Design of the Process

Joint fact-finding procedures can be tailored to almost any consensus building effort. They should be used, however, only when they are fully incorporated into a process—when explicit ground rules have been developed for conducting the joint research and when participants have agreed on a way to incorporate the results of this effort back into the deliberations of the consensus building group. In addition, the full range of stakeholders should be involved in the design and delivery of the process.

Joint fact-finding should increase, not detract from, the fairness of a negotiation. For example, it would not be appropriate for a set of parties representing one view to pay for an outside expert, unless the arrangement were acceptable to all the participants (as in the AIM case). Also, a fact-finding process that is forced on participants or seems to have no connection to the main deliberations will only exacerbate the tendency for parties to polarize on the issues involved.

Availability of Human and Financial Resources

Joint fact-finding can be expensive and time-consuming, in part because it often involves selecting and hiring technical or scientific experts. The selection process involves a small consensus building effort in and of itself, and thus takes some time. The expert(s) chosen generally have to be paid a daily fee. In addition, sufficient time and funds must be available to ensure that all parties have a fair opportunity to have input into a fact-finding process. No single interest group's perspective should dominate simply because it has more resources. Joint fact-finding should be used only after participants carefully assess the human and financial resources necessary to carry it out and determine that those resource are available.

When Not to Use Joint Fact-Finding

In certain circumstances, it may not be appropriate to pursue joint fact-finding. In cases in which there are significant power imbalances among the parties, for example, and powerful parties are seeking to use joint fact-finding to reinforce that imbalance, it is not in the interests of some parties to pursue a collaborative effort. When there is a severe disparity in expertise, joint fact-finding may not be appropriate if ways cannot be found to equalize access to expertise.

If parties do not believe they can construct a fair fact-finding process that will be used to garner mutually beneficial data and information, it should not be pursued. When fact-finding cannot be effectively integrated into a dispute resolution or consensus building process, it may not be appropriate to introduce it. If there are not adequate financial resources to complete a thorough and satisfactory process, parties may elect to use existing information. Stakeholders should work to jointly develop a fact-finding process, but if they are unable to develop a mutually agreeable plan, they should perhaps proceed in another manner.

■ *Who Does the Fact-Finding?*

"Participants themselves may gather and analyze information, or they may hire outside experts."

In a consensus building process that includes joint fact-finding, participants themselves may gather and analyze information, or they may hire outside technical or scientific experts to do these tasks. This section explores these two options and includes a discussion of how best to select outside experts if the second option is chosen. We also examine the important role that neutral parties (e.g., mediators) can play as interlocutors on behalf of technically less knowledgeable groups.

Parties as Fact-Finders

Sometimes, participants in consensus-based negotiations possess scientific or technical expertise. In such cases, the parties themselves can address technical matters. Critical to the implementation of this approach is an agreement that a fact-finding component is needed. Participants may then choose to form a work group to investigate scientific issues, or the full negotiating group can be involved. Several important design issues should be considered if a work group is to be appropriately used.

1. The role and objectives of a fact-finding group must be clearly articulated. If all stakeholders agree about a work group's goals, they will likely accept the results that emerge from it. The full group must provide a clear mandate to any sub-work groups that are formed.
2. Participants in a work group should reflect the diversity of interests and perspectives in the overall group, so that the conclusions they reach will be credible to all parties. Sometimes, people representing one set of interests may not have the right expertise to send someone to a work group. In this case, they might want to ask one of their constituents, who does have the right knowledge, to take part.
3. A work group must have adequate time and resources to carry out its joint fact-finding tasks.

The use of participants to conduct joint research provides a side benefit: It increases the analytical capabilities and knowledge of all representatives, creating a more level playing field. In the AIM process, for example, it would have been almost impossible for the environmental interests to have adequate information about industry practices without joint fact-finding. This would have put them at an extreme disadvantage in the negotiations. Due to the joint data collection effort, one of the lead environmental representatives was able to use the raw data to develop a computer analysis of the potential VOC reductions that would be forthcoming from any proposal offered by other parties.

The structure of the joint fact-finding work groups is important. One option is to invite anyone who wants to join to attend. Another is to limit membership to only those with technical credentials. We would almost always opt for the first, although we would also work hard to ensure that the most technically sophisticated members of the group had agreed beforehand to join the work group. On highly technical and controversial issues, such as selecting a site and a disposal method for handling low-level nuclear waste, it is critical that a site selection task force includes the political representation of potential host communities, the lead scientists from federal and state agencies, and industry representatives. Although any number of consultants are capable of collecting the relevant information, ranking sites, and suggesting the "most appropriate" location for a new repository, the final siting recommendations will have no credibility unless the full range of stakeholder interests is directly involved (Susskind & Laws, 1994).

Using Outside Scientific and Technical Resources

Parties often opt to use outside help to gather and analyze data, particularly when they do not have sufficient expertise among them. A group may choose to use a single outside expert, a panel of experts, a consulting firm, or the resources of an academic institution.

Single Expert

In some cases, a single individual can be identified who has the appropriate expertise and will be acceptable to all parties. The NOCC in Maine, for example, chose one expert (an epidemiologist) to work with them to devise a cancer incidence study. Given the complex dynamics that typically characterize science-intensive consensus processes, however, it may not be possible to find one individual who is trusted by all parties or has sufficient breadth of expertise to be helpful.

Panel of Experts

Often, as a result of having to build a process that is acceptable to diverse participants and can handle the full range of issues involved, consensus building groups select a panel of experts. In these instances, attention should be paid to the process used to select the experts so that a range of opinions and methodological backgrounds is represented. In the New York Bight process, a very systematic approach was employed in selecting experts. When the mediation team interviewed stakeholders during the convening process, they asked interviewees to nominate scientists whose expertise could illuminate technical aspects of the issues at hand. This process yielded a roster of about 80 people from diverse specialties. Of this list, 40 were academics and 40 were agency staff or consultants. The parties were able to narrow the list once it was clear that PCBs were to be the focus of the negotiation. The mediation team and the parties then determined which experts were the most appropriate to assist in the joint fact-finding process. Ultimately, 23 scientists provided assistance to the project at various points.

Academic and Consulting Resources

In some cases, an academic institution or consulting firm can serve as a resource for fact-finding. In the AIM case, a consulting firm was retained to conduct the data collection and analyses. In a case like that, in which information gathering is the primary objective, a consulting firm can often provide the necessary services. Negotiators should remain directly involved in designing the scope of work and assessing and monitoring the results. Academic assistance is often more credible than consulting help, because university-based scientists are presumed to be working in the public interest while private consultants are presumed, often unfairly, to be motivated by profit. These presumptions must be tested and dealt with in each case.

In the New York Bight case, the experts who participated were recruited from many organizations, but the overall research effort was conducted under the auspices of the New York Academy of Sciences. At the end of the process, the academy endorsed the final report. Support of the academy throughout and at the conclusion of the process was critical to the positive outcome since it is held in such high regard by public officials in the region.

Selecting Outside Technical Experts

Once participants have decided what kind of expert(s) they need, they must define criteria for the selection of those experts, identify potential sources of candidates, and determine a fair process for selection. They should also develop a budget for technical services and identify potential sources of funding.

Criteria for Selection

Before a group can identify appropriate technical expertise, its members must determine what they want the expert(s) to do. In particular, they must assess what issues need to be addressed and what questions need to be answered. (These decisions are discussed at length in the next section.) This will help to define criteria for the selection of experts. Criteria might include type of expertise, level of experience, reputation, references, availability to complete the tasks in the desired time, ability to work within the budget, and experience in a multiparty, collaborative setting.

Sources for Candidates

Experts might come from universities, consulting firms, government agencies, or other private and public entities. Parties might identify potential candidates by talking to professional contacts, references from those contacts, or staff of appropriate professional associations. Computer-based searches of the World Wide Web offer another quick way to generate possible advisers, as do library searches aimed at generating a list of well-known authors on a topic.

Fair Selection Process

A consensus building group must design a fair selection process that allows for the identification of the most qualified and affordable candidates who will be acceptable to all parties. In some cases, the full group may wish to help choose the experts, but if there is adequate trust among the parties, a subgroup can perform this task.

Participants might begin a selection process by identifying an initial slate of candidates that meets the most important selection criteria. The next step would be to obtain bids from these candidates. Parties could then use the criteria again, in a more focused way, to narrow the list. They also might interview the most promising candidates, if time permits. Parties should discuss and try to come to agreement on the best potential candidate(s) through dialogue. Or they may wish to prioritize candidates individually or in caucus and then compare their results. If a polling process of some sort is used, it is best to take only straw polls. Final decisions should be made by consensus if at all possible.

Cost of Assistance

The cost of hiring outside consultants can be considerable. Parties need to identify a budget for the activities and possible sources of funds for covering the costs. Sometimes potential advisers will be willing to help a group sketch a range of budget options. A budget should include the full cost of completing the selection process, information gathering, data analysis, and development of decision options for the issues to be addressed. In some cases, it may not be possible to conduct full and thorough analyses given budget constraints, in which case participants will need to prioritize their information needs.

Sources of funding might include the parties themselves, a single party with adequate funds and enough interest to warrant coverage of the expenses, or private foundations. In the AIM case, the paint industry considered it so much in their interest to develop an adequate database that they paid for the services of a consulting firm to do the job. Sometimes a technical expert will be interested enough in the topic and the challenge of working in a consensus building setting that he or she will offer to work pro bono. In the NOCC case, for instance, the analyst was personally interested in the case and the consensus process and provided his services without charge.

Occasionally, only a few parties in a consensus building process feel they need additional information or outside technical advice, while others may feel it is not warranted. In this circumstance, a group may need to hire technical experts to assist the parties who want help to create a more equal level of knowledge and understanding of the critical issues. There is the danger, of course, of other parties bringing in opposing consultants, resulting in the old problem of dueling experts. To avoid this, parties should agree there is a need for the assistance, jointly design an acceptable selection process, and then establish common rules for how the assistance will be used. They may need the help of a mediator if they disagree strongly on any of these items.

■ *Building Lasting Agreements:*
  Steps in a Joint Fact-Finding Process

Joint fact-finding comes in many shapes and sizes. Parties entering into joint fact-finding at the beginning of a consensus process can integrate it into all stages of their negotiations. A joint fact-finding component can also be added later in a decision-making process, if critical information is found to be missing or if parties reach an impasse. In this section, we describe the critical steps in a joint fact-finding effort initiated at the beginning of a consensus building process.

The idea of undertaking fact-finding generally arises when participants realize that they need a deeper understanding to resolve a problem or find a way to deal with scientific uncertainty. In a joint fact-finding process, participants must determine (1) the issues of concern that require further information, (2) a process for gathering information and answering key questions, (3) the questions to be asked and the method of analysis to be used, (4) any limitations on the analytical methods to be used, and (5) the best ways of proceeding once new information is available.

Define Issues of Concern

Participants should begin a joint fact-finding endeavor by defining the problem or issue to be resolved. They might do this by having people state the issues of concern from their perspectives and the questions they believe need to be addressed to reach consensus. Parties may wish to brainstorm these issues and withhold criticism until all possible ideas are on the table. Once participants fully understand each other's perspectives, they can begin to delve further, through dialogue, to get at the underlying interests that drive those concerns. With a more complete basis of understanding, parties can begin to jointly identify the most crucial information gaps or uncertainties that exist and the issues that could be appropriately pursued in a fact-finding process.

This first step is often the most difficult. For example, in the case of efforts to site low-level radioactive waste repositories, getting agreement on what questions to ask is almost impossible. Opponents of nuclear power, who believe that by making it impossible to dispose of waste safely they can create additional pressure to close down power plants, will insist that the question that needs to be answered is, "How can a completely safe site and disposal technology be found?" Others, who take a narrower view of their task, will be looking for a disposal site that will meet federal and state requirements—requirements that do not call for zero risk.

Parties should also discuss potential frameworks for analyzing issues and how the information gathered will be used. To define a framework, parties should assess the information that exists on the problems or issues and then identify a mechanism for filling in gaps or resolving unanswered questions.

It is important during this phase that parties at the table discuss the potential for joint fact-finding with the constituencies they represent, so that the full set of issues likely to be of concern is identified at the outset. Such a list can be refined and narrowed over time, but problems are likely to emerge later in a process if a major topic of concern is missed at the beginning. In the case of environmental impact assessment, the process for considering the environmental damage likely to be caused by a proposed project, this initial step is called *scoping* (Jain et al., 1993). Scoping is done in a very public way to ensure that all the issues of concern to stakeholders are enumerated.

Define the Process for Gathering Information

In creating a process for gathering and analyzing information, participants must define ground rules, determine who will manage the process (e.g., a subgroup or the full group), select appropriate experts to assist (if necessary), determine confidentiality needs and reporting requirements, and, preliminarily, discuss how the information will be used in the consensus building negotiations. The selection of experts and the use of work groups to manage a process were discussed in the previous section; the other tasks in this step will be described here.

Ground rules should cover the roles and responsibilities of participants who will be involved, the expert selection process, confidentiality, reporting, and general intentions on how the information will be used. These should be circulated and agreed to by the parties before the fact-finding effort begins. Just like ground rules governing an overall consensus process, these guidelines help to clarify the "rules of the game," so that questions do not arise at the end of a process about how it was carried out.

These kinds of ground rules are not that difficult to formulate. For example, it is often helpful to have a ground rule such as "Participants in this joint fact-finding process agree not to distribute any information they receive until the group as a whole agrees on the timing and method of its distribution." This can avoid misinterpretation and further conflict.

Confidentiality may be necessary if the information to be gathered is proprietary or otherwise not public knowledge. Participants will need to determine how to use such information without compromising its confidentiality. In the AIM negotiations, for example, industry representatives reported data on their paint-manufacturing inputs and processes to a neutral party (acceptable to all the participants), who then prepared summary statistics. No single company's data could be identified, but the group had what it needed to engage in joint problem solving.

Parties need to determine how consultants or experts, if they are to be used, will report back to the consensus building group. Will they give a final oral presentation to a subgroup? To the full group? Should they also prepare a written report? How many interim reports or meetings are necessary? Interim reports enable group members to assess each step, so that they can handle any disagreements about methodology or assumptions as they arise and fine-tune the process. This helps to ensure that the results will be acceptable to the full group. It is also important to be clear that experts and consultants serve at the will of the group; in other words, they should proceed with data gathering and analysis only at the participants' discretion.

Group members should also develop preliminary agreements on how information will be used. For example, will it be used to develop policy or regulatory options? They must also figure out how it will be integrated into the consensus decision-making process. For example, in some regulatory negotiations the group has used the products of joint fact-finding to draft legal language. In others, the participants have used it to simply generate a statement of principles that the agency staff then used to draft a specific regulation. This should be clear before the group begins its joint fact-finding efforts.

Define the Questions to Be Asked and the Method of Analysis

The next step is to translate the general questions to be answered into specific questions to be asked of the experts. These are not the same thing. For example, the group may want to know which sites for a facility are available in a predesignated area, but the question to the consultant needs to be much more specific, asking about the detailed criteria used to evaluate each possible site. Questions can be developed in one of three ways: Representatives can jointly identify a comprehensive list, they can individually submit questions and then compile and sort them jointly, or a small subgroup can be charged with this task.

Parties must then decide what method(s) of analysis will be used. Some participants will have greater confidence in highly rigorous, quantitative methods, while others will prefer techniques of analysis that do not allege that complicated phenomena can be quantified. They may disagree, for example, over the use of a cost-benefit analysis that seeks to quantify the value of aesthetic impacts or the value of a human life. Another common method is the statistical analysis, which assists in plotting trends and can be used to forecast future events or the likelihood of certain things occurring. Risk assessment explores the hazards and exposure levels associated with various options. Case studies provide one-of-a-kind illustrations, while surveys can be used to compute and assess patterns and perceptions drawn from many cases.[3]

Methodological battles are quite prominent in many fact-finding situations. While the strengths and weaknesses of each method of forecasting and analysis are well-known to technical professionals, they often lead to esoteric debates that completely befuddle the general public. In these circumstances, a properly trained mediator can play an interlocutor's role: asking hypothetical and clarifying questions of an expert panel on behalf of the less technically skilled stakeholders. The most important thing is to help the fact-finding group to imagine beforehand what kinds of information it might end up with. The mediator should be able to help the group anticipate the form that the information will take and the extent to which findings and forecasts are sensitive to the way in which questions are asked. Indeed, it is always helpful to have a sensitivity analysis that shows all the participants how small changes in the data-gathering protocols form or in the choice of analytic assumptions can alter the results rather markedly.

As information is collected and an analysis conducted, the questions are often refined. This step should be accounted for in the design of a process.

Define the Limitations of Analytical Methods

"It is important to become familiar with the limitations of analytical methodologies."

It is important that those responsible for joint fact-finding become familiar with the limitations of various analytical methodologies. For example, statistical analyses should be accompanied by a clear explanation of the likely margin of error that, if large, can sometimes invalidate the results. Risk assessment may not cover key questions of interest because insufficient prior information exists to make acceptable forecasts. Cost-benefit analyses may not be meaningful if certain costs or benefits are not readily quantifiable. Some individuals find the very concept of risk assessments and cost-benefit analyses to be objectionable because monetizing all values violates their sense of what is appropriate. Case studies and surveys take time and money to conduct and may not offer results in a timely fashion. Moreover, the results are entirely dependent on the samples chosen, which can be easily manipulated. Parties should examine the potential limitations of each analytical method they choose and keep those limitations in mind when reviewing findings. Even with all these limitations, it is still better to proceed using joint fact-finding than to allow each party to procure an analysis that it alone finds attractive. Only when all the stakeholders struggle with these methodological deficiencies together are they likely to end up with a pool of information that they can build on. The goal is to have a believable database that is prepared in a transparent way. It is quite appropriate, once such a database exists, for the parties to interpret the data differently, driven by their varying interests.

Define the Best Way to Proceed

As the final products of a joint fact-finding effort are reported, parties should jointly receive and discuss them. The challenging work of integrating the findings into possible options for agreements then begins. Parties may need to develop contingent agreements based on several potential options, if one option does not clearly emerge as the appropriate basis for agreement. For example, if a forecast has been prepared and one set of stakeholders assumes that the worst case will occur while another set is more optimistic and assumes the "most likely case" will occur, the full group can formulate a proposal that spells out a contingent response in case the first group turns out to be right. In other words, they can have an agreement on the most likely case, but include in that agreement a clause saying that if the worst-case scenario turns out to be the correct one, then X, Y, and Z steps should occur and/or the group will reconvene to renegotiate the agreement. A group does not need to agree on a single forecast of future events to be able to suggest an appropriate way of proceeding.

Final reports from consultants or technical work groups may not reveal definitive "answers," in which case participants must decide how to proceed in the face of continuing uncertainty. In the NOCC case, stakeholders found that health data on the incidence of cancer in the area were still not complete or conclusive, but they were able to identify interim actions that would mitigate pollution problems. In cases such as this, parties may need to spell out joint monitoring procedures that can become part of their agreement. Alternatively, they may need to make decisions based on the information they have, even if it is incomplete.

■ Obstacles to Effective Joint Fact-Finding

Even the most sophisticated, comprehensive joint fact-finding effort does not always yield useful results. Stakeholders need to consider the following possible obstacles that may arise.

When parties have extreme differences in technical background, joint fact-finding can be very challenging. Those with less knowledge will have to work hard to become familiar with the issues. However, joint fact-finding itself does provide ways to close most knowledge gaps and, ultimately, achieve mutually agreeable solutions. To accomplish this, it may be important to offer less knowledgeable parties additional training or assistance. This offer should be made to all participants, but presumably only those who need it will accept it.

Joint fact-finding can be time-consuming and difficult to coordinate. Deadlines may make it impossible to complete the kind of joint fact-finding that is really appropriate. Representatives and their constituents need to be informed about deadlines and progress to keep expectations in line with reality.

In some cases, parties will not be able to agree on the selection of an expert. Too many technical professionals may have already "taken sides" on the issue. The group should be encouraged to work hard to accommodate each other's interests in the selection process. Sometimes it helps to seek assistance from outside the region, even though this usually adds to the cost.

Occasionally, when the most comprehensive, inclusive fact-finding process has been conducted and the analyses are complete, parties will not be able to agree on how to interpret the results. In this instance, they need to define points where errors may have been made along the way, determine if their mutual assumptions have changed and address those changes, or gather additional information. Sometimes the best that can be done is to prepare a written report highlighting the elements of the analysis and the disagreements that emerged.

One of the most difficult obstacles can be when results are inconclusive. As mentioned, some parties in the NOCC case were forced to accept the fact that attributing health effects directly to the area's pollution problems would require much more research and analysis than they could afford. Parties were still able to agree on interim measures to undertake to improve public health, however. Often, it helps to search for these kinds of "no regrets" proposals: actions that might (or might not) help solve a problem but that are worth doing for other reasons as well, like improving public health.

Finally, people involved in joint fact-finding often face critical junctures in which some conclusions can be drawn from an analysis, but by gathering more information the analysis could yield better results. They must struggle to determine how much information is enough. Typically, political, financial, or time-related constraints dictate when an analysis must conclude.

■ Conclusion

Joint fact-finding, and the appropriate use of technical experts, can play an effective role in many kinds of consensus building efforts. Joint fact-finding is most useful when the parties themselves serve as the experts or when the parties select and manage their own technical advisers. The success of joint fact-finding depends on whether the information generated is adequately integrated into the consensus building process. Fact-finding that proceeds independently from the will of all the parties may fail to yield useful results or durable agreements. If properly structured, however, collaborative fact-finding can contribute to more cohesive relationships among parties and a better understanding of differing views. Fact-finding, however structured, will not necessarily lead to agreements among parties with contending interests. It will, however—if done correctly—lead to the development of increased understanding of the systems involved or the impacts that policies, programs, or projects are likely to have.

■ Notes

1. Kai Lee's book *Compass and Gyroscope* (1994) and Connie Ozawa's text *Recasting Science* (1990) are both good general sources of additional information on joint fact-finding.

2. Volatile organic compounds (VOCs) are ozone-forming chemical compounds that contribute to smog. They are released from various consumer and commercial products, such as paints, when those products are used.

3. Gary King, R. O. Keohane, and S. Verba's volume *Designing Social Inquiry* (1994) provides excellent information on research methodologies.

■ *References*

Forester, J. (1994). Lawrence Susskind: Activist mediation and public disputes. In D. M. Kolb (Ed.), *When talk works: Profiles of mediators* (pp. 309-354). San Francisco: Jossey-Bass.

Jain, R. K. et al. (1993). *Environmental assessment.* New York: McGraw-Hill.

King, G., Keohane, R. O., & Verba, S. (1994). *Designing social inquiry: Scientific inference in qualitative research.* Princeton, NJ: Princeton University Press.

Lee, K. (1994). *Compass and gyroscope: Integrating science and politics for the environment.* Washington, DC: Island.

Ozawa, C. P. (1990). *Recasting science: Consensual procedures in public policy making.* San Francisco: Westview.

Susskind, L. E., & Laws, D. (1994). Siting solid waste management facilities in the United States. In F. Kreith (Ed.), *Handbook of solid waste management* (pp. 13.1-13.13). New York: McGraw-Hill.

10

MAKING THE BEST
USE OF TECHNOLOGY

■ *Connie P. Ozawa*

omputer technologies are fast changing our world. In his
1995 book *City of Bits,* MIT Dean of Architecture William
Mitchell describes teaching a class in Singapore without
leaving his office in Cambridge, Massachusetts. He declares
himself "telepresent" after opening a screen on his desktop
computer and seeing his classroom of students. A video monitor
beside his desk displays what the students see—Dean Mitchell,
who glances over at his own image and unconsciously adjusts his
tie, as he would looking into a mirror. Not only do the students
see and hear their professor, but he can see and hear them,
respond to their questions, and give immediate feedback to their
comments. The thousands of miles of land and sea separating
them dissipate.

The infrastructure for computer-based communications technologies is growing daily. Engineers are developing ways to pack
greater and greater computing capacity onto smaller and smaller
computer chips, software developers are creating new and increasingly user-friendly applications, and the costs of these technologies are continuing to drop. Today, computers enable busi-

The author thanks Peter Adler, Todd Barker, Gail Bingham, Frank Dukes, and John Helie
for their time, stories, and insights, and the many other practicing mediators and
facilitators who answered e-mail information requests.

nesspeople to manage office affairs from their laptops while sitting on planes 30,000 feet up in the air and schoolchildren to "chat" daily with grandparents living across the continent.

The number of computers in homes and offices is also rising steadily. In 1984, only 8 percent of U.S. households owned computers. This proportion rose to 15 percent by 1989, and to 23 percent by 1993. Over the same period, the percentage of persons 18 years of age and older who used a computer at home, the office, or school doubled, growing from 18 percent to 36 percent (U.S. Bureau of the Census, 1998). By 1994, more than one-third of households with incomes of more than $35,000 owned computers; of these, more than a third had modems (U.S. Department of Commerce, 1995). But statistics tell only part of the story. The "information superhighway" can be traveled not only in privately owned vehicles but also on public transit equivalents, through access to computers at public libraries, schools, and other community-based facilities (Friedland, 1996).

In the field of consensus building, the use of computer technologies is keeping pace with the "computerization" of the broader society. As a supplement to face-to-face meetings, computer-based communication modes are increasingly being used in consensus processes, particularly in federal agency-sponsored efforts. Even large-group teleconferencing has been used—for example, by the White House in its 1997 effort to jointly formulate the U.S. position on global warming before the international climate change summit in Kyoto, Japan (White House, 1997)—although it has not been widely attempted in lengthier, more intensive consensus building efforts. Amid the chorus of enthusiasm that often accompanies spectacular new technologies, however, there should be, in the realm of consensus building, a sobering voice of caution about their limitations and challenges. While the possibilities for new applications will continue to expand, these seductive technologies must not end up undermining consensus building efforts.

This chapter reviews opportunities for using currently available technologies as communication and analytical aids in consensus building and discusses some of the risks involved. It is organized around five aspects of consensus building: dissemination of and access to written materials; discussion, debate, and deliberation; analysis; decision making; and the drafting of written documents. The chapter ends with a summary of key concerns about the use of computer technologies in consensus building.

■ Dissemination of and Access to Written Documents

Consensus decisions that are generated without the involvement of all people and organizations with an interest in the issues (or responsibility for implementing the decision) are likely to be more fragile than those based on comprehensive participation. Throughout a consensus building process, therefore, the issue of who receives what kinds of information has repercussions for the depth and durability of a negotiated agreement. Computer-based communication technologies can be invaluable aids in disseminating information to stakeholders.

At the outset of a proposed consensus process, it is generally desirable for the broadest possible array of people to be notified, so that all key stakeholders can be identified. Depending on the process to be used, either all these stakeholders will be invited to participate or a representative set will be chosen to take part in deliberations.

Once the negotiation is under way, it is not only essential that all active participants receive relevant information, but it is also generally best for interested but nonparticipating parties to be kept abreast of a group's progress. The cost of duplicating and distributing written materials, however, often presents pragmatic constraints for information dissemination. Keeping participants and observers informed is expensive and natural-resource intensive. In a hypothetical case, even a modest 20-page meeting summary sent to 60 members of a consensus building group requires 1,200 sheets of paper. In many complex disputes, the number of interested individuals can range from 200 to 2,000.

In addition, the bearer of news is often as important as the news itself with respect to credibility, particularly in highly contentious debates. Designating a repository of printed information can become a highly politicized question, because of the implications concerning who has control over and access to documents. A government agency often serves as the repository, but in this era of low trust in government (Nye, Zelikow, & King, 1997), that option may not be adequate.

Computer Tools for Information Dissemination

"The World Wide Web and e-mail are perhaps the most useful technologies for disseminating information."

Two Internet-based computer applications—the World Wide Web (the Web) and electronic mail—are perhaps the most useful technologies for disseminating information. The World Wide Web is a part of the Internet, an electronic communications network that connects computer facilities around the world to each other. The Web has become popular in part due to its user-friendly graphic interface and ease of connection between *sites.* A site is a discrete information repository that typically is maintained by a single entity and has a cohesive design. A user logging on to the Web from one computer can link to any Web site at the click of a mouse button. Links from one Web site to another are called *hotlinks.* Hotlinks generally appear on a screen as images of buttons. Each "button" is labeled and provides an instant cyberspace connection to another Web site. A single site may have numerous *pages,* or subrepositories. So, for example, a manufacturer's Web site may include a page with product information, a page with distributor's names and addresses, a page with short bios of its senior executives, and so on. Because of its worldwide reach, the Web allows for an extremely broad distribution of materials.

Electronic mail, or e-mail, is a more personalized form of computer-based communication. An e-mail *address* is an electronic pathway to a particular Internet *mailbox* where messages are stored. Access to a specific mailbox is possible from any Internet-linked computer that has the appropriate e-mail software, but is restricted to an individual user by a gatekeeping password. Any person with an e-mail account can send a message to any other person in the world with an e-mail account, as long as he or she has the correct address. E-mail distribution lists and message management systems (often called listservs, after the proprietary name Listservs™, a popular version of this type of software) enable one e-mail message to be sent to many recipients simultaneously. In contrast to the Web, on which users must actively seek out posted information, e-mail messages sent individually or via a listserv arrive directly at a recipient's electronic mailbox.

The Web and e-mail can be used to assist convenors and facilitators with four discrete functions relating to information dissemination: (1) notifying the public of an upcoming consensus building process and seeking out appropriate participants during convening, (2) distributing materials to participants during a process, (3) enabling participants in a consensus process to share information with their constituents, and (4) keeping the public informed about the progress of a consensus building process.

Supporting the Convening Process

Before a consensus building process is convened, a notice about it could be posted on the Web. Many government agencies, from the municipal to the federal levels, maintain Web sites to inform the general public of upcoming and ongoing events and activities. The site of the city of Portland, Oregon, for example, contains the city council's schedule of public meetings, agendas, and past meeting summaries (City of Portland, OR, 1998). A notice about an upcoming public consensus process could be posted on a page of a government site, such as Portland's, as well as on the sites of other relevant organizations (e.g., the chamber of commerce and a local advocacy group).

Alternatively, an independent Web site could be created for a consensus building process itself—a site that has a name, format, font, and graphics of its own and is not merely a page on one stakeholder's Web site. This independent site could then be hotlinked to other sites that are of interest to prospective participants and the public to help "lead" people to the independent site. For example, the city of Portland's site could be hotlinked to the independent site of a state-sponsored consensus building process. The cost of creating an independent Web site and making documents available to all Internet users is usually no more than the cost of hiring a technician to design and maintain the site and load documents. Independent sites are most useful in processes that are expected to include large numbers of participants and last a long time (to justify the cost of setting up and maintaining the site), and in those cases that are so polarized that the process must not be associated with any particular group's own Web site.

A Web site designed for notification and public outreach could also allow individuals or organizations to electronically indicate to the convenor their interest in the process (i.e., via e-mail or by filling out an electronic form). This can greatly facilitate the convenor's task of identifying stakeholders, and therefore potential participants. Moreover, Web site visitors can easily forward a notice to others who may be interested in the process, giving the term *word-of-mouth* new meaning.

Notification can also be accomplished by posting messages to an appropriate listserv. For example, there may be a listserv whose members are officials in state environmental agencies, or one whose members work for citizens groups. Many listservs have nationwide memberships, however, and may not therefore be an appropriate venue for a notice about a site-specific or local-level consensus process.

Distributing Documents
to and among Participants

Once consensus building has begun, facilitators can use e-mail and listservs to send documents and messages to participants between meetings. Participants can also use these tools to communicate with each other and share drafts among themselves. Many facilitators routinely establish a database that includes participants' e-mail addresses. The facilitator can then send out memos, agendas, meeting minutes, and notices of Web postings by e-mail or listserv. As e-mail becomes as familiar and routine as the postal service, dissemination tasks will become increasingly efficient and timely.

Web sites also can be used as document repositories for a consensus building group. Documents can be posted on a site for viewing, printing out, and/or downloading to a user's own computer. Because of the aspatial nature of cyberspace, potential sensitivities regarding the location of document repositories in a particular consensus building effort can be minimized. An independent Web site probably does this best, because creating a page on a stakeholder's site poses the same problems as physically storing information at a stakeholder's office. The relative ease and low cost of establishing hotlinks to the independent site and the essentially unlimited nature of doing so means that the site can be "owned" by all participating groups whose Web sites are hotlinked.

Communication between
Participants and Their Constituents

A Web site can be customized to facilitate document distribution and communication between representatives in a consensus building process and their constituents. Such communication (electronic or not) is essential; it helps to ensure that constituents stay informed about a process throughout and ultimately support any consensus to which its representatives agree.

The official representatives to a process might use a special page on a site (independent or otherwise) to direct their constituents to particular documents, screening out what they believe is less relevant material and creating more efficient use of the constituents' time. The representative of a citizens group questioning the economic soundness of a proposed light-rail line, for example, might post only the documents concerning financial analyses. Documents about issues such as environmental impacts, transit equity, or long-term regional livability might not be included, creating a more "streamlined" set of materials for constituents to review.

If desired, Web sites can be created with restricted access. Passwords or user identification codes can be set in place to allow only designated individuals to enter a Web site or a portion of a site. This dedicated space might be used to share additional documents among a specific constituency or provide conferencing capabilities to assemble comments about negotiation priorities. For example, the members of an environmental organization involved in the light-rail discussion might like to share among themselves a report on the comparative environmental impacts of light rail versus enhanced bus service before bringing these issues to the wider group.

Keeping the Public Informed during a Process

During a consensus building process, a Web site can report matters specific to the process to the public. Relevant documents such as meeting minutes, agendas, schedules, working documents, and background resources can be posted on a Web site, allowing public viewing of these materials. Essentially, anyone with a computer, modem, and Internet service provider can procure these materials. Interested parties can read the documents on-screen or download them and print them out. Duplication and printing costs are transferred from the process sponsor to the user and are incurred only if the user determines that a hard copy of the material is needed.

Finally, one Web site can be constructed to provide both public notice and reporting functions as well as private, stake-holders-only pages. In a recent U.S. Department of Defense (DoD) multistakeholder dialogue concerning alternatives to the incineration of chemical weapons, a Web site was set up to give the public free access to press releases, official documents, and meeting summaries. In addition, secured areas on the Web site were constructed with access restricted to citizen representatives, federal and state regulatory representatives, DoD staff, and DoD contractors. The consensus building group's internal documents, such as draft reports and meeting summaries, were posted on the secured site. In this case, all written materials were disseminated electronically; hard copies were distributed by the convenors to only two or three participants (T. Barker, personal communication, July 1, 1998).

Access to Online Information

To lead people who have online access to a consensus group's Web site, the facilitator or a computer-savvy participant must sign up with the various search engines (e.g., Yahoo!, HotBot, and AltaVista) and, usually, provide them with *keywords* that relate to the site. Then, any user who does a search using one or more of the keywords will be directed to the site. Most search engine companies charge a small, one-time fee for this service. Hotlinks on related Web sites can also lead people to a site.

But computer technologies will achieve the goals of public notification and materials dissemination only to the extent that the public is connected to cyberspace. Indeed, the reliance on computer-based communication tools raises concerns regarding the notion of an "equal playing field" among those who ought to be included in and kept abreast of progress in consensus building dialogues. Access to the Web and e-mail varies across different segments of the population. A 1995 study by the U.S. Department of Commerce found, not surprisingly, that the poor (those with annual incomes less than $10,000) have the lowest percentage of households with computers (5 percent in rural areas and 8 percent in urban areas) compared with the wealthiest households (those with annual incomes above $75,000), of which 60 percent to 64 percent are equipped with computers. Similar though not as striking disparities exist with respect to race (fully one-third of rural households identifying as "Asian or Pacific Islander, non-Hispanic" own computers, compared with only 6 percent of rural black households) and age (those homes in which the head-of-household is more than 55 years old ranked lowest among all age groups in computer ownership). Although these disparities are troubling, the conventional alternative of placing documents in specially designated repositories in government offices or libraries does not provide equitable access either, since differences in geographic proximity, mobility, and political savvy may disadvantage certain groups. Electronic tools such as Web sites can thus enhance information dissemination, but should perhaps be used in combination with other methods.

Depending on the nature of the consensus building effort, disparities among participants in access and facility will be a greater or lesser concern. Until computers and Internet connections are as ubiquitous as U.S. Postal Service carriers, convenors and facilitators must always ask, "Who is not getting information but ought to be?" and make appropriate efforts to reach the desired individuals or groups. Inadvertently leaving one or two participants out of the information loop can create unnecessary tension within a group, as those overlooked may feel left "in the dark," creating suspicions and discomfort toward the process. In the DoD case, only a handful of the 35 participants were not equipped with appropriate technology. DoD provided all participants with the same word processing software, which made sharing and editing documents much easier. DoD was not able, however, to provide computers to the two or three participants who did not already have one. These individuals were encouraged to access the Internet through computers housed at "outreach centers" located near each chemical weapons site. Apparently, they did so readily (T. Barker, personal communication, October 9, 1998). The technological demands go beyond simply having a computer on one's desk; they include connecting the computer to an Internet server, loading appropriate software to enable exchange of information in compatible formats, and having the necessary peripherals, such as a printer. If a convenor wishes to rely exclusively on computer-based communications, as did DoD in this case, the convenor ought to take responsibility for ensuring all participants are equally well equipped.

■ Discussion, Debate, and Deliberation

The heart of consensus building is discussion, debate, and deliberation. Face-to-face interaction is often essential for achieving consensus, especially in situations in which trust among the participants is low. Nonetheless, communication technologies present opportunities for both broadening and deepening the exchange of views. These applications can be useful among the consensus building group itself as well as for stakeholding representatives to maintain two-way communications with their constituents.

Building consensus also requires the active involvement of each participating individual or organization. A common fear, often realized, is the inordinate amount of time a consensus process requires. As group size increases, the sheer number of hours for discussion is likely to increase, especially if group members represent discrete stakeholding groups or viewpoints. A skillful facilitator may help to structure exchanges efficiently in face-to-face meetings. However, attempts to rein in discussion are often at the cost of either limiting the number of speakers allowed floor time or restricting the length of time each speaker speaks. Either way, participants may not have time to share concerns and good ideas, thus hindering consensus building in the long run.

Within the dynamics of face-to-face meetings, a number of challenges arise. The floor may be used as a stage for overly dramatic speakers, and participants may use tactics such as grandstanding and posturing. Also, those more familiar with the meeting environment may dominate the dialogue. For example, in a public policy consensus building process, consider the relative comfort levels of a CEO of a *Fortune 500* corporation compared with a local neighborhood representative. The former participant is likely to be experienced and comfortable in speaking before large groups; the latter may be facing such an audience for the first time. Ensuring an acceptable balance of floor time among speakers can also be difficult. Finally, discussions are easily led offtrack or can lose focus as participants respond to tangential issues raised by previous speakers instead of addressing the points under debate.

The finite nature of face-to-face meetings also causes a certain pacing of the discussion. Put simply, the dialogue must continue moving. This need for movement creates a limited tolerance for silences in any portion of the meeting. Responses to speakers' comments must be offered within a specified time interval. If they are not, the agenda moves forward. A participant's comment on a point made previously often incurs inefficiencies; it takes time to reconstruct the context of the comment, and in the process, new disputes may arise over this reconstruction. Members of the group may also grow impatient with slower learners, putting social relationships and the process itself at risk. To complete agendas within allotted meeting times, conventions have been developed regarding acceptable silences following a call for questions or comments; in general, long silences are not tolerated. While a skillful facilitator may be able to minimize these kinds of challenges, computer technologies can augment a facilitator's work in important ways.

Augmenting Face-to-Face Meetings
With Computer-Based Technologies

Internet technologies such as listservs and Web conferences offer ways to break through the constraining time barriers of face-to-face meetings by enabling group discussions to continue between meetings. During meetings, equipment that projects a computer screen on a wall can be useful in helping to focus a discussion.

Listservs and Web Conferences

A listserv is an interactive Internet option in which the e-mail addresses of subscribers are compiled into a master electronic mailing list, such that any subscriber can send an e-mail message simultaneously to all other subscribers. The running dialogue that results when people share their ideas via a listserv is "heard" by all subscribers. If desired, listserv messages can be organized according to topics (or conversation *threads*) and placed on the Web for wider reading. Listservs can be created for entire consensus building groups, subsets of groups, or any other subset of persons.

Web conferences are areas of a Web site in which people can post messages and read other posts. Conversations are *threaded* together by topic.

Listservs and Web conferences allow participants to continue discussing topics raised in face-to-face meetings without time constraints. That is, "speakers" can key in for as long as is necessary for them to express their views. "Listeners" can receive messages at their convenience and respond when they choose. Listserv and conference discussions thus allow individuals more discretion in allocating time for active deliberations. Participants who are not ready to move forward from particular points have the option of continuing to discuss issues over the listserv or Web; others may choose to simply skim or skip over such exchanges.

"Using the Internet to continue discussions provides a written record of exchanges."

Using the Internet to continue discussions not only extends the meeting time available for dialogue and deliberation, it also provides a written record of exchanges. A written record authored by a speaker may have a powerful effect in terms of ensuring accountability. Extreme or ambiguous rhetoric may be self-censored because the dramatic value of such tactics is offset by the need to substantiate and stand by one's statements. Users may also edit the length of their statements, realizing the delicate trade-off between wordiness and effectiveness. On the other hand, facing a computer screen instead of a human face may have the contrary effect of enabling participants to rant and rave, making extreme statements. Participants may also feel less constrained by not facing listeners who might demand substantiation of stated points. In the RuleNet case (an on-line consensus building dialogue described later in this chapter and in Case 8), the facilitation team monitored and screened listserv messages. A few statements were judged by the facilitators as being potentially inflammatory or damaging to the group consensus building effort. These messages were returned to the sender for revision before being broadcast to all subscribers.

Internet options allow for discussions to be conducted either among a limited number of participants (as on a listserv) or openly to any Internet user (as on a Web conference with unrestricted access). In either case, the use of the Internet to extend discussion opportunities creates additional demands on the facilitator's role. The facilitator can be explicitly involved in the exchanges, monitoring the discussion as in face-to-face meetings, or exchanges can occur without direct intervention. In the latter case, the facilitator may retain the right to "listen in," just as in face-to-face meetings, for the purpose of understanding the substantive issues and to be helpful in building consensus. If listserv discussions are posted on the Web for general reading, it may become the facilitator's responsibility to catalog the various comments according to topics.

The facilitator also may need to keep track of who contributes to such discussions and who does not. This tracking, in fact, may be an essential task, since dialogues that are conducted without the participation of all members will fragment the group into subsets of people who no longer share a common knowledge base. Participants who have "stepped out of the room," so to speak, may be left behind as Internet discussions move others further along in their development of consensus. Individuals excluded from pivotal discussions may feel a loss of under-standing of issues or ownership in the process, putting at risk the ultimate potential for consensus. To avoid such situations, the facilitator may need to confirm that all members have "heard" critical discussion points. This would entail monitoring confer-ence and listserv discussions, extracting key points, posting sum-maries of the exchanges, and developing and implementing a method of confirming the receipt and reading of the messages by all participants. All these steps are technologically possible, but highly time-consuming.

In a national dialogue on ecosystem management, the facili-tation team used Internet exchanges between face-to-face meet-ings to move the group closer to agreement on points raised in the previous sessions. Using the *single negotiating text* technique (Fisher & Ury, 1981; Raiffa, 1982), the facilitators drafted and posted on a listserv their best approximation of an agreement. Participants then reacted to the draft through e-mail. The e-mail messages were archived on a conference site[1] for all participants to read. The facilitators then revised the draft agreement in accordance with the comments, and the most current version of the draft was used as the starting point for discussions at the sub-sequent face-to-face meeting. Because the facilitators were aware that not all participants actively contributed to the Internet-based discussion, they did not assume that the full group would support the revised document. The facilitators believed, however, that the exchanges did help to define a new, more effective starting point for each face-to-face discussion (T. Barker, personal communication, July 1, 1998).

Computer Projections

Within face-to-face meetings, computer technologies can also be used to enhance the quality of discussions. As a high-tech version of flip charts, a computer screen projected onto a wall can display a group's ideas and create a common focal point for the conversation. With eyes drawn to the screen, participants are physically as well as mentally engaged in a common effort. While a facilitator or an assistant works the keyboard, the dynamic nature of stringing together written words on a large screen commands the attention of participants and tends to keep the group focused. Computer projections have the added convenience of producing a record that can be printed out and shared immediately with others.

Inherent Risks

These applications of communication technologies are exhilarating in their promise, but they also bring new challenges and exacerbate old ones. While information and views can be exchanged relatively easily through listservs and other Internet options, it is virtually impossible to monitor who is listening and how well, unless the listener explicitly signals a response. Silence, in a listserv discussion, may be caused by a wide range of factors, ranging from hostility to passive disengagement to a withdrawal based on external demands on one's time. Unless conventions are established to signal when each participant has "left the room" (such as mutually agreed-on, explicit notification procedures for nonparticipation beyond a given length of time), absences are subject to (mis)interpretation.

Also, while a mechanism may be installed to report who has logged on, it is impossible to ascertain how closely each message was read. Moreover, no technology can gauge the reaction of the person who reads the message. In contrast to face-to-face meetings, the written word lacks emotive cues from both the speaker and the listener. For example, in face-to-face communications, a comment intended as humorous is readily understood as such when the speaker smiles and gives a little laugh. Any doubts as to the intent of the speaker are usually dispelled by the reactions of other listeners. The social setting and reactions of others provide important cues to individuals about the content and meaning of messages. In contrast, written messages—especially among those whose relationships with one another are newly developed—can easily be misinterpreted.

Some computer conventions have been developed in an attempt to temper the lack of emotive cues in e-mail messages. For example, the "smiley face" symbol can be used to note humor or friendliness, messages typed in all capital letters suggest that the writer is "yelling," and feelings can be expressed explicitly by writing out words such as *sigh* or *shrug* in parentheses. These conventions, however, still fall short of conveying human qualities important for mediating the tone of messages. Moreover, they are available only to the message sender. The sender writes with little current information about the mood or demeanor of his or her intended recipient(s). In face-to-face situations, speakers often tailor their messages to accommodate the mood of the listener(s), but this dynamic is lacking in computer-mediated communications. Communication technologies used to supplement face-to-face interactions hence present a host of new interpersonal communication challenges in consensus building.

The RuleNet project offers several insights into the use of technologies to extend opportunities for discussion (see Case 8). RuleNet was an experiment by the Nuclear Regulatory Commission (NRC) to conduct an entire federal rulemaking process over the Internet. The rule under consideration concerned fire prevention at nuclear power plants. Stakeholders ranged from citizen-neighbors of nuclear facilities to NRC regulators. More than 300 people registered for the process, although only about 20 participated on a regular basis. The project was run from Lawrence Livermore National Laboratory in Livermore, California. Internet conversations were monitored closely by the facilitation team. All listserv messages, for example, were received first by the facilitation team and screened before they were broadcast on the listserv. Potentially offensive remarks and profane language were returned to the sender for reconsideration. Interestingly, the physical isolation of participants in Internet conversations appeared to counter the moderating effect of putting one's words in print, as mentioned previously. That is, in contrast to fostering accountability, the relative anonymity of the computer medium may have encouraged participants to exaggerate their views and to state them more aggressively. The *complete* lack of face-to-face meetings in this case and not the medium itself may have been the major factor affecting online behavior (J. Helie, personal communication, April 14, 1998).

Because the volume of respondents on the system could potentially reach into the hundreds, if not thousands, the lead facilitator employed a number of assistants who "listened in" on the five different conference sites (divided along the five main topic areas under discussion) and filtered up to him pertinent information. The time and financial costs related to the monitoring of the Internet dialogue were thus substantial. How these resource demands compare with face-to-face consensus building is difficult to determine accurately. However, it is clear that on-line discussions require significant facilitator involvement and, also important, demand a new set of technical skills.

It would be remiss not to acknowledge the fact that changing the medium may change who participates and to what extent. There are often dramatic differences between the ability of individuals to articulate their views orally as opposed to through the written word. Obvious concerns arise in processes involving those for whom the language used is not their native tongue, but even among different types of professionals significant differences exist in the ability of individuals to express their ideas in written text as opposed to orally or through freehand graphics (such as pictures or schematics). The balance between face-to-face meetings and Internet-mediated discussions has implications for prejudicing a process in favor of writers over speakers, or vice versa. While providing opportunities for participants to express their views in a multiplicity of media is desirable to maximize information exchange among participants, the notion of "equal floor time" takes on new complexity.

Finally, the use of computer projections instead of flip charts can affect the dynamics of face-to-face interactions. Computer projections tend to draw all participants' eyes toward the screen, which may in fact be a weakness rather than a strength. Participants who are focusing on the screen are not following the facial expressions, hand gestures, or other body language of the speakers. Indeed, listeners may become oblivious to who is speaking, concentrating instead on the letters appearing on the screen. The effect is exaggerated by the fact that in most cases, the room is darkened to improve the readability of the projection screen. The use of computer projections within face-to-face interactions must be undertaken wisely and with these risks in mind.

■ *Analysis*

Decisions require analysis. Consensus building aims to develop a shared understanding of the basis for a decision. The more complex the issues and the greater the number of stakeholders involved, the more daunting is the challenge of dealing with analysis. Computer technologies can facilitate analysis in consensus building in three discrete ways: (1) as aids in conducting technical analysis, (2) as communication tools in discussions about technical aspects of specific issues, and (3) as individual and group decision-making tools. The first two points will be discussed in this section. The third point will be considered in the next.

Many complex, large-group consensus building processes are formed around issues that cannot be resolved without some type of technical analysis, such as financial projections; economic, social, or environmental impact assessments; or evaluations of economic feasibility. These types of analyses are often central to enabling participants to generate options, understand how their own concerns may be addressed by those options, and imagine and examine new scenarios. However, disagreements frequently arise over the acceptance of a given analysis because of differences concerning underlying assumptions, the validity of data sets, the interpretation of results, and other methodological details or because of skepticism regarding the source or sponsor of an analysis. When participants disagree about scientific and technical analyses, for whatever reason, consensus building flounders.

Confounding the complexity of dealing with scientific and technical analyses is the fact that participants often have widely divergent analytical capabilities depending on their training, education, and experience with respect to both the substance and the methodology of the analysis conducted. These differences may manifest themselves as variations in readiness to move forward in the discussion. Those who are comfortable with the meaning and implications of an analysis will be more willing to move ahead than those feeling uncertain or confused. Differences in the readiness of participants to move forward can be highly disruptive to a consensus building effort. In a public discussion in Oregon regarding the development of a municipal water treatment facility, for example, city engineers were more comfortable with the projected effectiveness of the purification technology than citizens less familiar with the technology or the chemistry of decontamination. City officials caught in the middle of the controversy stalled their decision and convened additional public meetings to solicit more input. As time passed, those already convinced of the technology's effectiveness grew increasingly impatient and began to imply that the citizens' resistance was based on emotional, aesthetic sensitivities rather than level-headed considerations (Nokes, 1998; Tims, 1998).

Even if participants have a basic understanding of a technical analysis, they may not be able to articulate their reservations. In some cases, unfamiliarity with the technical vernacular may impede a member's ability to explain his or her concerns. In other cases, participants may use language and terminology differently, creating severe communication difficulties. At the least, the process is slowed down as clarifications are made. At worst, the process moves forward with gross misunderstandings lurking under the surface of the conversation. Alternatively, an individual confused by the various technical arguments could simply refuse to continue the dialogue, causing the process to grind to a halt.

Computer-Based Analytical Tools

Effective use of scientific and technical analyses is a serious and complex concern that must be addressed in the overall design of a consensus building process. Computer-based communication technologies can be applied in targeted ways, however, to help facilitate a shared understanding among participants.

When one or more stakeholders raise doubts about a particular analysis due to methodological issues such as the choice of underlying assumptions, the definition of appropriate data sets, or the selection of modeling parameters, computer technologies can be brought in to clarify the extent to which these differences affect the results. While techniques such as sensitivity analysis (a calculation of the extent to which one value will change if either a baseline assumption or the data set is altered) have long been used, today's technologies allow this analysis to be conducted in new ways. In the past, sensitivity analyses were often conducted at the request of interested parties by trained technicians in isolation and the results were then reported back, but now technicians can load data and software programs onto transportable diskettes, and stakeholders, with minimal instruction, can undertake the analysis themselves. This improves the credibility of an analysis and imbues participants with a more visceral understanding of the material.

Moreover, these programs can be run on home computers and transmitted over the Internet, allowing participants to follow the implications of varying assumptions in the privacy of their homes or offices. The personalized nature of this approach allows individuals to set their own pace in wading through an analysis, repeating and pondering steps as needed until the individual feels comfortable with her or his understanding. Participants who differ in terms of their assessment of baseline conditions (e.g., the size and characteristics of a city's population in intercensus years) or projected rates of change (e.g., population growth rates) can manipulate these factors on their own and calculate the degree to which such differences affect the outcome. Without losing face or ground in a negotiation, members of a consensus building group can ascertain on their own the extent to which given assumptions affect the technical basis for the decision. Participants will arrive at meetings with a fuller understanding of technical issues and better prepared to discuss them. Potential disagreements can often be narrowed or even resolved in this way.

"Computer analyses can also be conducted in face-to-face meetings." Computer analyses can also be conducted within the context of a face-to-face meeting. Desktop or laptop computers can be set up so that small groups can work around individual consoles independently, or one computer can be projected onto a wall screen for the entire group to read. In either case, rather than any one individual or group "owning" a technical analysis, every member of the group can have input. Technical experts can either lead a group through an analysis or simply be on hand to provide assistance as needed. The collective ownership that results often prevents questions from arising about the legitimacy of an analysis. The hands-on nature of these tools creates a more intimate understanding of concepts and terminology, facilitating communication about analyses. If confusion over technical elements is the reason that certain individuals resist moving a discussion forward, analyses conducted in a face-to-face meeting can help to overcome such situations.

Such joint analysis can lead to resolutions. For example, in a land use development dispute in Hawaii, a spreadsheet program was used to help participants understand how varying proportions of affordable housing, higher-priced housing, and open space would affect the project's economic feasibility. Rather than the city planner or the developer's consultant explaining why various distributions of land uses were not feasible, the participants themselves were able to conduct the analysis. The meeting was held at a local university in a room equipped with several computers, which were loaded with identical software and data sets. Representatives from environmental groups, the local community, and farmers huddled around each station, plugging in numbers to test the financial implications of different housing and open space mixes. This exercise was undertaken after the opposing groups had developed a certain level of mutual respect. Specifically, the community had gained an appreciation and acceptance of the developer's need to recoup costs and generate some profit, and the developer acknowledged the community's desire to preserve open space and ensure continuing opportunities for small farms (P. Adler, personal communication, September 14, 1997).

Another example that illustrates the usefulness of computer technologies is a regulatory negotiation convened by the Environmental Protection Agency (EPA) regarding disinfectants and disinfection by-products in drinking water. In this case, stakeholders in the rulemaking negotiations—including federal and state agency officials, water suppliers, consumer advocates, environmentalists, public health officials, and chemical and equipment suppliers—involved more than two dozen technical experts to form a working group to provide relevant analyses and advice to the negotiating group. This technical working group included experts trusted by the full range of participating stakeholder groups. That is, every stakeholder could rely on at least one member of the technical working group for advice.

Members of the technical working group met with the negotiating group as well as on their own in preparation for plenary meetings. In the course of their work, they relied on computers both with and without Internet connections. The formal rulemaking negotiations usually occurred at meetings scheduled a month or so apart, and the technical experts were expected to respond to queries and conduct additional analysis between meetings. Using Internet connections, analysts working across the country from one another exchanged spreadsheets and data sets. Internet connections allowed one analyst to generate a piece of data and others to build on it in a truly collaborative fashion from more than a dozen different geographic locations. Had the experts relied on overnight mail (to exchange computer diskettes), their work would not have proceeded as speedily or cost-effectively.

Prior to meeting with the stakeholder representatives in the plenary sessions, the technical experts met face-to-face to prepare their joint presentations of requested technical information, such as the forecasts of compliance rates by water suppliers given varying proposed standards or the total costs of compliance given proposed regulatory options. On these occasions, the analysts would assemble around a table with their laptop computers before them; some would take notes on the discussion, others would call up spreadsheets and generate new ones, and still others would construct overhead slides to display at the next day's plenary session. Working collaboratively, the analysts would develop a strategy for best presenting the material to the plenary group for review.

The technical working group also conducted real-time analysis during plenary meetings. They would set up in a room adjacent to the negotiation floor, ready to modify model parameters, assumptions, or data sets in response to inquiries or requests by the stakeholder representatives. For example, the cost of compliance with new drinking water standards was a concern. The higher the standard, the greater the number of municipal drinking water systems that would fall out of compliance, and the higher the costs of achieving compliance. Relying on a database of examples of treatment streams from actual systems, and a "Monte Carlo" statistical program with its own sophisticated database, the analysts could take standards suggested by stakeholders in the plenary discussions, project how many systems would be in violation, and provide quick estimates of the consequent, overall costs of compliance. The technologies (as well as the trust that had developed among the analysts themselves and between the technical group members and the stakeholder representatives) enabled the timely delivery of highly relevant, technical information (G. Bingham, personal communication, May 11, 1998).

Another computer tool that is becoming increasingly available is the geographic information system (GIS). This spatially based system allows discrete data, such as census data, to be loaded into a computer, manipulated, and displayed in map form. The visual display of information is often a powerful tool for helping parties reach consensus in certain types of disputes, such as those involving land use. GIS technology allows for the easy creation of overlays in the same way that Mylar maps displaying different sorts of data were once used.

Consider, for instance, a decision regarding the siting of a new solid waste incinerator. A community might argue that it currently hosts a high burden of less desirable land uses and that a proposed site would aggravate an already unfair situation. Moreover, the community might contend that the proposed site is dangerously close to especially vulnerable populations, such as children and elderly persons. Various types of locally unwanted land uses (LULUs) or unwanted facilities identified by street address could be displayed on a map using GIS. Other types of land use information could then be added to the database to show their spatial relationships to the LULU sites. Schools, day care centers, hospitals, senior centers, and elderly housing facilities, for example, might be "layered" over the map of LULUs. In a single graphic, participants could see the spatial relationships of these land uses and any patterns that exist. This method of displaying information visually is not new, but the advantage of current technology is, again, that such analysis now can be conducted relatively quickly by persons with little training or, alternatively, in a group. GIS maps can be available in a matter of hours instead of days or weeks.

Inquiries are limited by the GIS database available, however. While municipalities, regional public service providers, and state governments are continually expanding these databases, as in any analysis, the results are only as sound as the original data. GIS data vary from locality to locality with respect to unit of analysis (e.g., census tract, neighborhood, or zip code), accuracy, and how up-to-date it is. Often, time and budget constraints require analysts to piece together a composite picture using data that have been collected using different methodologies at different times. Under such a scenario, the data bits are not equally valid from a methodological perspective, but the variation in quality is not evident from the GIS map. Therefore, applications of these computer technologies must be accompanied by discussions of the quality of data and other model parameters that are embedded within the powerful, graphic display of information provided through GIS. Otherwise, participants in a consensus building process may be misled by an erroneous visual image, unnecessarily adding obstacles to the development of a sound consensus.

These cautions pertain to the use of emerging computer technologies in analysis generally, as well. While these tools present welcome opportunities to make technical analysis more accessible and more comprehensible to participants in consensus building efforts, users must retain a critical stance toward the components of the analysis. In addition to the quality of data, the strengths and weaknesses of the models represented by particular computer programs and applications should be disclosed and considered. Models are abstractions of reality, in many cases ostensibly describing a set of dynamic relationships over time. However, the construction of a model requires a simplification of reality that may or may not be accurate. Some elements are highlighted, others may be omitted entirely. External factors may or may not be appropriately considered. Therefore, rather than wholeheartedly embracing any particular model because it is "user friendly" or easily manipulated by relatively untrained participants, users must remain skeptical and cautious. The facility of conducting analyses collaboratively should not overshadow the uncertainties that are embedded within an analysis.

■ Computer-Based Decision-Making Technologies

In a consensus building process that involves many participants, it may be desirable to take a reading of the group periodically to ascertain how close participants are to reaching agreement. In a conventional, majority-vote process, this reading often consists of taking straw polls on the various issues under consideration to gauge whether or not a given proposal has a chance of gaining sufficient support for passage. Straw polls are intended to be tentative and nonbinding, providing an indication of where the group stands without committing individuals to their choices. In a consensus process, straw polls can be used in a similar fashion, although because the objective is consensus rather than simply majority support, the voting process may be as obstructive as it is helpful in moving the group forward. Specifically, open polling, straw or otherwise, may inadvertently contribute to a premature locking in of positions among participants. Issues on which there are few dissenters may be considered "closed" by those in the majority, even if they are not officially settled by group agreement. And because issues are interdependent, attempts to reduce the number of issues under consideration ultimately can reduce rather than increase the possibility of resolution. As issues become closed to discussion, the potential for developing creative options by combining several issues or constructing acceptable packages of issues decreases. Approaching agreements as tentative until a comprehensive accord is reached is often a wiser way to proceed (Raiffa, 1982, p. 140).

Computer-Based Tools

Computer-based technologies provide an opportunity to poll participants in a consensus process without the risk of hardening positions prematurely. How can this be achieved? Using a questionnaire posted on the Web, participants can be asked whether or not they support a given alternative. If they do not support it, they can be asked to explain their objections or to suggest modifications. Participants enter their responses directly onto preformatted, electronic response forms. Software programs tally the results, identifying issues on which agreement exists but not disclosing the vote count on issues for which disagreement persists. Instead, the program simply provides the narrative explanations of continuing objections. No actual vote counts need be disclosed. Although some system of identifying voters is necessary to ensure the legitimacy of the poll (e.g., a password), the software program provides an option for protecting individual voting preferences, even from the facilitator. This approach can be convenient and low cost and can result in the quick tallying of results. It can also provide the facilitator with a clearer sense of how close a group is to agreement and which issues need work.

Such a program was used in the RuleNet project. In this case, participants were given a 24-hour window to self-administer a survey over the Internet. The facilitator had access to the results of the poll; the participants did not (J. Helie, personal communication, April 14, 1998). This arrangement may be preferable if the group wishes to avoid feeling "locked in" on particular alternatives—even those for which consensus exists. Periodic polling through computer communication technologies can be conducted throughout a consensus process, allowing the facilitator to gauge how close a group is to reaching agreement. It is particularly useful in large groups, for which such polling and tallying can comprise a significant task if performed manually.

A number of additional negotiation software programs exist that may in the future be successfully integrated into consensus processes. At this point, however, effective applications are rare. At the time of this writing, no software programs could be found that facilitators believed were productive aids in the development of consensus. Nonetheless, consensus building professionals are intrigued by the possibilities of modifying negotiation software programs for use in consensus building efforts, and the outlook for expanded applications as these tools are further developed and adapted is promising.

■ *Drafting Written Documents*

Written documents are a part of most consensus building processes. From meeting agendas to final agreements, group processes run more smoothly if care is taken to ensure that verbal agreements are inscribed. The written word provides a catalyst to achieve clarity and ultimately to signify a level of mutual understanding. Generation of these documents occurs in a variety of social configurations: An executive committee of a larger group may be responsible for setting and distributing meeting agendas, volunteers to an ad hoc task force may be asked to prepare briefings on lengthier materials, or an entire consensus building group may be directly involved in drafting a written agreement. Computer technologies may be applied in each of these contexts, with appropriate modifications.

A number of challenges arise in putting ideas down in print. Identifying key points, ordering the sequence of these points, and selecting appropriate language are just a few examples of steps that can be confounded when groups rather than an individual take up the "pen." One approach for overcoming the problem of "too many cooks" is to assign drafting to one person and then circulate that draft for review, addition, and revision. In certain circumstances, such an approach works fine. Setting agendas in this manner is not often cumbersome, for example.

A more common practice for drafting more complex documents, such as agreements, is to create a drafting group of three to five persons. Individuals in this group divide up responsibilities for sections of the document and submit drafts to an editor (usually a participant or the facilitator) who compiles the parts, edits, and suggests revisions before the draft is circulated to the full consensus building group for review.

In situations in which the issues at hand are contentious or when the written document must capture a complex logic and cover many issues, as is often the case in consensus building processes, drafting can require a substantial amount of time. If a draft is reviewed by all members of a consensus building group individually, the author(s) may have to go through a series of bilateral exchanges to clarify the intent of suggested changes. Some of these alterations may trigger additional changes as others respond to the revision, requiring yet another round of review. The primary author(s) may not share the comments with all participants (either intentionally or inadvertently), and if an individual's concern is not accurately or fully incorporated into the draft revisions to her or his satisfaction, that participant may move to thwart acceptance of the document. In some cases, the choice of written language may crystallize a lack of consensus that was not evident in oral exchanges. While such a discovery is ultimately beneficial for the overall consensus effort, it can be surprising, disruptive, and require additional meetings that can prolong a process. Also, some participants may view the writing of statements and agreements as an opportunity for stalling.

Using Computer Technologies in the Drafting Process

Computer technologies offer a number of options to assist in the drafting of written documents. An obvious advantage is the speed by which drafts can be circulated for review, but additional benefits exist as well. If the circulation of a draft concurrently to all members of a group is desired, e-mail can be used to transmit copies simultaneously. Participants can review a draft and send reactions and suggested revisions either back to the author or to the author and all participants. If the author alone receives the feedback, e-mail serves primarily as a convenient, time-saving, and resource-saving (no-hard-copies-required) device. The author is still faced with the challenge of synthesizing and harmonizing all comments. If responses are transmitted to all members simultaneously, individuals can build on one another's responses to each comment. Some respondents may simply put forth their reactions to specific points; others may attempt to revise portions of the draft (i.e., one paragraph or one short section), integrating their own concerns as well as those expressed by other members through their e-mail messages. Each participant receives not only the latest working draft but also has all the responses in his or her electronic mailbox. While this approach may be information rich, it can also become unwieldy, unless someone, such as the facilitator, attempts to sort the responses in some way. Alternatively, participants can be sent a draft in an agreed-on sequence and be asked to build on one another's responses, comments, and revisions. The latest working draft is essentially the single negotiating text, and electronic mailboxes contain the building blocks and history of its derivation.

When time is short, e-mail and facsimile can provide the necessary edge to meet a deadline. In one recent case, a multi-stakeholder group with nationwide membership was asked by the EPA to make recommendations on regulations concerning the consideration of children in risk assessments. After reaching a tentative agreement in face-to-face meetings and then disbanding, the group realized that their recommendations must be very carefully crafted so as to avoid misinterpretation by the agency. Specifically, the group did not want the agency to interpret its support for agency attention to specific risks to divert resources away from existing regulatory activities that the group believed were effective in reducing overall risks to children. The group quickly divided up the writing tasks—with individuals on a subcommittee taking responsibility for drafting one of the recommendations. The authors sent their drafts to one person who then consolidated the pieces and sent the complete document out by e-mail or fax to all members of the work group. A telephone conference call was held to discuss the draft, and a revised draft was sent out for a second round of review. The combination of technologies—e-mail, fax, and telephone conferencing—worked together to overcome the serious challenges of space and time (G. Bingham, personal communication, May 1, 1998).

"In face-to-face meetings, computer screen projections can facilitate the drafting of written documents."

In face-to-face meetings, computer screen projections can facilitate the drafting of written documents. While projections may be viewed as little more than high-tech flip charts, the ability to write clean copy with a few strokes of the keyboard significantly enhances clarity and understanding. The quibbling that often arises over the use of specific language can occur with all viewing and assessing the relative impacts of the different word choices. While the technique of recording suggestions as they are presented is not new, computer technologies facilitate the process. The attentive engagement of all participants is more critical than who controls the keyboard. Consequently, the projection should be sufficiently large for all participants to view easily, so that participants sitting in the back of the room don't tune out of the group drafting effort. Just as the flip chart is an effective tool for focusing participants' attention, a computer screen projection can help keep members on track. A caveat with this approach is that group writing, even with the ease afforded by word processing programs, is a slow, time-consuming endeavor. Members must weigh the relative advantage of dedicating their time together to writing, in light of other drafting options available, as opposed to the many other tasks before them.

■ Conclusion

Computer-based communication technologies offer significant potential for enhancing consensus building. Obvious advantages include time savings and increased convenience. E-mail, listservs, and Web sites can assist in the timely notification and distribution of materials, as well as extend opportunities for the exchange of ideas. Recordkeeping and information management are transformed from a process requiring meticulous notetaking, duplication, and filing to one involving an instantaneous electronic recording system ready for electronic filing. Convenors may realize considerable cost savings by reducing, and perhaps eliminating, copying and mailing. Geographically remote and less mobile participants can engage in discussions or collaborative work without incurring the cost and inconvenience of traveling.

Nonetheless, the introduction of new technologies invariably raises questions, some of which may be easily addressed, others of which may be more intractable. For example, inequities in access and skill in today's high-tech world are serious concerns. As the proliferation of computers and Internet connections continues and computer literacy rates rise, however, this worry will likely fade in importance. Other effects, such as whether "speakers" feel more or less accountability for computer-mediated messages, however, are more complex and less predictable. Without attempting to provide a comprehensive listing of the potential disadvantages of increasing reliance on computer technologies in consensus building, this section summarizes a few of the more conspicuous roadblocks to effective use, suggesting remedies in some cases and simply issuing warnings in others. The concerns fall broadly into three areas: representation and voice, the role of the facilitator and additional technical support, and the importance of social relationships.

Representation and Voice

The potential of computer technologies for extending outreach and access to information is tremendous. Publicizing consensus building efforts and providing information regarding publicly sponsored events can be done relatively quickly and at low cost through the Web, listservs, and e-mail. The proliferation of Web sites maintained by public agencies and private organizations is good news for outreach purposes, as notices of consensus building efforts can be readily posted on these sites.

While the potential for broadcast certainly exists, access is, in reality, limited. Those charged with outreach for specific consensus building processes ought to be aware of the potential biases of computer-based notification efforts. Access is restricted, first—rather obviously—to those with computer literacy and Internet connections. Early data show that definite patterns of usership exist, including noticeable differentials by ethnicity, socio-economic class, educational attainment, and age (U.S. Department of Commerce, 1995). If participation by people less likely to be computer users is desired, the convenor must take special care to ensure that those individuals or groups are adequately equipped with necessary hardware, software, and training. Even among a group of seasoned computer users, software incompatibility problems often arise. Convenors must check and double-check the technological infrastructure. Also, access to specific

Web sites is a function of individual awareness, motivation, and political astuteness. Simply putting the word out does not mean that those who ought to be involved in a consensus process will come forth of their own accord. For a variety of reasons, people often need to be asked. Broad participation is not ensured by open access, and computer technologies are not a panacea for the difficult challenge of bringing all potentially affected parties into a discussion. A letter or phone call may be an important complement to Internet publicity, just as a notice in the *Federal Register* is not an adequate invitation in many cases.

Even within a process already underway, the availability of various communication technologies will vary among the participants. No single technology standard will fit all processes. Process sponsors will need to be vigilant about assessing the degree to which participants have access to and fluency in various technologies and make accommodations as appropriate. In some cases, the anticipated benefits of computer-based communications may be sufficiently high that convenors may want to obtain resources for improving access to technologies for all participants. When participants do not rely on the same technologies, convenors will need to ensure that the amount of time allocated for various types of communications is adequate for all members given the technologies available to them. For example, written documents circulated in preparation for face-to-face meetings ought to be received by all participants early enough to allow for adequate review, regardless of whether the document is delivered electronically or through the postal mail.

In addition, the time savings created by computer usage will be allocated, deliberately or not. For example, computer technologies can speed up the exchange of information. Documents can be transferred almost instantaneously. These are tremendous time-saving devices, but who will appropriate the time saved? Will the extra time be claimed by the authors for document preparation or awarded to the recipients for additional review time? Or will the savings, in the end, prove illusory, as the time required for downloading and printing documents is multiplied by the number of readers who find that hard copies are imperative for careful and thoughtful reviews? In one consensus building process, a facilitator noted that downloading and printing one set of documents took six hours (T. Barker, personal communication, July 1, 1998)! Although such issues may at first appear trivial, their importance will grow when deadlines are imminent, and they ought to be discussed early on in a process, perhaps during the setting of ground rules.

Representation and voice in consensus building correlate strongly with access to information and the ability to respond meaningfully in a timely manner. How information is transmitted and the (un)evenness by which participants in a process receive it can have serious consequences. Convenors intending to incorporate computer-mediated communications into their processes must tread cautiously into this new terrain.

The Role of the Facilitator

Computer-based communication technologies provide valuable opportunities for additional information exchange and deliberations. It appears, however, that the wisest applications require a facilitator. Moreover, computer communications can create rather considerable demands on a facilitator and in many cases may require the addition of a computer technician (or two) to a facilitation team.

The range of tasks that need to be performed by a facilitator and their consequent demands is highly variable, but even straightforward applications can complicate a consensus building process. If Web sites are used for information exchange, for example, a facilitator may need to sort and weed out documents to prevent Web sites from becoming mere data dumps. This relatively minor function requires technical skills not commonly held by facilitators. If conversations occur on-line, a facilitator may need to take responsibility for ensuring that all participants are kept up to speed as the conversation moves beyond what was achieved in the face-to-face sessions. This task can become quite cumbersome, if not impossible, as the facilitator lacks the ability to read nonverbal cues and must develop a system of making discrete inquiries to "read" the comprehension level of each participant. A facilitator may also need to screen messages to avoid inflammatory remarks or comments that might prove destructive if unmediated. Notwithstanding the fact that screening messages constitutes a highly interventionist technique, the latter two tasks can be quite time-consuming for a facilitator. A facilitator may need assistance in monitoring online discussions and a team may ultimately spend more time monitoring and facilitating those conversations than the ones that occur in meetings.

Asking a facilitator to perform such functions on secured Web sites is a double-edged sword. While such conduct may be desirable from an efficiency perspective, the facilitator becomes privy to private discussions. This forces the facilitator into a shuttle diplomat role, willingly or not.

Perhaps one of the most perturbing aspects of computer-mediated communications in consensus building is the inability of the facilitator to employ the range of more subtle but powerful techniques that are available in face-to-face settings. For example, a facilitator commonly moves around the room during discussions, using his or her physical location to give cues to the participants. A facilitator's facial expressions (and those of other participants, for that matter) can also quietly reassure participants who may begin to feel uncomfortable in a given situation. In contrast, facilitators' interventions in electronic communication must be direct, discrete, and explicit. Exactly what the cost is in terms of a loss in the artfulness of facilitation has yet to be discovered.

The Importance of Social Relationships

Communication flows more smoothly between intimate friends than between relative strangers. The social relationships that have been established among participants undoubtedly affect the ease with which computer applications can be integrated effectively into consensus building efforts. Similarly, the extent to which a facilitator needs to be involved is a function of those relationships. Computer-based communications are a "cold" medium. The potential for misinterpretation of messages, let alone the sending of outright antagonistic ones, will be greater for those groups with a weaker foundation of shared knowledge and experience compared with those with a history of working together. The less familiar participants are with one another, the greater ought to be the facilitator's role in monitoring on-line discussions.

The best balance between face-to-face and computer-mediated exchanges is difficult to judge, however, without knowledge of the nature of the participants, their histories, and their relationships in the particular consensus building situation. As a general rule, while Internet services for information dissemination can be employed relatively confidently with minor adaptations to address non-computer-user populations, on-line discussions should be approached more conservatively. Facilitators, convenors, and participants ought to decide together at the beginning of a process the types and frequency of "virtual" exchanges they would like to build into the dialogue, and then integrate those understandings directly into the ground rules. Protocols for computer-based communications should be clearly spelled out to minimize the chances of missteps. The use of computer projections within meetings, whether for analysis or for developing written documents, should also be approached cautiously. Participants should know one another relatively well before allowing a projection screen to become the center of their attention, rather than the facial expressions and body language of the speakers and listeners.

Although early experiences with communication technologies in consensus building have proven promising, systematic data on the benefits and costs are sparse. It is difficult to assess the exact effects of different applications on a consensus building process. It is also worth noting that many of the examples used in this chapter involved participants of similar economic and educational status (largely professionals employed at the various stakeholding groups). Computer-based communications in a more diverse group may be more difficult. In any case, charting the best course for the future depends on gleaning lessons from experiences of the past, however few they may be, and discussing those lessons in the light of current concerns. Making the best use of computer technologies in consensus building processes hinges on the awareness and willingness of potential users to critically and fairly consider available technologies.

■ *Note*

1. The conference site used "command-line-user-interface" technology, which predated graphical or Web-based technology.

■ *References*

City of Portland, OR. (1998). [Online]. Available: www.ci.portland.or.us.

Fisher, R., & Ury, W. (1981). *Getting to yes: Negotiating without giving in.* Cambridge, MA: Houghton Mifflin.

Friedland, L. A. (1996). Electronic democracy and the new citizenship. *Media, Culture & Society, 18,* 185-212.

Mitchell, W. J. (1995). *City of bits: Space, place and the infobahn.* Cambridge, MA: MIT Press.

Nokes, R. G. (1998, May 29). Water proposal raises ownership issue. *The Oregonian.*

Nye, J., Jr., Zelikow, P., & King, D. C. (1997). *Why people don't trust government.* Cambridge, MA: Harvard University Press.

Raiffa, H. (1982). *The art and science of negotiation.* Cambridge, MA: Harvard University Press.

Tims, D. (1998, June 29). For now, Wilsonville nixes Willamette water. *The Oregonian,* pp. B1, B4.

U.S. Bureau of the Census. (1998, July). [Online]. Available: www.census.gov.

U.S. Department of Commerce, National Telecommunications and Information Administration. (1995). *Falling through the net.* Washington, DC: Author.

White House. (1997). [Online]. Available: www1.whitehouse.gov/wh/work/100697.html.

11

DEALING WITH THE PRESS

■ *James E. Kunde*

Americans have a love-hate relationship with the media. We rely on information from a wide range of news sources to keep us "in the loop" and help us make decisions about everything from how to vote to whether or not to carry an umbrella to work. We can (and do) get news at any time of the day or night. We watch 24-hour news channels, read the daily papers, surf the World Wide Web, and carry pagers that transmit continuous streams of information. Want to find out if Congress passed that tax cut? Want to know what the Dow Jones Industrial Average is this very moment? Want to know what the weather will be in Beijing tomorrow? No problem. In each case, we can find out in a matter of minutes. The fact is, we live in a media age.

At the same time, we decry media intrusion into the private lives of public figures and everyday citizens. We gripe about sensationalism and images of violence on the evening news. We are cynical and skeptical about what we see on TV, hear on the radio, and read in the paper (Lehrer, 1998). Some observers even consider the press part of a separate and somehow out-of-touch class of people—the "opinion elite" (Feldmann, 1998).

Those involved in consensus building also have mixed feelings about the press. Often, mediators and facilitators seek to avoid press coverage. They worry about inaccurate or biased reporting and the possibility that a news story will inflame an already heated debate. These appear to be valid concerns, because the press's interests and mediators' interests are often diametrically opposed. The press, after all, focuses on conflict. Conflict is interesting and newsworthy. When two congressional candidates take part in a debate, for example, the snippet that makes the evening news is inevitably the one angry, heated exchange that took place during an otherwise cordial interaction. Mediators and facilitators, on the other hand, seek to resolve conflict. They want to focus people's attention on what the disputing parties have in common and how they can reach mutually beneficial solutions. News coverage of a consensus building process that exaggerates a conflict distracts people from the possibilities for agreement.

At the same time, mediators and facilitators know that news coverage can benefit a consensus building process immeasurably. Reporters who provide responsible, balanced coverage can educate the public about the issues, legitimize an ongoing negotiation, and help to ensure that stakeholders are held accountable for implementing agreements. Indeed, sometimes mediators and participants *need* press coverage to generate support for a process, and may therefore actively seek it out.

This chapter argues that press coverage should not be feared or avoided. The benefits outweigh the potential downsides—but only if mediators and participants know how to deal with the press and if they take the steps necessary to ensure good coverage. (In any case, avoidance may not be possible. Reporters have a legal right to cover most public consensus building processes in any way they see fit.)

This chapter seeks to guide facilitators and participants as they interact with reporters during a consensus-based process, pointing out how they can make these interactions beneficial for all involved. The chapter has three sections. The first relates two short examples that illustrate the extremes of media coverage, showing how the press can either be a benefit or a detriment to a consensus process. The second section describes how to do a *media assessment,* a term we use to mean the process of thinking about whether press coverage is inevitable or desirable and what should be done about it. A media assessment is typically conducted by a facilitator as part of a conflict assessment.[1] The third section provides guidance on how to handle the press during and after a consensus building process.

■ Case Examples: The Extremes of Media Coverage

"Press coverage can be either a help or a hindrance to a consensus process."

Press coverage can be either a help or a hindrance to a consensus process, depending on how well mediators and journalists communicate and are able to work together. The following are two examples that illustrate the extremes.

The first example takes place in the late 1980s, in Montgomery County, Ohio, where the city of Dayton is located. At the time, criminal justice costs were rising dramatically all over the country, because of a combination of high crime rates, demographics (an increased number of teenagers), and growing "get tough on crime" sentiments. As a result, controversies became commonplace between county commission members, on the one hand, and elected judges, sheriffs, and prosecutors, on the other, over the level of spending on criminal justice. Judges frequently threatened to use (and sometimes did use) their authority to "order" funding allocations for court costs and jails beyond the amounts allocated by county commissions. Judges in Montgomery County had not yet exercised this authority, but had announced their intention to do so. In response, Montgomery County administrator Don Vermillion convinced the county commission to invite all elected officials to participate in a consensus building process to prioritize and allocate county funds. Carl Moore and I facilitated the effort.

In the course of designing the consensus process, Moore and I met with the editor of the *Dayton Daily News*, explained the process to him, and negotiated some "media ground rules." Among them, the editor agreed to assign only one reporter to cover the negotiations and to instruct the reporter not to go in and out of the room while deliberations were under way. This arrangement ensured that the reporter would follow the discussions step-by-step and would not disrupt the process. We contacted the managers of two local television stations and secured the same agreement.

The negotiations were a success—the elected officials reached agreement on spending priorities for the county. By following the ground rules, the newspaper reporter was able to get a full sense of how the process worked and explain it to the public in a clear, helpful article. The story that was written reflected the positive atmosphere among the negotiators and accurately described the in-depth, productive dialogue that took place (D. Vermillion, personal communication, November 5, 1998).

In fact, the story helped to win public support for the use of collaborative decision making on other issues of concern in Dayton. The multiparty gatherings to prioritize funding, which became an annual tradition, were expanded to include additional public officials, business executives, and community leaders and to address topics other than spending priorities. Out of these conversations emerged the idea of sharing certain sales tax receipts among the county and all of its municipalities, for economic development purposes. This remains one of the few regional tax-base-sharing programs in the country. Without the positive, accurate press coverage of that first consensus building effort, such results might never have been achieved.

The second example takes place Des Moines, Iowa in 1996. County officials there were also engaged in a budget controversy, but in this case a windfall caused the problem. Several years before, a nonprofit racing association had built a horse-racing track. It eventually went bankrupt. A sympathetic county Board of Supervisors bailed the track out with public money, however, and used bond funds to refurbish it. It went bankrupt again. This time, the Iowa legislature gave the county authority to install slot machines at the track. Soon the track was out of debt, the bonds were paid off, and revenues for the county reached $6 million per month—a totally unanticipated outcome. Soon elected officials, community leaders, business interests, and others were fighting over how to spend the money. Should it be used to fund the school system? New highways? A convention center? Libraries? Social services? Everyone had an opinion.

The county employed an outside facilitation team (made up of myself and two other mediators) to develop a process for seeking agreement on how to spend the budget windfall. With assistance from the Kettering Foundation, we developed a two-pronged effort. First, a group of about 25 local leaders was convened to seek consensus on a few realistic and desirable options for spending the money. Second, the public was asked to discuss and comment on those options. More than 1,300 people participated in this second part of the effort, which involved public meetings and surveys. The Board of Supervisors retained the final say over how the money would be spent, but agreed to take account of the recommendations that emerged from the process.

In the rush to get the effort started, we did not meet with local editors and station managers to explain the process. Instead, we let county officials visit with an editor at the *Des Moines Register*, the largest local paper. This was a mistake. The editor apparently did not trust the local officials. He felt that the process was a sham and that budget priorities had already been set, and the local officials could not dissuade him. They were not able to communicate the concepts behind the process very well and did not raise the idea of media ground rules. Thus, after the process began, stories began appearing in the *Register* that were critical of the process and that focused on (and thereby aggravated) differing opinions among members of the Board of Supervisors (Bowers, 1997a, 1997b). Even worse, reporters disrupted and nearly derailed the public involvement process, though perhaps not intentionally. Several times, reporters and TV cameramen entered a room while a meeting was under way and began to film the discussions. Conversation simply shut down as microphones were thrust into the participants' faces and cameras came in for close-ups. In all likelihood, the journalists did not intend to create difficulties, but their actions caused a great deal of anxiety among the participants and the facilitators. Finally, one of the facilitators met directly with representatives of the press to talk about methods of coverage, but by that time it was too late.

The process was eventually successful, in spite of the reporters' interruptions. Many members of the public expressed satisfaction with both the process and the results. In response to the overwhelming sentiment expressed at the public meetings, the county commission decided to spend most of the money on education. (Interestingly, the group of 25 local leaders favored spending it on highways and a convention center.) Reporters' behavior came close to undermining the effort, however, and clearly hampered the discussion.

■ *Conducting a Media Assessment*

"It is essential that facilitators assess the media situation before each process begins."

As these examples illustrate, the media have the power to either support or undermine a process. Facilitators and participants can, however, have a significant impact on how press coverage occurs. By reaching out to editors and reporters, as in the Dayton case, facilitators can help to ensure good coverage of a process and minimal disruption by reporters. It is essential that facilitators assess the media situation before each process begins and, if appropriate, design a strategy for handling the press. We believe a media assessment—the process of thinking strategically about whether or not press coverage is likely and deciding what should be done about it—should be conducted during the convening phase, as part of a conflict assessment.

This section describes the questions that facilitators should try to answer as part of a media assessment. While each situation is unique and demands a different approach, the same questions need to be answered to determine a strategy appropriate to a given situation:

1. Is press coverage desirable in this situation?
2. Is the press likely to be interested in covering this process?

If the answer to either question is yes, then

3. What media ground rules should be proposed to guide the behavior of participants and the press?
4. What media outlets should be contacted? Which individuals at each outlet should be approached?

Is Press Coverage Desirable?

A facilitator must begin by determining whether or not press coverage might be beneficial for a consensus-based process. To do this, the pros and cons of publicity should be carefully considered.

As the Des Moines case shows, press coverage can complicate a process tremendously. Indeed, the presence of reporters in a room during deliberations alters the behavior of participants. These behavior changes are best explained by a concept known in the speech and communications field as *self-monitoring*. Self-monitoring is a tendency to phrase statements describing facts or emotions in a way that anticipates how other parties will respond, rather than being completely candid.[2] The original focus of self-monitoring research was to illustrate how our perceived need for civility can be overdone and can interfere with our ability to communicate clearly. Self-monitoring is a tendency that can restrict group members' ability to deliberate effectively. In an agreement-seeking process, it is important for participants to be able to clearly communicate their interests so that opportunities for mutual gain can be discovered. If participants focus too much on how they say something rather than just saying it, they risk misrepresenting their interests, and their fellow participants may waste time trying to guess what they really mean. At the beginning of a process, when participants do not yet know or trust each other, some self-monitoring may be desirable; it can help to ensure that people do not offend each other.

A simplified test for individual self-monitoring behavior was developed several years ago (Snyder, 1987). It produces a score between 1 and 10. A score of 1 reveals an individual so direct and rude that he or she would probably offend people quite often. A 10, on the other hand, would indicate so much skill at deceiving others about facts or feelings that no one would trust the person. I have found that the most effective work teams in industry score an average of 3 on the test. Groups of elected officials, such as city council members, seem to average around 7.

The presence of the press—especially when it is very visible—induces high self-monitoring. For example, if participants think that their words may end up in the next morning's paper, they are less likely to suggest potential solutions that would result in mutual gains for all parties, because this might cause them to be seen by the public or their constituents as "selling out." They also would be less likely to suggest "outside the box" solutions, for fear of being ridiculed. Self-monitoring significantly impedes what management consultant Peter Senge refers to as "systems-level dialogue," in which group members focus on thoughtful analysis of a problem before solutions are considered. Systems-level dialogue is a condition critical to group work (Senge, 1996).

Press coverage can also complicate a process simply because consensus building is new, complex, sometimes lengthy, and not easily boiled down into sound bites, headlines, or 800-word articles. Unless a reporter is familiar with consensus building or is particularly thorough, press coverage may not do a process justice. In fact, reporters often aren't interested in "process" anyway; they are interested in outcomes. Unless a mediator or group spokesperson educates a reporter about how a good process *leads* to a good outcome, a reporter may not see the point in describing the process at all. Other aspects of consensus building may not be intuitively obvious to a reporter, and a mediator should take the time to explain them. For example, reporters may not understand that participants are representing larger constituencies and that special efforts have been made to mirror the full diversity of stakeholder perspectives. They may think and write, instead, that a negotiating group is an exclusive club trying to impose its solutions on the public. Claims such as these make it much harder for a group to "sell" an agreement if one is finally reached. Or reporters may not understand that uncovering and reviewing conflicting perspectives is a necessary and helpful activity on the path to reaching consensus. They may simply focus on the fact that the parties disagree. A news story that highlights conflicts without describing the larger process can lead the public to think that the negotiations are failing. Because consensus building is still relatively new, facilitators must work hard to ensure that journalists understand what is involved.

Participants in a collaborative effort may use the press in ways that are detrimental to consensus building. They may, for example, say things to reporters that, when published, inflame the situation. They may insult their fellow negotiators or try to characterize the views or opinions of others and get them wrong. They may leak information that is supposed to be kept confidential, such as draft reports or behind-the-scenes conversations, to bolster their negotiating positions or "kill" a process by eroding public support (Primack, 1998). All of these tactics can create animosity, diminish trust, and make reaching agreement much more difficult.

A public consensus building process in Chelsea, Massachusetts provides a good example of a situation in which a person detrimentally affected a process via the press (Case 3). Chelsea is a small city outside of Boston that had a long history of corruption and fiscal irresponsibility on the part of local officials. In 1990, with the city on the verge of bankruptcy, the state suspended Chelsea's local government and put the city under receivership. The appointed receiver was charged with developing a new city charter—in essence, replacing a malfunctioning democracy with a new and functional form of government. After some false starts, the receiver hired a mediation team to develop a consensus building process through which the residents of Chelsea would draft a new charter. A diverse, 18-member charter preparation team was organized. The team's members worked well with the press and the coverage was excellent; in fact, it was essential to securing broad agreement for the outcome. At one point, however, when the team was trying to decide whether a new city council should have 9, 11, or 13 members, a story appeared in the *Boston Globe* quoting an unnamed source as saying the new Chelsea city council might have 15 members. The team had never discussed this option. As it turned out, someone in the receiver's office had given the reporter an incorrect figure. (His motives for doing this were never determined.) As a result, team members felt as if the process was not legitimate—as if decisions about the new charter had already been made and their efforts were futile. The facilitators had to work hard, publicly and behind the scenes, to assure the team and the public that this was not the case.

Because press attention and coverage can create so many problems, mediators and participants sometimes want to know whether the press can be legally barred from a consensus building process. Typically, the press can be kept out of conversations among private citizens. But any time public officials are involved or a process is sponsored by a public agency, the media probably have a legal right to be present. (Chapter 13, on legal issues in consensus building, discusses this matter in more detail.)

In any case, despite all the complications, mediators and participants often *want* press coverage of a consensus building process. They may even seek it out. Why? Because responsible press coverage can help to ensure that the public—including the constituencies of the stakeholder representatives involved—is kept informed about the ongoing discussions. An informed citizenry is desirable for many reasons.

First, negotiators are often seeking consensus on issues that will affect all the residents of a community or region, or at least a broad cross section of them. The Chelsea group, for example, was developing a charter for the entire city. Ultimately, city residents would vote on the preparation team's recommended charter, and it was important that they be kept informed of the team's progress and not be caught off guard by the final product. The preparation team hired a communications consultant, in fact, to help publicize its effort. The team and the consultant worked together to ensure newspaper coverage and, several times, described the process and the emerging agreement on cable television call-in shows. As the Chelsea group discovered, press coverage is a quick and effective means of educating the public. Such coverage may also encourage citizens to come to meetings, contact representatives to convey an opinion on an issue, or even advocate for the outcome of a process.

A second benefit of press coverage is that it enhances the relationships between representatives and their constituents. In particular, it enables the members of stakeholder groups to follow the progress of a dialogue. As discussed in Chapter 6, on representation, participants often feel a tension between the need to represent their constituents' wishes and the need to be flexible enough to change their opinions based on new information or a better understanding of how their concerns might be addressed. They often go through a learning process that is difficult to explain to their constituents. The result is sometimes a shocked response from a stakeholder group at the end of a process: "You agreed to *what*?" Press coverage that keeps constituents up to speed on evolving negotiations helps carry constituents along the learning curve with their negotiators.

Finally, press coverage can help to ensure that an agreement will be implemented. The implementation of negotiated agreements often involves numerous organizations and levels of government, and it is sometimes unclear who is responsible for doing what (Pressman & Wildavsky, 1984). If the press describes the terms of an agreement and names the people and organizations responsible for carrying it out, implementers are more likely to be held accountable for meeting their commitments. In addition, press coverage can make implementation easier simply because it helps to build public support for a process, as in the Dayton, Ohio case. A widely supported outcome is less likely to be thwarted during implementation.

In the late 1970s, for example, the Kettering Foundation (in cooperation with the Carter White House and the Department of Housing and Urban Development) designed an experiment called the *negotiated investment strategy*. The process entailed the neutral facilitation of efforts to identify and prioritize local problems (e.g., low-income housing shortages, environmental problems, economic development needs) and focus federal, state, and local resources on dealing with those priorities. It was applied in St. Paul, Minnesota; Columbus, Ohio; and Gary, Indiana. Discussions in each city involved participants representing public and private sector organizations at the local, state, and federal levels. The process was very successful; it resulted in numerous actions by the various players that solved long-standing, seemingly intractable problems (Isidore, 1987). In fact, later evaluations showed the process was the "most implemented" federalled intervention during this period (Moore & Carlson, 1984). In each city, a major factor driving implementation was that the commitments made by participants during the process were widely reported in the press (Coke & Moore, 1979; see also "St. Paul Receives $40 Million," 1979). People are less likely to dodge responsibility for carrying out an agreement if they know they are going to be held accountable publicly.

Facilitators should take all of these advantages and disadvantages of press coverage into account when considering whether or not media attention is desirable. If discussions are meant to involve only private citizens (who do not want their conversation publicized), and the press does not have a legal right to attend meetings, a facilitator may decide that coverage is not warranted. If a process involves a diverse cross section of individuals and requires widespread public support to ensure implementation, a facilitator may want to seek media attention. The many "in between" cases will require a facilitator's best judgment. Because press coverage has so many benefits, and because the potential negatives can be mitigated with proper preparation, we believe that mediators should always plan for media coverage.

Is the Press Likely to Be Interested in a Process?

The second key factor to consider as part of a media assessment is whether or not the press is likely to be interested in covering a process. The fact is, journalists are not inclined to write about consensus-based efforts. I would estimate that the press has been interested in only about 25 percent of the consensus building projects on which I have worked. Counting only the cases in which public officeholders were involved, I would say the press covered about half.

Editors and reporters are bombarded with daily press releases and phone calls from people pitching story ideas. From among these, they must choose the topics they believe are most newsworthy. What they are looking for is *news*—that which is literally new, unique, controversial, or otherwise particularly interesting or which directly affects large numbers of readers or viewers. Journalists may well think a consensus building process is not newsworthy, either because it does not meet some tacit "standard" or because it is not explained in a way that catches their attention. Much about consensus processes—the endless hours of meetings, the fact-finding activities, the painstaking negotiations—seems tedious to most journalists. Also, processes that go on for many months are simply "old news" to them.

The press also may ignore consensus processes because coverage may require an extensive time commitment on the part of reporters. Because consensus building is new, complex, and involves so many players, it is not easy to cover. A good story will include interviews with people representing all sides of a controversy and (depending on the focus of the piece) perhaps sitting through hours of meetings to generate a clear understanding of the debate. Reporters can cover other, more straightforward stories in less time and with less effort.

Certain consensus building processes are less likely to draw press coverage than others. In my experience, for example, the big-city press is not likely to cover efforts involving suburban communities. Newspapers and television stations in these areas are more focused on events in the city than in the suburbs, probably due to staff limitations. I facilitated a consensus process in Dublin, Ohio, a large suburb of Columbus, that was much like the Montgomery County (Dayton) process described at the beginning of this chapter. Unlike my Dayton experience, no reporters expressed any interest in covering the Dublin effort. Processes that are particularly lengthy (many months or years long) are also less likely to garner coverage.

The press *is* likely be interested when a consensus building group is discussing a "hot" issue or when high-profile players are involved. The Des Moines gambling windfall case certainly met both of these criteria. It was a countywide controversy among diverse constituencies over how "extra" funding (an unusual occurrence) should be spent; it also involved 25 prominent local leaders. The Chelsea case fits the bill, too; it involved creating a new city government, which would affect literally every citizen, and all local political leaders had a stake in the result. A disagreement I mediated in Columbus, Ohio drew press attention in large part because the disputants were two of the wealthiest, most successful businessmen in the city. In that case, a swarm of reporters staked out the conference center during the mediation sessions. Business leaders, elected officials, and outspoken activists draw the media's attention to a consensus process, particularly when the debate concerns a newsworthy topic.

In addition, certain steps in a consensus building process may be more newsworthy, and thus more likely to draw press coverage, than others. Reporters may be interested, for example, in writing about the entry of a neutral facilitator into a controversy. The first meeting of a process may also draw interest, as might the release of a final report or notice of a settlement. But again, these events will be of interest only if the topic or the people involved are newsworthy.

To determine if the media are likely to be interested in a consensus building process, a facilitator should talk to the stakeholders during the conflict assessment about the media situation. Have the local papers or TV stations covered this issue before? Is it a hot topic locally? Are any of the people involved particularly prominent or notorious? These kinds of questions will help a facilitator assess whether or not the press will come calling.

If stakeholders do not want coverage and the press is not likely to come calling, the facilitator can conclude the media assessment; nothing more needs to be done. But if press coverage is desirable, inevitable, or both, more work will need to be done. In particular, a facilitator must think about setting media ground rules and talking to editors and station managers before a process gets under way. (Note that we do not recommend simply trying to avoid the press if coverage is not desired. If the press is interested, it is best to be prepared and try to get the kind of coverage that will be most helpful.)

Recommend Ground Rules for Participants and the Press

Ground rules are explicit agreements among participants about behaviors that will and will not be accepted. Two different types of ground rules are needed to ensure high-quality press coverage supporting the goals of consensus building. A facilitator conducting a media assessment must consider and make recommendations regarding both.

First, a facilitator should develop (and recommend in a written conflict assessment) ground rules that will guide a negotiating group's interactions with the press. These ground rules should include guidance on who will talk with the press (e.g., the facilitator, the chairperson, a designated spokesperson, a hired press consultant, all participants, or some combination thereof) and what they will say. Perhaps a facilitator will agree to talk only about process matters and not the substance of the debate. The chair, or two or three participants representing different viewpoints, might also be designated as spokespeople. They should be directed to represent the process and the discussions to the media in a way that is nonpartisan and fair to all. If a group decides that *all* participants should speak to the press as they see fit, they might include a ground rule that they should talk only about their own interests and perspectives and not try to characterize the views of others. Ground rules might also define who will be responsible for writing press releases and how often, and if or when draft reports or agreements will be released. A facilitator might recommend a ground rule stating that participants should not indicate the content of a likely agreement until that agreement has been formally accepted by everyone involved. A facilitator should review possible media ground rules with interviewees during a conflict assessment to get their reactions. All recommended ground rules should be discussed and revised by the consensus building group as a whole.

In the Chelsea case, the charter preparation team agreed to several ground rules regarding the press. For example, they agreed to avoid negotiating through the press. (The person in the receiver's office who went to the *Globe* with incorrect information was not covered by these ground rules.) They also identified three spokespeople who were empowered to talk to reporters. According to the case study, "These people could go to [reporters] and say, 'This is where we are in the process. These are some of the proposals on the table. These are some of the early decisions we're considering,' but they were not supposed to attribute particular statements to anybody."

Second, a facilitator or convenor should think about what ground rules to ask reporters to follow while covering a process. The term *ground rules* in this case refers to something like the old sexist idea of a "gentlemen's agreement." Press representatives will not want to make an explicit, unalterable, written commitment to cover an event a certain way, because that would jeopardize their independence. They may give a nod or an "OK, we'll try it," which is, in fact, very dependable. To insist on a more

"A facilitator or convenor should think about what ground rules to ask reporters to follow while covering a process."

formal commitment is to run the risk of alienating the media representatives.

Ideally, each press outlet will agree to assign one reporter to cover a process, have that person stay for the entirety of each meeting, and have the person commit to not "go in and out" repeatedly during a session, particularly with audio and video equipment in tow. In fact, it is best if the press agrees not to set up cameras and tape recorders in a meeting room at all, but rather to wait until after a meeting is over to take photos or video footage. This behavior will be the least distracting to participants, will reduce self-monitoring, and will ensure that a journalist gets a complete sense of the process. Reporters should also be asked not to conduct interviews with participants during breaks, but rather to wait until the end of a session (although sometimes concessions have to be made so reporters can meet their deadlines). In general, participants will forget the press is present if reporters and camera crews do not keep running in and out and do not intercept them at breaks. This arrangement also makes it possible for a reporter to gain full insight into all that is happening, which, when combined with in-depth interviews after meetings, can result in a clear and accurate account of the consensus building effort.

In most cases, reporters and editors will agree to abide by such ground rules. Often, however, after agreeing to them, an editor will not send anyone to a meeting but will instead have a reporter write a story based on postmeeting conversations with the facilitator and perhaps a few participants. This is not as effective as full-assignment coverage, but it is better than the "running in and out" model, which so often happens with overburdened reporters.

Determine Whom to Approach in the Press Regarding Ground Rules

The key to getting media representatives to agree to cover a process responsibly (or at all) and abide by ground rules is to approach the "right people" at newspapers or television stations. During a media assessment, a facilitator must carefully consider whom to contact and how.

To learn more about how best to approach media representatives, we interviewed three experienced journalists. All were employed by print publications that cover major metropolitan populations; one had also been a TV station manager. The interviewees were Paul Harral, executive editor for special features at the *Fort Worth Star-Telegram*; Ralph Langer, executive editor of the *Dallas Morning News*; and Gregory Moore, managing editor of the *Boston Globe*. Each was asked several questions about how the press should be approached and how they might respond to the suggestion that they abide by certain ground rules in covering a consensus building process. Their responses are summarized in Figure 11.1.

Paul Harral said he would respond favorably to a reasonable request to abide by ground rules. He said that in most cases, the managing editor is the person who should be approached initially. Harral added, however, that he would want any discussion of ground rules to also include the paper's editorial board and "a couple of key editors." He suggested that the purpose of the dialogue would need to be explained in some detail. "Don't push the concept of *third party* beyond *mediation*," he said, because "that's the term we all understand." While he said that the contact could be made through "reliable locals," he felt it would be better done by the "hired gun"—the facilitator. He felt that a facilitator should talk first with editors in the print media, and then go to the visual media. He suggested that TV stations usually follow the lead of the print media in such matters. Harral also said that there is "some precedent" for visual and print media agreeing to ground rules together.

Harral said that facilitators should talk to editors and reporters early in a process and keep them informed; the journalists will appreciate it and will work hard to publish accurate and well-informed stories. He said they would much rather know that a process was occurring from the beginning than find out after an agreement had been reached. Harral recalled a story he had been told regarding negotiations over the reconstruction of Interstate 30, which runs through downtown Fort Worth. The Bass brothers (the city's wealthy protagonists) were head-to-head with Eddie Chiles (then the owner of the Texas Rangers baseball team) over the design and location of the highway. Facilitator Jim Laue was brought in to mediate, which he did masterfully. The *Fort Worth Star-Telegram* did not know about the mediation until an agreement was reached. When Harral was recruited, he was told this story and admonished never to let the paper miss another impor-

	Ralph Langer, *Dallas Morning News*	Paul Harral, *Fort Worth Star-Telegram*	Gregory Moore, *Boston Globe*
Who in the press should be approached?	Managing or executive editor.	Managing editor, but include editorial board and other key editors.	Managing editor.
How should they be approached?	Look them in the eye and give context that "checks out."	Explain in detail, but clearly.	Don't try for too many ground rules.
Should print or electronic media be approached first? Will different media cooperate on ground rules?	Print, then TV. There is some history of getting all the media together to cooperate on ground rules.	Start with print, then go to visual; TV will usually follow the lead of newspapers.	Start with print. There has been good experience of cooperation on some high-profile issues.
Who should make the approach?	Prefer approach by *both* the neutral and a local who brought in the neutral.	Could be "reliable locals," but best done by the "hired gun."	Mediator has to be the one.
How much about facilitated problem solving will a press person know?	Familiar with the concept, have seen it being applied several times.	Don't push the concept beyond *mediation.* That's the term we all understand.	About 75 percent of journalists at managing editor level would quickly "get it."
How detailed should ground rules be?	Basic, straightforward.	Simple, but understand that "off the record" doesn't exist. We may agree to keep silent for a while.	Very important not to set too many ground rules.
Any final advice?	Be prepared to explain the context and have a good sense of the press coverage of the circumstance where the intervention is occurring.	A rising journalist who has come to the community to stay for a while will listen; one on his or her way to bigger places may have trouble with it. Know who you are dealing with.	There has been an example of cooperation in coverage in Boston in the 1996 Senate campaign between John Kerry and Bill Weld, in which the press covered an issue-focused debate.

Figure 11.1. How to Approach the Press: Thoughts from Newspaper Editors

tant article like that (P. Harral, personal communication, September 9, 1997).

Ralph Langer from the *Dallas Morning News* responded similarly, but added some different ideas. He said he would prefer to be approached by a facilitator as well as representatives of the local groups who had hired the facilitator. He agreed that the print media should be approached first and then the television stations. He stated that there was "some history" in Dallas of getting the press together and agreeing on basic ground rules for handling sensible coverage of a high-profile process. A final admonition from Langer was that it is important for a facilitator to "look you in the eye" and to be "straightforward" about the process and the issues in dispute (R. Langer, personal communication, September 11, 1997).

Gregory Moore from the *Boston Globe* was the final interviewee. He said he would respond positively to a request to follow ground rules because "we would get a better story." When asked about his familiarity with facilitated consensus building, he said he was "generally familiar" with the concept of consensus building and the role of mediators and facilitators. He guessed that about three-quarters of the managing editors around the country would quickly "get it." Moore felt strongly that the mediator needed to be the one to make the approach and explain the process. He said that there had been some experience in the Boston area with cooperation among press sources on high-profile issues. For example, during the 1996 U.S. Senate race between John Kerry and William Weld, the Boston-area press came together, agreed to follow some basic ground rules, and responsibly covered an issues-focused debate. He also said that responsible coverage is much more likely in "the post-O.J. Simpson environment." Moore cautioned, however, not to try to set too many ground rules (G. Moore, personal communication, September 18, 1997).

Based on the comments of Harral, Langer, and Moore, we can infer that the facilitator, perhaps with a few potential participants, should probably be the one to meet with the press, and the approach should be made during the convening phase (e.g., after the conflict assessment is completed and it is clear that a consensus building process is moving ahead). Community leaders may be able to make the approach on their own, but they should have some standing in the community and be able to fully explain the process.

Harral, Langer, and Moore also say that the managing editor of the major print media outlet is the person to approach first. I recommend asking interviewees in a conflict assessment process for their thoughts on which newspapers and TV stations should be approached and which editors should be contacted first. In some cases, if a prospective participant knows of or has had a good relationship with the reporter likely to cover the process, the facilitator could approach that reporter directly to discuss ground rules and coverage. If the reporter is not interested in covering the process, or balks at the idea of ground rules, the editor should then be contacted.

In meeting with an editor, a facilitator should acknowledge the media's right to cover public meetings in whatever way they choose. The facilitator should also clearly define the topic that is to be the subject of consensus building and the process that will be used. The neutral should also define his or her role as *mediator* and refrain from using jargon. The editors may need to be convinced that a consensus building process is worth covering. In talking with them, a facilitator should emphasize the importance of the issue to the community or region, the diversity of key stakeholders who will be involved, the uniqueness and benefits of consensus building, and so forth. If a facilitator wants publicity for an effort and the editors are skeptical of its importance, a real sales job may be required.

The facilitator should ask the editors if they will agree to follow some basic ground rules. A verbal agreement is all that should be sought. If there is a precedent for joint media ground rules (with TV stations), the facilitator should follow those. If not, the facilitator will need to meet with the electronic media one by one and diplomatically indicate what the print media have agreed to do. It is especially important to get a verbal agreement, if at all possible, to keep cameras and tape recorders out of the meeting room. It is a good idea to promise reporters a press conference involving several key participants after each session. In general, if the print media have agreed to not put cameras in the room, the electronic media will do the same.

Before contacting media representatives, a facilitator should be aware of one more issue: the relatively new concept of *public journalism* (also called *civic journalism*). Public journalism is based on the idea that reporters have a special responsibility to help the public understand the context within which to evaluate news (Charity, 1995; Rosen, in press). An advocate of public journalism would say, for example, that reporters should work to extract real public interests from surveys, and then ask candidates for public office to respond to those specific concerns, rather than just reporting the content of negative campaigning or a candidate's latest campaign promise. The *Wichita* (Kansas) *Eagle* and the *Charlotte* (North Carolina) *Observer* are often mentioned as papers with a commitment to public journalism. KERA, a Dallas-Fort Worth public broadcasting station, is a good example of public journalism in the broadcasting realm. One example of the effect of this standard was the *Charlotte Observer's* thorough and frequent coverage of a community visioning process in Charlotte-Mechlenburg County. The *Observer* was one of the leading partners supporting the consensus building effort, in fact (Miller, 1994).

Public journalism is currently dividing the field. Opponents are wary of having "standards" set for them that guide how events are supposed to be reported. But where it is responsibly practiced, public journalism seems to encourage an interest in and responsible coverage of deliberative public processes such as consensus building. It is useful for facilitators to know whether the editors they are contacting are proponents or opponents of the public journalism movement. Those who are advocates may be more interested in covering a consensus building process in depth.

■ *Dealing with the Press*
   during and after a Process

If a facilitator conducts a thorough media assessment and approaches editors and station managers based on the guidelines in the previous section, he or she will have set the stage for a good interaction with the press. This section provides additional guidance for dealing with the press during and after a consensus building process. It focuses on what a facilitator and participants ought to know about reporters to interact with them effectively, what to do during a process, and what to say at the end.

Know Something about Reporters

If mediators or participants expect to come into contact with reporters, they ought to know something about the business of journalism and the environment in which reporters work. The more they know about the field, the motivations of journalists, and the constraints under which reporters operate, the more they will be able to help reporters do their job well and so help to ensure good coverage of a consensus building process.

Many journalists are graduates of journalism schools, at which they gain academic training and field experience and are fully indoctrinated with the ethics of professional journalism. These ethics include mandates to tell "all sides of a story" (to be sure that coverage is not slanted) and to tell a story as they see it (not be unduly influenced by any single interest or viewpoint). Impartiality and autonomy, in fact, are as important to journalists as they are to mediators. This may be a useful point for a mediator to make when explaining to a reporter his or her role in a consensus building process; it will help the reporter understand the role and is a bit of common ground on which to start a good working relationship.

Someone selecting a journalism career is usually not motivated by monetary ambition. Journalists rarely get wealthy plying their trade, unless they become one of the very few who write a syndicated column or a best-seller. Journalists are often, rather, motivated by a desire to serve the public interest. Those who have long careers in the field tend to be curious about new ideas, quick to catch on, and very competitive.

Most reporters have a *beat:* a slate of issues they specialize in covering. One reporter might cover local politics, while another may specialize in crime stories, and yet another may write primarily about science and the environment. It would be helpful for a mediator to know what a reporter's beat is, so the mediator can focus on educating him or her on the issues about which the reporter is less familiar. A technology reporter, for example, may quickly catch on to the scientific issues involved in a consensus building process, but need help dissecting the political intricacies of the negotiation.

Journalists' lives are governed by deadlines. Most do not work 9:00 a.m. to 5:00 p.m., but rather whatever hours are dictated by their deadlines. They are almost always under pressure to get stories out and to do their part to help editors fill the paper (or magazine or news broadcast). Mediators and participants need to be respectful of these deadlines; they should try to return calls from reporters as quickly as possible and should not make unsolicited calls to reporters close to their deadlines.

Reporters typically develop lists of sources they can call for interviews or comments on a breaking story. These sources are invaluable in helping a reporter quickly assess all sides of a story and gain trustworthy insights into something about which he or she may know very little. It is helpful for mediators and group spokespeople to make themselves available to reporters—to become useful and trustworthy sources—to ensure that reporters understand consensus building and can write about it accurately.

Reporters always prefer to work on a story for which they have enough time and sources available to fully develop an accurate and insightful presentation. Therefore, mediators and participants alike should work to create a setting in which a reporter has access to complete information and enough time to develop a good story. Providing background information well in advance and making participants available for interviews on short notice, for example, will make a reporter's job easier.

Television stations operate along the same lines as print publications, although some differences are worth noting. For television stories, reporters must think more about the visual imagery to accompany the text; the best stories are not conveyed with just a talking head. Ideally, a TV piece will show action footage. Unfortunately, a shot of participants debating an issue is about the best they will get in a consensus building process. Mediators may need to work with TV reporters to determine appropriate times and places to film participants, however, since running in and out of meetings can be disruptive. Also, because television stories are typically much shorter and less in depth than newspaper or magazine pieces, TV reporters will have to distill a process description down to its most basic elements. Facilitators and spokespeople can help in this regard by providing succinct statements, press releases, and background material.

Weekly or monthly magazines and weekly newspapers normally will have the fewest time constraints and the most incentive to cover something in depth. Most mediators will attest to the fact, however, that these publications are typically not the ones interested in consensus building processes. This may be because they tend to be national in scope and so would only cover a process with nationwide implications. It may also be that mediators have not sought out the editors of magazines in an effort to try to stimulate coverage. Nonetheless, in most cases, a group will be dealing with daily newspapers and local TV stations.

Finally, it is important to note that there is a tremendous amount of competition among media outlets and among reporters to see who can beat the other to a story or who can get the best interview. Mediators should take care not to inadvertently exacerbate this competition, because it may hurt coverage of a process. For example, a facilitator who calls only one out of several interested journalists to report a breakthrough in a negotiation has just given that reporter a scoop. The other journalists will be miffed because the facilitator has ensured that that one news outlet will be the first to run the story. The news outlets that have been shut out may either run no story at all (because it will be old news by the time they can cover it), or may end up running a more negative story because they are not feeling very positively toward the mediator or the process. (This is not to say that the press writes negative stories to "get back at" people; we assume they do not. It simply does not seem wise to anger those who have such a strong influence on how the public perceives a process.) Mediators should, therefore, always contact *all* possible news sources with any information about what they are doing.

Dealing with the Press during a Process

"It is absolutely critical to be honest and give meaningful insight into why a process is going the way it is."

During a process, a facilitator (or designated spokespeople) should provide press briefings or interviews after each meeting, or at reasonable intervals along the way. In interviews and briefings, it is absolutely critical to be honest and give meaningful insight into why a process is going the way it is. It is also important to be optimistic—to convey to reporters that building consensus takes time and hard work but that even heated controversies have been resolved using consensus-based procedures.

Press releases with more detailed updates are also useful. They help to shape the media's interpretation of a process and can put into perspective events that might otherwise be misunderstood. For example, if a participant announces late in a negotiation that she cannot live with some provision in a proposed agreement, a press release could (if appropriate) convey optimism about the possibility of still reaching consensus.

It is also important that participants be reminded to follow the media ground rules and told not to try to influence the process through the press. If participants break the ground rules repeatedly, this may be a sign that the ground rules are not appropriate or that there are more fundamental problems involved.

If a newspaper article appears that a group perceives to be inaccurate or distorted, participants should discuss how they want to proceed. They could write an op-ed piece or a letter to the editor thanking the press for its coverage, but setting the record straight. If it is an error of fact, they could call the reporter or his or her editor and ask that a correction be run. Or, if it is not particularly egregious and does not need to be publicly refuted, they could simply ask to meet with the reporter to discuss the issue, so that the problem does not occur again.

What to Say at the End of a Process

At the conclusion of a successful process, a negotiating group may want to conduct a press conference and issue a press release. Participants should provide reporters with a copy of the written agreement or final report. It is important that reporters understand the context of an agreement and are given information in concise, easy-to-digest form. The use of visual aids helps.

Once in a while, despite every effort, a process does not produce an agreement that satisfies all participants. Or sometimes an agreement is reached, but it breaks down during implementation. How does a facilitator communicate with the press in either of these circumstances? First, it would be wise to get the leaders who suggested the consensus building process and the key stakeholders in the disagreement to come together as the process concludes to see if they can agree on a statement that accurately describes what caused the failure. Developing a single message helps stakeholders acknowledge their disagreements, sends a clear statement to the public, and paves the way for resolving the issue at some time in the future. The joint statement should be distributed to the press—preferably with the key parties present—so that the "bad news" gets out completely and quickly. If there is partial agreement, it should be announced at the same time.

It is important in these situations to handle "blame" carefully. If the parties can go through a positive parting process, blame may be restructured as simply "problems that remain" and the door can be left open to try consensus building again at a later date. A facilitator should connect the outcome with the situation at the beginning of the process, so that progress is noted and all constituencies can properly reflect on whether or not they are satisfied with the performance of their representatives.

A process may have failed because of the limitations of the facilitator. Participants may have decided their facilitator is biased, for example, and discontinued the negotiation. In such a situation, the facilitator should lay a path for another neutral to intercede later. A neutral's honest discussion with the press about his or her limitations gives credibility to both the neutral and the process.

If a process broke down because one or more of the parties had a better alternative than any option developed at the table, the facilitator should carefully explain the concept of BATNA (best alternative to a negotiated agreement) so the press can explain it to the public. The facilitator should not discuss any party's specific BATNA, unless that party has already revealed it to the press.

If a process broke down because of a "problem person" and that person's constituency is unaware of this, then a facilitator might consider finding a way for the press to report that message. A well-worded statement, such as "I was unable to gain the trust of so-and-so," or "I was never able to adequately bring so-and-so into the process," should work. It is not appropriate for a facilitator to hide poor performance by a participant. On the other hand, a facilitator should not aggravate honest differences or escalate the conflict further. If the up-front press interactions are handled well, a self-effacing approach will probably work and will lay a path for another attempt to reach agreement in the future.

■ Conclusion

Press interest in a consensus building process need not present a problem for a facilitator or a group. Instead of avoiding or

1. Be proactive. Assess the media situation as a part of the initial conflict assessment and determine an appropriate course of action.
2. If press attention is inevitable or desirable, determine some appropriate ground rules for participants for dealing with the press and for reporters to follow in covering the process.
3. Meet one-on-one and face-to-face with key editors and station managers before a process begins to explain consensus building and discuss ground rules. Acknowledge reporters' right to do anything they deem appropriate, and don't expect more than a "we'll see" response.
4. Know something about the challenge of being a reporter. Be as prepared for dealing with them as you expect them to be in dealing with you.
5. During deliberations, give thorough but concise press briefings and interviews at appropriate intervals, focusing on the process.
6. At the end of a process, organize a press conference and write press releases describing the process and the agreement(s) reached. If a group fails to reach consensus, handle "blame" in a manner that keeps open all reasonable paths for a later attempt at resolution.

Figure 11.2. Dealing with the Press: General Guidelines

ignoring the press, as is often the case, facilitators and participants should think ahead of time about whether or not they want press coverage, whether or not the press is likely to come calling, and what kind of press strategy they want to adopt. With good preparation, it is possible to have some measure of control over how a group interacts with the press.

This chapter outlines several key steps that should be taken to ensure responsible press coverage of a consensus building process. (These steps are summarized in Figure 11.2.) First, prepare a media assessment as part of the initial conflict assessment and determine if the press is likely to be interested in the story. As part of that assessment, develop possible media ground rules and identify the best press contacts to talk to about them. The best contact is likely to be the managing editor of the most prominent newspaper in the area. The facilitator should meet with that person directly, if at all possible, with or without other stakeholders, to explain the consensus building process and discuss proposed media ground rules. Assuming the print media agree, the facilitator should approach the electronic media, relying on past precedents if possible. The facilitators should make sure all parties know something about how reporters work and are prepared to help them do their job. Spokespeople should be available after each session for interviews. If consensus is achieved, a group should celebrate it and publicize it. If a process fails, the reason for failure should be clearly communicated, leaving open opportunities for subsequent dispute resolution efforts. This guidance, along with a four-leafed clover and rabbit's foot, might just ensure positive, accurate press coverage.

■ Notes

1. A conflict assessment helps mediators to determine who should be involved in a process, what issues should be addressed, how a process should be structured, and so on. It involves one-on-one interviews with a broad set of stakeholders. It is described in detail in Chapter 2.

2. For more information on self-monitoring, see "Impression Management" (Snyder, 1981) and *Public Appearances, Private Realities* (Snyder, 1987), as well as "On the Nature of Self-Monitoring" (John, Cheek, & Klohnen, 1996).

■ References

Bowers, F. (1997a, April 11). Polk GOP leader says supervisors manipulating forums about track. *Des Moines Register,* p. M3.

Bowers, F. (1997b, May 15). Schools feel lucky about casino funds. *Des Moines Register,* p. M2.

Charity, A. (1995). *Doing public journalism.* New York: Guilford.

Coke, J. G., & Moore, C. M. (1979, November). Experiments will test the procedure. *Nations Cities Weekly,* pp. 38-40.

Feldmann, L. (1998, September 23). How fault lines split on Clinton. *Christian Science Monitor,* p. 1.

Isidore, J. (1987, July 12). Plan modernizes downtown Gary. *Gary Post-Tribune,* p. 1.

John, O. P., Cheek, J. M., & Klohnen, E. C. (1996). On the nature of self-monitoring: Construct explication with Q-sort ratings. *Journal of Personality and Social Psychology, 71,* 763-776.

Lehrer, J. (1998, October 22). The trouble with journalism. *Boston Globe,* p. A23.

Miller, E. D. (1994). *The Charlotte Project: Helping citizens take back democracy, The Poynter Papers, No. 4*. St. Petersburg, FL: Poynter Institute for Media Studies.

Moore, C., & Carlson, C. (1984). *Public decision making: Using the negotiated investment strategy* [Unpublished pamphlet]. Dayton, OH: Kettering Foundation.

Pressman, J., & Wildavsky, A. (1984). *Implementation*. Berkeley: University of California Press.

Primack, P. (1998, October). Mediators and the press: A failure to communicate? *Consensus, 40*, 1, 3, 4.

Rosen, J. (in press). *What are journalists for? The adventure of an idea within the American press: 1989-1997*. New Haven, CT: Yale University Press.

Senge, P. (1996, April 9). *The leaders' new work*. Presentation and workshop sponsored by the Dallas County Community College District Foundation, Dallas, TX.

Snyder, M. (1981). Impression management: The self in social interaction. In L. S. Wrightsman & K. Deaux (Eds.), *Social psychology in the 80s*. Monterey, CA: Brooks/Cole.

Snyder, M. (1987). *Public appearances, private realities: The psychology of self-monitoring*. New York: Freeman.

St. Paul receives $40 million in U.S. funds. (1979, December 14). *Minneapolis Star and Tribune*.

12

DEALING WITH DEEP VALUE DIFFERENCES

■ *John Forester*

The topic and title of this chapter are "Dealing with Deep Value Differences." Perhaps the subtitle should read, "Trying to Do Better Than Fighting or Running for the Hills," for trying to resolve value-laden conflicts seems futile to many people. Our values, after all, appear to be intimately connected to who we are and aspects of the world we cherish, whether they involve the sacredness of land and water or the sanctity of life or private property. Values run deeper than *interests*. When we give up one interest—getting something done quickly, for example— we often try to make up for that by gaining on another interest— getting our results less expensively, perhaps. But when we give up something we value, we often feel we give up part of ourselves, and that's very difficult, very threatening, and hardly compensated by some gain somewhere else.

Because *values* seem connected to identity and not to simple choices between this good versus that one, this benefit and that one, they appear inherently personal, subjective, developed as a matter of tradition and socialization, and not amenable to change

Thanks for research and transcription assistance with this chapter go to Brad Mueller, Dorian Fougeres, and Kathrin Bolton. Thanks, too, for comments on earlier versions of the chapter go to Peter Adler, Susan Podziba, Mike Hughes, Ann Martin, Rachel Goldberg, Davydd Greenwood, and Jeff Seul.

by persuasion, rational argument, or even bargaining. Thus, we have the widespread public skepticism about the potential of dealing with value differences. If persuasion, rationality, and bargaining can't get someone to budge from a "value position," what in the world can be done when values conflict?

Unfortunately, the more we mystify value differences as ultimately personal, subjective, irrational, or spiritual, the more we pull the wool over our own eyes and simply fail to appreciate or understand those differences. The more we presume that values are so subjective that they are virtually undiscussable, the less likely will we be even to *try* to discuss them. The more our own rhetoric of "deep" and "fundamental" value differences presumes unbridgeable chasms between those who hold differing values, the more likely we will be to wring our hands and the less likely we will be to look for practical ways to live together, honoring rather than fearing, shunning, or obfuscating our real value differences. Deep value differences are serious, to be sure, but our common ways of speaking about them can often make our problems worse, not better.

Nonetheless, efforts to build consensus between those with differing values can produce unexpected results that seem almost magical to the parties involved. Although they begin with the presumptions that the others "will never talk to us" and that their value systems are so radically different that "we'll never be able to work something out with them," parties are often astonished to find themselves crafting real, productive, satisfying agreements. In British Columbia, for example, facilitated negotiations between Native tribes (called First Nations) and non-Native parties, including the government, interest groups, and industry, created an innovative community development trust fund in the face of long-standing conflict and mutual suspicion (see Case 10). And in the United States, where community conflict over abortion rights has led to escalating hostility, polarization, and, at times, deadly violence, a project called the Network for Life and Choice has used facilitated dialogues to explore common ground, build trust, develop respect, and even formulate collaborative action projects between those with opposing views (see Case 15). Many facilitators and mediators take pains to point out that these processes involve nothing magical at all; they take hard work, skill, sensitive exploration of issues, persistence, and creativity. Indeed, dealing with value differences takes not magic but competence—the deliberative abilities to listen, learn, and probe both fact and value together—which democratic citizens can refine and practice as they deal with their differences and so govern themselves (Forester, 1999; Gutmann & Taylor, 1992; Gutmann & Thompson, 1996).

This chapter explores the ways stakeholders and mediators can build consensus effectively when disputes involve deeply differing value systems or views of the world. Our aim is to clear up several widespread misunderstandings about value differences and to learn by listening closely to practitioners who have handled deep value conflicts successfully. In the first part of the chapter, we consider the puzzling difficulties and potentially crippling obstacles that disputes presenting deep value conflicts seem to involve. In the second part, we examine a fascinating Colorado case in which state public health officials, gay rights activists, conservative Christian groups, and others sought agreement on how to prioritize federal funds earmarked for HIV/AIDS care and prevention. The third part concludes with lessons and implications for consensus building practice.

■ *Value Differences and Consensus Building: Mediation Snake Oil?*

In the public realm, value differences often seem to be so personal, and so passionately espoused, that they seem irreconcilable. If one person believes that all land is sacred and another believes that all land is a potential commodity to be bought and sold, what kind of resolution can there be? Because many understand that changing people's values involves not just changing their preferences but changing who they are, changing their identities, public skepticism about resolving value conflicts seems reasonable enough. Still, that skepticism not only can encourage an "I told you so" resignation—"They'll never even talk to us"—but it can too easily mislead people and hide practical solutions from view. As we will see, in the face of deep value differences many practical resolutions may be possible, even if (or indeed because) asking parties to change their fundamental beliefs is neither necessary nor relevant to settling the dispute at hand.

But value differences do often appear irreconcilable to the public eye, and so when mediators come on the scene and begin talking about "negotiation," "joint agreements," and "consensus building," anyone who's still awake rightly begins to get suspicious. After all, if the value systems are irreconcilable, and this mediator is talking to us about reconciliation, agreements, or compromises, then either we're being "sold a bill of goods" or someone's going to get hurt—and in either case, we're likely to be poorer for the experience. "If I participate in consensus building, will I be pressured to compromise my principles? To betray my commitments, my integrity?" When values are at stake, public suspicions of morally dangerous compromises are reasonable and quickly forthcoming.

Similarly, when value differences are deeply felt, mediators' claims of neutrality will be suspect by any politically astute (if not cynical) public. Who in the real world is neutral? Who's kidding whom? Furthermore, when the values involved are about the sanctity of life or land, traditions, or the environment, mediators who speak of respecting all viewpoints equally seem more like political spin doctors with no values at all than helpful dispute resolvers.

In such cases, mediators talk the talk of consensus and mutual gains, but much of the public hears "consensus" as "induced betrayal." When mediators point to the possibility of reaching compromises, many in the public begin to feel resentful: "Betray my values? Who the hell are you? Why can't you take me seriously? No thanks!"

Mediators who speak of compromise may mean well, but they practice poorly. Failing to recognize the intimate nature of the parties' commitments to their values, these mediators begin with a procedural solution—a problem-solving process that they believe (sometimes rightly) they can implement—but they may unwittingly antagonize the very people with whom they wish to work. Sometimes they don't even know they've done it: "I'm just suggesting a *process*!" a prospective mediator might say. But environmentalists or tribal members or neighborhood residents hear it quite differently: "These mediators want to plug me in to a process, as if I'd negotiate about anything and just give away my grandparents' land. They're not taking me seriously, the hustlers—they're presuming that I'll just sell out whatever I believe in. They don't get it."

Not surprisingly, when government officials try to promote mediated processes, they often run into similar suspicions and problems. What they propose as a "neutral" and unbiased consensus building process can be interpreted by the public as anything but that. The public often has little love for government, little trust in city hall, and certainly no inclination to assume that officially sponsored dispute resolution processes will be unbiased. Will those processes really be indifferent to the interests of the politicians and the prerogatives of government agencies? " 'Neutral and unbiased,' ha!" the public may think.

In a complex political world, anyone with half an eye open will be right to worry that processes of compromise might just mean fancy-looking deal making. The noble language of "public involvement" and "stakeholder participation" is not likely to persuade affected citizens that any real participation and real public learning about issues and options will take place. A history of government secrets, planners covering up decisions already made, ineptly handled communication between decision makers and affected publics—all this has bred a public cynicism, and a political realism, that too easily preempts a critical and healthy democratic imagination and the civic capacity to recognize, learn from, and act well in the face of value conflicts.

So mediators, convenors, and consensus building participants alike have their work cut out for them. When values are at stake, they begin not with respect and public confidence, but in the glare of public suspicion and moral skepticism.

Threatened Interests versus Threatened Values: Different Strategies Required

To complicate matters further, people often are not clear and not honest—with others, with themselves—about what constitutes their values and what are simply needs and wants. Often, differences between what people care about—their apparently evolving, subjective interests—take on a very different and, practically speaking, an apparently more intractable complexion as more deeply secured values, or relatively fixed *commitments,* or worldviews. To dramatize or emphasize the seriousness of a concern we may feel as participants in a public process, we may present what we want, desire, or prefer—our *preferences*—as far less subjective, far less changeable than they are. And so we present them, intentionally or not, as more firmly rooted *needs,* precommitting ourselves to the severity of our wishes. Although differences in preferences may seem manageable, differences in needs often seem harder to reconcile without someone getting hurt. Similarly, when people have different interests, they might negotiate and come to some mutually agreeable accommodation. But when values conflict, disputes seem less amenable to resolution in the popular eye, and more sensitive negotiating strategies are required. For example, when we lose on our interests, we often ask if gaining on some other interests can compensate us. But when we lose cherished values, we feel morally compromised, betrayed, damaged, or sold out. Wrecking our trusted car creates problems for the composition of our possessions, but the insurance company might compensate us adequately for our loss. Wrecking structures we value deeply, however—our trusted marriage or the health of a loved one—changes the constitution of our lives and can hardly be compensated. So we speak of "making up for" the loss of a possession, but we speak of "mourning" and "working through" the loss of a loved one.

The point here, of course, is not semantics but practical expectations—practical strategies and options in consensus building. Faced with rival preferences in a negotiation, parties will try to devise counteroffers, but faced with deep value differences, they must respond differently, for a counteroffer proposed too quickly may appear to devalue, or fail to take seriously, what the other parties care deeply about. What can seem to be a quick, simple counteroffer can offend and humiliate another party, fuel resentment and distrust, and escalate a conflict further, making the job of negotiating successfully even harder.

Now sometimes none of this will matter. When you exaggerate the depth of your needs and I respond as if you're strategically misrepresenting or exaggerating in that way, we have old-style positional bargaining. This may not be pretty, but through small steps, listening and learning, inventing and improving on *mutual gain* options, we can resolve our differences effectively and efficiently.

But consider what happens when you're not exaggerating the depth of your value commitments involved, but I'm still responding as if you were. You're presenting cherished values ("Four generations of my family have farmed this land; it's who we are."), but I respond to them as if they're exaggerations or fabrications ("Look, there's lots of other land you'd like."). The result: You will very likely feel disrespected, humiliated, insulted, and, not least of all, very angry. This is not likely to help us solve our problems together! Or if you treat me as if I'm lying precisely when I'm telling you about what's really important to me, I'll feel disrespected, offended, and humiliated, and I'll be angry! Indeed, mix the attempt to express deep values on one side with suspicions of misrepresentation insinuated by the other side, and you get the recipe for explosions we too often see. The results are increased cynicism about the capacity of anyone—especially governments—to resolve disputes involving conflicting values and diminished hope that anyone involved in public disputes will listen respectfully and take value differences seriously (Susskind & Field, 1996).

Of course, we can face another trap here. Suppose you *are* indeed misrepresenting your desires as deeper needs, but I'm gullible, and I treat your representations as deeply tied to who you are. This combination threatens to limit our resulting agreements in ways that hold them hostage to the initial misrepresentations. If your demand for complete control (of the institution, land, process, etc.) is really *not* nonnegotiable as you have righteously claimed it to be, we are likely to *miss opportunities to generate mutually satisfying options*. We'll miss those opportunities because we may both really be willing to negotiate, to trade, more than we have so far, but your posturing and my gullibility keep us both from making further gains. ("It's nonnegotiable!" you say, and I affirm your posturing, "I hear you! OK," sealing us off, together, from exploring options of further negotiation that we'd both have preferred.) We congratulate ourselves about being tough bargainers, feel that we did as well as we could have, and both, unfortunately, miss the real opportunities before us. I remain thunderstruck to this day at the words of a University of California, Berkeley, administration official who, after several weeks of silence, readily agreed to meet with striking students and explained his lack of previous telephone contact with the student leaders with the stunning, "But you *said* your demands were 'nonnegotiable' !" The combination of posturing by the students and literalism on the administration's part here took a great toll, weakening the university's credibility and public support, rupturing faculty-student relationships, and damaging students' education.

Balancing Respect and Skepticism in Value Conflicts

Let's consider these problems of posturing and obtuseness more carefully. Let's say Smith and Jones find themselves face-to-face in a contentious consensus building process. What might happen? Figure 12.1 presents four elemental possibilities.

First, Smith can be expressing deeply held values, and Jones can respond as if that's just what Smith is doing. Most of this chapter is devoted to understanding what such a response might involve on the part of stakeholders and mediators.

Second, though, Smith can really be expressing deeply held values, but Jones, always on guard for duplicity and exaggeration, can respond as if Smith is just acting strategically—with the explosive results indicated. Here a difficult situation of value conflict escalates and becomes even more difficult.

Third, though, Smith can actually be acting strategically, but Jones, a bit too ready to acknowledge cultural differences uncritically, thinks that Smith is expressing deeply held values. Here both parties are likely to do less well than they might have, as the costs of posturing and attending to phony concerns distracts them from options that might serve their actual interests.

Fourth, Smith can be acting strategically and Jones can respond just as if Smith is acting that way. In this case, both parties are vulnerable to all the difficulties of positional bargaining and the dance of the "prisoner's dilemma": I'm afraid that you'll exploit me (if I tell you what I'm willing to trade, to concede), and you're afraid that I'll exploit you (if you tell me what you're willing to trade, to concede). As a result, we fail to make the trades that would make us both better off, and so rather than finding ways to "give in order to get"—the mutual-gain options—we generate only "lose-lose" compromises, if we get past impasse at all.

These four possibilities raise more than strategic concerns. They suggest that as participants in consensus building efforts, we'll do poorly if we don't understand that disputes in which "deep values" seem to be at stake can involve stakeholders' identities as well as their interests. Knowing that some "wants"

	Smith is expressing deep value commitments	Smith is posturing, treating interests as deep values
Jones takes Smith to be expressing deep values	*Result:* A deep value dispute requiring mutual recognition and practical, collaborative problem solving	*Result:* An inefficient, short sighted, hampered negotiation with mutually poor compromises
Jones takes Smith to be posturing, treating preferences as though they were deep values	*Result:* Anger, escalation, and resentment preempting recognition and problem solving	*Result:* Positional bargaining

Figure 12.1. How Parties with Real or Perceived Value Differences May Interact during a Consensus Building Process

are incidental and that some "values" are indeed deeply cherished, virtually part of who a person is, we need to listen carefully to others—to respect and not infuriate them—to assess how the values they espouse fit into broader patterns and commitments of their lives, patterns that did not just begin yesterday, presumably. We need to know that when others do not see and understand our basic values, we feel that they do not see and understand us; failing to respect the cherished quality of the values we espouse, we feel that they fail to respect us. So one lesson of Figure 12.1's possibilities is that if we are not careful, we can easily disrespect and offend others, which weakens our abilities to work together, to figure out together how to go on with this project, this property, this environmental concern. We need to understand others' commitments, their histories, the extent to which their previous commitments do or don't hold them hostage, the extent to which the values they espouse define their very identities or happen to have been embraced for the first time last week.

"Under the guise of 'respecting a difference in belief' we easily can be tempted to stereotype quite narrowly others' concerns."

Figure 12.1 also suggests that we need to resist two temptations. First comes the temptation of relativism ("their beliefs are fundamentally different; they'll never agree to anything we want"). When we find ourselves thinking in this way, we end up trapped and blinded by our own presumptions. We have moved, mistakenly, from the difference in another's beliefs to strong presumptions about their identity and motivations. Under the guise of "respecting a difference in belief" we easily can be tempted to stereotype quite narrowly others' concerns, their willingness to explore those concerns with us, and indeed their capacity to teach us about issues and options in ways we may find helpful. Instead of falling into this trap, we should be respectfully skeptical when we face others' claims that the lands they must have, the trees they must protect, or the properties they must be able to sell really reflect the manifestation of their deep commitments, their basic values.

Second, we face the temptation of taking this skepticism too far, of adopting an arrogant, economistic attitude. (Listening to the other's claims about the land, we think [or say], "Yeah, sure, but everybody has their price; what's yours?") Here of course we fail to recognize anything like a deep commitment that defines who a person is as well as what he or she desires. Here we presume that our way of measuring value—be it in terms of dollars or some other measure—can simply replace and transform what the other cares about. In so presuming, we are likely to throw fuel on the fires of conflict (Gurevitch, 1989). But we can do better, which we shall see as we consider the track record of accomplished mediators and consensus builders (Susskind & Field, 1996).

Handling Value Conflicts: Listening, Learning, and Telling Stories

Listen to experienced Canadian mediator Gordon Sloan, who convened an 18-month process involving negotiations among representatives from 14 sectors to formulate a land use plan for Vancouver Island. Sloan describes the initial presumptions of the parties quite poignantly.

They're *each saying exactly the same thing about the other.* That's a piece of information that they should know. It's handy to be able to tell them that, when they say to you, "You'll be able to trust what we say, but there's no way you can trust anything they say." It's *great* to be able to say to them in response that, "You won't believe this, but they used *exactly* the same words to describe their view of you." They're amazed. "They did?!? They don't think we're accountable?" They discover that there are *all kinds of assumptions that one value system makes about the other that have to be debunked.* (Forester & Weiser, 1996, p. 18)

As parties in public disputes and consensus building efforts, we see *that* someone is different, but we don't know much about *how* they are different. Seeing difference, we are tempted to presume not only what they think but what they will (or won't) do. But if we can recognize these pitfalls, we can recognize, too, a basic practical truth about dealing with claims about conflicting values: We need to learn about the other parties as well as about the issues in front of us. We fall into negotiation traps if we either take others' value claims too seriously (and so preempt exploration and search) or take those claims too lightly (and so fail to devise solutions that can actually satisfy the other's values). In both cases, we blind ourselves, restricting our ability to create options that satisfy our concerns and the concerns of others. Knowing that there is much that we don't know, we need to take practical steps to learn about the history and identity and character of the parties making mention of value differences.

When we listen to mediators reflect on their practice, we see that they must help parties overcome the presumptions that restrict their understanding and imagination of new options. Mediators work, in part, to help vulnerable, uncertain, and often fearful parties to learn about one another's perspectives and values. Listen once more to Gordon Sloan as he describes the widely shared presumptions held by the Vancouver Island stakeholders early on in their process.

> I couldn't simply say [to the parties], "You're going to have to negotiate, period," because that wouldn't mean anything to them. We had to demonstrate, and teach, and do some skills-based training for them to actually practice and role-play before they had a sense of what it meant to attempt to solve problems with people whose values were so radically different from theirs. And when I say, "theirs," I mean every group; every group shared that impression, that "It's us against them." It's this dichotomy that you run into all the time in mediation, but it's much more serious in multiparty public policy negotiations: "There's no way that the enemy will ever understand me," because "the enemy" is inherently evil, weak, out of touch, all those things.
>
> That being the case, "There's no way we'll ever come to terms." So the way to solve that, it seems to me, is to give people a chance privately and safely within their own sector

to air their own anxiety, to practice some of this stuff, and to have an experiential bite at seeing that they can do this—they can communicate effectively, they can deal with stupid behavior across the table effectively. Or at least they have a sense of what that would be like. That was very effective. (Forester & Weiser, 1996, p. 17)

Getting past the presumptions that parties bring to complex and contentious disputes is certainly not easy. Especially when values are at stake, careful and sensitive listening is more important, and perhaps more difficult than ever. With all the best intentions, parties may be more focused on the issues that concern them than the underlying interests they wish to satisfy. This is not surprising, but it means that mediators as well as parties need to probe, to learn, to resist taking anything literally, to search for what is really at stake, for the facts that matter. Mediators and parties alike can do that by listening critically, asking both "What if . . . ?" and "Why . . . ?" questions, as they try to explore the interests and values that underlie parties' expressed positions and work to explore hypothetical trades, packages of options, and resolutions. Focusing here on the clarification of interests, domestic and international mediator Jon Townsend suggests how such probing and exploration can work.

It's helpful for me to know what the difference is between an "interest" and an "issue." I have a prejudice, a bias, that says in most cases, . . . be it negotiation or mediation, most people come to the table with their issues, but they really have not thought a lot about what their interests are. In my experience, people don't negotiate on their interests. They hardly know their interests. They haven't thought about their interests. As a people, generally speaking, we don't think in terms of interests.

Let's say, I'm dealing with an employee. That employee wants a 10 percent increase in salary. Well, the proposal that he or she would make would be a 10 percent increase. The "issue" . . . is money. But the interest is financial security, and there might be a dozen different ways to help someone meet their financial security that may never have anything to do with the 10 percent increase. In fact, there may not even be any money ever given to that person.

My listening has helped, for me anyway, to have an understanding, since in my own experience people usually don't come to the table with their interests known. So I need to listen for that. . . . The thing that I guess I'm familiar with is that we can work for *issue resolution* through *interest satisfaction.* So we'll satisfy people's interests in order to get the issues resolved. So people still have to address those issues, because they're the surface things. . . . But the end result may be—and probably and usually is—about something a little bit deeper, about their *interests,* the "whys." "Whys" are so important to talk about; . . . it helps to listen. (Forester & Weiser, 1996, pp. 135-136)

Mediators suggest that they can learn, and help the parties to complex disputes to learn, too, in a wide variety of ways. Sometimes they make it possible for parties to step back from adversarial conflict to listen to one another's personal and specific stories, and let the richness and the detail of those stories suggest new concerns, reveal additional interests, and disclose underlying values (Forester, 1999). In the British Columbia case involving First Nations, Norman Dale writes of stories, for example, as "so important as a means for finding a way through long-standing cross-cultural conflict" (see Case 10). Noting not only that stories are "accessible to most everyone" and that "the indigenous cultures of America are noteworthy for [their reliance on] oral traditions," Dale makes an even stronger point: "Telling and listening to stories is particularly important because much of what preoccupies First Nations people involved in public policy issues is the unacknowledged and therefore unfinished business of the past." Telling stories is a way to acknowledge and deal with that past. In the case describing dialogue on abortion issues, Michelle LeBaron and Nike Carstarphen tell us, "Sharing stories had a bonding effect on participants and revealed underlying shared concerns, hopes, and values among the participants. Trust and empathy emerged in the group as participants adopted more relaxed postures and registered surprise at the similarities among them" (see Case 15). In complex public disputes, stakeholders, who often presume a lot about each other but actually know less, can learn a good deal by listening carefully to one another's stories (Forester, 1999).

Sometimes, too, mediators and facilitators can bring in outside consultants respected by all parties to shift the parties' attention from adversarial argument to relevant historical, legal, or technical concerns they share. For example, in workshops involving county and tribal government officials in Skagit County, Washington, facilitator Shirley Solomon and colleagues invited local community college staff to share historical material about the county in the days before and after white settlers came (Forester & Weiser, 1996). In a consensus building process in Chelsea, Massachusetts, in which a mediator helped community residents draft a new city charter, outside consultants were helpful in briefing residents on the technical and legal aspects involved in drafting the charter (see Case 3). Sometimes consensus building parties can come to see the issues before them in new ways because facilitators help them to see data in new ways. Referring to a contentious transportation-planning case, mediator Lawrence Susskind tells a striking story about how a slide show of parking garages around the country helped the parties to envision the issues of scale and visual and environmental impact in new ways (Forester, 1994). In other cases, such as workshops called "search conferences," participants cover the walls of their meeting rooms with a jointly produced "community history" on butcher paper, not just to involve all stakeholders in some more "hands-on," "get 'em up out of the seats" way, but to create a joint visual representation of shared concerns (Emery & Purser, 1996). In consensus-based planning processes, too, planners may use sketches and visual materials less to represent defined alternatives than to probe issues, interests, and feelings (Forester, 1999). In a curious way, the use of innovative visual representations seems to allow parties, at times, to focus a bit less on parrying one another's claims and a bit more upon a fresh source of ideas, specific concerns, and aspects of issues needing attention.

The *drama of mediation,* in fact, seems intimately tied to this struggle for discovery, these attempts of mediators to help parties learn in new ways, to help them understand in fresh and deeper ways *what they already are quite convinced they know all about.* As Sloan suggested, after orientations and preliminary training in dispute resolution processes, parties begin to move beyond their initial skepticisms that "they'll never talk to us!" As Townsend too suggests, parties can come to the table initially so focused on the issues at hand that they have not considered more carefully the underlying interests that they themselves really do wish to serve. In these processes of discovery, deliberation, and learning, the parties are losing nothing; they are asked to listen, not to give anything up. They are gaining in self-understanding and in the understanding of the others they must work with and the issues that affect their lives (Benhabib, 1995; Forester, 1999).

When value differences are involved in a case at hand, parties and mediators alike must recognize that the need to "probe, not presume" is more important than ever. Just because of the blinding power of cultural presumptions, they need to remember that they must learn about other parties whom they really do not know very well, about values and value systems they may, or may not, share. They need especially, in contentious disputes, to make space for a central insight that hinges on recognizing that humans are not perfectly rational, all-knowing beings: We always care about more than we can focus our thoughts on at any one time, and so we do ourselves a favor by finding safe ways of learning more about the concerns we do have, the unexpected implications of the actions we are considering, and the deeper motivations of the parties we are facing.

When value differences are at stake, especially when the understanding of those different value systems is not finely developed, parties and mediators can anticipate that "there's more to work with than meets the eye"; more to work with than they have yet anticipated, certainly more to work with than general public perception would suggest. Not letting their perception of deep value differences stop them from listening closely, they may find that hidden, or not yet expressed, interests of conflicting parties differ sufficiently so that they might yet "exploit their differences" to realize mutual gains. So a developer wishes to maximize numbers of units built and her return on investment; the environmentalist opposition wishes to maximize open space. Both need to ask carefully about options that might increase the density of units, enabling both the developer to build more units and the environmental advocates to preserve more open space.

These observations reflect an initial conclusion about traps that consensus builders fall into and more sound approaches they might adopt in the face of value differences. The shortest version of this conclusion, this lesson for practice, would be: "Look and see!"

The slightly longer version would be just as simple: When values conflict, assume the need for all parties to learn: about each other, about the issues at stake, about the practical options that lie before them. Recognize that indeed their *value differences* might be irreconcilable and might prevent them from reaching a mutually satisfactory, voluntary agreement about how to go on—but take that irreconcilability not as a premise, but only as a clearly demonstrated product of mutual discussions and attempts to learn. So in cases involving such ordinarily intractable issues as abortion and sacred lands, LeBaron, Carstarphen, and Dale show us how facilitated and mediated processes allowed parties with deeply conflicting values not only to listen and learn from each other but to devise practical, collaborative future actions. So, despite temptations to stereotype adversaries who espouse different values than theirs, parties in consensus building processes can and should commit themselves to learning first, testing their presumptions, even refining the agendas of discussion to enable them to satisfy underlying concerns as they discover them. *Value irreconcilability* is a possibility, of course, then, but it should be the *product* of a fair, inclusive, well-informed learning process, not a self-fulfilling presumption.

> "When values conflict, assume the need for all parties to learn: about each other, about the issues, about the options."

When parties make claims of "rights," similar considerations come into play. Sometimes those claims will be merely strategic, rhetorical ploys that are elements of power plays; sometimes those claims will seek to invoke actual legal entitlements. Just as no one should give up basic rights because they join a consensus building process, however, no one should automatically believe every claim to "rights." Like value claims, rights claims need to be *explored* by parties in light of available evidence, neither dismissed out of hand nor gullibly granted.

Suspecting that value differences are irreconcilable, parties need to look and see, to try to discover new opportunities for fruitful negotiation. If they discover those opportunities, so much the better. If they discover their differences are irreconcilable and that they can craft no concrete, acceptable moves, then they can turn to their alternatives. Even here they have a thin agreement; exploring practical options in a safe, facilitated process designed to explore new alternatives, they agree voluntarily that their differences are irreconcilable; they agree that they need to turn to the courts or another form of political conflict. The crucial point here is that value irreconcilability can be a real outcome, but it should be an outcome that is discovered through a real process of searching for alternatives; it should not be a presumption, tempting as it may be, that threatens to answer questions before they are asked, to bury desirable options rather than to create them together.

■ Setting Priorities for HIV/AIDS Prevention in Colorado: A Case Example

Fortunately, we have instances of public disputes in which skillful mediators have brought parties together and through the dangerous presumptions that "they'll never agree to anything we would agree to!" In the example that follows, we examine a deceptively simple case of mediation practice that involved deep value differences. We will listen carefully to the account of Mike Hughes, a planner-turned-mediator, reflecting on his work, which has a good deal to teach us about the possibilities of reaching practical agreements when value differences are involved (see Forester & Weiser, 1996, and Case 14; all quotes from Mike Hughes are from pp. 1019-1025 in this *Handbook*).

In an effort to build consensus on HIV/AIDS funding priorities for federal monies that come through the State Health Department in Colorado, Hughes facilitated and mediated a large and diverse group of citizens that included health officials, straight and gay activists, members of conservative Christian religious organizations, blacks, Latinos, and whites, employed and unemployed. The discussion involved 60 or more participants at regular meetings over many months.

After early difficulties recognizing speakers in turn and keeping discussions moving forward with many people in the room, Hughes and his comediators adapted a technique to improve the quality of the group's discussions. He explains:

[We] moved the chairs into concentric circles with a small table and four chairs at the center. And we made aisles that led to the center of the room so everyone could easily move from the back to the front.

With this setup, I could get out of the way and let people come to the table and talk rather than waiting for me to call on them. We explained the procedure to the participants: "When we are ready to open discussion on a topic, we will clearly mark the transition: Now it's time for discussion. Then we will get out of the way. If you've got something to say, come sit in a chair. There are four chairs, and four of you can talk with one another—loudly, so we can all hear it. When you're done, get out of the chair. If you see somebody waiting, make room for them. When we think that the discussion has wound itself to some sort of conclusion, or we want to ask if you have come to some consensus, we'll interject to move the process on. But when it's time to talk, it's time to talk. You don't have to be called on. You don't have to raise your hand."

They loved it. They took to it both because the structure made sense and because they sensed our responsiveness. Through the remainder of the work, we used this system.

By enabling freer and more interactive discussions, including, as we shall see, vivid and moving personal stories, this technique helped with the discussion of issues—up to a certain point. Then the going got tougher. After generating 13 clusters of needs, crafted down from 150 or more after many facilitated sessions, one of the issues of very basic value differences arose at the center of the discussions.

This wonderful participant—he was brilliant—came into the circle, and he said, "Here's a need that is missing. There is a need to shift the discussion of AIDS in Colorado from a moral issue to a public health issue, and I refuse to participate in moving this plan forward until we wrestle with that."

He made an eloquent speech about how moral barriers to effective AIDS education were killing people. . . . The whole room was captivated. Other people ran to the table and started talking with him. The folks from Focus on the Family and from Colorado for Family Values talked about why for them, this *was* a moral issue and the meaning their values had for them.

Faced with some parties referring to basic moral beliefs and others adamantly refusing to accept those beliefs, Hughes kept going, and his practice has a great deal to teach us. As he continues, he talks about how important the prior ground rules, precedents, and track record of the group were.

> His statements weren't accusatory. They weren't blaming. He didn't denigrate Amendment Two[1] supporters or folks who opposed certain prevention methods on moral grounds. He was angry, but his emotion didn't take the form of a personal accusation.
> Amazingly, no one broke the ground rules. People were speaking to one another respectfully. They were doing their best to listen to one another.

Hughes teaches us here about the importance of respect and recognition, even (or especially!) when deep value differences divide parties. Here the advocate was not accusatory, not blaming, not denigrating, and thus not attacking the other parties personally. As Hughes goes on, he shows us how the HIV/AIDS conversation focused on issues and practical options, not personal defensiveness or attacks.

> The person who began the discussion simply said, "[Amendment Two and the moral barriers] are in place, and because they're in place, this is the effect." It was depersonalized, meaning "not accusatory." But it was clearly personal from his own point of view. It was very much an "I message." "This is how I see it." It set the right tone.
> We came upon another issue later on, where people stood up and said, "All of you people . . . " It was a racial issue. "You white people all are . . . " The stereotypes flew out, and the room exploded. But that didn't happen on this one. He didn't say, "All you religious bigots . . . all you Bible thumpers . . . " Instead, he said, "These barriers are in place." He didn't say who put them there. He didn't point any fingers or make any inflammatory statements. He just spoke from his own beliefs and his own anger and his own pain at seeing people that he cares about die. It was emotionally very powerful.

Hughes tells us here that the discussion was personal, deeply felt, emotionally very powerful—but not personally aggressive, hateful, or verbally violent. The disagreements were fundamental, but the parties were indeed attacking what they took to be the problems at hand; they were not attacking one another personally. Indeed, because they respected their common ground rules—speaking one at a time, respecting each other, using appropriate language—and maintained a safe place in which to disagree, even fundamentally, they were able to move ahead, Hughes shows us, even when moving ahead meant taking exactly opposite views from one another. As Hughes explains, progress in the face of this deep disagreement led to a mediation within a mediation.

> In the ensuing discussion, others said, "Well, those aren't the facts. In fact, why people are dying is because we can't, in our culture, frame these things in moral terms, because we're losing the moral ground underneath us." These people were taking the opposite point of view. They said, "No, you don't understand, this must become a moral issue. If it isn't a moral issue, people will continue to behave in ways that put them in danger. It's when you have the moral underpinnings to keep you from behaving in those ways, *that's* when people won't die."

Hughes then continued with a familiar move of mediators and facilitators: bringing the very lack of consensus to the group for discussion and possible problem solving. Lacking consensus, lacking forward movement in the discussion, Hughes and his comediator turned to a mechanism the group had already discussed.

> We had ground rules about conflict resolution. When an issue couldn't be resolved within the group, we would resort to small-group mediation.
> For this conflict—the one about morality—the four people present included the person who had presented the issue, a person from Colorado for Family Values, and one person each for support of their point of view. Luckily, the person from Colorado for Family Values selected someone with a moderate stance from an organization called His Heart (a Christian organization that cares for people with AIDS). The person who presented the issue, from the Colorado AIDS Project, selected a colleague who was a collaborative, calm

presence in the group. From my point of view, these were wise choices.

Hughes has not helped the group to avoid the value conflict, but he has worked to help the group face it more efficiently. Turning to a mediation alongside the larger discussions, Hughes describes other crucial considerations in handling deep moral disagreements: the importance of selecting spokespeople with commitment, experience, and the ability to work with others, who will have a "calm presence" in a group when emotion runs high, when feelings run deep, and of course when time runs short! Far from being overshadowed by the depth of value disagreements, the personal qualities of negotiators matter a great deal, perhaps because personal integrity, identity, reputation, honor, and sanctity are involved—for these qualities allow parties to distrust less and focus more, to parry less and listen more carefully, learning practically as they go. Hughes goes on, giving away the end of the story before he tells how he got there:

> The five of us sat down between meetings with the large group and did a mediation, and we developed language that the four of them could live with. It was clear that what we were doing was writing a plan. Instead of getting mired in "I have to change your mind about this" kind of talk, we focused on "What words can we find together?" And they did it. We walked out of that mediation after two hours with a message that all four of them agreed to.

"The *wisdom of mediation* is achieving a consensus not on value systems but on practical options to support together."

Hughes does not suggest that anyone was a pushover here, that anyone gave up any issue of value commitment or belief. Quite the contrary—the success of the mediation involved not reconciling the parties' beliefs but enabling the parties' practical agreement on a detailed option. The mini-mediation created an agreement on a public statement—a plan, a public promise—that would represent the agreement and consent of all the parties. So this was no matter of mere "words"; they were writing a formal planning document that they expected to shape the policy and resource allocation of the State Health Department. Hughes teaches us here about what we can call the *wisdom of mediation*: achieving a consensus not on paradigms, value systems, or belief systems but on practical options to support together. But how did

Hughes do this? He continues, showing us crucially the importance once again of ground rules, safety, mutual respect, and recognition despite intense moral disagreement.

> The way I did it was to take the process that we were using for [the larger group] and compress it into [the] two hours. First I said, "We're going to begin at the beginning. Let's make sure we all know one another." We did introductions. I continued, "OK, let's get the ground rules clear. This two-hour session will work if: You talk one at a time. You respect one another. You use language that's appropriate. You avoid personal attacks." I laid out the familiar ground rules to make clear how careful we would need to be when we spoke to one another.
>
> I laid out a process. Each person would talk about the importance of a particular wording, so they could educate one another about their respective views. Then each would suggest options that would take into account the needs expressed. Finally, we went into problem-solving mode.

Here Hughes recapitulates a crisp and instructive practical approach. Rather than minimizing disagreement, he respects it and makes the case for a shared process of discussion that will allow each party to educate others about why this issue is so important. But he does more. Acknowledging difference and conflict, acknowledging the temptations to engage in personal attacks, stressing "how careful we would need to be when we spoke to each other," he points forward too. He tells the parties that even with their disagreements, moral as they may be (one rejecting another's sexuality as immoral, one arguing for the autonomy and dignity of that sexuality), the mediation process will ask them to propose concrete options about the issues at hand. Hughes makes a subtle and crucial point here. He does not ask the parties to change each other's beliefs or commitment, but to consider options that they find acceptable, within their value systems, for the issue at hand. Hughes says that he had been listening not just to what the parties disagreed about but to what they both cared about, even if they might express those interests in radically different ways. He goes on:

I knew that underneath the wording there was a common concern: to stop this disease from spreading. I knew that unless they really saw that they ultimately were aiming at the same thing, just aiming at it in absolutely opposite ways, that they were just going to keep aiming in opposite ways, and that they would not find language that the other one would find acceptable. Recognizing their mutual interest in creating a plan acceptable to each of their constituencies was key.

Hughes turns once more to what I have called the wisdom of mediation, the recognition that disputes may be settled by crafting a consensus on practical options that enable the parties to continue to disagree about fundamental values. The wisdom of mediation involves knowing what does not need to change while enabling participants to climb down from the abstract peaks of value systems, paradigms, and worldviews to get their hands dirty in a collaborative discussion of actual options they may endorse together. Hughes tells the story this way:

Once all four of them heard this message from the others—that they too wanted to stop the disease—it became a joint task. They suspended confrontation for long enough to discover that they could in fact find words that would be satisfactory for both sides, and they didn't have to give up their points of view. They also found that they could agree to disagree. That was part of it, acknowledging what they weren't going to change. Regardless, they had to write a document that both sides could live with. That was simpler, so I focused them on that.

The language they all agreed on was this: "There is a need to remove moral objections to HIV prevention and education that is appropriate to the behaviors of the target community." Now that's somewhat vague. But then they followed with, "For communities that include members with a range of moral perspectives, HIV prevention methods need to be appropriate to that range of moral perspectives by presenting multiple prevention messages." The subtext of this statement is, not everybody in any community is going to share every moral perspective. Therefore, if you give people prevention messages, they should encompass a range of moral points of view. In other words, prevention messages should present multiple options that correspond with those different moral perspectives.

The only way that we could get the gay rights activists to accept sentences two and three was to include sentence number one: "There is a need to remove moral objections to messages that are appropriate to the target community." In concrete terms, this means that for settings such as gay bars, you can use sexually explicit material. Why? Because in a gay bar, sexually explicit material is within that audience's moral parameters. But if you go into the schools, and you've got students who come from a fundamentalist Christian point of view, both those students and their parents would likely be uncomfortable with sexually explicit material. Thus, the wording encourages a range of messages that are tailored to a spectrum of moral perspectives.

In two hours they hammered this out: three sentences.

But the story did not end there. As the mini-mediation wound up, their work was immediately threatened. Hughes describes what happened as humorous, but the event is quite instructive, reflecting the importance of bounding discussions, maintaining the practical wisdom to focus on working consensus, not more abstract and general "beliefs" and "values."

It only became difficult at the very end. I said, "Look you're all done, the mediation's over, hurray for you. You get to go back to the group and say, We have a draft for you. Now let's all go home." But instead of leaving, everyone stood around and started talking about whether being gay is a lifestyle or not. They hit on the word *lifestyle* and suddenly started to have an argument. I interrupted and said, "I think it's a mistake for you to continue this conversation. I think you should get in your cars and go home." They laughed and shook hands and said, "You're right. We did well today. Let's go home." But I can tell you they were not going out for a beer together afterwards.

We would do well to learn from the character of this result. The parties "were not going out for a beer together afterwards," so their resulting relationships were anything but harmonious.

They had reached a workable and practical result, but they had not compromised their beliefs, values, or commitments. They immediately began to argue once they left the confines of the facilitated conversation, but they recognized that they had indeed made progress and that despite many remaining differences, that progress mattered: "You're right. We did well today. Let's go home."

They respected one another's efforts and reached a practical consensus, but they did not change one another's beliefs. They did not change one another's deep values. They did not reconcile belief systems or paradigms or commitments, and they had the wisdom, cultivated by the mediation process, to understand that their practical task was done. They had achieved a working consensus on practical options, and that consensus building mattered far more here than any more general and abstract doctrinal discussions. Their work was successful, far short of transforming cultures or belief systems, but far beyond personal attacks and destructive sniping, and far beyond impasse in the face of making practical recommendations to the State Health Department.

Lessons from the HIV/AIDS Case

Hughes's work in the HIV/AIDS priority-setting case illustrates several lessons about mediation in the face of deep value differences.

First, deep value differences themselves were *not* negotiated in the HIV case, and popular distrust of anyone promising to reconcile such differences—and change people's identities along the way!—is perfectly reasonable. Hughes shows strikingly, though, that even when deep value differences exist and are not negotiable, practical opportunities for dispute resolution may still exist, and these real opportunities should not be preempted with the presumption that "Oh, they'll never agree to anything we'd want."

Second, Hughes echoes other consensus builders who have used shared ground rules ("take turns," "no personal attacks," etc.) to protect the autonomy and safety of each party (Forester, 1994; Forester & Weiser, 1996). Even though the parties had significant moral disagreements, they were able to negotiate successfully without coercion.

Third, the parties brought deep differences, but they were able to leave, to walk away, as well. Their agreement appeared to be fully voluntary and was not made under duress. Their differences notwithstanding, the parties were able to craft working agreements about concrete priority setting; they were able to *specify* needs rather than to *generalize* about value doctrine.

Fourth, Hughes helps us to appreciate the value of stakeholder representation and its efficacy in formulating well-crafted, locally appropriate options. We don't know of the relative numbers of constituents; we see instead that the mediation process enabled parties to devise specific agreements that responded to their interests, interests that might well have been less carefully articulated by lobbyists, voting publics in referenda, or particularly well-organized constituencies applying pressure to politicians for "results."

Fifth, the HIV case suggests that concrete issues linking the parties can be resolved even when no simple economic or monetary trades are possible. Crucially important to workable agreements was a careful process that allowed parties to learn about each other's sensitivities, interests, and limits, a process that enabled parties also to craft options that responded substantively to the diverse interests represented in the process, even if weakly organized outside of that process.

Sixth, Hughes makes clear the importance of personal style and lack of posturing—on the parts of both the mediators and the parties. The parties did not posture unduly, taking positions for the sake of taking them, rather than trying to reach the ends they cared about. But he indicates, too, that they were not pushovers: They did not compromise, they did not cave, they did not sell out or betray the faith of their constituencies. Value differences certainly do matter, but Hughes suggests that they can be properly, respectfully, and effectively handled when parties abide by ground rules, listen carefully, think creatively, and articulate their own interests effectively too.

Seventh, Hughes helps us recognize the wisdom that Gordon Sloan introduced earlier. Given deep differences, parties on all sides might be tempted to think, "They'll never talk to us," but they may well be wrong, and the job of the mediator is to provide the context, occasion, and safe process in which parties can meet and speak to one another, listen to, and learn from one another.

Perhaps most important, we can derive a "moral" about the wisdom of mediation in the face of fundamental value differences from Mike Hughes's story: We should not expect parties to reconcile their *general* value systems, but we should, instead, explore very carefully how those same parties might still effectively resolve practical disputes over very specific, implementable options. To prevent *these traps of misplaced abstraction* (because we cannot agree about the nature of the universe, we then think we cannot agree to take turns talking . . .), mediators and convenors should enable the parties to meet, listen, learn, and decide together where they can and cannot make progress to their own satisfaction.

■ *Practical Implications: Consensus Building in the Face of Value Differences*

Hughes's example shows how skillful mediation can help disputing parties with deep differences to live together peacefully, even if not harmoniously. What general implications can be drawn, then, from the cases and ideas in this chapter, for the practice of mediators and consensus builders facing value-laden disputes? Consider several points.

First, without early agreements on ground rules that provide safety for consensus building participants, parties who tell their stories may only humiliate and antagonize one another further. But with such ground rules, parties with deep value conflicts can begin to recognize one another's history and concerns and start to explore new options for going on together. Creating and maintaining such "safe spaces," in which conflicting parties can listen attentively and respectfully to one another's stories, is an essential part of mediators' jobs, especially when deep value conflicts are at stake.

Second, as Gordon Sloan suggested, parties learn as they listen to one another's stories. Even though participants begin by presuming a great deal about issues and other parties, they find that they can also learn a great deal about both. They can learn, for example, that issues are often far more complex than they might have thought and that other parties are not as simple, thickheaded, and intransigent as they might have seemed.

In plenary and small-group discussions, through formal fact-finding and informal rituals of meals and other meetings, through direct questions and indirect explorations, facilitators and mediators can create rich and varied opportunities for parties to learn (Forester, 1999). Many forms of media and representation can help here: poetry and song, film and slide presentations, dramatic enactments and field trips, expert judgment and stories within other stories. In consensus building, apparently simple stories do real work, and parties that do not listen well risk missing the action—and the satisfaction. Barely glimpsing in the beginning what they still need to know, parties in effective mediations come to learn about the specifics rather than the generalities of the issues at hand. They learn about detail, not doctrine—about practical proposals, not public propaganda. When they begin to do that, the parties can explore specific options together; they can build a working consensus about practical steps forward, instead of pursuing vague agreements on far more abstract, if rhetorically potent, worldviews.

Third, when parties learn about the specific, detailed concerns of the other parties, they find out that some of those concerns are much easier to satisfy than others. They learn, crucially, that what's most important for another party may be far less important for them—and vice versa. With that understood, they discover that they can make offers that cost themselves little even as they benefit others significantly. They can then devise options that create mutual gains: not equally devastating compromises, but packages of "trades" that actually satisfy the concerns and interests the parties bring to the table. By getting to specifics—realizing the wisdom of mediation, avoiding the fallacy of misplaced abstraction—parties in consensus building processes can achieve not poor compromises but significant mutual gains.

Fourth, when parties tell stories, they tell a lot about themselves, too, their connections and histories, their cares and fears. Telling pointed stories, they are not entertaining; they are relating events that matter, even while disclosing their own identities, too, and revealing the senses of what they honor, what they owe to their constituents or elderly or ancestors, what they find incidental and what they find sacred. In the storytelling of parties, historical identity can be ignored and dismissed or recognized and acknowledged. So attentive parties listen to the person speaking as well as to their words, to the silences, cadences, and tone of what's said as well as to what's said most emphatically (Forester, 1989).

Fifth, though, consensus building may be impossible unless the party-to-party work of acknowledgment and recognition precedes the work of problem solving. As long as you're calling me a stupid jerk, I'm going to find it very hard to sit down with you to solve a problem you care about. Once parties begin to recognize that they both have complex histories and real problems that worry them, then and only then can they begin to work together to solve their problems effectively. When the value commitments of the parties differ significantly, mediators need to create opportunities for mutual listening and learning. In this work of learning about issues and one another, parties distinguish more important from less important issues; they distinguish between peripheral and central concerns. They put aside what need not be settled and focus on practical strategies. Recognizing their different histories of commitment, struggle, and often loss, parties together come to honor the past and explore how to create their futures.

Sixth, then, after recognition comes exploration, listening, learning, invention, proposals, creative work: not compromise, not betrayal of commitments, not giving up but *crafting practical options that work for both parties*. The developer singing the virtues of private property may still cluster units to maximize return, even as deeply committed open-space advocates maximize environmental amenity—all because clustering of the units provides a practical option that works to satisfy both parties. The rule here is simple but powerful: Probe practical options, don't presume shabby outcomes. Stress learning, not solution. Use a safe, protected mediation process to create and explore options.

With skilled facilitation, with the wisdom to focus on the specifics of practice rather than on the abstractions of worldviews, consensus building in the face of deep value conflicts may well be possible, empowering parties rather than resigning them to impasse, or business as usual. How to do it? In a nutshell, the best advice when facing deep value conflicts seems to be: *Don't* promise the "resolution of value conflicts" in the case at hand, because this will, quite rightly, sound like an oxymoron, a contradiction in terms, to much of the concerned public. *Do* promise

> "Consensus building may be impossible unless the work of acknowledgment and recognition precedes the work of problem solving."

joint learning, better information, exploration of solutions, analysis of options, the testing of future working relationships, and possible provisions for renegotiation in the future. *Do* remember: The wisdom of mediation can produce mutually beneficial agreements about how to go on together—not a compromised consensus on deep values, but a real, workable, and mutually beneficial consensus on practical strategies.

■ Note

1. Amendment Two was a ballot initiative that passed in Colorado that made it illegal for a local government to adopt an ordinance specifically to protect the civil rights of people who are gay or lesbian. It was overturned by the U.S. Supreme Court in 1996.

■ References

Benhabib, S. (1995). Global complexity, moral interdependence, and the global dialogical community. In M. Nussbaum & J. Glover (Eds.), *Women, culture, and development: A study of human capabilities* (pp. 235-255). Oxford, UK: Clarendon.

Emery, M., & Purser, R. E. (1996). *The search conference.* San Francisco: Jossey-Bass.

Forester, J. (1989). *Planning in the face of power.* Berkeley: University of California Press.

Forester, J. (1994). Lawrence Susskind: Activist mediation and public disputes. In D. M. Kolb (Ed.), *When talk works: Profiles of mediators* (pp. 309-354). San Francisco: Jossey-Bass.

Forester, J. (1999). *The deliberative practitioner: Encouraging participatory planning.* Cambridge, MA: MIT Press.

Forester, J., & Weiser, I. (Eds.). (1996). *Making mediation work: Profiles of community and environmental mediators.* Typescript, Cornell University, Department of City and Regional Planning.

Gurevitch, Z. D. (1989). The power of not understanding: The meeting of conflicting identities. *Journal of Applied Behavioral Science, 25*(2), 161-173.

Gutmann, A., & Taylor, C. (1992). *Multiculturalism and "the politics of recognition."* Princeton, NJ: Princeton University Press.

Gutmann, A., & Thompson, D. (1996). *Democracy and disagreement: Why moral conflict cannot be avoided in politics, and what should be done about it.* Cambridge, MA: Belknap Press of Harvard University Press.

Susskind, L., & Field, P. (1996). *Dealing with an angry public.* New York: Free Press.

13

LEGAL ISSUES IN CONSENSUS BUILDING

- *Dwight Golann*
- *Eric E. Van Loon*

ost participants in consensus building processes are private citizens acting out of a sense of civic responsibility. Very few have the specialized background needed to understand all the legal issues that may arise in a consensus process. Nonattorneys often feel unsure about how to respond to legal objections that are raised and are sometimes doubtful that a problem is serious. The goal of this chapter is to sort out the legal issues that are likely to come up during consensus-based efforts and suggest ways to respond to them. On the one hand, we want to demystify those objections that are not serious barriers. On the other, we hope to offer practical advice about how to handle legal concerns that cannot and should not be ignored.

With so many state legislatures, courts, and systems of legal rules[1] in the United States, it is impossible to offer a single answer to most legal questions. Responses are likely to depend on the state(s) in which a consensus building effort takes place and the terms of the ground rules that govern a process. Precise answers are also difficult for the more fundamental reason that lawmakers themselves are sometimes unclear; the laws they pass and the rules they write often create more ambiguities than they resolve. For some issues, no statute or regulation exists, forcing individual courts to make law on an ad hoc basis. As a result, it can take decades before a particular issue is addressed in the legal system—and even then the answer may vary from one place to another.

Despite these limitations, it *is* possible to provide general guidance on legal challenges that may arise in the course of consensus building. We have identified six categories of challenges. Many of the issues within these categories proceed from the fact that consensus processes often involve public officials, who are subject to special constraints because of their role in government.

1. *Relationship to government agencies and the courts.* Disputes that are the subject of consensus building are sometimes simultaneously the focus of legal proceedings before agencies or courts. This raises the question of how the two processes should be coordinated.

2. *Procedural requirements imposed by laws and regulations.* Government employees often must follow specific procedures, which may prevent them from making binding commitments during a negotiation. For example, agency officials usually cannot commit to change regulations as part of a settlement, because they must first consider comments from the general public.

3. *Substantive restrictions on the power of government representatives.* Some limitations on government negotiators cannot be resolved even by following the right procedures because they arise from fundamental constraints embedded in the U.S. system of government. An example is the concept of separation of powers. The head of a federal agency, for example, cannot make commitments that bind Congress to take action. Similarly, state agencies are limited in how they can control the activities of municipalities on topics such as education or zoning.

4. *Disclosure requirements and confidentiality protections.* Participants in sensitive negotiations often prefer to hold their discussions in private, and many states bar participants from revealing what was said during a mediation process. Other statutes, however, require that meetings in which public officials participate be open to citizens and the press. Because consensus

building is a mediative process that often involves public officials, both sets of laws may apply, creating confusion.

5. *Liability considerations.* Mediators and facilitators can be held legally liable for their actions in a consensus-based process and should therefore take appropriate precautions. Certain risky behaviors should be avoided, for example, and liability insurance should be obtained.

6. *Implementation concerns.* Once an agreement has been reached, everyone involved presumably wants to see it carried out. Nonetheless, implementation problems may arise over time, prompting two legal questions. One concerns the minimum requirements for a contract to be legally binding. For instance, must an agreement be written in "legalese" to be enforceable? The other question involves how to structure the terms of an agreement so that, if necessary, it can be enforced by court order.

In the pages that follow, we take up the legal questions that arise in each of these six categories, offering as clear a picture as possible of how such questions can be resolved. To not burden the chapter with technical legal discussions, we have included endnotes referencing legal texts that can provide more detail.[2]

■ *Relationship to Government Agencies and the Courts*

When people disagree on an issue of public policy, they may attempt to bolster their positions by commencing legal actions. For example, a neighborhood group in Santa Fe, New Mexico was opposed to a developer's proposal to build a new subdivision. The group filed a lawsuit challenging the city of Santa Fe's authority to provide the developer with the necessary infrastructure to build on the land. Although the suit was rejected by the court, the fact that the group was willing to sue reportedly increased the developer's willingness to bargain. The two sides, along with other stakeholders, entered into a consensus building process and ultimately reached agreement on the character and layout of the new development (Lampe & Kaplan, 1998). This example illustrates how legal action can sometimes improve a party's alternative to settlement, thereby increasing the party's negotiating power.

Whenever consensus building overlaps with a legal case, however, issues of coordination arise. Actions by a court or administrative tribunal may interfere with a negotiation process, or vice versa. Or a consensus building participant may use the existence of a lawsuit as an excuse to stall. If a dispute or adjudicatory decision is pending before a government agency, and that same dispute or decision is to be the subject of a consensus-based process, concerns may arise about the legality of allowing staff from the same agency to participate in the process. But the impact can also be positive. For example, the fact that a court or agency is on the verge of issuing a decision can be used by a facilitator to create the sense of urgency needed to settle a controversy. In effect, the parallel legal proceeding creates a "settlement event" that aids the consensus building process (Golann, 1996, pp. 4-5, 41-44). This section considers key questions regarding the relationship between consensus building efforts and activities in government agencies and the courts.

Please note that words such as *case* and *judge* are used in this section, and throughout the chapter, to refer not only to traditional lawsuits decided by courts but also to *adjudicative* proceedings that occur in government agencies. A proceeding is adjudicative if it decides the legal rights of specific persons, as opposed to setting policy or creating regulations that affect the public generally. Agency adjudications occur before administrative law judges, boards, and commissions rather than courts, but they pose the same issues of coordination as traditional lawsuits.

If a dispute is pending before a court or agency and is the subject of a consensus building process, how can these two proceedings be coordinated?

When an issue or dispute is the subject of a lawsuit filed in a state or federal court, or is the subject of a formal complaint or proceeding before a regulatory agency, the court or agency is sometimes said to have "taken jurisdiction" over the matter. If a proposed consensus building process seeks to address some or all of the issues that are pending before a court or agency, several questions may arise: Will a consensus process interfere with the pending legal proceeding? Will the process duplicate the efforts of the government body or court? What will happen if the results of the legal case and the consensus-based effort conflict?

In general, informal, ad hoc consensus building processes cannot usurp the authority and responsibility of courts and administrative agencies to resolve matters that are properly before them. That is, as a general legal matter, if some parties to a dispute do not wish to participate in a voluntary consensus process and want their dispute to be decided by a court or other government body, they cannot be prevented from rejecting consensus building and pursuing their legal options. If, on the other hand, all parties to a dispute are willing to attempt to resolve it through consensus building, they can request that the court or agency put the formal process on hold for a specified period of time to give them an opportunity to do so.

How can this be arranged? The same general guidance applies whether the decision maker is a court or agency. The parties before a court usually inform the court that they wish to seek a voluntary settlement and ask for a suspension of the legal proceeding. Sometimes all parties make this request jointly. At other times, one or more parties might present the formal request while the others merely indicate that they have no objection. A suspension can be either for a limited or an open-ended period of time. A facilitator should only approach a court with a request in coordination with the participants in a suit.

The most common way to approach a court is to contact the judge's clerk and ask for a *status conference,* that is, an opportunity to meet with the judge and the disputants to discuss the case's procedural status. At the status conference, the judge and the parties can talk about how to coordinate the activities of the two processes. The conference may occur in a courtroom or in the judge's private office (or *chambers*). The parties or the facilitator should be prepared to describe how the consensus building process relates to the legal case, the plans for carrying it out, and how much time is likely to be needed to reach a conclusion or give the judge a progress report.

A judge has several options. He or she may decide to suspend (or *stay*) a legal case for a period of time to permit a consensus process to go forward. Alternatively, a judge could order that preliminary legal work on a case take place, but that the trial itself be delayed. The latter option is less desirable, because preparing for court distracts people from and diminishes the energy available for consensus building. Also, the adversarial tone and mind-set that prevail in most litigation tend to undermine the more cooperative spirit that facilitators try to foster in a consensus process.

Although some judges and adjudicators are under pressure to move their cases to a conclusion, most are more than happy to give parties an opportunity to achieve a settlement among themselves. This, after all, saves the government's limited resources, including staff time; allows decision makers to avoid what are sometimes difficult decisions; and helps to eliminate the possibility of appeals filed by parties who are unhappy with a nonconsensual outcome.

If a dispute or decision is pending before a public agency, can government decision makers or technical staff participate in a consensus building process that seeks to resolve that dispute?

When a government body has suspended a legal proceeding or decision-making process while consensus building is attempted, the question of whether to include government representatives in the process—and who those officials should be—can sometimes become a sensitive legal issue. For example, a question may arise about whether U.S. Environmental Protection Agency (EPA) technical staff should be involved in a dialogue to build agreement on proposals for new EPA regulations. Or, if a public utility commission must make a ruling on a company's application to construct a new power plant, and a process is convened to build consensus on the siting of that plant, it may be unclear whether the commission's staff should take part in the conversations. In very technical environmental and utility matters such as these, agency staff expertise may be critical to a process; it can help participants address key issues intelligently and provide information about the "leaning" of the regulators on a hotly disputed matter.

Great care must be exercised, however, in deciding *which* government employees to invite to the table. In negotiated rule-makings or other *policy formation* processes, senior-level government officials may participate as long as they tell the other parties that any solution they agree to will be subject to the agency's formal ratification. Government officials directly responsible for deciding an *adjudicated* matter, however (such as those who must decide whether or not a proposed power plant complies with state siting standards), should not participate in agreement-seeking conversations on that same matter.

The reason for this distinction is that administrative judges and regulators who make adjudicatory decisions must follow procedural requirements and safeguards that help to ensure their impartiality in a case. Most relevant among these is the ban on *ex parte contacts,* which bars a decision maker from talking to disputants separately or privately. The idea is that an adjudicator could be influenced by data or comments offered by one "side" that the opponents do not have a fair chance to rebut. If an adjudicator were to participate in consensus building, he or she would likely receive information about a conflict through informal discussions, perhaps with some of the disputants absent. Then, if the group failed to reach agreement, and those people who are parties before the adjudicatory body elected to seek a ruling on the matter, the adjudicator could not in good faith make a decision confined to the official record before him or her, as the law requires. Also, if a regulator participates in crafting an agreement and then is required by the agency to review the agreement for compliance with legal standards, the regulator can hardly be considered impartial in reviewing his or her own handiwork. Thus, regulatory and judicial decision makers are generally not allowed to participate in consensus building efforts.

Although the ex parte rule imposes severe limits on agency adjudicators and some of their direct staff, consensus processes can often draw on the expertise of an agency's technical staff. Scientific and policy staff are often among the most knowledgeable about a disputed matter, and they may have strong feelings about how it should be resolved. A "consensus" reached without benefit of such experts may be ill informed or doomed to rejection later. Agency experts *can* be involved without harming a regulator's ability to rule on a disputed matter. An agency could designate technical staff to participate in a process, for example, and then segregate them from the regulatory staff who will advise the decision makers on the matter in question. Usually, both sets of employees are directed not to talk to each other about the case.

If the parties to a dispute are able to reach agreement in a consensus process (if, e.g., the parties in the power plant case were able to agree on where it should be sited), they can inform the judge or commission of their agreement, or they can jointly request that the adjudicator enter an order to implement it. In general, concerns about ex parte contacts can be avoided, either by giving all the parties to a legal case the opportunity to be present whenever an issue relating to the case is discussed with a judge or by putting information in writing and sending it to each litigant as well as the judge.[3]

■ Procedural Requirements Imposed by Laws and Regulations

Individuals can usually bind themselves to a settlement by a signature or handshake, but government representatives often cannot commit their agency to take (or not to take) action. The restrictions can be either procedural or substantive in nature. A *procedural* requirement means that certain steps have to be followed before a decision is final; thus, for example, agencies are typically required to solicit and consider comments from the public before they can change a regulation (Gellhorn & Levin, 1997, pp. 296-341). Governments also must follow certain contracting and procurement procedures, which have implications for their ability to hire dispute resolution practitioners. A *substantive* restriction, by contrast, limits a government entity's ability to act, regardless of what procedure it follows. Procedural issues are discussed in this section; substantive objections are dealt with in the next.

> *What special procedural requirements does the law impose on consensus building processes?*

Policy matters and disputes that come before courts or administrative agencies are often subject to elaborate and specific procedural requirements, which may be embodied in either law or regulations. Examples include the extensive and complicated rules governing public utility regulation and state environmental protection. In contrast, when the same issues are being addressed in a consensus process, very few legal requirements are likely to apply.

Two exceptions to this general rule warrant notice. First, a few states have limited procedural requirements that apply even to informal settlement processes. Although these state requirements are relatively rare, participants in a consensus process should ask an attorney early on to research what, if any, procedures might be required under the laws and regulations of the state where they are meeting or where a settlement will be implemented.

"Groups formed under the auspices of a federal agency may be subject to requirements of the Federal Advisory Committee Act."

Second, many consensus building groups formed to address national policy issues under the auspices of a federal agency are likely to be subject to the procedural requirements of the Federal Advisory Committee Act (FACA).[4] A consensus building group is generally subject to FACA if the group is used by a federal agency to provide advice or recommendations and includes participants who are not federal government employees. Exceptions exist for groups that are exclusively for "fact-finding" or "information exchange" purposes, for meetings with people who are providing individual rather than collective advice or recommendations, for meetings with federal officials for expressing group views (so long as the government does not use the group repeatedly as a preferred source of advice), and for subgroups of FACA committees. So, for example, a consensus building group formed to develop regulations for a federal agency (often called a regulatory negotiation or reg-neg) would be subject to FACA. In Case 9 in this volume, the 63 people involved in building agreement on regulations for the Indian Self-Determination and Education Assistance Act were formally organized as a FACA committee. If an ad hoc group is deemed to come under the auspices of FACA, its membership must be "balanced," and a number of steps are required to establish it formally. These steps include creating a charter, a "consultation letter," and a "transmittal memorandum," and notifying the public in the *Federal Register*.

Once a group has been established as a FACA committee, a number of procedural requirements apply to its operation. Meetings must be announced in the *Federal Register* 15 days in advance, and (except under limited circumstances) must be open to the public and provide an opportunity for input by nonmembers. In addition, every FACA committee must have a "designated federal official" for such tasks as approving agendas and minutes, providing documents and committee reports for public inspection, and maintaining financial and membership records.

When a government body is paying all or part of a group's facilitation costs, can a facilitator be selected without going through a formal public bidding process?

The government's competitive bidding requirements exist to prevent corruption and the waste of public funds, but they can also be cumbersome and time-consuming. When a public agency is funding a consensus building process, a question may arise about whether a facilitator or outside technical expert can be hired without adhering to these requirements. A related question is whether public bidding laws that give government decision makers the responsibility for selecting contractors also bar nongovernmental stakeholders from helping to select a facilitator.

In many processes, particularly negotiated rulemakings and policy dialogues, government funds are used to pay all or part of a facilitator's fees. Initially, public bidding requirements would appear to apply to selecting facilitators, imposing significant complications on the selection process. In practice, however, this is rarely an insurmountable barrier, because many of the laws that codify bidding procedures allow for flexibility under such circumstances. To check the specific requirements of the jurisdiction in which a consensus process is being conducted, it may be helpful to contact the office of the state attorney general and ask for the division that handles public contract disputes.

At the federal level, agencies such as the EPA have created flexible contracting arrangements (or *indefinite quantities contracts*) with dispute resolution organizations. These contracts are used to hire facilitators and fund consensus building efforts without going through the full federal procurement process. A second federal mechanism beginning to be implemented is the shorter-term "just-in-time" contract, which can be used by employees at both headquarters and regional offices and enables officials to procure mediation services on short notice. A third mechanism slated for implementation by the year 2000 for environmental disputes is a National Roster of Dispute Resolution Professionals, for use by the EPA but administered through the Udall Foundation/Udall Center for Studies in Public Policy at the University of Arizona in Tucson. Other federal agencies, such as the Federal Deposit Insurance Corporation, have also created rosters of mediators. These rosters enable government officials to select and secure a mediator without going through the procurement process.

From Massachusetts to Florida and west to California and Oregon, state offices of dispute resolution have also created rosters of preapproved facilitators, which enable them to contract with a mediator quickly to address disputes as they arise. The Massachusetts Office of Dispute Resolution and the Florida Dispute Resolution Consortium were two of the earliest. There are now more than 30 state offices, most of which manage rosters. State dispute resolution offices can usually be located by calling the state government's general information number, or by contacting the National Institute for Dispute Resolution in Washington, D.C.

■ *Substantive Restrictions on the*
  Power of Government Representatives

Some legal barriers are not merely issues of procedure; they involve substantive restrictions on the power of the government to act. For example, the government cannot "take" private property without paying fair compensation to the owner. It is conceivable that the terms of a settlement that required the government to restrict activities on private land so severely that its owners could not make any valuable use of it, or that granted the public a right of access (an *easement*) to the land, could require the government to pay the owners for the lost market value of their property (Glicksman & Coggins, 1995, pp. 55-63). Other rules are intended to prevent one branch or level of government from exercising powers that are reserved to another; thus, an executive branch official could not ordinarily commit a legislature to enact a law, nor could the official guarantee how a judicial action would be decided. Still others prohibit government bodies from handing their power or authority over to outside groups or individuals.

Government agencies sometimes cite substantive limitations as reasons why they cannot participate in consensus building or why they object to a proposed solution. Sometimes the objection is lodged by a private party. A polluter, for example, might oppose a proposal for a novel regulatory scheme on the grounds that the terms would violate the limitations on governmental authority. In legal terms, this limitation-of-powers issue may go by various names:

- An *undue delegation* problem, meaning that if the government joined a consensus building process it would be improperly handing over its official powers to a private group.
- An *ultra vires* or *separation-of-powers* issue, implying that an official or agency would be acting outside the limits of its legal authority.
- *Usurpation of power,* in the sense that an outside group— usually the participants in the consensus building process— would be taking over a role properly reserved for the government (Gellhorn & Levin, 1997, pp. 8-28, 32-34, 68-70).

Whatever the label, the practical options for resolving the objections are similar.

What can be done if a public official refuses to participate in consensus building on the grounds that to do so would violate the law?

If the objection is that participation itself would violate the law, the issue is fairly simple. By joining a consensus building process, an official is simply agreeing to talk with members of the public and to give consideration to any recommendations that are developed during a process. Merely communicating with members of the public is unlikely to be improper,[5] and an agreement to participate does not imply that the agency has agreed to be bound by the group's views.[6] Of course, a commitment to "consider carefully" a solution recommended by all or most of the people concerned about an issue may be the practical equivalent of agreeing to adopt it, but this is a political rather than a legal concern and should be addressed as such.

What if a participant cites these "limits to power" principles to object to a proposed agreement?

Usurpation, separation, delegation, and ultra vires objections are most likely to be raised when specific settlement options are discussed. A participant might argue, for example, that an agency could not agree to a settlement without violating legal doctrines that restrict governmental power.

If the problem is that a unit of government not present in the consensus process is the one that has the authority, the solution is simple, at least in theory: Get the missing player to the table.

A more serious issue arises when no one can legally commit the government to act. This is particularly likely when an official decision must be made by a commission, legislature, or other group of people. An agency representative might be unable, for example, to guarantee that a zoning commission would grant a variance or that a city council would amend an ordinance, because such decisions would require the vote of a multimember body. To some degree, this is merely a variant of an issue that arises frequently in traditional negotiations. Negotiators who represent groups of people or organizations, such as a corporation or neighborhood group, often do not have complete power to bind their constituents to an agreement. A private person or business can solve this problem by appointing a negotiator as its legal "agent" (Hynes, 1997, pp. 3-33, 99-114), but governmental powers often cannot be transferred to a single individual. There are two options for dealing with the problem of limited governmental authority.

1. Provide for *phased implementation* of the settlement; that is, require private parties to carry out their end of the bargain only after the government has done its part. In a land use dispute, for example, a community group might agree to dismiss a lawsuit only after a municipality carried out its commitment to make a zoning change.

2. Reach a *conditional settlement,* in which no one is bound to a deal until its terms have been formally ratified by the government participants.

In either case, the negotiators representing government decision makers should agree to use their best efforts to convince their colleagues or superiors to endorse a settlement. This is sometimes known as *recommendation authority.* In a reg-neg, for example, an agency convenes a group that represents all parties interested in a proposed regulation and asks them to seek a consensus on its content. Representatives of the agency often participate in, or at least listen to, the group's deliberations and will warn them if a proposal is likely to be unacceptable to the agency. If the group is able to reach consensus, its proposal is recommended by the representatives to their agency for adoption as a draft regulation to be put out for public comment.[7] Procedures like these strike a balance between giving meaning to a group's efforts and avoiding an improper transfer of official power to private citizens.

A variant of the undue delegation problem is the rule that to preserve the principle of separation of powers, one branch of government cannot exercise powers granted to another. Thus, an executive agency cannot usually commit a legislative branch to take action, nor could either one agree to a resolution that decides a case pending before a court. Many state constitutions impose separation-of-powers restrictions that are more severe than those under federal law (Gellhorn & Levin, 1997, pp. 32-34).

Separation-of-powers concerns are especially likely to arise when a consensus building process "stretches the envelope" and creates imaginative solutions. This was vividly illustrated during a pioneering effort to mediate a long-standing environmental dispute involving the construction of a flood-control dam on Washington's Snoqualmie River. For environmental reasons, the state's governor had repeatedly rejected plans to build the dam, but was facing increasing pressure from farmers and others to "do something." He responded by appointing two mediators to lead a search for a solution. The mediators decided at the outset to exclude government representatives from the process, reportedly out of fear that private citizens would not be able to bargain with officials on an equal basis. An imaginative agreement was eventually hammered out that involved resiting the dam to minimize its impact and imposing extensive land use controls. The governor endorsed the deal and began trying to implement it. The planned zoning changes, however, required action by two counties and 15 towns. Local government representatives, who had not been involved in the negotiations and were not subject to the governor's authority, were not anxious to put in place the proposed solution. As a result, the implementation of the Snoqualmie settlement was stalled for years (Dembart & Kwartler, 1980).

Another manifestation of the separation-of-powers concern arises in the area of spending. To ensure that strict control is maintained over the public purse, many states bar executive agencies from committing the state to spend money unless the legislature first appropriates the funds. As a result, if an agreement required public funding to be implemented, an agency would probably be unable to guarantee anything more than to advocate for the necessary appropriation. Similarly, a branch of government may not be able to legally bind even itself to take action in the future. Thus, for instance, legislative bodies cannot typically commit themselves not to amend a statute in a future year. The best response to a separation-of-powers concern is usually to bring representatives of all relevant branches of government to the table and, if necessary, reach a phased or conditional agreement like those described previously.

What other laws limit a government agency's ability to make binding commitments?

The ability of officials to agree to settlement terms is restricted even when a commitment would not raise delegation, ultra vires, or separation-of-powers concerns. Such limitations are too numerous and too idiosyncratic from state to state to discuss here, but an example would be state laws that bar administrative agencies from issuing regulations unless they have specific legislative authorization to do so.

One frustrating consequence of the wide variety of limitations on the power of government is that agency representatives who participate in a consensus building process may not be aware of the restrictions on their authority. As a result, they may agree in good faith to terms that they cannot legally carry out. Again, this is most likely to occur with "outside the box" solutions. The best protection against such frustrations is probably for government participants to check back with their offices periodically to learn whether terms being discussed in a consensus building process may pose a legal problem. In our experience, career government lawyers are the most likely to have encountered, and thus be able to identify and resolve, these sorts of obstacles. However, facilitators must balance the risk of tripping over a hidden constraint against the psychological reality that focusing too much on obstacles, particularly early on, will discourage participants from considering imaginative solutions.

■ *Disclosure Requirements and Confidentiality Protections*

Confidentiality and disclosure issues can arise at any point in a consensus process. At the outset, for example, some participants may insist that discussions be held in private, while others may argue that the law requires the public to be granted access. As a process continues, a media representative might assert a right to attend meetings that are being held in private. Or a participant in a public process might become so disruptive that other parties want him or her removed, but it may be unclear whether or not someone can legally be kept out of the room. If a consensus process is successful, participants may wish to notify a court or agency about the settlement, but without spreading the details in the public record.[8] Common questions on confidentiality and disclosure are answered in this section (Golann, 1996, pp. 361-377).

> *Can the public or the media legally be excluded from consensus building discussions? What should be done if outsiders request confidential materials exchanged during the process?*

People involved in disputes generally have the legal right to talk or negotiate with each other in private.[9] Neutrals may wish to speak confidentially with disputants in a mediation, because people are often more open to considering imaginative solutions if they can talk without their adversaries present. Thus, confidential "caucuses" are a key element of the mediation process.[10]

In consensus building, however, the presumptions governing privacy in negotiation are often reversed. Many consensus building efforts involve public issues, numerous participants, and government agencies. As a result, discussions are likely to be open to the public and the media. Consensus building negotiations are routinely reported in the press and may even be broadcast live on radio or cable television. In consensus building, then, privacy is often nonexistent. Indeed, the press and the public are likely to have a legal right to observe consensus building discussions in the following situations.

"The press and the public often have a legal right to observe consensus building discussions."

When a Process Involves a Public Official or Agency

When government officials are involved in negotiations, *sunshine* or *public meeting* laws,[11] enacted to promote citizen participation in government, may require that proceedings be open to the public. The terms of these laws vary from state to state. Some apply only when enough officials are present to make up a quorum of the negotiating group, while others have different triggers. Some laws also require that official notice be given of the time, place, and agenda of each meeting. FACA is a federal-level public meeting law. In the Native American Self-Determination reg-neg discussed earlier (Case 9), legal rules required that formal notice be given of the group's meetings in advance. A copy of such a notice appears in an appendix to that case. The point is that the very presence of government representatives in a consensus building process may require that the public, including the press, has access to it. Even when no official is physically present at meetings, the fact that a government agency is sponsoring or funding consensus building may require that documents generated or exchanged during the negotiations be available to members of the public for inspection and copying. The federal Freedom of Information Act[12] (known as FOIA and pronounced "foy-yah") and its state counterparts create broad rights of access to documents generated by or given to public employees, again to increase citizen access to the work of government. State and federal records-preservation laws may even bar officials from destroying certain records generated during a process without first obtaining official approval.[13] On the other hand, both sunshine and freedom-of-information laws typically contain exceptions that permit officials to discuss certain sensitive topics in private and shield documents that deal with these topics from public review. Examples include data about an individual's health or financial status, commercial trade secrets, and tactics in litigation.[14]

When a Facilitator Is Paid for or Directed by a Government Entity

Government entities sometimes agree to pay some or all of a facilitator's fees or expenses. Although such assistance can help disputants hire skilled neutrals, it is possible that a mediator paid from public funds will be considered a public employee for purposes of a sunshine or freedom-of-information law, creating the disclosure obligations discussed above. The attorneys or the ethics commission of the government body hiring the mediator should know when this situation would arise.

When Information about a Process or Its Result Is Filed in Court

The fact that a dispute is the subject of a court case is very unlikely, in and of itself, to expose consensus building discussions on the same topic to public or media access.[15] But if the parties to a consensus process ask a court to participate in their settlement, for example, by filing an agreement with the court so that it can be enforced more easily, this may open the agreement to public scrutiny. Even if a judge orders that a document remain confidential (*under seal*), a different judge, acting at some point in the future in the same or a different case, could decide that the document should be disclosed.[16] People concerned about confidentiality should keep consensus building meetings and associated documents out of courthouses, if possible.[17]

If we need to hold discussions in private, what steps are most likely to ensure confidentiality?

The ability to talk about sensitive issues behind closed doors may, in some cases, facilitate a negotiation process. Assuming that public access is not required by law, consensus builders may want to develop ground rules that assure participants that what they say will not be disclosed to outsiders without their consent. There is no perfect method to guarantee confidentiality, but several steps will help.

Court Orders

The strongest and surest guarantee of confidentiality is a court order. This device, known as a *protective order*, is a command issued by a judge that bars the parties to a lawsuit from doing certain things. For example, a judge might order the participants in an environmental legal case not to disclose geological information provided by a corporate participant. Judicial orders provide strong confidentiality protection because people are usually reluctant to anger a court, especially if they expect to appear before the same judge as parties in a lawsuit. The primary disadvantages are that court orders can only be issued if a dispute is actually pending in court, and they cover only the parties to a lawsuit, not outside stakeholders. In addition, many judges are reluctant to enter what they see as gag orders because of free-speech concerns.

Privileges

A legal *privilege* is a rule that bars a person from disclosing what another person has said. In most states, for example, conversations between doctors and patients and lawyers and their clients are privileged, meaning that these professionals are forbidden to disclose what their clients tell them without the clients' consent. Almost every state has created a privilege that restricts the participants in mediations, including both parties and mediators, from disclosing information revealed during the mediation process. If consensus building satisfies the definition of mediation in the state where it is held, then a legal privilege may bar the participants from talking to outsiders about what was said.

There is no general mediation privilege under federal law, however, so negotiators must rely on the privileges created by state statutes. Inevitably, the conditions for invoking the privilege and the extent of the coverage that it provides will vary from state to state. In a single consensus building process, what participants say in a meeting held in one state might be privileged, while information disclosed during a later discussion that occurs across a state line might not.[18]

Agreements

The most common way to ensure confidentiality is to have participants sign an agreement pledging to keep their discussions private. In a purely legal sense, both confidentiality agreements and legal privileges are weak, because there are few effective remedies if they are violated. Nonetheless, confidentiality agreements are often effective. To a surprising degree, even bitterly opposed parties respect clear ground rules once they agree to them.

It may thus be worthwhile to ask the participants in a consensus process to sign a confidentiality agreement such as the sample shown in Figure 13.1. It is important, however, to clarify the extent to which participants can share information with the people and organizations they represent. It is also important that everyone who may receive sensitive data during a process, including experts, informal advisers, and observers, sign the confidentiality document.

---

*If an outsider intrudes on discussions or a participant
becomes disruptive, what legal remedies are available?*

Consensus building is inherently inclusive, with a strong bias toward keeping angry and emotional people inside a process. Sometimes, however, a participant may lose control and become so disruptive that a process cannot continue. When this happens, the best advice for the facilitator is probably to adjourn the meeting temporarily and talk with the person, perhaps with help from someone whom the disrupter sees as an ally. If informal responses are not effective, it is possible to seek legal assistance.

If a process is being conducted in cooperation with a court, then a judge may be able to help restore order. A judge could

By my signature on this document, I agree to keep confidential and not to reveal to any person outside this process any information or documents that I receive, or to which I have access, as a result of this process. This Agreement does not, however, require me to keep confidential any information or documents to which I have access independently of this process.

I agree that I will not violate this Agreement in any manner, and understand that if I do, I will be subject to the same penalties and sanctions as the parties to the Agreement, and the attorney or party who has invited me to attend will be subject to the same penalties and sanctions as if they had committed the violation.

Figure 13.1. Sample Confidentiality Agreement

deliver a stern lecture to the offender, or could issue a court order conditioning the offender's further participation in the discussion on an agreement to comply with the ground rules. If judicial intervention is not available, the options for excluding intruders and disruptive participants are quite limited. After a disruptive person has been asked to leave, a security officer or police officer can be called to escort the person from the premises. If such a problem is anticipated, however, the rules of procedure for the meeting should set clear standards for how the meeting is to be conducted. If the ground rules for a process are vague, security personnel will likely be reluctant to play referee.

■ Liability Issues

People sometimes worry that by taking on a facilitator's role they will expose themselves to legal liability—in other words, that they can be sued for something they do, or fail to do, in carrying out their responsibilities. While it may be true that "no good deed goes unpunished"—in the sense that facilitation seems at times to be a thankless job—the risk of legal exposure to liability claims is very low. It can be lessened further by taking a few precautions.

What precautions should a facilitator take to avoid legal liability for his or her participation in consensus building?

The first point to make is that liability claims against mediators or facilitators are extremely rare: We know of no specific instance in which a mediator or facilitator of a consensus building process has been sued, much less held liable, because of his or her work. People should not be discouraged from taking on the role of facilitator by the remote possibility that they could be sued for their trouble. Nonetheless, as consensus building becomes more common, the risk of liability problems could increase. Therefore, a few basic precautions may be helpful.

Obtain Liability Insurance

Professional facilitators should consider obtaining liability insurance. Such coverage is available at surprisingly low cost, reflecting the fact that legal claims against neutrals are so rare. Members of the Society of Professionals in Dispute Resolution (SPIDR)—a nationwide professional organization based in Washington, D.C. that is open to nonlawyers—can obtain liability coverage on very good terms. Amateur facilitators should check with an insurance agent about whether their existing insurance, for example, the "umbrella" policies that are offered with homeowners' coverage, includes facilitation activities that are undertaken on a volunteer basis.

Ask for Immunity

Another common precaution a neutral facilitator should take is to ask parties to agree that the facilitator will not be held liable for his or her activities and will not be called as a witness in any legal case related to the dispute. A sample immunity agreement that will accomplish this appears in Figure 13.2.

Avoid Risky Behavior

The most likely source of a legal claim against a facilitator is a conflict of interest. If a facilitator has a prior relationship with a participant in a process, the facilitator should disclose that fact at the outset to everyone involved. A facilitator should be particularly careful to disclose any information that could suggest that he or she has a monetary interest in how the dispute is resolved, for example, if the neutral's spouse is employed by a company that could benefit from the outcome of the process.

Neither the Neutral nor his or her employees or agents shall be liable to any party for any act or omission, other than willful misconduct, in connection with any consensus building process that is conducted under this Agreement.

The parties agree not to call the Neutral nor any of his or her employees or agents as witnesses or experts in any pending or subsequent litigation or arbitration relating in any way to the dispute that is the subject of this negotiation. The parties and the Neutral agree that the Neutral and his or her employees and agents will be disqualified as witnesses in any such proceeding.

Figure 13.2. Sample Immunity Provision

In practice, of course, people are often selected to facilitate precisely because the disputants know and trust them: The very existence of a prior relationship is what gives people confidence in the facilitator's skills. As a result, experienced facilitators may find themselves making such disclosures regularly. The best rule of thumb is that even a tenuous relationship or connection should be disclosed immediately. Doing so will avoid later embarrassment, and a show of candor may actually increase many participants' comfort level with a neutral.

Apart from conflicts of interest, few specific rules govern how a facilitator must conduct his or her work. As discussed previously, facilitators should be careful about ex parte contacts with judges in legal cases that are related to a consensus building process. Facilitators should also be aware that if they are paid out of public funds they may become subject to special ethics rules that apply to public employees. Similarly, neutrals who receive cases through an organized program such as a court referral network may find themselves subject to specific duties imposed by the program.[19]

■ Implementation and Enforcement Considerations

Reaching an agreement may be the easier part of a consensus building effort; often the more difficult task is to convince officials and stakeholders who were not present during the negotiations to ratify the compromises reached by their representatives. At this point, a question may arise as to whether a neutral facilitator can properly become an advocate for an agreement that is reached. Also, when a settlement is successfully ratified, cooperation among the representatives may break down as implementation proceeds, raising the issue of whether settlement terms can be enforced in court.

Can a facilitator publicly support or advocate for ratification of an agreement reached through a consensus process?

At the conclusion of a consensus process, some participants may suggest that the facilitator become a public spokesperson on behalf of the group, communicating the agreement to the public or to a particular government agency or adjudicator. For example, if utility companies and other stakeholders have negotiated a settlement of an issue pending before the state public utility commission, some parties may ask the facilitator to present the agreement to the commission for approval. Other participants, however, may question whether this is an appropriate role for a neutral facilitator.

Facilitators can often serve as credible advocates of a consensus agreement. Although individual stakeholders or a representative group of participants could probably present the substance of the agreement equally well, the facilitator sometimes assumes the spokesperson's role to underscore the fact that an agreement takes account of a diversity of interests. The facilitator can answer questions from a disinterested perspective and can always call on participants to explain their own perspectives. If a consensus process was open to the public or was covered in the media, then the facilitator's public voice is usually taken for granted.

When a consensus building process has been closed to the public and conducted under strictures of confidentiality (similar to traditional mediation), and especially when the facilitator's role was exclusively internal and did not include involvement with the media, "the facilitator as public spokesperson" may appear improper or illegal, or at least inconsistent with principles of confidentiality and neutrality. This may be especially true when some participants have dropped out or when certain participants, although they have signed on to an agreement, have reservations about parts of it—and perhaps even hope that a reviewing authority will require refinements that will make it more to their liking.

Most confidentiality agreements will not preclude the facilitator (or any other participant) from communicating the terms of settlement, even when the consensus is less than complete. Typically, confidentiality requirements apply to the process in which consensus is negotiated, rather than to the final terms of a settlement. Sometimes parties do wish to keep their final agreement confidential, but these cases are comparatively rare. Indeed, in most circumstances a consensus agreement is submitted to a public authority for formal approval, or perhaps even for implementation. In addition, it is not illegal or improper, or a violation of neutrality, for a facilitator to assume a public advocacy role at the end of a process, as long as the participants so desire. If participants do not wish a facilitator to take on a public spokesperson role, the facilitator should remain in the background.

"Participants should be clear in the ground rules about the proper role for the facilitator."

To reduce the likelihood of this issue arising, participants should be clear and explicit in the ground rules about the proper role for the facilitator. When ground rules are unclear or do not address this issue, however, the participants as a group can decide at the appropriate time whether or not the facilitator should assume an advocacy role. If need be, the confidentiality agreement can be formally amended to provide explicitly for such activities. In short, neutral facilitators, as long as the participants support such a role, can be very effective in explaining and advocating for the adoption of a consensus agreement.

Can a consensus-based agreement be made legally enforceable?

Successful consensus building often culminates in an agreement in which the parties commit to take specific actions. However, legal issues can arise that affect the durability and enforceability of a settlement.

Legal Formalities

Participants often want assurances that a settlement will be implemented as planned and that no participant will renege on his or her part of an agreement. In these cases, it is helpful to adhere to the following basic guidelines to ensure that a settlement is enforceable in court, if the need arises.

- As soon as agreement is reached, write out the key terms in the form of an agreement or memorandum of understanding. A "handshake" deal may be legally binding in theory, but as a practical matter a written and signed agreement is much more likely to be implemented.[20]
- State clearly, in plain language, what each participant has agreed to do. A judge looking at an agreement should be able to understand from the document itself the essence of each party's obligations.
- Think about contingencies and changes in conditions that might frustrate implementation of the agreement. Either account for them in a settlement or create a self-contained process, such as mediation followed by binding arbitration, to resolve them quickly. Courts have the power to modify agreements to take account of unforeseen changes, but they will not always exercise this authority, and it is thus unwise to rely on that possibility.[21]

If a memorandum setting forth parties' agreement is (1) in writing, (2) states the key terms, and (3) is signed by the persons or organizations who will be bound by it, then no matter how messy or inelegant it may appear, most courts will treat it as a legally binding contract. Agreements need not include any "magic words" (e.g., *hereby* or *whereas*), Latin phrases ("nunc pro tunc"), or legal jargon ("party of the first part"), nor is it usually necessary to have parties' signatures notarized or witnessed.

Enforcement Tools

If parties do not voluntarily comply with an agreement, court enforcement may be necessary. Judges enforce contracts in two basic ways: (1) by requiring a party who is shown to have violated an agreement to pay money damages to another party who can prove that the violation caused monetary harm, and/or (2) by ordering a party to comply with its agreement in the future. The second remedy is known as *equitable relief* or *specific performance*; the orders that a court issues to enforce the deal are called *injunctions* and sometimes *restraining orders*. In most situations, an injunction is more effective than money damages because it prevents the violation from occurring again, but for various reasons courts are often reluctant to issue injunctions (Dobbs, 1993, pp. 78-85, 98-100).

Parties should think about how to frame a settlement so as to maximize the likelihood that a court will be willing to order a reneging party to honor its bargain. In general, the following conditions must be met.

- The person or organization that is needed to carry out an agreement must be legally bound by it. This involves the issue of limits on governmental authority discussed in earlier sections.

- The party must be capable of doing what the agreement requires. If there is an insurmountable obstacle that is outside a party's control (e.g., the party does not have the money needed to comply and cannot get a loan), a court will not order the impossible.

- The terms must be clear enough for a court to write a clear and unequivocal order to the violator.

- The task of supervising an injunction must not be a major burden on the court. If, for example, an agreement requires hostile parties to work closely together, or if there is no clear standard that the judge can apply to decide whether a party has performed its obligations, then a court will likely refuse to issue an injunction.

- Implementation of the agreement should not cause harm to the public or to people who were not represented in the negotiation process.

- If conditions are likely to change before the settlement is completely implemented, the agreement should take account of this, and if possible, a mechanism should be incorporated to adjust the terms to the new circumstances.

In the final analysis, the most effective way to guarantee implementation is usually not a lawsuit, which is almost always uncertain, slow, and expensive, but rather for all parties to carry out their bargain voluntarily. This is most likely to happen if the terms of a settlement are clear, the agreement provides benefits for everyone involved, and a process is provided to resolve quickly any disputes that arise during implementation.[22]

■ *Conclusion*

The goal of this chapter was not to provide comprehensive answers to every legal question that might arise about consensus building; that could easily fill a large volume on its own. Rather, our objective has been to identify the types of legal questions that might arise, to explain the fundamentals of the issues involved, and to steer readers in the direction of more comprehensive answers. Additional information can be found in the publications listed in the reference list, and from the various professional associations in the mediation and dispute resolution field.

Finally, it is worth remembering that consensus building is fundamentally about negotiation, not law. Despite the widespread growth of consensus building over the past 10 years, very few legal issues arising in consensus processes have been so important or long-lasting as to make their way into a court. Our hope is that the information in this chapter will allow facilitators and stakeholders to keep legal issues in their place and to focus on the truly difficult problem: creating an effective consensus.

■ *Notes*

1. In this chapter, the terms *law* and *rule* are used in a general sense to refer to all types of legal standards, including state and federal statutes, agency rules and regulations, local codes and ordinances, and court decisions.

2. Readers will find relatively concise, plain-language explanations of these issues in a series of paperback books published for law students by West Publishing Co. on various legal topics under the titles *[Legal Topic] in a Nutshell*. The book in this series that is most relevant to consensus building is Gellhorn and Levin's *Administrative Law and Process in a Nutshell* (1997).

3. In some situations, even sending a judge an unsolicited letter or document about the merits of a legal case can pose a legal problem. The concern is that such a filing might be interpreted as an "end run" around court rules that define how each side can present its arguments. There should not be a problem, however, with contacts about procedural issues, such as scheduling, or with any communication that all of the litigants agree may be sent.

4. Originally enacted in 1972 (P.L. 92-463), amended by the Government in the Sunshine Act in 1976 (P.L. 94-409), and codified at 5 U.S.C. 551 et seq., FACA has been administered by the General Services Administration (GSA) since 1977. The comprehensive GSA rule governing its management is found at 41 CFR Part 101-6.10 (Dec. 2, 1987).

5. One exception is where the official is involved in a judicial-type process. As explained previously, persons in such circumstances may be bound by the rule against ex parte contacts.

6. Thus, for example, a federal appeals court has held that it does not constitute "bad-faith negotiation" for an agency to repudiate a consensus recommendation as to the content of a regulation and propose an alternative version for public comment. See *USA Group Loan Services, Inc. v. Riley*, 82 F.3d 708 (7th Cir. 1996).

7. Congress enacted the Regulatory Negotiation Act of 1990, 5 U.S.C.A. sec. 561 et seq., to promote the concept of reg-neg and to resolve doubts about whether federal agencies can participate in such a process. For a discussion of reg-negs, see Harter (1982).

8. A somewhat related problem arose in the New York Bight Initiative case (Case 6). There, chemical companies who had participated in a successful consensus building effort were unwilling to sign on to the group's final report because of concern that factual findings in the report might be used against them in a pending lawsuit.

9. This right could fall under the legal rubric of a right to privacy, to control entry to private property, to be free from a "nuisance," or to avoid a breach of the peace. In practice, of course, a facilitator might encounter difficulty enforcing rights of privacy, for reasons discussed later in this chapter.

10. One example of the usefulness of private discussions in consensus building is the Massachusetts Military Reservation case (Case 7), in which the parties assembled a team of experts to analyze options for solving a severe groundwater pollution problem. According to the participants, the group's ability to discuss controversial scientific issues on an "off-the-record" basis was a key to success, because under conditions of confidentiality "people could hash out ideas and talk informally," without concern that they might contradict the official position of their employer.

11. Examples of such statutes include New York's Sunshine Law, N.Y. Pub. Off. Law sec. 100 et seq. (Consol. 1987) and California's Open Meeting Law, Cal. Govt. Code sec. 54950 et seq. (West 1983).

12. FOIA is printed at 5 U.S.C.A. sec. 552 (1977). For an explanation of its provisions, see *Freedom of Information Act Guide and Privacy Act Overview* (1992), available from the U.S. Superintendent of Documents in Washington, D.C.

13. For example, 44 U.S.C.A. sec. 3101 et seq. (1991) requires the preservation of certain federal government records.

14. For example, FOIA includes exemptions for such matters as trade secrets, confidential financial information, and personnel and medical files; see 5 U.S.C.A. sec. 552(b).

15. Thus, for example, a federal appeals court refused to grant a newspaper access to a court-sponsored settlement process, even though the process (a summary jury trial) occurred in a courtroom and resembled a traditional trial; see *Cincinnati Gas and Electric Co. v. General Electric Co.*, 854 F.2d 900 (6th Cir. 1988).

16. For example, in *Bank of American National Trust & Savings Association v. Hotel Rittenhouse Association*, 800 F.2d 339 (3d Cir. 1986), an appeals court overrode a trial judge's decision and ordered a confidential settlement agreement to be disclosed to a nonparty. Another example is the Florida Sunshine in Litigation Act, which bars court orders that have the purpose or effect of concealing a "public hazard"; see Fla. Stat. Ann. Sec. 69.081(3) (West. Supp. 1995).

17. For a good analysis of the issues involved in access to mediated settlements, see Menkel-Meadow (1993).

18. The mediation privilege laws of every state are catalogued and described by Rogers and McEwen (1994).

19. As one example of such a program restriction, mediators who accept cases from the Middlesex Multi-Door Courthouse in Cambridge, Massachusetts are barred from speaking with disputants before the mediation process formally begins.

20. One practical problem familiar to mediators is that if an agreement is not written down and signed it is much easier for an unhappy participant to later claim that what one side calls a settlement was merely a discussion or a draft, or that the agreement was to a different set of terms. Also, some oral agreements are legally unenforceable. State laws known as *statutes of frauds* bar courts from enforcing certain oral promises and unsigned documents. Examples relevant to consensus building include the general rule that an agreement to convey an interest in real estate and a promise that cannot be performed within one year must be set out in a document that is signed by the objecting party to be enforced by a court.

21. The Supreme Court has ruled that courts have the power to go back and modify final legal judgments, even when the judgment embodies a painstakingly negotiated settlement of a controversy. This is particularly likely to occur when the public interest is affected or public funds are involved; see *Rufo v. Inmates of Suffolk County Jail*, 112 S.Ct. 748 (1992). The moral is that if a

settlement does not include a mechanism by which its terms can be adjusted to meet changing conditions, the courts may be asked to do so.

22. For an example of a multistep dispute resolution clause that can be incorporated into a settlement agreement, see Golann (1996, pp. 353-356).

■ References

Dembart, L., & Kwartler, R. (1980). The Snoqualmie River dispute: Bringing mediation into environmental disputes. In R. Goldmann (Ed.), *Roundtable justice* (pp. 39-54). Boulder, CO: Westview.

Dobbs, D. H. (1993). *Law of remedies.* St. Paul, MN: West.

Gellhorn, E., & Levin, W. M. (1997). *Administrative law and process in a nutshell.* St. Paul, MN: West.

Glicksman, R. L., & Coggins, G. C. (1995). *Modern public land law in a nutshell.* St. Paul, MN: West.

Golann, D. (1996). *Mediating legal disputes.* New York: Aspen Law and Business.

Harter, P. J. (1982). Negotiating regulations: A cure for malaise. *Georgetown Law Journal, 71*(1), 1-113.

Hynes, J. D. (1997). *Agency, partnership and the LLC.* St. Paul, MN: West.

Lampe, D., & Kaplan, M. (1999). *Resolving land use conflicts through medation: Challenges and opportunities.* Cambridge, MA: Lincoln Intitute of Land Policy.

Menkel-Meadow, C. (1993, June). Public access to private settlements: Conflicting legal policies. *Alternatives, 6,* 85.

Rogers, N., & McEwen, C. (1994). *Mediation: Law, policy and practice.* Deerfield, IL: Clark Boardman Callaghan.

14

IMPLEMENTING CONSENSUS-BASED AGREEMENTS

■ *William R. Potapchuk*
■ *Jarle Crocker*

Stories told by mediators about past consensus building processes can sound remarkably like Martha Stewart reminiscing about last month's formal dinner party. Both talk about the importance of planning ahead, the difficulty of deciding who to invite, the need to have a shared understanding of the proper rules of behavior—even the quandary of how to "divide the pie" after a long discussion around the table. But chances are, neither the mediators nor Martha talks much about what happens after the meeting, or the party, is over.

That's because the aftermath often isn't very pretty. For Martha, there's the stack of dirty dishes in the sink and the problem of how to get the merlot stain out of the white loveseat. For the mediator, there's the problem of putting the agreements into practice. Indeed, the implementation of consensus-based agreements is often beset by challenges. Sometimes, after they leave the table, stakeholders find that they have divergent interpretations of what their agreement means. Other stakeholders may find that those they represent—their constituents—aren't at all happy with the outcome, putting everyone in a tight spot. Or a consensus building group may find that a funding source, which they were sure would help them see the deal through, has other priorities.

With the success of collaborative processes increasingly evaluated by the tangible results they produce, it's essential to think about how to "make the deal stick." The purpose of this chapter is to take up the challenges relating to implementation and provide prescriptive advice for overcoming them. (For advice about merlot stains, call Martha.)

Evidence of the challenges of implementing consensus-based agreements abounds. In the business world, a sobering study of corporate strategic-planning processes found that during the heyday of such initiatives in the late 1980s, fewer than 3 percent of the resulting plans were actually implemented (Westley, 1995). A significant problem in assessing the implementation of mediated and facilitated agreements in complex public policy issues is a lack of rigorous evaluation studies, questions about how to define success, and trouble quantifying results that are often highly qualitative in nature (Sipe, 1998).

One explanation for the difficulty in assessing the issues surrounding implementation is that consensus-based processes are being applied to a growing array of economic, social, and environmental issues. The use of a neutral party to mediate disputes was initially developed to assist labor-management negotiations in the 1950s (Burton, 1990). In those first cases, the stakeholders were easily identifiable, the issues clearly defined, and the authority for implementing agreements already established by law. Today, consensus-based processes are applied to everything from formal regulatory negotiations involving federal agencies to community "visioning" initiatives involving hundreds, and sometimes thousands, of participants.

■ *The Challenge of Implementation*

To frame the discussion that follows, it is helpful to build a simple typology of consensus-based processes that shows how the challenges of implementation grow with the complexity of the issues being addressed. A tight interdependency exists between the scope of problems tackled and the number of stakeholders involved. The wider the net is cast, the more individuals, organizations, and institutions will have an interest and stake in participation. In turn, implementation of agreements becomes more complicated as a greater number of stakeholders, policy arenas, and decision-making processes are woven together. This is illustrated in Table 14.1.

Two critical dilemmas for the implementation of consensus-based approaches to handle contentious issues cut across all of the processes illustrated in this table. The first core issue is that while new ways of making public decisions continue to spread in use and popularity, the mechanisms for their implementation are usually found in traditional institutions and processes. Consensus-based processes are often employed when there is a need to convene diverse stakeholders that do not often sit at the same tables, forge connections among related policy arenas that are otherwise isolated, and address the "soft" issues, such as the quality of relationships among stakeholders, often all shortcomings of the organizational infrastructure. However, because collaborative processes are often not institutionalized, the burden of implementing consensus-based agreements usually falls on these same "status quo" mechanisms. When addressing relatively straightforward situations, this is often not a problem. For example, in the facility-siting issue characterized in Table 14.1, the expectation for implementation, should an agreement be reached, is that the regulatory authority will grant the appropriate approvals and the institution proposing the facility will build it—a very reasonable expectation.

Imagine, in contrast, the coastal zone management dispute. Multiple municipal governments have land use authority and manage their own section of the coastline. The counties may manage the landfill and the roads, while the state Parks Department manages the public beaches, and the state Department of Natural Resources manages the sections of the coastal area preserved for wildlife. All of these entities could have an implementation role, and some may be able to shoulder the responsibilities more ably than others. In this case, like many others, the impetus for collaboration comes from the recognition that traditional mechanisms for making public decisions are not designed to address complex relationships among diverse stakeholders and intermeshed issues. However, the irony is that after consensus-based agreements have been reached, it is often these same institutions that play a significant role in implementation.

TABLE 14.1 Typology of Consensus-Based Processes

Example	Problem	Stakeholders	Agreement
Facility siting	Single issue in one problem area	Clearly defined and somewhat limited in number	Defined parameters for implementation characterized by clear problem definition and linkages among stakeholders
Urban water management conflict	Small number of issues in two or three problem areas	Clear core group of primary stakeholders, with unclear larger group of secondary stakeholders	Partially defined parameters for implementation characterized by complex linkages among individual issues and stakeholders
Coastal zone management plan	Many issues in many problem areas	Unclear number of primary and secondary stakeholders	Undefined parameters for implementation characterized by complex linkages among individual issues, broader problem areas, and multiple, often unconnected decision-making processes

The second core issue lies in the nature of what makes consensus-based agreements differ from those produced by "business as usual" public policy. At its best, collaborative decision making not only produces tangible policy outcomes but also less easily defined results such as new relationships among stakeholders, novel and shared understandings of the problems being addressed, and more constructive norms of behavior for individuals, organizations, and communities. Indeed, it is often these intangible factors of trust, reciprocity, and mutual support that hold agreements together (Putnam, 1993b). Successful implementation of agreements depends on creating fertile soil for these outcomes to grow and flourish, something that is not easily captured through implementation tips, memorandums of understanding, contracts, and other types of "paper" agreements. This dilemma can be especially acute in addressing environmental issues where individuals and organizations need to change ingrained behavior to make progress on an issue. In these instances, agreements need to go beyond specific policies to include a community "ethic" about how individuals, the private and public sectors, and others will interact with local and regional ecosystems (John, 1994).

The remainder of this chapter looks at the ways that facilitators, mediators, and stakeholders engaged in consensus-based collaborative processes can skillfully navigate a course that ends with the successful implementation of their agreements. The typical mediated decision-making process can be divided into three stages: prenegotiations, or getting the parties to the table; negotiations, the actual deliberations; and implementation, putting the outcomes into effect (Susskind & Cruikshank, 1987). The implications for implementation at each stage will be discussed, detailing the potential pitfalls that can occur, with an accompanying discussion of how to address the challenges that arise.

Before we begin, there is one important lesson to impart, perhaps the most important in this chapter. Consensus-based methods for making decisions are not linear. Sometimes, new stakeholders or issues are added halfway through a process, making it necessary to "loop back" and repeat earlier stages. In other instances, the process may be "uneven," with some stakeholders enjoying success working through some of the issues, while others remain stuck. Because the stages of the process and stakeholders are interconnected, many problems with implementation occur because of poor process design, well before any agreement is signed. In a chess match, the deciding move often comes a dozen turns before checkmate. The same is true in consensus building, and it can be difficult, if not impossible, to recover from a poor opening. By the same token, the game is won not by a single move alone but by a well-conceived and well-executed strategy. The following suggestions should be taken in this light—not as individual actions, but as a collective strategy for achieving success.

■ Before the Party Starts: Getting to the Table

Whether it's a dinner party, chess match, or consensus building negotiation, the opening can set the tone for the entire course of events. Problems that arise in this stage are especially difficult to address at the time stakeholders in a collaborative process are discussing implementation. If the negotiations are not initially derailed because of poor process design, land mines may not be uncovered until the stakeholders move to put their plans into action, and by then, it is often too late to undo the damage.

"Many an implementation plan falters because the right people were not at the table from the beginning."

Many an implementation plan falters because the right people were not at the table from the beginning. In some instances, this may happen because not enough planning and effort has gone into encouraging stakeholders to participate, making it difficult to achieve the "critical mass" necessary to leverage significant change. Another common problem is that participants are drawn from a lineup of the "usual suspects"—stakeholders picked because of their "insider" status or because they wield significant power or influence. Agreements that fail to reflect the authentic diversity of a community or organization are likely to fall flat.

Another question that should be addressed at the outset is how a proposed consensus building process should connect with other collaborative efforts, policy arenas, and events that can affect the results. Perhaps the ultimate horror of the host or hostess is to find out the night before the gala that two other parties have been scheduled for the next evening. The same is true for a mediator or facilitator. To take a worst-case scenario, the implementation plan resulting from a difficult regulatory negotiation can be annulled by the results of a parallel, but disconnected, legal decision that voids the agreement. The following are three basic principles that, taken together, offer an effective approach to getting a consensus building process up and running in a way that will address common implementation problems before they begin.

Focus on Issues of Representation and Participation

When thinking about whom to invite for a dinner party, a host will usually start with a list of friends who know each other, get along, and generally enjoy spending time together. Determining whom to involve in consensus building efforts is not so straightforward. Issues of representation and participation that most directly affect implementation are discussed below.

Perhaps the most common misstep made in representation is to involve only traditional stakeholders, under the assumption that they will make enlightened decisions that are in everyone's interest and that those decisions will therefore enjoy broad support. Unfortunately, even the most thoughtful and equitable agreement can collapse if it is tainted by the perception that it was made by an "inner circle" of stakeholders. Add the politics of race, class, and gender to the mix, and the difficulties that can result from failing to assemble a diverse group of stakeholders should be clear.

This lesson about the importance of representation is illustrated well by Case 12 in this volume, which describes a community strategic-planning process in "Middletown." In the initial stages of that process, stakeholders were limited to a small group drawn primarily from elected local officials. The implementation plan that initially emerged from this process called for significant actions to be taken by a wide range of nongovernmental organizations. Not surprisingly, those groups lacked the buy-in essential to motivate a reallocation of their already scarce resources. As a result, the first plan withered on the vine without the support of the stakeholders required to take action. Had the implementing organizations been at the table, they might have been able to structure a plan that would have achieved the same goals but more accurately reflected the capacities of the relevant organizations. The result might have been somewhat less ambitious, but such a plan would ultimately have been more successful because the stakeholders were committed to its implementation.

Similarly, it is important to address the issue of which people in each organization or system are considered representative. Common wisdom is to seek the most senior persons to ensure that the representatives can make commitments on behalf of their organizations. Indeed, this rule of thumb has become the norm in public policy consensus building. However, some observers have begun to challenge this approach to representation. Westley (1995), in an analysis of multiple environmental policy-making processes, argues that "many middle- and lower-level managers are deliberately excluded from the rich face-to-face discussions that forge the backdrop, the meanings, and the frames for policy discussions." He goes on to note that this exclusionary practice limits overall organizational learning, blocks innovation, and fails to address implementation. For example, in a national policy dialogue focused on the actions and programs of a federal agency, successful implementation may depend on the involvement of a representative from a regional office and the creation of a mechanism to solicit input from other regions, not solely the involvement of senior officials at headquarters. Especially when dealing with situations where successful implementation will require changed behaviors at all levels of an implementing agency, a greater number of perspectives at the table can lead to more responsive implementation plans. The more varied the views on the issue taken into account and the more different the definitions of the problem considered, the greater the chance that the actions that result from deliberations will share the support of a wide group of internal stakeholders. As a general rule, the higher the level of participation among those directly affected, the greater the legitimacy of the agreement, and hence the greater the chance of successful implementation.

Involving people from all levels of a stakeholder organization can create new issues such as the need to create "safe space" for those lower-level individuals who may feel (or actually be) vulnerable if they do not toe the party line. Furthermore, an increase in the number of representatives can make a process more unwieldy. The tiered process discussed below is one strategy for addressing this dilemma. Other models of large-scale processes have also been developed that involve hundreds or thousands of individuals. Initially used within organizations, these approaches have begun to be adapted to public policy contexts (Bunker & Alban, 1997; Emery & Purser, 1996; Weisbord & Janoff, 1995).

It is also important to attend to concerns about diversity. Participants in a consensus building process should reflect as much as possible the broader racial, gender, and class makeup of all stakeholders—those in decision-making positions, those responsible for implementation, those who may be affected by the agreement, and those who can block its implementation. One technique that can be used to address diversity issues is to imagine what groups or individuals affected by decisions that emerge will say. How will they perceive the stakeholders sitting around the table? Will anyone share or speak for their needs and interests? Are there representatives included who look like them? More important, process managers should ask individuals from the different stakeholder communities to assess all decisions about representation.

Closely related to questions about diversity and representation is the fact that there are often multiple sets of stakeholders who agree to be included. It is often advisable to build multiple "tiers" of participation, especially when it is anticipated that any resulting agreement will require a new way of thinking or behaving on the part of key stakeholders. A tiered process uses different methods to engage ever-widening circles of stakeholders, albeit in different ways. Primary stakeholders, or those most deeply involved, generally require intensive relationship building, including opportunities for face-to-face exchanges among the parties that further mutual education and encourage collaborative problem solving.

Work with secondary stakeholders often depends on the distribution of information and makes ample time for these stakeholders to provide input to their representatives. Crafting connections to the general public requires a media strategy, and perhaps techniques such as focus groups and opinion polls, to generate feedback and build the political will for change. (See Chapter 11 for more on developing a media strategy.)

Figuring out who needs (and wants) to be at the table is one thing; getting them there is something else altogether. Many consensus building horror stories start out with the mediator or facilitator talking about how a collaborative process was publicized throughout the community (in many languages, no less), and a diverse set of stakeholders struggled to develop a joint plan of action. As soon as the draft plan is announced, new stakeholder groups emerge and criticize the effort for not reflecting their interests and perspectives. At this point, the storyteller usually laments, "What went wrong?"

The reasons stakeholders choose not to participate, even in collaborative processes that directly affect them, are legion. For traditionally disenfranchised groups, past discrimination has led them to believe their voice simply will not be heard. Senior-level managers and elected officials claim they are too overloaded to participate—until someone makes a decision that traverses their turf. For everyday citizens, calls to participate in time-consuming and often highly complex processes fall on deaf ears. However, as soon as an agreement is reached to site a facility next door, participation in local politics (and in opposition to the carefully crafted implementation plan) suddenly becomes a burning interest.

There are two rules of thumb that convenors and facilitators ought to keep in mind. First, make it easy for stakeholders to say yes, and hard to say no, to invitations to participate. Hold meetings in places that are convenient and accessible. Explain the benefits of participation and why each person's contributions are important. Most important, make direct and personal contact with groups and organizations being recruited. Second, engage the stakeholders on their own terms. Especially in culturally diverse settings, be attentive to the appropriateness of the location of meetings, cultural assumptions about how decisions ought to be made, and how current issues are perceived through the lenses of past history. Also, remember that different stakeholders have a wide range of skills, knowledge, and capabilities. Make sure to provide the appropriate technical information (written in accessible terms), relevant training, and other resources that will help stakeholders work as equal partners. Finally, when new stakeholders emerge, work with previously identified stakeholders as well as the newcomers to jointly establish a path for moving forward.

Spread Ownership of the Process

At a proper dinner party, as Martha Stewart could attest, the guests should have as little responsibility as possible for planning, setting up, and taking care of the resulting mess; these are the jobs of a good host or hostess. In collaborative decision making, the opposite is true.

The perception of who "owns" a decision-making process and the results it produces will emerge from each and every communication and the way day-to-day activities are managed. All too often, institutions and governmental entities with significant levels of authority and power believe it is their right to dictate how the work of the group should proceed. The implicit message that other stakeholders often take away is that their views about participation do not count. Furthermore, these stakeholders often perceive that the process belongs to the initiator or convenor, not to them. Addressing questions of ownership can be critical to developing a solid commitment that will lead to implementation.

The importance of spreading ownership among stakeholders is well documented in the case of Chattanooga, Tennessee's Vision 2000 initiative (Case 11). In Chattanooga, an important source of early financial support for the community's work was provided by the local Lyndhurst Foundation. However, one of the foundation's concerns was that the visioning process be owned by the community. Rather than specifying funding details or issuing elaborate operating guidelines, Lyndhurst provided the majority of the operating budget for Chattanooga Venture, a diverse board of 60 people drawn from all over the city, to use in catalyzing the visioning process.

From the very beginning of the Vision 2000 initiative, groups and organizations from all sectors of the community shared responsibility for the design of the process. It should be no surprise that the resulting broad-based ownership of the final vision translated directly into a successfully implemented action plan. One evaluation of the Vision 2000 initiative found that the process created almost $800 million in new investments (or $2,778 per county resident), 223 new projects and programs, 1,381 new permanent jobs, and more than 7,300 temporary construction jobs (U.S. Department of Housing and Urban Development, 1993).

Several actions can be taken to create an atmosphere of joint ownership, encouraging all stakeholders to play a vital role in all stages of a collaborative process. First, include participants in the initial stages of process design. Remember, ownership of the process leads to ownership of the results. Many manuals on process design counsel that an important first step of consensus building is the creation of a small initiating committee of stakeholder representatives to work with all participants on issues of process design that can nurture ownership (Godschalk, Parham, Porter, Potapchuk, & Schukraft, 1994; National Civic League, 1997). Second, distribute the responsibility for managing the process among the stakeholders. If one organization provides most of the funding, look for "in kind" contributions from others to show support (and therefore ownership). Even largely symbolic moves, such as developing a letterhead listing all participating stakeholder groups (much as a board of directors is often listed on organizational letterhead), can contribute to a sense of shared ownership.

Understand the External Environment

There are several important rules for making sure consensus building efforts do not run afoul of forces at work in the larger political setting.[1] As any successful facilitator or policymaker can confirm, the first step is to identify potential political "land mines." These can include everything from internecine disputes among departments that make collaboration difficult to "turf" issues that divide stakeholders. In communities, classical political land mines often involve past events that still divide residents or create resistance to even talking with the opposing "side." In some instances, these may be issues or events that fall outside of the problem areas and stakeholders directly engaged by the process.

As part of a conflict assessment, the mediator or facilitator may want to interview stakeholders who are knowledgeable about the political terrain. (See Chapter 2 for details on conducting an assessment.) If the subject of the process is inherently "political," the neutral may want to encourage stakeholders to build in a discussion of political considerations as an early agenda item. These discussions are often most successful when they are conducted as a *force-field analysis,* in which participants seek to understand the forces for change and those opposed to change. Participants may also "map" the decision-making process, understanding the roles of key committees and caucuses. Analysis that focuses on each stakeholder's expression of is or her favorite (or least favorite) legislator can create more conflict and hard feelings.

A second suggestion is to engage officials from the outset. This does not necessarily mean directly inviting them to the table, although that might be appropriate in certain situations. Rather, it helps to build a constituency among elected officials, top-level management, and others for any agreement that emerges. Just as important, a diverse group of stakeholders committed to a consensus building process can form a powerful constituency that ensures their implementation plan stays on the political "map" in spite of changes that occur in political leadership.

Changes in the broader political environment can have significant effects on implementation. In Loudon County, Virginia, a set of stakeholders learned this lesson the hard way. Loudon, a fast-growing county that is home to Dulles Airport and a beautiful rural landscape, used an intensive, yearlong consensus building effort to prepare a new zoning ordinance. (The process was facilitated by the lead author of this chapter.) Prompt implementation hopes disappeared as, in rapid succession, the county administrator was fired, the assistant county administrator for development left, the planning director resigned, and seven of the eight members of the board of supervisors were defeated at the polls. (These changes were unrelated to the consensus-based process.) Several individuals from the consensus building group, in partnership with staff, persevered, leading to the adoption by the planning commission and board of supervisors of the consensus-based document two years later. However, many other agreements are not able to move forward when there are dramatic changes like these in the political environment.

Several strategies can be used to address such challenges. The best strategy is to schedule the consensus building effort so that it does not overlap with major elections. When that is not possible,

- engage incumbents and their opponents (through briefings, at a minimum, and in some circumstances by seeking commitments to support the consensus building process);
- engage key publics or constituent groups in building a broad-based political support for an agreement that can withstand changes in political leadership; and
- slow the process down during electoral season and then adjust it, as necessary, based on the results.

A second challenge is alignment. Often consensus-based processes cut across multiple policy arenas. In these instances, implementation can be stymied by related decisions of other policy-making bodies; they can also be disrupted by conflicts that spill over from other arenas.

Decision-making forums are *aligned* when their processes and results are coordinated, working to support and strengthen each other. For example, the past decade has seen a groundswell of human services "systems reform" initiatives (at all levels of government) that seek to promote interagency collaboration through pooled funding streams, staff "teams" drawn from different organizations, and greater community involvement in shaping policy (Schorr, 1989, 1997). In practice, this can be extremely difficult to achieve. Often decisions or actions made in different policy arenas are simply unconnected. As in the following example, agreements may call for actions, and at the same time, the parties may not have the authority or capacity to ensure compliance.

The difficulties that beset the implementation of the San Francisco Estuary Project (Case 5) demonstrate the problem of alignment quite nicely. In that situation, a large number of stakeholders were also engaged in three other multistakeholder policy dialogues to negotiate water policy at the regional and state levels. Furthermore, one of the key strategies—developing zoning tools to protect streams and wetlands that are part of the San Francisco Estuary—required action by 111 local governments in the 12-county region. Of the 111 jurisdictions, only 18 had existing provisions that addressed these issues. The consensus recommendations of the land use work group were adopted unanimously by the San Francisco Estuary Project's management committee (unlike other recommendations), but the structure of existing institutions blocked further action. Despite the clarity of the agreement, the stakeholders did not have an institutional or legal strategy worked out to ensure that all 111 municipalities amended their zoning ordinances to reflect the new agreement. While there were notable moves toward multijurisdictional cooperation, including the organization of educational activities by the Association of Bay Area Governments and the creation of an implementation committee to drive priority implementation projects, the sad fact is that many of those 111 jurisdictions did not put plans in place that reflected the consensus agreement. Many at the table were strongly opposed to creating a new regional regulatory framework or empowering an existing regional entity to take responsibility for implementation.

Sometimes, political decisions in other policy arenas can disrupt implementation. In 1991, the Atlanta Regional Commission and a core group of leaders convened a 10-county regional visioning process, Atlanta 2020. During the deliberations, the commission approved a controversial limited-access highway around Atlanta, angering many stakeholders who felt they were not adequately consulted about the decision. As a result, the credibility of the visioning process was damaged, eventually leading to an action plan that lacked the necessary support for implementation (Helling, 1998). Attempts at meaningful participation on one issue can be undermined when politics as usual is the dominant practice in other, related policy arenas. Often, leaders can be coached to recognize this phenomenon, but sometimes they can learn it only via the "school of hard knocks."

■ *A Menu for Success: At the Table*

The implementation of consensus-based agreements often hinges on whether stakeholders can translate their new shared commitments back into the work of their "everyday" organizations. Success in this regard depends on developing strategies when stakeholders are at the table that create durable agreements that can withstand challenges to implementation.

Many mediators believe that the relationships created among stakeholders can provide a lasting foundation of trust that undergirds implementation. While many accept such statements as intuitively true, a more complete analysis is essential to understand why relational dynamics really work. A variety of scholars and practitioners, building on the concept of social capital, have begun to delineate the different types of "capital" that can be created by public processes (Podziba, 1998; Potapchuk, 1996; Potapchuk, Crocker, Boogard, & Schechter, 1998). Gruber and Innes's work, which is among the most compelling, describes the interaction between *intellectual capital* (group understanding), *social capital* (relationships), and *political capital* (clout) (Gruber, 1994; Innes, Gruber, Neuman, & Thompson, 1994).

The underlying logic is that for an agreement to be durable and implementable, stakeholders must develop a deep and shared understanding of the situation, build new relationships characterized by trust and reciprocity, and generate sufficient commitment from individuals and institutions. If these conditions are met, resulting agreements will not only reflect the collective interests of the group but also be able to withstand challenges to implementation that may arise. Therefore, a strategy that "capitalizes" the process helps to establish a foundation for implementation.

Building Intellectual Capital

Clear and regular communication between representatives involved in deliberations and their constituents, conducted in a way that promotes shared understanding, is a primary element of most consensus building processes. Failure to build that understanding can cause problems ranging from misperceptions of the consensus building process to outright conflict that can hamper implementation. Building effective networks of communication that contribute to the development of intellectual capital is critical for two reasons. First, the constant conversation among participants promotes continued learning about each other and the issues under discussion. Second, conversation is a core component of building social capital, as discussed below.

The need for joint learning in successful consensus building has been noted by many authors (Dukes, 1996; Lederach, 1995; Senge, 1990). They also point to the role that fresh information plays in producing shared understandings. If new data are used solely to buttress already held positions, it suggests that a consensus building effort has not yet built sufficient intellectual capital to move forward collectively. Yankelovich (1991) uses related terminology; he suggests that one can recognize the qualitative shift in discourse as participants move from *opinion* to *judgment*. Opinion, he asserts, is a snapshot of what a person is thinking at a particular point in time. Judgment only emerges after deliberation, when one's ideas and assumptions have been tested and reexamined.

Strategies designed to promote shared understanding may only be effective if they reach beyond those at the table to foster dialogue among all those whose views differ. For example, there is always a danger that support among immediate representatives for an agreement will not translate into support among their constituencies. In other words, the intellectual capital created among the representatives at the table does not always translate well for those not directly involved. Often, the communication within a core group of representatives is not replicated in the broader circle of stakeholders. Presented with a final agreement for their approval, the larger constituency may criticize or reject the agreement, because they did not develop the deeper understanding that those at the table were able to attain. (See Chapter 6, on representation, for more on this problem.)

Sometimes the challenge is rooted in the way individuals express themselves. A problem with communication among stakeholders was one characteristic highlighted in the San Francisco Estuary Project process. In that case, a working group of scientists and policymakers found they rarely spoke the same language or shared similar assumptions about environmental and political issues. This kind of miscommunication can confound the strong agreement necessary to ensure action. In these situations, facilitators or other process managers may be needed to "translate" among different groups of stakeholders. In some instances, it may be advisable to engage outside experts to educate stakeholders on technical issues. Another approach is to identify "boundary crossers" in each group who can do the translating. These tend to be individuals with professional identities that straddle different "worlds," such as a forester working for a logging company who also used to be an employee of the state Department of Environmental Quality and can therefore "speak the language" of all the different stakeholder groups.

Managing Uncertainty

Often what separates stakeholders is not disagreement about what they know to be true, but divisiveness over what is not knowable. Both agreement and subsequent implementation often depend on the way in which uncertainty will be handled. Implementable agreements often specify ways of managing uncertainty to build support. For example, in a mediated agreement over a proposal to build a new mall, residents were deeply concerned that the construction of the mall would lower their property values. The developer was insistent that the presence of the mall (and a very upscale anchor store) would actually increase property values. Together, the stakeholders crafted an index of housing values for the surrounding areas. The developer then bought an insurance policy to reimburse homeowners who, if they sold their homes, might not realize the same appreciation in housing values seen in the surrounding areas. In this case, the insurance policy was never needed (Rivkin, 1987).

Similarly, people often hold differing views on likely patterns of development. In a conflict over a proposed road in Hampton, Virginia, citizen opponents were sure that the new road would attract still more traffic. While public officials did not totally disagree with this logic, they sought to identify a right-of-way for the road in case it were needed and to purchase it now rather than wait and be forced to buy the right-of-way at a higher price. Both sides agreed that they did not want to increase traffic on existing roads. The stakeholders finally agreed to add the road to the long-range plan, have the city establish the right-of-way, and purchase the property. They were able to address their differing views of the future by agreeing to maintain the right-of-way as a park until the traffic on the nearest arteries exceeded an agreed-on level. In this way, the road would follow development, not the other way around. The road has now been built (Plotz, 1991). In both situations, a deeper understanding of what cannot be known was used to shape an implementable agreement that sought to manage the uncertainty.

The specifics of what makes for a good agreement will vary depending on the issues and forum. What doesn't change is the need to help stakeholders gain a deeper understanding of each other's perspectives, interests, and the type of relationships necessary to sustain a consensus agreement on controversial issues. These efforts to build intellectual capital must start from the beginning of a process with a solid process design and extend past immediate implementation throughout the life of an agreement.

Building Social Capital

Much as a robust understanding needs to be nurtured among stakeholders, so, too, does the need to build strong working relationships. Harvard political scientist Robert Putnam has revolutionized our thinking about the importance of constructive social relationships in building agreements. Drawing from his 20-year study in Italy that analyzed centuries-old civic traditions

(1993a), Putnam expanded the notion of social capital, a term first used regularly by conflict theorist James Coleman (1957, 1990). Putnam (1993a) notes:

> "Social capital" refers to features of social organization, such as networks, norms, and trust, that facilitate coordination and cooperation for mutual benefit. . . . First, networks of civic engagement foster sturdy norms of generalized reciprocity: I'll do this for you now, in the expectation that down the road you or someone else will return the favor. . . . Networks of civic engagement also facilitate coordination and communication and amplify information about the trustworthiness of other individuals. . . . Finally, networks of civic engagement embody past success at collaboration, which can serve as a cultural template for future collaboration. (p. 36)

Building healthy stores of social capital among stakeholders is intimately connected to the successful implementation of consensus-based agreements. Perhaps the best example of this is the idea of the *negotiated investment strategy* (NIS). Conceived by the Kettering Foundation, the NIS was piloted in the late 1970s under the Carter administration to help cities convene stakeholders from the federal, state, and local levels to jointly negotiate strategies for city development. Each level of government organized a negotiating team, often including a fourth team of representatives from the private sector. These teams worked to build a robust picture of the needs and interests of all the stakeholders, and then met collectively to work out a strategy for city development that was mutually satisfactory. While the agreements were well conceived and in some cases pathbreaking frameworks for maximizing the use of federal, state, and local resources, the agreements failed to contemplate one crucial scenario: the election of Ronald Reagan as president. When he took office, nearly all of the funds the federal government had committed were no longer available.

Nonetheless, in each of the four cities where the NIS was piloted, there was virtually a 100 percent success rate in implementing the resulting agreements. Indeed, the NIS is often called one of the most successful experiments of its kind (Moore & Carlson, 1984). In evaluations conducted several years afterward, the original participants identified several factors that led to the positive results. The most-cited reason was that the NIS very consciously focused on building relationships among stakeholders who rarely sat down together, even when the decisions they had to make had significant impacts on each other. It was those relationships that accounted for successful implementation (Crocker, DuPraw, Kunde, & Potapchuk, 1996; Henton, 1981).

There is no single recipe for building the kind of social capital that leads to strong relationships among stakeholders. Techniques used in one community or organizational setting may fail in another for a host of reasons, including the history of past disputes, cultural barriers, the capacity of the stakeholders, and the lack of sufficient resources. In many cases, this kind of work calls for strong intervention by a facilitator or mediator. If, for example, there is little formal contact between environmentalists and the business community, it may be appropriate to structure a meeting between those stakeholders designed to increase understanding—before any substantive negotiating takes place. Indeed, the role of relationship building in addressing deeply rooted conflicts is amplified in international dispute resolution where a mode of practice has emerged to address this task (Fisher, 1997; Lederach, 1995).

Underpinning this analysis is an important lesson. When there is little need for an ongoing relationship and agreements can be easily implemented (e.g., by writing a check), one may need to attend to just enough relationship building to reach agreement. Should the parties have an ongoing relationship or the resultant agreement be expected to face a lengthy implementation process or multiple challenges, building strong working relationships and sufficient stores of social capital is likely to be essential to success.

Working in the Absence of Social Capital

In some settings, the history of mistrust, poisoned relationships, and deep differences is unlikely to be overcome through a single consensus building process. Strategies that rely on the development of social capital to undergird implementation are unlikely to be successful in these situations.

The most common approach when these challenges arise is to structure an agreement that specifically proscribes the desired actions of each party, often establishing incentives for compliance and penalties for noncompliance. In this type of agreement, nothing is left to chance. Each step should be described in detail, time lines should be clear, and responsibilities identified. Furthermore, these types of agreements often need a monitoring component as a further means of ensuring compliance.

Building Political Capital

"Who has the 'juice' ?" is among the first questions asked by seasoned negotiators. They want to know who can make things happen. Those who have the "juice" are often people who hold positions of authority and have substantial talent for "working the system." Many times these are individuals who have budgetary authority as well.

When such individuals are absent from a consensus building process, often the first step is to figure out how to get them to the table. Failing that, some will call off the effort, believing that nothing can be achieved. In understanding political capital, it is important to recognize that while in some cases it is essential to have a key individual involved, in many cases the political equation should be understood as $1 + 1 + 1 = 7$. This recognizes that while one person, say, a cabinet secretary, may be critical to committing an agency to act, consensus building often requires several entities to act together. Furthermore, the titular heads of those agencies may not have the time to commit to an intensive process. So, if three department heads, several steps removed from their respective secretaries, are able to craft an agreement, their combined voice is likely to be more powerful than any cabinet secretary alone.

In assessing political capital, it is important to consider passion and commitment as well. Busy decision makers often move from one meeting to another, with little time to prepare or to follow up unless the topic is a priority issue for them. Finding political capital is sometimes a matter of tapping into the passionate commitments of a key player. Without that energy, implementation will not have the support needed to withstand challenges.

Working in the Absence of Political Capital

While a theoretical argument can be made that all types of capital are equal, in practice political capital may be the most important. The absence of political capital often suggests that key stakeholders are missing from the process, which will make it difficult, if not impossible, to move forward.

Two approaches that diverge from this rule of thumb are important to note. First, as in the arena of international conflict resolution where a multitrack approach is a dominant framework, and intense, off-the-record workshops are used to build relationships and reduce misperceptions, there is an increasing use of these types of interventions in domestic policy issues. These approaches are not designed to generate agreements, but, rather, in some circumstances, to lay the groundwork for follow-on agreement-focused activities.

Second, some collaborative approaches recognize that political leadership will not move on an issue unless there is clear expression of public will. It may be necessary to mobilize and engage the general public in ways that sway the actions of leaders (Chrislip & Larson, 1994). For example, in Chattanooga's successful visioning effort, political leaders were neutral, at best, toward the process. In many cases, this lack of enthusiasm among key leaders would be the kiss of death for a process. The citizens involved in the many public forums in Chattanooga, through their numbers, enthusiasm, and commitment, ultimately swayed their political leaders into action, defying political wisdom. If the support of key public leaders cannot be gained, an agreement has little chance of being successfully implemented.

■ When the Music's Over: Closing the Deal

"Groups should strive to prepare documents that spell out exactly who has to do what (by when) to ensure implementation."

Significant stores of social, political, and intellectual capital are not a substitute for a well-crafted written agreement. Groups should always strive to prepare documents that not only specify the commitments that participants are making to each other but also spell out exactly who has to do what (by when) to ensure implementation. In some settings, this step will be relatively straightforward, while in others it will require fairly elaborate schedules of contingent actions (and the triggers or findings that will activate them).

In some cases, an agreement may be a prelude to still another process that can begin only when the first round of commitments is completed. For example, stakeholders in a policy dialogue that produced draft legislation may find that key legislators do not support core elements of the bill they have proposed. It is easy to imagine that stakeholders—having spent countless meetings fine-tuning and wordsmithing draft legislation—would be deflated and allow the bill to sink, because they had presumed their work would be recognized and passage would be ensured. If, on the other hand, the stakeholders had focused sufficient attention on implementation earlier in the process, they would have developed a shared understanding of the politics of the legislature, made decisions about how the bill ought to be sponsored, determined who should brief members of the legislature, and identified the events that would cause them to reconvene and renegotiate the substance of the bill. Recognizing a lack of support as an event that would cause them to reconvene, stakeholders then might find a means of bringing key legislators into their camp.

In thinking about implementation, participants must carefully consider the context in which they are negotiating. For instance, the best solution is of little value if no one can afford it. Some have described the role of the facilitator or mediator as the "agent of reality."[2] The agent-of-reality role should not put a damper on the enthusiasm of the participants, but should help the parties understand that the "process high" that occurs at the end of some consensus building efforts may lead to agreements that are fully acceptable to the stakeholders, but not implementable. A typical factor in this scenario is capacity. A neighborhood redevelopment strategy that requires a local community development corporation (which currently has a director and a part-time secretary) to rehabilitate 50 residential units in the next 18 months probably exceeds the capacity of that entity. Seriously contemplating the capacity of organizations that will have responsibility for implementing the agreement will preserve the credibility of those organizations over time.

To address this issue, stakeholders might develop best-case, typical, and worst-case scenarios that help them consider a wide array of contingent commitments. As they engage in this analysis, stakeholders may find that a key element of an implementation strategy is best memorialized as an informal understanding with an elected official. For example, a key legislator might be willing to lend behind-the-scenes support to an environmental initiative, even if it is opposed by industrial interests in her district, but would definitely not want this noted in a written agreement.

All negotiating groups should develop implementation strategies in the course of developing and finalizing agreements. Implementation strategies should consider the following.

- Whether new stakeholders are created through the tentative agreement who will need to be involved in implementation
- What formal approvals (e.g., a vote by the city council, a review by the general counsel's office) are needed, and how they will be obtained
- How to approach stakeholders not at the table, including constituents of those who are participating, to develop broad-based support for an agreement
- How to approach the general public and how a public education or media strategy can be used to reach the public
- What resources (e.g., financial, staffing, or otherwise) are needed to support implementation and how they will be obtained
- Whether there will be a series of ongoing decisions that require the participation of multiple stakeholders and, if so, how they will be made
- Potential changes in leadership at implementing entities and how these ought to be addressed
- What events can trigger renegotiation

Once the stakeholders have developed an implementation strategy, they should then be poised to finalize the product of their consensus building efforts. The written agreement should be fully understood by all of the stakeholders. In addition to spelling out the commitments of all relevant parties, a written product can include

a description of the process by which the agreement was reached;
a list of the people (and their affiliations) who participated;
a discussion of the implementation strategy;
detailed description of the commitments that have been made;

a summary of the deliberations, especially on the
   "tough" issues;
an explanation of the choices made by the stakeholders;
an executive summary; and
a place for all of the stakeholders to sign.

As the written agreement is finalized, it is important to explore whether there are rituals or special events that can build support for implementation. For example, public signing ceremonies can add visibility and make it more difficult for participants to back away later. Proclamations by a chief elected official can recognize an informal agreement (and implicitly suggest how the power and authority of that official could be used to enforce implementation). Community-based processes often include a celebration, thanking the participants who helped and acknowledging the importance of collaborative processes.

■ After the Party's Over: Moving Forward

Consensus building efforts require a handcrafted implementation strategy, responsive to the agreement and the context. Implementation, then, should follow the path laid out by the participants at the table. Because challenges may arise in implementation regardless of the situation, however, consensus building participants may want to consider the following common implementation procedures.

Referenda

Changes in political leadership can dramatically affect the implementation of an agreement. In Santa Barbara, California, where growth management was a highly contentious issue, pro-growth city councils alternated with antigrowth city councils. Attempts to address this important policy issue were stymied by the constant fluctuations in leadership. In a highly participatory, consensus-oriented update of its comprehensive plan, this community chose to dramatically limit growth, reducing the number of "buildable square feet" by a factor of 10. Concerned that the plan could be overturned by a new city council, the process managers proposed an advisory referendum, which won more than 60 percent of the vote. This expression of political will by the electorate gave the plan the stability it needed (Plotz, 1991).

Implementation Work Groups

> "New work groups may be needed to monitor implementation of the agreement and address any challenges."

As an agreement moves forward, new work groups may be needed to monitor implementation of the agreement and address any challenges that may arise. Such work groups should include representatives who are concerned about the operational side of things. Initially used in siting disputes where neighbors to a newly sited facility needed to work collaboratively with construction managers (Keystone Center, 1985), this approach is now used in a wide range of settings (U.S. Army Corps of Engineers, 1996).

Partnering

Pioneered by the U.S. Army Corps of Engineers for managing large-scale construction projects, partnering is a formal process in which the implementing organizations and monitors seek to build a partnership at the beginning of implementation and meet periodically to work on unforeseen issues and iron out differences. Partnering methodologies have been successfully applied in a wide range of settings (U.S. Army Corps of Engineers, 1996).

Building Partnerships and Governing Entities to Manage Implementation

Sometimes, the existing organizational infrastructure is inadequate to respond to implementation challenges. Furthermore, in many settings, the resources of numerous organizations must be brought to bear on the challenge. This recognition has spurred the creation of new entities whose primary role is to manage implementation, particularly the ongoing stream of decisions and policy issues that require joint attention. Commonly seen in the human services arena (Center for the Study of Social Policy, 1997; Schorr, 1997), these entities are increasingly being used in other arenas. For example, the Quincy Library Group in northern California and the Applegate Partnership in Oregon are both community collaboratives, each of which brings together a diverse set of organizations to work at the intersection of economic and environmental issues.

■ Conclusion

The skills and strategies needed to ensure implementation are much like those needed to guarantee success with other elements of the consensus building process. Attention to detail (e.g., Who can call this legislator by Friday?) is as important as being able to design a new organization. Furthermore, successful implementation rests not only in having a well-crafted agreement but also in nurturing the passion and commitment of the stakeholders to "make the deal stick."

■ Notes

1. Many of the legal questions relating to implementation are addressed in Chapter 13.

2. First credited to Wallace Warfield, of the Institute for Conflict Analysis and Resolution, George Mason University.

■ References

Bunker, B., & Alban, B. T. (Eds.). (1997). *Large group interventions: Engaging the whole system for rapid change.* San Francisco: Jossey-Bass.

Burton, J. W. (1990). *Human needs theory.* London: St. Martin's.

Center for the Study of Social Policy. (1997). *Creating a community agenda: How governance partnerships can improve results for children, youth, and families.* Washington, DC: Author.

Chrislip, D. D., & Larson, C. E. (1994). *Collaborative leadership: How citizens and civic leaders can make a difference.* San Francisco: Jossey-Bass.

Coleman, J. S. (1957). *Community conflict.* New York: Free Press.

Coleman, J. S. (1990). *Foundations of social theory.* Cambridge, MA: Belknap Press of Harvard University Press.

Crocker, J., DuPraw, M., Kunde, J., & Potapchuk, W. (1996). *Approaches to environmental decision making: An exploration of lessons learned.* Washington, DC: Program for Community Problem Solving.

Dukes, E. F. (1996). *Resolving public conflict: Transforming community and governance.* New York: St. Martin's.

Emery, M., & Purser, R. E. (1996). *The search conference.* San Francisco: Jossey-Bass.

Fisher, R. J. (1997). *Interactive conflict resolution.* Syracuse, NY: Syracuse University Press.

Godschalk, D. R., Parham, D. W., Porter, D. R., Potapchuk, W. R., & Schukraft, S. W. (1994). *Pulling together: A planning and development consensus building manual.* Washington, DC: Urban Land Institute, Program for Community Problem Solving.

Gruber, J. (1994). *Coordinating growth management through consensus-building: Incentives and the generation of social, intellectual, and political capital.* Berkeley: University of California at Berkeley, Institute for Urban and Regional Development.

Helling, A. (1998). Collaborative visioning: Proceed with caution. *Journal of the American Planning Association, 64,* 335-349.

Henton, D. (1981). *Rethinking urban governance: An assessment of the negotiated investment strategy.* Menlo Park, CA: SRI International.

Innes, J. E., Gruber, J., Neuman, M., & Thompson, R. (1994). *Coordinating growth and environmental management through consensus building.* CPS report: A policy research program report. Berkeley: California Policy Seminar, University of California, Berkeley.

John, D. (1994). *Civic environmentalism: Alternatives to regulation in states and communities.* Washington, DC: Congressional Quarterly Press.

Keystone Center. (1985). *Keystone siting process training manual.* Austin: League of Women Voters of Texas Education Fund.

Lederach, J. P. (1995). *Building peace: Sustainable reconciliation in divided societies.* Tokyo: United Nations University.

Moore, C., & Carlson, C. (1984). *Public decision making: Using the negotiated investment strategy* [Unpublished pamphlet]. Dayton, OH: Kettering Foundation.

National Civic League. (1997). *The community visioning and strategic planning handbook.* Denver, CO: Author.

Plotz, D. A. (1991). *Community problem solving case summaries* (Vol. 3). Washington, DC: Program for Community Problem Solving.

Podziba, S. (1998). *Social capital formation, public building, and public mediation: The Chelsea charter consensus process.* Dayton, OH: Kettering Foundation.

Potapchuk, W. R. (1996). Building sustainable community politics: Synergizing participatory, institutional, and representative democracy. *National Civic Review, 85,* 54-59.

Potapchuk, W. R., Crocker, J. P., Boogard, D., & Schechter, W. (1998). *Building community: Exploring the role of social capital and local government.* Washington, DC: Program for Community Problem Solving.

Putnam, R. D. (1993a). *Making democracy work: Civic traditions in modern Italy.* Princeton, NJ: Princeton University Press.

Putnam, R. D. (1993b). The prosperous community: Social capital and public life. *The American Prospect, 13,* 35-42.

Rivkin, M. (1987). *A review paper on the accommodation of diverse views in the public works improvement process.* Washington, DC: National Council on Public Works Improvement.

Schorr, L. B. (1989). *Within our reach: Breaking the cycle of disadvantage.* New York: Anchor.

Schorr, L. B. (1997). *Common purposes: Strengthening families and neighborhoods to rebuild America.* New York: Doubleday.

Senge, P. (1990). *The fifth discipline: The art and practice of the learning organization.* New York: Doubleday.

Sipe, N. G. (1998). An empirical analysis of environmental mediation. *Journal of the American Planning Association, 64,* 275-285.

Susskind, L., & Cruikshank, J. (1987). *Breaking the impasse: Consensual approaches to resolving public disputes.* New York: Basic Books.

U.S. Army Corps of Engineers. (1996). *Partnering guide for environmental missions of Air Force, Army, and Navy.* Fort Belvoir, VA: U.S. Army Corps of Engineers Institute for Water Resources.

U.S. Department of Housing and Urban Development. (1993). *Vision/reality: Strategies for community change.* Washington, DC: Author.

Weisbord, M. R., & Janoff, S. (1995). *Future search: An action guide to finding common ground in organizations and communities.* San Francisco: Berrett-Koehler.

Westley, F. (1995). Governing design: The management of social systems and ecosystems management. In L. H. Gunderson, C. S. Holling, & S. S. Light (Eds.), *Barriers and bridges to the renewal of ecosystems and institutions.* New York: Columbia University Press.

Yankelovich, D. (1991). *Coming to public judgment: Making democracy work in a complex world.* Syracuse, NY: Syracuse University Press.

CHAPTER

15

VISIONING

■ *Carl M. Moore*
■ *Gianni Longo*
■ *Patsy Palmer*

In the early 1980s, Chattanooga, Tennessee faced economic, social, and environmental problems that had been brewing for a long time. Early industrial growth had brought dozens of major industries to this small city, including the Tennessee Valley Authority, and with them the promise of economic well-being. But by the early 1960s, that promise remained unrealized. While the population of other Southern cities boomed, Chattanooga's slowed to a crawl. The city had few professional jobs to offer; most of the workforce was concentrated in the manufacturing sector. Meanwhile, years of industrial activity began to take its toll. In 1969, according to the U.S. Environmental Protection Agency (EPA), Chattanooga had the worst air quality of any urban area in the United States. By the 1970s, race relations between African American and white residents were strained to the point where violence was not uncommon. And in the late 1970s, a recession hit hard, as offshore production siphoned off a key source of economic activity (Case 11).

In the face of these diverse problems, many Chattanoogans felt that something needed to be done. But they were also pessimistic that anything would ever change. According to Dalton Roberts, a county executive in that era, "There was no leadership coming together to look at all of our problems and say, 'What are we going to do?' " (Cooper & Macksoud, 1993). No one thought that politicians could be trusted with the task of defining a new vision for Chattanooga's future.

The dilemma confronting Chattanoogans is not uncommon in American cities. Public policy consultant Barbara Rusmore (1998) helps to explain why. She theorizes that Americans live with

> a political system that discourages the kind of dialogue that might lead to a constructive vision. Our political process can seldom even arbitrate disputes. Instead, it creates disputes, separates people who might actually have something to gain from listening and working together, and fosters incremental, short-run action based on compromises between narrow interest groups. (p. 17)

In Chattanooga, a handful of local officials, business executives, and civic leaders sought to take action outside the political process. They joined forces to create a nonprofit organization called Chattanooga Venture, to "put the city on a successful track for the turn of the century."[1] The organization's first initiative was Vision 2000, which involved a new and, at the time, untested process called *visioning*. Ten years later, the organization sponsored another visioning effort, called ReVision 2000.

Visioning is a process in which people build consensus on a description of their preferred future—the set of conditions they want to see realized over time. Chattanooga conducted a broad and inclusive *community-wide* visioning process. (Visioning can also be used to develop a vision for a single organization, and to help an organization or community find a way to solve a specific, narrowly defined problem.) In a community-wide visioning process, a diverse cross section of residents work together to define the key issues facing a community and develop shared goals for addressing those issues. These goals can guide a community in developing new projects and programs in areas such as economic development, transportation, education, culture, the environment, recreation, race relations, social services, and so forth. Participants in visioning processes typically also draft recommendations describing how these goals should be achieved.

Nearly 15 years after Chattanooga's first visioning effort and five years after its second, the city continues to be one of the South's major industrial centers, but many of the problems that accompanied industrial development have been put to rest. The city has become a popular tourist destination and a retail and distribution center. The numerous projects spawned by the visioning effort have helped to revitalize the downtown area, clean up the environment, improve recreational opportunities, and provide needed human services. The projects have included, among others, a fleet of electric buses, an aquarium, the Tennessee RiverPark, a family violence shelter, and an organization that promotes the construction of affordable housing.

Delegations from cities across the nation travel to Chattanooga each year to see the "miracle" for themselves and to ask, "If they did it here, can we do it at home?" Indeed, Chattanooga's vision was so successful that many communities think the city had something special up its sleeve—more money, greater resources, better luck. *Governing Magazine* recently asserted that "visioning fever" is "a highly contagious bug that has been sweeping civic America in the late 1990s," in part because it has worked so spectacularly well in Chattanooga (Walters, 1998).

Is Chattanooga an exception, or do the elements for success reside in every town, city, or region where people are dissatisfied with the status quo? In this chapter, we explain how communities and organizations of all types can use visioning to imagine (and then work to create) their desired futures.

This chapter focuses on community-wide visioning, a process that can be applied in communities with anywhere from 50 to hundreds of thousands of residents. The chapter begins with an overview of the benefits and pitfalls of this kind of visioning. It also describes the preconditions for launching a successful process. The chapter then presents the key phases of a typical visioning effort. To illustrate how each phase works, we go behind the scenes of Chattanooga's second visioning process, ReVision 2000. (The first two authors of this chapter assisted in designing, facilitating, and training local facilitators for the ReVision 2000 process.) The chapter also explores how other communities with different histories, problems, and resources have used a Chattanooga-like approach. The chapter concludes with a description of alternative approaches to visioning, including a brief mention of how organizations can use visioning internally in the process of developing strategic plans.

■ The Benefits and Pitfalls of Visioning

In the past few decades, citizen participation in the political process has clearly declined. Decisions affecting communities are now made mostly by politicians and policymakers who respond more to expert advisers and special interests than to citizens, who have few channels for communicating their concerns and preferences. And it is not just politicians' fault. Members of the public, in many cases, have ignored their responsibilities as citizens. Assuming they have little influence anyway, they no longer search for ways to affect public decision making. Ironically, representative democracy may have dulled citizenship.

Even when government officials do try to solicit citizens' views and ideas (sometimes due to legal requirements for participation, sometimes because they think they can improve decisions in this way), they typically use an approach that fails to tap the public's knowledge and creativity. Agency officials, for example, often make preliminary decisions after consulting experts and weighing options. Then, they hold a public hearing and ask, "How do you like this solution?" This approach limits citizen influence to a thumbs up or thumbs down response to a nearly finished product.

"Rather than being asked, 'Do you like this decision?' citizens in a visioning process are asked, 'What do you want?'"

Visioning is an entirely different approach. Rather than being asked, "Do you like this decision?" citizens in a visioning process are asked, "What do you want?" Rather than sitting anonymously in a crowded auditorium at a public hearing, they are invited to join small-group discussions alongside their neighbors. And rather than being asked for their input near the end of a process, they are asked to contribute ideas at the beginning, before experts and policymakers narrow the range of options.

Visioning reinvigorates citizenship in the communities where it is used. Through a series of well-managed, facilitated meetings, individual citizens—a school principal, a small-business owner, a bank teller, a stay-at-home mom—come together to consider what their community should look like in the future. Those who participate in such dialogues often end up at the forefront of efforts to realize those goals through projects of various kinds.

In addition to mobilizing citizen participation, visioning processes give direction to public and private leaders. In the Chattanooga process, local elected officials and other public and private sector leaders were not "the engine of the train." Rather, they rode in the caboose, waiting to see where the public would take them. Once a new vision had been defined for the city, they were able to jump out in front and resume leading; at that point, they knew where the public wanted to go.

Visioning also provides a catalyst to leadership among what is now called "civil society." Most communities have plenty of talented people with good ideas, but what these people lack is "permission" to move forward—a broad-based consensus on the direction change should take. Community-wide visioning creates this permission, because it is shaped by the whole community. It also provides an impetus for actions by individuals that can help realize shared goals.

Finally, by promoting dialogue across traditional barriers, visioning paves the way for future cooperation and collaboration among a community's diverse stakeholders. Businesspeople find themselves defining a community's key problems and opportunities alongside the staff of grassroots environmental organizations, Republicans sit down with Democrats, and community philanthropists hear the views of low-income parents. When visioning is done well, participants learn about each other and about a process they can use to make collaborative decisions in other settings as well.

While visioning has many benefits, it can also have pitfalls. A successful community-wide process that engages the public and produces a useful document will create expectations that the public will be consulted in the same manner in the future. In addition, the vision itself raises the expectation that certain actions will be taken. If a vision remains mere words on a page, citizen skepticism about the value of public participation will only increase.

■ The Preconditions for Community-Wide Visioning

A community is ready for a visioning process when (1) many different groups are dissatisfied with the status quo; (2) there is an emerging sense that the community must "inherit a different future" than the one suggested by the status quo; and (3) attempts to instigate change have been blocked by one or more sets of interests. The immediate impetus for visioning is often a perception on the part of ordinary citizens and community leaders that the political system has failed to respond adequately to real problems facing the community. At this moment, political leaders lose "permission to act." Exasperated, community members conclude that change will come about only when citizens take greater control of the effort to improve a community's quality of life.

A community is not ready for visioning when citizens believe that public dialogue lacks the potential to produce good ideas. If apathy and civic disengagement are pervasive, it may be difficult to convene a successful process. At least some residents must recognize that change is needed and believe that it can be catalyzed by a public process.

We are often asked whether a "crisis" provides the right moment to initiate a visioning process. Behind this question lies the perception that citizens will not get involved unless a crisis is at hand. We believe, however, that the optimal time to initiate visioning is *not* when a community is facing an acute challenge. In such situations, participants tend to invent ideas that address only that challenge. They are less likely to open up their thinking to other issues important to their community's future.

■ The Phases of Community-Wide Visioning

Whether a visioning process takes place in a small farming community on the Great Plains or a densely populated, sprawling city on the eastern seaboard, it follows a similar succession of phases. The first phase focuses on getting organized and includes determining who will lead the visioning effort, developing a process design, and promoting broad-based participation. The second phase includes the visioning process itself. This process involves a series of substeps, including gathering ideas, drafting goals, educating, and voting. The third phase emphasizes follow-up and implementation. Each of these phases is discussed in detail below.

Examples of how each phase is applied are drawn from four locales. The first is Chattanooga's ReVision 2000. The three other examples took place in "Middletown"; Birmingham, Alabama; and Catron County, New Mexico. Each conducted visioning for different reasons, with different kinds of leadership, different participants, and different access to resources. By comparing these cases, we hope to illustrate the rich variation in the way visioning can be carried out.

Organizing for Visioning

Community-wide visioning can be initiated in a number of ways, for a number of reasons. It does not depend on a single agency or institution. In fact, many of the first visioning efforts in the United States were initiated by small groups of citizens— usually nonprofit, business, religious, and neighborhood leaders—who got together informally and decided that an inclusive dialogue could help their community to define and implement a more positive future. In many cases, they were motivated by a view that their local governments were out of step with the community's aspirations.

Compare the start-up efforts in Chattanooga with those in Catron County, New Mexico. In Chattanooga, the effort was initiated by a few community leaders, including the head of a local foundation, the chair of a group that was developing a riverfront revitalization plan, and several others. These leaders founded Chattanooga Venture after visiting several other cities around the country where community task forces had successfully recharged economic and social development. Venture spearheaded Vision 2000 the same year it was formed. Buoyed by the success of that effort, the organization launched ReVision 2000 10 years later.

Catron County's visioning process provides an interesting contrast. Catron County is one of the most rural places in the United States, and in the early 1990s tensions escalated among ranchers and loggers, U.S. Forest Service officials, and environmentalists over the management of the county's abundant forest and grazing lands. As environmentalists pushed for more stringent regulations to protect endangered species, several logging concerns closed down, causing a number of Catron County residents to lose their jobs. In an atmosphere of animosity and accusations, some residents began to fear for their physical safety.

One resident—a physician concerned about the effects of stress in his patients' lives—decided to pull together a group that could air the conflict and redefine the county's long-term goals collaboratively. With assistance from the New Mexico Center for

Dispute Resolution, he convened a diverse group of 20 people: the Catron County Citizens Group. This group became the focal point of a multiyear process involving intensive dialogue and sometimes effective problem solving on controversial issues. After almost a year spent educating each other about their perspectives on land use and other topics, this group launched a facilitated visioning process designed to include the entire community (Case 13).

While visioning can be mobilized by one concerned citizen or a small set of community leaders, it can also be initiated by government agencies. Increasingly, planning and development agencies are stepping into a leadership role, proposing and then helping to manage community dialogues about the future. For example, when government agencies set out to develop comprehensive plans for municipalities, counties, or regions, they often add a visioning stage to ensure that plans reflect citizens' long-term aspirations.

Whether the idea to launch a visioning process comes from an individual, a community organization, or a government agency, the proponent's first step should be to carefully consider whether visioning should be pursued. As mentioned previously, visioning does not make sense in all situations. If a community is absorbed in a narrowly defined crisis, or if stakeholders have no faith in the value of public dialogue, then an elaborate visioning process would probably be a poor use of time and resources.

To help determine whether or not visioning makes sense, proponents can gather information about how it has been used in other parts of the country, as leaders in Chattanooga did. Proponents should also identify the likely goals of a process and the key participants. Finally, they will need to investigate whether resources are available to support the costs of visioning, such as hiring a full- or part-time coordinator to manage logistics. Throughout these deliberations, an initiating group could consult with a trained facilitator. If the proponents decide to proceed, their next tasks are to consider leadership and process design.

Establishing Who Will Lead

An initiating group must clarify who will lead the community through visioning and who will handle the multitude of "on-the-ground" tasks essential to a successful effort. In almost every case, the best strategy is for the initiating group to broaden its membership and assume the role of a steering committee. It is essential to establish a steering committee that includes representatives of all the major stakeholding groups in a community. Otherwise, proponents will have a hard time garnering support. On the other hand, if a steering committee is too large (say, more than 25 members) then its meetings may become unwieldy and ineffective. The following criteria should be used in selecting people to serve on such a committee.[2]

- Members must be seen as credibly reflecting the various perspectives and experiences of the broader community. Any key stakeholder group in a community (e.g., the clergy, school teachers and administrators, health care providers) ought to be able to identify with at least one committee member.

- Some members should be perceived as having previously taken actions in the best interests of the community as a whole. That is, some individuals should have a reputation among the public at large for exercising power responsibly.

- Collectively, steering committee members must be a "constituency for change." The committee should include some leaders who will be able to leverage resources in service of implementing the results of the visioning effort. It should also include people who can, by virtue of their stature in the community, hold established authorities and organizations accountable for the implementation of recommendations.

- A group must include strong facilitative leaders whose primary focus is to promote and sustain a collaborative process rather than advocate for a particular point of view. In other words, it is necessary to have some people who are at the table because they have a commitment to the process or a passion for the betterment of the community, not because they are closely associated with a group that has a specific agenda.

The importance of multistakeholder leadership in a visioning process cannot be overemphasized. In Chattanooga, the board of directors of Chattanooga Venture functioned essentially as a steering committee during the two visioning efforts. It included more than 50 people representing dozens of different organizations and constituencies in the city. As a result of the board's diversity and credibility, the group readily secured broad-based participation and support for the visioning processes it championed.

In thinking about who will lead a visioning process, people often want to know what role elected officials should play. Elected officials may, in some cases, be the initial advocates for a visioning process, as they were in Middletown (Case 12). In the early 1990s, the city council in this Canadian community of 100,000 became worried about how the city would confront emerging social and economic problems with limited municipal resources. The council decided to organize a series of dialogues to generate ideas for a forward-looking economic development strategy. The press release announcing this visioning-type process explained the city's dilemma.

> We are facing significant challenges today. Resources are stretched, and simply increasing taxes and revenues to meet increased expectations is not possible in today's economic climate. In this environment, the need for community-based goals and objectives is critical to making our city an outstanding community.

Middletown is not the sole example of political leaders mobilizing community action. In many municipalities, a new generation of "facilitative leaders" are winning office, leaders who believe a key part of their role is to convene stakeholder groups in dialogues about what they would like their leaders to do. Sometimes, however, these leaders have to initiate visioning in the face of strong resistance from other elected officials, who say, "That's our job!" and insist that such a process would undermine their authority.

Instead of taking a lead role, elected officials can simply become one among many members of a steering committee. Catron County's process was initiated by the Catron County Citizens Group, one of whose members was a county commissioner, but the county commission had no formal role in starting or sponsoring the process.

We recommend, in fact, that elected officials *not* be given sole responsibility for the design and management of a visioning process. As Chattanooga demonstrates, there are real advantages to having the leadership come from outside government. When visioning is led by a committee that replicates the community's diversity, participants are more likely to view a process as being their own (rather than imposed on them by an external authority). The Middletown case is instructive in this regard. There, the city council sponsored the process and city councilors were heavily involved at each stage. In part due to the strong presence of elected officials, the citizens of Middletown did not feel ownership of that process nor did they stand by what it produced.

Forming a Staff

Volunteers on a steering committee will not be able to undertake the myriad tasks involved in planning and overseeing a multiple-meeting process involving hundreds, if not thousands, of people. They must, rather, focus on issues such as process design, fund-raising, retaining outside facilitation assistance, and using their stature to publicize the effort. Under almost all circumstances, therefore, visioning is better managed by a full-time or at least part-time paid coordinator. A paid coordinator should assume primary responsibility for executing the steering committee's decisions.

The staff of ReVision 2000 was invaluable. One talented, respected individual, knowledgeable about the community, was responsible for managing all the logistics. Asked her views on what makes for an effective coordinator, she said it should be someone who has no formal connections to local government, business, or the professional planning community.[3] This gives the person an important level of autonomy.

Designing a Successful Process

Another task of an initiating group (or a steering committee, if one has been convened) is to design the visioning process. Among the design issues that must be addressed are the following: how long the process will take, how many rounds of meetings are needed, what the agenda for the meetings in each round ought to be, and who will facilitate the sessions.

Most visioning processes start with an idea-gathering step that consists of large and small facilitated meetings attended by hundreds of residents. Participants at each gathering are asked to respond to a question or series of questions about the characteristics of the future they would choose for their community. The answers (sometimes thousands of them) are organized into categories. They are then distilled into progressively more specific products such as vision statements, goals, and development scenarios.

Although this sequence of steps is typical, the process used to gather and synthesize information will vary from community to community. The approach that a community designs should reflect the unique personality of that place, including its local political, environmental, and social characteristics.

A successful vision requires the participation of a great many citizens. Whether or not people come hinges in part on how well the process is publicized. Participation is also directly affected by the design of the process. Imagine, for example, if a steering committee scheduled most visioning meetings during daytime hours, and one of the few sessions scheduled during the evening conflicted with the school district's quarterly Parent-Teacher Association meeting. Potential participants with school-aged children and full-time day jobs would conclude that the sponsors were not serious about hearing their views. Similarly, if the meetings all took place far from public transportation routes, potential participants might conclude that a process was solely for wealthier residents with automobiles. Seemingly secondary decisions about scheduling, location, and format can have critical consequences for who attends.

Process designers must also anticipate the factors that can deter someone from participating. A few are worth mentioning. In a community with a dearth of political leadership, some residents may be apathetic. They may have made up their minds that the chances for major change are slight. In other cases, residents may have been disappointed by the outcome of earlier participation efforts. Whole groups may fear that they will not be treated fairly, particularly if they have long felt disenfranchised. And some residents will be reluctant to participate simply because they have no personal history of civic involvement, or because they like things the way they are.

To attract broad-based participation, then, the design of a process needs to reassure potential participants that

1. Rather than being lectured at, they will have an opportunity to contribute their ideas.
2. Their ideas will be recorded and respected, and none will be lost.
3. The process will ensure that those ideas are translated into concrete actions that some individual, business, public agency, or nonprofit organization will actually implement.
4. The process is being spearheaded by a group that will continue to be involved after the vision is clear and will work toward its implementation.

In short, the design of a process should give potential participants confidence that there are good reasons to get involved. It should persuade them that visioning will achieve real, concrete change.

The initiating group must also think carefully about how to design a process that gathers the right kind of information. A vision challenges the notion that "experts know best," by assuming that those who live in a place are the ones who ought to decide what should be done to maintain or improve it. Not every meeting, however, will automatically tap into that knowledge. Participants are unlikely to contribute their ideas unless they think a meeting offers a "safe" environment. In other words, participants need to feel they can voice their concerns and ideas without the risk of being ignored, ridiculed, or criticized by other participants or expert observers.

This has direct implications for process design. First, it is important to think carefully about who will facilitate community meetings, and how those facilitators should be trained. Facilitation is perhaps the single biggest factor determining whether meetings achieve a respectful exchange of views. Second, meeting agendas need to be developed with an eye toward ensuring that everyone has an opportunity to speak, but no individual feels put on the spot.

The use of expertise is another issue that those designing a visioning process need to consider. For example, a community that believes expanding open space is a priority for the future might want to consult with landscape designers. Process designers must find ways to use expertise to enhance the quality of a vision, without making participants feel that the final product is more the work of experts than of citizens. One way to do this is to fold in expertise at a later stage (perhaps after a first round of meetings), when stakeholders have developed a preliminary set of goals and are at the point of defining how to achieve them. Waiting to introduce expertise helps to ensure that it will not inhibit citizens' imaginations.

Finally, the design of a process should include some mechanism for tracking and documenting who participates. The public has become increasingly sophisticated about sampling techniques, and they may want to know who came out and whether they were representative of the whole community. In Chattanooga, people completed a brief questionnaire when they registered for the meetings, which created a record of who participated.

It may take a substantial amount of time and effort to work through these process design questions. In Birmingham, Alabama, an initiating committee composed of 50 community members met for more than a year to deliberate about the most appropriate way to develop a regional vision for 12 counties. The group looked to an experienced facilitator for help during this phase. Among other tasks, their meetings focused on establishing a shared set of values, debating the geographic boundaries to use, and selecting and hiring a consultant to assist in executing the process they designed. When the process was launched, the committee's inclusive membership and its thorough and careful planning combined to ensure balanced and widespread participation in the visioning effort.

Ensuring Broad-Based Participation

The last and perhaps most important step in the "organizing for visioning" phase is to get the public to participate. The members of an initiating or steering committee may feel daunted by the challenge of enticing people to join. A steering committee can brainstorm numerous strategies to increase the chances of a good turnout, however, and they should also consult with stakeholders for ideas. The total list should be fashioned into a publicity and outreach plan.

Publicity. Successful visioning requires a full-fledged public information campaign. Public information should be designed to catch the attention of community residents. A name (like Chattanooga's ReVision 2000, or Birmingham's Region 2020), a logo, and a few slogans can give the process a clear, recognizable identity.

More important, public information, whether disseminated on the radio, in brochures, or in newspapers, should do more than tell people where and when they can attend meetings. To be effective, it needs to entice people—to send a clear message about why it is important to participate. The message might be: "Help make [this town] a better place to live," or "Help build a great future for [this town's] children." Regardless of the words, it should communicate persuasively the idea that each citizen's opinion adds value.

The specific means for publicizing a process will differ in every community, depending on the resources available and the creative ideas of its planners. Chattanooga organizers had a generous budget for public relations. Other processes have been quite successful with promotional strategies that relied on much less funding. Some have piggybacked onto scheduled community events. In Catron County, New Mexico, organizers decided that their kickoff should occur at the Heritage Festival on July 4th, a well-attended community event.

Attracting press coverage is an essential part of a promotional strategy. In recent years, it has become a little easier to persuade the press that it has a responsibility to cover stories about cooperation. As part of an emerging commitment to "civic journalism," many reporters are more receptive to writing stories about community visioning; they even see it as a way to sell papers (Charity, 1995).

Outreach. An outreach plan should include strategies for how citizens from all parts of a community can be approached and invited to provide their input into a process. In Birmingham, where the visioning process involved 12 counties, 12 separate outreach committees were convened. Each was led by local leaders knowledgeable about the kinds of outreach that were likely to be most effective in their area.

Networks of existing community organizations—the Rotary club, church groups, the PTA, or local professional associations, to name a few—can be an invaluable resource for outreach. These organizations can use existing channels of communication, such as their newsletters, to inform their members about the goals of a process and the agendas and schedules for upcoming meetings.

Even more important, community-based organizations give a steering committee a way to reach to the public. If an organization's regular meetings are held on a schedule that dovetails well with a visioning process, then those meetings can become venues for visioning. Members of a steering committee or other volunteers can ask to use a part of a group's meeting time to facilitate a conversation and gather input for the vision. In this way, community members can participate in visioning without adding yet another meeting to their schedules.

Another effective outreach strategy is to appoint volunteer "captains." A captain's job is to ensure a good turnout for a given meeting. In Catron County, where the only newspaper widely distributed in the region was a "shopper's weekly," organizers of the process might have confronted empty meeting rooms had they not assigned volunteers to bring residents to meetings. At one meeting in the tiny town of Luna, New Mexico, more than 27 residents came, largely because one community member made a personal commitment to persuade them to come.

A predictable pattern in all kinds of public participation efforts, and one that a steering committee must be wary of, is overrepresentation by middle-class, middle-aged participants. It is difficult to get community members on the far reaches of a community's socioeconomic spectrum or the ends of the age spectrum to participate. Often, obstacles exist to securing the participation of politically marginalized groups, such as racial or ethnic minorities in some communities.

Including all of the diverse elements of a community in a visioning process takes careful planning and hard work. Again, one strategy is to take the process to the people: to organize meetings in locations and at times that are convenient for them. The processes in Chattanooga, Middletown, and Catron County tailored strategies for including hard-to-reach populations, such as senior citizens and high school students.

At a minimum, public information materials should encourage participation by emphasizing that meetings are open to all.

The materials should also anticipate fears that important decisions about the direction of change have already been made by a small group of powerful politicians. They should reassure their audience that visioning is a truly democratic process that places equal value on all participants' views regardless of their age, class, race, ethnic background, or relative political clout.

Conducting a Visioning Process

Once a steering committee has been established, a set of process design decisions has been reached, and publicity and outreach plans are being executed, the visioning process can begin. The four steps involved at this stage are gathering ideas, drafting goals, educating, and voting. These steps sometimes overlap.

Gathering Ideas

Gathering ideas is the first and most important step in the act of visioning. In multiple meetings held in various locations, residents should be asked to envision what their community has the potential to become. Ideas must be carefully recorded.

The major challenge is to get residents to articulate their long-term aspirations, unencumbered by their knowledge of the constraints of the present. An effective vision will look out over at least 10 years (often longer) and describe a desired end state. It will also define a path to achieving that end state. To be successful in gathering ideas about what this path should be, organizers must ensure that participants feel comfortable voicing their aspirations, even when friends, neighbors, and peers disagree. This requires both an effective meeting agenda and trained facilitators.

The purpose of every agenda should be to give participants an opportunity to talk with each other, often in small groups, about things they treasure, things they want to preserve, and things they want to re-create. In these conversations, they begin to sketch a vision. Good visioning sessions can yield thousands of ideas about the future of a community.

In Chattanooga, more than 2,000 people participated in two rounds of meetings—one round to gather ideas and one to formulate goals and action steps based on those ideas. During the first round, nine community meetings were held in one month, primarily during evening hours. In an effort to involve elderly residents and high school students—two hard-to-reach populations—one meeting was held at the senior center and another was held at the convention center, where high school students from throughout the area gathered.

Those attending the meetings selected one topic from among five: people, place, work, play, or government. At each meeting, they were asked to respond to a question that sought to draw out their ideas about what they wanted for the future. The facilitators asked the participants to develop their ideas one at a time, in a round-robin format. Every idea was recorded on a flip chart. When the lists were complete, the groups spent some time clarifying those ideas that were not immediately comprehensible. Then each group selected what they thought were the five most important items. The final product of the meetings was a list of ideas with an indication, based on the number of votes each received, of how strongly participants felt about each. The facilitators closed the sessions by letting everyone know that even those ideas receiving no votes would be considered during the goal-setting process. This first round of meetings resulted in a list of 2,559 ideas.

In Catron County, the idea gathering was begun at the Heritage Festival, where people were asked to write what they treasured about the county on "gold coins" they placed in a treasure chest. At the county fair a month later, they got a chance to review the treasures.

In keeping with visioning's goal of reinvigorating citizen involvement in a community, a steering committee will often ask residents to facilitate meetings. Their job is to create a safe environment that is conducive to productive thinking. Typically, volunteers are trained in facilitation and meeting management techniques. In the process of preparing volunteers to run meetings, the capacity of a community to manage collaborative decision making long into the future is enhanced. In ReVision 2000 in Chattanooga, more than 150 volunteers were trained to facilitate public meetings. In a visioning process conducted in Grand Island, Nebraska, a city with 50,000 residents, more than 250 people participated in facilitation training. Of these, only a small number ultimately facilitated visioning sessions; the rest learned the skills for future use.

Drafting Goals and Action Steps

Once a set of ideas has been collected, the ideas can be fashioned into tangible goals. Often, these goals become the basis for developing action steps: activities that organizations and individuals are assigned responsibility for carrying out.

The goal-drafting step can be handled in a number of ways. A common approach is to convene a small committee to generate a "first cut" at goals, and then hold a round of public meetings to improve and ratify them. This approach was used in Chattanooga. A small group made up of members of Chattanooga Venture's board, as well as other citizens active in the organization, met to review the more than 2,500 ideas recorded during the first round of public meetings. The group devised a set of categories that could be used to cluster the ideas, including education, beautification, crime and safety, downtown, health, housing, leadership, multiculturalism, riverfront, and youth, among others. Thus, for example, after the sorting was completed, the category "education" included all the various ideas about what Chattanooga's schools should be like in the future. The group's next task was to create preliminary goal statements for each category that captured the ideas in clear, simple language. One of Chattanooga's goals for education was: "Excellent public schools, K-12, which are well funded and actively supported by the community."

The board of Chattanooga Venture then conducted a second round of public meetings. Promotional materials were again used to encourage residents to attend. Every meeting was able to cover several categories by having participants split into breakout groups; each breakout group discussed one category. In each breakout session, a facilitator handed out a list of the ideas that had been generated during the Round One meetings. Participants were asked to read the list and write down recurring themes in the margins. The facilitator called on people one at a time and recorded the themes they identified on flip chart paper.

When all of the themes were captured on the flip charts, the facilitator then read the goal statement that had been generated by the drafting team from Chattanooga Venture. Participants were asked to evaluate how well the goal reflected the themes that the group had identified. Once a goal statement was agreed on, facilitators turned participants' attention toward deciding what concrete actions, programs, or projects might be implemented to accomplish the goal. An action item for the education category, for example, was "Involve the business community . . . in creating quality public schools for the 21st century." Using a straightforward process (individual idea-generation, round-robin recording of ideas, discussion to clarify the ideas, and rank ordering), each meeting concluded with a concrete product: a list of goals and action items that, when merged with the products of other groups addressing different topics, would become Chattanooga's new vision.

Catron County used a similar, but much smaller-scale process. After residents attending the two local fairs had identified what they treasured about the county, six visioning sessions were organized in four towns. In Luna, the best and only place to meet was the fire station, since the "downtown" had hardly a building in it. In two other towns, meetings were held at senior centers in an effort to reach elderly residents. In the town of Reserve, a classroom of students at Reserve High School participated. The meetings were facilitated by members of the Catron County Citizens Group. The facilitators shared the "treasure list" with participants, and then led a discussion about the kind of community participants wanted their children and grandchildren to inherit. A long list of potential goals was produced and the Citizens Group was given the job of synthesizing them and paring them down.

It is worth noting that participation often drops off between a first and a second round of meetings. Recognizing that the public has limited patience with a lengthy process, some communities have used a streamlined version in which all ideas, goals, and action steps are generated in one round of meetings.

Regardless of the approach a community uses to draft goals, process organizers should make sure that those goals capture public sentiment in language that is easily understood. In Chattanooga, organizers made an intentional decision not to simply have participants say "yea" or "nay" to goal statements prepared in advance. By having participants first look at the full list of ideas and identify themes, and then evaluate goal statements in light of those themes, citizens had to think carefully about whether the goals accurately captured all the relevant ideas. Other communities have achieved the same objective by using focus groups. These groups, composed of a diverse set of citizens, react to goal statements and advise organizers on whether or not those statements will be clear to the public. Focus groups often lead to tangible improvements in language.

Educating

Throughout a visioning process, it is important for organizers to educate the public about the process and key issues being discussed. Many people will not be able to attend public meetings, but well-designed educational materials can keep them abreast of the dialogue. If the public is fully aware of the process, then a vision document is much more likely to garner widespread endorsement.

The organizers of ReVision 2000 prepared a magazine with detailed information about their visioning effort. The magazine was mailed to every household in the county. In Grand Forks, North Dakota, where a visioning process was initiated to help the community rebuild after floods and fires, a four-page, color supplement was printed in the newspaper several days before the first meeting. The supplement was also distributed at the meetings. Other communities have successfully encouraged local newspapers to run feature articles on key issues that upcoming public meetings will address.

Catron County took yet another innovative step. Organizers there wanted to get community residents thinking about the key characteristics of their county before the visioning process began. Because there were no media outlets that could be tapped to distribute background information, they came up with another device: a quiz. As meeting participants arrived at the registration table, they were given a set of questions to answer. Residents were asked to estimate the county's population, the number of bars, the average income of residents, and the total number of cows in the county, among other things. At the beginning of the meeting, a moderator reviewed the quiz with the participants. As people discussed their answers, they developed a shared base of information about the physical and demographic attributes of their own community.

Voting

In some visioning processes, the public is invited to ratify the goals and action steps developed in visioning meetings. There are several benefits to including a ratification step. First, when citizens have a chance to vote on which goals and action steps will be incorporated into a final vision, the product will have greater community credibility, and residents will be more likely to hold each other accountable for its implementation. In addition, when residents have to choose from among multiple goals, they begin to develop an appreciation for the trade-offs involved in the realization of their preferred future.

How is voting typically organized? Chattanooga held a Vision Fair at Miller Plaza, an attractive downtown space. Citizens who came to the Vision Fair were given an opportunity to review the goals and actions that came out of the second round of meetings, and each cast votes in favor of the five actions they favored. In Grand Island, Nebraska, members of the public were given "Heartland Dollars" (akin to Monopoly money) and instructed to stuff their Heartland Dollars in mason jars placed in front of the goals they would most like to see implemented with taxpayers' money. Most voting procedures, like these, involve allowing participants to indicate their preferences by allocating a limited number of votes. Regardless of the procedure, many communities have chosen large commercial malls as the setting for their voting events—pedestrian traffic in and around a mall increases the likelihood of reaching many people quickly.

Implementing the Vision

A community-wide visioning process that does not lead to new projects, programs, or activities is probably not worth the effort. Yet it is hard to give specific advice about how a community can ensure that its vision will be implemented. Many factors affect which parts of a vision will lead to action, and these factors are not generalizable from place to place. The context matters greatly. New local issues, a shift in a community's political or economic landscape, or the emergence of a new leader can all play a part in determining what happens to a community's vision document.

Nonetheless, communities can and do develop strategies to facilitate successful implementation. Steering committees should begin thinking about which implementation strategies to adopt the day they begin designing their visioning process. When they don't, the likelihood of encountering obstacles to implementation is far greater. In Middletown, a multiphased visioning process produced Our Common Future, a plan addressing issues such as environmental quality, economic development, and opportunities for youth. While a few of the plan's good ideas were realized, many were never acted on. Implementation was hindered by weak support for the plan among municipal staff and fear among community organizations that the plan would duplicate and overshadow their work. In retrospect, some of those involved in the process speculate that these obstacles might have been overcome with more careful planning at the outset.

The first and most important strategy for ensuring implementation has already been discussed: Build broad-based interest and participation. This helps to ensure community ownership of a final product. The more residents feel they are part of a process, the more they will be invested in, and excited about, seeing it lead to tangible improvements. Also, visioning should be carefully designed to involve community leaders who must later become the champions of new projects and programs.

A second strategy relates to the content of the final vision document. It should point clearly in the direction of what needs to happen next. To do this, it must outline broad directions for change, goals that everyone can understand and explain to others, and many detailed, specific actions.

A third strategy is to assign individuals or groups the task of following through on different parts of the vision. Many communities have convened working groups to make these assignments. When their members include representatives of the public, private, and nonprofit sectors, these working groups can accurately match citizens' aspirations with the capabilities and resources of existing organizations. In Birmingham, seven such groups were formed to translate 34 goals and strategies into a coherent plan for action.

It is important to find ways to measure progress toward the realization of a community-wide vision. If citizens can see that a community is making headway, they will continue supporting implementation. Increasingly, communities are using *benchmarks* and *indicators* to measure progress. Benchmarks describe a starting point; they express where things were before implementation activities began. They provide a way of measuring the extent of progress over time. Indicators are a similar tool; they point to what one should look at when measuring change. For example, if one goal in a vision is to increase public access to affordable housing, the benchmark might be the number of units of affordable housing in the year before visioning began. The indicator might be the number of new units constructed annually.

Last, successful implementation requires sustained leadership from an organization that has made a public commitment to seeing the vision through. In Chattanooga, the sustained efforts of Chattanooga Venture through the implementation phase is what has made visioning there so successful. (A recent decision to house Venture at a nearby state university, and let its staff go, may slow the pace of innovation in the city.) In the absence of an established organization like Venture, an ad hoc steering committee can serve in this role. Such a steering committee must meet the criteria outlined earlier in this chapter, in the section "Establishing Who Will Lead."

While a vision can be helpful in planning, the primary purpose of visioning is to create a political mandate for change. A vision identifies what a constituency prefers, so those responsible for acting in the interests of the community, such as elected leaders, know how to act. What is most significant about the story of Chattanooga is not that a written plan was created based on the vision of the local citizens. It is that the process mobilized those who were already charged with acting in the interests of Chattanooga—including local officials and people representing community-wide agencies such as the United Way, the chamber of commerce, the public schools, and especially Chattanooga Venture—by telling them what their constituencies wanted them to do.

In *Cities and the Wealth of Nations,* Jane Jacobs (1985) talks about the difficulty of charting a precise course for planning. She notes in particular that the effort to develop "industrial strategies" to meet "targets" using "long-range planning" assumes falsely "that economic life can be conquered, mobilized, bullied" (p. 222). Because she believes there are real limits to how effectively one can plan for development and expansion, she believes the answer is to "manage the drift."

"Managing the drift" is exactly what needs to happen when a community-wide vision is being implemented. Plans aren't realized in a steady, predictable way. The best one can do is to be ready to seize unexpected opportunities and create new opportunities when they are slow to appear. Visioning was successful in Chattanooga because Chattanooga Venture managed the drift: It convened the right people, provided a safe place for ideas to incubate, and paid attention on a daily basis to emerging opportunities.

■ Variations in Visioning: Beyond the Community-Wide Approach

This chapter has taken an in-depth look at *community-wide* visioning, which is by no means the only way a community or group can envision its future. Table 15.1 describes and provides brief examples of a variety of alternative approaches a community or a subset of citizens might employ. Through the use of an example, this section explains one of those alternatives: the charrette. The section also briefly describes how visioning can be used by a single organization in a strategic-planning process.

A Charrette in Casper, Wyoming

A *charrette* is a short and intensive visioning process. Stakeholders convene in a series of meetings (lasting from one day to several weeks) to develop a plan for a major facet of community life, such as the downtown, recreation, or transportation.

In Casper, Wyoming in early 1998, residents were concerned about what would become of a large refinery site (owned by Amoco) that was about to be vacated. A major worry was that there would be an interminable and costly legal battle over environmental remediation of the site (since there was evidence of underground contamination and other problems). Citizens knew that companies, regulatory agencies, and citizen groups could spend a decade litigating this issue, followed by another decade before the cleanup was actually finished. Another refinery in the same town had been in litigation for more than 15 years, and the final remediation still had not been accomplished.

The refinery in question was adjacent to the city. Given the prime location, its abandonment would hinder the rejuvenation of the local economy, which had been decimated by the oil "bust" of the 1980s. A variety of ideas for how the site might be used had recently been proposed by citizens, but no action had been

(text continues on p. 585)

TABLE 15.1 Approaches to Visioning

Approach	Description	Example
American assembly	An informed constituency convenes to discuss a policy issue and to make recommendations about future action(s) on the issue. A typical pattern is for multiple stakeholder groups to answer common questions, a writer drafts a statement reflecting the points of agreement among the groups, and all stakeholders then meet and use parliamentary procedure to systematically revise and ratify the statement.	New Mexico First, a nonprofit organization, convened 150 people in a "town hall" meeting. The meeting was titled "American Indians in New Mexico and Their Neighbors: Building Bridges of Understanding." The participants met in small groups for two days of structured discussions. The agreements and recommendations from the small groups served as the bases for a draft consensus report that was made available to the participants prior to a plenary session. At the plenary session, all of the participants amended and then approved the draft report.
CEO process	Business leaders from major corporations in a community convene to address the economic vitality of that community.	More than a decade of economic crises in Cleveland, Ohio motivated business leaders there to commission a study on what could be done to improve the city's economy. The study recommended the formation of an organization composed of the most influential local business leaders. Based on the study, an organization was formed. Its executive director led the businesspeople in developing and executing strategies to bolster the local economy. A core strategy was to complete visible physical projects in the city to motivate interest in the community and a willingness to sustain the efforts necessary to achieve economic stability.
Charrette	Those who have a stake in an issue convene in intensive, interactive meetings, lasting from one day to several weeks, to develop a plan for that issue. Charrettes are typically used to address a large aspect of a community: the downtown area, recreation, transportation, and so forth.	In Casper, Wyoming, an injunction issued by a federal court created an opportunity to do something about a vacated refinery site. Key community leaders organized a group of 21 citizens who reflected Casper's diversity. The group educated themselves (and the general public) about the site and what might be done with it, about current planning in Casper, and about what other places had done to use brownfields wisely. The group then brainstormed possible futures for the site. Once they had a general vision, the group told a "design team" what they wanted. The design team, with the public looking on, developed options for the site. The citizens said which aspects of the options they preferred, and their preferences became the community's vision. This vision was the basis of a negotiation in which the refinery owners, residents, and government officials developed an agreement for the cleanup and redevelopment of the site.
Community-wide visioning	The entire community is invited to meetings and asked to envision a desired future for the community. There are no limits on the focus of their vision.	In Chattanooga, Tennessee, a nonprofit organization, guided by a large, diverse, and influential governing board, initiated a community-wide process that encouraged all citizens to attend public meetings to say what they wanted for the future of their city. (See chapter for detail on this effort.)

Civic infrastructure process	A select group of people is invited to study what should be done to improve the civic infrastructure of the community.	In Youngstown, Ohio, approximately 150 people—the alumni of a community-leadership organization and key local leaders—were invited to come together to study the city's civic infrastructure. They divided into teams, studied specific topics, and then reported to the full group. The teams were organized around the 10 components of civic infrastructure identified by the National Civic League: citizen participation, community leadership, government performance, volunteerism and philanthropy, intergroup relations, civic education, community information sharing, capacity for cooperation and consensus building, community vision and pride, and intercommunity cooperation. After the report-outs were completed, the group developed a short list of doable actions that, if accomplished, would improve the community.
Future search conference	Those with a stake in an issue meet intensively (up to two and a half days) to explore the "whole system" surrounding the issue, develop an ideal scenario of the future, and agree on action plans to work toward the realization of the future.	A regional planning agency in Colorado responsible for the state water-quality plan invited 48 people to meet for two full days and two nights to seek common ground on the future of water-quality decision making. Participants included representatives of agricultural, industrial, and recreation interests; local and municipal governments; federal and state agencies; water providers; and water and sanitation districts. At the "search conference," stakeholders identified trends and forces, analyzed the common history of the participants, identified a desirable future for water-quality management in the region, and decided how they would move from ideals to action (Rehm, Schweits, & Granata, 1992).
Healthy communities effort	A select group of people is invited to convene to determine what should be done to ensure the future "health" of a community.	In northeast Ohio, a County Healthy Communities Initiative was launched involving four area hospitals, nonprofit service providers, the religious community, and neighborhood leaders. A diverse group of 75 residents undertook a nine-month planning process to improve the region's health and well-being. They began with a set of values and a vision of their region as a healthy community. Over the course of the process, they worked to build a foundation for an integrated health care service-delivery system with the four hospitals and other service providers. They also formed a Youth Development Initiative, involving all youth-related efforts in a process that enabled them to set shared priorities and use resources wisely.
Key community leaders	A diverse, selective group of community leaders is invited to meet to identify issues that are critical to the future of the community and to develop plans to address those critical issues.	In Akron, Ohio, a diverse group of community leaders was invited to attend an annual, daylong meeting convened by a group called Goals for Greater Akron. At the meeting, the leaders worked in small groups to identify goals the community should work to achieve. The convening organization was then responsible for brokering activity to see that progress was made on accomplishing the goals.

(continued)

TABLE 15.1 Continued

Approach	Description	Example
Priority boards	A community or neighborhood convenes to decide on priorities for expending resources that have been allocated to it.	The Dayton, Ohio city government was facing a major revenue loss and thus had to cut back on services and capital outlays. At the same time, they created separate funds for neighborhoods. People in the neighborhoods were asked to make decisions about whether to restore some of the services or to use the resources in other ways. To do this, each neighborhoods formed a "priority board" to establish priorities. City staff assisted the boards. Eventually, priority boards became the process for determining all budget priorities in Dayton.
Study circles	Self-selected and/or invited citizens participate in small-group, democratic, highly participatory discussions on an issue of concern to the community.	Community leaders in a town in Ohio organized a study circle program to help citizens identify and address challenges facing the town. More than 70 people met in seven study circles, using materials that covered issues such as land use, town services, and community spirit. In their groups, citizens identified nine major areas of focus: education, young people and senior citizens, recreation, business support and development, historic preservation, land use/zoning/open space, roads and infrastructure, and waste disposal and cleanups. At an action forum following the study circles, citizens signed up for task forces to make improvements in the eight areas. The task forces are now in progress. National issues forums (NIFs) are a variation on the study circle approach. In NIFs, groups study alternative approaches to a key national or community issue and work their way through to an informed view of what should be done about the issue.
Scenario writing	A select group of people is invited to create alternative future scenarios for their community and to use the scenarios to agree on a desired future.	In Missoula, Montana, a carefully selected group of citizens was invited to help address the emerging issue of community growth. Four alternative scenarios ("stories") about how the future might unfold were developed. Informed by the scenarios, the group created a single vision of a desirable future that defined the characteristics and qualities of 10 critical aspects of that future: the natural environment, built environment, decision-making processes, sense of community, economy, education, relationships/partnerships, government, arts and culture, and social climate. They then developed strategic priorities and policy recommendations for achieving the vision.

taken. Company officials had not responded to the citizens' initiative.

Then, a group of people living and working adjacent to the site filed a lawsuit claiming property damage from refinery pollution. A federal judge gave an initial ruling that indicated Amoco would, indeed, be required to clean up the site as specified by the EPA. After the judge's ruling, a citizens group was approached by regional EPA officials and encouraged to become involved in determining the fate of the property. This group saw that the judge's initial ruling created an opportunity. In just three weeks, the judge was scheduled to hear testimony and rule on the initial complaint brought by the neighbors. The citizens group realized that Amoco might prefer to negotiate a settlement with Casper residents directly, rather than wait for the judge's second ruling. They had to act quickly. They also knew that they alone could not speak for the community about what should be done with the site.

Because the citizens group had a very brief window in which to initiate, design, conduct, and complete a visioning process, a comprehensive community-wide effort would have been far too time-intensive. In any case, the city had completed a related planning process just a couple of years earlier, although the results did not provide specific guidance for resolving the future reuse of the refinery property. Since they wanted to use visioning not to imagine every aspect of their community's future but rather to make a decision about the future use of a specific parcel of land, the citizens group needed a process that could be used to gather extensive information and ideas on just one subject.

The group thus hired the lead author of this chapter to assist with the design and facilitation of a charrette. Funds came from a variety of sources: Amoco, the city, the county, local residents, businesses, and the EPA. Once funds and a facilitator were in place, the group invited citizens to nominate themselves as participants, making it clear that the process would involve a great deal of time and personal commitment. Instead of picking the participants directly, the citizens group selected a larger, broader group to make those decisions. This may have helped to reassure residents that the design of the process was not controlled by a select few. Ultimately, this larger group selected 21 citizens representing the diversity of the community.

Called the Homework Group, the 21 citizens attended meetings almost every evening for two weeks. They heard presentations from all of the parties (including Amoco), from other cities that had faced similar reuse dilemmas, and from local residents who had opinions about what ought to be done with the site. After the presentations, the Homework Group met all day on a Friday and on a Saturday morning to develop a vision for the site. Over lunch on Saturday they told a "design team" (composed of an architect, two landscape architects, a developer, someone knowledgeable about civic infrastructure, and a scientist specializing in toxicology and site reclamation) what they thought would be desirable uses for the site.

After touring the parcel in question, the design team began working on alternative ideas and sketches for the site. They had access to maps of the site and to people who might be a resource in the design process, including the members of the Homework Group. Sunday afternoon, a little more than a day after being told what the citizens imagined for the site, the design team presented three reuse options. They received substantial feedback from the Homework Group on each. Less than 24 hours later, the design team prepared a proposal for a composite approach that they thought took account of the Homework Group's concerns. Just before noon on Monday, the Homework Group reviewed and agreed to their proposed design.

A small negotiating team representing the citizens group (unofficially) and the city and county (officially) made the composite design the starting point for a negotiation with Amoco. The negotiation resulted in an agreement that Amoco would provide a compensation package to the city in the form of a reuse plan for their site. Among the uses agreed for the large parcel were a site for performing arts, a botanical garden, sports fields, and an industrial park. The agreement also included additional funds and other assistance specifically geared toward making sure that the new uses would protect the environment and human health.

After the charrette, Amoco also negotiated with the Wyoming Department of Environmental Quality and with the EPA regarding a streamlined regulatory review that would speed up the remediation efforts. By finding ways to remove steps that often take substantial amounts of time—such as passing official papers back and forth between the agencies or pursuing litigation—the negotiation accelerated the completion of the reuse plan.[4]

Using Visioning within a Single Organization

"Visioning within an organization is essentially the same as for whole communities— on a much smaller scale."

Visioning is commonly used within organizations and groups —including corporations, nonprofit organizations, church congregations, PTAs, and others—to help them think about and plan for their future. It is often a central element of an organization's strategic-planning process. The process of visioning within an organization is essentially the same as the process we have described in this chapter for whole communities—on a much smaller scale. But three differences are worth noting.

A visioning process within an organization is typically initiated by the senior leadership in that organization: the board of directors, the executive director or president, or the management team. Even if the idea comes from elsewhere in an organization, visioning is not likely to take place without executive-level approval and support. In community-wide visioning, by contrast, the impetus often comes from a diffuse and diverse set of stakeholders who are not in formal leadership positions. In a community setting, it is often better if elected leaders are *not* involved at the outset.

The focus of an organizational visioning process is often more narrowly circumscribed. Senior leaders in an organization may define the range of issues that will be addressed and the people who will be involved in developing the vision statement. A visioning process in a corporation might focus only on "sales and marketing issues," for example, excluding other functions or broader concerns such as management structure and employee benefits. Community-wide visioning, as we have seen, is much more free ranging and all-inclusive.

Finally, an organization will generally do a thorough *environmental scan* prior to conducting a visioning process. That is, it will gather detailed information on both internal factors, such as the organization's heritage and culture, current structure, services and products, and constituents, and external forces likely to have an impact on the organization, such as rules, laws, trends, and competitors. Such information helps visioning participants understand the context and the constraints under which they are operating. Environmental scans are typically not done in community-wide visioning. In that setting, the "context" is too vast to assess, and participants will think more creatively if they do not concentrate on such constraints.

■ *Lessons and Principles for*
Community-Wide Visioning

From the experience of Chattanooga, Catron County, and the other communities described in this chapter, we can distill a number of lessons and general principles that can be applied to a community-wide visioning process in any town, city, or county.

- The timing must be right; there should be clear signs that a community is ready for a change. A community in the midst of a crisis should resolve that crisis before proceeding with a visioning process.
- A vision should be community driven. Even when conducted at the suggestion of a government agency, visioning should be led by a steering committee that can lend legitimacy and visibility to the process. A steering committee must reflect the economic, social, and racial makeup of a community and should include business and community leaders, elected officials, representatives of special interests, ordinary citizens, and those with facilitative leadership skills. A steering committee needs adequate time to design a process.
- If possible, a paid coordinator should be hired to assist the steering committee.
- Early on, organizers should work to build support for the process itself, in the form of endorsements from local leaders, a public information campaign, media coverage, and outreach efforts. Promotional materials should communicate that the process is for everyone who has ideas about the future; it is not a dialogue among experts.
- A visioning process must be inclusive and reflect the diversity of a community or region. The organizers must provide a place and a format that will encourage a positive and creative dialogue among the broadest possible cross section of community members.
- A visioning process must address all the issues facing a community (e.g., economic development, job creation, the

environment, recreation, education, social life). A vision should provide a complex, all-inclusive, far-reaching view.

- Once a process is announced to the public, there is value in moving quickly. In Chattanooga, ideas were gathered in February, goals were refined and actions were identified in March, and the public voting—the Vision Fair—was held in April.

- Local citizens should be trained to facilitate the process.

- The final results should be presented in a single document and distributed as widely as possible. The completion of a process should be celebrated with public events and ceremonies.

- A vision must be designed to lead directly to implementation. Without a commitment to implementation, a vision is incomplete and will not result in positive change. An organization outside of government should be in place to broker the implementation process.

A visioning process implemented following these general principles has a good chance of being successful in any town, city, or county. Chattanooga, after all, was not a "miracle." Visioning can be used in any community to catalyze change, provide leaders with a clear sense of what citizens want, and reinvigorate democracy.

■ *Notes*

1. References to Chattanooga that are in quotes, where no other reference is cited, are taken from Case 11 in this volume.

2. The phrasing for these criteria has been borrowed in large part from the Missoula, Montana scenario project (see Table 15.1), supplied to us by Jim Butcher.

3. As told by Karen McMahon, coordinator of ReVision 2000, to James E. Wanserski on August 3, 1998.

4. For more information about the charrette in Casper, Wyoming, see the articles by Jason Marsden (1998a, 1998b) and Jeff Tollefson (1998) in the *Casper Star-Tribune*.

■ *References*

Charity, A. (1995). *Doing public journalism.* New York: Guilford.

Cooper, E. M. (Executive Producer), & Macksoud, A. (Producer and Director). (1993). *Chattanooga: A community with a vision* [Film]. Warwick, NY: Leonardo's Children Production.

Jacobs, J. J. (1985). *Cities and the wealth of nations: Principles of economic life.* New York: Vintage.

Marsden, J. (1998a, May 8). Amoco offers $60 million. *Casper Star-Tribune,* pp. 1, 4.

Marsden, J. (1998b, August 14). Reuse plan revealed. *Casper Star-Tribune,* p. 1.

Rehm, B., Schweits, R., & Granata, E. (1992). Water quality in the Upper Colorado River basin. In M. R. Weisbord (Ed.), *Discovering common ground.* San Francisco: Berrett-Koehler.

Rusmore, B. (1998). Wise use and the limits of public lands. In K. Hess, Jr. & J. A. Baden (Eds.), *Writers on the range* (pp. 15-24). Niwot: University Press of Colorado.

Tollefson, J. (1998, March 31). New future for Amoco site? *Casper Star-Tribune,* pp. 1, 8.

Walters, J. (1998, May). Cities and the vision thing. *Governing Magazine* [Online]. Available: www.governing.com/5vision.htm.

16

COLLABORATIVE PROBLEM SOLVING WITHIN ORGANIZATIONS

■ *Christopher W. Moore*
■ *Peter J. Woodrow*

Every day, corporate executives, government agency officials, and leaders of nonprofit organizations must make difficult decisions and resolve disputes. The case of Kate Morgan, the director of a small nonprofit group called People for People, represents a typical example of the challenges leaders face.[1] People for People coordinates volunteer services for elderly people, single mothers, and people with disabilities in a large urban area. Recently, the board of directors determined that the organization lacked clear and comprehensive personnel policies. They directed Morgan to develop such policies within three months, in the form of a written manual for board approval.

Two years ago, People for People employed just 10 people. Morgan now has a staff of 45, who supervise close to 450 volunteers. As the organization has grown, staff members have increasingly asked for more involvement in setting the organization's direction and policies. Morgan knows that if she asks employees for their input on the personnel manual, she will hear widely differing opinions. Some staffers regret the loss of the family feeling in the organization and rail against "bureaucracy," while others celebrate the coming of age of a serious community institution. Morgan suspects that these two tendencies will be difficult to reconcile in developing the new policies. Morgan's dilemma is that she has a short time to develop the manual and a staff that insists on having a say in decisions that will affect them.

How should Kate Morgan proceed? Should she issue personnel policies of her own design? Should she seek input from others first, but still write the policies herself? Perhaps she could appoint a task force to develop draft policies for her consideration. Maybe the recommendations of a task force should be submitted to staff and volunteers for comment. Would organizational unity be served by seeking widespread approval for the draft policies before taking them to the board? Would that take more than three months? If Kate does not involve staff and volunteers, will she face a serious revolt?

Morgan does not want to see this issue escalate into a full-blown conflict. She has observed too many disputes, and the difficulty of handling them, in her own and other organizations. Now, if she could just figure out what to do. . . .

This chapter seeks to help leaders such as Kate Morgan determine when and how to apply consensus-based techniques to decision making and conflict resolution *within* an organization, such as a business, government agency, or nonprofit group. (Many of the other chapters in this book focus mostly on building consensus *among* organizations.) The principles of consensus building remain the same, whether they are applied within one organization or among many. However, the relationships among parties in the two types of processes may differ somewhat. Parties involved in an internal consensus building process may have considerable influence over each other, for example, since they are entirely dependent on each other to achieve organizational goals. The power dynamics, therefore, may be intense and pronounced. While power is always an aspect of interorganizational processes as well, the parties in those cases remain independent actors who can always withdraw from a negotiation. For most practical purposes, withdrawal is not an option in an intraorganizational situation, unless organizations split up or individuals quit. This chapter will explore the uses and challenges of consensus building in these intraorganizational circumstances.

The first section of the chapter discusses the use of consensus building approaches in decision making. During the past decade,

CEOs, managers, human resource professionals, and organizational development specialists have turned away from top-down, unilateral decision-making methods and developed innovative, consensus-based approaches. Through the use of these new methods, leaders and managers gain the active participation of people at all levels of their organizations and, ultimately, secure broad endorsement for important policies, procedures, and strategic directions. The guidelines in this section apply to situations in which issues are contentious, and may involve parties who hold divergent views, but the situation is framed as a decision-making problem, not a dispute.

The second section explains how leaders such as Morgan can use consensus building techniques to better handle disputes that arise in organizations. Such disputes may be interpersonal in nature, arising over issues such as performance, discipline, remuneration and benefits, discrimination, sexual harassment, and other such items. Or they may involve problems of cooperation, coordination, and competition among different programs or departments, or relationships with external entities such as customers, neighbors, or regulatory agencies. The section focuses primarily on the process of designing dispute resolution systems: procedures that can be used to handle conflicts or disputes. In this context, consensus building has two applications. First, the process of designing and approving a proposed dispute resolution system typically involves building consensus among potential users of the system. Second, in recent years, dispute resolution systems themselves have come to include consensus-based approaches—such as negotiation, facilitation, and mediation—for handling conflict. This section will review both of these applications.

The third section considers the role of managers and other leaders in intraorganizational consensus building, and it addresses some of the concerns managers and employees typically have about consensus processes. It discusses problems leaders may encounter as they promote collaborative decision making and dispute resolution and describes how to overcome those problems.

In the public, private, and nonprofit sectors, we find organizations large and small, new and mature, complex and simple, traditional and innovative. Each organization has a unique style of decision making and conflict resolution, and this chapter cannot possibly address all the myriad permutations. However, the need to make decisions and resolve disputes is common to people in all kinds of organizations. And consensus building, by its very nature, is flexible and dynamic. We invite readers to explore how and when consensus-based procedures will work best for them and their organizations.

■ Consensus-Based Decision Making in Organizations

In the past, many managers used "command and control" approaches to make decisions. They defined a problem themselves, collected and analyzed information, and then decided how the problem should be addressed. While this approach has worked and will continue to work effectively in some instances, it is not efficient or well suited for problems in which

- employees have strong expectations regarding participation in decision making,
- ownership of a solution by several parties is critical for successful implementation,
- logical and acceptable answers are not immediately clear,
- accurate data are nonexistent or contradictory,
- rules and regulations have produced enormous complexity (e.g., legal requirements regarding sexual harassment or environmental compliance),
- multiple parties with diverse views are contending for acceptance of their solution(s), and
- similar (but not identical) problems surface repeatedly in an organization.

"Involve people from diverse levels and departments within an organization in forging consensus."

If leaders or managers attempt to take unilateral action in situations such as these, they are likely to encounter strong resistance to their decisions or, lacking crucial information from those involved, make bad decisions. The most effective alternative to command decision making is to involve people from diverse levels and departments within an organization in forging consensus. Such involvement provides a greater chance for gathering all relevant information, draws on the creativity of many people, and reduces internal resistance.

Before discussing approaches used to build consensus, we will examine a case of intraorganizational consensus building involving a U.S.-Mexican joint venture.[2]

Case Example: Building a Partnership at Alianza

The experience of "Alianza," the fictional name of a real U.S.-Mexican joint venture in the telecommunications field, shows how consensus building can be helpful in developing long-term business partnerships, coordinating interdependent parts of organizations, and addressing and reconciling corporate and national cultural differences.

The telecommunications industry around the world is highly dynamic and competitive. To respond to this ever-changing market, business leaders feel compelled to develop, produce, and market new products continually; seek new markets aggressively; and coordinate the work of their various departments and teams better.

In the early 1990s, after the telecommunications industry in Mexico was deregulated, a large financial institution in Mexico and a major U.S. telecommunications company developed a partnership to market products and services in the new environment. Staff from both organizations formed joint teams to bring new products on line. Developing effective work teams is a challenge even within a single organization. The task is far more complicated when team members speak different languages, maintain divergent assumptions about decision making and work styles, and come from multiple organizational and national cultures. Managers at Alianza attempted to address these differences, but found themselves unable to establish a single set of behavioral and performance guidelines that satisfied everyone.

In an effort to take a fresh approach to these problems, Alianza secured the services of CDR Associates (the authors' organization of some 20 staff people).[3] Our job was to help the company design a consensus building process for crafting organizational agreements that would enable employees to work more effectively together. Alianza managers also hoped to develop ongoing procedures for addressing issues that might arise in the future. In a multiday retreat, approximately 30 managers and employees from several work teams met to formulate agreements on how to handle certain organizational issues. The first part of the retreat focused on identifying specific problems and building awareness and understanding of the contrasting work cultures of Mexico and the United States. The two groups uncovered conflicting work patterns and communication styles that were seriously hindering their interactions. The U.S. company had a hard-driving, high-intensity style characterized by extremely blunt communication, work hours lasting from early morning until late at night, and a linear approach to completing tasks. The Mexican corporation, in contrast, valued diplomatic and indirect communications. Mexican work hours started later in the morning and lasted until early evening, including a long lunch break. The Mexican group also tended to approach tasks in a less linear fashion, often working on several tasks at once.

The Mexicans perceived their U.S. colleagues as rude, demanding, and often burnt out from overwork. The U.S. group found it difficult to get a clear answer out of their Mexican counterparts, were critical of their more leisurely pace of work, and viewed their work patterns as chaotic.

The efforts of participants at the retreat to understand these dynamics established a basis for addressing specific problems. For example, the group established norms, expectations, and procedures regarding internal communications that people from both cultures could live with. These included norms regarding the timing and manner of communication, as well as mechanisms for providing feedback to each other on an individual and team basis. The joint group also developed accountability mechanisms that would inform everyone about progress toward deadlines on specific projects, so that employees would focus on outcomes rather than on work styles. The group also recognized that they could not address all possible problems during the retreat, but needed ongoing consultation and problem-solving procedures. By the end of the retreat, participants reached agreement on many of the issues they had identified and developed procedures for handling future differences.

Consensus Building in the Context of Organizational Decision Making

The Alianza case shows how consensus-based decision making can be applied within an organization, and it depicts conditions that are well suited for a consensus approach to organiza-

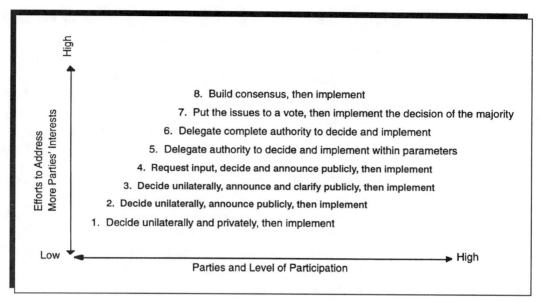

Figure 16.1 Stepped Sequence of Decision-Making Processes
SOURCE: Adapted from Doyle and Straus (1982).

tional problem solving. For another description of consensus-based decision making in an organization, see the God's Fellowship Community Church case in this volume (Case 16). In that example, a congregation worked together to determine how to regroup and move on after its pastor was forced to resign.

Organizations use a range of decision-making processes to address organizational problems. Figure 16.1 shows these processes in a stepped sequence that indicates the number of parties involved in decision making, the level and type of involvement, and the degree to which multiple interests are addressed.

Steps 1-3: Unilateral Decision Making

The first three procedures in Figure 16.1 are used by leaders or managers who act unilaterally, that is, without seeking input or approval from others. In all three cases, the person in charge makes the decision. But at each successive step, the person provides affected parties with increasingly more information about the issues and decision rationale, thereby enhancing the probability that the decision will be well received. Unilateral decision making is effective only when a decision maker has widely recognized or formally mandated authority to decide, a decision does not require significant input or support from affected parties, necessary information is available to make an informed decision, and those affected by a decision will readily comply with it. When these factors are missing, unilateral decision making may lead to new problems or conflicts.

Step 4: Request Input

A decision maker may choose to request information or advice before making a decision. Many mechanisms are available for seeking input, including informal meetings, focus groups, questionnaires, interviews, or simple requests for ideas. With more information from more sources, a decision maker can consider the perspectives of multiple parties, which increases the level of ownership those parties may feel about a final decision. Thus, this process is effective when a decision maker wants to maintain final authority, but feels that additional information will improve the quality and acceptability of the outcome. This process is dangerous if leaders are not truly interested in other people's ideas and suggestions. If a leader seeks input and then ignores it, those who offered their thoughts will feel disappointed or even betrayed. The process is also not ideal if there are widely diverging opinions in an organization that cannot be reconciled by a command decision. When leaders invite the expression of strongly held views and then must issue a "ruling," they risk alienating the "losers."

Steps 5-6: Delegated Authority

When a decision maker delegates his or her authority, the number of people involved in decision making expands. For example, a CEO might create a task force made up of managers and employees to develop a new health insurance plan. The CEO might limit the authority of the task force to negotiating a new policy with an existing provider, or the CEO could permit the task force to consider other providers, solicit information about employee opinions and needs, and make a decision regarding the provider and plan. Delegated authority allows more interests to be taken into consideration and increases stakeholders' sense of ownership of a decision. It also enables an organization to complete more tasks than can be handled by a single decision maker. Groups working under delegated authority run into trouble when their authority to decide is not clear (i.e., the parameters are not well-defined), their decision-making processes are inefficient, or those who granted them authority decide to take it away. Such groups can also encounter the same difficulty as a person making a decision with input, particularly if they solicit input, receive contradictory viewpoints, and then must make a decision they know will not meet everyone's interests.

Step 7: Voting

Voting allows even more people concerned about an issue to participate in making a decision. Voting can be either binding or nonbinding. A nonbinding straw vote reveals the preferences of voters, but does not constitute a final decision, even if there is a clear majority in favor of one option. Groups may use a straw vote to find out where participants stand on an issue (and possibly why), so they can develop a more acceptable proposal that integrates more interests and gains wider support. A binding vote commits participants to implement the will of the majority.

Formal voting is a win-lose process in which the will of the majority is imposed on the minority. In a voting process, the majority does not have to address the interests of the minority once they have secured 51 percent of the votes. However, the win-lose impacts of voting can be mitigated by increasing the percentage of votes needed for a decision from a simple majority (51 percent) to two-thirds or higher. This decreases the number of people who must submit to a decision that they did not support. Many groups also minimize the adverse impacts of majority rule by avoiding voting until proposals meet as many participants' concerns as possible.

Step 8: Consensus Building

In consensus building, people who will be affected by a decision work together to develop a solution that meets as many of their individual and collective interests as possible. This may even require a group to consider the interests of stakeholders who cannot be physically present in the room, such as future generations. In well-managed consensus building processes, participants are often able to craft superior agreements. Rather than imposing the majority's solution on a minority that benefits little from it, these agreements advance elegant solutions that bring gain to all participants. When all participants (or at least an overwhelming majority) accept a package of proposed solutions, they have reached a consensus decision. As discussed in "A Short Guide to Consensus Building" earlier in this volume, consensus does not necessarily mean unanimity—after searching long and hard for ways to make an agreement acceptable to all, a group may decide that the interests of one or a few stakeholders cannot be met without leaving other stakeholders worse off. At this point, the group might decide to accept overwhelming support as its final result.

When to Use Consensus Building

Consensus is not appropriate in all internal organizational decision-making situations. Experience shows that it is particularly effective in certain situations, such as when one or more of the following are true.

- *When no individual or group has the authority to make a unilateral decision, or when a unilateral decision-making process has failed.* At Alianza, powerful decision makers were present, but were unable to make and enforce a unilateral decision. Cultural differences inhibited the ability of employees to work together, and a decision maker could not simply command cooperation.
- *When no individual or group has adequate knowledge or information to make an informed or wise decision.* The Mexican and American employees at Alianza had to share information and assumptions before decisions could be made about how they would work together.
- *When highly divergent views must be reconciled to move forward.* Alianza employees had to discuss their differing views and work habits before they could develop new, mutually acceptable procedures for working together.

- *When unity among individuals in a team or organization is essential, or when a highly unpopular decision might lead to divisiveness.* To achieve the ambitious goals of the joint venture, Alianza needed to forge an effective multicultural team—which they could achieve only through consensus building.

- *When strong cooperation and support will be needed to implement an agreement.* Cooperation was fundamental to the resolution of cross-cultural tensions at Alianza. Implementation of new procedures would have been impossible without cooperation and support from both Mexican and American employees.

- *When decision makers are seeking an integrative and elegant decision.* Some leaders see themselves (or their organizations) as innovative, creative, even risk taking. Some may also perceive that business as usual will not move them forward or remove barriers to greater efficiency, competitiveness, or a more satisfied workforce. Traditional decision making cannot always generate innovative solutions, so other models for decision making and/or dispute resolution are needed—models that draw on the creativity of a wider group. As we will see in a case described later, Levi Strauss & Co. used consensus building to develop an improved conflict management system, in part because it took pride in being on the "cutting edge" when in came to employee satisfaction and productivity.

When Consensus Building Should Not Be Used

"It would be wrong to conclude that consensus building is the best way to make all decisions in an organization."

It would be wrong to conclude that consensus building is the best way to make all decisions in an organization. Leaders and managers should use a mix of the procedures listed in Figure 16.1, carefully considering when one procedure will be more effective than another. Consensus building procedures are not appropriate for all circumstances and probably should not be tried when one or more of the following situations exist.

- A decision has already been made, so a consensus building effort would be a sham.

- Adequate information is available or more input is not desired.
- Information collection will delay a decision without improving its quality, or additional data will only confuse or obscure a situation.
- It is clear that concerned parties can decide on their own.
- Crucial parties refuse to be involved in decision making, for whatever reason.
- An issue is not important enough to merit the time, energy, or expenditure of resources required to complete a consensus building process.

Consensus decision making requires a good-faith interest in the outcome of the process. If decision makers have already made a decision, going through the motions of consensus building will create discontent. Consensus also assumes that decisions can be improved through wider participation, because additional information or ideas can be incorporated. If the best and most creative ideas are already "on the table" and all of the relevant information is readily available, then little would be gained from a consensus process—unless the process might bridge divergent perspectives and build greater unity.

Consensus decision making also requires the inclusion of all organizational constituencies relevant to a particular decision. Some decisions will require the participation of all horizontal units (departments, divisions, etc.). For others, inclusion of vertical elements within the hierarchy will be more important. Some decisions will require both vertical and horizontal participation. For instance, a company might want to develop new policies regarding flexible schedules, maternity and paternity leave, and telecommuting. Since such policies could potentially affect all employees, a consensus building process would need to involve people from all units and all levels. In a union environment, a union might take the position that such policies involve fundamental conditions of work and might refuse to participate or demand reopening of contract negotiations. In that case, the company would have to determine how best to work with the union and, perhaps, whether and how to proceed without union involvement. In general, consensus building should not be used unless all appropriate constituencies are represented.

Consensus processes take time and effort. In most organizations, consensus building should be reserved for important, non-routine matters that warrant the expenditure of resources. Even organizations that place a high value on consensus decision making have had to learn when to use it and when to apply other decision-making methods.

■ Consensus Building and Dispute Resolution Systems Design

Now that we have seen how consensus building can be used in decision making, we will examine how it can be applied to help resolve disputes in organizations. Organizational leaders regularly face an array of conflicts: disputes between managers and nonmanagement employees; charges of discrimination and sexual harassment; disputes over the allocation of resources; and disputes with customers, neighbors, and regulatory agencies, among others. If poorly handled, these conflicts can generate significant costs for organizations, in terms of frustration, disappointment, poor performance, wasted time, a loss of creativity and productivity, a souring of relationships, and high employee turnover, not to mention the financial costs of attorneys hired to press or defend against lawsuits. Simply put, conflict affects an organization's bottom line.

Shrewd managers of large and small organizations are increasingly attempting to address the knotty problem of organizational conflict using an innovative approach called *dispute resolution systems design*. Dispute resolution systems design is a focused process for developing new or enhanced systems and procedures for dealing with a wide range of conflicts.[4] Consensus building may be used to design and develop broad-based support for new dispute resolution systems. In addition, the resulting systems themselves often incorporate consensus-based, voluntary conflict resolution processes, such as facilitation, mediation, and conciliation.

The Dilemmas of Organizational Dispute Resolution

Some disputes within organizations are resolved well using traditional methods, such as grievances, appeal panels, and arbitration. However, common problems with traditional dispute resolution systems include the following.

- Conflict resolution procedures, such as grievance processes, sometimes take too much time.
- Even the parties who "win" their disputes are often dissatisfied with the outcome.
- Many procedures do not provide any means for bringing parties face-to-face to address the real issues.
- In some cases, relationships among parties are actually worsened due to the dispute resolution process.
- No regular procedures exist for addressing certain kinds of conflict, such as interunit disputes or issues with customers, the public, or government agencies.
- People may refuse to use existing processes, because they consider them unfair, cumbersome, or likely to bring reprisals.
- At times, people overuse processes, overloading a system with grievances and causing a backlog of unresolved cases.
- Organizations lack ways to intervene in problems early and informally to prevent them from becoming difficult and protracted.
- Too many disputes escalate all the way to expensive adjudicatory processes, such as the use of arbitrators or law courts for resolution.

In two cases presented in this section, organizations engaged in dispute resolution systems design to develop new attitudes, skills, procedures, and structures for managing and resolving conflicts.[5]

Case Example: The Saskatoon Correctional Centre

CDR Associates was hired in 1994 to address a labor-management crisis following a strike at the Saskatoon Correctional Centre in Saskatchewan, Canada. CDR was asked to propose and implement a plan for improving the relationship between union employees and management staff, about 200 people in total. The aim was for union and management to learn to work together in a more cooperative spirit, decrease tension, reduce the degree to which people felt they were working in a negative or hostile environment, create systems to handle grievances and other conflicts in a proactive and constructive manner, and resolve specific disputes. This effort came in the wake of a confidential report by an independent evaluator hired by the Canadian government to assess conditions at provincial prisons. The report identified a number of serious concerns with the system and focused on the Saskatoon Correctional Centre as exhibiting particularly egregious problems.

CDR staff made five trips to Saskatoon over a six-month period to work with the Centre's staff and management on dispute systems design, mediation of specific conflicts, and conflict management training. On the initial visit, the CDR team talked with union and management leadership and other staff to get a full picture of the issues that needed to be addressed. They also held "office hours," during which any staff member could unofficially and even anonymously talk with the CDR team. The issues identified through this process included the following.[6]

- A fundamental lack of trust between management and the union at all levels, but particularly at the leadership level
- A backlog of close to 200 grievances
- A lack of appropriate settings for regular communication between the union and management, as well as unclear decision-making processes
- A lack of skills and informal processes for basic conflict resolution, resulting in unnecessary escalation of conflicts into formal processes (such as grievances)
- A history of highly contentious interpersonal animosities, some escalating into physical violence
- A recent bitter strike

Also during this visit, CDR helped to establish a steering committee for the project. It was composed of four members appointed by management and four by the union's Stewards Council. All members took their task—to look after the health of the entire institution, rather than to focus on their personal issues—very seriously and struggled to allot the time necessary to do the job well. Ultimately, the steering committee approved an intervention plan (developed with the CDR team), designed training programs and a new dispute system, negotiated the resolution of several key issues, provided frequent feedback to the CDR team, monitored the project's progress, and oversaw the implementation of recommendations that emerged.

The CDR team also worked closely with the highest-ranking union leader (the chief shop steward) and the prison's director, both individually and jointly, to improve their working relationship. The team helped them establish regular meetings, coached their communications, helped them clear up old tensions, and encouraged them to make agreements and follow through on them. As the relationships between their union and management constituencies improved, these two individuals found greater latitude for working together without being seen as betraying their group's interests.

A crucial element of the CDR intervention was working both to reduce the backlog of grievances and to redesign the overall system for resolving disputes within the prison. The team worked with representatives of union and management to review the backlogged cases one by one. They discovered that many involved overlapping and repeating issues regarding overtime, part-time staff, and seniority policies. In some cases, the labor and management representatives were able to come up with principles to guide decisions for a whole class of disputes (such as overtime) and then apply the principles to each appropriate case. CDR also directly mediated several difficult, long-standing cases that had become symbolic of the poor relationship between union and management. Although these cases involved only a few individuals directly, bringing the cases to closure provided a sense of hope that other problems could be addressed successfully.

To improve the overall working relationship between the union and management, CDR also facilitated a series of dialogues. They first worked separately on issues within the management team and within the Stewards Council. Subsequently, they facilitated joint meetings between the two groups. Over the six months, the participants in these meetings articulated a positive vision of the relationship both groups desired and worked together to solve problems.

The CDR team and the steering committee also worked on the system for resolving disputes. Essentially, the institution had only one mechanism for dealing with conflict: the formal grievance system defined by the union contract. This system was time-consuming, cumbersome, bureaucratic, and tended to escalate rapidly to arbitration. There were no regular means for union and management to address issues of interpretation of the contract or policy issues that fell outside the contract. Steering committee members identified aspects of the existing dispute resolution system that were working well and those that were not, and they generated ideas for improvement. Over several months, the group put together a proposal for a new conflict resolution system that encouraged people to resolve disputes quickly and at the lowest appropriate level.

The proposed system included an informal and voluntary mediation option, using mediators from the community, as well as a process for initiating an investigation or fact-finding procedure, again using outside neutrals. If parties chose to enter mediation, they did not lose their right to pursue a formal grievance at a later time. The steering committee was to oversee implementation of the new components, monitor the effectiveness of the system, and make recommendations for improvements over time.

The steering committee recognized that even with better systems, prison personnel lacked the skills for dealing with conflicts on a day-to-day basis. The first step in the new dispute resolution system called for "do-it-yourself" negotiation. If all employees could learn basic negotiation skills, they might be able to resolve most issues informally, without having to engage the formal conflict resolution system. In response to this perceived need, CDR provided a two-day basic conflict resolution course for all 200 prison employees.

At the end of the project, the steering committee decided that they should continue to work together on a regular basis to monitor relationships among union and management, oversee the new dispute resolution system, and provide a forum in which systemic sources of conflict could be identified and discussed. The steering committee also agreed to (1) provide information to all staff and management about activities designed to meet the goals of the project and (2) make recommendations for other activities that would promote and maintain constructive working relations at the prison.

Case Example: Levi Strauss & Company[7]

Levi Strauss & Co. has long been recognized as a company that tries to create a positive and productive work environment. As a means for advancing the goals in its business plan related to employee satisfaction and productivity, Levi Strauss initiated a dispute resolution systems design project. Its purpose was to develop new ways to address employee concerns, resolve disputes between peers and between employees and managers, and enhance the productivity of facilities. To develop broad support for the new dispute resolution system, the company engaged in an effort to build consensus among major constituencies within the company on the design of the system.

The first steps in the design process involved conceptualizing the project, identifying the organizational needs it would meet, and building support among senior management for the effort. A senior attorney in the company's legal department initiated these activities, drawing on her understanding of the personnel issues in the company and her experience with voluntary, collaborative methods of dispute resolution.

After senior management gave the go-ahead, coordination of the project shifted to a design team composed of managers and workers from all levels and numerous functional units within the company. The design team initiated a companywide conflict assessment, which identified major personnel issues and disputes within the organization, evaluated existing conflict resolution procedures, analyzed problems with these procedures, and compiled concerns voiced by employees about new procedures. A benchmark study of best practices in dispute resolution implemented by other companies was also conducted.

Upon completion of the assessment, the design team set out to build consensus on a new dispute resolution system. It ultimately developed a system that involved a four-step approach to resolving employee disputes.

- *Level 1:* Encourage direct negotiation or problem solving between the parties.
- *Level 2:* Provide coaching assistance for one or more parties from a Levi Strauss employee trained in conflict resolution strategies and skills, followed by a second round of unassisted negotiations.
- *Level 3:* Offer mediation by a trained, internal Levi Strauss mediator or mediation team, or an external mediator.
- *Level 4:* Provide arbitration by an external neutral who is acceptable to all parties.

To implement the new system, the design team created an implementation team. The implementation team, a diverse, cross-functional group like the design team, identified a set of pilot sites at which the new procedures could be tested. The pilot sites included a clothing design group in the company's headquarters, a sales office in New York, a sewing plant in Texas, and a finishing facility in Texas. Representatives of the pilot groups were brought together in a "pilot council," to ensure consistency between the sites. Coordination teams, composed of both managers and workers, were also established at each pilot site. All of these teams operated by consensus and were facilitated by group members. During this time, approximately 50 employees, from both management and labor, were trained at each site to be conflict management coaches, mediators, or trainers.

External consultants were used at various stages throughout the design and pilot implementation process. They helped the internal groups conduct the conflict assessment and benchmark study, consulted with the design team on the design of the system, developed educational and training materials to promote it, trained personnel in a range of cooperative conflict management procedures and skills during the pilot projects' implementation, developed an in-house training-for-trainers program, and acted as troubleshooters to address difficult problems.

Due to serious economic difficulties, Levi Strauss & Co. has recently reorganized its corporate structure and closed 13 plants, which has hampered full implementation of the dispute resolution system. Nonetheless, the effort has resulted in observable improvements in the way employees handle workplace conflicts and the resolution of a number of individual workplace disputes.

The Steps and Stages of Dispute Resolution Systems Design

"The best way to garner support for a new system is to provide for broad participation in its design."

For new dispute resolution procedures to succeed, they must enjoy the support of all potential users. The users must consider the new system fair, timely, and efficient. The best way to garner support for a new system is to provide for broad participation in its design—that is, to build consensus. The consensus building processes undertaken at Levi Strauss and the Saskatoon prison ultimately enabled those organizations to, in some degree, transform employees' relationships from conflictual to collaborative, develop common vision, and construct procedures that could be used to address current and future disputes. We will now examine the seven typical steps in a consensus building process used to design a new dispute resolution system.

It is important to note, however, that not all design or redesign processes follow these steps. In some cases, an organization will simply want to add a dispute resolution method, such as mediation, to a traditional grievance process. Since a major redesign is not required in that case, a brief consultative process may be sufficient. Smaller organizations may also be able to design dispute resolution processes in a less formal manner. For instance, when CDR Associates developed internal dispute resolution procedures, one of the senior staff drafted a new dispute resolution policy, circulated it to all staff for comments, revised it based on the feedback, and took a final draft to the full staff for approval. The more elaborate steps below are appropriate for larger, more complex organizations or institutions in which low levels of trust between managers and employees may require more deliberate and transparent efforts.

Starting the Initiative and Bringing on a Consultant

Dispute resolution systems design projects start somewhere and with someone. In many organizations, the effort is initiated by the legal department, since attorneys there may be aware of increasing legal costs from the use of arbitration and lawsuits to resolve personnel issues. The human resources department may also be active at this early stage.

At Levi Strauss, a senior lawyer, in consultation with senior management, got the process started. At the Saskatoon Correctional Centre, the initiative came from Saskatchewan province-level organizations above the centre. Key individuals at that level recognized that the prison was in need of external assistance. A provincial official and a provincial union leader jointly approached the prison director and the chief shop steward to explore options, and also solicited a proposal from CDR Associates (whom they knew from previous work in the province).

In the two cases, the parties who first catalyzed the efforts took initiative only after securing at least minimal support from senior management or, in the case of the union, approval from both officers and opinion leaders in the union. All stakeholders do not have to support a dispute resolution systems design initiative, but a critical mass of interested parties is needed for it to succeed. More than one initiative has failed because it was the brainchild of only one senior leader who did not build a constituency for the process. The role of the initiators in the two cases, however, differed tremendously once the process was launched. At Saskatoon, the director and chief shop steward remained integrally involved, both as individuals and as members of the steering committee. At Levi Strauss, the attorney stepped aside and an internal consultant from the organizational development department facilitated the diagnosis and design team meetings, where most of the initial work was accomplished.

Building the Design Team and Making an Intervention Plan

To manage a dispute resolution systems design initiative, many organizations form a *design team, steering committee, advisory group,* or *process design committee.* This group generally includes 5 to 10 representative stakeholders from throughout an organization, including all levels and functional units (e.g., departments or divisions). Design team members may be appointed by senior leadership or chosen by a constituency group (as in the Saskatoon case) or may be nominees or volunteers (as in the Levi Strauss case). It is better for a group to manage the process than an individual, because a group has more cumulative knowledge and will ensure that multiple viewpoints are considered. To be effective, design team members should

- enjoy the respect of their peers and constituencies and be articulate about their interests;
- collectively represent all parties who might have an interest in or use the system;
- be comfortable talking with people from different backgrounds, positions, and levels in the organization;
- be willing to strive for consensus decisions that will benefit the whole organization, not solely the interests of a particular group;
- have the authority to make recommendations or decisions; and
- be able to gain the support of their constituencies for agreements reached.

The responsibilities, authority, and reporting relationships of design teams are established in various ways. Sometimes they are defined by senior leaders in an organization, as at Levi Strauss. Other groups jointly negotiate their responsibilities, as in the Saskatchewan case. Some design teams receive a mandate from another group, such as a board of directors. Design teams can play a number of roles. They may act as

- sounding boards, listening to the views of groups and individuals;
- catalysts or door-openers, maintaining contact with key groups within an organization throughout a process, particularly for garnering support;
- situation assessors, collecting and analyzing information about existing systems;
- systems designers, choosing among dispute resolution procedures and organizing them into a comprehensive system;
- strategists, particularly considering how to build organizational consensus; and
- implementers of new systems.

It is important to define the roles and authority of a design team early in a process, so members understand what they are expected to do. At the same time, individuals and groups outside of the team should understand how the process will work, how final decisions will be made, and how they can provide their ideas and perspectives.

Design team members may change at different stages during a consensus building process. At Levi Strauss, people joined or left the design team during the design and planning stages of the process as the tasks and focus changed. However, enough members served throughout the process to preserve institutional memory and continuity.

The design team needs clarity about its tasks and how it will function internally. Once formed, design team members must define their overall goal and what success will look like; specify how they will make decisions; identify available information about procedures for resolving disputes, additional information needed, and ways to obtain it; perform a facilitative role within various units or constituencies, opening doors and overcoming barriers to completion of the design process; clarify the roles and responsibilities of internal and external consultants; and establish a project time line.

Diagnosing the Current Conflict Management System

A design team must conduct or arrange for an assessment of current dispute-handling processes. The assessment usually consists of two essential activities: information gathering and analysis. The goal of the assessment is to inventory existing systems, procedures, and personnel; evaluate how well systems are working; identify problem areas or conflict types that are not addressed at all; and clarify what changes, corrections, or additions might be desirable to achieve organizational goals. For instance, the assessment might reveal that existing systems handle conflicts between supervisors and employees well, but that there is no forum for addressing disputes between managers.

Design team members may collect information themselves, or they may ask a subgroup or internal consultant to do it. At times, a design team may ask an external consultant to conduct interviews, focus groups, or other types of surveys. At Levi Strauss, assessment tasks were shared among design team members and internal and external consultants. At Saskatoon, the external consultants collected a great deal of data and then brought it to the steering committee for discussion.

The procedures used to collect information vary. Levi Strauss, with its widely dispersed and diverse workforce, used questionnaires and focus groups. At Saskatoon, the CDR team used individual interviews, separate meetings with labor and management groups, joint labor-management discussions, and facilitated discussions within the steering committee. The process used must fit the culture of the organization (i.e., formal/informal, written/oral, personal/impersonal, face-to-face/anonymous), be trusted by employees, and produce accurate data about the current state of the organization.

Once data have been collected, the design team should review them, discuss themes, assess current strengths and weaknesses, identify the kinds of disputes to be addressed, clarify what needs to be changed, and build a consensus within the team concerning next steps. At this point, a group might forward its analysis to senior leadership, or, if they have the authority, proceed to the design stage. At Levi Strauss, the group held multiple consultations with leadership and constituencies outside of the design team, to build support and consensus, before proceeding with process design.

Designing a New System or
Revamping an Existing One

Once a design team has assessed the merits and problems of existing dispute resolution procedures, it is time to revise these procedures or create new ones. At this stage, dispute systems design consultants may prove very helpful, particularly because they can provide information about process options and the experience of other organizations. Both Levi Strauss and the Saskatoon Correctional Centre used the services of external consultants at this stage.

To begin the design process, a group should review the range of procedural options for resolving conflicts. Such procedures may either prevent or mitigate unnecessary or destructive conflicts, or manage and resolve them when they do arise (Moore, 1996a). Some of the conflict intervention procedures that are often considered are identified in Table 16.1 (from Moore, Delli Priscoli, Mayer, Wildau, & Smart, 1996).[8] The consultant should describe the uses of the procedures, outline their merits and weaknesses, explore potential applications, detail how they have been used by other organizations, and facilitate a discussion on the appropriateness of specific procedures for addressing problems and needs of the organization. Once design team members understand the range of procedures available to them, they must make appropriate choices and combine them in a system—often a sequence of steps.

Increasingly, companies, organizations, and agencies are choosing measures that anticipate the emergence of costly disputes and try to resolve them before they escalate. Procedures on the left side of Table 16.1, for example, include preventive, early, cooperative, and voluntary means for dispute resolution. These procedures aim to handle disputes in a timely and efficient manner and to assist parties in arriving at consensual decisions. (When an organization uses a consensus building process for designing and approving a new dispute resolution system, the result is often an increased use of consensus-based procedures for handling conflicts.)

The four-step approach developed at Levi Strauss emphasizes preventive and early resolution elements, including employee orientation sessions on cooperative conflict resolution expectations and procedures, a handle-it-yourself conflict resolution brochure, and call-in information lines. The system also includes cooperative dispute resolution procedures such as negotiation, employee coaching by peers trained in conflict analysis and resolution, and in-house mediation. Arbitration is provided as a last resort, but the company hopes that fewer than half a percent of all disputes will reach this step.

At the Saskatoon prison, the new elements were all early, informal, and voluntary procedures: better conflict resolution skills to encourage do-it-yourself negotiation, mediation, and investigation. The steering committee hoped that these measures would help prevent the filing of formal grievances. Although they did not revise the grievance process itself, they did provide a mechanism for reverting to mediation if both parties agreed.

Developing Support for the New System

Once a design team has reached a tentative agreement on new or enhanced procedures, it must take its proposals up to senior

TABLE 16.1 A Continuum of Alternative Dispute Resolution Procedures

Cooperative Decision Making	Neutral-Party Assistance with Negotiations or Cooperative Problem Solving			Neutral-Party Decision Making	
Parties Are Unassisted	Relationship-Building Assistance	Procedural Assistance	Substantive Assistance	Advisory Nonbinding Assistance	Binding Assistance
Conciliation	Counseling or therapy	Coaching/process consultation	Early neutral evaluation	Nonbinding arbitration	Binding arbitration
Information exchange meetings	Conciliation	Training	Minitrial	Summary jury trial	Med-arb
	Team building	Chairperson	Technical advisory boards/disputes panels	Advisory mediation	Mediation—then arbitration
Cooperative/collaborative problem solving	Informal social activities	Ombudsperson	Fact-finding	Private courts/judging	
Negotiations		Facilitation	Settlement conference		
		Mediation			

SOURCE: From Moore, Delli Priscoli, Mayer, Wildau, and Smart (1996).
NOTE: See note 8 in the text for explanation of the terms.

leaders, across to peers, and down to subordinates to get their input, additional concerns, suggestions for revisions or improvements, and ultimately, approval. This consensus building process may involve the preparation of memos, pamphlets, and draft concept papers; one-on-one conversations; small discussion groups; formal presentations; or large-scale meetings. The goal is to gain support for the design and build commitment to the proposed changes at all levels.

In Saskatoon, the new dispute system evolved over several months, providing ample opportunity for labor and management members of the steering committee to discuss the proposed changes with their respective constituencies. As a result, the proposal went through several iterations before the group agreed on a plan and implementation process. Levi Strauss built consensus by holding meetings between senior management and the design team, conducting small informal meetings on the plant floor at several facilities, and establishing local implementation teams.

At this point, resistance to change often surfaces. Some individuals or whole departments may feel threatened. For instance, the establishment of an ombuds office reporting directly to the CEO may be threatening to the human resources department. Or the legal department may fear a loss of control as more issues are handled through mediation. Union leadership may feel comfortable with traditional grievance procedures and resist change to less adversarial approaches. A design team must devise strategies for addressing these concerns. In some cases, one-on-one meetings with uneasy individuals will allay fears. In others, the group may need to renegotiate components of the proposed system to build a stronger organizational consensus.

Implementing the New System

The design team must now make detailed plans regarding adequate staffing to implement the program, assignment of responsibilities, and a time line and mileposts for activities to be initiated and completed. Typical tasks include case intake and screening, referral mechanisms, and a method for assigning cases to mediators. Implementation may also involve training people who will operate the new system, potential users, and in-house service providers. At the Saskatoon prison, the training program for all employees was a key component of implementation. In addition, the steering committee clarified its ongoing oversight role and developed a pool of external mediators.

Because implementation involved different tasks than the design process, Levi Strauss set up a new national-level implementation team and local coordination teams, composed of both managers and employees, at each facility where the project was introduced. These teams briefed all employees about the new procedures, arranged for half-day conflict resolution training programs, identified prospective coaches who could advise employees on constructive resolution strategies, and identified prospective in-house mediators and mediator trainers. Coaches, conflict resolution trainers, and mediators, drawn from both employees and management, participated in a 40-hour mediation and conflict management training program to prepare them to work with fellow employees. Case intake and referral systems, quality control mechanisms, and supervisory systems were also established.

Operating the New System

This stage involves ensuring that a dispute handling system functions smoothly and implementation problems are corrected. It also involves identifying, assessing, and addressing problems and disputes in the organization. At Levi Strauss, operations were managed largely by facility-based, management-employee coordination teams and dispute resolution coordinators. The teams took responsibility for overall policies and oversight of the initiative. The coordinators managed the intake of personnel cases and the assignment of coaches and mediators and generally supervised the mediation process. At one of the early training sessions at a blue jeans finishing facility, employees used the cooperative problem-solving skills they had just learned to resolve a problem in the finishing process that had plagued the company for years.

Dispute resolution systems are an important aspect of organizational life, since they help shape how people communicate with each other and work to handle their differences. For this reason, dispute resolution systems design processes are prime candidates for the use of consensus building procedures.

■ Roles of Leaders and Managers in Consensus Building

Managers play a powerful role in initiating, supporting, and sustaining consensus building efforts in modern organizations. Since this role is new for many managers, they have often been required to learn new skills so that they can succeed. Since the 1960s, especially in North America, managers have adopted more collaborative styles of leadership that engage people from multiple levels of an organizations in vision building, goal setting, program development, and day-to-day decision making. This new concept of management has been called *facilitative leadership.*[9] This shift preceded, and now runs parallel to, the development of collaborative, consensus-based approaches to management.

In fact, leadership roles at *all* levels of organizations are changing, particularly as consensus-based procedures are implemented for decision making and dispute resolution. Leading is no longer an exclusive function of those above; people also lead from below. "Facilitative leaders" may be found at all levels of an organization. So, while many collaborative decision-making and dispute systems design processes are initiated from above, leadership often then shifts to midlevel managers and other staff lower in an organization. In fact, broad participation and ownership by multiple levels within an organization are critical for success.

The dispute systems design initiative of Levi Strauss illustrates this well. Although the project was initiated by the legal department, the design team included managers and staff from diverse levels and units within the organization. The opinions of floor employees and managers were valued equally—because the ultimate plan had to be acceptable to all potential users.

Facilitative leadership does not arise only from inside of organizations. At Levi Strauss and Saskatoon, one or more external consultants provided systems advice, procedural options, and, when requested, facilitation assistance, as part of the effort to build consensus.

*Functions of Facilitative
Leaders in Consensus Building*

What do facilitative leaders—whether from inside or outside of organizations—do to help groups build consensus? We have identified 11 key roles that facilitative leaders perform in consensus building processes. We will examine each of these briefly.

1. *Process visionary.* Leaders are typically accepted as substantive visionaries who set specific goals for an organization. A less common function is that of a process visionary or *conceptualizer.* The leader as process visionary offers general goals, such as a more cooperative work environment, greater ownership of the way work is done, or increased voluntary settlement of disputes. These leaders then develop a vision of a process that can be used to move people in that direction. In the cases described, key leaders in management, the union, and the legal department suggested procedures for involving a cross section of the organization in consensus building.

2. *Champion.* Champions hold positions of both formal and informal authority and are advocates for new approaches (Kanter, 1983). As respected individuals, they are able to get others involved, marshal resources, and build support for new initiatives. In the Levi Strauss case, various members of the design team played the role of champion to build support for the initiative at different stages.

3. *Convenor.* In the convening role, leaders assess a problem and bring together the right people to address it. Convening is a critical task in a consensus decision-making or dispute systems design process, because the right people must participate or the process will fail to address the concerns and interests of all parties, and implementation will be at risk due to lack of support. The convenor generally holds a formal position of authority. At Alianza, the convenor was the senior manager in charge of marketing.

4. *Educator.* In this function, the leader educates peers, subordinates, and superiors about the task at hand, be it collaborative decision making or dispute systems design. In each of the

cases described, leaders from all levels helped to educate their colleagues about consensus building, the interests of various groups within the organization, and potential procedures that might address these interests. Leaders external to the organization, such as consultants, also play an important role as educators, especially in presenting procedural options for resolving disputes or building agreements.

5. *Facilitator.* Facilitators assist in group problem solving by promoting effective communication among participants, encouraging the exchange of information, and articulating emerging consensus decisions. Leaders may facilitate meetings or may simply participate as group members who offer procedural suggestions concerning how the group can better accomplish its task. Facilitative leaders may also recognize the need for external facilitation assistance, help secure group commitment for it, and recruit and select a facilitator. External facilitators are process experts who do not have a substantive stake in any specific outcome or solution. As an impartial and skilled resource, they can often design and conduct successful problem-solving procedures to address even the thorniest issues. External facilitators were used in each of the cases above. In addition, Levi Strauss used internal facilitators.

6. *Coach and trainer.* The facilitative leader informally coaches group participants to improve their performance or conducts formal training sessions to impart necessary skills and procedures. Most of the cases cited above included a training or coaching component, often conducted by an external consultant with appropriate skills. At Alianza, consultants presented training modules on cross-cultural communication and problem solving. In the Saskatoon and Levi Strauss cases, consultants presented formal training programs on collaborative negotiation procedures, the mediation process, conflict resolution strategies and coaching, and training-for-trainers.

7. *Troubleshooter.* Most consensus building initiatives include at least one major hurdle or glitch that is hard for the consensus building group to overcome without the assistance of a powerful facilitative leader. A leader might have to address such problems as the refusal of key persons in the organization to support a consensus building process, unexpected shifts in per-

sonnel or resources, internal group dissension, or significant changes in the external environment.

8. *Salesperson.* In a role similar to the champion, a salesperson "markets" consensus proposals to others in the organization (such as other senior- and midlevel managers) to gain support for implementation. Facilitative leaders may also oversee the "sales" activities of other group members. This role is important because the success or failure of a consensus building process often hinges on the active support of respected leaders and people in authority. For example, at Levi Strauss, the CEO hosted a special reception for the members of the dispute resolution systems design team, at which he expressed his strong support for the initiative. His visible endorsement of the process helped sell it to others in the organization.

9. *Incentive provider.* People participate most enthusiastically in consensus building when they feel there is something in it for them. Those taking active roles in a design team or guiding a decision-making process need tangible benefits. Important incentives include the satisfaction that a new procedure effectively meets individual or organizational needs, the enjoyment of working successfully with other group members, public recognition, opportunities for advancement, or other more tangible rewards. Facilitative leaders often provide incentives that encourage top-level performance. At Levi Strauss, managers publicly recognized the contribution of individuals and teams at the end of each phase of the project.

10. *Project manager.* In every successful consensus building project, someone, or a small group, acts as project manager: coordinating team activities, making sure everything runs smoothly, and seeing that a group accomplishes its task. A facilitative leader often performs this role.

11. *Decision-making group member or design team member.* At initial meetings, a facilitative leader may help to define the mandate of a group and identify parameters for decision making. After that, a leader often becomes a full and equal participant in a consensus building process, either to represent a specific group of interests or to voice personal concerns. This participation

requires a leader to put his or her decision-making authority aside to allow group consensus building to occur. However, he or she may continue to voice opinions and be an advocate for individual views or interests. In each of the cases described in this chapter, senior managers participated as group members and helped the groups arrive at mutually acceptable decisions that satisfied the interests of stakeholders at all levels in the organization.

Problems, Barriers, and Dilemmas in Consensus Building

People often express concerns about the desirability of undertaking a consensus building initiative. This section provides answers to some of the most common questions and concerns regarding the use of consensus-based methods inside organizations.

Questions and Concerns of Senior- and Midlevel Managers

"Isn't decision making my job?" and *"Do I lose my authority if I agree to participate in consensus building processes to make decisions or resolve disputes?"* Final approval of all major decisions usually rests with the chief executive of an organization, or with other managers to whom decision-making authority has been delegated. However, more creative, effective, and acceptable proposals can often be developed by representative groups. These recommendations can then be submitted to senior decision makers for consideration and, potentially, approval and implementation. Consensus building is designed to enhance the quality and acceptability of a decision, not to overturn organizational authority to make final decisions.

"What happens if I don't like the outcome of a collaborative problem-solving process? Do I have to accept it and live with it?" In consensus building, every participant, including leaders and managers, has an opportunity to voice opinions and advocate for interests. For consensus to be reached, all opinions must be considered and all interests satisfied to the greatest extent possible. It is management's responsibility to articulate its interests clearly to ensure that the outcome will address those interests. If

all key interests are not met (including management's), there will be no consensus for managers to accept or reject.

"Doesn't consensus building take a lot of time? We can't do consensus building on every issue or we will never make any decisions." Consensus building is not appropriate for all decisions—only those that meet the criteria in the section "When to Use Consensus Building" earlier in this chapter. Any comprehensive decision-making process takes time, and consensus building does too. Most decisions have a decision-making phase, a selling or persuading phase (in which support is solicited from those affected by a decision), and an implementation phase. Command decisions may be made quickly, but often take a long time to implement because people affected by the decision, or those who must assist with implementation, must be convinced to support it. Consensus decision making may have a longer decision-making phase, but the selling and implementation phases are frequently shorter, because support is developed during decision making and does not have to be sought later. So, in the long run, consensus building may be more efficient and rapid than command decisions.

"How can we involve subordinates when they do not understand the big picture and do not have the expertise needed to make an informed decision?" Managers should involve people in a consensus decision process who have an interest or stake in the outcome—or who are in a position to block implementation. Participants do not have to have specific expertise on the issues in question. Consensus building is a mutual education process in which participants share information; therefore, all parties generally gain a more complete grasp of the issues during the process. Although people lower in organizations may not perceive the big picture in the same way as senior executives, they usually understand one or more components of the problem—often better than their superiors. Securing input from all levels of an organization helps to create a wiser, better, and more acceptable decision than if participation and insights from any significant part of the organization are excluded.

"Can I initiate a consensus building process without gaining the support of my superiors?" Ideally, a consensus building process should enjoy at least minimal support from all levels in an organization before proceeding. With this support, all participants are more likely to accept the outcome. Midlevel managers who initiate such a process should clarify the merits of shared decision making with both superiors and subordinates and make efforts to secure the support of champions from all levels before beginning.

"Initiating and supporting a consensus building process is not an abdication of responsibility."

"Won't my superiors see consensus building as an abdication of my responsibilities?" The responsibility of leaders is to guide good decision making within their organization—whether by making a decision themselves or promoting wise decision making by others. If a manager initiates and supports a consensus building process, this is not an abdication of responsibility. It may, in fact, be the wisest course of action. In addition, a skilled proponent of consensus will not erode his or her power. Rather, others in the organization will come to recognize the leadership and power associated with adept consensus building as a different source of authority—not power *over* others but power *with* others.

"Should we hire an external consultant to help guide our decision making or dispute systems design process? Will it really be worth the effort or money?" Expertise in conducting consensus building with large numbers of people, in developing consensus decision-making procedures, and/or in dispute systems design is rare among personnel in most corporations, government agencies, and nonprofit organizations. This is especially true in organizations without a history of shared decision making. Consultants with expertise in consensus building can be of significant assistance to organizations—with resulting time and cost savings—because they are familiar with approaches and procedures that are likely to succeed. External assistance can often speed up a decision-making process and lead to more rapid implementation. After an organization learns new ways of making decisions or successfully implements new systems, external consultants are typically no longer needed.

Concerns of Employees and Unions

Reservations about consensus building processes are not the exclusive domain of managers; union members and other non-management employees may also have concerns and questions.

"If we participate in a consensus building process, aren't we just doing management's job without being recognized or paid to do so?" Union members and other employees participate in consensus building processes to exert influence on the outcome of critical issues in an organization. By participating, employees are not doing management's job; rather, they are shaping decision making by promoting their concerns and interests directly. Although employees are not usually paid extra to participate in consensus building, they may receive benefits such as public recognition; increased status in an organization, employee association, or union; and/or opportunities for professional enrichment.

"How can we trust that management will respect our views and ensure that we are not expending a lot of energy for nothing?" There is no guarantee that management will accept the results of a consensus process. However, if management has given initial approval for a process, a representative group has reached a consensus agreement or recommendation, and the group has considered the interests of managers, it is highly likely that management will accept and implement the decision or recommendations. When management rejects a consensus recommendation, managers jeopardize their credibility as advocates for or participants in future cooperative efforts.

"Won't the direct involvement of employees in a consensus building process weaken the role of the union as the representative of the employees?" Employee involvement in consensus building does not necessarily weaken the role of unions. In fact, joint decision making provides opportunities for unions to engage with management in decision making far beyond what is possible in collective bargaining and contract administration meetings. Consensus building in a unionized setting should involve union officials and other informal union leaders, to ensure that all views are heard and that employees approve agreements.

Typically, collective bargaining agreements include provisions regarding the handling of grievances. In unionized settings, therefore, the procedures described previously regarding the design of dispute resolution systems must include strong union participation and buy-in. At times, by joint union-management agreement, new procedures can be defined as supplementary to the contract to avoid opening contract negotiations. If the new procedures are successful, the groups can decide if they want to include them in the next full round of contract talks. Similarly, many labor-management contracts now include provisions for labor-management councils, which take a variety of forms. These councils can serve as consensus building mechanisms, functioning much as the steering committee did in the Saskatoon case.

"How can we use consensus building in the context of unequal negotiating power or influence?" Consensus building is a process that attempts to satisfy the interests of *all* involved parties and not just those of the most powerful party. In consensus-based decision making, all parties are encouraged to advocate for their interests, listen to the interests of others, and seek solutions that address and satisfy as many of those interests as possible. Although managers and other employees may command different amounts and sources of power (and consensus building does not change that), the consensus building process provides an opportunity for educating others about everyone's concerns—an opportunity that would not normally be available to a weaker party. Groups that feel they have little power at the beginning of a consensus process are often pleasantly surprised by both the process and outcome. They find not only that others listen to them but also that their interests are seen as legitimate and are addressed in final agreements or recommendations. Moreover, power is dynamic in consensus building. When seemingly weaker parties prepare well and make good proposals, they can increase their power in a negotiation.

Other Problems and Concerns

"How can consensus building be introduced in an organization with a long history of hierarchical and top-down decision making?" An organization with a history of top-down decision making may find it more difficult to introduce consensus-based

procedures. However, numerous organizations with these traditions have successfully implemented consensus programs. In general, the transition often occurs because management has discovered that top-down decision making (at least on a specific issue in question) has not resulted in desirable outcomes and that a new approach is needed. Hierarchical organizations often try consensus building on a case-by-case basis, with a narrow mandate for a decision-making group. Usually, they attempt the process on less critical problems first, and then expand its use to more important issues once it has proven successful.

"An existing issue or conflict is so serious that development of new consensus-based procedures is not possible at this time. What should we do?" Organizations that are embroiled in serious conflict often find it difficult to develop new dispute-handling systems or to institute new decision-making procedures. In such cases, the organization is advised to address the conflict first—possibly using consensus-based processes, such as mediation—and then develop more institution-wide procedures. The Saskatoon case illustrates this well. The union and management leadership, with assistance from the CDR team, worked on their relationship and on outstanding grievances before tackling larger policy issues.

■ Conclusion

The cases cited in this chapter show that consensus building can help to achieve significant organizational change. Consensus-based decision making can result in decisions that are better, more fully supported, and more easily implemented than top-down decisions. The use of consensus processes to design dispute resolution systems results in problem-solving procedures that effectively handle all kinds of disputes, whether they are programmatic, intra- or interdepartmental, labor-management, or personnel related. The systems often emphasize and use consensus-based dispute resolution procedures, such as negotiation, peer coaching, facilitation, and mediation, in contrast to more traditional systems developed through top-down decision making. Successful implementation of a consensus building process can be greatly enhanced by the active involvement of people in leadership positions. Such leadership is not confined to the highest levels;

those who lead from the middle and from below provide crucial energy and creativity for building broad consensus on new approaches and systems that meet the challenges of the modern organization.

■ Notes

1. The case of Kate Morgan and People for People is hypothetical, although it is loosely based on a composite of real situations.

2. In a joint venture, two or more companies engage in an economic enterprise together, and each provides investment capital, human resources, and/or intellectual capital.

3. Although we have drawn on the experience of CDR Associates in writing this chapter, most (if not all) firms working in dispute resolution could recount similar experiences. Several other consulting firms worked on portions of the consensus building, decision making, and dispute systems design projects in the Saskatchewan and Levi Strauss cases presented in the second section of the chapter.

4. Other excellent sources of information on designing dispute resolution systems within organizations include the 1988 book by Ury, Brett, and Goldberg called *Getting Disputes Resolved* and a 1996 volume by Costantino and Merchant titled *Designing Conflict Management Systems.*

5. All three cases described in this chapter involve fairly large organizations. While the degree of complexity and difficulty may be less in smaller organizations, the same general principles apply.

6. Note that all of these problems concern the staff and management of the prison; issues regarding prisoners were not included.

7. For an expanded discussion of the Levi Strauss experience, see Case 17.

8. Many of the terms in this table are self-explanatory or defined elsewhere in this book. Others may require explanation. *Conciliation,* for example, is a process of building positive social relationships between disputing parties through site visits, casual conversations, facilitated workshops, and so forth. A *minitrial* is an abbreviated, nonbinding trial, often conducted by a retired judge, that provides parties with detailed data about the legal merits of each party's case. The purpose of a minitrial is to better prepare parties to negotiate a settlement. Neutrals on *technical advisory boards* and *nonbinding disputes panels* review conflicting data and information central to a dispute and suggest ways to reconcile the differences. In an *advisory mediation* process, an impartial party first provides process assistance to help parties seek resolution but, if a negotiation reaches impasse, will offer a nonbinding, advisory opinion on how the case should be settled. A *settlement conference* is a pretrial procedure used within the court system in which parties' attorneys, and sometimes the disputants themselves, seek a mutually agreeable solution. A settlement judge or referee presides over the conference. A *summary jury trial* is very similar to a

real trial; it includes a judge, jury, testimony, evidence, and so forth, but the process is abbreviated (typically taking less than a day) and the verdict is nonbinding. The idea is to give parties a realistic assessment of how a jury may decide a case, perhaps encouraging them to settle out of court. *Arbitration* is a private, quasi-judicial process in which disputants present their arguments and evidence to a neutral party who then issues an opinion. Arbitration can be either binding or nonbinding. In *"med-arb,"* parties seek to reach agreement through assisted mediation, but agree to submit to binding arbitration (conducted by the mediator) should they reach impasse. *"Mediation—then arbitration"* is essentially the same process, except that the mediator and arbitrator are different people. *Private courts* or *private judging* are trial-like procedures that are typically overseen by former judges who issue nongovernmental, binding rulings. The process is often quicker and less costly than a public court trial (Moore et al., 1996b).

9. For additional information on facilitative leadership, see Rosabeth Moss Kanter's *When Giants Learn to Dance* (1989) and Robert Greenleaf's *Servant Leadership* (1977).

■ *References*

Costantino, C. A., & Merchant, C. S. (1996). *Designing conflict management systems: A guide to creating productive and healthy organizations.* San Francisco: Jossey-Bass.

Doyle, M., & Straus, D. (1982). *How to make meetings work.* New York: Jove.

Greenleaf, R. K. (1977). *Servant leadership: A journey into the nature of legitimate power and greatness.* New York: Paulist.

Kanter, R. M. (1983). *The change masters: Innovations for productivity in the American corporation.* New York: Simon & Schuster.

Kanter, R. M. (1989). *When giants learn to dance: Mastering the challenges of strategy, management, and careers in the 1990s.* New York: Simon & Schuster.

Moore, C. (1996a). *Conflict prevention as an element of dispute resolution systems.* Unpublished manuscript. Boulder, CO: Author.

Moore, C., with Delli Priscoli, J., Wildau, S., Smart, L., & Mayer, B. (1996b). *Dispute resolution systems design: Resource manual.* Boulder, CO: CDR Associates.

Moore, C., Delli Priscoli, J., Mayer, B., Wildau, S., & Smart, L. (1996). *An executive manual on alternative dispute resolution.* Ft. Belvoir, VA: U.S. Army Corps of Engineers.

Ury, W. L., Brett, J. M., & Goldberg, S. B. (1988). *Getting disputes resolved: Designing systems to cut the costs of conflict.* San Francisco: Jossey-Bass.

EVALUATING CONSENSUS BUILDING

■ *Judith E. Innes*

C onsensus building is a comparatively new but increasingly popular way of making choices, addressing problems, and developing strategy in complex and controversial situations. It is often used as a supplement, or even an alternative, to decision making by legislatures, chief executives, bureaucracies, and courts. Consensus building has not yet, however, achieved the recognition or public acceptance enjoyed by these familiar institutions. Not many people understand how consensus building works, much less what it accomplishes when it is most effective. Evaluations of consensus building—evaluations that assess its strengths and weaknesses, help determine when it should be used, compare it with traditional decision-making procedures, and so forth—can help build public understanding of and trust in consensus-based processes.

Evaluations can also fulfill numerous other purposes. Mediators and facilitators who design consensus processes, for example, might find evaluations helpful in determining which strategies and methods are likely to work most effectively, under which conditions, and for which tasks. Potential participants need in-

This chapter draws extensively on the paper "Consensus Building and Complex Adaptive Systems: A Framework for Evaluating Collaborative Planning" (Innes & Booher, in press-b). The author is indebted to David Booher for his advice and ideas on this chapter.

formation about how and when consensus building is effective so they can decide whether or not to get involved. Public and private agencies, interest groups, and business organizations called on to lend staff time or financial support also need an informed way to reach this decision. Once deliberations are under way, funders, convenors, and participants may want to assess how a process is working and make midcourse corrections. After a process concludes, interested but nonparticipating parties may want to know what the outcomes were. Those who study public policy making and organizational development need to understand how and why consensus building is similar to or different from the alternatives, develop theory and evidence to define *best practices,* and establish when and why consensus building is (or is not) successful. Evaluations can help meet all of these needs.

This chapter argues that good consensus building can produce high-quality agreements and commitments to action that other methods of deliberation and choice would have been unlikely, or even unable, to produce on their own. It makes the further case that even when a consensus process does not result in formal agreements, it can produce valuable results for a community or organization—results such as new working relationships, trust among formerly contending parties, and increased knowledge and understanding about an issue. These latter consequences, which are too often unrecognized by those assessing consensus processes, make consensus building very difficult to evaluate. They also take on particular importance when we look at them in the light of a complex systems perspective. The chapter briefly describes complexity science and explains how it can provide a new framework for evaluating consensus building. Relying on concepts drawn from the complexity sciences, best practices developed by dispute resolution professionals, ideas drawn from social theory, and an extensive body of research on consensus building practice, the chapter outlines two sets of criteria—one dealing with process and one with outcomes—that should be applied in evaluating consensus building.

The chapter then describes three general types of evaluations of consensus-based efforts: (1) midcourse evaluations, which are conducted partway into a negotiation to assess progress and make process improvements; (2) end-of-process evaluations, which are done just as an effort concludes to find out about the satisfaction of participants and identify the first-order outcomes; and (3) retrospective evaluations, which are conducted well after a process is over to identify the value and stability of agreements, the durability of relationships, and other second- or third-order (i.e., long-term) effects, or to compare consensus-based processes with each other or with other decision-making methods. Finally, the chapter outlines the key research methods recommended for gathering evaluation information, including the use of surveys, in-depth interviewing, focus groups, and direct observation.

The San Francisco Estuary Project

This chapter draws extensively on the case of the San Francisco Estuary Project (SFEP, Case 5), a five-year consensus building effort funded by the National Estuary Program and chaired and staffed by the U.S. Environmental Protection Agency (EPA). In this project, hundreds of stakeholders took part in technical advisory and issue-based committees to develop a Comprehensive Conservation and Management Plan (CCMP) for the San Francisco Bay and delta. These committees, as well as a 49-member management committee, were assisted by professional facilitators. SFEP participants included representatives of businesses, agricultural interests, local governments, environmental organizations, citizens groups, and numerous state and federal agencies (e.g., the U.S. Army Corps of Engineers, the U.S. Fish and Wildlife Service, the California Department of Water Resources). It was an extraordinarily complex effort, in part because the estuary extends into 12 counties and touches four major metropolitan areas.

SFEP is a useful case for the purposes of this chapter because it continued long enough for a full range of consequences to develop and it started long enough ago for second- and third-order effects to have emerged. (The group reached agreement on the CCMP in 1993.) In addition to the CCMP, the project produced a "state of the estuary" report and an agreement on the use of a unique new indicator, the isohaline index, which uses salinity to assess the capacity of the bay and delta to support biodiversity. Although many participants and observers regarded the CCMP and the state of the estuary report as not particularly innovative or significant, the process did have important consequences. The isohaline index, for example, became the basis for the state's decision to increase the amount of water released into the delta in dry years. Many of the stakeholders learned a good deal about important technical issues. New relationships were formed among stakeholders who had been in bitter conflict. SFEP participants gained skills and experience that they brought to other, related consensus building processes that were established later. In fact, by 1997, consensus building had become the norm in the water policy arena in California, due in part to the example of the SFEP.

■ What Consensus Building Can Accomplish

"Consensus-based discussions can have secondary effects, such as better relationships and learning." Participants in consensus-based discussions can reach good agreements that meet their needs and interests. But such discussions can also have secondary effects, such as better relationships and learning, that may prove to be even more important in the long run. These effects must be considered in evaluations of consensus building to get a complete and accurate sense of the value of consensus-based efforts. This section looks at a few of the many positive outcomes that can result from consensus processes.

High-Quality Agreements

Consensus building efforts, if designed and implemented well, can produce agreements among stakeholders who would otherwise not even talk to one another. These agreements are typically of higher quality than decisions made through majority-rule voting or litigation, because they satisfy the interests and concerns of all parties and are based on the knowledge and expertise of those parties. Such agreements can also be more durable; implementation is less likely to be thwarted by unhappy stakeholders, because the interests of all stakeholders have been taken into account. Agreements are more likely to *be* fair and to be *regarded as* fair. They are likely to be grounded in carefully tested, widely agreed-on technical information, not on information that is trusted by only one set of stakeholders. Also, because consensus building involves dynamic group discussions, it is more likely to produce innovative ideas (Susskind & Cruikshank, 1987).[1]

It is important to note that consensus building *can* produce low-quality agreements—agreements that offer little improvement over the status quo, represent only a superficial consensus, are unfair, or are grounded in false or inadequate information. But consensus processes that are designed according to the guidance in this book and the criteria set forth in this chapter should produce high-quality agreements.

Beyond Agreements

Consensus building processes, whether or not they result in an agreement, typically produce numerous secondary consequences that are sometimes more important than any agreement. For example, consensus building can result in new relationships and trust among stakeholders who were either in conflict or simply not in communication. These people may begin to work together on other issues and, in so doing, solve problems in mutually satisfactory ways. In the SFEP, for example, a Corps of Engineers representative got to know some Sierra Club leaders and, from then on, contacted them prior to finalizing project designs for dredging or construction to talk about how projects could be made more environmentally acceptable. As a result, many Corps of Engineers projects were modified, and conflict between the Corps of Engineers and environmental organizations was greatly reduced.

A consensus building effort may also result in the formation of a new project, partnership, or organization. Because of the SFEP, for example, the Aquatic Habitat Institute (a quasi-governmental research agency) was restructured to coordinate the monitoring of the bay's water quality.

Learning is another important second-stage consequence. In any well-managed process, participants and their constituents come to have a much better understanding of the technical issues involved in a controversy. In the SFEP, for example, participants jointly learned about the most important causes of the bay's declining water quality and the extent of the loss of fisheries. Consensus building participants can also learn about the concerns of other stakeholders and the conditions and constraints under which they operate. As a result, they often develop a more realistic and sympathetic understanding of others' interests and of how others might respond to proposed solutions or options. In fact, participants in group processes can achieve both single- and double-loop learning. In single-loop learning, they discover better ways to accomplish their goals and, as a result, change their strategies. In double-loop learning, they conclude that their goals are unrealistic or they discover that if they rethink their objectives, they can meet more of their real interests than they had hoped. Double-loop learning involves going back to the beginning and starting the dialogue over with new assumptions (Argyris & Schon, 1974). In consensus building, double-loop learning can lead to surprising alliances among parties and can end paralyzing conflict.

New relationships and trust, new partnerships and organizations, and joint learning are all examples of shared social, intellectual, and political capital (Gruber, 1994; Innes, Gruber, Neuman, & Thompson, 1994). Such capital provides value to individual stakeholders as well as to a larger community. Even when formal agreements turn out to be difficult or inappropriate to implement, or when such agreements seem to offer only modest changes from the status quo, a consensus process can still have important results if it has produced one or more of these kinds of capital.

Consensus building must therefore be seen not only as a method to move a community forward on controversial issues (although it is very good at accomplishing that) but also as a way to build the practices of civil discourse. It is a way to teach participants what they share and how they can work together long after a group disperses. Ultimately, consensus building needs to be evaluated as a way to build the capacity of citizens to communicate, understand, and cooperate.

■ *Existing Evaluations of Consensus Building*

The evaluations of consensus building conducted to date have not adequately assessed the full set of long-term and secondary effects outlined in the previous section (and described in more detail later in the section on criteria). Evaluations were often conducted too early for these effects to be identified, or researchers simply chose not to take them into account. The value of consequences such as learning, new practices, and new institutions has only recently begun to be acknowledged. Some researchers have, however, used multiple data-gathering methods, which allowed them to address a variety of questions and make the kinds of case comparisons that can provide meaningful evidence about the benefits and limitations of consensus building.[2]

Although existing evaluations are not comprehensive, a substantial body of experience does exist from which to develop a framework for conducting thorough evaluations of consensus building. Much of this experience is recorded in the general methodology literature on evaluation,[3] and many of the evaluation studies most pertinent to our purposes focus on mediated dispute resolution or negotiation rather than consensus building, per se. Also, many relevant studies are technical reports, theses, or monographs, none of which are widely available (Amundsen, 1998; Corburn, 1996; Elliott, 1993; Moss, 1997). A number of articles have been published, however, that describe criteria and principles for framing an evaluation or theories that can be tested (Campbell & Floyd, 1996; Harter, 1997; Menkel-Meadow, 1997; Susskind & MacMahon, 1985). The Society of Professionals in Dispute Resolution (1997) has developed guidelines for dispute resolution that are, implicitly, evaluation criteria; most of them correspond to the criteria offered in this chapter. Similarly, the elements of a framework for consensus building developed in Canada could be used as criteria (Canadian Roundtables, 1993).

Published evaluations have used a variety of research methodologies. Many have used surveys or in-depth interviews to assess participants' levels of satisfaction and their perceptions about what was achieved (Brett, Barsness, & Goldberg, 1996; Elliott, 1993; Helling, 1998). Others have compared a small number of cases with each other, using surveys, interviews, and written records to evaluate techniques and outcomes (Bowman, 1988; Susskind & MacMahon, 1985; Wheeler, 1993).

Some evaluators have, by analyzing written records, developed quantitative indicators to compare mediated with unmediated disputes (Coglianese, 1997; Sipe, 1998). This type of study, however, can only include variables that are readily measurable and obtainable from records, such as the time spent on a process or whether or not parties reached a settlement. It does not provide much understanding of the quality of the outcomes. Also, if these studies do not include extremely large numbers of cases (200 to 300) and do not provide qualitative information about each case, their conclusions can be misleading. A case in point is the 1997 study by Coglianese, which purports to demonstrate that negotiated rulemaking took longer than traditional methods of developing federal regulations and did not reduce litigation. These conclusions were made by comparing the formal records of 17 cases of negotiated rulemaking with traditional rulemaking. The 17 cases were not comparable with the conventional rulemaking set, however, because most of them involved more controversial issues. Indeed, they were selected for negotiation because they were particularly difficult and unlikely to fare well in the ordinary rulemaking process (L. E. Susskind, personal communication, June 9, 1998). The study only speculates on why they were selected, rather than finding out. Also, the technique the author used to estimate the duration of each process was inappropriate (Harter, 1997). If the author had compared matched cases (in which negotiated processes were paired with similar but nonnegotiated examples), used larger numbers of examples, or gathered other forms of information, his results would have been more meaningful.

■ The Challenge of Evaluating Consensus Building

"Consensus building challenges typical thinking about success and failure, which makes it difficult to evaluate."

Why haven't more comprehensive evaluations of consensus building been done? In large part, it is because consensus building challenges typical thinking about success and failure, which makes it difficult to evaluate. Conventional ideas about decision making and evaluation may fail to capture the unique values offered by consensus building and, if applied, may lead an evaluator to see failure where there is success and vice versa. This section discusses some of the challenges of evaluating consensus building.

The Challenge of Evaluating Agreements

The most obvious (and common) criterion for evaluating a consensus process is whether or not it produced an agreement. Certainly, this is an important measure. At times, however, an agreement may be reached but the process could be regarded as a failure. Agreement does not mean much, for example, if it is superficial and conflict breaks out again soon. Nor is it valuable if a proposal is poorly informed, infeasible, or unlikely to produce the results that participants anticipate. For instance, an agreement to increase water flows to improve biodiversity in San Francisco Bay would have been a failure if the scientific data to support the relationship between biodiversity and flows were flawed. Agreement for the sake of agreement is not success. Quality matters. This is true for consensus building more than conventional decision-making forums because consensus processes are not typically formal and institutionalized; if people are to trust new, informal, and ad hoc processes, they must see that these processes produce quality outcomes.

Another way to think about success is to ask, "Did we accomplish our goal?" In consensus building, this criterion is not of much value. Often participants do not have a shared goal, other than perhaps reaching an agreement. Rather, each party is typically focused on meeting his or her own interests. Also, a process may start with a broad or ambiguous purpose that cannot be measured or that participants may not define in a common way. Alternatively, a group may start with one broad objective and then choose to alter it in the course of a dialogue.

Another possible evaluation criterion is whether or not agreements are implemented. But in some cases, implementation might represent failure—for example, if later scientific evidence contradicts a group's original conclusion but an agreement forces action nonetheless. And it is not necessarily evidence of failure if an agreement is not implemented. Even when an agreement was well informed and backed by stakeholder commitment, implementation can be affected by many unforeseeable factors, such as budget shortfalls, expensive emergencies such as earthquakes, or the election of a new government.

Finally, even a process that does not reach agreement may well be a success, because consensus building results in so many other valuable consequences. Participants may learn more about an issue, each other's interests, and possible solutions, for example.

The Challenge of Assessing Outcomes Other Than Agreements

Agreements, therefore, are not the only outcome that should be considered in an evaluation. An evaluator who looks only at an agreement will miss the other important results of a process such as improved relationships, new collaborative activities, and so forth. It is difficult to identify and document these other outcomes, however, in part because they may not be identifiable until long after a process is over. And these consequences are difficult, if not impossible, to measure quantitatively, even when they are quite significant.

It is also challenging to find ways to attribute outcomes directly to a particular consensus-based process. Consensus building is typically used in complex situations, in which many activities are taking place simultaneously and external conditions keep changing. A project or partnership that is established a year or two after a consensus process concludes may be the combined result of that process and many other factors. It is often impossible to determine conclusively that the consensus process caused it.

For example, several important consensus building efforts followed the SFEP. First, the governor formed the Bay-Delta Oversight Council, a consensus-based group charged with revisiting the water flow proposals of the SFEP (and including a different mix of stakeholders). At the same time, the federal government organized a group of agency representatives to look at the use of the isohaline index and to consider applying the isohaline standard recommended by the SFEP. These two groups were then merged to form a new consensus building effort called CALFED. CALFED prepared a bond measure for statewide water projects and habitat conservation that was supported by all major state interests—it was one of the few bond measures to pass in California in 1996. CALFED also built agreements among agencies and other interests that some believe signal an end to

California's legendary water wars. SFEP was at least partly responsible for the creation of these successful spin-off processes.
SFEP had demonstrated to the water community and the governor, for example, that consensus building can be powerful. Also,
a number of people who had learned negotiation and collaboration skills in the SFEP turned up in some of these later processes.
Clearly, other factors contributed to the creation of CALFED,
such as the president's interest in having federal agencies collaborate with state agencies. So the events cannot be uniquely attributed to the SFEP, but the linkages can be traced through careful
inquiry.

The Challenge of Evaluating Process

It is not enough to evaluate consensus building solely on the
basis of outcomes; the process itself matters. If an agreement—
even a "good" agreement—was not arrived at by a process that
was fair, open, inclusive, accountable, or otherwise legitimate, it
is unlikely to receive support from all participants, much less from
outsiders. Unlike traditional decision-making methods, consensus building is not supported by the force of law or tradition. Its
participants are usually not elected or formally appointed. Therefore, its outcomes may not be as readily accepted as legitimate as
those made through traditional means. Consensus building thus
stands or falls on the acceptability of the process used, and it
needs to produce good solutions *through* good processes. When
process criteria are met, stakeholders who have not achieved their
goals may still support an agreement because they feel their voices
were heard and their interests were incorporated as much as
possible.

In any case, a process that ignores a vulnerable interest, fails
to take important facts into account, or does not challenge
unnecessary constraints will probably not produce a good solution. For example, a regional transit-planning effort in the San
Francisco area that did not include representation of the inner-
city poor failed to provide service that would link these residents
to jobs in the suburbs. It also resulted in less nighttime service,
which reduced poor residents' accessibility to late-shift jobs. This
result was not good for the poor or the economy in the view of

some critics.[4] A good process—one that included representatives of all stakeholders—would likely have produced a better agreement.

Process is also important because much of what consensus building accomplishes, such as new levels of trust, shared knowledge, alliances, personal networks, and working relationships, is the product of a collaborative and mutually respectful process. Our research (Innes et al., 1994) has shown that processes that meet the criteria in this chapter are most effective in producing these intangible benefits.

Process may be very difficult to assess. A simple survey of participants or a measurement of outputs will probably not provide a meaningful assessment. Either could lead to a conclusion that a process was unsuccessful when it was actually successful or vice versa. For example, participants responding to a survey could say they were satisfied with a process when they were actually manipulated and misled, or they could say they were dissatisfied when they actually accomplished a great deal but had unrealistic expectations.

■ Complexity Science as the Basis for a New Evaluation Framework

Because consensus building is complex and challenges traditional thinking about success and failure, evaluations of it must be carefully constructed. Also, as we have seen, there is little in the existing literature that directly addresses how best to handle these challenges. The remainder of this chapter, therefore, sets forth a new framework for conducting comprehensive evaluations of consensus building. The bases for this new framework are emerging ideas about the universe as a complex, organic system. *Complexity science,* as these ideas are collectively known, is useful for helping us to understand the crucial role that consensus building plays in society today. This understanding, in turn, provides the basis on which we propose criteria for evaluating consensus processes. This section explains complexity science, the next outlines a comprehensive set of criteria for evaluation, and the last two describe the types of evaluations that can be done and methodologies, respectively.

The Universe as Organism

Advances in biology, physics, computer science, and mathematics have begun to reveal a way of understanding the universe as a complex, adaptive system. Complexity science contends that the world is not like a machine, as scientists long assumed, made of parts interacting in a predictable way according to knowable laws. Instead, these scientists say the world works much more like a living organism, growing and evolving. A machine is designed to do a specific task, and it cannot do anything else, but an organism can *adapt and change* in response to information in its environment. It can develop new activities and evolve as it "learns" about that environment. This learning occurs as individual *agents,* which might be, for example, molecules in the human body, ants in an ant colony, or a bit of computer code in a larger program, search the environment and then individually respond to feedback from it by changing their patterns of action. The ants, even with their tiny brains and limited sensory capacity, quickly mobilize large numbers to attack a bit of food left on the kitchen counter once they come across it. Individual molecules form and evolve in response to their environment, adding and subtracting components in a random way at first, but with the most effective forms persisting or developing further. As changes are introduced into the environment or as new patterns of molecules or ant behavior appear, the other elements of the system respond and change as well. Thus, a system made up of very dumb individual components can, as a whole, show tremendous intelligence, learning capacity, and an ability to adapt. This process so thoroughly mimics an organism that one complexity science writer has termed it a *web of life* (Capra, 1996).

Self-Organization

Scientists have discovered that this type of adaptive, self-organizing process is a highly efficient way of accomplishing many tasks in a complex, uncertain, and changing environment. Such a process can do things that are either impossible by mechanical or command-and-control methods or inordinately time-consuming. The most familiar example is probably the highly "intelligent" computer chess programs, which today can win against all but the greatest chess masters. As long as programmers designed chess programs that tried to consider all possible moves and identify the best one at each stage, the results were poor. Once they discovered how to build learning into the programs, the computers became significantly faster and more powerful.

An experiment done by a computer scientist with an audience of several hundred people provides another simple illustration of this remarkable and counterintuitive efficiency of the self-organizing system. All members of the audience were given paddles with one red side and one green side. A large computer screen was set up in front of the group that could show the patterns of the colors displayed by the audience. The audience was instructed to form the letter Z with green paddles. It took a minute or two for the participants to adjust their paddles such that they saw the letter Z appear on the monitor. When they tried a second letter, the result emerged more quickly (Kelly, 1994). Both efforts happened significantly faster and more efficiently than if a set of rules for paddle usage had been developed, explained, and handed out. Instead, each individual agent, or member of the audience, worked out what to do individually by watching his or her neighbors and the monitor. Thus, a kind of simultaneous learning based on feedback proved to be an efficient method for producing a desired collective result.

Complex, self-organizing systems depend on distributed intelligence rather than on a single controlling mechanism. That is, they form and evolve not because there is a single intelligence telling each agent what to do, but because each agent, whether it is an ant or molecule or a person, acts individually on the basis of feedback it gets from its immediate surroundings. Although each agent is capable of responding only in the most limited ways to limited information, the system as a whole is very intelligent.

The Edge of Chaos

An intelligent, adaptive, learning process can emerge in nature when the environment is unstable, although not completely chaotic. In totally stable environments, equilibrium powerfully hinders change. Highly chaotic environments, on the other hand, produce only random responses, and systems cannot settle into patterns. Thus, the intermediate state—the "edge of chaos"—is the setting that is most conducive to innovation. Individual agents respond to the challenges of this near-chaos environment through experimentation or random search until they find productive strategies. If they are networked together, the feedback can flow from agent to agent, affecting each of them and increasing the potential for the system of which they are all part to move to a higher performance level. For such systems, one cannot draw a clear distinction between the system and its environment because these coexist in a symbiotic way, with each having an effect on the other.[5]

Consensus Building from the Perspective of Complexity Science

Complexity science provides a lens through which we can see and identify the most valuable contributions of consensus building in our complex and rapidly changing society. It also helps us to develop criteria for the kinds of processes most likely to produce good outcomes.

It is clear that the world today is in the edge-of-chaos state, ripe for creativity and adaptation and unlikely to support the old ways of doing business. The signs of this state are manifested in many ways. A change in Hong Kong's stock market destabilizes the global financial system. From the local up to the international level, individuals with different values and cultures are in conflict. Science, experts, and professionals are no longer seen as offering guarantees of truth. Trust in government is low. Authority and power are dispersed in many, if not most, nations. The quantity and speed of communication have increased dramatically and, in the process, created an increasingly complex environment for decision making. Uncertainty and change have become the norm.[6] Under these conditions, getting something complex done, even when a powerful agency or corporation has designed and planned it, is very difficult. In addition, social, economic, and technological changes are happening so rapidly that strategies a community or organization learned a few years ago are no longer effective.

In these circumstances, mechanistic, top-down analysis and decision making do not work well, but self-organizing systems depending on distributed intelligence are likely to be effective.

Certainly, successful businesses today depend on flexible linkages with other businesses and a combination of independent and coordinated action (Saxenian, 1994). Similarly, leaders in the field of organizational development argue that team-based approaches that empower participants are the most effective path to innovative organizations capable of adapting and moving forward (Senge, 1990).

"Consensus building creates a self-organizing learning system."

Consensus building is well suited as a response to these conditions of change, complexity, and uncertainty because it creates a self-organizing learning system: It links together stakeholders in a way that is not unlike the feedback systems among the agents described by complexity scientists. This learning system helps to build capacity in terms of knowledge, relationships, and strategy among these agents, and this capacity in turn helps to support the development of more productive patterns of action in communities and organizations. Consensus building is a way of creating a complex, adaptive human system to respond to the environment we face. The collective intelligence of a consensus building effort can, like an ant colony or the neural networks in the brain, offer more intelligence and effective joint action than the cleverest policymaker or analyst.

Implications for Evaluation Criteria

Using a complexity science perspective, we can infer the sorts of processes that can be most effective in a complex, uncertain world and the kinds of outcomes and consequences that are most important. A complexity perspective suggests, for example, that a high-quality consensus process should be self-organizing and evolving, good at gathering information from the environment, experimental and creative, and effective at making connections among participants. It suggests that desirable outcomes include learning, innovation, and changes in the patterns of action in response to environmental challenges and problems. Many of the process and outcome criteria proposed in the following section grew in part from the notion that what consensus building does best is help organizations and communities adapt constructively and creatively to the issues they face and the larger environment in which they operate.

■ *Criteria for Evaluating Consensus Building*

This section outlines criteria for evaluating consensus-based processes. These criteria are grounded significantly in the idea that consensus building is a method for creating a self-organizing, adaptive system for a complex, changing, and uncertain context. They are also grounded in research on the practice of consensus building, including our own work (Innes et al., 1994), and they correspond in most respects to the guidance on practice that is offered in this volume and by the international organization of dispute resolution professionals (Society of Professionals in Dispute Resolution, 1997). The ideas underlying the criteria have also been influenced by the work of social theorist Jurgen Habermas, who has proposed a concept of communicative rationality to guide the processes of dialogue and collective learning that is remarkably parallel to the best practices of consensus building (Fox & Miller, 1996; Habermas, 1981).

Criteria about Process

The first set of criteria relates to the nature of a consensus process. While no process will fully meet all these criteria, the set of criteria is offered as a goal and a standard against which to assess a process. The more fully the following criteria are met, the more effective a consensus building effort is likely to be.

The consensus building process includes representatives of all relevant and significantly different interests. Proper representation is essential to ensure that a discussion is well informed about the positions and perspectives of the various parties, that it is regarded as fair and legitimate by those who are not present, and that the learning that takes place can be communicated to outside constituencies and the public. A process that meets this criterion will be more swiftly and smoothly implemented than one that does not. SFEP did not include many representatives of water interests from southern California, for example, so the governor would not support SFEP's conclusions until they were discussed and approved by those interests.

The process is driven by a purpose that is practical and shared by the group. The purpose may be to develop an agreement on how to manage a resource, how to use a piece of land, or the content of a new budget. The purpose must be broad enough to allow people with differing perspectives to share it, but concrete and important enough to assure members that their energy is well spent working on it.

It is self-organizing. A consensus process should allow participants to set their own ground rules and determine their own tasks, objectives, and discussion topics. If these elements are imposed by an outside party or bounded by "standard procedures," participants will not feel that they own the process. Without that sense of ownership, they may assume a less active role in the learning and decision making taking place. Also, the process will likely fail to respond to key needs within the group and will function less effectively than it could. The SFEP group was only partially self-organizing and so was not as efficient or effective as it could have been. The National Estuary Program required that the group prepare a plan and a "status and trends report" and gave them five years to accomplish these tasks. They did complete these two reports, but many participants did not think the documents were particularly innovative. The group's most important contributions, in fact, were tasks they were not asked to do, such as developing a set of management options for the bay and an isohaline salinity index.

It follows the principles of civil discourse. Consensus building should include face-to-face discussions in which all participants are respected and listened to, have equal access to information, and are able to learn about each other's interests. In this type of dialogue, each participant has the opportunity to assess the sincerity and legitimacy of the others, assess the scientific accuracy of information, and understand what others are saying.[7] Participants can assess each other's sincerity by getting to know each other both around the table and in informal contacts (e.g., meals and breaks). Effective facilitators make sure participants' statements are understood by others. Participants' credentials need to be laid out early on as each explains his or her interests. These principles not only ensure that a process is fair and its conclusions have legitimacy but also that it can work like a self-organizing, adaptive system. Such systems depend on individuals being empowered to act autonomously and in an informed way and to make choices that they deem appropriate. If individuals are manipulated or ignored by other participants in a dialogue, the collective result will be less desirable.

It adapts and incorporates high-quality information. All participants must be aware of and learn from facts, scientific knowledge, and firsthand experiences relevant to the issues. This often happens through joint fact-finding, in which stakeholders and experts work together to collect and analyze information. Any data must be focused in ways that make sense to a group, members' questions and doubts need to be answered, and all parties must be able to accept the methods of collection and analysis as neutral and accurate (Innes, 1998). Joint fact-finding was what lent so much power to the isohaline salinity index in the SFEP. Almost everyone accepted the index, and as a result, it was influential even when the SFEP ended. Joint fact-finding must uncover and make use of the best-quality information, because a complex, adaptive system depends on each individual's ability to make informed choices.

It encourages participants to challenge assumptions. A creative, adaptive process must enable and encourage stakeholders to think "outside the box." Participants must be able to ask whether a law can be changed, whether a problem can be defined differently, or whether a related topic needs to be taken up. They need to be able to experiment, explore, and challenge accepted practices. Participants with less power need to be able to question existing power structures or show how these are harmful to them. All stakeholders need to be able to propose ideas that may seem crazy to others at first. One of the greatest benefits of consensus building is its capacity to identify new directions and ideas that would not otherwise be considered by an agency official or a chief executive, both of whom must make decisions within existing institutional and resource constraints. Complex systems are at their most effective when they produce new patterns that allow them to perform in unanticipated ways.

It keeps participants at the table, interested, and learning. No process can work if it fails to keep the players engaged. Drama, humor, informal social interaction, the empowerment of participants, and positive and constructive discussion are all important in ensuring this engagement. These elements are also essential for making a consensus process a continuous, joint learning project in which individuals are eager to take part and as a result of which they can change their views and actions (Innes & Booher, 1999).

It seeks consensus only after discussions fully explore the issues and interests and significant effort was made to find creative responses to differences. The effort to listen and incorporate the knowledge and concerns of participants is essential to the creativity of a process and to its effectiveness in adapting to external conditions.

As a practical matter, it is unlikely that any process will meet all these criteria. It may be impossible to get a key stakeholder to the table, resources may not be available to conduct extensive joint fact-finding, or time limits may prevent a full exploration of issues. Some groups may be constrained by legal or procedural requirements that prevent them from being fully self-organizing, challenging assumptions, or having an inclusive set of stakeholders. Many of these obstacles, however, are not insurmountable. A city council, for example, which is not self-organizing and operates under numerous procedural constraints, can set up a separate, self-organizing task force to address a controversial issue. A consensus group can raise funds from local foundations to hire technical experts, or can make use of the resources of local universities. All consensus building groups should do everything possible to meet all these criteria, since each one measures important dimensions of success.

Criteria to Assess Outcomes

Consensus building should be evaluated by the type and quality of its outcomes as well as its processes. These outcomes include short- and long-term results and second- and third-order effects. Desirable outcomes mirror the outcomes of a complex, adaptive system. A good consensus building process meets at least some of the criteria described in this section. A process that achieves many of the outcomes is probably better than one that achieves few, but the outcomes may vary in importance depending on the situation. The relative importance of each criterion in each case ultimately will have to be judged by those affected by the results.

The process produced a high-quality agreement. An agreement should meet the interests of all stakeholders. Its design should reflect sufficient thought, dialogue, and commitment to make it feasible, implementable, and stable. It should resolve differences in ways that take advantage of opportunities for joint gain. It might also provide for ways to change an agreement in response to new conditions. A high-quality agreement is flexible and adaptive.

It ended stalemate. If group members reach agreement, they have effectively ended stalemate. But even if they do not reach consensus, they may no longer be paralyzed by distrust, anger, and conflict. After a process is over, they may continue their efforts to reach agreement, act more constructively and cooperatively, or even move forward without a formal agreement. Stalemate is a dangerous state from a complex systems perspective because a system will collapse if it cannot adapt.

It compared favorably with other planning or decision methods in terms of costs and benefits. The costs include out-of-pocket financial outlays, participants' time, in-kind contributions, and length of time required to achieve results. The benefits are those outlined in this list.

It produced feasible proposals from political, economic, and social perspectives. Agreements and proposals should be designed to fit actual conditions and meet participants' needs and concerns. The proposals should be ones that can be acted on and should solve the problem(s) at hand. Action and change are important to move a complex system forward.

It produced creative ideas for action. Innovative ideas can help to resolve problems and foster learning and growth. Even new ideas that do not work out as hoped or are not implemented can help to change the ways of thinking that led to stalemate or conflict.

Stakeholders gained knowledge and understanding. By the end of a process, stakeholders should understand more about the issues and more about other stakeholders' viewpoints, interests, and circumstances. This learning can lead to change in stakeholders' attitudes toward other stakeholders, ideas about actions they should take to meet their own interests, and actions on matters related to the issues that brought them together.

The process created new personal and working relationships and social and political capital among participants. Networks and linkages are critical to ensure that a complex system can be responsive and adaptive. Information must flow freely among participants for the most effective results. A successful consensus process leaves a legacy of relationships among diverse parties, which permits continuing exchange of information, cooperation, and understanding.

It produced information and analyses that stakeholders understand and accept as accurate. A consensus process may produce facts, models, forecasts, histories, indicators of key phenomena, or narratives about a problem and its causes or consequences. Improved data and information gleaned through joint fact-finding is a crucial part of the collaborative learning process.

Learning and knowledge produced within the consensus process were shared by others beyond the immediate group. A good consensus effort is one in which the representatives at the table have kept in close touch with the stakeholder groups they represent, kept them up-to-date on the discussions, and introduced stakeholders' concerns into the dialogue. A good process is also one in which the knowledge and ideas generated at the table spread to others in a community or organization (both during and after a process), whether by word of mouth or deliberate outreach and communication. SFEP, for example, established a major outreach effort during the process and shortly afterward formed a group called Friends of the Estuary to build public support and secure funding for implementation of the CCMP. In addition, a broad group of interested advocates and agency staff became involved for years afterward in monitoring and assessing the progress of the estuary.

It had second-order effects, beyond agreements or attitudes developed in the process, such as changes in behaviors and actions, spin-off partnerships, collaborative activities, new practices, or even new institutions. An effective consensus effort sets in motion a cascade of changes. Some participants may discover common ground with others and work together to accomplish tasks unrelated to the consensus group's agenda. Participants may, in the future, make fewer unilateral decisions regarding complex or controversial issues and instead seek to build consensus for action. In fact, consensus building may gradually become more the norm, as it has in the field of water policy today in California. Because consensus building gives participants new skills, the process contributes to the rebuilding of civil discourse in communities where communication has broken down.

It resulted in practices and institutions that were both flexible and networked, which permitted a community to respond more creatively to change and conflict. A process might change the agendas or activities of public agencies or interest groups. The isohaline index developed by the SFEP, for example, was adopted by federal agencies for regulatory purposes. SFEP also produced a long-term process to facilitate networking and information sharing among advocates and concerned players whose interests are affected by water quality in the estuary. A consensus effort might also spawn a new generation of people with skills in and an interest in using consensus building. It could provide the foundation for long-term partnerships between stakeholders.

It produced outcomes that were regarded as just. The outcomes must be well-informed and fair to the stakeholders, but they must also be regarded by society as just and desirable. Thus, a process that solved a problem at the expense of a powerless set of people would not meet this criterion, nor would one that provided the most benefits to players who seem undeserving.

The outcomes seemed to serve the common good or public interest. A community should understand the outcomes of a public consensus process as beneficial to its welfare, in a broad sense. Serving the parochial interests of stakeholders at the table may be in the public interest, because it reduces conflict and allows stakeholders to operate more productively. If, however, a group produces outcomes that harm the larger community, this would not be a positive result even if the stakeholders at the table are satisfied. For example, if stakeholders in the SFEP agreed to meet their interests by fencing off the estuary and preventing public access so they would not have to change their own practices, the process would not be seen as advancing the common good.

The outcomes contributed to the sustainability of natural and social systems. A good consensus effort produces proposals that will protect resources, but not sacrifice the economy. It finds creative ways to build a mutually supportive relationship between the environment and the economy and take advantage of the full range of human resources in a community. Sustainability is ultimately the ability of a system to adapt creatively to change and stress. The learning that takes place in consensus processes builds the capacity of key players in a community to understand and work toward sustainable systems in a continuous way.[8]

If a consensus building effort meets the process criteria laid out previously, it is also likely to meet most of these outcome criteria. An inclusive process, for example, is likely to produce outcomes that are just and serve the common good because it includes such broad representation that the only acceptable strategies will be valuable to the community as a whole (Innes, 1996). In addition, a process operating by the principles of civil discourse and integrating high-quality information is more likely to produce feasible and implementable agreements.

■ Evaluation Options

"To conduct a meaningful and useful evaluation, an evaluator needs a set of explicit criteria."

To conduct a meaningful and useful evaluation, an evaluator needs a set of explicit criteria like those just described, along with data-gathering methods and a study design appropriate to the intended purposes and audience. The purposes can be, for instance, trying to improve a particular process, trying to assess the value of consensus building compared with alternative methods of deliberation and choice, or building theory about how and under what conditions consensus building is or is not successful. The audiences can include the participants in a particular process, elected officials or public agencies, professional organizations of mediators, scholars and researchers, or the general public. The scale can range from a group conducting a self-evaluation during one meeting to a long-term, systematic, comparative study of dozens or even hundreds of cases. The cost could range from almost nothing to several hundred thousand dollars. An evaluation can be conducted early in a process or several years after it is over. This section describes three general types of evaluations, each of which fulfills different purposes: midcourse evaluations, end-of-process evaluations, and retrospective evaluations.

Midcourse Evaluations

After a few months or more of a consensus process, it may be desirable to assess how it is going. Members of a group may be dissatisfied or skeptical about whether they are making progress. Funders may need to decide whether to continue supporting a process. Stakeholder organizations may want to assess whether their representatives' time is being well spent. A facilitator may sense concerns within a group about his or her technique, but may need an outsider's opinion on what to do differently.

Midcourse evaluations typically assess the degree to which process criteria are being met, the satisfaction of participants, and whether a group is focusing on the right tasks. It might ask, Are representatives at the table communicating with their stakeholder groups? Do all participants feel well-informed and empowered? Are participants engaged and interested? Why or why not? Identifying and remedying process problems at an early stage can help to ensure more satisfactory outcomes and can keep stakeholders at the table. Midcourse evaluations can also anticipate outcomes by finding out whether participants are learning and seeing possibilities for agreements or joint activities.

End-of-Process Evaluations

An evaluation conducted within a month or two of a final meeting—when the experience is fresh in everyone's mind—can give funders, convenors, participants, and outside observers an objective assessment of what a group accomplished. Funders, convenors, and participants may want to know if time was well spent, if they should stay involved through the implementation and monitoring phases, and if they should try this type of process again. Facilitators and others who plan to continue to work in consensus building will want to know the degree to which process criteria were met and how process failures may have affected outcomes. This information can be used to improve their own and others' practice. The academic community may also be interested in conducting end-of-process evaluations, particularly those linking process to outcomes. They may seek to publish the results in scholarly or professional journals on dispute resolution, environmental policy, urban affairs, business, or other fields in an effort to contribute to the theory of consensus building.

In end-of-process evaluations, first-stage outcomes—such as learning and changed attitudes among participants, new activities, and agreements reached—can be identified. Any planned next steps or follow-up processes can also be identified as outcomes. These outcomes need to be described in very specific terms (e.g., "three environmental organizations joined with farmers' groups to develop legislation on pesticides"). This sort of evaluation should reveal what additional outcomes are anticipated and show the directions of change that are already evident.

Retrospective Evaluations

Retrospective evaluations of consensus building—those that are conducted one to five years after a process is completed—are important for a broad audience of political leaders, dispute resolution professionals, interest group leaders, planners, scholars and theorists, organizational development experts, and well-informed publics. Retrospective evaluations allow for the comparison of multiple cases and the identification and documentation of second- and third-order effects.

This section describes three basic kinds of retrospective evaluations: (1) evaluations that look at the second- and third-order outcomes of a single consensus process, (2) those that compare two or more consensus-based efforts, and (3) those that compare a consensus building effort with a similar controversy that was resolved using traditional decision-making methods.

Almost certainly, those who will have the time, money, and incentive to do any type of retrospective evaluations will be researchers, consultants, and scholars who receive research grants or contracts. Some organizations or agencies may conduct them as well, particularly if they are considering adopting consensus building as a standard procedure for complex or controversial issues. Convenors or funders may hire an evaluator to do an in-depth assessment of a single process they sponsored, so they can decide whether and how to support such processes in the future. Evaluations that compare consensus building in different issue arenas, look at questions of design and appropriate conditions for instituting a process, or compare consensus building with traditional decision making are most appropriately supported by state or federal governments or foundations. Findings from these types of studies are useful for determining whether and how consensus building can be most effective. The audience for these studies is broad and can be reached through journals and professional meetings, as well as through workshops, training programs, and professional education.

Retrospective Evaluation of a Single Process

To identify second-stage consequences, retrospective evaluations of a single process should take place at least a year after a process is completed. These evaluations should trace the effects over time of an effort on the participants and their relationships to each other. They should also identify events and activities that can be at least partially attributed to a process, as well as the institutions that emerged or changed because of formal agreements or other understandings that developed during the deliberations. Where possible, evaluations should be conducted five or more years after the end of a process, to tap into many of the longer-term consequences and to find out how the learning has spread. After all, once people learn something new or develop new working relationships, it takes time for identifiable consequences to appear.

Comparison of Multiple Consensus Building Processes

Evaluations that compare two or more similar consensus building processes well after they have been completed provide the opportunity to examine the effectiveness of different consensus building techniques and strategies. Such studies could compare the process designs, facilitation techniques, joint fact-finding efforts, and project management structures that were used.

These evaluations can help facilitators, mediators, and even convenors to improve the practice of consensus building. Such evaluations can also test the crucial proposition put forward in this chapter that a consensus building effort that meets the appropriate process criteria will also meet the relevant outcome criteria.

Comparison of Consensus Building with Traditional Decision Making

Studies comparing consensus building with other methods of policy making and planning can help answer the following important questions: What does multiparty consensus building do better or worse than elected bodies following *Robert's Rules of Order,* well-informed chief executives advised by expert analysts, or advocacy processes that play out in the courts? What are the costs and benefits of consensus processes in comparison with these alternatives? Which use more resources? What is the comparison of accomplishments with costs in time, uncertainty, and out-of-pocket funds across cases? Which approaches produce changes that are more lasting or solve problems more effectively?

In this type of evaluation, an evaluator could compare the costs of a consensus building effort with the expenditures in a similar controversy spent on litigation, lobbying, and media campaigns. The costs that must be considered include cash outlays, salaries, volunteer time, and in-kind support, as well as the costs of delayed decisions (e.g., to businesses and the environment). Any evaluation that seeks to assess societal costs must include the expenditures of all players. Care should be taken to measure the complete costs of conventional decision-making processes, which may be less obvious than the costs of consensus building because we take them for granted. For example, it is important to count the staff salaries of various public and private players who may be involved in ongoing litigation, research, or other activities designed to make the case they want to make about an issue. The benefits also need to be compared across decision methods. One needs to compare the full range of outcomes of a consensus effort with the immediate and second- and third-order effects of the other methods. For example, it would be useful to know which approach resulted in better working relationships among parties. Another benefit to compare has to do with the degree of certainty associated with a type of deliberation; an evaluator might want to ask how confident participants feel at the end of a process that agreements reached will be adhered to.

Making comparisons across decision methods is tricky and can at best produce approximate answers to these questions. No decision-making process is a pure case of consensus building, bureaucratic procedure, or judicial or executive decision making. Decisions in the real world are typically made using a complex mix of these methods. The methods may influence each other in ways that no one can identify, much less separate for analytic and comparative purposes. The best option is to choose cases for comparison that offer the clearest distinctions possible—that is, compare cases that are mostly consensus building with those that are mostly made by some other method. Even if these distinctions can be made and cases can be carefully and credibly matched for comparison purposes, the comparison may still be questionable because consensus building is not randomly applied to cases. It is often chosen as a decision-making method because of the predilections and attitudes of key players, the history and nature of the controversy, the intractability of the dispute, and so forth. Therefore, issues that are the subject of consensus building are likely to have been different to begin with from those that are handled in more traditional ways. Differences in settlement rates, length of time to reach agreement, and implementation may be due as much to these factors as to the consensus process itself. One could get around this with large samples of similar cases, if they existed—but they do not. The best way to compare consensus building with other methods may be to analyze the handling of a single situation before and after consensus building is introduced.

If done well, evaluations that compare consensus building to other methods can help identify which kinds of conditions and problems are best suited to consensus building and which call for more standard decision methods. These evaluations should help produce a better understanding of when an issue is ready for consensus building; whether the scale, complexity, and level of controversy associated with an issue make it appropriate for consensus building; and whether existing levels of social capital and habits of collaboration in a community make it a good method to use.

Retrospective Assessment of the
San Francisco Estuary Project

An assessment that was done of the second-order effects of the SFEP offers a valuable model for others (SFEP, 1996). Although it was not a systematic evaluation of the process, or even a rigorous effort to link the second- and third-stage effects to the project itself, it does demonstrate how one can identify and document the cascade of changes that may take place in the wake of a large-scale consensus building effort.

Three years after the SFEP management committee reached agreement on the CCMP, SFEP staff tracked down public and private implementation activities that had been instituted since the CCMP was released. They focused on activities that were designed to protect or improve wetlands, aquatic resources, or habitat, or otherwise meshed with the plan's strategy. The resulting evaluation report included a detailed, 60-page table that identified each of the plan's proposed actions and described implementation efforts to date. For example, one proposed action noted in the table was to "ensure that Basin Plans encourage water reclamation and reuse." Next to it in the table, in a column labeled "Initiatives," the report notes that the state's Water Management Planning Act was amended to require districts to prepare water recycling plans. In an "Implementation" column, the table notes that one of the stakeholders—the state Water Board—adopted statewide goals for water reclamation. A fourth column notes current roadblocks to progress, such as the need for water agencies to coordinate with sanitary districts to do recycling. The last column, titled "New Frontiers and Possible Priorities," calls attention to the ways players are going beyond the original mandate of the plan. It notes that an effort is being made to integrate water reclamation and wastewater discharge standards in the state's inland surface waters plan.

This evaluation report took months to prepare and was based on staff interviews with stakeholders, relevant agencies, and private groups. To test the accuracy of the report, an all-day workshop was held with the original participants and interested members of the public. The report was revised and amended based on workshop participants' comments.

While this report does not and cannot directly draw a causal link between the CCMP and each of these activities—indeed, it notes that many of the activities were undertaken without explicit intent to implement the plan—it does show the degree to which the intent and spirit of the plan are being carried out. It is likely that many, if not most, of the activities in the table have to some degree been undertaken or influenced by one or more SFEP participants. The fact that the CCMP was agreed to with such a broad consensus and that it became the EPA's guiding document is significant to the various agencies that are involved in water management activities, as most of them must deal with the EPA. The existence of the plan itself creates a certain status and legitimacy for activities consistent with it, even though the plan did not have the force of law. Relatively few activities are likely, in any case, to be uniquely produced by a consensus process such as the SFEP, because it took place in such a complex public policy context and engaged so many players.

A full-fledged retrospective evaluation of the SFEP would have to be considerably more in-depth than the assessment that was conducted. It would need, for example, to assess the degree of individual and institutional learning that resulted from the process. The SFEP chairperson discovered during the process that the management committee was too big and diverse to be productive. After the SFEP was over, he organized and designed a separate consensus building process to discuss dredging issues, and in that case he recommended creating a much smaller steering group. That process was ultimately successful in resolving bitterly contested dredging controversies. A more complete evaluation would also likely show that SFEP participants took different positions in later decision processes than in the SFEP because of what they had learned.

A full retrospective evaluation would also look at the progression of any innovative ideas, findings, or agreements that came out of a group. In the case of the SFEP, it would be important to trace and document the uses of the isohaline index of salinity and the degree to which stakeholders, agencies, or courts applied the index in their decision-making processes. This index did become significant after the SFEP concluded when federal agencies adopted it as a way of assessing whether there was sufficient water released into the San Francisco Bay. Ultimately, the acceptance of this indicator by numerous agencies and interests helped to force a reluctant governor to agree that more water should be released into the delta and bay in dry years.

A complete retrospective analysis would also look at the design of a process. For the SFEP, an evaluator might ask whether the combination of multistakeholder technical advisory committees and issue-based committees worked well or not. How well did their work feed into the management committee's deliberations? Did the SFEP's public advisory committee succeed in educating the public about the issues and generating support for the SFEP's work?

This type of analysis can also look at the incentives for participation and for reaching agreement as factors affecting success. In the SFEP, for example, the environmentalists and the farmers did not have strong incentives for reaching agreement, because each knew they could take their case into other decision-making arenas at the state and federal levels. Local governments had little incentive to participate, in part because they had insufficient resources to send staff to the meetings. (The SFEP was only one among dozens of regional decision-making processes going on simultaneously.) Nonetheless, all these stakeholder representatives ended up supporting the CCMP. A good retrospective evaluation could sort out the reasons why.

An evaluator could also do a comparative evaluation; he or she could compare the SFEP with the Sacramento Water Forum, a similar consensus process that also focused on water management. The Sacramento group used a public relations consultant to design and manage public processes, for example. The effectiveness of this method could be compared with that of SFEP's public advisory committee. Other process design, facilitation, and participation issues could also be compared. An evaluator could also examine what tasks the groups took on and which were the most and least productive, how large the steering committee should be, and when joint fact-finding should be conducted.

■ *Gathering and Analyzing Data*

"The ideal evaluation combines quantitative evidence with more qualitative information."

After deciding what general type of evaluation to do and when in a process to do it, the next step is to determine what kinds of information to gather and how to gather it. An evaluator may want to gather objective, quantitative information (e.g., about the length of a process, the percentage of cases in which agreements are reached, or the number of participants who are satisfied with the results), or richer but more ambiguous qualitative information (e.g., about events, relationships, perceptions, and attitudes). Both types of information can be gathered by conducting surveys, analyzing written records, observing meetings, interviewing participants, and/or using focus groups or other group discussion methods. Each of these data-gathering strategies has different advantages and disadvantages, which need to be assessed in light of an evaluation's objectives and the resources available. Some information-gathering methods are relatively simple and inexpensive, while others require more expertise, effort, and time. Some methods are best suited for gathering objective, "hard" data, but these tend to oversimplify and tell only a limited part of the story. Other methods can provide rich narratives and detailed descriptions of processes or outcomes, but such information is difficult to sum up and compare across cases. The ideal evaluation combines quantitative evidence, which reveals how common or extensive a characteristic or result is, with more qualitative information, which describes the flavor of a process and the dynamics involved in reaching outcomes. For example, an evaluator might combine quantitative information from a survey of participants that reveals what percentage instituted new activities as the result of a process, with qualitative information about the nature of these activities and the ways representatives persuaded their stakeholder organizations to implement them. This section discusses five research methods and the purposes for which they are best suited: surveys, group methods, interviewing, observation, and documenting outcomes.

Surveys of Participants

A formal survey of participants or stakeholders is often an important component of an evaluation. A survey involves asking everyone in a given category (e.g., participants, observers, funders) a standard set of questions in the same way (e.g., in person, by phone, or in written form). This standardization allows the results to be summarized in a quantitative form. A survey might reveal, for example, that "30 percent of participants were either satisfied or very satisfied with the outcome of a process" or "a higher percentage of women than men thought the process was fair."

A survey might be done midway through a process, but it is best conducted soon after a process ends, when it can address issues related to outcomes and when participants' memories are still fresh. Surveys are most useful for evaluating consensus building groups with at least 20 to 30 participants. A group this size is too large for conducting in-depth interviews with each participant, but large enough for meaningful patterns to emerge in responses to a survey.

A survey's cost can range widely, from a few hundred dollars (for a questionnaire with four or five questions that is administered to 30 people) to many thousands of dollars (for a survey with 30 or 40 questions that is administered to 200 to 300 people). A survey of SFEP participants would be at the high end of the scale, because it would need to query the hundreds of people who participated in a variety of ways over the course of the five-year process. Also, a rather complex and carefully crafted questionnaire would be needed to remind people of the context of the process without biasing their answers.

In a survey, participants who have direct experience with and can speak knowledgeably about a process can say how it worked for them. They can be asked to report on their own behavior, including, for example, how often they communicated with their constituents. They can be asked about the aspects of the process that seemed to work well and poorly. They can also provide information about outcomes in which they have played a part or have direct knowledge, such as whether they have begun to do any consensus building in other arenas or have developed partnerships with other participants. They can be asked what, if anything, they learned from the process and how their attitudes toward the issues or the other stakeholders have changed.

It is difficult to develop a survey instrument whose results will reflect an accurate picture of participants' attitudes. It requires designing questions that are unambiguous and easy to answer. If respondents are to fill out the survey themselves, it has to be laid out properly and written in simple language. A phone survey must be administered by trained interviewers. Every survey instrument must be pretested on a few participants to see if they understand it and respond appropriately, and it must be redesigned as needed. For all but the most simple of surveys, professional assistance should be obtained to design the questionnaire, administer the survey, and analyze and write up the results.

The benefit of surveys is that they can distill complicated information from a variety of people into a simple, quantitative form, and they can be completed fairly quickly. The disadvantage is that surveys tend to oversimplify—they do not get at the complexity of a process and its outcomes. Also, they represent the opinions and perceptions of people who may not remember events accurately or who may have only partial knowledge of a situation.

Group Methods

Some of the most useful information-gathering techniques are those in which an evaluator generates discussion among a group of people to solicit their views. These can be used for getting feedback from participants about how a consensus process is working or did work. These methods are particularly suited to self-organized, midcourse evaluations conducted by a facilitator or chair of a group. If an evaluation is to address the effectiveness of the facilitation, however, it should be conducted by a professional evaluator or other skilled outsider.

The evaluator asks participants questions such as "What aspects of this process are working best?" and "What is the biggest problem in this process?" In one approach, participants can be asked to provide brief, anonymous written responses to these questions, either ahead of time or during an evaluation meeting. The evaluator sorts through the responses and, with the group gathered around a table, writes the main comments on a flip chart for all to see, perhaps clustering them by category. At this point, the evaluator facilitates a discussion of the comments. Typically, some time is spent understanding the key points, then discussing the possible reasons behind the responses, and then developing ideas about how to build on the strengths mentioned and eliminate the problems.

This method can be relatively inexpensive and involve only the time to prepare for and conduct the discussion and possibly to write up and distribute the conclusions. It can be used to give participants a safe and anonymous way to criticize a process and provide everyone with the chance to discuss the causes of problems and possible solutions. Members of a group, for example, might say that a facilitator is not treating some of them fairly, or might want to criticize his or her way of organizing the issues. The group might, as a result, set up a committee to give feedback to the facilitator, or might even hire a different facilitator.

These discussion methods are part evaluation and part action research,[9] in that they are designed to engage a group in learning about what is and is not working from each other's point of view. This sort of evaluation helps a consensus process to become an effective, self-organizing, learning activity.

If anonymity of responses is not necessary, one can use focus groups for important parts of the evaluation. Focus groups are subsets of individuals who are brought together for a one- to three-hour discussion and asked for their opinions and thoughts on a topic. Focus groups are used for many research purposes, from marketing studies to evaluations. In consensus building, they are useful for both midcourse evaluations and end-of-process analyses. In these cases, focus group participants may include a subset of people involved in a consensus process, a set of interested observers, or even potential users of the consensus group's results, depending on the evaluation objective.

In a focus group session, a facilitator typically poses questions to the group and facilitates a discussion on the answers they give. For example, a focus group might discuss how well the environment was protected under the SFEP's management plan for San Francisco Bay. Group members would probably express some differences of perceptions and opinions, although they might also agree on some issues. The researchers would learn by listening to the conversation on audio- or videotape or in some cases watching it in person.

Focus groups do not result in "bottom line" answers like a survey might. They will not reveal, for example, what percentage of participants felt a certain way or how they would rate the outcomes on a scale of 1 to 10. Instead, this method produces a nuanced and complex understanding of how participants viewed the issues and what went on during a process. The results help an evaluator to piece together a story of what happened in a process and why. They also help evaluators to understand the different ways participants evaluate what happened. The discussion itself leads participants to "think aloud," develop more sophisticated perspectives, and provide more thoughtful answers than they could in a survey. Focus groups can be a relatively inexpensive and efficient method for gathering rich information, although experts are typically required to design and manage the sessions and summarize the results.

Interviewing

Perhaps the most valuable information about a consensus building effort will come from in-depth interviews with participants, sponsors of a project, staff, and observers. Interviews can be conducted during a process, just after its conclusion, or several years later.

To conduct in-depth interviews, an evaluator should prepare an *interview protocol:* a list of basic questions, to be asked of every interviewee. The questions asked should be open-ended; that is, they should encourage an interviewee to talk at length about whatever topic he or she feels is relevant or important. This is in contrast to closed-ended questions, which require a yes or no (or other short) answer. If more than one person will conduct the interviews, it is critical that the interviewers work together beforehand to develop a shared understanding of the objectives, so that the results can be comparable. In addition, interviewers need to be taught how to develop a good rapport with an interviewee, ask open-ended questions that encourage interviewees to think, and follow up on key topics. In a case like the SFEP, a protocol might include questions about the techniques the facilitator used, the participants' experience in the process, and the group's agreements. If an interviewee says that he did not like the facilitator or some other aspect of the process, the interviewer should pursue this; he or she should try to find out why and identify the point in time when the participant reached this conclusion.

Since open-ended interviews take one to three hours each, it is typically not feasible to interview everyone. Because the purpose of interviews is not to document percentages or otherwise "score" the answers, it is not necessary to be exhaustive. It *is* important, however, to interview participants representing the full range of interests to get an insider's insight into and understanding of a process and its outcomes.

All respondents, of course, are selective in what they say. The evaluator's job will be to make sense out of the various, sometimes conflicting stories and assessments and to provide an overall interpretation and narrative explaining what went well, what did not go well, and why differences of opinion may exist. Interviewers may have to talk to more and more people until a clear story begins to emerge.

Interviews are useful for a variety of reasons. Even though the results of interviews are not easily quantifiable, as those of a survey are, an interview provides a wealth of detail and nuance that is simply not possible with a survey. Indeed, interviewees' responses are likely to be so idiosyncratic and complex that a survey would not capture them. Interviews with the facilitator and staff of an effort will give an evaluator a relatively accurate description of a process, the amount and kind of preparation that went into meetings, and the types of techniques that were employed to build consensus. Interviews with key players give an evaluator information about why those participants joined a process, and why they did or did not stay at the table. Did they feel empowered or treated equally? Were they confused and when? What aspects of the process made a difference or changed their views? Interviews can be well suited to finding out what participants learned and how the learning occurred, how they view the process and the other participants, how their organizations reacted to the process, and how they changed. In the course of an interview, a respondent can bring up points that did not occur to the evaluator but that may be critical to understanding what went on and how or why a process worked.

Open-ended interviews are also essential for tracing the second- and third-order effects of a consensus process. Typically, stakeholders do not at first think about what led them to take new actions, and it may be necessary for them to talk through the possibilities with an interviewer to become aware of what they have learned or how they have changed. Such interviews could be used not only to find out whether a process, for example, helped interviewees to create new working relationships but also to get them to explain exactly when and how it did this. It can explore what was innovative about a proposal from the participants' perspective and find out how and when the proposal was created. In these interviews, an evaluator gets a history and overview of the process and procedures as well as stories that illuminate what happened.

The disadvantages of interviews are that they are inevitably subject to an individual interviewer's skills, and the interpretive part of the effort is difficult to do well because of the complexity of the findings. Nonetheless, interviews produce a story that can be very illuminating and can communicate to many people what happened and why.

Observation

Although it is possible to learn a good deal about a process through interviews, surveys, and so forth, the ideal way for a neutral evaluator to gather information is to observe a consensus building process in person. An evaluator could observe an entire process from beginning to end to do a complete end-of-process or retrospective evaluation. Obviously, this sort of approach must be planned early on in an effort. But observation can also be helpful during a process; a brief visit by an experienced and knowledgeable observer in the midst of negotiations can result in important feedback for a facilitator and participants.

For a more detailed, end-of-process evaluation, an observer should attend and take detailed notes on as many meetings of a consensus building group as possible. It is also helpful for an observer to attend staff or steering committee meetings, where the planning is done for the larger meetings. If the evaluator is conducting a scholarly study of consensus building, it is important that the observation be done as thoroughly and systematically as possible. Sometimes, participants will not be comfortable allowing an outsider to observe particularly sensitive negotiations or caucus meetings. An evaluator should assure participants that their confidentiality will not be compromised, but even that assurance may be insufficient in some cases to gain access.

Observation is a useful tool because participants and facilitators seldom can remember exactly what they did during a process, much less pinpoint what went wrong, why, and when. A careful observer, however, can identify the methods being used, what was said, and what roles the participants were playing when a new idea appeared, a conflict was resolved, or a breakthrough was made. An observer can pick up the energy level and collective attitude in a room and record the actual sequence of events.

Relatively little evaluation has been done thus far involving direct observation, in part because it is time-consuming and therefore difficult to fund. Also, there is so much to watch and hear that it is difficult to keep complete, useful records. With more experience in observing consensus building dialogues, evaluators and researchers will refine their methods.

Documenting Outcomes

In an end-of-process or retrospective evaluation, outcomes can be identified through interviews, focus groups, and surveys, but it is important for an evaluator to do additional work to obtain concrete evidence about the existence and quality of these outcomes. This work should include developing a checklist of possible outcomes and inquiring about them to those inside and outside of a process. Care should be taken to identify outcomes that might be considered positive, like agreements, and those that are negative, like new animosities between parties. The list of possible outcomes can be based on the outcome criteria outlined previously in this chapter, and it can be amended after discussions with participants and observers about which outcomes are particularly important or likely. The evaluator should, wherever possible, seek measurable and specific results of a process. Outcomes might include jointly developed and agreed-on information, like the state-of-the-estuary report done in the SFEP, or indicators like the isohaline index. It might include spin-off efforts, new institutions, and second-stage collaborative processes. The qualitative aspects of these efforts (not just the number of each) are most important. For instance, what value did the new institutions or collaborative processes have? What activities did they engage in? What agreements did they produce? Each outcome is significant, and it is preferable to sum up and characterize the different kinds using examples rather than attempting to reduce them to statistics. When making comparisons across cases, the outcomes can be categorized and classified for easier reporting and for associating types of outcomes with types of processes.

■ Who Should Conduct an Evaluation

While some limited evaluation can be done by a group and its facilitators and other staff, in most cases a trained researcher or evaluator should be hired. The evaluator should not have close connections to the organizers of the process, nor should he or she be affiliated with a particular "side" of the issues in question. Neutrality and professionalism are important if the evaluation is to be meaningful and trusted. Participants have to be able to trust the evaluator and be willing to be honest with him or her about both positive and negative opinions of the process. An insider is therefore typically not appropriate to do the job. The exception to this principle is that reflective self-evaluation by facilitators can be a useful component of a larger effort involving other types and sources of information.

Professional evaluators might be found at a university, private consulting firm, or government agency. An evaluator from a local university may be able to delegate much of the work to graduate students. Government agencies and large companies that do monitoring or quality assessment may be able to provide evaluation services. Private sector consulting firms are also available to do evaluation work, and they can draw on teams with specialized skills to conduct surveys or manage focus groups. Wherever the expert evaluator is housed, he or she can either conduct the evaluation, train the consensus building group's staff to do much of it, or simply provide advice to the staff or key participants on aspects of it that require technical expertise, such as questionnaire design and report write-up. For end-of-process evaluations, a group should hire an evaluator before the process is complete so he or she can do some direct observation and be ready with surveys, interviews, or other methods as the process is winding down. While an evaluation team should work closely with the leadership and facilitators of a process, if not also with the group as a whole in designing the study and identifying the important questions to address, the credibility and accuracy of the evaluation will depend significantly on the expertise, credentials, and perceived neutrality of the evaluator.

■ Concluding Comments

Evaluation is an important part of ensuring that consensus processes can serve their most important function as self-organizing, learning processes that help to move a community or organization forward. Consensus building at its best not only helps participants reach agreements, it teaches them to communicate constructively, helps them to create meaningful information, and helps them to develop an understanding of the issues and of the other participants. It provides the opportunity for innovating and resolving issues by helping participants see things in new ways. Consensus building is very much the tool for the fragmented, conflictual societies of our time because it offers the opportunity to create shared perceptions, values, and actions when it is done effectively. Consensus building is still in its early stages as a means of making community choices, and around the world people are learning it by trial and error. Systematic evaluation must play an important part in moving consensus building into its next phase and in helping communities understand what it can accomplish and how it can work.

■ Notes

1. We have looked at how this dynamic process brings out creativity and generates innovative solutions. The informality and safe environment of a consensus building dialogue can encourage participants to build new scenarios and put together ideas to create new concepts (Innes & Booher, 1999).

2. These include a study on negotiated rulemaking sponsored by the Administrative Conference of the United States (Kerwin & Langbein, 1995); a master's thesis from MIT comparing 16 mediated land use dispute cases with a matched set of conventional cases (Amundsen, 1998); a second master's thesis from MIT comparing 15 mediated cases of land use disputes in Canada (Moss, 1997); and the author's monograph on 13 cases of consensus building in growth and environmental management (Innes et al., 1994). A forthcoming evaluation involving 400 interviews and 100 cases is in preparation under the sponsorship of the Lincoln Institute of Land Policy. A preview of this study is currently available (Matsuura, 1998).

3. The most up-to-date and usable overview of this literature and an outline of evaluation methods are in *Utilization-Focused Evaluation* by Patton (1997).

4. This point is taken from an analysis of the Metropolitan Transportation Commission's collaborative transportation planning process, research in progress by Innes and Gruber.

5. A number of books provide good introductions to complexity science for the nonscientist (Capra, 1996; Holland, 1995; Kauffman, 1995; Kelly, 1994; Waldrop, 1992).

6. Manuel Castells (1996, 1997, 1998) has eloquently described the logic of this rapidly evolving global society in his trilogy.

7. These are principles Habermas (1981) outlines and that are sometimes known as conditions of ideal speech.

8. This idea linking sustainability to complex systems thinking and consensus building has been further developed in "Metropolitan Development as a Complex System: A New Approach to Sustainability" (Innes & Booher, in press-a).

9. This is a term to describe research that is conducted not just for the enlightenment of a neutral observer but for the explicit purpose of changing the participants in the study as well.

■ References

Amundsen, O. M. (1998). *Evaluating the use of mediation in land use decision making.* Master's thesis, Massachusetts Institute of Technology, Cambridge.

Argyris, C., & Schon, D. A. (1974). *Theory in practice: Increasing professional effectiveness.* San Francisco: Jossey-Bass.

Bowman, P. A. (1988). *The Keystone process: An evaluation of its test cases.* Dallas, TX: U.S. Environmental Protection Agency, State Programs Section (6HHS) Hazardous Materials Branch.

Brett, J. M., Barsness, Z., & Goldberg, S. (1996, July). The effectiveness of mediation: An independent analysis of cases handled by four major service providers. *Negotiation Journal,* pp. 260-269.

Campbell, M. C., & Floyd, D. W. (1996, February). Thinking critically about environmental mediation. *Journal of Planning Literature,* pp. 235-247.

Canadian Roundtables. (1993). *Building consensus for a sustainable future: Guiding principles.* Canada: Roundtables on Environment and Economy in Canada.

Capra, F. (1996). *The web of life: A new scientific understanding of living systems.* New York: Anchor.

Castells, M. (1996). *The information age: Economy, society and culture: Vol. 1. The rise of the network society.* Cambridge, MA: Blackwell.

Castells, M. (1997). *The information age: Economy, society and culture: Vol. 2. The power of identity.* Malden, MA: Blackwell.

Castells, M. (1998). *The information age: Economy, society and culture: Vol. 3. End of millennium.* Malden, MA: Blackwell.

Coglianese, C. (1997, April). Assessing consensus: The promise and performance of negotiated rule making. *Duke Law Journal,* pp. 1255-1349.

Corburn, J. (1996). *Pursuing justice in environmental decision-making: Deliberative democracy and consensus building.* Master's thesis, Massachusetts Institute of Technology, Cambridge.

Elliott, M. (1993). *Carpet policy dialogue assessment.* Final report to the U.S. Environmental Protection Agency, prepared under contract to RESOLVE. Consortium on Negotiation and Conflict Resolution, Georgia Institute of Technology, Atlanta.

Fox, C. J., & Miller, H. T. (1996). *Postmodern public administration: Toward discourse.* Thousand Oaks, CA: Sage.

Gruber, J. (1994). *Coordinating growth management through consensus building: Incentives and the generation of social, intellectual, and political capital* (Working Paper Vol. 526). Berkeley: University of California, Berkeley, Institute of Urban and Regional Development.

Habermas, J. (1981). *The theory of communicative action: Reason and the rationalization of society* (Vol. 1, T. McCarthy, Trans.). Boston: Beacon.

Harter, P. J. (1997). Fear of commitment: An affliction of adolescents. *Duke Law Journal, 46,* 1389-1428.

Helling, A. (1998, Summer). Collaborative visioning: Proceed with caution! Results from evaluating Atlanta's Vision 2020 Project. *Journal of the American Planning Association, 64,* 335-349.

Holland, J. (1995). *Hidden order: How adaptation builds complexity.* Reading, MA: Addison-Wesley.

Innes, J. E. (1996, Autumn). Planning through consensus building: A new view of the comprehensive planning ideal. *Journal of the American Planning Association,* pp. 460-472.

Innes, J. E. (1998, Winter). Information in communicative planning. *Journal of the American Planning Association,* pp. 52-63.

Innes, J. E., & Booher, D. E. (1999, Winter). Consensus building as role playing and bricolage: Toward a theory of collaborative planning. *Journal of the American Planning Association, 65*(1), 9-26.

Innes, J. E., & Booher, D. E. (in press-a). Metropolitan development as a complex system: A new approach to sustainability. *Economic Development Quarterly, 13*(2).

Innes, J. E., & Booher, D. E. (in press-b). Consensus building and complex adaptive systems: A framework for evaluating collaborative planning. *Journal of the American Planning Association.*

Innes, J. E., Gruber, J., Neuman, M., & Thompson, R. (1994). *Coordinating growth and environmental management through consensus building.* CPS report: A policy research program report. Berkeley: California Policy Seminar, University of California, Berkeley.

Kauffman, S. (1995). *At home in the universe.* London: Viking.

Kelly, K. (1994). *Out of control: The rise of the neobiological civilization.* Reading, MA: Addison-Wesley.

Kerwin, C., & Langbein, L. (1995). *An evaluation of negotiated rule-making at the Environmental Protection Agency Phase I.* Washington, DC: Administrative Conference of the United States.

Matsuura, M. (1998, July). Mediation, and mediators, get an "A." *Consensus, 39,* 4.

Menkel-Meadow, C. (1997, August). Symposium on alternative dispute resolution. *UCLA Law Review, 44,* 1871-1933.

Moss, D. R. (1997). *Evaluating the use of mediation to settle land use disputes: A look at the Provincial Facilitator's Office of Ontario.* Master's thesis, Massachusetts Institute of Technology, Cambridge.

Patton, M. Q. (1997). *Utilization-focused evaluation: The new century text.* Thousand Oaks, CA: Sage.

San Francisco Estuary Project. (1996). *CCMP workbook: Comprehensive conservation and management plan for the bay-delta: Implementation progress 1993-1996.* Oakland, CA: Author.

Saxenian, A. (1994). *Regional advantage: Culture and competition in Silicon Valley and Route 128.* Cambridge, MA: Harvard University Press.

Senge, P. M. (1990). *The fifth discipline: The art and practice of the learning organization.* New York: Doubleday.

Sipe, N. (1998, Summer). An empirical analysis of environmental mediation. *Journal of the American Planning Association,* pp. 275-285.

Society of Professionals in Dispute Resolution. (1997). *Best practices for government agencies: Guidelines for using collaborative agreement-seeking processes.* Washington, DC: Author.

Susskind, L., & Cruikshank, J. (1987). *Breaking the impasse: Consensual approaches to resolving public disputes.* New York: Basic Books.

Susskind, L., & MacMahon, G. (1985). Theory and practice of negotiated rulemaking. *Yale Journal on Regulation, 3,* 133-165.

Waldrop, M. M. (1992). *Complexity: The emerging science at the edge of chaos.* New York: Simon & Schuster.

Wheeler, M. (1993). Regional consensus on affordable housing: Yes in my backyard? *Journal of Planning Education and Research, 12,* 139-149.

PART 3

CASES AND COMMENTARIES

INTRODUCTION TO THE
CASES AND COMMENTARIES

■ Michèle Ferenz

P art 3 of this *Handbook* presents case studies that illustrate how the theory and general rules of practice presented in the preceding chapters have fared in the heat of real-life situations. Each case tells a story, in whole or in part, of a dispute resolution process and describes the lessons learned. The application of consensus building tools in the wide variety of settings described here—from complex, multiparty public policy debates to intraorganizational dialogues, and from the local to the national scale—demonstrates the rich potential of collaborative approaches. The themes that emerge from these examples parallel those elaborated on by the chapter authors, each of whom referred to one or more of the case studies.

The selection of the case studies was made with an eye toward obtaining a broadly representative sample, with variation across issue area, geographical location, and level of decision making. The cases differ, too, in style and tone; each attempts to convey an atmosphere as well as factual circumstances. Some accounts walk the reader, step by step, through every stage of consensus-based decision making. Case 1, "Activating a Policy Network: The Case of Mainport Schiphol," for example, is organized that way. It describes a classic development dispute triggered by ambitious plans to expand Amsterdam's Schiphol Airport in the 1980s. The prospect of turning Schiphol into an international air hub promised great economic gain to the Netherlands but threatened to worsen environmental conditions in surrounding urbanized areas. Long-festering tensions erupted over the issues of airfield extension, configuration of the runways, noise abatement, and the regulation of night flights. In response, a host of affected municipal, provincial, and national government agencies and business interests tried to forge an integrated development plan for the Schiphol region.

Case 2, "The Northern Oxford County Coalition: Four Maine Towns Tackle a Public Health Mystery," also deals with a dispute involving potential trade-offs between economic prosperity and human and environmental health, but the context is rural New England: A group of residents in Northern Oxford County, Maine came together to explore possible links between emissions from a local paper mill and levels of air pollution and cancer rates. Over a two-year period, a coalition of concerned residents, health care providers, small businesses, the mill managers, and government officials sponsored a series of scientific investigations and developed an action plan. The case study focuses on the stakeholder analysis that preceded the joint efforts, the setting of objectives and ground rules, and the design of a joint fact-finding process.

Case 3, "The Chelsea Charter Consensus Process," describes how a new city charter was designed collaboratively in a city torn by corruption. The process, which engaged the entire citizenry, helped Chelsea, Massachusetts, transition out of state receivership to financial stability and the restoration of community activism. The case highlights important issues of representation and legitimacy, and it offers firsthand reflections of the mediator on the most daunting challenge of her career.

Case 4, "Affordable Housing Mediation: Building Consensus for Regional Agreements in the Hartford Area," chronicles a collaborative effort to address a housing crisis faced by Connecticut communities in the late 1980s. The result of this mediated negotiation was an agreement, the Fair Share Housing Compact, requiring the 29

communities involved to meet ambitious affordable housing targets. The compact has been successfully implemented in most of the communities involved.

Case 5, "San Francisco Estuary Project," describes the evolution of the Comprehensive Conservation and Management Plan (CCMP) aimed at improving the health of the estuary. The account details the extraordinary technical and political complexities of this multiparty dialogue. In this case, the important outcomes included not only a written agreement but also the education of the participants, the creation of new networks, and relationships needed to ensure implementation. The case raises important questions about how to evaluate consensus building efforts.

The remaining cases are less comprehensive. They explore one or two aspects of consensus building in greater depth. In essence, they provide a snapshot of a particular phase or feature of consensus building. Case 6, "Resolving Science-Intensive Public Policy Disputes: Reflections on the New York Bight Initiative," describes an elaborate joint fact-finding process. This process examined the technical consequences of various ways of managing a heavily polluted ocean region adjacent to New York Harbor. The process involved a panel of scientists and a negotiating group of 22 resource managers and demonstrates quite nicely how scientific knowledge can be integrated into consensus building in the public arena.

Similarly, Case 7, "Negotiating Superfund Cleanup at the Massachusetts Military Reservation," also grapples with joint fact-finding. Here, though, the central concern is a public outcry over a proposed response to the contamination of a regional water supply. The military did not pay sufficient attention to the likely impacts of its proposed cleanup on hydrological and ecological systems. This led to the creation of a team of technical experts and an elaborate consensus building process among these experts that took place in the public eye.

Case 8, "RuleNet: An Experiment in Online Consensus Building," focuses on the use of information technologies in negotiated rulemaking. It describes a 1996 pilot project launched by the Nuclear Regulatory Commission (NRC) that used the Internet to involve stakeholders in revisions of fire protection regulations. The case highlights the promise that Internet applications hold for consensus processes, as well as some problems the NRC encountered in its venture into cyberspace.

Case 9, "Regulatory Negotiations: The Native American Experience," also describes federal rulemaking—the largest ever, in fact. But its underlying theme is the role that socioethnic and cultural differences play in such processes. The case outlines the development of regulations, with the active participation of tribes, to implement the Indian Self-Determination and Education Assistance Act. This act gives tribes the authority to contract with the federal government to operate federal programs. Particularly sensitive issues of concern were sovereignty, the neutrality of the mediators, and the logistics of meeting management.

Case 10, "Cross-Cultural Community-Based Planning: Negotiating the Future of Haida Gwaii (British Columbia)," delves deeply into the psychological scars wrought by past injury and current power imbalances, and how these must be addressed in designing a consensus building process. The case tells the story of the creation of a jointly managed fund for the development of Native and non-Native communities in British Columbia. It especially highlights the need to confront history before moving into a problem-solving mode.

Case 11 and Case 12 present accounts of two different visioning processes. The former, "The Chattanooga Process: A City's Vision Is Realized," shows how a core group of enterprising citizens can galvanize fellow residents. The latter, "From City Hall to the Streets: A Community Plan Meets the Real World," by contrast, points out the many stumbling blocks that sometimes doom such a process. Here the focus is on what can go wrong during implementation.

A series of cases focuses on fundamental value disputes—situations in which stakeholders perceive their most cherished principles, if not their very identity, to be at risk. In such polarized situations, relationship and trust building take on overriding importance. Case 13, "The Catron County Citizens Group: A Case Study in Community Collaboration," describes how a continuing dialogue diffused a potentially violent dispute over the use of public land in what came to be known as the "toughest county in the West" (New Mexico). Case 14, "Facilitating Statewide HIV/AIDS Policies and Priorities in Colorado," describes a process that produced HIV prevention strategies in the state of Colorado. That effort included a wide range of stakeholders, from persons afflicted with AIDS to members of conservative religious groups. Case 15, "Finding Common Ground on Abortion," relates the experiences of pro-life and pro-choice activists brought together in a series of meetings to share their perspectives with each other.

All of the above cases deal with ad hoc groups, whose members did not share institutional affiliations but rather came together to resolve a problem they had in common. Our final two cases, by contrast, deal with consensus building within permanent organizations that are confronting a moment of crisis. Case 16, "Organizational Trauma Recovery: The 'God's Fellowship Community Church' Reconciliation Process," describes the efforts of a religious congregation to reestablish cohesion and vitality after its founding pastor was removed for inappropriate sexual conduct. Case 17, "Building Consensus for Change within a Major Corporation: The Case of Levi Strauss & Co.," describes the design and implementation of an innovative employee dispute resolution program.

Each of the 17 cases in this part of the *Handbook* is accompanied by reflections offered by one or more experts from a variety of disciplinary perspectives. The insights of the commentators, who are without exception leading thinkers in their fields, are offered in the form of brief observations evoked by particular passages in the cases.

Howard Raiffa, who wrote the ground breaking book *The Art and Science of Negotiation* (1982, Harvard University Press), provides a decision scientist's perspective on Case 1 and Case 7. In his commentary on Case 1, Raiffa zeros in on the role of facilitators. He also lauds the Dutch temperament and raises doubts about whether the process would have had a positive outcome elsewhere. With respect to Case 7, Raiffa discusses attitudes toward risk and explains the relationship between resource expenditures and reductions in pollution levels.

William Moomaw, an environmental scientist who is currently Professor of International Environmental Policy at the Fletcher School of Law and Diplomacy, comments on Cases 6, 7, and 8, all of which have a strong scientific component. He provides insights into the internal divisions among scientists and advice about the form and content that expert opinion ought to take. He also puts a human face on the scientific elements of the case studies.

Max H. Bazerman, Professor at the Kellogg Graduate School of Management, adds the perspective of a social psychologist. His commentaries on Cases 2, 10, and 13 repeatedly touch on the themes of mediator neutrality and the idea of "expanding the pie."

Mark Kishlansky, Professor at Harvard University and a specialist in seventeenth-century British history, applies a historical lens to Cases 1, 3, and 11. He focuses on governmental structures, decision making, and political change.

Sally Engle Merry, an anthropologist at Wellesley College, offers her reactions to Cases 4, 10, 11, 16, and 17. Many of her remarks reflect a deep concern with the obstacles to cross-cultural communication.

Jane Mansbridge, a political scientist teaching at the Kennedy School of Government at Harvard and author of the acclaimed book *Beyond Adversary Democracy* (1983), comments on Cases 3 and 12. She traces the link between "collective action problems" and corruption and makes frequent reference to issues of stakeholder representation and process legitimacy.

Charles F. Sabel, a political economist teaching at Columbia Law School, provides commentaries on Cases 1, 2, and 4. Sabel takes Case 1 as an opportunity to explore whether the essence of consensus building lies in the discovery of new solutions or the mere settlement of conflict. He uses Case 2 to present an analogy between the consensus builder and "the peace-making gunslinger who is the mythic hero of the American Western." Case 4 offers Sabel a point of departure for a discussion about consensus building as either a complement to or substitute for government action.

Carrie J. Menkel-Meadow of the Georgetown Law Center adds a legal perspective to Cases 3, 5, 7, 9, and 15. Her discussions contrast the informality and flexibility of consensus processes to more structured legal environments.

Finally, focusing on the moral problem that is at the core of Case 14, Daniel Markovits of Yale Law School explores the distinction between interests and values, and between compromise and consensus.

1

ACTIVATING A POLICY NETWORK
The Case of Mainport Schiphol

■ Peter Driessen

When we consider how to approach social problems in general and environmental problems in particular, we think first and foremost of government. Of course, one of government's major functions is to bridge social divisions by guiding social developments. Yet governments play an ambivalent role in Western societies. In practice, they perform a dual task. Besides acting as arbiter in the social arena, a public authority usually takes part as a player in the game, even performing on separate administrative levels simultaneously (Tjeenk Willink, 1980). In the role of arbiter, government is supposed to profile itself as an institution that weighs interests by exercising its argumentation and authority and can make choices on that basis. In the role of player, we find governments that take an active stance in defending the interests of certain social groups. These governments tend to maintain close and multifaceted ties with private organizations. Actually, the "government" is composed of many government organizations. Each represents a particular interest. And each of these assumes certain delegated tasks and responsibilities related to these interests. Accordingly, the capacity of governments to resolve social problems is fragmented. ➡

This case is reprinted from "Activating a Policy Network: The Case of Mainport Schiphol" by P. Driessen, pp. 19-35 in P. Glasbergen, *Managing Environmental Disputes: Network Management as an Alternative*, 1994, with kind permission from Kluwer Academic Publishers.

∽ COMMENTARY

This is an account of a success story. It illustrates how an interactive negotiation process was able to harmonize environmental, economic, and developmental concerns in the extension of Amsterdam's Schiphol Airport. I certainly concur with the author that "the planning of airfields has a high potential for conflict." Analytically, the problem is complicated. There are a myriad of conflicting objectives (financial, economic development, national prestige, environmental degradation, quality of life of the abutters, housing stocks) and the various stakeholders have violently opposed trade-offs. There are numerous crucial uncertainties where experts honestly disagree. The whole problem is exacerbated by political realities and violently opposed ideologies. Still, a compromise was made that seemed to satisfy not all, but most, stakeholders. I'm not sure, however, that an analogous process would have been successful in the United States.

—Howard Raiffa, *Decision scientist*

∽ COMMENTARY

The case contains a commentary, better than any I could provide, in the form of an epilogue that brings the story up-to-date. From this observation alone, you will correctly conclude that things turn out better, or worse (or some combination of the two), than the author, reflecting on the expectations of the participants, expected. Since one of the principal aims of consensus building is to solve otherwise intractable problems by detecting possibilities that normally go unnoticed, the surprise, for better or worse, is a sign that something went wrong. As you read the account, resisting the temptation to jump to conclusions, try to discern the systematic flaw that turned an effort to extend the range of social vision into what was, in certain respects, a shortsighted project.

—Charles F. Sabel, *Political economist*

Obviously, conflict is inherent in this dual role. These unavoidable conflicts could be resolved easily if there were a hierarchical relation between the variety of government organizations. Formally, hierarchy is not entirely absent in the Dutch state system. Yet in practice, the administrative bodies are fairly independent, each carrying out its own tasks and responsibilities. Thus, the different government bodies are not tied into the kind of hierarchical relations that would permit them to approach complex social problems by working through a linear process of increasing control. Given this situation, it is imperative that the parties involved form working relationships that increase the opportunities for problem solving. This assumes that the policy network becomes activated. The government bodies involved should be urged to arrive at a joint approach to the issue by setting up a structured process of interaction and communication.

This manner of activating the policy network has a chance of succeeding only if the concerted effort yields benefits for each of the parties separately. Therefore, an activated network must have the potential for win-win outcomes: All parties will expect to end up better off than if they had not participated.

This chapter analyzes a case in which a policy network was activated in an attempt to resolve an incoherent and fragmented act of government. This case involves a dispute about plans to expand Amsterdam's Schiphol Airport. This airport, which has a function for national, continental, and intercontinental air traffic, is situated in a highly urbanized area. Because of its presence, the quality of the surrounding environment has been under pressure for years. Nonetheless, there are ambitious plans to expand the airport. The increasing competition of other West European airports plays a significant role in these plans. As far as the Dutch government is concerned, Schiphol should grow into a mainport. In other words, it should become an airport that acts as a hub for continental and intercontinental air traffic. This development is deemed to be in the national interest. On the one hand, there is a national economic interest at stake. On the other hand, the plans trigger an environmental dispute, manifesting itself for the most part at the regional level. The population living within a 10- to 15-km radius of the airport would be subject to severe nuisances, consisting of noise and stench among other aggravations. Furthermore, the risk of hazard is highest in precisely this region. ⮞

⮞ COMMENTARY

One of the key features of the Amsterdam case was the prefigured decision of the central government to expand the airport into an international hub. This meant that all of the participants were forced to discover their "win-win" outcomes within the context of developmental growth. No group or agency could gain by foot-dragging or by actively seeking to derail the process. This gave the policy network immediate advantages and disadvantages. The multiple agencies of the Dutch government already knew the outcome of their process, which restricted interagency conflict. The municipal governments and citizen groups were negotiating within the context of striking the best deal possible. The disadvantages were equally evident: The process would be considered illegitimate from the start and the public would regard it as imposed rather than negotiated.

—Mark Kishlansky, *Historian*

Let us get to the heart of the matter. From an environmental perspective, restrictions should be imposed on airline activities. From an economic point of view, these activities are extremely valuable. The stalemate between the economic interests of the state and the environmental interests of the region has existed since the 1950s. Subsequent efforts to resolve it have been to no avail. Various government bodies and private organizations are involved in this dispute. In the late 1980s, one of the government authorities took the initiative to activate the policy network as the first step toward addressing the issue in a coordinated fashion. The following exposition reveals the approach taken to motivate the organizations involved to join the concerted effort. The analysis emphasizes the way in which participating actors achieved win-win outcomes. In addition, the analysis also elucidates the different roles played by government bodies in the decision-making process.

■ Issues Involved in Planning Airports

For decades, attempts to expand existing airports have led to administrative ordeals in many countries throughout the world. ••

∽ COMMENTARY

As an aside, in 1970, Ralph Keeney and I were asked to give partisan advice to a behemoth government agency in Mexico, the counterpart of the Ministry of Transport and Public Works in the Netherlands, which was about to enter into intergovernmental negotiations on the modernization of the existing airport in Mexico City or on the development of a new airport 25 miles north of the city. The issues and uncertainties were not much different from those of Schiphol. It became quite clear to us that our clients had already made up their minds about what was best and wanted to use our analysis not for internal decision purposes but to convince the other government agencies of the merits of their preferred alternative. As our analysis with them unfolded, trade-offs articulated, uncertainties examined, as static strategies became more dynamically intricate, our clients became slowly convinced that their preferred strategy was not very good for them or the nation. At first, they resisted what the analysis seemed to be saying, but they then succumbed to the logic of it and acted accordingly. So you see, I come to this case with the feeling that the Schiphol problem is very complicated and good analysis should be part of the negotiation process.

—Howard Raiffa, *Decision scientist*

On the one hand, growth is an economic issue. Clearly, the need to expand airports is primarily the result of a growing world economy and the concomitant demand for additional airport capacity (Zehender, 1987). In this connection, one of the main aspects of airport planning is the ability to project future demand for air transport (both passenger and freight). On the other hand, planning of airfields also involves an important environmental issue. Airports have significant impacts on their physical surroundings. The influences are many and diverse. All over the world, noise is considered to be the biggest problem. This is most acute for airports situated near major population centers. Besides noise, air pollution and safety are major concerns. Finally, an expanding airport attracts industry. Moreover, the rising volume of incoming and outgoing passengers and freight makes it necessary to improve the infrastructure. In turn, these improvements may lead indirectly to new environmental problems at the regional level. ••

⌘ COMMENTARY

The other factors involved in airport expansion were national prestige and improved quality of life for members of the community. This would occur through enhanced passenger services as well as economic dimensions of growth. Forward planning necessitated expansion, as there would likely be denser populations, higher demand for air transport, and greater competition for air commerce. On the other hand, the environmental arguments against expansion were stable. Noise and stench were already at intolerable levels for local residents.

—Mark Kishlansky, *Historian*

Airlines are, for the most part, commercial ventures. Yet in many countries, government intervention in the airline sector is remarkably large (Doganis, 1992). Often, this takes the form of a controlling interest in the firms that run the airports. In some cases, it even takes the form of state enterprises. This may be explained by the economic impulses through the backward and forward links of the airline industry. It should be borne in mind that an airport is not only a place where passengers and freight are received, handled, and transferred onward. Besides an infrastructural facility, an airport is primarily a commercial service and as such can act as an economic growth pole (Kramer, 1990). Particularly with respect to large airports, airline interests are directly associated with the economic interests of the state, which need governmental protection.

Numerous publications throw light on what the planning of airfields actually entails. To name a few, studies have been conducted on London's third airport (Hall, 1980) and Paris' second (Barraqué, 1993); the new airports in Tokyo (Radford & Giesen, 1984) and Munich (Kretschmer, 1984); and the expansion of the airports in Frankfurt (Rucht, 1984) and Bremen (Strubelt & Adam, 1993). These studies reveal that the planning of airfields has a high potential for conflict. Often, many parties are involved in disputes, which usually derive from controversies between government and citizens (who are concerned about the quality of their environment), between government and firms (which sometimes incur damage to their economic interests), or between various government bodies (as a consequence of divergent interests or an ambivalent division of competence). The studies cited above also identify three important characteristics of these disputes.

First, research plays a key role in these controversies. This pertains to research on, for instance, the need to build a new airport or expand the existing one, or it may concern the most desirable infrastructure in and around the airport. The research may deal with the profitability of operation, it may investigate the economic impact of the airport, or it may consider possible negative effects on the environment. Of course, research may not play an "objective" role in the decision-making process. Nonetheless, it still plays a role in the conflict of interests. This is expressed in the dissent over research results and the frequent request for a second opinion.

A second feature is that legal proceedings are often brought to bear in an attempt to force a breakthrough in the dispute. ⊷

ᴄ᾿ COMMENTARY

Legal proceedings are usually seen as inimical to consensus building despite the fact that they use a form of dispute resolution structurally akin to binding arbitration. Legal decisions can be a positive part of consensus building in that they represent bedrock positions that each side must accept and from which other issues can be resolved. Because lawsuits are expensive, time-consuming, and usually involve winner-take-all outcomes, they are rarely seen as integral to long-term consensus building. Indeed, the threat of lawsuits usually signals the breakdown of negotiated settlements, and are an action of last resort.

—Mark Kishlansky, *Historian*

Legal proceedings are mostly initiated by those parties who have no access to the formal decision-making process or who cannot exert enough influence by way of discussion and negotiation.

Third, in connection with the above points, these disputes are rarely resolved in a manner that is satisfactory to all parties. The outcome is often a long, drawn-out delay in work on the project, a hopeless stalemate in the decision-making process, or cessation of the project. These scenarios may also be classified as lose-lose or win-lose situations.

■ *The Development of Schiphol Airport*

For many years, conflicts have beset the planning of Schiphol Airport, located adjacent to the city of Amsterdam. A debate has been going on since the 1950s regarding how and how much the further development of the airport should take into account the negative effects on the environment. Noise nuisance is a key issue in this debate. In the meantime, many investigations have been carried out, plans have been published, and legal proceedings have been conducted. None of these efforts,

however, have led to a solution to the problem. The dispute about the expansion of Schiphol continually receives new impetus from economic developments. In recent years, these impulses have been felt more acutely. The airline industry is in flux, especially because of the trend toward "internationalization." Not only airports but also airlines have to meet tougher international competition. In this way, the international component of business management is becoming increasingly important.

In the near future, competition between the European airports is expected to become stiffer. In part, this is due to the creation of a single European market for air transport. Competition will tend to concentrate the intercontinental traffic at a limited number of European destinations. The Dutch government seeks to bolster Schiphol's position to secure the airport's future as a motor for the Dutch economy. Thus, Amsterdam is supposed to occupy a key position in continental and intercontinental air traffic.

In 1992, Schiphol ranked fifth among European airports in terms of number of passengers (after London, Paris, Frankfurt, and Rome); in terms of freight, Amsterdam came in fourth (after Frankfurt, London, and Paris) (NV Luchthaven Schiphol, 1993). Schiphol handled 19.1 million passengers and 695,000 tons of freight in that year. Amsterdam's biggest competitor is Paris. The possibilities for expansion at London's Heathrow Airport (presently, more than three times the size of Schiphol) are already limited. The airport at Frankfurt is expected to gradually relinquish some of its capacity to a new central airport in Berlin. And Brussels' Zaventem Airport is already behind in development. In contrast, Charles de Gaulle Airport near Paris still has wide room for expansion.

The fervent competition between airports is fueled by the increasing competition between carriers. A trend is emerging toward ever-larger companies in the industry and more cooperation between them, which leads to economies of scale. Naturally, an airport can corner a bigger piece of the market if it can host several big airlines (the *mega-carriers*).

■ The Policy Network

From the beginning, various government organizations have been involved in the development of Schiphol Airport. The main players are three ministries. The Ministry of Transport and Public Works is by far the most important actor in the policy network. This ministry is formally responsible for airport planning, and its jurisdiction is circumscribed in the Aviation Act, which regulates the development of airfields as well as the abatement of noise nuisance. Thus, the Ministry of Transport and Public Works is responsible for the economic development of the airport as well as (an aspect of) environmental quality. Second, the Ministry of Housing, Physical Planning and Environment is also involved. This ministry implements policy regarding the rest of the environmental effects of the activities of the airline industry, namely, air pollution, stench, and hazard. Moreover, this ministry is responsible for physical planning in the Netherlands. Finally, the Ministry of Economic Affairs plays an important role. This ministry pursues further economic development in the region of Schiphol. ➴

➴ COMMENTARY

The involvement of overlapping government agencies in the policy network posed particular problems in the development of a consensual decision. Though the three Dutch government agencies with jurisdictional authority over airport expansion necessarily accepted the mandate for airport expansion, each had more at stake than achieving this outcome. Interagency rivalry and power would have to play a critical part in the positions the ministries adopted and the coalitions they built during negotiations. This fragmentation of government would have had even greater impact if the decision on expansion had been open-ended. It might have been possible for opposing groups to ally with one ministry or another on jurisdictional rather than policy grounds.

—Mark Kishlansky, *Historian*

Lower tiers of government also play a role in Schiphol's development. The province of North Holland and the municipalities surrounding the airport are the authorities most deeply involved. The province is responsible for environmental policy and planning for the region. The surrounding municipalities have a variety of interests. To varying degrees, all enjoy the benefits and endure the aggravation of having the airport close by. The benefits take the form of firms that locate in the vicinity of the airport, thus creating more jobs and income in local taxes. The aggravation takes the form of noise, stench, air pollution, and other activities that degrade the environment. The municipality of Haarlemmermeer is a special case, because the airport lies within its territory. Accordingly, this municipality is authorized to create a land use plan for the airfield.

Finally, two enterprises play a crucial role in the policy network: NV Luchthaven Schiphol (Schiphol Airport, Inc.) and KLM. The former is the company that operates the airport, and it is entirely state owned. The national government holds about three-fourths of the shares in this company, and the rest is owned by the municipalities of Amsterdam (22 percent) and Rotterdam (2 percent). KLM, the major Dutch carrier, is partly owned by the state (about one-third of the shares) and has a large stake in the expansion of the airport. Thus, the government has a strong influence on the major Dutch air transport companies. This is why the interests of air transport are considered national interests that warrant governmental protection. As noted above, this situation is similar to that found in many other Western countries.

■ Impasse in Decision Making

In the policy network described above, diverse interests come into play. Their tasks and responsibilities are dispersed over many actors. To date, it has not been possible to reach consensus within this network on the future development of Schiphol Airport. As pointed out earlier, tension between growth of the airport and urban expansion in the surrounding area has been building up since the 1950s.

For years, there has been a lack of clarity on the developments impinging on Schiphol (de Maar, 1976; Driessen, Glasbergen, & Spek, 1993). First of all, there was uncertainty about noise nuisance. It took a long time for noise to be acknowledged as a problem and to find a way of calculating the level of distress. A system was developed in the Netherlands to measure noise nuisance in the mid-1960s. However, there is still no agreement on how it should be applied. For instance, there is some discussion about how to determine the threshold value for maximum admissible noise nuisance. Furthermore, opinions differ on setting a specific norm for night flights. The disagreement revolves around the degree to which departing and arriving airplanes disturb the sleep of nearby residents, and whether such disruption is detrimental to public health. With regard to both of these discussions, it should be pointed out that setting norms will automatically decrease the options for expanding the airport (unless, e.g., it is decided to demolish some buildings). But restrictions on expansion also impose limits on the airport's function as an economic growth pole. Second, there was uncertainty about how rapidly air traffic would increase and the degree to which technical developments in aeronautics would be able to help reduce noise levels. In this regard, the question arose whether aircraft that make less noise would be built in the future.

Both of these uncertainties had an effect, especially at the municipal level. In the

1960s and 1970s, municipalities in the surrounding area did not have sufficient information on the long-term development of Schiphol or on the possible consequences of growth of noise nuisance. In those days, there was a severe housing shortage in the Netherlands, and it was acute in the region where the airport is located. That housing shortage demanded a quick response. In that context, urban extensions steadily encroached on the airfield; with hindsight, this was not a good solution. A complicating factor is that in the past, hardly any discussion took place between the various actors. There was insufficient insight into the problem and no consensus on how to resolve it. Not surprisingly, every actor basically set his or her own course. In a sense, Schiphol developed in a vacuum. No dialogue took place with the surrounding area, and the neighboring municipalities extended their residential areas without consulting the airport authorities. Only in the mid-1970s were both developments—the extension of the airport and the growth of the urban agglomeration—more closely linked. But by that time, the problem of noise had taken on major proportions. Construction of four takeoff and landing runways had been completed, and the largest urban extensions in the area were already in place.

Finally, it should be noted that the problems concerning Schiphol could not be resolved within the context of the existing policy network. As pointed out earlier, the Ministry of Transport and Public Works occupied a pivotal position in this network. It was responsible for both the economic development of Schiphol and the abatement of noise nuisance. In the Netherlands, environmental policy—and thus noise abatement—constitutes a primary task of the Ministry of Housing, Physical Planning and Environment. Accordingly, at the end of the 1970s, it was agreed that noise produced by aircraft would be regulated by the Aviation Act, for which the Ministry of Transport and Public Works was responsible. Yet this ministry also proved unable to balance the interests of the air transport industry and those of the environmental movement. A wide-ranging plan—the Outline Plan for Civil Aviation Airfields—was designed to resolve the problem of noise. However, this plan was never fully implemented. In addition, the growth of Schiphol was designated as being in the interest of the nation. The objections that had been raised with regard to noise were apparently considered less important. For a long time, it was firmly believed that measures to prevent noise nuisance would prematurely curtail Schiphol's options for expansion. This attitude reflects a preference for technical solutions. In this vein, it was initially expected that technological innovations would keep the noise level of future aircraft much lower; thus, the problem would largely go away by itself.

In the mid-1980s, decision making on the extension of the airfield had reached a deadlock. The parties could not agree on how much the airport should be allowed to grow, nor could they agree on how to tackle the environmental problems. In particular, the parties involved held different opinions on the future configuration of the runways, the abatement of noise nuisance, and regulation of night flights. The NV Luchthaven Schiphol also made ambitious plans in the mid-1980s—in the wake of the economic recession—to eventually make Schiphol one of Europe's mainports (Commissie Van der Zwan, 1986).

■ *Breaking the Impasse by Activating the Policy Network*

In 1988, the Dutch government made a crucial statement in an important national memorandum on physical planning. In this document, the government posited that in the light of the recent economic revitalization, the development of Schiphol into a mainport should be fostered. The rationale was that development in this direction would provide a major impulse for employment. Yet Schiphol should only be allowed to grow along these lines if its development was accompanied by improvement in the environmental quality in the surrounding areas. The elusive goal to bridge the gap between economic growth and improvement of environmental quality was thought to be within reach by taking a coordinated approach to the problem. To that end, an integral plan had to be made for the Schiphol region. At the very least, this plan would have to include a perspective on the development of the airport up to the year 2015 (Vierde Nota, 1988).

This statement gave new impetus to the effort to resolve the problems related to the airport. The primary responsibility for the tasks proposed in that landmark document was the Ministry of Housing, Physical Planning and Environment. ➤

☙ COMMENTARY

The leadership role assumed by the Ministry of Housing, Physical Planning and Environment appears to have been fortuitous rather than preconceived. Because this ministry was likely to be the strongest voice for environmental concerns, the fact that it took the initiative in orchestrating the process preserved the environmental voice, on the one hand, and co-opted it to expansion, on the other. As the author later notes, "Because people realized that the project would be carried out no matter what . . . many parties chose to cooperate."

—Mark Kishlansky, *Historian*

This ministry had never played a leading role in the policy network. Nonetheless, authorities at the ministry decided to break through the administrative barriers to further development of the airport. This was to be achieved by designing an organizational framework for the discussion whereby the coordinated approach would be given a concrete form. In other words, the ministry took the initiative to activate the policy network. This move reflected the ministry's desire to bring into the foreground the environmental interests at play. This goal could be achieved only if the ministry were to take an active role at an early stage in formulating the new plan. Because of this initiative, the Ministry of Housing, Physical Planning and Environment acquired a dual function in the project. It had to take care of setting up the project and managing it, and it also had to secure the input of environmental interests in the decision making. ➤

∞ COMMENTARY

From my perspective, and acting with hindsight, I applaud the leadership taken by the Ministry of Housing, Physical Planning and Environment in activating the policy network. That ministry played a dual role: one, as an interested party, and two, as a convenor, chair, and facilitator of the planning process. I found it interesting that, as revealed shortly, it was the parties represented in the steering committee that "ruled the roost" and shared in the "all gain" results. There is a lesson here for other negotiations: If you want to share in the joint gains, get included!

—Howard Raiffa, *Decision scientist*

At first, this raised suspicion among other government bodies. The initiative to start such a project had been taken away from the Ministry of Transport and Public Works. Moreover, the latter ministry had a strong affiliation with one of the project's two aims. Other parties wondered whether they would be able to take a neutral position in the ensuing discussion. But their initial wariness soon gave way to a realistic attitude. Because people realized that the project would be carried out no matter what—it had the backing of a government decree—many parties chose to cooperate. They felt it was better to jump into the fray rather than wait out the game on the sidelines. Then, too, they recognized that as lone operators, none of the parties would be able to break the deadlock in decision making about the expansion of the airport.

The organizational structure that was set up for this project consisted of a project group and a steering committee. The latter comprised eight organizations: the Ministry of Transport and Public Works; the Ministry of Housing, Physical Planning and Environment; the Ministry of Economic Affairs; the province of North Holland; the municipalities of Amsterdam and Haarlemmermeer; NV Luchthaven Schiphol; and KLM. The project group first had a much broader base. So as not to alienate other municipalities that might be important discussion partners in the stages of brainstorming and implementation of the plan, it was decided to include these parties in the project group. It soon proved, however, that the parties represented in the steering committee ruled the roost, while the others were gradually shunted onto a sidetrack. With hindsight, this was not surprising, because only a select few could book "all-gain" results. ∞

∞ COMMENTARY

Again it is instructive to note the ad hoc nature of the structures for problem solving. The creation of a policy committee composed of all interested groups and of a steering committee of essential power brokers gave way to the omnipotence of the steering committee alone. It is not clear that the members of the policy committee who were eventually excluded from decision making were those who could not "book 'all-gain' results," or were simply those not powerful enough to block or advance progress. Nevertheless, a process that excludes interests that cannot be part of a win-win solution will have difficulty building consensus or achieving compliance. Again, in this case the imposed nature of the outcome (in principle though not in detail) had an effect on which groups could be comfortably encompassed in decision making.

—Mark Kishlansky, *Historian*

As soon as all parties had agreed to participate in the project, a joint statement of intent was drawn up in the form of a covenant specifying the aim of the project, the policy standpoints, the organizational structure, and the financing of that organization. Furthermore, this document clearly explained why cooperation was essential. It argued that the tension between economics and the environment could be relieved only by reaching consensus. At the same time, the covenant also attested to the existence of mutual rivalry. As a case in point, the Ministry of Transport and Public Works and the province of North Holland added a statement to the covenant elaborating on their own interests and stance on policy. In doing so, they set the stage for the negotiation process that was yet to be started.

After the necessity of cooperation was acknowledged by all parties involved, the formulation of plans could begin. As the plans were being hammered out, consensus had to be reached between the parties on a development perspective for the Schiphol region, and on measures to actually implement this perspective.

The plans were formulated in three stages—the three different strategies that were deployed to come to agreement between the parties.

- The *cognitive* stage was directed toward gathering and exchanging information.

- The *productive* stage was directed toward decision making on the main points of discussion.
- The *formalizing* stage concerns final decision making and the creation of social and political legitimacy for the plan.

It should be borne in mind that the clustering of these activities was not determined beforehand; rather, these stages were only distinguished afterward.

■ The Cognitive Stage in the Process of Formulating a Plan

The strategy followed by the project leaders at this stage was to bring the various parties closer together by conducting investigations and exchanging information. It was assumed that sharing information might contribute to a better understanding and more appreciation for each other's standpoints. And that, of course, was expected to help the parties reach consensus.

The activities in this stage centered on a project program, a research program, and the development of three scenarios. An important function of the project program was to chart the diverse standpoints. In addition, an inventory was made of bottlenecks and gaps in knowledge as a first step toward finding solutions. On the basis of the project program, it was decided to continue by way of a research track and a scenario track. In the research track, 13 investigations were delegated. For each of these, an advisory committee was recruited from members of the project group. By drawing the interested parties into active participation in the investigations, it was hoped to maximize agreement on the research results. A separate group was cre- ated to develop scenarios. This group made three projections, each corresponding to the number of passengers that could be transported per year and the concomitant number of flights departing and arriving at the airport. Calculations for the year 2015 put the high scenario at 60 million passengers, the middle scenario at 40 million, and the low one at 20 million. ➡

∞ COMMENTARY

I found the initial proposal to work simultaneously on several scenarios quite appropriate, as was the decision to concentrate on the accumulation of information for subsequent decision making.

There seemed to be no need for a professional facilitator in the cognitive stage of deliberations. All was orderly while information was being collected, analyzed, and disseminated. That's not always the case. A facilitator with problem-solving, analytical skills could often contribute to structuring the problem.

—Howard Raiffa, *Decision scientist*

∞ COMMENTARY

The decision to create research groups and scenario groups brought the process of decision making forward by linking empirical information to potential outcomes. While this first stage generated contention, it actually had the effect of narrowing the issues of dispute and creating coalitions around potential scenarios seen as more or less favorable to the different interests. While this did not result in reaching an agreement, it nevertheless moved the process forward and gave way to concrete disputes over an actual plan rather than general disputes over principles.

—Mark Kishlansky, *Historian*

In this stage, there were already signs that the parties were forming coalitions. The municipality of Haarlemmermeer and the province of North Holland together comprised the environmental coalition. These parties attached most importance to a high-quality environment in which to live. The mainport coalition consisted of the Ministry of Economic Affairs and the Ministry of Transport and Public Works, along with the municipality of Amsterdam, NV Luchthaven Schiphol, and KLM. These partners rallied around the economic interests of the airport. The Ministry of Housing, Physical Planning and Environment was in limbo, pulled by two opposing sets of demands: to manage the project as best as possible, and to defend the environmental interests. Obviously, this ministry did not fit neatly into one of the coalitions.

When the investigations and scenario studies were finished, the project leaders set out to write a draft plan. This plan was met with a rain of criticism and, understandably, was not released. This setback indicated that the time was not ripe for decision making. The material was extremely complex and the parties still disagreed on many issues. Many points proved to be unclear or subject to differences of opinion. For instance, the following were still under discussion: adjustment of the system of take-off and landing runways, setting norms for noise nuisance, setting a specific norm for night flights, possibly using high-speed rail links as a substitute for continental flights, relocating air transport activities to other airports, and manner and degree of financial commitment to the agreements yet to be made. In view of the dissent in the steering committee on the initial draft plan, the project leaders decided to switch to a different approach. This decision also marked a clear transition in the process of formulating the plan.

■ The Productive Stage in the Process of Formulating a Plan

The next stage was no longer concerned with increasing the supply of information. Instead, the parties sought to digest what they had and to arrive at a decision. A facilitator was recruited for this new "game," which was aimed at decision making. ∞

∞ COMMENTARY

The first efforts at resolution revealed the fault lines among the interests on the steering committee; it is interesting to note that it was only at that point that a facilitator was brought into the process. The risks involved in not using a facilitator earlier were minimized in this case because there was little chance the negotiations would break down in the wake of the government mandate to develop a plan of expansion. In other cases, the use of a facilitator at the fact-finding stage is critical to ensure the integrity of the research being done or potential scenarios being created. Similarly, in the Amsterdam airport case the facilitator could focus immediately on the bottlenecks in the process rather than attempt to deal first with peripheral issues on which agreement was more easily secured. There was no need to build momentum toward closure as closure was already presupposed.

—Mark Kishlansky, *Historian*

The task of the "outsider" was to guide the negotiations between the parties. This slot was filled by a person who held an independent position with respect to the parties involved and was also well informed on the issues. ∞

∽ COMMENTARY

Evidently, in moving from the cognitive stage to the decision-framing stage (I prefer *framing* here to *making*), emotion heated up and a professional facilitator was introduced—someone skilled in running meetings efficiently, in the conduct of human relations, and in negotiation processes. It is not clear whether the facilitator had staff support and whether the facilitator had analytical, problem-solving skills. Did the facilitator generate substantive proposals for the consideration of the negotiation parties? Or did the facilitator assume a more passive role?

—Howard Raiffa, *Decision scientist*

The approach taken by the facilitator was aimed at bringing the main bottlenecks to the fore. In that way, opportunities arose to reach agreement, at least on key points, between the parties. The approach was characterized by the creation of a strong interaction between the project group and the steering committee. The latter was confronted with issues that the project group had pared down to size. The steering committee reviewed the issues and approved the solutions offered by the project group. In the event that approval was withheld, the issue was sent back to the project group, where renewed attempts would have to be made to reach consensus. Thus, a cyclical process came about. The approach consisted of five steps.

Step 1

First, an inventory was made of the most important points for discussion. This was done with the aid of blank sheets of paper taped to the wall, on which possible topics were posted. Using colored stickers, members of the project group could indicate their assessment of the topics. They had to name the topics that would require a state-ment. In this fashion, the main issues were distilled. The following points for discussion emerged from the inventory: configuration of the runway system, abatement of noise nuisance, a regulation for night flights, the relocation of activities to other airports (e.g., training flights), the substitution of high-speed trains for continental flights, infrastructure around the airport, development of industrial premises, taking action on air pollution, financing of the measures, and procedures for decision making once the plan has been established.

Step 2

Subsequently, the problem had to be defined for each topic. Certain problems were split up into subsets. An attempt was made to give a precise description for each of these (sub)problems.

Step 3

When the inventory was complete, members of the project group were asked to offer a solution for the various problems. As a rule, the members with the deepest involvement in a problem and the most divergent opinions were supposed to write a joint memo on the question. In case they could not agree on certain aspects, the differing insights could be expressed.

Step 4

Ultimately, this approach resulted in a number of memos on the problems that emerged during the inventory round. These reports identified some possible directions for solutions. The documents were circulated among the members of each project group for their comments. Then the memos and the notes made on them were collected. At that point, the facilitator set about rewriting them in the form of reports on decision points. These reports were organized in the following way. A proposition was formulated for each topic. It was accompanied by proposals for a direction in which to find a solution and, where possible, proposals for concrete decisions. The following information was provided on each topic:

- formulation of the first draft plan,
- the problem for which a solution should be sought,
- one or more directions for a solution, and
- proposals for a decision on content or procedures.

Step 5

The reports on decision points were finally submitted to the steering committee for a decision. In case the committee was unable to approve any of the proposals, that particular topic was sent back to the project group, accompanied by the committee's comments, and the procedures were repeated. This stepwise approach was repeated in three rounds. In these three cycles of decision making, all the discussion points were dealt with. Consensus was reached on the main thrust of these points. Thus, the approach was successful and led to a new draft plan on which all parties agreed. ➤

➤ COMMENTARY

I think it is fair to say that the five steps described here, the "productive stage in the process of formulating a plan" were conducted in a spirit of what I call fair, open, truthful exchange (FOTE). It was great that this was the case and it's a tribute to the Dutch. Such amicable accord of process may not be so readily achievable in other cultures. From my negotiation perspective, what the facilitator did in Steps 1 to 4 was to generate a template (a framework for decision making) describing the key issues that needed to be resolved and suggested resolutions for these issues. Presumably, the parties shared their preferences with each other, and I assume they did not posture or play strategic coalitional games. Great!

It is at the close of Stage 4 and 5 that the process seems fuzzy to me and where it is lucky that agreement was achieved. I am left with the impression that each issue was resolved separately by the steering committee by consensus. This seems surprising to me. I would suspect that a good deal of logrolling would have taken place. "I will give in on issue X if I can get my way on issue Y." I also would have guessed that coalitions would have formed in these claiming procedures.

—Howard Raiffa, *Decision scientist*

∽ COMMENTARY

The staged process of focusing around disagreements and refining compromises allowed the facilitator to bring competing interests together. The use of mixed groups with opposing viewpoints led to constant face-to-face bargaining in the small groups. Competing interests would state alternate plans and then be forced to find common ground among them. This is a technique that often works when individuals are highly motivated to find agreement, but it can also lead to irreconcilable positions on major issues.

—Mark Kishlansky, *Historian*

■ *The Formalizing Stage in the Process of Formulating a Plan*

Up to that point, the discussion and negotiation process took place within a closed circuit. In fact, only the parties represented in the project group and the steering committee had the opportunity to influence the development of the plan. Once the draft plan was made public, the process of consensus building came into a new phase. At that point, the central aim was to gain social and political legitimacy. Concretely, this meant that the plan had to be opened up to public discussion, and the reactions had to be taken into account in the final version. ∽

∽ COMMENTARY

Now comes disclosure to the public. The facilitator deserves a lot of credit for presenting choices in a way that did not polarize the public. Perhaps even more credit goes to the Dutch temperament. In the United States, life would have been more complicated. Maybe not as complicated as was the case in Israel and the Palestinian Authority when Oslo accords were made public, but something like that typically happens when quasi-secret deliberations are made public and the "losers" can identify themselves. In the United States, the "losers" have a fluid mobility to organize into blocking coalitions.

—Howard Raiffa, *Decision scientist*

∽ COMMENTARY

Attempting to build consensus after the hammering out of the various compromises is the most interesting part of the Amsterdam airport case. Normally, efforts at consensus building would take place before the actual processes of decision making had gone very far. In this case, the decision to exclude participation from the public and to restrict the number of options that the government would allow to be considered had the effect of inverting a normal consensus building. What is interesting, however, is that these decisions did not prevent efforts at achieving agreement.

—Mark Kishlansky, *Historian*

And when this was done, the plan had to be submitted for approval to Parliament, the provincial executive of North Holland, and the municipal councils of Amsterdam and Haarlemmermeer.

This stage was extremely complex for two reasons. First, it proved that the "closed circuit" approach had a major drawback: The citizens of the region were suddenly confronted with a plan they had hardly heard of before. In fact, few people even knew it was in preparation. Not surprisingly, there was a great deal of criticism of the approach taken. The psychological effect was adverse; the plan was generally received with suspicion. The authorities were accused of making a deal with industry and of having ignored the interests of the local residents.

Second, the parties in the steering committee decided to organize a separate public discussion for each of their constituencies and to hold political consultation. The government authorities in particular were of the opinion that this was not a joint responsibility of the steering committee but a task that each tier of government should perform independently. The rationale was that each authority knew best how to inform its populace. As a result, the public discussion did not proceed in a coordinated fashion, and each government resorted to its own method of public discussion. For instance, both the province of North Holland and the municipality of Haarlemmermeer held public hearings to give the population the chance to respond to the plan. The municipality of Amsterdam, by contrast, chose an entirely different approach. Instead of inviting the public to react to the plan, the municipal council held a survey among 35 selected organizations. The questionnaire was constructed such that the respondents would be confronted with the whole range of opposing forces: on the one hand, the force in favor of developing the airport into a mainport, on the other, the force for improving the quality of the residential environment. One example is that environmental organizations were requested to consider the economic consequences of not extending the airport. And representatives of industry, by contrast, were asked how developing a mainport would affect the quality of the local environment. This approach prevented the respondents from using the survey to defend their own interests exclusively.

In view of the purpose of this stage, another strategy had to be found to retain the consensus already achieved. The facilitator's main focus of attention at this point was the steering committee. The project group was only expected to complete a few investigations and recommendations. In this stage, the facilitator had to keep in mind that each party might take criticism of the plan as a lever to reopen discussion on memos that had already been submitted. Therefore, the facilitator sought to prevent the parties from deviating from the main course and thus undermining any compromise already reached. Accordingly, his approach was first to keep the parties in continual contact, whereby everyone had the maximum information on progress in the discussions on content. This led, for instance, to frequent bilateral discussion. Second, the facilitator took upon himself the task of writing the final text of the plan. All the standpoints and motions emanating from the political consultations were compiled, organized, and translated into draft texts. These drafts were repeatedly rewritten in response to remarks from the steering committee. ➤

☞ COMMENTARY

What emerges from this final stage is the realization that consensus is secondary to maintaining the integrity of the sets of compromises created by the steering committee. For this reason, the facilitator found it necessary to become an open advocate for the agreement rather than an agent of the process. Writing the final text of the plan gave the facilitator power to shape the final agreement in ways that may not have been anticipated when the role was first defined. This is an example of how open-ended processes sometimes create the best opportunities for bringing opposing interests together.

—Mark Kishlansky, *Historian*

This approach was also successful. The original plan was revised at certain points, but the consensus remained intact. Agreement was reached on reduction of noise nuisance and hazard. This was accomplished, for instance, by changing the system of runways on the airfield (constructing a fifth runway and changing the angle of an existing one); other key changes were the exclusion of noisy aircraft and the substitution of high-speed train connections for continental flights. Furthermore, agreement was reached on setting a threshold for noise nuisance and on providing additional sound insulation for dwellings in the vicinity (the process of insulating against sound had already been started in the 1980s). With regard to the rest of the environmental effects (stench, safety, and air pollution), agreement was reached on the aims, while concrete measures were left to a later stage of plan elaboration. ☞

☞ COMMENTARY

Sidestepping the details of contentious issues is a common technique in efforts to build or maintain a consensus. It is predicated on the assumption that people co-opted into the process will ultimately compromise details rather than derail an entire agreement. This probably fails as often as it succeeds. It takes a shrewd facilitator to assess which critical details will shatter the process entirely.

—Mark Kishlansky, *Historian*

The whole package of measures would permit the airport to grow to roughly 40 to 45 million passengers per year by 2015; eventually, the environmental load would be reduced.

On the basis of the plan, the parties involved drafted a covenant containing the main agreements. The covenant had the status of a statement of intent. It explicitly mentioned that the perspective expressed in the plan would be carried out jointly by the parties. Moreover, it reported that the plan would be elaborated further by way of various procedures before implementation could be started.

It should be borne in mind that in the case reviewed here, the parties reached agreement on a long-term development perspective. A perspective of this nature was desirable to build a unified front for further negotiations on actual steps to be taken. And this perspective specifies the main directions for future expansion for the airfield. Clarity on these options is imperative for the parties representing the economic interests. And for the parties dedicated to defending environmental interests, assurance was given that the major environmental problems caused by air transport will be dealt with.

In the next few years, this development perspective will have to be worked out as measures for implementation. Therefore, the parties were unable to make hard-and-fast agreements. At this stage of the discussion, neither government bodies nor private organizations could afford to promise concrete results. In the stage of plan elaboration, it will prove whether the consensus built among the parties is actually durable.

■ *Further Analysis of the Process of Activating the Policy Network*

The case reviewed here demonstrates that government bodies and private organizations need each other to devise an effective approach to environmental issues. In the past, it proved impossible to resolve the dispute over extension of the airfield. In many respects, it was a no-win situation. When acting independently, none of the parties was able to come any closer to achieving its goal. To break the deadlock, the policy network was activated by starting a structured process of interaction and communication.

The case of Schiphol leads to the conclusion that the process of activating a network proceeds by stages. These have been discussed at greater or lesser length in the above section and are also treated in the literature on activating networks (Soeters, 1991). These are the *initiative, cognitive, productive,* and *formalization* stages.

In the initiative stage, attention is primarily focused on mobilization of the parties who should be included in tackling the problem. This is the stage in which the ideas of common interest and interdependence are noticed by one of the parties. The initiator then seeks to involve other parties in a structured process of interaction and communication. In this process, it is imperative to convince the various parties of the added value to be derived from a concerted effort and the benefits to be gained by the individual parties. The strategy to be deployed at this stage should therefore make it clear that autonomous development—that is, development without a concerted effort—is not attractive to any of the parties involved. This stage can lead to a joint statement of intent in which the necessity of acting in concert is endorsed by all parties.

Subsequently, both the cognitive and the productive stages emphasize activating the processes of interaction and communication between the parties. These two stages should lead to convergence between the diverse definitions of the situation. Moreover, the actors should harmonize their moves. In both stages, special methods must be applied to get the parties to actually come to an agreement.

The cognitive stage is directed at the exchange of information and new ideas. Its aim is to influence the way the parties perceive the problem. At this stage, joint investigations and information exchange projects are set up. In this way, the parties can get acquainted with each other. The aims of this stage are to make an inventory of the problems, to reach agreement on the precise wording of these problems, and if possible, to determine goals for the projects. The strategy should be to start an open dialogue as a way to help the various parties show more understanding for each other's standpoints. More knowledge about the issue and a deeper appreciation of each other's interests could encourage the parties to reach consensus.

In the third stage of the process of activating the policy network, there is a concerted "production" effort. Decisions on the main issues are conscientiously prepared. They form the basis for compromise: on directions in which to find solutions, on measures of implementation, and on financing. In fact, the willingness of the various parties to follow through is determined in this productive stage. This is precisely the point at which it becomes clear what sacrifices have to be made and what benefits may be distributed; alternatives for behavior will be restricted and/or broadened. Usually, this is when it will first be clear whether win-win outcomes are actually feasible. The negotiations between the various parties will be ruthless at this stage. Therefore, the strategy of using an (external) facilitator to methodically structure the negotiating process will pay off in this stage (Susskind & Cruikshank, 1987).

In the last stage, formalization, agreements are recast as a plan and possibly also a covenant. At the same time, the plan has to be formally recognized. Its social and political basis can be confirmed by subjecting it to procedures for public discussion and administrative decision making. In this stage, a transition takes place from internal decision making to external legitimation. On the basis of the definitive arrangements

that are ultimately made, new dependency relations emerge between the parties.

■ *Conclusions*

This chapter has discussed the main characteristics of the process by which networks are activated. This process was illustrated by sketching a dispute surrounding the extension of an airfield, namely, Amsterdam's Schiphol Airport. The core of this dispute is that environmental policy would require restrictions on air transport activities—due to objections regarding noise nuisance, stench, hazard, and air pollution—whereas these activities are extremely important from an economic point of view. In this situation, it is inconceivable that the activities taking place in and around the airfield would be forced to stop completely. Accordingly, the environment would continue to be subjected to some degree of stress in the future. The question arises how environmental aims can be harmonized and what role the government can play in this effort.

This case illustrates that the government plays various roles in resolving the problem of planning for an airfield. Earlier, I used the term *dual role* in this connection. The government takes the role of an arbiter in the social arena, while also taking part as a player in the game. The latter role is also taken by a government body that pursues purely private interests. Air transport is a case in point; this is an area where public and private interests are closely interwoven. This dual role generates conflicts that are not easily resolved, due to the absence of a hierarchy in government organization. The result is often a lack of coherence in governmental acts. This problem is all the more urgent because the government's need to direct developments has increased considerably over the past few years. Social problems are increasing in complexity and scale. Environmental issues form a good example of this trend. The good intentions to do something about these problems can usually not be achieved. This is because in practice, the capacity of the government to control developments remains limited.

In the case described here, we also observed that government control can be increased by activating networks. In this way, the coherence of government policy can be enhanced: Government organizations are encouraged to set up a joint approach to the problem, together with private organizations. The controversies between public and private actors did not arise in this case. The approach described here even led to a breakthrough in the decision-making impasse. The success of activating a network in this case depended on four factors. First, it was demonstrated that autonomous development, being the continuation of the current situation, was not appealing to any of the parties involved. In other words, it was a lose-lose situation. Second, it was made clear that the parties involved were not able to break the deadlock on their own and bring the resolution of the problems any closer. All parties acknowledged that they needed each other to arrive at a fruitful approach to the issue. Third, in a more or less intuitive manner, the planning process evolved such that in each stage—initiative, cognitive, productive, and formalization—appropriate strategies were applied to promote consensus between the parties. Fourth, a perspective was developed for the future of the region, in which environmental and economic goals were related to each other. This development perspective

was taken as a package deal by the parties involved; it was a package with which each of them would eventually win more than they stood to lose.

Let us return to the question posed at the beginning of this section. Indeed, the government can play a dual role in harmonizing environmental and economic goals. First of all, in the role of manager, the government can try to organize decision-making arrangements between the actors with the most interests at stake. In this role, the authorities will have to attempt to bridge the conflicts of interest between public and private actors. This can be done, for instance, by setting conditions on further development to the benefit of all parties. In performing this role, the emphasis lies on communication and guidance. This chapter has given depth to that role, elaborating on the way in which the policy network was activated and on how the interaction and communication processes between the parties involved were shaped. Second, complementary to its first role, government can act as arbiter to combat excesses. In this role, the authorities will carefully monitor the compliance with agreements on reduction of the environmental load. Moreover, they will have to ensure that every possible effort will be made to prevent further deterioration of the environment in the vicinity of the airfield. Thus, network management does not neutralize the dual role of the government. In fact, it adds a new role to the interplay. The government takes on a third task: to manage the organization of decision-making arrangements between the various actors. This third role represents an attempt to compensate for the conflicts of interest inherent in government's traditional roles of arbiter and player.

■ *Epilogue*

It might be logical to conclude that the method employed to activate a policy network was successful. A plan for the extension of Schiphol Airport emerged, and a consensus was attained between all concerned parties. The crucial question, however, is whether this consensus subsequently led to resolution of the problem. Unfortunately, this is not the case. The problem of reconciling economic and environmental interests is an infinitely complex one in which technical and social factors play an important role. The aviation sector is an economic growth engine, which in the past rarely concerned itself with the quality of the environment. Change in attitude and action in this sector requires time and the exertion of considerable social and political pressure. Instead, in the Schiphol decision-making process, a compromise was sought that fit within the existing mental framework of the parties. The most important lesson of the aftermath of this case is that consensus building is not a onetime venture. It is an ongoing process of problem solving that must take account of new developments as they emerge. ●◆

◌◦ COMMENTARY

There, after a bit of meandering, you have it: An effort at social exploration of new approaches turned out to be an exercise in the management of dissent. This result reveals a tension in the idea of consensus building as problem solving. Problem solving as the discovery, through practical deliberation, of new solutions (which the participants could not, given their "existing mental framework," have imagined but for their commitment to investigate their differences)? Or problem solving as the fixing or arbitration of conflict so that each of the parties satisfies enough of the original demands to make it worthwhile—for the moment at least—to proceed with the deal? The emphasis in the cases is on the first interpretation, but as this story shows, despite exhortations to openness and inclusiveness, it is easy enough to settle for the second. (Political scientists might be tempted to think the Dutch government, and entities working closely with it, could be especially prone to this interpretation because of the country's long experience with split-the-difference, interest-balancing neo-corporatism. But keep in mind that collective bargaining functioned for decades by similar principles in the United States, and consensus building can, in some variants, be thought of as a way of applying the nonlitigious forms of dispute resolution familiar from the collective bargaining regime in its heyday to other realms.) Presumably, a more precise idea of what I call in Case 2 *rolling* or *rippling representation* would at least suggest standards and tests of openness that would warn of the danger of such self-defeating closure. Without such standards, surprises of the kind described here are consensus building accidents waiting to happen.

—Charles F. Sabel, *Political economist*

After the plan had seen the light of day, the Dutch government formally assented to the extension of the airport. Key assumptions were that the airport could grow to a maximum of 44 million passengers and 3.3 million metric tons of freight per annum and that this capacity would be reached around the year 2015. Requirements regarding noise, air pollution, nuisance by way of odor, and external safety were also promulgated, and a fifth runway planned, which was to be situated so as to reduce the discomfort of nearby residents.

It has become obvious in recent years, however, that the assumptions on which these projections and decisions were based were not realistic. The airport experienced a much speedier growth than anticipated, and the rapid development threatens to undermine efforts to maintain environmental standards. The fifth runway is being challenged in court by various environmental groups. These groups had not been involved in the consensus process, and they oppose any increase in air traffic. Furthermore, new research established that the quality of the environment surrounding the airport is actually worse than previously assumed.

As a result of these new developments, Schiphol continues to dominate the political agenda; instead of consensus, new conflict situations arise and trust in the government's ability to fill the roles of arbitrator and manager has eroded. For all the stakeholders, it has become obvious that a more fundamental approach is desirable. Everything is once again open to discussion, including the country's need for a second airport. On this issue, a more comprehensive and inclusive debate is taking place than was the case with the expansion of Schiphol.

■ References

Barraqué, B. (1993). Roissy—Charles de Gaulle Flughafen. In H. Zillessen, P. C. Dienel, & W. Strubelt (Eds.), *Die Modernisierung der Demokratie* (pp. 97-113). Opladen: Westdeutscher Verlag.

Commissie Van der Zwan. (1986). *Schiphol naar het jaar 2000*. Amsterdam.

de Maar, H. G. (1976). *De uitbreiding van Schiphol: hoe de komst van het straalvliegtuig invloed heeft gehad op het bestuur*. Deventer: Kluwer.

Doganis, R. (1992). *The airport business*. London: Routledge.

Driessen, P. P. J., Glasbergen, P., & Spek, E. N. (1993). *Evaluatie van het ROM-gebieden-beleid*. The Hague, Netherlands: Deelstudie Schiphol en omgeving.

Hall, P. (1980). *Great planning disasters*. London: Weidenfeld and Nicolson.

Kramer, J. H. T. (1990). *Luchthavens en hun uitstraling. Een onderzoek naar de econo-mi-sche en ruimtelijke uitstralingseffecten van luchthavens*. Utrecht.

Kretschmer, W. (1984). Fallstudie: Grossflughafen München II. In D. Rucht (Ed.), *Flughafenprojekte als Politikum: Die Konflikte in*

Stuttgart, München, und Frankfurt (pp. 100-194). Frankfurt: Campus Verlag.

NV Luchthaven Schiphol. (1992). *Schiphol in cijfers*. Amsterdam.

Radford, K. J., & Giesen, M. O. (1984). *The analysis of conflicts over the location of airports near major population centres*. Research Report No. 87. Toronto.

Rucht, D. (Ed.). (1984). *Flughafenprojekte als Politikum: Die Konflikte in Stuttgart, München, und Frankfurt*. Frankfurt: Campus Verlag.

Soeters, J. (1991). Management van Euregionale netwerken. *Openbaar Bestuur, 10*, 12-27.

Strubelt, W., & Adam, B. (1993). Entscheidungsprozesse um Flughafenplanungen—am Beispiel des Flughafenausbaus in Bremen. In H. Zillessen, P. C. Dienel, & W. Strubelt (Eds.), *Die Modernisierung der Demokratie* (pp. 135-155). Opladen: Westdeutscher Verlag.

Susskind, L., & Cruikshank, J. (1987). *Breaking the impasse: Consensual approaches to resolving public disputes*. New York: Basic Books.

Tjeenk Willink, H. D. (1980). *Regeren in een dubbelrol*. The Hague, Netherlands: Commissie Hoofdstructuur Rijksdienst.

Vierde Nota over de Ruimtelijke Ordening. (1988). Deel d: Regeringsbeslissing, Tweede Kamer, vergaderjaar 1988-1989, 20490, nrs. 9-10.

Zehender, S. M. (1987). Airport site selection. *Airport Forum, 17*(2), 32-39.

2

THE NORTHERN OXFORD COUNTY COALITION

Four Maine Towns Tackle a Public Health Mystery

- Sarah McKearnan
- Patrick Field

I n February 1991, a popular New England television news show ran a segment called "Cancer Valley." The story depicted a rural American community's worst nightmare. It suggested that the people living in Northern Oxford County, Maine were experiencing extraordinarily high rates of cancer, and it implied that air emissions from a local paper mill might be responsible. Images of local residents walking through cemeteries, with the mill's billowing smokestacks looming in the distance, struck an alarmist tone.

The television show amplified a debate that had been under way for some time in four rural towns surrounding, and economically dependent on, the mill: Rumford, Mexico, Peru, and Dixfield (hereafter referred to as the four-town area). For many residents of the towns, the television show lent credence to suspicions that an abnormally high percentage of their family members, friends, and neighbors had contracted cancer. Others were angry, opposing the claim that there was a health problem in their community. These residents warned that the label "Cancer Valley" could unjustly tarnish the community's reputation and hinder economic development for a long time to come. Still others were equally concerned that the controversy over cancer rates would force the mill to close, breaking the valley's economic backbone.

In the midst of the controversy, the mill was indignant about the charges leveled against it. Mill managers pointed out that they were in compliance with all existing federal and state regulations concerning air quality. They were quick to note that the mill had recently invested more than $50 million in technologies designed to reduce both the odor and the toxicity of the wastes emitted through the mill's stacks.

Although many residents had very real fears of high cancer rates, few data were available to substantiate or alleviate those fears. Likewise, data on the quality of the air in the four towns were limited. In the absence of credible information, the controversy seemed sure to produce an extended series of attacks and counterattacks. In a set of communities small enough that people recognize each other at crosswalks or in the supermarket, this kind of protracted debate was sure to be painful. But what could any one person do? What, if anything, could the community do collectively?

With leadership from the Maine Department of Environmental Protection (DEP) and the U.S. Environmental Protection Agency (EPA), town residents on different sides of the debate came together in 1994 to initiate a community-based consensus building process. They called their group the Northern Oxford County Coalition (NOCC).

The 25-member coalition met over two years, with support from the Consensus Building Institute (CBI), a nonprofit provider of nonpartisan facilitation assistance. Many stakeholder groups participated, including concerned residents of the towns (including some employed by the mill), health care providers, small businesses, the mill management, local and state elected officials (including members of the Maine legislature), and state and federal agencies responsible for protecting human health and the environment.

Over two years, the coalition gradually overcame distrust and recriminations to complete several fact-finding and action-oriented projects. The members

- jointly designed a study to investigate cancer rates in the valley,
- initiated a community-wide radon-testing program through which 400 homeowners tested their homes for the cancer-causing gas,
- worked with agencies to evaluate recent air-monitoring data and to design a continuing air-monitoring program,
- held a public forum on dioxin and pollution prevention,
- wrote and distributed an action plan with numerous recommendations in the form of a community newsletter, and
- organized a new "Healthy Communities" coalition to continue the work of the NOCC.

In addition to conducting studies and organizing forums, the NOCC allowed residents with differing viewpoints, incomes, and interests to build more trusting and collaborative working relationships. This case study does not seek to retell the complete story of the NOCC. Rather, it explores in depth several aspects of the work undertaken by the NOCC, including getting started, investigating cancer rates jointly, and taking actions to ensure that the coalition's recommendations would be implemented. The case study also identifies key lessons about the process of building consensus in a community setting. ◆◆

◆ COMMENTARY

Of the cases in this *Handbook* that I have read, this one most fully reveals the surprising resemblance between the self-understanding, perhaps even the working fantasy, of the consensus building facilitator/negotiator and the peace-making gunslinger who is the mythic hero of the American Western. Of course, the consensus builder uses words, never bullets, to resolve disputes, and the gunslinger in the end has to expect to meet violence with violence of his own. But this difference of means aside, consider the similarities: Both figures come from afar to towns driven by inveterate faction (the farmers or merchants against the ranchers in the Western, the industrial interests against the townspeople here). Both are welcomed because they promise to create peaceful order, and both are suspect because their peace-making powers are somehow derived from suspect commerce with the wider world. (Honest folk won't trust anyone who is as quick on the draw as the gunslinger, and neither will they trust a fast-talking fancy dan who might conjure agreement from confusion or ignorance.) The crucial struggle for both is to identify and rally those who want to live in peace—and perhaps, will put themselves at risk to attain it—from those who live to fight. Gunslinger and consensus builder have both seen enough of life to expect surprises—ennobling and demeaning—as parties on all sides discover what respect for oneself and others requires. In the end, after the Western shoot-out and the consensus builder's single-text negotiation, both heroes leave town, and with it a prospect of a lasting peace that they, in their quest to best conflict, are unlikely to know themselves.

The point of this comparison is not, of course, to establish some moral equivalence between the two figures but rather to call attention to features of both settings that the focus on the respective heroes blends out. Above all, what both accounts neglect is the role that institutions—laws, various agencies of public administration—play in structuring conflicts, and shaping their resolution, and how the resolution of conflict in turn reshapes the institutions. This inattention to institutions accords well with the founding assumption of both stories: that the intervention of outsiders is necessary just because the institutions of order, if they ever existed, have broken down. From this perspective, the real story of institutions begins with the peace making, and the compacts in which that process results, hence the shot of the judge or law book in the closing frames of the Western or mention of the first disputes resolved by the newly built consensus in the cases collected in this *Handbook*.

But how well does the assumption of an institutionally impoverished, if not empty, place of conflict accord with the facts? A crude way to assess the goodness of fit between assumption and circumstance is simply to ask whether the stories of conflict resolution told here have the compactness and self-sufficiency that the analogy with the Western suggests. If they do, then consensus building, in addition to its other accomplishments, builds its own institutions. If not, if, in other words, "outside" institutions of government keep intruding into the story or become entwined with it, then some other, more encompassing point of view—one that treats consensus building as part of a larger story of changes in the contemporary forms of public decision making—is worth considering.

No single case—no matter how detailed—can, of course, by itself decide such large questions about the utility of a general frame of analysis. Nonetheless, the story of the Northern Oxford County Coalition is particularly informative as a kind of limiting case. On the one hand, in myriad ways that are left to the reader to detect, it describes the reality of small-town conflict that underpins the parallels between Western myth and modern dispute resolution. On the other, it has a surprise ending that casts doubt on the utility of that parallel even in the settings where it appears most useful. I'll have more to say about that ending, but only when the smoke clears.

—Charles F. Sabel, *Political economist*

■ *Background*

With metropolitan Portland an hour and a half to the south and a vast sweep of undeveloped forest lands just an hour to the north, the four towns of Rumford, Mexico, Dixfield, and Peru lie clustered around the confluence of the Swift and Androscoggin Rivers. At 15,000, the population of the towns is predominantly blue collar, and includes many families that have lived "in the valley" for generations. The mill as a physical and economic presence in the valley is impossible to ignore. It lies on an island in the center of Rumford, its six "smoke" stacks and giant mill buildings overshadowing the brick tenements and small-town main street. The mill provides jobs for 1,600 workers and directly or indirectly employs nearly 35 percent of the region's workforce (Beckley, 1994, p. 189). A local journalist commented:

> We have been dependent upon a paper mill for the last seventy five years or so. . . . Sure as hell they are the lifeblood of the community. We would blow away if it wasn't here, so we need it desperately. They pay well. And basically the whole town respects and supports them, I think. (Beckley, 1994, p. 193)

The mill has a long history in the four towns. The first facility was constructed in 1897 by the Rumford Falls Paper Company. Over the years, many smaller mills came and went, but this large facility took hold in the region's paper products industry. From 1976 through 1996, the mill was owned by one of the largest forest products companies in the world (Corburn, 1996, p. 24). For many years, the company that owned it enjoyed a positive relationship with the community. Many town residents made a good living at the mill. But a series of strikes in the early 1980s frayed goodwill and put distance between workers and mill managers. Then, amid a growing national environmental consciousness, some town residents began vocalizing concerns about mill emissions and local disease rates, further widening the rift among various constituencies.

■ *The Impetus for Consensus Building*

A local public hearing organized by the Maine DEP triggered the creation of the NOCC. The mill had applied for a license to increase its emissions from existing boilers. This occasion became the setting for a dramatic confrontation between the mill and town residents. Nearly 125 people attended. Many came to proclaim their complaints and fears about the impacts of mill pollutants and leveled the charge that neither the Maine DEP nor the mill was doing enough to protect health in the valley.

The Maine DEP faced a difficult dilemma. On the one hand, the mill was meeting emissions limits established by federal and state statutes. In particular, emissions were well under the Clean Air Act's allowable ceilings for criteria pollutants such as sulfur dioxide, nitrous oxide, and particulate matter. In fact, recent technological improvements at the mill had substantially cut the levels of criteria pollutants coming from the mill's stacks.

On the other hand, preliminary monitoring in the areas surrounding the mill had recently shown levels of air toxics that exceeded state health guidelines. Air toxics (also known as hazardous air pollutants) are a class of pollutant that encompasses literally hundreds of chemicals emitted from a variety of sources. For many years, the health risks of air toxics were not well understood, and they were not regulated. In the 1990 Clean Air Act amendments, Congress directed the EPA to begin regulating air toxics, but these regulations had not yet been developed when the NOCC began its work. ⇥

⇥ COMMENTARY

Very generally speaking, problems of this sort are becoming the rule, rather than the exception, in environmental regulation. Legislation has typically limited the emissions of particular pollutants, such as the sulfur dioxide and nitrous oxide mentioned here, from large and discrete point sources, such as the mill's stacks. Non-point source pollution, such as the effluents from households or corner dry cleaners, or the nitrogen or phosphorous sometimes contained in the runoff from farms, is only now being regulated, even though the aggregate effects of such pollution may be devastating to the environmental or public health. Conflicts over non-point source pollution can be especially rancorous because the polluter can often claim, fairly, to have incurred great expense to comply with the law, while the affected population feels menaced not only by the omnipresence of pollution but also by the other side's ability to exploit legal technicalities to escape further responsibility.

—Charles F. Sabel, *Political economist*

Dennis Kechel, director of the DEP's Bureau of Air Quality Control at the time, decided that since the situation did not call for *regulatory* action, he would instead organize a consensus building process. While he wasn't sure exactly what the outcome might be, he felt strongly that there needed to be some community forum where stakeholders could address their concerns. ⇥

∞ COMMENTARY

If problems of non-point source pollution had been less familiar at the time of the story, the official might have been much more hesitant about taking exploratory and potentially provocative action. Today, many federal and state initiatives have begun to address the problem, and an agent on the spot might well begin by establishing some relation with one of these.

—Charles F. Sabel, *Political economist*

After meeting separately with the various potential stakeholders, the DEP hired a facilitator from Colorado and convened the first multistakeholder meeting in February of 1994. Four meetings were held in the first six months. During this period, the EPA came forward with a grant of $80,000 to support the work of the newly formed group. The going was tough in these early meetings. Participants came to the table frustrated and angry and could not agree on what they should do together. One participant said:

Every time I came home from the meetings I would think that this is a coalition that hasn't coalesced. There was no agreement on what should be done, how it should be done, and there were viewpoints expressed that ranged from "There are no problems in the valley" to "You can knock on any door and someone in the family had died of cancer." . . . It seemed like no one knew what the plan was.

Concerned that the coalition might dissolve, the EPA approached CBI. CBI offered to work with the coalition on a pro bono basis for the first year, in part so that the EPA's grant could be used to support substantive investigation the coalition might decide to undertake.

Public agencies thus played a key role in jump-starting the NOCC. ∞

∞ COMMENTARY

To return for a moment to the institutional void that is the natural habitat of the paladin of the Western and the consensus builder: Saying that the public agencies helped in "jump-starting" the NOCC is an artful way of getting government institutions into the story, and then right out again. The suggestion, to my mind, is that the government officials, overtaxed by the situation, pass the mantle of authority to consultants and consensus builders (just as the aging sheriff in the Western, outgunned by the rampaging ranchers or the gang of desperados, pins a star on the paladin and then retires into the background).

—Charles F. Sabel, *Political economist*

In the atmosphere of outright hostility among stakeholder groups, no one within the four towns could propose that everyone sit down at the same table: That proposal would have been rejected outright by the others. Furthermore, none of these groups really knew about community-based consensus building used elsewhere. the DEP was in a unique position to seize an opportunity. Although some were skeptical of the DEP's motives and sympathies, many citizens in the area saw the DEP as the entity accountable for air quality in the region. Citizens expected the DEP to do *something*. The EPA's financial support not only made the process feasible, it also helped bring people to the table by showing that a public agency (almost four hours' drive away) was attentive enough to citizen concerns to provide resources for fact-finding. Even though the mill might also have had the ability to supply funding, such a contribution would probably have threatened the legitimacy of the process. Other local institutions with a greater degree of perceived neutrality (e.g., local governments, the hospital) simply did not have the means to provide funding.

■ Section 1: Conducting a Stakeholder Analysis

When we arrived at the Peru Town Hall during a heavy snowstorm in April 1993 to offer our assistance, we met a group that was skeptical about whether anything positive could emerge from a collaborative process. The coalition had spent four meetings trying to sort through competing visions of what kinds of projects should be the focus of their work. We proposed doing a *stakeholder analysis,* an assessment that would help us to identify the range of stakeholder groups; assess whether the coalition's current membership was inclusive of the towns' broader interests; summarize the concerns of current NOCC participants as well as other stakeholders; and formulate, if possible, an agenda for a midsummer retreat and a draft long-term work plan. With few other potential sources of help, the group agreed to give CBI a try. ➛

∽ COMMENTARY

As CBI entered the picture, how did it manage the expectations of the parties? Many parties had expectations for solutions and clear scientific results. Yet the problems to be studied are not easy ones. Part of the role of the facilitator should be to manage expectations of the process at the front end.

—Max H. Bazerman, *Social psychologist*

A month later, we headed to Rumford to interview 48 stakeholders in their homes and offices. From the interviews, we identified eight stakeholder groups: state and federal agencies, local government, small and large businesses, organized labor, interested citizens, health care providers, environmental advocacy groups, and state nongovernmental organizations (NGOs) concerned about public health and the environment.

We found that both across and within these different stakeholder groups, there was a wide range of views about whether the four-town area had elevated cancer rates. For example, one stakeholder voiced the view that there was *no* conclusive evidence to suggest that various forms of cancer were more prevalent in Rumford compared to elsewhere. Another suggested that while there might not be scientific evidence of higher cancer rates, people's personal experience provided strong support for this conclusion. He noted that most families up and down his street could report a case of childhood leukemia, adult lymphoma, or other kind of cancer. ◦•

◦• COMMENTARY

A critical issue facing CBI appears to be divergent expectations on the part of the differing parties to the dispute about the facts: Did the mill cause increased rates of cancer? The consensus builders appear to have approached the problem by trying to get all the parties on board in terms of process, hoping that outcomes would follow. In contrast, Raiffa (1982) and others (Gillespie & Bazerman, 1999; Lax & Sebenius, 1986) have argued that the use of contingent contracts can be used to take advantage of differing expectations. At the risk of oversimplification, if the mill claims that it is not creating cancer and a citizens group claims it is, if the parties can agree on an independent scientific assessment, each side should be willing to bet on its a priori beliefs about the outcome of the scientific assessment. Many such bets are possible. The use of contingent contracts offers a very different approach to resolving disputes under uncertainty. The focus is on a process that fixes the outcome based on a contingency that is learned after the agreement is reached. I offer this idea as an alternative, one that builds a process around outcomes, in comparison to the current model, where consensus building was the core goal, with an assumption that a good process leads to a good outcome.

Contingent contracts can be an excellent mechanism for using negotiator differences to build integrative agreements. Instead of arguing over differences concerning the likelihood of some future event taking place, parties can make a contingent contract. In the Northern Oxford County Coalition case, the bet could have been based on the independent scientific assessment.

—Max H. Bazerman, *Social psychologist*

REFERENCES

Gillespie, J., & Bazerman, M. H. (1999). *Bets.* Working paper.
Lax, D., & Sebenius, J. (1986). *The manager as negotiator.* New York: Free Press.
Raiffa, H. (1982). *The art and science of negotiation.* Cambridge, MA: Belknap Press of Harvard University Press.

There were similar differences of opinion about the issue of air quality. Some emphasized how much air quality had improved in the valley over the past few decades, noting that just a few decades ago, clothes hanging on a clothesline would turn black from the dirty valley air. Others painted a very different picture of a rural place with the air quality problems of a densely populated city. In addition, many people had concerns about the NOCC. Some worried that its meetings were dominated by loud and unpleasant arguments among a few vocal critics and defenders of the mill. Others felt the NOCC would not lead to any real change—it would simply be a lot of talk.

Despite these differences of opinion, we found that many stakeholders thought the NOCC might be worthwhile. They had long been frustrated that debates about air quality and public health occurred in a vacuum of factual information, and they recognized that the NOCC might be able to get people working together to gather credible data. There was broad agreement that the NOCC's first task should be to "put on the table" all the existing studies about air quality and public health, so everyone could review them together.

Based on these findings, CBI drafted a 12-page assessment recommending that the NOCC hold a summer retreat, consider expanding membership to include other groups such as local health care providers and concerned citizens, and move forward in developing a clear work plan.

Benefits of a Stakeholder Analysis

From the perspective of the facilitation team, the stakeholder analysis was critical in laying the foundation for a collaborative dialogue for a number of reasons. First, the effort created a means for people to voice their concerns, something they may not have felt comfortable doing with a neighbor or a local employer. For example, among those we interviewed were a number of millworkers who felt that the mill management had been negligent in protecting worker health. Some even felt that their own health might have been impaired by overexposure to toxic chemicals. The stakeholder analysis gave them the opportunity to get all of those concerns out in the open, without fear of reprisals.

The written report also functioned as a corrective lens: It revealed that there were actually commonalities in stakeholder views that had been obscured and distorted in the anger. For example, all stakeholders said they cared about long-term enhancement of public health of the valley. The report also mapped the disagreements, but since it made no individual attributions, it did so in a way that shifted the focus from *people* expounding differing views to the *substance* of those views. By looking closely through this lens, stakeholders in the four-town area could begin to build a more focused, multifaceted picture of what the conflict was all about.

The stakeholder analysis was also an aid in identifying who should be at the negotiating table. By asking existing NOCC members who might be missing from the dialogue, we kept casting the net wider. In our report, we identified four groups that seemed underrepresented: local health care providers, local citizens, small businesses, and the Maine Bureau of Health. The coalition then helped design a plan for adding representatives of these groups: A public meeting was held to invite new citizen representatives to join, the local hospital was asked to designate someone who could represent nurses as well as hospital management, and coalition members placed calls to local businesses in an effort to drum up interest in participating. These efforts yielded several new NOCC members.

Finally, we believe the stakeholder analysis helped us gain a foothold in a small rural area inclined to be suspicious of "outsiders." No one in Rumford had ever heard of the Consensus Building Institute. Cambridge, Massachusetts, home to CBI, was almost a four-hour drive from Rumford, and surely perceived by some as a bastion of academic pretension and liberal activism. Moreover, another outsider, the EPA, had proposed that the coalition use CBI's services. Because the EPA was itself the target of some suspicion among community members, it wasn't surprising that the agency's support for hiring us did not translate into instant trust on the part of community members. We believe that one-on-one conversations with stakeholders on their own turf enabled us to take the first steps toward building legitimacy and trust in the community. It was an opportunity to get to know coalition members one at a time. Moreover, it helped to demonstrate that we could be nonpartisan—that we could listen without judgment, and summarize views without compromising anyone's privacy. ◄►

◄► COMMENTARY

These points are indeed so central to the consensus building process that they bear immediate restatement. The stakeholder analysis is at the heart of this new kind of public problem solving precisely because it creates a setting in which the definition of the problem to be solved can be elaborated even as the circle of those who can or should contribute to its solution is (re)drawn, and vice versa. Contrast this with the normal procedure of representative democracy, in which the legislature, representing the citizens, defines the problem and delegates its solution to an administrative agency (which may in turn decide to include certain "affected interests" in its considerations of solutions).

The contrast is particularly evident with regard to the ideas of representation that underlay the two systems. In representative democracy as we know it, of course, the citizens of territorial jurisdictions have interests and elect representatives to advance them. In the deliberations characteristic of consensus building problem solving, citizens concerned about the solution of some problem participate directly in articulating possible solutions, and in enlarging or redrawing the circle of participation. This can happen, as here, simply by asking some participants to propose additional, underrepresented ones, but it can happen as well when nonparticipants decide to participate (or ask for invitations to join the deliberations) because of actual or potential effects on them of initial rounds of decision making or discussion. If the kinds of public problem solving described in this *Handbook* spread, the relation between this novel form of *rolling* or *rippling representation* and the traditional representation of interests will pose great questions for the understanding of our Constitution and democracy. It would surely be self-defeating to halt the use and development of the consensus building techniques until these large problems are resolved, assuming they can be, but it would be recklessly optimistic to assume that there are no such long-term problems simply because the techniques demonstrably work in many situations where traditional ones do not.

—Charles F. Sabel, *Political economist*

■ *Section 2: Getting Organized*

Getting the NOCC to work on its first project was not easy. The NOCC meetings that took place before the stakeholder analysis had been acrimonious. Many of the emotions that worked their way into insults and accusations grew out of events long since passed: charges of the mill covering up toxic releases; charges that vocal citizens had personally and unfairly attacked the mill's environmental manager in front of his family at the 1993 permit public hearing. Stakeholders had an understandably hard time putting the past behind them; the consequences for individual relationships were evident at each of the NOCC's early meetings.

To make matters worse, the NOCC's first four meetings did not produce a clear direction for the group. Members still had very different ideas about which problem should be the coalition's main focus. Cancer rates, respiratory illness, and pollution prevention were all proposed. Somehow, the NOCC needed to find a focus in the midst of this intense distrust and high emotion, and get to work. The early meetings and the stakeholder analysis had helped parties to vent, but the key to moving forward was reaching three framework agreements on how to work together and on what. These were a set of ground rules, an overarching mission, and a detailed, month-by-month work plan.

Laying Down Ground Rules

The stakeholder analysis clearly revealed that NOCC members had a lot of misgivings about what future NOCC meetings would be like. Many felt that past meetings were dominated by a few. Interviewees voiced concern that the coalition had been hijacked by a few "extremists" and those with more moderate viewpoints would stay away from coalition meetings.

After the stakeholder analysis had been completed and presented to the coalition, our first task was to help the group reach agreement on ground rules that would ensure that NOCC meetings were constructive. We brought to the coalition draft

ground rules based on what we had found worked well in other consensus building processes.

One section of the draft addressed how members should communicate with each other. There was a rule suggesting that only one member should speak at a time, and no member should interrupt anyone who had the floor. Another ground rule disallowed personal attacks, and a third committed members to speak their own views rather than the views of others at the table. Taken as a group, these ground rules sought to ensure an environment of respectful communication, so that members would not shy away from speaking openly for fear of being ignored, ridiculed, or unfairly criticized. They also sought to keep the group as a whole on track, avoiding the kind of hostile and distracting interactions of the past.

Another section of the ground rules delineated the role and responsibilities of coalition members. All members should come to meetings prepared to represent not only themselves or their organization but all of the members of their stakeholder group. The ground rules explained that this meant members should commit to keep in touch with their constituents. It also meant bringing these viewpoints back to the negotiating table and helping other NOCC members reach a better understanding of them. This ground rule posed a special obstacle for "citizen" representatives on the NOCC who had no organized process for communicating with the members of their "group," which could encompass the entire population of the four towns.

There were also ground rules that laid out the role of other key participants in the process: the facilitator, alternates who would come to meetings when regular members couldn't make it, and the media. And there was a section that described how the NOCC would make decisions. It memorialized the idea that the group would aim to reach agreements that met the interests of *all* stakeholder groups. It also introduced a very new, and for many, counterintuitive, idea that any agreement on a specific issue would be tentative until the coalition had reached agreement on multiple issues. Holding off on final consensus would allow participants to craft an agreement that allowed for trade-offs across issues, thus more effectively incorporating the participants' different interests and priorities in a complete package.

We expected that reaching agreement on the ground rules would pose a major hurdle. It was the first major agenda topic we floated with the NOCC, and it meant committing to rules that not everyone had abided by in the past. To us, as "experts" in process, the decision seemed momentous. Given the level of anxiety we had heard in our interviews, we were quite surprised when our draft was met with silence. No one had much to say, and the draft was approved with very few changes.

At that early stage, most people in the room were more interested in debating the "real" issues than debating how to debate the issues. Ground rules were foreign and untested, and it was still difficult for some members to grasp what a difference they might make. As one participant said at the NOCC retreat: "Enough of this 'nicey-nice' stuff: Let's move on to the real issues."

Over time, however, the group began to take more interest in the ground rules. After one year of meetings, we began hearing complaints that the rules were not being observed consistently. There was a concern that a few NOCC members tended to grandstand rather than negotiate in good faith, and that they peppered the discussion with comments that were accusatory or derogatory. This, the concerned stakeholders asserted, prevented many from participating in the group discussions. Some NOCC members also told us that they thought we weren't doing enough to enforce the ground rules.

We took this as our cue to ask again if the rules fit the needs of the coalition, or if additions or changes might be needed. This time, very few NOCC members sat silent. Their experience working in a consensus building mode had given them a new appreciation of the importance of ground rules, and new insight into what kinds of restrictions and responsibilities would create the most productive meetings. For example, one member proposed a new rule enabling anyone to call a "time-out" during a meeting with the two-handed T signal used by referees. The time-out signal provided a way for an NOCC member who felt a few were dominating the discussion to alert the facilitator and request an intervention. We believe this ground rule shifted the dynamics of NOCC meetings. By transferring some of the responsibility for identifying ground rule violations to the members themselves, it made them feel that those rules were theirs rather than ours. With the new time-out rule in place, we found that NOCC members who had rarely participated in meetings began offering their views. Along with this time-out rule, the group adopted a "disagreements list." Contentious items that tended to bog down conversation could be remanded to this list and added as a specific item to later meeting agendas. This allowed for work to move ahead without ignoring areas where parties had fundamental differences of opinion.

Once the revised ground rules were in place, an interesting change took place: There were few instances thereafter when we needed to interrupt the course of the conversation to enforce them. The group began to use humor and friendly teasing more often, as a way to diffuse conflicts and personality clashes. The NOCC at first ignored a set of ground rules imposed on them by us as outsiders. Over time, as the group learned together, however, they saw the real need for ground rules, crafted the rules to meet their needs, and internalized them in a way that established a code of conduct from within the group. We learned a simple but valuable lesson: Effective ground rules have to be built through experience. ◆

∞ COMMENTARY

If you thought I was introducing needless complexity into the discussion by suggesting the novel, self-constructing, or self-reflective character of consensus building, the discussion of ground rules and their revision in the preceding paragraphs should convince you that the actors are way ahead of the commentators on this one. Not only do the participants begin to demand effective policing of the original, vague procedural rules, they also invent a time-out procedure that allows the participants themselves to shape the flow of discussion in a way that prevents domination by the logocrats and gives rise to norms of intervention that ultimately make recourse to the time-out "rule" that the actors themselves devised and apply all but unnecessary. This example enlivens the useful remarks on how to set an agenda and ground rules found in "A Short Guide to Consensus Building."

—Charles F. Sabel, *Political economist*

Developing a Mission Statement

Establishing ground rules was helpful (especially over time), but the NOCC still needed a destination. The next task was to define a purpose that everyone could support. Unfortunately, no common purpose announced itself. Stakeholder groups held different views about what constituted the "problem": cancer rates, the mill's emissions, lack of public education on the dangers of smoking, or pollution from small businesses, cars, and households, to name a few. What could the NOCC do? The EPA pushed us and the group to devise a mission statement.

Several pieces of a mission statement emerged from the stakeholder analysis.

First, every stakeholder was ready to affirm an interest in seeing the quality of life in the valley improved. While there were many and sometimes sharply differing perspectives about the status of public health and air quality, everyone agreed that improving both was fundamental to ensuring a high quality of life in the region. Last, everyone wanted a clearer understanding, based in scientific fact, about public health and air quality in the four towns. These became the building blocks of a mission statement. After several rounds of negotiation, the coalition reached consensus: "The Northern Oxford County Coalition has been established to improve the quality of life in the valley by protecting and promoting public health and enhancing air quality."

It's worth pointing out that although the mission statement captured agreement that we had heard clearly articulated in our interviews, hammering out the exact language was a time-consuming process. A good part of three meetings was taken up negotiating a few simple sentences. For example, there was a lively debate among members of the NOCC as to whether the phrase "enhancing economic opportunity" should be included in the first sentence. For some, including this phrase was akin to unraveling the commitment to protecting worker or citizen health. Behind every such debate, there was a complex subtext about how different phrases might or might not be interpreted.

Charting the Course: Developing a Work Plan

With the ground rules and mission statement in place, the next hurdle was developing an agreeable work plan. In some ways, this was the most difficult of the three agreements to develop because it committed NOCC members to a course of action and, at least temporarily, excluded other activities. At first, we tried to produce the plan through face-to-face meetings. We convened a retreat in a motel outside Rumford to begin forging a preliminary document describing what the NOCC would do by when. We quickly realized, though, that it would not be possible to make this a group project. Having just worked through the ground rules and the mission statement, many members were impatient with all the "process" talk. They wanted to get down to work.

We realized that we needed to prepare a first draft, and invite people to react to it.

Initially, we felt anxious about this task, since we knew no more than any NOCC member about how epidemiologists might assess whether there is a cancer problem in a community, or how air quality experts would judge the quality of the air people breathe. We needed to come up with a plan for how the NOCC could explore the big-headline questions that were being bandied about in coffee shop conversations, union meetings, and Rotary luncheons. But specific activities needed to be based on an understanding of what was technically and scientifically feasible. So first, we went back to the results of the stakeholder interviews to clarify what kinds of questions the coalition might want to ask as part of a joint fact-finding process. Second, we got on the phone with expert epidemiologists, toxicologists, and air-monitoring experts to ask how would one go about answering the questions, Are cancer rates unusually high in our community? Where could we find the necessary data, and how long would it take to analyze?

We had trouble recommending to the NOCC what subject members might tackle first. In our initial interviews, many had listed their worries about cancer as their highest concern. But some members were reluctant to support such an investigation. Representatives of the EPA and the Maine DEP argued that studying cancer was too difficult because of its multiple forms and the vast uncertainty about its causes. They also pointed out that because cancer has such a long latency period, current cancer rates would not be a good indicator of the valley's present environmental conditions. They suggested that an investigation into respiratory illness might better indicate the current status of the valley's public health and environmental quality. Still other

NOCC members, the health care providers among them, thought that the NOCC should focus first on helping residents see the need for healthier lifestyles.

In the end, we recommended that the NOCC launch its work with a study on cancer incidence, designed by NOCC members with the help of an epidemiologist. ❧

❧ COMMENTARY

I think that the decision to develop the study with NOCC members as part of the scientific team is an interesting decision. It is certainly consistent with the spirit of consensus building. Yet it runs against the notion of using comparative advantage in getting a task done. Why would NOCC members be doing the work, rather than overseeing the work of a university-based team? On the other hand, it is interesting to think about the process advantages of having the NOCC directly involved.

—Max H. Bazerman, *Social psychologist*

The Maine Bureau of Health had a large, multiyear database of cancer cases in the state, so completion of a study analyzing cancer rates seemed feasible. But more important, cancer was a strongly felt concern among the citizen representatives. It seemed that pursuing any other issue would be seen as a diversion if not an outright denial of the problem. Even though there were compelling reasons why a cancer incidence study might not be the most pragmatic choice, we felt that many stakeholders from the four towns would commit to the process only if they felt it addressed their fundamental concerns. Once the coalition had grappled with the mystery of local cancer rates, it might be possible to take on other issues, such as air quality monitoring, or smoking habits.

We then produced a draft work plan for one year. It proposed a set of activities for both the full NOCC and a set of subcommittees. We added subcommittees as a means of breaking down complicated tasks (e.g., assess air quality in the four towns) into manageable projects that could be carried out by a smaller number of NOCC members (e.g., review monitoring data collected in 1991 and 1993). We also hoped that subcommittees would be smaller and thus more informal, encourage more discussion among participants, discourage grandstanding, and help build better relationships among the participants.

The plan laid out a preliminary structure for the group's work, set a deadline for the deliberations, and pointed toward a concrete final report that would summarize the work of the group and be distributed to the valley's residents. But the details of the work plan kept evolving almost as soon as it was printed. The plan called for the cancer incidence study to be done in three months. It took eight. ❧

∽ COMMENTARY

The time passage is interesting. It is common for plans that are projected to take a fixed amount of time to take two, three, and four times as long. Why? In this case, lives were potentially at stake. I would argue that many consensus building initiatives take substantially more time than predicted and that this creates process and outcome problems.

It is fascinating that we all know that it takes longer to build a house than planned, longer to complete a project than scheduled, and longer to write a paper than promised to an editor. So why do we not adjust over time? Psychological research shows that we have a bias toward optimistic illusions. Unrealistic optimism is the tendency to believe that our futures will be better and brighter than those of other people (Taylor, 1989). Taylor reports that people expect that they are more likely to graduate at the top of the class, get a good job, obtain a high salary, enjoy their first job, get written up in the newspaper, and give birth to a gifted child than reality suggests. We also estimate that we are less likely to have a drinking problem, get fired, get divorced, become depressed, or suffer physical problems. Taylor notes that we persist in believing that we can accomplish more in a day than is humanly possible and that we seem immune to the continued feedback that the world provides on our limitations.

We see the same pattern in the domain of negotiations. Rod Kramer (1994) found that 68 percent of the MBA students in a negotiation class predicted that their bargaining outcomes would be in the upper 25 percent of the class. These students also expected that they would learn more than their classmates, with more unique results, and that they would contribute more to the class experience.

The net result of this unrealistic optimism is poor planning and failed expectations.

—Max H. Bazerman, *Social psychologist*

REFERENCES

Kramer, R. M. (1994). *Self-enhancing cognitions and organizational conflict.* Working paper.
Taylor, S. E. (1989). *Positive illusions.* New York: Basic Books.

The plan was too ambitious. Ensuring that the plan was inclusive created an irresistible temptation to fold in more activities than could be accomplished in a year. Moreover, our initial time estimates did not take account of how much time it would take for the group to develop an efficient work style, how long it would take to wade through complex technical information, and how much time experts and agencies would be able to spend on NOCC projects.

Changes in the priorities and interests of NOCC members also caused the work plan to evolve. For example, as the cancer incidence study gave members more insight into how public health data could be accessed and analyzed, some NOCC members became more interested in launching a study of respiratory illness. Also, as NOCC members learned more about potential causes of cancer, NOCC members devised new ideas of what to work on, such as a radon-testing program for homeowners in the community. All of these ideas required that the NOCC adjust its original work plan.

The work plan was important. A shared understanding of where the group was headed prevented it from becoming sidetracked, confused, and, ultimately, unproductive. However, had the coalition held fast to its original plan, it would have been less effective in maintaining a direction that was in line with the available resources and time, as well as the interests of coalition members. In addition, all this effort showed us and the NOCC an important role of the facilitators in such a community-based process: Not only our neutrality but also our time and access to potential resources were essential to assisting the NOCC.

■ *Section 3: Tackling an Investigation of Local Cancer Rates*

Coalition members had decided to make their first task an effort to gather and analyze data from the Maine Cancer Registry. Their objective was to determine if cancer rates were abnormally high in the four-town area and, if rates did turn out to be high, to identify the reasons why. Carrying out the task seemed daunting. With the exception of the NOCC's representative from the Maine Bureau of Health, neither the members of the coalition nor the facilitators had been involved in previous efforts to apply epidemiological research methods to an assessment of local disease rates. In fact, it's probably safe to say that while a number of community stakeholders had done an impressive job of educating themselves over the years about environmental and public health issues, none had designed and carried out a scientific investigation of any kind.

The challenge went beyond our collective status as technical novices: The subject matter was controversial, highly charged with concerns about sickness and death. Some stakeholders were convinced that a virtual cancer epidemic was under way, and others were equally adamant that this claim was unfounded. It was hard to imagine how NOCC members could get to the point where they might agree on an interpretation of jointly gathered data. The NOCC launched its study of cancer incidence without really knowing where it was headed. ✺

✺ COMMENTARY

Evidently. But did the members of the NOCC recognize that they didn't know? Did the consensus builders? If both recognized this early on, it is unlikely that the group would have foundered around in search of a precise project for as long as we will see it did. If only one of the two had clear ideas about the ambiguity of the goals, what hampered communication with the other? I raise these questions because it is now hardly unusual (but not, perhaps, routine) for parties facing environmental problems to acknowledge their ignorance even in affirming the importance of their common dilemma, and to begin attempts at a solution with an open-ended study that aims to specify the problem to be solved. Many efforts to address non-point source pollution, to return to the earlier example, grow out of such studies. Perhaps the NOCC was so divided that by this time, it would be impossible to agree to such a broad investigation even if the techniques for organizing one had been widely known. Or it may have been that, focusing on local problems, .he consensus builders neglected to take advantage of techniques for addressing open-ended, diffuse problems emerging outside of Northern Oxford County. The conclusion to the case study will leave us puzzling about that.

—Charles F. Sabel, *Political economist*

☞ COMMENTARY

It is interesting to see this successful consensus building process in an environment where the process was created "without really knowing where it was headed." This is very counterintuitive to a management school professor. If you do not know what the goal is, how can you know if you were successful? Yet the authors provide some good answers. If the process creates a better community dialogue, more publicly acceptable data, and a better environment for future discussion, it is clear that much success was achieved. At the same time, the issue of specifying objectives on the front end remains an interesting issue for consensus builders.

—Max H. Bazerman, *Social psychologist*

There was, however, a collective determination to get to the bottom of a public health mystery.

Choosing an Expert

It was clear from the beginning that the cancer incidence study was going to be a complicated and time-consuming task. The first step was to assign the bulk of the work to a subset of NOCC members who cared about cancer incidence, who had a background that would prepare them for the work, and who were committed to putting in the time needed. The Technical Subcommittee (TSC) was formed to initiate and oversee the study. As a group, TSC members represented the key stakeholder groups represented on the NOCC, including citizens, the union, the mill, and the state and federal public agencies.

One of the first questions the TSC asked is: What kind of expert assistance do we need to carry out this study, and where can

we find it? Members of the TSC quickly realized that one or several people trained in epidemiology would be best equipped to help. The mill and the union each had experts to recommend, but the TSC decided that the best route would be to identify a single "outside" expert chosen by the whole group. One possibility was to ask the Maine Bureau of Health to provide an expert, because it was the agency's Cancer Registry that would supply the data for the study, but there were worries about how credible a Bureau of Health expert would be. An earlier study, abandoned in the late 1980s due to funding limitations, had left a bad taste in the mouth of some coalition members. They charged the bureau with covering up alarming health data about cancer and respiratory illness in the four-town area.

With no obvious expert in sight, it became important for us to assist the committee in identifying potential candidates. The TSC had a few suggestions of people we could contact in the state of Maine. We volunteered to contact these individuals and to make some additional inquiries. Telephone calls to universities in New England and New York turned up a number of scientists willing to advise the NOCC. Then the TSC convened to review the résumés.

What happened produced an important lesson for the NOCC. By the end of this TSC meeting, members decided to recommend that the NOCC retain Dr. Bill Barnes (not his real name), a highly qualified epidemiologist from a respected New England university. They reached the decision quickly and efficiently. They also agreed to invite Dr. Barnes to the next TSC meeting to present methods for analyzing Rumford's cancer rates, and they further agreed to invite him to a meeting of the full coalition just one week later. But then the plan began to unravel.

As we soon found out, Barnes had given a video deposition as an expert witness in a suit brought against the mill on behalf of sick workers. The mill's representative at the table did not know this. Just one night before the next TSC meeting, several representatives of the mill called CBI and insisted that Dr. Barnes be dismissed. The mill appealed to us, asking how they could trust this expert. They apologized for not realizing this sooner, but said they had no doubt he would be the union's expert and would not provide the kind of nonpartisan advice that would be make the cancer study credible.

Because this was at a very early stage of the coalition's work, members were quick to be suspicious of each other's intentions. When the mill's representative brought his request to the TSC meeting, some TSC members were furious, demanding to know why the mill was backtracking from an earlier agreement. With Dr. Barnes waiting outside, NOCC members argued about what to do. Some members insisted that Dr. Barnes was perfectly capable of being neutral and that the mill was stonewalling the initiation of a study to uncover facts about cancer. Others supported the mill's request, noting that it was understandable why the mill was concerned about Dr. Barnes's neutrality. ➥

➥ COMMENTARY

Barnes's lack of full disclosure is certainly shocking to this reader. The authors are self-critical for not asking. Yet professionals have certain obligations, and my view is that Barnes failed his.

—Max H. Bazerman, *Social psychologist*

In the end, the subcommittee decided to follow through on the decision to have Dr. Barnes give a general presentation on epidemiology at the next NOCC meeting, but they agreed that a new technical adviser should be found immediately after. We encouraged the committee to talk about some criteria that could be used to ensure that members' preferences would be accounted for in the selection process. They agreed with the mill's proposal that technical advisers to the NOCC should not have had any past involvement in litigation involving any of the constituencies represented in the group. We then recommended a new step in the selection process (and in hindsight one we wished we had thought of earlier): Each potential adviser would be asked to fill out a detailed disclosure form identifying any prior connection they had to the NOCC's members and affiliated organizations.

Over the next week, we scrambled to locate additional advisers who would have the same depth of experience as Dr. Barnes but who would also be credible to all of the NOCC's constituencies. During the discussion over new résumés, NOCC members again raised sharp objections to the mill's eleventh hour protest. But the group was able to reach consensus on the selection of Dr. Daniel Wartenberg, an epidemiologist from Rutgers University. Dr. Wartenberg had no prior involvement with any of the parties and was viewed by everyone as having the ability to offer nonpartisan advice. He was also generous in his offer to assist the NOCC; he was interested in participating in a community-based process and asked only for a small stipend and travel expenses.

The incident with Dr. Barnes was important in the development of the NOCC. First, it taught everyone the value of investing time up front to ensure that experts brought on to advise the group were cred-

ible in the eyes of all members. While initially it was hard for those who were skeptical of the mill's intentions to be responsive to their request, in the end they recognized that a technical expert wouldn't be effective unless he or she had a vote of confidence from all stakeholders. Second, it showed everyone, and especially the mill, what it meant to build consensus. The negotiation over who to choose was the first test of the group's ability to listen seriously to the concerns of a single party, and to alter the course of a decision to ensure that those concerns were addressed.

Gathering and Analyzing Data

When the NOCC began its cancer incidence study, we all thought the process would be relatively straightforward. All the data were already in the Cancer Registry. Many NOCC members assumed that if the NOCC just looked at the number of cases in the four-town area, the answer of whether too many people were falling sick or dying from cancer would be readily apparent. ••

☞ COMMENTARY

Hmm. Looks like the consensus builders, while helping the laypeople to manage the experts, are going to get some lessons in the ambiguities of expertise themselves.

—Charles F. Sabel, *Political economist*

It wasn't long into the process of working with Dr. Wartenberg that the group began to understand the complexity of designing an epidemiological investigation. Dr. Wartenberg came to the Rumford area and met with the TSC several times. During

those meetings, he pushed the group to agree on a purpose for the investigation. The discussion revealed the fact that members had different ideas about what they hoped to learn. Some members wanted to explore the linkages between cancer cases among workers and exposures to toxic chemicals emitted from the mill. Others thought that the first step should be to examine rates of cancer, to determine if there were elevated rates worth worrying about.

In response to what he heard about the different agendas among TSC members, Dr. Wartenberg reviewed an inventory of potential research methodologies, from a community health survey and a case control study to an analysis of local prescription use. For each, he explained the advantages and disadvantages, including the ease of obtaining the data, the degree of uncertainty in interpretation, the cost and time involved, and the power of the methodology to answer questions that were important to members of the TSC.

After discussing these options, TSC members agreed that an investigation of cancer incidence using Cancer Registry data would be the best option. This was not an easy decision; it was difficult for some stakeholders to accept that at least at this stage, such an investigation would not pinpoint causes of cancer but only the rates of cancer as compared with other places. Luckily, one of the TSC members was a consultant to the labor union with significant expertise in epidemiology. She helped to buffer the message from Wartenberg; as she supported his observations and advice, she helped to shore up labor's comfort with his neutrality. Her involvement helped us to learn that sometimes a combination of neutral *and* partisan expertise is necessary to bring credibility to joint fact-finding.

Further discussion about the merits and limitations of the TSC's approach surfaced some serious concerns among TSC members about the quality of the data in the Maine Cancer Registry. Some members were worried that cancer cases might have been underreported to the Cancer Registry

in its early years. With Dr. Wartenberg's help, the TSC built into the study design a quick test to help assess the possibility of significant underreporting. NOCC members also worried that other cases remained undocumented because residents of the four towns had been treated in other states. The TSC's representative from the Bureau of Health played a key role at this juncture, helping the group understand the strengths and limitations of the registry's cancer database.

There were many other methodological issues that needed the group's attention. What would the rates in the four-town area be compared with? After all, rates would only be "high" or "low" if they were compared with rates from somewhere else. The group reviewed various options, including comparing local cancer rates with rates (1) in other similar Maine towns (perhaps a mill town), (2) in the remainder of Oxford County, (3) in the state as a whole, and/or (4) in the entire United States. While some members liked the idea of comparing Rumford cancer rates with a similar mill town, the group raised two concerns. One, if the rates ended up quite similar, did this mean there was no problem, or did it mean that both towns had elevated cancer rates, perhaps associated with the mills? Two, how would another town feel if NOCC members dredged up that town's data on cancer incidence without its explicit permission? Dr. Wartenberg also emphasized the advantages of comparing Rumford with a database with a significant number of cases: Such a comparison would increase the likelihood that the results would be statistically significant.

The TSC spent three or four meetings making decisions such as these and eventually developed a methodology for the study. The subcommittee brought its proposed study design to the full NOCC: an investigation of average cancer rates for 22 different kinds of cancer in men and women for the period 1983 to 1992, and a comparison of those rates to rates with the state of Maine and in a national white database called the U.S. SEER white population database (the Surveillance, Epidemiology, and End Results program of the National Cancer Institute). The NOCC approved the study design with a few minor changes. With Dr. Wartenberg's help, the TSC then prepared a data request to the Maine Cancer Registry.

When the data arrived, Dr. Wartenberg prepared statistical tables for the TSC (and eventually the NOCC) to review. The tables showed that the rates for all cancers combined for both males and females in the four-town area were elevated when compared with those of Maine. It showed that males had a statistically significantly elevated rate for cancers of the respiratory system, male genital system (primarily the prostate gland), and lymphomas. Females were shown to have a statistically significantly elevated rate for cancers of the endocrine system (primarily thyroid) and for cancers of the colon. In addition, a number of other types of cancer were elevated in females, but not to a statistically significant degree.

Interpreting the Data and Writing the Report

While the "facts" seemed straightforward enough, the next step was to interpret the data and to summarize the results in a report for the full NOCC and finally for all residents of the four towns. This was perhaps the most challenging part of the cancer incidence study. To develop the content of a cancer incidence report, the TSC had to work toward agreement on how to present the data. But it soon became clear that interpreting the data was not an objective exercise.

For example, some NOCC members thought the report should say that some of the higher rate ratios (a number that compares the local cancer rate with the state or national rate) warranted concern and further investigation. Other TSC members were equally insistent that epidemiologists would not typically be concerned about ratios unless they indicated cancer rates two to three times the state average. They pointed out that elevations less than two times were as likely "noise" as they were indicators of real problems, especially with such a small data set (thousands of people rather than millions). This led to a long discussion about whether the TSC should include in its report a benchmark that signaled when the community ought to be concerned about that cancer. Some thought that any rate ratio that was elevated should be of concern. Others thought the subcommittee should not raise concern unless the rate ratio was two to three times greater than expected. And still others argued that the TSC should just present the numbers and let the readers decide. ➤

➤ COMMENTARY

The argument over criteria level is interesting, and the result of the consensus building process. Again, it raises the question of specifying more of the task on the front end. Could, perhaps, the community better agree on levels that warrant action if those were specified before the data were in?

—Max H. Bazerman, *Social psychologist*

Reaching an impasse on this issue, the TSC decided to have its draft report peer reviewed. If the TSC couldn't resolve these questions, perhaps advice from three professional epidemiologists would help. Interestingly, these experts each had different answers in response to the TSC's question about when a community should be concerned about a specific rate ratio. In fact, the peer reviewers' responses reflected the range of opinions held by TSC members.

Turning to peer reviewers did not produce an agreement. But TSC members discovered that what seemed a local, highly partisan dispute was also a disagreement among scientists across the country. This helped the subcommittee gain an appreciation for the difficulty of drawing precise, universally shared conclusions about technical issues. From this new vantage point, they could agree to our recommendation that they abandon the quest for a singular consensus on how to interpret the rate ratios for the community, and instead agree to *describe* the range of views among them in the body of their report.

Throughout these meetings, Dr. Wartenberg was a steady voice in favor of moving beyond debates about interpretation. Put simply, his question to the group was: So, what now? Now that you have this incidence data, you can struggle to craft the right word or phrase to describe it. But what will the TSC recommend to other NOCC members about what should be done to respond to these results? The group accepted this advice, and it worked with Dr. Wartenberg to hammer out detailed options for action, including an inventory of possible follow-up studies that could be done to investigate rates that were statistically significantly elevated, as well as better cancer-screening and detection programs in the four towns and public education to encourage people to adopt healthier lifestyles.

In the end, the TSC struggled for many weeks to reach a final consensus on the language in the complete report. Late in the process, one member in particular insisted on several revisions to the report. After multiple rounds of negotiation, the TSC decided that it was not possible to meet this member's interests and still ensure that the report was responsive to the interests of others. TSC members decided to report out to the NOCC that they had reached a consensus of 9 out of 10 members, and the dissenting member was invited to attach a letter explaining his concerns to the text of the report. Some members of the subcommittee were disappointed that they failed to reach unanimity, but they also recognized that everyone had worked hard to improve the report as much as possible from the standpoint of each member. ☙

☙ COMMENTARY

"9 out of 10" raises the issue of defining consensus. This topic is explicitly treated in Part I of this *Handbook*. Once again, it is interesting to think about specifying necessary agreement levels on the front end.

—Max H. Bazerman, *Social psychologist*

Taking the Report
to the Full Coalition

Throughout the process of collecting data, analyzing them, and writing the cancer incidence report, the NOCC met to hear reports from the TSC about its progress and to provide input. Still, when the final report was presented to the full coalition, additional negotiations were needed.

Some NOCC members were frustrated that the report was only an incidence study; it did not include any analysis of what might be causing the elevated rates. Others were frustrated that the report didn't make a clear statement about whether or not there was a cancer problem in the valley. For those who had long been convinced that cancer rates were sky high in the four towns, it was hard to fathom why the TSC couldn't say that there was a confirmed health problem wherever there was a local cancer rate that was statistically significantly higher than the same rate statewide. At this point, the TSC assisted Dr. Wartenberg in educating the larger group. TSC members talked about the fact that statistical significance is just one of the many factors that scientists weigh when evaluating cancer incidence, and they pointed out that scientists often disagree in their conclusions about what to be concerned about. The TSC banded together at that moment, as they worked to persuade the NOCC that what was important was reaching agreement on what all stakeholders could do to follow up on these incidence data, both with further research and with concrete actions to improve public health. ∞

∞ COMMENTARY

Here, in an eddy in the stream of the narrative, is the core of the scientific and practical problem facing the NOCC and many other such groups. The scientific problem is that ratios of the incidence of cancer, or any other disease, in two areas are meaningless without information about the characteristics and behaviors of the populations in the respective territories. Suppose, for example, that the incidence of lung cancer is much higher in Pollution City than in Pristine County but that everyone over 12 years of age smokes in Pollution City, while there are no smokers at all in Pristine County. Is the high lung cancer rate caused by pollution? By smoking? Or is it the exposure to some combination of smoking and pollution, for at least a certain number of years, that causes lung cancer in Pollution City? The practical problem is that investigation of the causal chains that run together in such complex exposures requires attention to environmental issues, occupational and other behavioral patterns, and careful monitoring of the population's health. Because it is impossible to study everything at once, priorities have to be set, and the best way to do that is to follow the leads provided by early studies, without losing sight of the need to gradually gain deep knowledge of the whole context of the original problem. Dr. Wartenberg apparently got all this, and much more, across by displaying what was known at each moment and then "moving beyond debates about interpretation" by asking, "What now?"

—Charles F. Sabel, *Political economist*

Despite frustrations on the part of a few members, the NOCC ultimately did reach agreement on the report, "A Report on Cancer Incidence in the Rumford Maine Area." They also decided to leave the letter outlining concerns by the one TSC member attached to the final document. The main motivation for working hard to bridge remaining differences was a shared desire on the part of NOCC members to get the cancer incidence data out to residents of the four towns. Copies of the cancer incidence report were distributed informally by NOCC members, placed in the town libraries, and sent to health care providers and community organizations. The NOCC also organized a briefing about the report for physicians in the area.

The whole investigation, from the day the TSC was convened, had taken eight months. The process was limited in its outcome but extremely valuable for NOCC members. It was limited because the study did not establish causal relationships between elevated rates of cancer and its causes. It did not definitively state that there was, or wasn't, a cancer problem in the four-town area. For those suffering from cancer, it provided neither vindication nor relief.

However, by doing their own study, NOCC members were able to gather and analyze real data on cancer, and draw their own conclusions. For the first time, the four towns had concrete, credible information on cancer rates in their area. The report provided a credible source of information to the community because it had been developed by not one, but several, stakeholder groups. Dr. Dieter Kreckel, a local physician at the Rumford Community Hospital and a member of the NOCC, stated in the NOCC's final action plan: "Putting our heads together to do a study on cancer rates was a big accomplishment for the NOCC and for this community. This is a subject people care a lot about. Our results should give everyone a more accurate and believable picture of cancer incidence."

Equally as important, NOCC members learned about both the possibilities and the limitations of scientific analysis. These new insights were a direct product of learning by doing, a process that was made possible by a technical expert who understood the role he should play in a community-based consensus building process. Rather than presenting a fully articulated methodology and asking for the group's permission to execute it, he helped the group develop its own methodology.

Rather than announcing the conclusions he had drawn from the analysis of the data, he talked about the heterogeneity of scientific interpretation, told the group members what he thought, and then encouraged them to draw their own conclusions. **❧**

❧ COMMENTARY

Notice that just as the NOCC participants learned to remake their ground rules by working with consensus builders who are demonstrably convinced that ground rules must be corrigible to be effective, so they learn to put expertise to uses of their own devising by working with an expert whose knowledge includes understanding of its own limits. Feel free to draw from this observation optimistic conclusions regarding the possibility of a form of directly deliberative democracy in which problem-solving participation blurs the traditional line between experts and laypersons.

—Charles F. Sabel, *Political economist*

■ Section 4: The Middle and Last Phase—Reaching beyond the Negotiation Table

After completing the cancer incidence study, the NOCC initiated several new fact-finding projects aimed at developing a better sense of air quality in the region. An Air Quality Subcommittee with representatives from the mill, the Maine DEP and EPA, labor, town governments, and concerned community residents was formed.

The Air Quality Subcommittee did a careful review of monitoring data gathered by the DEP in 1991, 1993, and 1995 at four monitoring sites in the valley. The data raised some concerns about levels of air toxics, which were at the time not controlled by federal regulations. In particular, 3 air toxics out of 40 measured—benzene, chloroform, and 1-3 butadiene—were found to have concentrations that raised concerns given health-based guidelines already developed by the Maine Bureau of Health. The level of chloroform was particularly unsettling. Unlike the other two pollutants, its main source was the mill, and the mill had recently made some technological changes to its bleaching process that many thought would reduce levels. The Maine DEP agreed to collaborate with the NOCC to design a more thorough, year-long air-monitoring program. The group provided the DEP with suggestions on when to begin and end the monitoring, and where to place monitoring devices.

Because the NOCC had learned from the cancer incidence report that radon might contribute to lung cancer, the NOCC also undertook a residential radon-testing program. Through this program, 400 homeowners in the four towns tested their homes for radon using test canisters do-nated by the EPA. Boy Scouts helped assemble the kits and the instructions for homeowners. The four town halls helped to distribute and collect them. An EPA-contracted lab analyzed the results, which were sent out to homeowners along with confidential letters. When a public meeting was held to share the overall results (individual results were kept confidential), more than 60 citizens showed up to find out what the NOCC had learned, ask questions, and speak with state-certified vendors who offered radon remediation.

These projects were the main focus of the NOCC's work up until its concluding six months. As the NOCC matured, it was clear that members were developing a better understanding of technical issues related to public health and air quality. Evidence of this cropped up repeatedly at NOCC and subcommittee meetings. At several points, a member spotted mistakes in mathematical calculations and data inconsistencies. Another member who had no formal scientific background continually surprised us when he quizzed agency experts in detail about their methodology for gathering air samples.

Although it seemed that the NOCC was making real progress in developing a better understanding of the status of public health and air quality in the area, we wondered if the broader community had learned much. Representatives who worked for established organizations like town offices, the mill, or the hospital could communicate easily through existing channels like staff meetings, internal briefings, and company newsletters. But NOCC members who represented average citizens of the four towns had no simple means to talk with those they represented. Sure, they could talk at a town meeting or at Freddie's Restaurant, but was that enough? One NOCC member said candidly that she rarely talked to other citizens about NOCC issues: "A few of them will ask questions and I'll answer them to the best of my ability. But I am not going out campaigning. I haven't got that kind of time" (Cluck, 1997). Time was clearly a problem. Members were giving a lot just by coming to meeting after meeting. This was a donation of three hours a night at least twice a month for two years (not to mention the work in between meetings). In addition, while NOCC members were becoming educated consumers of public health and air quality data, the sheer complexity of the information made educating others a tall order.

We wondered, how could the larger community gain from the hard work of NOCC members? And who would implement the recommendations that the NOCC was developing if the NOCC closed up shop? In the last six months of its life, two key developments helped to transfer the momentum built up by NOCC members into an ongoing, institutionalized community collaboration: the negotiation of a consensus action plan for widespread distribution and the formation of a new, ongoing health-based coalition.

The NOCC's Action Plan

NOCC members had agreed from the outset that they should produce some kind of final product, but most of the NOCC (and us) had only a vague conception of what that might mean. As the NOCC learned more and more, the final report became increasingly important. One member who owned a local Laundromat in the town of Mexico said at every meeting, "How are we going to get all this informa-

tion in one place, in a form where people can read it and understand it?"

A NOCC member who worked for the EPA invited a community education specialist from her office to advise the coalition. Working with this specialist, NOCC members decided that their report should be in the form of an oversized newsletter. Each section would describe a different part of the NOCC's work: cancer incidence, radon, air quality monitoring, and respiratory illness, to name just a few. Each section would also include recommendations to government agencies, local businesses, and individuals.

The NOCC agreed to form a drafting subcommittee with representatives from each stakeholder group to take charge of the writing. The NOCC also accepted our offer to generate "first cuts" at each section for the drafting committee to review and improve. This proved to be effective. First, we could devote time to the drafting process that NOCC members just didn't have. Second, we had access to a storehouse of documents describing the NOCC's work (which had already been approved by the coalition). Third, putting words on paper, as we learned from the cancer incidence report, was a highly charged activity. It was important to have a neutral produce a "single text" for review and improvement by the full group.

We worked for three months with the drafting committee to produce a complete report. The process moved forward slowly as the drafting committee struggled to find language that met everyone's interests. Sometimes, entire meetings were spent hashing through a few words or sentences. In these moments of impasse, having learned from the drafting of the cancer incidence report, we recommended that the committee describe the range of views, rather than trying to forge a singular consensus view.

While the NOCC was able to delegate the bulk of the writing work to its drafting committee, finalizing the newsletter with the entire NOCC was challenging. NOCC members often wanted to renegotiate language that others thought had already been approved. In part, this was the natural result of having so many cooks work on the soup. But in addition, NOCC members were realizing that they needed to be more active than ever in representing their constituencies' interests. After all, these agreements were going into print. We aimed to strike a balance between encouraging the group to consider every change that seemed truly critical to one or more members and continuing to push so that drafting did not become a process without end.

In the fall of 1997, the NOCC mailed out its 12-page newspaper-sized newsletter to more than 7,000 households. It was rewarding for members to see a culmination of all of their hard work—a final product chock-full of graphs, charts, and text that did not exist before. The NOCC held a press conference, complete with the heads of EPA Region I and the Maine DEP. The local and regional print and television media cov- ered the story. The final report signaled the close of the NOCC's work, but also signaled that there was plenty left to do—others would need to pick up where the NOCC left off.

The Healthy Communities Coalition

Once work was under way to develop recommendations for the final report, we had some confidence that the results of the NOCC's work would not go unnoticed. But we still worried about what would happen when the coalition's funding ran out and we drove home to Boston for the last time. Would there be any momentum for further work to improve air quality and public health once the NOCC stopped meeting?

The subject of what might live on after the NOCC became a preoccupation of the Public Health Subcommittee, which had been charged with deciding what kind of studies the NOCC should recommend to follow up on the group's analysis of cancer incidence. About $10,000 of NOCC funds remained. How could this money best be spent?

The NOCC had boiled down further public health action to several possibilities. The options included funding an asthma survey; further, focused cancer studies; and/or a start-up grant for a Healthy Communities program. The Public Health Subcommittee had learned about the Healthy Communities program through a presentation by the subcommittee's Bureau of Health representative. Based on the World Health Organization's model to address health problems in developing countries, the Healthy Communities program could provide a vehicle for a range of local stakeholders to further assess public health in the broadest terms: They could look at environmental health, public safety, recreational opportunities, and even economic health. Other Maine communities had successfully used the program. One community developed a child literacy program and built a public swimming pool. Another nearby community had purchased a van to bring health promotion, prevention, and education to its outlying areas. ➥

⊂➣ COMMENTARY

Whoa, whoa. All of a sudden, just as the story is ending, it seems that NOCC and the consensus builders were never as isolated as it seemed. Other communities in Maine, learning, via the World Health Organization, of experiences in developing countries, had already put in place the kind of open institutional structure that could accommodate the kinds of exploratory investigation and action that were proving successful, but hard to stabilize, in Northern Oxford County. How did all this learning go on? Do (at least some of) the Healthy Communities programs in fact do the kinds of things that NOCC has come to regard as essential to solving the problems it set out to address? Or is the succession from NOCC to Healthy Communities program just an expedient that allows an inconclusive project to pass away with dignity? If the new institution is more than a face-saving device (and my own experience of similar programs suggests it well can be), could NOCC have benefited from earlier collaboration?

But to ask such questions is to begin to elicit another version of the story, a version that takes for granted that Northern Oxford County, precisely because it is not alone in facing ambiguous problems that overtax many contemporary institutions, has a lot to learn from what others in its situation are doing, and perhaps a lot to teach them as well. This other story would be as much about consensus building among communities as within them, and as much about the construction of new institutions as about the rules for operating in the void left by the disorganization of the old. It would be more a story of how a whole people can solve the mysteries that trouble them—look back to the subtitle of this case—than about how a town turned to (peaceable) outsiders to restore the peace.

—Charles F. Sabel, *Political economist*

Excited about the program, the Public Health Subcommittee sponsored a luncheon, paid for by NOCC funds, and invited NOCC members, local banks, local social service providers, ministers, school administrators, hospital board members, and others to hear about the program. The luncheon was a success in terms of the number who attended—more than 40 community leaders—and the enthusiasm expressed by the community at large about the Healthy Communities program. During the luncheon, the state coordinator of the program remarked, "We've never had so many people in a community turn out for the first event. This is terrific."

But Healthy Communities needed money. The program would require a part-time, paid coordinator; office space; and other resources. The Public Health Subcommittee first, and then the NOCC as a whole, wrestled with what to do. Some stakeholders were interested in trying to learn more about asthma and other respiratory illnesses. Others wanted follow-up with more cancer studies. Others advocated for helping start up the Healthy Communities program. It would provide a vehicle to carry on the NOCC's work—many of the activities left undone could be passed on to the new coalition. Without such a vehicle, these proponents argued, who would track the study and who would be there to receive the results? Nonetheless, some expressed concern that the broader mission and membership of such a coalition would water down the original intent of the NOCC, focusing efforts on teenage pregnancy, for instance, rather than on environmental protection.

After discussion, the group unanimously decided to forward the remaining NOCC funds to the new coalition. In a final press release upon the completion of the NOCC's final report, a posterboard-size mock-up of the check was handed over to the new Healthy Communities program coordinator. In addition, the mill also offered up $5,000. In the meantime, the subcommittee had worked with the assistance of CBI to prepare several grant applications. The Healthy Communities coalition —named the River Valley Healthy Communities Coalition—was ready to carry on the work of the NOCC.

■ Epilogue

The NOCC was never able to definitively refute or confirm the original television report about "Cancer Valley." Nor was the NOCC able to provide much relief to the families of those with cancer. But the work started by the NOCC in regard to air quality did lead to good news. First, as the coalition was finishing its work, the mill announced it would alter its bleaching process, eliminating all use of elemental chlorine, a significant source of chloroform and a potential source of dioxin. After a year of DEP air toxics monitoring supported and molded by the NOCC, the community learned that chloroform levels had indeed dropped significantly after the mill's action.

And one year after the NOCC held its final banquet, the Healthy Communities coalition was still going strong. The mill had continued to keep the coalition informed of ongoing environmental changes at the mill. The coalition had sponsored an educational event for physicians and other local health care providers on the latest techniques for diagnosing and treating asthma. The coalition had won a $30,000 grant to reduce smoking. The coalition had established a new committee to develop, finance, and build a multipurpose community center and pool. The coalition was working to expand membership from 45 to 100 organizations and to raise additional funds.

While there were probably a number of factors that contributed to the formation and forward momentum of this new Healthy Communities coalition, we believe the NOCC laid the essential groundwork. The NOCC created a forum where residents of the four towns could use fact-finding and deliberation to explore issues that were a source of painful, protracted conflict in their community. As members worked on these issues, they began to see each other differently. It was no longer just Mill versus Labor, for example; it was a group of people with different interests, fears, and concerns who could work together constructively despite their differences. Over the course of the two years, the NOCC also mobilized state agencies and showed the community how to link up to resources in Augusta, Boston, and even as far away as Washington, D.C.

When it came time to think about how to close out the NOCC's work, the fruits of this process were evident. Although it had been hard work for everyone, it had ultimately persuaded NOCC members that consensus building could work. They made a tough decision to channel their remaining funds into developing a new coalition that would support continued collaboration among community members. Several NOCC members decided to take on leadership positions in the new coalition, and other residents of the four towns were waiting in the wings, ready to get involved. ➤

∽ COMMENTARY

In summary, this is a fascinating case describing an interesting consensus process. It certainly provides much useful guidance, yet it highlights central issues that need to be debated as the consensus building field develops.

—Max H. Bazerman, *Social psychologist*

■ *References*

Beckley, T. M. (1994). *Pulp, paper, and power.* Unpublished doctoral thesis, University of Wisconsin–Madison.

Cluck, V. (1997). *The Northern Oxford County Coalition: An analysis of representation and communication.* Unpublished master's thesis, Massachusetts Institute of Technology, Cambridge.

Corburn, J. (1996). *Pursuing justice in environmental decision making: Deliberative democracy and consensus building.* Unpublished master's thesis, Massachusetts Institute of Technology, Cambridge.

CASE

3

THE CHELSEA CHARTER
CONSENSUS PROCESS

■ Susan L. Podziba

Democracy requires that citizens participate in their governance. A strong democracy effectively engages its citizens. Conversely, a weakened democracy denies access to its members and is operated by a small number of individuals. This is a story of a democracy that went astray, and an attempt to set it back on track. It is a chapter in the history of Chelsea, Massachusetts, a city of 28,000 residents located just north of Boston on a land mass, only 1.8 square miles, divided by a bridge.

In 1990, the city of Chelsea would have met most criteria for a malfunctioning democracy. Two of its past four mayors were incarcerated on federal corruption charges, and a third pleaded guilty to a grand jury but avoided punishment because the statute of limitations for his offenses had expired (Claiborne, 1994). Municipal officials were unable to deliver basic services such as trash disposal and snow removal, and after years of falling test scores, the city hired a local university to manage its schools.[1] It clearly had a patron-client gov-

---

A longer version of this case, titled *Social Capital Formation, Public Building and Public Mediation: The Chelsea Charter Consensus Process* by Susan L. Podziba, was published in 1998 by the Kettering Foundation (200 Commons Road, Dayton, Ohio, 45459). In addition, material for this case was excerpted from an interview with Podziba conducted by John Forester (1998), "Collaborative Civic Design in Chelsea, Mass: A Profile of Susan Podziba" in J. Forester (ed.) *Mediation in Practice: Profiles of Community and Environmental Mediators*, working paper, pp. 203-236, Ithaca, NY: Cornell University, Department of City and Regional Planning. Podziba designed and implemented the Chelsea Charter Consensus Process. She served as mediator during charter negotiations and led a process team that included Roberta Miller, an expert in municipal governance, and Mark Morse, a professional charter drafter.

ernment; those who "knew someone" were served and often got city jobs. Finally, as it headed for bankruptcy with a $10 million deficit on a $40 million budget, shortly after a $5 million state bailout, the state legislature, with the governor's approval, suspended Chelsea's local democracy and placed the city under state receivership. ❧

❧ COMMENTARY

Corruption is a form of free rider problem in which the immediate participants benefit but the overall public good of legitimate government is diminished. If there were as many people who understood the logic of the free rider problem as those who understand the logic of supply and demand, it might (I am not sure of this) be easier to explain to those who take part in corruption why it is not a good idea.

Many middle-class and professional people simply assume that bribe taking, cronyism, and the like are bad. But others see this stance as simply a form of Victorian prissiness. The case assumes throughout that the citizens of Chelsea by and large opposed the corruption in city hall ("many Chelseans felt shut out of local government and lost faith in the city's ability to govern itself"). But the government was consistently voted back into office. We don't hear much in this case from the majority who voted for the incumbents. Yet the many Chelseans with patronage ties to that government or other reasons for voting for it must have been more numerous than the many Chelseans who felt shut out. The many with ties may have preferred both the material benefits and the access to government that those ties conferred to improvements in the schools and a balanced budget.

—Jane Mansbridge, *Political philosopher*

The Chelsea Charter Consensus Process, which took place from October 1993 through June 1994, was a public consensus building process designed to engage a politically disillusioned community in the formation of its new local government. The Chelsea Charter of 1994 became effective after it was approved by the Massachusetts State Legislature and signed into law by the governor. Special elections were held to elect a city council, and the city was released from receivership in July 1995 after the council hired a city manager. The work to restore Chelsea's democracy involved reengaging citizens who had given up on their city and engaging the city's newcomers, who historically had been closed out of city hall.

■ *Background on Chelsea*

Since the turn of the century, Chelsea, Massachusetts has been an immigrant city. A first stop for Poles, Ukrainians, Russians, Jews, and other Europeans, most moved to suburbs after accumulating some wealth. The most recent immigrant groups to settle in Chelsea have been Hispanics and Asians, who account for 40 and 15 percent of the current city population, respectively. Over the years, Chelsea has had to contend with the inherently conflicting values, traditions, and interests of its diverse population.

In 1990, Chelsea was placed into state receivership as a result of financial mismanagement and corruption among its municipal officials. A critical element of the mission of the receivership, as outlined in the statute that created it, was to recommend to the governor a new form of government for the city. This was of serious import because its 1903 city charter, under which Chelsea was governed prior to receivership, had been revised by over 2,000 special acts of the Massachusetts State Legislature, all of which contributed to a blurring of the lines of authority between the mayor and the Board of Aldermen and their interactions with the city's boards and commissions.

At the time the state legislature voted to put Chelsea into receivership, city hall was run by a clique. To access "public" services, one needed to know the "right people." Hiring practices hinged on a system of patronage rather than skills. As a result, many Chelseans felt shut out of local government and lost faith in the city's ability to govern itself. Others, with limited or no experience with democracy, simply expected little in the way of services. Chelsea represented a particularly severe degeneration of political responsibility and citizen alienation. Its government, like other dysfunctional cities across the United States, was "perceived as so autonomous that the public [was] no longer able to control and direct it" (Harwood Group, 1991, p. iii). ∞

∞ COMMENTARY

From the perspective of many ordinary citizens, a bribe can increase freedom. You benefit, the cop benefits, and no one seems to lose. Patronage makes sense too. If you bring in your family to vote, or work for the right people at election time, it seems both just and reasonable to get some form of payment for your effort. The surface freedom and justice obscure the larger collective action problem: If *everyone* acts this way, the result is not what almost anyone wants.

In an earlier era of immigration, accessing public services always meant knowing the right people. In this earlier system, however, public officials had an incentive to reach out to citizens to ask if the officials could do anything for them. Big-city political machines had a communications network (although highly biased by race and ethnicity), based on the precinct and even on the block. Even today, in working-class areas, single-member districts are likely to produce more working-class aldermen and more aldermen who see their main job as bringing back specific material benefits for the district, while at-large elections are likely to produce more professional aldermen and more aldermen who see their main job as making overall policy for the city.

It is important, then, not simply to label as *corruption* the mechanisms that have tied immigrants and working-class people more closely to government. Nevertheless, in the long run corruption usually delegitimates a government, making it far harder to collect taxes voluntarily or tap for common purposes into the altruistic, other-oriented feelings people may have for their community.

—Jane Mansbridge, *Political philosopher*

When Lewis H. Spence was appointed state receiver of Chelsea in 1991, he faced the daunting task of replacing a political machine, notorious for corruption and mismanagement, with a municipal government that would truly serve the needs of an ethnically diverse, factionalized, and disillusioned population. Although he had the authority to simply draft a new city charter, as his predecessor had done,[2] Spence believed that if the new government was to survive, the people it was to govern would have to create it. To this end, he enlisted the help of a professional mediation team, headed by the author of this case study, and initiated the Chelsea Charter Consensus Process. ✏

✐ COMMENTARY

The democratic processes that existed in Chelsea had not broken down, that is, corporate officials were still elected for fixed terms by a majority of registered voters and they were still subject to legal constraints as evidenced by the number of officials prosecuted and convicted. What had broken down was the willingness of Chelsea's citizens to use the powers inherent in majority rule to effect reform. It was the intervention of the state that initiated the process whereby Chelsea created a new charter, and that intervention was precipitated by a fiscal rather than a constitutional crisis. This top-down pressure naturally created special problems for generating bottom-up participation in a politically torpid community divided by ethnicity, nationality, and class. The decisions by the receiver to use a mediation team and by the team to attempt to use consensual methods to encourage participation were also imposed on the community.

—Mark Kishlansky, *Historian*

✐ COMMENTARY

Consensus processes, often facilitated by private mediators, need to be properly and legally authorized and legitimated. Often, they work better than the governmental systems already in place, but there is always the dilemma of the appropriate legal relationship between effective, informal processes and formal laws, whether constitutions, state legislation, city charters, zoning laws, or other regulatory schemes. In the case of the Chelsea Charter Consensus Process, the appointed state receiver "enlisted the help of a professional mediation team," clearly raising the issue of what happens when public officials draw in private consultants to help facilitate what should be public, deliberative, and democratic processes. Though the best of these processes, like the Chelsea Process, are open and involve the public—indeed, they are so good because they often involve the public more than conventional governmental processes do—there is still the difficulty of formal legal and political legitimacy to be reckoned with.

—Carrie J. Menkel-Meadow, *Legal scholar*

■ *The Chelsea Charter Consensus Process*

The Chelsea Charter Consensus Process (Chelsea Process) was designed to reopen city hall to all residents of Chelsea and to create a new, thriving democracy in the city. Rather than leave decision-making responsibilities solely to municipal officials, the Chelsea Process sought to engage citizens. To accomplish this, the process needed to reach deep into a disenfranchised community and confront the suspicions and frustrations spawned by former city administrations.

The key assumptions of the Chelsea Process were that the people of Chelsea had valuable information to offer in the development of their city charter and that the act of providing and integrating such information would strengthen both the charter and the citizens, thereby strengthening the city's future democracy. An example of how the unique knowledge of its citizens strengthened Chelsea's charter is the fact that the Chelsea Charter of 1994 prohibits anyone "convicted of a criminal offense involving misconduct in elective or appointive office, trust, or employment" from holding elective, appointive, or employment positions in the city.[3] This is an unusual element for a city charter, but Chelsea residents knew they needed to protect the city from past corrupt officials such as a charismatic former mayor whose prison term was soon ending. ◆◆

◯➤ COMMENTARY

The reformers, it seemed, had to put into the Chelsea charter a special provision preventing the voters from electing anyone who had previously been convicted of a criminal offense involving misconduct in elective or appointive office. They particularly feared that a majority of voters might like the former mayor because he was "charismatic." It is not clear from the case study that the views of the majority of voters, who presumably might well have voted for the ex-mayor if they had not legally been prevented from doing so, were well represented in the consensus process. If they were, it would be useful to know how they reacted to the process, and what kinds of arguments made them see how destructive the patronage process could be overall.

Ironically, both the left and the right on the political spectrum have until recently often denigrated worries about corruption. The left has been highly conscious of the way the Progressive reformers of the early twentieth century in the United States were inspired in their attacks on corruption in part by fear and scorn of immigrants, with their "dirty" ways and "dirty" politics. Business interests in the cities also often benefited from efficient, transparent government run by people of their own class and values. Many Progressive anticorruption reforms, accordingly, had the intentional effect of reducing the power of the working class. Registration requirements reduced the number of legitimate immigrant voters. At-large elections reduced the number of working-class aldermen as well as aldermen with close personal ties to working-class voters. City manager systems reduced the possibilities of patronage. Recognizing the way these anticorruption reforms served business and professional interests at the expense of the working class, many analysts from the political left have not been enthusiastic opponents of corruption.

At the same time, on the political right, free market libertarians have seen corruption as one way that the energetic, entrepreneurial, free-wheeling individual can avoid the heavy hand of the bureaucratic, rent-seeking state. If governments primarily use their power to take the citizens' taxes for personal profit or, more subtly, to build the bureaucratic class (of social workers, teachers, school janitors, city clerks, etc.), and if regulations are primarily integral plans of a monopoly structure established by existing businesses and unions, then a bribe in the right place to avoid a tax or circumvent a regulation is a warranted blow for individual freedom and market efficiency.

—Jane Mansbridge, *Political philosopher*

The Chelsea Process commenced with approximately 40 interviews with community leaders: formal leaders and informal opinion makers. Interviewees ranged from sitting aldermen to heads of community organizations to the city Santa Claus. The interviews had multiple goals. First and foremost was to learn of the perceived causes of Chelsea's problems, why the city was put into receivership, the hoped-for elements of its new government, and what would be required for the new government to last over time. The information generated during the interviews revealed a spectrum of opinions regarding Chelsea's past. Almost all called for fiscal responsibility as a crucial element of the new government, and many also insisted that city services be provided uniformly throughout the city. Some interviewees felt that fiscal mismanagement led the state to suspend Chelsea's local democracy while others believed that "the state took it over so that Massport could site an [airport] parking lot in the city." Still others stated, "We have no problem."

In addition to gathering information about the city, the interviews allowed leaders of the community to be personally apprised of the process, and initiated the creation of relationships between the mediator and the community. The interviews

served as an opportunity to let people know the mediator and her assumptions regarding her role and the process. In Chelsea, information travels quickly by word of mouth, and the interviews were an opportunity for the mediator to give real information to community leaders, who then passed it throughout the city.

In accordance with the goal of seeking to enable the community to govern itself, Chelsea residents were trained to serve as facilitators to run community meetings. This allowed a local face to be cast on the process. It was assumed that residents would be more open with their friends and neighbors and that the process would belong to Chelsea, not a stranger. The use of local facilitators also helped with the multicultural and multilingual nature of the city.

At the outset of the process, a public forum was held in the high school gymnasium. After a brief explanation of the process, citizens were divided up at round tables, each of which included a local facilitator. Around each table, some in English and some in Spanish, residents of Chelsea discussed why their city was in receivership, what its new government should be able to accomplish, and what form of government was most likely to be able to achieve and sustain the kind of government they yearned for. "Would a mayor be able to do it? Or would a city manager hired by an elected council be a better option? Should they have a smaller or a larger legislative body?" ◆

◆ COMMENTARY

Governmental consensus processes allow more systematic information gathering. Scientifically created surveys, polls, interviews, focus groups—all the tools of well-educated and technically astute consultants and facilitators—often produce better information than patronage or interest-driven government processes. Public forums, such as the one in the high school gymnasium conducted here, may be effective precisely because they occur outside of the usual corridors of power and corruption, whether real or perceived. Thus, there may be reinvigorated participation and truer democracy at work. Nevertheless, there is still the question of representativeness of nonelected participants and accountability to local nongovernmental organizations, as well as to unaffiliated citizens. The success of a process like that conducted in Chelsea is that it engaged and educated new citizens in a community with so many immigrants. It also drew together, to a large extent more successfully than the formal democratic process, ethnic groups that might not meet well in other circumstances.

—Carrie J. Menkel-Meadow, *Legal scholar*

◆ COMMENTARY

Who was invited? Who came? These kinds of events often exclude those who have little time or fear speaking in public (or, in the case of the Asian residents of Chelsea, perhaps could not speak either English or Spanish fluently).

—Jane Mansbridge, *Political philosopher*

The facilitators also ran two sets of community meetings for a total of approximately 45 meetings. The first set was designed to explore their neighbors' ideas about good government and the future of Chelsea. ◆

◆ COMMENTARY

As a matter of American political theory, one could read the stories of citizen consensus processes as continuous with the active group life noted by Alexis de Tocqueville over 150 years ago, with newly diverse and invigorated interest and citizen groups forming around new issues: funding, education, health care, physical safety, and security.

—Carrie J. Menkel-Meadow, *Legal scholar*

Later in the process, the facilitators led meetings to get input on the draft charter. To enable people to talk in their usual surroundings, since they were unlikely to attend separate charter meetings, the community meetings were held at local social clubs, churches and synagogues, elderly housing residences, even drinking clubs and private homes. ↠

↞ COMMENTARY

This is an important point. In a consensus process, which takes more time than many people have, it is advisable to make access to the process as easy as possible. Since the process is often threatening to the many who are not comfortable with public speaking, meetings should be in as small scale and comfortable, homey places as possible.

—Jane Mansbridge, *Political philosopher*

Early process activities resulted in clarifying the community's concerns about its local government and identifying individuals who could participate as citizen decision makers in discussions of the mechanics of governance. Throughout the Chelsea Process, a diverse range of activities was initiated to explore and draw out the thoughts and concerns of the community. There were ward meetings and public forums. Newsletters and a survey questionnaire, in English and Spanish, were sent to every household. A charter hot line was set up, and cable television programs were aired on the subject, including numerous call-in shows and a program featuring a panel of local government experts. ↠

↞ COMMENTARY

The survey questionnaire sent to each household is a good idea, even if few people actually fill it out. It extends the group members who feel they have been consulted, although their ideas may never be represented. Similarly, the great and varied mix of approaches makes it more likely that the process will tap different kinds of groups, and different opinions within different groups. The public leadership of different political and ethnic groups does not always speak accurately for the concerns and the political positions of the members of those groups.

It would have been a good idea to have done more outreach to the Asian community. Precisely because they were so hard to involve, extra effort would have been warranted. Whenever some groups are hard to contact, it is worthwhile, if one can afford it, to hire someone of the appropriate background or ethnicity to make the initial contacts and do as much of the recruiting as possible. Although Susan Podziba seems an excellent facilitator, having an American white woman trying to recruit from a nationally mixed Asian community seems a recipe for failure.

—Jane Mansbridge, *Political philosopher*

In addition to the professional mediation team, the process was supported by a communications consultant, who drafted some newsletters; the city attorney, who provided legal opinions when necessary; the receiver's chief of staff, who helped access state charter resources; and the former chairman of the Aldermanic Subcommittee on Governance, who provided insight on the local political pulse.

The Charter Preparation Team

The Charter Preparation Team was charged with preparing Chelsea's new city charter, based on the public input generated through a host of public participation venues. Seventy candidates had been recommended by Chelsea residents for service on the team during the community leader interviews, community meetings, call-in-cable shows, public forum, and on the charter hot line. ⋙

⋙ COMMENTARY

The use of community leaders was a vital attempt to establish a form of representation different from one person/one vote. It was important that the civic structure of the community was represented in ways other than through local officials, and it was equally important that those who took part in the consensual process saw themselves as speaking for others directly. This would allow both for the softening of individual desires and of individual personalities once the decision-making process was under way. Nevertheless, it is instructive that the mediation team did not identify crucial constituencies without which the process could not take place. This meant that no group could wreck the consensus building process by withdrawing and that the failure of participation by particular groups—an especial problem in Chelsea—would not defeat the process. The absence of Asians from the Charter Preparation Team could never have occurred if the team had been appointed from outside, but was a natural result of open recruitment in the initial stages of the Chelsea Process. In this case, it appears that the absence was the result of disinterest rather than militancy.

—Mark Kishlansky, *Historian*

To select the team, a selection committee reviewed the complete list of candidates relative to criteria such as a commitment to securing the best form of government for the city of Chelsea, a willingness to look at issues citywide rather than from a narrow agenda, a willingness to learn about and operate by consensus, and a willingness to learn about and discuss mechanics of governance. A proposed team was published in the local paper to allow members of the community to suggest revisions or additions to it. ⋙

∞ COMMENTARY

The criterion of looking for individuals who were willing "to look at issues citywide rather than from a narrow agenda" undoubtedly eliminated radical groups and the extremes on the different sides of the issues in the city. This was probably a realistic and constructive move. Its effects in muting dissent should, however, be noted.

—Jane Mansbridge, *Political philosopher*

The selection committee, a group of three individuals, was itself chosen according to specific criteria. They were individuals considered to be highly moral by Chelseans, and included a Cuban pastor, the editor of the local newspaper, and the founder and director of an alternative high school program. The three narrowed the list from 70 candidates to 18. ∞

∞ COMMENTARY

Note the critical importance of individual morality. Whenever governmental legitimacy has broken down, a great deal of the legitimacy of any outcome rests on the character and morality of the leadership. After a revolution or a long struggle for independence, citizens can sometimes use time spent in jail, for example, as a cue to a leader's genuine dedication to the common good. Taking publicly a political stand that will incur a jail sentence sends what economists call a "costly signal" of the genuineness of one's intentions. Those who supervised this process were extremely wise in looking for individuals whose own character, known to many in the community, could give legitimacy to the process.

—Jane Mansbridge, *Political philosopher*

∞ COMMENTARY

Despite wanting to enthusiastically support the energy and effort that go into these more effective ad hoc—though facilitated—processes, one still has to wonder who "chooses" the players? "They were individuals considered to be highly moral." Who puts the consensus builders and facilitators in charge of community values? Or choice of representatives to the process? So, while the important counter-governmental processes of group and community meetings, work task forces, and new participation are important in these processes, who is granted authority and how do we know it is "legitimate"? Though the facilitators of this process tried hard to reflect the diversity in Chelsea, they were unable to keep representatives from the Asian community active in the process. So how do we judge whether the process and its outcomes are truly representative of the community? With only 30 percent voter turnout in the approval of the city charter, how are we to judge the efficacy of a presumably more democratic government?

—Carrie J. Menkel-Meadow, *Legal scholar*

A particularly difficult issue was the question of elected officials serving on the team. On the one hand, the charter eventually had to pass a special election during which the endorsement of those who could draw electoral support would be helpful. On the other hand, in informal discussions, the politicians themselves expressed an awareness that they were widely perceived to be a part of the problem. As one stated, "If you have too many of us, the people are going to hate it." Based on conversations with elected officials, the team eventually included three aldermen and one Chelsea School Committee member.

The final 18-member team, which, in addition to the politicians, included 12 ordinary citizens, a state representative from the Executive Office of Communities and Development, and a representative of the receiver, represented virtually all sectors of the city.[4] Some of the citizens had continued to participate in local affairs during the city's decline and the period of receivership. Others were returning to public life,

having previously opted out of municipal affairs. Still others had never before been involved in local affairs. At least one member had never set foot inside city hall. Most team members had limited knowledge of the mechanics of governance.

At its preliminary meeting, the Charter Preparation Team members received a report outlining the input from the community meetings, interviews, and public forums. They shared stories of their personal and political lives in Chelsea, negotiated ground rules, and were briefed on issues of local governance by the professional charter drafter hired to assist in translating their decisions into charter language. Soon after, a panel of previous and current municipal officials from other cities and towns gave presentations to the team about how their municipal governments functioned. In a televised session, the team questioned the panel about the decision-making processes in mayoral and council-manager forms of government. ❧

❧ COMMENTARY

Sometimes these sessions have a greater effect than one might think, via word of mouth. Most important, if something is said in such a session that many people would object to, it is quite likely that at least one person who will object will be watching, they can spread the word, and eventually the disagreement will become public.

—Jane Mansbridge, *Political philosopher*

After two months of meetings, the team presented an initial proposal to the community. It called for a council-manager form of government, a 13-member city council of 10 district and 3 at-large councilors, with two- and four-year terms, respectively. The proposal was presented to the community through ward meetings, a

public forum, and a call-in cable television show. Since turnout at the snowy winter ward meetings was low, a survey was sent to all registered voters. Approximately 10 percent returned the survey. Information obtained from the community supported the general direction of the initial proposal. ❧

↜ COMMENTARY

Was there any way of knowing anything about the geographic residence or class background of those who returned the survey? Often a few questions on area of residence or years of school completed can help those who try to make sense of these kinds of surveys understand how much they are skewed to those with a college education. If a group really wants to find out relatively accurately what opinion is "on the ground," it is usually a good idea to hire a professional survey outfit. Random digit dialing, for example, may miss those without telephones, but it is a relatively cheap process, with a far more reliable outcome than a mailback survey, which winnows out a highly self-selected group.

—Jane Mansbridge, *Political philosopher*

During five months of almost weekly mediated meetings, the Charter Preparation Team deliberated over every aspect of the charter—from the form of government to the selection process of key municipal officials to whether or not God should be mentioned in the preamble. The most contentious issue was the composition of the school committee. Though all shared the goal of getting more parents with children in the Chelsea public school system onto the school committee, they disagreed on the composition—at large or by district—that would lead to the desired result. Some felt that district representation would make it easier for parents to run because they would have to campaign only in their neighborhoods. ↝

↜ COMMENTARY

It is common knowledge in political science that at-large elections produce more professional-class (and White and female) representatives, and single-member districts produce more working-class (and Black and male) representatives. At-large elections are more likely to produce representatives concerned with citywide policy questions. Single-member districts are more likely to produce representatives concerned with getting benefits for the district.

—Jane Mansbridge, *Political philosopher*

Others felt that at large would be easier because, for the sixth and seventh slots, one would need an overall fewer number of votes. In every case, the team engaged in extensive deliberations to weigh a series of options. The charter, as a whole, is a complex set of choices, accomplished through deliberation and integrative bargaining.

Upon completion of the draft city charter, a newsletter summarizing the charter was sent to every household in the city and published in the local newspapers. The following month, 20 facilitated community meetings, a public forum, and several call-in cable shows were held to answer questions about the charter and generate community input.

The input from this final round of community meetings was compiled by the mediator, who matched all the feedback to the relevant sections of the charter. The team then used this annotated version of the draft charter to consider every concern registered by the community.

As a result of the community's responses to the draft charter, several key decisions were reconsidered. For example, the proposed 13-member city council was reduced to 11, and the proposed four-year term for at-large city councilors was reduced to two years. The final charter, which represented a consensus of the Charter Preparation Team, was made available throughout the city, and members of the team held a number of call-in cable television shows to inform the citizens of the changes made to the original draft as a result of the input it received from the community. Charter revisions were also printed in the local newspaper, the *Chelsea Record*.

The Charter Is Approved

Shortly after the final charter was completed, a special election was held to give the community an opportunity to approve or reject the charter prepared by the team. ➥

∞ COMMENTARY

Having a special election rather than an election timed to coincide with a presidential, congressional, or mayoral election ensures a relatively low turnout with, therefore, a considerably greater percentage of professional- and upper-middle-class voters and a lower percentage of working-class and lower-middle-class voters than in the citizenry as a whole.

—Jane Mansbridge, *Political philosopher*

Throughout the process, the receiver told the community that if the citizens approved the charter, he would recommend it to the governor as the city's new form of government. The charter was approved by a 60-40 margin with a 30 percent voter turnout, and it was subsequently approved by the state legislature and the governor.

At the time Chelsea was placed under receivership, large segments of the community had become effectively disenfranchised from the political process. By creating avenues for public deliberation in the charter's development and by engaging citizens as decision makers, the Chelsea Charter Consensus Process was able to explore and contain the diverse concerns of the community. Individuals from virtually all segments of the community engaged in deliberative discussions and voiced their interests, and those interests were woven into the fabric of their new city charter.

■ The Impact of the Charter Preparation Team on the Process

The Charter Preparation Team members were personally affected by the Chelsea Process and had a tremendous impact on the city as a whole. During the preliminary meeting of the team, members placed themselves on a Chelsea time line to describe their entry into the city, both personally and politically. This exercise began with a giant time line marking some of the most momentous points of Chelsea's history: Abraham Lincoln's and George Washington's visits to Chelsea; important battles in the Revolutionary War fought there; the major fires, one in 1903 and another in 1974, that destroyed substantial parts of the city. The mediators asked people to place themselves on the time line: When did they move to Chelsea? When did their families move to Chelsea? When did they become politically active in Chelsea? This sharing of stories "broke the ice" among team members and brought into view their shared devotion to Chelsea, their common public goal of preserving its existence, and, often, their families' similar immigrant histories, though at different points in time.

Next, the team developed, by consensus, the ground rules that would govern deliberations. The successful completion of a product—the ground rules—modeled a new way of deliberating. At the beginning of the process someone said, "In Chelsea people scream at each other. They'd never agree to disagree, they just disagree. And disagreements have long lives. They hold grudges forever." At its conclusion, someone else commented, "What we really did was find a new way to discuss an issue." ➥

The ground rules included a consensus decision rule, but empowered the mediator to call for a vote if, after prolonged discussion, it was clear that it would be impossible to reach consensus. An item could pass only by an extraordinary majority of 80 percent. The package of decisions that was the complete charter, however, had to be adopted by a true consensus of the team. ➥

The use of a consensus decision-making rule rather than a simple majority rule greatly contributed to the Charter Preparation Team's ability to deliberate. In a simple majority situation, a group can proceed with a decision despite the objections of as much as 49 percent of its membership. Over time, the people comprising this 49 percent are likely to stop participating as they realize that such a forum does not provide adequate opportunities to satisfy their concerns. In a consensus situation, each participant must listen carefully and work to understand the interests and concerns of the others. A participant's lack of consent to a proposal effectively vetoes that proposal and triggers additional deliberation until a consensus emerges. A Hispanic man, who was part of an organization that was inclined toward protests and lawsuits against the city, said, "I really like this process—not because I get everything I want, but because I get a fair hearing."

Throughout their service, Charter Preparation Team members found that in-dividuals both perceived and valued issues differently. This was apparent from the outset, even on the charter preamble, which the mediator began with to create momentum for the process with the hopes of a quick consensus victory. A question was raised about whether or not God should be mentioned in the preamble. One woman felt that she was representing the atheists in Chelsea, and another woman, who was a born-again Christian, insisted that God be included in the charter. As the issue took on great significance, the mediator distributed examples of preambles from other charters, the Massachusetts Constitution, and the U.S. Constitution. Between meetings, the mediator worked out language that was agreeable to the two women at the extremes. Although the woman who wanted God mentioned offered language that the other woman agreed to, the former rejected her own words during the next team meeting. The team eventually agreed, by consensus, to include the phrase "Under God with religious freedom" in the preamble. ◦➤

◦➤ COMMENTARY

The tabling of issues is one of the key techniques for establishing consensus, especially at the beginning of the process. As more issues are resolved consensually, momentum builds to settle the rest in the same fashion. Moreover, the tabling of especially contentious issues at the beginning allows individuals to develop trust and to become a group.

—Mark Kishlansky, *Historian*

◦➤ COMMENTARY

Tabling an issue of great contention is a time-honored method for helping to resolve disputes. Many centuries ago, during the Putney debates in England, as Cromwell's army sat outside London, members of the different factions argued over whether, when they seized power, they were going to extend the franchise to all men who owned a certain amount of property (a radical proposal) or keep the franchise as it was. Repeatedly, as tempers wore thin, members of both factions called for a break in the deliberations, so that the individuals concerned could consult both their inner lights and God. Until the middle of the sixteenth century, the English parliament made most of its decisions by consensus, and frequently tabled for a while the matters on which agreement could not be reached. The Society of Friends, who have taken the process of consensus further than almost any other long-standing group, often tables its most contentious matters—returning to them when tempers have cooled, more information has been gathered, and people have been able to talk with one another out of the public limelight.

—Jane Mansbridge, *Political philosopher*

Many substantive issues revealed great differences among the team members. The major issue in dispute was an at-large versus district composition to the school committee. Others were concerned about the relationship between the city and nonresident business owners; still others emphasized the need for a public process to hire key city officials, such as the police chief and city manager. All these matters were discussed in great detail and decisions were informed by the community input the team received, and the "packages" the team could agree to based on trade-offs of various options. Toward the end of the negotiations, when the school committee composition was decided in favor of at-large members by an 80-20 percent vote, a team member called the mediator to tell her he would oppose the charter. The mediator immediately drove to his organization and reviewed with him other elements of the charter that

he wanted and some that he had fought hard for, for example, a city manager and no mayor, an expanded council, and public processes for major city hires such as the police chief and city manager. At the end of the meeting, the team member agreed to stay on the team and support the charter.

Throughout its almost weekly meetings over a period of five months, the team was sustained by its members' abilities to deliberate according to a true definition of public deliberation. "There was an orderly exchange of opinions and experience such that people came to understand each other a little, and the motives that impelled each of them, and the different values that sustain them" (*A Public Voice*, 1993, p. 6). As a result, they made responsible decisions that were rooted in the concerns and interests expressed by all members of the team and informed by the community. ◆

◆ COMMENTARY

Consensus well conducted has this vitally important effect. People feel heard. Indeed, they are heard. The power of each individual to veto both ensures a hearing and relieves the sometimes anger-provoking anxiety that one will not be heard. When consensus is not well conducted, however, the minority can feel many kinds of subtle pressure to go along. This pressure has the opposite effect, of making one feel that not only was one not heard but also no one even knew that one wanted to be heard. In these situations, people in the minority often bite their tongues and leave—and feel deeply bitter afterward.

"Having one's voice heard" is important to people—often more important than getting what one wants. Tom Tyler (1990) shows that even convicted criminals are more satisfied with their sentences when they have had what they consider a fair trial. Satisfaction with the process predicted overall satisfaction even more than did satisfaction with the outcome. And what a fair trial often meant to them was a process in which their side of the story got heard.

As the scale of the decisions required to manage our cooperative lives gets larger, and as designers of institutions (e.g., schools) focus on the advantages of bigness, the crucial advantage of the small setting, which allows many people to have a say, gets lost. The best part of the Chelsea Process, in my view, was the part that brought the discussion into people's neighborhoods and homes. The more a process can (1) take the discussion where people are, (2) allow people the chance to formulate their ideas on the issues, (3) let people's ideas and needs be heard, and (4) give people a chance to reformulate their ideas after listening to others, the more the outcome will make sense in fact. In addition, the more these processes take place, the more everyone involved will feel heard, will feel validated, and will become more able to live with the eventual decision.

—Jane Mansbridge, *Political philosopher*

REFERENCE

Tyler, T. R. (1990). *Why people obey the law.* New Haven, CT: Yale University Press.

The increased visibility of trusted Chelseans contributed to sustained public participation in the Chelsea Process. As the process went on, the team members assumed all responsibility for public appearances. The mediator ceased all public appearances once Chelseans took the helm. They appeared on cable TV shows, made presentations to groups such as the chamber of commerce, and spoke before the Board of Aldermen. The Charter Preparation Team meetings were open to the public and, therefore, the media, but the team identified three spokespersons who discussed current proposals on the table and progress in decision making, but did not attribute particular statements to anyone. ⌁

⌁ COMMENTARY

It seems to me that the difficult challenge in local governmental consensus building situations is how to recognize and legitimate significant advances in creativity of outcomes and increased participation. These improvements come from using the "tools" of professional facilitation in integrative bargaining (e.g., the creative time line and stories, public forums, focus groups) over those of a tired bureaucracy or failed local government. Without "fossilizing" these new processes by making them more formal, we attempt to deal with the formal legitimacy issues. In my own experience with these processes, when they are working well, parties will adhere to internally agreed-on procedures and ground rules. But when someone is unhappy, they will "take it to the streets," the media, or—even worse—lawyers, to tie up, in litigation and publicity, questions about the legitimacy of processes, violations of state, local ethics-in-government statutes, or formal regulatory requirements. It is hard to achieve total buy-in, and without formal protections renegades from the process, or those who become substantively unhappy, have many tools they can use to derail a process that has no formal legal standing. As a lawyer-mediator, I can't resist also wondering how these processes will fare as "authorized," legitimated processes in formal law or whether we are better off working informally first and worrying about complying with legal technicalities later. (See Chapter 13, on legal issues in consensus building.)

—Carrie J. Menkel-Meadow, *Legal scholar*

■ *The Issue of Legitimacy*

At the start of a consensus process, it is not unusual for reluctant participants to assume that key decisions have already been made. Typically, such skepticism wanes once the process is under way and people actually see the impact they can have on the outcome. Not surprisingly, Chelsea's skepticism was persistent.

The community was initially skeptical of its own ability to "build something." During the community leader interviews, many individuals spoke of the culture of the "stupid kid from Chelsea," which meant that one should not expect much from the city's residents. This attitude was further described as a "tear-down mentality," that is, when anyone in town began to do well, people contributed to character assassination of that person. In one instance, in declining to serve on the Charter Preparation Team, a woman said, "I won't be helpful. I can only be divisive, argumentative, and obstructionist."

As a response to the city's skepticism, the Chelsea Process provided numerous entry points for public participation, which combined to inform and remind the community that something different was happening in the city, something that they were invited to participate in and, in fact, could

barely escape. A momentum was created that spoke of legitimacy, of change, of hope, of reason to participate. Each separate entry point gave individuals opportunities to participate in the ways that most suited them. Some chose active public participation, some chose passive ways such as watching television or reading a newsletter. Some engaged in informal conversations, which had an immeasurable impact on the process and the community.

One tool the mediation team used to demonstrate the legitimacy of the Chelsea Process was a pictorial process map. It was brought to meeting after meeting to show Chelseans all possible points of entry for offering input that would affect the substance of the charter. It clearly illustrated the elements and sequence of the process. From the map, citizens could trace their participation and know of future opportunities. The process map, along with the revised proposals developed by the Charter Preparation Team, confronted the skeptics with concrete evidence contrary to their suppositions.

Most important for the legitimacy of the process, the receiver lived by his word. He did not insist on particular decisions within the charter. His representative on the Charter Preparation Team had equal standing with all other members. The receiver had his opinions, and he shared them, but he never intimated that the charter should reflect his opinions over those of the community. Even with the divisive issue of the school committee composition, the receiver put the legitimacy of the process ahead of particular substantive decisions. In a private conversation with the mediator, the receiver suggested that the community would benefit from a school committee elected by district. However, he accepted the Charter Preparation Team's decision of a school committee elected at large. ◆

○ COMMENTARY

The goal of the receiver was to encourage participation and to establish a sense of communal ownership for the new charter. He was, of course, protected by the overriding laws of the commonwealth and the need for legislative approval of the finished product. Nevertheless, the receiver understood that inputs rather than outcomes were the key to restoring a sense of civic responsibility in the community. Consensual decision making is especially effective when there are many equally viable outcomes. Whether a council has 11 members or 13, or whether school committee members are chosen at large or by district, is less significant than whether those participating in the process of decision making feel that they are making choices.

—Mark Kishlansky, *Historian*

The legitimacy of the Chelsea Process enhanced individuals' determination to influence the eventual outcome. The community learned of its impact on the negotiations of the Charter Preparation Team in a number of ways. First of all, each team member received a lengthy summary of all the input generated during the first set of community meetings and community leader interviews. An abbreviated version was mailed to all households as a newsletter titled, "Chelsea People Talk about a New City Government." At least one person commented that the piece "quoted me almost verbatim." Community members began to feel heard. As the process was legitimized in the eyes of the community, it was secured from the former clique-in-power, those who perceived a loss from increased public involvement, who stood ready to exploit any infraction.

Residents saw examples of how the information they provided had guided the Charter Preparation Team's discussions. In the draft charter, for example, the team had proposed a 13-member council to replace the nine-member Board of Aldermen of the old charter. The consensus of the community was that 13 would be too cumbersome, and the Charter Preparation Team revised its proposal to 11 councilors. Term lengths were also revised. Originally, the team suggested two-year terms for district councilors and four-year terms for at-large councilors. Members of the community felt that this would create power imbalances among the councilors and recommended that all have two-year terms, despite the original concern that two-year terms provided less stability than four-year terms. The team adopted the community recommendation of two-year terms for all 11 city councilors.

Members of the community actually came to Charter Preparation Team meetings with written proposals for its consideration! In addition, they typically offered suggestions, rather than making demands. ⬦

⬦ COMMENTARY

Consensual processes have to be learned, especially when groups contain members who have excelled in adversarial, democratic processes. Building a consensus is not the same as building a majority. Modern majoritarian practices thrive on creating differences rather than commonalities. This is especially true when representatives practice identity politics, defining their group against other groups. Even the tactics of coalition building are of limited value in consensual politics. Thus, the author observes that by the end of the process people "offered suggestions, rather than making demands," an indication that the experience of achieving consensus had changed assumptions about political participation and was making inroads on the learned behavior of community representatives.

—Mark Kishlansky, *Historian*

A number of incidents tested the legitimacy of the Chelsea Process and caused residents to question whether they were right to hope and believe they could have a role in shaping Chelsea's future. As the Chelsea Process moved toward actual decision making, those elements in the community seeking to derail the process became more active and destructive. For example, as the community moved toward consensus on a council-manager, rather than a mayoral, form of government, individuals in Chelsea who wanted to be mayor opposed the process. They were politically astute enough to know that they could not publicly say they wanted a mayoral form of government. Instead, they desperately sought to delegitimize the consensus process by exploiting the old tendencies of the city regarding outsiders and the likelihood of being deceived. ⬦

⬦ COMMENTARY

The difficulty experienced by the Charter Preparation Team in protecting its process was that behind the consensus building of the new charter was a conventional majority-rule vote on its acceptance by the community. Thus, politicians excluded from the process could use traditional means in an effort to defeat the work of the preparation team. It is clear that the public relations effort directed against deliberate misinformation had to come from the mediation team rather than from the preparation team. This was an important aspect of protecting the work of the preparation team, but it is another example of the impact of the top-down process in the Chelsea case. One of the conventional difficulties of consensual processes is the diffusion of leadership within the group. It is instructive here that the mediator assumed the role of leader at crucial moments in the process.

—Mark Kishlansky, *Historian*

In one instance early in the process, an alderman reported, on television, that he had been to the State House and saw people printing Chelsea's new charter. His allegation clearly implied that the Chelsea Process was a sham. His comments, though pure fabrications, resounded throughout Chelsea. To protect the legitimacy of the process, the Charter Preparation Team selected four of its members to go to the next Board of Aldermen's meeting. They made public statements regarding the work they were doing on the charter, the issues under discussion, the options under review, and when the community could expect a draft charter. The legitimacy of the process, articulated by a Chelsea public, thus countered the rantings of an individual.

Another threat arose during discussions of the composition of the city council. The team had been discussing the options of 9, 11, or 13 councilors, when an article appeared on the front page of the *Boston Globe*'s Metro section, which quoted an unnamed source "familiar with the decision-making process" as saying there might be as large as a 15-member council. The Charter Preparation Team had never entertained the option of 15. At the next team meeting, many of its members themselves questioned the legitimacy of the process. Some thought they were being used to create support for decisions that had already been made in the receiver's office.

The mediator, whose role evolved into the protector of the process, went to the next meeting with a memo clarifying the receiver's intentions. A section of the memo read, "I have received assurances that there is no 'predisposed charter.' The receiver expressed to me his continuing confidence in this process. He believes that the charter you develop will accurately represent the wishes of the community and thus is likely to be supported by the voters in a special election." Midway through the meeting, the Charter Preparation Team felt assured that the process continued to be legitimate. In addition, when the identity of the source of the *Boston Globe* article was traced to the receiver's office, the mediator discussed the problem with the receiver's chief of staff. At the next receiver's office staff meeting, the receiver told his staff, "None of you are to talk to reporters about this governance process at all, or you're gone."

A third attack came just prior to the public circulation of the draft charter. Another alderman, at another televised meeting, said that she had received a copy of the charter in her mailbox, and it was dated December 1, 1992—almost two years prior to the start of the Chelsea Process. "This proved," she said, "that it was a done deal." The document she had in hand was actually contracted for by the previous receiver and was rejected by the second receiver and the Aldermanic Subcommittee on Governance (of which she was a member) because it had been written without any public involvement. It was also markedly different from the draft completed by the Charter Preparation Team. In response, the Charter Preparation Team wrote a letter to the alderman asking her to publicly clarify her remarks. Behind the scenes they negotiated with her for a public apology to the team, they wrote a letter to the editor of the local paper, and two team members went to the next Board of Aldermen's meeting to again describe the work of the team. ➻

∞ COMMENTARY

Behind-the-scenes discussions are useful for many reasons. First, out of the public forum, people are much less likely to hold on to a position just because they have previously committed themselves to it. You lose face when you change your mind in public, but in private you can reconsider. Second, the potential for humiliation in a public forum raises anxieties in a way that is not usually good for the processes of thought. Third, once you have said something in public, it is not easy to take it back. An insult that slips out in anger in public is heard by all, and nothing the original speaker can do will remove it from the memories of everyone there. An insult that slips out in private can be immediately (or even a little later) retracted and an apology given, with far less permanent harm being done. People who have been insulted in public can remember the slight until their dying day. Behind-the-scenes negotiation allows intermediaries trusted by all parties to go around and talk with opponents individually, finding out what is most important to them and seeing if some other solution to their needs can be reached. Most important, a one-to-one conversation allows back-and-forth discussion of an issue, whereas the public form, which provides for as many as possible to have a say, encourages position taking and makes it hard for those concerned to fashion a solution that meets all the concerns of everyone involved.

Behind-the-scenes discussions are, however, often suspect. When trust is at a minimum, all parties often want to see everything that happens. "Sunshine" (in the sense of fully public deliberations) creates legitimacy while it destroys many of the conditions for thoughtful negotiation.

—Jane Mansbridge, *Political philosopher*

These attempts to create distractions from the goal of the Chelsea Process were met with conscious and deliberate actions. Without swift and accurate responses, the perception of the legitimacy of the process and, therefore, ongoing participation would have suffered. Maintaining the legitimacy of the process was a high priority for the mediator. To do so, she created opportunities to describe and identify process milestones. When there were actual attempts to derail the process, the mediator worked with those responsible for the process in the community to quickly develop and implement strategic responses. However, nothing the mediator could do was as powerful as the local public defending the process. The Charter Preparation Team became a powerful force in the community. Even those opposed to the process dared not attack the team's legitimacy. ∞

∞ COMMENTARY

As the mediators of this process realize, legitimacy of the process is a high priority of mediators. Where tools developed in private settings are used in more public and regulated settings, mediators and facilitators have to be especially careful that democratic principles are observed. How decision rules are to be arrived at and implemented is crucial, and there must be enough public commitment to the process to be regarded as legitimate by governmental decision makers as well as by the governed. The supreme political irony, of course, is that often these creative processes have achieved greater democratic participation than older, more formal, processes, but the new process can be easily derailed by a few unhappy and legalistic parties. This, of course, goes to the importance of maintaining representativeness and participation by all the key stakeholders. In the case of some regulatory agencies, like zoning boards or other bodies, it is useful to get some preprocess approval of acceptability. I have mediated public disputes in which legislators, government agents, boards of directors, and others have participated in various ways, in part to ensure some formal governmental acceptability. This will not always be possible.

—Carrie J. Menkel-Meadow, *Legal scholar*

■ *Community Ownership and Commitment beyond the Process*

A successful public consensus building process results in community ownership of the outcome and a commitment to its implementation. Sustained participation throughout the process leads to a product that reflects the unique characteristics of the community involved. Strong participation by Chelsea residents maintained the process, and there is evidence to support both the assertion that the charter reflects local interests and that there exists a strong commitment to its implementation. ∞

∞ COMMENTARY

It is easy for mediators to confuse the use of consensual decision making with the building of a consensus. It is clear from the entire account of the Chelsea Process that participation was restricted to a very small group of Chelsea residents, a group that largely excluded elected officials and accidentally excluded one of the largest ethnic groups in the city. Moreover, the charter was accepted by a narrow majority of a small percentage of voters. Less than a fifth of Chelsea's citizens endorsed the work of the Charter Process, hardly grounds for believing that the process built a consensus rather than that a consensual process built a charter.

—Mark Kishlansky, *Historian*

The Charter Preparation Team gradually claimed ownership of the charter long before it was complete. As a result of its members' hard work, the charter had a decidedly local flavor to it. For example, the charter requires an extraordinary majority (8 out of 11) to hire and fire the city manager, it explicitly bars convicted felons from holding elected office, and it makes absolutely no mention of a mayor—not even a ceremonial mayor. These decisions reflect the pain Chelseans had experienced because of former corrupt officials. ●●

∽ COMMENTARY

It is instructive that only in the three-quarters supermajority necessary for the selection and removal of the city manager is there any carryover between the processes that were used to create the charter and the processes by which the charter governs the community. It is not clear from the account whether there were ever any suggestions during the drafting process that aldermen use consensual methods to determine certain kinds of resource allocations, like school funding or budgeting. In this case, the process was not viewed as a model for future government but rather as a technique for gaining participation, raising morale, and educating citizens. These are not insignificant goals or achievements, but it remains unclear how they will affect issues like cronyism, corruption, and inefficiency in local government in the future.

—Mark Kishlansky, *Historian*

In one instance, state custom prevailed over local preferences, a mistake that contributed to the 40 percent "no" vote in the special election. The word *voters* needed to be given precise meaning in the definitions section of the charter. Many wanted the definition to include "citizen of the United States of America." Due to time pressures, the Charter Preparation Team accepted the proposal to adopt the words of the Massachusetts Constitution: "as defined by the laws of the Commonwealth, including but not limited to residency, age and citizenship requirements of voters" (Chelsea City Charter, 1994, Section 9-4 [l]). As a result, some in Chelsea exploited rifts between old and new immigrant groups by arguing that "the charter doesn't even define voters as U.S. citizens." This was especially important because of a prior proposal to allow noncitizens to vote in local elections.

The consensus process officially ended when the Charter Preparation Team signed the top sheet of the charter, attesting to their consensus, and presented it to the receiver. After it was passed in the special election, approved by the Massachusetts State Legislature, and signed into law by the governor, the commitment of the community beyond the consensus building process became clear.

To begin with, 44 candidates ran for 18 elective offices. In the previous election, two of nine aldermanic seats were uncontested. In the first election guided by the new charter, citizens elected the most diverse legislative body in the city's history. The 11-member council included four women and three minorities (one woman): two Hispanics and one African American. Previously, the Board of Aldermen had two women and two minorities (one woman). ●●

∽ COMMENTARY

Again, no Asians seem to have been elected. It is unclear from the case whether any even ran for office.

—Jane Mansbridge, *Political philosopher*

As an "only in Chelsea" would have it, a man who won an at-large city council seat declined the position to maintain his Conservation Commission appointment. According to the charter, the resulting vacancy was to be filled by the next top vote-getter in the at-large race. The seat was therefore to go to a Hispanic woman, leaving as the runner-up a Caucasian man, who had been an alderman in the previous term. When he tried to interpret the charter in a way that would allow him to assume the vacant position, members of the Charter Preparation Team weighed in and publicly discussed the intent of the vacancy section of the charter. The former alderman backed down, and Chelsea-watchers expressed hope at the change in community conduct. Having discussed, deliberated, and decided every detail of the charter, the Chelsea residents of the Charter Preparation Team became protectors of the charter.

■ *Limits of the Process*

With the city in receivership and the receiver's absolute support, the Chelsea Process was temporarily protected from politics as usual, with locally elected officials limited to an advisory role. Some members of the Board of Aldermen attempted to derail the process that they perceived as threatening to their power. They did so through strategies of deceit, misinformation, and, finally, negative campaigning prior to the special election. Had they real power to pass ordinances, however, they might have successfully sabotaged the process. Therefore, a city akin to Chelsea that is not in receivership would likely face greater difficulty in using a public consensus building process to draft a city charter.

In addition, although Chelsea's local democracy had been suspended, political forces at the state level continued to operate. During the process, these forces had little clout because of the consensus decision-making rule—there were simply too many people from too many political and social sectors to try to control. However, there is evidence to suggest that this was not the case after the election of the new, 11-member council. Some of those elected had strong ties to state officials, who may have been able to wield some influence over the selection of the city manager.

Thus, politics as usual and power relationships have a potentially great impact on a consensus process that seeks to enable a city to govern itself. The power-clique that benefits from limited participation will seek to protect its "turf." Receivership can simplify this matter during the process but cannot intercede once the new political system is up and running. ∽

∽ COMMENTARY

As the mediators of the Chelsea Process realize, one of the most important aspects of democratic consensus processes in local government is to ensure that the energy created by these unique forms of integrative problem solving is sustained. The first time any new process is used, there may be great enthusiasm and participation, but what happens when the facilitators and mediators go home? In an ideal consensus building process, the participants have been educated to new ways of citizen involvement. They have learned how to negotiate, how to form and deal with coalitional politics, and how to represent themselves. But in a community like Chelsea, typical of many in the United States, how can the accretion back toward corruption or the dominance of a particular economic or other political force continually be resisted to ensure continued democratic participation? Where elective politics have failed, we are now trying out a variety of alternative processes for empowering local communities. The challenge remains to keep these processes vital, flexible, real, truly representative, and legitimate without simultaneously imposing too much formalistic structure.

—Carrie J. Menkel-Meadow, *Legal scholar*

■ *Epilogue*

On September 11, 1997 the front page of the *Boston Globe* Business section led with the headline "7-story, $13 million hotel planned for Chelsea" (Kindleberger, 1997). According to the article, the hotel, to be developed by a national, Houston-based corporation, will be a "symbol of the hard-luck city's renaissance."

Since the end of its receivership, Chelsea has balanced three municipal budgets, produced an ambitious capital improvement program, increased its tax base, opened new schools, and reduced its crime rate. It has stabilized financially and administratively, and past daily crises have given way to general routine. According to the city solicitor, "It's boring here now!"

Observers regard city hall as professional and as having the capacity to translate city council decisions into constructive policy and action. The residents seem to have had a hand in this turnaround. Said Guy Santagate, the city manager, "While I can't document it, I feel that people are more involved today" (Gentile, 1996).

Chelsea's residents are showing newfound political will and cooperation. Since the adoption of the new charter, the number of neighborhood associations has grown from 2 to 10. These associations are credited with pressuring the city to begin a Quality of Life program, which involves numerous city departments. Chelsea's citizens also appear set to win a political battle fought to keep an asphalt plant from locating in the city. The residents want a cleaner industry. In the past, such a plant would probably have moved in, and people would have announced their familiar refrain, "We always get dumped on." Today, they are effectively putting forward a unified political will.

However, Chelsea does not lack political challenges. In November 1997, the city held its first municipal elections since the end of the receivership. (The 1994 elections were held prior to the end of the receivership.) A number of the elected candidates had not run for elective office in the past, but included in that group is a former police captain, tried on corruption charges, and ultimately convicted of tax evasion. The charter prohibits someone convicted of violating the public trust during city employment from taking office. Since his election, city hall has requested a legal finding from the state attorney general based on the charter provision.

Another challenge ahead will be selecting a replacement for the city's outgoing police chief, a sophisticated criminal justice executive of national stature. Observers say there will be political pressures to choose an insider, just as there will be political pressures to hold a fair and open selection process.[5]

In sum, the evidence suggests the Chelsea Charter Consensus Process did succeed in increasing positive political activity among Chelsea residents. ⬦

∞ COMMENTARY

The use of consensus building processes in the political arena is both the most promising and the most potentially problematic of all its applications. Where, as in Chelsea, the conventional democratic processes had failed, through corruption, nonuse, alienation, patronage, and budget problems, alternative processes are clearly necessary. Here they have been (so far) successful at building alternative institutions, training new leaders, and demonstrating new ways of making decisions. Consensus building processes, then, are particularly useful in local government settings, be they full governmental and legislative processes, block grant budget allocations, environmental and zoning siting issues, labor-management disputes, or even in single-crisis management situations. They can enable populations to reengage in democratic deliberations and participation in the political system. They can balance interest groups and invite new players and stakeholders to the table, and they can educate and empower new generations of leadership.

—Carrie J. Menkel-Meadow, *Legal scholar*

However, the learning continues as Chelseans are confronted with an ongoing set of choices that will influence whether the city will continue to be livable and attractive for development or whether it will repeat its past destructive ways. ⬦

∞ COMMENTARY

Many features of Chelsea's "livability" are nonexcludable goods. They are best supplied by a populace that willingly pays taxes, reports crimes, attends PTA meetings, and volunteers. That willing cooperation must, however, be supplemented by the actions of a legitimate government that exercises sufficient coercion on the noncooperators that the cooperators are not taken for suckers.

—Jane Mansbridge, *Political philosopher*

∞ COMMENTARY

I regard the use of consensus building processes in local government as one of the most exciting, yet difficult, developments in the American democratic process. How adaptive our formal system of government is to full participation and creative, integrative solutions and how energetic our overburdened, hardworking citizens can be remains the challenge of the future.

—Carrie J. Menkel-Meadow, *Legal scholar*

∞ COMMENTARY

Consensus has many drawbacks as a decision mechanism. It takes a lot of time. It lends itself to repetition, as new entrants join or new facts arise, and the repetition not only loses more time but also undermines patience and morale. Consensus creates great temptations for imprecision. To get an agreement everyone can live with, participants find language that means different things to different people. Consensus sometimes leads to deadlock, a win for the status quo. Some forms of consensus create subtle pressures on the minorities to go along, so that they may not even be aware of their combined strength. These forms usually also leave little historical record of minority concerns, intensity, and numbers.

In this case, however, these drawbacks seem to have been outweighed by the advantages of consensus. A consensus process that secures the genuine agreement of every party concerned is the most legitimate decision procedure imaginable. It guarantees not only acquiescence but at least cognitive commitment. In cases where every party concerned has also participated in forging the consensus, it guarantees emotional commitment as well. The process often also builds emotional bonds between participants, making them more likely from then on to make the others' goods their own. Moreover, having paid so much, in energy, time, and emotion, to bring the consensus about, cognitive dissonance makes it likely that those who have made the investment will value the outcome, usually more than others who have not made the investment. Consensus done well will also produce unity, encourage mutual caring and listening, and elicit more information than other processes. Consensus makes the most sense when legitimacy, commitment, unity, mutual caring, and synergistically created information are extremely important.

The most efficient forms of cooperation to produce nonexcludable goods are those that can build primarily on voluntary commitment to do one's share, and need only a minimum of coercion to discourage shirking. If consensus is the best, or one of the best, ways of building that voluntary commitment, we might conclude that it is better to build more consensual procedures into our everyday governing structure than to have to set up extragovernmental bodies in an ad hoc fashion in times of crisis or special need.

—Jane Mansbridge, *Political philosopher*

■ Notes

1. Boston University, headed by John Silber, entered into a 10-year contract with Chelsea to manage its entire school system. This contract was approved by the Chelsea School Committee, an elected body.

2. Lewis H. Spence served as deputy receiver during James Carlin's eight-month term as the first receiver.

3. See Chelsea City Charter of 1994, Section 2-9 Prohibitions. In November 1997, a former Chelsea police captain, who was convicted of tax evasion that stemmed from corrupt activities, was elected to the city council. He was prevented from assuming this position by the attorney general, based on a request from city officials.

4. The only group that did not formally participate on the Charter Preparation Team was the Southeast Asian community. Both a Vietnamese man and a Cambodian man agreed to be on the team, but came only to the preliminary meeting. It is the mediator's sense that if time had not been as constrained, additional inroads into the Asian community could have been made. The summary of the draft charter was, in fact, translated into Khmer and distributed throughout the Cambodian community.

5. Authority to interpret Massachusetts city charters rests with the attorney general.

■ References

Chelsea City Charter. (1994).

Claiborne, W. (1994, September 7). Bringing a battered city back from the brink: Consensus-building process inspires citizen involvement and a new charter in Chelsea, Mass. *Washington Post.*

Gentile, M. (1996, January). Consensus helps Chelsea, Mass., forge new city charter and return to self rule. *Consensus,* p. 1.

Harwood Group. (1991). *Citizens and politics: A view from Main Street America.* Dayton, OH: Kettering Foundation.

Kindleberger, R. (1997, September 11). 7-story, $13 million hotel planned for Chelsea. *Boston Globe,* Business section, p. 1.

A public voice . . . governing America. (1993). Dayton, OH: Kettering Foundation.

■ *Further Reading*

Mathews, D. (1994). *Politics for people: Finding a responsible public voice.* Chicago: University of Illinois Press.

Miller, K. (1989, October/November). "Negotiated investment" pays off for two regions. *Consensus,* p. 1.

Putnam, R. D. (1993). *Making democracy work: Civic traditions in modern Italy.* Princeton, NJ: Princeton University Press.

Susskind, L., & Cruikshank, J. (1987). *Breaking the impasse: Consensual approaches to resolving public disputes.* New York: Basic Books.

4

AFFORDABLE HOUSING MEDIATION

Building Consensus for Regional Agreements in the Hartford Area

■ Lawrence Susskind
■ Susan L. Podziba

The project that is the subject of this case study is the result of a 1988 Connecticut state program that initiated a consensus building process to address the housing crisis in the area. After scores of housing bills died in legislative committees, a compromise bill passed, creating a pilot program to encourage municipalities, with the help of mediators, to negotiate regional affordable housing plans. As required by the legislation, the secretary of the Office of Policy and Management, together with the commissioner of housing, sponsored two pilot projects—one in the Capitol Region (Hartford) and one in the Greater Bridgeport Region—to increase housing opportunities for low- and moderate-income families. The legislature allocated $50,000 to pay professional mediators who could assist the communities in reaching consensus. By law, the compacts had to be unanimously adopted by all communities in a region, otherwise, there could be no agreement.

In the Capitol Region, which is the focus of this case study, representatives of the 29 communities reached an agreement on a fair share housing compact that would increase affordable housing by as many as 6,400 units over the next five years. Similarly, the Greater Bridgeport Region's representatives from six communities reached an agreement to provide more than 3,000 units of affordable housing under a five-year plan. Every community in both regions committed to supply a specific number of units of affordable housing. The compacts were negotiated over six-month periods, and the negotiations were followed by local ratification processes.

Municipal, regional, state, and private interests were all taken into account in the compacts. Home rule was respected, while the need to respond to regional housing problems was met. The compact stresses flexibility. Each municipality can pursue an approach to providing affordable housing that will maintain its character and respect the unique constraints it faces.

To begin the statewide pilot program in Connecticut, a request for proposals to participate was sent to all 18 regional planning agencies in the state by the Connecticut Office of Policy and Management (OPM). To be seriously considered, an agency had to supply letters of support from the mayor or first selectman of every city and town in the region. Five regions submitted complete applications. A committee composed of officials from the OPM and the Connecticut Department of Housing (DOH) chose the Capitol Region and the Greater Bridgeport Region for the pilot program.

Once the two participating regions were identified, the OPM organized a search committee to select mediators to assist with the regional negotiations. The search committee included representatives from the OPM, DOH, the Capitol Region Council of Governments, the Greater Bridgeport Regional Planning Agency, and member towns from both regions. Prospective mediators were asked to submit draft work plans and qualifications. After follow-up interviews with a short list of candidates, a team from Endispute, Incorporated, of Cambridge was selected to mediate the negotiations in both regions.

Although originally planning to choose different mediation teams for each region, the search committee selected the Endispute team for both, convinced that the overlap would allow a sharing of information on approaches that succeeded or failed in one region, insight that could save time for the other region. In the Capitol Region, Lawrence Susskind and Susan Podziba served as the mediators.

The selection process was difficult, in part, because most of the members of the selection committee had no experience with mediation. As a result, they had difficulty formulating the questions to ask the potential mediators. Second, they wanted a guaranteed product in a fixed time frame. The potential mediators knew only that the communities were looking for negotiation assistance. This made it difficult to prepare a precise work plan or schedule. During the interview sessions, the prospective mediators suggested possible scenarios, expounded on their past experience in similar situations, answered questions, addressed concerns, and, in essence, educated the members of the search committee about the process they were about to initiate.

A case study of one of the two pilot projects follows. It includes both descriptions and analyses of the negotiations in the Capitol Region. ➻

∽ COMMENTARY

Of the consensus building cases I have seen, this one comes closest to depicting the new forms of problem solving as an instrument and complement to the reform of public administration, rather than as a freestanding substitute for it. Consider from this vantage point the contrast between this story of affordable housing in Connecticut and the account of the investigation of putatively high cancer rates in Northern Oxford County, Maine that I analogized to mythic peace making in the American Western (see Case 2).

In Maine, the consensus builders are called in by a lone official, the director of the Bureau of Air Quality Control in the state's Department of Environmental Protection, and financed by an ad hoc grant from the Environmental Protection Agency. After "jump-starting" the consensus building, the official presence recedes to the point of invisibility, and institutionalized civilization reappears only at the end of the story, when the Northern Oxford County Coalition is folded into an emerging program on the self-monitoring of community health fostered by the World Health Organization.

In Connecticut, in contrast, the state legislature authorized the secretary of the OPM, together with the commissioner of housing, to select the two best proposals for increasing the supply of affordable housing from those submitted by various regional consortia of the local governments, and then to entrust operating direction of the winning programs to outside consensus builders. The consensus builders are in this case, therefore, best seen as general managers of experimental reform projects designed, in very general terms, by the legislature and specified, at somewhat higher resolution, by the immediate protagonists: the regional consortia of governments around Hartford and greater Bridgeport, which submitted the winning proposals.

In saying this, I don't mean to make of the consensus builders mere instruments of settled government policy. They were, after all, being asked to manage programs that were regarded as experimental precisely because no one could say in advance what goals ought to be set or what means chosen for obtaining them. Management of programs that have as their purpose the ongoing determination of their means and ends is certainly not traditional management, and still less bureaucratic public administration in any familiar sense.

But even if the consensus builders were not a mere tool of the government, neither were they the artificers or architects of the situation. The government in the Maine case was close to clueless. In Connecticut, it knew very well where to look for clues for new policies, and even where to look for "managers" of a new kind to make best use of the partial, available information, and uncover more. In principle, moreover, the government might at the time have constituted some internal unit to manage deliberations within and among the regional consortia. Or, assuming that this type of managerial task was then beyond its reach, government may have learned—not least through collaboration with the consensus builders—how to accomplish such things now. Is there any reason, after all, to think that government can learn enough about the limits of old forms of organization to authorize (competitively chosen) pilot projects, bring in outsiders to demonstrate new kinds of consultative management, and—having thus opened public administration in ways that would have been unthinkable a generation ago—yet be unable to learn to effect such management within its own ranks?

On this interpretation, *consensus building* is part of a larger movement that connects groups of citizens with concerns for particular areas of policy with corresponding government entities in a collaborative search for surprising answers to the problems that join them: answers that are politically practicable in part just because their novelty puts them outside the bounds of familiar conflicts of principle and self-interest. The story of affordable housing in the Hartford and Greater Bridgeport areas illustrates the power of that collaboration by showing how, with relatively simple means—competitive choice of pilot projects, consensus building deliberation with project groups, and pooling of results across them—it is possible to uncover novel and workable solutions while forming the political determination to try them in practice.

—Charles F. Sabel, *Political economist*

■ Description of the Compact Negotiations

The Capitol Region committee was composed of representatives from the 29 communities in the Hartford area and three agencies: the state OPM, the state DOH, and the Capitol Region Council of Governments (CRCOG). The municipalities that took part in the negotiations were Andover, Avon, Bloomfield, Bolton, Canton, East Granby, East Hartford, East Windsor, Ellington, Enfield, Farmington, Glastonbury, Granby, Hartford, Hebron, Manchester, Marlborough, Newington, Rocky Hill, Simsbury, Somers, South Windsor, Suffield, Tolland, Vernon, West Hartford, Wethersfield, Windsor, and Windsor Locks.

Although some communities had more than one person attending the negotiation sessions, one individual from each community was designated the spokesperson who represented the group for the purpose of determining consensus.

At the beginning, the committee had no specific direction and no clear concept of the product that would result from the negotiations. Through discussion, the group decided to produce a compact, containing a commitment from each community to supply a specified number of affordable housing units over a five-year period.

Beginning the Negotiations: A Preliminary Meeting

Endispute and CRCOG convened a preliminary meeting to explain the consensus building process to all the municipal representatives in the Capitol Region. The goal was to generate a list of the municipalities' concerns relative to affordable housing and to begin developing protocols that would govern the negotiations.

At the start of the meeting, each representative explained his or her community's interest in creating affordable housing opportunities and the limitations it faced. Some of the issues raised at this meeting included shortages of open land, environmental constraints, and a lack of public utilities, limiting the number of multiunit dwellings a town could build. Other concerns raised were the need for fairness in allocating responsibility across the region, maintaining community character, and respecting local autonomy.

Many suburban representatives were concerned about being forced to supply housing for residents of Hartford's shelters. However, the Hartford representative set a congenial tone at the outset of the negotiating when she stated, "If each community would take care of its own residents, Hartford's burden would be eased."

In other words, if fewer suburbanites moved into Hartford's less expensive housing, thereby reducing upward pressure on rents, the city would be better able to provide for its own residents. Once she made this statement, a number of the representatives from the suburban and rural communities felt more at ease. They did not feel they were being pressed to "solve Hartford's problem," only to tend to their own needs. ❧

❧ COMMENTARY

Although the suburban representatives may have heaved a sigh of relief that they were not going to be asked to take on Hartford's problems, the underlying inequalities in income and housing prices that created the affordable housing crisis remained. If each community, rich and poor, takes care only of itself, there will be no collective benefit to the poor communities produced by collaboration with the rich. For such a system to improve the quality of life for poor people, there needs to be some evocation of a larger collective good that would encompass rich as well as poor by improving the quality of housing for the poor.

—Sally Engle Merry, *Anthropologist*

Ground Rules

To ensure that the participants and the mediators understood their respective roles and responsibilities, ground rules were needed. These covered such things as the expected level of, and responsibility for, outreach to the public; decision-making rules that the group would adhere to; interactions with the media; summaries of the meetings; the relationship of the pilot program to other government housing activities; and limits on the mediators' activities.

In essence, the ground rules were designed to encourage mutual understanding among the representatives and an atmosphere of joint problem solving. For example, the municipal representatives agreed to seek consensus rather than make decisions by a majority vote. This meant that if one community objected to a particular point, a change had to be made to accommodate that community. Votes were never taken. Given that the regional fair housing compact had to be adopted unanimously by all the municipalities, consensus was the only plausible decision-making rule. However, this meant that any municipality could have effectively ended the negotiations at any point in the proceedings by deciding not to be part of the compact.

With respect to the media, the ground rules explicitly stated that representatives were free to make statements to the press regarding their own opinions, but they were restricted from attributing statements to others involved in the compact negotiations. If an article or news story misrepresented a representative, that individual promised to report such an occurrence to the group. (Indeed, this occurred on one occasion, and the representative reported the actual statements he had made.)

Bimonthly Meetings

Beginning in January 1989, negotiating sessions were held every two weeks for six months. During the "off" weeks, the subcommittee met to draft proposals for presentation to the larger group. Meetings were held in the South Congregational Church in Hartford, and, fortunately, no funerals were scheduled during the Wednesday morning meetings. (We were told by the church at the outset that funerals would take precedence over compact negotiations!) Each meeting generally focused on one or two issues, such as municipal targets for housing units or the definition of affordable housing.

Negotiations

From the early discussions at the preliminary meeting and individual follow-up phone calls,[1] an *agenda of concerns* was developed. The agenda of concerns included the following categories: definition of affordable housing, formula for determining targets, environmental and land use constraints, maintaining community character, "affordable housing for whom?" question, "what is a regional approach?" question, possible solutions, funding for new initiatives, and statutory deadline. It incorporated all the interests and concerns raised by the representatives and provided a focal point for future meetings and discussions.

At the outset of negotiations, the representatives grappled with the definition of affordable housing. They discussed what was meant by *affordable,* identified target populations, and assessed both regional and local needs for additional housing units. The Capitol Region ultimately adopted the state's definition: Affordable housing is affordable when residential costs are not greater than 30 percent of gross household income and that income is below or equal to the regional median income. (In 1989, median family income in the Capitol Region was $45,500 according to statistics provided by the U.S. Department of Housing and Urban Development.)

The discussions of the definition of *affordable* began an ongoing education process for participants regarding the target population for affordable housing units. Many came to the negotiations equating affordable housing with public housing and were shocked to find that most municipal employees, and often the representatives' own children, would benefit directly from the housing opportunities actually intended by the state. ❧

❧ COMMENTARY

This turnabout captures nicely the provocatively disorienting power of problem-solving deliberation. Delegates arrive at a meeting expecting to reenact an old fight over the respective rights of welfare recipients and suburban homeowners. They discover, instead, an unexpected connection between the situation of some of their own children and those on welfare. Of course, the connection cuts both ways: Many suburbanites will decide to define their contribution to the protection of the vulnerable as the protection of their own children, friends, or neighbors. But others will begin to wonder if worlds until then taken to be utterly distinct might not be connected in yet other ways they have only begun to suspect. Either way, as we will see, "affordable housing" comes, suddenly and surprisingly, to be a problem relevant to every community, and once this commonality is acknowledged, the tools developed to address the problem in one setting can be applied, with new effects, in others.

—Charles F. Sabel, *Political economist*

Once the committee members understood and agreed on the definition of *affordable* and the scope of target populations, the representatives developed a statement of principle, which became the preamble to the compact. The committee continued to revise the preamble throughout the negotiations as additional concerns were raised.

Toward the close of the negotiations, Hartford's representative proposed the addition of an antidiscrimination paragraph to the preamble. This led to an intense debate over whether the committee should adopt a principle of *nonexclusion* or *nonpreference*. A principle of nonexclusion would allow anyone meeting the income criteria to apply for a housing unit in any community. However, a municipality would be free to set eligibility criteria, including criteria that granted a preference for local residents in ranking the applicants. Nonpreference, on the other hand, would disallow such preference. Several representatives felt strongly that a town should be able to give preference to its residents if the units are built with town revenues. Hartford's representative, however, felt that such preference requirements in suburban communities would restrict housing mobility for Hartford's residents. The limited affordable housing opportunities in suburban areas would also force newcomers to move into the city, thereby pushing Hartford's housing costs even higher.

The Hartford representatives circulated a proposal that would have allowed towns to give preference to residents for 50 percent of the units and keep 50 percent available to the public at large. This was rejected out of concern for how constituents would react to a blatant nonpreference clause in the compact. Instead, the smaller towns agreed to a nonexclusion clause. This meant merely that towns could not explicitly exclude anyone applying for housing in their community because of the applicant's place of residence. ➤

➤ COMMENTARY

As this discussion indicates, the issue of which community would provide affordable housing for which other community's members was indeed a key problem. There was clearly a desire on the part of the Hartford representative to provide housing options for its residents in the suburbs and not to make affordable units available only to existing members of a community. It appears that the suburban towns won, retaining their ability to give preference to their own residents if they so choose. Despite the emphasis on consensus building, here the wealthier suburban towns prevailed over the city with its poorer population. Situations of unequal power pose challenges to consensus building strategies. Developing a collective sense of responsibility, finding some trades that will benefit both, or imposing a decision seem to be the primary ways of bypassing this difficulty. In this situation, however, there were clearly efforts to split the difference, to come up with intermediate positions such as the 50-50 proposal, which might have produced a more consensual outcome.

—Sally Engle Merry, *Anthropologist*

The most difficult question concerned the numerical targets, or goals, each community would be expected to achieve. A working group met and developed no fewer than 16 options describing fair share allocation formulas. Several formulas stressed a local approach to tallying each community's unmet housing need. Other formulas began with an estimate of regional need and allocated proportionate shares to each locality. The municipalities quickly chose a formula that began with an estimate of local need and gave them credit for past affordable housing efforts. This option, as it turned out, stipulated the lowest targets for all the municipalities except Hartford. To accommodate Hartford and gain its support, the representatives agreed to let Hartford meet a lower percentage of its local need than the other communities. ➛

➛ COMMENTARY

Lest you think that this sort of indeterminacy, and the kinds of debates over indicators and measures of progress to which it gives rise, is a feature of public administration that distinguishes it from the world of private enterprise, where profit provides a sure guide to action and measure of progress: The more private firms make operations transparent by having project teams provide rich information to suppliers, clients, and, of course, each other, the more measures of performance (growth rate, market share, proportion of products introduced in the past five years, and on and on) proliferate, and the more debate about which potential measures (and the goals with which they are associated) are indeed relevant to the firm's situation itself becomes an integral part of the discussion of broad strategic questions. Thus, debate about whether a company should sacrifice current profits to increase market share or innovation rate is central to debate over what kind of company it wants to be, just as debate over formulas for allocating the burden of supplying affordable housing is central to clarifying different understanding of affordable housing.

On reflection, this connection between performance measures and strategy is unsurprising. If you start with very general goals (increase affordable housing, build a competitive minivan), you will naturally be debating large goals when you debate specific subtargets, and vice versa.

—Charles F. Sabel, *Political economist*

Each community eventually agreed to meet at least 25 percent of its local shortfall. The city of Hartford, however, was asked to meet only 12.5 percent of its local shortfall. No community was expected to meet a target greater than 35 percent of the annual average number of building permits issued in the previous five years. This capped the number of units for four of the largest municipalities (below the 25 percent level). The communities also agreed to specific subtargets for very low-income households (annual income below 50 percent of the regional median income); low-income households (annual income between 50 and 80 percent of regional median income); and moderate-income households (annual income of 90 percent to 100 percent of regional median income). This approach led to the formula discussed in detail below.

Before finalizing the targets, the group turned its attention to possible strategies that communities could use to meet their targets. The Greater Bridgeport Region Affordable Housing Compact Committee had created an extensive "menu" of strategies designed to increase affordable housing opportunities. This menu was revised and adopted by the Capitol Region and focused on five different approaches: production, regulatory changes, leadership, taxation policies, and financing mechanisms. ●●

∽ COMMENTARY

A lot just happened all of a sudden, and without being able to say exactly what or why, I want to freeze the frame and speculate on the goings-on. First, the Greater Bridgeport wing of the project, mentioned at the outset but in the background since then, has just made an entrance. Second, we learn that while the consensus builders in the Hartford area were discussing goals and ways to measure them, the group in Bridgeport was making an inventory of means. Third, revised and grouped into five broad categories (regulatory changes, taxation policies, etc.), this "menu" of strategies is adopted by the Hartford group and will allow customization or contextualization of affordable housing policy to suit the needs of different locals in that region.

This is, as I see it, significant, because it underlines an aspect of consensus building as collaborative exploration of possibilities that is—for reasons connected to Western-hero aspects of the consensus builders' self-conception, as well as the trajectory of the reform of public administration—underexposed in this and other cases: the need to pool local experiences so that problem solvers in one area can learn from the experience of problem solvers in another (and also to establish various kinds of public accountability, more in a moment on this). So long as government was, as in Maine, next to clueless about how to reorient itself in the face of problems too complex for central and uniform resolution, projects of the consensus building type were likely to arise in isolation from one another, more or less in response to the vagaries of particular, farsighted or desperate officials. Comparing projects would have been a distant prospect, because there were few projects to begin with, and fewer still that were, accidentally, comparable. The focus on the local, defined as a place rich in history but wanting in institutions, that goes with the self-conception of the peaceable paladin could only reinforce the proclivity to focus energies inward.

Once, however, government begins—however haltingly—to foster consensus building in a systematic way, creating many potentially comparable projects by design, then comparison of experience across participating areas or units is necessary for the same reason that the exploration of difference is imperative with any one of them: It reveals possibilities and tensions that otherwise would go unnoticed, and so sparks the discussions from which innovative solutions—the ones that point beyond current blockages—are fashioned. Thus, the Connecticut legislature presumably thought that it would not only be politically expedient but also significantly informative to have two regions included in the pilot project, rather than one. By the same token, the legislature was probably, as noted, trying not only to save money but also to encourage the exchange of information by hiring one consensus building consultancy to manage both areas. Hence, deliberately or not, the legislature created the conditions that gave rise to the division of labor between projects that ultimately proved so useful in Hartford. How, if at all, does consensus building as portrayed in this *Handbook* need to be reconceived to take full advantage of such possibilities as government starts to provide them, or to help find alternative ways of pooling experience when programs do not directly encourage it?

—Charles F. Sabel, *Political economist*

Discussions of strategy revealed an overwhelming desire for each community to select approaches that meet its special needs. As a result, each community was allowed to select from the menu the strategies that it preferred. Because the compact communities had committed to meeting their numerical targets in a way that incorporates environmental, economic, transportation, and infrastructure constraints, the array of techniques the communities intend to use is quite diverse. For example, one town might construct new housing while, in another, subsidies for residents in existing units might be sufficient to reach the target. One community may stress home ownership while another may prefer rental units.

Implementation

Each compact municipality agreed to be accountable to the others. The Policy Board of CRCOG will monitor implementation of the compact. The agreement contains provisions for midcourse correction since issues may arise during implementation that were not foreseen in the negotiations.

To ensure implementation, the representatives stressed the need for technical and financial assistance from the state and federal government and the private sector. In response, the state of Connecticut set aside $5 million of its 1990 DOH budget specifically to assist compact communities. While this was considered a helpful start,

Capitol Region communities plan to lobby the state legislature for $7.5 million per year in housing assistance funds for the life of the compact.

Even with this higher level of state support, many communities must depend on private sector assistance to meet their goals. Most will reexamine their zoning regulations and consider density bonuses to developers who are willing to create mixed-income developments or, in some other way, ensure the long-term affordability of a percentage of newly developed units. Towns that own land may create land trusts and hire private developers to build affordable housing on town land. While such units will sell at market rates, long-term affordability can be ensured through continued town ownership of the land, which will be leased to home buyers. Highly developed towns will focus on rehabilitating existing units or substandard units. They may convert unused public buildings, such as schools, or other buildings they can acquire, such as old factories, into housing for low- and moderate-income households.

Ratification

According to the legislation that created the affordable housing pilot program, the compact could not become binding until the local governing bodies of all 29 communities formally ratified it. For some, this meant seeking a vote at the town meeting.

Others had to achieve city council approval.

The compact originally set January 31, 1990 as the deadline for ratification. By January 24, 1990, 20 of the 29 Capitol Region municipalities had approved the compact, 4 had defeated motions to approve it, and 5 had not yet acted on it.

At a January 24 meeting, the Policy Board, the body charged with monitoring implementation of the compact, voted to extend the ratification deadline to March 31, 1990 because many of the municipalities had new administrations as of January 1. This gave towns that had not yet voted on the compact an opportunity to do so. The Policy Board members also hoped some of the communities that had voted against ratification would reconsider.

By March 2, all of the Capitol Region municipalities had voted on the compact. It was approved by 25 municipalities and rejected by 4. One of the communities that had previously rejected the compact reversed its vote, but another town rejected it. The four that ultimately rejected the compact were East Hartford, Bolton, Windsor, and Windsor Locks.

Thus, according to the unanimous-decision rule set out in the act that established the Regional Fair Housing Compact Pilot Program, the Capitol Region compact could not be implemented. However, CRCOG's Executive Committee and the Policy Board wanted to move forward with the compact. On February 28, the CRCOG Policy Board unanimously adopted the following resolution:

> The CRCOG Policy Board supports an amendment to Public Act 88-334 to allow for establishment of a regional housing compact among 75 percent of the municipalities in the compact region.

The state Select Committee on Housing then drafted a bill incorporating the recommended changes. Municipal representatives who participated in the compact negotiations testified in support of the bill. The executive director of the Greater Bridgeport Regional Planning Agency requested the decision rule be changed to 65 percent given that only four of the six Greater Bridgeport municipalities had ratified the compact by that time.

In April, the bill passed to change the rule to require 65 percent approval of the member communities. The CRCOG Policy Board and the Regional Planning Commission then adopted the compact as part of its regional plan. As a result, 25 Capitol Region municipalities are developing their affordable housing plans as agreed to in the compact. Work has also commenced to develop regulations to govern the Infrastructure Trust Fund. This fund was created by the same act that established the pilot program and will provide resources to compact communities for their housing programs. ◆◆

◌◆ COMMENTARY

Again, this discussion shows the importance of renegotiating all the categories to reach a consensual agreement. The key to developing affordable housing plans seems to be developing a broad range of alternatives through which particular communities can meet their goals. Moreover, when agreement was not unanimous among the towns who participated in the negotiations, even the ground rules under which the project began were changed. Instead of requiring unanimous agreement, the conditions were changed by the legislature to accommodate a 65 percent agreement rate among constituent towns. It is the ability to keep everything open to renegotiation and to find new ways to split apart issues and redefine them that seems critical in this process.

—Sally Engle Merry, *Anthropologist*

■ *Analysis*

Representation

In most circumstances, a mediator begins a case by identifying the stakeholding parties (whose presence helps to ensure the durability of any eventual agreement) and securing their commitment to participate. In this case, the legislation outlined specifically the full range of participants: representatives from each municipality, from the regional planning agency, and from the OPM and the DOH. When the mediators asked whether the scope of the participants should be broadened beyond the original group, the OPM and DOH officials resisted. The local representatives saw no reason to include nongovernmental organizations at the table. The mediators suggested that interest groups such as housing advocates, antidevelopment groups, labor unions, the chamber of commerce, and perhaps the American Civil Liberties Union (ACLU) could be invited, but the representatives preferred that interest groups not be included. The governmental stakeholders pointed out that they were the only ones named in the legislation. ❧

❧ COMMENTARY

In this little skirmish over who is to be at the discussion table, we catch a glimpse of the larger, emergent conflict between what I called, in the Maine case, the notion of *rolling* or *rippling representation* associated with consensus building problem solving and familiar forms of representative democracy. The consensus builders start with an open-ended list of participants: labor unions, the chamber of commerce, and "perhaps" the ACLU. Aside from a general idea of maximizing relevant diversity (housing advocates, antidevelopment groups), there is no well-formed principle of inclusion or exclusion and, especially, no particular deference to elected officials. The elected officials, on the other hand, think that their election as local representatives and their nomination in the legislation authorizing the pilot projects give them impeccable and (nearly) exclusive rights to participate in the affordable housing deliberations. Are the consensus builders extending democracy by pressing for the inclusion of groups and viewpoints that might otherwise be ignored, or are they distending it by undermining the respect for the legitimacy of the vote and the legislative enactment?

This is, I think, a bad question, in the way of a false dichotomy, because it suggests that democracy has an essence that is either honored or defaced by the one vision of representation or the other. A more useful way to size up the situation, as I hint in the remarks on the Maine case, is to suppose that the very fact that discussion of these apparently contradictory alternatives could be so matter-of-fact is itself a small sign of a larger reorientation in the idea of democracy itself, away from territorial representation of interests and toward the kind of direct, practical deliberation that does the work in consensus building. But whatever the eventual trajectory of development, it is unlikely that the heterogeneous mix of principles that comes to light in this little debate about who's in and who's out will prove stable.

—Charles F. Sabel, *Political economist*

∽ COMMENTARY

A critical issue in all negotiations, of course, is who is at the table and who is not. Here, the beneficiaries of affordable housing and their advocates were not present, except as observers and in the public forum. How different would the process have been if there had been poor people desperate for housing in the negotiations, who might have told their stories of crisis and difficulty? What if they had described everyday problems of divorce, racial discrimination, arson, or aging in a way that evoked the sympathy of others around the table? If the goal is to build consensus, as it is in this process, it is both tempting and dangerous to keep those who would not go along away from the table.

—Sally Engle Merry, *Anthropologist*

The participants did agree to create other avenues to encourage participation by interested parties, such as public hearings and elaborate notification procedures, and to attract observers to all the negotiation sessions. People associated with the Urban League, the Hartford Neighborhood Coalition, and the Hartford Chamber of Commerce attended most of the meetings. However, these nongovernmental officials and others who observed the negotiation were offered no decision-making authority. If they did not agree with a particular proposal that all the committee members agreed to, the observers' only option was to convince at least one member of the negotiating committee to dissent.

A public forum was held one evening at the State Legislative Office Building in Hartford to gain still further input from "outside groups." About 50 people attended and raised issues such as the desirability of increasing municipal housing goals, targeting lower-income populations,

and addressing housing discrimination more aggressively. These issues were discussed at the next meeting of the compact negotiations, and revisions in the draft agreement were made to respond to all of the points raised at the forum.

Many of those who spoke at the public forum had attended the compact meetings and understood the consensus building process. As a result, the comments were introduced in such a way that the group could incorporate them. For example, the executive director of the Hartford Neighborhood Coalition announced her support for a proposal on local preference that had previously been offered by the Hartford representatives to the compact negotiating committee. The proposal was that 50 percent of a locality's affordable units would be available to local residents, and the other 50 percent would be available to anyone who applied. This was an indication of her familiarity with the process. On the other hand, an ACLU lawyer spoke and stated that preference should be abolished completely. The lawyer did not understand the

agreements that had gone on within the negotiating group. ◆◆

◌ COMMENTARY

Well, perhaps. But whatever this particular ACLU lawyer did or didn't understand about discussion within the negotiating group, the ACLU as an institution is, as I understand it, dedicated to connecting individual or local struggles for civil liberties to an extension of those liberties nationally (via reinterpretation of the state and federal constitutions), which in turn sets the stage for still more expansive local fights, and so on. The upshot is that part of what it means to be an ACLU lawyer is to worry, automatically, about the general implication in constitutional principle of local decisions or precedents. In this case, of course, a reasonable worry from this standpoint would be that, in agreeing to some principle of local preference in the allocation of affordable housing, one might be creating an obstacle, way down the road, to the full racial integration of the largely white suburbs. From the consensus building perspective, such worries about distant implications of principle come at the expense of problem solving in the here and now, and so betray a lack of understanding of what consensus building is about.

Here again I think it would be wrong to pick one side or the other in the dispute. Should concern with the "correct" interpretation of general and ambiguous principles (such as a right against discrimination) paralyze exploration of alternatives that might give surprising practical effect to the great idea? Plainly not. Should local decision making proceed in complete indifference to its implication for the emerging framework of background understandings that will, sooner or later, come to reshape local decision making itself? Plainly not. The way around this second false dichotomy is to find some method of connecting local decision making to broader discussion of possible changes in the background rules, and so establish a kind of accountability of each local to the others and the nation as a whole. Consensus building as depicted here neglects this possibility, for the same reasons, I think, that it neglects information pooling across projects more generally. Indeed, determining what general conclusions to draw from different local solutions is one of the main tasks of information pooling. This is not the place to show how such information pooling could address constitutional questions. But the intuition is that some progress in pooling would make it possible to give a fuller account of the ACLU lawyer's dilemma and suggest more fruitful ways of addressing it.

—Charles F. Sabel, *Political economist*

This may have been the same position held by the Hartford Neighborhood Coalition representative, but she had observed how issues were traded within the group in an effort to satisfy the concerns of all the participants.

Another important representation issue was the process used to select negotiating committee members from each locality. All representatives were designated by their chief elected officials. In some cases, especially the smaller rural communities such as

Marlborough and Suffield, the first select-man represented his own town. A member of the Hartford City Council and the city's director of housing and development represented Hartford. Many towns were represented by town planners. Others were represented by citizens who were either active in their communities or had direct interests in affordable housing (e.g., a developer of affordable housing with a background in public service, and a real estate broker). Thus, the group was quite diverse: Some had housing expertise, others were skilled in the art of politics, and still others were new to both fields and had to be educated by the group. The mediators sought to downplay differences in relative authority among members of the group. All were treated equally. To equalize the perceived status of the representatives, everyone was addressed by his or her first name, and name cards indicated only the person's name and the town he or she represented.

In many ways, the diversity of the group helped the negotiations. Different individuals had expertise to offer at particular sticking points. For example, housing experts were able to formulate the definition of affordable housing and inform the group about general rules of thumb regarding housing affordability for each income level. These members also explained different methods of financing housing development, indicating what had worked and what had failed in Connecticut. The politicians, on the other hand, wanted to skip over the planning issues they felt were politically inexpedient and demanded that other issues be given special consideration regardless of their technical significance. All in all, the diversity created a helpful dynamic.

The choice of individual representatives greatly affected the negotiations. Since personality and personal agendas shaped a great deal of the interaction, some representatives, for instance, were less than helpful. At least one citizen played a blocking role and tried to subvert the negotiations by asking the same questions all the time and causing the group to go in circles. When the group spoke about targets, she insisted it address strategies. After it addressed strategies, she still refused to discuss targets. At several points, the group went out of its way to satisfy her requests, which often made little sense and had little direct bearing on the compact. While her concerns were carefully addressed, she still refused at the last minute to initial a statement of support for the compact, committing to bring it back to her community for ratification. As a result, the CRCOG director of community development contacted the town's first selectman, who himself signed the statement of support.

Selection of the Mediators

The mediator selection process was difficult because, like many others interested in negotiated policy dialogues, the members of the search committee did not have a clear idea of the role of the mediators. Those who interviewed prospective mediators did not quite understand the process they were getting into or the skills they were seeking. In fact, the terms of the contract (i.e., a six-month limitation and a request for a precise work plan before the first meeting) were akin to a patient calling the doctor on the phone and asking for a cure before mentioning even general symptoms. The mediators had not seen the patient, so to speak, so it was difficult to guarantee an outcome in an explicit time frame.

This is a major issue for others who may want to implement a similar compact negotiation. The search committee's concern was well-founded: They wanted to know what they would be buying. However, the mediators were forced to somewhat predict the service they would be offering when, in fact, the nature of that service depends on the specifics of the case. Although mediation has never been applied to affordable housing in quite this way before, the search committee wanted to know that the process would fit the time frame and the budget, which were preset. The mediators were able to provide a generic work plan, but it included an explanation of the ways in which it might have to change. While the mediators agreed to a fixed-price contract, they also indicated that they would take responsibility for raising supplementary foundation funding if it were needed.

Organizational Protocols

Setting organizational protocols served two major functions. First, it led to agreed-on rules for governing the negotiations. The rules covered representation, dealing with the media, the decision-making process, and other essential procedural matters. This step was important because many of the representatives had no experience with consensus building, which is much easier, for example, if all the participants agree ahead of time not to attribute opinions to others when talking.

Second, the discussion of ground rules allowed the participants to engage in consensus building for the first time around procedural issues that were relatively non-controversial. During these early sessions, the representatives came to understand how the group could function without relying on *Robert's Rules of Order* or taking votes. Each representative quickly saw that

his or her contribution affected the outcome. Thus, the negotiations over ground rules illustrated to the participants that the outcome was theirs to control.

Political Leverage

The Connecticut cases were especially interesting because participation in the process was purely voluntary. No lawsuit was hanging over their heads; the legislation did not force anyone to take action. As is always the case, the possibility of future legislation mandating affordable housing exists, as does the possibility that advocacy groups might file a lawsuit, but at the time the negotiations were convened, these threats seemed minimal. In many ways, this is the best time to mediate a dispute, that is, before the parties reach an impasse. However, it also means there is little political leverage to use on recalcitrant negotiators. Some participants had a hard time estimating the impact of not reaching agreement. Indeed, some representatives believed from the beginning to the end of the negotiations that while housing opportunities should be made available to people of all income levels, their own communities should not be forced to accept a share of this responsibility.

Neither the legislation nor the participants from the state agencies provided any guidelines regarding what the compact needed to include. Some thought it could simply be a statement of support for increasing the affordable housing stock in the region. Others thought it had to include specific housing plans for each municipality, including the strategies each would use to meet its numerical target.

Mediators cannot provide political leverage. While mediators can use existing sources of leverage to move negotiations toward intelligent agreements, they cannot create leverage where there is none. For this reason, the compact took the shape that it did. It reflects the willingness of the representatives to voluntarily address the affordable housing crisis in Connecticut. The participating communities voluntarily agreed to make a best effort to meet specific goals. This is consistent with Connecticut's tradition of strong home rule. The municipalities did not want to be forced to take action by the state, so they willingly entered into a voluntary agreement among themselves.

Significance of an Institutional Law

CRCOG served as the host for the consensus building process. For many years, CRCOG has been responsible for preparing regional development plans. The council had also prepared an affordable housing needs assessment for the region. CRCOG's participation added an aura of credibility to the process because the representatives had worked with the council in the past. CRCOG also provided an enormous amount of technical data in a very timely fashion. When CRCOG volunteered to play an active role in helping to monitor and implement the compact, the participants accepted. This solved the problem of how to link the informally negotiated compact with the formal mechanisms of governmental authority.

Fair Share Allocations

The Capitol Region's negotiating committee spent close to one-third of its formal meeting time considering the question: What is a municipality's fair share of responsibility for affordable housing? The answer to this question had to satisfy the political needs and interests of 29 diverse communities, ranging from a large central city to small rural communities with little or no infrastructure to support public services. The formula also had to account for past efforts to provide affordable housing. For example, the city of Hartford would not accept a formula that required it to accept the lion's share of responsibility for affordable housing since it had already provided most of the region's affordable housing supply.

In working group or subcommittee sessions, municipal representatives developed a host of options—16 in all—to present to the full committee for discussion. Between the working group meeting and the committee meeting, CRCOG produced housing projections using each formula. Thus, the options were presented to the committee as general policies along with corresponding numerical targets for each community.

The formula options were divided into five categories: regional, local, local/regional, percentage of affordable housing stock, and number of municipal employees.

The *regional* approach would distribute responsibility for affordable housing evenly throughout the entire region with no attention to housing need within each locality. First, the number of households in which income falls at or below the regional median income and more than 30 percent of that income is spent on housing would be calculated. Then, a municipality's fair share would be based on its percentage of the region's total number of households. The options within this category dealt primarily with crediting communities for past affordable housing efforts. These included the following: no credit at all, equal credit for all post-1980 affordable units, and credit for all post-1980 affordable units but only one-half credit for elderly housing (which is much easier to site than family housing). Another possible variation would increase the overall regional need by the number of potential first-time home buyers. These were defined as households that were not currently spending more than 30 percent of their income for rent, that could afford mortgage payments, but that could not raise enough money for a down payment on a house.

The *local* approach would require each community to supply affordable housing units equal to the number of households in its community defined as needing affordable housing. The *local/regional* approach suggested the communities adopt a formula that added 10 percent of the regional need, as determined by the regional approach, to their locally derived need. This compromise option sought to redistribute some of the regional need across all the municipalities while keeping the major focus on local need. Both the local approach and the local/regional approach included the same options for dealing with credit and potential home buyers as those mentioned above.

Not surprisingly, the need to credit communities for their past efforts was suggested primarily by those representatives from communities that had made significant efforts to supply subsidized housing in the past. Two options were formulated in this category. The first would require each municipality to determine *what percentage of its housing stock was affordable.* Each community's fair share would then be calculated as the number of units required to reach and maintain an affordable housing stock equal to an agreed-on percentage of

the community's total housing stock. The alternative would require that a certain percentage of all future development in each municipality be affordable.

Still another, possibly the most politically salient formula, was based on the *number of municipal employees* in each town whose salaries were below median income. That number would represent the municipality's numerical goal for the compact. This option reflected the fact that in many communities, municipal employees can no longer afford to live where they work. It also provided an easy way to break through the public's often negative response to affordable housing. In fact, one community had recently approved plans to build housing units for local police officers. A variation was to increase such municipal targets by adding one-half the number of volunteer firefighters, police officers, and emergency service workers in each community.

After reviewing all the proposed options, the group agreed in principle that each municipality should make a best effort to satisfy at least 25 percent of its local shortfall in affordable housing over the next five years. The city of Hartford was required to meet only 12.5 percent of its local need. The local approach was adopted because it was politically palatable. Some representatives argued in support of the local/regional approach because they wanted the compact to redistribute regional responsibility. Others argued that since they were trying to meet only 25 percent of local need (over a five-year period), it did not make good political sense even to bring up regional need, since local residents would undoubtedly oppose any attempt to redistribute regional responsibility. ➥

∽ COMMENTARY

Again, the question of who is at the table emerges as a critical factor. Since Hartford has the largest need while the suburbs generally are less in need and uninterested in housing Hartford's poor population, the ratio of city to suburban representatives sitting around the table probably helped to shift the discussion from a regional approach to a local one. Under the former, the suburbs would have had a larger obligation to provide affordable housing than under the latter.

—Sally Engle Merry, *Anthropologist*

If the local approach were strictly applied, Hartford would have been responsible for 50 percent of all new units resulting from the compact. Hartford, the central city with the greatest number of moderate- and low-income residents, would benefit most from regional redistribution, and therefore strongly supported the regional option. To accommodate Hartford, the committee agreed to reduce Hartford's responsibility to only 12.5 percent of its locally derived target. The locally based formula benefited the other 28 communities. To satisfy Hartford's and their own interests, they all agreed. The 25 percent and 12.5 percent figures represented about 5,000 new units if the compact were successful, and this was an enormously ambitious goal.

The earliest agreement was in principle only. Many other issues needed to be resolved before any representative would sign off on a specific number of units. These issues included explicit credit for past contributions to the regional affordable housing stock and ways to modify targets that could not be met because of particular "community characteristics." With little discussion, the committee agreed to count all past efforts to increase the affordable housing stock. Just exactly what was included in this move was later revisited in detail.

Many communities submitted modified proposals seeking to alter the formula to benefit either their community or the region as a whole. For example, Canton's sewer lines were at capacity and the town had voted down funds for expanded treatment capability. Therefore, there was no possibility of linking new units to existing sewers and the town could not build high-density developments. For this reason, the town requested that its goal be reduced from 84 units over five years to 6 units per year. The committee rejected this proposal.

Somers, a small rural town in the northern part of the region, requested an exemption because it is home to the state's 2,000-bed maximum security prison. As its representative suggested, "We already supply affordable housing to 2,000 inmates." The committee also rejected this request.

As it turned out, no one could muster enough support to create individual exemptions. Many felt that each municipality could come up with good reasons for lowering its goals, but that the wide range of strategic options available for meeting individual targets meant that no matter what the characteristics of a community, each should be able to reach its affordable housing goals.

The committee did, however, consider possible changes in the formula that might be applied to all the communities. The town of Bloomfield proposed that municipalities be given credit for their "nearly affordable housing." The proposal suggested that municipalities with more than 20 percent of their total housing sales below $100,000 receive credit equal to one-half of their percentage of sales at or below $100,000. To accommodate this suggestion, a representative from Glastonbury proposed that all towns receive partial credit for housing units that sold below $100,000. Thus, even if a town had only 10 percent of its housing stock below $100,000, it would receive a 5 percent credit toward its total local target. At first the proposal passed easily, but later in the negotiations, an alternative was suggested that threatened this early interim agreement.

The Windsor proposal, as it came to be known, suggested that municipalities be credited for all Connecticut Housing Finance Administration (CHFA) mortgages issued for one- to four-family residences between 1980 and 1989. In concept, this proposal assumed that such mortgages represented a municipal contribution to affordable housing.

These Bloomfield and Windsor proposals created some difficulty for the committee, which was complicated by a further Hartford proposal. During the compact negotiations, Hartford's city council met and issued instructions to its committee representatives. The crux of the resulting Hartford proposal was the following: inclusion of a nondiscrimination clause in the compact's preamble; minimum goals for each of the categories of very low-, low-, and moderate-income housing; and a 7,000-unit minimum for affordable units created as a result of the compact. Hartford felt that if fewer than 7,000 units were created, it might do better if it tried to force new state legislation for mandatory affordable housing.

With time running out, still other proposals were submitted. Newington requested the goals be based on rental units only because homeowners spending more than 30 percent of household income chose to do so. This proposal was summarily rejected, since it would have required completely revamping the formula, which the representatives had spent weeks trying to finalize.

Using the 25 percent and 12.5 percent of local need targets—even with credit for past affordable housing efforts and the application of the Bloomfield proposal— some participants still felt they had an unrealistically high number of units to achieve. For example, West Hartford's target represented 116 percent of its annual new construction for the previous few years. All committee members agreed that such a goal was both unreasonable and politically unfeasible.

A number of proposals were suggested to remedy this situation. Possibilities included a cap on targets so that no community would be expected to exceed 30 percent to 50 percent of its annual production rate over the previous few years. Some representatives rejected this proposal because their towns had experienced periods of high growth in the past five years that they did not expect to repeat, yet their targets would reflect these boom years. After much discussion, including strong pressure from the Hebron representative, a real estate expert who assured the committee that anything beyond 35 percent of new housing starts was pure folly, the group agreed to accept a universal 35 percent cap on all local targets. This primarily affected the larger municipalities in the region.

The 35 percent cap also reduced the overall goal for the region, and Hartford begrudgingly lowered its floor for affordable units resulting from the compact from 7,000 to 5,000. However, Hartford representatives made it clear that for less than the 5,000 units agreed to, they would withdraw from the negotiations—effectively destroying the chance for a regional housing compact.

At the time of the public forum, the numerical targets were still not finalized. The remaining issue was whether the Bloomfield proposal or the Windsor proposal would be applied. The Bloomfield proposal resulted in greater redistribution of the units among the smaller towns in the region. It also kept the total number of units resulting from the compact above 5,000.

The effect of the Windsor proposal, on the other hand, was to greatly increase the number of units in the larger towns. With a 35 percent cap, the total number would be slightly less than 5,000. An option floated was to increase the cap to 40 percent, which resulted in the largest towns taking on an additional few hundred units. Oddly enough, the Windsor representative continuously insisted that those towns with little or no affordable housing should do the most, and those with past affordable housing efforts should be rewarded. His proposal would have the completely opposite effect, yet he could not see this.

The group had set the day before the public forum as the time to finalize the targets. At the end of the meeting, with Windsor the only holdout against the Bloomfield proposal, a group of representatives confronted the Windsor representative. Many left the session thinking that he had agreed to drop his proposal, but he said he only agreed to *consider* dropping it. In a discussion with the lead mediator following the meeting, he stated that he stood by the Windsor proposal.

For the public forum, the draft compact that was distributed contained ranges for each municipality's goal representing the Windsor and Bloomfield proposed numbers. The response of the public was that the goals were too low in general. Many housing advocates present applauded the regional cooperation reflected in the compact, but argued that the region needed to aim for a greater number of units to meet the housing crisis. After the public forum, all the representatives present agreed that anything less than 5,000 units would be perceived as less than a serious effort.

The group had one meeting left to finalize the targets. After that, the mediators' contract was up. The Windsor representative did not come to the last meeting, and his alternate came with no authority to withdraw the Windsor proposal. Clearly, a successful blocking effort had occurred, much to the frustration of the group.

Thus, they had no choice but to accommodate the Windsor proposal in some way. In the end, representatives were given a choice of either number. Many accepted the Bloomfield number—which was higher—to honor the 5,000-unit floor. The representatives agreed that *ranges* be adopted as goals to give each local governing body a role in actually deciding its municipal target. Those who had already accepted the higher number were not given a range. For some, the range represented the difference between the Bloomfield and Windsor proposals. For others, it represented a capped and noncapped number relative to annual housing starts.

The range was a politically salient resolution to the fair share allocation issue. To begin with, it accommodated the Windsor representative and achieved consensus among the representatives. Second, it brought local officials into the decision-making process. Many felt this would result in reframing at least some of the local debate; that is, discussions would focus in part on which target they should choose rather than simply whether they should accept or reject the compact. Finally, as a result of using ranges for targets, the total number of units resulting from the fair housing compact was increased to between 5,000 and 6,421. This addressed the concerns of the housing advocates, who felt that the total number of units was too low.

The focus of the fair share allocation discussions leaped from fairness, based on formula alternatives, to political feasibility. The representatives easily and quickly engaged in the give-and-take of negotiation, as illustrated by their immediate agreement to reduce Hartford's local goal. This amicability and willingness to accommodate the interests of others continued throughout the negotiations.

As the targets crystallized, the participants judged their potential obligations in light of what they thought their constituents would accept. Until they reached reasonable levels, representatives were forced to develop arguments to justify reductions in their targets. In the end, the fair share allocations represented the most the representatives thought they could deliver. In fact, many felt they may have stretched too far and were greatly concerned about their towns' responses.

The negotiated fair share allocation of responsibility for affordable housing has the imprint of the 29 representatives. Clearly, no planner or legislator would have developed a similar formula. Woven through this formula are the opinions and concerns of almost all the representatives. As a result, each representative was able to agree to support the compact during ratification.

A similar formula developed and imposed by someone else (i.e., planner, judge, or legislator), even one leading to similar targets, would have less of a chance for successful implementation. Because this was a voluntary effort and represented an agreement among the elected officials of all the towns, it has a good chance of being implemented. ❧

❧ COMMENTARY

The complexity of the agreement is very important in providing local control over this process, and it was the result of extensive local input. As the authors point out, it was not what a top-down planner, judge, or legislator would have done. Yet it reflected the concerns and interests of the people sitting around the table. At the same time, these individuals were also in intermediary positions, representing their towns to the discussion and the discussion to their towns. This is frequently a stressful position to occupy and one that affected several of the participants' abilities to make agreements since they had to sell them to their constituencies back home. It is not clear what the towns stood to gain by participating in this negotiation and making these agreements; there appears to be a legislative stick and perhaps also governmental funds as carrots.

—Sally Engle Merry, *Anthropologist*

Representatives' Link to Authorities

As stated previously, the municipal representatives in the Capitol Region were very diverse. They included city council members, first selectmen, town planners, town managers, and citizen activists ranging from real estate developers to interested people with no background in housing. This diversity resulted in some representatives being empowered to negotiate on behalf of their local governing bodies and others being less closely linked to local authorities. The first selectmen and members of municipal government could be held accountable for staying in close touch with elected bodies. Indeed, the elected officials were much more careful in their commitments, basing them on their political acceptability. Many checked back with their governing boards and brought back comments for the group to address. Other representatives did not keep lines to their legislative bodies open. They negotiated as representatives, but did not have the same support.

Each representative was reminded regularly to approach local authorities and community members for input. In an attempt to ensure this connection, participants were asked to invite elected officials to a compact meeting so they could offer their comments and insights. It was also helpful for other officials to observe the negotiations and see how decisions and agreements were reached. Twelve invited guests from eight municipalities attended at least one of the negotiating sessions.

The pilot program was a new experience for all who participated, including the mayors of the towns. Some considered it very important and so either represented their towns themselves or chose particularly talented people to do so. Others saw it as just

another regional committee and, therefore, took less care in choosing representatives. It is of great importance that participants be chosen carefully. The more skilled the representatives, the better the negotiation process, and, therefore, the better the outcome.

The Roles of the Mediation Team

The mediation team was composed of experts in both consensus building processes and affordable housing issues and strategies. As a result, the mediators were able to carefully craft the consensus building process to fit both the specifics of housing issues and preexisting assumptions about public policy making. For example, not only did the process have to be open and fair, it had to be perceived as such. That is, the representatives had to understand that they were shaping a policy that balanced the substance of housing needs with political feasibility.

The mediators performed a range of tasks, from delving deep into the substance of affordable housing issues to molding proposals in work group sessions to managing personality problems. Throughout the process, the mediators worked hard to keep the representatives focused on the particular agenda items of the meeting. Often, participants preferred to discuss the constraints their towns had with respect to siting affordable housing. The mediators created and sustained a positive atmosphere and momentum so that the representatives emphasized what they could do rather than what they could not do. To this end, the mediators stressed the group's goal and the state's commitment to let the communities voluntarily address a regional problem.

The mediators employed a variety of strategies to gain the trust of the representatives. Most important, they made it absolutely clear that their role was to facilitate discussions, not to impose solutions. At the start of the negotiations, some of the representatives thought the mediators were hired by the state to lead them in a particular policy direction. However, as the committee members' comments and suggestions were incorporated into the draft compact, they realized the committee had complete control over the outcome.

The mediators used the *single-text* method of negotiation, whereby written proposals generated in work groups are revised by the participants until consensus is reached. At the earliest possible point, a draft compact was developed, consisting of all the previous interim agreements, and blank spaces were left for issues that had not yet been discussed. The negotiations then centered around the remaining issues, such as monitoring the compact and revising the other points until the group reached a final consensus. This proved to be a successful method of operation, because it helped maintain the group's focus and momentum. It also allowed the mediators to help the representatives look for mutually beneficial trades that furthered many of their varied interests.

The mediators avoided getting involved in political disputes or making judgments. Instead, the mediators helped untangle such disputes or show that they were not useful to the discussions. For example, there were strong value differences among the representatives. Some felt that the municipalities and the state should help moderate- and low-income families obtain affordable housing. Others thought that people who expected such assistance were lazy. Nothing would have convinced anyone of the other's position, though the representatives might have spent all their time discussing these value judgments. The mediators kept the discussions focused on the political forces that made it feasible for the committee to develop an affordable housing compact as a cooperative venture among local governments.

The major lessons illustrated by the case were these:

1. Representation is important—mediators may have to help representatives stay in touch with their formal governing bodies.
2. Ground rules are not enough for managing the press—mediators may need to take an active posture vis-à-vis press releases and meeting with the press.
3. It is important to have a convening presence (such as CRCOG) on-site and to have technical data and resource people available because they can save a lot of time and money.
4. Inventing options and creating packages is an important role of the mediators.
5. Subcommittees are crucial for inventing and creating options.
6. There is a need for a postnegotiation presence for the mediators.

■ Conclusions

The Capitol Region negotiations produced an informed consensus. The interests of 29 municipalities and several state agencies were met. With the help of a mediation team, difficult technical and political obstacles were overcome. While ratification is still a potential problem and implementation will depend on a series of economic and political forces beyond the control of the participating communities, the negotiations were a success.

The key to agreement, first, was finding a formula that represented a set of principles that all the participants could endorse, and then refining that general principle to take account of the special and different needs of each participant.

The success of this multiparty, multi-issue negotiation hinged, in large measure, on the ability of the mediation team to create a sense that the process, as well as the outcome, was fair to everyone involved. ❧

❧ COMMENTARY

It is significant that the mediators moved the discussion from shared principles to specific features of agreements, rather than vice versa, and that the result was a simple principle of increasing affordable housing joined to a complex menu of strategies and systems of counting. The negotiation process clearly drew on a substantial body of information about housing, land use, zoning, local regulation, and local government that the mediators brought to the table as well as the participants—who contributed to a somewhat variable extent. The intervention of the mediators is intriguing, although not as elaborated as it might be. How did the mediators handle obstructionist individuals? What does the demand for consensus mean to the way the process goes forward and these people were treated? To what extent did the mediators structure the discussions and keep them in focus, providing concrete options and alternatives rather than allowing a free flow of discussion?

Looking at this agreement from the perspective of an anthropologist, it is striking that this process and document are both framed in a very particular language and culture. The compact is phrased entirely in the language of planning, strategies, statistical techniques for defining what affordable housing means and measuring the shortfall. It relies on a body of statistical information about populations and incomes. There are other possible ways of imagining this discussion and its outcome. There might be narratives of searches for housing, frustrations with the quality of housing particular people found, or collective histories of communities' past good or bad experience incorporating housing options for people with fewer resources, for example. There might be stories of racial discrimination, divorce and housing hardships, job loss and migration. There might be local stories about extended kin groups, local religious and voluntary organizations, or civic associations that created a sense of community in particular towns and defined a town's identity. There is no sense in this document of the desires of consumers of this housing or of the kinds of options that they might like. This is, instead, a document produced by more or less reluctant providers seeking by and large to preserve what they have.

Would there have been greater sympathy for the consumer with an expanded process? Would the solutions have looked different with consumers as well as providers around the table? How, in the absence of the consumer, was this person or family envisioned? It is significant that when the participants realized that their children might be eligible, they changed their attitudes. Yet the position of the recipient was represented only statistically here, in a single discourse of numbers rather than in the complexity of an individual life. Whether such people are lazy or deserving thus could not be answered and remained a background point of disagreement. This discussion is not intended as a criticism of the process but as an analysis of the language and structures that defined it.

—Sally Engle Merry, *Anthropologist*

■ *Epilogue*

The Capitol Region Fair Housing Compact on Affordable Housing took effect on May 23, 1990 after it was ratified by 25 municipalities and incorporated into the *Plan for Development of the Capitol Region of Connecticut.* The original legislation that created the compact negotiations required the compact to be incorporated into the *Plan* only after it was ratified by all 29 communities that comprise the Capitol Region. After three communities rejected it, representatives of the participating municipalities convinced the state legislature to amend Public Act 88-334 to require ratification by only two-thirds of the participating communities. (A 26th community later ratified it.)

As a result of the affordable housing compact negotiations, 26 Capitol Region municipalities created 4,657 new housing opportunities for very low-, low-, and moderate-income families and individuals during the compact's five-year period of performance. The communities succeeded in reaching their goal of creating between 4,583 and 5,637 new affordable housing opportunities in the region between July 1, 1989 and March 31, 1995. During that period, according to the *Capitol Region Fair Housing Compact Annual Report* (September 1995),

> new housing opportunities, equal to 102% of the minimum goal and 83% of the maximum goal [were created]. Progress for individual municipalities ranged from accomplishing 12.5% of the local goal to exceeding the five-year maximum goal. New affordable renter and/or owner units [were] built in 19 communities; mortgage assistance programs in conjunction with the Connecticut Housing Finance Authority, the Farmers Home Administration, and the Connecticut Department of Housing created affordable home ownership opportunities in each of the 26 towns; and rental assistance programs expanded affordable housing opportunities in 24 municipalities.

In addition, 21 towns voluntarily amended their zoning regulations in support of affordable housing strategies. For example, many communities adopted zoning mechanisms such as density bonuses, cluster zoning, accessory apartments, allowing apartments over commercial space, and eliminating or lowering minimum-floor and -lot requirements. ◆◆

◆◆ COMMENTARY

Notice that in addition to creating 4,657 "new housing opportunities," the project produced an active inventory of affordable housing strategies whose practical availability (those who contemplate adopting one can easily get advice from those who have done so already) is arguably changing the very meaning of affordable housing in ways the participants, consensus builders among them, are just beginning to register. Is all this just tinkering with existing policy, or radically transforming the way locals provide housing for the vulnerable?

—Charles F. Sabel, *Political economist*

At the end of the five-year life of the compact, the Capitol Region began work on its Regional Housing Policy. It was incorporated into the *Plan for Development of the Capitol Region of Connecticut* on January 28, 1998. It takes a more regional approach regarding its affordable housing goals than did the compact's numerical goals for each municipality.

However, the Regional Housing Policy clearly builds on the efforts of the compact. As did the compact, the policy rests on the assumption that affordable housing is a regional problem. Similar to the compact, the policy is an agreement among the communities of the region and relies on CRCOG as its institutional base for implementation and assessment. Finally, the new policy recognizes and respects that different communities will require different strategies for providing affordable housing and in some ways reflects the compact's use of a menu of strategies to choose from based on the unique characteristics of each municipality.

In sum, the affordable housing compact negotiations were successful in achieving the goal of creating almost 5,000 new affordable housing opportunities and in defining affordable housing as a regional problem and a long-term commitment to coordinated actions among municipalities.

■ Note

1. During the individual phone calls, representatives expressed many concerns. Some spoke of their support for affordable housing throughout the region and stressed that every community would have to play a role in alleviating the regional housing crisis. Others expressed support for housing, but fear of integration. Still others feared changes in community character. Indeed, one representative said, "Do you want to take our football field and turn it into high-rise buildings?"

SAN FRANCISCO ESTUARY PROJECT

■ Judith E. Innes
■ Sarah Connick

The San Francisco Estuary Project (SFEP) was part of the National Estuary Program (NEP), which was designed to bring all the stakeholders in an estuarine system into a consensual agreement on the state of the estuary and a plan for its restoration and management.[1] The scope and complexity of the issues addressed by the SFEP, the size of the affected area, the range of technical information needed, the number and diversity of players, and the political and economic powers engaged by the process presented major challenges for the process and its participants.

At the end of five years, the SFEP produced a consensually adopted Comprehensive Conservation and Management Plan (CCMP) recommending numerous actions for improving the health of the estuary. This plan, however, may be a less significant achievement than other results of the process, including agreements on technical descriptions of the estuary and methods of measuring water quality, new networks of relationships among participants, educa-

The San Francisco Estuary Project case study was originally published in *Coordinating Growth and Environmental Management through Consensus Building*, by Judith Innes, Judith Gruber, et al. (University of California: California Policy Seminar, 1994), and is reprinted by permission. In the first version, interviews were conducted by Michael Neuman and Judith Innes, and the case was written by Judith Innes. The version that appears here was updated by Sarah Connick. The authors are grateful to Scott McCreary for providing comments on the original version, which were helpful in further developing the case.

tion of participants about the estuary and each other's responsibilities, and other consensus processes that built on this one. Although, when the plan was adopted, there were complaints that the consensus was "thin" and the prospects for implementation were uncertain, there is no doubt that the SFEP has changed the practices and politics of water management in California.

■ Context

The SFEP was contentious for many reasons, but most of all because it entered the highly conflictual arena of California water politics. In California, agricultural and urban interests in distant parts of the state hold rights to and depend on diversions of water that would otherwise flow through the estuary. In the estuary, freshwater flows mix with the waters of the Pacific Ocean, producing a gradient of less-and-less salty water as one moves upstream. The estuary's ecosystem, including a number of endangered species, depends on this gradient. Thus, in the SFEP, water rights and water quality came to be posed as conflicting values.

The link between water quality and flows also presented problems around how to set boundaries for the SFEP that in turn affected stakeholder selection and which topics would be on the table. In the bay and delta, water quality management and water

diversions are regulated by independent sets of agencies, criteria, and regulatory processes. The State Water Resources Control Board (SWRCB) is responsible for making water rights decisions, involving trade-offs between water uses and the protection of aquatic resources. Other state and federal agencies have responsibility for operating water projects and protecting water quality and endangered species. The SWRCB's decision-making process was separate from the SFEP, however, and under way as the SFEP got started. The separation of the decision making on flows led to conflicts and disagreements over who were the appropriate stakeholders. For example, if flows were to be addressed by the SFEP, how should the interests of the distant water users be represented?

In addition to the SWRCB and SFEP processes, water rights and water quality issues were being reviewed in two other arenas. A federal process to set water quality standards for the bay-delta was already under way. In addition, in the course of the SFEP, the three major groups having water interests in the state—agricultural and urban water users and environmentalists—established an informal "tripartite process." Their aim was to reach agreement quietly among themselves, out of the spotlight. Many of the same individuals and organizations were involved in all four parallel processes, and therefore had ample opportunity to influence water policy outside the SFEP. ∞

∞ COMMENTARY

This case study demonstrates an increasingly troublesome, but common, challenge to consensus building efforts: multiple, parallel, and simultaneously occurring processes. To paraphrase from an important scholarly article about the social construction of disputing, multiple processes present challenges of "framing" and "gaming," as well as the more common issues of "naming, blaming, and claiming" (Felstiner, Abel, & Sarat, 1980-1981). To the extent that participants in issues as complex as those presented by the San Francisco Estuary Project can use different processes with different constituencies, with different issue definitions, and with different legal requirements, manipulations of processes, both public and private, can hinder the accomplishment of "resolutions" or substantive progress, while the different "processes" are "gamed" and used to thwart any forward movement. Thus, the use of multiple processes may advantage those who prefer the status quo or those who would prefer to delay some activity.

There are some solutions to these problems. In consensus building exercises that run parallel to lawsuits (such as in environmental cases like the SFEP situation), it is sometimes possible to get a stay from a court to temporarily halt the litigation while a broader base of stakeholders participate in a mediation or other consensus building exercise. In other cases, regulators or legislators may be asked to join at the beginning of a process so that appropriate legislative or regulatory approvals can be "promised," if not fully delivered, at the beginning so as to preempt at least some parallel processes. Coordination, by facilitators or convenors of parallel processes, is also sometimes possible and always useful, if for no other reason than to help frame the issues, and "police the agenda," so they remain somewhat stable across multiple meetings and processes. But if these or other "solutions" are not available, gaming or manipulation of multiple processes is a real danger to consensus building. In a recent case I mediated, for example, the parties used the press, despite confidentiality agreements, to create a public "parallel" process when they wanted to sabotage the private process.

—Carrie J. Menkel-Meadow, *Legal scholar*

REFERENCE

Felstiner, W., Abel, R., & Sarat, A. (1980-1981). The emergence and transformation of disputes: Naming, blaming and claiming. *Law & Society Review, 15,* 631.

The conflicts among the parties were fundamental. Environmentalists, agricultural and urban water users, business groups, and development interests had been operating in a highly adversarial mode for many years. The intensity of feelings was high, and many of these bitterly opposed parties had not sat around a table together before. In addition, the various agencies having responsibilities related to the estuary have an array of differing and sometimes conflicting missions. Among the state agencies, the Department of Water Resources plans, constructs, and operates water supply projects; its constituents are primarily agricultural and urban water us-ers. The SWRCB and the Regional Water Quality Control Boards are regulatory agencies that address water rights and water quality issues. The California Department of Fish and Game is responsible for habitat and species protection. Federal agencies such as the Environmental Protection Agency (EPA), the Fish and Wildlife Service, and the Bureau of Reclamation also represent an equally wide range of perspectives. In addition, local governments have responsibility for land use decision making. Relationships among the various agencies are not always easy. By all accounts, Governor Deukmejian was reluctant to nominate the San Francisco Estuary for the NEP in 1987 because of the tremendous inherent political difficulties.[2] Due to the state's lack of enthusiasm, the EPA took the lead in organizing and staffing the project, although formally project sponsorship was shared by the EPA and the state as required by law. The EPA's role as lead agency raised suspicions among some state agencies that the project was a "conspiracy" to allow federal agencies to set standards and control state agencies' actions.

■ The SFEP Structure and Process

The NEP provides for the convening of a management conference to assess trends, collect and characterize data, and develop a comprehensive plan for the restoration and management of an estuary. It specifies that, at a minimum, the members of the conference should include representatives of federal, state, regional, and local agencies having jurisdiction within the estuarine zone, and representatives of affected industries, educational institutions, and the general public. Based on this guidance and experience elsewhere, the EPA established a Management Committee (MC) consisting of federal, state, regional, and local agencies, and other organized interests. A Sponsoring Agency Committee consisting of representatives of four state and federal agencies was established ostensibly to oversee the project. In practice, however, the MC provided the overall direction for the project and served as the final decision-making body. Two other committees were created to assist the MC. The Public Advisory Committee (PAC) consisted of citizen representatives and provided a means for public participation. The Technical Advisory Committee (TAC) consisted of scientists and engineers drawn from agencies, universities, and other research settings. It was responsible for providing information and advice on science- and technology-related matters and, in particular, for assisting in the characterization of the estuary.[3] The chairs of the TAC and PAC also served on the MC. In all, about 120 people served on these committees, and many of the same agencies and interest groups were represented on each. ➡

∽ COMMENTARY

Bringing to the fore the variety of conflicts in the various constituencies—such as urban-agricultural, water rights-water quality, federal-state regulatory agencies, environmental-business interests—and recognizing that these conflicts or different values themselves might cut across participating agencies demonstrates some of the strengths of consensus building exercises. Out-front identification of conflicting interests while involving those separate interests in a common task or set of tasks (creation of scientific standards, statement of the problem, etc., before "solutions") provides the possibility of working across conflicting interests. Bringing all parties to a table simultaneously has the risk of alliance and coalition formation and strategic play, but it also often surprises by allowing cross-interest alliances and coalitions on particular issues, rather than fighting the "big issues" in the more conventional adversarial mode. Alliances on different issues can lead to trades and can disrupt historical two-party fighting as well (such as long-standing environmental-business interests). The perhaps more limited standard of success, by reaching some consensus on at least a definition of *water quality,* is the kind of accomplishment that can occur in this kind of setting.

—Carrie J. Menkel-Meadow, *Legal scholar*

At the outset, the EPA appointed about 20 people to the MC. It expanded itself several times in recognition of the need to include additional viewpoints, and by the end of the process had 49 members. Members were primarily staff of public agencies and interest groups and some citizen representatives. The MC also included several local elected officials, but only two or three participated regularly. It met bimonthly in half-day meetings, and more frequently and with longer meetings toward the end of the process. Twenty to 30 members attended on average, with as many as 35 or 40 members attending when important issues were on the table.

The issue of how to define the boundaries of the problem affected stakeholder selection. For example, one state agency official felt the MC had a regional bias toward the bay-delta and that it did not include adequate representation of statewide interests, that is, the water users who are geographically distant from the estuary but depend on its water. In contrast, the notion of including southern water users infuriated one environmental representative who felt the SFEP was about the estuary and there was no reason to include others. Similarly, some business and development representatives thought there was too much emphasis on environmental issues and not enough on socioeconomic impacts. The MC acknowledged these diverse opinions, but agreed its focus would be on how to protect the estuary. The MC members' thinking was that the statewide perspective was brought by the state agencies on the MC who were responsible for balancing state and regional needs. In addi-

tion, southern California water wholesalers and state water contractors were represented on the PAC. Thus, the southern water users were represented in the SFEP, albeit indirectly.

At the outset, there was no general agreement on the nature of the estuary's problems; some parties did not even agree that there was a problem. Over the course of the first year, the MC worked together with the TAC and PAC to identify and frame the issues, and then convened subcommittees to address them in detail. Subcommittees initially were formed to address aquatic resources and wildlife, land use, wetlands, pollutants, and dredging. A subcommittee on local government was also formed, but disbanded after a time. Later in the process, two more subcommittees were formed on flows and water use. Each subcommittee had representation from a range of interests, and included people with technical and nontechnical expertise. The subcommittees also had overlapping memberships. It was in the smaller groups that much of the substantive debate occurred and where participants built much of their shared understanding and consensus. Over the course of about three years, the subcommittees worked in concert with staff and consultants to develop status and trends reports in their issue areas and to recommend actions for inclusion in the CCMP.

Participants had a variety of motivations for coming to the table and staying there. A number of parties who were wary of environmental regulation were there explicitly for self-protection. With the EPA leading the project and a total of $7.5

million available for the project over five years, there was significant potential for things to happen, both good and bad. As one agency representative said, "If we do not participate, decisions might be made that go against our mandates." When asked, "What kept you at the table?" another agency official replied,

Fear. Feeling that we had so much at stake that we had to be there. We talked about walking [i.e., leaving the process in protest] in some dramatic fashion . . . but it was hard to say we are not going to play. The SFEP clearly had substantial institutional structure . . . clout . . . recognition. ◆◆

◐ COMMENTARY

In addition to differing parties or constituencies, this process illustrates how people can sit down at a consensus process with different motivating factors. While some will do so out of an optimistic expectation to actually resolve a problem, negative motivators may also be important, such as the fear expressed here by some parties that did not want to be excluded from the process or the substantive outcome that might be achieved. In any process like this, it is important to recognize that different motivations may encourage parties to participate (as in mediation, some parties want cheap or faster resolution, while others want creative, party-tailored solutions) and that is the good side, but the skilled facilitator must always be aware that different motivations can also result in different behaviors—fear may not produce the same proposals as desire to see a fair resolution. The skilled facilitator must keep the variety of motivations in mind when organizing processes of communication, establishing methods for brainstorming, and evaluating solutions and decision criteria and rules.

—Carrie J. Menkel-Meadow, *Legal scholar*

Many environmentalists were reluctant to participate because of their view that consensus building allows too much compromise. One commented, "The environment always loses. The other interests weaken the goal of protection." For several environmental groups, it was a compromise just to be at the table instead of bringing lawsuits or lobbying for new laws and regulations. ◆◆

◐ COMMENTARY

I am always troubled when participants view consensus processes as "compromises." In this case, environmentalists complain that consensus processes prevent or inhibit the enforcement of legislation through lawsuits or lobbying for new laws, as if those processes don't produce compromises too. More important, there is a fallacy here in the thinking process that all "consensually" arrived at solutions either are immoral or are unprincipled compromise. I have written (Menkel-Meadow, 1984, 1995), as have several philosophers (Golding, 1979; Kuflik, 1979; Pennock & Chapman, 1979), that compromise is not a necessary part of a solution that attempts to meet the need of all sides, and that even where there is compromise, it can often be morally, as well as practically, and Pareto, superior to other outcomes. "Litigation romanticists," as I have called them, often assume that if they litigate they will win. More than 90 percent of all lawsuits conclude without a win-lose trial; most (more than 65 percent) "settle" for something short of "total victory." More important, particularly in the environmental field, a court or legislative victory does not always lead to perfect compliance and execution of the laws. While the SFEP also clearly still has implementation issues to deal with, consensual processes are still more likely to lead to compliance or at least the process for ongoing implementation negotiations.

Participants who claim they do not like compromise assume that they must give something up to get concessions from the other side when this is not always the case. It may be, for example, that adherence to arbitrarily set standards may "move" not because of a concession but because of a new understanding of what is necessary to meet scientific requirements. Furthermore, consensus processes make clear that a multiplicity of constituencies may look at problems through the lens of different interests—all of which may have validity, if differently valued validity.

—Carrie J. Menkel-Meadow, *Legal scholar*

REFERENCES

Golding, M. (1979). The nature of compromise. In J. R. Pennock & J. W. Chapman (Eds.), *Compromise in ethics, law, and politics*. New York: New York University Press.

Kuflik, A. (1979). Morality and compromise. In J. R. Pennock & J. W. Chapman (Eds.), *Compromise in ethics, law, and politics*. New York: New York University Press.

Menkel-Meadow, C. (1984). Toward another view of legal negotiation: The structure of problem solving. *UCLA Law Review, 31,* 754.

Menkel-Meadow, C. (1995). Whose dispute is it anyway? A philosophical and democratic defense of settlement (in some cases). *Georgetown Law Journal, 83,* 2663.

Pennock, J. R., & Chapman, J. W. (Eds.). (1979). *Compromise in ethics, law, and politics*. New York: New York University Press.

Participants also indicated their other principal reason for attending was to get to know the others and learn about their concerns. TAC members used their meetings as opportunities to exchange scientific information and get updated on one another's research.

Issue Subcommittees

The issue subcommittees had varying success. Agreement was reached on pollution, dredging, and land use. Substantial agreement was reached on aquatic resources, although a minority report was produced on this topic. Two subcommittees—wetlands and land use—ran into particular difficulties.

Wetlands

Wetlands proved to be the most contentious issue. Builders and farmers lined up against environmentalists over how to define a wetland and on whether the policy goal should be "no net loss" or restoration and increase of wetlands. One problem was a lack of technical certainty. It was unclear which wetland types were more critical for the estuary given its current status. Also, environmentalists distrusted wetland restoration policies because of the technical uncertainties of success. Developers and farmers sought a limited and precise definition of a wetland, and preferred a no-net-loss policy to requirements for protecting them all. Another difficulty was a general feeling of resentment among business and some local representatives that socioeconomic issues were not being given adequate attention or priority.

Process was also a concern. A previous wetlands process in which most of the participants had engaged had fallen apart, leaving the participants unhappy with one another. Despite the earlier experience, the wetlands subcommittee worked without a facilitator and members wrote the report themselves. They were unable to reach a consensus, however, and a minority report was included in the final CCMP.

Land Use

The land use subcommittee was also contentious, but ultimately reached a consensus. It was one of the last of the original subcommittees to be organized. Staff and professional and university-based consultants developed technical reports on demographics and the potential impacts of land use intensification for the group. From a policy perspective, however, many difficult issues remained. A central issue dividing participants was regional government. Some participants contended that the formation of a regional government would do much to solve many land use problems. Others, especially local officials, opposed the notion of a new layer of government. The conflict in the subcommittee mirrored debates that were going on in several state-

wide arenas outside the SFEP, including in the state legislature. Another difficulty was that the subcommittee's task was not well-defined and its membership was stretched thin. Several of the more concrete land use issues, such as wetlands and pollutants, already were being addressed in other subcommittees, and participants were putting their energy into those efforts. Thus, the land use issues remaining for the subcommittee were essentially those around planning.

Although the subcommittee's consultants produced informative reports, the conflicts around land use continued to impede participants' progress toward a consensus. Thus, toward the end of the subcommittee process, the SFEP hired one of the consultants, Scott McCreary of CONCUR, to facilitate meetings. Over a four-month period, involving just two meetings of a subcommittee subgroup, the consultant together with staff wrote the status and trends report on land use, and the land use management options. The use of a facilitator in this case clearly was useful. According to one participant who also served on the wetlands subcommittee, the process was not as "gut wrenching as the wetlands, in which the group wrote everything from scratch." The subcommittee's report and recommended actions were adopted unanimously by the MC.

Perhaps because of the inherently difficult nature of land use issues, however, the subcommittee's efforts received mixed reviews at the time of the adoption of the CCMP. Although the land use section was adopted without a minority report, the participants whom we interviewed—environmentalists, local representatives, and business interests—all felt that overall the section was weak. The lack of enthusiasm from all sides may simply reflect that genuine compromises were achieved—that as one individual commented, it got "watered down for consensus purposes." Although most parties interviewed found the facilitation helpful, the process apparently did not get beyond this mutual-adjustment effort to a mutual-gains position or sense of shared mission.

Flows, Water Use, and Aquatic Resources

Initially, the SFEP organizers decided to set aside the intensely controversial issue of water flows in the estuary. Flows and water rights issues were being addressed by the SWRCB in its hearing process, which was expected to result in a decision well before the SFEP was to be completed. The organizers' thinking was to use the information that would be developed by the SWRCB rather than to attempt to debate the same issues in the SFEP. At the outset, there was also a concern that some of the key players might not come to the SFEP table if flows were on the agenda. Even without the flows issue on the table, the SFEP had numerous issues on which to work.

Two years into the SFEP, however, the SWRCB process clearly had stalled. The plan to incorporate its findings into the CCMP was not going to work. Moreover, the aquatic resources subcommittee had concluded it could not complete its work without discussing flows. Many participants had been complaining about the difficulty of completing the estuary project without addressing flows in an integral way. Environmentalists threatened to quit the SFEP and sue the EPA. Thus, in 1990 the MC convened a flows subcommittee, consisting of carefully selected members including environmentalists and water

agency representatives. In private meetings, the subcommittee designed a series of technical workshops. It also created a smaller subcommittee on water use and supported original research.

After about a year, the flows subcommittee merged with the aquatic resources subcommittee, and together they developed a comprehensive action plan. Although there was substantial support for their plan, it was accompanied by a minority report in the CCMP. The major controversy around the issue was complex and much was at stake. Views were polarized, with some members of the subcommittee taking a rigid position and apparently saying, "Don't take our water." Environmentalists accused the SWRCB of having an unfair policy of supplying water to all those with contractual and other rights, and only sending residual water into the estuary. One SWRCB representative contended,

> The SFEP was not just a bay issue. The water rights they were dealing with were used by the entire state. Thus, it is a water rights issue, not just a water quality issue. Flows are not directly a water quality issue like discharges. It is not just the amount of water, but the timing, where and how, and the facilities.

The SWRCB's responsibility was to balance interests. State agency representatives also had to recognize that the governor might not accept results that took too much water from the state and federal water projects. While the subcommittees did not solve the political problem of competing demands on the water, they reached agreement on the point that flows were linked to water quality and on the idea of a conservation strategy. Other issues would have to be worked out in other arenas.

The Role and Use of Technical Information

In retrospect, the technical role of the SFEP may be the most important contribution to the policies and practices of water management for the estuary and to improved coordination among the agencies. The process of developing technical information provided opportunities for mutual learning among scientists and between scientists and laypersons. In addition, it resulted in the development of an innovative measure of estuarine health. ∞

∞ COMMENTARY

Perhaps the greatest contribution of consensual processes in such complex scientific environments is the exchange of information across scientific specialties and the relationships that develop between people schooled in different disciplines. The cross-, or as I like to call it, *trans-*, disciplinary learning that occurs when scientific experts must speak to each other across a "to be solved together" rather than adversarial "expert witness" problem-solving structure can have added value beyond the particular problem being worked on. For example, while the estuary problem looked like it was about water rights and water quality, it became clear it was also about development, economic security, jobs, wildlife and wetlands preservation, governmental sovereignty, and control issues, all of which have to be accounted for and accountable for a solution to be workable. We have learned from litigation that the "science" that is produced by contesting and adversarial experts is not always the best (Goldberg, 1994; Jasanoff, 1995). And to the extent that even scientific "decisions" are affected by important social processes and organizational behavior, it is important that we learn how to deal with and evaluate the scientific and human layers of decision making in the interactive environments in which they occur (Vaughn, 1996, 1998).

As the comments in this section of the case study make clear, "facts" are not always facts: Their interpretations depend on human processes that often need clarification, explanation, and facilitated understanding, all of which can often occur with facilitated dialogue. To the extent that scientists and decision makers need "bridge builders," often a cofacilitation team may be appropriate in highly complex disputes or regulatory problems like the SFEP: one with some technical expertise and a coleader with "process" or "educational" expertise. Errors of judgment, science, or politics are most often made when groups of similar disciplines insulate themselves within their own knowledge bases or their own internally derived ethical or accountability standards. Consensus processes can provide that external review or reality check that may be absent when a system becomes too closed (see Badaracco, 1997, for some examples of the need to consult multiple layers and communities when making difficult choices).

—Carrie J. Menkel-Meadow, *Legal scholar*

REFERENCES

Badaracco, J. (1997). *Defining moments: When managers must choose between right and right.* Cambridge, MA: Harvard Business School.

Goldberg, S. (1994). *Culture clash: Law and science in America.* New York: New York University Press.

Jasanoff, S. (1995). *Science at the bar: Science and technology in American law.* Cambridge, MA: Harvard University Press.

Vaughn, D. (1996). *The* Challenger *launch decision: Risky technology, culture, and deviance at NASA.* Chicago, IL: University of Chicago Press.

Vaughn, D. (1998). Rational choice, situated action and the social control of organizations. *Law & Society Review, 32,* 231.

The EPA first constituted the TAC by inviting scientists and engineers having relevant expertise from a variety of agencies, and research and educational institutions. The committee later expanded itself to include additional science and engineering expertise. Despite several requests, it did not enlist an economist, attorney, or social scientist. Effectively, the membership reflected a policy decision that the TAC was to focus on science and the characterization of the estuary. Academics participated initially, but soon found little incentive to stay. As they and some other researchers dropped out, the committee consisted increasingly of agency and interest group staff. The TAC's contributions were brought into the larger SFEP process through the issue subcommittees on which TAC members served, and through a set of facilitated workshops.

The status and trends reports developed by the subcommittees over the course of four years reflected a mutual acceptance of information and put a stop to endless adversarial arguments in which no one could agree on the basic facts. One of the TAC members described the difference between adversary science and how the TAC operated this way:

It is almost a joke how technical information has been abused in this area. The state water board runs quasi-judicial administrative hearings. Lawyers bring their own technical experts; they cross-examine the scientists and find typos in their articles and raise the question of whether the whole article might not be riddled with mistakes. There is no question of peer review. Moreover, differing opinions are equally weighted. So if 99 percent of the scientific opinion supports one view and only a few people support another, they are weighed equally. We tried in the TAC to use scientific standards to determine what could be accepted.

Developing the reports was not an easy task, however. By design, the exercise was intended to be purely scientific. In practice, however, it proved difficult to make a clear distinction between technical and nontechnical issues. In essence, they jointly constructed the information they could agree on. According to one member,

The status and trends reports were originally meant to be technical only. We tried to be factual in what we put there. But then there was a debate. . . . [A technical person from an environmental group] wanted to include conclusions on how badly the bay was doing. We did not do it because it was not factual. There were polarities among members, though all are scientists. You have not only environmental advocates but also people from agencies who work for the discharger community, saying, "You cannot draw those conclusions." . . . Debates were over what could be concluded or said, or over caveats that were needed. You can speculate, and you can have differing interpretations that are legitimate. One of the scientists would end up pointing out where there was little argument over conclusions.

The difficulties that arose around the attempt to distinguish between technical and nontechnical information illuminated a certain culture clash between many TAC members and others involved in the process. The issue subcommittees supervising the preparation of the status and trends reports consisted of scientists and managers. The scientists wanted the reports to be limited to scientific characterization, while the managers insisted on including a set of "management options." One TAC member noted, "Scientists don't like to talk politics." A frustrated member complained,

The MC decided there should not be separate technical and lay subcommittees on the same topic. These mixed groups did not want to use scientific criteria of relying on peer review and findings that have been well established. They wanted to rely on anecdotal evidence and common sense, gripes, and they wanted to talk about management options. Some scientists

felt they could not be tainted with hearsay and dropped out.

Managers had similar frustrations. One commented that the status and trends reports were "useful because they got the scientists to agree on some findings. They think of themselves as gods in their fields and fight over hypotheses and try to block each other's views."

Although the process was time-consuming and sometimes frustrating, overall it appears the exercise had beneficial effects for long-term communication among participants, and for developing a common understanding of the issues and their implications. Although little *new* information was developed, much was done to sort and organize existing information so it could be understood and used. One of the participants with little scientific background expressed a common view:

The status and trends reports were good—a valuable resource for the future research. Now things are written down. The inventory of research gaps was good. The reports put the information into ordinary language and made the scientific findings accessible to people.

Some lay participants acknowledged having learned some science. And one engineer found the experience of working with the managers changed him:

Suddenly I became exposed to political realities. I used to work in an experimental mode. You get all the factors right and then systematically carry out the task. I discovered the world was not like that. It has taken me years to change from the rational, logical thinking of an experimental scientist. For example, I used to think if we laid out the monitoring program and ran through it, people would like it. I did not realize people change their minds a lot and, over time, in any case, do not even see the same problem any more. ➥

❧ COMMENTARY

This case study reveals so well how so-called scientific rationality must be melded with "political or managerial realities" to be enacted or effective. Consensus processes, so far, where they have worked, have been the bridges between different disciplines, with different "standards of proof," rules of decision, and methods for approaching problems. Modern-day problems are all multilayered and require a coordinator to "keep all the meat in the sandwich." In this case, a new scientific standard of water quality emerged from this "political" and "scientific" process conducted over time with multiple participants.

—Carrie J. Menkel-Meadow, *Legal scholar*

The SFEP made its most important technical contribution in the development of an innovative water quality index that could be used for monitoring the estuary's health. The SFEP convened a group of scientists, representing environmental protection and water diversion agencies and interests, to develop a science-based consensus on the impacts of freshwater diversion on the estuary's biological resources. They hired Dr. Jerry Schubel, a water scientist and director of a marine institute at the State University of New York at Stony Brook, to facilitate four workshops. Within the first hour of meeting, the group concluded it would not deal with quantitative measures of flows because they could not be made sufficiently precisely. Instead, it focused on how to measure water quality, much to the frustration of a state water agency representative who contended that the EPA must have manipulated the process so it could attend to its agenda of setting new water quality standards.

Whatever the case, the scientists reached substantial agreement on a new indicator of water quality for the estuary, the 2 parts-per-thousand (ppt) salinity index, also known as X2, although some state water agency representatives did not join the consensus. A technical participant explained,

> We have chosen 2 ppt as the surrogate for knowing where the mixing zone is. This zone is rich, where a lot of life is generated and high concentration of food. . . . Typically, this zone, most agreed, should be near Suisun Bay because if it goes further back into the delta where there are deep channels, then it does not have the beneficial effects it does in the shallow area.

The scientists achieved a high degree of consensus on the salinity index, although there was some disagreement about the appropriate location for the mixing zone.

The broad acceptance of this indicator had a number of important coordinative and political results. First, it formally established agreement that water quality and flows are linked in a fundamental way, since the location of this salinity level is affected by the amount of water flowing through the estuary. This agreement was a major breakthrough, not because it was a surprise but because it provided a relatively scientific and legitimate criterion for the argument. Second, the index came to be more or less understood and regarded as important by the lay members of the MC. Even if the SWRCB would not adopt it as an official measure of water quality, other agencies likely would. For environmental agencies, it was a potentially powerful tool to challenge water user interests.

Finally, and most important, the general acceptance of this indicator was a measure of the degree to which the SFEP members had come to reconceptualize the problem of the estuary as an ecological system in which they all played a part. When they began, some said there was not even agreement that there was a problem, and each of the groups saw it somewhat differently. The choice of a system or outcome measure like the salinity index, rather than an input measure such as end-of-the-pipe discharges, represents a recognition that the estuary's health is a collective and complex problem requiring collaborative decision making and action.

Staffing

The SFEP was well staffed, with as many as 19 people at some point on at least a part-time basis. They were largely EPA employees, with some additional personnel borrowed from state agencies. A variety of consultants were also hired to assist in various tasks.

Staff generally assisted the committees rather than taking an active, leading role. According to a principal staff director,

> The role of the staff was to facilitate group interaction and provide infor-

mation. They provided administrative support and made the agendas with the chair of the group they worked with. The small work groups left the lobbying and the networking to the staff to handle. Staff did its work one-on-one with the small groups to explain the new changes in the documents on the controversial issues. There was a phone tree, and one staff member handled several MC members. Sometimes they just passed along information, such as administrative things. Other times, it was more like education or lobbying.

According to a number of respondents, a level of trust among members and between members and staff was developed in the small groups, and carried through the rest of the process.

Although, even when asked, not many of our respondents said the staff were biased, there clearly was a problem in having staff come from the EPA. Most we interviewed reported that the staff tried to serve members equally with information. Nonetheless, the environmental protection orientation of the EPA created problems. One of the managers of the process said,

> Nonenvironmentalists did not trust staff because they regarded them as pro-environment. Environmentalists wanted staff to be advocates. Our staff are typically pro-environment advocates in the first place.

To provide a greater sense that the project was not being unduly driven by the EPA, the staff were housed in the offices of the Association of Bay Area Governments. Two or three of the nonenvironmentalist players complained that the staff lobbied members. One said, "Staff was biased, should have been more neutral." Remarkably, though no one disputed that staff advocated for environmental protection, most accepted it as legitimate, given the legislative purposes of the project.

Consensus Process and Facilitation

The MC was chaired by Harry Seraydarian of the EPA, who ran meetings largely in a consensus building way. Remarkably, according to our respondents, even participants who distrusted the EPA accepted his chairing as fair. Nonetheless, they found he "represented his agency when he needed to." Key EPA staff sometimes felt their loyalty split between their boss and the overall direction given to them by the MC, particularly when the chair disagreed with the MC. As the five-year deadline for plan completion approached, issues became more focused and resolving them more difficult. The MC decided to hire an outside facilitator to help it complete the CCMP, which the staff had begun to write. The SFEP selected two people who worked together to facilitate the meetings.

The size of the MC and its diversity made the meeting process difficult. The early organizers' commitment to be inclusive had led to the large size, which clearly was not efficient for working out complex issues. While the relationships may not have become warm among participants, by the end of the process they were trading jocular insults among one another, regardless of their position or role. The meeting process seemed to equalize the participants' opportunity to be listened to, in much the model prescribed by the literature. One midlevel agency participant observed,

> The SFEP got us sitting around the table. I noticed that the power and

prestige of individuals faded as people sat there over time. The deputy director of [a major state agency] . . . had no more clout than the [an environmental group]. . . . The organization behind the person faded after a while and it became just two people—bricks banging into each other. . . . The monoliths were no longer there, but you had strong individual personalities.

Participants generally were pleased with the facilitators, who they felt helped the MC move along. One of the facilitators ran the meetings, keeping to a strict schedule and making sure agreements were reached if possible. The other operated a computer equipped with a large display screen that allowed everyone to see wording changes as they were made. Those we interviewed had some ambivalence around the group's focus on the language of the plan, which was promoted by the use of the display technology. Although they found it helpful as a way of keeping track of where the group was, they felt the focus on wording sometimes obscured the underlying interests. One member commented,

> It tended, at times, to focus on trivia. Yet it was a clearly good way to move the process along. The focus was on the language and not on the content of the policy.

The criterion for establishing that there was a consensus was, de facto, 100 percent agreement. The facilitator alleviated the tension around this "voting" procedure by using a "six-finger" rule that gave members more than one option for expressing their views. A member would hold up anywhere from one to six fingers to signify his or her view of a proposed idea. The scale went from one finger, representing "I fully agree," to four, "I do not like it but I will not block consensus," to five, "There is no way I will agree to this," to six, "I won't agree but perhaps further discussion can resolve it." This procedure gave participants a way to express their views, without necessarily having to be obstructionist. As a practical matter, however, over time it became dichotomous. Was a member's vote five fingers or something else? And could the five be changed to another number? A development representative said, "Everyone was relatively happy with the finger voting system, which was relatively good. The facilitator used straw polls often, which worked well." She felt, however, that in the SFEP, "consensus meant majority rule and did not mean 100 percent unanimity"—meaning the six-finger rule could mask some dissent.

Adoption of the CCMP

The last meeting of the MC was devoted to adoption of the CCMP. One hundred percent agreement was needed and there were still some "no" votes. The deadline set by the federal legislation was 5 o'clock that afternoon. As time passed, the facilitator hurried the committee along, finding words they could agree on, without pursuing the underlying reasons or meaning. Agriculture and the building industry were especially dissatisfied. Some members had difficulty with a recommendation that the salinity index should be used as a means of assessing ecosystem health. It was worked out that the recommendation would be to "consider" use of the index as an indicator, but a minority report was also prepared on this topic. In an ironic twist, the ground rules provided an incentive to agree to adoption of the plan even if one did not agree fully with its contents. One could

prepare a minority report to be included in and disseminated with the plan only if one became a signatory to the document. There were also problems around the insufficiency of the information on the plan's cost implications, on which debate had to be cut off due to a lack of time.

Full consensus was reached amid cajoling and teasing of reluctant members, loudly expressed worries of some members about the support of the constituencies they represented, and clear indecision until the last moment by key state agency officials who said they would not have supported the plan if other substantial groups had not. The official vote was 100 percent, but in conversations after the meeting it seemed to represent little commitment or enthusiasm by at least some players, such as building and business groups, farming interests, and state water agencies. There was a clear tension in the room between the desire to see a product from five years of work and ambivalence about aspects of that product. Nonetheless, the CCMP covered many issues that had been resolved and most players bought into most of the plan.

Prospects for Implementation of the CCMP

At the time of adoption of the CCMP in the spring of 1993, there was great uncertainty among participants about whether and how the plan would be implemented, or indeed how it would make any difference. Most participants focused on the plan itself and the potential for implementation as the test of the SFEP's success or impact. Participants expressed concern that because of the 100 percent consensus requirement, the plan's contents were either the lowest common denominator or stated so generally that issues would have to be

fought out again in implementation. Because the plan did not have the force of law,
some thought it would end up sitting on a
shelf, collecting dust. No one claimed it was
a radical piece of work. One participant
asserted that 90 percent of what was in the
plan was going to happen anyway and that
other things might happen just because
they were good ideas. ⦿

⦿ COMMENTARY

The "exit" interviews in this case study demonstrate that the process produced
thoughtful reflection and feedback. Participants seemed to learn that how consensus
was defined mattered and that something less than 100 percent agreement might have
been more effective. A customized voting system attempted to deal with priority
setting, yet some felt there was still a need to establish more of a culture of cooperation
and collaboration. Astute participants can learn from one process what the barriers
or hindrances to resolution are and learn for the next episode how to involve all the
important stakeholders, how to establish communication rules, governing and managerial units to cross technical areas, and how to develop language that is general
enough for transdisciplinary understanding but specific enough to solve concrete
issues.

—Carrie J. Menkel-Meadow, *Legal scholar*

Participants saw a number of other problems for implementation of the plan. In
addition to the consensus being thin, the
plan set no priorities, did not identify lead
agencies, and contained insufficient information on the social and economic costs of
the proposed actions, particularly for local
governments. Where the money would
come from to support implementation actions was also uncertain. The plan contained proposals for developing revenue
sources in support of implementation, such
as surcharges on water users and real estate
transfers. These proposals, however, would
require support of the governor and the
legislature.

A major cause of concern was that the
plan had not acquired sufficient commitment among the state agencies. More important, there was an evident lack of support from the governor's office, whose
concurrence was required by law. Would he
sign the plan given its financial implications
and, more important, its challenges to the
water supply that serves the southern farmers and urban areas? Even though they had
signed on to the CCMP, some participants
urged the governor to reject at least those
portions of the plan on which there were
minority reports.

Although many participants felt the governor's approval of the CCMP would be
critical to the success of implementation,
along with active support from the agencies
and other communities represented, the
MC chair could see ways the plan could
have an effect in any case:

> Some see the purpose of the CCMP as
> an enforcement tool and look for the
> teeth. I want to use the plan as a basis
> for implementing actions, but not as a
> club. We sent the plan to agencies and
> asked which parts were priorities from
> their view. It went to all relevant agen-
> cies with a request to identify costs and

actions already committed to so we can decide on the next steps. We are working to have regional water quality boards take the lead on implementation. We expect to have a new implementation committee including some interest groups, along with agency people.

■ *Epilogue*

In November 1993, Governor Wilson issued his concurrence, which was modified by a number of conditions he appended to the plan. The EPA administrator officially approved the plan several weeks later. The governor opposed any new revenue sources to support implementation. He also registered specific conditions in regard to water rights, endangered species, wetlands, the need for setting priorities, and

the use of the salinity index. With regard to the latter, he specified that his concurrence was based on the understanding that the CCMP "neither requires nor recommends" use of the salinity index as a water quality "standard." Around the same time, he also instructed the Bay-Delta Oversight Council (BDOC) to revisit the SFEP proposals on flows and water quality. The governor had appointed BDOC following the EPA's disapproval of a 1991 state plan to reduce the salinity of the delta. Like the SFEP, BDOC is a consensus group, but it reflects a very different notion of the boundaries of the problem and the appropriate stakeholders. Two-thirds of the participants represented farming and urban water interests in southern California that would be affected by the proposals to increase freshwater flows to the bay. ◆

◆ COMMENTARY

Of course, ultimately a process and a problem as complex as this may come down to the decision of one person—a governor, in this case, or a president—which may limit what groups can accomplish. Nevertheless, to the extent that a group-based consensual process is truly participatory and involves enough of the stakeholders, developing commitment to the process and the outcomes reached and reducing the adversarialism and "demonization" of the other sides, single-veto officers—like governors or presidents—may not be able to reject the outcomes of a process that has brought previously contending parties to some kind of agreement or commitment. While underlying positions may not be changed, parties may come to realize they are better off for having learned from the other side and achieving the "possible" than remaining intransigently committed to positions that will prevent anything from happening at all.

Though the jury is still out on the implementation of the outcomes of the estuary project process, it is clear that at least some groundwork ("waterwork") has been laid for talking across disciplines and attempting to manage complexity. Parties do seem to have learned that while winning may be good, the risk of loss and no action is potentially worse. If we are to manage complexity, we have to try to find ways of bringing people together in different ways. Whether multiple, ongoing processes will help or further complexify the environment remains to be seen, but at least 5 years to some realistic proposals is faster than the 10 to 20 years that complex environmental litigation and regulation often takes.

—Carrie J. Menkel-Meadow, *Legal scholar*

Meanwhile, four key federal agencies got together to further refine the salinity index and consider applying the standard suggested by the SFEP. Reflecting the amount of political and technical support underpinning the salinity index, these agencies officially proposed use of the 2 ppt isohaline criteria as a dynamic measure of bay-delta water quality in December 1993. This process, in loose combination with several other concurrent efforts, helped lay the groundwork for the development and signing of the 1994 Bay-Delta Accord. The accord is considered by many to represent a truce in California's water wars. It lays out an agreement for managing the delta that would be followed until a more comprehensive decision could be made through another collaborative process—the CALFED Bay-Delta Program. By the time of the signing of the accord, all parties had developed sufficient confidence in the viability of the salinity index as an indicator that it was included explicitly in the agreement, and it is now used in the management of the bay-delta. CALFED is now considering the use of the index on a permanent basis for long-term restoration and management of the bay-delta ecosystem. In 1996, as a result of the CALFED collaboration, all the major state interests supported a statewide bond measure for water projects and habitat restoration. This measure was one of only a few supported by voters and provided funding that is now being used for bay-delta restoration and protection under the auspices of the CALFED program.

Five years after the signing of the CCMP, the SFEP stakeholders are continuing to implement the recommendations of the CCMP. The stakeholders built mechanisms for coordinating their efforts into the plan, most of which are being followed as planned, although some adaptations have been made to accommodate unanticipated conditions. One of the most notable outcomes of the SFEP process has been the development of additional collaborative processes to address implementation issues.

CCMP implementation is coordinated through a 30-member committee, which receives broad oversight from a five-member executive council. The original vision was that the implementation would be carried out through a variety of subcommittee and working group efforts involving relevant agencies and other stakeholders. In practice, a small staff also has been retained under the auspices of the SFEP. In concert with their agency partners, the staff provide a focal point for the coordination, fund-raising, and public outreach activities. In a unique collaboration among agencies, SFEP staff is housed in the offices of the Regional Water Quality Control Board, funded by the EPA, and officially employed by the Association of Bay Area Governments, which also handles the fiscal administration. All SFEP projects are supported by grants from the EPA and state and local governments. This year it will receive grants totaling nearly $2 million in support of specific implementation actions.

The work of two other entities—Friends of the Estuary and the San Francisco Estuary Institute—is also critical for the implementation of the CCMP. Friends of the Estuary is a nonprofit corporation established in 1991 as an outgrowth of the SFEP. Friends was established originally as a way to build public support for the CCMP and obtain governmental and nongovernmental funding to supplement the estuary project. Today, it is responsible for promoting and coordinating the public involvement and education programs.

The San Francisco Estuary Institute (SFEI) is a nonprofit, technical organization that operates externally from any individual stakeholder and at the collective direction of all of them. As such, it is able to provide technical expertise in which all of the stakeholders have trust. The SFEI conducts research and monitoring; evaluates, interprets, and manages data; and disseminates this information to agencies, universities, school systems, and the interested public. The regional monitoring program is one of the innovative ideas generated in the SFEP process that is now operating with success under the auspices of the SFEI. The program is funded by the 77 public and private organizations that discharge treated wastewater, cooling water, or urban runoff or are involved in dredging activities in the bay. Many of these organizations also provide expertise or logistical support to the program; a number of federal and state agencies also contribute funds or in-kind services to the program.

The Friends of the Estuary and the SFEI boards of directors and the implementation committee have overlapping membership through which direction to these organizations and the SFEP is loosely coordinated. In addition, the SFEP, Friends, SFEI, and their agency counterparts work closely on a variety of projects. For example, one of the two areas in which the CCMP did not contain consensus was wetlands management. The implementation committee decided that before much could be done with regard to wetlands management, a set of goals needed to be developed. The agencies having regulatory interests in wetlands created a collaborative process to develop a consensus on the areas and types of wetlands needed in the bay. The San Francisco Estuary Ecosystem Goals Project draft report was published in June 1998 and contains goals and recommendations for wetlands management. Although the project

operates primarily under the auspices of the SFEI, it is a truly collaborative effort involving a number of agencies and organizations, and well over 100 individuals.

The SFEP and SFEI have been involved in a variety of other collaborations with agencies and stakeholder organizations to focus attention on CCMP implementation issues. For example, in 1996, the SFEP organized a workshop on ballast water exchange and exotic species invasions. Similarly, the SFEP collaborated with several state and regional agencies and the EPA to develop a guidebook for city and county governments on ways to help improve the estuary. Every two to three years, the SFEP in collaboration with its partners organizes a "State of the Estuary" conference. These conferences focus on the scientific, management, and policy issues relating to the health of the estuary, and they draw large audiences of people with diverse interests.

About a year after the completion of the CCMP, the SFEP staff found itself facing several problems. One was that the CCMP contained many actions, but no priorities. In addition, the SFEP was required to submit a report to Congress, but had no way of tracking progress. Based on a series of interviews with stakeholders, staff started developing a chart indicating where progress had been made on the various action items and by whom. Then in August 1996, it convened a workshop to set priorities for bay-delta action over the next five years. Seventy-five representatives from federal, state, regional, and local governments and business and environmental groups reviewed the progress chart and participated in facilitated discussions. Out of these discussions came a list of 10 priorities, which now guide the SFEP staff and stakeholders as they implement the CCMP. In October

1996, the SFEP published the *CCMP Workbook,* an impressive compilation of progress made on each of the CCMP recommended actions. The *Workbook* served as the SFEP's report to Congress and is considered such an effective communication tool that its format has been adopted by several other estuary projects around the country.

The experience gained in the SFEP has contributed to the development of several other consensus-based processes, the most directly related of which is the Long-Term Management Strategy (LTMS) for materials dredged in the San Francisco Bay. As an outgrowth of the SFEP dredging subcommittee, the Army Corps of Engineers and the EPA convened representatives of the agencies having regulatory authority over dredging in the bay, together with navigation interests, fishing groups, environmental organizations, and the public. They hoped to overcome the "mudlock"—the legal disputes and bitter conflict—that had paralyzed dredging management. The organization of this process included a steering group smaller than that used in the development of the CCMP. It also separated the policy group from other participants, but nonetheless sought wide participation. The LTMS organizers made these structural adaptations as a result of their SFEP experience. The LTMS has achieved a number of policy agreements. A final Policy EIS/Programmatic EIR was released in late 1998 and includes as the preferred alternative plans for reuse of dredge materials. In addition, LTMS agencies have established a "one-stop" interagency office for applicants seeking dredging permits. This office also allows the agencies to coordinate better their day-to-day dredging decision-making and environmental protection responsibilities.

■ Assessment

The SFEP has made and continues to make lasting changes in the way agencies and other stakeholders work to accomplish their goals in the estuary. As a first-order outcome, the public and private stakeholders continue to coordinate their actions and make progress on implementing the actions of the CCMP. As second- and third-order outcomes, the learning that has taken place in engaging in consensus-based collaborations has spawned further collaborations. Relationships built through the SFEP have proved useful in addressing concerns in related areas. As a result of experience in the SFEP and a variety of other processes, collaboration is seen now as a more effective way to address the complex, interlinked issues facing California water policy makers. In the words of the MC chair, "I can say we have gotten better coordination through consensus process, though we did not necessarily have consensus on everything." All our evidence supports this.

The CCMP

Officially, the SFEP achieved consensus on the CCMP, with brief minority reports in two areas. In other words, a great many issues and policy directions were agreed to. Although some said the consensus was thin on some points, some language was vague, and the governor only agreed to it with conditions, the CCMP remains the adopted plan for the estuary. It is an official document that has weight for administrative decision making and for legal challenges by watchdog groups. While it does not have teeth in the sense that particular parties can be forced to act in particular ways, many parties have acted as it says because they have decided it is a good idea.

Personal and Professional Networks

Participants representing most of the key players influencing the water quality in the estuary developed working relationships and communication networks with one another, as well as an understanding of each other's perspectives. Many of them use these relationships and understandings to do their estuary-related work; they call each other and coordinate informally over issues before they become conflicts. One agency participant observed,

> I now have networks into 40 different groups representing different values or at least points of view. If they have frustrations they can call me. I get called a lot. I call them a lot too. I am on the phone with the Sierra Club almost every day. I ask them what I can do to help. I try to find out what they are doing and to see what I can do consistent with my agency's objectives, to help.

Agreement on the Nature of the Water Quality Problem

Participants came to a basic agreement on the existence and characterization of the estuary's water quality problem. This agreement moved the debate away from one relying on adversary science, in which participants could hide their views behind arguments over evidence and data quality. They produced a major document, compiling a consensually agreed-on scientific description of the estuary, in a form accessible to managers and the public. They moved from a set of narrow, parochial views of the estuary as a place where pollutants are dumped, shipping is conducted, and endangered species try to survive to an understanding of the estuary as an ecological system where the many activities interact in complex, and not fully understood, ways.

Agreement on the Salinity Index for Measuring Water Quality

They largely agreed on the salinity index as an indicator of estuarine health and a principal monitoring tool. This index is now largely accepted as a legitimate indicator of water quality because of the debate SFEP participants went through, and agencies now rely on this measure. These were achievements from a scientific viewpoint as they brought the management methods more in line with current science, but they also represented a political achievement that set up conditions for effective long-term coordination. The selection of this indicator and wide acceptance by stakeholders of the conception of the estuary as a system in which all have a stake were tantamount to an agreement that future estuary management would require collaborative problem solving.

Spin-Offs and Related Projects

The LTMS, San Francisco Estuary Ecosystem Goals Project, and federal agency consensus effort on the salinity index were all direct outgrowths of the SFEP. Each was designed differently to take into account the nature of the issues at hand and to reflect the organizers' learning about the strengths and weaknesses of collaborative processes from their experience in the SFEP.

In addition to spin-off collaborative decision-making processes, the SFEP resulted in a number of collaborative institutions. For example, the SFEI was developed as a nonprofit organization to coordinate and carry out research and monitoring. With representatives of agencies and stakeholders on its board of directors, the SFEI operates as an external and trusted scientific group.

Changes in Participants' Formal Positions on the Issues

We were not able to find that participants had changed their positions on major issues under dispute. However, some understandings and actions changed. For example, the new monitoring strategy now provides for less intensive monitoring of individual discharges, and more comprehensive monitoring of ambient conditions in the estuary. One participant said, "Basically, no one changed their point of view," but felt people "did get a better understanding of the issue. For example, I better understood the seriousness of the problem and the issues of the delta and Suisun Bay."

Boundaries of the Problem and Alternative Decision Arenas

The biggest challenge confronted by the SFEP was that decision making relative to the estuary was being carried on simultaneously in several arenas. Although people continued to participate in the SFEP, they knew they had alternative places where they could try to undo decisions made in the SFEP. The availability of such alterna-

tives lessened their commitment to the process and meant there was not as much incentive for participants to reach agreement as there would have been if the SFEP were *the* place where decisions were made.

This problem was linked to some fundamental difficulties in setting boundaries on the problem. There were continuing disagreements in regard to the scope of the problem and the appropriate stakeholders, and around whether the project would address socioeconomic impacts in addition to environmental quality issues. These continuing issues around the boundaries of the project raised questions about the legitimacy of the process and led to uncertainty among the participants about its importance. It also placed the governor in the position of having to choose between two unresolved and conflicting agendas: that of the CCMP and that of the water users.

Local Government Buy-In

One major limitation of the estuary project was that it did not succeed in getting effective local government participation or commitment to action. It did not even really offer much in the way of strategy pertinent to local governments, although local governments would be critical players in many implementation actions. For example, the land use and the wetlands section of the report would depend to a considerable degree on the voluntary cooperation of local governments or the creation of some type of regional government.

In general, participation from local governments was low. Some larger municipalities sent technical staff, but few elected officials attended. One explanation was that these officials did not really see it as worth their while to attend. The attitudes of many participants reflected little understanding of the multiple responsibilities and agendas of cities and their strained financial condition. Since the city leaders were not there they could not explain themselves, nor could they influence the implementation strategy to make it manageable for themselves or ensure local governments would have an incentive to take action.

The Consensus Process

Respondents gave the consensus process mixed reviews. It accomplished certain things as discussed above, but its accomplishments were limited by several factors. First, the early decisions to include every player and to define consensus as unanimity meant that inevitably some things could never be agreed on, even with almost everyone behind them. It also meant that some decisions really were the lowest common denominator. It meant too that the MC ended up being large and unwieldy. Finally, the decision to work out the language of the final report in MC meetings may have been a mistake. Although parts of the plan were drafted by subcommittees and staff, the facilitators' efforts became focused on "wordsmithing." The development of agreed-on language inevitably became more important than establishing in-depth understanding or real agreement in principle. This focus may have contributed to the sense of many players that agreement was thin.

The absolute deadline probably helped the group move to as much consensus as it did, but also truncated the process abruptly before key decisions about implementation could be made. At the last meeting, the most difficult implementation issues—costs and the identification of responsibili-

ties—were scarcely addressed, much less resolved. Those agreeing to the plan may have changed their minds had the implications of these issues been clear.

Consensus may be a slow process, but it had important political consequences in the views of most participants. One participant noted, "The SFEP might make working on implementation and legislation over the next five years easier due to the work of the last five years." Another observed, "The consensus aspects generated a lot of community support for the SFEP. The strength of using consensus was political. But the process has not gotten support outside the estuary." One participant, who was often in disagreement with others, remarked, "It kept people at the table constructively."

Participants also griped about the process. One, who came only to protect her interests and was always considering walking out, said, "I think the only thing we agreed on was that we hate this." In the first meeting of the implementation committee in 1994, there was substantial sentiment expressed that they did not want to use the consensus process they used in the MC. One critic asked herself, "Are we arriving at consensus for the sake of consensus itself? Are we really moving forward? Is the environment benefiting?" Her worry was that "people get so wrapped up in it and felt this need for consensus so much . . . they will do whatever it takes to get it." One environmentalist, who was the only participant we found with this view, said, "I would rather it not be a consensus project. Voting, majority rule would result in a stronger document for the resource. Environmental aspects were weakened in order to gain consensus."

The same critics also saw benefits. The environmentalist acknowledged that if "that sort of thing [i.e., consensus] gets the governor to sign the plan, then it may have been good." The other concluded, "Consensus is the thing to do. I think that consensus is a good thing. I think consensus is here to stay." In the end, even the few strong critics supported the idea of consensus building as a strategy even if they disagreed with certain aspects of how it was carried out.

The philosopher among our respondents—a technical person whose eyes had been opened to many new perspectives—offered the most thoughtful overall assessment of the SFEP, its results, and its effects on him:

> We are all in this together is what we have learned. None of us has the resources any more to overwhelm the others. We can't compete in a win-lose situation any more because the cost of losing is so high. We have to try for win-win solutions. Goodwill is an important ingredient in all this. The SFEP is a good example of how goodwill was developed over time. Interest groups had argued over the toys and scientists each said their own type of science needed to be done. There was at the outset no consensus on what were the issues, or what needed to be studied. SFEP changed that. We started seeing ourselves as a neighborhood making decisions about our backyard. You realize you cannot have everything. *Now the no-action solution is no longer acceptable.* The process requires energy and time, but it takes us in the direction it should for a democratic society.

■ Notes

1. The National Estuary Program was established by the 1987 amendments to the federal Clean Water Act (§ 320) and modeled after the Chesapeake Bay Program. It is administered by the EPA.

2. The governor also nominated Santa Monica Bay at the same time. For a description of the Santa Monica Bay Estuary Project, see Innes, Gruber, Neuman, and Thompson (1994).

3. See Tuohy (1993) for a full outline of the TAC activities.

■ References

Innes, J., Gruber, J., Neuman, M., & Thompson, R. (1994). *Coordinating growth and environmental management through consensus building.* Berkeley: California Policy Seminar.

Tuohy, W. S. (1993, April-June). Characterizing the San Francisco Estuary: A case study of science management in the National Estuary Program. *Coastal Management, 21*(2), 113-129.

■ *Further Reading*

Arandale, T. (1994, March). A guide to environmental mandates. *Governing.*

Association of Bay Area Governments. (1995, December). *Improving our bay-delta estuary through local plans and programs.* Oakland, CA: Regional Water Quality Control Board/San Francisco Estuary Project.

Friends of the Estuary. (1995). *Annual report 1995.* Oakland, CA: Author.

McCreary, S. T., Harnish, L., Tibbott, E., & Warren, B. (1993). *Options for strengthening existing institutional arrangements for watershed protection of the San Francisco Estuary.* CONCUR/PERC Working Paper No. 93-06. Berkeley, CA: CONCUR.

McCreary, S. T., Langenthal, J., Neuman, M., Buice, M., & Warren, B. (1993). *A prototype system for classifying watersheds in the San Francisco Estuary region.* CONCUR/PERC Working Paper No. 93-05. Berkeley, CA: CONCUR.

McCreary, S. T., & Tietke, C. (1993). *A first look back at the San Francisco Estuary Project.* CONCUR Working Paper No. 93-02. Berkeley, CA: CONCUR.

McCreary, S. T., Twiss, R., Warren, B., White, C., Huse, S., Gardels, K., & Roques, D. (1992). Land use change and impacts on the San Francisco Estuary: A regional assessment with national policy implications. *Coastal Management, 21,* 219-253.

San Francisco Estuary Project. (1991, February). *Status and trends report on land use and population: The geomorphology, climate, land use and population patterns in the San Francisco Bay, Delta and Central Valley drainage basins.* Oakland, CA: Author.

San Francisco Estuary Project. (1992, June). *State of the estuary: A report on conditions and problems in the San Francisco Bay/Sacramento-San Joaquin Delta Estuary.* Oakland, CA: Association of Bay Area Governments.

San Francisco Estuary Project. (1992, August). *The effects of land use change and intensification on the San Francisco Estuary.* Oakland, CA: Author.

San Francisco Estuary Project. (1993). *Managing freshwater discharge to the San Francisco/Sacramento-San Joaquin Delta Estuary: The scientific basis for an estuarine standard.* Oakland, CA: Author.

San Francisco Estuary Project. (1993, March 31). *Regional monitoring strategy.* Oakland, CA: Author.

San Francisco Estuary Project. (1994, June). *Comprehensive conservation and management plan.* Oakland, CA: Author.

San Francisco Estuary Project. (1996, October). *CCMP workbook: Comprehensive Conservation and Management Plan for the bay-delta implementation progress 1993-1996.* Oakland, CA: San Francisco Bay Regional Water Quality Control Board.

San Francisco Estuary Project. (1997). *State of the estuary, 1992-1997.* Oakland, CA: Author.

State Water Resources Control Board, California Environmental Protection Agency. (1993, April). *Water Right Decision 1630: San Francisco Bay/Sacramento-San Joaquin Delta Estuary.* Draft. Sacramento: Author.

Tuohy, W. S. (1994. January-March). Neglect of market incentives in local environmental planning: A case study in the National Estuary Program. *Coastal Management, 22*(1), 81-95.

U.S. Environmental Protection Agency. (1987, January). *Summary report of survey findings for the Bay/Delta Project to Office of Marine and Estuary Protection.* Washington, DC: Tetra Tech.

U.S. Environmental Protection Agency. (1989, August). *Saving bays and estuaries: A primer for establishing and managing estuary projects.* Washington, DC: Author.

Wakeman, T. H., III. (n.d.). *Partnerships in decision making within the San Francisco Bay/Delta.* Unpublished draft.

6

RESOLVING SCIENCE-INTENSIVE PUBLIC POLICY DISPUTES

Reflections on the New York Bight Initiative

■ Scott McCreary

The New York Bight Initiative was one of the first studies to explicitly design a collaborative decision-making process to take account of the shortcomings in the way traditional administrative, legislative, and judicial processes handle science-intensive issues. It was carried out from 1986 through 1988 under the auspices of the New York Academy of Sciences (NYAS). The substantive focus of the Bight Initiative was the management of pollutants in what the National Oceanic and Atmospheric Administration called "one of the most stressed marine ecosystems in the United States,"[1] the ocean region adjacent to New York Harbor known as the New York Bight.

From a process standpoint, it emphasized the procedures for joint fact-finding, and the linkage between fact-finding and the effective negotiation of a single-text document.

The Bight Initiative consisted of four main phases: a prenegotiation phase devoted to establishing the logic for intervention and framing issues for investigation; a 10-meeting series of mediated negotiations within which the joint fact-finding activity was focused; a postnegotiation ratification phase; and, finally, a documentation phase of the results of the case.[2]

The New York Bight Initiative was built on three key features:

1. Direct dialogue among a panel of scientists and a plenary negotiating group of 22 resource managers, resource users, and other interested parties.
2. An extensive joint fact-finding effort to review and present relevant technical information and evaluate the technical consequences of policy alternatives.
3. Mediated negotiation of an 80-page single-text document through five successive drafts, including five chapters of findings and one chapter of management strategies.

The balance of this case study addresses several topics. First, the logic for intervention is defined and how issues were framed for investigation is explained. The section following that explains how scientists were recruited to participate in the Bight Initiative and details the various roles scientists played. Then, how the joint fact-finding process worked, and how that work supported the development of a single-text agreement, is described. Last, the ratification phase of this single-text process is described.

■ *Framing Issues for Investigation*

The process began at the initiative of the author, then a doctoral candidate at MIT's Department of Urban Studies and Planning, who teamed[3] with the Science and Decision Making Program at the NYAS to prepare a successful proposal to the William and Flora Hewlett Foundation for financial support. The initial period consisted of strategic planning, stakeholder analysis, and issue identification.

We identified 30 key resource agencies and managers and recruited them to provide advice on strategic planning. This core group included representatives from federal, state, and local environmental protection agencies and from the Port Authority of New York and New Jersey, as well as a range of fishing, conservation, and maritime interests. Many of these actors shared responsibility for one or more aspects of resource management, yet have worked in largely separate decision-making venues. Strong, productive working relationships existed among a handful of groups. Other sets of groups had distinctly polarized relationships. For example, representatives of environmental protection organizations and the wastewater treatment agencies had disagreed strongly over the appropriateness of continued dumping of sewage sludge in the New York Harbor region. As well, the environmental interests had joined with the fishing industry in sharp disagreements over how best to dredge and deepen New York Harbor, given the likely resuspension of sediments laden with contaminants. While some strong coalitions existed among small groups of these organizations, there had been few, if any, prior efforts to pull together the full range of agencies with decision-making responsibility into a coherent effort to resolve these management issues.

At the time, citizens groups and resource agencies were in the process of developing specific proposals to restore the bight. The NYAS was concerned that unless these proposals took account of the strong competing interests at stake and were based on the best available science, poorly designed solutions might result. The academy did not seek to push particular models for action. Rather, it hoped to promote agreement by improving communication and cooperation among scientists, policymakers, and the public. In particular, the following issues were to be addressed in the consensus process:

- Is the bight stressed? What are the criteria for making this assessment?
- Is there a need for a bight restoration and management strategy?

- Which issues should be addressed first?
- How can consensus be developed to propose and implement a bight strategy? ⚬➤

⚬➤ COMMENTARY

None of the questions posed in the four bullets has a unique scientific answer. The concept of a stressed ecosystem needs clarification, and the question of the need for restoration and management is one of policy, not science. Science can help set priorities for what to do, once the policy decision is made as to the extent that society wishes to restore an ecosystem. Science may be useful in building a consensus for a bight regional management strategy, but science cannot determine that strategy.

—William Moomaw, *Environmental scientist*

An initial meeting confirmed that there was a high level of conflict and considerable scientific uncertainty inherent in bight management. The more than 30 participants agreed that the bight needed to be managed in a way that went beyond single issues, single disciplines, single interest groups, and single political jurisdictions. Some members of the core group expressed a willingness to fund a broad consensus building effort, but asked the academy to poll bight users and managers extensively to provide greater clarity about the most pressing bight management issues, the obstacles to effective bight decision making, and their level of interest in participating as potential negotiators in the emerging Bight Initiative. ⚬➤

⚬➤ COMMENTARY

Disagreement over facts and interpretation of science is often an impediment to agreement. There are three dimensions of scientific uncertainty that are recognized within the scientific community. The first arises because measurements or observations are insufficient to adequately bound the interpretation. Often, the necessary measurements have simply not been made. The second form of uncertainty may arise because of conflicting measurements, for example, one study finds high levels of PCBs in fish whereas another finds low levels. The third type of uncertainty arises not from issues of adequate data but rather from disagreements over competing or incomplete theoretical frameworks. The resolution of uncertainty within the scientific community may be accomplished through additional research. However, disagreement over uncertainty in developing consensus for policy implementation may not be resolvable since uncertainty is often used in this context to prevent action from being taken.

—William Moomaw, *Environmental scientist*

Over the following autumn and winter, our team conducted a conflict assessment during which we prepared a detailed survey instrument and interviewed close to 100 resource users and managers in the bight. A 10-page interview guide included a mix of open-ended and close-ended questions. Interviews were preceded with a letter explaining the agency's interest in promoting resolution of science-intensive disputes in the New York Bight. Open-ended questions touched on the respective roles in bight management, comments on traditional mechanisms for resolving conflicts between competing uses, and comments on obstacles to effective use of scientific information in bight management.

Perhaps the most important part of our interview guide asked respondents to consider a list of 23 bight management issues and rank order the top five issues. We asked respondents to consider whether (1) the issue was pressing; (2) the issue was characterized by elements of scientific or technical disagreement; and (3) the issue might be clarified or resolved through dialogue among scientists, decision makers, and representatives of key interest groups.

A total of 71 ranked questionnaires were returned to the academy. No single issue emerged as the unanimous choice, but five issues were mentioned by more than half the respondents. The question of assessing risks to the environment posed by contaminants topped the list. Human health risks and a classification of contaminant concentration by source were also major concerns. We established that a focus on the sources, fates, and effects of a class of contaminants would allow us to touch on issues rated high by a very large number of respondents.

The findings discussed above, along with the results of the open-ended interview questions, were described in a document mailed to key stakeholders in June 1986. One part of the report identified and discussed some of the obstacles that respondents perceived as inhibiting effective use of scientific information. They included the following:

- Some data are considered inaccessible to decision makers and the public.
- Parties may be unwilling to consider information that undermines their position.
- Testing protocols and standards are not sufficiently coordinated among agencies.
- Scientific uncertainty and disagreement frustrates effective use of information.
- Data are collected without following an issue-based research agenda.
- Media and elected officials may not make the best use of scientific information.

We reported these findings at a follow-up meeting in July 1986 and were encouraged to develop a formal proposal to submit to potential stakeholders and foundation funders. Through continued interaction of a small steering committee between July 1986 and October 1986, we refined the focus to the sources, fates, and effects of PCBs (polychlorinated biphenyls), a group of chlorinated organic compounds. PCBs were chosen as the focus because of a well-documented persistence in the environment, their tendency to bioaccumulate in fatty tissues, their responsibility for both carcinogenicity and reproductive impairment of a wide variety of marine organisms, and health effects in humans. Of particular concern were the potential risks to people who consume striped bass and bluefish contaminated with PCBs. PCBs enter the New York Bight from a variety of sources. Despite broad agreement over these basic statements, the relative importance of the sources, the extent of the biotic effects, and the real importance of health effects were widely contested and would thus lend themselves to a process devoted to joint fact-finding.

■ Involvement of Scientists and Technical Experts

A central premise of the New York Bight Initiative was to make possible the face-to-face interaction of policymakers and resource users.[4] Accordingly, our team designed and executed a process devoted to joint fact-finding. Our proposal called for a 5-meeting pilot process (which later grew to a 10-meeting series), with particular emphasis on joint discovery and evaluation of the most up-to-date scientific information. We envisioned a panel of scientific advisers working with negotiators in direct dialogue. Our proposal also called for the development of a single negotiating text to sum up the findings of the deliberations. This single text was to note areas of agreement and disagreement and would develop policy recommendations.

Variations on the proposal were sent to 14 prospective funders; of these, 11 agreed to provide support. The Office of Coastal Resources Management agreed to fund the joint proposal of the New York and New Jersey Coastal Programs. Private funders included the Towboat and Harbor Carriers Association, the Monmouth-Ocean Development Council, and the Exxon Foundation. Agency funders included the Port Authority of New York and New Jersey, the New York City Department of Environmental Protection, the Interstate Sanitation

Commission, and the Long Island Regional Planning Board. Altogether, the NYAS spent one year raising $85,000 from external sources and agreed to provide matching resources in the form of staff time and space to support the initiative.[5]

Once funding was in place, our team turned to the challenge of recruiting scientists. Identifying and engaging the help of these expert panelists was a two-phase process. In the first phase, as part of the conflict assessment, we assembled a large pool of candidate experts. In our stakeholder interviews, we asked respondents to name scientists whose expertise could conceivably help illuminate technical aspects of major bight issues. This yielded a roster with about 80 individuals (40 academics and 40 agency staff or consultants) with diverse specialties.

The second phase began once PCBs, which persist in the environment and accumulate in biota, were chosen as the focus for attention. Beginning in the 1930s, PCBs were manufactured for industrial uses, especially for electrical equipment because of their heat transfer properties and low combustibility. PCBs were used widely in chemical applications during the 1960s. Later, Monsanto, the original manufacturer, started using PCBs only for electrical equipment and other uses of PCBs were curtailed. General Electric was among the companies that bought the product and manufactured equipment, which used PCBs. Some of this equipment subsequently discharged PCBs into the environment.

We set out to locate scientists who could give an initial briefing to the negotiating group on some of the sources, fates, and effects on the marine ecosystem of PCBs. As work progressed, we redoubled our recruiting efforts for scientists with expertise in toxicology, human health effects, and sedimentology. This effort was iterative as the fact-finding activity continued through the first 8 of the 10 meeting series. By the end of the Bight Initiative, we had enlisted a total of 23 scientists.

We used two overarching selection criteria in recruiting scientists. The first, consistent with the aims of the Bight Initiative and the mission of the academy, was that they be able to generate the best, most up-to-date scientific information. We considered the possibility that negotiators could be given "veto power" over which experts were recruited. However, we rejected that as an inflexible approach that might preclude the best available information from entering the process and stifle an open exchange of views.

The second was to draw on people who would be viewed as credible by the negotiators. We tried to gauge this with a review of recent literature, conversations with negotiators, and, as the fact-finding process progressed, discussions with some of the first scientists recruited. Often, one scientist in a particular specialty was able to lead the academy to colleagues whose expertise could be useful. Several negotiators—both industry officials and environmentalists—also recommended experts who were tapped. Finally, in a few instances, scientific advisers also represented their agencies.[6]

The NYAS used some rather general guidelines to confirm that panelists would be suitable. Our team looked for people with advanced degrees (all but two had doctorates) who had worked and published for several years on their respective subjects. We also asked panelists whether they had previously been involved in "science advising for policy," though we did not expect them to have previous experience in a process with the structure of the Bight Initiative. ◆

◆ COMMENTARY

Adversary science or *advocacy science* is based on the debate model favored by lawyers. It involves having scientists present only the scientific data and theory that bolster a particular side of an argument. This approach has become particularly dominant in environmental debates, and it conflicts with the goal of science to evaluate objectively all evidence before coming to a conclusion concerning cause and effect.

—William Moomaw, *Environmental scientist*

The academy's neutral, nonpartisan standing and its strong scientific reputation[7] helped immeasurably in recruiting panelists for the Bight Initiative. A further element of attraction was the novelty of the process and its potential value for moving the policy debate along. The fact that the academy is housed in the old Woolworth family mansion on the Upper East Side proved to be a draw for some experts, as well. In a few cases, the academy offered to pay a modest per diem and travel expenses,[8] but in most cases this was not necessary. ◆

Eighth Workshop—Text Revision in Working Teams—August 1987

The August workshop will have two major objectives: (1) refining management options developed at the July 26 meeting, and (2) refining sections of the draft text on biological effects. Your greatest contribution will probably be in helping the group refine and critique draft management suggestions, and in offering an overview of efforts to clean up New Bedford Harbor for comparative purposes.

You should be forewarned that the group is a contentious one; in the words of one scientific adviser, members are "a bunch of prima donnas." Some individuals will no doubt take pains to point out how New Bedford and the Hudson/Raritan-Bight are different. But do not let this dissuade you from participating fully.

Figure 6.A. Excerpt from Letters of Invitation to Scientists to Serve as Scientific Advisers for the Bight Initiative in a Later Stage of the Process

∽ COMMENTARY

The question of who funds science or a scientifically based process has become a major issue. Are funders intent on buying a particular outcome, or are they genuinely interested in obtaining the outcome dictated by the scientific findings? The choice of the New York Academy of Sciences as a neutral convenor was critical for attracting scientists to the process and in achieving credibility of the final recommendation.

—William Moomaw, *Environmental scientist*

Once a scientist agreed to serve as a panelist, the NYAS team offered brief guidance in writing, as illustrated in Figure 6.A. These instructions evolved as the focus shifted from initial briefings to in-depth fact-finding, and later to the revision of negotiated language.

As the sequence of mediated negotiations was getting under way, several roles were envisioned for scientists. One was to identify relevant information and comment on its validity. A second was to explain cause-and-effect relationships. This was crucial to the Bight Initiative, since the causal sequence of sources → fates → effects of PCBs was chosen as the frame for analysis. Another important role of scientists was to help evaluate alternate policy recommendations and forecast their implications. Still another key charge was to help clarify the basis of scientific disagreement and uncertainty.

The scientists accomplished these tasks in a variety of ways. One mechanism was to offer scientific briefings and participate in subsequent question-and-answer sessions in which we helped participants to "cross-examine" scientists. Another was to invite scientists to draft initial versions of portions of the negotiated text. Related tasks were to comment on interim drafts summarizing findings, and to join policy makers in deliberating the merits of policy alternatives.

Role of the Mediator in Facilitating the Interaction of Negotiators and Scientific Advisers

The Bight Initiative demonstrated that, to be effective, a mediation team must fulfill a whole series of tasks to facilitate the involvement of scientists and technical advisers. Two of these have already been identified: recruiting scientists and then providing clear "terms of reference" for the briefing or dialogue tasks expected of them. ⟿

∾ COMMENTARY

It is extremely important that the tasks of the scientists were clearly stated and that the expectations of their contributions were made clear from the beginning. Many scientists are uncomfortable with questions about what should be done and are often better at assessing the implications of alternative policy recommendations than they are at suggesting appropriate policies.

—William Moomaw, *Environmental scientist*

Some other tasks are those of a secretariat. These included preparation of detailed agendas and packets containing relevant supporting materials for each day's workshops. These packets typically included short biographies for scientists, memoranda summarizing relevant scientific literature on a topic or an outline of policy options, and copies or excerpts of relevant scientific articles.

Our team accomplished our goal of bringing high-quality, up-to-date information to the deliberations. Moderating those discussions was a major task of the mediation team. Mediators introduced scientists and related their expertise to the task at hand. Then, as scientific advisers proceeded with their presentations, the mediators tried to discern when some presentations were becoming too technical or jargon laden. In other instances, the mediation team asked the experts to clarify their terms: "In other words X." Or, "So that means that Y."

Nevertheless, we had to identify and then work to overcome several obstacles to effective dialogue. In particular, we needed to perform several kinds of coaching and intervention in the preparation and presentations of technical advisers. In particular, we (1) anticipated and restructured overly complex presentations, (2) sought to eliminate unnecessary caveats about expertise, (3) encouraged greater tolerance for nonscientists, and (4) redirected the orientation of the scientists from a focus on research to policy action.

Anticipating and Restructuring Overly Complex Presentations

The mediation team found that scientists often present themselves as though they were addressing a scientific conference of their peers. This is no surprise, since this is the professional norm for most scientists. A recurring problem in the early briefings was that scientists tried to be overly comprehensive, swamping the participants with more information than they could readily handle. For instance, one scientist, when asked for a concise, 20-minute overview of PCB fates, presented 45 slides in 45 minutes. Another scientist, speaking on synergistic effects of PCBs and other contaminants, tried to be concise by packing his remarks with technical terms. We responded by giving ever-more specific instructions and coaching to scientists as the 10-meeting sequence proceeded.

Avoiding Unnecessary Caveats about Preparation or Expertise

In other cases, scientists' self-presentations cast doubts on their expertise or preparation. For example, the NYAS team recruited an aquatic toxicologist to summarize reported effects of PCBs on marine organisms. She prepared an excellent summary in the form of a concise memorandum as requested. But she preceded her professional review of scientific articles by noting, "I didn't really do a literature search." In fact, this investigator did do an informal literature search: She reviewed about 25 scientific articles and summarized them, but may not have turned up and abstracted every conceivable citation. Even though she had a very thorough grasp of her subject, the effect of her rigorous use of the term *literature search* and subsequent disclaimer was to undermine her credibility with the group. The mediator hoped that the panelists would elect to incorporate a summary of her findings in tabular form, listing the effects of PCBs in different aquatic organisms. The panelists instead initially favored including none of her material. Drawing on this lesson, we urged scientific panelists to accurately recount their expertise and level of preparation, but not to denigrate their own experience.

Encouraging Tolerance for Nonscientists or Specialists in Other Disciplines

Some scientists lacked tolerance for laypersons who "ask questions with obvious answers." One scientist, while eager to ensure the scientific accuracy of the discussions, treated a young environmental representative in a condescending style, stating at one point, "I hate it when my students interrupt me before I finish." The unfortunate result was to alienate the negotiator. Two other scientists went further and asserted that fellow scientific panelists with other backgrounds were unqualified to comment on certain subjects. To avoid such incidences, we stressed our fundamental objective of elevating the level of understanding among Bight Initiative negotiators. In instances where scientists appeared to be talking down to negotiators, the mediator tried to get parties to adopt a more conciliatory, collaborative posture.

Redirecting a Preoccupation with Research over Policy Action

Several scientists displayed a tendency to recommend more research rather than commenting on more tangible management options. Scientists varied in their willingness to recommend or propose revisions to policy actions in the face of scientific uncertainty, particularly if the subject matter extended beyond the bounds of their expertise. Our mediation team kept scientists focused on the job of summarizing relevant information and offering prescriptive advice. We repeatedly reminded scientists that while recommendations for new research and analytic tasks were welcome, their charge also included identifying and forging consensus on policy alternatives. ▪▶

∽ COMMENTARY

When faced with a gap in knowledge, conflicting data, or ambiguous theoretical frameworks, the natural response of the scientist is to ask for more research. After all, this is what they do. On the other hand, it is also important for policymakers to recognize that in some cases, additional measurements or analysis of existing data is necessary to resolve an issue. For example, one contentious issue in PCB-laced sediments is the argument over whether removing these sediments by dredging will stir up the PCBs and increase the amount of biologically available chemicals in the water column. A short-term, carefully monitored test at a limited site could provide a straightforward answer that would guide policymakers as to the relative degree of risk involved in using dredging as a remediation option. To my knowledge, such tests still have not been undertaken, and the "risk from dredging" remains a scientific uncertainty that paralyzes remedial action.

It is extremely difficult for scientists to shift from their role as scientific investigator to that of policy adviser. The rewards in science are for discovering greater complexity and for identifying more subtle effects within a narrowly drawn field of expertise. After all, the more obvious things have already been discovered. Scientific disciplines are deep rather than broad, and the practitioners spend many years mastering the techniques and vocabulary that allow them to practice within their chosen field. Laypeople are clearly seen as incapable of understanding such complex and advanced ideas. Caveats are the norm, and scientists are often loathe to step outside their turf of expertise and greatly resent it when anyone else steps across the boundary into theirs. Maintaining credibility with one's scientific peers is exceedingly important to scientists, and there is often disdain for scientists who either simplify their findings or whose work is used as a basis of policy, because the precision and accuracy of the findings are of necessity diluted or compromised to some degree. By way of contrast, effective policy prescriptions must be simple, at the cost of less precision, and the implications must be transparent and obvious to the nonscientific policymaker and public. The role of a facilitator to clarify the explanations of scientists is essential.

—William Moomaw, *Environmental scientist*

We quickly learned that it was sometimes necessary to allow a scientist a 5- or 10-minute monologue on an arcane subject before he or she was able to focus clearly on policy alternatives. Giving scientists "air time" yielded the dual benefits of establishing the legitimacy of their expertise and allowing them to summarize the key implications of a complex idea. Sometimes, this venting took place in writing: Scientists prepared lengthy briefing papers, which were modified to fit the needs of the participants. For instance, one expert wrote three or four pages on the physical features of the bight; he then worked with other advisers to boil the results down to a one-and-a-half-page document.

The tasks of recording meeting highlights and preparing meeting reports also assisted the exchange of information. Because participants knew they could count on receiving detailed meeting summaries, they were able to focus on the dynamics of the discussion without taking copious notes. The mediation team used both personal computers and large sheets of wallpaper to summarize the deliberations.

Assisting scientists and negotiators with the task of packaging information in an appropriate format was a major task of the mediation team, as detailed in the next section. This involved working closely with technical illustrators as well. The mediators needed to develop strategies for fairly representing information subject to scientific and technical disagreement.

■ *Specific Examples of Joint Fact-Finding and Information Sharing*

Creating a format to enable participants to engage in joint discovery and review of relevant information was a principal feature of the New York Bight Initiative. Joint fact-finding began at the initial meeting in January 1987 and continued through August 1987. This work spanned scientific briefings, group deliberations, and drafting of findings. This section presents several examples of the joint fact-finding activity. The following discussion touches on packaging of information in a useful format, dealing with the burden of proof, and steps to clarify and narrow scientific disagreement and uncertainty. This section concludes with observations on benefits of joint fact-finding.

Packaging Information in a Useful Format

A key finding of the New York Bight Initiative is that the format in which information is presented is as important as the information itself. Organizing information

in an appropriate way is crucial to the development of joint understanding of a problem.

Scientists can help provide the essential content, but providing the context or frame of the information became the responsibility of the mediation team. Simply stated, scientists (or any technical experts) working alone cannot always furnish the information in the most useful format. "Packaging" information in a clear, appropriate format required the joint effort of scientists, the mediation team, and negotiators. Appropriate packaging of information in a single text also requires careful attention to phrasing and sequence of prose.

Example 1: Defining, Documenting, and Illustrating PCB Movement through the Ecosystem

One issue we tackled in the joint fact-finding phase of the Bight Initiative was to document PCB sources and movement through the ecosystem. The starting point was a briefing by Dr. Joel O'Connor of the National Oceanic and Atmospheric Administration in which he described approximate quantities of PCBs in the Upper Hudson River, the Lower Hudson River, and the Hudson-Raritan Estuary, as well as the changes in these volumes over time. Negotiators urged the NYAS to continue synthesizing available information on this subject. To comply with this request, the NYAS mediation team and Dr. O'Connor jointly assembled the PCB Sources Subcommittee to be drawn from a mix of Bight Initiative negotiators and an expanded group of scientific advisers. ➥

∽ COMMENTARY

Task-specific groups like the PCB Sources Subcommittee are narrowly focused scientifically. Developing such groups fits better with many scientists' comfort level than organizational structures that are more broadly based.

—William Moomaw, *Environmental scientist*

In getting the PCB Sources Subcommittee under way, Dr. O'Connor circulated a modified draft of the summary table he had presented at the initial briefing to about a dozen colleagues who had published peer-reviewed articles, Ph.D. dissertations, or technical reports on PCB sources in the Hudson-Raritan ecosystem. Based on comments and corrections from these experts, a third version of the table was compiled. Subsequently, these scientists were invited to attend a PCB Sources Subcommittee meeting. The purpose of this gathering was to prepare an up-to-date synthesis and answer questions of the nonscientist negotiators.

Our mediation team proposed several ground rules, which the PCB Sources Subcommittee accepted. These included the following: (1) The group would focus specifically on sources; (2) scientific experts would serve as nonpartisan advisers—they would not represent one particular view over another; (3) interaction between scientific advisers and Bight Initiative negotiators was strongly encouraged; and (4) the group would move as far toward consensus as possible. In addition, the subcommittee established the important principle that information included in the summary table must be linked to a specific published article, technical report, or personal communication of data from the scientist who gathered it. ∽

∽ COMMENTARY

It is extremely important to scientists to base findings on securely documented information, of which peer-reviewed scientific articles are the most respected. Insisting that all references in the tables be linked to specific articles, technical reports, or identified scientists not only satisfies scientific credibility criteria for scientists but also ensures policy makers that they are using credible scientific input and not just opinions of individual scientists. The public is also well served by this transparent approach in that individuals, corporations, and public-interest organizations who were not involved directly in the process can have access to the information that was used in the policy-making process and make their own judgments as to its appropriateness or credibility.

—William Moomaw, *Environmental scientist*

We structured the agenda to begin with the creation of a joint working vocabulary. This involved drafting and revising working definitions of key terms—such as *source, flux,*[9] and *volatization*[10]—used to describe sources of PCBs and their movement through the ecosystem. Building this list of key terms in itself was a single-text negotiation exercise: One scientists would propose a definition, we would write it on flip chart paper, and another would propose a revision, which in turn would be subject to further change.

Reaching agreement on these working definitions gave the subcommittee not only a common language but also an important sense of momentum. It was determined that information on resources and fluxes be listed for two time periods: 1959-1979 and 1980 to the present (this break point was appropriate because flux of PCBs declined markedly after 1980). More important, the subcommittee undertook to prepare a "PCB budget": a table that showed sources, reservoirs (resting points), and fluxes (movements) of PCBs through the system. The subcommittee also agreed that each possible source of PCBs should be listed for each segment of the river, even if some data were missing. The next draft result was a 12-page table with many gaps.

At the negotiators' request, Dr. O'Connor joined with Dr. John Sanders, a sedimentologist based at Columbia University, to prepare a more concise version of the table, and together they boiled it down to four pages. In all, 25 scientific studies were referenced in the PCB budget.

The PCB Sources Subcommittee agreed that the four-page table should be included in the single-text document, but pointed out the need to present information on PCB sources in other formats. To more clearly communicate the nature of the problem, the subcommittee developed several paragraphs of text to summarize the key findings. Included were the following:

- Land disposal sites and electrical equipment are almost certainly the largest PCB reservoirs. Sediments of the Hudson River and estuary system are probably the next largest reservoirs.

- PCB levels in the system are dynamic. Available information indicates that PCB transport in sediment down the Hudson River has declined considerably between 1970 and the early 1980s and has since leveled off.

- The most obvious features of PCB flux in the region are that they are dominated by historic discharges of the General Electric Company. Although GE discharges of PCBs declined dramatically and have virtually ceased, flux of PCBs continued.

- Potentially significant loadings—such as industrial discharge, sewage treatment plant (STP) effluent, combined sewer overflow, and urban runoff—are not adequately measured.

The New York Bight Initiative demonstrated that technical information needs to be presented in multiple formats to make it accessible and understandable. For example, negotiators agreed that a figure was needed to show how PCBs move through the system. ➻

➻ COMMENTARY

It is useful to present information in multiple formats even within the scientific community. Hence, data tables, graphs, and diagrams can play an essential role in clarifying the basis for decision making to all constituencies.

—William Moomaw, *Environmental scientist*

Some negotiators suggested creating a flow diagram. In struggling to make a flow diagram geographically precise, they arrived at the idea of creating a series of block diagrams keyed to specific reaches of the river and estuary. The negotiators began sketching illustrations, but soon found that they lacked the patience and skills to implement their suggestions. Our mediation team offered to pass on the task to a technical illustrator who was on the staff at the NYAS. Figure 6.B shows excerpts of the figure in its final form.

Example 2: Summarizing the Existing Regulatory Framework for PCBs

The NYAS team and the negotiators completed a similar sequence of tasks to put information on PCB regulations into a useful format. In brainstorming text on PCB management, negotiators suggested that a matrix be prepared to summarize regulations that pertain to each PCB source.

The NYAS team sought help from the attorneys who edit *Environmental Regulation Reporter,* an authoritative periodical on environmental law and regulations. The

editors produced a dense, 12-page manuscript and obligingly traveled to a Bight Initiative negotiation session to present their analysis. Despite the mediators' efforts to portray the work in a favorable light, the Bureau of National Affairs (BNA) editors met with a rude reception from some negotiators, who rejected the lengthy prose format as inappropriate and reaffirmed their desire to see information summarized in a tabular format.

Negotiators wanted to see regulations grouped according to several subjects:

- the ban on uses;
- standards involving drinking water, fish consumption, and allowable PCBs in navigable waters;
- regulations pertaining to specific PCB inputs or reservoirs;
- laws guiding the cleanup of spills; and
- laws guiding the cleanup of in situ PCBs.

With the help of the NYAS team, the negotiators' needs were related to the BNA attorneys, who responded with a revised matrix. ●○

⌒ COMMENTARY

Agreeing on data to put into a table is often an arduous task. Science is not so much a democracy of ideas but rather a consensus as to what is established and what is not. As critics are often keen to point out, just because the scientific community "agrees" on a set of facts or on a particular interpretation does not make it so. It is always possible that the lone dissenting scientist is correct after all. Having said this, it is still important to recognize that the lone dissenter has available to him or her a peer-reviewed process for presenting the alternative view. This process subjects the dissenter's view to testing by others to determine whether or not it should become the new paradigm.

—William Moomaw, *Environmental scientist*

In the end, four different tables were created: General Regulatory Framework (for

an excerpt from this table, see Table 6.A), Restrictions on Industry Discharge, Con-

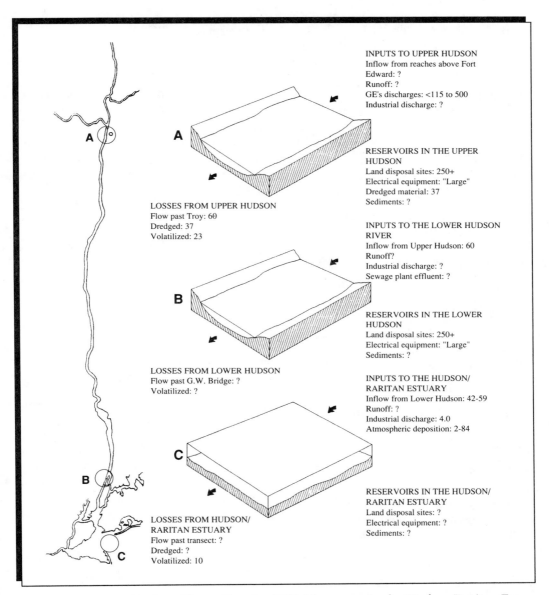

INPUTS TO UPPER HUDSON
Inflow from reaches above Fort
Edward: ?
Runoff: ?
GE's discharges: <115 to 500
Industrial discharge: ?

RESERVOIRS IN THE UPPER
HUDSON
Land disposal sites: 250+
Electrical equipment: "Large"
Dredged material: 37
Sediments: ?

LOSSES FROM UPPER HUDSON
Flow past Troy: 60
Dredged: 37
Volatilized: 23

INPUTS TO THE LOWER HUDSON
RIVER
Inflow from Upper Hudson: 60
Runoff?
Industrial discharge: ?
Sewage plant effluent: ?

RESERVOIRS IN THE LOWER
HUDSON
Land disposal sites: 250+
Electrical equipment: "Large"
Sediments: ?

LOSSES FROM LOWER HUDSON
Flow past G.W. Bridge: ?
Volatilized: ?

INPUTS TO THE HUDSON/
RARITAN ESTUARY
Inflow from Lower Hudson: 42-59
Runoff: ?
Industrial discharge: 4.0
Atmospheric deposition: 2-84

RESERVOIRS IN THE HUDSON/
RARITAN ESTUARY
Land disposal sites: ?
Electrical equipment: ?
Sediments: ?

LOSSES FROM HUDSON/
RARITAN ESTUARY
Flow past transect: ?
Dredged: ?
Volatilized: 10

Figure 6.B. Excerpts from Figure Showing PCB Movement in the Hudson/Raritan Estuary and New York Bight, 1957 to 1979

trol on Specific PCB Inputs and Reservoirs, and Spill Notification Requirements. Each table described the PCB source or reservoir, the applicable regulatory standard, its citation in the federal code of regulation, and the date it took effect.

The concise presentation of restrictions on PCB manufacturing, use, and cleanup led negotiators to draw the overall conclusion that PCBs are thoroughly regulated. However, negotiators chose not to delve into discovery of concrete information on the extent of compliance with the regulations.

TABLE 6.A A Product of Joint Fact-Finding: Excerpts from PCB Regulations Tables—General Regulatory Framework

Action	Effective Date	Regulation/Legal Authority
Manufacture, processing, distribution banned	Jan. 1, 1979	40 CFR 761/Toxic Substances Control Act (TSCA)
Ban on uses	Phaseout began Oct. 1, 1984; final Oct. 1, 1990	40 CFR 761/TSCA
Designated as hazardous substances	March 13, 1978	40 CFR 116/Federal Water Pollution Control Act (Clean Water Act); Sections 311 (b)(2)(A) and 501(1)
Proposed recommended maximum for drinking water set at 0	50 FR 46936	Would amend 40 CFR 141.50/ Safe Drinking Water Act
Limit of 2 ppm set for fish intended for human consumption	August 20, 1984	FDA
Listed as hazardous substances that may subject applicants for NPDES permits to additional requirements	July 18, 1980	40 CFR 122, Table 2D-4, Clean Water Act
Ambient water criterion for PCBs in navigable waters set at 0.001 micrograms per liter	Jan. 12, 1977 (compliance date Jan. 12, 1978)	40 CFR 129.105(a)(3)/ Clean Water Act

Dealing with the Burden of Proof

The outcomes of many technically intensive disputes hinge on the question of which side should bear the burden of proof (Brooks, 1984). In other words, in the context of the Bight Initiative, does one need to produce a "smoking gun" linking PCBs to effects observed in the field, or is "circumstantial evidence" sufficient to motivate action?

COMMENTARY

The question of who should bear the burden of proof has been addressed in recent years by appealing to the precautionary principle and the reduction of risk in the face of uncertainty. Those responsible for the creation of the alleged problem often argue that unless there is proof of harm (the definition of which they must approve), they should not be held liable for any costs associated with remediation or compensation. Those who perceive a risk to themselves or to the environment argue that if there is evidence of risk (by their definition), then prudent action must be taken to reduce that risk. Scientists drawn into such debates, and beyond their initial presentation of evidence, usually play only an ineffective role in resolving the burden-of-proof argument.

—William Moomaw, *Environmental scientist*

The question of who should bear the burden of proof arose repeatedly in the fact-finding phase of the Bight Initiative. Port and chemical industry representatives repeatedly pressed regulators and environmental interest groups to point to conclusive evidence linking PCBs to environmental damage. Conversely, environmental groups pressed for aggressive action in the cleanup and remediation arena. Although negotiators did not arrive at any overarching principle, they did address the issue in several ways. Through the work of scientific advisers and the active mediation of the NYAS team, the tone of the final text reflected an evenhanded approach. Neither cluster of interests succeeded in shifting the burden wholly to the "other side."

The following pages present an example of our efforts to help negotiators confront the burden-of-proof question as it bore on the important challenge of determining whether laboratory studies of biological effects are relevant to real effects in the field and, more generally, how to characterize plausible environmental effects based on circumstantial evidence.

Determining Whether Laboratory Studies of Biological Effects Are Relevant to Effects Observed in the Field

The joint fact-finding phase of the Bight Initiative involved negotiators and scientific advisers in the consideration of available data. As a result, one of the tasks for negotiators was to determine whether laboratory studies of effects of contaminants are relevant to effects observed in the real environment. This variation on the burden-of-proof question arose during the negotiation of language summarizing biological effects of PCBs on fish and other biota. •◦

◦◦ COMMENTARY

The difficulty of extrapolating laboratory findings to the field is extremely vexing. In the laboratory, the researcher has control of many variables and can therefore identify specific factors and their influence when other conditions are held constant. In the natural environment, exposure is to multiple natural and man-made chemicals under a variety of conditions. Some of these other chemicals may act synergistically to produce enhanced adverse health effects, while others may act antagonistically to diminish or obscure adverse health effects. Even if a chemical in the environment is potentially harmful, humans may not be exposed to it because it is sequestered in some way. Sorting out the effects of a particular chemical or set of chemicals and determining their exposure route are often very expensive, and relatively few comprehensive studies are undertaken. Often, those opposing action will state that "despite laboratory studies, there is no evidence of harm to humans or to wildlife under real-world conditions, and hence no action is needed." Scientifically, the lack of a study is not a reason to assume that no risk exists, especially if there is laboratory evidence to the contrary. The compromise wording in the report is a rare example of a statement that is scientifically accurate as well as being politically acceptable.

—William Moomaw, *Environmental scientist*

Negotiators recognized that isolating the effects of PCBs from those of other contaminants in urban water bodies is almost impossible. How, then, should the text summarize laboratory studies that show damage caused by PCBs at very low concentrations and may mirror the effects thought to exist in the field?

NYAS mediators asked Dr. Judith Weis, an aquatic toxicologist from Rutgers University, to review articles she had compiled on the subject and to brief negotiators on her findings. In the preparatory briefing packet, the mediation team asked whether some version of the data summarized by her should be included in the single-text document. Dr. Weis suggested that the following wording might be appropriate: "In laboratory studies, deleterious effects of PCBs on reproductive habits have occurred at levels of 1 ppb [parts per billion] or less. European field studies of flatfish and seals strongly suggest that PCBs are responsible for reproductive impairment. However, in the Hudson River, there are no data that conclusively relate PCBs to reproductive impairment."

To avoid incorporating findings in the text that ran contrary to their values and interests, some negotiators insisted on a stricter standard. Geraldine Cox of the Chemical Manufacturers Association and Dan Curll of the Towboat and Harbor Carriers Association took a strong position against including any version of Weis's summary. They initially argued that if the studies did not show a causal linkage between PCBs and damage to fish in the Hudson River and the bight, then no version of the material should be included. Nick Stevens of the Interstate Sanitation Commission and George Lutzic of the New York City Department of Environmental Protection retorted that excluding the material would constitute suppression of information.

Dr. Joseph O'Connor (not Dr. Joel O'Connor, mentioned earlier), another scientific adviser, tried to help the group out of the jam by suggesting some alternate language, although Weis took exception to portions of his wording, as is evident from the following exchange:

O'Connor: Consider an excerpt from the recent NOAA report on PCBs in Atlantic bluefish: "Despite laboratory evidence describing PCBs as highly toxic at low concentrations there are few published data showing evidence of ecological effects due to PCBs in natural systems. However, some studies provide evidence that PCB effects in natural systems may be subtle and difficult to isolate from the effects of other environmental contaminants." The NOAA report continued: "We know of no data demonstrating that PCBs in natural environments are the direct cause of chronic or acute toxicity."

Weis: I must take issue with this last statement. That assertion makes light of good correlations between some of the lab studies and European field studies of flatfish and the study of seals. A fair, evenhanded treatment must mention these items. Then, the text should note that these effects were not shown in the Hudson. I could live with that.

In the end, parties agreed to include a shortened version of Weis's summary, citing the most important studies and listing the major biological effects. After some further consideration, the parties also agreed to incorporate a more general conclusion from O'Connor's language in the text:

Lack of evidence conclusively linking adverse environmental or ecological impacts with PCBs is not proof that PCBs are toxicologically benign. Adequate studies have not been conducted in the Hudson/Raritan-Bight to rigorously establish whether observed ecological effects can be specifically attributed to PCBs, or to synergistic effects of PCBs with other contaminants, or to other causes.

Finally, negotiators came to agreement around two high-priority research items to help deal with technical uncertainty: to conduct a tiered study of PCB movement through the sediment and water column of the Hudson/Raritan-Bight system, and to document congener-specific research on the movement of PCBs through various environmental compartments, including edible seafood and other selected biota.

Clarifying and Narrowing Areas of Disagreement and Uncertainty

The most complex and controversial element of the joint fact-finding effort dealt with representing the evidence linking PCBs and health effects in humans, a subject on which there has been broad disagreement in the scientific community. ⬦

∽ COMMENTARY

The difficulty of coming to consensus over health effects is often tied as much to the legal and motivational effects of such findings as it is to scientific uncertainty. Once human health effects are established, defection from within the industry group is likely to occur, and regulatory action by government becomes a much more likely outcome. Since health effects are the one factor that can swing support for an issue to one side or the other, there is much less willingness to give ground on any single piece of information that would undercut one's position or undermine one's interest.

—William Moomaw, *Environmental scientist*

Accordingly, the NYAS team did not expect to settle this high-stakes public health debate in the context of a dialogue on coastal water quality. Nevertheless, the NYAS mediation team was determined that the text should accurately portray existing information and the specific extent and basis of scientific disagreement over the interpretation of available data. Together, the negotiators and advisers tackled a litany of contested subjects: carcinogenicity of PCBs and pathways to humans, mechanisms of carcinogenic action, developmental toxicity, human absorption and metabolism, epidemiology, and accidental poisoning.

Our mediation team helped negotiators address this problem by arranging briefings from three scientific panelists who could offer different perspectives on the issue. Stephen Safe of Texas A&M University discussed noncancer health effects and commented on some of the uncertainties inherent in attributing health effects to PCBs. James Cogliano of the Environmental Protection Agency's (EPA's) Cancer Assessment Group discussed the elements of cancer risk assessment. Michael Connor of Battelle Laboratories helped place PCBs in the larger context of other contaminants.[11]

Stephen Safe's presentation summarized some of the noncancer health effects attributed to direct ingestion of or contact with PCBs, including chloracne, changes in liver functions, and impairment of visual functions. This information seemed to be readily accepted by most negotiators. Safe's briefing also explained that one basis of existing PCB regulations that classify PCBs as suspected environmental carcinogens is the Yusho poisoning incident, in which Japanese families ate rice oil accidentally contaminated with PCBs and dibenzofurans, another suspected carcinogen. In addressing the links between PCBs and cancer, Safe emphasized the synergistic effect of PCBs and dibenzofurans, and he suggested that dibenzofurans, rather than PCBs, may have been the true "bad actor."

Cogliano emphasized that the Yusho incident was only one piece of evidence considered. His talk and associated briefing paper explained that PCBs are classified by the EPA as probable human carcinogens based on a series of key studies on animals; they are not classified as known human carcinogens. Cogliano's briefing also touched on developmental effects of PCB exposure. Cogliano constructed his calculations of cancer risk in step-by-step fashion on an overhead projector for all negotiators to see. He fielded aggressive questions by chemical industry and Port Authority representatives, who harped on the uncertainty inherent in forecasting cancer risks. Still, it was evident that this candid presentation of the reasoning behind the agency's determinations was very much appreciated even by negotiators such as a senior Port Authority official, who exclaimed, "This is great!" Geraldine Cox was adamant that the conservative assumptions embedded in the EPA's methods be clearly expressed in the single text. Port interests wanted risks

of PCBs placed in the context of relative risk. As detailed below, the NYAS mediators used several strategies to deal with these concerns.

The dialogue over health effects of PCBs in humans differed from less controversial discussions of PCB sources and regulations in several ways. No amount of discussion was able to produce a single version of the "facts" that all negotiators could agree was accurate. Rather, the give-and-take in the briefings and deliberations of negotiators revealed the presence of substantial technical disagreement and uncertainty on the question of health effects of PCBs. Negotiators from the chemical industry sought to share information from studies other than those summarized by the scientific advisers with the intent of including this material in the text.

At this juncture, the NYAS team discussed with other negotiators how to handle this "volunteered" information. We worked with negotiators to adopt several protocols to avoid freezing development of the single text in its tracks. First, negotiators agreed that findings had to be documented in published literature (preferably peer-reviewed journals) to be included in the negotiated text. (Participants agreed to make an exception to this ground rule for the comments of two scientifically trained negotiators, Geraldine Cox and Ellen Silbergeld.)

Three other drafting strategies were used:

1. express the assumptions or rationales used to support a particular forecast of health risk,

2. identify specific uncertainties inherent in health risk assessment, and

3. express the range of interpretations associated with specific data sets.

Express the rationales or assumptions in support of an estimate of health risk:

[Finding 9, Carcinogenicity and Pathways to Humans]

"EPA's methods reflect the consensus view of several respected scientists in the regulatory and scientific communities. They are consistent with recent findings of the Office of Science and Technology Policy, which stated that when the precise mechanism of cancer induction is not known as with PCBs, then a straight-line projection is a reasonable and prudent method to use. The rationale—that it is reasonable, for practical purposes, to regard an agent for which there is sufficient evidence of carcinogenicity in animals as presenting a carcinogenic risk to humans—reflects the views of the International Agency for Research on Cancer (IARC), World Health Organization."

Express uncertainties associated with the forecast of risks:

[Finding 10, Carcinogenicity and Pathways to Humans]

"Critics of EPA's methods, including many respected health professionals, point out that extrapolating linearly (as in EPA models) may be much too conservative. Specifically, they criticize extrapolating from very high doses—such as the maximum tolerated doses—to low dose human exposure even for those carcinogens that are mutagens. Such analysts suggest that the agency should present an array of slopes to show maximum, most probable, and minimum risks for PCBs. In this way, a sensitivity analysis on their data could be provided (Cox, 1988). However, EPA counters that at present, no methods are available to enable this sort of sensitivity analysis."

Express the range of interpretations associated with scientific observations:

[Finding 13, Carcinogenicity and Pathways to Humans]

"A range of professional opinion exists as to appropriate interpretation of published data on occupational exposure, additional poisonings, and animals studies.

"In a recent article (1987) Renate Kimbrough, when at the Centers for Disease Control, reviewed about 120 published articles on occupational exposure, accidental poisonings, and animal studies. She concluded that 'no conclusive evidence thus far reported shows that occupational exposure to PCBs causes an increased incidence of cancer.'

"Staff of EPA's Cancer Assessment Group generally concur with this finding but also notes that existing human data are not sufficient to allow conclusions to be drawn about the presence or absence of carcinogenic effects of PCBs (James Cogliano, personal communication).

"EDF's staff toxicologist Ellen Silbergeld (personal communication) dissents from Kimbrough's conclusion. In her view, existing evidence strongly suggests a link between PCBs and cancer in humans. Moreover, she believes that since PCBs and dibenzofurans are the empirical mix, they should be considered together in health risk assessment."

Figure 6.C. Drafting Strategies to Clarify and Narrow Areas of Scientific Disagreement

Judicious use of each drafting technique helped produce a balanced and technically sound discussion of human health effects. Examples of each approach are given in Figure 6.C.

These strategies were used several times over the 10-meeting process in which five successive drafts were produced, culminating in the final ratified agreement (although most of the 220 or so findings incorporated in the single-text agreement were less controversial and therefore less time-consuming to negotiate).

Using Joint Fact-Finding to Build a Single-Text Document

At the third meeting of the series, we asked negotiators to split into two groups and to develop a draft outline, or table of contents, for the ultimate work product. With minor differences, the two groups both envisioned a logical sequence of sources, fates, and effects of PCBs and wanted to include a chapter of policy recommendations. Thus, a decision was reached early in the process that the final text should include both findings and recommendations. (As discussed below, an alternative strategy would have been to produce two separate, but cross-referenced, documents and to seek ratification of only the policy recommendations.)

Review of draft findings and tentative formulations of policy options continued at Meetings 4 through 8. By Meeting 8, we had a complete draft of all chapters. Over the months of September and October, we then developed three successive drafts. Our team served as the secretariat, producing and revising the drafts. We brought a pair of portable computers and laser printers to the negotiating sessions, and we were able to develop several important sections in real time as negotiators pressed ahead with their work.

Often, information presented in scientific briefings constituted "raw material" for a negotiated single text. A table showing PCB levels in fish, for example, was included almost verbatim. In this way, joint fact-finding set the stage for negotiation over policy options. Time and again, negotiators made reference to key findings in

framing their arguments about management options. It was apparent that our joint fact-finding efforts had helped create a more "even playing field" for participants who ordinarily have unequal access to technical expertise or scientific information.[12] The process had helped participants build their understanding of complex issues in manageable, stepwise fashion. Organizing the deliberations of the negotiators around sources and effects of PCBs, followed by effects on biota, and, finally, effects on human health created a logical structure for the single-text document.

The final single-text document had the following structure: The document begins with a ratification page listing the signatures of the heads of 18 participating organizations.[13] Next, an executive summary recaps about 30 key findings and management recommendations. The next five chapters report the negotiators' findings. Recommended management strategies are reported in the sixth chapter. Seven appendixes present more detailed information. Presented in a desktop published format, the body of the text is 47 pages, and there are 28 pages of appendixes.

Chapter 1 of the text presents an overview of the Hudson/Raritan Estuary and the New York Bight and explains the chemistry and historical use of PCBs. The second chapter, on biological effects, reports on both human health and biota. The human health discussion reviews the links between PCBs and cancer in humans, the development of toxicity, and reports of some important epidemiological studies. The discussion of the effects on biota summarizes PCB levels in fish reported by three government agencies; reproductive impairment and other effects on biota are also reviewed.

Chapter 3 of the text summarizes sources and movements of PCBs. This chapter includes the tabular presentation of inputs, reservoirs, and losses of PCBs. Chapter 3 of the negotiated text also reviews the fates of PCBs—their transformation by physical, chemical, or biological processes. Chapter 4 briefly discusses socioeconomic effects of PCBs on fisheries, port operations, and tourism. Chapter 5 presents an overview and comment on the existing management structure. The chapter includes a detailed summary of the regulatory framework, restrictions on industry discharge, control on specific PCB inputs and reservoirs, and spill notification requirements. Also included in Chapter 5 is a comparison of the respective methods used by the states of New York and New Jersey to sample, analyze, and interpret PCB levels in species of edible fish.

The recommended management strategies that follow are organized into management principles, management options (sorted by high and medium priority, and options that face major obstacles), and suggestions for public education. Specific recommendations are included for source reduction, more consistent monitoring of environmental trends, and coordinated issuance of health advisories to warn people about consuming PCB-contaminated fish. Promising new decontamination technologies were identified—including UV/ozone, naturally adapted microbes process, and supercritical water oxidation—that merit investigation as alternatives to more traditional methods of PCB decontamination, such as incineration. ➥

∾ COMMENTARY

Disagreements over appropriate recommended actions reflect the parties' interests. Agreeing even to source reduction may not only be expensive for the releasers of chemicals but may also be seen as acknowledging that the release of the chemicals is dangerous. Similarly, not insisting on removal undermines an environmentalist position that the chemicals are dangerous.

—William Moomaw, *Environmental scientist*

■ Challenges in Ratification of the Single-Text Agreement

From the inception of the Bight Initiative, we envisioned that negotiators would have to "sell the agreement back home" and demonstrate that they were truly speaking for their organization when they acceded to the document. Unfortunately, we did not think through in detail the mechanics of moving this ratification process along. As a result, we did not anticipate or emphasize the eventual ratification of the document in

the ground rules we wrote to structure the process. By the fifth meeting of the process, negotiators agreed that they wanted to press for ratification of the final work product, but this commitment was a bit soft, and, as a result, proved difficult to enforce later in the process.

Our mediation team continued explicit discussion of ratification at the October 10, 1987 meeting when we brought forward the second complete draft of the text. We specifically asked negotiators how close they were to being able to recommend ratification to their respective organizations, and what specific changes they would need to make this recommendation. Several detailed responses were received, and we distributed two subsequent versions of the document to all parties. Based on a number of conference calls in which negotiators expressed their intent to ratify the final document, we envisioned a definitive response within 90 days, and we felt confident that most groups would ratify in 45 days when we mailed out the final text for review and ratification in December 1987.

In fact, the ratification process for the New York Bight Initiative stretched over a very long period of time—six months—and consumed several weeks of time on the author's part. By April 1, 1988, over half the groups had ratified the document, and by the end of April 1988, there were 16 ratifiers. The ultimate result of this process was to bring forward signatures of 18 of the 22 members. Signatories included all of the initial core group: the EPA, New Jersey Department of Environmental Protection, New York State Department of Environmental Conservation, and the city of New York, as well as a range of port, fishing, and environmental groups. Interestingly, although the port organizations had sometimes aligned themselves with the chemical industry, they all ratified the final document. Similarly, all of the local and regional environmental groups signed the document. Four groups did not ratify the document, however: the Environmental Defense Fund (EDF) and the coalition from the chemical industry. ❧

❧ COMMENTARY

It is interesting to note that the nonsigners were all interests that have been and are in the future likely to be legal protagonists in court over this and other similar issues.

—William Moomaw, *Environmental scientist*

In hindsight, the factor that had the greatest bearing on ratification was the decision to recruit to the negotiating table representatives of the industry that manufactured and used PCBs. These parties— GE, Monsanto, and the Chemical Manufacturers Association—were not members of the original core group of the Bight Initiative but were invited to join our group after PCBs were chosen as the focus for attention. These organizations were (and still are 10 years later; see Revkin, 1998[14]) involved in high-stakes discussions and litigation about redemption of PCB spills in the Upper Hudson River. They were concerned that findings in the single-text document might be used in courts and other forums. This was true even though we had spent 10 months trying to accurately represent a range of opinions about the most contentious issues. Perhaps we could have structured the ground rules to deal with the use of information in other forums, but even with such assurances, it is not at all clear that the recalcitrant parties would have signed the document. Again, we did not anticipate this late-inning hesitancy because the parties were so cooperative during the early work of the Bight Initiative. EDF's comments were twofold. First, a concern was expressed that the final single text understated the linkage between PCBs and cancer in humans—notwithstanding the fact that the final text clearly stated divergent views on this matter. The second concern was that the document did not "read" like the proceedings of a scientific panel—that its findings were somehow not crafted in a sufficiently scholarly manner, or that the disparate topics were treated in too fragmented a fashion.

As the series of 10 full plenary sessions of the Bight Initiative wound up, we set in motion a process to secure ratification of the document. A final drafting subcommittee meeting was convened in Washington, D.C. on October 26, 1987 among the four dissenting organizations: EDF, GE, Chemical Manufacturers Association, and Monsanto. The intent was to undertake a selective rewriting of the portion of the document dealing with carcinogenicity and pathways to humans. At this stage, we already had agreement on some 200 specific findings; it did not seem overreaching to hope we might close this last gap between recalcitrance and ratification if a few key parties could "agree to disagree." Recognizing the divergent views that would be represented around the table, the mediation team anticipated that a greater effort to fully characterize the professional views of the negotiators—that is, to fully disclose the degree of disagreement on this particular issue—might move the parties closer to ratification of the overall document. The result of this rewriting was to more clearly state certain findings, link findings more explicitly to cited literature, and explain key assumptions associated with specific studies. Although parties expressed appreciation for the final effort by the mediator, this final meeting did not move the parties from their views that they did not want to ratify the final document.

One tactic that might have increased the odds of full ratification would have been to segment the single text into two documents: a summary of technical findings and

a section on management options. After all, the latter were negotiated through five successive drafts; represented a balanced mix of analytic, environmental management, and research tasks; and were carefully structured to convey order of priority and to acknowledge opportunities and obstacles for implementation. In the end, they were not particularly controversial.

Similarly, the vast majority of the 220 findings were not controversial. The "big ticket items" on which substantial divergence of views persisted, even with the extensive fact-finding effort, were (1) the links between PCBs and cancer in humans, and (2) the proper stance toward decontamination and remediation technologies, particularly whether to endorse continued on-site containment versus dredging and application of new remediation technologies.

As our mediation team was readying the final report for distribution, some of the dissenters contacted Heinz Pagels, executive director of the NYAS, and suggested that because the document was "flawed," the academy should not publish it. Dr. Pagels countered that the report was a sound piece of work, and published it on the academy's letterhead.

■ *Epilogue*

Retrospective interviews with former NYAS colleagues, Bight Initiative negotiators, and scientific advisers suggest that the Bight Initiative has had four sets of significant implications:

1. A rich process model was established and documented to guide subsequent intervention in science-intensive environmental policy disputes.

2. An information base was established for use in subsequent bight environment decision making.

3. Policy recommendations were stated to create a foundation for both immediate implementation and for further refinement and development of policy options for subsequent resource management decisions.

4. Important professional relationships and networks were established.

Process Model

First, the Bight Initiative established a valuable process to guide subsequent intervention in science-intensive environmental policy disputes. The Bight Initiative has particularly informed CONCUR's[15] model of practice in the design of joint fact-finding processes to resolve about 20 complex, science-intensive disputes. Examples include projects involving comparative risk assessment, regional flood protection and habitat restoration, hydropower relicensing, and remediation of contaminated sites (Crane Valley Project Committee, 1997; Guadalupe River Flood Control Project Collaborative, 1998; Louisiana Department of Environmental Quality, 1991; McCreary, 1995; Thompson, Templet, Gamman, McCreary, & Reams, 1994). The Bight Initiative has also informed the subsequent practice of several of the negotiators and technical advisers. For example, Joseph O'Connor, one of the scientific advisers to the Bight Initiative, brought some of his experience as a scientific adviser to later work at the Aquatic Habitat Institute in California, which focused on assembling technical information in support of management decisions for San Francisco Bay.

Use of Information Gathered and Synthesized

The compilations of stakeholder groups and the synthesis of technical information produced by the Bight Initiative have been used in several ways, primarily in conjunction with the policy recommendations of the Bight Initiative. The kickoff of the Bight Initiative anticipated by two years the National Estuary Program, created by the 1987 amendment to the Clean Water Act. The National Estuary Program's purpose was to promote the development of comprehensive management plans for estuaries of national significance threatened by pollution, development, or overuse. Responding to the request of the governors of New York and New Jersey, the New York Harbor was accepted into the program in 1988. In 1987, Congress also required the EPA to prepare a restoration plan for the bight. Because the harbor and the bight are linked in so many ways, the EPA and the Management Conference agreed to make the Bight Restoration Plan a product of the Harbor Estuary Program.

Recommendations Implemented as the Basis of Subsequent Management Actions

The recommendations of the Bight Initiative have been pursued in various ways. Recommendations concerning unified testing of PCB levels in fish were pursued by the respective agencies from New York, New Jersey, and the National Marine Fisheries Service. Other recommendations created the foundation of further policy development through the New York-New Jersey Harbor Estuary Program, a multiagency consortium, which in turn produced the *Final Comprehensive Conservation and*

Management Plan (1996). The *Plan* includes seven elements, which address broad policy areas, including management of toxic contamination. The management of toxics element, the longest portion of the *Plan,* gives considerable weight and emphasis to management of PCBs. This *Plan* element includes 13 specific objectives, of which 5 address PCBs specifically and another 4 apply directly to PCBs. Many contain recommendations quite similar to those stated in the Bight Initiative's single text: developing unified testing protocols for PCBs in fish, conducting congener-specific analyses of PCBs, updating mass balances to track the movement and volume of PCBs in the river system, and reducing down-river transport of PCBs.

Personal Networks and Relationships

The Bight Initiative established and cemented numerous personal networks and relationships. As the New York-New Jersey Harbor Estuary Program was getting under way, the New York State Department of Environmental Conservation contacted the author to obtain a summary of the stakeholders identified through the Bight Initiative, as well as our analysis of these stakeholders. Many of the participants active in the New York Bight Initiative still remain very active in management matters in 1999. From the author's perspective, important long-term professional relationships were begun with both Marc David Block and—when Marc left the team due to health reasons—John Gamman, then a fellow MIT doctoral student. This marked the beginning of a collaboration that has grown into the foundation of our present firm. I have subsequently called on several members of the scientific panel in some of my later work on estuarine and water quality issues. The NYAS has also continued its institutional sponsorship of scientific dialogues pertaining to the estuary, and several of the scientific advisers active in the Bight Initiative have recently contributed to these programs.

■ **Notes**

1. Cited in a letter of invitation by Heinz Pagels, executive director of the New York Academy of Sciences, to stakeholders invited to a first organizational meeting in June 1985.

2. The results were submitted, along with an analysis of four other cases, as the author's doctoral dissertation to MIT's Department of Urban Studies and Planning (McCreary, 1989).

3. Members of the team initially included the author, Dr. Janice Perlman, Marc David Block, and Marlene Mallner. Later, Perlman left the academy and Block became less active in the project, and the author recruited MIT colleague John Gamman to join him in the final mediated sessions.

4. This model stands in contrast to two other prevalent models for injecting scientific advising into environmental decision making: the

blue ribbon panel and the adversary science model prevalent in litigation and traditional public review and comment processes.

5. The one-year gap is unusually long, and reflected the need to raise funds to support continued work.

6. Thomas Belton of the New Jersey Department of Environmental Protection's Office of Science and Research also served as a second negotiator behind Lawrence Schmidt, head of the Planning Office.

7. The NYAS was founded in 1838, has members in 80 nations and all 50 states, publishes *The Sciences* and its own *Annals of the New York Academy of Sciences,* and has taken very few positions on public policy issues.

8. About three-quarters of the scientists had home institutions in the New York metropolitan area, although the NYAS also invited experts from Woods Hole Oceanographic Institution and Battelle Laboratories in Massachusetts, Texas A&M University, the Environmental Protection Agency, and the Bureau of National Affairs in Washington, D.C.

9. Movement of PCBs at some rate; mass of PCBs that passes a given rate per unit of time.

10. Conversion from liquid or solid to gas; process by which PCBs enter the atmosphere.

11. The actions of two negotiators—Geraldine Cox of the Chemical Manufacturers Association and Ellen Silbergeld of the Environmental Defense Fund—though not formal scientific advisers, also had a major impact on this section of the document as will be shown below.

12. However, it should be stressed that while a resource pool helps give groups equal access to information, it cannot completely compensate for differences in professional training, preparation, or access to staff assistants.

13. Ratification is briefly discussed in the next section.

14. In addition to the Revkin article, 49 other articles were published in 1998 in the *New York Times* on PCBs in the Hudson River or the Hudson-Raritan Estuary/New York Bight.

15. CONCUR was cofounded by myself and John Gamman. The firm provides services in environmental policy analysis, mediation, and negotiation training.

■ *References*

Brooks, H. (1984). Resolution of technically intensive public policy disputes. *Science, Technology & Human Values, 9*(1), 39-50.

Crane Valley Project Committee. (1997). Phase 1 agreement of the Crane Valley Project Committee. *Progress report and interim recom-*

mendations to the Federal Energy Regulatory Commission on the relicensing of the Crane Valley Project. Berkeley, CA: CONCUR.

Guadalupe River Flood Control Project Collaborative. (1998, July). *Agreement to make a recommendation for construction, operation, and maintenance of the Guadalupe River Flood Control Project.* Prepared under contract for the U.S. Army Corps of Engineers, the Santa Clara Valley Water District, the City of San Jose, and the City of San Jose Redevelopment Agency. Berkeley, CA: CONCUR.

Louisiana Department of Environmental Quality. (1991, November 30). Project report of the Louisiana environmental action plan to 2000. *Vision statement, final ranking of environmental issues, and guiding themes for implementation. The negotiated single text of the public advisory and steering committees.* Baton Rouge: Author.

McCreary, S. (1989). *Resolving science-intensive public policy disputes: Lessons from the New York Bight Initiative.* Doctoral dissertation, Department of Urban Studies and Planning, MIT, Cambridge.

McCreary, S. (1995). Independent fact-finding as a catalyst for cross-cultural dialogue: Assessing impacts of oil and gas development in Ecuador's Oriente region. *Cultural Survival Quarterly, 19*(3), 50-55.

New York-New Jersey Harbor Estuary Program (including the Bight Restoration Plan). (1996). *Final comprehensive conservation and management plan.*

Revkin, A. (1998, July 24). Toxic chemicals from 1970s still pollute Hudson, study says. *New York Times,* Metropolitan section.

Thompson, R., Templet, P., Gamman, J., McCreary, S., & Reams, M. (1994). A process for incorporating comparative risk into environmental policymaking in Louisiana. *Risk Analysis, 14*(5), 857-861.

■ Further Reading

McCreary, S. (Ed.). (1988). Managing PCBs in the Hudson Raritan Estuary and the New York Bight. In *The negotiated single text of the New York Academy of Science New York Bight Initiative.*

McCreary, S. (1989, August 15). *Resolving science-intensive public policy disputes: Lessons from the New York Academy of Sciences joint fact-finding and single text negotiation procedure.* Prepared under the auspices of the American Academy of Arts and Sciences.

New York Academy of Sciences. (1986, July). *Findings from stakeholder interviews and surveys.* New York Bight Initiative.

New York Academy of Sciences. (1987a, January 21). Initial joint fact-finding: PCB sources, fates, and effects. *Meeting summary.* New York Bight Initiative.

New York Academy of Sciences. (1987b, February 19). *Meeting summary*. PCB Sources Subcommittee, New York Bight Initiative.

New York Academy of Sciences. (1987c, March 31). Joint fact-finding: PCB sources, fates, and effects. *Meeting summary*. New York Bight Initiative.

New York Academy of Sciences. (1987d, May 26). Workshop: Developing a single text document. *Meeting summary*. New York Bight Initiative.

New York Academy of Sciences. (1987e, June 15). Developing a single text document. *Meeting summary*. New York Bight Initiative.

New York Academy of Sciences. (1987f, July 15). Developing a single text document. *Meeting summary*. New York Bight Initiative.

New York Academy of Sciences. (1987g, July 21). Developing a single text document. *Meeting summary*. New York Bight Initiative.

New York Academy of Sciences. (1987h, August 18). Developing a single text document. *Meeting summary*. New York Bight Initiative.

New York Academy of Sciences. (1987i, September 10). Managing PCBs in the Hudson Raritan Estuary and the New York Bight: Second draft single text. *Meeting summary*. New York Bight Initiative.

New York Academy of Sciences. (1987j, October 10). Managing PCBs in the Hudson Raritan Estuary and the New York Bight: Third draft single text. *Meeting summary*. New York Bight Initiative.

New York Academy of Sciences. (1987k, October 27). Managing PCBs in the Hudson Raritan Estuary and the New York Bight: Fourth draft single text. *Meeting summary*. New York Bight Initiative.

New York Academy of Sciences. (1987l, December 10). Managing PCBs in the Hudson Raritan Estuary and the New York Bight: Fifth draft single text. *Meeting summary*. New York Bight Initiative.

NEGOTIATING SUPERFUND CLEANUP AT THE MASSACHUSETTS MILITARY RESERVATION

■ Edward Scher

■ Short History

The soils and the groundwater that lie beneath the Massachusetts Military Reservation (MMR) are saturated with the toxic remnants of more than 50 years of active military use. The MMR has been used as an armed forces base since 1911 (*Plume Response Plan,* 1994, p. 2-1). The reservation is 34 square miles (approximately 22,000 acres) and borders the towns of Bourne, Falmouth, Mashpee, and Sandwich on Cape Cod in Massachusetts, approximately 70 miles south of Boston. The military, in the standard practice of the day, built and used unlined landfills; poured

excess jet fuel off into the ground; and serviced large numbers of tanks, trucks, and other vehicles with their gas, oil, and hydraulic needs. Over time, petroleum products, aviation and motor fuels, solvents, spent acids, laboratory chemicals, and wastes leached down through the sandy soil and into the Upper Cape's aquifer—the area's sole source of drinking water. In the late 1970s, prior to any detailed knowledge of the extent of contamination, the town of Falmouth discovered an alarming problem: A recently installed municipal well was literally foaming like dishwater. Given that an old base wastewater treatment plant sat upgradient from the town well, known as the Ashumet

Valley well, the assumption was quickly made that the plant was to blame. The municipal well was immediately shut down, with the result that the town lost 25 percent of its water supply.

Spurred on by such a disconcerting discovery and its adverse consequences, the Department of Defense initiated an Installation Restoration Program (IRP) on the site of the Otis Air Force Base (a part of the MMR) in 1982. The Air National Guard was put in charge of the IRP. By 1986, the IRP had expanded to an investigation of the entire reservation, including areas controlled by the Army and the U.S. Coast Guard. By 1987, 73 possibly contaminated "study areas" were identified on base, 43 of which eventually required further evaluation.

As study progressed at the reservation, citizens became increasingly alarmed about the quality of their water supply. In 1986, the National Guard Bureau agreed to provide replacement costs for the lost Ashumet Valley well as well as to pay for residences with private wells to hook up to town water (which is safer because it is more closely monitored). In 1986 and 1987, the town of Mashpee had private wells in an area known as Briarwood tested for potential contaminants. Sampling results found levels of trichloroethylene (TCE) and tetrachloroethylene (PCE) that exceeded state and federal drinking water standards in seven wells. In 1989, the U.S. Environmental Protection Agency (EPA) proposed that the MMR be placed on the national priorities list of the Comprehensive Environmental Response Compensation and Liability Act, more widely known as Superfund.

As investigation continued and public concern increased, more and more atten-

tion became focused on cleaning up the base. No sooner would the military get a handle on one problem, establishing source areas of pollution and the possible related groundwater contamination, then another unpleasant surprise would arise elsewhere. For instance, in early 1990, after the MMR had been placed on the Superfund priority list, yet another major site of contamination was discovered. A summer camp adjacent to the MMR offered the town of Mashpee land to drill a new municipal water supply. Once again, the water was contaminated. Another test well 1,000 feet away yielded the same result. That well's water contained 3,000 parts per billion (ppb) of benzene. The federal drinking water standard for this toxin is 5 ppb. To make matters worse, ethylene dibromide (EDB), a potent carcinogen, was also detected at levels significantly above federal and state standards. Rumor had it that you could light this water on fire. The town of Mashpee had inadvertently drilled into a new *plume* of groundwater contamination. A plume, as defined at the MMR, is a body of groundwater containing contaminants that exceed safe drinking water standards established by the U.S. EPA. This plume came from leaks in a pipeline that was used to transport fuel from the Cape Cod Channel, across town land, onto the base.

Ten plumes had been identified by 1994 (yet another would be discovered in the fall of 1996). Some were caused by runoff from storm drains. Some were caused by existing or old landfills. Others were caused by chemical spills of one kind or another. The IRP was charged with identifying, investigating, delineating, and, ultimately, cleaning up this entire extensive contamination.

∽ COMMENTARY

The specific chemicals listed are extremely toxic in the very high concentrations identified. The relevance of this kind of technical information is often debated, but the levels are so high here that it is difficult to imagine an argument that these substances did not cause a significant risk.

—William Moomaw, *Environmental scientist*

■ *Project Crises*

On January 22, 1996, the prime engineering contractor to the IRP released a partially completed design for the containment of seven plumes of groundwater contamination at the MMR. This design included large-scale pump-and-treat systems that would pull water from wells installed into the plume, treat the plumes above ground through carbon filtration, and then reinject the treated water back into the aquifer (also known as extraction, treatment, and reinjection systems, or ETRs). Although the design was only 60 percent finished, it met with extraordinary opposition from regulatory agencies, the public, and even from within the military. The resistance came as a shock to the IRP's engineering contractor and the Air National Guard, the military agency responsible for managing the cleanup, because of the considerable effort it had made in securing public acceptance of its cleanup goal: total and simultaneous containment of the plumes.

In fact, before turning to engineer a containment plan, the Air National Guard had avidly sought to build political consensus. "The community, represented by local elected officials and activist groups" (*Plume Response Plan,* 1994, p. ES-2), the Massachusetts Department of Environmental Protection (DEP), the EPA, and the Air National Guard had all participated in the preparation of the guidelines used to develop the design, known as the Plume Response Plan. From the view of many residents, activists, and regulatory agencies, the goal of total simultaneous containment of the contamination guaranteed that the military would clean up the plumes to an acceptable level. From the Air National Guard's perspective, meeting the mandate would ensure public and regulatory support for its efforts. Parties viewed total containment and treatment of contaminated groundwater as a "fail-safe" objective; no matter what, the military would be forced to solve the problem. ∞

∽ COMMENTARY

It's critical at the beginning to formulate the right problem to be addressed. In the MMR case, the goal was immediately accepted: total and simultaneous containment and cleanup of all plumes. Restoration to the pristine state. That's a great slogan to energize the troops, but the problem formulation may distort the search for practical, constructive ways to ameliorate the problem. At an extreme, it may be ridiculously expensive to clean up the mess. The aim is to enhance the quality of life of the Cape

Codders by improving the health and safety of its residents, enhance the environment and the ecology of the region, and maintain or improve property values. Perhaps this could best be achieved in not cleaning up all the plumes to the same degree, but controlling the directions of the plumes, bringing in other sources of pure water, or improving the ecology and environment by other means that are more efficiently done. I don't know the answers, but I suspect the quest for pristine restoration is too inhibiting a goal. Goals, prematurely announced, may be dysfunctional in a way akin to positional bargaining in negotiations. Goals have a tendency to prejudge the nature of the problem.

Not always, but often, there is a so-called J-relation between the percentage reduction of some pollutant and the resources required to achieve this reduction. (See the accompanying figure.) There is often a critical point where further reductions become frighteningly expensive. Moving from level A to B in the figure may involve huge resources that perhaps could be expended elsewhere, like reduction of another pollutant. Without knowledge of the graph, the goal selected might be achievement of the reduction level B or better without understanding the cost-effectiveness relationship. The aim of the exercise is to balance measures of effectiveness and costs. Goals, prematurely set, often interfere with this mission.

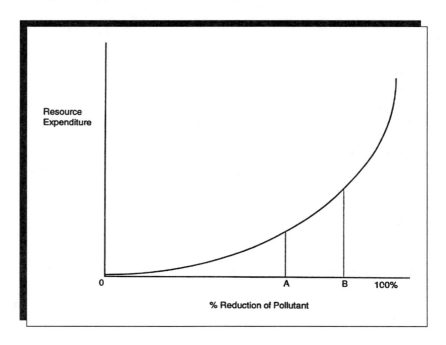

In an uncertain world, the choice between alternative A or B results in a choice between the risk profiles associated with each alternative. For each alternative there is a set of possible resulting outcomes, and for each of these outcomes there would be a multidimensional consequence. Choice between risk profiles, especially in the context of a Superfund cleanup, is horrendously complicated. Analysis entails two distinct aspects that can be separated: assessments of the uncertainties involved and evaluations of the consequences. By formalizing the problem of choice, experts, knowledgeable about the physical problem, can be asked assessment questions about the uncertainties without mixing in evaluative concerns about trade-offs. Without a formal structure, asking experts what alternative should be chosen is asking them to synthesize their assessments and evaluations and this is what the public should want to avoid. It's my impression that the problem was not sufficiently structured to enable experts, knowledgeable about science, to stick to their comparative advantage and to provide an input to the public to help in their evaluative tasks. Furthermore, if scientific experts stick to their assessment task, it becomes easier to seek peer review of their inputs. Of course, in a democratic society, scientific experts may want to inject their evaluative opinions, but they should then don a new hat for the public to see.

—Howard Raiffa, *Decision scientist*

But as it turned out, the "60 percent design" would have required pumping 27 million gallons of groundwater per day. This was more than the entire Cape pumped for its daily water needs. For some part of the public, the sheer magnitude of the proposed system appeared too large and incomprehensible. ➷

➷ COMMENTARY

Numerical information is of little meaning to the policy debate until it is put in context. Demonstrating that the 60 percent solution involved pumping and purifying groundwater at the same rate as required to supply all drinking water on the Cape was an effective way to put the proposal into context for the public and decision makers. It clarified the scale of the project both physically and economically, and it made the original remediation proposal look foolish to the public.

—William Moomaw, *Environmental scientist*

To ecologists, the design seemed to threaten ecological disaster on the Upper Cape. Wetlands would dry up. Endangered species in vernal pools would die. The shores of ponds, precious for boating, fishing, and swimming, would expand into mud flats as the ponds themselves shrank. Salt water from the ocean surrounding the Cape would intrude into the aquifer. Others worried about treated but still slightly contaminated water returning to the ponds and the safety of the piping between the pumping wells and the treatment plants. In February, only a few weeks after the 60 percent design had been released, the IRP, with concurrence from the EPA and DEP, delayed the issuance of the 95 percent design. Progress on the design of a cleanup plan ground to a halt. As John DeVillars, regional administrator for EPA Region I, told the *Cape Cod Times*, "The cure was worse than the disease" ("Broken Trust," 1997). ➷

∽ COMMENTARY

The Massachusetts Military Reservation cleanup is a good case study of the issues that often occur in Superfund cases. Although initially the parties thought they had engaged in a consensus process with the appropriate political parties, the solution proposed seemed drastic and insensitive to other parties. Ecologists were concerned about pumping too much water for cleanup and feared that such a "solution" would have deleterious effects on the ecology of the Cape ("the cure was worse than the disease"). Complex, stalemated lawsuits may provide interesting opportunities for trying out new dispute resolution processes.

—Carrie J. Menkel-Meadow, *Legal scholar*

What could the parties do to break this stalemate? Disappointment and frustration were high. Cape citizens had waited almost 15 years for the cleanup, and what they had found themselves in instead was an engineering and political morass to top off the contamination beneath them. New politically acceptable and technically sound solutions were not at all obvious, especially since the IRP, with encouragement from the DEP and EPA, had already attempted to build consensus by organizing various citizen action teams. The idea behind these teams was that they would allow local government officials and citizens to have a say in the investigation and cleanup of the base. In 1986, the Technical Environmental Affairs Committee had been created. In 1993, the Senior Management Board (SMB) and joint process action teams (PATs) were formed. The SMB included senior-level regulatory officials from the military, DEP, and EPA, as well as a representative selectman from each of the four towns. PATs, chartered by the SMB, were created to give citizens forums for voicing their concerns and influencing decision making. One PAT in particular was designed to focus on the technical issues of plume management, the Plume Management Team (PMT). It would seem that this intense level of citizen involvement would have been enough. In fact, the PMT had been instrumental in preparing the failed Plume Response Plan in June 1994.

Inherent in the total simultaneous-containment approach, intended to build broad-based support for the program's objectives, were serious blind spots. Secondary effects of remediation, such as the ecological impacts of pumping so much groundwater to the surface for treatment, were not adequately considered, in part because of the rush to move quickly from studying and planning to execution. The technical complexity of containing and treating the plumes was underestimated, and the potential impact of engineering solutions on hydrological and ecological systems went largely unexamined. In binding itself to the mandate set by the regulatory agencies and concerned citizens, the military created a situation in which it was difficult to identify, much less address, the potentially significant collateral damage wrought by pursuing the stated goal. The military had restricted participation in the remediation design process to the goal development stage. The mandate that thus emerged was then used by technical experts to guide the design of the cleanup plan. This approach limited the involvement of the public as well as outside experts in the development and review of the cleanup design. The design that emerged was viewed as a failure by the same groups that had approved the criteria that guided it. ⊷

This case study charts the course of events that led the Air Force, EPA, DEP, and local residents and officials from this 60 percent design impasse to an agreed-on decision-making process for selecting, plume by plume, the conceptual remedial designs for the engineered systems that would clean up the plumes. The case study describes the formation of a team of technical experts called the Technical Review and Evaluation Team (TRET) and the TRET's assistance in helping the IRP, EPA, and DEP develop a technical "road map" for moving beyond the 60 percent design impasse. It covers the time period from March 1996 through July 1996. ⊷

■ *Breaking the Impasse*

The Technical Review and Evaluation Team

In mid-March 1996, responding to the 60 percent design crises, high-level officials at the Department of Defense, EPA, and DEP created the TRET. This technical team, to be composed of experts across various agencies, would review the current design, investigate alternatives, and analyze impacts to the environment and surrounding communities. The aim of this initiative was to, as quickly as possible, seek out a viable plume containment project that met both regulatory requirements and public acceptance.

In May 1996, just four months after the crises had begun, the TRET released a final report. Its recommendations on how to proceed with plume containment received support from most of the opponents to the 60 percent design, and partially on the strength of this support, efforts to clean up groundwater at the MMR would finally begin in earnest. The TRET process relied on a collaborative, multidisciplinary effort. TRET members interacted with public representatives throughout their decision-making process. The participation of experts from a wide range of technical and institutional backgrounds was central to achieving a technically sounder outcome. Unlike the 60 percent design, the TRET's recommendations acknowledged the technical uncertainties surrounding the treatment methods and tried to balance the goal of remediation against the danger of secondary effects.

The formation of the TRET initiated a new design approach. It provided a means for stakeholders to sort through complex, incomplete, and sometimes inconsistent information and find a technically and politically acceptable way forward. The TRET served, in one sense, as an ad hoc think tank, an incubator for the formulation of new ideas and reformulation of older ones. The goal of the TRET and the stakeholders' interaction with it was to

> provide a viable plume containment project that meets Guard, regulatory, and community acceptance without delaying the schedule for award of the containment project this summer [1996]. The project must clean the plumes to acceptable levels without unacceptable impacts to the environment. (*White Paper,* 1996, p. 1)

The TRET involved all the parties—public, regulatory, military, and contractors—in the decision-making process. There were two participatory tracks. The first was the membership of the group itself, which was both multidisciplinary and interinstitutional. The internal workings of the TRET were described by one participant as "50 experts in a building one step above an Army barracks with the risk assessment people in one corner and the hydrological people in the other. It was very chaotic" (March 26, 1997 interview). The second track was the use of open forums to interact directly with the broader community and public advisory groups. This contact was important in keeping the public informed, ensuring that the TRET responded to its needs and building credibility for the process and experts.

TRET Membership and Interaction

In determining TRET membership, the military, EPA, and DEP recognized the need for representation of a wide array of technical and scientific specialties. Many of the IRP's engineering firms' problems stemmed from the absence of risk assessors and ecologists on their design team. The TRET was composed of hydrological, ecological, and human health groups. The ecological group included experts in both ecological risk (risks posed to the ecology from contamination) and ecological impacts (potential impacts from the engineered solution on the ecology). Although membership revolved, a diverse group (approximately 15 experts in the hydrological and 25 members in the ecological and human health groups) participated on the TRET (Public Comments Record, 1996, p. 14). The wealth and diversity of expertise on the TRET helped ensure technical validity in the various aspects of the design process and encouraged an outcome that balanced the orientations of different fields.

The institutional representation on the TRET in turn helped address the interests of the various stakeholders and build support for the recommendations. The same diversity of opinion that exists between scientific disciplines exists between different institutions—even between experts in the very same field. In reviewing the perspectives on environmental risk among 1,011 scientists and engineers, Barke and Jenkins-Smith (1993) found that "percep-tions of risk and its correlates are significantly associated with the type of institution in which a scientist is employed." The body of literature on risk perception corroborates this finding. Two, among many, possible reasons for these differences are organizational culture (people like to work with like-minded people) and institutional focus (i.e., advocate, regulatory, or research). Limiting the institutional representation in a decision-making process, therefore, can be an impediment to addressing the technical, as well as political, perspectives of all parties. ➵

➢ COMMENTARY

Perceptions of risk by scientists are tied not just to their institutional affiliation, but there are strong correlations with discipline and interest of an employer. Ecologists often perceive greater risk than do engineers. It is unclear whether this is because they have studied the vulnerability of the environment more or because people drawn to a study of the natural world are inherently more sympathetic to protecting it. Engineers may be more prone to believe in technological fixes.

—William Moomaw, *Environmental scientist*

TRET members represented more than 20 different military, regulatory, and research agencies, as well as various consultants (Public Comments Record, 1996, p. 14). Each of those institutions, through its representatives on the TRET, had an opportunity to express its interests and review the work of the group. Part of the TRET's success was due to the explicit effort to get the members to check their "institutional agenda" at the door. ➵

➢ COMMENTARY

The difficulty of agreeing on the basis of expert opinion rather than in terms of an institutional agenda in part reflects an institutional belief system that is difficult to park at the door, but it may also reflect the difficulty of agreeing on a level of proof.

—William Moomaw, *Environmental scientist*

Still, members were responsible for monitoring the progress of the TRET not only in light of their own "expert opinion." Their presence on the TRET gave others in their home institution a direct link to the TRET, building credibility and further expanding the circle of exchange of ideas, information, and opinion. The TRET thereby internalized, and sought to balance as much as possible, the conflicts and tensions that characterized the problem it had been charged with solving. From the stand- point of buy-in, the presence of a repre- sentative assured institutions that their in- terests were being addressed. The TRET benefited by having credible advocates who could return to their constituencies and explain the decisions that were made. ❧

❧ COMMENTARY

The ultimate "success" (not really known yet) of the TRET process is an illustration of contrasts between how the legal system and consensus-based processes operate. First, the attempt to reengineer a solution that would both meet technical regulatory requirements and satisfy public interest groups required a multidisciplinary approach. Technical expertise was combined with input from other participants and stakeholders to ensure that several goals were met at once: "Clean the plumes to acceptable levels without unacceptable impacts to the environment." Legal institutions like courts have a difficult time using multidisciplinary approaches. Although experts may testify or give advice, they often do so for a particular "side," and this adversarial commitment may blind experts to the good ideas or solutions of the other side or, at the simplest level, block communication across sides, even from within the same discipline. A consensus building process that puts multidisciplinary experts and laypersons on the same side of trying to solve the problem allows for more creative solutions, information sharing, and explanations of goals and technical aspects of a problem across disciplines, especially where, as here, multidisciplinary approaches are necessary to meet multi- plex, not single (winner take all) goals.

—Carrie J. Menkel-Meadow, *Legal scholar*

Still, TRET membership continuously raised challenges. For one, members of the TRET were expected to act independently of their organizations, to openly and hon- estly express their professional opinions. However, some TRET members felt torn between the strategic policy directions their organizations were promoting and their own best, professional opinions. Some felt this "two hats" problem limited the agency members' ability to brainstorm ideas openly and to evaluate suggestions from a purely apolitical, substantive stand- point. Second, the membership, particu- larly at the staff level, changed from week to week, making it difficult to build effi- ciently a shared understanding of the prob- lem and stable agreement on viable solu-

tions. The military provided new technical consultants that needed to be brought up to speed. Agencies, wrestling with priori- ties and limited resources, moved some off of this project onto others, and drew other expertise from off of other projects to the TRET.

Furthermore, while the military and the agencies were exceptional in generally al- lowing the TRET a great deal of freedom to work out viable solutions, this lack of oversight created ongoing uncertainty as to the TRET's roles, responsibilities, and overall mission. TRET members feared that if their opinions ultimately strayed too far from agency policy, their ideas and their influence would be discounted if not out- right rejected. ❧

∽ COMMENTARY

As participants get committed to solving a particular problem in a consensus building situation, they may feel the tension of "representing" two interests: the interests of the particular problem on which they are working and their institutional loyalties (and job requirements). These "agency" problems are no strangers to lawyers, but in consensus building environments there may be many agent-principal relationships, and conflicts of interest probably need to be monitored by the parties on an ongoing basis, both for ethical and instrumental reasons (to avoid post hoc attacks on the process and its results).

—Carrie J. Menkel-Meadow, *Legal scholar*

Ultimately, to address some of these problems, the TRET appointed a four-member steering committee of respected senior scientists in human risk, ecological impact, and hydrogeology known as the "TRET leads." An Air National Guard environmental engineer was also borrowed from another site to help coordinate between the TRET and the military.

Despite such difficulties, the overall tone was positive. For the first time, people were interacting face-to-face and off the record. ∽

∽ COMMENTARY

The TRET process illustrates the importance of face-to-face meetings of those actually involved in problems, rather than reliance on agents (like lawyers or other representatives) who negotiate without the principal's active participation. The use of facilitated "caucuses" or "off the record" meetings allows parties to test and try out proposals or to discuss things that would not be possible in totally public and formal settings.

—Carrie J. Menkel-Meadow, *Legal scholar*

The TRET was neither deliberating in front of an audience in public meetings nor in official regulatory management meetings. The TRET met day in and day out, sequestered away from the main IRP program in their own underequipped, but separate, building (an old barracks). Despite the shortage of computers, faxes, and space, one participant remembers that "the nice thing was that it was away from the regulatory process—people could hash out ideas and talk informally" (March 26, 1997 interview). This informality was the key to building understanding and reconciling the different perspectives of TRET members. Working closely as a multidisciplinary team, members began to understand their colleagues' views and look for ways of meeting everyone's needs. ∽

◌ COMMENTARY

The consensus building process used in the TRET proceedings was ongoing over a long period of time. While lawsuits may take a long time, in terms of discovery, information gathering, and hearings, end-state events like trials or hearings tend to dramatically rigidify positions and produce artificial closure or end points in the conclusions reached. The continued (over a long time) interaction of interested parties allowed trial "balloons" of different solutions to be floated, tested, debated, discussed, and thought about between sessions and with consultations with interested parties. Formalistic hearings seldom present the opportunity for this kind of continuous flow of information in and out of the formal process before decisions, rulings, or positions become final and binding.

—Carrie J. Menkel-Meadow, *Legal scholar*

As one member explained, TRET was composed of people chosen "for their experience, not their institution's agenda. Interaction and frank discussion were what made TRET work" (February 27, 1997 interview). The persuasiveness of an argument was a function of the power of the rationale behind it and of the availability of supporting data, not relative to the proponent's position. ◌

◌ COMMENTARY

With more than 20 different kinds of institutions, constituencies, agencies, and consultants participating in the process, different kinds of ideas and solutions must necessarily be considered. As the case study describes it, the process itself became a kind of "holding vessel" or "incubator" of ad hoc, tentative, and contingent ideas and formulations that could be floated among the different groups for consideration. More formal processes tend to produce single solutions, seriatim, which are then ruled right or wrong (courts) or voted on (zoning bodies or regulatory agencies). The need to explain things across different expert disciplines often serves to clarify and simplify as well as to bring to the fore what each discipline can or cannot contribute to a solution. The matrix, rather than the yes/no, win/lose, pro/con chart, is a more accurate visual description of what happens when choices are opened out by the contributions of different disciplines.

The very act of working jointly on a problem, across disciplines, allows the parties to "check their 'institutional agenda' at the door" and to give them an interdisciplinary stake in solving a particular problem. In more conventional adversary processes, this is virtually impossible as parties almost never check their party/side agenda at the courthouse door (or even the settlement door).

—Carrie J. Menkel-Meadow, *Legal scholar*

The TRET was assisted by a team of four facilitators from the Consensus Building Institute of Cambridge, Massachusetts. The facilitation team was brought on board the project at the same time as the TRET was created. The team facilitated some TRET meetings, met with the TRET leads to resolve process problems, helped provide an interface between the TRET leads and high-level officials, and assisted the TRET in interacting with the public. More broadly, the facilitation team was playing an in-depth and somewhat unusual role in the project through facilitating the TRET as well as facilitating the citizen action team meetings, and mediating among the key agencies and local officials and activists all at the same time. Although facilitation "ramped up" with the creation of the TRET, facilitation was not new to the project. One of the facilitation team members had been assisting one citizen team for almost two years with the financial support of the DEP. ⊷

⊷ COMMENTARY

The TRET process makes clear how important it is to have skillful facilitators manage such combinations of people and types of meetings. While often judges or agency personnel may try to facilitate settlements of environmental cleanups or other complex matters, they may not be particularly skilled in coalitional bargaining, technical confidentiality requirements, meeting management, and group interaction. Without skillful meeting and group management, such processes can become dangerous, releasing confidential information that exacerbates a dispute or public reaction. A dispute that could be making progress is thus made contentious and adversarial.

—Carrie J. Menkel-Meadow, *Legal scholar*

⊷ COMMENTARY

The TRET was assisted by a team of four facilitators from the Consensus Building Institute. These facilitators presumably were experienced in helping with the internal processes within TRET and in externally communicating with the public. These facilitators are experts on human relations, on how to run meetings, on how best to negotiate to generate mutual gains. All indispensable, but not enough. I may be wrong, but I don't think these facilitators were experts in problem-solving techniques. They are not trained in operations research, in decision analysis, in modeling, in statistical analyses, in research on collective decision making. It would be nice if the facilitators had these skills as well. The Cape Cod disaster is a complex problem that screams out for good analysis; loads of experts were involved on hydrogeology, on ecology, even on economics, but no experts on the methodology of complex decision making. So that's my major constructive comment. There is a need for a trained, professional, problem-solving staff. We should identify groups that could perform those functions and build up a track record of constructive experiences. The authors report that the TRET served as an ad hoc think tank. What's needed is a think tank that's less ad hoc; there's the need for facilitation groups that can help structure the policy- and decision-making process as well as help with human relations interactions. These facilitators should transfer learning from one case to the next.

—Howard Raiffa, *Decision scientist*

Engaging the Public: Interaction between the TRET and the Public

Reaching the general public, or choosing adequate public representatives, can be a challenge. The communities in the four towns adjacent to the MMR, however, were well organized. This was due in part, perhaps, to the 15-year political struggle over the plumes at the MMR. Along with elected and appointed public officials, the Air National Guard recognized nine locally based special interest groups such as the Association for the Preservation of Cape Cod and Upper Cape Concerned Citizens (Public Comments Record, 1996, Figure 1). These public representatives took part in various public advisory committees as well as in public meetings. There was the Plume Containment Team that had developed the original Plume Response Plan. It had evolved somewhat (and assumed the name of Joint Process Action Team, or JPAT) because members of other citizen teams dealing with public outreach and long-range water supply issues were invited to participate in Plume Containment Team meetings. Last, all of these citizen teams were chartered by an advisory board, the SMB. ∞

∞ COMMENTARY

The TRET process used an outside "feedback" mechanism that is virtually impossible in more formal legal settings. By holding regular meetings with a broad base of public groups and issuing fact sheets and press releases, sharing of information with the interested parties can prevent "surprises" and can encourage both participation and "buy-in" to the eventual solutions. Often, top-down imposed solutions by courts or regulatory agencies may be resisted simply because some interested parties not formally invited into the process may feel excluded, even if they are not treated badly by the ultimate outcome. We know from research in procedural justice (Lind & Tyler, 1988) that parties evaluate legal proceedings for process fairness, regardless of outcome; in other words, the process matters just as much, if not more, than the outcome achieved.

—Carrie J. Menkel-Meadow, *Legal scholar*

REFERENCE

Lind, E. A., & Tyler, T. R. (1988). *The social psychology of procedural justice.* New York: Plenum.

Some of the citizens on the teams had an expertise (medical, engineering, legal, scientific) that they brought to bear on the problem. Many, through their exposure over time to a variety of issues, gained a sophisticated understanding of both the technical and procedural intricacies of cleaning up a Superfund site. A few of the representatives on the SMB had been active in the cleanup almost since the pollution was first discovered in the late 1970s. ∞

∞ COMMENTARY

It is important to recognize that members of the community may also come with expert knowledge or training and can have insights into even the technical aspects of the project.

—William Moomaw, *Environmental scientist*

Almost all of these people were volunteers who donated two to four hours of their time in meetings as often as once a week. These representatives exerted a large influence by publicizing the story and making information available to their constituencies. A few were skilled activists and politicians, quoted frequently in the local and regional press, working behind the scenes to influence decision makers in various agencies.

The TRET engaged these representatives, as well as the broader public, through open meetings held, at a minimum, once a week. These were supplemented by press reports and fact sheets on technical and process issues frequently released by the military. TRET members participated in meetings of the various community advisory boards and in town meetings, which usually drew 50 or more citizens. Through this outreach effort, the TRET was tapped into the political leadership, local knowledge, and technical expertise of the educated lay public. As with the group's internal membership, the TRET endeavored to involve the full range of citizen stakeholders, elicit their concerns, and inform them of the TRET's work. For instance, over 25 different conservation organizations and local experts, such as shellfish wardens and county conservation commissioners, contributed information to the ecological database that TRET members were organizing (JPAT meeting minutes, 1996).

One of the central tasks of the facilitation team was to assist the TRET in working with the public. The facilitation team would provide feedback in the preparation for and debriefing of presentations at public and citizen team meetings. As the TRET prepared for open gatherings in the affected towns to explain their ongoing work, the facilitation team called on SMB selectmen to help shape the agenda. The facilitation team also staged dry runs of the public presentations with the TRET and elected officials, ensuring that the experts would address the strongest concerns and interests of the towns in language understandable to laypeople as well as scientists.

The Role of Experts

A consensus approach recognizes the need for decisions to reflect a plurality of views and the collective character of social and political life. Ideally, parties are given equal opportunity to deliberate on all aspects of the issue at hand and their contributions are given equal consideration. However, when faced with highly technical questions, participants typically rely on experts to explain technical matters and, at times, to use their own "best scientific judgment." How, then, should experts convey their information, ideas, and beliefs? It is up to technical experts to fit their expertise into discussions of complex problems in a way that appropriately acknowledges uncertainty and disagreement and engages all parties in what remain value-laden judgments (Woodhouse & Nieusma, 1997, p. 24). The burden on the experts is the same as that on any other participant in the conversation. They must elucidate the reasoning behind their opinions in a way that is intelligible to all. Technical experts should be seen as advisers, not as unassailable authorities. ➥

➥ COMMENTARY

It is essential that technical experts provide not just answers but also an explanation of the basis and assumptions on which their responses are based. This transparency brings a sense of credibility to the proceedings that is otherwise lacking, especially when experts disagree on either the substance or interpretation of particular data or information.

—William Moomaw, *Environmental scientist*

The two-track approach of the TRET was created to tackle the highly technical nature of the plume containment design under severe time constraints. Those who participated as members of the TRET had specific expertise: hydrology, ecology, geology, and so on. However, in making value-laden judgments there are no experts (Woodhouse & Nieusma, 1997, pp. 24-25). A consensus approach calls for a "conversation" in which experts and other parties all participate as equals, and information is both shared and questioned. In dividing the deliberation into two tracks— one primarily of technical experts and one of various, diverse stakeholders, including but not limited to the technical experts— the TRET took a somewhat hierarchical or technocratic approach, more similar to the IRP design team. However, the TRET was distinctly different. ➥

➥ COMMENTARY

In making value-laden judgments there are no experts. But, I would like to add, there are experts who can help people in the process of deciding, who can help people sort out their value-laden basic judgments and to help synthesize them with their assessments of uncertainty.

—Howard Raiffa, *Decision scientist*

➥ COMMENTARY

While there are no unassailable experts in making value-laden judgments, it is questionable whether all parties are participating as equals. What is most important is that parties, regardless of their level of expert knowledge in a particular field, be open to working with others of differing expertise in coming to a solution that is technically, economically, and politically feasible.

—William Moomaw, *Environmental scientist*

The different subgroups within the TRET met daily throughout the monthlong development of the final report, encouraging hydrogeologists, ecologists, and human health risk assessors to challenge and shape one another's thinking. These daily meetings were successful in spite of the heterogeneity of experts' views, because a "workshop" atmosphere predominated in which different members tried to understand each other's perspectives and carried on a continuous dialogue. For instance, for the first time ecologists were explaining to hydrologists why the maintenance of groundwater and pond levels was crucial to ecological health. The hydrologists' heightened understanding of ecological concepts, and vice versa, was a direct result of the double role each member played as both teacher and student.

TRET members extended these practices to public meetings. They not only presented their work and responded to comments but also engaged with participants in genuine deliberations. TRET members asked for help in finding and understanding data; they acknowledged uncertainty and the diversity of opinions that existed. This pattern of interaction kept ideas on the table for elaboration and reevaluation. The explicit effort to engage the community challenged the conventional view of knowledge as "linear" and as the exclusive domain of formally trained experts. Their use of these meetings to ask participants questions and to brainstorm helped forge a new relationship between technical advisers and the broader public that brought greater flexibility to the process. Feedback from the public reduced the chances that new blind spots (technical or political) would arise. Because parties were more fully educated and directly involved in the development of solutions, they understood the trade-offs and limitations necessary to reach the final collective goal.

The TRET Final Report

The TRET's final report recommended that each of the plumes be addressed singly (as opposed to simultaneously as in the 60 percent design). Two important messages distinguished this new approach: It asked people to take a more measured response to the individual risks posed by each plume. The TRET recognized that "plumes cannot be managed individually without acknowledgment of the inter-connectedness of the aquifer system" (*Toward a Balanced,* 1996, p. 13), but at the same time each plume had distinctive characteristics that should inform design and decision making. It also highlighted the need to balance the desire to solve the problem quickly and comprehensively with the uncertainty that attends the cleanup. Consistent with this exhortation, the final report called for an "incremental" approach.

Based on the findings presented in the TRET final report, the military and its contractors prepared the Strategic Plan for the cleanup of the MMR groundwater plumes, which was delivered to the EPA and DEP on May 15, 1996. The central feature of the overall plan was the Comprehensive Plume Response Plan, which was the direct successor of TRET (*Comprehensive Plume Response Plan,* 1996, p. 4.2.4). This Strategic Plan specified containment actions for two of the plumes; for the others, it identified data gaps and specified ways to close these before proceeding to action. This new plan embraced many of the "guiding principles" identified by the TRET, such as taking a balanced approach by weighing all the impacts of action (and no action) and using an "iterative" approach. The TRET had set all concerned parties on a new and more feasible trajectory for decontaminating the plumes. As one town elected official remarked, "There's a major change in this Strategic Plan from the original plan that we looked at, which was just to do containment on everything and to believe that we know enough to accomplish that. We know now that we did not know enough to just go out and contain all the plumes" (Pre-Final Draft of the Massachusetts Military Reservation Installation Restoration Plan, 1995, p. 72 of comments received, Comment No. 143). ❧

❧ COMMENTARY

Perhaps most important, as a difference from the formal legal process, the TRET process allowed a more contingent solution to emerge than would typically result from either an adjudicated outcome or a settlement. The parties agreed to containment actions for two, rather than all of the contaminated plumes, so that effects could be measured and reevaluated. Thus, the multidisciplinary participation of experts and public officials, as well as interested parties and laypeople, brings to light the considerable knowledge gaps that have to be filled as real-world solutions are tried and evaluated. Keeping the process intact, with enough of the same actors, may be a challenge, but the recognition that remediation needs to be done iteratively and gradually, for constant monitoring and reevaluation, is one of the advantages of such processes over the more formal and conclusive processes of courts and agencies that must definitively rule and "end" their deliberations.

—Carrie J. Menkel-Meadow, *Legal scholar*

With the release of the Strategic Plan, the TRET had met the goals set out at its inception. A review of the TRET was performed by the Consensus Building Institute in July 1996. The Consensus Building Institute found that many participants credited the TRET with getting the containment effort back on track and rebuilding credibility for the IRP's cleanup effort. It did so by providing independent, multidisciplinary review of technical work coupled with an effort to integrate value-based considerations through public outreach and review. In just over two months, the crisis over the 60 percent design had given way to a publicly acceptable Strategic Plan and budding trust in the military's effort to contain and clean up plumes at the MMR. It is impossible to wholly ascribe this movement to the TRET; many crucial technical and political boundaries also shifted during this tumultuous period. What is certain, however, is that much credit is given to the TRET by the public, regulatory agencies, and military. ❧

∽ COMMENTARY

The learning points from such a process for environmental decision making are these: Ongoing, dynamic processes may be more flexible and ultimately more acceptable and legitimate than one-shot lawsuits or agency proceedings. Multidisciplinary expert solution seeking that cuts across "two-sided" adversarial processes may create more synergistic coalitions across institutions and "sides" that enable more creative solutions to be suggested without attribution or "ownership" by a particular side in a dispute. Complex problems like Superfund, multiparty site responsibility, and environmental externalities require complex matrixlike processes and solutions, rather than two-sided, polarized litigation sides, which may produce overly rigid and unacceptable on/off solutions. Skilled and expert facilitators may be necessary to organize data, people, and processes that operate on multiple tracks simultaneously. Contingent, testable, and flexible solutions may be the only way to attempt to deal with modern complex problems, as we build in contingencies and try to evaluate the effects of remediation efforts to prevent cures that are worse than the disease.

All of this suggests that consensus building techniques and processes have great promise in the area of environmental cleanup. The one major obstacle that must be theorized, as well as dealt with in practice, is the relationship of such important flexible and informal processes to the legal requirements of regulatory and enforcement statutes and processes that command certain outcomes, as well as processes to ensure legitimacy within a democratically structured government. To the extent that this case study demonstrates governmental, as well as public, acceptability and legitimacy, it is a model of a possible process. Other uses of such consensus processes that have relied more on private parties and processes may stir up more opposition and concerns about the relationship of public commands to private accommodations (for further exposition of these difficult tensions in the use of consensus building techniques in regulatory settings, see Jody Freeman's 1997 article).

—Carrie J. Menkel-Meadow, *Legal scholar*

REFERENCE

Freeman, J. (1997). Collaborative governance in the administrative state. *UCLA Law Review, 45*(1), 1-98.

∽ COMMENTARY

This is a beautifully exposited and instructive case study. Suppose, for example, a similar catastrophe were to arise in some other state. What are the lessons to be learned from the MMR case in Cape Cod?

Although the MMR case seems hopelessly complex, I daresay that many Superfund cleanup tasks involve many of the same features: A crisis triggers the concern of the public; there is an outcry to do something quick; money is no object; get something done! no half measures; there are a myriad of interdependent scientific uncertainties, and so-called experts are suspect because of their biases; the public needs to rely on experts whom they do not trust; there are many objectives that cannot be simultaneously optimized; horrendous trade-offs must be made; interest groups will have to holler to be heard; the negotiation process is rife with distrust, strategic misrepresentation, and coalitional dynamics; no matter what is agreed on as a compromise, it will be viewed as a sellout by various interest groups, lots of ex post facto group regret; and there will be groups of net losers who will want to sabotage the agreement.

—Howard Raiffa, *Decision scientist*

■ *References*

Barke, R. P., & Jenkins-Smith, H. C. (1993). Politics and scientific expertise: Scientists, risk perception, and nuclear waste policy. *Risk Analysis, 13*(4).

Broken trust: The regulators. (1997, January 7). *Cape Cod Times.*

Comprehensive Plume Response Plan. (1996, June). Prepared for the Installation Restoration Program.

JPAT meeting minutes. (1996, April 10). Available: http://www.mmr. org:80/stakhlder/jpat.

Plume Response Plan. (1994, June). Prepared by the Plume Management Process Action Team.

Pre-final draft of the Massachusetts Military Reservation Installation Restoration Plan. (1995, July 3).

Public comments record, January 1 to May 15, 1996. (1996, October 4). Draft. Prepared for the Installation Restoration Program by Waste Policy Institute.

Toward a balanced strategy to address contaminated groundwater plumes at the Massachusetts Military Reservation. (1996, May). Final report of the Technical Review and Evaluation Team.

White paper: Peer Review Team charter. (1996, March 14). Draft. Air National Guard.

Woodhouse, E. J., & Nieusma, D. (1997, Spring). When expert advice works, and when it does not. *IEEE Technology and Society Magazine, 16*(1), 23-29.

8

RULENET

An Experiment in Online Consensus Building

- Michèle Ferenz
- Colin Rule

When William J. Olmstead was a law student in Topeka, Kansas, he was frustrated at his inability to attend public hearings on affirmative action rules. His school refused to pay for the trip to the District of Columbia. Many years later, Olmstead himself had moved to Washington, where he occupied a senior position in the legal counsel's office of a major federal agency. Sitting in the heart of power, he was still bothered by the limitations inherent in the conventional regulatory process. He aimed to make the process more open and inclusive. *Negotiated rulemaking,* a consensus-based practice that directly involves stakeholders in forging administrative rules, had grown in popularity as a form of national policy setting. But full, early, and active public engagement was

still a ways off. Computers, Olmstead believed, might help cover some of that distance.

Thus began an experiment that came to be known as RuleNet, an electronic conference on proposed modifications to existing fire protection rules conducted by the Nuclear Regulatory Commission in early 1996. This case study will explore the technical and political dimensions of RuleNet. We begin our account with a contextual overview of the actors and issues that played a role in shaping the pilot project. We proceed with an outline of RuleNet's technological attributes to provide a concrete sense of how the computer tools structured interactions among the participating parties. We then detail the factors that contributed to what is widely characterized as RuleNet's mixed success. We conclude with a discussion of the strengths and limitations of online consensus building, based on the demonstration project.

■ *The Challenge of Regulating Nuclear Power: A History of Controversy*

More than 100 commercial nuclear power plants operate in the United States, generating approximately one-fifth of the country's electricity needs. The agency responsible for licensing and oversight of these facilities is the U.S. Nuclear Regulatory Commission (NRC), which was established as an independent body in 1974 to assume the regulatory functions formerly carried out by the Atomic Energy Commission (AEC). The mission of the new organization was defined as directing "the Nation's civilian use of byproduct, source, and special nuclear materials to ensure adequate protection of public health and safety, to promote the common defense and security, and to protect the environment" (U.S. NRC, 1997).

From its inception, the NRC has enjoyed little smooth sailing. Both its origins in the womb of the AEC and its organizational culture have contributed to persistent misgivings about the agency's independence from its licensees. The AEC was an avid promoter of nuclear development, and the NRC staff is strongly identified with a "priesthood of engineering" that doesn't always take seriously the risk-related concerns of a skittish public. Over the years, charges of regulatory capture have been aired repeatedly in Congress and in the media, where the NRC was often characterized as the "fox guarding the hen house." In the mid-1980s, the NRC found itself on the agenda of the U.S. House of Representatives Committee on Interior and Insular Affairs; 10 years later, it was on the cover of *Time* magazine (Pooley, 1996, p. 46). Each conducted its own brand of special investigation, and concluded that the NRC had "demonstrated an unhealthy empathy for the needs of the nuclear industry to the detriment of the safety of the American people" (Subcommittee on General Oversight, 1987). ◆

◇ COMMENTARY

The history of nuclear power has become one of controversy, but in its early days, discussions were a closed shop. It was only when problems began to arise in the industry and trust was lost that the need for more public input was realized. The creation of a separate regulatory agency, the NRC, was seen at the time as a way to restore credibility to the secretive, top-down management system that had grown increasingly arrogant. Organizations such as Science in the Public Interest and vocal critics such as Barry Commoner and Linus Pauling had set the stage by successfully demonstrating that the secrecy surrounding nuclear weapons testing had led to flawed actions and cover-ups. This problem was not limited to the United States. The Chernobyl accident in the Soviet Union was the midwife of glasnost, or openness, that eventually spelled the end of the Soviet system and empire a decade later.

—William Moomaw, *Environmental scientist*

But demands for greater accountability and transparency from the public have been matched by complaints from manufacturers and operators of nuclear energy plants. In the 1970s and 1980s, the construction of more than 100 planned reactors was deferred or aborted. No orders have been placed since 1978 and some plants have shut down prematurely (Aron, 1997, p. 3). Representatives of the economically battered industry blame costly delays and failures of entire projects partly on inconsistencies and inefficiencies in the NRC's regulatory process. They decry its voluminous and ever-evolving guidelines. They also criticize what they describe as an excessive emphasis on strict compliance with administrative rules, an approach that, they allege, fails to discriminate between problems with severe and minor safety implications.[1]

Among the more hotly contested of a host of controversial nuclear-related issues is that of fire protection regulation pertaining to nuclear reactors. An unwieldy body of prescriptions has burgeoned in this area since a 1975 fire at the huge Brown's Ferry station in Alabama damaged essential equipment, causing the worst nuclear accident in the United States before Three Mile Island. •⊸

⌘ COMMENTARY

The Brown's Ferry fire caught the public's imagination because it was started by a workman's candle being used to check for drafts from the channels through which electric control cables passed through the containment shell. Suddenly, nongovernmental organizations (NGOs) and the public felt they could comment intelligently on what had previously been a highly technical field that was only accessible to nuclear physicists and other scientists.

—William Moomaw, *Environmental scientist*

To avoid future disasters, in 1981 the NRC implemented a regulatory framework to prevent, detect, control, and extinguish fires in nuclear plants. That framework was codified at 10 CFR 50.48 and CFR Part 50, Appendix R.[2] But as soon as it was promulgated, it was subjected to a rare legal challenge by industry and only barely survived judicial scrutiny. In subsequent years, reinterpretations of the underlying rules and thousands of exemptions granted to licensees produced a potpourri that made it daunting even for the regulators themselves to figure out the licensing basis for a particular plant.

The vast confusion that has reigned in the realm of fire protection is exemplified by the troubled history of Thermo-Lag 330, a plasterlike fire retardant material used by a majority of American nuclear plants. Thermo-Lag is used to coat electrical circuitry that controls emergency reactor shutdown. Appendix R requires that critical cables be insulated by barriers rated to withstand fire damage for three hours (or for one hour, in the presence of detection and automatic fire suppressant systems). Throughout the 1980s, Thermo-Lag was widely touted as the substance that best met such specifications, despite a series of test findings that should have raised concerns. In the early 1990s, the long-simmering Thermo-Lag issue erupted, creating huge headaches for the NRC and nuclear operators. Among other things, the agency staff was berated by the NRC's own in-house inspector general for sluggishness in reviewing Thermo-Lag-related problems. In the end, the NRC acknowledged a pattern of product failure, declared Thermo-Lag "inoperable," and ordered its licensees to take remedial action. ❧

❧ COMMENTARY

The slow realization that Thermo-Lag might be a problem is echoed in the recent findings that fire retardant material in aircraft is insufficient to contain fires adequately. The bureaucratic responses are similarly slow as were those of the NRC.

—William Moomaw, *Environmental scientist*

By the fall of 1996, fire safety system overhauls were completed in less than half of the affected nuclear power units ("Faulty Insulation," 1996). In part, the slow progress during the intervening period was due to the significant financial burdens that the replacement of Thermo-Lag entailed. The total cost of replacing the material was estimated at $500 million—a further blow to an industry that was already buckling under strong competitive pressures. Trying to find a way out of the debacle, the NRC maintained that, given adequate alternative precautions, Thermo-Lag usage was of "low safety significance." On these grounds, the agency once again granted a series of exemptions—a move that stoked the ire of nuclear watchdog groups. The NRC also started paying increased attention to other aspects of fire protection—such as nuclear plants' fire hazard analyses, penetration seals, and lube oil collection systems—and indicated that it was prepared to contemplate changes in the fire protection regulatory framework more generally. The declared objective of such a redrafting exercise would be to make rules less prescriptive and more performance based.[3] The bitter debate over the cost and policy implications of fire safety regula-

tions was far from resolution when a senior lawyer at the NRC decided to make a splash—and picked the weighty fire protection issue to do so.

■ The Genesis of RuleNet: Great Expectations

Over the past few years, national policymakers have attempted to "use the Internet to bring government to the people"[4] by making available electronically a wide range of federal information and services. But the NRC was the first federal agency to use sophisticated, interactive computer technology to involve stakeholders in the development of administrative rules. The pioneering spirit behind this initiative was William J. Olmstead, the agency's associate general counsel for licensing and regulation, who is universally described as entrepreneurial and visionary. Olmstead was a strong believer in alternative dispute resolution (ADR) and had served a two-year term as the head of the Administrative Conference of the United States (ACUS), an independent government agency charged with improving the procedural fairness and efficiency of federal regulatory programs. During his tenure as executive director of

ACUS, Olmstead had frequent interactions with mediator John Helie, then director of ConflictNet, a provider of ADR resources online. (Helie has since left ConflictNet to create Mediate.Com, a mediation information and resource center on the Web.) The idea of an electronic forum for regulatory negotiation germinated in the exchanges between the two men, and came to fruition in the mid-1990s in the shape of RuleNet.

RuleNet was Olmstead's answer to the Clinton administration's call for innovative and cost-effective governance. That call was given institutional force in the form of the National Performance Review (NPR), an ongoing effort to streamline bureaucracy under the leadership of Vice President Al Gore. The NPR had previously developed a system called REGNET, a program using computer networks to disseminate information relevant to federal regulations under consideration. Riding the same wave, the NRC first instituted the use of electronic bulletin boards, where interested parties could "post" comments on a proposed rule. That system was too rudimentary for the participants to interact directly among themselves or with the agency. However, a more ambitious design was the logical next step. Over the course of 1994, the idea of an online rulemaking process matured within the NRC and plans for the creation of an appropriate communications system advanced.

The substantive focus of the online rulemaking was a matter of some debate within the NRC. In selecting a topic, the staff grappled with the tension between strong appeal and manageability. The former prevailed when the choice fell on the question of whether, and how, performance-based regulations could be made applicable to fire safeguards in nuclear reactors. In early 1995, the nuclear industry had submitted a petition for rulemaking, known as Appendix S to 10 CFR Part 50, which was to replace Appendix R in whole or in part. Arguing that advances in fire-modeling and risk-forecasting techniques allowed for the identification of appropriate, situation-specific performance criteria, the proposed amendment called for greater regulatory flexibility in reaching fire safety objectives. The NRC had already solicited and received public comment on the petition in the conventional way. Olmstead (1996) saw the maturity of the fire protection issue as an advantage inasmuch as

1. There was a clearly defined topic of interest to the technical regulated community so that significant useful participation could be anticipated.

2. There was a baseline in the traditional paper-notice-and-comment process with which to compare results. ➥

➥ COMMENTARY

The criteria for choosing the fire issue seem sound. The subject of the rulemaking contains a range of highly technical and nontechnical issues such that people with a wide variety of specialized knowledge could be expected to participate. The issues are focused enough to be manageable, and having a prior paper record allows comparison with traditional approaches. A major advantage of the online process is the ability to provide rapid response to issues raised and questions asked by the participants in the consensus building process.

Olmstead and his colleagues on the NRC legal team expected that an online negotiation could enhance the quality of both the administrative rules that the agency devised and the process for generating them. RuleNet was designed as a three-month pilot project (with roughly six weeks devoted to the development and adaptation of appropriate online technology and six weeks allocated for the dialogue itself). Among its goals was testing the propositions that stakeholder discussions via the Internet could help speed up regulatory action and reduce its contentiousness. Proposals, Olmstead suggested, could be submitted and revised based on rapid feedback, while discord could be addressed as it emerged, before it festered and positions hardened. Above all, the Internet was touted as having the potential for broadening participation and democratizing decision making: No longer would regulatory negotiations be dominated by a small circle of power brokers and experts. Theoretically, anyone could weigh in—as long as he or she had an opinion and a modem.

The NRC published a vision statement in November 1995 that outlined the concept behind RuleNet. According to this document, the process would consist of several phases that moved from stating the problem, to imagining solutions, to formulating more concrete proposals, to debriefing and evaluation. It identified several decision-making mechanisms that would be available, such as caucusing, voting, and "consensus evaluation." It also envisioned recruiting professional neutrals to facilitate the online dialogue. As the technology design team based at Lawrence Livermore National Laboratories explained, the RuleNet system was intended to "encourage participants to share dialogue rather than to posture or express positions . . . the real

value is not in people's knee-jerk reactions, but rather in the case-based and on-line expertise" (Information Technology and Security Center, Lawrence Livermore National Laboratory, 1996, p. 25).

Appropriately, RuleNet was inaugurated with a "virtual meeting" in cyberspace on January 5, 1996. A facilitated video conference discussion involved audiences gathered at one Sprint location and a handful of Kinko's copy stores across the country. A transcript was fed to the Internet, through which still more participants could follow the proceedings on their home or office computers with a delay of only a few minutes. Web users could also electronically interject comments and questions from their home or office computers. Despite the fact that NRC Chairman Shirley Jackson was on hand to give her imprimatur, the kickoff event was grander in design than in execution. The Kinko's copy shops made for rather cramped quarters and many of the messages that poured in merely stated that the record had stopped scrolling across the screen. The *New York Times* caught some of the involuntary humor in the scene in the following rendition:

> "Press 'more' at the bottom of your screen," the facilitator, John Helie, advised, speaking to the camera. The comment was put on the Web. "Of course," he added, "They'll probably have to click on 'more' in order to get that information." (Wald, 1996, p. D-2)

The multimedia kickoff was an apt preview of things to come. On the one hand, it was a demonstration of the power and promise that the use of technology holds for consensus building. On the other hand, few new adventures proceed without hitches—and RuleNet would prove to be no exception.

■ *The Technology Underlying RuleNet*

Information technology is dazzling. Sometimes people exposed to it understand it too little and entrust it with too much. Obviously, the promoters of RuleNet focused heavily on computer capabilities. But the RuleNet team members' strong attention to tools also clouded their awareness of some flaws that slipped into the design of the consensus building process. The main stumbling blocks were not technical; in fact, technical problems were relatively minor irritants along the way. Rather, in the general excitement, the temptation to charge ahead without full consideration of the dynamics of the fire protection dispute proved irresistible and, ultimately, problematic. Political realities ended up getting in the way—realities not anticipated by some unflappable technological optimists on the NRC staff who assumed, for example, that "the software will summarize points" (interview with Elin Whitney-Smith, Washington, D.C., August 1998). In retrospect, Francis Cameron, special counsel for public liaison at the NRC and a close Olmstead associate, observed that it is apparent that some consensus building practices, such as convening, are equally important in an online setting. "Doing it electronically doesn't mean that you shouldn't have the focus, drive, and systematic effort you usually put into a consultative process."

The Tools of RuleNet

The address of the RuleNet World Wide Web site was http://nssc.llnl.gov/RuleNet. The visual image that graced its home page was a colorful drawing representing a power plant, a single-family house, and the nation's Capitol building, all interconnected through a whirl of telephone wires. Computer engineers at Lawrence Livermore National Laboratory (LLNL) had previously developed Internet software called NetForum, a multicomponent program used for electronic conferences and other interactions by a variety of clients. NetForum was adapted to suit the specific needs of RuleNet participants, as defined by the NRC. An LLNL team accomplished this through the design of tools that helped focus the dialogue, summarize information, and identify peripheral issues that should be brought into the center of the discussion. They became the primary means by which the facilitators and the technical support staff guided the flow of the negotiation and urged the group closer to consensus. Among the Web-based tools were the following:

- A "participant tool" allowed anyone to register for the NetForum and participate in discussions.
- "Frequently asked questions," or FAQs, provided some background information to the participants, as well as spelled out the "rules of engagement" that postings on the site had to follow. This allowed for doubts raised by participants to be clarified immediately, a marked improvement over the traditional paper process in which queries from the public are answered only with the release of the final rule, if ever.
- The "news tool" reported information about NetForum and ensured that participants knew when new postings appeared on the site; it also allowed participants to be up-to-date

on the progress made by different, parallel discussion groups.

- The "reference tool" allowed participants to contribute a document or to browse documents that had been sent in by other participants or loaded by the NRC. Appendix R, for example, was searchable in full text form.

- The "forum manager tool" arranged the postings of the participants and facilitators so as to make the dialogue easier to follow. All of the postings could be sorted by author, date, position on the issue being discussed, or subject.

- "RuleNet Commons" was a discussion forum open to everyone, including people who were not registered on the site. Additionally, it provided a place where postings deemed not appropriate by the moderator of Net-Forum could be posted.

- A "moderator tool" gave the moderators the power to review postings before they were posted to the NetForum space. If a posting was too inflammatory, it could be returned to the composer with a suggestion that it be rephrased. ⇌

⇋ COMMENTARY

The set of reference and discussion management tools, frequently asked questions, and other innovations should enhance any consensus building process whether available through the Internet or otherwise. The informational features should provide reassurance—or set off alarms—for those who are just browsing, and raise the level of those participating to a higher level. Is there any way of assessing whether that happened?

—William Moomaw, *Environmental scientist*

Another important feature of the Rule-Net technology was that it could operate as a "listserv" discussion in addition to a World Wide Web-based forum. In other words, once participants had registered, they could receive or write new messages in their e-mail programs instead of having to log on to the RuleNet site every time they wanted to intercede. While less fun and flashy than the graphics-enhanced Web page, e-mail technology adds convenience and immediacy to the communication.

Dialogue Structure and Content

Participants were meant to gear up for the discussion by perusing through a vast array of documents and position papers posted on the RuleNet site. The dialogue itself proceeded in three phases: an issue identification phase (January 5-16, 1996), a comment synthesis and proposal development phase (January 17-26), and an analysis and drafting phase (January 27-February 9). A facilitation team was on hand with a range of expertise; John Helie was recruited to serve as the lead mediator. Two "moderators" with extensive editorial and computer experience operated at his flanks. Site maintenance and trouble-shooting were the responsibilities of technical staff at LLNL's Information Technology and Security Center (IT&S), where the NetForum program originated.

For efficiency's sake, the discussion was organized into separate "threads"—the cyberspace equivalent of breakout groups—each of which was focused around a specific question or proposal drafted by the facilitators. Feedback was catalogued and evaluated using a "consensus evaluation tool," a device that allowed stakeholders to register their approval or disapproval on a proposition, and the strength of their preferences and convictions. At any time, Helie could write a proposed consensus statement that would appear on the screen of all the registered users when they logged on. The participants would respond with a number from 1 through 6, with 1 representing complete agreement and 6 amounting to strong objection. The average would indicate the areas of strongest disagreement. Users selected a number between 4 and 6, who were asked to follow up with a list of "sticking points"—issues that they thought required resolution before they could move down the numerical scale. These lists were visible only on the administrator page, which was not accessible to the regular participants. Helie would then put out a new statement that sought to incorporate the concerns raised by dissenters. The lower the average rating, the closer the group moved toward "consensus." If a group discussion appeared focused and harmonious, Helie would post a proposition that was likely to generate a lot of low scores. He could then call for a vote with the assurance that a majority would be in agreement. ➥

➣ COMMENTARY

The use of rolling weighted polling of positions is a technique that probably worked better in an Internet format than it possibly could in a face-to-face encounter.

—William Moomaw, *Environmental scientist*

In addition, graphics were built into the technology of NetForum to represent the thrust of a message in the main forum map. The participants themselves chose among the symbols that could accompany a comment. Among the icons appearing next to each contribution were

- a question mark: to request clarification;
- a large letter *A* for Answer: for contributions responding to posted questions;
- a shining lightbulb standing for "promising practice": to present actions taken in other situations that might offer a good way to realize a recommendation or address an issue;

- a large thumbs-up indicating agreement: to offer support of a proposition or argument set forth by someone else;

- a small speech balloon (as in a cartoon) with the words *Yes, but* inside it: to qualify a preceding comment by offering exceptions to or extensions of the argument it advances;

- a large yin-yang symbol: to offer alternate ways to implement a proposal or recommendation;

- a large thumbs-down indicating disagreement: to directly challenge a prior message;

- the word *New* in colorful letters: to begin a new line of discussion under an overall subject heading; and
- the word *None* in colorful letters: to indicate that the writer held no position on the specific issue being discussed. (Information Technology and Security Center, Lawrence Livermore National Laboratory, 1996, p. 27)

Looking at the entire flow of a particular discussion as calibrated by these icons, the moderators could assess the general mood and identify areas of agreement, controversy, or confusion.

■ Phases of the Dialogue

Phase 1

The dialogue began with a 10-day exploratory period. This time was allocated to problem definition and for the public to review the provided background information and ask clarifying questions. The initial queries put before the participants were very general in nature. One example was: "What are the pros and cons of allowing licensees to adopt revised regulations on their own schedule, and piece by piece instead of all at once?"[5] Extensive discussion ensued on this topic, and eventually the eight people who had been actively engaged in the back-and-forth used the "voting tool" to register their sentiments. It was clear from the results that there was a broad range of opinions among the participants but that the majority leaned toward opposition.

The second question aimed at listing the key elements of a potential performance-based fire protection rule. Proposals included training in fire safety for on-site personnel, leakage of significant doses of radiation, disposal of nuclear waste, "safety-centricity" of managers, and licensees' commitment to openness and public engagement ("Options," 1996). A second consensus evaluation determined that the participants were of widely different opinions on this question as well.

Consensus evaluations were held on several additional questions, such as the following.

- How should the NRC go about ensuring that the new performance-oriented requirements actually work? What mix of modeling, risk assessment, validation and verification, and licensing will work the best, both for NRC and the licensees? (12 responses)
- Should a revised regulation cover only those systems necessary to achieve safe shutdown (with the rest of the fire protection-related requirements addressed elsewhere), or should it cover requirements for all functions related to fire protection? (17 responses)
- Should requirements for areas less important to the safety of the plant be relaxed/eliminated? Will a probabilistic risk analysis result in better focus and coherence in NRC's regulations by allowing resources to be used more effectively? ("Options," 1996, pp. 9-10) (48 responses)[6]

Phase 2

In Phase 2, participants were asked to brainstorm and propose solutions to the issues raised in the first phase. Based on the contributions that had been gathered, the RuleNet team crafted six questions designed to elicit proposals for alternatives to existing regulations. To carry on effective, simultaneous discussions, six virtual parallel "working groups" were created at this stage. In summary, the themes of the mini-forums were the following.

- What alternative approaches are available for dealing with the deficiencies in the fire protection rule? Should any rulemaking take place within the framework of a new "performance-based" rule?
- If some areas of fire protection were recognized as being of higher priority, what are some areas where benefits would accrue to licensees? If pilot programs were approved, what would be their framework and scope?
- If a prioritized approach is approved, what are some categories judged to be of higher safety significance?
- Assuming that a performance-based rule were adopted, what are regulatory alternatives for implementing such an approach? Are there examples that demonstrate the differences, and perhaps the respective benefits, of performance-based versus prescriptive rules?
- Recognizing that critics have pointed to problems in using probabilistic risk

analyses (PRAs) in the fire protection area, what alternatives are available for using PRAs in this field?
- If NRC's fire protection rules were to be changed, what risk-based performance alternatives are available to ensure that the facility's safe-shutdown methodology is adequately protected from the effects of fire?[7]

Each area of inquiry spawned a series of comments, structured in the forum map as a vertical chain or thread. Topics that attracted little interest were eventually dropped. But none of the miniconferences drew a very large audience: Almost half of all the messages sent came from the same handful of participants (including Olmstead, one very vocal independent fire consultant, and the designated industry representative). These exchanges were often highly detail oriented. Furthermore, in all of the parallel discussions, the same small and dedicated core of active participants chimed in. The electronic forum, then, may have generated its own problems of exclusivity but it also allowed people to be in multiple "rooms" at the same time—something that would be impossible in the physical world. ➙

☞ COMMENTARY

Organizing in phases and producing six parallel threads or virtual working groups is more likely to be a fruitful approach using this technology. Participants can cruise back and forth between threads, which would be impossible in real time.

—William Moomaw, *Environmental scientist*

Phase 3

At the end of these first two phases, the RuleNet team summarized the outcome of

the online talks in three key areas. One of these policy positions was quite crisp and strong in tone, one was tentative, and one was entirely noncommittal. The wording depended on the degree of polarization on each issue that had emerged in the prior discussions. The recommendations that resulted were the following.

Fire protection requirements. "Fire protection features should be 'graded' according to the relative importance to plant safety . . . the fire threat for each fire area should be defined, and protection provided based on the threat rather than equal protection across the board."

Risk and fire modeling. "Risk information and fire modeling can be beneficial to develop a regulation to focus licensee activities on safety-significant activities in order to improve the cost effectiveness of plant fire protection programs without adversely affecting safety. However, to develop such a rule would require the necessary risk and fire models."

Regulatory flexibility. "No participant advocated that rulemaking was necessary as a solution to a public health and safety deficiency in the existing rule. Rather, some participants endorsed rulemaking as necessary to provide licensees with more flexibility in implementing fire protection regulations (although there was no agreement on how this should be done). Other participants thought that certain benefits could be achieved by working within the existing rule, for example, by ensuring that staff interpretations of the existing rule were consistent or by ensuring that NRC enforcement guidance recognizes that not all fire protection requirements are equal in contributing to safety. Others did not believe that licensees could demonstrate that they were complying with the existing rule, and therefore, no rulemaking should be undertaken until this demonstration is made."

These synopses were posted to the RuleNet site for participant review. A "caucus tool" had been devised to allow for separate consultations. Use of that option was actively encouraged at that point, but none of the stakeholders took advantage of it. Once again, a few participants dominated the discussion. Fifteen of the 25 fire protection-related contributions came from one person. Many of the other messages were informational requests more than substantive observations.

That does not mean no one was checking in, however: A fourth question dealing with the effectiveness of RuleNet itself triggered a lively discussion—41 messages—which highlights that the process was of significant interest. Evaluations were overwhelmingly positive and lauded the fact that RuleNet opened up government proceedings to public participation and scrutiny. Others emphasized that a cost analysis should be undertaken before the concept of online negotiations was further integrated into the regulation-setting process. ➥

∽ COMMENTARY

The positive response of participants is encouraging. It suggests that the process made them feel that their voices were being heard and that their interventions were having an effect. This is often not the reaction when parties introduce testimony in a static form and must wait for the rulemaking to learn if any of their input was heard or used.

—William Moomaw, *Environmental scientist*

Ground Rules

In many consensus building efforts, the exercise of defining ground rules collectively is the first step toward building trust and, it is hoped, an agreement. But in Rule-Net, the stakeholders had no role in process design. Most important, they had no input into what meaning to ascribe to *consensus* in the RuleNet setting. No clear decision rule was ever formulated or ratified by the participants. Furthermore, little effort was made to educate participants about the meaning and value of consensus-based decision making. Perhaps inevitably, some people missed the point: "They wrote summaries of the comments—leaving out the ones they didn't like—and called that 'a consensus,' " said one reactor engineer. "The consensus stuff was unnecessary. I mean, don't tell me what I'm telling you."

The RuleNet discussion was guided by one iron ground rule, though: No offensive language, no capitalization (which was construed as shouting), and no anonymous postings were admissible. When a comment was received from a participant during a real-time chat session, it immediately went through a content control device, known as a "Bozo filter," that checked it for certain words. The postings that cleared the automatic filtering were forwarded to the moderators, who acted as the final line of defense. If they encountered a potentially problematic posting, they would engage the author in a one-on-one dialogue. Although there was some grumbling about First Amendment rights, participants generally agree that the filtering mechanism was very successful in keeping nasty comments out of the public domain, and hence in keeping the tone courteous and professional.

■ Stakeholder Resistance: Many "Cruisers," Some "Lurkers," Few "Participants"

As we have seen, the choice of a high-profile safety issue as the subject of RuleNet was quite deliberate. Indeed, it had profound impact, especially in terms of stakeholder participation. The initial fear of the organizers was that they would be overwhelmed with contributions (a subject such as emergency planning has in the past elicited as many as 3,800 comments from the public at large) before they could eliminate the technological bugs in the system. But moderator Elin Whitney-Smith suggested they consider the opposite scenario: "You really have a problem if you have a party and no one comes." Her point was well taken, for the community of people who know and care about the intricacies of fire protection at nuclear power plants is a very restricted one. Framed in highly technical terms, the RuleNet debate left emotional, big-picture policy questions, such as the desirability of commercial nuclear power, out of bounds. The result was a process for the initiated few: reactor operators, antinuclear activists, fire protection engineers, and a handful of consultants and academics who specialize in fire safety concerns.

Usage statistics were compiled by the staff at LLNL to categorize the types of users of the RuleNet system. They created four different profiles: participants, registered lurkers, unregistered lurkers, and cruisers. Participants were active contributors to the system, lurkers spent time on the system but did not post messages, and cruisers came through the site on only a few occasions and did not spend a significant amount of time. This analysis showed that for the full duration of the RuleNet project (November 20, 1995 to February 9, 1996), there were 28 participants, 6 registered lurkers, 313 unregistered lurkers, and 387 cruisers. An analysis of the e-mail addresses of the people passing through the system shows that the majority (14,165) of hits came from "gov" domains, slightly less (11,385) came from "com" domains, and a much smaller number (1,403) from "edu" domains. Only 20 registrants were active, regular participants (defined in terms of both frequency and substantive nature of their input)—and even they were a partial representation of the stakeholder categories that set the tone in the larger fire protection debate. For a number of different reasons, people affiliated with the nuclear industry, public interest groups, and the NRC contributed hesitantly or not at all.

At the outset, the weather didn't cooperate either: In early January 1996, an extraordinary snowstorm blanketed the capital, as if to prove, as John Helie put it, that "virtual reality still has some very messy ties to reality." Along with the cold spell, a government furlough kept people in their homes, where many did not have access to the Internet. The RuleNet dialogue shriveled as a consequence. During this lull, a memorandum was circulated that dealt the process a further setback. The Nuclear Energy Institute (NEI), an industry advocacy group that represents all nuclear plant operating licensees, issued a letter discouraging individual utilities and other industry organizations from participating in RuleNet. Fire experts and legal support staff operating in plants around the country were asked to follow the discussions and funnel their feedback to an NEI representative, instead of giving their input directly to the entire conference. This injunction was largely adhered to, as evidenced by the registration data: 24 percent of registrants identified themselves as having some relation with the commercial nuclear industry or the private sector. However, with one exception (a person who never received the memorandum asking him to stay off the site) these members did not post messages.

Doubtless, the NEI attempted to control the flow of information to avoid splits in the industry position as well as potentially embarrassing revelations about safety violations. If anyone could speak out freely, the industry group's internal decision-making structure risked being bypassed and undermined. Dissension among its ranks would thus potentially be made public before the organization itself had a chance to deal with it. But the NEI also substantiated its objections with reference to indeterminacy in the RuleNet process: "We believe that there are a number of significant questions that need to be resolved in the RuleNet pilot effort," the letter explained. "For example, NRC's disposition of communications among participants, qualification of participants, potential influence by special interests, conduct of private versus open caucuses among participants, and representation by organizations versus individuals, etc. are some of the questions that have not been addressed by the RuleNet procedures."[8]

Aside from questions about the credibility, authority, and expertise of individual contributors, NEI's main concern regarded the legal status of the RuleNet record. The official comment period on the fire protection rulemaking petition had expired. In fact, one of the documents that served as a departure point for RuleNet was one that contained NRC staff recommendations on the issue based on paper comments received in mid-1995 ("Options," 1996).

Just how would the RuleNet contributions fit into the existing administrative proceeding? Would they supersede the paper process or be treated as an adjunct? In fact, was the objective of RuleNet to produce a draft rule or was it merely an additional opportunity for affected parties to exchange information and find some common ground?

The rationale put forth by the industry for its partial boycott of RuleNet leaves some critics cold. Peter Craine, counsel for special projects at the NRC, while agreeing that some terms of RuleNet were ill defined, zeroed in on the heart of the matter—the question of representation: "It's about democracy," he said. "It's like saying, 'Of course only landowners should be allowed to vote; do you want some peasant to have an equal say in this?' " But participation was not forthcoming from nuclear watchdog groups either, despite the fact that they were not muzzled by some umbrella organization. Some activists charged that the NRC had already made up its mind on fire safety and would manipulate Rule-Net to garner support for its position. Others objected to the use of computers in rulemaking, dismissing the exercise outright as a toy for "techies."[9] Still others bemoaned the lack of educational reference tools, such as links to glossaries, necessary for ordinary citizens to make sense of the mass of jargon-laden information.[10]

Last but not least, the NRC itself was not united in its enthusiasm for RuleNet. The technical staff doubted that RuleNet could cover any ground other than the well-worn paths that they had traveled with industry and nuclear watchdog groups on the fire safety issue so many times in the past. Given the abstruse nature of nuclear safety requirements, "We could send signals to the entire galaxy and not get more thoughtful input," said Gary Holahan, director of Division of System Safety and Analysis in the Office of Nuclear Reactor Regulation. Such profound skepticism was compounded by a hierarchical organizational culture that puts a premium on slow and painstaking deliberation. "It is very unusual for us to be giving written feedback to the world," said the NRC's chief fire engineer, Steven West. "There is a formal process for deciding even if we answer a question. RuleNet is wilder." Under normal circumstances, as many as 10 people may be involved in drafting a response to a query from the public—a standard operating procedure not conducive to the immediacy and spontaneity of expression that an online dialogue requires. In spite of repeated assurances, staff members felt uncomfortable broadcasting their own views, especially if these did not coincide with those of their superiors. "RuleNet seemed to propagate informal personal subjectivism," echoed Holahan. "It was an alien way of doing business." ◆

∽ COMMENTARY

The reaction of the NRC officials is very interesting. The degree and speed of response is different for them under RuleNet processes. But then this degree of consensus building may also be new to them.

—William Moomaw, *Environmental scientist*

Beyond the political ramifications of RuleNet, there were also practical constraints that dampened participation; a number of regular contributors cited time as a key limiting factor.

■ The Role of the Neutral: Mediation and Moderation

The RuleNet process needed the facilitation services of experienced conflict managers to urge the dialogue forward and to minimize frustration and name-calling. To be entirely effective, however, these process experts would have required substantial assistance from fire protection engineers familiar with the language, science, and theory of the field. The challenge of integrating technical expertise into the consensus building process, difficult in face-to-face situations, was complicated further by the text-only environment of online interaction.

The primary task of the facilitation team was to "take the temperature" and synthesize the main ideas that emerged in discussion. If controversy erupted on a particular topic, a report to that effect would be prepared for the newsletter (though the NRC itself retained final editorial control over the newsletter's content). Helie and the moderators attempted, through natural topic aggregations, to break down the complex technical questions into manageable topics. Navigating the legal and technical minutiae that make up NRC regulations was no small feat, however, and help was often not readily available: "It was like going to Mars and not knowing what Martians look like when they are having a good time," recalled moderator Chris Berendes.

In a virtual world of vertical discussion threads, as opposed to a real world of three-dimensional rooms, facilitators can easily get lost, overpowered by the prose of other contributors. To surface reasons for disagreement and crystallize consensus, a strong hand may therefore be required of online facilitators, not the light touch of the people who filled these roles in RuleNet. This appears to have been no fault of their own, but rather the result of a lack of clear definition of their role at the outset and conflicting expectations about who should take the lead: the dispute resolution process experts or the NRC fire engineers.

Third-party intervention online poses challenges different from those found in face-to-face negotiations. Some responsibilities, such as ensuring that all have an equal opportunity to speak and keeping time, fall by the wayside; other tasks can assume a great deal more importance. NRC lawyer Cameron observed that "when the process falls apart in cyberspace over a period of time, the lack of a facilitator doesn't seem as immediately critical as in face-to-face where it is obvious when things unravel." Still, an electronic conference has to be just as carefully monitored to keep discussions on track—perhaps more so, because many of the subtler cues based on body language will get lost between the lines. "In a normal process," Cameron continued, "you know what people bring to the process in terms of eloquence, intelligence, and emotionality. Instead, here you're never really sure who will be doing what." The Bozo filter was successful in eliminating verbal abuse from the discussion, but RuleNet provided little evidence that online communication is inherently less confrontational. Successive comments in a thread were as likely to diverge as to converge, with participants sometimes fixating on minute points of disagreement in another's contribution. Mutual trust may also be harder to build between parties staring at a screen instead of into each other's eyes. "It's the old line 'I want to know if you smile when you say that,' " said Robert William Bishop, general counsel of NEI. ∾

∾ COMMENTARY

The role of the facilitator may be different in the RuleNet context, in that he is responsible for so many simultaneous threads and dimensions of the discussion. Capturing agreement is still a major role that needs to be played. The use of Bozo filters and other devices appears to have succeeded in lowering the temperature of exchanges so that substantive issues could be discussed, and a consensus built.

—William Moomaw, *Environmental scientist*

■ *Outcome of RuleNet: An Assessment of the Pilot Project*

RuleNet was neither an unqualified success nor an abject failure. Certainly, no major progress could be recorded in the task of overhauling fire protection regulation. In the summer of 1998, the NRC was still firing off reminders to utilities that Thermo-Lag deficiencies have to be corrected. Meanwhile, the controversy over the desirability of performance-based rules continues unabated—consensus is elusive both within the NRC and among the various pro- and antinuclear interests that have faced off on this issue. In a dramatic shift from its previous position, the nuclear industry announced that it was no longer interested in new rules. The reason given for this about-face was reduced confidence in the adequacy of the new modeling and risk assessment techniques that had been the centerpiece of the proposed Appendix S. Antinuclear activists continue to push for the NRC to abolish the myriad exemptions.

The NRC, caught in the uncomfortable middle, determined it should await the development of a new fire code by the National Fire Protection Association (NEPA) before taking further steps. That trade association is expected to develop a proposed standard by 2000. In the interim, nuclear plants that still use Thermo-Lag deploy a very low-tech countermeasure against potential blazes: Workers patrol important reactor areas on an hourly basis to detect incipient conflagrations.

In terms of concrete, substantive results, therefore, RuleNet turned up little. Few surprising opinions or creative solutions were offered, and few minds were changed. Then again, the brief process was never realistically expected to resolve an entrenched, technically complex dispute with strong political overtones. "It was Benjamin Franklin on the first balloon," NRC lawyer Craine summed up. Given the cocktail of intense emotions and antithetical positions, nuclear policy generally is rough terrain for consensus building—and fire protection rules have a particularly bitter history. RuleNet's aspirations were more modest: a "baby step," as Olmstead called it, in the direction of revolutionizing negotiated rulemaking through the introduction of new, computer-based collaborative tools. By that yardstick, RuleNet accomplished its mission. With Olmstead's untimely death in 1998, the NRC lost the most determined promoter of the use of the World Wide Web as a forum for regulatory activity. But evidence that the pilot has indeed left its mark is that others are contemplating following in his footsteps: Moni Dey, a senior reactor systems engineer, for example, is hoping to use the Internet to conduct a peer review of a major report on fire safety analysis.

As mentioned above, respondents to a survey on RuleNet immediately after the conclusion of the project gave mostly positive feedback. A staff analysis partly based on these reactions asserted that the electronic rulemaking process had proved "superior to traditional notice-and-comment rulemaking from the perspective of allowing a fuller elucidation of the parties' positions" ("RuleNet," 1996). Still, it appears clear that at least in the short-term future, an online process can be useful as a supplement, not a substitute, to traditional rulemaking procedures.

From a technological perspective, RuleNet may have been ahead of its time: The tools used were state-of-the-art at the time RuleNet occurred. But the development of online technologies is advancing at a rapid pace, and what is available only two years later makes the NetForum software used in 1996 look very primitive. Common online tools such as chat rooms, audio, rudimentary videoconferencing, whiteboards, and team document authoring software have all emerged in the past few years. Some of these tools might have proven very useful in the RuleNet experiment.

A handful of important lessons emerge from the RuleNet experiment that can help shape future online consensus building efforts:

Policy issues may lend themselves better to electronic debates than complex, technically demanding or science-intensive questions. The subject of RuleNet was such that the lay public had neither the expertise nor the interest to contribute. Instead, its target audience was the usual cast of highly trained specialists. ◆◆

◆◆ COMMENTARY

I am surprised that one conclusion is that more technical issues such as fire standards at a nuclear reactor are less well dealt with in this format than are less technical policy issues. The opportunity to answer technical misconceptions without interrupting the flow of the ongoing dialogue would seem to give a Web-based process an advantage. The ability of those with concerns to participate is very much a technology choice question. Perhaps there needs to be a training system for those who wish to participate that is designed from the perspective of users and not providers. This is an example of the "computer manual problem."

—William Moomaw, *Environmental scientist*

Technology is a prop; it is not a substitute for the careful preparation and execution of a consensus building process. From convening to issue framing and from virtual meeting management to process evaluation, each step should be planned strategically to ensure buy-in from key stakeholders, sustain their commitment through the process, and make good use of the final output. Above all, the objectives of the process must be clearly spelled out, and the outcome should hold a clear place in the legal and administrative setting that is the context for such negotiations.

The choice of technologies is not neutral. It can have a significant impact on the extent of participation. E-mail is less sophisticated than the Internet, but it may still be accessible to a wider range of people. There is also a distinction between *pull* and *push* technologies: The former rely, as in RuleNet, on the target audience to seek out the pertinent Web site and repeatedly log on to participate in a dialogue; the latter label applies to features intended to draw stakeholders in and keep them up-to-date through automatic e-mail announcements and solicitations for reactions.

Mediators who operate in an online context should try to be assertive. Active management of the discussion and frequent interventions by the neutral lend the structure that an online dialogue requires as much as face-to-face interventions.

online processes can be resource intensive. Information technology reduces the need for mounds of paper and steep fares. But despite the speed and ease of long-distance electronic communication, it is not free. The NRC paid the LLNL an estimated $300,000 for the software required to run RuleNet. Beyond direct monetary expenses, an online consensus process also requires a significant time commitment from serious participants. One danger, therefore, is that a process of adverse selection kicks in. Because, as Vincent Brannigan, a professor of fire protection regulation at the University of Maryland pointed out, "The people on the Net may be all those who are not busy otherwise." Key stakeholders should therefore ideally be allowed to dedicate a part of their workday to an online process that is relevant to their own professional lives and/or to their employers. Obviously, that is possible only if these stakeholders have Internet access from their workplace, a requirement that was not met at the time of RuleNet even for some senior fire engineers of the NRC.

Technology-driven processes can make demands on people that run counter to the standard operating procedure or culture of the organization they work for. Unless this dynamic is recognized and adequately addressed, key stakeholders may not offer input as often or openly as would be desirable.

■ Notes

1. See, for example, testimony by Joe F. Colvin, president and chief executive officer of the Nuclear Energy Institute (NEI), and by James T. Rhodes, chairman and chief executive officer of the Institute of Nuclear Power Operations (INPO), before the Senate Environment and Public Works Environment Subcommittee on Clean Air, Wetlands, Private Property and Nuclear Safety, July 30, 1998.

2. 45 *Federal Register* 76611, November 19, 1980; 46 *Federal Register* 44735, September 8, 1981, as amended at 53 *Federal Register* 19251, May 27, 1988.

3. 57 *Federal Register* 4166 (February 4, 1992) and 57 *Federal Register* 55156 (November 24, 1992).

4. Jim Van Wert, senior adviser for policy planning at the Small Business Administration (quoted in "Gov.net," 1996, p. 43).

5. From the RuleNet Web site: http://nssc.llnl.gov/RuleNet/Discussions/Topics_I.html.

6. From the RuleNet Web site: http://nssc.llnl.gov/RuleNet/Discussions/Topics_I.html, October 1998.

7. From the RuleNet Web site: http://nssc.llnl.gov/RuleNet, October 1998.

8. Letter by William H. Rasin, NEI, to the NEI Nuclear Strategic Issues Advisory Committee, dated December 1, 1995.

9. Robert Pollard, nuclear safety engineer of the Union of Concerned Scientists (cited in "Nuclear Agency," 1996).

10. Eileen Queen, spokeswoman of the Union of Concerned Scientists (cited in Wald, 1995).

■ *References*

Aron, J. (1997). *Licensed to kill? The Nuclear Regulatory Commission and the Shoreham Power Plant.* Pittsburgh: University of Pittsburgh Press.

Faulty insulation draws heavy fine. (1996, October 14). *Engineering News-Record, 237*(16), 9.

Gov.net: Government turns to the Internet to win back public faith. (1996, April 29). *Government Computer News, 9*(15).

Information Technology and Security Center, Lawrence Livermore National Laboratory. (1996, June 28). *RuleNet. FIN L-2501 Task 9, 25,* 27.

Nuclear agency taps Internet for rulemaking. (1996, November 20). *Newsbytes News Network.*

Olmstead, B. (1996, May). *The design and experience with RuleNet.* Paper presented at the NCAIR Electronic Dispute Resolution Conference, Washington, DC.

Options for pursuing regulatory improvement in fire protection regulations for nuclear power plants. (1996, October 2). *SECY-96-134.*

Pooley, E. (1996, March 4). Nuclear warriors. *Time Business/Special Investigation,* p. 46.

RuleNet. (1996, August 29). *SECY-96-188.*

Subcommittee on General Oversight and Investigations of the Committee on Interior and Insular Affairs of the U.S. House of Representatives. One Hundredth Congress. First Session. (1987, December). *NRC coziness with industry; Nuclear Regulatory Commission fails to maintain arms length relationship with the nuclear industry. An investigative report.*

U.S. Nuclear Regulatory Commission, Division of Budget and Analysis, Office of the Chief Financial Officer. (1997). Mission statement. *Information Digest, NUREG-1350, 9,* 2.

Wald, M. L. (1995, November 24). Nuclear agency to use Internet to receive ideas for new rule. *New York Times.*

Wald, M. L. (1996, January 15). Agency tests a new kind of public hearing. *New York Times,* p. D-2.

CASE

9

REGULATORY NEGOTIATIONS
The Native American Experience

■ Jan Jung-Min Sunoo
■ Juliette A. Falkner

This negotiated rulemaking process has been a model for developing successful Federal and tribal partnerships in other endeavors. The consensus process allowed for true bilateral negotiations between the Federal government and the tribes in the best spirit of the government-to-government relationship.

—Secretaries Bruce Babbitt (Department of the Interior) and Donna Shalala (Department of Health and Human Services), commending the Indian Self-Determination and Education Assistance Act amendments' negotiations (*Federal Register*, 1996)

The views presented here are those of the authors and do not necessarily reflect the views of the federal government. The authors wish to acknowledge the helpful commentary and analysis offered by many of the participants in the negotiations. Especially helpful were comments offered in discussion and/or in writing by Buford L. Rolin (Health Director, Poarch Band of Creek Indians), Michael Anderson (Deputy Assistant Secretary, Indian Affairs, Department of the Interior), Commissioner Linda Gonzalez (FMCS), Commissioner John Wagner (FMCS), Katherine Grosdidier, MBA (President/CEO Southcentral Foundation), and Lloyd Benton Miller (Sonosky, Chambers, Sachse, Miller, Munson, & Clocksin). Besides author Jan Jung-Min Sunoo, the cofacilitators from the Federal Mediation and Conciliation Service were Commissioners Pete Swanson, Beverly Reinhart, and Linda Gonzalez.

■ Overview

In 1996, 63 people—48 representing Indian tribes and tribal organizations throughout the country, and 15 representing more than 10 federal agencies and offices—completed the largest negotiated rulemaking ever. By adhering to a consensus process, the participants designed a regulatory framework that years of typical negotiating had failed to accomplish. In addition, the process became a model for future dialogues with Indian tribes. ⬤

⬤ COMMENTARY

The use of consensus building processes in negotiated rulemaking (reg-neg) has been a much-touted (Harter, 1982), as well as controversial, endeavor. Add the usual dilemmas of public regulation, interest groups, "capture" or conflict and participation, the difficulties of the relations between the federal government and Indian tribes, and the cultural differences between the government bureaucracy and the many interested tribes, and we would likely have some insoluble process issues for developing acceptable regulations for a bipartisan contracting process. This largely successful reg-neg process involving over 63 participants—including two federal departments and 48 Indian tribes—demonstrates how skillful, respectful, and task-oriented facilitators can make a difference in what might otherwise be an acrimonious and formless or unnecessarily adversarial process.

—Carrie J. Menkel-Meadow, *Legal scholar*

REFERENCE

Harter, P. J. (1982). Negotiating regulations: A cure for malaise. *Georgetown Law Journal, 71,* 1.

■ Historical Background

In 1975, Congress passed the Indian Self-Determination and Education Assistance Act (Public Law 93-638). This act gave Indian tribes authority to contract with the federal government to operate federal programs such as schools, health facilities, construction projects, and so on that would serve their tribal members and other eligible persons. These contracts became known as "638 contracts" after the act that enabled them. The act's purpose was to shift the responsibility of service delivery from the government to each tribe or tribal organization so that the tribe would have improved services and more autonomy. However, by 1988 Congress determined that instead of 638 contracts improving services to the tribes, the federal government had created a complicated bureaucratic maze, making it more efficient for the government to continue to operate contractible programs itself. For example, the government took an average of six months to process a 638 contract proposal, instead of the 60 days required by the act. To correct these problems, Congress revised the act and directed the Department of the

Interior and the Department of Health and Human Services to develop regulations over a 10-month period with the active participation of tribes and tribal organizations.

Advisory versus Negotiating Capacity of the Two Parties

Despite the 10-month deadline, the two departments and the Indian tribes did not reach agreement on draft regulations until 1990. During this time, the departments sponsored several regional negotiation sessions throughout the country. Tribal representatives were offered an opportunity to present their issues to a panel of federal employees. However, these employees did not always have the full negotiating authority of their agencies. In several instances, agreements the federal team reached with the tribal representatives were overturned by superiors in Washington, D.C. More important, after the 1990 compromise had been reached, the departments continued to work on the proposed regulations without tribal input. When a new administration took over in 1993, a decision was made to publish the draft regulations. On January 20, 1994, five years after the original deadline, the draft regulations were published. In the preamble, the new administration noted the lack of tribal participation since 1990.

Tribal reaction to the proposed regulations was extremely negative. Tribes, tribal organizations, and national Indian organizations criticized both the content of the 1994 proposed regulations and their length; the regulations ran over 80 pages in the *Federal Register*. In response to this criticism, the Departments of Health and Human Services and the Interior began holding regional meetings. Because the tribes had been excluded from the decision-making process leading to the proposed regulations, the departments agreed to create a formal advisory committee under the Federal Advisory Committee Act of 1990 (FACA).

While the tribes and the departments discussed formation of the committee, Congress began its own investigation into the rulemaking and administration of the act. In October of 1994, Congress, skeptical of the departments' rulemaking efforts and management of the 638 contract programs, decided, again, to amend the Indian Self-Determination and Education Assistance Act. However, this time Congress severely limited the areas subject to regulation and required the departments to develop any regulations jointly and with the active participation of Indian tribes under the guidance of the Negotiated Rulemakng Act of 1990. In addition, Congress required final regulations to be published within 18 months or the departments would lose their rulemaking authority. The deadline was May 25, 1996.

The Advisory Committee

By the time the October 1994 amendments passed, the two departments and the tribes had come to agreement on the membership process for the Advisory Committee. Because of the act's recent amendments, the tribes and the departments agreed that this committee would be responsible for recommending to the departments what regulations, if any, should exist. To ensure that the tribes had adequate representation on the Advisory Committee, the departments and the tribes agreed to allow two tribal representatives from each

Bureau of Indian Affairs and Indian Health Service area (organizational subunits of the departments) for a total of 48 tribal representatives. To avert past negotiating problems with federal officials, the departments agreed that they would be represented by individuals with full and binding negotiation authority for their agency or office. The Department of the Interior chose nine negotiators, and the Department of Health and Human Services chose six negotiators. In late January 1995, pursuant to FACA, the departments published the proposed list of tribal and federal negotiators in the *Federal Register.*

The Negotiators

The tribal negotiators ran the full gamut, from sophisticated Indian attorneys who had many years of experience writing Indian law and close ties with many U.S. senators and Congress members to tribal councilmembers from rural areas of North America. In between were members of organizations such as the National Indian Health Board, medical and educational facilities of all sizes, construction contractors, social workers, and teachers.

The federal negotiators were, for the most part, experienced in administering and interpreting the existing laws and regulations concerning the Department of the Interior's and the Department of Health and Human Services's interaction with the Native American tribes and tribal organizations. They represented a number of different bureaus under the two departments, such as the Bureau of Indian Affairs, Bureau of Land Management, National Park Service, Indian Health Service, and Minerals Management Service. As with the Native American negotiators, there were often dif-

ferent perspectives and interests championed among the negotiators on each side.

Finding an "Acceptable Neutral"

In February 1995, the departments finalized the list of negotiators. However, the tribes and the departments wrestled with finding a facilitator. The past rulemaking experiences left many with the impression that a neutral facilitator would be helpful, and various lawyers, tribal leaders, and private mediators were considered for the position. However, no one could agree on who was most qualified. Most of the lawyers and tribal leaders who had been suggested either had no experience with large negotiated rulemakings or were not considered neutral. Independent mediators were expensive and required a federal procurement contract, which took too long to finalize.

The 18-month deadline was approaching and no facilitator had yet been chosen. After discussing the problem with the then Administrative Conference of the United States (ACUS), it was suggested they contact the Federal Mediation and Conciliation Service (FMCS). The FMCS responded to the plea for help.

The FMCS is a small, independent federal agency that employs about 200 experienced labor mediators. The FMCS was founded in the 1940s by Congress under the Taft-Hartley Act to give labor unions and companies an alternative to striking to resolve their differences. Its staff currently mediate close to 6,000 cases per year. At the time of the departments' contact, some mediators had experiences in dispute resolution encompassing cross-cultural, multiparty, environmental, community, court, and international work. But no one had actual experience working with a rulemaking body of this size. The idea of working with such a large committee representing the interests of over 500 tribes and tribal organizations across the country, as well as two separate departments with all their internal agencies, seemed daunting to say the least.

To compensate for the large size and diverse interests on the committee, the FMCS selected four experienced mediators, two women and two men of diverse ethnic backgrounds. The lead facilitator was a middle-aged, third-generation Ko-

rean American who had a great deal of experience in intercultural situations. The second team member was a Mexican American woman in her 30s with previous federal experience. The third was a Euro-American male, the only mediator who actually had previous experience working on regulatory negotiations. The final member of the FMCS team was the most experienced of the group, a middle-aged Euro-American woman who was well respected as a mediator in her area. ✒

✒ COMMENTARY

When four experienced labor mediators from the FMCS took on the function of facilitating a reg-neg process that had been stalled for about 20 years, they demonstrated the ability to "jump cultures" themselves, illustrating for the parties the ability to move from one discipline to another and to learn from others. By learning the language and culture of the Indian-federal government contracting process (*638 contracts, waiver procedures, declination procedures*), the facilitators modeled that parties could learn, and take the perspective of others. Even though the parties had different interests, they themselves already shared a culture—even if a legalistic and "artificially" created one. Thus, this reg-neg both demonstrates what good facilitation can do and, at the same time, exposes the dangers of "capture"—the process itself may create its own internal culture that may be less permeable to outsiders who see private deals being cut. On the other hand, using facilitators who are outside of the parties' cultures, as done here, often serves to keep the parties honest with each other (by having to explain things to the outsiders) and thus assure at least some accountability to those outside of the process. "Outsider" facilitators also can maintain neutrality and use process expertise that does not get "captured" in its own way by the substance at issue.

—Carrie J. Menkel-Meadow, *Legal scholar*

Since the late 1980s, the FMCS had specialized in *win-win negotiations* or, as they later became known, *interest-based negotiations*. By 1996, the FMCS had scores of successful experiences under its belt in the labor management arena, and growing confidence that interest-based negotiations were a genuine evolutionary step forward in the field. Thus, it was only

natural to advocate this process over the traditional adversarial-oriented negotiations that had characterized exchanges between tribes and the U.S. government over the past century.

The facilitators were confident that the federal participants would find them acceptable; the FMCS had a 50-year history with federal agencies. The main question was whether the tribes and tribal organizations would find the FMCS acceptable. The facilitators' first task would be to win the confidence of the tribal representatives, whom they suspected might look askance at the "neutrality" of a federal agency mediating between tribes and federal agencies. Because of the pressing time line, the lengthy process of formal bidding and interviews of the convenor were put aside for the first meeting, and the tribal representatives agreed to let the FMCS "audition" for the sake of getting the show on the road. All parties reserved the right to seek another facilitator if the FMCS did not live up to their expectations. ∞

∞ COMMENTARY

The use of FMCS mediators (themselves a diverse group of facilitators) illustrates other issues of neutrality: whether a federal agency can be perceived as neutral and fair enough to work with parties when one of them consists of other federal bodies. That these mediators were successful in their facilitation role demonstrates that often neutrality and quality may not be necessary and sufficient conditions for each other—quality may be demonstrated in the moment and with the particular personnel who are chosen to do the work. Neutrality, as an elusive quality to be aimed for in mediation/facilitation (Gadlin & Pino, 1997), really means absence of bias or partiality toward the parties, not without total relationship to either the parties or to the substance of the dispute. Thus, different segments of the government or even an organization like a corporation, labor union, or university can sometimes serve others (with a combination of "neutrality" and organizational knowledge).

—Carrie J. Menkel-Meadow, *Legal scholar*

REFERENCE

Gadlin, H., & Pino, E. W. (1997). Neutrality: A guide for the organizational ombudsperson. *Negotiation Journal, 13,* 17.

As it turned out, the first meeting went well. Everyone could see that the FMCS facilitator role was one of process and not content. They also felt reassured by the ground rules that were collectively developed. With that concern put to rest, the FMCS was hired to do the facilitation for the negotiations.

Expectations of the Federal Agencies

As the first joint Indian/federal meeting drew near, the federal team prioritized its issues and defined a narrow set of goals for the first meeting. The federal team agreed on the following objectives:

- Demonstrate commitment to the process
- Affirm authority to negotiate on behalf of the federal agencies they represented
- Approve facilitators
- Choose federal/tribal cochairs
- Develop protocol/guidelines for the rulemaking process

- Develop short-/long-term agenda
- Demonstrate need for regulations and suggest model for resolution

In addition, the federal team agreed that it should not control the first meeting's agenda. Instead, the federal team submitted a draft agenda to the committee and welcomed changes. The federal team wanted to convey to the tribal representatives that this was an inclusive process. At the same time, the federal team realized that the parties would have to move quickly.

The motivations for this principled approach from the federal team seemed to be political as well as personal. There was a lot of pressure from a new Congress and a new administration to see these negotiations work. Similarly, there was guarded hope from the tribal constituencies that after the recent pro-Indian amendment to the act, Indian self-determination might finally be meaningfully defined. The two chief spokespersons for the Department of the Interior and Department of Health and Human Services were both relatively new to their posts and committed to improving their departments' relationship with the tribes. They believed this new way of negotiating would provide a positive step in that direction.

Expectations of the Tribes and Tribal Organizations

Initially, there was a great deal of skepticism from tribal representatives that this negotiation would be any different from past frustrating attempts to reach a federal agreement. Not only was there general impatience after the past 20 years of negotiations, but there were also many diverse opinions among the tribal representatives themselves.

A vocal minority of the tribal representatives maintained that they would be better off without any regulations, since the law (largely authored by one of the tribal attorneys at the negotiations) was written in a way favorable to tribal rights. If no consensus were reached on regulations, the law would stand without regulations, and some thought this would be a more favorable result for the tribes. Hence, some of the tribes felt they were in a win-win situation with regard to the government. If they could not reach a favorable agreement, then at least they would be able to sue the federal agencies in court with a strong law (pertaining to contracting with the government) to back them.

Other tribal representatives felt strongly that the chance to define the way the federal government and tribes and tribal organizations developed contracts was a once-in-a-lifetime opportunity. Once and for all, the operation of these entities could be clarified, and the likelihood of a distant federal official exercising discretion over 638 contracts could be reduced.

■ The Negotiations

Groundwork by the Facilitators

The federal mediators posed the following questions to federal team members to test their commitment to the regulatory negotiation process. Would the level of decision making given to the federal negotiators be high enough to enable meaningful negotiations? Would consensus achieved in the full committee be upheld by the Secretaries of the Department of the Interior and

Department of Health and Human Services? And finally, would sufficient financial and logistical support (e.g., clerical, administrative, transportation, and accommodations) be pledged for the effort? The FMCS received satisfactory responses on all counts.

In addition, the facilitators anticipated that the cultural issues unique to a predominantly Native American committee would play an important role in the success of this negotiated rulemaking. Fortunately for the dynamics of the negotiations, several of the federal negotiators were Native Americans. Although these negotiators sat "across the table" from the tribes, they could empathize with many of the concerns of the tribes and tribal organizations.

Because of his relative lack of experience working with Native American negotiations, the lead facilitator from the FMCS researched Native American styles of conflict resolution. Besides reading articles and books on the subject, he also consulted an expert in the field of Native American peacemaking, Dr. Diane LeResche, an Alaska Athabaskan. The following guidelines were suggested to the tribal and federal cochairs in informal discussion. There was no formal discussion with the full committee about these practices, but they were sounded out quietly with cochairs and gradually became part of the negotiation's culture.

- Begin each day with a prayer. This practice was based on the practices of Native American meetings, and it seemed to set a respectful and positive tone between the federal and tribal representatives at the beginning of each day.
- Offer a last day's prayer before everyone goes home. This also seemed to

be a bridge-building ritual. Even after multiple days of long and intense negotiations, a communal prayer—whether in English or a Native tongue—affirmed the positive work that had taken place.

- Anticipate many different levels of comfort in negotiating with the federal government. As noted previously, some tribes had much experience in formal settings and others had very little.
- Be comfortable with periods of silence.
- Draw out the opinions of the quiet participants. Some people will not share opinions unless they are asked; silence does not always mean agreement.
- Do not go forward until everyone in the room understands what is happening. It is a value among many tribes to not proceed until everyone is comfortable and understands where the group is headed. This may tax the patience of facilitators and negotiators if they are very goal and results oriented.
- Problem solving among some tribes is more holistic and circular than among some Euro-American groups. Ambiguity is more easily tolerated. Hence, be prepared to begin to solve one problem, then shift to another halfway through the first, and then come back to the first when the second is almost resolved, and then have both problems pull toward resolution simultaneously in the end.
- A good, friendly sense of humor is respected.
- Respect toward the elders is universally expected.

- The Native American participants will know who should be designated as leaders within their group. They will not have to vote to choose them.
- Build in some social time (breaks, evening receptions, going out to eat, celebrating someone's birthday, etc.) to give people informal time to build relationships, foster communication, and ease any tensions that might exist.

This advice turned out to be instrumental as the facilitators tried to guide 63 committee members—each of whom had veto power—toward consensus on regulations so complex that the government's first drafting of them had reached 80 pages. ➭

➭ COMMENTARY

Although "researching" the cultures and cultural issues of disputants is always a good idea, including prefacilitation interviews with key actors and participants to become informed about both general and more specific issues that are likely to come up, I am a bit concerned about the dangers of "essentializing" cultures when this is done. For those of us in the dispute resolution and negotiation field, there remains a spirited debate about whether there really are nationalistic, gendered, racial, cultural, or simply more individual or personal differences in negotiation styles or behaviors (see, e.g., Gadlin, 1994; Kolb & Coolidge, 1991; Rubin & Sander, 1991). Here, with 48 different Indian tribes, there is a danger of essentializing Native American cultures into "one" culture for disputing purposes, which may mask cultural variations among tribes, just as there might be differences among the federal departments involved as well. The Department of the Interior, for example, might have a different "institutional" culture than the Department of Health and Human Services, for purposes of engaging in a reg-neg process about the delivery of services by Native Americans. The danger of essentializing cultures in consensus building environments is that it can lead to too much expected or projected behavior. To the extent that individuals do not conform to expected cultural behaviors, that is a good thing for seeking consensus and building communication across as well as within groups. While acknowledging that there may be many more constituencies and groupings than one originally hoped to deal with, varieties of "cross-cutting" behaviors can actually help the process by diminishing rigid assumptions about how parties or groups will react to particular proposals or ideas.

—Carrie J. Menkel-Meadow, *Legal scholar*

REFERENCES

Gadlin, H. (1994). Conflict resolution, cultural differences and the culture of racism. *Negotiation Journal, 10,* 33.

Kolb, D., & Coolidge, G. (1991). Her place at the table: A consideration of gender issues in negotiation. In J. Rubin & W. Breslin (Eds.), *Negotiation theory and practice.* Cambridge, MA: Program on Negotiation.

Rubin, J. Z., & Sander, F. E. A. (1991). Culture, negotiation and the eye of the beholder. *Negotiation Journal, 7,* 249.

First Formal Convening of the Parties

The first meeting between the 48 tribal and the 15 federal representatives took place on April 11, 1995, in a Holiday Inn in Arlington, Virginia. The meeting began with a benediction by a respected tribal representative, words from agency officials, and self-introductions of all 63 representatives. Participants were then asked to share what expectations they had for the negotiations. This took about 90 minutes and was followed by a presentation by a tribal attorney of the history and significance of the Indian Self-Determination Act of 1994.

The tribal representatives consisted of laypeople, tribal leaders, CEOs of tribal health centers and educational programs, spiritual leaders, and attorneys. It was evident from the first day that all tribal representatives took their responsibility to their constituency very seriously. They often stopped the negotiations to ask questions if they felt things were moving ahead without clarity.

After lunch, the lead facilitator from the FMCS and a representative of another government agency, ACUS, gave a presentation about negotiated rulemaking. The interest-based problem-solving approach became an important part of the group norm for negotiating. In the coming months, frequent references would be made to "sharing information," "You're making a demand there, let's discuss interests, like the mediators taught us . . . ," and similar comments that demonstrated a shift in negotiating style.

Getting Agreement on Protocol

The tribes and tribal organizations and the federal agencies caucused to select cochairs and begin work on the protocol for the negotiations. Even at this early stage, frustration was beginning to surface. Some representatives were anxious to get into the content of the negotiations and felt too much time was being wasted on such "process" issues as defining consensus, setting protocol, and establishing ground rules. Eventually, the group deferred to the greater experience of the facilitators on these matters. ◆◆

◌ COMMENTARY

This case study illustrates one of the classic tensions in facilitation work: how much time to spend on the negotiation of and explanation about process. As Sunoo and Falkner ably describe, there is an impatience by parties who want to get started and begin "chewing" on the substance. Yet it is often a mistake to start too soon without adequate explanations about roles, responsibilities, and those all-important ground rules: confidentiality, rules of behavior, definitions of *consensus*, protocols for decisions, feedback, and so forth. Here, the parties had to choose ground rules of procedure and behavior, select cochairs (work task representatives), and select subjects for task-oriented work groups. The group members developed principles derived from their own negotiations and "cribbed" from past multiparty facilitations (demonstrating the importance of keeping case histories and institutional memory on what has been used before), including principles for such matters as participation, meeting structure, decision making, agreement, personal safeguards, schedules, and roles (of facilitators, cochairs, and work groups). While this case study illustrates the commonalities of many multiparty facilitations, it also demonstrates the importance of adapting process protocols to each individual dispute, conflict, or matter to be facilitated. Here, the parties chose important processes to include spirituality (opening and closing prayers), different cultural assumptions about decision making and consensus (silence, contrary to the law, does not imply assent), and relations between smaller work groups and the larger plenary sessions. A flexible combination of tried-and-true processes with individual adaptation to the matter at hand may require some up-front time in process planning, but the benefits often include a particularized "constitution," which can be referred to when conflicts and substantive disputes threaten to derail the process later.

—Carrie J. Menkel-Meadow, *Legal scholar*

Within the tribal caucus, much discussion took place regarding the definition of *consensus*. What should the committee do when all 63 members could not agree on an issue? Would a vote of 75 percent then suffice as consensus? The facilitators persuaded the group to conceptualize consensus as 100 percent agreement by all present when a quorum exists. With regard to an impasse, facilitators suggested, that bridge could be crossed when it was reached. This approach—not dwelling on negative possibilities—was one of the recommendations of the Native American experts. ∞

∞ COMMENTARY

I am a little concerned that the facilitators used language indicating that they "persuaded" the parties to adopt their definition of consensus. In its pure form, facilitation should not include imposition of facilitators' views on the parties, especially as to something as important as the definition of an acceptable agreement process. Just as the question of how an impasse would be handled was put on hold, it might have been instructive to "reserve" decision rules until the first decision point arrived and then have the parties deal with it in context. For some engaged in consensus building or facilitative processes, "rules of decision" are better arrived at in context—in the particular, rather than in the abstract. For others, it is important to have such ground rules as what constitutes *consensus* defined as early and clearly as possible for reference when things get tough. Yet facilitators need to be aware of the fact that some groups like to make rules, in advance, in the abstract (constitution making) while others prefer to make them in the concrete settings in which they are needed (common law development).

—Carrie J. Menkel-Meadow, *Legal scholar*

On the second day, sample ground rules and protocol from another negotiated rule-making were shared with the group, modified somewhat, and accepted. These protocols covered the areas of participation (who was qualified to negotiate); meetings (open, minutes, agendas, under what laws, caucus protocol); decision making (consensus, work groups); agreement (goal of the negotiations to come up with a final recommendation for the Secretaries of the Departments of Health and Human Services and Interior); safeguards for committee members (no personal attacks or prejudiced statements, act in good faith to reach consensus, share information); schedule; facilitator (agreed to use the FMCS and defined the role of the facilitator as taking no positions on issues before the committee and to serve at the will of the committee); and cochairs (four tribal cochairs and two federal cochairs, cochair meetings open to committee members) (see Appendix A).

Organizing the Work

A proposal for breaking the complicated law into six work groups was put forward by a tribal attorney. The tribal and federal representatives then adjourned to their respective caucuses to decide if the division of work made sense, and who would sign up for which work groups. The six work groups clustered the topics under the following: Federal Tort Claims Act, the Contract Disputes Act of 1978 (41 U.S.C.601 et seq.), declination and waiver procedures, appeal procedures, reassumption procedures, discretionary grant procedures for grants awarded under Section 103 of the act, property donation procedures arising under Section 105(f) of the act, internal agency procedures relating to the implementation of this act, retrocession and tribal organization relinquishment procedures, contract proposal contents, conflicts of interest, construction, programmatic reports and data requirements, procurement standards, and property management standards. All but three of these permitted regulatory topics are addressed in this rule.

Once the group reached consensus on the structuring of the work, representatives signed up for the work groups in which they had the most knowledge and desire to participate. There was a palpable loosening of tension in the room as the delegates went from list to list; finally, the negotiations were beginning to address the nuts and bolts of why they were there. Because some delegates enrolled in multiple work groups, the cochairs rarely scheduled more than three work groups to meet simultaneously, and people had to choose their priorities as the groups went forward with their work. The other limitation on restricting the number of groups meeting at once was simply the finite numbers of facilitators and note takers.

Each work group functioned with one facilitator, one scribe (secretary with computer), and two cochairs (federal and tribal) who set the agenda. There was variation in facilitator directiveness in each work group. Sometimes the meeting was chaired by the cochairs, and sometimes by the facilitator. This balance depended on the level of technical discussion, the personalities of the facilitators and cochairs, and the dynamics of the work group. In all cases, however, the primary role of the facilitator was to act as the guardian of the process, and he or she often needed to intervene to bring the negotiations back to an interest-based/problem-solving process.

An important key to keeping the participants motivated was regular updates on the status of progress made in the work groups. As each work group finished its draft of a section of regulation, it was tallied on a "status sheet" as "Draft Finished." As the drafts were approved by the full committee, they were marked "Approved in Ses-

sion" (see Appendix B). Thus, steady progress was evident and spirits were kept up.

Structuring the Consensus Process: A Major Key to Successful Negotiations

As each work group came to consensus
on discrete parts of the regulations, it
would submit completed sections to the
plenary session for large-group approval.
Work groups could not present any product
to the large group unless they themselves
had reached consensus on it—an important
rule established early in the negotiations.
The rationale behind this thinking was the
following:

- The delegates most knowledgeable
  and most passionate about an issue
  would naturally participate in the appropriate work groups.
- If there were differences among tribal
  representatives on an issue, they
  would first be thrashed out in the
  larger tribal caucus before consensus
  with the federal representatives in the
  work groups could be reached.
- If there were differences among the
  federal representatives, a similar process would occur. They would come
  to agreement in the larger federal caucus before stating a position in their
  work group.

In fact, this process worked exactly as
planned. Unless someone had missed a caucus meeting, misunderstood the wording,
or saw another aspect to the situation that
he or she had overlooked previously, work
group recommendations that made it to the

full committee were generally passed without difficulty.

Sensitive issues demanded a great deal
of discussion time within either the Indian
or federal caucuses. The party that was
waiting for a response would often begin to
get impatient the longer the caucus lasted.
The facilitators, who were generally permitted access to these caucuses, would then
have to assure the waiting parties that progress was being made, without divulging the
specific content of discussion. It became
part of the culture of the negotiations to
respect the right of both parties to engage
in caucuses whenever they felt it was necessary.

The committee agreed to the following
Suggested Protocol for Approval of Work
Group Recommendations:

1. Work groups present their recommendations.
2. Questions of clarification only are
   asked first to make sure everyone
   understands the recommendations.
3. Questions of content are raised after the section is explained. These
   are listed by facilitators on the flip
   chart and addressed one by one.
4. The group and work group cochairs
   decide whether concerns should be
   answered in large-group or tribal
   and federal caucus, or should be
   referred back to the work group.
5. If there is agreement, then the recommendation is adopted by consensus.

These protocols worked well as a whole.
When a proposal was presented that might
be controversial to federal representatives,
it was presented to the full committee by a
federal member of the work group. The
opposite was true if a recommendation

emerged from the work group that might be problematic to tribes and tribal organizations. It then became the responsibility of that work group member to "sell" the work group's recommendation to skeptics on his or her own side.

Although the possibility existed for stronger and more sophisticated negotiators to "strong-arm" weaker and less sophisticated negotiators, blatant power plays and divide-and-conquer tactics were rarely experienced either within or between federal and tribal constituencies.

Technical Expertise and the Facilitators

One difficulty recognized early on by the facilitators was the fact that they had seriously underestimated the high level of technical and legal jargon spoken by the very knowledgeable and content-savvy participants. In many cases, the negotiators had been working with certain contracts and laws for years, and terms such as *638, block grants, retrocession, procurement standards, Federal Tort Claims Act, internal agency procedures, waiver procedures, declination procedures,* and *programmatic reports and data requirements,* while familiar to contractors, program administrators, and lawyers, were quite foreign to labor mediators. At first, this necessitated much questioning, explanations, and corrections of the notes that facilitators wrote on flip charts. After several sessions and some homework by the facilitators, however, this ceased to be a problem.

Crises

Throughout the process, experiences from the past haunted the negotiators. At one point, the tribal team threatened to walk out of the negotiations because the Office of Management and Budget (OMB) would be reviewing the regulations; the tribes believed that OMB had undermined previous regulatory attempts. Under Executive Order 12866, OMB is responsible for reviewing all "significant" regulations, and the federal agencies were bound by this process. OMB respected decisions of the negotiated rulemaking committees, but was authorized to review the regulation and ensure it met various legislative and executive mandates. After a long and heated discussion, the federal agencies agreed to include the tribes in formal discussions with OMB.

The federal government was committed to writing the regulations in clear, simple language—known as "plain English." The tribes had previous experience with federal representatives rewriting (and altering) agreements that had been made out in the field. For this reason, suspicion arose when a federal negotiator recommended putting the entire set of regulations into a plain-English format. Many of the attorneys on the committee were unfamiliar with this process, and tribal members were concerned that the spirit of the committee's decisions would be lost. However, a federal attorney and a tribal cochair showed the rest of the group the benefits of plain English, and this writing style was adopted.

It was apparent that some members of the committee were uncomfortable with various aspects of the negotiations. For example, some expressed anxiety about the draft regulations. Would they appear weak or inflexible to their own constituency? Again, participants had to be reminded that they each possessed absolute veto power: Nothing would go forward from the committee until all had given their approval.

Others were concerned about the final regulation. During the last negotiation session in Denver, it appeared to the federal team that the tribes were exercising "ownership" of the regulations, prompting concern that their department's role in the rulemaking and eventual implementing was not being recognized. When the federal team attempted to assert authority there was a tremendous backlash. After separate caucuses, the mediators determined that each side wanted recognition for its efforts and assurance that the other side would support the final regulations.

The committee encountered substantive issues on which it could not agree. During the proposed rule, the committee published these issues in the preamble and invited comments from the public and each other. This allowed each party an opportunity to cool off and review the suggestions from commenters. Unfortunately, this process was not possible for the final rulemaking, because the federal agencies could only publish binding decisions in their regulations. To provide all parties with the opportunity to voice their concerns, the tribes and federal team members prepared reports to the Secretaries. A joint consensus report written by the tribal and federal representatives summarized the issues agreed to by the entire committee.

Both the tribal and federal teams also filed a smaller report, stating their position on the issues on which no agreement could be reached. The reports were presented to the chiefs of staff for both departments. The tribes and tribal organizations had had incentive to reach agreement on as many issues as possible, because any place that consensus was reached was virtually ensured of being approved by the Secretaries, whereas anything *not* agreed on would be left to the discretion of the Secretaries. In the end, the departments made some decisions in the tribes' favor and some in the government's favor.

■ Outcomes of the Indian Self-Determination Negotiated Rulemaking

The negotiations ended on time with all but four issues resolved. The four issues did not hold up the overall implementation of the regulations. The entire committee of 63 members had successfully consented to 34 pages of very detailed regulations written in plain English that would now guide tribes and tribal organizations and federal contractors in negotiating contracts between the Departments of the Interior and the Health and Human Services. Tribes and tribal organizations who wished to contract with the federal government to provide health services, education, and construction projects for Native peoples would now have an easily comprehensible set of procedures that was consistent for two federal agencies and clear to novice Indian contractors as well as to new federal administrators.

In summary, significant outcomes include the following:

- Largest negotiated rulemaking to date. Sixty-three committee members—each with full veto power.
- First negotiated rulemaking binding two departments (Department of the Interior and Department of Health and Human Services) to the same regulations.
- Used full consensus for all decisions.
- Created a model for future dialogues with the tribes.

- Became benchmark for future negotiated rulemakings for Department of the Interior and Department of Health and Human Services.
- Developed and improved relationships between the negotiators that persisted beyond the rulemaking and assists with resolution of other problems.
- Expressed satisfaction by tribal and federal agency representatives using the regulations.

■ Factors Contributing to a Successful Negotiation

Much of the open and positive nature of the negotiations can be attributed to several fortunate external factors that supported a positive outcome. These included

- Political pressure/time deadline.
- Common knowledge base and familiarity with issues.
- Clearly defined areas to negotiate.
- Balance of power. Both sides had the absolute power not to reach agreement.
- Real negotiations versus "consultation." In the past, tribes were not really negotiating but were merely being asked for feedback. Subsequent decisions were then made after the federal representatives were by themselves back in Washington, and the tribes would sue or take political action to protest.
- Authority to make decisions. The committee included high-ranking federal and tribal representatives. It

was made clear at the outset that if federal representatives at the table consented to a decision, it was 99 percent certain that their respective Secretaries would sign off on it.

Additionally, there were several significant internal factors that also supported a positive outcome:

- Many of the parties knew each other.
- Knowledgeable and respected tribal and federal steering committee. The steering committee members were notable for their mutual respect and candor with each other, and their genuine goodwill toward seeking a successful end to the negotiations. They offered positive intellectual as well as moral leadership and kept the negotiations consistently on the high road. There was very little gamesmanship and a lot of honest struggle.
- Strong consistent facilitation. The FMCS committed four experienced mediators to all the meetings. Each individual work group, some of the tribal and federal caucuses, and all of the plenary sessions were facilitated. The consensus building process and ground rules were consistently reinforced and adhered to throughout the yearlong negotiations.

■ FMCS Contribution

The facilitators from the FMCS helped the negotiators set and keep to protocol and ground rules. This type of monitoring created a safe environment for the negotiations to take place. The guardians of the process, facilitators met countless times to assess the morale of the group and whether conflicts were brewing. They helped to maintain social cohesion, advise the steering committee, and steer the negotiations away from land mines because of their proximity to both parties. The federal mediators often sat in tribal as well as federal caucuses and were able to understand the frustrations both sides experienced. As one tribal representative put it, "When we would get really frustrated, it was just comforting to see you guys so confident and optimistic about these negotiations all the time!"

Participants felt the responsibility to do their best to stay focused, constructive, and open-minded. The authors feel that a cultural bias toward harmony also helped keep negotiations on track. Accepting genuine consensus as the only decision-making process and giving all 63 delegates veto power truly empowered and sobered all participants to act in a statesmanlike fashion. ∞

∞ COMMENTARY

The significant success of this reg-neg process demonstrates some of the key features of successful facilitation. The smaller work groups keep people task and issue focused, as well as concretely directed at particularities of issues to be resolved rather than arguing about global or historical issues (in this case, e.g., there could have been much energy spent on how long and destructive the previous decades of regulation activity had been). To the extent that everyone works hard in the task groups, mutual respect and deference to other groups' work product also allow some efficiencies to develop in decision making and rules of decision. Using caucuses, within groups, across groups, with or without facilitators, also is a technique that allows the airing of confidential concerns that can be dealt with, in addition to allowing cross-group communication by delegated representatives.

Finally, the educative function of consensus building processes is demonstrated here by the attention paid by the facilitators to educating the participants about interest-based negotiation. In its best practice, a good reg-neg, consensus building, or negotiated process leaves the parties better off to deal with each other in the future by virtue of what they have learned, and in the case of the federal government and Native American tribes negotiating delivery of services contracts, it is more than likely that there will be future interactions that will have been aided by this process experience.

—Carrie J. Menkel-Meadow, *Legal scholar*

NOTE

1. I prefer to stay away from "win-win" language. Many negotiations and facilitations, especially those in the legal system, will not be win-win. They don't need to be "win-lose" and are often better than what a court can accomplish, but in my experience, I have found that saying "win-win" to the parties may set up unwarranted expectations that everyone will be better off than they were before.

Sometimes that is true, but often it is also true that the parties are better off than if they had done nothing or used some other process, but they may still have to do something they don't want to or trade something or otherwise "give" something that is not purely a better end state than when they began.

■ Reference

Federal Register. (1996, June 24). Vol. 61, No. 122, p. 32483.

APPENDIX A
Indian Self-Determination Negotiated Rulemaking Committee: Organizational Protocol

■ *Preamble*

The Indian Self-Determination Negotiated Rulemaking Committee has been established pursuant to P.L. 103-413 and is further detailed in a Committee Charter approved by the Secretary of Health and Human Services and the Secretary of the Interior.

The Committee is charged with the development of regulations to implement amendments to the Indian Self-Determination Act.

1. *Participation*
   A. *Attendance at meetings.* Each Committee Member for each party must make a good faith effort to attend each full negotiating session. The Committee Member may be accompanied by such other individuals as that Member believes is appropriate to represent his/her interest. In the event that an alternate Committee Member attends a meeting based upon consultation and agreement by the respective Area, Merry Elrod, Acting Director, Division of Self-Determination Services shall be notified for travel reimbursement purposes.
   B. *Constituents' interests.* Committee Members are expected to represent the concerns and interests of their constituents.
2. *Meetings*
   A. *FACA.* The negotiations will be conducted under the Federal Advisory Committee Act (FACA) and the Negotiated Rulemaking Act of 1990 (NRA).
   B. *Open meetings.* Negotiating sessions will be announced in the *Federal Register* prior to the meeting and, consistent with FACA requirements, will be open to the public. Members of the public will be given opportunities at various times throughout each meeting to make comments, raise questions, or submit materials for the record.
   C. *Minutes.* The committee shall observe the requirements of the Charter regarding minutes, records, and documents. In addition, approved minutes will be maintained and distributed to the Committee and Tribes by the representatives of the HHS and DOI.

D. *Agendas.* Meeting agendas will be developed by the Designated Federal Officials (DFOs) and Tribal Co-Chairs.

E. *Caucus.* A break can be declared at any time by any party. Parties will be asked for an estimate of the time needed for the caucus. Internal procedures will be determined by each respective caucus.

3. *Decision Making*

A. *Consensus.* The Committee will operate by consensus of the Tribal Co-Chairs and DFOs after consultation with their respective caucuses. (Note: The genesis of this language is unclear. The Committee actually operated by consensus of the full Committee and not merely consensus of the Tribal Co-Chairs and DFOs.)

B. *Work Groups.* Small Work Groups may be formed by the Committee to address specific issues and to make recommendations to the Committee. Work Groups are open to any Committee Members or the Member's designee, plus such other individuals as the Committee believes would enhance the functioning of the Work Groups. Work Groups are not authorized to make decisions for the Committee as a whole. All Committee Members will be notified of all Work Group meetings by the DFOs and Tribal Co-Chairs.

4. *Agreement*

A. *Product of negotiations.* The intended product of the negotiations is a preliminary report and proposed regulations in the form of a written statement developed by the Committee on behalf of the Secretaries of DOI/HHS and Tribal representatives. The Secretaries agree to use the Committee's preliminary report and proposed regulations as the basis of their Notice of Proposed Rulemaking. Prior to a publication, the DFOs will provide the Committee with notice and an opportunity to comment on any changes in the proposed regulations.

B. *Final rule.* The Committee will review all comments received in response to the Notice of Proposed Rulemaking and will submit a final report with recommendations to the Secretaries of DOI/HHS for promulgation of a final rule.

5. *Safeguards for the Committee Members*

A. *Good faith.* All members agree to act in a good faith effort to reach consensus in all aspect of these negotiations by encouraging the free and open exchange of ideas, views, and information. Specific offers, positions, or statements made during the negotiations except for those made by DFOs may not be used by members outside the negotiations without approval of the Committee. Personal attacks and prejudiced statements will not be tolerated.

B. *Information.*

1. The members of the Committee agree to exchange information in good faith.

2. Members of the Committee will provide information called for by this paragraph as much in advance of the meeting at which such information is to be used as possible.

6. *Schedule*

Negotiating sessions will be held regularly as determined by the Committee. Unless extended by Congress, the deadline for the negotiations is 18 months from the date of enactment of Public Law 103-413.

> May 11-13, 1995 Denver, CO
> (Work Groups meet 5/8 to 3/10/95)
> June 13-15, 1995 Reno, NV
> July 10-12, 1995 Anchorage, AL (or Seattle)
> Aug. 9-11, 1995 Tulsa, OK

7. *Facilitation*

FMCS staff under the leadership of Jan Jung-Min Sunoo will serve as the facilitators and will work to ensure that the process runs smoothly. The role of the facilitator often includes developing draft agendas, facilitating Committee and select Work Group discussions, working to resolve any impasses that may arise, preparing meeting summaries, assisting in the location and circulation of background materials the Committee develops, and other functions the Committee requests. The facilitators will take no position on the issues before the Committee and serve at the will of the Committee.

8. *Co-Chairs*

The four Tribal Co-Chairs shall be selected by the Tribal representatives of the Committee. DFOs are Michael Anderson, DOI, and Tony Itteilag, HHS. The role of the Co-Chairs usually includes developing draft agendas, chairing Committee and Work Group discussions, working to resolve any impasses that may arise, preparing meeting summaries, assisting in the location and circulation of background materials the Committee develops, and other functions the Committee requests. The Co-Chairs will represent positions of their caucuses and serve at the will of their caucuses. The

Tribal Co-Chairs and/or other Tribal representatives of the Committee may be authorized to negotiate the Tribal positions with the DFOs and shall report the results of any negotiations to the full Committee for further action. Meetings of the Co-Chairs shall be open to the Committee Members.

APPENDIX B
Status of Indian Self-Determination Drafts, August 21, 1995

	Approved in Session	Draft Finished	None
Group I			
Draft Conflict of Interest			X
Programmatic Reports and Data Requirements	8/11/95		
Procurement Standards	8/11/95		
Property Management Standards	8/11/95		
Financial Management Standards	8/11/95		
Lease of Tribally Owned Bldgs. by Secty.	8/11/95		
(add in subsection "h" and "I")		X	
Property Donation Procedures		X	
Group II			
Construction			X
Group III			
Reassumption Procedures	8/11/95		
Retrocession and Tribal Organizations	8/11/95		
Relinquishment Procedures			
Group IV			
Federal Tort Claims Act	8/11/95		
Contract Dispute Act		X	
Internal Agency Procedures		X	
Insurance (fold into FTCA?)		X	
Group V	(recommends no regs in this area)		
Group VI			
Appeal Procedure (Draft 7, 8/11/95)	8/10/95		
Waiver Procedure (Draft 12, 8/11/95)	8/10/95		
Review and Approval of Contract Proposals (Draft 7, 8/9/95)	8/10/95		
Declination Procedure (Draft 13, 8/11/95)		X	
Initial Contract Proposal Contents		X	

CASE

10

CROSS-CULTURAL COMMUNITY-BASED PLANNING

Negotiating the Future of Haida Gwaii (British Columbia)

■ Norman Dale

O ver the past two decades, explicit negotiations have become the most favored means of resolving long-standing conflicts between Canada's Native peoples (generally referred to as First Nations) and non-Native parties, including governments, other communities, interest groups, and industry. The present case study describes one such experience. The setting was modern-day British Columbia, primarily on islands known as Haida Gwaii or the Queen Charlottes, off that Canadian province's northwest coast. The challenge was economic planning, which, as of 1990, centered around a $38 million expenditure program to alleviate

difficulties arising from a recent decrease in forestry opportunities.

This planning took place in the aftermath of the most publicized environmental conflict to date in British Columbia: the struggle over logging South Moresby, the southernmost third of Haida Gwaii. I was appointed community liaison for the economic-planning process and began my work in February 1990. Over the next year, the Haida and other communities negotiated the transformation of a primarily top-down and one-time spending version of economic development into a community-controlled model.

This chapter tells the story of my first-hand experience in the creation of the Gwaii Trust, a nonprofit entity funded by the Canadian government and managed by the community. It begins with a general account of the geographic and historical setting including a recent, bitter controversy over logging. I then describe more specifically the South Moresby Agreement, which set the stage for discussions about the economic future of Haida Gwaii. Next is the entire deliberative process of the negotiations. The case begins at a point where direct face-to-face meetings among parties were seen as unlikely at best. It documents the struggle of getting people to the table and, then, the actual "table negotiations." The remaining pages describe the denouement, and the communication and cooperation that took place as the parties sought to gain acceptance for their agreement.

This case focuses on selected defining moments and on my role and actions at these critical times. These milestone events did not occur during the actual sit-down meetings, generally seen as the centerpiece of negotiations. Rather, they took place well before a negotiating table was even envisioned and, then, well after a formal "accord" was coproduced. The closing section of this chapter summarizes principal lessons of the experience.

■ Geographic and Historical Setting

In conflicts involving First Nations and other cultures, accounts of geography and especially history are often themselves problematic. Indeed, as the Haida Gwaii case reveals, disagreement about a region's "story" can be the defining factor in conflict between parties.

The region's physical setting can be described with little or no controversy: an archipelago of islands located 60 miles off the mainland of British Columbia. Haida Gwaii is made up of more than 200 islands. The principal ones are still known by "settler names": Graham Island on the north side of Skidegate Channel where five of the six distinguishable communities are, and Moresby Island to the south.

The communities of Haida Gwaii became key parties in the controversies. One can characterize them as two cultural communities comprising the Haida Nation and the non-Native community. Alternatively, and as would appear on a map, one can speak of six communities: the two Haida villages of Old Massett and Skidegate, and the four others, Massett, Port Clements, Queen Charlotte City, and Sandspit. Of these, only Sandspit is on Moresby Island.

Most Canadians refer to these islands as the Queen Charlotte Islands or simply the Charlottes. But to the indigenous people, as well as to an increasing number of their supporters, the islands are Haida Gwaii. For First Nations, names are enormously significant and convey implicit messages about ownership. Thus, amidst the Haida's assertion of rights (including land title) over the past 15 years, strong advocacy has developed to make Haida Gwaii the favored name.

Characterizing the relevant history is even more problematic than naming the land. Said (1975) observed that "the point at which a storyteller chooses to begin is the first step in the intentional construction of meaning" (p. 1). Not surprisingly, the Haida "begin" their story earlier than the non-Haida, resulting in a sharp discrepancy between each group's respective histories. This was significant for the mediation process to come, since each community draws on its history to explain its political and economic prospects.

For non-Haida, the period in question was the recent decade of turmoil over logging and the fate of South Moresby that embroiled Island communities and extended nationally and internationally. In 1985, dreams of creating an extensive protected wilderness had collided with the cutting plans of a major forest company. The dispute quickly moved to physical confrontation, including sustained roadblocks with Haida and environmentalists, on one side, and loggers, mainly from Sandspit, on the other.

In 1987, a resolution was imposed from the outside. Bilateral negotiations between the provincial government of British Columbia, which had extended the cutting privileges based on its ownership of the land,[1] and the federal government concluded with the South Moresby Agreement. This created a National Park reserve ending all future logging and providing, in compensation, a Regional Economic Development Initiative.

It would be misleading, however, to end with this account of the historical setting. For the Haida, the struggle for South Moresby was but the latest of a series of intrusions occurring steadily for more than two centuries. From their perspective, the trouble began no later than 1774 when Spanish explorers became the first European visitors to Haida Gwaii. For many years thereafter, visits by outsiders in quest of furs and gold created a pattern of fragile cross-cultural relations, not entirely different from those in the 1990s.

The Haida were known by other First Nations as ferocious warriors and slave takers whose raids took them as far south as modern-day Washington state. In their early contacts with Europeans, they were considered shrewd traders—ever-ready to thwart incursions in their territory (Fisher, 1977). A British captain, George Dixon, traded with the Haida and found them "highly capable"; however, he declined invitations to visit for fear of being "instantly butchered." His caution was well-founded in light of the Haida's "subsequent record of attempting to overpower trading vessels without provocation" (Fisher, 1977, p. 78).

The Haida subsequently suffered hardships typical of the nonmilitary subjugation of First Nations. First came horrific disease epidemics, notably the scourge of smallpox, which is believed to have reduced the Haida population from 6,000 to 800 between 1835 and 1885 (Duff, 1964). This assault was compounded by missionary conversions eroding faith in traditional customs; enforced residential schooling that doggedly suppressed Native language and culture; the prohibition of the traditional politico-religious ceremonies of the potlatch; and the confinement of the communities to tiny reserves,[2] leaving all other traditional lands up for grabs by a surging wave of European settlers. These acculturative forces unquestionably created social and individual trauma that persisted over the generations. It is this legacy that the Haida, including the representatives in the present case, consider a minimal "history lesson." ∞

∞ COMMENTARY

How much context is necessary to move into a situation and work toward building consensus? The anthropological perspective is that a great deal is needed. In this case, for example, the history of Haida incorporation into Canada; its nineteenth-century loss of population; and the subsequent Canadian undermining of Haida beliefs, religious life, and cultural practices are clearly essential points for understanding this situation. Moreover, burgeoning First Nations activism in defense of land and cultural rights in the past two decades is also critically important in understanding the Haida position. As this activism increases, the Haida people will continue to change the way they assert their claims. Therefore, essential features of context include the surrounding conditions of the conflict, the cultural understandings that each group of participants brings to the conflict, and the historical processes by which this present situation has emerged.

Context also incorporates the logging interests, the pressures on the government to log this region, and the political and economic factors that led to the South Moresby Agreement. Many critical questions are not answered here that are essential to understanding the context. What is the position of the group that wishes to log the forests? What is its power base? How is it related to local logging communities, to the Canadian government, and to transnational economic interests? Why did the South Moresby Agreement offer $38 million in development aid to the region? In what ways is it vulnerable to First Nations resistance? Small groups like First Nations communities tend to exercise moral suasion and power through public opinion rather than direct economic and political force. As a result of the indigenous peoples' activism of the past two decades, there is greater willingness to resist losses of land and autonomy and far stronger transnational linkages to provide inspiration, ideas, and access to world opinion.

None of these groups is uniform. There will clearly be differences within all of these constituencies about how strongly each wishes to push for its interests. Within First Nations communities, for example, there is often disagreement about how strongly to assert claims and how much to resist the benefits offered by government or private industry in exchange for surrendering these claims. There is a long history of distrust of government and many experiences of betrayal. Tackling consensus building in a situation of this kind without knowledge of the historical and broader contemporary context of a conflict of this kind risks irrelevance or even complete failure of the project.

—Sally Engle Merry, *Anthropologist*

■ *The South Moresby Agreement's Provisions for Economic Development Planning*

The South Moresby Agreement (SMA) signed between the governments of Canada and British Columbia in July 1988 set the stage for economic development planning. Subsequent cross-cultural negotiations followed a course quite different from the paradigm for development process explicit in the SMA. However, the potential for economic opportunity was a direct result of that intergovernmental understanding.

Part I of the SMA concerned parks that were to be created separately for the land portion and the marine side of South Moresby. Its details are not germane here, except for one glaring omission: the Haida Nation. Despite having played the pivotal role in the protest leading up to the agreement, the Haida were not included in its formulation or given an explicit place in its implementation.

Part II of the SMA, the Queen Charlotte Islands Regional Economic Development Initiative, is key to our story in two important ways. First, the initiative provided for funds worth $38 million in Canadian dollars. Second, the Regional Economic Development Initiative presented an unusually transparent model of top-down development and planning, one that allowed communities to see how far from their desired practice the SMA really was.

The top-down perspective was most evident in the SMA's view of senior government planners, on the one hand, and of communities, on the other. Federal and provincial representatives were assembled as the Planning and Coordination Committee. This committee's primary responsibility was to prepare the strategy for expenditures, all of which were to be made within eight years of the SMA signing (South Moresby Agreement, Part II, Section 31[1]).[3] The procedure envisioned that the Planning and Coordination Committee would prepare plans for the most effective use of the money, after which "the plans [would] be implemented by the responsible government department, ministry, or agency" (South Moresby Agreement, Part II, Section 35[e]).

Wording of the SMA's section on local participation reveals the highly subordinate role seen for the Island communities:

In pursuance of its planning function . . . the Planning and Coordination Committee, with respect to the planning phase of the Initiative, *may* seek the participation . . . of a Queen Charlotte Islands planning advisory committee composed of representatives, resident in the Queen Charlotte Islands, of groups who have an interest in the economic development of the Queen Charlotte Islands *where the Planning and Coordination Committee considers that such participation would contribute* towards the effective exercise of *its* planning function. (South Moresby Agreement, Part II, Section 34[3], emphases added)

The "Queen Charlotte Islands planning advisory committee" came to be known as the Residents' Planning Advisory Committee, or RPAC, during the process. Input from the communities to senior government planners was to be entirely at the discretion of the latter. Nowhere in the provisions for the Regional Economic Development Initiative was there mention of the Haida as distinct from any other "residents." The actual evolution of the process, however, was very different from the framework outlined by these provisions.

Before describing the events occurring between 1990 and 1994, I will elaborate on the role that I was supposed to play. ••

∽ COMMENTARY

This is the first of many places in this case where the author insightfully comments on his role and his lack of neutrality. Dale clearly departs from the common view of neutrality as a critical component in mediation. Yet ample evidence suggests that such departure is necessary for effectiveness. I note this issue now, but return to it in response to Dale's reflections at the end of the case.

—Max H. Bazerman, *Social psychologist*

The Planning and Coordination Committee (hereafter, P&CC) commissioned a team of consultants known as "the Secretariat," which was to coordinate a preliminary economic strategy. This task would have involved both the subcontracting of economic sectoral research and the coordination of public consultation. The Secretariat was set up in Vancouver, 500 miles southeast of Haida Gwaii, but merely city blocks from the offices of key P&CC members. Only the team member known as the "community liaison" would actually work and live on the Islands. Initially, this was my designated role. The Secretariat's "terms of reference" described my job as a "community economic development liaison consultant" and set forth the following responsibilities:

- To provide information about the Queen Charlotte Islands Regional Economic Development Initiative;

- To assist residents in maintaining a liaison with the Planning and Coordination Committee;

- To coordinate activities and ensure effective communication between other government agencies that may become involved in the Economic Initiative and the Residents' Planning Advisory Committee;

- To provide assistance to research consultants involved in the preparation of the economic development strategy and to coordinate their communication with the Residents' Planning Advisory Committee; and

- To provide whatever assistance the Planning and Coordination Committee considers appropriate to enable the Residents' Planning Advisory Committee to fulfill its terms of ref-

erence. (From "Canada: British Columbia South Moresby Agreement, Planning & Coordination Committee, Terms of Reference: Role and Responsibility of the Contractor.")

Note the absence of words such as *mediation, facilitation,* and *negotiation* that would imply proactive community involvement in framing the Islands' economic future.

As a trained mediator who had worked on similar projects directly for other First Nations, I believed, from the start, in neither the philosophy nor the feasibility of such top-down planning. Likewise, the head of the Secretariat was involved because he saw possibilities for empowerment through collaboration. Unabashedly, I had little intention of faithfully playing a role that—rather openly on the Islands—I referred to as "keeping the kids at play while the big guys down south do the real work."

Back in Vancouver, I did not "wear" this perspective in plain sight for the client. Instead, I adopted an ethically fragile position: It is better to work as a covert "change agent" than to leave the task to others whose philosophy fitted the formal client's (i.e., the P&CC's) expectations.

■ The Negotiation of Community-Based Planning

Months after my work began on Haida Gwaii, I conceptualized the case as something akin to *negotiated investment strategies*: multiple parties deciding together on the use of funds for their various communities. We were negotiating an accord about the use of the Regional Economic Development Initiative. But in early 1990, the challenge was more fundamental than a simple conversation about money. The interaction between parties was tentative and rudimentary; there was no talk of anything like negotiations. Later discussions revealed, inter alia, deep needs for change in the way that the parties saw each other and the place they now shared as home.

As with any public policy consensus process, there were a number of phases in the negotiations that produced the Gwaii Trust community development fund. These can be broken down as follows:

1. Getting to the table (January 1990 to August 1990)
2. Negotiating an accord (September 1990 to December 1990)
3. Building acceptance for the Gwaii Trust concept "beyond the table" (January 1991 to April 1992)
4. Preimplementation planning through the Gwaii Trust Interim Planning Society (April 1992 to May 1994)
5. Implementation—which goes on to this day (May 1994 on)

This case, however, is not organized in accordance with these phases. Instead, the focus is on key episodes and intervals that took place primarily during the first three phases. A key theme that emerged from this case study is the importance of context to ongoing negotiations.

Imagining the Possibility of Negotiations

At the beginning of 1990, the prospects were poor for a dialogue between the Haida and the non-Haida communities. The idea of a permanent trust fund instead of a government-driven, one-time expenditure program had already occurred to sev-

eral community leaders. But government agencies were planning to spend the money themselves, and the lack of solidarity among the Islands' communities made this approach appear simple and attractive.

Seats on the RPAC were open to the two Haida communities (Skidegate and Old Massett), but these had been occupied only by council-appointed observers. Old Massett had little used even this limited avenue of participation. The Haida stance was clear: They wanted full and equal participation on what was in essence the decision-making group—the P&CC. During 1989, there had been little movement in respect to these demands. In January 1990, Haida leaders issued calls for a major revamping of the P&CC.

I arrived in the midst of this deadlock. My very first assignment was to compose a brief and noncommittal response. Even agreement to say essentially nothing at all was hard to obtain among RPAC members. They were uncertain of how to react, given community concern about Haida assertiveness.

By early 1990, the Regional Economic Development Initiative was already running well behind schedule. Construction of the harbor was to have begun in 1989 and the remaining initiatives put in place by 1990. Neither was on the horizon. Thus, the public was restless and pressure on the P&CC and RPAC was building.

The Leadership Workshops and Their Consequences

Prior to my involvement, the P&CC had decided that RPAC needed a series of "leadership development" workshops. The premise was a common one: This untutored group of local people needs collaborative skills as well as greater understanding of cross-cultural relations, negotiations, planning processes, and tourism development. These workshops, held through the spring of 1990, yielded a rich trove of stories.

The first of the workshops focused on cross-cultural relations and was delivered by a consultant from eastern Canada and a Native from another tribe. The presenters made a strong emotional impact as they told RPAC about the history of residential schools where Native children, uprooted from their communities and families, had been subjected to acculturation. In essence, this workshop created greater receptivity for the Native struggle in general and the Haida position in particular. Months later, when RPAC prepared for critical negotiations with the Haida, I was able to invoke some of this empathy.

"There Is a System. . . . It Works"

The second workshop was led by two guests presenting on a territory-wide grassroots planning process, Yukon 2000. I pause here to confront a puzzle: If the P&CC was committed to the top-down process, why did it invite presenters from a process that was explicitly bottom up? Why did P&CC members lay before their loyal advisers a model so different from their own? I regret not having asked them at the time.

Months later, when the hierarchy had been radically altered and political masters were applauding the results, everyone on the P&CC claimed that they had wanted RPAC to play a more assertive role. But that is rewriting history a bit. At the same time that RPAC was hearing about Yukon 2000, there was strong pressure from the P&CC to get endorsement of a work plan fully consistent with the SMA's top-down version of planning.

As the Yukon 2000 workshop drew to a close, several RPAC members waxed enthusiastic. One member asked pointedly, "Just what process *is* the Secretariat planning to use?" As a member of that Secretariat, I responded with a straightforward and grim description of the top-down process. They had heard it before, but now the difference between what was planned and what could be envisioned was all too clear. The discussion turned to a vivid and excited interchange about democratizing economic planning for the Islands.

The sole Haida observer, Gitsga, was in attendance. Also present was the supervisor of the new National Park reserve. I had noticed nonverbal cues of discomfort from Gitsga as the ardent dialogue about planning carried on. As chair for the session, I asked him to share his views. What followed was one of the most dramatic moments of my entire involvement in this case.

Gitsga spoke briefly but with visible anger about how, once again, as had been the case for more than a century, white people were ready to surge ahead without considering the Haida's views or interests. After asking rhetorically whether RPAC had heard anything at the cross-cultural workshop, Gitsga ended by saying, "You want to create a system for deciding what to do with this land. But there is a system here already. It works." With those words, he stood, said that he could no longer be part of RPAC and left. Gone was the bubbly enthusiasm over grassroots planning.

I excused myself and went out to Gitsga, who was already pulling away in his truck. I asked him if there was anything I could do. He reiterated his anger and his decision not to be involved as an observer any more. I returned to a still stunned and somber group. One member articulated the question that was on everybody's mind: "What the heck was that all about?"

Having just spent three years employed by First Nations, I had some thoughts about Gitsga's outburst and I shared them with the group. ◑

◐ COMMENTARY

The author clearly brings to his role in the negotiations an extensive background in First Nations issues and sympathy with First Nations peoples' historically marginalized position in the Canadian state. Without his past experience, his response to Gitsga's resignation would probably have been quite different, and the Haida voice in the negotiations would in all likelihood have been greatly diminished, perhaps replaced by periodic skirmishes after the agreement was completed. The author makes clear in his account that he is not neutral—equally committed to both sides—but is dedicated to shifting the SMA process from one of imposition to one of negotiation. His background in mediation and work with other First Nations clearly equip him with a particular body of knowledge and experience that shapes the way he intervenes. An economist from Toronto with no First Nations experience would bring a different body of knowledge and skills to this assignment.

Thus, the particular skills, background, and knowledge of a facilitator are of critical importance in his or her actions. Without the author's particular strengths and efforts, it is highly likely that Gitsga would never have returned to RPAC. It is intriguing that the organization that envisioned a top-down process of economic development nevertheless hired a person with a background in mediation and work with First Nations and Native land claims to be the community liaison consultant, suggesting some ambivalence about simply imposing a development plan on an unconsulted and unwilling community.

—Sally Engle Merry, *Anthropologist*

Basically, I linked the personal powerlessness felt by so many Natives to the continuing scant recognition of their political system. As I found out later, my observations offended the Parks Canada superintendent, who reported the following observation back to the P&CC: "Mr. Dale made a series of wholly uninvited criticisms of federal and provincial policy." This feedback had ramifications for me and for the Secretariat, but at least some RPAC members were better able to make sense of Gitsga's behavior. Moreover, my public disagreement with the Parks Canada superintendent made RPAC membership realize that I saw them, more than the governments, as my employer.

Gitsga's resignation could have been seen as a very major setback. I chose instead to see his departure as an opportunity to undermine any complacency within RPAC. The following day, I visited Gitsga at his home. I did not refer to what had happened or ask whether he would change his mind. He told me about how he grew up and his ongoing work as an artist. I told him about my time with the Kwakiutl First Nations and gave him a copy of the book I coauthored on Native land claims (Cassidy & Dale, 1988). Only as he was seeing me to my car did he say, "Let me know when the next meeting is . . . I may come."

Bare Rock or Wasco?

Prior to the third leadership workshop, a regular meeting of RPAC was convened to talk about the Secretariat's emerging work plan. RPAC members were still enthusiastic about a grassroots process and were now even more motivated by the challenge of building a bridge to the Haida. Prior to the meeting, I had informed each of them that there was a chance that Gitsga would rejoin.

A seemingly small event had recently been covered in the local weekly newspaper; this event would have an enormous and unexpected impact on our proceedings. Close to our mid-Islands meeting ground, at a place called Tlell, a large rock protruded from the intertidal sandflats. An anonymous metalworker-artist had decided that this bare rock needed adorning. He forged a five-foot metal stick figure that held a spyglass, and placed this figure on the rock. Another anonymous person removed it, and then the artist put another one up. People wrote letters to the editor offering various positions. Environmentalists said the sculpture bothered the eagles; others liked the little mariner on the rock.

As RPAC members, including Gitsga, arrived for our meeting, a good-humored conversation arose about the sculpture with approximately equal pros and cons bandied about. Then Gitsga spoke. "The Haida don't like it but not because of the eagles. The rock is sacred. It is the Wasco." Gitsga went on to say that he had "a big problem" when people just went ahead and did what they liked with the landscape. To the Haida, he said, the Islands are not a blank sheet waiting to be written on. Warren Foster, the RPAC member from Sandspit—the community most divided with the Haida—waded into the discussion. He said that in all the years he'd lived on the Islands, he'd never heard anything about the Wasco rock. "Are you saying that we can't do anything on these Islands because everything has its own story?"

Gitsga replied that not everything was storied or sacred. "Then," asked Foster, "how are we supposed to know?" "Just ask," responded Gitsga. The conversation turned to how little interpersonal discussion between Haida and non-Haida had taken place, despite years of living in close vicinity. Conversations about values and the meaning of places were especially infrequent. Gitsga then told the story of the Wascos, giant sea dogs that were large enough to catch killer whales. These amazing creatures had kept Haida villages well fed until a jealous sorcerer conjured up a sea storm. The rough seas exhausted the Wascos, and they turned into the great rocks along the shore near Tlell (for a written version of the story, see Barbeau, 1953, pp. 305-306).

At first, as this talk of the rock and the Wasco continued, a couple of members signaled that we should get on with the meeting. But as the story of the Wasco and its cultural significance unfolded, no one wanted to stop. Without prompting from me, most of the members began to link the incident of the rock to the concerns Gitsga had expressed so dramatically two weeks earlier. The storied place of the Wasco rock was just like the "the system that works" that Gitsga had referred to then. These concepts were outside the ken of non-Haida; only time and care would lead to greater understanding and, thereby, greater respect. One member summed it up as follows: "I guess we're going to have to move real slow in everything from now on if we're going to have any hope of understanding." ∞

⌘ COMMENTARY

The story of the rock, which is both a bare outcrop and Wasco the spiritual sea dog, is a wonderful illustration of the existence of different cultural frames of meaning. In this case, local Euro-Canadian residents and Haida looked at the same object and saw something different. Understanding these different frameworks is crucial to consensus building. Interpretations have implications for action. Whether or not a person wants to decorate the rock with a statue depends on whether she sees it as a rock, a revered spirit of a sea dog, or a roost for eagles. It is not only Haida interpretations that shape this conflict; indeed, most of the interpretive frameworks are not Haida. For example, the SMA is framed in the language of economic development, not spiritual growth or environmental preservation. Its enactment is arranged through a system of consultants, committees, and experts, all of whom write reports and meet regularly. Both the organization of the process and its forms of knowledge and categories of action are deeply rooted in a bureaucratic, European way of talking, organizing, and thinking about problems.

—Sally Engle Merry, *Anthropologist*

⌘ COMMENTARY

In many environmental disputes, a key element is the recognition of issues that have "sacred" value. Ignoring the sacredness of issues is to ignore what matters to a party—which goes against virtually all useful models of negotiation. On the other hand, there is a counteracting tendency to view anything sacred as undiscussable. Yet lack of discussion eliminates the search for trades, which is necessary for finding efficient agreements. Bazerman, Gillespie, and Moore (in press) suggest that the label of sacredness may inhibit negotiators' abilities to find, or even contemplate, trade-offs. When issues acquire a sacred stature, people lose the ability to think in sophisticated ways about or even consider trade-offs that involve those issues (Tetlock, Peterson, & Lerner, 1996). They may avoid decisions in which values must be traded off against each other, defer the decisions to others, or pretend as if the conflict doesn't exist. Dale does an excellent job of managing the tension of recognizing the importance of sacred issues, without going overboard in a way that would eliminate the possibility of future trades.

—Max H. Bazerman, *Social psychologist*

REFERENCES

Bazerman, M., Gillespie, J., & Moore, D. (in press). The human mind as a barrier to wise environmental agreements. *American Behavioral Scientist*.

Tetlock, P. E., Peterson, R., & Lerner, J. (1996). Revising the value pluralism model: Incorporating social content and context postulates. In C. Seligman, J. Olson, & M. Zanna (Eds.), *Values: Eighth annual Ontario symposium on personality and social psychology*. Hillsdale, NJ: Lawrence Erlbaum.

As long as my work continued on the Islands, the story of the bare rock that was also a revered sea monster remained a touchstone for RPAC. This story went hand in hand with the larger story—how hard it was to fathom each other's frames of reference. A decision was made to direct the P&CC not to proceed with the Secretariat's work plan until RPAC could find a way to work with Haida leaders. RPAC also asked Gitsga to work with me to set up a "feast" so that the two sides could become better acquainted. From my perspective, this was a direct outcome of the dialogue about the rock.

Over the course of the next month, there was considerable interchange among Gitsga, RPAC, and myself about how to best plan a feast for the committee and the Haida leadership. The latter, mostly viewing RPAC as a "redneck" group, at first dismissed the notion. Feasts in Pacific Northwest coast culture often confer recognition on the hosts (Drucker, 1965). In addition, the Haida insisted on their status as a government, and consequently sought to negotiate only with other governments, not "stakeholders." Thus, what may have seemed incomprehensible reluctance to RPAC was actually consistent with both ancient precepts and modern political "optics." Fortunately, Gitsga and I were available to interpret the initial lack of response to RPAC's invitation. We found an opportunity in the final leadership seminar for what might be called "politically safe feasting."

The Tourism Workshop: The Parties Begin to Connect

The final leadership seminar was planned for June and centered on tourism planning. The SMA had called for the creation of a "world-class tourism destination" featuring the new national parks. Few Islanders, Haida or otherwise, were pleased with this externally determined priority. Yet they recognized that given the Islands' unique natural and cultural features, inevitable change would come—perhaps even in the form of opportunity.

A Native American from Hawaii, George Kanahele, had been invited to lead the RPAC tourism seminar. Because Kanahele was a visitor from another indigenous group, the Haida leadership saw a feast held in his honor as a necessity. At last, this presented the ideal opportunity for holding an RPAC-sponsored feast. A seminar given by Kanahele would be followed by a feast catered by Haida cooks and paid for by RPAC. In anticipation of the arrival of a prominent Native visitor, senior Haida leaders became deeply involved in the planning. The chair and several other members of RPAC met for the first time with these leaders at the relatively informal setting of the "Kanahele feast."

Talk of angry withdrawals, shared myths, personal revelations, and feasts may seem colorful asides to the real negotiating process. This, I submit, was not so on Haida Gwaii nor is it so for any serious, long-lasting public conflict involving cultural differences. To the contrary, this is the very heart of conflict resolution. ➥

❧ COMMENTARY

Dale insightfully notes the role of the nonbinding, noncommitting meeting of the parties. The question is, what role does this discussion play? One notion is an affective connection—which I certainly endorse. However, recent research shows that nonbinding discussions can have a significant effect on reducing egocentric interpretations of what would be a fair resolution (Wade-Benzoni, Tenbrunsel, & Bazerman, 1996). Essentially, nonbinding discussions allow each side to put itself in the shoes of others—something we all know to be a good idea, yet too infrequently practice.

—Max H. Bazerman, *Social psychologist*

REFERENCE

Wade-Benzoni, K. A., Tenbrunsel, A. E., & Bazerman, M. H. (1996). Egocentric interpretations of fairness in asymmetric, environmental social dilemmas: Explaining harvesting behavior and the role of communication. *Organizational Behavior and Human Decision Processes, 67,* 111-126.

Brokering the "Obvious" Solution

By the week after the Kanahele feast, both RPAC and Haida leaders were independently beginning to focus on the funds for regional development. The SMA had provided $38 million for regional development. The P&CC still held the view that disbursement of these funds should be decided on the basis of economic sector studies. Almost by definition, this would mean work by professionals unlikely to be found on the Islands.

Underlying the above approach was the assumption of Haida nonparticipation, which was now crumbling. Still, the P&CC needed some sense of the local population's wishes regarding expenditures. To persuade the P&CC that the new contacts could provide valuable input, some shared vision would need to emerge.

The Haida-RPAC relationship was too tenuous to even think of jointly setting spending priorities. In 1989, RPAC had made public a "shopping list" of possible expenditures. In reaction, the Haida made clear that any relationship they had with the National Parks agency would be destroyed if "one penny was spent." My discussions with RPAC members, Haida leaders, and other residents revealed a general feeling that the $38 million was, in any event, evaporating. Seeing no concrete progress, many Islanders outside RPAC and the elected councils convinced themselves that the money was no longer available, despite my assurances to the contrary. Others had the more accurate concern that inflation was eroding the value of this money.

With an eye toward increasing the Haida role in planning, RPAC did explore one project possibility. A recent fire at the Queen Charlotte Islands Museum had badly charred a number of old totem poles, leaving them virtually unsalvageable. RPAC suggested funding a project that would allow Haida artists to make modern re-creations of the burnt poles. Gitsga sounded out the Haida leadership. They declared themselves to still be opposed, in principle, to spending prior to clarification of the Haida role in economic planning. However, Gitsga reported privately that some leaders appeared pleasantly surprised that RPAC had even generated such an idea. Images of the other were changing—on both sides.

In early summer, the fear of losing the $38 million by erosion or senior government caprice grew stronger. An idea previously discussed by RPAC and others resurfaced: The money could be put in an interest-bearing account pending the completion of an economic development plan. The P&CC had rejected this idea in 1989, but now the president of the Council of the Haida Nation, Miles Richardson, Jr., anxiously campaigned for such a fund. While the groundwork was laid for this "obvious solution," the P&CC pressed the Secretariat to produce the long overdue work plan. This plan was to include a timetable and a process for the preparation of sectoral studies.

Wayne Tebb, the director of the Secretariat, was in a precarious position. I was reporting that RPAC would not even look at a work plan prior to provisions for direct Haida involvement. The P&CC was informing Tebb that he was in default of contractual obligations and that he had better submit a plan. Reluctantly, Tebb forwarded a draft of a work plan to both RPAC and P&CC. RPAC refused to comment. It was at this point that Robin Dodson, the federal cochair of the P&CC, took bold action. He informed me that his committee would disband RPAC if it did not comply with the P&CC's request for comments on the work plan.

At a special RPAC meeting, I was directed to relay once again to the P&CC that RPAC was not in a position to review the plan. I was also instructed to mention that RPAC was now in touch with Miles Richardson, Jr. and had earned Haida support. Naturally, both Gitsga and I made sure that the Haida leadership did in fact concur with RPAC's position. RPAC also invited the P&CC to come to the Islands for an emergency meeting. The principal agenda item would be the renewed demand for a trust account to protect the $38 million principal.

When I conveyed the RPAC response to Dodson, he was surprisingly calm. Months later, Dodson told me that the P&CC had indeed been divided over RPAC's direction and that some had wanted my contract terminated. Dodson opposed this perspective; by conveying an order that would be refused by RPAC and unacceptable to the Haida, Dodson predicted his opponents in P&CC would eventually "get in line" with the communities. The prospect of a full consensus among Island communities was increasingly attractive; the alternative was to start from scratch if the current RPAC and community liaison were replaced. Both the Islands' communities and federal and provincial politicians were becoming impatient with delays in implementing the Regional Economic Development Initiative. Some suggested that the whole park deal be scrapped if Canada could not deliver on its economic development commitments.

Apparently, Dodson's gambit worked. A visit by the cochairs and several other P&CC members was set for early August. Separate meetings would be arranged with the Haida leadership and RPAC.

In the weeks leading up to the P&CC visit, RPAC members and the Haida held caucuses to further consider the concept of a trust fund. Face-to-face negotiations between these groups would be necessary at some point; for now, we aimed for a one-time session, provided that a trust was deemed feasible by Canada and British Columbia. We obtained agreement in principle that a joint meeting would be held soon after the P&CC visit. Meanwhile, in the caucuses, a compelling concept emerged: that the trust be made permanent and placed under joint Haida/non-Haida community management. Both sides could find powerful incentives to this arrangement. The annual interest generated by a principal of $38 million would be considerable, and could be dispensed through development grants by a joint management authority. When the P&CC met with the Haida and then RPAC in early August 1990, they heard a similar refrain: The principal must be protected forever. ◆

☞ COMMENTARY

Dale nicely highlights the role of a shrinking pie on negotiations. To the extent that a settlement was delayed, the parties lost the interest on $38 million—clearly, an incentive to settle. However, it is also important to note that if one of the sides is more concerned about this interest, this provides a distributional advantage to the other side.

Jim Sebenius has recently argued for a presettlement process in such cases, where the parties reach a tentative settlement but do not gain the advantage of settlement until the details are solved. Thus, Sebenius might argue that a tentative agreement could have been suggested where the structure was put in place for a settlement, the interest was held in escrow, and the parties would benefit only when final agreement was reached. Such presettlements are difficult, and Sebenius has noted the failure to reach such agreements in the 1994 baseball strike and the airline pilots' strike of 1996-1997 (Lax & Sebenius, 1997).

—Max H. Bazerman, *Social psychologist*

REFERENCE

Lax, D., & Sebenius, J. (1997, February 24). A better way to go on strike. *Wall Street Journal*, p. A22.

Federal Chair Dodson knew well that a daunting challenge lay ahead: convincing the federal government to turn over $38 million to small communities with a combined population of less than 6,000. Informal discussion between Dodson and senior officials in Ottawa revealed concerns that the action was without precedent. The federal government, officials claimed, gave targeted grants, not money for someone else to put in the bank. Yet this was not entirely accurate. In fact, much to the annoyance of Island communities, the government had placed funds in trust for major forest companies whose activity had been curtailed by the creation of the park. Compensation took the form of interest-bearing accounts. RPAC and the Haida now asked only for treatment as fair and generous as that received by these large corporations. ◆

☞ COMMENTARY

The disparity in the treatment of funds reveals the enormous difference in economic power between forest companies and local communities, both Haida and non-Haida. Such power differentials are always critical to the way agreements are formed and provide an essential part of the context of subsequent agreements. However, it seems that in the context of the contemporary Canadian state, Native peoples have access to a kind of moral authority despite their lack of economic power. From an ethnographic perspective, considerations of power, like issues of culture, are always central issues.

—Sally Engle Merry, *Anthropologist*

It was clear that the P&CC would support a trust account, provided the Haida and RPAC could directly negotiate the details. Given the lack of constructive relations, it seemed unlikely that one session would be sufficient. As convenor, I identified the incentives that could lead to continued meetings between the parties. Two weeks before the meeting, I met with Miles Richardson, Jr. and his key advisers, who informed me of the Haida's one "nonnegotiable" condition for management of the trust account: that they would permanently hold the right to name the chair of any managing body. On the other hand, he did agree to equal representation and to working by consensus rather than voting.

Preparing to Negotiate

Shortly thereafter, RPAC named its delegates to the meeting. (They included one delegate from each of the four non-Haida communities.) I scheduled a premeeting briefing and discussion session and prepared a detailed presentation on the management of the Islands' economy. I included themes that built directly on shared experiences including the residential school stories, the myth of the Wasco rock, and how whites had generally wrested control from the Haida since the times of first contact.

My emphasis was on disempowerment. I drew parallels between the RPAC communities' current feelings and the Haida's experience over a much longer time period. I thus set the stage for consideration of the Haida demand to name a chair for the proposed trust fund. This arrangement would represent the Haida's first opportunity to lead a new institution on the Islands in over 150 years.

The discussion of the Haida demand was heated, but no RPAC member rejected it out of hand. They pondered how they would "sell" the concept back home, agreeing to characterize the deal as a limited recognition of Haida self-governance, an act of good faith, and, above all, a bargain essential to accessing badly needed funds. Quid pro quos were felt to be in order. The most promising arena for such a trade concerned the Sandspit harbor project.

The SMA's Regional Economic Development Initiative explicitly promised this project to Sandspit, the community most affected by the end of logging in the new National Park reserve. Thus, this large capital project threatened to absorb $8 million or more "off the top" of the overall Regional Economic Development Initiative fund. Two of the three non-Haida communities supported Sandspit's right to funds for harbor construction. But with the discussion now including the Haida, Sandspit's bitter opponents in the logging controversy, the harbor's claim was certain to move to center stage.

In response to the Haida insistence on naming the chair, RPAC negotiators agreed to stand behind a Sandspit demand that discussions of the Regional Economic Development Initiative fund be kept separate from the viability of the harbor project. RPAC would not ask the Haida to agree to devote money to the harbor, instead placing the issue outside the scope of discussions.

The federal government's interpretation was the exact opposite: They saw the SMA as a total of $38 million, inclusive of harbor funding. Deep fiscal deficits were a major public concern across Canada. The SMA already exceeded $100 million when compensation to forest companies and park construction costs were factored in. Only enormous and concerted effort—among old adversaries on the Islands—could increase this level of funding.

My hope was to build momentum about the concept of a permanent trust managed by the community, without getting hung up on the size of the initial principal. Then mountains might be moved, including the federal government's aversion to increasing the funding for Haida Gwaii. Canada's lack of timely fulfillment of promises in the SMA could provide leverage for full funding of the community trust and the harbor project. This would occur, however, only if there was a united front locally.

Face-to-Face "Nonnegotiations"

The "onetime" meeting was held in Skidegate, a Haida village, in September 1990. The explicit purpose of the meeting was "to explore the possibility for creating a permanent jointly managed community trust fund." No commitment to proceed further than "exploration" at that one meeting was implied by anyone's attendance.

The Haida were represented by their highest-ranking elected officials: the president and vice president of the Council of the Haida Nation and the chief councilors from Old Massett and Skidegate. After the initial introductions, Richardson stated the Haida's demand to name the chair of any permanent management entity. The representative from Sandspit replied that he would accept such an arrangement. The Haida were visibly surprised. Other RPAC members spoke in concurrence, committing to the idea in principal and pledging to take it back to their constituencies.

Without framing his comments as a counterdemand, Sandspit representative Warren Foster spoke next. He stated that Sandspit had been promised a harbor and that some issues bearing on that project's funding remained open. He explained that he sought only "noninterference" between the fund and the harbor planning. The Haida did not react. Tempers remained in check, and this was the major relief and achievement of this first encounter.

By the end of the meeting, all present recognized that further sessions would be desirable. Richardson reiterated that these sessions could not be seen as negotiations. The Haida Nation, he reminded the group, was a government and therefore only ne-gotiated with governments. He pointed out that all Haida in attendance were vulner-able to potentially vicious criticism for even meeting with an advisory body like RPAC.

Wording can be critically important at times like this. RPAC agreed that our ses-sions were not to be called negotiations. At my suggestion, RPAC also offered to re-quest a letter from the governments of Canada and British Columbia using the terminology "exploratory discussions." This would give the Haida added comfort with what for them were unprecedented consultations. At the conclusion of the meeting, I was asked to prepare a rough plan for a series of "nonnegotiating" ses-sions aimed at producing an under-standing. We began to refer to those present as the "Group of Eight."

Reaching an Accord in the Group of Eight

Through the autumn of 1990, the Group of Eight met approximately every three weeks. My task was to develop a working draft, essentially a single negotiat-ing text that addressed critical choices and issues. For the most part, these de facto negotiations were the easiest part of the Haida Gwaii process. The exception was the harbor issue; here, the only area of agreement was to leave it alone.

Sandspit representative Foster had been appointed to RPAC by Duane Gould, the elected regional director for Sandspit on the Skeena–Queen Charlottes Regional District. Gould wanted nothing less than explicit Haida support for the harbor as a condition for a shared community develop-ment fund. Both Foster and I spent consid-erable time arguing with Gould that this kind of support would never be forthcom-ing. Foster argued persuasively that the

storm the Haida had raised in the logging-versus-park controversy was indicative of what would happen if they openly opposed the harbor. By this time, the harbor was under assault from environmentalists for its potential impact on marine wildlife. Haida opposition could only make things worse.

One of the Haida negotiators sought to explicitly exempt the $38 million from des-ignation for the harbor, a demand that was unacceptable to RPAC. In the end, all par-ties agreed to a "without prejudice" clause, which was essentially a postponement. The quid pro quo of agreeing to a Haida-appointed chair was duly noted as a reason to accede to this clause.

In early December, the parties agreed to the Accord on a Community Development Fund. Unlike most negotiated settlements, the final product was not signed. The Haida's reluctance to negotiate with non-government entities required innovative "ratification." The chair of RPAC and the Council of the Haida Nation sent separate letters of approval for the accord. RPAC's letter went to the P&CC, while the Haida's letter went to the federal minister respon-sible for the SMA.

Reenergizing Postagreement Commitment: The PEI Presentation

Standing back from the Gwaii Trust ne-gotiations, one is impressed by the brevity of direct negotiations compared with what preceded or followed. It took seven months to get to the table, three months to produce the Accord on a Community Development Fund, and almost three more years before the Gwaii Trust was formally created as a nonprofit society with money in the bank. The story of those three years is beyond the scope of this case study. Thus, I will deal primarily with the year following the com-pletion of the accord, including the design of an implementation mechanism. Like the prenegotiations phase, this proved to be a challenging period.

As I reflect on the events of 1991 and 1992, it is puzzling that it took so long to produce a workable plan. The end product, the Gwaii Trust now in operation, is really no different from what was outlined in the accord. Unquestionably, the issue of the harbor tended to flare up every so often and set back cooperative planning. But in my opinion, the seemingly slow progress had more to do with the evolution of trust. As some of us said at the time, "Without 'small t' trust, no 'large T' trust!" This region had been divided by a long and bitter controversy over logging, and a much longer period of cross-cultural tension stretching from the late eighteenth century. Now, in this milieu, we wanted to create an organization based on the exercise of equal and cooperative control. ⇌

⇌ COMMENTARY

Significant to the context of the present situation is the success of the Haida in opposing logging in the past, although the author does not describe this role or the specific features of the logging conflict. It appears, however, that the Haida have a history of political success. This shifts the terms of the present negotiation. Moreover, the possibility of involvement by environmental groups, which sometimes have considerable resources and political clout, also shapes the present dispute. There are indications in this case study that the relative power of the parties incorporates moral authority as well as economic power. Moreover, transnational processes are also relevant: The movement for Native sovereignty, so central to Haida negotiations, is part of a global movement of indigenous peoples whose interconnections were indicated by the arrival of a Native Hawaiian leader who was given an important feast in the middle of this conflict. The environmental movement, now clearly transnational, is a force in this conflict as well.

—Sally Engle Merry, *Anthropologist*

In the first few months after the Accord on a Community Development Fund, energies sagged or were diverted to other matters. The satisfaction of forging a preliminary design seemed almost enough. The parties decided to continue as a planning body using the same representation and process that had created the accord. Yet in the first quarter of 1991, no meetings could be arranged. The involvement of top Haida elected officials provided the advantage of legitimacy, but these officials were devoted to numerous matters of importance to the Haida Nation. We needed to reinvigorate the energy of the Group of Eight.

In April, I came across some promotional material for a conference about rural economic development. The conference promised to explore how other regions managed the challenge of setting development priorities; I believed RPAC and the Group of Eight would benefit from attending. The conference was set for July on Prince Edward Island (PEI), which was also where I was from. I had already decided to go, and I suggested that one or two RPAC/Group of Eight members might wish to accompany me. Instead, they all wanted to go. As the delegation—and the costs of traveling across Canada—swelled, it seemed fitting to take a more active role at the conference. I suggested that we formally share our experience, raising the following question: Given a substantial source of funds for rural development, what are options for their expenditure?

The trip to PEI proved to be a significant milestone in the development of trust and the Gwaii Trust. Just traveling and socializing together helped bind the parties, and a strong working relationship emerged between Sandspit representative Warren Foster and the chief councilor for Old Massett, Michael Nicholl Yahgulanaas. Free from their other responsibilities, the group was able to focus entirely on the status of the accord. To prepare for the conference, the group first needed to find a way to make a common presentation.

We convened informally over a meal on a Sunday afternoon to design the Haida Gwaii/Queen Charlottes Development Fund workshop, which was scheduled for the following afternoon. Very soon, we discovered strikingly different versions of the group's shared history, and old tensions began to surface. At this point, I wondered if we were back again really "talking about the Wasco." I suggested we "coauthor" an integrated version of the community fund's history to test our ability to resolve differences within the group.

The Group of Eight spent the rest of Sunday (until about 11:00 p.m.) and Monday morning preparing a 15-minute talk. Events and feelings were aired about the 1985 South Moresby logging blockade. Group members shared (perhaps for the first time) their unhappiness when the issue was taken off the Islands by senior federal-provincial negotiations. "Shared economic powerlessness" emerged as a unifying theme. Stories unfolded—about individual experiences in residential schools, the physical appropriation of Native art pieces, and the adoption of Native symbols into mainstream culture. Several members were moved to tears.

For the Group of Eight, there was pride in having listened to and spoken of such different versions of history. Substantive learning had occurred about perspectives that neither saw in the heat of the South Moresby conflict. A consensus building tool had been mutually discovered: using narrative to unearth issues unapproachable in a solely rational manner. ➥

➥ COMMENTARY

Several times in this case study, consensus building moved forward through retellings of shared past experiences, positive as well as painful, and through recognition of differences in the way these events were understood and interpreted. It is notable that this author finds such narrative moments of critical importance but that others involved in the negotiation tended to think them irrelevant or a waste of time. This shows that what seems irrelevant from a bureaucratic, task-focused perspective is actually fundamental to building the understanding and trust that precede cooperation, particularly when there are extensive histories of hostility and injury. As anthropologists have long noted, in most parts of the world and even in smaller communities in the urbanized West, it is well understood that social relationships of trust must precede discussions about problems and actions; it is only in the recently created impersonal world of Western bureaucracy that a belief has emerged that such relationships are unnecessary and can be bypassed in the interest of efficiency.

—Sally Engle Merry, *Anthropologist*

Once again, we had a touchstone to help overcome difficult moments as the accord was implemented.

Renewed by their work together, the group called on Foster and Yahgulanaas to return west via Ottawa and to engage in some intensive lobbying. During this trip, the group also came up with the name "Gwaii Trust," which solved the ever-present issue of wording by combining highly meaningful Haida and English words.

The Long Journey to the Gwaii Trust Continues

The period of making the Gwaii Trust a reality stretched out for several more years. My involvement continued until April 1993, when the first $5 million were deposited by the federal government into the Gwaii Trust Interim Planning Society (GTIPS), the Gwaii Trust's forerunner.

For a long time, we pondered the design of a public consultation process on the setup of the trust. In the end, each community formed its own public process, but called on GTIPS members for assistance. We also devoted immense effort to lobbying the provincial and federal governments to create an "interim trust." Contention over Sandspit harbor continued, partially because of the Gwaii Trust but also because of unrelated environmental concerns.

In 1994, the government of Canada finally allotted the full $38 million to the Gwaii Trust and another $10 million to Sandspit for the construction of the harbor. The Gwaii Trust was incorporated in September 1994, followed by the selection of representatives to the board from each community. ◆

◆ COMMENTARY

This is an interesting example of expanding the pie. The source of the expansion was the Canadian government—it appears to have paid the extra $10 million. This is common in complex disputes. The Israel-Egypt agreement is commonly cited as a prime example of integrative bargaining: Israel got security and Egypt got ownership. This hides the fact that the United States chipped in billions of dollars to make all of this occur. Gillespie and Bazerman (1997) provide multiple examples of such parasitic integration: where the extra resources are obtained from a party outside the immediate dispute, who may well have an interest in seeing an agreement.

—Max H. Bazerman, *Social psychologist*

REFERENCE

Gillespie, J., & Bazerman, M. H. (1997). Parasitic integration. *Negotiation Journal, 13,* 271-282.

■ *Conclusions*

A Place for Stories and Histories

Consensus building must rely on well-planned, well-executed, face-to-face negotiations. For most complex and controversial public policy issues, sound expert analysis plays a major role in shaping the possibilities for agreement. But something else is often needed, especially when the parties have been at odds for generations and come from disparate cultural traditions. In a case like Haida Gwaii, "methods" that complement but also transcend highly rational processes are particularly compelling.

The resolution of this case certainly depended on the core techniques of mediated consensus building. But I did not dwell here on the "table negotiations," in part because the present volume provides readers with a toolkit of approaches and techniques. Instead, I placed more emphasis on the intragroup dynamics that took place away from the table. These events often generated the enabling moments of the process and in my view were the most important "interventions."

On at least three occasions, the parties gained momentum by *dealing with history* in highly personal, narrative, and even emotional ways. I refer particularly to discussions about the Wasco and the PEI presentation, as well as the "pep talk" given to RPAC prior to their first negotiating session with the Haida. The use of personal and collective stories was key to at least the first two.

Why are narratives about the past so important to navigating long-standing cross-cultural conflict? At the most general level, stories can be found in all cultures

worldwide; they are a common denominator valued by all ethnicities and ages. Relatively few people learn the rules of specialized modes of discourse such as legal argumentation or Western scientific debate. But nearly all of us, beginning as very young children, are immersed in stories—whether of fiction or family tales. Stories are thus an inseparable possession and truly constitutive of our identity (Randall, 1995).

Indigenous cultures of America are noteworthy for having relied on oral rather than written traditions. In Canada, belated recognition of the importance of oral history has now even reached the Supreme Court. In a landmark ruling, Supreme Court justices concluded that Aboriginal oral history holds significance equal to more conventionally acquired evidence, including scientific testimony. The justices recognized that much of the Aboriginal culture's message exists as narrative rather than written documentation. Practitioners in the field of consensus building should be no less respectful.

Finally, First Nations people are often preoccupied with the unacknowledged and therefore unfinished business of the past—a mind-set with significant ramifications for public policy.

> It is important for First Nations peoples to tell their stories—and most of those stories are about the past relationship between First Nations and European non-Aboriginals. For First Nations peoples, history defines the present; it is not something to set aside in pursuit of a better tomorrow. Stories about collective historical experiences reveal a relationship that is the basis of our current thinking about what did or could work in addressing the problems

we face. . . . For First Nations peoples history keeps coming up and it probably always will. (Mercredi & Turpel, 1993, pp. 13-14)

Observations about My Role

Looking more broadly at key episodes, it may be helpful to sum up the nature of my role. This summary should not leave the impression that my role was by any means the predominant one. Without the courage of Gitsga, the audacity and open-mindedness of Warren Foster, and the risk taking of all the community leaders, there would be no Gwaii Trust. Still, in keeping with the purpose of the present volume, it is important to lay out what I believe were my most salient contributions. In sum, they appear to be

- cross-cultural sensitivity that allowed me to move between and interpret different cultural frames;
- the ability to seize opportunities to build cross-cultural empathy;
- the willingness to be close friends with the people who ultimately became negotiators;
- and, of course, the patience to attend to the myriad process details that arise during multiparty consensus building processes.

It was also critical that I lived in these Islands for a relatively long period of time, allowing me to make friends and to deeply appreciate the strength and the texture of people's narratives. In this context, I believe a mediator flown in from time to time would have been less likely to bring about a settlement.

In closing, I must return to one issue. When first employed by the P&CC, there was a discrepancy between the P&CC's expectations and my intended actions. As I confessed earlier, I was not interested in playing my contracted role, which I characterized above as "keeping the children playing" while the "real work" gets done. How can I account for what I did? A far cry from "best practices" for the would-be mediator!

One justification is as follows: The planning model first presented in the SMA was inappropriate and ineffective. If carried out "successfully," this plan would have continued the debilitating pattern of removing critical decision making from community control. More likely, I felt, it simply would not have worked, leaving everyone locked in struggle over the use of the $38 million. Had I been candid with the P&CC at the outset, I might not be telling this story now. Is it acceptable to conceal one's intentions from powerful parties so as to gain access to the situation? Hardly.

Regardless of who hired me, I sought an economic development plan that was both fair and likely to be implemented in good faith. I believed that only consensus among those principally affected by a decision would likely produce this kind of positive outcome. And so I framed my role as helping build consensus among Haida Gwaii communities, which, in turn, put them in a strong position to advocate for a more inclusive plan. Notwithstanding this rationale, the thoughtful reader will share my unease at the choices often faced and made in achieving consensus outcomes. ❧

∞ COMMENTARY

Kolb (1983, 1994) found that while mediators routinely espoused neutrality, they also believed in "interventionist" mediation.

When mediators are queried about their roles, they tend to respond by making a normative distinction between passive and active mediator roles. The image of the passive mediator is the silent observer, someone who confines his activities to providing coffee and sharpening pencils. The active mediator is one who, through his efforts, makes a major contribution to the achievement of settlement. The forms of this major contribution may vary. Descriptions of them include applying pressure, channeling communications, allowing the parties to save face, persuading and leading the group in its task accomplishment and social relationships. (Kolb, 1983, p. 24)

The issue of neutrality was central to different views of mediation advocated by Stulberg (1981) and Susskind (1981). Stulberg argued that mediators should be neutral, lacking clout, and unconcerned about the outcome (p. 94). Stulberg argued that such neutrality was essential for developing trust between parties and mediator. Susskind argued that such neutrality was unobtainable in most complex disputes and that aiming for it would be a barrier against effectiveness. Lawrence Susskind argued that success often required active intervention by the mediator:

> The [successful] mediators were willing to inject themselves into the substance of the disputes. They were not content to facilitate and encourage discussion among the parties. In that regard, they were activists. They had personal views about the appropriate scope and content of the agreements that were emerging. They did not take sides in a way that might have jeopardized their credibility with the parties, but they were not neutral in the usual sense. They worked behind the scenes, between meetings and during meetings, to find elements of agreement that could be treated separately, items that could be traded, issues that could be packaged, and ways in which the momentum of the negotiations could be used to pressure holdouts. (Susskind, 1981, pp. 39-40)

Moore (1986) argued that mediators cannot and should not be neutral with regard to the process. According to Moore, neutrality becomes less of a practical operational procedure than an ideal that mediators aspire to. Sara Cobb and Janet Rifkin (1991) argue that there are three different conceptions of neutrality at work in mediation:

"Impartiality" as "that which ensures against bias," where the mediators' role is "to either dismiss their opinions, values, feelings, and agendas or to separate them from the mediation process . . . to avoid coercing the parties and thus imposing the mediator's solution or values upon them" (p. 42).

"Equidistance," which concentrates on keeping the relationship between the parties equal even though at any one moment the mediator may favor one side or the other (pp. 42, 46).

"A practice in *discourse*," where the "mediators participate by shaping problems in ways that provide all speakers not only an opportunity to tell their story but a discursive opportunity to tell a story that does not contribute to their own delegitimization or marginalization" (p. 62).

While Stulberg (1981) and Cobb and Rifkin (1991) offer useful information for thinking about neutrality in the abstract, it is clear that Dale's view of the task is closest to the Susskind view of mediation. Dale is well aware of this as the case develops. In fact, he argues that his behavior was "a far cry from 'best practices' for the would-be mediator!" I would disagree with his conclusion and argue that departures from stricter notions of neutrality have been necessary for the success that Dale partially created.

—Max H. Bazerman, *Social psychologist*

REFERENCES

Cobb, S., & Rifkin, J. (1991). Practice and paradox: Deconstructing neutrality in mediation. *Law and Social Inquiry, 16*.

Kolb, D. (1983). *The mediators*. Cambridge, MA: MIT Press.

Kolb, D. (1994). *When talk works*. San Francisco: Jossey-Bass.

Moore, C. (1986). *The mediation process*. San Francisco: Jossey-Bass.

Stulberg, J. (1981). The theory and practice of mediation: A reply to Professor Susskind. *Vermont Law Review, 6*.

Susskind, L. (1981). Environmental mediation and the accountability problem. *Vermont Law Review, 6*, 85.

■ *Epilogue*

The Gwaii Trust was established as a nonprofit society under the laws of British Columbia in September 1994. A permanent board was established that follows exactly the organizational structure negotiated half a decade earlier. A small staff and permanent office have been put in place in Massett, one of the two Haida communities. The Haida continue to have the sole right to appoint the chair, but that does not imply that only Haida have filled that position. For over a year, the Haida sanctioned as chair a non-Native resident elected from Sandspit, the community that has historically been least sympathetic to the assertion of Aboriginal sovereignty.

The Gwaii Trust is now worth more than $40 million and yields annual planning and project funding of approximately $2 million (Canadian). These funds have for the most part been plowed back into the principal, but several programs have been initiated whereby, at last, Island communities, groups, and individuals are benefiting from the money from the SMA. This includes a scholarship fund for Island students, a small capital grants program available equitably to all communities and community groups, and infrastructure and community economic-planning funding. Indeed, I have been asked back to Haida Gwaii twice to facilitate Sandspit's community economic development planning process, funded entirely by the Gwaii Trust.

As important as money has been the benefit to the Islands in terms of a slow but steady bridging of the divide among communities. In 1997, the Council of the Haida Nation approached the Gwaii Trust for grants in aid of paying down long-accumulated legal bills associated with the legal battles of the mid-1980s over South Moresby. It was a difficult moment in the Gwaii Trust's brief and early history. Yet after considerable debate, this unusual one-time request was agreed to and a very moving ceremony and feast were held for the passing of a check of more than $100,000.

This Islands Community Stability Initiative (ICSI) was initiated in 1995 with equal representation from the six communities and the Council of the Haida Nation. It has forged a consensus on a wide array of strategies aimed at achieving a more stable and higher degree of benefits to Island communities from local natural resources. The model of equal representation from the six communities and the Council of the Haida Nation has been closely followed, and several of the ICSI board members are "veterans" of the Gwaii Trust.

While on Haida Gwaii in 1998, I was able to tour the Sandspit harbor, which was completed at last in late 1997. The harbor was built with many problems and further delays—but none originated, as one might have expected 10 years earlier, from any opposition by the Haida or other Island communities. While there, I met separately with both of the lead participants in the

Wasco discussion back in 1990. Gitsga continues to be among the Haida's leading artists, drawing forth the images of storied creatures (including the Wasco) from silver, cedar, and argillite. Warren Foster still repairs radiators of the huge, heavy-duty vehicles used in timber harvesting. Yet both separately offer mediation services within their communities, each having pursued further training in alternative dispute resolution.

There is additional evidence of the improvement in intercommunity relations. The model of the Gwaii Trust organizational structure has been emulated in an Islands-wide initiative to take greater control of forest resources and management. ∞

∞ COMMENTARY

Dale offers many insightful observations. It is clear that he played a critical role in creating this agreement. His reflections offer an interesting opportunity to peek inside a real mediation and compare the result to a number of academic observations.

—Max H. Bazerman, *Social psychologist*

∞ COMMENTARY

An intriguing feature of this situation is that confronted with potentially divisive and unresolvable questions such as the choice between funding the harbor project or fully supporting the Gwaii Trust with the total amount of funds, the author attempted to move the discussion to process and shared concerns rather than posing an either/or proposition. In the end, the solution was to expand the pie rather than to divide it up, but a critical part of this ultimate success lay in the ability to move around and past a potential deadlock by refusing to engage the issue on these terms. There was clearly an ongoing pattern of give-and-take from both sides, as well as a sidestepping of apparently intractable issues that could not be handled by smaller exchanges. The mediator reframed demands and found new ways to think about them to bypass the obvious conflicts of interest. Particular strategies of this kind are clearly essential aspects of the consensus building process.

The author raises concerns at the end about the role he played in this situation. He clearly was neither "neutral" nor committed to carrying out his employer's agenda. Instead, he appears to be committed to an idea of justice that recognizes past injuries against the Haida and their historic rights in the region. He is also committed to an idea of effectiveness that assumes that unless the local group participates in making the agreement, it will be hard to implement. His concerns suggest a way to think about the "neutrality" of mediators. It is possible to see the mediator as neutral toward the parties in a personal sense yet committed to the norms of the community as a whole and to its sense of justice. This commitment may lead the mediator to favor the interests of one group over another. Anthropological accounts of mediation in many parts of the world indicate that mediators are typically respected, senior individuals who stand for the sense of justice and normative ordering of the entire community. They can mediate among groups with whom they have ongoing social ties because their primary commitment is to the normative system of the whole community rather than to the interests of any particular group.

Applying this model to a legally plural situation such as the one described in this case study is clearly more difficult. There is a Canadian normative system and sense of justice, a Haida one, and probably a distinctive, local Euro-Canadian one. Perhaps the story-telling episodes that involved rethinking history and the past relations among these groups were crucial because they provided opportunities to bridge the gaps between the ideas of justice within each community. This process helped to create a shared vision of justice for all of them. On the basis of this shared vision, it was possible to establish and implement the agreement. Even the Canadian government came to accept this vision since the government agreed to pay the promised trust funds plus additional money for the harbor project.

In this situation, as in much of the rest of the world, mediator neutrality meant commitment to a larger sense of justice rather than merely to maintaining equal distance between the two parties. And in this situation, as in much of the rest of the world, the long-term commitment of the mediator to the community, evidenced by his sustained residence in the community, was critical to achieving this stance.

—Sally Engle Merry, *Anthropologist*

■ Notes

1. The ownership of the lands by the province actually was and remains as of the late 1990s in dispute with the Haida Nation. As subsequent discussion in this chapter will indicate, this is a major point of contention between the Haida and other parties, especially the senior governments.

2. In Canada, the term *reserves* is used equivalently to *reservations* in the United States.

3. One key provision of the SMA regarding these expenditures was that "certain initiative projects" were to be undertaken, including a recreational harbor to be built at Sandspit (South Moresby Agreement, Part II, Section 32[1][a]). This community had been the leading opponent of creating a park due to fears of economic losses when logging ceased in South Moresby. The harbor was its compensation. The question of how this commitment would affect the overall funding for the Islands became one of the most stubborn issues throughout the planning of the Gwaii Trust. This difficulty will be considered in the text below.

■ *References*

Barbeau, M. (1953). *Haida myths illustrated in argillite carvings.* Bulletin No. 127. Anthropological Series No. 32. Ottawa: National Museum of Canada.

Cassidy, F., & Dale, N. (1988). *After Native claims?* Lantzville, BC, Canada: Oolichan.

Drucker, P. (1965). *Cultures of the north Pacific coast.* San Francisco: Chandler.

Duff, W. (1964). *The Indian history of British Columbia: Vol. 1. The impact of the white man.* Victoria, Canada: Provincial Museum.

Fisher, R. (1977). *Contact and conflict: Indian-European relations in British Columbia, 1774-1890.* Vancouver: University of British Columbia Press.

Mercredi, O., & Turpel, M. E. (1993). *In the rapids: Navigating the future of First Nations.* Toronto, Canada: Viking.

Randall, W. L. (1995). *The stories we are.* Toronto, Canada: University of Toronto Press.

Said, E. (1975). *Beginnings: Intentions and method.* New York: Basic Books.

11

THE CHATTANOOGA PROCESS
A City's Vision Is Realized

■ John Parr

O ver the past 10 years, Chattanooga has become a much-cited
example of successful collaborative, consensus-based decision making and
action. An in-depth look at Chattanooga in
1996 uncovered a community that aspires
to a different way of doing business. This
case study focuses on the Chattanooga
Process, in which citizens are engaged at
multiple levels of policy planning and
implementation. Over the past 15 years,
Chattanooga has worked at both the institutional and personal levels to help citizens
internalize a more inclusive, cooperative
approach to civic decision making. The
Chattanooga region is not free of prob-

lems, but it has pioneered techniques that
in most places are only talked about.

This case study will begin with a brief
snapshot of Chattanooga today, then travel
back in time to provide context and key
historical moments. Through different avenues, the city's character and formative
influences will be described—by definition,
an imprecise task. What is the Chattanooga
Process, and how did it happen? After exploring the city's centerpiece, Vision 2000,
this case study reviews Chattanooga's ongoing challenges and accomplishments and
concludes with a section on lessons for
other cities.

The research for this case study was conducted by the James MacGregor Burns Academy of Leadership at the
University of Maryland as part of its project titled "Boundary Crossers: Community Leadership in a Global
Age." Copies may be obtained from the Burns Academy of Leadership, 301-405-5751.

■ *Chattanooga versus Urban Sprawl*

In 1995, Chattanooga citizens were becoming increasingly disenchanted with the character of real estate development. During the past two decades, the area had seen a 12 percent increase in population—and a 93 percent increase in land gobbled up by development. Ann Coulter, executive director of the Regional Planning Agency, realized that people in the region were frustrated, but unaware of other options. All seemed resigned to a future clogged with traffic jams and urban sprawl. Community leaders anticipated that an attempt to change development standards would generate resistance, unless new ideas were presented in a way that was easily understood. ••

∽ COMMENTARY

The assumptions of this writer are that growth should be regulated by a regional planning agency that can overcome opposition to regulation by presenting "new ideas . . . in a way that was easily understood." This view suggests that there is an unarticulated consensus that land should not be gobbled up by developers and that "urban sprawl" does not serve the needs for affordable housing, dispersed school districts (which means more local control), and new health care facilities out of the central city among other social services.

—Mark Kishlansky, *Historian*

Ann Coulter took an approach typical of the *Chattanooga Process* (a term coined by the author). Coulter is a long-term resident of Chattanooga, who absorbed this city's culture through volunteer activities. The story of her approach to development in Chattanooga illustrates both the community's "modus operandi" and a related fact: that for its residents, collaborative problem solving is almost second nature.

First, planners involved residents at the beginning stages of policy formulation and development—not with a public hearing or an invitation to look at completed maps, but by asking citizens to participate directly and interactively. In addition to written questionnaires, planners used visual preference surveys, in which participants are asked to rank pictures of different types of developments. More than 2,500 people participated in sessions conducted at major employment centers, neighborhood groups, civic and professional organizations, and public library branches or through television broadcasts and video copies. The Regional Planning Agency used national consultants to assist them, but primarily relied on the local public to guide their work. ••

☞ COMMENTARY

The use of outreach techniques like the visual preference survey enables ordinary citizens to have input into planning decisions at an early stage, but the tabulation of the preferences of 2,500 citizens is not the same as developing a consensus. It is noteworthy that this process identified the important constituency as individuals rather than as interest groups in Chattanooga (although we are not told how the preferences in the visual preference surveys that individuals ranked were initially established). Presumably, they represented realistic alternatives that coincided with vested interests within the planning, environmental, and development communities. Nor is it clear how choosing from among a number of predetermined developments relies on the ideas of the local public.

—Mark Kishlansky, *Historian*

The second step has been the incorporation of survey results in an updated, comprehensive, long-range plan by the Regional Planning Agency. The third step will be to use the plan to rewrite zoning and other regulations. In this manner, future development should be consistent with the preferences expressed by a broad cross section of residents. This process takes a number of years to execute, but is thought to minimize controversy and acrimony in the long run.

In Chattanooga, this commonsense, reasonable approach is not mere theory, but established practice: the vehicle for solving problems over and over for the past two decades. From recovering the river to revitalizing the downtown to creating affordable housing, Chattanooga's list of collaboratively solved problems is impressive.

■ *A Bit of History*

A thumbnail sketch of Chattanooga's history, decade by decade, provides context for this city's ambitious vision. After the Civil War, soldiers from the North noted the city's central location and its train and river access and envisioned rich industrial possibilities. They were not disappointed: Deposits of coal, iron, and clay were soon discovered and exploited. Today, many wealthy families are descendants of Yankees who emigrated to Chattanooga to seek their fortunes.

In the 1930s, Chattanooga became the site of the Tennessee Valley Authority headquarters. This event brought electricity, as well as a spurt of economic growth. Later, the city's fortunes took a turn; in the 1950s, its population growth was slow compared with similar-sized cities in the South. While Chattanooga grew 15 percent, Nashville grew 24 percent, and Columbia, South Carolina grew 40 percent. ☞

By 1960, Chattanooga had the highest percentage of its workforce in manufacturing of any Southern city, and a paucity of white-collar jobs. While the Sun Belt expansion led to booms in Southern cities in the 1960s and 1980s, Chattanooga failed to benefit. Most disturbingly, the city endured increasingly contentious race relations. A damaging controversy over school busing rocked the city, and a 1971 race riot resulted in the death of one African American resident and injuries to many more. In 1980, an all-white jury acquitted two Ku Klux Klan members of shooting four African American women, and several businesses were firebombed. Chattanooga continues to have strong concentrations of African Americans and poor Appalachian whites. Chattanoogans, like most Americans, encounter socioeconomic and racial divides as they work to develop community programs and projects.

Beginning in the 1980s, neighborhood leaders regrouped, determined to improve Chattanooga's image and diversify its economy. Chattanooga is a popular tourist destination, a retail and distribution center, and one of the South's major industrial cities.

■ *Origins of Chattanooga's Collaborative Approach*

In 1969, a young Jim Brown was eating dinner with his parents when he heard a television news broadcast. Walter Cronkite stated that Chattanooga had received a dubious distinction: Its air quality was the worst of any city in the United States. Chattanooga's air was dangerously polluted in a number of categories: ozone, particulates, and nitrous oxides from the production of TNT at the Volunteer Ammunition Plant.

The federal Department of Health, Education and Welfare (a division of it was a precursor of the Environmental Protection Agency) suggested an Air Pollution Control Board. But Chattanooga did something special. Key industrial and civic leaders not only set up a control board but also started a major effort to educate the public on health issues. The entire community responded, supporting tough changes and accepting the impact these restrictions had on the local economy. Within five years, Chattanooga had met or exceeded all air quality standards.

Council member David Crockett described the air pollution problem as a "heart attack" for the community. In retrospect, Chattanoogans see the disciplined, proactive response as setting the tone for much that has taken place in Chattanooga over the past 20 years. Leaders got together, announced the problem, and helped the populace develop a local solution. In this way, Chattanooga created an air quality board and made large investments in new technologies. Today, as other cities whine about federal standards and then fall short, Chattanooga is in compliance with every federal air quality standard. ∞

∞ COMMENTARY

The analysis of how Chattanooga responded to its air pollution problem is made in terms of the will of the community developed by education on public health issues. Why this should have worked in Chattanooga is not specified. The closing of the Volunteer Ammunition Plant was obviously the single largest contributor to clearer air in the region, and the loss of manufacturing jobs another. Neither can be traced directly to the will of the community to solve the problem posed by air pollution. The assertion that "leaders got together, announced the problem, and helped the populace develop a local solution" again suggests that goodwill is sufficient to solve difficult, often intractable, problems. The author believes that individuals such as Jim Brown rather than structured processes of problem solving were decisive in the Chattanooga experience.

—Mark Kishlansky, *Historian*

Brown, like numerous other Chattanoogans, has made a personal commitment to improving the region's quality of life. He serves as executive director of the Tennessee River Gorge Trust, an organization that has protected 14,000 acres since its inception. He has developed programs to get young people, particularly minorities, involved in preservation and restoration programs. Like numerous other Chattanooga residents, Brown volunteers for a range of task forces and committees.

The exemplary management of the air quality issue and the dedication of people like Jim Brown provide clues to understanding Chattanooga's present-day success. However, there is one final chapter to this story: the Moccasin Bend Task Force. While it may seem remarkable that a river

revitalization organization would have an impact on an entire community, this group's commitment to finding a civic process that worked had unforeseen ramifications.

By the end of the 1970s, Chattanooga was in a recession, factories were obsolete, and offshore production was sapping the city's economic lifeblood. There was no plan for the community's future. A handful of community leaders including Rick Montague, director of the Lyndhurst Foundation, future mayor Gene Roberts, and future city council member Mai Bell Hurley sought information about how other communities were pulling themselves together.

At the time, Rick was the citizen chair of the Moccasin Bend Task Force. This group was preparing a plan to revitalize the riverfront; by chance, their consultants, Carl Lynch and Associates of Cambridge, placed a strong emphasis on public participation. Consequently, Eleanor Cooper, a local, was brought on board to help facilitate the outreach and involvement. The task force held more than 65 public meetings. "We went to wherever people were: We didn't ask them to come to our meetings, we went to them," said Montague.

As the Moccasin Bend master plan was being developed, a subgroup began research on cities that were successfully negotiating challenges similar to Chattanooga's. They identified Indianapolis, and put together the first of the city trips that were to become standard. Travelers included business leaders, local elected officials, and foundation and nonprofit leaders. During the visit, the 25-year-old Greater Indianapolis Progress Committee (GIPC) caught the attention of the delegation. This nationally recognized committee was started by a group of private sector leaders who felt Indianapolis needed a mechanism for reaching consensus on civic issues. When the small group of Chattanoogans returned, they resolved to create a similar organization. The result of their efforts was Chattanooga Venture. ∞

∞ COMMENTARY

One important contribution to the Chattanooga Process was the use of outside consultants and the willingness of local leaders to adapt programs from other communities rather than to rely on local traditions and historical arrangements. The use of established consulting firms like Lynch and Associates and the appropriating of Indianapolis's task force approach to local problems was a key development. The fact that the initiative was taken by private citizens directing a community-based foundation was also significant. Nongovernmental organizations (NGOs) played a crucial role in the revitalization of Chattanooga, and many of the original foundation leaders ultimately became part of city government.

—Mark Kishlansky, *Historian*

Chattanooga Venture's last major project was the 1993-1994 ReVision 2000, which created a new set of goals for the community. The principles they adopted reflect Chattanooga's evolving community ethos:

- Create a process open to all.
- Recognize and preserve every idea.
- Rely on the wisdom of the community.

- Respect both the simplicities and complexities of the community.
- Eliminate barriers to sincere and honest dialogue.
- Understand the strengths and limitations of community building.
- Seek workable solutions.
- Insist on diversity.
- Accept responsibility for the consequences of the vision.
- Promote trust.

The following section will explore the current factors contributing to Chattanooga's progressive community vision. These factors include the interaction of government, business, and civic involvement; broad-based training in facilitation; the role of the media; and involving young people in community activities.

■ *The Three-Legged Stool of Civic Infrastructure*

Former senator Bill Bradley, now chair of the National Civic League, describes civic infrastructure by using the analogy of a three-legged stool. All communities have a business sector, government institutions, and a civic sector. For a community to be healthy and stable, argues Bradley, all "legs" must be more or less the same length. That is, it takes more than just good elected officials, strong business leadership, or active citizens alone for a community to effectively cope with change. The following section explores how Chattanooga has built on its strengths in each of these areas.

Business: Leading the Charge toward Sustainability

At first blush, Jim Vaughn seems the typical Type-A personality: career chamber of commerce president; conservatively dressed, gregarious, with a quick smile and a hand out to greet you. His office, though, holds clues to the contrary. In one corner is Al Gore's *Nature in Balance;* on another

shelf rests David Rusk's *Cities without Suburbs.* These books are not just for show; Vaughn has read and understood them. "We are going to build the future of Chattanooga by balancing the economy, ecology, and equity," he says with conviction, and it's hard to find a reason to doubt him.

The specific actions of the Chattanooga Chamber of Commerce give substance to Vaughn's claims. The largest business organization in the region, the chamber is responsible for a number of initiatives:

1. In 1996, it devoted its annual planning session to urban sprawl. The chamber supports a change of ordinances and codes to encourage mixed-use and infill development and to reduce the amount of parking lot creation.

2. It opposed highway widening in the downtown area and pushed the state transportation department to fund impact studies of such proposals.

3. It supported a half-cent sales tax for economic development and schools, approved by the voters in 1996. The tax paved the way for redeveloping the city's South Side and a former U.S. Army ammunition plant. Both locations are earmarked for companies involved in environmental technologies.

4. It opposed new wood chip mills on environmental grounds.

5. It supported new state university programs for a master's degree in environmental sciences and a doctoral degree in environmental engineering. ➥

∽ COMMENTARY

The role of the Chattanooga Chamber of Commerce is stressed in demonstrating that it has not always acted in ways associated with business interests but rather appears to have attempted to balance business and community needs. What is unclear is why a group devoted to optimizing business interests would take what is regarded as an enlightened stance on development and environmental issues.

—Mark Kishlansky, *Historian*

An example of business community action is RiverValley Partners, Inc., a public-private partnership that performs economic development recruitment and expansion activities. Its promotional materials outline a broad range of community initiatives, from low-income housing development to downtown's electric buses to riverfront projects. It also has recruited environmentally conscious industry—and this search paid off. DuPont, for example, expanded operations even as it closed plants in other communities around the country.

The electric buses downtown exemplify the entrepreneurial approach of businesspeople in Chattanooga. The community decided that a key to downtown revitalization was the availability of free shuttle buses. Concern about air quality made traditional diesel buses problematic; the community looked into electric buses and found they were manufactured in only one place in the nation. Thus, Advanced Vehicle Systems, Inc. (AVS) was created in Chattanooga. AVS is now one of three electric bus manufacturers in the United States and ranks number one in sales.

Civic: The Network of Collaborators and Consensus Builders

A discussion of community in Chattanooga must begin with Chattanooga Venture. To prepare for the turn of the century, government, business, and civic leaders created Chattanooga Venture in 1984. They hoped to engage the larger community in shaping the city's future.

Chattanooga Venture could be described as a *community-building intermediary,* a term coined by Angela Glover Blackwell, former head of the Urban Strategies Council in Oakland, California and now head of Policy-Link. A handful of these organizations exist around the country, and they demonstrate the following key properties:

- Ability to convene diverse factions around a problem-solving agenda.
- Capacity for quick impact, due to experienced, independent leadership and a staff of talented generalists.
- Desire to engage community residents at many levels.
- Focus on systems change, with a recognition that recommendations are not enough and concrete resources are necessary for reform to succeed.
- The energy to start new ventures and provide staffing to get these organizations up and running.

Chattanooga Venture is now housed at Chattanooga State Technical Community College. The board meets every quarter to determine whether Venture should once again go to work on a specific issue. Serving as Venture's home is important for the college, says its president, Dr. James Catanzaro: "I am always trying to figure out how to merge the assets of the college with the assets and needs of the community." Though currently without a full-time staff or specific agenda, Chattanooga Venture could be returned to active duty with little trouble. ❧

❧ COMMENTARY

The use of Chattanooga Venture as an organization of intermediaries providing staff support and intellectual infrastructure for community-based initiatives is a vital component of the city's success in involving its citizens in community development. Its association with the local university is an innovative feature, especially as Chattanooga State is a regional college and many who come into contact with Chattanooga Venture as students will build on that experience as citizens. Well-developed community organizations make it easier for NGOs and government agencies to conduct two-way communication, to channel criticisms and complaints, and to involve community groups in early stages of planning.

—Mark Kishlansky, *Historian*

It could be argued that through its success, Venture put itself out of a job. The hundreds of programs, projects, and organizations Venture spawned and the lessons Chattanoogans learned from participation now form the basis of community operations. Gerri Spring, who ran a Neighborhood Network started by Venture, says, "Communities need a safe haven for ideas to germinate." A look around Chattanooga reveals receptiveness to new ideas in almost every organization in the community.

The foundation community, particularly the Lyndhurst Foundation, contributed significantly to these accomplishments. Each project described here has been dependent, in some fashion, on foundation resources. More important than money has been the Lyndhurst leadership. Rick Montague, the organization's first full-time executive director, recalls, "We were interested in Chattanooga's future, but we were concerned that people would feel that the agenda was all set and paid for by the foundations."

Lyndhurst helped start Chattanooga Venture and provided major underwriting of general operating costs. This was instrumental to Venture's success, according to Eleanor Cooper, Chattanooga Venture's executive director during its heyday. "Because of Lyndhurst's support of the operating budget, Venture wasn't beholden to anyone and it allowed it to put together an extremely diverse board of 60 people," says Cooper. Chattanooga did the visioning work so many communities have done across the country. The difference was, Chattanooga did this work more boldly and thoroughly than anyplace else in the country.

Government: The Caboose on the Civic Train

No one talks about government as a leader of the Chattanooga Process, but in fact this city's government has been a critical partner. Longtime mayor Gene Roberts, while not a creator of the Chattanooga Process, was consistently supportive. In fact, the collaborative Chattanooga Process permeated the city's bureaucracy and benefited from strong leadership from throughout the community.

City government's ability to work with the community is demonstrated in its approach to Parks and Recreation. Every aspect of this system is built on flexible partnerships. For example, neighborhood "sports associations" run a city ballpark, take care of scheduling, and are in charge of concessions. An OutVenture section offers affordable opportunities for young people and families to go canoeing, backpacking, hiking, and white-water rafting all over the southeast. In addition, the section offers "outward-bound" training for inner-city youth.

Over the next few years, an initiative will create a 75-mile network of greenways that links parks with each other and with the river. Larry Zehnder, deputy administrator of the Department of Parks and Recreation, directs this project, among others. He is a parks and recreation professional with 24 years of experience in cities throughout the southeastern United States. Zehnder's descriptions of these programs suggest a mix of community organizer and privatization advocate. About the greenway effort, for example, he says, "Citizens are driving this—they will make it happen, not us." Zehnder explains the department has no one on staff qualified to carry out the effort. But he sees no reason to panic. Instead, Zehnder contracts with the Trust for Public Lands to work with citizen task forces. He obtained funding from foundation and corporate sources.

Possibly one of the reasons there is so much activity outside city hall's domain is that until 1989, Chattanooga had an archaic commissioner form of government in which at-large elections chose people to run specific departments. This antiquated method was successfully challenged as violating the Voting Rights Act. While it has been rightfully replaced, frustration with this outmoded style may explain why there has been so much private activity. Today's governance system includes a nine-member council elected from districts, and a directly elected mayor. Four of the nine council members are African Americans, giving that community a strong voice in government.

The city council has two particularly outstanding members, Mai Bell Hurley and David Crockett. With her white hair and energetic style, Hurley evokes the quintessential "little old lady in tennis shoes." In fact, Hurley is a sophisticated activist who served as chair of the Chattanooga Venture board of directors during its early years. Now she brings that same aggressive yet collaborative style to the city council. Crockett, an early retiree from IBM, is best described as a civic entrepreneur. A fiscal conservative, he built a record of powerful solutions to challenges facing the community. Hurley and Crockett were the driving force behind a city charter amendment that consolidated the city school system into the county system—confronting a volatile issue with true political courage.

Any consideration of government in Chattanooga must include the federal government and the Tennessee Valley Authority (TVA). TVA staff have been key participants in projects related to the river and the environment; in addition, their construction of a large office downtown catalyzed revitalization and they helped with start-up grants for the electric bus effort. The staff at TVA seeks engagement within the community. TVA's Linda Harris is with the Clean Water Initiative, where she spends time in schools helping students understand the importance of clean water. In 1990, she organized the Earth Day celebration, attended by 10,000 people.

■ *Institutionalizing Consensus-Based Decision Making*

Collaborative problem solving is employed by almost all the institutions in Chattanooga. The success of the Chattanooga Venture initiative played a significant role in "spreading the gospel." Early on, key organizers realized that they could have long-term impact if they trained people in collaborative techniques.

Thus, 50 people received in-depth training and became part of a "facilitators bank." Similarly, more than 150 people were trained as facilitators for the ReVision Chattanooga effort. Participants were not only CEOs and government leaders but also "regular" citizens. As trained residents moved from organization to organization, and neighborhood to neighborhood, the techniques they learned traveled with them. By osmosis, people involved in Venture's projects learned the value of collaboration. ➥

➥ COMMENTARY

The use of facilitators and instruction in collaborative methods is one of the more innovative of the initiatives taken by Chattanooga Venture. Regrettably, we are not given an in-depth look at either the training process or the ways in which it operated to make collaboration rather than conflict the basic mode of community-based town planning.

—Mark Kishlansky, *Historian*

As we have seen, foundations also played a key role in institutionalizing collaborative problem solving. The Lyndhurst Foundation's funding decisions convey the message that collaborative initiatives deserve particular support. The Community Foundation of Greater Chattanooga's "Grant-Making Philosophy" contains the following statement: "Give priority to projects which utilize existing community resources and foster collaboration, communication, and cooperation."

Chattanooga has the standard leadership development programs, which introduce people to others they wouldn't normally meet and expose participants to community issues and institutions, but their programs also include training in facilitation. And one key to Chattanooga's success is that it has leaders everywhere. They are carrying out projects ranging from the Westside Community Development Corporation to downtown revitalization to the Family Violence Shelter—and importantly, they are not only the people officially at the top. Years of citizen-focused processes have cultivated an innate sense of how to build contacts and obtain resources for project start-up. According to Linda Harris of TVA, "A lot of mutual respect and trust has been built because so many of us have worked on so many different projects over the years. We don't have to ask if it is OK to contact someone—you just pick up the phone and do it."

■ The Media's Role in Consensus Building

Chattanooga has two dailies with a joint operating agreement. The papers do not aspire to civic or public journalism, but do provide solid coverage of events affecting the community, from elections to potential development projects. Pat Wilcox, managing editor of the *Chattanooga Times,* commented on the relationship of the paper to the community: "Leaders in Chattanooga are so creative at bringing in stimulating speakers and running highly participatory processes on issues that it is easy for the media to cover these activities and give our readers a real sense of what is happening." The *Times'* features on different neighborhoods appear in the news section, not relegated to "lifestyle," as is the practice by many papers elsewhere. In addition, the paper's editorial page promotes issues relating to sustainability and the environment.

There is a noticeable difference between the tone of news coverage in Chattanooga and that of other cities. Here is one example: The largest health care institution in Chattanooga is the privately owned Erlanger Medical Center. Early in 1997, the medical center downsized, cutting its work-force by almost 500 employees. In doing so, however, the center used a process that involved everyone from top administrators to doctors to service personnel. The front-page headline in the *Times* the next day was "Erlanger Shaves Work Force by 456." In most other places, more inflammatory language would have been used (e.g., by using *slashes* instead of *shaves*). The *Times,* like most of the rest of Chattanooga, is "with the program."

Overall, the media do not take a strong leadership role in the community. Their coverage of issues, however, promotes understanding of community debates, possible options, and how to get engaged, if people want to.

■ Bringing Young People to the Table

Most communities struggle with how to engage young people in community decision making. For communities to remain vital, some portion of leadership must come from within. In the 1970s, Rick Montague noticed that most of Chattanooga's bright young people were leaving for college and never coming back. At the time, he was teaching at a local private school; 18-year-old Chris Crimmons was one of his students. Increasingly concerned about Chattanooga's brain drain, Montague tried to convince Chris to stay in his hometown. Chris loved Chattanooga, but at that time, all he and his friends wanted to see was this city's disappearance in the rearview mirror. They wanted a life where there was opportunity and excitement. Montague prevailed, however, and soon Crimmons was a key leader of RiverValley Partners, Inc., a public-private partnership dedicated to the Tennessee River front.

Perceptions have changed in Chattanooga. Today, most young people don't think about moving away—as demonstrated by the following interchange at the School of the Arts and Sciences. Eight student leaders of various races were asked where they planned to be in 10 years. All but one immediately answered, "Chattanooga." The lone dissenter said, "Hey, I'm only a freshman! I don't know what I'm going to do with my life." More typical was a student who confidently predicted her life path. She would go to medical school, and then return as a pediatrician. In 10 years, she would be practicing medicine in a facility that would include a day care center.

When pushed about their feelings, students talk about being involved in the community. For example, students ran the largest forum for candidates during the spring 1997 city elections. Students also describe being asked to serve on advisory committees and to design programs targeting youth. Adults have tried to set the following example: Work collaboratively, be inclusive, work hard, and have fun.

■ The Chattanooga Process and Vision 2000

This section explores the Chattanooga Process and Vision 2000 in greater detail. ❖

∽ COMMENTARY

The Chattanooga Process described here is certainly inspiring. The basic program of business, civic, government, and foundation collaboration in developing priorities and locating leaders to carry them through seems to be the key feature. Involving young people is another key principle. It would be intriguing to find out how it works in practice. How does it deal with the differences in priorities and preferences that inevitably emerge? How are leaders located and encouraged? How are decisions made, particularly when different interest groups have different views? Bringing people with different priorities together is clearly a first step, but how these people interact and make decisions is critically important. Perhaps one clue to the way the process functioned in practice is the observation that potential leaders are invited to participate in goal setting early in the process so that they can help to set the goals and feel more "ownership" of the process.

—Sally Engle Merry, *Anthropologist*

An analysis of the successes of Chattanooga since the late 1970s unearths a set of themes conducive to civic business. Here are some key components of the Chattanooga Process, in the words of various Chattanoogans:

- "Any idea is worth exploring. At the beginning, all possibilities get a respectful hearing."
- "Success will occur if we all sit down and put our heads together; that way, we can reach a common agenda."

- "There must always be a specific, but open-ended, agenda for public participation."
- "The collective good is always the goal, and that means the good of *all* citizens."
- "Preventing future problems and creating systemic change are always priorities in the process."

- "We always bring in the best people in the country to speak, advise, and participate."
- "When necessary, we visit other communities that have been successful to find out the nuances of how and why a solution worked there, and what to avoid." ∞

∞ COMMENTARY

The "key components of the Chattanooga Process" are a list of commonsense principles for establishing trust and goodwill on the part of participants. How they operate in specific, complex problem solving remains unclear. "Any idea is worth exploring" is a principle of respect, especially toward nonprofessionals and ordinary citizens, but its limits are quickly reached in any real-life situation. Given budget and scheduling constraints and the complexities of urban planning, few ideas are worth exploring even if many can be heard. "The collective good is always the goal" is a principle that assumes there is a single collective good that can be agreed on, though it is conflict over what constitutes the good of the commonwealth that is at the root of most intractable problems. Part of the charm of the Chattanooga Process is that it does not recognize intractable problems: "Success will occur if we all sit down and put our heads together."

—Mark Kishlansky, *Historian*

Chattanooga has taken processes and approaches used by other communities and maximized their power. This has occurred through institutionalizing progressive concepts, and helping citizens integrate these concepts into their everyday activities. Conversations with residents ranging from high school students to business leaders result in an eerie feeling: All appear to have the same computer chip implanted in their brains.

As described above, Chattanooga makes decisions by involving a broad base of people to help define, and then solve, a problem. The best example of this kind of collaboration is the initial work of Chat-

tanooga Venture's Vision 2000 in 1984. This group's impact has been truly astonishing, as the facts and figures below reveal.

Vision 2000's major goals were as follows:

Development of the riverfront
Revitalization of the downtown
Advancement in human relations
Improved public education
More affordable housing stock
Improved cultural facilities
City elections by district
Environmental initiatives

Increased job opportunities

Positive community image

Accomplishments in response to these goals include

The Tennessee RiverPark

Chattanooga Neighborhood Enterprise

Family Violence Shelter

Human Rights/Human Relations Commission

Tivoli and Memorial Auditorium renovations

Tennessee Aquarium

Walnut Street Bridge restoration

The statistical breakdown of Vision 2000 activities is also impressive:

Total number of projects/programs: 223

Total number of jobs created: 1,381

Related construction jobs: 7,300

Total number of people served: 1,551,000

Total financial investment: $793,303,813

With a population of 285,536 in Hamilton County, Vision 2000 investment amounts to $2,778 per person, with private investment at $2,083 and public investment at $695. More than 1,700 people participated, resulting in a community Commitment Portfolio of 40 goals for the city by the year 2000. Vision 2000 was a broad-based, public participation process in which diverse citizens were asked the following key question: "What are your goals, hopes, and dreams for Chattanooga?"

Many communities have attempted similar efforts without Chattanooga Venture's results. What was different here? The answer lies in techniques of implementation. Chattanooga Venture used the goals outlined by its citizens as a road map to determine what projects, task forces, and fledgling organizations it would help create. Chattanooga Venture was not the implementer, but often served as an incubator for interested people to get a project started. By 1992, of Venture 2000's 40 goals, 37 had been either completed or partially completed. The public embraced the effort, as did the region's leaders, and public-private partnerships formed with an eye toward making the visions reality. In 1992, Chattanooga Venture conceived of ReVision 2000 and again invited the community to offer its ideas. This time, citizens responded even more readily, encouraged by the successes of the past several years.

More than 2,600 people participated in ReVision 2000, generating 2,559 ideas in nine community meetings. These ideas were translated into 27 goals and 122 recommendations in a second round of five community meetings. Will Chattanooga blaze through with the same spirit of achievement that marked Vision 2000? In Chattanooga these days, no one is betting against it.

■ *Chattanooga: Challenges and Accomplishments*

The Chattanooga region has not openly tackled the issues of race and economic disparity. However, the Chattanooga Process has been used to both involve a variety of residents of different races and socioeconomic groups and help minority and disenfranchised populations. For example, the Westside Community Development

Corporation (WCDC) operates in the African American neighborhood on the edge of downtown. Initially a partnership between public housing residents and the Junior League of Chattanooga, WCDC has an aggressive agenda of job creation and retention, small-business development, job training, and child care development. •◦

◦• COMMENTARY

Although issues of race relations were identified early as one of the challenges that faced Chattanooga, little in Chattanooga Venture was directly related to these problems. The Vision 2000 goal of eliminating substandard housing as well as creating zones of affordable housing was not race specific although it did aid the black community. We have no information as to how many African Americans participated in either Vision or ReVision 2000 or how their distinct interests were met by the Chattanooga Process. It is instructive that few private venture initiatives involved education and local schooling, other than the establishment of a college scholarship program for low-income students. Local schools are one vital area in which government cannot be the "caboose on the civic train," and it would be interesting to learn if the techniques developed to address other community-based problems have had a positive effect on schooling.

—Mark Kishlansky, *Historian*

In 1996, the organization transformed a closed school into a community center for agencies and community-based organizations. It also developed a venture with Midland Foods of Memphis to train residents in concessions. With their new skills, residents will be employed at food cart businesses at the RiverPark.

Foundations, private sector organizations, and government agencies contributed to the success of these ventures. Not surprisingly, WCDC's annual meeting drew a gym full of people from these entities. From their demeanor and interaction with others, it was clear that their visit was not pro forma.

Vision 2000 identified affordable housing as a key issue facing the community. To help educate the community, James Rouse of the Enterprise Foundation was brought to town as a consultant. In 1986, community and neighborhood leaders created a new institution inspired by his ideas: Chattanooga Neighborhood Enterprise, Inc. (CNE). This nonprofit organization focuses on providing all Chattanoogans with appropriate and affordable housing. It aims to eliminate substandard housing through the development, financing, renovation, and management of decent facilities in low- and moderate-income neighborhoods. Between 1986 and 1996, the organization invested more than $100 million, and over 3,000 units were produced or rehabilitated. CNE is the rental property owner/manager for more than 300 units; its homeownership education programs have reached over 1,500 families. CNE currently serves over 40 new families a month.

There has been a conscious effort to ensure that new public spaces do not become identified as "turf" for any particular ethnic group. On the river are fishing programs; here, older African American men teach young people of every background how to fish. Music, arts, and cultural festivals celebrate all races and cultures. A Saturday afternoon spent at the RiverPark will find visitors of all ages and races.

Young people have a prominent place on the agenda. Together We Can is a program sponsored by the Community Foundation of Greater Chattanooga in cooperation with city government and the public school system. Any low-income student who graduates in accordance with a certain minimum standard from a Chattanooga high school is eligible for a scholarship to a higher-education institution. As of fall 1996, 165 students were attending college with assistance from this scholarship. That number will increase dramatically as the fund's principle reaches $21 million in 1999.

Chattanooga's chapter of the Urban League facilitates policy development in the areas of children, race relations, and empowerment. The Urban League's broad range of activities includes pre- and post-purchase homeownership counseling, pot-luck dinners with other racial and ethnic groups, and sensitivity training for teachers around racial issues. Eighty-three-year-old George Key serves on the boards of the Urban League, Chattanooga Venture, and a number of other nonprofits. He speaks with excitement about Chattanooga's direction, because "we have people from all walks of life, including the power structure, working together to make sure that job opportunities keep increasing and race relations keep improving."

■ Following in Chattanooga's Footsteps

Chattanooga's lessons are transferable to other communities, in part because city leaders have carefully documented their work. At last count, delegations from more than 90 cities and countries have come to witness accomplishments in Chattanooga and to examine how goals became a reality.

Chattanoogans often modestly ascribe their success to their small size: 150,000 in Chattanooga and 300,000 in the region. Jim Brown sees Chattanooga as a place that is "small enough to know each other, and big enough to pull the resources together." Undoubtedly, size makes the going a little easier, but the elements of the Chattanooga Process could be used anywhere. Luckily for the rest of us, Chattanoogans love to share the "secrets" of their approach.

One such secret: Chattanoogans work tremendously hard to get the right people at the table before the visioning and consensus building starts. Mai Bell Hurley describes her encounter with a young entrepreneurial businessman who wanted to give something back to the community. Immediately, she invited him to participate in Vision 2000. When affordable housing became a priority, this businessman used his skills to create Chattanooga Neighborhood Enterprises. Too often, communities have to mobilize people *after* goals have been specified—usually without much public input. Without ownership of the process, it is unlikely that people will participate in implementation.

Eleanor Cooper points out three strategies critical to collaborative community problem solving:

- Involve both leadership and grass roots at every stage.
- Continuously educate the community about new approaches.
- Make the process experiential (people learn more from walking on the Riverwalk than from hearing a consultant give a speech about riverfront development).

Of course, no city operates without some rancor and competition. But community involvement and participatory planning are not hollow phrases in Chattanooga. They are, instead, the basis for important community decisions. In many communities, the message is: "Don't rock the boat." Success is achieved by allowing the power structure (a few men in a back room!) to remain intact. In Chattanooga, however, success has been redefined. Young professionals are "rewarded" if they can apply the principles of Chattanooga Venture to their organizations.

In the words of Chattanooga City Council member David Crockett, citizens want a community "that is cleaner, greener, and safer; that values human and natural resources; and that provides an economic system that will keep our children here." In Chattanooga, that vision was jointly created and implemented by government, business, and nonprofits, resulting in literally hundreds of completed projects.

Rick Montague says, "Every community needs a place where people with different agendas can come together to share ideas and work together." Chattanooga seems to have designated a number of such places. More important, this community has brought to life a true culture of collaboration. ❧

❧ COMMENTARY

Can this process be replicated elsewhere? Involving grassroots people along with business, government, and foundation leaders in goal setting and program development was a key part of the process in Chattanooga and clearly can be done in other cities. But did it also take the sense of despair and the 1970s crisis in air quality to galvanize leaders to change? Was an economic transformation of the region necessary to fuel the developments in urban planning and housing? Would this have worked equally well with a less supportive media establishment? These contextual features of history, economy, politics, and culture are critically important in the anthropological analysis of a process of this kind.

There are indications in the case study that the situation in Chattanooga was not entirely unique. Chattanooga drew on the experience of other towns such as Indianapolis and is now widely sought out as an example. The collaboration of business, government, foundations, and grassroots people has clearly been successful here, and such grassroots collaboration has succeeded in other towns as well. Clearly, this process can be replicated in other cities, even though the details will vary with the local situation. A thorough and detailed social analysis is necessary to decide when and where it is possible to use this vaguely defined Chattanooga Process.

—Sally Engle Merry, *Anthropologist*

FROM CITY HALL TO THE STREETS

A Community Plan
Meets the Real World

■ Kate Connolly

> According to the premises of strategic planning, the world is sup-
> posed to hold still while a plan is being developed and then stay on
> the predicted course while that plan is being implemented.
>
> —Henry Mintzberg, "The Fall and Rise of Strategic Planning"
> (1994, p. 110)

The premises of strategic planning are often at odds with the way the real world works. Indeed, it is not uncommon to see a strategic plan just "sit on the shelf" without proceeding to the implementation stage. Worse still, a strategic plan may reach the implementation stage even though the priorities it outlines are so broad they are almost impossible to carry out. Just how challenging a well-intentioned plan can be is evidenced in this case study, which re-counts my firsthand experience with the attempts of a small city in Canada to implement its community-based economic development strategy.

The objectives of the strategic plan I helped implement involved the improvement of many aspects of life in the city of Middletown.[1] They ranged from the revitalization of Middletown's downtown areas and the development of its physical infrastructure to the enhancement of the city's human services and the strengthening of its transit system. The plan's objectives were to be accomplished through a bold new collaboration among community organizations, the corporate sector, and government quite unlike anything the city had seen.

Despite some successes, the final results fell far short of what city officials had hoped to achieve. Nevertheless, Middletown learned critical lessons from its experiment with strategic planning that continue to inform its economic development efforts. These lessons may be particularly useful for other municipal officials and community leaders struggling to improve the quality of life in their towns.

■ The Need for a Strategic Plan

Middletown is a city of approximately 100,000 people. A variety of ethnocultural groups, including immigrants from European countries such as Germany, Poland, and Portugal as well as from Far Eastern countries such as the Philippines, make up the city's current demographic profile. Originally settled by the Scottish in the late eighteenth century as the three communities of Oakdale, Johnstown, and Palmyra, the area was consolidated into the city of Middletown in the early 1970s. Because this consolidation was provincially legislated (i.e., at the state level) and did not come about through a mandate of local support, many of Middletown's residents still harbor loyalties to the smaller communities to which they trace their historic roots. With its many parks and trails, and its rivers forming natural corridors throughout the city, Middletown has retained at least some of the small-town atmosphere that characterized its constituent communities.

Inevitably, as Middletown moved into the 1990s, concerns about the environment, the economy, transportation, and the impacts of growth began to surface. After going through a painful restructuring in the 1970s and 1980s during which the city shifted its primary economic base away from manufacturing (the production of textiles had been a mainstay for the community) and toward high-tech industries, Middletown found that although more jobs had been created, these jobs required education and training that many of its residents lacked. Furthermore, an underdeveloped retail sector provided workers with few alternatives for employment after a number of manufacturing plants closed down.

As a result, unemployment rose while opportunities for youth dwindled. Crime, too, became a growing concern. Compounding these problems were increasing pollution and a lack of unity among the three original communities. Clearly, the city needed a broad-based strategy for improvement.

■ Championing the Creation of a Strategic Plan

One group that recognized Middletown's growing struggles was the Economic Development Advisory Committee (EDAC) to the Middletown City Council. EDAC's members were mostly residents involved in industry, business, and commerce who had been appointed to the committee by the city council as volunteers. Members of EDAC had no voting rights on the city council, but were expected to make informed recommendations to the council about economic matters involving the entire community.

For the members of EDAC, most, if not all, of the community's problems were related in some way to Middletown's economic health. What their city needed, EDAC members believed, was a long-term economic development strategy that relied on the active leadership of community organizations from all three towns, such as neighborhood associations, human service agencies, arts groups, civic clubs, and the like. That the strategy should be community based seemed like a logical choice, since Middletown had a rich history of community involvement and leadership. On March 22, 1993, the Middletown City Council unanimously adopted a recommendation to prepare the city's first community-based economic development strategy.

The strategy was built on the idea of *partnership development,* which meant that the Middletown City Council and the community at large would share responsibility for the development and implementation of the plan. The city council was to coordinate the overall initiative, while community organizations would be responsible for the actual planning, funding, and implementation of concrete economic development projects. Partnership development also meant that community organizations would work with one another and with the private sector to achieve the plan's goals, sharing costs and resources. Never before had community groups in Middletown been expected to take up so much responsibility for economic development. The following quote (from a press release sent to local and regional newspapers by the city council prior to its adopting the recommendation) hints at the community's new responsibilities:

> We are facing significant challenges today. Resources are stretched, and simply increasing taxes and revenues to meet increased expectations is not possible in today's economic climate. In this environment, the need for community-based goals and objectives is critical in making our city an outstanding community. We believe this process will be crucial to our success in the future.

At this point in the process, the city council approved funds to have a strategic plan developed, anticipating that some additional funding would be provided through a provincial grant. The next step was for EDAC to work with community representatives from all three "core" (downtown) areas of Middletown to determine the specifics of the plan.

■ Developing the Plan

In fall 1993, EDAC members formed a volunteer steering committee, the Community Leaders Roundtable (CLR), that would help develop the official strategic plan. They also hired an outside consultant to work with the CLR. Comprising participants from more than 50 community organizations, CLR members represented a broad cross section of the city's special interest groups, including organized labor, education, tourism, neighborhood associations, seniors, the environment, industry, faith communities, the chamber of commerce, human service agencies, real estate, the arts, health, agriculture, disability issues, and sports.

To ensure that the residents of Middletown knew about, understood, and contributed to the development of the strategic plan, EDAC staged televised phone-in shows with Mayor Susan Hudson, public forums, and town hall meetings that allowed residents to ask questions and voice their opinions. It also sent a survey to residents asking questions about the quality of life in Middletown and led brainstorming sessions with various community groups on the same questions asked in the survey.

The CLR reviewed all the input gathered from approximately 600 residents and many community organizations and created draft action plans that were to inform the final economic development plan. It also held a series of weekend workshops during which its members, elected representatives of the Middletown City Council, and department heads from the municipal bureaucracy contributed to the draft action plans. It was during these weekend workshops that the visioning process occurred and CLR members began articulating their excitement about the plan. A writing committee appointed by EDAC then took the suggestions that emerged from the CLR and drafted a final plan, named Our Common Future (OCF), for submission to the Middletown City Council. ➥

➥ COMMENTARY

A political scientist immediately asks: Are all elements of the community adequately represented in the consulting process? A citizens advisory council, in most cities, will consist primarily of middle-class individuals, often of the dominant race or ethnicity, and of business interests.

Although proportional representation of the conflicting interests is required in democracy to legitimate *adversary* decisions (decisions in matters of fundamental conflict, properly decided not by consensus but by majority rule or proportional allocation), proportional representation of different perspectives is *not* required in a consensual process based on common interests. Rather, consensus requires at least *threshold* representation (sufficient representation for the perspective to be adequately heard) of all perspectives that could contribute importantly to the ongoing decision. Threshold representation could require more or fewer representatives than proportional representation (Mansbridge, 1983).

In Middletown, therefore, we must ask: Are there important perspectives whose representatives would not be likely to phone in to a television show hosted by the mayor, or to attend a public forum or town hall meeting? Poorer people are often intimidated by public speaking; so are people who do not use words frequently as part of their daily work and people whose native language is not the one in which the public forum is being conducted. The perspectives of these people usually need to be actively solicited. One cannot expect them to step forward in a public space.

—Jane Mansbridge, *Political philosopher*

REFERENCE

Mansbridge, J. (1983). *Beyond adversary democracy.* Chicago: University of Chicago Press.

■ *Our Common Future*

EDAC presented OCF to the city council as a strategic plan "for all sectors, based on the belief that economic growth, environmental health, and social well-being are inextricably linked . . . a strategy for the

long term with bold expectations that cannot all be met tomorrow or next year." ◆

✎ COMMENTARY

Consensus requires underlying common interests. One of the common failings of consensus procedures is, therefore, to assume common interests inaccurately. Here the belief that economic growth, environmental health, and social well-being are "inextricably linked" seems to have been at the assumed root of the process rather than the result of skeptical investigation of the accuracy of that belief. The goals of economic growth and environmental health often conflict, as when economic growth requires using nonreplaceable natural resources or creates pollution. Similarly, economic growth can conflict with social well-being, as when that growth requires or creates inequality in wealth. Finally, environmental health can conflict with social well-being when environmental health is defined as the health of the earth and the planet and not the health of the humans on that planet.

One might begin a process such as this by simply saying that the process will consider only those measures in which economic growth, environmental health, and social well-being do not conflict and will rule out of consideration all other measures, no matter how important they might be. In this case, however, it seems that the possibilities of conflict among these goals may not have been adequately explored. The participants, committed to consensus or at least to a nonconflictual process, may have imposed from the start a simple "belief" that these goals were inextricably linked. Such an assumption from the beginning may have made it hard for conflicting perspectives to be heard.

Whether or not it was true in this case, the imposition of a common-interest perspective, even when such a perspective inaccurately reflects the reality as many of those affected are likely to experience it, often appears in communities that are committed to consensus or for some other reason want to avoid overt conflict.

Such communities need actively to build in safeguards to solicit divergent opinion. Straw polls of the participants in the process can perform this function. So can professional opinion polling among the affected population (with questions, including open-ended questions, worded not to generate agreement but to test and solicit disagreement). So can facilitating divergent lines of communication with the decision makers.

—Jane Mansbridge, *Political philosopher*

The city council unanimously endorsed the plan during its formal deliberation on October 24, 1994.

Designed to be read and understood by the average citizen, the final plan was 16 pages long. It consisted of six broad objectives and 43 action plans, some of which were more concrete than others. Each of the 43 action plans fit somewhere under the six overarching objectives, which supported "strong community leadership, a vibrant and diverse economy, improvements to the physical infrastructure, strong downtown core areas, sufficient human services, and quality-of-life features and amenities." The action plans described specific goals, such as "Build volunteerism through improved communication and promotion," and sometimes concrete projects, such as "Establish a single civic focal point that includes a city administration building."

The strategic plan also outlined several measures of progress for each broad objective and the action plans under it. For example, some of the measures of progress for the objective of developing strong community leadership included increased voter turnout, increased volunteerism, and increased numbers of youth in leadership positions.

Although the city council endorsed OCF in October 1994, it was 10 months before the provincial government approved the funding for its implementation. The funds allocated amounted to $150,000 total for two years. The municipality, on the other hand, offered a good deal of in-kind support (e.g., office space, office equipment, secretarial support) as well as $100,000 for the first year.

As OCF suggested it do, the Middletown City Council next established a Strategic Plan Implementation Roundtable (SPIR) to lead, coordinate, and encourage the implementation of the plan. SPIR was supposed to "recommend priorities for implementation . . . seek out groups of community partners to take responsibility for specific actions . . . establish working groups as required [and] . . . monitor the strategy's overall implementation."

SPIR comprised Mayor Hudson, the chairs (elected officials) of the three standing committees of the city council (Planning, Engineering & Public Works, and Public Services), the chief administrative officer (CAO) for the city, and 12 citizens drawn from a range of "community partners," that is, organizations from various sectors that, it was hoped, would agree to provide in-kind, volunteer, or financial resources in support of the implementation effort.

■ The Implementation Phase

To set the work of SPIR in motion, the CAO asked me to come on board as project manager for SPIR as of April 1, 1995. I was, at the time, superintendent of community programs for Middletown's recreation division, a job that entailed supervising the operations of—and developing formal policy for—programs on everything from the arts to youth recreation. This position, plus my earlier work as Middletown's community development coordinator, made me a good fit for the position.

The project was staffed by me as the full-time project manager, and by a part-time project assistant who came from outside the municipal government. My duties as project manager were to develop a communications plan (brochures, public presentations, etc.), work with community partners to get them fully involved, coordinate the fund-raising campaign, and generally handle the day-to-day operations of the project (correspondence, reports, etc.).

Housed in the Office of the CAO/Mayor in the central administrative offices at city hall, SPIR met once a month, with additional meetings when needed. The two SPIR cochairs also met with me at least one other time each month to discuss emerging issues and plan the agendas for future meetings.

The first task that we faced was the prioritization of action plans to be implemented. Although one might consider this a simple task, it was not: The objectives and action plans of OCF addressed a wide range of needs and community interests, all of which had been identified as important by residents.

We had to take into consideration that some action plans required a heavy infusion of financial and other resources. Also, the implementation of a number of the action plans required the creation of complex partnerships between various levels of government and numerous public and private sector organizations.

Eventually, a number of criteria informally emerged to guide the decision-making process in choosing the priorities for immediate implementation. SPIR was especially interested in choosing action plans that would "yield high public visibility, provide opportunities for partnership development, and have meaning and relevance for many Middletown residents." Guided by these criteria, SPIR ended up choosing the following action plan as the focus of its immediate attention:

> Develop a new core revitalization strategy that encourages investment; celebrates the uniqueness of the three historic communities of Oakdale, Palmyra, and Johnstown; and promotes, among other things, residential intensification, tourism, heritage preservation, and the renewal of existing infrastructure.

This choice was particularly challenging because, as mentioned earlier, the city had not one but three downtown core areas, and all were struggling at the time. A number of stores were empty, movie theaters and other amenities that traditionally draw people into downtown areas were lacking, and the preferred shopping venue had become a commercial "strip" geographically equidistant from all three areas. What was good about this particular action plan was that it conceivably involved all members of the community and had the potential to draw in many partners from both the private and the nonprofit sectors.

At this point, project staff launched a public education campaign that updated municipal employees and community organizations about the status of OCF and the choice of core revitalization as the most critical action plan. The operative phrase in the educational campaign was, "We all have a place here, and we all have a role." We used brochures, public presentations, advertising on buses, and weekly newspaper articles to market the message. It was assumed that the broader community would "jump on the bandwagon" and get involved in what was seen as an exciting new initiative of great benefit to the community.

The next step was to hold a community forum, to which approximately 75 individuals and organizations were invited. The forum, which was held in January 1996, provided an opportunity for the various partners to articulate specific initiatives on which they would collaborate. It was at this stage that the city council expected community organizations to take the lead in the core revitalization effort. Some partnerships that were formed at this time did eventually yield productive results.

One year into the implementation phase, however, it became apparent that the assumptions that had guided the creation of the strategic plan were markedly different from the realities being experienced by SPIR members. Most of the community partners were not jumping on the bandwagon. In fact, no committee or roundtable or individual had really thought much about how to get the community partners to commit to develop concrete projects or what exactly that would entail.

SPIR certainly couldn't demand anything from those of its members who represented community organizations. Neither did it have its own resources to dole out. The members of SPIR were supposed to be "champions" of the implementation process, but we were never sure what that meant. Because, in many ways, the community partners had no clear guidelines to follow for the building of concrete projects, most of them never did move forward with core revitalization plans or activities.

■ One-Year Assessment

Once it became apparent that community implementation of OCF was not taking place as expected, SPIR decided that it needed to pause and take a reflective look at its progress to date, assess what issues were emerging as barriers to implementation, and outline its next steps.

To assist with this review process, the consultant who had worked with EDAC to guide the development of the strategic plan was contracted in May 1996 to facilitate a review workshop with the members of SPIR. The focus of the review workshop was threefold. First, the members of SPIR assessed how the community had changed since the plan was developed in ways that were relevant for the plan's implementation. Second, progress of the implementation effort was reviewed. Third, an approach to implementation over the coming 12 to 18 months was developed.

After considerable discussion, the group came up with a new concept for an expanded SPIR. The main challenges that the expansion was designed to address were the need to broaden the community's involvement and the need to ensure that there was no duplication between the work being done by SPIR and that of other citizens advisory committees to the city council (such as those dealing with the environment, core revitalization, the economy, or riverbank trails). The group also discussed the need to broaden the volunteer base and

develop mechanisms to communicate with and acknowledge the efforts of volunteers.

After SPIR expanded to include 36 community representatives, it held a number of forums with its new members to pick action plans for short-term implementation, instead of focusing on core revitalization as a single, long-term goal. Through a series of prioritizing exercises held in November 1996, SPIR members selected five action plans from OCF and then broke into working groups to identify specific activities that could be undertaken to fulfill each action plan. They also identified community partners needed to assist with the implementation of each plan.

For example, one of the action plans selected focused on increased opportunities for entrepreneurship. Specific activities that the working group identified as necessary to implement this action plan included developing a network of agencies that promote entrepreneurship, creating a list of services those agencies provide, and consolidating information about services into a comprehensive brochure.

It was not long after the one-year assessment that it also became increasingly apparent to me that if many of the objectives in the strategic plan were to be implemented, additional sources of funds other than those provided by the city council would be required. SPIR members and I decided that a community fund-raising campaign was needed, and so we began to consider campaign options.

■ Fund-Raising Campaign and Project Shutdown

To support the action plans chosen for short-term implementation, SPIR developed a fund-raising campaign titled "Buy into Middletown—Share in Our Future." The idea was to encourage families, community groups, and businesses to donate money for projects by purchasing a nonredeemable "share." Modestly priced at $2.00 Canadian per share, it was anticipated that all residents could, conceivably, participate. SPIR took a creative approach to winning the participation of residents, such as having contributors sign their names on the side of a city bus that traveled throughout town to various special events and festivals.

The campaign kicked off at a local school and received some very positive press from two of the three community newspapers. An opinion columnist from the third newspaper, however, wrote, "Pardon me for being a pain in the old stock market, but doesn't it make more sense to invest two bucks in the community program of my own choosing? Put it where my heart is, rather than where some committee's mouth is?" In the article, the columnist also quoted a resident as saying, "I'm already paying for the strategic plan with my taxes. Asking the public to buy shares is redundant at best" (Local newspaper, June 1, 1997). ❧

❧ COMMENTARY

These words provoke a larger question on why the municipality was not perceived to represent the community: Why was it necessary to go beyond the established municipal authority, which already had the power to collect taxes for the public good? The conclusion that "a great deal more public education about the changing role of government would need to occur" seems to miss the point.

—Jane Mansbridge, *Political philosopher*

Although a number of letters to the editor to that particular newspaper opposed the negative position the columnist had taken, the questions raised in the column dogged SPIR throughout the rest of the campaign. Whatever the cause, after this point, raising private money for the project became more and more difficult. I had hoped that service clubs, for example, would make an inquiry about projects that they could support financially. I made presentations to most of the 54 service clubs in town and followed up with a letter requesting financial support, but very few responded.

Despite these difficulties, SPIR eventually met the campaign goal of raising $25,000, which the city council then matched. These funds went to kick-start projects related to the original core revitalization action plan, such as an organic farmers' market, a music festival, and a historic preservation database. Ultimately, SPIR members learned that a great deal more public education about the changing role of government would need to occur before a community fund-raising campaign of this nature could be launched again.

After the conclusion of the fund-raising campaign, the project known as Our Common Future slowly wound down. It was a plan that had been conceived with much hope and had ultimately affected the community in a positive way. Unfortunately, there was neither time nor money enough to conduct a comprehensive tracking report on the results of the initiative, which were, in their own way, substantial.

I left the project as a full-time employee on April 1, 1997, then served as a part-time consultant until December 31, 1997, when I left the municipality permanently. Eventually, funds in the city budget earmarked for the project were eliminated. The Middletown City Council ended its role in the project by explaining to the public that now that the community had been educated about the strategy, it could continue to implement action plans of its own choosing. Although there is currently no formal or structured implementation of OCF, the strategy continues to serve as a touchstone for many agencies and community organizations in Middletown.

■ Results

One may begin to wonder what concrete results, if any, were produced after four years of planning and implementing OCF. Most of the action plans were never actually carried out as described in the strategic plan, and none of the larger, more expensive projects, such as the building of an arts facility, was completed. It is important to emphasize, however, that OCF did in fact accomplish a number of things—some visible, some more process oriented.

For instance, a number of the community partners completed projects of direct benefit to Middletown as a result of the formation of new partnerships within the same special interest group (such as those providing supports for business entrepreneurs), among different special interest groups (such as tourism developing programs with seniors), and across sectors (such as a nonprofit association partnering with a local business).

The creation of cross-sectoral partnerships and collaborative relationships among community groups was itself a major paradigm shift for which OCF should receive credit. What OCF was saying is that it is through a partnered, collaborative effort that we can truly realize the community's potential and meet the community's priorities. Partners who seemingly had nothing in common learned through OCF that indeed, they did have shared interests and could creatively partner around joint projects meeting joint needs. ➥

∞ COMMENTARY

This kind of interchange among those who previously assumed they had nothing in common is one of the huge benefits of a process like this. It cannot be overemphasized. Indeed, those who have never taken part in a process like this find it hard to envision the cognitive connections that can be made and the emotional bonds that can be formed, even between past adversaries. It is also extremely hard to articulate this kind of interchange with a reasonable concern that conflicts of interest not be swept under the table. But good facilitators and negotiators can do it.

—Jane Mansbridge, *Political philosopher*

Many of these partners had never met or worked together previously. In the SPIR forums held to encourage community partners to work together, community representatives were heard to say things such as "I'm not sure why I was invited," "I'm not sure why they would have us at the same table," and "What do riverbank trails have in common with special events and festivals?" All of these partners, who at first thought they had wandered into the wrong room, became actively involved in brainstorming new ideas and initiatives for core revitalization.

For example, the organizers of the Middletown Farmers Market worked with representatives of both the Downtown Business Improvement Association and the music festivals. These partners determined that by adding music, mime, and other entertainment to the Saturday morning markets, the Farmers Market would take on a whole new ambiance. The market would be "a happening," rather than merely a place to buy fruits and vegetables. It was anticipated that the benefits of this initiative would include more patrons at the Farmers Market, more customers for the other shops and cafes in the downtown core areas, and an additional venue to showcase local arts endeavors.

OCF also paved the way philosophically for municipal partnership efforts that had never been attempted before. For example, one of the partnerships that the municipality struck with the private sector was the development of an ice park. The municipality leased some industrial land to the project's developers and, in return, was able to purchase ice time on a weekly basis at a reduced rate. These hours were then allocated to youth hockey groups at the municipal rate. The ice park is a high-quality facility and has provided the community with two additional ice rinks with no annual operating cost to the taxpayer.

In addition to community partnerships, many projects were carried out with the help of money donated through the fundraising campaign. A major portion of the riverbank trail was completed through a partnership with a youth service agency. While funding for equipment and supplies was provided by the "Buy into Middletown" campaign, other government funding provided a minimum wage for some teens who lived in an "at-risk" neighborhood in Middletown.

The teens, under the supervision of the chairman of the Riverbank Trail Committee, spent their summer clearing and developing a portion of the riverbank trail for public use. One of the teens said, "I used to do stuff that would be called vandalism, but now I know what goes into a project like this. If I ever catch anyone ruining what we've built, I will be really upset."

■ *In Retrospect*

In retrospect, most if not all of the problems that lessened the impact of OCF stemmed from the unrealistic expectations and incorrect assumptions that informed the development and implementation of the initiative. ➥

➥ COMMENTARY

The goal, to borrow from Jürgen Habermas, is a deliberation in which power, in the sense of the threat of sanctions and the use of force, is absent. Such a goal is in fact unachievable, because power permeates the world in which we live. We cannot even speak without using language that encodes power imbalances of all kinds.

But the fact that we cannot achieve the goal should not keep us from trying to approach it. The ideal, like lots of ideals ("Love thy neighbor as thyself" or "Be perfect, as thy heavenly father is perfect"), should be thought of as what political theorists call a *regulative* ideal: a goal at which to aim, without expecting that one will achieve the ideal in all its fullness. It would have been useful to find some way in which those who feared that their sector would later be punished in future dealings with the city council could express their views indirectly, without attribution.

Some members also hesitated to express their views because they thought they did not know enough about the subject. Scholars of participation in the 1970s in the United States found, for this reason, a dominance of the professionals in the field on almost every "participatory" or "citizen" board they studied. Some of this dominance is reasonable. In a procedure designed to reach the right decision, those with greater knowledge of the matter at hand should have more influence than those with less. But this reasonable dynamic often keeps those with a different perspective or a perception of conflicting interests from speaking at all. Again, whether making decisions by consensus or majority rule, groups need actively to facilitate the input of minority views. Groups that have some mechanism for actively soliciting minority opinion (e.g., a trained leader specifically allocated this task) are more likely, in laboratory studies, to arrive at correct and also more creative decisions (Hall, 1971).

—Jane Mansbridge, *Political philosopher*

REFERENCE

Hall, J. (1971). Decisions. *Psychology Today, 5,* 51-88.

Those expectations and assumptions involved questions about who would lead the project, how it would be funded and what resources it required, how much public support it had, and how long it would take to complete.

From the beginning, there was an assumption on the part of EDAC, the Middletown City Council, the CLR, and SPIR that the community itself would somehow produce dedicated leadership, funding, and other support to complete the specific projects identified under each action plan. The only problem was that the community didn't know about or understand this expectation until far into the implementation of OCF, when it became clear that neither the government nor the community had the resources necessary to carry out the kinds of tasks that the plan outlined. How these underlying assumptions developed and the effect they had on OCF is examined below. ◆

◆ COMMENTARY

One dynamic common to many organizations (and even social movements) that rely on volunteer efforts is the problem of overpromising. To induce people to spend the time at planning meetings (in this instance), organizers usually suggest that great things will come of the planning (or the voter registration drive, or the effort to pass a constitutional amendment, in the case of the Equal Rights Amendment in the United States). But it is hard, very hard, to make great things come about. Sometimes (seemingly not in this case, but in others) it turns out that many people are relatively happy with the status quo and do not want great things, thank you very much. In this case, implementation simply required resources that the voluntary groups did not have. Oscar Wilde is reputed to have commented, "The trouble with socialism is that it takes too many evenings." The same is true for any project that relies on volunteer time.

—Jane Mansbridge, *Political philosopher*

A Lack of Government Understanding, Support, and Resources

Because the city council had unanimously endorsed OCF, there was an assumption by the CLR and SPIR that the city council not only understood the role and purpose of a community strategic plan but also broadly supported it. The reality, however, was that in the minds of city council members, the community strategic plan remained one of many plans on the table for their consideration and held no greater or lesser importance than, for example, the Master Plan of Parks, Recreation, and Open Space or the Official Plan for Land Use. When I started my position as project manager, I was surprised at how little city council members understood the intent of the strategic plan, their role in its implementation, and the new way of doing business it prescribed.

Furthermore, one of the ways that the "world as we know it" did not stand still during the actual implementation of the plan was the political change in provincial leadership. The provincial government, which was elected shortly after the start of the plan's implementation phase, had campaigned on a program of fiscal restraint, debt reduction/elimination, and tax rebates. Within months of the new leadership coming into power, radical cuts in provincial funding were experienced by local organizations, which needed to restructure, redefine, and reengineer their operations to provide an acceptable level of service to the community with a significantly reduced budget. This downsizing of various groups could not have come at a more inopportune time for OCF.

The community volunteers involved in the plan's implementation also assumed that because the city council had adopted the plan, municipal staff were aware of its existence, supported the plan, and would commit time to assist with its implementation. Again, because OCF was just one of many plans and projects on the table, few department personnel actually got involved in the implementation effort. Municipal staff were also experiencing the same financial constraints felt by the city council. The elimination of transfer payments from the province to municipalities meant that staff needed to do "more with less."

A Lack of Community Ownership, Leadership, and Resources

According to OCF, the community was supposed to feel "ownership" for Middletown's economic development plan and, therefore, take up a leadership role in completing individual projects under each action plan. While groups did not oppose the plan, most did not understand the role and responsibility that had been assigned to them. Even with numerous discussions, orientation sessions, and workshops with various boards of directors throughout the community, active involvement and leadership on the part of community partners was minimal. There are a number of explanations for this failure that go all the way back to the formation of the plan itself.

First, while the development of the strategic plan had included a broad public consultation process, only about 75 residents contributed directly to the strategy's design. This number included members of the original Community Leaders Roundtable, the writing committee from EDAC, EDAC itself, the city council, and some city staff. Compared to the population at large, this number represented a very small portion of the Middletown community. In addition, the project lost momentum after the CLR completed development of OCF and disbanded—CLR members had been genuinely excited about the plan and should have been kept together and involved in the project.

Second, although the presence of so many elected officials on SPIR suggested broad support by the city council for OCF and helped the project during capital budget discussions, it also gave a contradictory message to the community about who owned the plan. In addition, the project staff should probably have been housed in a community facility external to city hall to make the statement that OCF was a community, rather than a municipal initiative.

Third, some of the resident members on SPIR were hesitant to disagree or debate issues in opposition to the views of the elected representatives because of a personal lack of confidence about their knowledge base and/or their ability to contribute to the process. Some members seemed to believe that the public officials were more informed about the various issues under discussion. There was also a sense of fear among resident members that the special interest groups they represented might later be "punished" in future dealings with

the city council, which, unfortunately, turned out to be the case for at least one of the groups involved.

The plan also required, to some extent, that the special interest groups set aside their priorities to contribute to the greater good. Some community organizations and individuals felt threatened by the strategic plan, believing that it duplicated their own mandates or planning initiatives. Some potential partners seemed unable to understand that they could contribute to the process. Collaborative action was a new concept to many community organizations, and its benefits were not always appreciated.

Another obstacle that impeded the progress of SPIR and the community representatives who served on it was the lack of clear instruction about what SPIR members were really expected to do. All the members showed up at meetings, discussed any concerns I had put on the agenda, and then went home until next month's meeting. We were all unable to define what real "action" on the part of SPIR members would be. If they didn't understand their personal role in implementation of the plan, how could SPIR members help their own organizations spearhead and fund specific projects?

But what was perhaps one of the most serious weaknesses of the economic development plan was that the community partners who were being encouraged to participate in the plan's implementation were volunteer-based organizations. While these groups supported OCF philosophically, in many instances they were already stretching their volunteers beyond the point of elasticity just to fulfill their own missions. Assuming additional commitments in support of the community strategic plan was beyond their capacity and means. Many simply did not have the human and financial resources to enable them to participate, and the project itself had no resources to support these organizations.

"But it's in the plan" was a phrase invoked like a mantra. Some of the community partners, who had long waited patiently for municipal support, believed that seeing their project identified in black and white on the pages of OCF would ensure immediate funding support. It soon became clear, however, that funding was one of the issues that had lacked sufficient attention in the development of the plan. This oversight in planning came to haunt much of the implementation effort.

Unrealistic Expectations about the Length of the Initiative

Of all the incorrect assumptions held by the city council and community members about OCF, the one that had the most serious consequence for the success or failure of the initiative involved its duration. There was a widely held assumption that even though the strategic plan was developed as a long-term strategy, there would be tangible, visible results immediately. Riverbank trails would be completed, an arts center would be constructed, and public transit would improve.

The truth is that community development and capacity building can involve major paradigm shifts for all members of the community. This change in thinking does not happen quickly—there is a phenomenal amount of education required to help the groups understand the new paradigm and why they should support a community-wide initiative and not just their own initiatives. I think that if the project could have continued as it was meant to continue, the partners could have been brought together to live out the philosophy of the plan.

Lessons Learned: Implementing Community-Based Initiatives

The following lessons can be distilled from Middletown's experience attempting to implement OCF:

- Identify starting assumptions at the outset and continually reexamine what beliefs about the project are being held by major players.
- Identify reachable, realistic goals from the outset and make sure those goals are understood and agreed on by participants.
- Accomplishing objectives for this type of initiative is rarely possible without some financial support. Clarify the financial requirements of your plan and demand that an appropriate economic analysis be completed for any objectives that are to be accomplished.
- Identify which partners are needed and exactly what they are going to be asked to contribute. A great deal of time can be wasted trying to bring a reluctant partner on board. Devote time to building alliances with those who are instrumental and those who want to be involved.
- Be sensitive to the territory and power concerns of the partners who are being asked to participate. They have mandates, agendas, negotiables, and nonnegotiables, and these issues need to be respected.
- Package progress and accomplishments in ways that your various audiences can understand.
- Choose some achievable first steps that can be experienced as "wins" for everybody because such wins can

boost buy-in, commitment, and enthusiasm.

- Remember the importance of demonstrating congruence between what is said in documentation and what is done in practice.

- Remember that the implementation of a community-based initiative is an iterative, fluid process requiring those involved to demonstrate flexibility, adaptability, and resiliency. ❧

❧ COMMENTARY

The Lessons Learned section is excellent. One comment on the fourth lesson ("Identify which partners are needed . . . "): Sometimes the originally reluctant partners turn out to be key to effective implementation. This is a hard call to make, but be careful that you don't limit the group only to "those who want to be involved" when those who do not want to be involved hold potential veto power or have access to critical perspectives that will be necessary for an effective decision.

—Jane Mansbridge, *Political philosopher*

It is impossible to truly measure how the vision identified in OCF has changed how our community operates or to what degree it is responsible for the many examples of partnership that we see operating in Middletown today. Perhaps that question is of little importance. What is important is that a new community paradigm was introduced and has been adopted by many groups within the community. Some very tangible projects were implemented and continue to be implemented. This has not only benefited the community but is a continuing source of pride for those volunteers involved in the completion of these projects. For that alone, Middletown can feel a tremendous sense of accomplishment.

■ Note

1. "Middletown" is not the actual name of the city involved in this case study. All proper names of people and places have been changed.

■ Reference

Mintzberg, H. (1994). The fall and rise of strategic planning. *Harvard Business Review, 72*(1), 107-114.

13

THE CATRON COUNTY CITIZENS GROUP

A Case Study in Community Collaboration

■ Melinda Smith

I n the early 1990s, Catron County, New Mexico had gained national notoriety as the "toughest county in the West." To-day, it is recognized for its success using collaborative problem-solving processes to bridge wide divisions of attitudes and values about public land use issues. The three-year period starting in the summer of 1995 is the focus of this case study. The events described are part of an ongoing story, with an outcome yet to be determined.

Catron County is one of the most remote and isolated counties in the lower 48 states. At nearly 7,000 square miles, it is the largest county in New Mexico. Over 75 percent of its land is under federal domain,

including a major portion of the Gila National Forest. A scant 2,500 people live in the vast expanse of land from the plains of St. Augustin to the alpine peaks and canyons of the Gila wilderness area. Ranchers and loggers have been dependent on these public lands for their livelihoods, some for more than three generations.

Like many western rural communities, Catron County faced dramatic changes during the past decade due to environmental pressure. Logging and grazing were restricted due to federal land management agency policy changes. A gridlock of federal regulations, lawsuits, and counterlawsuits reflected the escalating conflict among environmental groups, the county government, the Forest Service, and the cattle and timber industries.

In 1993, the Mexican spotted owl was listed as an endangered species by the U.S. Fish and Wildlife Service. As a result of appeals by environmental groups, logging was drastically curtailed. The Forest Service was required to consult with the U.S. Fish and Wildlife Service for each potential timber sale to ensure that the sale would not interfere with owl habitat. Before 1990, 30 million board feet of timber were being cut annually in the Gila National Forest. By 1995, timber cutting was reduced to 1 million board feet, and by 1998, virtually no timber sales, other than those done under forest restoration and salvage sale projects, were being offered by the U.S. Forest Service.

The only large-diameter lumber mill in the county, located in the town of Reserve, closed in 1993. This Stone Forest Industries mill was no longer economically viable. Thirty jobs were lost; given Reserve's population of 500, this loss was significant. The mill had temporarily closed two years before, putting 95 people out of work.

Some were forced to move away to find employment.

During this same period, ranchers experienced restrictions in land management practices by the Forest Service—also a result of pressure from environmental activists. The provisions of the National Environmental Policy Act (NEPA) and the Endangered Species Act were enforced more strictly by Forest Service rangers. This resulted in herd reductions and closer scrutiny of ranchers' management of their allotments, including restoration of land damaged by cattle grazing. Ranchers' problems were compounded by falling beef prices, drought, and increasing competition from elk for forage.

These changes left loggers and ranchers frustrated, afraid for their livelihoods and the well-being of their families, and increasingly angry at the federal government and environmentalists. The National Association of Counties listed Reserve, the county seat, as "an endangered community." With 25 percent of its residents living below the poverty level, Catron County's unemployment rate was 10.8 percent in 1995. ➥

⌘ COMMENTARY

Smith confronts the first of a number of psychological barriers in this very interesting dispute. The loggers are anchored to the past. Little recognition is given to the fact that for decades they were able to use federal lands without paying market rates. However, given that logging on federal lands at very low rates existed for many years, the loggers assume that this should continue forever. It is easy to see analogies to many other environmental disputes. Fisheries are being threatened at a rate even worse than our forests. When moderate cutbacks could have solved the problems, the fishers would not act voluntarily. Like our loggers in Catron County, they based their notion of what is appropriate on a false anchor: the way the world was.

—Max H. Bazerman, *Social psychologist*

Views of Loggers and Ranchers

Jim Thompson, who ran a local log-hauling business, reflected on these changes: "There's more spotted owls than people in this county now. I'm a log hauler—had to leave to make a living—affected me just like people in the Northwest. It just plumb put us out of business—threw us on the welfare lines. We don't stoop to drawing welfare so we just leave and find a job if we can. Don't do this county any good when we have to leave to make a living."

Skip Price, a longtime rancher in Apache Creek, hung an inverted American flag—a sign of distress—near the entrance to his ranch. He commented, "Our protest is with the environmental end of it. We woke up one day and it was on us. It gets to people, telling you how to run your business. And they don't even know what they're talking about. You're going to fight it, you're going to protest."

Glenwood rancher and former county commissioner Hugh B. McKeen, whose family has ranched in Catron County for three generations, observed, "This was the most peaceful place on earth. It didn't matter how much money you made. Nobody bothered you. You didn't have the Army Corps of Engineers getting after you about the river. You had no Endangered Species Act. You had a very good life, free of regulations." McKeen recalled a relative who tried to commit suicide and asserted that "with all the environmental suits, all the bureaucratic pressures on ranchers, and the difficulty people have just trying to make a living in these small towns, there's a portion of them that are going to shoot themselves or shoot somebody else. It's a reality." ✏

✏ COMMENTARY

A second psychological barrier confronting the intervention team is exhibited here by Mr. McKeen. Mr. McKeen's perspective is heavily influenced by egocentric interpretations of fairness. That is, he has a very specific reference point on what is fair: what existed that was favorable to his own interests. Notice that he doesn't compare to a time when the rivers were pure and untouched by humans. He doesn't consider the perspective of other species, and how they preferred things the way they were before humans. Rather, he compares the current situation to his unlimited human exploitation of the land.

—Max H. Bazerman, *Social psychologist*

Fed up with increasing federal regulations, the Catron County Commission retaliated, and in the process the county gained national attention as the leader in the county rights movement. A spate of local ordinances was passed that reflected the county's frustration with federal control over the citizens' resources and lives. The county commission wrote its own land use plan for the Gila National Forest and passed an ordinance calling for the arrest of any federal official—implying Forest Service employees—who imposes the "will" of the federal government on the "custom and culture of the people." The county commission passed a nonbinding resolution requiring all households to possess the "firearm of their choice." Another ordinance required "environmentalists" to register with the county prior to doing any assessments on land within county borders.

The Environmental Perspective

Environmentalists believed public lands were dominated by the ranching and logging industry, whose top priorities were not ecological preservation. Since the arrival of ranchers, hunters, and miners in southwestern New Mexico in the 1850s, species including the grizzly bear, the Mexican wolf, the jaguar, and the river otter have disappeared. According to 1995 Forest Service studies, 58 percent of the Gila National Forest's grazing allotments scored "D." The Gila River basin, according to zoologist W. L. Minckley, is the only riparian area in the world where every native fish species is endangered, threatened, or eliminated.

Kieran Suckling, executive director of the Southwest Center for Biological Diversity (SWCBD), described the modified clear-cutting being practiced in the 1980s in the Gila. He recalls touring a timber sale after the cut: "All the big trees were cut and the ground was ripped up by tractors. It looked like a war zone." After a careful study of the species and management policies for old-growth forests, the group decided that ecosystem management had to happen at a regional level. The SWCBD initiated an onslaught of lawsuits against the Forest Service that involved enforcement of the Endangered Species Act and the listing of species. Its injunction shut down logging in Arizona and New Mexico from August 1995 to December 1996. In

October 1997, the SWCBD filed a lawsuit to compel the Forest Service to reduce cattle on 90 riparian areas in Arizona and New Mexico.

Increased tension between adversaries resulted in physical symptoms of stress, and even the fear of violence. Elena Gellert, longtime environmentalist and resident of Luna, recalled "a dangerous kind of undercurrent that could have erupted any time." Gellert remembered: "I went to public meetings where I spoke in favor of the Endangered Species Act, and listing certain species, and that was at a meeting where there were threats of using bullets and shooting. I remember leaving that meeting being concerned for my vehicle, concerned for my own safety. I was very concerned for the safety of the people who are now the Southwest Center for Biological Diversity."

The Forest Service and Larger Community

The Forest Service, for its part, found itself caught in the middle between the resource industries, county government, and the environmentalists. It became the target of lawsuits from both sides. While ranchers and loggers claimed that the Forest Service went too far in restricting their grazing and timber activities, environmentalists asserted that the Forest Service had not gone far enough in enforcing federal environmental law. Compelled to spend thousands of dollars responding to appeals and lawsuits, the Forest Service was limited in the funds it could spend on forest restoration.

Forest Service employees felt the tension so profoundly that they hired a counselor to assist them and their families. Mike Gardner, district ranger for the Reserve District, described the atmosphere: "You're wondering if you're coming home each night, especially when there is so much rhetoric about guns and every family having a gun and things like that. A lot of people who work for the Forest Service and myself felt threatened."

Concern for the physical and emotional health of the community prompted Mark Unverzagt, the only physician in the county, to seek outside help. Dr. Unverzagt, or "Dr. Mark," was seeing increasing numbers of patients with anxiety and depression, regardless of their position in the land wars. He was treating more drug and alcohol problems and encountering higher rates of spousal abuse and family violence. The health of Catron County's citizens was being affected by conflict, disruption of the economy, and "outside forces" over which the community felt no control. Dr. Unverzagt believed the physical well-being of the community was in jeopardy.

Mark Unverzagt had come to Catron County in 1993 with his young family. Although a newcomer, Dr. Unverzagt gained the trust and respect of the residents he served. In 1995, he decided to take action. He called the New Mexico Center for Dispute Resolution (NMCDR), a nonprofit mediation center based in Albuquerque, to seek assistance. He had heard that the NMCDR was experienced in mediation and violence prevention work, and he hoped these techniques could be applied to the situation in Catron County.

■ *Convening the Catron County Citizens Group: July–December 1995*

The NMCDR recommended bringing people together to begin dialogue on the issues that divided them. As a first step, people were invited who knew and trusted Dr. Mark. The NMCDR reasoned that this group would likely accept Dr. Mark's leadership as they grappled with complex issues and strong emotions.

Dr. Mark identified about 20 people, including rancher Hugh B. McKeen and his wife, Margie; Forest Service ranger Mike Gardner; environmentalist Elena Gellert; then mayor of Reserve Harold Dykstra; then county extension agent Doug Baird; Howard Hutchinson, coordinator of the Coalition of Counties of New Mexico and Arizona; county treasurer Jan Porter; and several other ranchers, Forest Service employees, clergymen, environmentalists, and community leaders. This group has remained the nucleus of the Catron County Citizens Group (CCCG). Since July 1995, the group has ranged from 15 to 50 people and has met monthly. It began as a dialogue group to create a forum for discussion, and evolved into a planning and action group engaging in collaborative processes. ⟿

○ COMMENTARY

It is interesting that the early goals of the group were all process oriented, and this continued throughout much of the case. An alternative possibility is that the parties could have agreed that no party would be asked to make an agreement that was worse than their BATNA (best alternative to a negotiated agreement) or the group could have agreed to search for opportunities for joint gain. While process issues were critical, it is useful to raise the question of whether content opportunities were missed while pursuing process concerns.

—Max H. Bazerman, *Social psychologist*

The first meetings in the summer and fall of 1995 were sometimes tense, but participants seemed grateful for the opportunity to vent their frustrations. Dr. Mark or Harold Dykstra acted as convenors, and John Folk-Williams of Western Network and I served as facilitator and recorder. Harold Dykstra expressed the following goal for the first gathering: "To encourage everyone to voice their honest opinions without fear of being criticized and to begin working together to stop the spread of misinformation and to begin building trust." The group generated ground rules, including the following:

1. Listen to all in a respectful manner.
2. Engage in open and honest discussion.
3. Talk to others outside the group in a way that respects all views.

By September 1995, the group developed a mission statement, motivated in part by the curiosity and skepticism of people in the larger community. The mission of the group was written and submitted for publication in the weekly real estate advertising circular. This circular was then mailed to every post office box in the county. The group hoped to educate the residents about the purpose of the group and invite them to participate. The mission statement read as follows:

The mission is to come together to openly and honestly discuss and deal with the diverse situations we face, finding common ground from our different points of view to ensure an economic, social, and environmentally sound future for us all.

Despite differences, the group quickly established common ground. Shared interests included the need for economic devel-

opment and diversification, the maintenance of rural lifestyles and values, the importance of sound land stewardship, and the importance of participation in the decisions that affected the county. Participants were grateful for a forum to deal with these issues. Reserve district ranger Mike Gardner expressed it this way: "It was five years of pretty harrowing times with nobody really coming to your aid. Nobody saying, you know, 'Attaboy Mike, hang in there, things are going to change pretty soon.' Now with this group, I feel like I'm not just dealing with somebody with opposing views from mine or somebody saying things intentionally to make me mad."

Our role as facilitators was to ensure that meetings were productive and balanced. We also assisted the group as it used processes to achieve its goals. Early on, I asked for assistance from my colleagues at Western Network, an environmental dispute resolution firm based in Santa Fe. Staff members John Folk-Williams and Richard Pacheco were cofacilitators for the first 10 months of the process. Carl Moore, then also of Western Network, replaced his colleagues after the first year.

Designing processes to deal with the complex agendas of the participants was challenging and circuitous. There were false starts, dead ends, and many uncertainties during this long and multifaceted intervention. Gaining the trust of the group and acceptance as outsiders was critical to our continued presence. Dr. Ben Daitz of the University of New Mexico School of Medicine (also a friend of Dr. Mark's) provided initial funding to the NMCDR. This grant covered facilitation and travel for the first six months. However, our continued presence depended on raising additional funding through our own organizations.

The group agreed to allow Dr. Daitz, a documentary filmmaker, to film the meetings. He wanted to produce a film that would record the progression of events in Catron County. Some group members were initially uncomfortable with the idea of being filmed, but that discomfort dimin-

ished over time. Most people got used to the camera; besides, Dr. Daitz had also been involved in community health care and had inspired a baseline level of trust. ∞

∞ COMMENTARY

The intervention of the filmmaker is quite interesting. It is quite possible that the filming had a positive influence on the discussion, since people do not want to be seen on videotape being unreasonable. The famous Canadian documentary *Final Offer* detailed the negotiation process between General Motors and the Canadian branch of the UAW. *Final Offer* suggests that little inhibition occurred as a result of filming. However, when there was a change in management within Canadian GM, the new executive refused to continue with the filming. The experimental literature on constituency effects suggests that constituencies make bargainers tougher. We do not have data on the impact of filming.

—Max H. Bazerman, *Social psychologist*

"On the Ground" Projects

During the first six months, group members engaged in mutual education of their diverse points of view. The county rights advocates pressed their agenda of taking control of the public lands; they recounted increasing difficulties in working with the Forest Service. Hugh B. McKeen expressed these sentiments this way: "The people in this county need to set their own destiny— they need to make the decisions about the land they live on. The county movement is saying we can do a better job of management on public lands—better for the wildlife, better for the watershed, better for the environment, better for the economy." Group members like McKeen wanted to pursue a project that would transfer public lands to county control for 20 years. However, the group as a whole was persuaded to pursue a fresh agenda.

In 1995, six months after the first meeting, the group took on several "on the

ground" projects, both as a learning tool and a means to collaborate on projects. McKeen had proposed a piñon/juniper removal project on his Cedar Breaks allotment. (The trees were taking over grassland.) He proposed that reseeding would create more habitat for wildlife and grazing for cattle. While there was some disagreement about the long-term benefits of this project, the group agreed to initiate the process and identified a committee to work on it.

The procedures set forth in NEPA would be applied to the piñon/juniper project. This way, the group could learn together about NEPA's requirements and, according to some, reveal its overly regulated and protracted procedures. The second project, proposed by the Forest Service, entailed the transfer of public land to the county for the purpose of a business park. The NEPA process was also required for this project; the Forest Service suggested that the county take responsibility for streamlining the process.

Because of intervening agendas and other obstacles, neither project was completed quickly. The Cedar Breaks project was undergoing a scoping analysis as of January 1998. The regional forester approved 300 acres of land that could be considered for the business park project. A memorandum of understanding between the county and the Forest Service allowed the county to have cooperating agency status in the project.

■ *Broadening the Dialogue and Setting an Agenda: January–June 1996*

In early 1996, the group decided to expand the circle of participants. Each group member agreed to bring an additional county resident to the February meeting. By this time, four group members had participated in a facilitation training sponsored by the NMCDR and were asked to facilitate part of the meeting agenda. This was done to build local leadership and skills within the group.

At the February meeting, nearly 50 people crammed into the meeting room of the Presbyterian Church. After dividing into small groups, they brainstormed about their concerns and desired outcomes for the community. The list they compiled included the following:

- job availability,
- youth opportunities/parental and community support of youth,
- environmental issues and land management,
- the lack of cooperation between communities and divergent groups,

- diversification of economy,
- reduction of social polarization between long-term and new residents,
- reduction of hostility and development of tolerance for different views,
- maintenance of culture and acceptance of change,
- control change that happens and diminish negative influences,
- maintenance of work ethic,
- public education about land management from the local perspective,
- relief of tension/stress,
- good conflict resolution,
- a more effective decision-making process about land management, and
- people in the county deciding the future of the county.

Several members took the list and formulated group priorities, which the group endorsed in March. These priorities, listed below, set the agenda and structured the working committees of the group.

1. Education—including educating each other about different points of view and values, as well as the public about the issues and conflicts the county is experiencing.
2. Dispute resolution—finding processes for resolving differences and preventing threats of violence or destructive behavior.
3. Land stewardship—finding common ground for maintaining healthy range and environmental conditions everyone can agree on.
4. Economic development—developing new sources of revenue for the county and its residents.
5. Youth development—creating a means for full participation of the

county's youth in the current process and the future of the county.

The participants decided that they would commit to an additional year's work and then assess their progress. While never explicitly agreeing to make decisions using a consensus process, we as facilitators worked to ensure that decisions were made with the approval of all participants. The group also decided to involve the public in larger numbers. Thus far, they had resisted a public involvement process because they wanted to solidify the group's identity and purpose. More important, they were concerned that meetings might deteriorate into shouting matches.

Funding and Capacity Building

While the group was engaging in dialogue and self-definition, the NMCDR, along with the University of New Mexico School of Medicine, was writing proposals to pursue additional funding. A grant from the Hewlett Foundation allowed Dr. Daitz to continue his filming, and support from the SURDNA Foundation in March 1996 enabled me to continue as process consultant. More important, the SURDNA Foundation also provided funds for the group to hire its own local coordinator to manage meetings, publicity, projects, and committees. The idea of a local coordinator had been suggested by the facilitators and seconded by the group.

A hiring committee was put together to recruit the group's first coordinator, Gail Phetteplace. Gail and her husband, Alan, were newcomers to the county; she benefited in some ways from this "outsider" status, since she was perceived as neutral by the community. She had the energy, social skills, and organizational savvy to maintain

the group's momentum. The hiring committee soon became the steering committee for the CCCG, with Gail reporting to the steering committee. Capacity was being built for group self-governance. Instituting potluck dinners before each monthly meeting also contributed positive energy and cohesion to the group.

But in the April 1996 meeting, tensions again began to mount. The group had invited staff from the forest supervisor's office in Silver City to provide information about a proposed salvage timber sale, the H.B. sale, and to address the NEPA requirements in the grazing permit renewal process. Ranchers were facing herd reductions in their renewal of permits. In addition, loggers and those who would benefit from timber sales were frustrated by the efforts to prevent the H.B. sale. Adding to the tense atmosphere was an incident that took place in Eager, Arizona.

Incident at Eager

A Reserve Forest Service ranger and regular group attendee saw a sign on the Catron County courthouse door advertising a meeting of permittees in neighboring Eager, Arizona. The meeting's featured speaker was Karen Budd-Falen, an attorney and property rights advocate. Those gathered wanted to pursue litigation against the Forest Service for restricting grazing permits. At the meeting were several Catron County commissioners, and county officials and permittees including several members of the CCCG. The aforementioned incident unfolded in this way: A member of the CCCG recognized the Forest Service ranger, and went over and told him to leave. The ranger was told it was a closed meeting. He then went into the hallway, still within earshot. Several ranchers, none from Catron County, proceeded to escort the ranger out of the building in an allegedly rough manner. The ranger went to the police and reported the incident.

This story ignited the group and consumed two hours of discussion at the April meeting. The CCCG group member who had told the ranger to leave was outraged because he felt he had been wrongly accused of violence. The treatment of the ranger fueled everyone's fears of violence and propelled the group to issue a statement. After much negotiating, a statement was prepared that (1) reiterated the group's denunciation of violence as a means of resolving the public lands debate; (2) exonerated the rancher from any involvement in the Forest Service employee's forced expulsion from the meeting; and (3) upheld the ranger's right to be at the meeting, given the public notice. A copy of the statement was sent to the permittees' association in Arizona.

In addition, the group agreed anew to a set of behaviors, including (1) hearing all sides with respect and speaking the truth, (2) having direct communication before categorizing people, and (3) respecting everyone's value to each other and to the community.

Despite the heightened emotion at this April meeting, the group was able to use its time with Forest Service officials. A list of suggestions to deal with land use issues was generated. They included the following:

1. Hire independent scientists to do studies.
2. Develop processes for mediating disputes.
3. Find uniform methods of analysis by both the Forest Service and the Bureau of Land Management.
4. Involve the state Fish and Game Department in the processes.
5. Gain a better understanding of NEPA.
6. Increase understanding of standards and the land management plan.
7. Develop more cooperative monitoring on the ground between the Forest Service and the community.

The CCCG accomplished at least some of these ideas. They invited an expert to provide a four-hour seminar on the NEPA process and how it applied to land controversies. Mediation was explored as a process for resolving grazing issues, as described in the next section. To increase common understanding of forest and range conditions, the group decided to initiate a series of field trips in the county to discuss the specifics of land conditions.

The Environmentalists Come to the Table

At the same time that grazing issues were heating up, timber issues were heading for major conflict. The H.B. salvage sale was a proposed sale of burned timber on Eagle Peak, an old-growth forest area in the Reserve Forest Service District. The SWCBD opposed the sale because of its commitment to old-growth forest; in particular, the sale would involve building roads. The SWCBD was planning an encampment on Eagle Peak if the sale was to proceed, mobilizing scores of activists. We decided to contact Todd Schulke, the SWCBD's New Mexico staff person. We wanted to discuss his potential involvement in the CCCG, and whether the H.B. sale could be brought to the table.

Todd Schulke was a former resident of Reserve. He had done restoration and habitat research until the tension in Catron

County prompted him to relocate in Pinos Altos, south of Catron County. After discussions with SWCBD leadership, he agreed to attend the group meetings in the spring of 1996.

While several local environmentalists regularly attended meetings, none was affiliated with the groups engaged in ongoing litigation against the Forest Service. The presence of a representative of the SWCBD was essential to increased mutual understanding between environmental activists and their adversaries. As dispute resolution practitioners, we also hoped to bring some of the conflicts from the courtroom to the negotiating table. About his involvement in the group, Schulke stated, "My intention is to develop understanding and trust in each other so at least there is enough common ground that we can move together."

The group attempted unsuccessfully to negotiate the issues of the H.B. sale. Eventually, the sale was mooted by the Department of Agriculture's decision to restrict salvage logging to roaded areas. Accepting that there could be no agreement about the salvage sale, Mike Gardner proposed that the group turn its attention to other potential timber sales that involved small-diameter timber.

Riparian Tours

In May and June 1996, the group organized two tours to provide on-the-ground education about riparian conditions and practices. Group members were given an opportunity to have an impact on standards and guidelines for the Gila Forest land management plan. While there was not full agreement on the factors leading to riparian recovery, the tours created a common language for discussing issues.

■ Taking Action and Making Agreements: July 1996–June 1997

Exploring the Use of Mediation

Conflict between ranchers and the Forest Service stemmed in part from communication and interpersonal problems. For this reason, we encouraged the group to explore the possibility of mediation. The enforcement of environmental impact assessments on grazing allotments also created a host of conflicts involving data collection, analysis and interpretation of range conditions, and other Forest Service procedures related to permit renewal and monitoring. A mediation committee was assembled and held an exploratory meeting to examine potential dispute resolution processes.

The committee identified three levels of conflict around grazing issues: (1) interpersonal and procedural conflicts between rangers and ranchers, (2) substantive and procedural issues requiring the use of NEPA, and (3) larger public policy conflicts. Among the types of interpersonal conflicts that appeared suited to rancher-Forest Service mediation were

preferential treatment;

communication styles;

keeping agreements;

expectations of ranchers and Forest Service rangers;

monitoring after grazing permits are signed;

perceptions of punitive action;

personality conflicts;

differences in attitudes, cultures, and backgrounds of Forest Service personnel and ranchers;

lack of trust; and

uneven power perceptions.

Other issues involved substantive matters and the application of NEPA. These often required the presence of third parties, including environmental interests, and were identified as follows:

data collection and interpretation for condition of resources,

ownership of permit and improvements,

season of use,

number of livestock,

environmental interests and communication about them, and

permit terms and decision making.

Ranchers and Forest Service employees identified a conflict that they thought would be suitable for mediation. This conflict involved three ranchers and two Forest Service employees. One mediation session and a follow-up session were held, conducted by a staff mediator from the NMCDR with assistance from a mediator with the U.S. Department of Agriculture mediation program. The mediation was viewed as a qualified success. The parties came together and talked more candidly than ever before. Misinformation and rumors were confronted and cleared up, and the Forest Service employees reaffirmed their commitment to work with the ranchers.

What didn't work as well was that not all of the important parties were at the table. One ranger, for example, didn't feel comfortable discussing the issues in this type of forum. In general, the ranchers seemed hesitant to press for their needs when confronted with the assumed power of the Forest Service. The process can work, but there needs to be adequate education of the parties. Preparation time must be devoted to interviewing parties face-to-face prior to the mediation, and trust established to get all the parties to the table. For example, more might have been done to balance power so that the ranchers would be more satisfied with the outcome. It is clear that mediation is an appropriate intervention for many types of rancher-Forest Service disputes. However, it takes resources and commitment to fully implement such a program.

For the second type of conflict identified by the group (substantive and procedural conflicts), a mediation process needed to be designed that would incorporate the NEPA process, because these are disputes that require public input. With the input of a NEPA specialist and Forest Service employees, a process was designed to facilitate 10-year renewals of grazing permits. The goals of grazing permit mediation would be the following:

- Find common ground on a grazing management plan for the permittee among interested parties, including the permittee, the Forest Service, and environmental interests, plus the interdisciplinary team required by NEPA.
- Resolve conflicts in range and riparian conditions on grazing allotments.
- Allow participants to exchange points of view and build respect for their different perspectives.
- Strengthen relationships between parties.
- Avoid the costs of appeal and litigation.

Several concerns temporarily inhibited this pursuit. First, there was some concern that the process might violate the Federal Advisory Committee Act (FACA). Furthermore, it was presumed that this type of mediation would require public involvement, in particular, the participation of an environmental activist group engaged in litigation against the Forest Service. The willingness of such a group to participate in a permit renewal mediation process was questionable. If adversarial methods hold more promise for environmental activists, there is little motivation to negotiate.

Community Visioning Process

From the start, the CCCG recognized the need for a larger public involvement process. Many members felt that in addition to focusing on conflict resolution, they needed to get community consensus on a vision for the future. In the summer of 1996, a committee was assembled to implement a community visioning process. With the assistance of Carl Moore of Western Network, the CCCG initiated a series of public meetings in which citizens identified the treasures, threats, and opportunities facing the county. Four steps were taken:

1. In the summer and fall of 1996, Catron County residents were asked to identify what they treasured in the county. They did so through two public forums: the annual Heritage Festival and County Fair, where the CCCG maintained a booth. Over 400 responses were gathered.
2. Twenty CCCG members and other community residents were trained in facilitation skills in preparation

for the first round of public meetings.
3. Public meetings to create a list of desired visions of the future were held in the fall and winter of 1996. These meetings were cofacilitated with trained community members. Over 200 residents attended five meetings held in the communities of Luna, Glenwood, and Reserve and at the senior centers in Quemado and Reserve. Students at Reserve High School also participated in the process. The treasure list was shared, and each of the groups developed its visions and goals for the future.
4. The steering committee of the CCCG then synthesized the hundreds of newly generated ideas into a list of proposed goals.

The next step was to take the proposed goals back to the communities for prioritization. The CCCG would then act as a catalyst with other community groups and perhaps county government—creating plans to make the goals a reality. However, all these "next steps" were put on hiatus. Some members wanted to work on projects already undertaken to demonstrate the group's efficacy to the community. Furthermore, grazing and timber issues continued to be compelling. The CCCG decided to revisit the community visioning process at a later time.

New Organizational Structure

By October 1996, the group retooled its organizational structure. The steering committee included an additional environmentalist, and the committee structure was streamlined. Some of the ad hoc committees that had been created were renamed, and all were given a point-person to communicate with the coordinator. Committees now included the watershed improvement committee (formerly the timber committee), the economic development committee (formerly the business park committee), the community process committee, the mediation committee, and the youth committee. A number of members had long been interested in community and youth development projects and didn't want CCCG's entire focus to be timber and grazing.

By this stage in the genesis of the group, there were several significant additions to the regular attendees, including Adam Polley, the new county manager; Larry Patton, the attorney who defended the famed Diamond Bar Ranch against the ultimately successful attempt to remove all its cattle; Cricket Cox, property rights activist; Dr. Crandell Young, the new school superintendent; Vic Jenkins, forest consultant to the county; and Lyn Condo, a logger and small-mill operator. Attorney Patton commented on his participation: "Lawsuits should be at the end of the process."

Youth Project

Continued interest in a youth project resulted in a proposal to a local foundation. A program to bring mediation and collaborative processes to the schools was funded in November 1996. An expanded youth committee, made up of CCCG members and a number of teachers and administrators, met to plan program implementation. They decided to have high school students trained as mediators; they, in turn, would train elementary school students. The program would enable schools in Reserve to incorporate peer mediation into disciplinary policies. The program's second component was to provide secondary students with an opportunity to conduct research. The economic, environmental, and demographic data gathered by students would inform the group as it conducted its community visioning and planning processes.

One student completed a project on the history of agriculture in the county, demonstrating the change in conditions over the past 20 years. Another project involved the creation of a Web page to provide information about hunting and tourism in the county. While the projects were successful, neither the students nor their work were fully integrated into the goals and activities of the CCCG. This was due in part to the groups' decision to put the community visioning process on hold, since the resource issues were viewed as having greater urgency. In addition, the students had difficulty attending the evening meetings of the CCCG. While the group understood the importance of youth involvement in the group, the means to achieve it were not fully present.

Negotiation of Forest Health Projects

CCCG members point to the negotiation of two forest and range improvement projects as concrete accomplishments. In the fall of 1996, the Forest Service proposed several logging projects that the group might negotiate in lieu of the H.B. salvage sale. The group went on a two-day field trip to survey the sites. The first project, the T Bar Grasslands, entailed thinning of ponderosa pines from a grassland. This project wouldn't attract lumber companies because of the size of the logs, and all agreed that it would improve the condition of the grasslands.

The project that did cause significant controversy was the Apache Forest Improvement Project. The Forest Service proposed cutting 450,000 board feet to thin a 125-acre stand of ponderosa pines that had a high fuel load and serious mistletoe infestation. According to the Forest Service, tree density had increased two to three times over the past 100 years. Veteran Forest Service silviculturist Donal Weaver identified the goals of the project as (1) retaining the old-growth overstory, (2) reducing mistletoe invasion, (3) thinning tree density, (4) increasing forage, and (5) providing forest products for small industry.

The SWCBD objected to the project because trees larger than 16 inches in diameter were targeted for cutting. Two trips were made to the site to discuss the issues. On the first trip, it was agreed that the Forest Service would mark for cutting all of the trees in the prescription but would flag those that were 16 inches in diameter and above. On the second trip, the group would discuss the flagged trees and determine whether their removal would help or hinder forest health.

Although only 114 trees were flagged, Todd Schulke of the SWCBD said he would hold firm on the 16-inch cap. Schulke acknowledged that this was a politically motivated position, not an environmental one. He commented, "One thing that's underestimated is how far we're sticking our necks out being out here and advocating some of this stuff. We've got the Sam Hitts [environmental activist] of the world thrashing us . . there are some political realities." Others felt the cap was arbitrary and scientifically unjustifiable. From an economic perspective, the restrictions on logging were devastating the county.

County manager Adam Polley responded, "You're looking at Reserve. . . . You're looking at a group of people losing their living. If you want that on your conscience, that's great."

Don Weaver came forward to emphasize the group's progress in bringing former adversaries together. He stated, "To have Todd out here and trying to work with us and at least admit that there's a need for logging of some sort is a pretty big step. We just need to keep working together. . . . We're a long ways from where we were a year ago, which was nowhere." The Forest Service and others wanted assurance that the 16-inch cap was not setting a precedent. With that assurance, the group agreed to move ahead with the sale. Logger Lyn Condo emphasized that 7- to 20-inch-diameter trees were economically beneficial and marketable to small operators like himself.

While the group agreed that this was a small project, it built trust and was necessary to the health of the forest. Cricket Cox commented on the process: "I'm encouraged that we're beginning to get past the rhetoric and getting to the issues. It's been a long struggle." Mike Gardner summed up the sentiment of the group: "Any project where we have the agreement of the community, the chances it could be held up are minimized. A diverse group coming up with a desired future condition for an area—this group has to band together. This is the future of public lands management."

This was the first timber sale of the decade that had not been appealed. From a dispute resolution perspective, this negotiation had all the elements of good process: social learning, mutual respect, agreements in principle, achievement of individual goals and a common agenda, and an open door for future negotiations.

■ *The Conference and the Aftermath: July–December 1997*

The Conference

When funding was initially sought for the Catron County project, we planned a dissemination conference to share our experiences with similar groups in the West and with policymakers. A grant was obtained from the Robert Wood Johnson Foundation for this purpose. Originally, we imagined the conference would take place after the completion of the documentary film and at an end point in the intervention. However, both the film and the process were taking longer than anticipated. The conference needed to happen before the end of the funding period and could serve as an excellent educational tool for the group and the community.

The steering committee worked with us to plan and implement the conference. Three other collaborative groups in the West were invited to share their stories: the Malpai Borderlands Group of Arizona/New Mexico, the Ponderosa Pine Partnership of southern Colorado, and the LEAD Partnership of California and Oregon. The conference was held in July 1997. We gathered at Reserve High School to talk about the challenges, frustrations, and successes of collaborative processes emerging in the West. More than 45 Catron County residents participated, joined by 60 others from 12 states and the District of Columbia.

Groups told their stories on the first day, followed by commentary from invited speakers Alston Chase, environmental writer; Luther Propst of the Sonoran Institute; John Schumaker, dispute resolution specialist with the Bureau of Land Management; and New Mexico Senators Bingaman and Domenici. The second day provided an opportunity for the group to actually experience collaborative problem solving. Two workshops posed resource conflicts in the county, the H.B. salvage sale and a grazing allotment dispute. Participants analyzed the conflicts and attempted to resolve them through collaborative, not adversarial, means.

Not all the conference participants were sanguine about collaborative processes in resource management. The biggest critics were representatives of environmental groups, including Gila Watch, Forest Guardians, and the Sierra Club. They claimed that these processes don't represent national interests and inappropriately place decision making about public assets in the hands of place-based interests. There was concern that the environmental perspectives were inadequately represented and that local environmental activities were not equipped to negotiate the interests of national groups. ◆

◆ COMMENTARY

It is interesting to see that the more extreme environmental groups were left out of the agreement and became critics. This raises the important issue of what the consensus builder should aim for in terms of inclusion: majority rule, consensus, or a unanimous agreement. A majority-rule procedure can too easily leave too many parties out of the process, and implementation then fails. Getting a unanimous agreement is often impossible. Consensus can mean a number of different variations of things between majority rule and unanimity. The most common use of consensus is that a majority agrees and the minority agrees to go along. Another notion, closer to the current case, is that all the major interests are on board, and fringe elements on one/both sides remain in disagreement.

It is interesting that it is common for interventions to occur without the mediator/facilitator specifying the rules of agreement (what does it take for the group to agree?). I think that this issue is worthy of thought. In Conoco's famous failed exploration project in Ecuador, Concoco made the mistake of agreeing to extract oil from the rain forest only if all parties were on board. Not surprisingly, the Rainforest Action Network and other more left-leaning environmental groups announced that they objected. Having made a public statement giving these parties veto power, Conoco sold its land to a far less environmentally friendly corporation, who extracted the oil with far less environmental concern than Conoco had been willing to commit to making. The point is that the exclusion of extremists is often necessary in consensus building. We see the same pattern in peace processes in Ireland and Israel.

—Max H. Bazerman, *Social psychologist*

In general, however, the presenters were very well received. One conference participant commented: "The conference was for me a terrific opportunity to learn more about what I regard as among the best examples of conflict transformation at work. . . . The Reserve folks, and the other partnerships, are at work at much more than a series of tightly argued 'settlements.' This is a community transforming relationships and structures." Most of the CCCG felt the conference was a success, bringing the county some rare good press. It provided positive momentum for the continued work of the group.

Group Governance and New Directions

In the aftermath of the conference, the group again examined its purpose and direction. In the fall of 1997, the group considered the possibility of obtaining nonprofit status to procure funding for ongoing projects. The group also revised its mission statement, adding the words "to take action on projects" to emphasize getting things done in addition to talking. Gail Phetteplace resigned her job as coordinator and was replaced by Bob Moore, a 20-year resident of Glenwood and former Forest Service contractor. The group had several new projects on the table, including an ecosystem management project and developing and marketing small-diameter-wood products.

As process consultants, our role had evolved during the first two years of the process. We no longer facilitated the monthly meetings. Our activities included coaching the coordinator and the group about process issues and providing resources and training. We ensured that essential stakeholders were participating and that discussions and negotiations integrated the diverse interests represented in the group.

In assessing the group's work to date, some members held that the CCCG had been a successful forum but the power to implement decisions was not within the group's purview. Others felt that the group was indeed implementing projects. As one member put it, "We're taking baby steps, but we were so polarized before and now we are making progress."

The Grazing Lawsuit

New fissures in the group appeared in November 1997. Word got out that the SWCBD had filed a lawsuit attempting to limit grazing on the Gila National Forest and forests in New Mexico and Arizona; this suit would compel the Forest Service to comply with the Endangered Species Act by consulting with the U.S. Fish and Game Department. The lawsuit threatened to remove cattle from as many as 70 allotments in Catron County. At the November meeting of the CCCG, the county manager walked out—frustrated with both the lawsuit and the lack of warning about it.

By December, tension was high. Bob Moore and I went to Tucson to discuss the potential participation of SWCBD staff at CCCG meetings. At a time when trust was being strengthened among members of the group, the lawsuit was like a slap in the face. To clarify the meaning of the lawsuit, we requested that Kieran Suckling and Peter Galvin—key staff involved in the litigation—enter into a dialogue with the group. I hoped that by connecting personally with CCCG members, the SWCBD leadership would be more inclined to negotiate issues in the future. Suckling and Galvin said that they would like to make time in their schedules to attend several meetings, but couldn't be regular participants. So far they have not attended any meetings.

Time and priorities played a role in the absence of the SWCBD leadership, but questions still remained about their position. At the December 1997 monthly meeting, Todd Schulke, who had not worked on the lawsuits, agreed to explain what he could. He affirmed that the SWCBD wanted the Forest Service to adhere to the requirements of the Endangered Species Act. He clarified that the SWCBD was interested in ecological bottom lines and not removal of cattle. He also said that he was part of the CCCG to explore alternatives to litigation. No group had declared it would stop suing while attempting to collaborate, so why would the SWCBD? ∞

∞ COMMENTARY

Mr. Schulke's position is a useful reminder of why parties participate in consensus building: They believe they can get something better than their BATNA. Mr. Schulke clearly specifies that his group's BATNA is working just fine and that he is not willing to give up the fallback option of the BATNA. This highlights the need for interventionists to pay attention to the content of the parties' interests as well as the facilitation process. In an article I wrote with colleagues (Gibson, Thompson, & Bazerman, 1996), following the logic of Raiffa (1982), we argued that third parties should seek

1. An agreement if and only if the parties can better achieve their goals through negotiated agreement rather than coming to impasse.
2. An agreement that is maximally efficient. That is, there should be no acceptable alternative agreement available more beneficial to both parties.

3. A full consideration of the distribution of the disputed resources by the disputants.

Mr. Schulke's perspective highlights the need for these decision analytic considerations.

—Max H. Bazerman, *Social psychologist*

REFERENCES

Gibson, K., Thompson, L. L., & Bazerman, M. H. (1996). Shortcomings of neutrality in mediation: Solutions based on rationality. *Negotiation Journal, 12,* 69-80.

Raiffa, H. (1982). *The art and science of negotiation.* Cambridge, MA: Harvard University Press.

Members expressed a need for truth. The SWCBD pledged to do a better job of keeping people updated on its intent and actions. The SWCBD, Todd Schulke reiterated, was supportive of the CCCG's experiment and was interested in working with the CCCG to obtain outcomes not attainable by lawsuits. However, the SWCBD's bottom line was the viability of certain species. ••

---

๑ COMMENTARY

Again, I am impressed with Mr. Schulke's intuitive negotiation approach. While being very happy with his BATNA (winning in court), he is happy to be part of the consensus building process, if that allows his group to get more than what it can get through his BATNA. This nicely highlights the mixed-motive nature of consensus building. The goal is to try to build the pie, while realizing the distribution also matters and each party needs to achieve a resolution equal to something greater than each party's BATNA.

—Max H. Bazerman, *Social psychologist*

From the county's point of view, loss of the cattle industry would have serious financial consequences. According to ranchers, the environmental movement was attacking a way of life; they were fighting for a lifestyle, not just a job. To bridge the divisions between the environmentalists and the county, we visited with the county manager. We listened to his concerns about resource management controversies, and we encouraged his continued participation in the group. He subsequently returned to meetings on an intermittent basis.

■ *Coming Apart and Pulling Together: January–August 1998*

While grazing issues divided the group, common ground was easier to find on forest health issues. The group identified a number of forest-thinning projects that would improve the health of the forest as well as create marketable timber. A number of local loggers joined the group to discuss these projects.

Working in tandem with the CCCG, the Forest Service hoped to create a sustainable yield of timber projects to keep local loggers in business. One such project within the Negrito ecosystem would have the capacity to yield 90 million board feet of lumber. When word of projects of this size reached the Tucson leadership of the SWCBD, fresh divisions grew between the SWCBD and the CCCG. The SWCBD's Internet newsletter excoriated the Forest Service for the magnitude of its plans. Todd Schulke stated that his group was operating on a "narrow line of common ground" and that this volume of timber was way on the other side. Even the terms *timber sale* and *board feet* created mistrust.

The Forest Service explained that this number was merely a projection. Schulke acknowledged that the SWCBD had overreacted because of past directives coming from the Washington office of the Forest Service. The tensions finally eased after the group vowed to communicate more effectively. Group member Don Weaver suggested, "Next time there's a question, let's sit down and talk about it before we sling mud." Mike Gardner added, "When we get out on the ground, we might find some common ground."

Establishing Criteria for Future Forest Health Projects

Constructive work began by the Watershed Improvement Committee. This committee, working on timber issues, included four local loggers, a rancher, one of the county commissioners, several Forest Service employees, and Todd Schulke representing the SWCBD. In April, the committee defined criteria for identifying a forest health project. Any project undertaken should

- be located in previously roaded areas only;
- serve the needs of local operators;
- reduce density of timber;
- be part of an integrated and long-range treatment plan;
- serve an economic need and be economically viable;
- guarantee that investments will be worthwhile;
- keep small mills operable; and
- provide sufficient volume by size groups

After defining the criteria, the committee used resource maps of the Negrito ecosystem area in the Gila National Forest. These maps showed a range of factors, including tree density, mistletoe infection levels, and threatened and endangered species locations. After applying the criteria to several different areas of the ecosystem, a 5,000-acre area called Sheep Basin was found. It had moderate to high tree density and moderate mistletoe infection areas, and no threatened or endangered species. Although there were other areas in greater need of treatment from an environmental perspective, and still others that offered a greater ratio of larger-diameter trees (9-16 inches) to smaller trees (5-9 inches), the Sheep Basin area satisfied the greatest number of criteria. The committee planned a field trip to the area.

In June, about 15 CCCG members went to five Sheep Basin locations to discuss timber removal. The group soon acknowledged that this project would be more complex than the Apache project, since the ecosystem needs required a comprehensive watershed improvement project. Evident needs included protecting mature trees, controlling mistletoe, integrating fire into the treatment, dealing with range issues and cattle removal after fires, and confronting the impact of a large elk presence in the area. Other players, including the New Mexico Fish and Game Department, needed to come to the planning table.

The Grazing Conflict Deepens

The progress the group made with timber projects was overshadowed by deepening divisions in the grazing issues. By April, an out-of-court settlement on the grazing lawsuit was made between the Forest Service and the plaintiffs, the SWCBD and Forest Guardians. The Forest Service agreed to remove cattle from the most vulnerable stream sides in the Gila National Forest and other forests in Arizona. Ranchers and others in the group felt betrayed and anticipated the beginning of the end of ranching in Catron County. The Forest Service maintained that if it hadn't agreed to cattle removal from riparian areas, it might have been compelled to remove all cattle from the allotments named in the lawsuit.

In an attempt to manage the heightened divisions in the group, the April, May, and June meetings were devoted to identifying critical range issues and discussing mutually acceptable group actions. Working in small groups, participants identified the following issues that most concerned them:

- impact on rights, lives, and livestock economy;
- external forces, unfair politics, management without representation, management by judicial system;
- laws and regulations;

- social equity;
- ecosystem condition;
- wildlife issues (threatened and endangered species, elk, and wolves);
- livestock;
- need to know data and underlying agendas;
- inadequate science and information;
- no incentive for good management; and
- relationship between good management and open space.

As process designers we were challenged by the growing anger among some members of the group, by the inherent inability to resolve national issues at the local level, and by the splintering of views and values caused by the grazing agreement. Short of getting the SWCBD and Forest Guardians involved in formal negotiations with ranching and county representatives, which was highly unlikely, we found ourselves at a perplexing juncture.

At the May meeting, several ranchers brought up the prospect of civil disobedience in response to the removal of cattle from riparian areas. After some discussion, Bob Moore got the group back on track by revisiting the group's mission. He reminded participants that contemplation of unilateral action had to be taken outside of the group without the CCCG's influence or endorsement.

The Southwest Center for Biological Diversity Leaves the Table

In June, Todd Schulke stated that he had very little support from the SWCBD for continuing with the CCCG because of the grazing controversies. In addition, he announced his resignation from the SWCBD as a staff person; he was beginning a new job with the Southwest Forest Alliance (SFA) based in Santa Fe. He didn't expect the SFA to give him the latitude to participate in the group. However, Schulke expressed his interest in keeping in touch with the group and the Forest Service, and providing input on the forest health improvement projects.

So after over two years of involvement, the CCCG lost the formal participation of the SWCBD. Through the ups and downs of the group, Schulke continued to contribute to the community he had fled not many years before. He had attended meetings and field trips, negotiated points, expressed his views, and explained the policies and actions of the SWCBD. Schulke's departure was significant but not fatal to the group's authentic collaborative process.

Rally at the Courthouse in Reserve

Meanwhile, anger about the grazing issues turned to direct action. Several of the group members helped plan a July rally at the county courthouse in Reserve. Somewhere between 20 to 50 people gathered to request that the county commissioners pass a proclamation that the Forest Service and the environmentalists were acting against the ranching community. The commissioners responded with a weak version of the rally participants' request. Another rally was scheduled in Silver City to the south.

Some CCCG members were concerned about a misperception held by county residents: that the CCCG had organized the rally. After Bob Moore received numerous phone calls inquiring about the rally sponsorship, he felt compelled to issue a press release, which stated in part:

The rally is not sponsored by CCCG, but rather by a group of citizens who are frustrated with how current land management decisions are being made.

The CCCG is comprised of individuals and organizations representing an array of interests with some members supporting the upcoming rally and others who do not. . . . CCCG's mission is to serve as a forum to enable people with different views to openly and honestly discuss issues that concern our community; to find common ground in order to take action on projects that ensure an economic, social, and environmentally sound future.

Once the rally has passed, we will sit down at the table with heightened awareness and work on advancing wise management decisions for our natural resources through the process of collaboration. Over the past three years, CCCG has made strides that clearly demonstrate the value of the collaborative process. We need to keep working together and leverage our past accomplishments to promote direction for future accomplishments.

After the rally, the group pulled together to plan a collaborative learning experience on riparian issues. The Regional Forester, based in Albuquerque, agreed to visit the county with members of the Forest Service regional wildlife and range staff. A field trip was planned to discuss good riparian management, the impact of elk on stream sides, and upland watershed management. This field trip was the most ambitious of those sponsored by the CCCG, since all of the state and federal land management agencies were to be represented. The anticipated outcomes of the session were to identify pilot projects, gain interagency cooperation, and create some common ground among the diverse interests.

Future Directions

Another productive step was taken through the leadership of the group coordinator, Bob Moore. Moore obtained a rural economic development grant from the Forest Service to conduct a feasibility study for a small-diameter mill. He planned to evaluate the local forestry resources, research potential products and markets, assess appropriate mill capacity and technology, and address the benefits to the community and the environment. By the end of the summer of 1998, the CCCG had withstood internal divisions and had charted a positive course for the immediate future.

■ Lessons Learned

The insights gained from our extended involvement in the Catron County process are consistent with accounts of other community collaborative processes. Some of the lessons recounted here add to the growing body of knowledge on this topic.

Duration. These processes take much more time than anticipated. They can become long-term changes in decision-making governance rather than short-term dispute resolution interventions if groups have the commitment, time, and resources to do so. For example, the Applegate Partnership in southern Oregon has been meeting weekly for six years.

Multiple issues and process approaches. The nature of the Catron County case is complex. It did not focus on one particular land use conflict but on multiple issues, conflicts, and needs. The process has been organic; as neutrals we were experimental and adaptive in the process directions we

pursued. Some were successful, others not. There is no blueprint for addressing this type of community conflict. It is important to remain flexible, letting the group guide and set the agenda.

Outside facilitation and process design. For the Catron County process to work, it was important to have outside neutrals assisting in facilitation and process design. Although a number of collaborative groups exist without the help of dispute resolution practitioners, professional assistance and oversight can help groups achieve sound process practice. Some CCCG members remarked that without outside assistance, the group would not have been able to sustain itself.

Recognition of the scope of what is possible. The number of federal policy issues that were outside the power of the group was a source of frustration and feelings of powerlessness. It is important to encourage groups to recognize and act on tasks that are feasible to accomplish.

Inclusiveness. It is critical to have all of the appropriate stakeholders fully participating in these processes. Environmentalists involved in appeals and litigation are particularly essential. If groups and interests are not represented, then decisions made by collaborative groups can be undermined by those not present. Moreover, the opportunity for collaborative learning and the building of social capital is compromised.

Environmental participation. The participation of environmental groups is dependent on their viewing consensus processes as avenues for achieving their goals. The challenge is in getting local, regional, and national representation. A critical constraint is the lack of skilled environmental activists in rural communities—especially those with the capacity to participate over a long period of time.

Local convenors. The success of CCCG was due in part to local convenors, since they had the credibility to bring the parties to the table.

Local capacity building. Building local capacity is important for the long-term success of interventions of this nature. Developing local leadership and facilitation skills, promoting social learning, and helping groups develop some form of sustained governance is critical. Moreover, having a local coordinator to organize and manage the group's work was valuable, increasing capacity as well as the level of trust.

Trust and relationship building. Trust can only be built over time. Experiences that can strengthen relationships include field trips, potluck dinners, and the mutuality of grappling with issues and reaching concrete outcomes.

Project focus. Focusing on specific on-the-ground projects helps groups negotiate conflicts and move away from ideology and positions.

Funding and other resources. Obtaining funding to support long-term assistance in facilitation and process design is essential, especially when hostilities are extensive.

National and community interests. Both community and national interests must be addressed in collaborative processes about public lands management.

Agreement on the science. There is a need to find common ground in the science of ecosystem health, identifying scientific principles to help inform decision making.

Community health. Tying community health, economic development, and ecosystem health to a larger vision of community will help consensus groups achieve collective and long-term goals.

There is a need to study a range of consensus groups to begin to assess processes and outcomes. If best practices can be identified and described, communities initiating collaborative strategies will benefit from the wisdom of those that came before. Catron County, like its counterparts in other rural western communities, is seeking "a politics appropriate to the stewardship of nature and community" (Snow, 1997). Creating a sustainable economic base while practicing sound ecosystem management is our collective challenge. ✍

∾ COMMENTARY

Smith does an excellent job of highlighting what was learned by what the facilitators did in the Catron County dispute. I encourage interventionists to also ask what they could have done differently to be even more effective.

—Max H. Bazerman, *Social psychologist*

■ *Reference*

Snow, D. (1997). Empire or homelands? A revival of Jeffersonian democracy in the American West. In J. A. Bade & D. Snow (Eds.), *The next West: Public lands, community, and economy in the American West* (pp. 181-204). Washington, DC and Covello, CA: Gallatin Institute and Island Press.

14

FACILITATING STATEWIDE HIV/AIDS POLICIES AND PRIORITIES IN COLORADO

- Michael A. Hughes
- with John Forester and Irene Weiser

This case describes a consensus building process for HIV prevention strategies in the state of Colorado. The case came my way in 1994 and was a significant professional accomplishment: A very large (110 participants), diverse, and impassioned group reached consensus. Over an eight-month period, my involvement in this life-or-death topic profoundly influenced my approach to subsequent work.

This case will be presented both chronologically and thematically. Woven throughout the descriptions of meetings I mediated are many of the tenets and challenges inherent to consensus building. The following pages will describe how relationship building, common language, celebration, and rigorous consensus checks enriched our process. They also include details of several disputes within the meetings, as well as their resolution.

■ Background

In the early 1990s, Colorado's state health department received a directive from the Centers for Disease Control (CDC). From that point forward, health department funding for HIV prevention would be linked to how successfully the agency was able to gain community-based input in the area of HIV prevention strategies. The CDC funds the health department directly, and also provides funds that pass through the health department to community organizations doing AIDS prevention work.

The CDC set goals for a new project, Coloradans Working Together (CWT). This project was supposed to develop a plan for statewide prevention; it was also supposed to comment on and, if possible, to concur on the state health department's application for funding. In light of the CDC directive, the health department sought to engage the multitude of groups affected by the epidemic: gay men, African American and Hispanic populations, relatives of those infected, and professional service providers such as health care professionals and social workers.

This project took place in the atmosphere of Amendment Two, and people were painfully aware of the deep political divisions in Colorado. This amendment proclaimed that it would be illegal for any local government, city or county, to adopt an ordinance explicitly protecting the civil rights of people who are gay or lesbian. Amendment Two was a ballot initiative. Its passage led to boycotts and a legal battle that went to the U.S. Supreme Court, where the amendment was finally overturned.

■ The Ad Hoc Process

In 1993, at the request of Colorado's state health department, the National Civic

League became involved in the planning stage of CWT. This preliminary work—jointly conducted by the Civic League and the health department—was called the Ad Hoc Process. Its aim was to design community planning for HIV prevention in Colorado, statewide, and to set the stage for CWT.

Members of the Ad Hoc Process hoped to lay the groundwork for a public participation process that could bring potentially antagonistic groups to the table. They envisioned a process that would create enduring strategies for HIV prevention. First, they focused on stakeholder identification: Who cares about HIV prevention? Which groups are out there doing it? Where do they get their money? What do they need to be effective?

The Ad Hoc Process also focused on participation. Ad Hoc Process participants were aware that any plan unfavorable to the people who put Amendment Two on the ballot could be stopped in its tracks. Participants said, up front, "We have to get different religious points of view. We have to get different political points of view. We have to open the doors and mean it when we open the doors." More than anything else, participants didn't want to spend a lot of time and effort and then end up with something that couldn't be implemented. The political debate did not need to be inflamed one step further. ↩

↩ COMMENTARY

Conflicts of value are harder to resolve than conflicts of interest. Part of the reason for this is that values matter more to people than interests do (and matter to them more intimately) and are commensurately harder for them to sacrifice. John Forester discusses this feature of values in Chapter 12 of this *Handbook,* and I shall not add to his remarks here. Instead, I shall focus on another feature of values: the contrast between interests and values, which is equally important in making value conflicts particularly intractable. Consensus building in the face of value conflicts is particularly difficult and lies at the center of the problems Mike Hughes faced when he tried to build consensus in the Colorado HIV/AIDS project.

—Daniel Markovits, *Ethicist*

They recruited religious evangelicals and politically conservative, religious fundamentalists—not too many, but some. They tried to cover the political spectrum, with an awareness of who could stop this plan from being implemented. To achieve this kind of balance in Colorado, invitations must be sent to Colorado Springs, to Colorado for Family Values; in short, the people who put Amendment Two on the ballot. Despite the efforts of Ad Hoc Process participants, the religious right and Amendment Two advocates were underrepresented. Many of them viewed the health department as partisan, dominated by the political left. The health department director is appointed in Colorado by the governor—a Democrat. The governor has not dramatically advocated for gay rights, but he was well known to be anti-Amendment Two. I think the religious right believed that the deck was stacked from the beginning. There was a lot of skepticism on their part.

CWT had to represent a number of interests and points of view. The health department in Colorado was politically on the left in terms of AIDS prevention: It emphasized school-based education and condom distribution and was beginning to move toward anonymous testing—all of which are controversial. In the context of a broad political spectrum, HIV prevention activists and the health department were aligned pretty closely. However, activists in Colorado saw the health department as conservative. These community-based groups wanted more and faster ac-

tion in the fight against AIDS. Finally, various minority groups felt that funds had been unfairly diverted from their communities. They hoped to gain more autonomy and decision-making power regarding service delivery. At times, these groups were critical of the health department for tightly maintaining fiscal control and for going slowly in changing prevention programs.

Ad Hoc Process participants did a great deal of talking about what a good process would be. They talked about openness and confidentiality and how to balance those two things. They discussed ground rules, the number of meetings to be held, and "What is collaboration? How do you do it? What makes it go?" All their discussions underscored just how much conflict there was in the area of HIV prevention. The National Civic League hired us (CDR Associates) as a subcontractor to mediate what they expected to be a very charged policy dialogue.

Before they completed their work and disbanded, the Ad Hoc Process participants drafted a request for proposal for facilitation and mediation services. Then they turned over the process and the facilitation team to the CWT Coordinating Committee. The Coordinating Committee's role was to serve as the "memory" from the Ad Hoc Process, providing guidance and direction as well as monitoring progress. This committee consisted of veterans of the Ad Hoc Process as well as some new players. All told, the group included about a dozen of the most prominent AIDS activists in Colorado, including those doing HIV prevention in the state health department, gay rights activists, and AIDS prevention and AIDS care specialists. The membership reflected the diversity of the larger group, CWT; there was some balance of ethnicity, a pretty good balance of men to women, and a pretty good balance of gay to straight.

■ *The Process Takes Off*

The policy dialogue began with an organizational meeting. It was a huge kickoff, with a great deal of publicity. We had 110 people in the room; the energy was incredible. Internally at CDR, and again with the Coordinating Committee, we discussed the feasibility of mediating with so many active participants. Had the process design been ours, we would have chosen some kind of stakeholder representative group. The Coordinating Committee could have done the negotiating, with the 110 others watching and providing input in a different way. But the Ad Hoc Process had guaranteed the most open process I've ever seen. When I said that we would find a way to get consensus from 110 people, a part of me didn't believe it. I knew we would have to develop mechanisms for the process unlike any I'd used before.

Meeting number one established the foundation of our work together. My cofacilitator—Derek Okubo from the National Civic League—and I introduced ourselves. I also briefly reviewed my preferred style of facilitation: You're in charge and I'm here to safeguard your process. I always try to let groups know what I'm doing as the facilitator, and why I do what I do. Finally, I described my idea of consensus: an agreement reached after struggling with all interests to find the best solution ("best" mean-

ing the solution that satisfies the most important and the widest range of interests).

We knew we couldn't have 110 people introduce themselves efficiently. So we split participants into groups of five or six. After they spent some time talking, the plan was for one person to stand up and say, "These are the names of the people who are sitting here. This is Pete and Bill and John and Joe and Sam and Dolores. And among the six of us, the thing that we have in common about being here is . . . ."

I told them that in their small-group introductions, people should state explicitly if they did not want to share particular information with the larger assembly. That way they could maintain confidentiality. The Coordinating Committee and I were hoping that they would go to the heart of their life circumstances: "I'm here because I'm sick," or "I'm here because somebody I love is sick." But we didn't want to put people on the spot in front of 100 strangers.

Their reaction gave me great confidence. They looked at me like I'd lost my mind and said, "No, that's not a big deal. We'll talk about what we want to talk about." And for the most part, people were willing to disclose personal information. One person stood up and said, "This is so-and-so and she's a prostitute. She has AIDS." I think the truth is that people who are used to working in this arena—talking about sex, talking about death, talking about disease—have learned not to hide. It's part of the activism to speak out rather than remaining silent.

We did some team building. We convened a diversity panel in which every shape, size, color, and preference that we could imagine was represented. Someone from the African American community began the discussion. She stood up and spoke to these questions: Who is my community? What has been the effect of this virus on my community? What don't you know about my community that I want you to know? We had a member of the Latino community and a Native American. We had gay people, straight people, bi-people. We had people who were HIV positive but didn't have full-blown AIDS. We had people who did have AIDS. We tried to cover all the bases; one guy stood up and said, "I think I'm supposed to represent white straight people," and he got a huge laugh. He was from the Denver Department of Health. From the beginning, his message was about people's differences. He stated that acknowledging these differences—in life experiences, in political perspectives, and in socioeconomic backgrounds—would be crucial to the success of this project.

Although there was an open atmosphere and we were off to a good start, there was a lot of resistance when we started to talk about the process. A flood of questions arose: What does it mean to participate, and how many meetings are there likely to be? Where will meetings be, and how long they will take? What are the ground rules, and where are the data going to come from, and what's the purpose of this anyway? What's the CDC after, and what agenda is the health department going to push? There was lots of skepticism and discussion about whether this process was authentic: Who was missing from it? What would its outcome be? While a few questioned the process, most were quietly taking it in and at times meeting number one was ominously quiet. The suspicion, fear, and anger around HIV prevention would not instantly dissolve. People were absorbing what folks from the Ad Hoc Process were telling them. I observed moments of one-way communication and passivity, and

speculated that most participants were not ready to take ownership of the process.

■ Finding a Common Purpose: Relationship Building and Use of Language

People were sure of one thing: If this group was going to be able to work together, its members were going to have to embrace the group's larger mission. In developing a plan, they would have to go beyond their own personal agendas. They couldn't think in the back of their minds, "Look, my agency wants this money. That's why I'm here." People expected a lot of turf battles and struggles over money. To help build the sense of shared purpose, we created a statement of shared purpose called What We Believe. Among the values were parity, a commitment to give everyone an equal place in the process; inclusion, a promise to value everyone; and representation, a guarantee to draw all points of view into each decision.

We hoped to help people see that what they needed to accomplish for the state of Colorado was bigger than their own goals and, it was hoped, inclusive of their unique priorities. We certainly didn't accomplish this goal at the first meeting. But something equally important occurred: People began to feel as though they knew each other. We used a number of techniques to help people learn each other's names and establish rapport.

I also introduced the idea that much of what we would do together centered around the development of mutually acceptable vocabulary and grammar. We would focus on creating language for the plan that, we hoped, the whole group could live with. That way, we would move away from "I have to change your mind about this" and move toward "Well, what words can we find together?" We had to shift from confrontation to the collaborative development of language.

■ *Warning Signs and Stumbling Blocks*

The biggest challenge to teamwork was the probability of a high level of conflict, so we set about building systems to cope. A whole set of ground rules related specifically to dispute resolution. ◆

◈ COMMENTARY

Value conflicts are driven not by each side's single-minded pursuit of its own interests but rather by each side's single-minded attempt to promote its own view of everybody's true interests. The central character in a value conflict is not the egoist, who cares only about his own interests, but rather the egocentrist, who cares only about his own point of view. And accordingly, the key to resolving value conflicts is not to get each side to care about the other's interests but rather to get each side to respect the other's point of view.

Partly this poses a psychological problem, and the techniques Mike Hughes employed in mediating the conflict about AIDS—which included rearranging the room to allow for self-regulated group discussion, developing signals by means of which all members of the group could simultaneously approve or disapprove, and giving members of the groups tangible, physically discardable symbols of dispute—are ingenious psychological solutions to this problem. But the problem of getting each of the disputants to respect the other side's point of view is also a moral problem, not least because when consensus building is not morally justified then the psychological tricks used to achieve consensus will be chicanery only and can succeed only at the cost of leading people to betray their values.

There do not exist fixed or guaranteed methods for solving the moral problem. Nevertheless, any successful solution to the problem of getting each side to respect the other's point of view will contain two essential elements, and so it is worth investigating these as a way of learning how to build a successful, stable consensus. First, each side will learn to respect the other's point of view only if it makes a sustained effort to understand the other side's values from the inside. Hughes's repeated insistence that people who spoke at the mediation meetings should begin by describing how and why they came to be there was part of such an effort. Often, the best way to learn to respect someone's values is to understand how a decent, reasonable person could come to hold them. Second, it will help each side to learn to respect the other's point of view if both sides make a mutual, public commitment to a set of procedures for administering the mediation effort, procedures Hughes calls ground rules. It is important for all sides to accept such procedures and abide by them because doing so gives the opposing sides at least one set of ideals in common and also demonstrates to each side that the other side's values are at least compatible with holding a reasonable discussion (and deserve to be respected for this reason even if for no other).

—Daniel Markovits, *Ethicist*

When disputes arise, what do we do? When we can't deal with it as a whole group, where does it go? I did a one-hour training segment on how to raise conflict productively. When you're angry about something, or when you see your interests are not being attended to in some way, what do you do about it?

I gave participants 10 key ideas in this area:

1. Take care of yourself. Relax, breathe, and make yourself comfortable before tackling controversial issues.
2. Carefully consider timing. When is the best time to raise an issue?
3. Be clear with yourself about your real concerns.
4. Use "I" messages. Avoid blaming, finger-pointing, and so on.
5. Focus on the future. Communicate the way you want things to be, rather than dwelling on what you don't like about the present.
6. Frame concerns in terms of your interests, rather than making demands: "Here's the interest I'm trying to meet. . . ."
7. Assume that other viewpoints are possible.
8. Don't propose your favorite answer too soon.
9. Don't escalate conflict by insisting you are right.
10. Everyone has a right to the way he or she feels. Work to accept other people's strong feelings as well as your own.

It took time for participants to internalize these principles and begin to put them to use. In the beginning, participants didn't raise difficult issues in the meetings; instead, negative feelings carried over after the meetings. Participants called us to say, "You know, I don't trust the health depart-ment to do this" or "You know, the health department's too much in control of this" or "There were too many speakers from the health department." These misgivings eventually worked their way through the grapevine to the Coordinating Committee. People were grumpy about the presenters and the data. There had been some attrition, and we talked about that as a group. People said, "You know, that's the truth of it. That's how this is going to work—people will drop out."

In general, we stressed that people were going to have to talk openly and raise sensitive issues. We also made an effort to anticipate what wasn't going to work, and to make adjustments. There was one obvious thing that the Ad Hoc Committee, the Coordinating Committee, and the facilitators missed: We scheduled meetings from 8:00 a.m. to 5:00 p.m. Now, I'm notorious for getting caught up in the subject and resisting taking a break. But we learned right away that eight hours was way too much for somebody who has AIDS, or for somebody who is trying to fight the infection and stay well. Participants needed to spend less time each day, so we multiplied the number of days.

We cut the schedule back to 10:00 a.m. to 4:00 p.m., with, at a minimum, a mandatory 15-minute break in the morning, an uninterrupted hour for lunch, and a mandatory 15-minute break in the afternoon. We kept saying to the group, "Does this work for you? Is this the right purpose for this group? Are these data to your liking? You know, it's yours: You have to take ownership of this. This is your process." We did everything that we could think of to encourage feedback. At the end of every meeting, we asked, "What went wrong? What didn't work? What do we need to change?" I talked to people informally individually during breaks and at lunch.

■ *Sessions Two and Three*

We started off meeting once a month, then moved to every other week. Meeting number two introduced the epidemiological profile: These are the people who have been sick. These are the people who are getting sick. These are the rates of infection for different communities. A needs assessment, based on interviews with AIDS prevention organizations, was also explained. The presenters were from the health department or members of the Ad Hoc Process. The discussion that followed uncovered resistance to both the process and the data.

In session number three, there was discussion about whether the health department was just paying lip service to new strategies for HIV prevention. Would this process really make a difference, and would that difference result in money flowing in new directions than in the past? Was the health department prepared to lay off staff to get money out into the community? Health department staff were in the room, and they fielded hard questions about whether the prevention plan would be implemented according to recommendations.

The third meeting was rough, both in terms of the process and the substance. We tossed problems back at the group: "So, if you don't like the data, can we go get more? What would the data cost? Who would go get them? Who would you trust to have them?" We worked through some of those issues so that we could move forward in the next meeting.

At this point, our group was down to 60 or 70 people at each meeting. Some of the original 110 had come only to confirm that their own interests were represented. For example, people said, "Well, you know, if ACT UP (a gay rights activist group) is here,

I don't have to come." Or "If there are enough members of the Latino community here, then I don't have to come." After the kickoff, some people had gone their merry way. But we still felt that we had reached pretty far into the community and had attracted a wide spectrum of people.

In the third meeting, the power in the meeting shifted, and I felt a huge transfer of ownership happening. We stopped talking in Meeting 3 about anything that had come before. The Ad Hoc Process stopped, didn't exist any more. From here on out, anything that happened with this process was in the participants' own hands. One way I recognized this shift was that in Meeting 3, they came after me. Big surprise! I have learned from these large-group efforts that the facilitator is often a lightning rod. If you don't want that role, don't pick up the marker! Don't be a mediator if you can't accept the idea of being a target.

In the opening meetings, we set up the room in such a way that all 110 participants faced in the same direction. That way, the presenters could reach the whole group, and communication would go through the facilitator. The room was small, and we were elbow to elbow. The seats were theater style, with several big arcs of chairs. I was calling on people from my spot in the front of the room. When 40 or so hands went up, I would say, "I'm going to start over here on the right side of the room and I'm going to keep coming around, and I'll catch up so those of you that are way over on the left side of the room, you'll go first on the next question."

As I'm sweeping across the room, of course, new hands come up. By the time I got over to the other side, somebody went berserk and said, "I'm going to talk now, let me in!" I then acknowledged that the facilitation wasn't going very well. They said, "Yeah, you're too slow. You're not calling on us fast enough. You're not letting us talk." Suddenly, it was all my fault. I said, "Yeah, we've got to fix this process, and you've got to fix me and make sure that I'm doing this well." I knew we had to respond to their reaction to the facilitation. It became clear that we needed to structure our work so that all participants were thinking at once and working together. We would need to mix and match open discussion, small group, and individual work. We also decided to assign tasks both during and between sessions. Some objectives would have to be accomplished off-line, with subsequent opportunities for group discussion. And in the larger meetings, we needed a new structure. For the next meeting, we moved the chairs into concentric circles with a small table and four chairs at the center. And we made aisles that led to the center of the room so everyone could easily move from the back to the front.

With this set up, I could get out of the way and let people come to the table and talk rather than waiting for me to call on them. We explained the procedure to the participants: "When we are ready to open discussion on a topic, we will clearly mark the transition: Now it's time for discussion. Then we will get out of the way. If you've got something to say, come sit in a chair. There are four chairs, and four of you can talk with one another—loudly, so we can all hear it. When you're done, get out of the chair. If you see somebody waiting, make room for him or her. When we think that the discussion has wound itself to some sort of conclusion, or we want to ask if you have come to consensus, we'll interject to move the process on. But when it's time to talk, it's time to talk. You don't have to be called on. You don't have to raise your hand."

They loved it. They took to it both because the structure made sense and be-

cause they sensed our responsiveness. Through the remainder of the work, we used this system.

This method worked beautifully much of the time, but it was not without its downsides. At least twice, I was much too far away. I was down the aisle in the back of the room, and I should have been at the table with them. After some tough going, I suggested a modification. We had a room with mostly teal green chairs, but there were a few that were ugly pink. I suggested that we use green chairs for the four discussion seats, and add a fifth one—ugly pink— for the facilitator. That chair belonged to me or the cofacilitator. When necessary, we could sit down in it and mediate the conversation.

■ Visual Tools and the Use of Celebration

Throughout the process, we used a visual consensus check: You hold your thumb up if you're in agreement, even if you are willing to go along but you're not ecstatic. You hold your thumb sideways if you're not quite sure, or you want to ask a question, or you want more data. Thumbs down means, I'm not in consensus and you can't go forward without me. We'd gotten used to doing this kind of consensus check on wording and on process. We'd work through the thumbs down, and then we'd work through the thumbs sideways. When everybody could hold their thumbs up, we'd move on. We used this method a thousand times if we used it once.

We all rode an emotional roller coaster in the months we spent together. Celebration and exuberance came not from me, but from the participants and the Coordinating Committee. We played music at a lunch break. With some instruction and encouragement from one participant, people took each other arm in arm and danced around the room. One of the members of the Coordinating Committee was in an improvisational acting group, and she got the whole group involved in acting exercises at a break. She picked people out of the group and said they had to pretend, with gestures only, to demonstrate that they were angry or afraid or even constipated. It was hysterical. The dancing and other planned and impromptu team-building events had an important common element—touch.

In one of our first meetings, we asked the participants to get in pairs. We gave each pair a piece of paper and a pen. We asked the two to put their hands together on the pen and, without speaking to each other, to draw a picture. Each pair quickly discovered the need to cooperate and to give one another power over the pen and over the picture itself. Each person found ways to signal his or her partner through the simple release of pressure on the pen or a slight touch. The pictures were funny and hopeful, giving all of us one more opportunity to laugh and to look ahead. The act of drawing together, hand in hand, while trying to find answers to a disease passed from one person to the next through intimate contact was a powerful one. Contact could be part of healing as well.

As our work went on, it became clear to me that this group needed an opportunity to celebrate something, anything, because they were dealing with very depressing things: life and death, disease and destruction. In late fall, we actually lost one of the members of the group to AIDS. We grieved together over that. If we were going to grieve together over Joe's death, we certainly ought to celebrate together as well.

■ A Plan Emerges, Things Heat Up

The substantive core of the plan began to take shape at the fourth meeting. The CDC had strict guidelines about the content of this plan. For example, it mandated that we articulate the most important needs in HIV prevention in Colorado. Our group was challenged to identify populations affected by the epidemic—and to prioritize those populations. What an awful thing to ask people to do, to choose one group over another, but that's what they demanded: a ranking of jeopardized people. The group also had to identify preferred strategies for preventing the disease in those populations.

We started with needs. We asked each individual to generate a list, and ended up with something like 150 different needs. At lunch, we scrambled to organize the list as a point of departure for discussion. We told the group that before the next meeting, volunteers would further pare down these needs: remove the redundancies, categorize them, and make this list more manageable.

The small group was able to compress the 150 needs statements into 13 by lifting them to a level of generality that captured what was underneath. Of course, we hoped not to lose the nuance, but we needed these 13 as broader categories. As the discussion continued, a participant who would eventually contribute the 14th need spoke up. This wonderful participant—he was brilliant—came into the circle, and he said, "Here's a need that is missing. There is a need to shift the discussion of AIDS in Colorado from a moral issue to a public health issue, and I refuse to participate in moving this plan forward until we wrestle with that."

He made an eloquent speech about how moral barriers to effective AIDS education were killing people. His statements weren't accusatory. They weren't blaming. He didn't denigrate Amendment Two supporters or folks who opposed certain prevention methods on moral grounds. He was angry, but his emotion didn't take the form of a personal accusation. The whole room was captivated. Other people ran to the table and started talking with him. The folks from Focus on the Family and from Colorado for Family Values talked about why for them, this *was* a moral issue and the meaning their values had for them. People engaged in the discussion with renewed intensity. They started working on different levels, dropping down in those chairs and talking to each other person to person. The guy who started the discussion kept one of the four chairs for quite a long time. Then he got out, other people came in; later he was invited back.

Amazingly, no one broke the ground rules. People were speaking to one another respectfully. They were doing their best to listen to one another. The person who began the discussion simply said, "[Amendment Two and the moral barriers] are in place, and because they're in place, this is the effect." It was depersonalized, meaning "not accusatory." But it was clearly personal from his own point of view. It was very much an "I message." "This is how I see it." It set the right tone.

We came upon another issue later on, where people stood up and said, "All of you people. . . ." It was a racial issue. "You white people all are. . . ." The stereotypes flew out, and the room exploded. But that didn't happen on this one. He didn't say, "All you religious bigots . . . all you Bible thumpers . . ." Instead, he said, "These barriers are in place." He didn't say who put them there. He didn't point any fingers or make any inflammatory statements. He just spoke from his own beliefs and his own anger and his own pain at seeing people that he cares about die. It was emotionally very powerful.

COMMENTARY

Whereas interests are things people generally pursue for themselves (hence the term self-interest), values are things people pursue not just for themselves but for everyone (indeed, this is part of what it is for them to be values). This distinction may be seen, for example, in the difference between money, on the one hand, and religious salvation, on the other. Money serves a person's interests, and a person may want money just for herself. But religious salvation is a value, and part of what it means to believe in religious salvation is to want religious salvation for other people also, or at least to want religious salvation to be available to other people.

—Daniel Markovits, *Ethicist*

In the ensuing discussion, others said, "Well, those aren't the facts. In fact, why people are dying is because we can't, in our culture, frame these things in moral terms, because we're losing the moral ground underneath us." These people were taking the opposite point of view. They said, "No, you don't understand, this must become a moral issue. If it isn't a moral issue, people will continue to behave in ways that put them in danger. Once you have moral underpinnings to keep people from behaving in those ways, *that's* when people won't die."

☞ COMMENTARY

This important feature of values—that those who hold them want to apply them to people generally and not just to themselves—makes value conflicts particularly resistant to consensus building. It renders ineffectual key tools in the consensus builder's arsenal, tools that generally form the core of the consensus builder's efforts to resolve conflicts of interest. The most important of these are the idea of sympathy for others and the related idea of fairness. These two ideas come together in the golden rule—that you should do unto others as you would have others do unto you—and so it is useful, when investigating the peculiar problems that value conflicts present in consensus building, to examine how the golden rule works to help build consensus in conflicts of interest and how it fails to build consensus in value conflicts.

In a conflict of interest, for example, between people who want to use a river for quiet fishing and people who want to use the river for noisy motorboat races, it is often helpful to ask each party to imagine himself or herself in the other's shoes. Applying the golden rule in this way helps sensitize each side to what the other stands to lose; it drives home the thought that it's only fair for the two sides to resolve their dispute by meeting somewhere in the middle. No one should have to sacrifice everything when others sacrifice nothing. In this way, a consensus can be built.

But in a conflict of values, for example, between the fishers and boaters united as sportspeople, on the one hand, and religious people who believe the river is sacred and do not want it to be defiled, on the other, the technique of the golden rule and the ideas of sympathy and fairness that lie behind it will prove ineffectual. If the religious people are asked to imagine themselves in the position of the sportspeople, they will say that while they too like water sports it is simply wrong to defile a sacred river for passing earthly pleasure. And if one suggests to the religious people that it is unfair for their preferences to dominate the sportspeople's preferences, they will answer that the sacredness of the river is not a mere preference but rather a spiritual fact, one that is bad even for the sportspeople to ignore. Indeed, the religious people will add that it cannot be unfair for them to do what is best even for the sportspeople, that it cannot be unfair to save the sportspeople from suffering at the hands of their mistaken preferences, and that their efforts to keep the river unspoiled reflect their concern for the sportspeople as much as their concern for themselves.

Similarly, if one asks the sportspeople to sympathize with the religious people, they will say that they would not want to sacrifice solid humanist and utilitarian values in the name of what is in fact merely a religious illusion. And if one asks the sportspeople about fairness, they will say (as the religious people said) that it cannot possibly be unfair for them to save the religious people from so irrational a sacrifice as suffering at the hands of their mistaken beliefs and that they want to make water sports available to the religious people also and not just to themselves.

In a value conflict, each side understands sympathy and fairness through the lens of its own values, so these ideals can't help resolve the conflict and build consensus because they are among the forces that drive the conflict. Each side tries to impose its values on the other out of sympathetic concern for what it believes is truly best for the other side, just as each side tries to impose its values on the other side because it believes that abandoning the other side to false values would be unfair. And indeed, this is precisely the problem Coloradans faced at the most delicate and critical points in the HIV/AIDS mediation: A member of the Colorado AIDS Project insisted that the epidemic had to be understood as a public health problem and not as a moral issue because to do otherwise was to disrespect those who were dying of the disease or were already dead; a member of Colorado for Family Values replied that the only way to properly respect the dying and to save others from similar deaths was to make AIDS a moral issue. Each side believed in being sympathetic and fair, but they couldn't agree about what these ideas involved.

—Daniel Markovits, *Ethicist*

When the discussion had reached the point where people were beginning to repeat themselves, we would step in. We might say, "Look, this discussion hasn't led us to some kind of consensus point of view, that's clear. So what do you want to do with that conflict? You have to account for this in the plan. You have one person who is not with you unless the plan says something about this. We're going to have to do something. We're going to have to write a 14th need statement. Or we're going to have to find some other way to resolve it. So, what mechanism?"

■ *Small-Group Mediation: Morality and the 14th Need*

We had ground rules about conflict resolution. When an issue couldn't be resolved within the group, we would resort to small-group mediation. For this conflict—the one about morality—the four people present included the person who had presented the issue, a person from Colorado for Family Values, and one person each for support of their point of view. Luckily, the person from Colorado for Family Values selected someone with a moderate stance from an organization called His Heart (a Christian organization that cares for people with AIDS). The person who presented the issue, from the Colorado AIDS Project, selected a colleague who was a collaborative, calm presence in the group. From my point of view, these were wise choices.

The five of us sat down between meetings with the large group and did a media-

tion, and we developed language that the four of them could live with. It was clear that what we were doing was writing a plan. Instead of getting mired in "I have to change your mind about this" kind of talk, we focused on "What words can we find together?" And they did it. We walked out of that mediation after two hours with a message that all four of them agreed to.

The way I did it was to take the process that we were using for CWT and compress it into two hours. First I said, "We're going to begin at the beginning. Let's make sure we all know one another." We did introductions. I continued, "OK, let's get the ground rules clear. This two-hour session will work if: You talk one at a time. You respect one another. You use language that's appropriate. You avoid personal attacks." I laid out the familiar ground rules to make clear how careful we would need to be when we spoke to one another.

I laid out a process. Each person would talk about the importance of a particular wording, so they could educate one another about their respective views. Then each would suggest options that would take into account the needs expressed. Finally, we went into a problem-solving mode. Attending carefully to language was a task they were willing to accept. After all, we had already wordsmithed 13 needs. We had taken out commas and worked on the grammar and substituted one word for another. So they knew how to approach the 14th need, and they went at it.

I proposed this approach because I knew that underneath the wording there was a common concern: to stop this disease from spreading. I knew that unless they really saw that they ultimately were aiming at the same thing, just aiming at it in absolutely opposite ways, they were just going to keep aiming in opposite ways and would not find language that the other one would find acceptable. Recognizing their mutual interest in creating a plan acceptable to each of their constituencies was key. Once all four of them heard this message from the others—that they too wanted to stop the disease—it became a joint task. They suspended confrontation for long enough to discover that they could in fact find words that would be satisfactory to both sides, and they didn't have to give up their points of view. They also found that they could agree to disagree. That was part of it, acknowledging that they weren't going to change. Regardless, they had to write a document that both sides could live with. That was simpler, so I focused them on that. ∞

∞ COMMENTARY

Together, mediation practices give the conflicting parties experiences and reasons they can share and grounds for respecting each other's points of view. Around this they can begin to build a consensus even though their values conflict. And this kind of consensus, the kind built on shared reasons and based on mutual respect, is the kind most worth having. To be sure, a compromise resolution of the conflict may sometimes be secured even without achieving these ends, as part of what John Rawls (1985, p. 247) has famously called (in a related context) a mere *modus vivendi*. But such a compromise is much less than a true consensus because it is based on each side's prudential assessment of how best to promote its own peculiar values rather than on a set of values and reasons all sides share. Such a compromise is a truce in the conflict, but it is best described as a part of that conflict. Adapting Clausewitz's famous phrase, one may say that in that case, compromise is a mere continuation of conflict by other means. It is a compromise that all sides prosecute against one another rather than endorse together, a compromise without trust or community, and without the obligations and motivations trust and community generate. Even when such a compromise is in place, it is not an ideal but only a technique to be discarded as soon as it is no longer useful: Its slogan remains "who is not for us is against us," and its attendant attitudes and modes of action are ruthlessness and manipulation. This will tend to make compromise without consensus unstable, although how unstable is a practical question. I suspect, however, that such compromise will generally be unacceptably unstable, in which case consensus that reaches beyond being merely a prudentially motivated compromise turns out itself to be prudentially necessary.

—Daniel Markovits, *Ethicist*

REFERENCE

Rawls, J. (1985). Justice as fairness: Political not metaphysical. *Philosophy & Public Affairs, 14*(2), 223-251.

The language they all agreed on was this: "There is a need to remove moral objections to HIV prevention and education that is appropriate to the behaviors of the target community." Now that's somewhat vague. But then they followed with, "For communities that include members with a range of moral perspectives, HIV prevention methods need to be appropriate to that range of moral perspectives by presenting multiple prevention messages." The subtext of this statement is, not everybody in any community is going to share every moral perspective. Therefore, if you give people prevention messages, the messages should encompass a range of moral points of view. In other words, prevention messages should present multiple options that correspond with those different moral perspectives.

The only way that we could get the gay rights activists to accept sentences two and three was to include sentence number one—"There is a need to remove moral objections to messages that are appropriate to the target community." In concrete terms, this means that for settings such as gay bars, you can use sexually explicit material. Why? Because in a gay bar, sexually explicit material is within that audience's moral parameters. But if you go into the schools, and you've got students who come from a fundamentalist Christian point of view, both those students and their parents would likely be uncomfortable with sexually explicit material. Thus, the wording encourages a range of messages that are tailored to a spectrum of moral perspectives.

In two hours they hammered this out: three sentences.

It became difficult only at the very end. I said, "Look you're all done, the mediation's over, hurray for you. You get to go back to the group and say, We have a draft for you. Now let's all go home." But instead of leaving, everyone stood around and started talking about whether being gay is a lifestyle or not. They hit on the word *lifestyle* and suddenly started to have an argument. I interrupted and said, "I think it's a mistake for you to continue this conversation. I think you should get in your cars and go home." They laughed and shook hands, and said, "You're right. We did well today. Let's go home." But I can tell you they were not going out for a beer together afterwards.

They went back to the big group with their draft, and I stood on my head to praise the four of them. I wanted to send the message that they shouldn't take this kind of breakthrough lightly. If we hadn't been able to resolve this one, the extreme factions on each side might have dropped out, and the credibility of the plan would have been damaged. As it turned out, the exact wording didn't stick. The larger group changed it. But we celebrated the four of them. We all knew that this issue could have blown the whole group apart.

Things fell into place after the group decided on the 14 need statements. But there was more hard work after that, because we had to prioritize those needs. We also had to identify populations within each category and prioritize those. We had groups that developed strategies to meet the needs for each population, and again—prioritization of strategies.

■ The Racial Divide

The task of prioritizing populations triggered a discussion about race, oppression, and homophobia and what it meant to be hated or ignored. At that moment, having the table and those four chairs was almost not enough. Prioritizing populations raised questions about whether the well-being of African Americans or gay men or Latinos was a higher priority than for some other group. This highly charged confrontation made the "Is this a moral issue?" discussion look manageable by comparison. There were a lot of tears shed. It was sad, both because the group was pulling itself apart and because the issues themselves were painful to begin with.

Early in this part of the agenda, a man stood up and said, "All of you white people. . . ." The stereotypes flew out, and the room exploded. Participants aired their beliefs about how funds had been allocated: They believed that prevention money had been allocated disproportionately and that communities of color had not gotten funding commensurate with their rate of infection. I couldn't bring myself to stop this frank discussion about how hard it was to choose one group's needs over another's. Opinion is still divided about whether that meeting was a good or a bad thing. I have to take the mediator's role and say it was both.

I later learned that the discussion was very uncomfortable for a lot of people. They saw it as divisive and destructive, rather than ultimately healing. People came up to me and said, "Stop this thing!" A couple of people got out of their chairs and came over to me and said, "You're the facilitator, make this stop." (They were white.) I said, "I can't. If I stop this I will add insult to this injury." Then I added, "But if you think this should stop, there are chairs up there in the middle of the room. You stop it. You're part of this. Take a role in the discussion and see if it's best that we stop it." I let the interchange go, and the group kept going, until people were emotionally and physically exhausted.

For some, the discussion about race was too much. They believed that the acrimony drove a wedge in the group. I think it simply named the wedge that was already there and gave them a chance to talk it out. At the next meeting, people stood up and said, "I hated that. I thought that was painful and awful." Then other people stood up and said, "Yes, it was painful. Yes, it was awful, but I needed to do what I did in that meeting and I needed to have that conversation, and it was time well spent."

■ *Picking Up the Pieces*

I had thought long and hard about how to open the next meeting. By happenstance, I had been reading a book called *The Soul of Politics,* by Jim Wallis. A quote from that book hit me over the head, and I wrote it down. I showed it to one of the people on the Coordinating Committee and I said, "I think this is what happened in the last meeting." He said, "That's it, absolutely, and I'll read it at the next meeting." What Vic read was:

> Compassion. The word compassion literally means to suffer with, to put yourself in someone else's position, to walk for a little while in his or her shoes. Compassion always begins with listening. The listening that leads to compassion is the beginning of understanding. In America we build walls we desperately hope will keep people away from us. But these same walls are ultimately unable to prevent us from experiencing the consequences of abandoning our neighbor. The walls divide us but they don't protect us. Those illusory but oppressive walls must be broken down and nothing does that better than the experience of listening directly to the people on the other side of the wall. Getting close

enough to see, hear, touch, smell, and taste the reality of others is what always makes the difference. In listening to the stories of those so seemingly different from us, we find similar but unexpressed voices inside ourselves. Hearing one another's stories is the beginning of new understanding and the foundation of compassionate action. (Wallis, 1994, pp. 162-163)

In reading this quote, Vic made room for everybody to express different points of view about what happened. That was a very wise 30 minutes we took out of the agenda. People had a chance to decompress and let go of anxieties over what had happened in that difficult meeting.

Then we tried to pick up the pieces. We still had to get these populations prioritized. And participants rose to the occasion. They were able to say, Look, let's step back from this, and let's get this right. Let's make sure that we are understanding why you would put a group in the highest priority, and why you would put a group in a second level or higher priority, and why you would put the group in simply a high-priority population. We talked about the criteria. We talked about their concerns. They made those difficult decisions and reached consensus on every priority.

Before the last meeting, we gave people a draft of the plan and asked people to identify any reservations they might have. On sticky Post-it® notes, people had to write down the specific page number and the specific wording they wanted to change to make the plan acceptable to them. We stuck all these Post-it notes up on the wall. Everybody went and read them, and we worked through them at the last meeting. One by one, barriers to consensus came down from the wall.

People were nervous. There was a lot of anxiety about whether or not we'd get consensus. The Coordinating Committee members responded this way: They made worry beads for everyone. (These beads were the kind you hang on Christmas trees—segments of 8 or 10 plastic beads.) If we started to get stuck a little bit, people would run up and grab worry beads. If we were making progress, they would throw their beads back in the bowl. People started hooking worry beads together, putting them around their head, and weaving them into their clothing. Every now and then we'd hit a tough barrier to consensus. We'd get through it, changing the wording. People would hold their thumbs up, and start tossing the beads away.

At the end, I said to the group, Thumbs? and they started to hold up their thumbs. Then, one person said, "No," in a very loud voice from the back of the room. I thought, "Oh, we *don't* have consensus. There's something else—what haven't we done?"

But this person said, "No, don't hold your thumbs up, *stand* up."

I looked around and said, "Is that OK?"

And everybody said, "Yeah, let's stand up."

People started getting out of their chairs, and the next thing you know, not one person is sitting down. I said to the group, "Well, I think you've done it. You have consensus." And a cheer went up in the room, and people started to hug one another and shake hands and celebrate. And all of a sudden the beads started flying through the air. There was a huge shower of beads in the middle of the room, and I'm standing and I'm watching these beads float through the air and land in the middle of the room.

They were able to come to consensus on the plan, something that many people had thought impossible. Even I had doubted they could throw the doors open, let anybody come in, and still get real consensus. People were ultimately able to agree to a ranking of populations, lined up under the needs statements. Groups were prioritized as highest, higher, and high. They did it! At the project's conclusion, they had jointly worked out a document that described needs, populations, and strategies.

■ Reflections on the Process

One stroke of genius that had come from the Ad Hoc Process, from the health department, and from the CDC was this: The plan wouldn't be a onetime effort. People dedicated to HIV and AIDS work saw the need to do long-term, sustainable work in the planning arena. For this reason, CWT created one more CDC goal: We are going to take time to heal wounds. That was their exact phrasing, time to heal wounds. Participants promised each other that when we hit a painful subject, we would take the time to work through it, and heal as a community. They spoke about the depth of people's pain, and how best to offer relief. It was a *promise* they made to each other.

This was important, too, for me personally. I have a friend who has AIDS, a close friend. I'm executor in the will and will be a primary caretaker when it comes to that time. We're not there yet, thank goodness. More than 10 years we've known each other. And I've lost other friends to AIDS as well. This made it hard for me to keep my nose where it belonged, to be a good mediator and not a participant. There were a couple of times when I could feel myself slipping, feel myself being pulled in.

I can say without reservation that this work is the most important I've done in my professional life. With this group, we reached each other's deepest wounds—and were able to regroup and move on. I came to care deeply for the participants and for the Coordinating Committee members. I came to care deeply about the work they accomplished. While facilitators ostensibly adopt neutral stances, I believe my emotional engagement with participants was critical.

Any good I was able to do as a mediator came directly from being involved with them emotionally every step of the way. As the work progressed, the participants were able to raise difficult, emotional issues in large part because we were able to create a safe environment. To the best of my ability, anger and pain were attended to with compassion.

As a human being, to remain detached from participants' sadness would have been unthinkable. As a mediator, to remain at a distance from the CWT members would have made me inaccessible at critical moments of the deliberation. This realization has colored my subsequent work in this field. I cross freely into that more vulnerable place, trusting that empathy and personal connection enrich—rather than compromise—mediation of consensus building processes.

■ Postscript

It is October 26, 1998. Today, I had the chance to talk to Bob, the current CWT coordinator. He is now preparing for CWT's sixth year of community planning. A CDC study of prevention programs before and after CWT confirms that funding has changed significantly in response to the plan. CDC staff have invited Bob to share the success story and help those in other states who struggle for the elusive consensus we built. He acknowledges that each year requires hard work to keep the spirit of cooperation alive and to solve the next problem. But most important, in Bob's opinion the delivery of HIV services is much improved in Colorado.

■ *Reference*

Wallis, J. (1994). *The soul of politics: A practical and prophetic vision for change.* New York: New Press; Maryknoll, NY: Orbis.

15

FINDING COMMON GROUND ON ABORTION

- Michelle LeBaron
- Nike Carstarphen

In the United States and Canada, few issues are more divisive and polarized than abortion. Images of the conflict fill our heads: angry demonstrators waving placards showing aborted fetuses or botched back-alley abortions, clinic-defense and Operation Rescue volunteers screaming at each other, limp activists being dragged to waiting vans by police, hate mail and threats, fortified clinics, and doctors in danger.

As the conflict rages on, a growing number of concerned citizens—pro-choice and pro-life together—are forming local dialogue groups in an effort to find some common ground. Many of these dialogue efforts are facilitated by the Network for

Life and Choice, a project of a nonprofit organization in Washington, D.C. called Search for Common Ground. This is their story.

The characters in this story come from all over North America, from the front lines of the abortion conflict, to the back rooms where strategy is devised, to households touched by the abortion issue. Two of the best known are Andrew F. Puzder and B. J. Isaacson-Jones. Puzder helped write the Missouri law that gave states the authority to restrict abortions. Isaacson-Jones, the former executive director of Reproductive Health Services of Missouri, was the plaintiff in the well-known abortion case *Webster v. Reproductive Health Services*. Puzder

The evaluation of the Network for Life and Choice was supported by a grant from the Kellogg Foundation to the Network.

and Isaacson-Jones were adversaries in the abortion debate and were often pitted against each other in the St. Louis press.

Through a process of dialogue, however, each discovered that the other had come to abortion activism through concern about the large number of unintended pregnancies and poor women and children. Before long, they were collaborating on a Missouri Senate bill that would provide more adequate assistance and treatment for pregnant women addicted to crack cocaine (Wirpsa, 1996). Puzder and Isaacson-Jones also became a driving force behind the common ground movement and the 1992 establishment of the Network for Life and Choice. In 1995, they coauthored a policy paper on adoption that was published by the Network for Life and Choice Steering Committee. These two individuals exemplify the power of direct communication and mutual respect.

Since the Network was established, many other concerned citizens have followed in the footsteps of Puzder and Isaacson-Jones. More than 100 of them came together in Madison, Wisconsin in 1996 for the first annual conference on abortion dialogue. Participants from both sides of the conflict took part in workshops and seminars. For many, it was their first abortion dialogue experience; for others, it was an opportunity to meet like-minded dialogue supporters and strengthen the common ground movement. Those at the conference experienced "ahas"—laughter, tears, sorrow, joy, and empathy—and also took part in traditional conference networking. National press coverage reflected the opinion of many attendees that they were participating in the transformation of an important social issue.

This case study describes the Network's national-level efforts. It begins by outlining the judicial and legal frameworks that have

shaped the abortion issue in the United States. Against the backdrop of escalating social and political struggle, the birth of the common ground movement is described. The case study then traces the activities of a typical common ground group, drawn from a composite of actual experiences, through four phases: formation of the group, a workshop, postworkshop dialogue, and moving to action. The final sections address the limitations of the common ground process and the role of the media. Overall, the case seeks to illustrate how the common ground process provides an opportunity for constructive action regarding abortion; it is a welcome development in the face of widespread discouragement and deadlock.

■ *Abortion: Judicial and Legislative Hot Potato*

The abortion conflict has both religious and secular dimensions. Groups define the conflict in different ways, but essentially the struggle is one of morality, identity, and control. Those who believe the right to life holds the supreme place in our hierarchy of values are opposed by those who believe the rights to privacy and choice are paramount. The right-to-privacy argument scored a victory in 1973 when the Supreme Court, in *Roe v. Wade,* determined that women had a constitutional right to abortion. Ever since that decision, pro-life supporters have felt they were battling uphill against a moral wrong, and pro-choice supporters have felt an urgent need to defend women's hard-won rights.

While courts and legislatures in the early years after *Roe v. Wade* favored pro-choice positions, this trend reversed during the 1980s. Legislatures began to limit the use of state and federal funds to support abortion services. The 1989 Missouri case *Webster v. Reproductive Health Services* came close to overturning *Roe v. Wade*. Increased state and federal legislative action has continued with proposals to outlaw abortion altogether, to restrict its use, or less often, to extend abortion rights. Prospective legislators are now pressured to publicly state their position on abortion.

In this judicial and legislative climate, the conflict continues to be framed as win-lose. The identities of the "winners" and "losers" keep changing with each new decision and law. Thus, both sides keep fighting. To "live and let live" given the current regulatory, legal, and social conditions would be perceived by many pro-life advocates as losing and by many pro-choice advocates as insufficient. Abortion activists, media representatives, and public leaders discuss abortion using sensationalized images and adversarial rhetoric. These tactics have contributed to the escalation of the conflict into violence.

■ *Abortion and Consensus Processes*

The conflict over abortion poses a monumental challenge to advocates of consensus processes. It tests the efficacy of consensus building within the context of radically opposing worldviews and values. Proponents on both sides are unlikely to change their core views; thus, it would be unwise to use consensus processes with such an end in mind. Our core beliefs and values are intimately related to the way we create meaning and form our identities. Respect for differences in these key areas must thus be at the center of consensus processes seeking empowerment and recognition for all parties.

The Network for Life and Choice met this challenge by designing a process for dialogue among pro-life and pro-choice supporters. After initially responding to abortion-related incidents in Buffalo in 1992, the Network has used this process in at least 20 cities, including Boston, Cleveland, Denver, Minneapolis, Philadelphia, Toronto, Norfolk, Virginia, Pensacola, Florida, and Washington, D.C. Currently, the Network has more than 2,100 members.

The originators of the Network, Mary Jacksteit and Adrienne Kaufmann, drew on their experiences as a labor arbitrator/attorney and a Benedictine nun/educator, respectively. Using as a basis a pro-choice/pro-life dialogue model developed by Kaufmann, they designed a process focused on building relationships, trust, and community. Initially, they set aside the question of common ground on the issue of abortion itself, and focused on personal stories, shared heroines and heroes, and the correction of misperceptions of the other. Dialogues have since gone on to address many issues, including the status and welfare of women and children, the feminization of poverty, adoption options, unwanted pregnancies, and community safety and harmony.

Dialogues seek to prevent further intergroup polarization and abortion-related violence and to search for areas where joint action is possible. They are not designed to change the views of participants, nor do they seek new, objective information that can help participants reach a compromise.

The goals of the Network are to enable pro-choice and pro-life supporters to come together for constructive dialogue and for the exploration of cooperative activity in areas of joint concern; to assist and support local community efforts to create and sustain pro-life and pro-choice dialogues and collaborations; and to serve as a national network and resource for common ground efforts. Collaborative ventures coming out of pro-choice/pro-life dialogue groups have included papers on adoption, commu- nity initiatives to prevent teen pregnancy and promote family life education, and a set of principles for sexuality education presented to a state legislature. ➻

➻ COMMENTARY

The use of dialogue or public conversation processes in such divisive issues as abortion, affirmative action, hate speech, and sexual harassment is growing by leaps and bounds throughout this nation. This case study of the process used by the Network for Life and Choice presents only one example of a variety of organizations engaged in similar efforts to find "a third way" between those who are deeply polarized with respect to these difficult public policy issues. To the extent that these processes stand outside of the formal legal, legislative, and policy-making processes that by definition require determinate and rigid end-state solutions, they offer hope for seeing that many modern social and legal problems ultimately cannot be solved in dichoto- mous ways.

The dialogue process has been useful both because of the different procedures and ways of communicating it encourages among participants, and because it offers the potential for connection to action programs and policy solutions that can explore more mediate or complex solutions to seemingly intractable problems.

—Carrie J. Menkel-Meadow, *Legal scholar*

In 1995 and 1996, we were engaged by the Network's founders to formally evalu- ate the Network's national work and to explore the impact of Network participa- tion. Each Network session concludes with a brief, on-site questionnaire; our work would supplement these data with greater depth and perspective. We collected infor- mation through direct observation and interviews with Network directors, steer- ing committee members, local organizers, and participants from several North Ameri- can cities.

We sought to answer these key ques- tions: How is the dialogue process work- ing? Which elements of the process are critical? How has the dialogue process emerged differently in various contexts? What is the experience of participants in dialogue groups? What is the impact of dialogue on how participants view others and the issue of abortion? What are the implications of these findings for future initiatives? Our findings suggest that the dialogue process is a valuable contribution to public policy dispute resolution, with potential for wide application to divisive social issues.

The examples in the remainder of this case are drawn from the six workshop sites included in our evaluation (sites remain undisclosed to protect the confidentiality of participants). The examples reflect workshops as they were in 1996. Network activities continue to follow this format, with developments and changes appropri- ate to local conditions and evolving process needs.

■ *Forming a Common Ground Dialogue Group*

People reach out to the Network for Life and Choice for many reasons. Some feel the conflict is impeding social action for those who need help the most, such as poor women and children. Others are concerned about the increasing psychological, emotional, and occasionally physical violence in their communities. Some see the conflict as a stalemate, hurting friendships, dividing people of faith, and even causing family members to stop talking with each other. Most people are also motivated by the desire to understand one another, to listen and be heard.

The Network responds to invitations from individuals, formal or informal groups, religious institutions, and organizations who want to try the common ground approach. Some groups form rapidly and recruit Network assistance right away. Other groups organize locally and meet for some time before they invite the Network to assist them. (Throughout this case study, a distinction is made between *groups,* which are planning bodies and common ground dialogue groups that exist for various lengths of time, and *workshops,* which are one-day dialogue events.)

Network staff offer assistance ranging from giving advice over the phone to hands-on help in planning and facilitating groups. They have helped to assess local conditions, gauge the history and climate surrounding the conflict, and lead discussions with those involved in work related to abortion. As the Network gained press coverage, the number of requests for its help increased dramatically. To aid communities who wish to develop a common ground group, Jacksteit and Kaufmann

(1995) wrote a manual, which has been distributed to more than 200 individuals and organizations.

Occasional resistance to help from the Network arose from the following sources: the high-profile nature of a national organization, the perception that the Network was a liberal organization, and resistance to outsiders. Jacksteit and Kaufmann responded to these fears with dialogue about their philosophy and the group's needs. Confidence rose when prospective participants read the Network manual, which outlined what to expect from dialogue processes and workshops.

Groundwork for Dialogue

Common ground dialogues and workshops reflect local needs and conditions. Dialogue groups and workshops differ in size, context, type of participants, degree of formality, goals, and manner of origin. For example, some workshops were developed in a crisis atmosphere and focused on defusing hostility and violence. Others developed in a calmer climate and had broad goals as they sought collaborative action. Some groups developed with the intent of being an ongoing group, while other groups formed primarily to hold onetime events.

Despite the differences that have marked the development of common ground groups, there were several steps all groups were advised to take in creating a workshop dialogue process: invite a balanced group of pro-life and pro-choice organizers, develop a common purpose and agenda, develop a set of ground rules, and plan facilitator training sessions.

The first step was to form a strong nucleus with a balance of pro-choice and pro-life supporters of similar status. For example, when the head of the local pro-choice organization was part of the group, it was important to recruit the head of the local pro-life group. This was a difficult task, but it was essential to the ultimate success of the initiative. The groups ranged from 4 to 12 people, who served as the primary convenors, organizers, and planners. These core groups then recruited dialogue participants in a number of ways, including word of mouth, newspaper announcements, church bulletins, telephone calls, and written invitations. A primary objective was to gather a group balanced in numbers and status.

It was the core groups' responsibility to develop a common purpose, agenda, and ground rules and to begin the process of trust building. For example, the mission statement of the core group in Cleveland read as follows: "To bring together in a safe environment pro-choice, pro-life, and other concerned people who wish to share common ground on issues surrounding abortion; to build trust so that meaningful, respectful dialogue may take place; to take action on issues as consensus develops; and to be a positive and effective voice in society" (Jacksteit & Kaufmann, 1995, p. 57).

The Network advised groups to allow the goals of the group and any follow-up to develop naturally. Groups generally sought increased understanding and closer relationships at the beginning of their process, only later developing action plans or results-oriented goals. This makes sense given the void of genuine dialogue among activists in many communities. The Cincinnati-Covington dialogue group developed its statement together. The members called themselves People Listening People Caring: A Pro-Life Pro-Choice Group Seeking Common Ground, and they developed three guiding ideals: "We are one in the spirit of caring and compassion," "We listen with open hearts and open minds," and "Life has value and inherent dignity." They also created a mission statement that reflected these ideals:

> We, the members of People Listening People Caring, are a group of people who gather to discuss the issues surrounding abortion. Coming from different perspectives, we seek to look beyond our differences, to see each other as caring, compassionate people. We seek not simply to be understood, but also to understand. We reject the intolerance and violence which too often characterize the current debate; we meet in the hope of finding answers which uphold the dignity of all human life. We recognize that the pursuit of truth is often long and difficult; nonetheless, we dedicate ourselves to this pursuit. (Jacksteit & Kaufmann, 1995, p. 55)

Developing ground rules regarding behavior was essential to the dialogue groups. Many participants had negative experiences or expectations about dialogue with others. Ground rules created a safe environment and helped ensure that the dialogue process would be constructive. Typical ground rules included respectful language and behavior toward all in attendance, speaking for oneself and not one's constituency group, a commitment to attempt to understand and be understood, a pledge to refrain from efforts to convert or convince, and confidentiality—meaning that no names would be ascribed to comments from dialogue meetings. Some groups used a facilitator for their planning meetings to enhance productivity, enforce the ground rules, and monitor balanced participation.

Planning for Dialogue Workshops

The success of dialogue workshops was dependent on careful advance work. With Network guidance, the planning groups assessed local conditions, recruited participants, developed workshop goals appropriate to the community, decided on workshop content and structure, created a set of ground rules for the workshop, and selected and trained facilitators. The workshops had one lead facilitator—generally one of the Network directors—as well as experienced local facilitators for the small-group discussions. These local facilitators were usually familiar to committee members or came recommended to them. The Network held two- to three-hour training sessions for the small-group facilitators shortly before each workshop day.

Everyone who expressed an interest in participating learned in advance the purpose of the workshop and expectations for each of them. Written invitations and discussions with planning committee members were part of the recruitment effort. In addition, most groups required participants to register in advance of the workshop.

The registration form asked people to sign off on ground rules and to indicate whether they were pro-choice or pro-life. This process helped ensure realistic expectations; it also allowed organizers to determine the requisite number of small-group facilitators and balance participation evenly between pro-life and pro-choice supporters. The number of participants in

dialogue workshops ranged from 4 to 50. Some groups preferred to initially limit participant numbers, expanding their efforts after a successful pilot workshop.

Dialogue workshops were tailored to the needs of local communities. A typical structure included a daylong format with an opening session that set the tone of the process, a morning session devoted to small-group interaction, a large-group discussion of a questionnaire on abortion and social values, a second small-group session in the afternoon, and a closing session summarizing and synthesizing the events of the day and considering the future implications for participants. The following section takes the reader through a typical dialogue workshop.

■ Conducting Workshops: A Typical Day of Dialogue

It was Saturday morning at 9 o'clock. Workshop participants and facilitators made their way into a community center. There was a chill in the air, intensified by the presence of known and unknown adversaries. Participants were uncertain about what they could accomplish in one day. Some felt there was a great deal at stake; others were worried that the workshop would induce illusory harmony, and real differences would be laid aside.

The facilitators' goals in the opening session were to establish a safe and positive atmosphere. They welcomed the group and asked everyone to introduce themselves. On this particular day, Network founders Adrienne Kaufmann and Mary Jacksteit were present; in addition, there was one local facilitator present for every four participants in attendance. Adrienne and Mary led the large-group discussions, and the local facilitators led the small groups.

At the outset, participants were encouraged to mention their reasons for attending and their role (e.g., pro-choice participant, pro-life participant, facilitator). Common reasons for attending were curiosity about how the organizers would structure and lead the meeting, interest in learning about opposing perspectives, desire for new ways of dealing with this volatile issue, interest in frank talk with people on the other side, and a desire to discover common ground. Mary and Adrienne reviewed the ground rules and briefly went over the agenda for the day. Although the participants were familiar with the common ground approach from the registration materials, Mary and Adrienne spent time further explaining the workshop's philosophy and key interests: dialogue, not debate; discovering hidden common ground; exploring a continuum of views; and using connective thinking.

Adrienne and Mary elaborated on the difference between dialogue and debate. They explained that debate polarizes people into two groups, creating winners and losers. In a debate, people try to convince each other of the rightness of their position. Dialogue, on the other hand, acknowledges the connections among all persons—for example, those present might share community, faith, and/or citizenship, regardless of their points of view. Participants were asked to look beyond labels and stereotypes and to try to understand each other rather than convert each other. As Adrienne pointed out, "When an issue is explosive and relationships are already highly strained, dialogue is more likely than debate to lead to understanding and trust. This is accomplished through sharing personal stories and asking genuine questions."

A real understanding of what dialogue was and wasn't allowed participants to feel more secure about their interaction within the group. Many participants felt considerable risk and vulnerability in coming to the workshop. Other reservations included the perception that engaging in dialogue accorded the other side legitimacy. Viewed from this stance, dialogue was a "sellout" or a sign of weakness. Others feared that dialogue might lead them to change their beliefs. As one participant put it, "I don't want to give up my pro-life belief that life begins at conception. I don't want to be tainted in common ground mush. I feel comforted hearing that I'm not being asked to give up or compromise my beliefs."

Adrienne and Mary presented the image of two interlocking circles to visually depict the idea that all participants have both divergent and convergent experiences, concerns, beliefs, values, and goals. When parties are polarized, common ground generally goes unrecognized. This workshop, explained the facilitators, provides a space and a framework for people to uncover those areas of commonality. The goal is not compromise in search of a middle position. Rather, a focus on genuinely shared values and concerns can take parties to a meta-level that transcends the substance of the conflict. This type of sustained focus reduces polarization and the demonization of each side by the other and tends to increase trust and respect. ➡

∽ COMMENTARY

The common ground movement starts from a different orienting position than most efforts to foster debate on controversial issues. Rather than beginning with the clear differences in the right-to-life or right-to-choose sides of the issue, the common ground movement assumes some commonalities among humans who differ on the desirability or legality of abortion. Thus, by setting up ground rules for respectful conversation and specification of personal attributes or views of the speakers at meetings, the dialogue process hopes to clarify the commonalities of people who have different views about some things but who might agree about other things, for example, the need to eliminate violence at abortion clinics. To the extent that there is no expectation of changing views, the more common forms of debate, argumentation, persuasion, and general adversary conflict[1] are muted, if not entirely eliminated, and the goals of meetings are quite different. Whether motivated from a crisis moment to stop the violence in clinics or to more generally search for action-oriented solutions like improving adoption opportunities, preventing teen pregnancy, and promoting family life and sex education, these dialogue meetings are not designed to decide "big questions" finally or even to persuade particular policymakers or judicial decision makers.

—Carrie J. Menkel-Meadow, *Legal scholar*

NOTE

1. For descriptions of how agonistic argument has come to dominate our discourse in the family, education, politics, law, and the media, see Tannen (1998) and Menkel-Meadow (1999).

REFERENCES

Menkel-Meadow, C. (1999). The limits of adversarial ethics. In D. Rhode (Ed.), *The ethics of practice*. New York: Oxford University Press.
Tannen, D. (1998). *The argument culture*. New York, Random House.

Another metaphor Mary and Adrienne used as part of the common ground approach was a continuum. In the dominant discourse on abortion, the issue is delineated in a win-lose, bipolar way. However, even within deep-rooted conflicts, the views of each side fall along a spectrum. The facilitators noted that when people identify themselves as pro-life or pro-choice, others perceive them to be at the far ends of the continuum. In fact, their views on abortion and related social issues might fall somewhere in between. The idea of a continuum was meant to foster curiosity about other participants and their ideas. Participants were told they would have the opportunity to ask questions that would elicit the nuances of views along the continuum.••

↷ COMMENTARY

The abortion dialogues have helped spawn the development of a whole new process, which is not, strictly speaking, a "consensus building" process but seeks explicitly to avoid decisions, agreements, and "end states." Instead, these processes explore complexity and underscore "thinking along a continuum" rather than in a binary mode. Learning to set agreed-on ground rules and procedures allows the structured expression of deeply opposed views and permits guided questioning and probing of the bases of those views.

—Carrie J. Menkel-Meadow, *Legal scholar*

The dialogue process drew forth subtle differences within perspectives. The idea of a continuum appealed to many participants because they felt uncomfortable with labels: "I felt intimidated by the . . . labels. There's too much labeling which keeps one from being able to get to the person. I want to get away from the labels and don't want people to label me. I want to share my unique gifts and personality, not just my label. I want you to hear what's in my heart, my soul."

Finally, Adrienne and Mary introduced the use of connective thinking. This type of thinking focuses on the strengths and pieces of truth in a speaker's words, rather than on weaknesses or flaws. Listeners are urged to find connection with their own experiences, thoughts, and feelings. As Mary and Adrienne noted, "Over time, the practice of connective thinking in a group can lead to the creation of a web of shared knowledge woven from the threads of truth contributed by its members. Connective thinking fosters the building of constructive relationships and the development of community because it ties together the best wisdom of each member of the group" (Jacksteit & Kaufmann, 1995, p. 10). The experience of dialogue helps all participants to see how their views converge.

Before breaking into small-group discussions, participants completed an opinion survey, which included a range of statements about abortion and societal values. Everyone was asked to fill out the survey twice, first responding with their views and then as they thought members of the opposing group would respond. The survey used a 5-point scale from *strongest agreement* to *strongest disagreement*. Sample statements were "Abortion is an appropriate method of birth control," "Abortion is a violent procedure for terminating a pregnancy," "I feel certain about when life begins," "Sexual activity among consenting adults is acceptable outside long-term commitment," and "U.S. public policy should have as a major concern giving support to families raising children." The participants were informed that the questionnaire results would be reported after lunch. They completed the survey and moved into small groups. The first hour had gone by.

Morning Small-Group Interaction

Participants spent 90 minutes in small groups with equal numbers of pro-life and pro-choice supporters. Local facilitators guided each group. They sought to set a positive tone, maintain the ground rules, keep a focus on the agenda, ensure equal speaking time, encourage active listening, and elicit responses to facilitate understanding.

In this more intimate setting, participants were asked to introduce themselves again. People voiced their concerns about participating, as well as what they hoped would happen. Some feared the opinion of their family and friends; others worried about their churches. One participant put it this way: "I am a Roman Catholic. I'm in the middle, I can't decide, but I lean toward pro-choice. . . . The Church is talking about excommunication of people who don't follow its teaching or who associate with certain organizations" (LeBaron & Carstarphen, 1997). As participants shared feelings of risk and vulnerability with each other, they began to build trust.

The small-group facilitators outlined the work of dialogue, emphasizing active, noncritical listening. Next, they asked all participants to identify their heroes or heroines and to explain the reasons for each choice. After each person spoke, the facilitator asked someone on the other side of the conflict to reflect back what he or she heard. This exercise helped participants feel comfortable talking with each other, improved communication skills, revealed common values, and helped prepare for talk about more sensitive topics.

Small-group facilitators asked participants one particularly important question: "How did you come to your present beliefs about abortion?" People shared very personal experiences and broader political or pragmatic reasons for their current beliefs. Some stories were filled with pain—unplanned pregnancies, legal and illegal abortions, adoptions, inability to care for children, rape, childhoods of abuse and neglect. Most stories were filled with emotion. Again, listeners were helped to ask clarifying questions and to reflect back understanding.•➤

➤ COMMENTARY

With skillful facilitators, participants are asked to consider why they feel the way they do (learning to express and listen to the rich personal experiences that affect strongly held beliefs in such controversial areas), to explore "the gray areas" in their own thinking (exposing the uncertainties or more permeable boundaries around strongly held views), and to ask questions of each other (rather than to simply make strong declarative statements), all of which are designed to teach people to empathize with each other, even across huge philosophical and political divides. Whether they can change each other's views about the moral values informing positions on abortion, such guided conversations do lead to jointly crafted mission statements (reducing violence, rejecting intolerance), which can lead to particular action outcomes (joint monitoring of abortion clinics, joint presentations at schools and health clinics).

—Carrie J. Menkel-Meadow, *Legal scholar*

After all had spoken, the small-group facilitators asked participants to identify common themes in the stories. In some of the small groups, participants discovered they had arrived at very polarized positions via similar paths and values. Simple, stereotypical labels were replaced with images of complex, human individuals with varied experiences, moral struggles, and beliefs. Participants expressed surprise at the similarities among them, and most reported feeling closer to their counterparts.

Morning Wrap-Up

At the end of the morning, participants came back together to reflect on their small-group experiences. Many identified the small-group discussions as a highlight of the workshop. Participants' comments included the following:

> I saw how little either side wants abortion, yet how polarized the debate has become around the issue of abortion. I also saw that the abortion conversation has grown to take over other conversations that need to take place.

> I liked the personal stories because it made me reflect on why I hold my beliefs and gave me the chance to hear others' experiences and why they have their beliefs.

> The question of how we came to the positions we hold was a very important strategy because it made us reflect on experiences which are true, not focusing on philosophical reasons for our beliefs. People's ideas don't happen in a vacuum. This opened up minds.

The atmosphere in the room at this point was markedly different from that earlier in the morning. Participants' eyes looked wider, and their postures were more relaxed and receptive. Trust and empathy were clearly building. To honor this emerging trust, participants were asked not to discuss the day's topic during lunch. It was suggested that they get to know each other in ways unrelated to the abortion issue.

Analysis of the Questionnaire

After lunch, Adrienne and Mary presented the results of the questionnaire in four columns: how each group described its personal beliefs and how each group believed the other would respond. Displayed side by side, the questionnaire findings showed where there were areas of close agreement and where there were real differences. The findings also showed the misperceptions each group held of the other.

For the most part, participants acknowledged the stereotypes they had harbored. To everyone's surprise, all felt misunderstood, and all wrongly attributed to others stronger views than they actually held. Many described relief at finally being seen as unique individuals rather than part of a group holding one monolithic view. The participants were also excited to discover common ground around which they might be able to work in the future. By seeing differences and commonalities in a tangible, visual form, participants could take in the information in a different way. They began to see themselves in the "other"— and entertain the possibility that the "other" might be like them, and therefore trustworthy.

Afternoon Small-Group Dialogue

After receiving the results of the questionnaire, participants returned to their original small groups for another 90-minute dialogue. Events in the afternoon small-group dialogues varied greatly in the early years of the Network. In the original workshop design, the questions asked in the afternoon session included, "How have you personally experienced being misunderstood or stereotyped, and how has it affected you?" "What is the best you think can come out of common ground?" "What are areas of common ground that you think you could work on together?" and "How has the violence surrounding the abortion conflict affected you?" Groups differed in the extent to which participants wanted action-oriented discussion as opposed to continued sharing of personal stories.

Closing Session

Following the last small-group session, participants joined together for a final hour of dialogue. During this session, small groups reported on their discussions, stimulating a large-group discussion. Mary and Adrienne then led a discussion on the challenges of leaving the meeting and reentering the community. This topic included consideration of how constituents and supporters might view their participation in the dialogue.

This discussion reflected the reality that many participants were questioned before and after coming to the workshop by members of their constituency group. In fact, many participants reported that they felt more harassed by members of their own group than by members of the other group. These experiences are common to many people who have dared to speak with "the

enemy" in a variety of conflict situations. Other reentry issues such as the need to preserve confidentiality and rules about press contacts were discussed, giving participants an opportunity to engage in some problem solving together.

The final activity was an inclusive closing ritual to make the day feel complete. Participants were asked to generate an image or metaphor expressing how they experienced the day. This closing allowed participants to convey feelings and insights into their own experience concisely and creatively. The day was variously described as weaving a tapestry, making a quilt, planting a garden, or learning to dance.

■ Evaluating the Workshops

Participants' experiences in the workshops have been very positive. Of the more than 50 participants we interviewed, only one reported a negative experience. All the others described the workshops in such terms as "inspiring," "carefully orchestrated," "authentic," "transforming," and as "a source of creative possibility." Dialogue was celebrated as a good way to bring together human beings, sharing laughter, meals, and personal trials. Comments from participants have included the following: "Any effort to bring people together who are dealing with intense feelings and issues is healthy at a fundamental human level"; "The dialogue puts the issues and people into a more personal light, which makes it harder to dismiss others as just being lunatics"; and "I have been involved in it ever since then. It is a very impressive model."

∞ COMMENTARY

I am a firm believer in a well-run dialogue process to inform, build trust, and complexify what many prefer to keep simple and acrimonious. As this dialogue process spreads from use in such controversial issues as abortion and affirmative action, it is an interesting challenge to imagine other issues that would similarly benefit from such approaches. In higher education, some of us have already experimented with such methodologies in classes dealing with the issues of race and gender, sexual harassment, the death penalty, hate speech, and the Western canon of literature debates that have polarized campuses. To the extent that the dialogue process is useful at the individual level as well, its techniques can be applied to family counseling, marital mediation, and employee-employer relations—all areas in which "agreements to disagree" may be appropriate.

Public conversations and dialogue processes offer a fully "process-oriented" approach to controversial issues, differing from more conventional consensus building processes by not being task or outcome focused, but by facilitating those most difficult of human arts: communication and understanding.

—Carrie J. Menkel-Meadow, *Legal scholar*

When asked why the workshops were so successful, participants listed the focus on dialogue rather than debate, the facilitators, the structure and format of the workshops, and the goodwill of other participants. They especially appreciated the use of small groups, the specific questions, the questionnaire, agreed-on ground rules, and the neutral location of the workshops. All these factors contributed to building trust, understanding, empathy, and a culture of common ground. As one participant said, "It's very healing to hear and to be heard . . . completely and successfully . . . by a person of the opposite political perspective" (Wirpsa, 1996).

Participants appreciated the equal representation of both sides and the involvement of moderates, not radicals. Whether or not participants were really moderates or only perceived as such is difficult to say; participants in fact ranged from those who have never been active in the abortion conflict to those who have been labeled as radicals

by the media. We suspect that the nature of the workshops enabled people to be more moderate than they would have been otherwise. On the other hand, some dialogue groups have had more trouble when those with extreme views participated.

As noted above, facilitators were seen as key to the success of the workshops. Participants identified three important contributions of facilitators: providing a safe environment, maintaining focus, and facilitating in an impartial and unbiased manner. One person interviewed said he would not attend such a meeting without a facilitator. He felt that it was too difficult to talk about such emotional issues without some guidance.

■ Follow-Up Dialogues

While the initial focus of common ground workshops is on putting a face of humanity on the abortion conflict, groups have not stopped there. Some participants want to continue sharing and exploring their individual values and beliefs to deepen their understanding of each other. In other groups, topics for discussion at ongoing dialogue meetings developed out of concerns identified during the workshops. Topics have included reducing rates of unplanned and teenage pregnancies, promoting adoption, making society more "child friendly," and encouraging sexual responsibility in young men.•◦

◦ COMMENTARY

When we held a dialogue/forum at UCLA on affirmative action, we sought representation of a diversity of views along a spectrum and a diversity of people to express those views. A skilled facilitator asked all participants to explain where and how they thought affirmative action was appropriate and where and how their own views were formed or based on personal experience. Those participating ranged from an Asian male opposed to affirmative action in every setting, to a white male who favored it in education but not in contracting, to a white female who favored it everywhere, to an African American male who favored it in education, employment, and contracting. All participants were then asked to consider what more information they needed from other perspectives to inform their own views and what unknown facts or information would change their minds. Each participant was asked to express the "less certain" aspects of his or her own position. Such dialogues expose the variations in positions (such as the continua on which different forms of abortion might be distinguished) and, in fact, often expose how poorly our formal institutions resolve these issues by having to dichotomize them. Given the great richness and variety of views on affirmative action at the University of California, for example, it is sad and unfortunate that the ultimate decision about this issue remained an on/off voter decision through a rigid referenda process (though tinkered with and challenged post hoc in the courts).[1]

Thus, for such difficult and polarized issues, the combination of personal behavior rules (respectful listening, no name-calling or personal attacks), use of questions rather than declarative statements, recognition of continuum or "connected" thinking (rather than binary or polarized thinking), and the relation of experience to "rationally" held views can lead to, as the present authors describe it, "a web of shared knowledge," if not agreement. In some cases, they lead to further exploration of issues, continued meetings to serve as a "cooling off" center for those who want to help prevent escalation, and, at best, action plans for mediate solutions like community education, monitors, or adoption centers.

—Carrie J. Menkel-Meadow, *Legal scholar*

NOTE

1. For fuller descriptions of both the affirmative action dialogue process at UCLA and the polarized legal debates, see Menkel-Meadow (1996), Amar and Caminker (1996), Spann (1997), Sturm and Guinier (1996), and Ayres and Cramton (1996).

REFERENCES

Amar, V., & Caminker, E. (1996). Equal protection, unequal political burdens and the CCRI. *Hastings Constitutional Law Quarterly, 23,* 1019.

Ayres, I., & Cramton, P. (1996). Deficit reduction through diversity: How affirmative action at the FCC increased auction competition. *Stanford Law Review, 48,* 761.

Menkel-Meadow, C. (1996). The trouble with the adversary system in a post-modern, multi-cultural world. *William & Mary Law Review, 38*(5), 34-36.

Spann, G. (1997). Proposition 209. *Duke Law Journal, 47,* 187.

Sturm, S., & Guinier, L. (1996). The future of affirmative action: Reclaiming the innovative ideal. *California Law Review, 84,* 953.

■ Moving to Action

Ongoing dialogue groups have taken collaborative action to address issues of common concern in their communities. Some groups, such as those in Buffalo and Washington, D.C., sponsored additional workshops to bring new people into the common ground process. Other groups sponsored a larger common ground event. For example, the San Francisco group worked together for eight months to plan a weekend retreat for 31 women from the community.

Some groups took on advocacy activities at local and national levels. For example, the Wisconsin group explored the issue of sexuality education and arrived at a set of joint principles, which they then presented to state legislators. The Cincinnati group, People Listening People Caring, made its mission statement available to the public and offered to help other dialogue groups get organized. In several cities, pro-life and pro-choice supporters made joint public appearances to reduce the potential for violence in their communities. They wanted to demonstrate that pro-life and pro-choice adherents can work together on community issues.

■ Limitations of the Common Ground Process

The common ground process has been overwhelmingly successful. However, some workshop participants and groups have experienced difficulties. Three main problems have been reported: poor facilitation, moving to action too quickly, and frustration and tensions between those who want to "talk" and those who want to "do something." In a few isolated cases, participants thought local facilitators displayed bias or exerted too much or too little control over small-group discussions. As in other types of third-party intervention, the skill of the facilitator is key to an effective process. This suggests the need for more screening and training of small-group facilitators. Currently, local facilitators receive a two- or three-hour training the night before a workshop event. Facilitators might also be helped by participating in a dialogue workshop before facilitating a group.

As described previously, early dialogue workshops included afternoon discussions of possible joint activities. Many participants found this move toward action too quick given that they had barely begun to talk with one another. Therefore, later workshops included more time for relationship building. On the other hand, some dialogue groups that met for six months or more reported tensions within their group between those who were satisfied and those who wanted to "do something." Some ongoing participants reported that they lacked a sense of concrete progress over time. Some experienced burnout. For others, the satisfaction of improved relationships more than compensated for the lack of tangible outcomes.

Participants cited various reasons for their groups' difficulty in moving toward action. These included different motivations for participating in a dialogue group (i.e., relationship vs. task goals); lack of trust or agreement about particular actions (e.g., how to reduce teen pregnancy); an insufficient number of participants; and vulnerability with their constituency should they engage in public actions with "the other side." Ongoing groups are addressing these tensions in several ways. They are forming action-oriented subgroups; continuing dialogue on particular issues to build trust, leading eventually to action; and recruiting new participants, including "activists" and "extremists" in some cases.

■ The Role of the Media

The media often escalate conflict in public disputes. The Network is very aware of the media's potential for having both a negative and positive effect on the abortion conflict. The Network has advised common ground dialogue groups about how to help the media become a tool for constructive dialogue about abortion. Typically, the Network has restricted media access to dialogue workshops to maintain participants' confidentiality and ensure comfort in talking openly. Participants are also asked to agree on what statements will be made to the media and who the sources will be. One dialogue group wanted to publicize its positive experiences, but spent a difficult year negotiating a joint press release. Other groups have held press conferences about their dialogues and joint action.

The Network and local groups have sought to educate interested journalists through written and verbal communication and a documentary film that features a dialogue between pro-choice and pro-life women. Occasionally, group members sought out journalists who they felt would genuinely understand the process and goals and who would be impartial in their reporting. Few reporters have been granted permission for direct access to dialogue workshops or meetings. Those who attend must agree to the ground rules by which participants abide, especially confidentiality. On occasion, they are asked to come as real participants in dialogue workshops rather than as reporters.

Journalists were invited to report on the Reach for Common Ground First National Conference held in Madison in 1996. The Network and local organizers carefully briefed reporters prior to the conference. They made the requests described above, including abiding by conference ground rules, respecting people's privacy, and being willing to leave conference sessions if there was a strong objection to their presence. At the beginning of each session, facilitators reminded participants about the media's presence. They provided opportunities for people to rearrange themselves if they didn't want to be filmed, and to voice other concerns about the media presence. If objections arose, the facilitators mediated arrangements that considered both the participants' concerns and reporters' needs to cover the conference.

These arrangements included agreements to have visual images or audio only, and opportunities for willing participants to speak to reporters after sessions. This conference also included a plenary session on media coverage of abortion. Some participants felt the media presence inhibited what they said. Most participants, however, welcomed the media coverage. In their eyes, media coverage illustrated the importance of the common ground approach, helped people feel they were part of a larger movement, and contributed to "getting the word out."

The Network's and local groups' efforts to work with the media paid off. Instead of headlines that solely emphasize the polarized nature of the abortion conflict, stories reporting agreement have been found in the pages of the *New York Times, Washington Post, Washington Times,* and numerous other newspapers. Headlines such as "Abortion Foes Reach Accord on Adoption" (Holmes, 1995), "Abortion Sides Find Common Ground" (Price, 1996), "Adversaries of One Mind: Common Ground Exists Even in Our Most Vexatious Disputes" (Raspberry, 1995), "Agreeing to Disagree: Abortion Advocates and Foes Gather to Talk and Listen" (O'Hanlon, 1996), and "A Weekend without War over the Abortion Issue: Wisconsin Conference Seeks Shared Goals" (1996) illustrate how the common ground approach has shaped both media coverage and public debate.

Media coverage of the dialogue workshops, ongoing groups, and joint actions has helped publicize the possibility of bridging the great divide between pro-life and pro-choice supporters. As in most protracted conflicts, people assume that adversaries have nothing in common and have no hope for mutual positive regard. With increasing public awareness, more people are seeking out common ground groups or are starting their own. The Network has received many inquiries from people who heard about its work in the newspaper, on television, and on the radio.

■ Coming Full Circle: Addressing the Issue of Abortion

Even when common ground dialogues yield considerable joint action, the question of whether the abortion issue is closer to resolution still remains. We believe the abortion issue transforms incrementally each time it is talked about, felt, and acted on. One participant reported that since his involvement, he feels immediate concern for "the other side" when legislative or judicial victories occur on "his side." This empathy may lead to a brand of advocacy that keeps the humanity of the opposition in mind, inhibiting violent tactics.

As trust deepens, dialogues allow for questions such as "Do you have a question of genuine curiosity to ask someone on the other side?" Using this question, participants in ongoing processes have asked what pro-life advocates do for women and children, and how pro-choice advocates support those who have had traumatic experiences with abortion. They have also explored the limits of activism (e.g., the range of acceptable tactics and approaches), birth control and contraception, and sources of moral authority.

These dialogues are difficult. They sometimes disappoint participants who hope that they will, after all, come to common ground on the abortion issue itself. ••

↩ COMMENTARY

There are important limits to these processes that must be acknowledged. First, for those seeking complete reconciliation or action, there will be disappointment. Even exposing the variations in views on affirmative action did not forge permanent alliances for political action to depolarize the issue in the heated political and legal climate in California.[1] For those who dislike "just talking," dialogue processes often do not result in tasks accomplished, outcomes, solutions, or action plans.

Second, there are issues that many feel so strongly about that continua and connected thinking represent inappropriate compromises: If one supports abortion, one may not want to compromise on late-term abortions being different, or if one is opposed to abortion, recognize that rape, incest, or other undesirable pregnancies are different. To the extent that right-to-life advocates are also in favor of the death penalty they may not want to look for the connections that "sanctity of life" might entail.

Third, and related to this concern, if one sees the "humanity" of one's "opponents," how does one continue to fight for or advocate for deeply held principles? Or, to put the converse, to the extent that dialogues expose our experiential and other personal differences, we may actually exacerbate the differences among us (seeing class or life choices in the abortion controversy fueling other conflicts like whether there should be government-supported child care or whether women should stay at home). Much of the dialogue process assumes that more information will lead to more trust and understanding, perhaps underestimating the possibilities that more differences and disputes will be revealed as well.

—Carrie J. Menkel-Meadow, *Legal scholar*

NOTE

1. When I was trying to express a more nuanced view in a MacNeil-Lehrer televised debate with the proponents of Proposition 209 in California, my views were immediately polarized by the media, which seem to need to create dramatic debate formats, and by "the other side," which seemed to need to attack to make its point.

For example, pro-choice participants often nurse a fond wish that pro-life advocates will recognize the need for some abortions, while pro-life activists nurture a similar wish that pro-choice advocates will acknowledge the wrongness of abortion. When these hopes are not realized, participants either renew their dialogue efforts or lapse into frustration. Frustration is less likely to stifle dialogue once close relationships have formed, however. The sustained desire of participants to come together testifies to the power and potential of the common ground approach for use with value-driven public disputes.↩

☞ COMMENTARY

For me, the great satisfaction of such processes is the realization that empathy and sophisticated analysis brought together can demonstrate just how multifaceted and complex most of our most disputed issues are—polarized thinking is not helpful to resolving human problems. In my most utopian moments, I hope that dialogue and public conversation processes can make evident to lawmakers, journalists, and educators that polarized thinking is not the best way to analyze or solve problems and that more complex, gradual, or mediate solutions are often better policy choices and more accurate of the reality that most problems present.

—Carrie J. Menkel-Meadow, *Legal scholar*

■ *References*

A weekend without war over the abortion issue: Wisconsin conference seeks shared goals. (1996, June 3). *New York Times,* p. A10.

Holmes, S. A. (1995, August 18). Abortion foes reach accord on adoption. *New York Times,* p. 17.

Jacksteit, M., & Kaufmann, A. (1995). *Finding common ground in the abortion conflict: A manual.* Washington, DC: Common Ground Network for Life and Choice, Search for Common Ground.

LeBaron, M., & Carstarphen, N. (1997, June). Conference evaluation report. Prepared for the Kellogg Foundation and the Network for Life and Choice. *Negotiation Journal, 13*(4), 341-362.

O'Hanlon, A. (1996, October 27). Agreeing to disagree: Abortion advocates and foes gather to talk and listen. *Washington Post.*

Price, J. (1996, October 29). Abortion sides find common ground. *Washington Times.*

Raspberry, W. (1995, September 15). Adversaries of one mind: Common ground exists even in our most vexatious disputes. *Washington Post,* p. A25.

Wirpsa, L. (1996, June 28). Listening key as foes seek common goals. *National Catholic Reporter,* p. 5.

16

ORGANIZATIONAL TRAUMA RECOVERY

The "God's Fellowship Community Church" Reconciliation Process

■ David Brubaker

"God's Fellowship Community Church" is a medium-sized (about 850 members) evangelical Christian congregation located in a western state and affiliated with a Reformed Protestant denomination. Established by a well-known minister in the late 1970s, the congregation grew to more than 1,800 members within a decade. Allegations of ethical misconduct against the founding pastor ultimately led to his resignation in 1990, leaving a deeply divided and wounded congregation. This case study profiles the congregation's recovery process following that traumatic period (from 1990 to 1997), including my intervention as a consultant in 1993. It concludes with implications for consensus building processes in deeply di-

vided organizations, including the need for procedures to respond to leadership ethical violations.

■ Background

The founding pastor of God's Fellowship Community Church was a gifted minister with an uncanny ability to grow a church. The God's Fellowship congregation was first established in 1976, and by 1989 had mushroomed in size, building a striking new facility along the way. But rumors of inappropriate conduct by the minister soon began to surface, and in 1989 they exploded into the open. The resulting trauma would include a difficult investigation process, the departure of the pastor and many members, and an ongoing recovery process within the congregation he founded.

On a bright spring morning in 1989, a stunned congregation listened to its pastor of 13 years announce his impending divorce. While the pastor took a leave of absence, the local church board began a serious investigation of rumors that had persisted for years. In addition to the pastor's marital problems, a series of "leaks" from other women had led to heightened public scrutiny. Two lay leaders flew to the regional headquarters of the denomination to deliver several allegations of misconduct against their pastor. The allegations included inappropriate and unethical relationships with several women in counseling, misuse of church funds, and deception and manipulation in church governance. Based on these charges, the local church board voted to bar the pastor's return to the pulpit.

The Regional Committee of the denomination interviewed the pastor next. This committee links the denomination and its member congregations over a several-state area and has authority over the local church boards. During this meeting, the pastor denied all charges and claimed he was the target of an attempted takeover of power. Viewing the situation as a local church conflict rather than alleged pastoral misconduct, the Regional Committee overrode the church board and—to the disbelief of many—returned the pastor to his pulpit.

The Sunday of the pastor's return was like a triumphal entry. The pastor's supporters had covered the church in welcoming yellow ribbons. As the pastor claimed exoneration on all charges, his core of supporters and others joined in a standing ovation. His victims and those bringing their allegations remained seated in shock and dismay. In the following weeks, chaos and division characterized the congrega-

tion's interaction. Three groups could be identified: the ardent supporters of the pastor, those strongly opposed to his continuing ministry, and the concerned and confused majority who did not have enough information to take sides. In deference to the pastor's privacy very little information had been given to the broader congregation about the allegations against him.

The Regional Committee that had received the charges convened a congregational meeting designed to hear from all sides. Although it opened with a hopeful prayer, the meeting soon degenerated into a free-for-all. A reading of the charges was met with boos and catcalls, and those bringing the charges were labeled as unforgiving. Those who had more information about the seriousness of the allegations were again stunned by the response. Following the meeting, two key church staff members resigned, a majority of elders refused to serve communion, and many members prepared to leave the church.

Shortly after this unsatisfactory meeting, word was received that the Regional Committee had set a date to try the pastor on three counts of pastoral misconduct. Preparation began for a hearing where both the prosecution and defendant would bring witnesses and evidence. As the trial date approached, even greater polarization occurred between those for and against the pastor. Personal loyalty combined with a difficulty accepting the allegations drove the emotions of some church members, as the pastor's offenses became increasingly hard to ignore.

Days before the hearing, the pastor pleaded guilty to two of the three charges in pretrial depositions. He confessed to inappropriate relations with a counseling client and to lying to the congregation, church board, and regional officials. The admission of guilt brought immediate suspension and a prohibition against further ministry in the church he had founded. The local congregation was instructed to provide the pastor's full salary and benefits during his six-month suspension.

While the suspension brought some reduction of conflict, the vague statement of charges left much to individual interpretation. Some wondered if the pastor was being treated too harshly, while others believed the official statement of charges to be a whitewash. Many who distrusted the pastor saw the Regional Committee as naive and vulnerable to the pastor's manipulation. The initial wholesale support of the pastor, followed by an abrupt and ambiguous reversal, did little to inspire confidence in the committee's leadership.

The week following the end of the pastor's six-month suspension, selected members of the local church received a letter inviting them to attend the inaugural service of the pastor's newly founded church just several miles down the road from God's Fellowship. At this service, attendees were promised the real story behind the allegation and suspension. In the same

week, the pastor recanted his confession in an open letter to the Regional Committee, stating that he had pleaded guilty only to save his pension. He was immediately deposed as a "minister of the Lord" in their denomination by the Regional Committee.

Church membership "voted with their feet" in response to these dramatic events. Of its membership of 1,800, about 300 people followed the pastor to his new place of worship. Three hundred members left for other churches, and an equal number stopped going to church altogether. Meanwhile, the remaining members of God's Fellowship took stock of all that had occurred. While some were ready to put the trauma behind them, others were still hurting. Many relationships were strained as a result of the internal conflict, affecting long-term friendships and even family members. Those victimized in the process expressed a loss of faith in pastors, churches, and (for some) even faith in God. An atmosphere of depression prevailed in a church where "fellowship" had been the norm. ✪

✪ COMMENTARY

Helping a community learn to live and work together after a traumatic incident of internal attack or betrayal by a leader is one of the major contemporary challenges facing the world. As communal conflict becomes one of the dominant sources of tension and violence in modern politics, the need to figure out how to work toward reconciliation and healing in such situations becomes ever greater. The crisis this congregation faces is in this way analogous to the trauma confronting South Africa or Rwanda in the aftermath of apartheid and genocide. In all of these situations, there is deep distrust and anger about past injuries.

Although the betrayal of trust described here took place within a Christian religious framework, nonreligious situations can produce similar traumas. Indeed, the crisis in American society following evidence of presidential misconduct in the Watergate affair of the 1970s was not entirely different. And there are parallels with the deep division in the nation over the war in Vietnam. The model of reconciliation described here has broad applicability well beyond the specific case of a church conflict arising from the sexual misconduct of a charismatic founding leader.

—Sally Engle Merry, *Anthropologist*

During the subsequent two-year period of interim pastors, a meeting was held between leaders of the denomination and leaders of God's Fellowship. The purpose was to air hurts and concerns regarding recent events, with the hope of some healing. The meeting was tense and difficult and resulted in continued rupture between the denomination and the congregation.

In 1991, "Pastor John" was called to God's Fellowship on a permanent basis. Sensing that the church's life was still restrained by past trauma, the new pastor and lay leaders sought help by sending two representatives to the Ministry of Reconciliation Conference, sponsored every two years by the Lombard (Illinois) Mennonite Peace Center. The conference in 1992 included a special track on pastoral sexual misconduct, and the representatives found much there of relevance. They learned that organizations go through identifiable stages in recovering from the trauma of leadership misconduct. They also learned that some churches can languish in a kind of funk when the recovery process is thwarted.[1]

The work of Larry Graham, professor of pastoral theology and care at Iliff School of Theology in Denver, Colorado, was presented at the conference. Graham identified the following four stages out of his work with a Mennonite congregation that had experienced pastoral sexual misconduct:

1. *Precursor-secret phase:* In this stage, which can last for years and even decades, rumors of "inappropriate relationships" may arise but are rarely pursued. The principals know of the secret and others may suspect it, but life continues with a facade of normalcy.

2. *Discovery-chaos phase:* When an allegation actually surfaces, the denial described above is broken and the organization moves into a stage of chaos. This stage may last for months and is characterized by confusion and conflict.

3. *Awareness-polarization phase:* While the above phase typically endures during an investigation of the allegations, the awareness-polarization phase describes the organization's dynamic as further information is made available. Graham observed of the Mennonite congregation that "a number of members left the church, either because they did not think the congregation did enough to confront the minister and gain justice for the victims, or because they believed it victimized the minister and generally overreacted to the situation."

4. *Recovery-rebuilding phase:* Those who remain in the congregation are left to do the work of recovery and rebuilding. Inevitably in a sexual misconduct case, relationships have been damaged and trust has deteriorated, even among those who may have taken the same "side" in the earlier confusion. It was at this stage that my involvement with the God's Fellowship congregation began.[2]

■ *The Reconciliation Process*

The symptoms of a depressed and divided church fit what these two representatives were experiencing at God's Fellowship. The representatives spoke with one of the conference presenters (the author of this case study, David Brubaker), who was later retained to assist the congregation in healing. Although they experienced some persistent internal resistance to any overt healing process, the leadership of God's Fellowship determined to undertake a recovery/reconciliation process. (Those against the process thought it best to let time heal the wounds without directly dealing with them.)

The congregation's leadership determined that the purpose of the process would be "to establish the peace, purity, and unity of the greater [church] family through a ministry of reconciliation which seeks God's fullest reconciliation with Christ and each other." The leadership of the congregation also established five goals for the reconciliation process, as follows:

1. To remember and consider reappropriating important aspects of our church's earlier life, mission, and ministry that were lost in the discipline of our former pastor and subsequent events.
2. To restore a favorable attitude and relatedness with various levels of our denomination and reconnect with its rich history and theology.
3. To provide a vehicle for healing damaged relationships with current and former members of our congregation.
4. To uncover systemic dysfunction in the church and learn healthy patterns regarding authority, power, clarity in boundaries and communication, and attitudes that promote truth, justice, respect, and openness interpersonally.
5. To enable victims to continue their healing process by receiving the church's regret and affirmation for their courage, by helping them deal with justice issues, by finding resources for help, and by being assured that steps are being taken to protect others from any future victimization.

The strategy to achieve these goals included the formation of a Reconciliation Task Force, accountable to the church board, and the recruitment of an outside consultant to assist in the reconciliation process. An associate pastor recruited by Pastor John named "Pastor Bob" was approved to head the task force. The consultant, myself, began telephone conference calls with the task force in preparation for an on-site visit in February 1993. It quickly became clear that consensus building for this group would focus on the nature of the recovery/healing process, rather than on a particular outcome.

The five members of the Reconciliation Task Force were selected by the church board, and included one elder and one deacon. The composition of the task force reflected the diversity of the congregation, including some who were sympathetic to supporters of the founding pastor. An overarching criterion for membership was that the nominee be generally respected in the broader congregation. The response of the congregation was low-key but supportive. Members did not know quite what to expect from this new task force.

■ The First Reconciliation Weekend

On the third weekend of February 1993, I flew to the city where God's Fellowship is located to work with the congregation. The format of the weekend was as follows:

- Friday: Meet with the Reconciliation Task Force and the church board to finalize plans for the weekend.

- Saturday: All-day open meeting for the congregation.
- Sunday morning: Short report on Saturday's meeting and workshop in adult Sunday school.
- Sunday afternoon: Develop recommendations for improved organizational functioning with board members.

The Saturday open meeting began with a welcoming and prayer, and then Pastor Bob (the chair of the Reconciliation Task Force) read a brief opening statement that summarized the history of the most difficult period, mid-1989 to mid-1990. This summary statement reviewed the previous pastor's problems—sexual misconduct and financial irregularities—and was accepted as accurate by most members of the congregation.

Pastor Bob clarified the purpose of the day's events, with a focus on the desire for genuine reconciliation based on honesty and openness. Following his comments, I assumed the role of facilitator for the remainder of the day. Approximately 95 persons (of the 650 worshipping members then involved in the congregation) attended the open meeting.

I followed an outline that had proved successful in previous "trauma debriefing" sessions with congregations where sexual misconduct by a leader had occurred. The basic outline includes the following components:

1. *Congregational history.* This phase provides an opportunity for participants to revisit both high and low points of the congregation's history, reminding them of past resilience. It also assists the consultant in identifying long-established organizational "habits." Participants at God's Fel-

lowship recounted warm memories of the early years of exciting growth in the congregation. As they described key decision-making times, I identified a tendency (or "habit") of deferring to a strong leader rather than engaging all interested members in discussion and decisions.

2. *Congregational stages.* Based on the model that Larry Graham developed, I presented the four stages congregations typically pass through in their response to allegations of sexual misconduct or abuse against a leader. (These are described above.) When I shared these stages with the God's Fellowship congregation, participants agreed that their own experience paralleled the Graham model. They also expressed relief at the "normalcy" of their reactions.

3. *Congregational sharing and decision making.* Using three basic ground rules and respectful but tight facilitation, I then encouraged participants to share their reactions when they learned of the allegations, and how those reactions may have changed over time. The three ground rules I normally set are "no interruptions," "no quoting of participants outside the room without their explicit permission," and "speak for oneself, not for others who aren't present." A general guideline I offer is to be "hard on the issues but soft on the people" during discussion. If the polity of the congregation and the timing of the recovery process so indicate, then a decision-making process about next steps may also be initiated.

4. *Congregational "grieving."* No matter how serious the leader's offense, some members will deeply appreciate his or her contributions to the congregation. If a decision has been made or is reached to ter-

minate the leader's tenure, then an opportunity for grieving will need to be given. One way to permit such expression is to encourage participants to identify strengths of the leader, and ways in which he or she will be missed by them. ❧

∞ COMMENTARY

There are two distinctive features of the process Brubaker adopted. One is the exercise of focusing on the organization's past strengths and habits, on revisiting a sense of its history. The organization thus strives to develop some collective sense of "culture" as a basis for reconciliation across the chasm of conflict and suspicion. The other distinctive feature is congregational "grieving," the expression of individual experiences of injury and pain shared with others along with the opportunity to let the pain and grief go in a public, ritualized gesture.

Such gestures are more effective if the offender has confessed and apologized, but in this situation the pastor did not. Thus, the situation confronting the congregation resembles that facing the Truth and Reconciliation Commission in South Africa: Forgiveness was expected from victims but confession and a request for forgiveness was often not forthcoming from perpetrators. Can justice be served by a unilateral forgiveness of an injury in the absence of confession and repentance by its agent? In this case, church members were seeking to forgive one another as well as the pastor, and apparently the opportunity to do so, along with some confession and release, was emotionally powerful. Subsequent reconciliation meetings included opportunities for confession and forgiveness as well, even though this was never accomplished with the founding pastor. How to handle such a situation is a dilemma that constantly confronts attempts at reconciliation when offenders refuse to acknowledge responsibility.

—Sally Engle Merry, *Anthropologist*

Neutralizing History

After considerable sharing on the Saturday of the Reconciliation Weekend, I led participants through an exercise designed to enable naming and letting go of past painful events.[3] I first distributed several 3- by 5-inch cards to each participant, and invited them to write down one or several memories from the recent trauma that still were difficult for them. Once the writing had stopped, I made an observation: "Some of you might be ready to let go of painful memories, which you could symbolize by naming what is on your card and then handing it to me."

Many participants expressed strong emotions as they came to the front, read the content of one or several of their cards, and then handed them on to me. One lay leader came to the front and said he thought he had dealt with his own issues about the congregation's trauma, but discovered that he still had things that were unresolved. Other participants affirmed (through nods and even applause) both the reality of the pain that was described on the card and the choice to let go of it. Some participants held on to their cards, noting (with my support) that the time wasn't yet right for them to let go of them. I encouraged those who kept their cards to later find a ritualized way of release, such as burning the card. The general experience was of confession, letting go, and forgiveness.

In the end-of-the-day group evaluation, participants overwhelmingly described the "neutralizing history" part of the day as the highlight. While they reported that affirming their history, naming their losses, and understanding the phases of congregational response to misconduct were all helpful, it was the letting go that had the greatest emotional impact. All told, the day appeared to bring some progress toward achieving Goals 1 (to "remember and reappropriate") and 3 (to "heal damaged relationships") that the congregation had established. The only reported regret was that more current and former members did not participate. (I have consistently found that 15 percent to 20 percent of a congregation's active members will choose to participate in such a meeting. Significantly, these participants normally include the key lay leaders of the congregation.)

Systemic Issues

On the final day of the Reconciliation Weekend (Sunday), I met with the leadership group of the congregation to debrief Saturday's open meeting and to discuss issues that still needed to be addressed. I reviewed five major areas of systemic functioning (identity, boundaries, performance standards, communication, and power[4]) with the church board and invited them to rank their congregation's performance along a spectrum in each area.

The pastors and lay leaders reviewed these five areas and reached consensus on where they might place the congregation's current functioning. They agreed that in the past, communication patterns had not been adequate and power had been used in authoritarian ways. The leaders agreed to address these "congregational habits" that needed to be changed, consistent with their stated Goal 4 (to "uncover systemic dysfunctions in the church and develop healthy patterns").

■ Ongoing Reconciliation Efforts

In addition to the internal healing process that was initiated in 1993, congregational leaders recognized the need to address fractured relationships with previous staff and with the denomination. Pastor John and the Reconciliation Task Force planned a second "reconciliation event" for a weekend in February 1994, this time to address the painful break with a former associate pastor, who resigned after confronting the previous senior pastor and then being marginalized in the congregation.

With coaching from me but without any outside facilitator present, the session followed a similar outline to the February 1993 open meeting. After a prayer and establishing of ground rules, Pastor Bob read "A Brief Summary of History" of the congregation's turmoil. Pastor John then gave time to "grieve the past in appropriate ways," thanked the previous assistant pastor and his wife for their faithfulness, and asked their forgiveness for the congregation's sins and mistakes in the process. On behalf of the congregation, Pastor John asked the couple, "What do you want or need from us? What will set you free?"

This second reconciliation event proved as powerful for the congregation—and their former associate pastor—as had the first. Pastor Bob wrote me a short note with a copy of the outline they had used for the day, noting that "God richly blessed it." During the evening meeting with the associate pastor, both the pastor and his wife wept deeply. The couple had sold their home at a great loss, and moved from the area against their wishes. The following day, a Sunday, this pastor preached at God's Fellowship and served communion.

A third event occurred in February 1995, also with a previous associate pastor who had lived through the trauma of 1989-1990 but attempted to maintain a neutral stance on the allegations. (Although his neutral stance was taken at the advice of denominational leaders who urged him to "minister to both sides," such a stance had generated significant tension in the congregation.)

A fourth goal had yet to be addressed— "to restore a favorable attitude and relatedness with various levels of our denomination." Disappointment with the denomination's handling of the ethical misconduct crisis had given way to disillusionment and feelings of abandonment by many in the congregation. But a new, younger denominational leader had recently been appointed, and congregational leaders decided to initiate a reconciliation process with the denomination through him. The congregation planned a fourth weekend (in May 1995) "to dialogue with [the leader and his spouse] about the past crisis and the denomination's part in it."

On a Saturday morning, 25 members of the congregation gathered in the fellowship hall with the denominational leader and his wife for candid dialogue. Pastor John's summary of that day includes the following:

> During the meeting, affirmations and disappointments were shared. Sins on both sides were confessed and forgiveness was sought. Issues were raised regarding polity and power abuse, and denominational inexperience and inability to respond and help. The chaos

and confusion of this experience was very frustrating.

> During the meeting, an analogy was made between the Oklahoma City bombing (which had occurred just a month earlier) and the crisis at our congregation. There was shock, denial, anger, loss of innocence, many victims, many walking wounded, short-term and long-term effects, but in the case of the church, not many rescue workers. Some felt betrayed or abandoned by the denomination. [The denominational leader] affirmed our congregation's intentional efforts at reconciliation. He received all that was said graciously and responded appropriately.

■ Breakthroughs in the Process

Because my only on-site visit with the God's Fellowship congregation was the first reconciliation weekend in 1993, my firsthand impressions are limited to that weekend. As I summarized in my "consultant's report" back to the congregation, "Significant personal and corporate release occurred during the 'neutralizing history' session on Saturday, February 20. Many reported a feeling of becoming 'unstuck' from this phase of the congregation's history—and thus free to move on to another phase." In a letter to me dated March 1, 1993, Pastor John wrote, "We claimed that date [February 20] as a new beginning for us in our life as part of the body of Christ." Equally powerful moments apparently occurred during the second and third weekends with the associate pastors and the fourth weekend with the denominational leader.

■ *Lessons Learned*

As a consultant who has been privileged to accompany this congregation for the past five years, I have experienced their process as one of reconciliation and "rebuilding consensus" rather than as mediation. Reflecting on God's Fellowship Community Church's journey, I would offer the following observations.

1. There is no greater trauma for an organization than betrayal by its founder. I have dealt with a number of other pastoral sexual misconduct cases in the past decade, all of which were very traumatic for congregational members. However, a betrayal of trust by the congregation's founder understandably threatens the very foundation of the system.

2. Admission of responsibility by the offender is a helpful, but not absolutely necessary, part of the recovery process. The founding minister who committed the misconduct took no responsibility for his misdeeds. In addition to such denial, he continued to actively discredit those who raised concerns. This behavior contributed to the ongoing trauma and division in the congregation. Nevertheless, the congregation (under new leadership) assumed the responsibility to plan its own reconciliation and recovery process.

3. The recovery process from major organizational trauma takes a very long time. Several writers have observed that the recovery process from a personal sexual trauma (such as rape) can take from 5 to 10 years. I have observed that organizations recovering from the trauma of betrayal by a key leader average about 7 years to move

beyond the major impact of that betrayal. (These estimates assume a deliberate recovery process—organizations that are unable or unwilling to openly deal with such trauma often find the impact goes underground and persists for generations.)

4. It is not necessary for all organizational members to participate in the recovery process, although leadership support and participation are critical. Only 15 percent of the active membership of the God's Fellowship congregation participated in the first reconciliation weekend, but participants included nearly all of the key leaders and church staff. The healing within a small number of participants permeated much of the larger system; the positive impact as a result of leadership involvement continues to work its way through the entire congregation.

5. The skill and will of internal organizational leaders are the key factors in successful reconciliation processes. I recently analyzed about a dozen organizational interventions and determined that the most consistent variable in successful interventions was the presence of several well-functioning leaders (lay or clergy) in the leadership team. The God's Fellowship congregation was blessed with a number of skilled leaders who were willing to take risks to openly address a gaping wound.

6. An outside consultant can be a valuable asset to the degree that he or she resources (rather than replaces) internal leadership. It was the internal leadership of God's Fellowship that planned and implemented the reconciliation process, albeit in consultation with me. Although I facilitated the first reconciliation weekend, internal leaders planned and facilitated the

second, third, and fourth events. The amount of consultation I provided diminished over time. For the first event, my assistance was very intensive and on-site; by the fourth event, it was negligible. The 1993 event seemed to provide a process framework that internal leaders successfully adapted for the three follow-up events.

7. The faith tradition and spirituality of an organization can be powerful allies in the reconciliation process. Perhaps because of their evangelical tradition and the deep personal spirituality of their leaders, the God's Fellowship congregation infused every one of their reconciliation events with prayer, Scripture, and meditation. The simplest way for me to describe the breakthroughs that the congregation experienced is that "the Spirit moved," an admission, perhaps, that what happened was more than what mere humans could plan.

8. The personal costs for the "after pastor(s)" can be immense. The pastor who follows a colleague whose misconduct has traumatized a congregational system will himself or herself pay an enormous price, due to the loss of trust and damaged relationships in the system. Pastor John recently told me that when he first arrived at God's Fellowship six years ago, "the congregation was in the anger stage. We've been in the depression stage for most of the past five years. Only now can people talk about [what happened] without either obsessing on it or avoiding it. Most of the folks who were at ground zero (when the allegations broke) have left—the price they paid was much more than they anticipated."

■ Implications for Consensus Building

I propose that the God's Fellowship trauma recovery process offers an example of successful consensus building following major intraorganizational conflict. Never is consensus building more needed (or more difficult) than following a time of significant ethical violation by an organizational leader. Although "consensus" proved impossible to achieve in the midst of the chaos of allegations and denials, new congregational leaders implemented a multiyear consensus building process in 1992. Consensus, for God's Fellowship, meant first achieving a measure of healing and movement toward closure on past trauma, and then recovering and developing a vision for future ministry.

In more recent years (since 1995), the focus of congregational leaders has shifted from recovery from past trauma to re-visioning the future of the congregation. Congregational leaders have used some of the same methodologies that proved successful in reconciliation events (small planning teams, all-day retreats, open meetings) for setting congregational vision and goals. The "seven year rule" of organizational recovery processes seemed to apply almost perfectly to the God's Fellowship congregation, meaning that only by 1998 did energy and future focus begin to manifest themselves.

■ Procedure Development

A final major area of learning for God's Fellowship has been the need for stronger procedures to deal both with ethical violations and interpersonal conflict. By February 1995, the congregation had completed new procedures for reporting and responding to allegations of sexual misconduct, particularly against those in leadership positions. The church board developed a "restoration team" in 1996 to deal with a particular internal incident. The quality and comprehensive nature of the congregation's response to the 1996 incident illustrated for me the degree of both healing and learning that had taken place since 1990.

■ Final Comments

The current senior pastor at God's Fellowship (Pastor John) called to inform me that he had shared this case study with his current associate pastor (Pastor Bob) and two key lay leaders. He suggested some minor changes to improve the case study, and then made the observation below. His comments reveal how a "standard" process—reconciliation—can be internalized and transformed according to the worldview of its users.

The significant issue is deeper than the clinical terms that surface in this document. There certainly were intellectual, procedural, emotional, and even character issues. But there was more. The polarization was exacerbated by our inability to identify and confront spiritual evil at work. Blame that belongs to spiritual evil was diffused and aimed at average church members, faithful denominational leaders who were confused, and committed congregational leaders.

The fact that we could not name it and confront it as evil (we named it as "dysfunction" and as "emotional tension/disorder") greatly complicated the reconciliation process. This was more than discovering that our previous, gifted senior pastor was only human. The reconciliation process is significant because it has been used by God to break the power of our traumatic encounter with the evil involved in the misconduct of our founding pastor. We are seeing reconciliation, healing, and a new beginning. ◆

◆ COMMENTARY

The pastor's response to the written case study is revealing. He interprets the crisis in a different way than the facilitator, using a different cultural framework. The pastor says that the significant issue is deeper than the "clinical" terms of the document and that the conflict was the result of the working of a spiritual evil along with other emotional and intellectual issues. The pastor interpreted the event as a manifestation of the force of evil, and he felt that had the event been understood as a traumatic encounter with evil in the form of the pastor's misconduct rather than as "dysfunction" or "emotional tension," reconciliation would have been less complicated. In other words, the interpretive framework of the facilitator, using largely psychotherapeutic terms, was somewhat different from that of the pastor, who understood the roots of the conflict as the forces of God and evil.

This example is a valuable reminder that the same event can be interpreted in very different ways depending on one's overarching cultural framework. Such a perspective is fundamental to the way anthropologists analyze social situations. Where Brubaker saw dysfunctional communication, the pastor saw the acts of Satan. These are not mutually exclusive frames of interpretation, but they are significantly different and lead to different ways of understanding the conflict. And they imply different kinds of solutions. In conflict situations, the coexistence of different cultural frameworks for understanding the situation seriously impedes effective intervention and peace making. It makes a huge difference if one sees the source of this conflict as a charismatic leader with a sexual dysfunction rather than as an act of Satan against which all saved Christians must be vigilant and combative.

—Sally Engle Merry, *Anthropologist*

■ *Notes*

1. The author acknowledges the assistance of Steven Gold, Ph.D., one of the two congregational representatives who attended the Ministry of Reconciliation Conference in 1992 and who also prepared a draft chronology on which the "Background" section in this case is based.

2. Graham suggests that there may also be a fifth stage, which he dubs *resolution-transformation,* but that he did not witness with the congregation he accompanied. Although he affirms many of the steps the congregation took to deal with the allegations, the offender, and his victims, Graham observes that "there has been a premature desire to move on, to suppress painful, unwanted feelings and issues" ("Healing the Congregation," 1991). He concludes his paper by acknowledging that "the recovery process is long, complicated, and difficult. When corporately owned, and when engaged in a spirit of compassion and justice, it can deepen and enrich the ministry of the church to its members and to the larger world."

3. The "neutralizing history" exercise was first explained to me by Barbara Date of Menno Simons College in Winnipeg.

4. The five areas in which organizational health can be assessed are as follows:

   a. Identity: The spectrum ranges from "socially isolated" on one end to "socially invisible" on the other. A healthy organization strives to maintain a clear identity that communicates organizational values to outsiders yet welcomes dialogue about those values.

b. Boundaries: At one extreme are rigid and closed boundaries, and at the other are boundaries that are so blurred as to be meaningless. A healthy organization tends to establish clear but permeable boundaries, allowing people to enter and leave the system in healthy ways.

c. Performance standards: Completely closed ("incestuous") organizations tend to have shame-based standards driven by perfectionism, while completely open ("irrelevant") organizations often exhibit an "anything goes" attitude toward performance. Healthy organizations, by contrast, establish clear performance standards but have a high tolerance for mistakes.

d. Communication: The spectrum here ranges from distorted communication in an incestuous organization to meaningless communication in an irrelevant organization. Healthy organizations value clear, direct communication and establish a variety of ways to maintain it.

e. Power: In incestuous organizations, power relationships are inevitably highly authoritarian and paternalistic, whereas in irrelevant organizations power is so undefined that it may be impossible to discern. In healthy organizations, power is clearly distributed according to role, and there are checks and balances to ensure that the system responds to abuses of power.

■ Reference

Healing the congregation. (1991, Spring). *Conciliation Quarterly,* *10*(2).

17

BUILDING CONSENSUS FOR CHANGE WITHIN A MAJOR CORPORATION

The Case of Levi Strauss & Co.

- Judy Mares-Dixon
- Julie A. McKay
- Scott Peppet

Levi Strauss & Co. (LS&CO) is the world's largest producer of brand-name clothing and the second largest maker of jeans in the United States, behind VF Corp., maker of Wrangler and Lee. The company was founded in 1853 in San Francisco when Levi Strauss produced his first pair of "waist high overalls" for miners in need of sturdy pants. The company is still privately owned by Strauss's descendants, the Haas family.[1] LS&CO employs approximately 30,000 people. In 1996, its sales reached a record $7 billion, and in 1997 sales totaled approximately $6.9 billion. The company is known for its philanthropy, family business tradition, team approach to manufacturing and management, and generosity toward its employees. In February 1998, for example, LS&CO received the first annual Ron Brown Award for Corporate Leadership from President Clinton for its record of corporate responsibility and community-based initiatives.

LS&CO has traditionally prided itself on its consensus-based management approach. As *Business Week* reported in 1994,

1994	Alternative Dispute Resolution Design Team convened
1995	Information gathered from focus groups around the United States Management approves design of CRP
1996	Implementation Team created Core Team created
1997	Pilot Council convened Training begins at Pilot Sites Pilot Sites begin piloting CRP
1997-1998	Downsizing begins; plant closures announced

Figure 17.A Time Line of Conflict Resolution Program (CRP) at Levi Strauss & Co.

CEO Robert Haas "is out to make each of his workers, from the factory floor on up, feel as if they are an integral part of the making and selling of blue jeans. He wants to ensure that all views on all issues—no matter how controversial—are heard and respected" ("Managing by Values," 1994, p. 46). For example, when a major reengineering of product development and distribution systems was needed in 1994 to respond to changing fashion trends, LS&CO approached the problem in keeping with its consensus-based vision. More than 6,000 employees were asked to provide advice on what LS&CO should do differently, and with those data, nearly 200 managers spent a year planning the reorganization. The company's Diversity Council, which represents African Americans, Asians, Hispanics, women, and other groups to top management, also played a role in the decision-making process.

Motivated to actualize and further the consensus-based and people-oriented vision at LS&CO, in 1994 the company began to examine its internal practices and procedures for resolving nonunion employee conflicts. At the initiative of an early and vocal champion—Joann M. Russell, associate general counsel—LS&CO embarked on a project to study its existing dispute resolution systems; identify avenues for change; and design, implement, and evaluate a new set of processes for managing disputes. In 1997, with the help of outside consultants from CDR Associates, LS&CO had a new conflict resolution program (CRP) in place in four pilot sites across the United States (see Figure 17.A). ↩

↩ COMMENTARY

An organization's initial process of assessment needs to identify major problems and sources of tension before proposing a solution. This project followed that approach, but it addressed only one source of tension: the relations between workers. It did not consider relations with employers. Such an approach is likely to debilitate a dispute management system. Unless the power structure of an institution is incorporated into the conflict resolution process, it risks becoming a marginal system for trivial or insignificant problems while major issues having to do with the allocation of power are handled elsewhere or not at all. Indeed, the end of the chapter implies that management was relatively uninvolved in the process, reinforcing my suspicion that the processes bypassed the hierarchical relations of power in the company and ended up handling relatively minor problems. These are minor problems in that they do not affect large numbers of workers, but they can be of major importance to particular individuals involved in them, of course.

—Sally Engle Merry, *Anthropologist*

Just as the piloting phase of the CRP was rolled out, however, LS&CO began to respond to economic changes overtaking the company. Despite the overall success of LS&CO, the company has faced increased competition from designer jeans and store brands over the past few years, and its revenues have declined. Analysts attribute part of the company's loss of market share to LS&CO's refusal to move North American production overseas, which results in higher costs and thus higher consumer prices. In February 1997, LS&CO announced that it would lay off 20 percent of its salaried workers, or 1,000 people, to reduce overhead. In November 1997, LS&CO announced that it would close 11 of its 37 North American plants in 1998, laying off 6,400 manufacturing workers, or 34 percent of its North American workforce. In August 1998, the company reorganized its management structure, switching from a function-based structure—sales, merchandising, brands—to brand management centered on two market groups: youths (ages 13-25) and young adults (ages 25-35). And in September 1998, the company announced proposed plans to close four facilities in Europe, which could eliminate more than 1,500 jobs or a fifth of its European workforce, and two finishing facilities in the United States because of overcapacity caused by declining demand for jeans.

This case study chronicles the development and implementation of the new dispute resolution system at LS&CO and the impact of these structural and workforce changes over the past year. It focuses on three questions throughout:

- How were consensus-based approaches used in the design and implementation of the CRP?
- In what ways were consensus-based processes built into the new CRP at LS&CO? and
- What barriers and dilemmas did LS&CO encounter during the design and implementation process, and how were they addressed?

The case study is organized chronologically, beginning with the initial impetus for change and progressing through the information collection, design, implementation, and evaluation phases of the CRP project. It ends with a discussion of the project's key findings and lessons.

■ *The Initial Impulse for Change*

LS&CO has long had a foundation of values that management disseminates widely to employees. Included in that statement are a mission statement; an "Aspirations statement"; and specific aspirations related to teamwork and trust, diversity, ethical management, communication, and empowerment. Several of these core principles motivated the creation of the CRP at LS&CO. For example:

- The mission statement includes that "our work environment will be safe and productive and characterized by fair treatment, teamwork, open communications, personal accountability, and opportunities for growth and development."
- The Aspirations statement includes that "we want our people to feel respected, treated fairly, listened to, and involved. Above all, we want satisfaction from accomplishments and friendships, balanced personal and professional lives, and to have fun in our endeavors."
- The communication Aspiration states that LS&CO's leadership should foster "an environment where information is actively shared, sought, and used in ways that lead to empowerment that works, improved performance, and meaningful feedback."
- The empowerment Aspiration notes that LS&CO hopes to promote "ways of working in which responsibility, authority, and accountability for decision making are held by those closest to our products and customers, and every employee has the necessary perspective, skills, and knowledge to be successful in his or her job. We all share the responsibility for creating the environment that will nurture empowerment at all levels of the organization."

- The business vision Aspiration states that "the Company will support each employee's responsibility to acquire new skills and knowledge in order to meet the changing needs of our business."

To ensure that LS&CO's Aspirations are understood and embraced, the Aspirations statement hangs on office and factory walls.

In 1994, Associate General Counsel Joann Russell convened the Alternative Dispute Resolution Design Team to identify how employee disputes were being handled within the company and to explore possible alternatives that might better align with LS&CO's mission. No crisis precipitated the project, nor was LS&CO responding to litigation costs or the loss of a major lawsuit. Those at LS&CO involved in the creation of the CRP underscore the importance of the aspirational values in the original support for designing a nonunion dispute resolution system. They stress the importance to LS&CO's management of actualizing these values. "I saw myself as a bridge to enable and empower others," Russell recalls. "I relied on my own interest and enthusiasm to inspire, instigate, and challenge. What I wanted was for people to realize their own vision." The team hoped that a new conflict resolution system might bolster LS&CO's corporate culture by helping employees to develop an appreciation for the learning opportunities that disputes can present, increase worker satisfaction and productivity, and help to actualize the company's Aspirations.

Those originally involved in the project recognized an inherent tension within the values championed by LS&CO's management: The Aspirations statement challenged employees to communicate about differences openly and productively, but it also encouraged getting along and treating each other with respect. How were both goals to be realized in a given interaction? How could employees bring up difficult subjects in a very busy and task-oriented workplace and overcome the tendency to translate "being aspirational"—an LS&CO slogan—into "making nice" rather than discussing conflicts openly? Others had surfaced this tension within LS&CO's Aspirations statement before. For example, F. Warren Hellman, a San Francisco investment banker and an LS&CO director, has said, "There's a danger that this [the aspirational vision] will degrade into a touchy-feely, I-don't-want-to-offend-you, creativity-stifling style of management" ("Managing by Values," 1994, p. 48). The early champions of the CRP hoped that a new approach to conflict—and the culture change within LS&CO that the CRP could produce—would address this tension.

To guarantee broad knowledge of and support for the project, members of the team were drawn from all divisions of the company. Russell identified key stakeholders throughout the company who should be included in a cross-functional design effort. These stakeholders represented the following areas at LS&CO: the prevention, safety, and health organization; human resources representatives from the field offices, headquarters, and global human resources; sales; the two primary brands, Levi's® and Dockers®; finance; communications; legal; operations and sourcing (including two plant managers); and the business continuity group (charged with ensuring that production would continue even after a natural disaster or other contingency). Personnel from each of these areas either volunteered for or were asked to join the Design Team. The team's first and primary task was to perform a needs assessment to identify gaps between organizational needs and existing dispute resolution capacity.

■ Building Support and Gathering Information

From the outset, the Design Team sought support from all levels of the company for the new CRP. At one level, Joann Russell and others sought out other managers and executives and promoted the idea of a new conflict resolution system within the executive hierarchy. In March 1995, a group of sponsors was selected that included the presidents of the Levi's and Dockers brands, the vice president of operations and sourcing, the vice president of human resources, and the executive vice president of global human resources. This group agreed to work with Russell to provide resources for the project and support the CRP when it ultimately went for approval to the leadership of LS&CO nationwide.

The Design Team initially conducted a series of focus group discussions in 12 company locations across the country. To ensure a representative sample of the workforce, random focus group participants were selected according to a profile based on years of service, gender, function, and language. Each focus group consisted of 10 to 15 individuals who were asked questions about LS&CO's current system for resolving conflicts and what they thought a new system should look like. Approximately 400 employees were interviewed in total. Input was also solicited regarding how employees and the company should share responsibilities under the new CRP.

The Design Team then collected and analyzed the focus group data. Several themes or lessons emerged from the focus groups.

First, field employees working in manufacturing plants reported different experiences with conflict than salaried employees working in office settings. Field employees said that they relied on the chain of command for resolving conflicts, whereas salaried employees felt that no real process for resolving conflicts existed. When asked how they learned to use the chain of command, employees in the plants consistently reported that they relied on the employee handbook or gathered information during employee orientation. Others learned to turn to their supervisors through word of mouth or by observing other employees in conflict situations.

Those field employees that used the chain of command as a conflict resolution mechanism did so inconsistently. Because no clear dispute resolution process existed, employees involved in conflicts often bypassed lower-level managers and looked for help from more senior management. As a result, lower-level managers were often the last to find out about conflicts in the workplace. And some employees who did turn to their managers reported that managers tried to decide disputes unilaterally. Several managers said that they did not know the extent of their responsibilities as conflict managers.

Second, employee fears about the current approach to conflict were widespread. Employees feared retaliation if they reported problems to either supervisors or indiscreet colleagues. Employees hoped for a system in which most conflicts could be resolved face-to-face without the involvement of management, and internal to the company. For example, field employees felt that a peer review process would not be acceptable unless conflicts involving personal and sexual harassment issues were excluded from the process, because too much information would leak out of the process and back into the workplace.

Finally, the focus groups uniformly expressed employees' desires to be trained in conflict resolution skills and concepts. Employees recognized that they lacked the skills to handle disputes productively (or, as often, they realized that their coworkers lacked such skills). All sought information and experiential training in managing conflict better. And many hoped that their new skills and the new CRP would resolve disputes in a more timely manner. ❧

❧ COMMENTARY

This case illustrates what any good ethnographer knows: To change a situation, it is essential to understand how it works in the first place. The approach here is a grassroots effort to design conflict resolution systems tailored to the particular situation. Focus groups and employee consultation were critical to learn about the particular features of the situation and to design an appropriate and workable program. Two key features of the situation emerged as a result of this anthropological approach: the differences between office workers and factory workers, and the cultural and linguistic diversity among the employees. Both were essential to the final plan.

—Sally Engle Merry, *Anthropologist*

■ Designing the Conflict Resolution Program

With the focus group data in hand, Joann M. Russell and others on the Design Team set out to create a new CRP for LS&CO.

The Design Goals

Based on the information gathered in the focus groups, the Design Team created a set of requirements for the new CRP. These included the following.

Early intervention. Conflicts would need to be addressed early and by employees directly. If the CRP allowed disputes to be resolved nearer their source, the Design Team hoped to empower employees by giving them control over when and how problems could be addressed. For those employees who were unwilling or unable to engage in direct, face-to-face problem solving, the system would provide support and assistance from a coach or mediator.

Easy-to-use information. Employees would have to become familiar with the mechanics of the CRP and be directed to its resources. When the CRP was eventually pilot tested, LS&CO developed a brochure titled "Understanding More about Resolving Conflicts" that explained the CRP process, provided definitions of relevant terms, and directed employees to the appropriate resource for additional information.

Equal access. Training and information about the CRP and conflict resolution skills would have to be available in all four principal languages spoken by LS&CO employees in the pilot sites: English, Spanish, Vietnamese, and Lao.

Choice and flexibility. The CRP should be flexible and allow employees to schedule coaching or mediations at different times and on different shifts to accommodate varied schedules. Moreover, an employee should be able to seek help from anyone—a manager, supervisor, employee mediator, or coworker—in the form of coaching or feedback. This freedom of choice would allow those with different styles and preferences to seek assistance tailored to their needs. For example, whereas one employee might look for coaching from a friend who could offer support and listen empathetically, another might prefer a coach to suggest solutions, offer critical feedback, and illustrate different ways to approach the conflict situation.

Commitment of resources. Employees should be permitted to use work time to manage conflicts. There should not be lengthy bureaucratic delays if employees seek more formal help within the CRP; coaching or mediation should be available within days or hours.

Confidentiality. Everyone participating in the CRP should maintain confidences at all times.

The New LS&CO Conflict Resolution Program

With these goals in mind, the Design Team set out to craft a systematic and structured approach to conflict. The team came up with a relatively simple four-level approach:

CRP Structure	Percentage of Conflicts Expected to Be Resolved at Each Level
Level 1: Face-to-face conflict resolution	90
Level 2: Coaching (return to Level 1)	7
Level 3: In-house mediation	2.5
Level 4: Arbitration	0.5

At Level 1, employees were to raise conflicts face-to-face and negotiate a resolution of their disagreements locally. The Design Team expected that 90 percent of conflicts could be resolved in this way. To ensure the success of this first level, the CRP would have to include a training component for *all* employees, so that each employee would have new skills to manage conflict more productively.

At Level 2, employees who could not resolve their conflicts face-to-face would be encouraged to seek the assistance of a coach. A coach would serve as an informal counselor and sounding board, rather than as an advocate or champion. The coach would give feedback and help the disputants identify their own contribution to the problem under negotiation. This stage of the CRP required that employees be trained in both "being a coach" and "getting a coach." Rather than have a formal roster of designated coaches, the Design Team expected employees to seek out their coworkers, managers, and friends for help. The team expected that of the 10 percent of disputes that reached Level 2, all would return to Level 1 after coaching and 70 percent would be resolved there. ◖

◖ COMMENTARY

The use of an intermediate level of intervention between one-on-one negotiation and mediation—the coach—is an innovative and promising idea. It has the potential for providing a way of dealing with conflicts to a person who is afraid or unwilling to confront the other person in a mediation session.

—Sally Engle Merry, *Anthropologist*

Level 3, the mediation stage, was intended for those few disputes that were not resolved face-to-face and with coaching. Independent in-house mediation seemed a perfect forum to address employees' desires for a confidential and low-risk process that did not necessarily involve management in employee disputes. Employees would be referred to a mediation coordinator in their location, who would explain the mediation process, give the parties a list of trained in-house mediators, assign the dispute for mediation, and track the results.

Level 4, the arbitration stage, was added to accommodate cases with legal implications that might demand a more formal resolution process. The Design Team assumed that some disputes—particularly those involving legal issues—would skip Levels 1 through 3 and proceed directly to arbitration or proceed through the system and eventually require arbitration. The arbitration stage was never formalized or implemented at the pilot sites.

Excluded Disputes

The CRP project was meant to augment, not replace, existing dispute management processes at LS&CO. For example, LS&CO had a variety of labor-management procedures for unionized workers, including a formal grievance process. Union-related disputes were never expected to enter the new CRP, and ultimately the CRP was not piloted at any unionized sites. The Design Team expected to pilot the CRP in a nonunionized setting and then consider whether it or some variation of it could be integrated into the union processes.

Similarly, the Design Team assumed that "structural" conflicts were also excluded. Employees with complaints about LS&CO's compensation or benefits package, for example, would not be able to initiate mediation with the head of the human resources department. And an employee with a complaint about the closure of a factory could not seek mediation with the CEO. Such structural decisions and conflicts were beyond the bounds of the CRP.

Management Approval

With their design complete, the Design Team sought and obtained approval from upper management for the design and for implementing the CRP at four pilot sites. The conflict resolution process was approved by the sponsors in March 1995, and by the U.S. Leadership Team at the end of 1995. In October 1996, the U.S. Leadership Team reconfirmed its commitment to the project, and in 1997, the sponsors similarly recommitted because several new members had been added due to restructuring.[2] ➤

☞ COMMENTARY

Basic to an anthropological analysis of a social situation is an understanding of the underlying power relations. It is important to ask how the project fits into the power structure of the company. One goal of the project was helping employees to manage their own disputes to relieve the burden on management. Yet management was reluctant to limit its authority. Is it possible to do both? It seems unlikely. Management might surrender control only over those disputes it considers trivial. But what if these so-called trivial problems include employee grievances against management? Moreover, although some conflicts involve only employees, others are a product of the situation within which employees are working. They may be the result of management decisions. To turn problems caused by management policies or work conditions back to the workers themselves to resolve does not empower these workers. Nor does it facilitate getting to the underlying sources of the dispute, one of the goals of the program. Instead, it can actually relieve management of responsibility for conflicts.

—Sally Engle Merry, *Anthropologist*

■ Implementation

To implement the CRP, an Implementation Team was formed. The Implementation Team, like the Design Team, was a cross-functional group composed of representatives from the same stakeholders within LS&CO that Russell had originally identified as important for the design effort. Some Design Team members carried over to serve on the Implementation Team and ensure consistency between the two efforts. Other members were new to the CRP project.

The Core Team was organized almost organically, coming together to meet the needs of implementing the program rather than in response to a directive from management. The team had four members: Joann M. Russell, Beth Doolittle, Donna Uchida, and Ollie Calvert. The team's tasks included building and maintaining support for the CRP within the organizational hierarchy at LS&CO, ensuring consistency in the offerings and program implementation across the four pilot sites, helping to design and evaluate the materials used in training, and overseeing the piloting phase of the project. In some sense the Core Team functioned as the "working group" of the Implementation Team. Whereas the Implementation Team met once a month or once every six weeks, the Core Team handled the implementation phase on a more day-to-day basis. For example, when the four pilot sites were selected, each member of the Core Team was designated as a primary contact for one pilot site, although all four members worked as a team to meet with site leadership, present information, and help manage the implementation process.

Identifying Pilot Sites and Creating the Pilot Council

LS&CO employs a very diverse workforce. The Implementation Team recognized early on that the success of the CRP hinged in part on the team's ability to solicit the involvement of employees from the major ethnic groups represented within the company, including those speaking Spanish, Lao, and Vietnamese as their first language; to include the views of both management and field employees; to incorporate in the CRP different views toward cooperation, competition, and conflict; and to manage contrasting beliefs about what constitutes an acceptable approach to conflict and the use of third-party intervention.

From the project's beginning, the Design Team had hoped that pilot sites would volunteer, rather than be volunteered, to test the CRP. Russell and others had worked to keep management from implementing the program too quickly or in a "top-down" fashion. Instead, the Design Team hoped that as the goals of the CRP became known throughout LS&CO, pilot sites would step forward.

In late 1996, the Implementation Team began thinking about what would constitute a successful set of pilot sites. Four sites ultimately volunteered or were chosen: the New York Regional Sales Office, the San Francisco Product Development group, the El Paso, Texas Airway sewing facility, and the Amarillo, Texas finishing center. In evaluating which sites to use, the team considered several criteria, including geographic diversity, business function diversity, workforce diversity, and size:

Geographic diversity. The pilot sites were located in California, New York, and Texas.

Business diversity. The pilot sites represented several types of LS&CO business units, including a sales office (New York), a design group (San Francisco), a sewing plant (El Paso, Texas), and a finishing facility (Amarillo, Texas).

Workforce diversity. The workforces in the four sites varied tremendously. New York and San Francisco, for example, were primarily management sites, and El Paso and Amarillo were primarily "local payroll" or field employees. Language diversity was also an issue. In El Paso, employees spoke Spanish only, English only, or were bilingual. In Amarillo, the same language diversity existed, and some Asian American employees were most comfortable speaking in Vietnamese or Lao. In San Francisco and New York, such language diversity was not an issue, but the corporate cultures varied tremendously. ❧

❧ COMMENTARY

The design team clearly recognizes the importance of incorporating cultural diversity into its plan. But what exactly does this mean? Is it sufficient to have conflict resolution available in several languages? Or are there more fundamental differences among people from different cultural backgrounds in the way they deal with conflict? Some groups are far less comfortable with asserting their claims and making complaints than others. Moreover, some cultural groups have a far more developed sense of rights and entitlements than others. The approach to these groups will have to be different. Those who find rights-based thinking less compatible may need more encouragement to use conflict resolution mechanisms for their problems and require different forms of presentation. It would be helpful to present a series of concrete examples of the kinds of problems that the conflict resolution system can deal with to members of each cultural group to make clear what the new process offers and for which kinds of difficulties it is appropriate.

However, what constitutes a cultural group is itself very ambiguous. Immigrants from Cambodia who have grown up in the United States typically have a different understanding of rights and conflict than do their parents who had been raised in Cambodia. Men and women often differ in their willingness to assert rights and make claims. Social class shapes a person's sense of autonomy and control over the world in many ways. Each of these aspects of diversity intersects with the others, so that a system needs to be tailored to the complexity of identities based on ethnicity, language, gender, class, and length of time living in the United States. Anthropologists now recognize that the older meaning of the term *culture,* in the sense of a homogeneous, integrated, and bounded way of life shared by a group of people, is no longer accurate for describing the fluid, interconnected, and contested nature of the practices and beliefs by which social groups are organized in the modern world. Indeed, many question whether such a concept was ever adequate, arguing that social groups have long influenced and dominated one another and that homogeneity was always the product of contestation and power struggles.

—Sally Engle Merry, *Anthropologist*

Size diversity. The four pilot sites varied in size. The design group in San Francisco contained approximately 60 employees, and the sales office in New York approximately 100, whereas the two plants in Texas employed approximately 600 to 700 employees.

As soon as the four sites were selected, the Core Team began working with leadership at each site to establish local CRP implementation teams. The Core Team aimed to have local employees at each site manage the implementation process. In El Paso, Texas, for example, a local team of 10 employees led the implementation efforts. Its tasks included explaining the CRP to employees, conducting the mediator selection process, selecting local trainers, and monitoring the training process.

As employees volunteered at each site and local implementation efforts got under way, the Core Team created a new entity: the Pilot Council. The purpose of this new team was to bring representatives from each of the four pilot sites into contact with each other to ensure consistency between the sites. The Pilot Council consisted of the four Core Team members and eight pilot site representatives, two from each location. Management at each of the four sites chose a manager to sit on the Pilot Council. In addition, the Core Team recruited a second representative from each site. This second person generally was someone more involved with implementing the CRP at the pilot site. In addition, this second representative often had more direct contact with the field employees in the El Paso and Amarillo sites.

The Core and Implementation Teams aimed to use a consensus building approach throughout the implementation phase. In structuring the implementation effort, for example, responsibility was handed over to

the local implementation teams at each pilot site. Although the Core Team and the Pilot Council made recommendations to these local groups, the local employees were expected to reach decisions about how implementation should occur. Local implementation teams conducted the initial employee orientations at the various sites and were heavily involved in the training efforts as the CRP unfolded.

For example, the Core Team provided each pilot site with a communications strategy for explaining the CRP to local employees. The Core Team sent the local implementation teams draft e-mails, cafeteria tent cards, and flyers that could be used to make general announcements about the CRP, to request mediator nominations, to notify prospective mediators of having been selected, and to make general announcements about employee training. The local implementation teams, however, were expected to adapt these materials to fit the needs of their site. In one production facility, for example, the implementation team decided to conduct an unannounced skit in the employee cafeteria to demonstrate the need for conflict management training. Team members simulated an employee-employee conflict, and then modeled how a third party could help work through the disagreement. The team knew that because of the diversity of languages and cultures represented in the plant, a demonstration would be more effective than written explanations of the CRP.

Mediator Selection

When the pilot sites were selected, the Core Team then sought to identify employees to serve as mediators for Level 3 of the CRP. The process of selecting mediators at each of the pilot sites was a key step in transferring ownership of the CRP to the employees. Rather than choose mediators from the top down, the Core Team assembled a template of characteristics—including the ability to keep confidences, garner respect, analyze issues in a dispute, listen well, communicate clearly, and separate oneself from a conflict—for employees to consider in nominating mediators. Employees at the pilot sites were then asked for their nominations. In the smaller sites—New York and San Francisco—nominations were collected easily through e-mail. In El Paso and Amarillo, a flyer was created, translated into Lao, Vietnamese, and Spanish, and distributed to employees. The employees then nominated mediators.

After receiving the nominations, managers at the pilot sites reviewed the nominations to consider whether those nominated could carry the additional workload of being a mediator. Ultimately, the nominated mediators ranged in age from 25 to 60,

occupied a variety of positions from production workers to management, and included individuals with eighth-grade educations and others with advanced degrees. Although the pool of mediators did not contain a representative number of managers, the Implementation Team recommended adding one or two managers to the mediator pool at each site, and pilot sites uniformly agreed.

The Core Team hoped to train more mediators than needed for each of the four sites. In this way, the team could consider each individual after the mediator training and determine who should serve as a mediator, who needed more training, and who would not be well suited to mediate. The Core Team enlisted CDR Associates, a collaborative decision-making and conflict management consulting organization, who provided the mediator training, to recommend which participants should be named mediators for the CRP. ➥

➥ COMMENTARY

A central part of the program was the selection and training of mediators. This kind of training frequently has a broader, ripple effect in conflict management processes, informally spreading the use of mediation to wider groups of people. But did people use the mediators in a more formal way? It has often proved far easier to recruit and train mediators than to attract cases to these mediators. This program apparently "empowers people by giving them the courage and tools to approach their managers and supervisors," in one manager's words. But has this been accomplished, and if so, how? Since the emphasis is on teaching employees to deal with one another rather than with managers, how did the program staff shift the focus from problems among employees to problems with management? Did this come from teaching about conflict as a process, from giving it a name and legitimacy? Although tantalizing, we don't really know how much this program accomplished without a more thorough evaluation.

—Sally Engle Merry, *Anthropologist*

Training

The Implementation Team considered various approaches to training the employ-

ees at the pilot sites to use the new CRP. It examined other training efforts that had occurred within LS&CO on other initiatives and saw that in most cases training

TABLE 17.A Training Approach (who conducted—approximate number of employees trained)

Location	Conflict Resolution Training	Mediation Training	Number of Mediators Selected
New York, NY	CDR—105	CDR—16	14
San Francisco, CA	CDR—60	CDR—12	8
El Paso, TX	CDR—Train the Trainers LS&CO—620	CDR—30	17
Amarillo, TX	CDR—Train the Trainers LS&CO—700	CDR—30	22

began at the top of the organization and then was expected to filter down over an extended period of time as managers trained their employees, and so on. Because of its consensus-oriented approach and determination to respond to the requests of those who participated in the focus groups, the Implementation Team decided to pilot a different training model: Its goal was that all employees at each pilot site would receive eight hours of training in conflict resolution within one month of the rollout at that site. The team felt that without broad training of all employees, the culture change needed to make the CRP work would not occur.

As the pilot sites began implementation, LS&CO retained CDR Associates to train LS&CO employees in conflict resolution and mediation skills and concepts. CDR Associates and the Core Team tailored the training to meet the needs of the four pilot sites. Four training modules were designed. First, all staff at a site would attend a one-day conflict resolution training that explained the new system, discussed how the pilot would work, and taught the interpersonal skills needed to engage conflict

productively. Second, those elected by the pilot site employees to serve as employee mediators would attend a one-week mediation training at their pilot site that would give an in-depth introduction to mediation skills and concepts. Third, for the larger sites—El Paso and Amarillo—CDR Associates would offer a "train the trainers" workshop to prepare LS&CO's employees to conduct the one-day conflict resolution session for the remaining employees. Finally, refresher courses were created to keep conflict management skills fresh in the minds of employees at the pilot sites. Employees were to receive a four-hour refresher course six months after their initial conflict resolution training.

In the two smaller pilot sites—San Francisco and New York—CDR Associates did all the necessary training. In San Francisco, CDR Associates offered the one-day conflict resolution training to approximately 60 staff members, and the mediation training to 12 (see Table 17.A). In New York, CDR Associates trained approximately 100 staff members in conflict resolution and 16 in mediation. In El Paso and Amarillo, CDR Associates trained LS&CO's trainers to handle the larger numbers of employees in the one-day conflict resolution training. CDR Associates trained approximately 30 mediators in each of those sites. (CDR Associates ultimately held one refresher course in New York and two at the El Paso, Texas site.)

The training focused on typical conflicts experienced by employees and managers at LS&CO. These included performance problems; complaints brought under the Americans with Disabilities Act; and disputes involving harassment, race conflict, language problems, and issues of gender, age, religion, power differences, or personality conflicts.

The objectives of the one-day conflict resolution training course were anchored in three domains: concepts, skills, and attitudes toward conflict. The concept and skills objectives were designed to equip employees with the ability to both understand and use the four-level CRP. The third component was designed to shift employees' traditional beliefs about conflict and conflict resolution.

- *Concepts:* The concept objectives included a theoretical overview of the causes of conflict and strategies to de-escalate conflict, an overview of conflict styles and how to deal with widely varying styles, effective communication techniques, competitive and cooperative approaches to problem solving in teams and between teams, strategies for selecting and using a coach, and an explanation of the mediation process.

- *Skills:* The skills objectives sought to develop the employees' ability to raise difficult issues, frame problems in solvable terms, deal with emotion, reach across language and cultural barriers, and otherwise prepare for face-to-face negotiation and mediation.

- *Attitudes:* These objectives challenged employees to examine their approaches to conflict, to recognize the importance of building trust in relationships, and to embrace a collaborative model of problem solving.

Throughout the design and implementation of the training programs, both CDR Associates and the Core and Implementation Teams sought to use a consensus building approach with involved stakeholders. The training modules, although created and reviewed centrally, were tailored to meet the challenges and demands of those "on the ground" at the pilot sites. At one site, for example, the majority of mediators chosen to attend the initial training spoke only Spanish. At the request of those working with the CRP at the pilot site, CDR Associates, the staff at the pilot site, and members of the Core Team assembled and translated all of the training materials into Spanish, arranged for simultaneous translation, and recruited Spanish-speaking coaches for the mediation practice sessions. The Spanish-speaking mediators received the clear message that they were part of a new, groundbreaking effort and that they did not have to wait until the problems had been worked out by their English-speaking peers to play a part in it. ➥

☞ COMMENTARY

The most intriguing feature of this experiment is, I think, the way it empowers mediators. The people selected to be mediators were pleased, they learned new skills, and employees were encouraged to seek them out instead of just complaining to a friend. As in many other situations, it appears that selecting and training mediators is the major outcome of the intervention. It certainly appears to be that way in this case. Although such an outcome may not fit with the express goals of the intervention, it is an important way of creating grassroots leadership beyond the immediate goals of enhancing conflict resolution capability. It needs to be recognized as an accomplishment in its own right.

—Sally Engle Merry, *Anthropologist*

■ *Evaluation*

The Design and Implementation Teams recognized early on that both quantitative and qualitative evaluation efforts should take place throughout the CRP project. As a result, quantitative statistical data were gathered at different points in the implementation process. For example, employees were asked to complete a short written questionnaire prior to attending the one-day conflict resolution training, and then completed the same questionnaire again at the end of the training. Employees filled out a similar questionnaire prior to beginning their six-month refresher course.

An external consulting team was hired to analyze the data. Key findings included the following:

- Prior to the CRP training, about one-half of employees felt that their co-workers had inadequate conflict resolution skills. Two-thirds of employees felt that LS&CO had done little to help with conflict resolution. Most people said that they either avoided or were reluctant to raise a conflict with a manager or supervisor.

- After the training, employees were more confident in their conflict management skills and in their ability to discuss difficult issues.

- Mediations did occur in some pilot sites. In El Paso, Texas, for example, six mediations were conducted. The mediated disputes tended to focus on work issues and work processes, such as production methods or the perception of favoritism, rather than on interpersonal relationship-type disputes.

In addition, the Core Team conducted focus groups to gather qualitative data after the initial training plan was complete. Although not all employees at all sites received refresher training, the team sought to gather information from those who had been through a refresher course. The team aimed to interview approximately 10 percent of the employees who had been through the CRP training. Employees made a variety of comments about the impact of the CRP and training on their work:

A lot of times we'd talk without thinking. Now we think and then we speak and then we act.

Those trainings that they've given us have helped a whole lot . . . because they've taught us to have more patience with people. They made us see that yelling doesn't get us anywhere. . . . They should have done it from the first day we started work—from that day on.

Now with the training they have given us, you speak more peacefully to people.

I used the skills at first, but over time it's slipped and I don't do it as much anymore.

Employees also reported a variety of fears, including that upper management wasn't supporting the program adequately or sincerely; the CRP didn't align sufficiently with LS&CO's Aspirations; the process didn't seem confidential enough; and some employees remained unreceptive to talking about conflicts.

Although the long-term effectiveness of the system remains unproven, the qualitative and quantitative information collected through written questionnaires and focus groups provided valuable insight into what was achieved, how the system was used, and what adaptations needed to be made. Overall it seems clear that

- there were observable behavioral changes in the way employees addressed and managed conflict;

- employees primarily used Level 1 and Level 2 of the CRP, and Level 3 to a lesser extent; and

- continued support at the upper and middle levels of management is imperative to ongoing success at the pilot sites.

Although not all pilot sites experienced behavioral change to the same degree, there was an overall sense that employees were assuming more responsibility for their problems, were listening more carefully to each other, were moving away from a "he said, she said" approach to conflict, and were using the skills they developed in the training courses. Jesse Butler, a mediator at one pilot site, noticed subtle changes in the behavior of his colleagues. "They speak up, challenge things, and act with more confidence," he reported. And human resources manager Ed Chamblin said, "The conflict management process empowers people by giving them the courage and tools to approach their managers and supervisors." His perspective changed as well. "For myself, the process evolved from 'yeah, it's a nice thing' into something I now see as essential. Employees with a conflict can remedy it, and then return to being productive." Isela Ramos, an Implementation Team member and mediator, witnessed what she termed "an awakening" among employees.

Initial evidence showed that employees were making use of the CRP. Lisa Bolster, a mediator and trainer, described how people seek a coach: "Before, when people wanted to talk about a problem, they would approach someone, usually a friend, primarily for the purpose of blowing off steam. Now people can use their own criteria to consciously select a coach. Because the coach serves in a more formal role, people are supported and encouraged to work toward solving their problem."

■ The Onset of Economic Turmoil at LS&CO

LS&CO began to announce plans for restructuring just as the CRP was being implemented in the four pilot sites. Approximately halfway through the training at the San Francisco site, LS&CO announced the merging of the San Francisco design group pilot site into a larger entity. The Core Team then faced the choice of training all of the members of the new, larger group or abandoning San Francisco as a pilot. Because of the complexities of the restructuring situation, the site was dropped from the CRP. Then, in November 1997, LS&CO announced 11 plant closings in North America, including the El Paso Airways pilot site. This not only sent the El Paso employees into turmoil but also raised doubts about the viability of the pilot project. Finally, on September 28, 1998, LS&CO announced the closure of two finishing facilities in the United States, including the Amarillo, Texas pilot site. ↔

↔ COMMENTARY

It appears that during the implementation process, as employees were being encouraged to accept more responsibility for solving problems, they had to grapple with job insecurities caused by company downsizing. Employee conflict resolution processes cannot get at the source of such a problem. Moreover, it seems that managers were relatively unrepresented as mediators and so did not get engaged themselves in helping to work out problems that their actions might have caused or could ameliorate.

—Sally Engle Merry, *Anthropologist*

No official decision has been made regarding the future of the CRP project. Many of the original sponsors and Core Team members have left LS&CO or have transferred to new positions and no longer work on the CRP project. A final report regarding the piloting effort is being prepared, but has not been completed. At this time, both the New York pilot site and the Amarillo, Texas site continue to use the conflict resolution skills acquired through the CRP training effort. Although no mediations have been conducted in the New York office, employees there continue to adapt conflict resolution skills to both their internal interactions and their interactions with external customers. And although the Amarillo site is scheduled to close in November 1998, employees continue to schedule mediations in the plant's final weeks.

"We knew the employees would have ample opportunities to apply their newly acquired conflict resolution skills," said Mike Hughes, one of the CDR Associates trainers. "We couldn't imagine how large and difficult the conflicts would be or how valiant their attempts to rise to the occasion." As LS&CO began to acknowledge its economic difficulties and employees braced for changes in the structure and composition of the workforce, those working with the CRP at the pilot sites began to see employees using their new skills in the context of very difficult conversations about their economic future at LS&CO. One instance was particularly noteworthy: Employees became aware of the company's plans to identify domestic manufacturing sites for closure on the same day as a one-day refresher course at one of the pilot sites. In addition, a class action lawsuit filed by employees against LS&CO was concluded on that same day in the same location. The court's decision in favor of the employees sparked controversy at the pilot site. Some employees organized pro-company rallies, and others spoke out against the company. Many employees feared that the lawsuit would prejudice LS&CO management against the pilot site and lead to the facility's closure. The Implementation Team, the Pilot Council, and the Core Team recognized that the refresher training provided an opportunity to address these fears constructively. The trainers devoted time to a one-on-one role play in which employees played characters holding opposing viewpoints about the court case. This gave employees an opportunity to apply their newly acquired skills to a very real and difficult issue in their workplace.

■ Lessons Learned

LS&CO learned important lessons from designing and piloting the CRP. These lessons can be organized around the three questions posed at the outset of this case study.

How were consensus-based approaches used in the design and implementation of the CRP?

Several key lessons regarding building consensus for a dispute system design initiative emerged early on in the project:

A design initiative should respond to a need perceived by many, not a few, within the company. At LS&CO, the initial focus group data showed convincingly that many employees within the company were eager for change in this area. This not only made it easier to garner the support of management for the project but also aided the presentation of the CRP to employees. Rather than being perceived as a top-down initiative from headquarters, the CRP was seen as a response by headquarters to "bottom-up" feedback from employees.

Those spearheading a design project must "walk their talk." LS&CO already enjoyed a consensus-based culture and vision. Had employees or management perceived that those on the CRP project were not living up to the consensus-oriented ideals of the project, most on the Core Team believe that support would have vanished.

Whenever possible, those who will be affected by the design effort should be consulted about the direction it takes. The Project, Core, Design, and Implementation Teams constantly checked in with focus groups, employees, leaders at the various pilot sites, and those selected to be mediators to ensure that all were included as the CRP unfolded. This not only led to changes in the way the CRP was designed but also ensured buy-in at the implementation phase.

Champions within the company are needed to lend initial credibility to the project. At LS&CO, Joann Russell was the primary champion in upper-level management. Her ability to enlist the support of other executive and upper-level managers proved vital to the success of the CRP.

Leaders representing different ethnic or cultural communities within the organization must be included in all phases of the process to secure acceptance of the system, adapt and translate materials, and encourage broad participation. At LS&CO, this meant working with the diverse workforce, including those speaking primarily Lao,

Vietnamese, or Spanish, to ensure that all felt included and considered. Materials were translated into multiple languages, trainings were offered to different populations in their primary language, and leaders of different ethnic groups were asked for input and feedback.

A top-down implementation strategy should be avoided in favor of bottom-up, volunteer-based, local implementation efforts. Whenever possible, the Core and Implementation Teams sought to use consensus building techniques to build commitment rather than ensure compliance. The Core Team sought volunteer pilot sites, for example, rather than ordering rollout from the executive level. Throughout the process, this approach ensured that more employees were invested in and committed to the project.

Individuals from different cultures must be represented in the CRP to ensure that all employees feel included. At LS&CO, this was particularly important. The mediator selection process, for example, allowed employees to nominate their mediators. This was done in part to ensure that different ethnic groups and cultures within the company would feel represented in the mediator pool.

The CRP was structured to encourage employees to resolve disputes locally and on their own rather than by escalating a dispute up the chain of command. In addition, employees were given a choice of who would serve as their mediator should their dispute enter Level 3. All of these structural aspects of the LS&CO system were designed to increase employee ownership of and buy-in to the CRP.

In what ways were consensus-based processes built into the new CRP at LS&CO?

Several steps were taken at LS&CO to align the new CRP with LS&CO's existing consensus-oriented culture and vision. These included the following:

Offering conflict resolution training to *all* employees affected by the new CRP. When establishing the expectation that employees will be responsible for managing conflict on their own, they must be provided with the support and resources to do so. LS&CO's existing Aspirations statement about training—that "the Company will support each employee's responsibility to acquire new skills and knowledge in order to meet the changing needs of our business"—ensured management support for this broad training approach.

What barriers and dilemmas did LS&CO encounter during the design and implementation process, and how were they addressed?

Although a consensus-oriented approach suggests that local implementation teams should be invited and expected to roll out a new dispute resolution system as much as possible, such teams also need centralized support and assistance. The Implementation Team discovered that handing over control of the CRP to local teams was difficult initially. Pilot sites needed technical and logistical support on matters ranging from how to create a project plan to how to convene a project team. Thus, the Core and Implementation Teams had to tread a fine line between offering a helping hand and dominating the implementation process.

Organizational upheavals can block or hinder the establishment of a corporate dispute resolution system. LS&CO experienced serious economic turmoil at the same moment that the CRP was being unveiled, and the former overtook the latter. At the same time, however, those involved in the CRP effort remain convinced that the skills training received by those at the pilot sites facilitated the change process at those sites. Mediators and others used their skills to address issues ranging from production guidelines to plant closures. Thus, to some extent the CRP effort was seen as a benefit, rather than a liability, during the restructuring and downsizing effort at LS&CO.

A dispute resolution system must be justified to management in terms of business needs and goals. From the outset, LS&CO's management saw the ways in which a new CRP could further LS&CO's corporate vision. At the same time, when economic trouble began, it was difficult to justify time commitments for training and ongoing implementation activity in the face of strong economic pressure on the company.

To ensure that a CRP project continues despite economic turmoil or corporate restructuring, some mechanism must be devised to create continuity in sponsorship and bridge the program from the old management to new management. As the original sponsors left LS&CO, there was little means or time to demonstrate the efficacy and vision of the CRP to those filling new positions in the corporate hierarchy. Without such a bridge, the future of the CRP is uncertain.

A dispute system design effort must both align with and find constructive ways to challenge the corporate culture in which it will be embedded. As noted, the CRP was championed as bolstering LS&CO's aspirational vision of open communication, employee support, and consensus building. At the same time, the CRP training had to urge employees to interpret the LS&CO Aspirations to mean that talking about conflict could be productive and that "being aspirational" did not mean avoiding conflict. Thus, the design and implementation efforts both integrated into and challenged LS&CO's corporate culture. Ironically, since the restructuring and downsizing at LS&CO, the company's aspirational and consensus-based culture has begun to change. According to employees at LS&CO, consensus-based management is no longer the favored or espoused approach. Thus, in many ways the CRP effort may no longer fit with the espoused culture of the organization.

■ Summary

Deciding how to define *success* is difficult in considering the dispute system design project at Levi Strauss and Company. At one level, the CRP was successfully designed and implemented as planned, and employees reported both learning a great deal and changes in the behavior of colleagues within the company. At the same time, because of economic upheaval the CRP is currently on hold and may never be fully realized. How then to determine whether the CRP was a successful program?

Regardless of the current or future status of the program, those involved in designing and implementing the program—including Core Team members, field employees, and consultants—all point out one way in which the CRP project was an unqualified success: It was a consensus building effort that consistently included stakeholders and was responsive to their concerns. Those involved "walked their talk." People remember the project with fondness because of this congruence between the message and the means of the CRP. And those still working on the project at LS&CO remain hopeful about its future because of the seeds planted through the consensus building efforts of those involved in the original program.

■ Notes

1. LS&CO has always been primarily family owned. The company was privately held for its first 118 years. In 1971, the company went public, but the Strauss family retained a controlling interest. Even after 1971, the company remained closely held and shares were traded only infrequently. In 1985, the company repurchased most of the outstanding shares, returning LS&CO to mostly private status. And in 1996, the company reclaimed all outstanding stock by buying out remaining shareholders.

2. As corporate restructuring and downsizing began in 1997, the makeup of the group of sponsors changed. The president of Levi's brand changed, as did the vice president of human resources. In addition, a third new brand—SLATES® dress pants—was added, and the president of that brand was added as a sponsor.

■ Reference

Managing by values: Is Levi Strauss' approach visionary—or flaky? (1994, August 1). *Business Week*.

SELECTED BIBLIOGRAPHY

This selected bibliography offers a modest listing of books that would comprise a basic library on consensus building. Many, but not all, of these titles are referenced in the chapters and case studies in this volume.

Arrow, K. J., et al. (Eds.). (1995). *Barriers to conflict resolution.* New York: Norton.

Bacow, L. S., & Wheeler, M. (1984). *Environmental dispute resolution.* New York: Plenum.

Bazerman, M., & Neal, M. A. (1992). *Negotiating rationally.* New York: Free Press.

Bellah, R. N., Madsen, R., Sullivan, W. M., Swidler, A., & Tipton, S. M. (1985). *Habits of the heart: Individualism and commitment in American life.* Berkeley: University of California Press.

Bush, R. A. B., & Folger, J. B. (1994). *The promise of mediation.* San Francisco: Jossey-Bass.

Carpenter, S. L., & Kennedy, W. J. D. (1988). *Managing public disputes.* San Francisco: Jossey-Bass.

Costantino, C. A., & Merchant, C. S. (1996). *Designing conflict management systems: A guide to creating productive and healthy organizations.* San Francisco: Jossey-Bass.

Crowfoot, J. E., & Wondolleck, J. M. (1990). *Environmental disputes: Community involvement in conflict resolution.* Washington, DC: Island.

Doyle, M., & Straus, D. (1982). *How to make meetings work.* New York: Jove.

Dukes, E. F. (1996.) *Resolving public conflict: Transforming community and governance.* New York: St. Martin's.

Fisher, R., & Brown, S. (1988). *Getting together: Building a relationship that gets to yes.* Boston: Houghton Mifflin.

Fisher, R., Ury, W., & Patton, B. (1991). *Getting to yes: Negotiating without giving in* (2nd ed.). Cambridge, MA: Houghton Mifflin.

Fisher, R. J. (1997). *Interactive conflict resolution.* Syracuse, NY: Syracuse University Press.

Golann, D. (1996). *Mediating legal disputes.* New York: Aspen Law and Business.

Goldberg, S. B., Green, E., & Sander, F. (1985). *Dispute resolution.* Boston: Little, Brown.

Gray, B. (1989). *Collaborating: Finding common ground for multiparty problems.* San Francisco: Jossey-Bass.

Kaner, S. (1996). *Facilitator's guide to participatory decision-making.* Philadelphia: New Society.

Kolb, D. M. (1994). *When talk works: Profiles of mediators.* San Francisco: Jossey-Bass.

Kramer, R. M., & Messick, D. M. (Eds.). (1995). *Negotiation as a social process.* Thousand Oaks, CA: Sage.

Kritek, P. B. (1994). *Negotiating at an uneven table.* San Francisco: Jossey-Bass.

Lax, D. A., & Sebenius, J. K. (1986). *The manager as negotiator: Bargaining for cooperative and competitive gain.* New York: Free Press.

Lewicki, R., & Litterer, J. (1985). *Negotiation.* Homewood, IL: Irwin.

Mansbridge, J. (1983). *Beyond adversary democracy.* Chicago: University of Chicago Press.

Mnookin, R., & Susskind, L. E. (in press). *Negotiating on behalf of others.* Thousand Oaks, CA: Sage.

Moore, C. W. (1996). *The mediation process: Practical strategies for resolving conflict* (2nd ed.). San Francisco: Jossey-Bass.

Ozawa, C. P. (1990). *Recasting science: Consensual procedures in public policy making.* San Francisco: Westview.

Raiffa, H. (1982). *The art and science of negotiation.* Cambridge, MA: Harvard University Press.

Rogers, N., & McEwen, C. (1994). *Mediation: Law, policy and practice.* Deerfield, IL: Clark Boardman Callaghan.

Rothman, J. (1997). *Resolving identity-based conflict.* San Francisco: Jossey-Bass.

Rubin, J. Z., Pruitt, D. G., & Kim, S. H. (1994). *Social conflict: Escalation, stalemate, and settlement* (2nd ed.). New York: McGraw-Hill.

Schwarz, R. M. (1994). *The skilled facilitator: Practical wisdom for developing effective groups.* San Francisco: Jossey-Bass.

Susskind, L., & Cruikshank, J. (1987). *Breaking the impasse: Consensual approaches to resolving public disputes.* New York: Basic Books.

Susskind, L., & Field, P. (1996). *Dealing with an angry public.* New York: Free Press.

Ury, W. L. (1993). *Getting past no: Negotiating your way from confrontation to cooperation.* New York: Bantam.

Ury, W. L., Brett, J. M., & Goldberg, S. B. (1993). *Getting disputes resolved: Designing systems to cut the cost of conflict.* Cambridge, MA: Program on Negotiation Books.

Weisbord, M. R., et al. (1992). *Discovering common ground.* San Francisco: Berrett-Koehler.

Index

Abel, R., 803
Abortion case, 681, 1031-1050
    as an example, 464, 475
Absent parties, 22, 38, 105, 147
    computer technology and, 403
    considering views of, 263-269, 270
    decision making and, 602
    implementation and, 532, 536, 547, 548
Abusiveness, management of, 315-317
Academic resources for experts, 388-389
Access:
    to technology, 409
    to the process, 750, 759
Access to information:
    disparities in, 409, 429-431
    equality in, 1071
    restrictions on, 407
    technology for, 403-409
Accountability, 68, 218
ACLU. *See* American Civil Liberties Union
Action plans, 973-974, 976-978
Action research, 666
Action steps, in visioning, 575-577
Active listening, 28, 44, 1040, 1041.
    See also Listening
ACUS. *See* Administrative Conference of the
    United States
Ad hoc assemblies:
    case studies on, 685-1050
    decision-making track and, 163
    key problems for, 20

"Short Guide" for, 20-35, 55-57
Ad hoc versus permanent groups, xiv, xix-xx
    in clarifying responsibilities, 40, 42, 43-44
    in convening, 36, 38, 39-40
    in deciding, 51-52
    in deliberating, 49
    in implementing, 53-54
    in organizational learning and development,
        54-55
Adaptation, and complexity science, 643-646,
    647
Adjudicative proceedings, 498
    See also Legal issues
Administrative agencies. *See* Government
    agencies
Administrative Conference of the United States
    (ACUS), 904
Adversary science, 29, 46, 376, 379, 834
Advisory boards, 216(figure)
Advisory groups, 224, 367, 611, 697, 903-904.
    See also Federal Advisory Committee Act
Advisory mediation, 616(table), 629(n8)
Advisory meetings, 69-70
Advisory role, acceptance of, 55-56
Advocacy science. *See* Adversary science
Affirmative action, 1045
Affordable housing, in Chattanooga Process
    case, 966
Affordable housing mediation case, 680,
    774-799
    compared to NOCC case, 775

Affordable housing mediation case, as an
    example:
  for representation, 271
  for roles, 199, 200, 203, 206, 209, 217
Age, and access to technology, 409
Agencies, government. *See* Government
    agencies
Agenda setting:
  assessor recommendations on, 121
  by ad hoc assemblies, 25-26
  by permanent groups, 41-42
  ground rules on, 227
  in case studies. *See* Catron County case,
      pp. 992-993; *and other specific cases*
  meeting management and, 295-298
  tasks in, 220
  value differences and, 478
  visioning and, 569, 573
  See also Issues
Agendas:
  as maps, 295
  as "sandwiches," 297-298
  for process design committee, 152-166
  institutional, 866, 869, 870
  modification of, 31-32, 48
Agents:
  in complexity science, 643-645
  of reality, 549
Agreement:
  checking for, 312-313
  criteria for seeking, 1002-1003
  letter of, 107
  mapping areas of, 117-119
Agreements:
  best possible, 339
  components of, 550-551
  confidentiality and, 512, 514, 519
  contingent, 333, 359-360, 396, 520
  dissenting views in, 336, 369-370
  evaluation of, 639-640, 651
  facilitators as advocates for, 518-519
  first-round, 360
  form of, 77, 196
  formal mechanisms for, 34, 53, 520
  government agencies as parties to, 507-510
  implementable, 223-224.
      See also Implementing
  informal, 52, 520
  intangible factors in, 531
  legal enforceability of, 520-522
  legislation built on, 549
  managing uncertainty in, 543-544
  not equivalent to success, 639-640

on PDC agenda flow, 154-166
proscribed actions in, 546-547
quality of, 634-635, 639, 651
ratification of. *See* Ratification
reaching, strategies for, 82-83
reaching, tasks for, 222-223
sealed, 512
tentative, 937
testing of, 32, 49-50
thin-ice, 351, 368
up-front, 311-312
AIDS/HIV case. *See* HIV/AIDS case
AIM (architectural and industrial maintenance)
    case, 380, 381-383, 390, 393
Airport planning case. *See* Mainport Schiphol
    case
Algorithmic approach, 309
Alianza case, 595-596, 600, 601, 621
Alignment to other forums, 539-541.
    See also Parallel processes
Alternate representatives, 23, 39, 721
Alternative decision arenas, 823
Alternative dispute resolution, 882
Alternative solutions, 222. *See also* Options
Ambiguity, as barrier, 204
American assembly, 582(table)
American Civil Liberties Union (ACLU), 784,
    785
Americans with Disabilities Act, 1079
Amsterdam airport case.
    See Mainport Schiphol case
Analysis:
  in conflict assessment, 116-120, 129
  interpretation and, 732-733
  technology for, 417-423
Analytical methods, in joint fact-finding,
    394-396
Anger, 930-931, 1017, 1053
  meeting management of, 315-317
  turned to action, 1006
Anthropological perspective:
  on context, 925-926, 968
  on culture, 925-926, 968, 1062-1063,
      1075
  on language, 797
  on mediators, 949
  on power, 1073, 1075
Applegate Partnership case, 171-172, 174-175,
    185, 552
Approach to consensus building, selection of,
    77-79, 157
Appropriateness, determination of:
  factors in, 66-70

in consensus-based decision making,
  600-603, 624
initial screening for, 175
meeting management and, 293
visioning and, 561-562, 564, 588
See also Conflict assessments; Feasibility;
  Initial screening; Initiation of
  consensus process
Arbitration:
  definition of, 630(n8)
  intraorganizational situations and, 615,
    616(table)
  legal issues and, 1072-1073
Architectural and industrial maintenance (AIM)
  case, 380, 381-383, 390, 393
Aspirations:
  idea gathering and, 573-574
  unrealistic, 333, 345-355, 708
  See also Expectations; Visioning
Aspirations statement, 1068, 1069, 1084
Assessments:
  conflict. *See* Conflict assessments
  of dispute resolution system, 613-614
  of media, 439-454
  of needs, 1069-1070, 1083
  See also Evaluations
Assessors, 100, 106-107, 114
  dilemmas handled by, 130-135
  See also Facilitators; Mediators
Assumptions, untrue, xvii.
  See also Misperceptions
Atlanta case, 199, 200, 202, 206, 209, 213, 217
Attitudes, in meeting management, 305-310
Attribution, avoidance of, 31, 47-48
Authority:
  constituents and, 795
  decision making and, 162, 623, 916
  delegation of, 598-599
  for recommendations, 508
  giving up of, xx
  initial screening of, 178
  intraorganizational, 1073
  moral, 938, 941
  procedural constraints and, 70
Authorship, individual, 31, 47-48

Babbitt, B., 173
Bandwidth, 160
Barriers. *See* Obstacles
BATNA (best alternative to a negotiated
  agreement):
  explained to the media, 459

preparation stage and, 329, 330
process, content, and, 989
producing consensus and, 350, 351, 366
satisfaction with, 1002, 1003
success and, 12
Bazerman, M. H., commentaries by:
  on case 2, 717, 718, 725, 726, 728, 729,
    732, 733, 741
  on case 10, 927, 933, 935, 937, 943,
    946-948
  on case 13, 986, 987, 989, 991, 1000-1003,
    1008
Beat, reporter's, 455
Behavior:
  changes in, as outcomes, 652-653
  disruptive, 55, 315-317, 319-320, 514-515
  expectation and, 80
  meeting management and, 305-310
  See also Ground rules
Behind-the-scenes discussions, 763, 764, 869.
    See also Nonbinding discussions
Belief in success, xxxix-xl, 305-306
Beliefs and values. *See* Values
Benchmarks, 579
Best alternative to a negotiated agreement.
    See BATNA
Best possible agreement, 339
Best practices:
  conflict assessment and, 102
  evaluations and, 90, 632, 1008
  producing consensus and, 329
Betrayal, 1053, 1060
Birmingham case, 571, 579
Blame, 459, 1062
Blocking actions, 793. *See also* Holdouts
Body language:
  computer technology and, 414-415, 416,
    433, 894
  power of, 314
  See also Nonverbal cues
Booher, D. E., 650, 672(n1)
Boomerang technique, 313
Boundaries:
  in systemic functioning, 1058
  of employee conflict resolution, 1073
Bozo filter, 891, 894
Brainstorming, 81-82, 221, 300
  in ad hoc assemblies, 30
  in permanent groups, 47
Breakthroughs, 1059. *See also* Transformations
Bridgeport Region, 773, 774, 781
Briefings, press, 457. *See also* Media, the
British Columbia case. *See* Haida Gwaii case

Broadening of responsibilities, 269-272
Brown, J., 954, 955, 967
Brown's Ferry fire, 881
Budgets, 75, 390. See also Funding
Burden of proof, 844-847
Business, in civic infrastructure, 957-958
Bylaws, as precondition for success, xviii.
    See also Ground rules

Canada's Native peoples. See Haida Gwaii case
Capacity building:
    complexity science and, 646
    funding and, 993
    implementation and, 549
    local, 1008
    tasks in, 229
    time needed for, xviii
Cape Cod Superfund case. See Massachusetts
    Military Reservation case
Capital:
    as outcome, 636, 652
    implementation and, 541-548
Capitol Region Council of Governments
    (CRCOG). See Affordable housing
    mediation case
Captains, in visioning, 572
Carlson, C., 445, 545
Carpenter, S. L., xiii, 102, 209
Carstarphen, N., 475, 478
Case study methods, 394, 395
Cases, court. See Courts
Casper, WY case, 581, 585-586
Categories of stakeholders, 92, 110, 156
Catron County case, 681, 985-1009
Catron County case, as an example:
    for convening, 63, 68, 182-183, 188, 192
    for visioning, 79, 563-564, 566, 571, 572,
        574, 576, 577
Caucus groups, for options generation, 82
Caucusing, facilitated, 22-23, 38-39
CBI. See Consensus Building Institute
CCMP (Comprehensive Conservation and
    Management Plan). See San Francisco
    Estuary Project case
CDR Associates, 595, 604-607, 610, 611, 614,
    628, 1078, 1079
Celebration, 551, 589, 1019-1020
CEO process, 582(table)
Ceremonies for closure, 551, 589
Chairs. See Committee chairs
Chamber of Commerce, 957, 958
Champions, 620, 970-972, 976, 1083

Change:
    complexity science and, 643-646, 647
    resistance to, 54
Chaos, and complexity science, 644-645
Charlotte Islands. See Haida Gwaii case
Charrettes:
    definition of, 581
    for visioning, 216(figure), 581, 582(table),
        585-586
Charter case. See Chelsea charter case
Chattanooga Process case, 681, 951-968
Chattanooga Process case, as an example:
    for implementation, 537, 548
    for visioning, 79, 557-589
Check-in procedures, 162. See also Ratification
Checking for agreement, 312-313
Chelsea charter case, 680, 743-772
Chelsea charter case, as an example:
    for convening, 181-182, 192, 196
    for media handling, 442-443, 446
    for outreach, 89
    for political dynamics, 74
    for representation, 189
    for roles, 199, 200, 202, 207, 208, 213,
        214, 218
    for value differences, 476
Children, implications for, 267, 268, 270.
        See also Young people
Churchill, W., 372
Circles of stakeholders:
    conflict assessment and, 21, 36-37, 108
    definition of, 12-13
    implementation and, 533, 535, 543
Citizens advisory group (CAG) case:
    absent parties in, 267-268
    common ground in, 271
    technical complexity and, 253-261
City hall to the streets case.
        See Middletown case
City management, cases on. See Chattanooga
    Process case; Chelsea charter case;
    Middletown case
Civic engagement, networks of, 545
Civic infrastructure:
    components of, 957-961
    process for improvement of, 583(table)
Civic journalism, 454
Civic renewal process, 216(figure)
Civil discourse, 636, 648
Claiming value, 12
Clarifying responsibilities:
    implementation and, 536-538
    in ad hoc assemblies, 24-27

in permanent groups, 40-44
matrix overview of, 14-17
meeting management and, 297, 298-302
Clarifying roles, 93-96, 298-302, 620-623.
    See also Consultants; Experts; Facilitators;
    Mediators; Practitioners; Recorders
Class context, 754
Closed-ended questions, 112-113
Closure:
    ceremonies for, 551, 589
    decision rules and, 366-368, 371-372
    less than unanimous agreement and,
        363-371
    to joint fact-finding, 398
    See also End stage
Coaches, 621, 1072
Coastal Zone Act (CZA) case, 100-101,
    105-106, 110, 116-117, 123, 132, 135
Cobb, S., 946
Coglianese, C., 637, 638
Cogliano, J., 847, 848
Cognitive stage, in policy network activation,
    696-698, 704-705
Coleman, J. S., 545
Collaboration:
    characteristics of success in, 207
    power of, 775-776
    principles of, 154, 290
Collaborative decision making, as process,
    216(figure)
Coloradans Working Together (CWT).
    See HIV/AIDS case
Command-and-control decision making, 594
Commitment:
    change and, 260
    contingent, 549
    government agencies and, 509-510
    implementation and, 537, 541-542, 547
    incomplete, 260
    meeting management and, 310
    resources and, 982-983, 1071
    responsibility for, 34, 52, 184
    seriousness of, 51
    testing of, 907
    values and, 467
    work plans and, 220
Committee chairs:
    appointment of, 24-25, 40-41
    role of, 94
Committees. *See* Executive committees; Process
    design committee; Subcommittees; Task
    forces; Task groups; Work groups

Committing, separated from inventing, 28-29,
    45, 331-332
Common good, 653
Common ground, 269-272, 973
    process of, 1031-1049
Communal conflict, 1053
Communication:
    absent parties and, 263-269, 403
    barriers in, 204
    common ground and, 269-272
    in producing consensus, 333, 336, 345-355,
        358
    in systemic functioning, 1058
    in technical complexity, 253-263
    intellectual capital and, 542-543
    practitioner skills in, 236
    practitioner tasks in, 224-225, 228-229
    process and, 216, 217
    relationships and, 214
    technology for. *See* Computer-based
        technology
    with constituents, 275-282.
        See also Constituent-representative
        relations
    with diverse counterparts, 246-253
Communicative/interactional process, 217
Community-based practitioners, 200-201, 206,
    231, 233
Community-building intermediaries, 958, 959
Community forum, 216(figure)
Community group representatives, 226-227
Community-wide visioning. *See* Visioning,
    community-wide
Comparisons of cases, for evaluation, 637, 651,
    657-659
Compassion, 1026-1027, 1036
Competitive bidding, 504
Complexity:
    as barrier, 204
    conflicting objectives and, 686, 688, 707,
        1007
    implementation and, 528-529
    in process design, 160
    management of, 253-263, 275-276, 836-839
    of analysis, 417
    of solutions, for complex problems, 877
    practitioner selection and, 233
    practitioner tasks and, 223, 225, 229
Complexity science:
    best practices and, 632
    for evaluation framework, 642, 646-671
    nature of, 643-646

Comprehensive Conservation and Management
  Plan (CCMP). *See* San Francisco Estuary
  Project case
Compromise, xxi, 277
  beliefs and, 1038
  instability of, 1024
  morality and, 806-807
  policy network activation and, 701, 703
  value differences and, 470, 488, 490, 491
Computer-based technology:
  challenges in, 402, 409, 414-417, 422-423,
    429-433
  disparities in access to, 409
  for ad hoc assemblies, 27
  for analysis, 417-423
  for decision making, 423-425
  for document dissemination and access,
    403-409
  for drafting documents, 425-428
  for finding practitioners, 235
  for graphics, 165
  for permanent groups, 43
  for technical versus policy issues, 896
  growth in, 401-402
  in rulemaking case. *See* RuleNet case
  logistics of, 96
Computer projections, 414, 416, 428
Computer science, 643-644
Conceptualizers, 620
Conciliation, 616(table), 629(n8).
    See also God's Fellowship Community
    Church case
CONCUR, 808, 854
Conditional settlements, 508
Confidentiality:
  agreements on, 514-515, 519
  balanced with openness, 1013
  ground rules and, 1013, 1036
  in conflict assessment, 100, 108, 111, 116
  in joint fact-finding, 393
  legal issues and, 510-514, 519
  media and, 1047
  program design and, 1071
  reasons for, 56
Conflict analysis, 103
Conflict assessments:
  analysis in, 116-120, 129
  approaches to, 102-103, 157
  definition of, 10-11
  development of, 101-102
  dilemmas and debates in, 130-135
  education in, 130-131
  for ad hoc assemblies, 21-22
  for permanent groups, 36-38
  for science-intensive disputes, 832
  future of, 135
  implementation and, 538
  information gathering in, 113-116
  interviews in, 21, 37, 64, 108-116
  introductions in, 107-113
  need for, 104-106
  phases in, 107-130
  practitioner tasks in, 219
  process design and, 63-64, 99, 120-128, 138
  recommendations of, 100, 120-128, 129
  report writing in, 103, 104, 128-130
  terminology of, 103
  who should conduct, 106-107, 138
  See also Environmental scans; Stakeholder
    analysis
Conflict resolution program (CRP) case.
    See Levi Strauss case
Conflict resolution systems. *See* Dispute
    resolution systems
Conflict, usefulness of, 306-307
ConflictNet, 883
Conflicts of interest, 131-132, 516-517, 869
  compared to conflicts of value, 1012-1013,
    1022
Congregational reconciliation case.
    See God's Fellowship Community Church
    case
Congregational recovery stages, 1054, 1056
Connective thinking, 1040, 1045, 1049
Conoco case, 1001
Consensus:
  defining of, 303. *See also* Decision rules
  definition of, 327
Consensus building:
  as an ongoing process, 707, 870
  as complement or as substitute for
    government action, 683
  as new solution or as conflict settlement, 707
  barriers to, 119, 180
  barriers to, dealing with, 55-57
  barriers to, types of, 203-204
  benefits of, xvii-xviii
  complexity science view of, 645-646
  core elements of, 212
  definition of, 6-7
  general approaches to, 77-79
  intangible factors in, 531
  key problem in, 12
  misperceptions about, xx-xxii
  model of, 212-218
  phases of, 138-139

preconditions for, xviii
principal aims of, 686
process versus substance of, xviii
"Short Guide" to, 1-57
stages of, 329-336, 531
status quo mechanisms for, 529
steps in, 20-55
terminology of, 5-13
typology of, 528-529, 530
uniqueness of each situation in, 61-62
untrue assumptions and, xvii
variety of issues covered by, xviii-xix, 61,
   270-271, 528, 679
variety of outcomes from, 634-636
Consensus Building Institute (CBI), xiii, 373(n),
   712, 716, 719, 870
Consensus building phase, 138-139.
   See also Deliberating
Consensus newsletter, 235
Consequences. *See* Outcomes
Conservation and Management Plan (CCMP).
   See San Francisco Estuary Project case
Constituent-representative relations, 253, 261,
   263, 270, 290
   aspirations and, 333, 345-355
   authority in, 795
   credibility and, 867-868
   evaluation and, 652
   ground rules and, 721
   harassment in, 1043
   intellectual capital and, 542-543
   joint fact-finding and, 392
   legitimacy and, 761
   media coverage and, 444
   ratification and, 272-282
   stressful, 794
   technology and, 406-407
   vulnerability and, 534
   See also Representation; Representatives
Constituents:
   ad hoc assemblies and, 34-35
   advice for, 280-282
   involvement of, 88-89, 95-96
   mandate framed by, 280-281
   outreach to, 192
   permanent groups and, 52-53
   technical complexity and, 261, 263, 275-276
   See also Representation; Representatives
Constraints, environmental scans of, 587
Constructive nature of deliberation, 27-28, 44
Consultants:
   in intraorganizational situations, 609, 613,
      614, 615, 619, 625

joint fact-finding and, 388-389
meeting management and, 302
value differences and, 476
See also Experts; Process consultants
Consultative workshop, 216(figure)
Content, versus process, 291
Context:
   environmental scans of, 587
   importance of, 925-926, 929
   initial screening of, 178-179
   process and, 215, 229
   understanding of, 232(table)
Contextual influences, 70-75
Contingent agreements, 333, 359-360, 396,
   520
Contingent commitments, 549
Contingent options, 31, 48
Contingent solutions, 875, 876
Continuum, thinking along, 1039, 1040, 1045,
   1049
Contract Disputes Act of 1978, 912
Contracts:
   in conflict assessment, 107, 108, 133
   legal issues and, 504
   roles, functions, and, 298
   sole source, 234
Convening:
   activities in, 205-207
   by government agencies, 195-196
   definition of, 10, 205
   dispute resolution systems design and,
      610-616
   example of failure in, 172-174
   example of success in, 171-172
   implementation and, 532-541
   importance of, 171-174
   in abortion case, 1037
   in affordable housing mediation case,
      774-775, 796
   in Catron County case, 989-992
   in Chattanooga Process case, 952, 954-956
   in Chelsea charter case, 748-751
   in God's Fellowship Community Church
      case, 1055
   in Haida Gwaii case, 929, 930
   in HIV/AIDS case, 1012-1014
   in Levi Strauss case, 1068-1070
   in Mainport Schiphol case, 694-696, 699
   in Middletown case, 970-972
   in MMR case, 866-869
   in Native American case, 903-907, 910
   in New York Bight case, 830-833
   in NOCC case, 716-720

in RuleNet case, 882-884
in SFEP case, 804-807
initial screening in, 174-184
matrix overview of, 14-19
of ad hoc assemblies, 20-24
of permanent groups, 36-40
participants identified in, 185-190
practitioners' role in, 205-207
process planning in, 195
report from, 103
roles in, 93-94, 170-172, 205-207, 225
steps in, 169, 174-195
technology for, 405-406
visioning and, 563-573
who should carry out, 180-181
See also Appropriateness; Conflict
     assessments; Funding; Ground rules;
     Process design; Representation
Convening analysis. *See* Conflict assessments
Convening assessment, 103.
     See also Conflict assessments
Convenors:
commitment of, 184-185
computer technology and, 404, 428,
     429-430
conflict assessment and, 100, 107, 132-133
effective participation and, 187
implementation challenges for, 536
in intraorganizational situations, 620
meeting management and, 292
process design and, 147
representation of, 190
role of, 93-94, 170, 225
speaking with one voice, 190
terminology for, 205
See also Convening
Conventional problem-solving approach, 77-78
Conversation:
absent parties and, 263-269
central role of, 251, 252, 270
common ground and, 269-272
domination of, 315
in technical complexity, 253-263
intellectual capital and, 542
judgments, experts, and, 874
threads of, 412, 887, 889
values and, 464
Web conferences and, 411-414
See also Communication; Stories
Coordination:
implementation and, 540, 549, 819, 821
legal issues and, 498-500
Coordinators, for visioning, 567, 588

Core elements, 212
Core principles, 1068
Core revitalization strategy, 975-976
Core tasks, 218-230
Cormick, G., 102
Corruption, 743-770
Cost-benefit analysis, 394, 395, 651
Costs:
conflict assessment of, 128
evaluation of, 651, 658
initial screening of, 179-180
legal issues and, 504
of computer technology, 408, 416
of conflict assessments, 113, 114, 134-135
of convening, 10
of evaluations, 654-655, 664
of joint fact-finding, 385, 390-391, 397, 398
of practitioner services, 237
of resources, 193
of Web conferences, 897
process design and, 75
See also Funding
Council on Foundations, 194
County rights movement, 987
Court orders, 513
Court referrals, 517
Courts, 496, 497-502
confidentiality and, 512, 513
enforceability and, 520-522
procedural requirements on, 502-505
CRCOG (Capitol Region Council of
     Governments). *See* Affordable housing
     mediation case
Creating value, 11-12
ratification, justification, and, 274
steps for, 330-333
through packaging, 28-29, 45
See also Joint (mutual) gains
Creativity:
in decision making, 601
in joint fact-finding, 379
in outcomes, 651, 653
in problem solving, 221
in processes, 649, 650
in ratification, 272, 274, 276, 277
value differences and, 491
See also Thinking outside the box
Credibility:
in constituent relations, 867-868
in convening, 171, 175
in joint fact-finding, 379
in practitioners' roles, 200
in process design, 141, 145

in process initiation, 63
in representation, 22, 38
in science-intensive disputes, 834, 837, 838, 840
legal issues and, 789
meeting management and, 308
of analyses, 419
of local convenors, 1008
See also Legitimacy; Trust
Criticism, withholding of, 30-31, 47
Crocker, J. P., 541, 546
Cross-cultural community-based planning.
    See Cultural context; Haida Gwaii case
Cross-trading. See Trading across issues
CRP (conflict resolution program) case.
    See Levi Strauss case
Cruikshank, J., 372(n2), 531, 635
Cultural context, 70-72, 536, 797
    ambiguity in, 1075
    decision making and, 600, 601
    essentializing and, 909
    facilitator selection and, 904-906
    in case studies. See Haida Gwaii case;
        Native American case; and other
        specific cases
    institutional, 909
    interpretations and, 933, 1062-1063
    intraorganizational, 70-71, 1057, 1085
    representation and, 751, 754, 767, 771
    technical information and, 812
Culture, meaning of, 1075
CWT (Coloradans Working Together).
    See HIV/AIDS case
CZA case. See Coastal Zone Act

Dale, N., 247, 248, 250, 475, 478
Data:
    for evaluations, 662-670
    interpretations of, 383
    organization of, 322
Dayton case, 437-438
Deadlines, 229, 783
    in joint fact-finding, 397, 824
    in the media, 455-456
Deadlocked positions, 204
Debate:
    compared to dialogue, 1038
    See also Deliberating
Deciding:
    by ad hoc assemblies, 32-33
    by permanent groups, 49-52
    matrix overview of, 14-17

See also Agreement; Commitment;
    Joint (mutual) gains; Records
Decision making:
    compared to advisory role, 55-56
    evaluations of, 658-659
    fallback mechanism for, 163, 303-304
    hierarchical, 594, 627-628
    in ad hoc versus permanent groups, 51-52
    intangible factors in, 531
    policy network activated in, 692-708
    status quo mechanisms for, 529
    technology for, 423-425
    timing of, 701
    unilateral, 653
Decision making, intraorganizational:
    concerns about, 623-628
    consensus-based, 594-603
    consensus-based, when/when not to use,
        600-603, 624
    new approaches to, 593
    stepped sequence in, 597-600
    unilateral, 594, 597-598, 600
Decision-making track, 162-163
Decision rules:
    determination of, 303-304
    for Web conferences, 891
    mixed procedures in, 756-757
    persuasion and, 911
    reaching closure and, 366-368, 371-372
Defensiveness, 308-309
Defining the problem. See Problem definition
Definitions, 5-13
Delaware Coastal Zone Act (CZA) case,
    100-101, 105-106, 110, 116-117, 123,
    132, 135
Delegated authority, 598-599
Delegation of powers, undue, 506, 508
Deliberating:
    absent parties and, 263-269
    at end stage, 333-372
    by ad hoc assemblies, 27-32
    by permanent groups, 44-49
    dispute resolution systems design and,
        614-617
    diverse counterparts and, 246-253
    evaluations of, 648-650
    implementation and, 541-548
    in abortion case, 1031-1047
    in affordable housing mediation case,
        778-782, 789-794
    in Catron County case, 991-995, 998-999,
        1001-1006
    in Chattanooga Process case, 961-965

in Chelsea charter case, 753-755, 758
in God's Fellowship Community Church
    case, 1056-1059
in Haida Gwaii case, 928-940
in HIV/AIDS case, 1014-1028
in Mainport Schiphol case, 698, 699-704
in MMR case, 869-875
in Native American case, 907-915, 916
in New York Bight case, 836-851
in NOCC case, 734-735
in RuleNet case, 884, 885-890
in SFEP case, 807-814, 815-816
legal issues and, 510-515
matrix overview of, 14-17
meeting management for, 287-322
technical complexity and, 253-263
technology for, 410-417
value differences in, 463-492
visioning and, 573-578
See also Inventing; Modifications;
    Prior relationships; Single-text
    procedure; Subcommittees
Delli Priscoli, J., 615
Demands, compared to interests, 6
Democracy:
    Churchill on, 372
    in science, 283(n10), 842
    problem definition and, 863
    representation in, 720, 784-785, 972
    Web conferences and, 884, 893
Democracy restoration case.
    See Chelsea charter case
Democratization of science, 283(n10)
Demonstration projects, 142-143
Des Moines case, 438-439, 446
Design. See Dispute resolution systems design;
    Process design
Development, organizational.
    See Organizational development
Development, process. See Process design
Dialogue:
    common ground and, 1032, 1033-1047
    compared to debate, 1038
    determining appropriateness and, 67-68
    for ad hoc assemblies, 20
    for permanent groups, 36
    legitimacy and, 1038
    phases for, 888-890
    policy, 216(figure)
    See also Deliberating
Disagreements:
    consensus and, 256, 259
    freedom for, xxii, 352

information and, 383
list of, 722
mapping areas of, 117-119
meeting management and, 310, 315-317,
    320-321
moral, 480-487
transformation in handling of, 756
values and. See Value differences
without being disagreeable, 28, 45
Disclosure:
    by experts, 729, 730
    of disagreements, 853
    requirements on, 510-512, 517
    See also Confidentiality
Discovery, and value differences, 476, 477,
    478. See also Exploration
Discussion management. See Meeting
    management
Discussions. See Deliberating; Dialogue
Disempowerment, 938. See also Power
Disillusionment, 1059
Display technology, 414, 416, 428, 815
Dispute resolution agencies, 234, 505
Dispute resolution systems:
    diagnosis of, 613-614
    in ad hoc assemblies, 35
    in permanent groups, 53, 54
    intraorganizational, 593, 603-619, 627,
        628
    procedures for, types of, 614-616
    strategy in, 336
Dispute resolution systems design:
    activities in, 209-211
    concerns about, 627, 628
    definition of, 209, 603
    dilemmas of, 603-604
    examples for, 604-610
    need for, 204
    steps in, 610-619
Dispute systems designers, 200, 209-211.
    See also Process designers
Disruptive behavior
    legal issues and, 514-515
    meeting management and, 315-317,
        319-320
    response to, 55
Dissemination conference, 1000-1001
Dissemination technology, 403-409
Dissent, acknowledgment of, 336, 369-370, 372
Distributed intelligence, 644, 645
Diversity:
    communication and, 246-253
    decision making and, 600, 624-625

idea generation and, 870
implementation and, 534-536
pilot site selection and, 1074-1075
social-cultural context and, 71
value of, 306-307
visioning and, 561, 572, 588
Document technology:
for dissemination, 403-409
for drafting, 425-428
DoD. *See* U.S. Department of Defense
Double-loop learning, 636
Doyle, M., 322(n), 372(n2)
Drafting:
strategies for, 848-850
technology for, 425-428
Drama of mediation, 476
Drift, management of, 580-581
DuPraw, M., 546
Dutch airport case. *See* Mainport Schiphol case
Dynamic/transformative process, 217-218

E-mail:
emotive cues and, 415
for ad hoc assemblies, 27
for document drafts, 427
for information access, 408
for information dissemination, 404, 406
for permanent groups, 43
representation, voice, and, 429
Ebb/flow of the group, 314-315
Economic context, 74-75, 1081-1083
Economic planning cases. *See* Haida Gwaii
case; Middletown case
Edge of chaos, 644-645
Editors, 450-453. *See also* Media, the
Education:
implementation and, 975, 977
in conflict assessment, 130-131
in intraorganizational situations, 620-621
in process design, 141, 143
in visioning, 577
interest-based negotiation and, 917
ongoing nature of, 778
participant preparation and, 84-85
See also Training
Education phase, 79, 81
Effects. *See* Outcomes
Elected officials, involvement of, 226, 753,
784, 805, 823, 982. *See also* Politics
Electronic bulletin boards, 883
Electronic communication.
See Computer-based technology

Electronic mail. *See* E-mail
Elliott, M., 637
Emotions:
dealing with, 338-340, 482
producing consensus and, 333, 336
value differences and, 482
Emotive cues, 414-415. *See also* Body language
Empathy, 339-340
Employees. *See* Intraorganizational situations;
Labor unions
Empowerment, 1077, 1080.
See also Disempowerment; Power
End-of-process evaluations, 632-633, 655-656
End stage:
challenge of, 328-329
dealing with obstacles in, 337-371
strategies for, 327, 333-336
Endangered species. *See* Applegate Partnership
case; Catron County case
Endangered Species Act, 986, 987, 988
Endgame. *See* End stage
Endispute, Incorporated, 774, 776
Enemies, xxi
Energizers, 319
Enforceability of agreements, 520-522
Enlarged thinking, 252
Environmental cases. *See* Applegate Partnership
case; Casper case; Catron County case;
Citizens advisory group case; Coastal
Zone Act case; Haida Gwaii case;
Mainport Schiphol case; Massachusetts
Military Reservation case; New York Bight
case; Northern Oxford County Coalition
case; Regulatory negotiation cases;
San Francisco Estuary Project case;
Snoqualmie River case; Vancouver
Island case
Environmental scans, 587. *See also* Conflict
assessments
Equidistance, 946. *See also* Neutral parties;
Neutrality
Equitable relief, 521
Escalation:
as barrier, 204
of interventions, 314
Estuary project. *See* San Francisco Estuary
Project case
Ethical misconduct case. *See* God's Fellowship
Community Church case
Ethics, 517
Ethnic diversity, 189. *See also* Cultural context
Evaluations, 35, 53, 90
challenge of, 632, 638-642

framework for, in complexity science, 642,
    646-671
limitations of, 528, 636-637
methods for, 637-638, 662-670
of case studies. *See* RuleNet case,
    pp. 895-897; *and other specific cases*
of meetings, 290
of outcomes, 224
of technical evidence, 261
options for, 654-662
problem solving and, 222
published, 637-638
purposes of, 631-632
types of, 632-633, 654-662
visioning and, 579
who should conduct, 670-671
See also Assessments
Evaluations, criteria for:
    about outcomes, 639, 650-654
    about process, 647-650
    complexity science and, 646
    guidelines as, 637
Evidence, technical, 261
Evil, 1062, 1063
Ex parte contacts, 501-502, 517
Exaggerations, and value differences, 468-469
Exclusion from meetings, 510-511.
    See also Open-meeting laws; Sunshine laws
Executive committees:
    formation of, 24, 40-41
    process design and, 156
Executive director, 161
Expectations:
    as motivation, 806
    behavioral, 80
    discovery and, 778
    goals, agenda, and, 906-907
    in seeking common ground, 1039
    management of, 717
    unrealistic, 979-980, 983
Expenditures. *See* Costs
Experience:
    of practitioners, 235
    pooling of, 781-782
Experts:
    capacity building and, 229
    community members as, 873
    computer technology and, 419
    cost of, 390-391
    disagreement among, 253, 376-377, 385,
        730, 733, 812
    evaluations by, 671
    evaluations of, 649

facilitators as, 299
for ad hoc assemblies, 29-30
for permanent groups, 46-47
legal issues and, 500, 501, 502, 504
meeting management and, 317-318
multidisciplinary efforts by, 866
process design and, 143, 166
questions asked of, 394-395
recruitment of, 833-835
representatives' tension and, 253-263
role of, 95, 299, 302
selection of, 387-390, 397, 729-730
visioning and, 569-570
See also Consultants; Joint fact-finding;
    Technical complexity
Exploration:
    of interests, 330-331
    of value differences, 474, 491, 492
    See also Discovery
Extended peer community, 263
External assessment, 174.
    See also Conflict assessments
External assistance versus internal assistance,
    230-233
External interactions versus internal
    negotiation, 244. *See also* Representatives,
    tension for

FACA (Federal Advisory Committee Act), 72,
    503-504, 511, 903
Face-to-face meetings:
    computer-mediated meetings compared to,
        414-416, 433
    computer technology and, 402, 410-422,
        433. *See also* Computer-based
        technology
    dimensions of success in, 290, 291
    management of. *See* Meeting management
    problems in, 291, 315-321
    value of, 289-290, 869
Facilitated caucusing, 22-23, 38-39
Facilitation:
    activities in, 207-208
    as precondition for success, xviii
    compared to mediation, 9, 208-209
    definition of, 7, 207
    dispute resolution and, 616(table)
    need for, 204
    success and, 207
    visioning and, 569
    See also Mediation
Facilitative leadership, 7, 619-623

Facilitative tools, 310-321
Facilitators:
    attitudes of, 305-310
    bank of, 961
    behaviors of, 305-310
    compared to mediators, 208-209
    computer technology and, 404, 406,
        411-413, 416, 431-432
    implementation challenges for, 531, 535,
        536, 538, 546, 549
    in intraorganizational situations, 621
    in process design, 143
    in producing consensus, 336, 339-340,
        347-351, 368
    legal issues for, 504, 512, 515-519
    media and, 439-453, 458-459
    meeting management by, 290-322
    mind-sets of, 305
    selection of, 7, 231-233, 299
    selection of, and contracts, 504
    selection of, and cultural context, 904-906
    skills lacking in, 144
    terminology for, 205
    tools of, 310-321
    training of, 961
    value differences and, 490
    See also Coordinators; Mediators;
        Neutral parties; Practitioners
Facilitators, role of, 4, 94, 170, 207
    as advocates, 518-519, 703
    as agents of reality, 549
    as peace-making gunslingers, 713, 716
    as process guides, 298-299
    clarification of, 24, 40
    expertise and, 871
    ground rules on, 519
    in managing expectations, 717
    in relationship element, 226, 227, 228
    in substance element, 220-222
    in Web conferences, 894-895
    technology and, 431-432
Fact-finding, joint. See Joint fact-finding
Fairness, 759, 776, 987
    quality and, 634
    sympathy, values, and, 1022-1023
Faith, 1061
Fallback mechanism, for decision making, 163,
    303-304
Fears:
    as motivation, 806
    of being co-opted, 196
    of conflict resolution process, 1070, 1081
    of majority rule, 747

    of punishment, 982
    of violence, 988, 989, 994
Feasibility, 119-120, 1007.
    See also Appropriateness; Conflict
        assessments
Feast, in Haida Gwaii case, 934
Federal Advisory Committee Act (FACA), 72,
    503-504, 511, 903
Federal agencies. See Government agencies
Federal Mediation and Conciliation Service
    (FMCS), 904-905, 916-917
Federal Register, 503
Federal Tort Claims Act, 912
Felstiner, W., 803
Field, P., 373(n), 469, 472
Field trips, 86
Filmmaker, 990, 991
Final products:
    determination of, 294-295
    of design process, 154-155
    of joint fact-finding, 393, 396
    of visioning, 579, 589
    ownership of, 579
    See also Agreements; Outcomes; Reports;
        Results
Financing. See Funding
Fire protection regulations. See RuleNet case
First Nations. See Haida Gwaii case
First-round agreements, 360
Fisher, R., 11, 372(n2)
FMCS. See Federal Mediation and Conciliation
    Service
Focus groups, 535, 614, 666-667
    intraorganizational, 1069-1070, 1080
    See also Polling
FOIA. See Freedom of Information Act
Force-field analysis, 538
Forecasts, technical, 262, 276, 395
Forester, J., 384, 465, 472, 474, 475, 476, 477,
    479, 488, 490
Forestry issues. See Catron County case
Formalizing stage, in policy network activation,
    696, 701-704, 705
Frames, 212-213, 933
Framing:
    of representative's mandate, 280-281
    of technical findings, 263
    parallel processes and, 802-803
    re-, 254
Freedom of Information Act (FOIA), 511-512
Freedom of information laws, 511-512
Frustration, and meeting management, 288,
    318-319

Funding:
  in Catron County case, 993, 1000, 1001,
    1008
  in Chattanooga Process case, 959
  in Middletown case, 971, 974, 976
  in New York Bight case, 833, 835
  in Northern Oxford County Coalition case,
    739-740
  initial screening of, 179-180
  locating sources of, 23-24, 39
  resource needs and, 193-194
  strategies for, 194
  See also Costs
Future generations, implications for, 267, 268,
  270
Future risk, 355
Future search conference, 583(table)

Gaming, and framing, 802-803
Gender representation, 156, 535
Geographic context, 156, 754, 924, 1075
Geographic information system (GIS), 422-423
Gibson, K., 1002
Gila National Forest. See Catron County case
GIS. See geographic information system
Goal frames, 212
Goals:
  assessor recommendations on, 121
  determination of, 77
  dysfunctional, 862
  in conflict, 973
  in convening, 176-177
  in visioning, 558-560, 575-577
  meeting management and, 295
  ownership and, 963
God's Fellowship Community Church case,
  597, 682, 1051-1064
Golann, D., 498, 510
Goodwill, 825, 964, 1044
Government:
  dysfunctional, 743-745
  fragmented, 687, 691
  in civic infrastructure, 959-961
  roles of, changing, 977, 981
  roles of, dual, 685-686, 687, 705-707
  See also Politics
Government agencies:
  convening by, 172-174, 175
  legal issues and, 496, 497-512
  political capital and, 547
  procedural requirements on, 502-505

  roles of, conflicting, 685-708
  substantive restrictions on, 505-510
  visioning and, 564
  See also Intraorganizational situations
Graham, L., 1054
Graphic road maps, 137, 148
  benefits of, 151-152
  examples of, 149(figure), 150(figure),
    159(figure)
  PDC agenda flow and, 157-159, 162,
    164-166
  See also Process maps
Grazing issues. See Catron County case
Grievances, in unionized settings, 627
Grieving, 1020, 1056-1057, 1058
Ground rules:
  as fundamental process component, 79
  as precondition for success, xviii
  assessor recommendations on, 123-128
  components of, 26
  development of, 80-81
  diversity, communication, and, 252
  emotions and, 339
  examples of, 124-127(figure), 303, 1017
  for ad hoc assemblies, 26, 31-32
  for permanent groups, 39-40, 42-43, 48
  for producing consensus, 347, 371-372
  imperfect representation and, 347
  in case studies. See Chelsea charter case,
    pp. 756-757; and other specific cases
  in joint fact-finding, 393
  in meeting management, 302-303
  in value differences, 484, 487-488, 489
  issues addressed by, 88-89, 95-96, 123, 214,
    519, 851
  media and, 89-90, 228, 437-439, 447-453,
    721, 777, 1047
  modification of, 31-32, 48, 722
  practitioners and, 227-229, 519
  respect and, 1039
  signing of, 26
  trust, comfort, and, 68-69
  types of, 227
Groundwater containment. See Massachusetts
  Military Reservation case
Group members. See Participants;
  Representatives
Group memory, 223, 300, 321-322.
  See also Records
Group methods in evaluation, 665-667.
  See also Focus groups
Groups, compared to workshops, 1035

Habermas, J., 647, 673(n7), 979
Haida Gwaii case, 681, 923-950
Haida Gwaii case, as an example:
    for preparation, 85
    for process design, 65
    for process initiation, 63
    for representation, 247-250
    for roles, 199, 200-203, 206, 209, 212-213,
        215, 217, 218
    for value differences, 464, 475
Handshake agreements, 520
Harral, P., 450-452, 453
Hartford case. *See* Affordable housing
    mediation case
Healing, 1026, 1028, 1054-1063
Healthy communities approach, 583(table)
Healthy Communities program, 738-740
Helie, J., 883, 886, 887, 894
Heuristic approach, 309-310
Historical context:
    in case studies. *See* Haida Gwaii case,
        pp. 924-926; *and other specific cases*
    influence of, 75
    See also Prior relationships
HIV/AIDS case, 681, 1011-1029
HIV/AIDS case, as an example:
    for meeting management, 306, 307-308,
        309, 312-313
    for representation, 250-252, 271
    for value differences, 479-489
HMO case. *See* Regional Health and Human
    Service Task Force case
Holdouts, 6-7, 33, 50
    blocking action used by, 793
    creating more joint gains and, 340
    dispute resolution and, 336
    legal issues and, 852
Horizontal versus vertical elements, 602
Hotlinks, 404, 408
Housing, affordable, 966. *See also* Affordable
    housing mediation case
Hughes, M., 250, 479-489

IAP2. *See* International Association for Public
    Participation
Idea gathering, for visioning, 568, 573-574
Idea generation, 635, 649, 651, 652, 870.
    See also Creativity; Deliberating
Identity:
    in systemic functioning, 1058
    values and, 473, 491.
        See also Value differences

Identity-based disputes, 215, 218
Illustrations, technical, 839, 841-842, 843
Immunity, 516
Impartiality, 106, 232(table), 946.
    See also Neutral parties; Neutrality
Impasses:
    dispute resolution for, 333, 336
    uncertainty and, 355-363
    See also Obstacles
Impatience with process, 910, 1046
Implementation advisory group, 224
Implementing:
    as major phase, 139
    by ad hoc assemblies, 34-35
    by permanent groups, 52-54
    capacity for, 549
    dispute resolution systems design and,
        617-618
    government limitations and, 507-510
    in abortion case, 1046
    in affordable housing mediation case, 781,
        782, 789, 797-799
    in Chelsea charter case, 765-769
    in Haida Gwaii case, 941-945, 947-948
    in Levi Strauss case, 1074-1079
    in Mainport Schiphol case, 704, 707-708
    in Middletown case, 974-983
    in Native American case, 915
    in New York Bight case, 854-855
    in NOCC case, 737-741
    in SFEP case, 816-821, 822-823
    legal issues and, 507-510, 518-522, 532-533
    matrix overview of, 14-17
    phased, 507-508
    politics and, 73, 535, 538-541, 547-548
    procedures for, 223-224, 551-552
    process steps and, 83-84
    strategies for, 550, 551-552
    visioning and, 578-581, 589
    See also Ratification; Relationships
Implementing, challenges of, 527-532
    in closing the deal, 548-551
    in negotiations stage, 541-548
    in prenegotiations stage, 532-541
    procedures and, 551-552
Incentive provider, role of, 622
Inconclusive results, 397-398
Indefinite quantities contracts, 504
Indian Self-Determination and Education
    Assistance Act, 503, 902, 903, 910
Indian tribes. *See* Native American case
Indicators, measurement, 579
Individual authorship, avoidance of, 31, 47-48

Inequalities:
  in access, 409, 429-431
  in power, 625, 779-780
  in socioeconomics, 777
Information:
  access to. *See* Access to information
  as outcome, 649, 652
  as resource, 192
  freedom of, 512
  management of, 403-433
  multiple formats for, 841-843
  quality of, 649
  technical compared to nontechnical, 812
Information needs, 598
Information superhighway, 402.
    See also Internet
Information technology. *See* Computer-based
    technology; Technology
Initial screening, 173-174
  guidelines for, 175-184
  upon completion of, 184-185
Initiation:
  of dispute resolution systems design,
    610-611
  of policy network activation, 694-696,
    704-705
Initiation of consensus process:
  for ad hoc assemblies, 20
  for permanent groups, 36
  for visioning, 563-573
  motivations in, 202-203
  start-up phase and, 138, 139
  who can participate in, 63
  See also Convening; Prenegotiations stage
Injunctions, 521
Innes, J. E., 541, 636, 642, 647, 649, 650,
    672(n1)
Innovation:
  chaotic environments and, 645
  in decision making, 601
  in outcomes, 635, 651
  in processes, 648
Institutional agendas, 866, 869, 870
Institutional barriers, 204
Institutional culture, 909
Institutional representation, 866
Institutions, new, as outcomes, 635, 653,
    822-823
Insurance, liability, 516
Intellectual capital, 541, 542-544, 636
Interaction Associates, 140, 322(n)
Interaction Method, framework for, 298

Interactional/communicative process, 217
Interest-based negotiations, 905, 917
Interest groups, 82, 187, 982
Interests:
  compared to demands, 6
  compared to positions, 6, 330
  compared to values, 463, 467-468, 488,
    1012-1013, 1021-1022
  definition of, 6
  exploring of, 330-331
  in process design committee, 145-146
  key, identification of, 92
  trading of, 27-28, 44
Interlocking activities. *See* Parallel processes
Intermediaries, in community building, 958,
    959
Intermediate participation status, 268
Internal assistance versus external assistance,
    230-233
Internal negotiation versus external
    interactions, 244.
    See also Representatives, tension for
International Association for Public
    Participation (IAP2), 184, 235
International issues:
  decision making in, 595-596
  dispute resolution in, 546, 548
  treaty negotiations in, 135-136(n)
Internet, 235, 404-408, 411-414.
    See also E-mail; Listservs; RuleNet case;
    Web conferences; Web sites
Interpersonal problems, 214
Interpretations:
  analysis and, 732-733
  cultural context and, 933, 1062-1063
  diversity of, 377, 383, 397, 810, 831
Interpretive frames, 212
Interventionist mediation, 946
Interventions:
  as tools, 310, 313-321
  escalation of, 314
Interviews:
  exit, of participants, 817
  in evaluations, 614, 637, 667-669
  in mediator selection, 774
  in stakeholder analysis, 717-719
  information gathering in, 748-749
  with the media, 457
Interviews, in conflict assessment, 21, 37, 64,
    832
  arrangement of, 113-114
  conduct of, 114-115

identification of parties in, 108-112
protocol for, 112-113, 114-115
Intraorganizational situations, 591-594
case studies on, 604-610, 1051-1086
concerns and questions in, 623-629
decision making in, 593, 594-603
dispute resolution systems design in, 593, 603-619
roles in, 619-623
visioning in, 587
See also Permanent groups
Introduction, letter of, 107, 108, 109(figure)
Inventing, separated from committing:
in ad hoc assemblies, 28-29
in permanent groups, 45
producing consensus and, 331-332
Isaacson-Jones, B. J., 1031-1032
Issues:
assessment of, 100, 103.
See also Conflict assessments
control of, 178
defining of, 76
framing of, 177-178, 212-213
identification of, 177-178, 392.
See also Problem definition
nature of, 66-67
See also Agenda setting

Jacksteit, M., 1033, 1035, 1036, 1037-1043
Jacobs, J. J., 580
Joint fact-finding:
advantages of, 377-380
as alternative to adversary science, 376
as one of many processes, 216(figure)
diverse interpretations and, 377, 383, 397
for ad hoc assemblies, 29-30
for permanent groups, 46
in MMR case, 866, 872-875
in New York Bight case, 833, 835, 839-851
in NOCC case, 725, 727-735
in SFEP case, 810
methods of analysis in, 394-396
obstacles to, 397-398
producing consensus and, 331, 359
quality in, 649
steps in, 391-396
tasks in, 220-221
when not to use, 385
when to use, 380-385
who does, 386-391
See also Experts

Joint (mutual) gains:
conflict assessment and, 117
creation of, additional, 333, 334-335, 340-345, 349-350
creation of, steps for, 330-333
fair standards to divide, 333, 335-336, 350-351
inventing options for, 28, 45
maximization of, 12
maximization of, in ad hoc assemblies, 32-33
maximization of, in permanent groups, 49-50
prior relationship and, 49
tasks in, 222
value differences and, 468, 470, 490
Joint problem solving, 216(figure)
Joint statement of intent, 696, 704
Joint technical analysis, 419-420
Journalists. *See* Media, the; Reporters
Judges. *See* Courts
Judgments:
movement from opinion to, 542
nonobjective, 261-263
value-laden, 874
Just-in-time contracts, 504
Justification, and ratification, 273-274

Kaufmann, A., 1033, 1035, 1036, 1037-1043
Keeney, R., 688
Kennedy, W. J. D., 102, 209
Kettering Foundation, 438, 444, 545
Key community leader approach, 583(table)
Kishlansky, M., commentaries by:
on case 1, 687, 689-691, 694, 696-698, 701, 703
on case 3, 746, 751, 756, 758, 761, 762, 765, 766
on case 11, 952-956, 958, 959, 961, 964, 966
Kramer, R. M., 726
Kreckel, D., 735
Kunde, J., 546

Labor unions:
decision making and, 602, 626
dispute resolution systems design and, 605, 617, 627
Langer, R., 450, 451, 452-453
Language:
cultural context and, 72, 905, 908

focus on, 815, 824
in science-intensive disputes, 840-841, 846
in win-win situations, 917-918
intellectual capital and, 543
process and outcome framed in, 797
relationship building and, 1015-1016
suspicion and, 914
training and, 1079, 1083-1084
Late arrivals, 32, 48
Lawsuits. *See* Legal issues
Lax, D., 11, 12, 937
Leadership:
  development program for, 961
  facilitative, 7, 619-623
  for implementation, 580
  in policy network activation, 694, 695
  in reconciliation, 1055-1060
  meeting management and, 301-302
  misconduct of, 1051-1062
  support from, 196, 1083
Learning:
  as outcome, 635-636, 649, 652
  complexity and, 807, 810, 812
  complexity science and, 643, 644, 646
  cultural context and, 905
  goodwill and, 825
  implementation and, 818, 821
  intellectual capital and, 542
  joint fact-finding and, 378, 735
  legitimacy and, 762
  meeting management and, 309-310
  ongoing nature of, 769
  organizational. *See* Organizational learning
  projects as, 991
  representatives' tension and, 253, 260, 276, 277
  trans-disciplinary, 810
  types of, 636
  value differences and, 473-478, 488, 489-492
  See also Listening; Stories
LeBaron, M., 475, 478
Legal issues, 56, 66, 495-497
  agreement enforceability and, 520-522
  arbitration and, 1072-1073
  confidentiality and, 510-514, 519
  courts and, 497-502, 512, 513, 520-522
  disclosure and, 510-512, 517
  government agencies and, 497-512
  holdouts and, 852
  implementation, and, 507-510, 518-522, 532-533
  implementation, credibility, and, 789

legitimacy and, 746
liability and, 515-517
media and, 443
procedural requirements and, 502-505
process design and, 72-73
substantive restrictions and, 505-510
Web conferences and, 892-893
win-lose conflict and, 1032-1033
Legal processes, compared to consensus processes, 864, 865, 868-872, 876, 877
Legitimacy:
  as a goal, 701
  conflict assessment and, 105
  dialogue and, 1038
  genuine agreement and, 770
  government and, 746, 752, 759, 769
  justification, ratification, and, 274
  of convenor, 36
  of other participants, 43-44
  participant selection and, 185, 186
  process and, 146, 648, 759-765
  promotion of, 218-219
  representation and, 972
  stakeholder analysis and, 720
  See also Credibility
Letter of agreement, 107
Letter of introduction, 107, 108, 109(figure)
Levels of involvement, 156, 158-165
Levi Strauss case, 682, 1065-1086
  as an example, 601, 608-622
Liability, 56, 515-517, 865
Liability insurance, 516
Limitation of powers, 506, 507-509
Linking of issues, 341
Links, between Web sites, 404
Listening:
  active, 28, 44, 1040, 1041
  compassion and, 1026-1027
  polarizing issues and, 1040, 1041
  skills in, 28, 44, 307
  value differences and, 472-479, 489, 491
  See also Learning; Stories
Listservs, 27, 43, 429
  for deliberations, 411-414
  for information dissemination, 404, 406
  RuleNet and, 886
Lobbying, 73
Local decisions, and precedents, 786
Locally unwanted land uses (LULUs), 422
Locations. *See* Sites
Logging issues. *See* Applegate Partnership case; Catron County case
Logistical choices, 96-97, 1084

Long-term relationships, 49, 53-54.
    See also Relationship building
Looking tough, xxi
Lose-lose situations, 470
Losing face, xxi
Loyalties, xix-xx
LULUs. *See* Locally unwanted land uses
Lynch and Associates, 956
Lyndhurst Foundation, 959, 961

Mailing lists, 27, 43, 404
Maine public health mystery. *See* Northern
    Oxford County Coalition case
Mainport Schiphol case, 679-680, 685-709
Mainport Schiphol case, as an example:
    for process steps, 80, 81, 82, 83, 84
Majority rule, xxii, 5, 599
    fear of, 747
    implementation and, 1000-1001
    legitimacy and, 762
    meeting management and, 303
    powers inherent in, 746
Management track, 161-162
Managers:
    concerns of, 623-625
    consensus builders as, 775
    decision making and, 594-603
    dispute resolution systems design and,
        603-619
    roles of, 619-623
Mansbridge, J., commentaries by:
    on case 3, 744, 745, 747-750, 752-759,
        764, 767, 769, 770
    on case 12, 972, 973, 977-981, 984
Maps:
    agendas as, 295
    conflict assessment and, 104, 117
    for RuleNet dialogue, 887, 889
    need for, xviii, 137
    of agreement and disagreement, 117-119
    of stakeholder interests, 219-220
    process, decision making, and, 538
    process, legitimacy, and, 760
    See also Graphic road maps
Marginal studies, 258-259
Markovits, D., commentaries by, 1012-1013,
    1016, 1021-1024
Massachusetts Military Reservation (MMR)
    case, 680-681, 859-878
Massachusetts Military Reservation (MMR)
    case, as an example:
    for joint fact-finding, 380-382

for legal issues, 523(n10)
for representation, 251, 262, 274
Matrix:
    in "Short Guide," 14-19
    of conflict assessment findings, 117-119
Maximization of joint gains, 12, 32-33, 49-50.
    See also Joint (mutual) gains
Mayer, B., 615
McCreary, S., 854
McKearnan, S., 103, 123, 128
McKeen, H. B., 987
McKinney, M., 373(n)
Measurement:
    of performance, 780
    of progress, 579
    See also Evaluations
Media, the:
    and the process, at the end, 458-459
    and the process, during, 457-458
    contacts in, 449-453
    coverage by, benefits of, 443-444
    coverage by, examples of, 437-439
    ground rules and, 89-90, 228, 437-439,
        447-453, 721, 777, 1047
    handling of, 89-90, 133-134, 454-461
    handling of, guidelines for, 460-461
    handling of, implementation and, 535
    in abortion case, 1047-1048
    in Chattanooga Process case, 962
    in Chelsea charter case, 777
    in Middletown case, 971, 977
    in Northern Oxford County Coalition case,
        721
    legal issues and, 443, 510-511
    mixed feelings about, 435-436
    outreach and, 192
    process design committee and, 166
    visioning and, 570-571
Media assessments:
    definitions of, 436, 440
    need for, 439-440
    questions to ask in, 440-454
Media strategy. *See* Media, the, handling of
Mediate.com, 235, 883
Mediation:
    activities in, 208-209
    advisory, 616(table), 629(n8)
    arbitration and, 616(table), 630(n8)
    as one of many processes, 216(figure)
    as precondition for success, xviii
    compared to facilitation, 9, 208-209
    definition of, 8, 208
    drama of, 476

in dispute resolution, 616(table)
in-house, 1072
need for, 204
practitioners' role in, 208-209
wisdom of, 484, 485-487, 489
See also Facilitation
Mediation Information and Resource Center,
235
Mediation privilege, 513-514
Mediators:
compared to facilitators, 208-209
conflict assessment and, 106, 131-132
implementation challenges for, 531, 535,
538, 546, 549
in joint fact-finding, 395
legitimacy and, 765
liability and, 516-518
media and, 453, 455-457
political leverage not supplied by, 789-790
selection of, 231-233, 774, 787-788,
1076-1077
skills lacking in, 144
terminology for, 205
training of, 1077-1079
value differences and, 466-467, 473-487,
490
Web conferences and, 897
See also Coordinators; Facilitators;
Neutral parties; Practitioners
Mediators, role of, 4, 8-9, 94, 795-796
as agents of reality, 549
as protectors of the process, 762, 763
as targets, 1018-1019, 1026
clarification of, 24, 40
distance, detachment, trust, and, 1028
in convening, 170, 206, 207
in facilitation, 208
in mediation, 208-209
in relationship element, 224-229
in science-intensive disputes, 836-839
in substance element, 220-224
neutrality, and, 8
neutrality, intervention, and, 927, 928, 931,
946-949
Meeting management:
after the meeting, 321-322
before the meeting, 292-305
during the meeting, 305-321
importance of, 290-292
need for, 287-289
producing consensus and, 329
technology for, 410-417
Web-based tools for, 885-886

Meeting problems, 291, 315-321, 410
Meeting schedules. *See* Time frame; Timetables
Meeting sites. *See* Sites
Memorandum of understanding, 520
Memory. *See* Group memory; Records
Menkel-Meadow, C., 524(n17), 637
commentaries by, on case 3, 746, 749, 752,
759-760, 765, 768-770
commentaries by, on case 5, 802-807,
810-811, 813, 817, 818
commentaries by, on case 7, 864, 865,
868-872, 876, 877
commentaries by, on case 9, 902, 905, 906,
909-911, 917-918
commentaries by, on case 15, 1034,
1039-1041, 1044-1046, 1049, 1050
Merry, S. E., commentaries by:
on case 4, 777, 779, 783-785, 791, 794,
797
on case 10, 925-926, 931, 933, 938, 941,
942, 948-949
on case 11, 963, 968
on case 16, 1053, 1057, 1062-1063
on case 17, 1066-1067, 1070, 1072, 1073,
1075, 1077, 1080, 1082
Metaphors, in seeking common ground, 1038,
1039, 1043
Methodological issues:
computer technology and, 418
in evaluations, 662-670
in fact-finding, 394-396, 731-732
Midcourse evaluations, 632, 655
Middletown case, 969-984
Middletown case, as an example:
for implementation, 533
for visioning, 79, 566, 567, 572, 579
Minitrials, 616(table), 629(n8)
Minutes:
compared to visual records, 9-10
meeting management and, 321-322
Misperceptions, xx-xxii. *See also* Assumptions,
untrue
Misrepresentation of values, 468-469
Missing stakeholders, 22, 38, 105, 147.
See also Absent parties
Mission statements:
in abortion case, 1036
in Catron County case, 990
in Levi Strauss case, 1068
in NOCC case, 723-724
Mitchell, W., 401
MMR. *See* Massachusetts Military Reservation
case

Moccasin Bend Task Force, 955-956
Modeling, technical, 262, 263, 276
Moderators of Web conferences, 886-887,
   894-895
Modifications:
   of agendas, 31-32, 48
   of ground rules, 31-32, 48, 722
Monitoring:
   ad hoc assemblies and, 34-35
   deadlines and, 783
   implementation and, 547
   Internet deliberations and, 413
   joint fact-finding and, 396
   permanent groups and, 53
   practitioner tasks and, 224
   self-, and the media, 440-441
Montague, R., 955, 959, 962, 968
Moomaw, W., commentaries by:
   on case 6, 831, 834-836, 838, 840-842,
      844-845, 847, 851, 852
   on case 7, 861, 863, 865, 867, 873, 874
   on case 8, 880-883, 886, 887, 889, 890,
      893, 895, 896
Moore, C. M., 437, 445, 545
Moore, C. W., 102, 106, 112, 114, 136(n3),
   209, 372(n2), 615, 630(n8), 946
Moore, G., 450, 451, 452-453
Moral authority, 938, 941
Moral disagreements, 480-487.
   See also Value differences
Morality:
   compromise and, 806-807
   participant selection and, 752
   values and, 1016, 1023-1025
Most likely case, agreement on, 396
Motivations:
   differences in, 805, 806
   in initiation stage, 202-203
Multiple formats, for information, 841-843
Mutual gains. See Joint (mutual) gains

Narration. See Stories
National Environmental Policy Act, 986
National Roster of Dispute Resolution
   Professionals, 505
Native American case, 681, 901-922
   as an example, 72, 503, 511
Needs, 467-468, 488
Needs assessment, 1069-1070, 1083.
   See also Conflict assessments
Negotiated investment strategy (NIS), 444-445,
   545, 928

Negotiated rulemaking, 879, 901, 902.
   See also Native American case;
   RuleNet case
Negotiation software, 425
Negotiations stage:
   implementation and, 531, 541-548
   See also Deliberating
Negotiator's dilemma, 12
Network for Life and Choice. See Abortion case
Networks:
   building of, 822, 855
   of civic engagement, 545
   See also Policy network; Relationships
Neutral parties, 7, 8, 40
   cultural context and, 904-906
   dispute resolution procedures and,
      616(table)
   evaluations by, 671
   in conflict assessment, 103, 106, 131
   in convening, 170, 175, 181-184
   in process design, 63-64
   in Web conferences, 894-895
   meeting management and, 298, 299
   persuasion by, 911
   representativeness and, 186
   selection of, 183-184, 230-238
   skepticism about, 466-467
   staff as, 814
Neutrality:
   departure from, need for, 927, 928, 931,
      946-949
   key principle of, 218
   of experts, 729
   of technology, 897
   quality and, 906
   tension generated by, 1059
New York Bight case, 680, 829-858
New York Bight case, as an example:
   for joint fact-finding, 379, 388-389
   for legal issues, 523(n8)
Newark Collaboration Process, 139-142, 146,
   147, 156-159, 167-168
Newspapers, 449-453. See also Media, the
Newsworthiness, 445-447
Nicaragua, 210-211
NIS (negotiated investment strategy), 444-445,
   545, 928
Non-point source pollution. See Northern
   Oxford County Coalition case
Non-unanimity rule, 367-368.
   See also Decision rules
Nonbinding discussions, 935.
   See also Behind-the-scenes discussions

Nonlinearity, 531-532
Nonobjective judgments, 261-263
Nonverbal cues, 247, 930.
    See also Body language
Northern Oxford County Coalition (NOCC)
    case, 680, 711-741
    compared to affordable housing case, 775
Northern Oxford County Coalition (NOCC)
    case, as an example:
    for conflict assessment, 105
    for joint fact-finding, 378, 380, 387-388,
        390, 396, 397
    for process design, 64, 72
    for representation, 267
Note taking, 115. See also Recording
Nuclear Regulatory Commission (NRC).
    See RuleNet case
Number:
    of interviewees, 110
    of PDC members, 146
    of stakeholders, 528-529
Number, of participants:
    advice on, 92-93, 226, 534
    in case study groups, 815, 904, 1014
    wide variety in, 122
    See also Complexity
Numerical information, effective presentation
    of, 863

Observation, for evaluation, 669-670
Observers:
    beneficiaries as, 785
    in Web conferences, 413
    role of, 95-96, 302
    rules regarding, 25, 41
    See also Media, the
Obstacles, 326-327
    dealing with, 55-57, 337-371
    in implementation. See Implementing,
        challenges of
    in intraorganizational situations, 623-629,
        1084-1085
    in joint fact-finding, 397-398
    initial screening of, 180
    potential, noted by assessor, 119
    types of, 203-204
    See also Value differences
O'Connor, J., 839-841, 846, 854
Off-the-record meetings, 869.
    See also Behind-the-scenes discussions

Officials, elected. See Elected officials
Oklahoma case, 85, 91
Olmstead, W. J., 879, 882, 884, 896
Ombudsman, 106
Online consensus building case.
    See RuleNet case
Online information, 408-409.
    See also Computer-based technology;
    Internet; Web sites
Online rulemaking. See RuleNet case
Open-ended interviews, 667-668
Open-ended questions, 112
Open-meeting laws, 56, 72.
    See also Sunshine laws
Open mindedness, 252, 260, 261, 281.
    See also Perspective; Transformations
Open participation, 91
Open polling, 424
Opinion to judgment, movement from, 542
Options:
    contingent, 31, 48
    development of, 79-80, 81-82
    generation of, methods for, 81-82
    generation of, tasks in, 221, 222
    joint fact-finding and, 396
    practical, and value differences, 484,
        485-487, 489, 491
    substantive issues and, 213
    testing of, 29, 45
    See also BATNA; Inventing
Oral reports, 128-129
Oral versus written traditions, 944
Organism, universe as, 643
Organizational culture, 70-71, 1057, 1085
Organizational development, 54-55
    matrix overview of, 16-17
Organizational health, 1063-1064(n4)
Organizational learning, 54, 1058-1059, 1085
    matrix overview of, 16-17
    See also Learning
Organizational meeting, 22, 38
Organizational trauma. See God's Fellowship
    Community Church case
Organizations, new, as outcomes, 635
Orientations, 191. See also Training
Outcomes:
    determination of, 77, 154-155, 294-295
    evaluation of, 639-640, 650-654, 670
    importance of, xxi-xxii
    ownership of, 765, 766, 915
    secondary, 634, 635-636

variety of, 634-636, 761
See also Final products; Reports; Results
Outreach:
mechanisms for, 192
planning of, 89
ratification, justification, and, 274
technology for, 404-406, 407-408, 429
visioning and, 571-573
Outreach track, 165
Outside parties as experts, 387-391.
See also Experts
Outside parties as practitioners, 7, 141, 905
necessity of, 713
versus internal parties, 230-233
See also Practitioners
Outside-the-box thinking, 332, 441, 509, 649
Overlapping activities. *See* Parallel processes
Overpromising, 980. *See also* Expectations
Overspecialization in science, 865
Overwhelming support, 7, 32-33, 50
Ownership:
implementation and, 981, 982
of final product, 579
of outcomes, 765, 766, 915
of technical analysis, 419
Ownership, of consensus process:
evaluation of, 648
goal setting and, 963
implementation and, 536-538
process design and, 62, 120, 137, 141-142,
167
shifting to, 1018
Oxford County Coalition. *See* Northern
Oxford County Coalition case
Ozawa, C. P., 398(n1)

Packaging:
assessor recommendations and, 121
in ad hoc assemblies, 28-29
in permanent groups, 45
in useful formats, 839-843
producing consensus and, 332-333, 334,
335, 372
value differences and, 490
Panel of experts, 388
Parallel processes:
awareness of, 73
conflict assessment and, 127-128
coordination of, 498-500
implementation and, 532-533, 539-541,
548-549

problem boundaries and, 823
separate decision making and, 802-803
settlement events and, 498
Parliamentary procedure, xxii, 5.
See also Robert's Rules of Order
Participants:
as fact-finders, 386-387
assessor recommendations on, 121-122
definition of, 171, 329
identification of, 90-93, 185-190
number of. *See* Number, of participants
preparation of, 84-85, 187, 191, 329-330
relationships among. *See* Relationship
building; Relationships
training of, 397, 429, 536, 589
See also Representatives; Stakeholders
Participants, selection of, 225-227
criteria for, 751-753
for visioning, 565, 568-569
implementation and, 532, 533-536
Participation:
for visioning, 565, 568-569, 570-573
forms of, 91-92
multiple entry points for, 760
tiers of, 535. *See also* Circles of stakeholders
tracking of, 570
Partnership building, 172, 192, 971
Partnerships:
as outcomes, 635, 652-653
implementation and, 552
in civic infrastructure, 958-960
strategic planning and, 971, 975-979
Passion, 547. *See also* Commitment; Emotions
Patronage, 744, 745
Patton, B., 11, 372(n2)
PCB case. *See* New York Bight case
PDC. *See* Process design committee
People for People case, 591-592
Performance measures, 780
Performance standards, 1058
Permanent groups:
case studies on, 1051-1086
compared to ad hoc assemblies, xxxvi,
xli-xlii, 35. *See also* Ad hoc versus
permanent groups
"Short Guide" for, 35-57
See also Intraorganizational situations
Perspective:
broadening of, 269-272
taking of, and absent parties, 266-267
See also Open mindedness
Phased implementation, 507-508

Phases, in consensus building process, 138-139, 157-158. *See also* Consensus building, steps in
Pilot programs, 1074-1076
Plain English, 914
Planning:
    in convening, 195
    limitations in, 580
    strategic, 969-984
Plinio, A., 140, 147
Podziba, S., 373(n), 541, 774
Points of view, 145. *See also* Interests
Polarizing issues, and common ground, 1031-1049
Policy dialogue, 216(figure)
Policy network:
    activation of, 685-709
    factors for success of, 706
    process stages for, 696-704
Political attacks, 763
Political capital, 541, 547-548, 636, 652
Politics:
    consensus applications to, 769, 770
    corruption in, 743-770
    cross-cultural planning and, 930, 931, 934, 935-939
    implementation and, 538-541, 547-548, 816-821
    participant selection and, 189
    policy network and, 686-708
    process design and, 73-74
    protection from, 767
    scientific rationality and, 813
    strategic planning and, 981, 982-983
    technology and, 885, 894
    visioning and, 558, 560, 562, 566
    See also Elected officials; Government
Polling, 599, 816
    implementation and, 535
    technology for, 424, 887
    See also Straw polls
Pollution cases. *See* Massachusetts Military Reservation case; New York Bight case; Northern Oxford County Coalition case
Pooling of experience, 781-782
Portland Web site, 405
Positional bargaining, 204
Positions, compared to interests, 6, 330
Postnegotiations stage. *See* Implementing
Posturing, 470-472, 488
Potapchuk, W. R., 538, 541, 546
Power:

absence of, 931, 938, 979-980
body language and, 314
in systemic functioning, 1058
intraorganizational, 592, 625, 627, 1066-1067, 1073, 1075
moral authority and, 938, 941
unequal, 625, 779
Power-based disputes, 214, 215, 218
Practicality of options, 484, 485-487, 489, 491
Practices, new, as outcomes, 652-653, 653. *See also* Best practices
Practitioners:
    characteristics of, 235-237
    community-based, 200-201, 206, 231, 233
    core tasks of, 218-230
    external sources of, 7, 141
    external versus internal sources of, 230-233
    legal issues and, 504-505
    selection of, 230-238
    selection of, criteria for, 231-233
    selection of, legal issues and, 504-505
    terminology for, 205
    See also Facilitators; Mediators
Practitioners, role of:
    in convening, 205-207
    in dispute systems design, 209-211
    in facilitation, 207-208
    in mediation, 208-209
    in process element, 215-218, 229-230
    in relationship element, 214-215, 224-229
    in substance element, 213-214, 219-224
Prayer, 908, 1056, 1058, 1061
Precautionary principle, 844
Precedents:
    local decisions and, 786
    setting of, agreement on, 26-27, 43, 56-57
Preferences, and values, 467-468
Preliminary proposals, 30
Prenegotiations stage, 531, 532-541. *See also* Convening
Preparation:
    in seeking consensus, 329-330
    of participants, 84-85, 187, 191, 329-330
    See also Training
Press, the. *See* Media, the
Press briefings, 457
Press conferences, 458
Press releases, 457-458, 566
Presumed liability, 56. *See also* Liability
Presumptions, and value differences, 472-474, 477-478
Prevention tools, 310-313, 317, 319

Principles:
    abandoning of, xxi-xxii
    core, 1068
    for trust, 964
    of collaboration, 154, 290
    of neutrality, 218
    of visioning, 588-589
    precautionary, 844
Prior relationships, building on, 49, 179, 721.
        See also Historical context;
        Relationship building
Priority boards, 584(table)
Prisoner's dilemma, 470
Privacy, 419, 511, 513-514, 1052.
        See also Confidentiality
Privileges, legal, 513-514
Probing, and value differences, 474, 477, 491
Problem definition:
    alternative decision arenas and, 823
    as a first step, 76
    critical nature of, 861-863
    joint fact-finding and, 220-221, 391-392
    representation and, 805
    scope of, 154
    subproblems and, 699
    Web conferences and, 888
Problem solving:
    approaches to, 77-78, 157, 309-310
    expertise in, 871
    processes and, 216
    tasks in, 221-222
Problems, challenging. *See* Obstacles
Procedural feasibility, 69-70
Procedural requirements, and legal issues,
        502-505
Procedures:
    dispute systems design and, 211
    ground rules and, 80
    misconduct and, 1061-1062
Process consultants, 138, 141, 143-144, 154.
        See also Consultants
Process context, 70-75
Process definition, 392-394.
        See also Problem definition
Process design:
    as major phase, 138, 139
    building support for, 166-167
    complex agendas and, 990
    conflict assessment and, 99
    contextual influences in, 70-72
    for employee conflict resolution program,
        1070, 1071-1073, 1083

    for joint fact-finding, 384-385
    for visioning, 567-570
    implementation and, 537-538
    in case studies. *See* Abortion case,
        pp. 1035-1037; *and other specific cases*
    maps of. *See* Graphic road maps
    PDC in. *See* Process design committee
    practitioner selection and, 232(table)
    preliminary, by assessor, 120-128
    steps in, 76-97
    variety of, 216
    who should participate in, 63, 145-146
    See also Convening; Dispute resolution
        systems design
Process design committee (PDC):
    agenda flow for, 152-166
    benefits of, 141-143
    charter of, 144-145
    dispute resolution systems and, 611-618
    formation of, 146-148
    graphic road map and, 148-152, 157-159,
        162, 164-166
    need for, 138, 140
    number of members in, 146
    primary responsibility of, 148
    process consultant and, 141, 143-144
    purpose of, 144
    who should be on, 145-146
Process designers, 231-233.
        See also Dispute systems designers
Process element:
    complexity of, 233
    core tasks in, 229-230
    in consensus building model, 215-218
Process guide, 298
Process initiation, 62-63
Process management, 232(table)
Process management group, 161
Process manager, 161
Process maps, 538, 760.
        See also Graphic road maps
Process ownership. *See* Ownership,
        of consensus process
Process planning, 195
Process review, 348-349
Process steps, components of, 79-90
Process visionaries, 620
Processes:
    access to, 750
    agenda items and, 297
    compared to content, 291
    compared to substance, xviii

crossovers in, 766
defining of, 392-394
evaluation of, 90, 641-642, 657
evaluation of, criteria for, 647-650
ground rules on, 227
impatience with, 910, 1046
implementation and, 528-529
joint fact-finding and, 392-394
meeting management and, 297
nonlinearity of, 531-532
preventions and, 312
protection of, 762, 763, 767
responsibility for, 297, 307-308
success and, 290
typology of, 528-529, 530
variety of, 216
Productive stage, in policy network activation, 696, 698-700, 705
Professional organizations, 235, 389.
    See also names of organizations
Professional practitioners. *See* Practitioners
Project manager, role of, 622
Projections, computer, 414, 416, 428
Promotional efforts. *See* Media, the; Outreach; Publicity
Proposals, single-text procedure for.
    See Single-text procedure
Proprietary information, 56
Prospective negotiated rulemaking, 102
Protective orders, 513
Protocols:
    for interviews, 112-113, 114-115, 667-668
    to govern activities, 80. *See also* Ground rules
Proxies, 23, 39, 162. *See also* Stand-ins
Psychological barriers, 986, 987, 1016
Public health mystery case. *See* Northern Oxford County Coalition case
Public hearings, 216(figure)
Public journalism, 453-454
Public meeting laws, 511.
    See also Sunshine laws
Public outreach. *See* Outreach
Publicity:
    process design and, 166
    technology for, 405-406, 429
    visioning and, 571, 588
    See also Media, the; Outreach
Purpose:
    determination of, 293
    evaluation of, 648
    mission statement and, 723-724

Putnam, R. D., 531, 544
Puzder, A. F., 1031-1032

Quality:
    evaluation and, 634-635, 639-640, 649, 651
    neutrality and, 906
Queen Charlotte Islands. *See* Haida Gwaii case
Questions:
    in interviews, 112-113
    in seeking common ground, 1041
    reflected back to the group, 313
Quick fixes, 164, 983
Quizzing and educating, 577.
    See also Education

Race issues, 156, 535
    access to technology and, 409
    discussion, healing, and, 1025-1026
    economic issues and, 965-966
    See also Cultural context
Radical groups, 752, 1044
Radioactive waste. *See* Citizens advisory group case
Raiffa, H., 11, 413, 424, 718, 1002
    commentaries by, on case 1, 686, 688, 695, 697, 699-701
    commentaries by, on case 7, 861-863, 871, 874, 877-878
Ranchers and loggers. *See* Catron County case
Ratification:
    ad hoc assemblies and, 34-35
    as justification process, 273-274
    challenges in, 851-853, 940
    decision-making track and, 162
    goals and, 578
    legal issues and, 518, 782-783, 798
    permanent groups and, 52-53
    political dynamics of, 73
    representatives' tensions and, 272-282
    visioning and, 578
Rawls, J., 1024
Readiness. *See* Appropriateness
Receivership, 744-746, 767
Recognition, and value differences, 481, 491
Recommendation authority, 508
Recommendations:
    from conflict assessment, 100, 120-128, 129
    from process design committee, 144-145, 155
    See also Reports

Reconciliation case. *See* God's Fellowship
    Community Church case
Recorders:
    in process design, 143
    responsibilities of, 24, 40, 88
    role of, 95, 299-301
Recording:
    definition of, 9-10
    guidelines for, 300-301
    meeting management and, 299-301,
        321-322
    on tape, 88, 114
    power of, 300-301
    visioning and, 570, 574, 575
Records:
    analysis of, for evaluations, 637-638
    of Web conferences, 892-893
    preservation of, 511-512
    technology for, 412, 428
    visual, 9-10, 33, 50-51, 88
Recovery case. *See* God's Fellowship
    Community Church case
Referenda, 551
Reflection of questions back to the group, 313
Refocusing of the group, 313-314
Regional Health and Human Services Task
    Force case, 325-326, 331, 332, 337-371
Regulations, 500-501. *See also* Government
    agencies; Legal issues
Regulatory Negotiation Act of 1990, 523(n7)
Regulatory negotiation cases, 420-422.
    See also Native American case;
        RuleNet case
Relationship building, 85-86
    conflict assessments and, 104
    convening and, 179
    deliberating and, 49
    implementation and, 53-54
    in case studies. *See* HIV/AIDS case,
        pp. 1015-1016; *and other specific cases*
    joint fact-finding and, 380
Relationship element:
    complexity of, 233
    core tasks and, 224-229
    dispute systems design and, 211
    in consensus building model, 214-215
Relationships:
    as dimension of success, 290
    computer technology and, 432-433
    constituent. *See* Constituent-representative
        relations
    focus on, in processes, 216

implementation and, 541, 544-547
long-term, 49, 53-54. *See also* Relationship
    building
new, as outcome, 635, 640, 652, 978
prior, 49, 179, 721. *See also* Historical
    context
to other efforts. *See* Parallel processes
values and, 463-492
with government agencies, 496, 497-502
with the media, 437-459
Relativism, and value differences, 471-472
Renegotiation, 550
Reopener procedures, 35, 53
Replication of successful approaches, 956, 965,
    967, 968
Reporters, 439-457. *See also* Media, the
Reports:
    of conflict assessment, 103, 104, 128-130
    of design planning, 154-155, 166-167
    of joint fact-finding, 393, 396
    See also Recommendations
Representation:
    computer technology and, 429-431
    evaluation of, 647
    imperfect, 346-351
    implementation and, 533-536
    in case studies. *See* Affordable housing
        mediation case, pp. 784-787;
        and other specific cases
    in democracies versus consensus building,
        720
    ratification and, 852
    rolling, 707, 720, 784
Representative participation, 91-92
Representativeness:
    convening and, 185-187, 190
    implementation and, 534-536
    need for, 268-269
    practitioner tasks and, 225-226
Representatives:
    advice to, 275-280
    alternate, 23, 39, 721
    as opportunists, 252
    assessor recommendations on, 121-122
    authority linked to, 795
    constituents and. *See* Constituent-
        representative relations
    definition of, 171
    facilitative role of, 278-279
    identification of, 22-23, 69, 280
    in process design committee, 145, 146
    mandate to, 280-281

of government, 500-502, 504-510
path to becoming, 241-244
qualities of, 280
relationships among. *See* Relationship
    building; Relationships
selection of, 93, 225-227
selection of, and meeting management,
    293-294
shift from opinion to judgment by, 542
shift in role and understanding of, 270-272,
    273
understanding by, active role in, 259-263
understanding experience of, 245-246
See also Participants; Stakeholders
Representatives, tension for, 244-245
    absent parties and, 263-269
    common ground and, 269-272
    diverse counterparts and, 246-253
    in intermediary role, 794
    meeting management and, 302
    ratification and, 272-282
    shifting role and, 270-272, 273
    technical complexity and, 253-263
Request for information, in decision making,
    598
Request for proposals (RFP), 184, 234-235,
    1013
Research, joint. *See* Joint fact-finding
Research needs, 87
Resource adviser role, 95
Resource needs:
    constituents and, 279-280
    guidelines for meeting, 190-194
    implementation and, 536
    initial screening of, 179-180
    See also Costs
Resources:
    commitment of, 1071
    for joint fact-finding, 385
    for Web conferences, 897
    strategic planning and, 975-979, 982-983
    See also Funding, 975
Respect:
    in intraorganizational situations, 626
    value differences and, 470-472, 481, 482,
        484, 1069
    values and, 1016, 1021, 1024, 1033
    See also Trust
Responsibilities:
    abdication of, 625
    broadening of, 269-272
    clarification of. *See* Clarifying responsibilities

collective, 779
conflicting, 803
fairness in allocation of, 776
for agenda items, 297
for committing, 34, 52
for conflict assessment, 21, 36
implementation and, 536-538
in politics, 744, 745
meeting management and, 297, 298-302,
    307-308
representatives, consultants, and, 257
strategic planning and, 971-972
See also Agenda setting; Computer-based
    technology; Ground rules;
    Mailing lists; Observers; Roles
Restraining orders, 521
Results:
    achievement of, 290
    inconclusiveness of, 397-398
    See also Agreements; Evaluations;
        Final products; Implementing;
        Outcomes
Retrospective evaluations, 633, 656-662
ReVision 2000 case. *See* Chattanooga Process
    case
Revisions, consolidated improvements in, 31,
    48
RFP (request for proposals), 184, 234-235,
    1013
Rhetorical/stylized process, 216-217
Richardson, R., 373(n)
Rifkin, J., 946
Rights-based disputes, 214-215, 218
Rights claims, 478
Rippling representation, 707, 720, 784
Risk:
    assessment of, 394, 395
    avoidance of, 516-517
    burden of proof and, 844
    dialogue and, 1038, 1041
    legal liability and, 515-517
    perceptions of, 866
Road maps. *See* Graphic road maps
Robert Wood Johnson Foundation, 1000
Roberts, D., 557
Robert's Rules of Order
    alternative to, xxii-xxiii, 3-57, 788
    evaluations and, 658
    limitations of, xiv-xv, 3-5
    majority rule and, xxii, 5
Roles:
    clarification of. *See* Clarifying roles

convening and, 170-171
meeting management and, 298-302
of government, conflicting, 685-708
See also Convenors; Consultants;
    Facilitators; Mediators; Practitioners;
    Recorders
Rolling representation, 707, 720, 784
Rolling weighted polling, 887
Rosters:
of experts, 388
of practitioners, 234, 505
Rulemaking cases. *See* Native American case;
    RuleNet case
RuleNet case, 681, 879-899
as an example, 412, 424-425
Rusmore, B., 558
Russell, J. M., 1066, 1068, 1083

Sabel, C. F., 282(n4)
commentaries by, on case 1, 686, 707
commentaries by, on case 2, 713-716, 720,
    723, 727-728, 730, 734, 735, 739
commentaries by, on case 4, 775-776, 778,
    780-782, 784-786, 798
Sacredness, 933
Sacrifice, shared, 351
Safe, S., 847, 848
Salespersons, role of, 622
Samoan circle, 323(n5)
San Francisco Estuary Project (SFEP) case, 680,
    801-827
San Francisco Estuary Project (SFEP) case, as an
    example:
for evaluation, 633-635, 640-641, 647-649,
    652, 653, 660-670
for implementation, 540, 543
for research needs, 87
Sarat, A., 803
Saskatoon case, 604-608, 611, 612, 614, 615,
    618, 619, 621, 628
Scenarios:
development of, 584(table), 697
for contingent commitments, 549
Schedules. *See* Time frame; Timetables
Schulke, T., 1002, 1003, 1004
Schwarz, R., 372(n2)
Science-intensive disputes:
models for, 833, 854, 855-856(n4)
specialization and, 838, 865
technology for, 896
See also New York Bight case

Scientific expertise. *See* Experts; Technical
    complexity
Scientific rationality, 812, 813
Scientific uncertainty, 376, 377, 831, 838,
    847-850
Scoping, 392
Screening, initial. *See* Initial screening
Sealed agreements, 512
Search conferences, 476, 583(table)
Search engines, 408
Search for Common Ground, 1031
Sebenius, J., 11, 12, 937
Secondary outcomes, 634, 635-636
Self-monitoring, 440-441, 449
Self-organization, 643-644, 645, 646, 648
Senge, P., 441
Sensitive information, handling of, 232(table).
    See also Confidentiality
Sensitivity analysis, 418-419
Separation of powers, 506, 508-509
Settlement conferences, 616(table),
    629-630(n8)
Settlement events, 498
Sexual misconduct case. *See* God's Fellowship
    Community Church case
SFEP case. *See* San Francisco Estuary Project
    case
Shared sacrifice, 351
Shift:
from opinion to judgment, 542
in role and understanding, 270-272, 273
Short-term demonstration projects, 142-143
Shuttle diplomacy, 228, 289
Signature page, 369-370
Signing ceremonies, 551
Simultaneous processes. *See* Parallel processes
Single-loop learning, 636
Single-process evaluations, 657
Single-text procedure:
as a general approach, 78
definition of, 11
in ad hoc assemblies, 30-31
in case studies. *See* New York Bight case,
    pp. 840-841; *and other specific cases*
in permanent groups, 47-48
Internet deliberations and, 413
options development and, 82
tasks in, 222-223, 228-229
Sites:
access to, 750, 759
for interviews, 114
for meetings, 97, 304, 536, 750, 759, 1044

on the Web. *See* Web sites
pilot, 1074-1075
visits to, 86
See also Space considerations
Situation analysis, 103.
    See also Conflict assessments
Six-finger rule, 815-816. *See also* Visual tools
638 contracts, 902-903
Size, membership. *See* Number
Skepticism:
    conflict assessment and, 120
    legitimacy and, 760
    role and, 203
    value differences and, 465-467, 470-472
    See also Suspicion
Sloan, G., 472, 473, 476, 488, 489
Smart, L., 615
Smart trades, 343-345. *See also* Trading across
    issues
Snoqualmie River case, 508-509
Snyder, M., 441
Sobel, G., 373(n)
Social capital, 541, 544-547, 636, 652.
    See also Relationships
Social context, 70-72. *See also* Cultural context
Social dynamics, 214-215
Social relationships:
    computer technology and, 432-433
    See also Relationships
Society of Professionals in Dispute Resolution
    (SPIDR), 102, 184, 235, 516, 637, 647
Socioeconomics, 777. *See also* Economic
    context; Social context
Socioethnic context. *See* Cultural context;
    Social context
Sole source contracts, 234
Solomon, S., 476
South Moresby Agreement, 925, 926-928
Space considerations, 304-305, 1016,
    1018-1019. *See also* Sites
Special master, 106
Specialization, in science, 838, 865
Spence, L. H., 746
SPIDR. *See* Society of Professionals in Dispute
    Resolution
Spin-out track, 163-164
Spirituality, 1061
Spokespeople, 456, 518. *See also* Media, the;
    Publicity
Sponsors, role of, 94, 170, 804, 1085.
    See also Convening; Convenors
Stakeholder analysis, 103, 294, 719-720.
    See also Conflict assessments

Stakeholders:
    categories of, 92, 110, 156
    circles of. *See* Circles of stakeholders
    definitions of, 12-13, 171, 293-294, 329
    identification of, 156, 179
    missed in selection process, 22, 38, 105, 147
    skepticism of, 120, 203
    See also Participants; Representatives
Stalemates, 651
Stand-ins, 265-266. *See also* Proxies
Standards, to divide joint gains, 333, 335-336,
    350-351
Start-up phase, 138, 139. *See also* Convening;
    Initiation
Statistical analysis, 394, 395, 421, 732, 734
Status conference, 499
Status quo, satisfaction with, 981, 1002
Steering committees:
    for dispute resolution systems design,
        605-608, 611
    for visioning, 565, 567, 572, 578, 588
    role of, 161
Steinglass, R., 373(n)
Stepped sequence of decision making, 597-600
Stereotypes, 471-472, 478, 481
Stories:
    compassion and, 1026-1027
    in abortion case, 1041-1042
    in Haida Gwaii case, 924-926, 932-934,
        942, 944-945
    in HIV/AIDS case, 1026-1027
    value differences and, 475, 480, 489-491
    See also Learning; Listening
Strategic actions, 470-472, 478
Strategic moments, 310
Strategic planning, 969-984
Straus, D., 322(n), 372(n2)
Straw polls, 32, 50, 423-424, 599, 816.
    See also Polling
Structure of the consensus process, steps in,
    76-97. *See also* Process design
Study circles, 584(table)
Stylized/rhetorical process, 216-217
Subcommittees:
    in ad hoc assemblies, 29-30
    in case studies. *See* San Francisco Estuary
        Project case, pp. 805-812; *and other*
        specific cases
    in options phase, 82
    in permanent groups, 46-47
    in process design, 147
    task force track and, 164
    See also Work groups

Subgroups, organization of, 86-87.
    See also Subcommittees; Work groups
Substance:
    ground rules and, 80
    process and, xviii
Substance element:
    complexity of, 233
    core tasks and, 218-224
    in consensus building model, 212-213
Substantive restrictions, on government repre-
    sentatives, 505-510
Suburban communities, media coverage of, 446
Sunshine Act, 523(n4)
Sunshine laws, 56, 228, 511, 512, 523(n4)
Superfund cleanup. *See* Massachusetts Military
    Reservation case
Surveys:
    as evaluation methodology, 637, 663-665
    joint fact-finding and, 394, 395
    of visual preference, 952, 953
Suspension of legal proceedings, 499-500
Suspicion, 467, 469, 914. *See also* Skepticism
Susskind, L., 261, 372(n1), 372(n2), 373(n),
    469, 472, 476, 531, 635, 637, 638, 774,
    946
Sympathy, fairness, and values, 1022-1023
Systemic functioning, 1058
Systems, in complexity science, 643-646
Systems-level dialogue, 441

Tape recording, 88, 114
Task force track, 164
Task forces, 86-87, 216(figure)
Task groups, 82, 147. *See also* Work groups
Taylor, S. E., 726
Technical analysis, technology for, 417-423
Technical complexity, 253-263, 275-276
    complex solutions and, 877
    fact-finding and, 378, 395.
        See also Joint fact-finding
    handling of, 836-839
    meeting management and, 317-318
Technical experts. *See* Experts
Technology:
    computer-based. *See* Computer-based
        technology
    disparities in access to, 409
    display, 414, 416, 428, 815
    negotiated rulemaking and. *See* RuleNet case
    pull versus push, 897
Television stations:
    contacts at, 449-453

visual imagery needed by, 456
    See also Media, the
Temporary groups, xiv. *See also* Ad hoc
    assemblies
Tension for representatives.
    See Representatives, tension for
Tentative agreements, 937
Testing:
    of agreements, 32, 49-50
    of commitment, 907
    of options, 29
Thermo-Lag 330, 881, 882, 895
Thin-ice agreements, 351, 368
Thinking along a continuum, 1039, 1040,
    1045, 1049
Thinking, connective, 1040, 1045, 1049
Thinking outside the box, 332, 441, 509, 649.
    See also Creativity
Thomas-Larmer, J., 134, 188
Thompson, L. L., 1002
Threads of conversations, 412, 887, 889
Thumbs up/down/sideways, 312-313
Time frame:
    computer technology and, 410, 411, 412,
        416, 430-431
    first-round agreements and, 360
    in capacity building, xviii
    in consensus process, 96, 122, 624
    in convening phase, 206
    in joint fact-finding, 385, 397, 398
    in process design, 145, 165
    in visioning, 589
    mediator selection and, 774, 787
    meeting management and, 297, 319-320
    practitioner tasks and, 220, 224, 229
    unrealistic expectations about, 983, 1007
Time-out rule, 722, 723
Timetables:
    for ad hoc assemblies, 25-26
    for permanent groups, 42
Timing:
    as procedural constraint, 69
    decision making and, 701
    dispute resolution systems and, 628
    issue identification and, 177
    political dynamics and, 539
    visioning and, 588
Tools:
    facilitative, 310-321
    Web-base, 885-886
Townsend, J., 474, 476-477
Tracking of Internet deliberations, 413,
    891-892

Tracks of activity, 156, 158-165
Trading across issues:
    creating more joint gains and, 334-335,
        340-341
    packaging and, 332
    searching for options in, 343-345
    value differences and, 490
Training:
    convening and, 187, 191
    dispute resolution systems design and,
        605-606
    experience and, 236
    for facilitators bank, 961
    implementation and, 536
    in computer technology, 429
    in intraorganizational situations, 621,
        1070-1072, 1076-1082
    in joint fact-finding, 397
    language and, 1079, 1083-1084
    visioning and, 589
    See also Education; Preparation
Transformations:
    crucial nature of, 756
    in process ownership, 1018
    in reconciliation, 1059, 1062
    in relationships, 216(figure), 1025, 1028.
        See also Relationship building
    meeting management and, 289
    no expectation for, 1039
    polarization and, 1042, 1048
    power of problem solving and, 778
Transformative/dynamic process, 217-218
Transformative relationship building,
    216(figure)
Transparency, 28, 45
Trauma recovery case. See God's Fellowship
    Community Church case
Treaty negotiations, 135-136(n)
Trials, 616(table), 629-630(n8), 1052
Tribal partnership case. See Native American
    case
Troubleshooters, 621-622
Trust, 67, 68
    as outcome, 635
    building of, 720, 814, 999, 1008, 1033,
        1034
    implementation and, 531, 541, 941
    importance of, 990
    in conflict assessment, 111, 132
    in convening, 175, 195, 196
    in intraorganizational situations, 626, 1053,
        1061
    in joint fact-finding, 383-384
        in process design, 141, 142-143
    legal issues and, 517
    media coverage and, 441
    practitioners' roles and, 200
    principles for, 964
    value differences and, 468
    See also Credibility; Legitimacy; Respect
Trust account case. See Haida Gwaii case

Udall Foundation, 505
Ultra vires, 506
Unanimity, 6-7
    decision making and, 600
    implementation and, 1000-1001
    in ad hoc assemblies, 32
    in permanent groups, 50
    less than, dealing with, 363-371
    limitations of, 815-816, 824
    producing consensus and, 327-328, 351,
        363-371
Uncertainty:
    complexity science and, 646
    dealing with, 355-363, 847-850
    judgments and, 873, 874
    management of, 543-544
    scientific, 376, 377, 831, 838, 847-850
Unconditionally constructive deliberations, 27,
    44
Undue delegation of powers, 506, 508
Unilateral decision making, 594, 597-598, 600,
    653
Unions, labor. See Labor unions
Universe as organism, 643
University System of Georgia, 210
Unmet interests, 333, 334
    dealing with, 337-345
Unrealistic aspirations, 333, 345-355, 708
Unrealistic expectations, 979-980, 983, 1007
Unrealistic optimism, 726
Unverzagt, M., 989, 990
Up-front agreements, 311-312
Ury, W., 11, 372(n2)
U.S. Department of Defense (DoD), 408, 409
U.S. Nuclear Regulatory Commission (NRC)
    case. See RuleNet case
Usurpation of power, 506

Value:
    claiming of, 12
    creating of, 11-12
    packaging for, 28-29, 45

Value conflicts. *See* Value differences
Value differences, 463-465
  common ground process and, 1031-1049
  dealing with, example on, 479-489
  dealing with, strategies for, 467-479,
    489-492
  exploration, discovery, and, 474, 476, 477,
    478, 491, 492
  ground rules and, 484, 487-488, 489
  interests and, 1012-1013, 1016, 1022
  irreconcilability and, 478, 479
  learning and, 473-478, 488, 489-492
  listening and, 472-479, 489, 491
  metaphors for, 1038, 1039, 1043
  obstacles in, 465-467
  probing and, 474, 477, 491
  real versus perceived, 470-472
  respect and, 470-472, 1016, 1024, 1069
  skepticism and, 465-467, 470-472
  stories and, 475, 480, 489-491
  sympathy, fairness, and, 1022-1023
  temptations to resist in, 471-472
  wisdom of mediation and, 484, 485-487,
    489
Value-laden judgments, 874
Values:
  compared to interests, 463, 467-468, 488,
    1012-1013, 1021-1022
  dissemination of, 1067-1069
  generalities, specifics, and, 488, 489, 490
  misrepresentation of, 468-469
  needs and, 467-468, 488
Vancouver Island case, 472-474
Verbal abuse, 891, 894
Vermillion, D., 437, 438
Vertical team bargaining, 229
Vertical versus horizontal elements, 602
Victims, 1052, 1053
Violence, fear of, 988, 989, 994
Virtual exchanges, 433.
  See also Computer-based technology
Vision 2000 case. *See* Chattanooga Process case
Visionaries, 620
Visioning, 78-79, 157, 163
  as process, 216(figure)
  cases on. *See* Catron County case;
    Chattanooga Process case;
    Middletown case
  intraorganizational, 587
  nature of, 558-560
  primary purpose of, 580
  variety of approaches to, 581-587
Visioning, community-wide:

  alternatives to, 581-587
  applicability of, 559
  benefits of, 560-561
  lessons for, 588-589
  phases of, 562-581
  pitfalls in, 561
  preconditions for, 561-562
  principles of, 588-589
Visual imagery, for television, 456
Visual maps. *See* Graphic road maps
Visual materials, and value differences, 476
Visual preference surveys, 952, 953
Visual records, 9-10, 33, 50-51, 88
Visual tools, 815-816, 1019-1020
Voice, and computer technology, 429-431,
  890
Voices being heard, 758-759, 890.
  See also Listening
Voting:
  decision making and, 599
  representation and, 755
  six-finger rule for, 815-816
  tool for, 888
  visioning and, 577-578
  See also Decision rules; Polling
Vulnerability, and dialogue, 1038, 1041

Wallis, J., 1026-1027
Wartenberg, D., 730-734
Wasco, 248-249, 932-934, 938
Water management. *See* San Francisco Estuary
  Project case; Snoqualmie River case
Web-based tools, 885-886
Web conferences:
  for ad hoc assemblies, 27
  for deliberations, 411-414
  for permanent groups, 43
  RuleNet and. *See* RuleNet case
Web sites:
  facilitator functions on, 431-432
  for information dissemination, 404-408
  for Mediate.Com, 883
  for Mediation Information and Resource
    Center, 235
  for polling, 424
  representation, voice, and, 429, 430
Weighted polling, 887
Weis, J., 846
Weiser, I., 472, 474, 475, 476, 479, 488
"What if?" testing, 29, 45
Who should . . . :
  attend meetings?, 293-294

be approached in the press?, 449-454
conduct conflict assessments?, 106-107, 138
conduct evaluations?, 670-671
do convening activities?, 180-181
do joint fact-finding?, 386-391
do process design?, 63, 145-146
initiate consensus processes?, 63
lead visioning efforts?, 564-567
take responsibility for agenda items?, 297
See also Responsibilities; Roles
Wildau, S., 615
Willingness to negotiate, 67-69
Win-lose situations, 1032-1033, 1039
Win-win situations, 687, 688, 905, 917-918
Wisdom of mediation, 484, 485-487, 489
Within-organization situations.
See Intraorganizational situations
Work groups:
as fact-finders, 386-387
for implementation, 552, 579
ground rules on, 228
in case studies. See Native American case,
pp. 912-914; and other specific cases
in options phase, 82, 780

in Web conferences, 889
task force track and, 164
See also Subcommittees
Work plans, 220, 724-727.
See also Agenda setting
Workshops:
as alternative to consensus process, 69
as one of many processes, 216(figure)
compared to groups, 1035
for determining appropriateness, 68
for preparing participants, 85
in abortion case, 1035, 1037-1045
World Wide Web. See Internet;
Web conferences; Web sites
Worry beads, 1027-1028
Written agreements, 520, 548-551.
See also Agreements
Written documents:
technology for, 403-409, 425-428
versus oral tradition, 944

Young people, 962-963, 979, 998.
See also Children, implications for

ABOUT THE EDITORS

Lawrence Susskind is Ford Professor of Urban and Environmental Planning at Massachusetts Institute of Technology. He was the first Executive Director of the Program on Negotiation at Harvard Law School, where he still serves as Director of the MIT-Harvard Public Disputes Program. Professor Susskind is founder and President of the Consensus Building Institute and author of 14 books including *Breaking the Impasse* (with Jeffrey Cruikshank, 1987), *Dealing with an Angry Public* (with Patrick Field, 1996), and *Negotiating on Behalf of Others* (with Robert Mnookin, 1999). He is an experienced public dispute mediator, having assisted in the resolution of more than 50 complex disputes. He has also presented workshops and seminars to more than 35,000 corporate executives, public sector managers, and citizen activists.

Sarah McKearnan is an experienced mediator/facilitator of multiparty dialogues. She was Senior Associate at the Consensus Building Institute for five years, where she assisted state- and local-level groups in building consensus on environmental and economic issues including facility siting, land use, pollution prevention and remediation, and public health risks. She also facilitated a regional strategic-planning process on human service programs and policies. She serves on the faculty of the International Programme on the Management of Sustainability. She is also a trainer of negotiation and consensus building skills for public, private, and nonprofit organizations. She has authored negotiation simulations, consulting reports, and articles on the history and practice of dispute resolution in academic journals and magazines. She formerly served as editor of "Practitioners' Notebook" in *Consensus*, a quarterly news publication published by the MIT-Harvard Public Disputes Program.

Jennifer Thomas-Larmer is a writer and editor in the dispute resolution field. She is coauthor of *Negotiating Environmental Agreements* (with Lawrence Susskind and Paul Levy, forthcoming) and is editor of "Practitioner's Notebook" in *Consensus,* a publication of the MIT-Harvard Public Disputes Program. She has edited numerous consensus-based reports developed by multistakeholder dialogue groups, including those sponsored by the U.S. Department of Health and Human Services and the Center for Strategic and International Studies. Clients have also included the President's Council on Sustainable Development and the National Recycling Coalition, among others. She previously worked as a facilitator at the Keystone Center in Washington, D.C., where she mediated policy dialogues on endangered species protection, nutrition labeling, agriculture, industrial eco-efficiency, and other issues. She holds an M.S. in natural resource policy from the University of Michigan.

ABOUT THE CONTRIBUTORS

Max H. Bazerman is the Thomas Henry Carroll Ford Visiting Professor of Business Administration and Bower Fellow at Harvard Business School. He is also the J. Jay Gerber Distinguished Professor of Dispute Resolution and Organizations at the Kellogg Graduate School of Management at Northwestern University. Previously, he taught at the Sloan School of Management at Massachusetts Institute of Technology, Boston University, and the University of Texas and was a Fellow at the Center for Advanced Study in the Behavioral Sciences in Stanford, California. He is the founder and Director of the Kellogg Environmental Research Center. His research focuses on decision making, negotiation, and the natural environment. He is author or coauthor of more than 100 research articles, and author, coauthor, or coeditor of nine books, including *Why Smart People Make Dumb Money Moves* (forthcoming), *Judgment in Managerial Decision Making* (4th ed., 1998), and *Negotiating Rationally* (with M. Neale, 1992). Professor Bazerman received his M.S. and Ph.D. from Carnegie Mellon University.

David Brubaker is the owner of Conflict Management Services, a mediation, consulting, and training organization based in Casa Grande, Arizona. He is currently a board member of the Arizona Dispute Resolution Association and is a past board member of the National Conference on Peacemaking and Conflict Resolution. He has been active in the dispute resolution field since he served as Associate Director of the Mennonite Conciliation Service from 1986 to 1988. During that period, he edited their newsletter, *Conciliation Quarterly,* and developed and edited the tape series "When You Disagree . . . ." Since 1988, he has published in the Alban Institute's journal *Congregations, Christianity Today,* and *Conflict Resolution Notes.* He holds an MBA from Eastern College and is a Ph.D. candidate in the Department of Sociology at the University of Arizona.

Chris Carlson is Codirector of the Policy Consensus Initiative, a nonprofit organization that works with state officials to establish and strengthen consensus building and conflict resolution efforts. She has been active in the conflict resolution field for more than 15 years, serving as mediator, facilitator, trainer, and consultant. She was formerly Executive Director of the Ohio Commission on Dispute Resolution and Conflict Management. Prior to her work at the Ohio Commission, she was Program and Legal Officer at the Kettering Foundation. She has also been Cochair of the SPIDR Environment/Public Disputes Sector and Cochair of the committee that produced the *Best Practices for Government Agencies* report, and she has served as a local elected official.

Susan Carpenter is a mediator, trainer, and author. She works with the public and private sector to address controversial issues at the local, state, and national levels. Her practice includes mediation, collaborative planning, and consensus building. She also teaches others to use mediation, negotiation, consensus building, and facilitation tools. She was the founding Director of the Program for Community Problem Solving in Washington, D.C. and Associate Director of ACCORD Associates in Boulder, Colorado. She holds a doctorate in future studies from the University of Massachusetts and taught for two years in Ethiopia as a Peace Corps volunteer. She is the author of numerous articles and coauthor of *Managing Public Disputes* (1988).

Nike Carstarphen is dedicated to intergroup reconciliation and peaceful social change. She specializes in facilitating dialogue and problem-solving processes, and training in conflict resolution, prejudice reduction, and intercultural communication. She has worked with government agencies, nonprofit organizations, police departments, schools, and at-risk youth in the United States and abroad. She is currently conducting an evaluation of peer mediation programs in northern Virginia schools. Her publications include articles in *Negotiation Journal* and *Teaching and Change,* and presentations at numerous conferences. She has taught courses in peace and conflict resolution at American University (AU) and George Mason University (GMU). She has an M.A. in international affairs from AU and is completing her Ph.D. dissertation at the Institute for Conflict Analysis and Resolution at GMU.

Sarah Connick is a doctoral candidate in environmental science, policy, and management at the University of California, Berkeley. Her research focuses on the use of consensus building processes in the making of California water policy. Prior to entering this graduate program, she directed environmental science policy studies for the Water Science and Technology Board of the National Academy of Sciences in Washington, D.C.

Kate Connolly has been active in the public sector for 25 years, both on a municipal government level and with numerous non-profit organizations. Her professional activities have focused primarily on community development, but her work has also involved women's advocacy, the implementation of community strategic plans, and public policy analysis. She earned a bachelor's degree in sociology from the University of Windsor (Ontario) and a master's degree in public administration from Queens University (Ontario). She is currently working toward a joint Ph.D. in urban and regional planning and recreation and leisure studies at the University of Waterloo, Canada. She owns a consulting firm specializing in organizational, community, and policy development.

Jarle Crocker is Program Associate with the National Civic League's Program for Community Problem Solving (PCPS). He has been Adjunct Professor of Communication at George Mason University for four years, teaching classes in interpersonal and small-group communication. As a facilitator, trainer, and consultant on community collaboration, he has focused on issues related to public participation in local government decision making, systems change initiatives for local government, intergroup conflict in schools, and the resolution of community conflicts over resource use, environmental justice, and related ecological issues. He received a degree in political science from the University of Pittsburgh and is currently a Ph.D. candidate at the Institute for Conflict Analysis and Resolution at George Mason University. His publications include "Challenging Huntington" in *Foreign Policy* (with Richard Rubinstein, 1994) and the PCPS working papers *System Reform and Local Government: Improving Outcomes for Children, Families, and Neighborhoods* and *Building Community: Exploring the Role of Social Capital and Local Government*.

Norman Dale is Senior Planner and Administrator for the Oweekeno-Kitasoo-Nuxalk Tribal Council, an organization representing shared interests of three tribes in British Columbia. He completed several years of graduate study at Massachusetts Institute of Technology's Department of Urban Studies and Planning and holds an M.S. in marine ecology from Nova Scotia's Dalhousie University. He is coauthor of *Building Consensus for a Sustainable Future: Putting Principles into Practice* (published by the National Roundtable on Environment & Economy, Ottawa, Canada) and an earlier book about Native land claims. He has written several articles on the use of alternative dispute resolution in fisheries conflicts, and he serves on the editorial board of *Consensus,* a periodical of the MIT-Harvard Public Disputes Program. He has also served as coastal policy adviser to several Canadian provincial governments, Canada's Department of Indian & Northern Affairs, and First Nations. He is a member of the Society for Professionals in Dispute Resolution and is on the board of the British Columbia Coastal Communities Network. He lives on the Nuxalk Indian Reserve in Bella Coola, British Columbia.

Peter Driessen graduated in urban and regional planning from the University of Nijmegen, the Netherlands. He is now Associate Professor of Environmental Studies at Utrecht University. Most of his research is related to the relationships between environmental planning and physical planning and with network management. His recent publications include "The Scope of Co-operative Management: Concluding Remarks" in *Co-Operative Environmental Governance: Public-Private Agreements as a Policy Strategy* (1998), "Performance and Implementing Institutions in Rural Land Development" in *Environment and Planning B: Plan-*

ning and Design (1997, vol. 24), and "Innovative Decision-Making on Infrastructure and Environment: Experiments with Network Management in the Netherlands" in *European Spatial Research and Policy* (1996, vol. 3, no. 2).

John R. Ehrmann has been involved in the application of collaborative processes in public and private sector settings for almost two decades. He has extensive experience facilitating national- and international-level legislative and regulatory dialogues and negotiations dealing with environmental policy issues and other topics related to sustainable development. He has provided facilitation services to the President's Council on Sustainable Development, the National Commission on Superfund, and policy dialogues on the Clean Air Act, Endangered Species Act, and Safe Drinking Water Act, among many others. He also served as Project Director for several advisory councils that addressed the implementation of multiple environmental statutes. He also facilitates internal organizational processes, including strategic planning, organizational development, advisory committees, and processes designed to further collaborative decision making and sustainable development. Dr. Ehrmann is a founding partner of the Meridian Institute, a nonprofit dispute resolution organization. He holds a Ph.D. in natural resource policy and environmental dispute resolution from the University of Michigan's School of Natural Resources and Environment.

Michael L. Poirier Elliott is Associate Professor of Urban Planning and Environmental Policy at Georgia Institute of Technology. His specialties include public policy dispute resolution and environmental management. He currently serves as Director for Research at the Consortium on Negotiation and Conflict Resolution and Codirector of the Southeast Negotiation Network. In these capacities, he mediates and facilitates public consensus building processes, designs dispute management systems, and conducts research in policy implementation and conflict management. These activities have focused on resolving disputes over solid and hazardous waste, siting and managing locally unwanted facilities, risk management policy, resource management, and growth management. Dr. Elliott also provides training and dispute systems design consultations in Estonia, Germany, Kazakhstan, Nicaragua, and Israel. He has also conducted over 40 training workshops in public policy conflict management and negotiation. He has published numerous articles on dispute resolution and coauthored a book, *Paternalism, Conflict and Co-production* (1983). He received a master's degree in city planning from the University of California, Berkeley and a Ph.D. in urban and regional studies from Massachusetts Institute of Technology.

David Fairman is Senior Associate at the Consensus Building Institute (CBI). An experienced mediator and facilitator, he has assisted groups in building consensus on environmental, economic development, human services, and facility siting-related policies and projects. He also provides negotiation training and education services for public, private, and nonprofit organizations. He directs CBI's Workable Peace Project, which teaches teenagers to understand and manage conflict between groups, and serves on the faculty of the International Programme for the Management of Sustainability. He has authored numerous negotiation simulations, consulting reports, journal articles, and book chapters. He holds a Ph.D. in political science from Massachusetts Institute of Technology and is a member of the Society for Professionals in Dispute Resolution.

Juliette A. Falkner is Director of the Office of the Executive Secretariat and Regulatory Affairs of the U.S. Department of the Interior. She graduated from Albion College in Albion, Michigan. In 1985, she received a Fulbright scholarship to study European labor politics in Germany. She received her J.D. in 1990 from the Washington and Lee University School of Law. She is a member of the Arizona State Bar. Prior to joining the Department of the Interior, she served as a judicial clerk to U.S. District Judge Stephen M. McNamee in Arizona.

Michèle Ferenz is Senior Associate at the Consensus Building Institute and a doctoral candidate in the Department of Urban Studies and Planning at Massachusetts Institute of Technology. Her research focuses on environmental management and conflict resolution in the Middle East. She has worked for CBS News, the *New York Times,* and the *International Herald Tribune* in Italy. She has also worked as a consultant for the Charles R. Bronfman Foundation on a project fostering economic development in the Middle East. Her publications include "The Design of a Palestinian-

Israeli Water Commission: A Best Practices Approach" (published in 1995 as part of the Environment and Natural Resources Program Discussion Paper Series by the Belfer Center for Science and International Affairs, Kennedy School of Government, Harvard University).

Patrick Field is Senior Associate at the Consensus Building Institute and mediator/facilitator with extensive experience facilitating multistakeholder dialogues on environmental policy and management issues, including public health, risk management, air and water pollution remediation, and energy. He cofacilitated the Northern Oxford County Coalition (NOCC) process with Sarah McKearnan. He is coauthor of *Dealing with an Angry Public* (1996) as well as numerous consulting reports, negotiation simulations, and journal articles. He also provides training in negotiation, facilitation, and consensus building to public sector clients in the United States and Canada. He received his master's degree in urban studies and planning from Massachusetts Institute of Technology. He is also a member of the Society of Professionals in Dispute Resolution.

John Forester is Professor and Chair of the Department of City and Regional Planning at Cornell University. He received his Ph.D. from the University of California, Berkeley. His research interests include the micropolitics and ethics of planning practice, including the ways planners work in the face of power and conflict. For the past decade, he has been producing "profiles" of planners, mediators, and participatory action researchers in the United States and abroad. His previous published work includes *Planning in the Face of Power* (1989), *Making Equity Planning Work: Leadership in the Public Sector* (with Norman Krumholz, 1990), *The Argumentative Turn in Policy Analysis and Planning* (edited with Frank Fischer, 1993), and *The Deliberative Practitioner* (1999).

Dwight Golann is Professor of Law at Suffolk University in Boston, where he teaches mediation and dispute resolution. He is the principal author of *Mediating Legal Disputes* (1996), co-winner of the CPR Institute Award for best book in the dispute resolution field in 1996. He chairs ADR programming for the Litigation Section of the American Bar Association (ABA), and formerly served in that capacity for the Business Law Section of the ABA. During 1998, he was Visiting Scholar at the Program on Negotiation at Harvard Law School. He is an active mediator, serving on the panels of the CPR Institute, the New York Stock Exchange, and other forums. He was formerly a civil litigator, and while on academic leave served as Chief of the Government Bureau and Trial Divisions for the attorney general of Massachusetts, directing the defense and settlement of all civil litigation for the commonwealth. He is an active ADR trainer and has led seminars on mediation and negotiation throughout North America and Europe.

Michael A. Hughes is Partner at CDR Associates, where he specializes in public policy mediation. He has extensive experience in conflict resolution, facilitation, and training in the public sector, where he has conducted regulatory negotiations, policy dialogues, and site-specific mediations. He uses those same principles to assist private companies, nonprofit organizations, and government agencies to effectively recognize, raise, and resolve their own conflicts. He holds a master's degree in city planning from the University of Pennsylvania and a bachelor's degree in political science and sociology from the University of Denver. He is a member of the American Institute of Certified Planners. He received leadership training through the University of Colorado Center for the Improvement of Public Management's Rocky Mountain Program, and he was trained in mediation by CDR Associates.

Judith E. Innes is Professor of City and Regional Planning at the University of California, Berkeley, where she has been on the faculty since 1974. She is also Director of Berkeley's Institute of Urban and Regional Development, an interdisciplinary, campuswide research unit. She is author of *Knowledge and Public Policy* (1990) and editor of *The Land Use Policy Debate in the United States* (1981). She has published many articles in planning and public policy journals on the role of information in policy processes and on the design of policy-making and implementation systems. Professor Innes's recent research has focused on collaborative planning and consensus building in growth management, environmental planning, and transportation. She is also Director of the University-Oakland Metropolitan Forum, a partnership between the university and the city of Oakland, which has developed new visions of the city, done research, and completed collaborative projects. She has a Ph.D. in urban studies and planning from Massachusetts Institute of Technology.

Mark Kishlansky is the Frank B. Baird, Jr. Professor of English and European History and Associate Dean of the Faculty of the Arts and Sciences at Harvard University. Previously, he taught for 16 years at the University of Chicago, where he was a member of the Committee on Social Thought. A specialist in seventeenth-century British history, he has written extensively on political structures and political change and coined the usage *consensus politics* to describe the nature of political decision making in the early seventeenth century. Among his books are *The Rise of the New Model Army* (1979), *Parliamentary Selection: Social and Political Choice in Early Modern England* (1986), and *A Monarchy Transformed* (1997). He is coauthor of *Civilization in the West* (3rd ed.) and *Societies and Cultures in World Civilizations* (1994) as well as editor of *Sources of the West* (3rd ed., 1997), *Sources of World History* (2nd ed., 1998), and *Political Culture and Cultural Politics in Early Modern England* (1995).

James E. Kunde, in his 30-year career, has worked as a city manager, a program director for a national foundation, a scholar and instructor in public administration, a director of innovation programs, an instructor in group process techniques, and a facilitator and mediator. While at the Kettering Foundation, he directed the development of the *negotiated investment strategy,* a highly successful experiment involving a negotiated approach to the expenditure of federal, state, and local resources in specific communities. He is currently Executive Director of the Coalition to Improve Management in State and Local Government, located at the University of Texas at Arlington in the School of Urban and Public Affairs. The coalition was developed to link the directors of national organizations of governmental officials together around common concerns to achieve excellence in public management.

David Laws is Lecturer in the Department of Urban Studies and Planning at Massachusetts Institute of Technology and a faculty associate at the Harvard-MIT Program on Negotiation. His research focuses on the development of deliberative practices and institutional arrangements in the public sphere. Recent publications include "Research for Policy and Practice" in *Integrating Knowledge and Practice* (with Martin Rein, 1997), "The Practice of Fairness" in *Environmental Impact Assessment Review* (1996), "Talking with the Future: Sustainability and Stewardship as Intergenerational Dialogue" in *National Forum* (with Lawrence Susskind), "Responsibilite transgenerationnelle et decisions publiques" in *Communications: Generations et filiation* (1994), and "Siting Solid Waste Management Facilities in the U.S." in *Handbook of Integrated Solid Waste Management* (with Lawrence Susskind, 1994, McGraw-Hill). He holds a Ph.D. in urban studies and planning from Massachusetts Institute of Technology.

Michelle LeBaron is Associate Professor of Conflict Analysis and Resolution at George Mason University in Virginia. She draws on her experience as a lawyer and a therapist in developing innovative scholarship, pedagogy, and practice in the conflict resolution field. In her previous position as Director of the Multiculturalism and Dispute Resolution Project at the University of Victoria, Canada, she published research and training resources for intercultural conflict resolution. She has worked in several countries around the world to design training and interventions in public policy, environmental, family, intercommunal, commercial, and organizational conflicts. Her current work focuses on gender, culture, and psychological dimensions of conflict. She holds an M.A. from Simon Fraser University and an LL.B. from the University of British Columbia.

Gianni Longo is a founding Principal of ACP Visioning & Planning, a consulting firm with offices in New York City and Columbus, Ohio. For the past two decades, he has pioneered the development of programs designed to involve citizens in decision-making processes. In 1984, he conceived and developed Vision 2000, a program of community goal setting in Chattanooga, Tennessee. This program, at the time the first of its kind, is credited with stimulating more than $790 million in development projects in that community. Subsequently, Mr. Longo has assisted communities and institutions throughout the country, including Chattanooga again (ReVision 2000), Washington, D.C.

(a transportation and land use vision), and Myrtle Beach, South Carolina (a vision for a Comprehensive Plan), to name a few.

Jane Mansbridge is the Adams Professor of Political Leadership and Democratic Values and Faculty Chair of the Women and Public Policy Program at Harvard University's Kennedy School of Government. She is author of *Beyond Adversary Democracy* (1983) and *Why We Lost the ERA* (1988), corecipient of the American Political Science Association's Kammerer Award in 1987 and the Schuck Award in 1988, editor of *Beyond Self-Interest* (1990), and coeditor with Susan Moller Okin of the two-volume collection *Feminism* (1994). Her current research includes work on representation, trust, the relation between coercion and deliberation in democracy, the public understanding of collective action problems, and the mutual interaction between nonactivists and social movements.

Judy Mares-Dixon is Partner at CDR Associates in Boulder, Colorado. She has extensive experience in mediating organizational disputes, community disputes, disputes involving cross-cultural issues and issues of discrimination, and family disputes including divorce and child custody. She has a background in civil rights. She is also a trainer and consultant in facilitation and dispute systems design. Her clients include Levi Strauss & Co., United Airlines, the U.S. Army Corps of Engineers, MediaOne, and Lucent Technology.

Daniel Markovits received his B.A. in mathematics at Yale University and then was awarded a Marshall Scholarship, which enabled him to return to England, where he was born. He received an M.Sc. in econometrics and mathematical economics from the London School of Economics before moving to Oxford, first to Balliol College and then to Christ Church, where he was elected Senior Scholar of the House in 1994. At Oxford, he studied philosophy, first for a B.Phil., which he received in 1994, and then for a D.Phil., which he will complete in the spring of 1999. During his last years at Oxford, he was simultaneously enrolled at Yale Law School, where he will receive his J.D. in the year 2000.

Scott McCreary is cofounder and Principal of CONCUR, Inc., a California-based firm specializing in environmental policy analysis, planning, and mediation of agreements on complex natural resource issues. He earned his doctorate from Massachusetts Institute of Technology's Department of Urban Studies and Planning with an emphasis in environmental policy and conflict resolution. He has also served as Associate of the MIT-Harvard Public Disputes Program. He previously held research appointments at the Woods Hole Oceanographic Institution and the University of California Berkeley Center for Environmental Design Research. He also serves as Lecturer in UC Berkeley's Department of Landscape Architecture and Environmental Planning, and annually teaches the courses "Negotiating Effective Environmental Agreements" and "Facilitating and Mediating Effective Environmental Agreements" at that university. He has mediated more than 30 agreements on a wide range of issues, including statewide water use planning, statewide risk assessment, regional land use planning, flood protection and habitat restoration, regional water supply, wetlands management, and remediation of contaminated sites.

Julie A. McKay is Program and Training Specialist at CDR Associates in Boulder, Colorado, where she works as a mediator, trainer, and coordinator of conflict resolution programs. She first practiced community-based mediation in 1988 and subsequently trained Better Business Bureau staff and volunteers throughout the country in mediation, arbitration, and communication skills. She also served as a mediator of consumer disputes. She earned an M.A. in international peace studies in 1993 from the University of Notre Dame and is also certified as a Training Specialist by Georgetown University.

Carrie J. Menkel-Meadow is Professor of Law at Georgetown Law Center in Washington, D.C. Prior to taking this position in 1996, Professor Menkel-Meadow was Professor of Law at UCLA for 17 years, serving also as Codirector of UCLA's Center on Conflict Resolution. She has served as a visiting professor at the University of Toronto and Stanford Law School and as a clinical professor at the University of Pennsylvania. A national expert on alternative dispute resolution, the legal profession and legal ethics, clinical legal education, feminist legal theory, and women in the legal profession, she has written and lectured extensively in these fields. She sits on numerous boards of public interest organizations and the editorial boards of journals in dispute resolution, law, social science, and feminism. She often serves as a mediator and arbitrator in public and private settings and has trained lawyers and mediators in the United States and abroad. She holds a J.D. from the University of Pennsylvania and an LL.D. (Hon.) from Quinnipiac College of Law.

Sally Engle Merry is Professor at Wellesley College. She received her Ph.D. in anthropology from Brandeis University in 1978. She is author of *Urban Danger: Life in a Neighborhood of Strangers* (1981), *Getting Justice and Getting Even: Legal Consciousness among Working-Class Americans* (1990), and *Colonizing Hawai'i: The Cultural Power of Law* (1999) and coeditor of *The Possibility of Popular Justice: A Case Study of American Community Justice* (with Neal Milner, 1993). She has published numerous articles and review essays on legal ideology, mediation, urban ethnic relations, and legal pluralism. She was President of the Law and Society Association from 1993 to 1995 and President of the Association for Political and Legal Anthropology from 1996 to 1998. She is currently working on a project on the cultural dimensions of violence against women in local and global spaces.

William Moomaw is Professor of International Environmental Policy and Director of the International Environment and Resource Policy Program at the Fletcher School of Law and Diplomacy at Tufts University. He is also Director of Tufts Institute of the Environment, which initiates and coordinates interdisciplinary teaching, research, and outreach across the university. His research explores the intersection of science and public policy and the ensuing development of international and domestic policy for scientifically based issues such as global climate change, stratospheric ozone depletion, air pollution, acid deposition, and chemical contamination. He previously taught at Williams College as Professor of Chemistry and as Director of the Williams College Center for Environmental Studies. He also directed the World Resources Institute's Climate, Energy, and Pollution Program. He earned his Ph.D. in physical chemistry from Massachusetts Institute of Technology.

Carl M. Moore is Professor Emeritus at Kent State University, where he taught and conducted research in argumentation theory and small-group behavior for 26 years. During that time, he also worked in 35 states and 10 countries, coaching communities in how to conduct community-wide goal setting and visioning, facilitating organizational decision making, directing the development of strategic plans, conducting retreats and evaluations for community leadership programs, and training people how to facilitate. His original contributions to the field of consensus building include the *negotiated investment strategy, budget expenditure reduction process,* large-scale conference design (such as for the White House Conferences on Balanced National Growth and Economic Development and Small Business), and the friendly use of *interpretive structural modeling.* He cochaired the gubernatorial commission that created the Ohio Office of Dispute Resolution and Conflict Management and has worked for many years, primarily with the Kettering Foundation, on strategies to help locally elected officials to use collaborative approaches.

Christopher W. Moore, Partner at CDR Associates in Boulder, Colorado, has worked in the field of decision making and conflict management for more than 20 years and is an internationally known mediator, facilitator, dispute systems designer, trainer, and author in the field of conflict management. He holds a Ph.D. in political sociology and development from Rutgers, the State University of New Jersey. He is author of *The Mediation Process: Practical Strategies for Resolving Conflict* (2nd ed., 1996), which is recognized as a standard text on mediation. He has helped to resolve disputes involving public policy development, negotiated rulemaking, a full range of environmental issues, organizational restructuring, collective bargaining, intra- and interdepartmental differences, personnel grievances, ethnic relations, and charges of discrimination. He has also assisted in the development of personnel dispute resolution systems for clients as diverse as Levi Strauss & Co., U.S. WEST Communications, the Royal Canadian Mounted Police, and the U.S. Army Corps of Engineers.

Connie P. Ozawa is Associate Professor in the School of Urban Studies and Planning at Portland State University, where she teaches graduate courses in negotiation, environmental policy and planning, and planning theory and practice. Before coming to Oregon in 1994, she was Associate at the Program on Negotiation at Harvard Law School and taught courses on negotiation and dispute resolution at Massachusetts Institute of Technology, Harvard University, and Tufts University. She has provided negotiation training to groups including South Pacific Island state diplomatic service professionals, teachers union representatives, health services providers, and environmental and community activists. She is author of *Recasting Science: Consensus-Based Procedures in Public Policy Making* (1991). She earned an M.A. from the University of Hawaii and a Ph.D. from Massachusetts Institute of Technology.

Patsy Palmer is a facilitator and writer in Florida. Her professional interests are in facilitating complex, multiparty decision making about community and public policy issues. She received a master's degree in conflict resolution from Antioch University in September 1998. She also holds a bachelor's degree in journalism from the University of Missouri and a master's degree in theological studies from Harvard Divinity School. She had earlier careers in journalism and government, working for Gannett and Knight-Ridder newspapers, President Jimmy Carter, the Florida Legislature, and two Florida governors.

John Parr is a cofounder and Principal of the Center for Regional and Neighborhood Action, a Denver-based nonprofit organization dedicated to linking the energy at the neighborhood level with regional strategies that involve collaboration among government, business, and nonprofit organizations to improve the quality of life of all residents. He is an attorney with extensive experience in strategic planning, mediation, urban planning, and sustainable development. He was Codirector of a project titled Boundary Crossers: Community Leadership in a Global Age. He has written and spoken extensively on collaborative community problem solving. He is Chair of the Institute for the Regional Community and the Pew Civic Entrepreneur Initiative, a Fellow of the National Academy of Public Administration, and a Commissioner of the Denver Urban Renewal Authority. He has been President of the National Civic League and an adviser to Denver Mayor Federico Peña and Colorado Governor Dick Lamm.

Scott Peppet is Lecturer on Law and Senior Fellow on Negotiation at Harvard Law School, where he has taught negotiation and dispute system design. He is coauthor of a forthcoming book with Robert Mnookin and Andrew Tulumello, *Bargaining in the Shadow of the Law: How Lawyers Can Create Value in Negotiation,* and author of several articles. His current research interests include how dispute resolution systems within organizations facilitate or inhibit organizational learning.

Susan L. Podziba specializes in public sector mediation and consensus building and is known for designing processes to fit the unique characteristics of given conflicts. In addition to being a Principal and Mediator at Susan Podziba & Associates, she is Visiting Lecturer at Massachusetts Institute of Technology's Department of Urban Studies and Planning. Her past projects include the design and implementation of consensus processes to develop a city charter for Chelsea, Massachusetts, which was under state receivership; an environmental management plan for Casco Bay, Maine under the U.S. Environmental Protection Agency's National Estuary Program; and a plan to reduce the incidental takings of marine mammals as required under the Marine Mammal Protection Act. She is Past President of the New England Society of Professionals in Dispute Resolution and a former Associate of the Public Disputes Project of the Program on Negotiation at Harvard Law School. She has a master's degree in urban planning from Massachusetts Institute of Technology and a bachelor of arts degree from the University of Pennsylvania.

William R. Potapchuk is Executive Director of the Program for Community Problem Solving (PCPS), a division of the National Civic League. PCPS helps communities develop and manage collaborative approaches to decision making, service delivery, intergovernmental relations, and community change. He has extensive experience as a facilitator, mediator, and consultant on collaborative systems. He has worked on major projects for the Annie E. Casey Foundation, the U.S. Department of Housing and Urban Development, and the Federal Transit Administration. He is the former Associate Director of the Conflict Clinic, Inc., now the Applied Practice and Theory Program at the Institute for Conflict Analysis and Resolution at George Mason University

(GMU). He holds an M.A. in political science from the University of Missouri and is currently pursuing a Ph.D. in conflict resolution at GMU. He has worked with coauthors on *Pulling Together: A Planning and Development Consensus Building Manual* (1994) and the PCPS working papers *Negotiated Approaches to Environmental Decision Making in Communities: An Exploration of Lessons Learned* and *Building Community: Exploring the Role of Social Capital and Local Government.*

Howard Raiffa is the Frank P. Ramsey Professor of Managerial Economics, Emeritus, at Harvard University, a post he has held for more than 30 years. He was also Chairman of the National Academy of Sciences' National Research Council Committee on Risk and Decision Making. Previously, he held teaching and research positions at Columbia University, Stanford University, and the University of Vienna. He served for several years as Director of the International Institute for Applied Systems Analysis in Laxenberg, Austria. He has been awarded several honorary doctorates: from Carnegie Mellon University, Northwestern University, and the University of Michigan, and Ben-Gurian University. Professor Raiffa received the Lanchester Prize for his book *Decision with Multiple Objectives: Preferences and Value Trade-offs,* with Keeney (1976). Some of his more recent books include *Decision Making: Descriptive, Normative, and Prescriptive Interactions* (1988), *The Art and Science of Negotiation* (1982), and *Smart Choices* (1999). He holds a Ph.D. from the University of Michigan.

Colin Rule graduated from Haverford College in 1993 and is currently studying public policy, at Harvard University's John F. Kennedy School of Government as a Kennedy Fellow, and dispute resolution, at the University of Massachusetts–Boston. He worked for the National Institute for Dispute Resolution in Washington, D.C. and has published articles in *Peace Review, The Fourth R,* and *Consensus* and authored *The Planning and Design of Student-Centered Collegiate Conflict Management Systems,* which was published by the National Association for Mediation in Education. He also served as a Peace Corps volunteer in Eritrea from 1995 to 1997 and is the cofounder of Shine-A-Light, a nonprofit organization that works with street children in Central

America. Currently, he is Business Manager for *Consensus,* a quarterly newspaper focusing on public policy dispute resolution.

Charles F. Sabel is Professor of Law and Social Science at Columbia Law School, a post he has held since 1995. He was formerly the Ford International Professor of Social Science at Massachusetts Institute of Technology. His recent publications include *A Constitution of Democratic Experimentalism* (with Michael C. Dorf, 1998, revised version forthcoming), *Worlds of Possibility* (ed. with Jonathan Zeitlin, 1997), *Ireland: Local Partnerships and Social Innovation* (with the LEED Programme of the OECD, 1996), *The Second Industrial Divide: Possibilities for Prosperity* (with Michael Piore, 1984), *Work and Politics: The Division of Labor in Industry* (1982), and numerous articles on economics and social organization. He received his Ph.D. in government from Harvard University.

Edward Scher, Associate at RESOLVE Center for Dispute Resolution, located in Washington, D.C., is currently helping to facilitate a negotiated rulemaking associated with the U.S. Environmental Protection Agency's drinking water regulations. Previously, Mr. Scher was Associate at the Consensus Building Institute. He also served as a Peace Corps volunteer in Uruguay, where he assisted local community groups in their efforts to promote natural resource conservation on the coast of the Rio de la Plata. He holds a master's degree in city planning from Massachusetts Institute of Technology and a B.S. in environmental studies from George Washington University.

Melinda Smith is the founding Executive Director of the New Mexico Center for Dispute Resolution, where she created a range of mediation programs in community, youth, and juvenile justice settings and authored and edited manuals on youth mediation used throughout the United States. She has done extensive training in the Middle East in conflict resolution and human rights education. She has served as Cochair of the National Association for Community Mediation and a member of the *Mediation Quarterly* editorial board. She is affiliated with the national firm Public Decisions Network and with a public policy dispute resolution group at the University of New Mexico. Her prior experience includes directing a civic and law education program for the State Bar of New Mexico, teaching at universities in Algeria and Iran, and managing federal programs for the Ramah Navajo tribe. She holds an M.A. from the University of Michigan.

Barbara L. Stinson has more than a decade of experience designing, facilitating, and analyzing collaborative processes. She has helped individuals and institutions in the public and private sectors pursue innovative approaches to identifying problems and solving conflicts, particularly on air quality, transportation, land use, and natural resource management issues. She facilitates internal organizational processes including strategic planning, organizational development, and processes designed to further collaborative decision making and sustainable development. She is a founding Partner of the Meridian Institute, a nonprofit organization providing neutral services in a variety of problem-solving contexts. Ms. Stinson has mediated and facilitated a variety of multiparty consensus processes, including the EPA's National Low Emission Vehicle Program and Endangered Species Act Implementation Dialogue. She has provided internal assistance to the EPA, American Forest and Paper Association, S.C. Johnson Wax, and the American Lung Association. She has a master's degree in city planning from Massachusetts Institute of Technology and a bachelor's degree in environmental conservation from the University of Colorado, Boulder.

David A. Straus is Chairman of the Board and a founder of Interaction Associates, LLC, an international consulting and training firm. Under his guidance, Interaction Associates has become a recognized leader in organizational development, group process facilitation, training, and consulting. He is responsible for major change efforts in a wide variety of organizations, including those in the health care and service industries, and has worked with social action partnerships in Newark, New Jersey, and Palm Beach County, Florida. Since its founding, Interaction Associates has consulted and provided training services to more than 1,000 clients, including 175 of the *Fortune* 500 corporations, government agencies, and nonprofit organizations in North and South America, Europe, the Middle East, and Australia. He earned bachelor's and master's degrees from Harvard University. Under grants from the National Institute of Mental Health and the Carnegie Corporation, he has conducted research in creativity and developed training programs in problem solving. He also coauthored the best-seller *How to Make Meetings Work* (1982).

Jan Jung-Min Sunoo is Regional Director for the Western Region of the Federal Mediation and Conciliation Service, which covers the 13 western states including Alaska, Hawaii, and the Pacific Rim. Before his appointment to his current position, he worked as a federal mediator in the greater Los Angeles area for nine years. He also worked in the Teamsters Union, where he was a truck driver and shop steward at United Parcel Service before being elected to a business agent position. He has held teaching positions at San Francisco City College and the City College of New York, and he has practiced clinical psychology at the Watts Health Center in South Central Los Angeles. Appointed by L.A. Mayor Tom Bradley to the Los Angeles Human Relations Commission, he headed up projects related to improving interethnic tensions, and he continues to be a well-known resource in the area of cross-cultural conflict resolution.

Eric E. Van Loon, Senior Mediator with JAMS/Endispute in Boston, has more than 10,000 hours of experience in facilitation, mediation, arbitration, and dispute resolution training. He specializes in complex, multiparty, high-stakes disputes and has conducted consensus building processes on issues such as electric industry deregulation, sports stadium construction, and a national safe drinking water negotiated rulemaking. He is experienced in cross-cultural dispute resolution, having mediated consensus among Indian gaming, business, and Indian education representatives. He is a member of a number of state and federal dispute resolution panels. Previously, he served in a variety of Massachusetts state government positions including Assistant Secretary of Environmental Affairs, Undersecretary of Economic Affairs, and Massachusetts Mediation Service Advisory Board Chair. He has also been an adjunct Lecturer at both Boston University School of Law and Harvard Graduate School of Education, and he previously headed a national, nonprofit educational and advocacy group. He is a graduate of Harvard Law School and the University of North Carolina at Chapel Hill and holds a master's degree from the London School of Economics.

Irene Weiser is a former veterinarian, whose interests in doctor-patient communication have led her far afield. To develop the communication skills she thought important for practice, she has volunteered as a rape crisis counselor, a "buddy" to people living with AIDS, and since 1992, a mediator at the Community Dispute Resolution Center in Ithaca, New York. At the time of the interview with Mike Hughes (see Case 14), she was a graduate student in education at Cornell University. She recently left academe to pursue a career in human services. Her interest in mediation remains strong, however. Most recently, she was trained in transformative mediation by the U.S. Postal Service and has been approved to work for them as a mediator of employment disputes.

Peter J. Woodrow, Program Director for CDR Associates in Boulder, Colorado, has more than 20 years' experience as a mediator, facilitator, trainer, and consultant. He has mediated and facilitated multiparty environmental, organizational, and public policy disputes, and he has developed and implemented international programs in consensus building, problem solving, and decision making in Eastern Europe, Asia, and Africa. He holds a master's degree in public administration from the John F. Kennedy School of Government, Harvard University. He has provided custom-designed training programs and dispute resolution systems design consultation to government agencies, corporations, and nonprofit groups. Clients have included the Western Governors Association, the U.S. Environmental Protection Agency, and the Alyeska Pipeline Service Company, among many others. In addition to his career in conflict management, he has worked intermittently for 30 years in international development and relief in Asia and Africa and is coauthor of *Rising from the Ashes: Development Strategies in Times of Disaster* (2nd ed., 1998).

The Consensus Building Institute, Inc.

The Consensus Building Institute, Inc. (CBI) is committed to refining the art and science of consensus building. A nonprofit organization, CBI was created by leading practitioners and theory builders in the field of consensus building. CBI was established in March 1993 and received its 501(c)3 not-for-profit status in September of that year.

■ *CBI's mission is to:*

1. undertake and publish the results of independent studies and assessments of consensus building and dispute resolution efforts in the United States and abroad;
2. assist public and nonprofit agencies and institutions in the United States and abroad in their efforts to develop and employ consensus building and dispute resolution in performing their public-interest functions; and
3. conduct workshops, seminars, and other training programs, and develop and disseminate instructional materials and practice guides, designed to advance public understanding of the theory and practice of dispute resolution and consensus building.

During the past five years, CBI has provided training and facilitation services to a broad spectrum of domestic and international public agencies, including the U.S. Environmental Protection Agency; the U.S. Department of Energy; the Massachusetts Military Reservation; the Dutch Ministry of Housing, Spatial Planning, and the Environment; the United Nations Commission on Sustainable Development; United Nations Framework Convention on Climate Change Secretariat; and ambassadors to the World Trade Organization.

■ *CBI organizes its activities*
   around three guiding principles:
   _____

1. Consensus building is an extremely important societal resource. Indeed, agreement (and the action it enables) constitutes a kind of social capital. We must develop this resource in a rigorous and systematic way.
2. Consensus building can and should be applied to the broadest possible range of problems, in all levels of government, in all kinds of organizations, and among all kinds of stakeholding interests, not only in the United States but in countries around the world.
3. Effective training is an essential building block in consensus building, and people of widely varying backgrounds and age groups can benefit from appropriately designed training.

The Work of CBI

■ *CBI is involved in four kinds of activities:*
   _____

1. Assistance to public agencies and officials

   CBI's founders have been involved in the design and implementation of consensus building efforts at the local, state, and national levels. We draw on this extensive experience to help government entities develop new consensus building and dispute resolution capabilities.

Our established fields of specialization include health and environmental standards (acceptable levels of risk), infrastructure and facility siting, land use and sustainable resource development, health care and human resource management, organizational redesign, and intergovernmental relations.

2. Consensus building internationally

Consensus building approaches are broadly applicable in all parts of the world and to the full range of international issues. While care must be exercised to take account of cultural differences, CBI has had success in applying consensus building techniques in different parts of the world. The international arena is fraught with conflicts. It involves multiple parties—nations, private actors, and nongovernment organizations—all of whom are demanding a voice. CBI is engaged in the assessment of numerous multilateral negotiations and institutional interventions designed to prevent or resolve conflict.

Our established fields of specialization include formulating multilateral environmental treaties, the management of sustainable development, achieving compliance with international agreements, and the facilitation of informal policy dialogues involving the highest level officials and nongovernmental actors.

3. Documentation and evaluation of current practice

CBI supports practical studies to determine what works (and what doesn't) in the field of dispute resolution and consensus building. Are established techniques and institutional arrangements effective? Are innovations in the field achieving what was intended? CBI has undertaken numerous studies for a range of public agencies, foundations, and nonprofit organizations.

Our Board of Directors includes some of the country's best known researchers in the consensus building field. We are also linked to the MIT-Harvard Public Disputes Program at Harvard Law School and the Environmental Policy Group at MIT.

4. Design and evaluation of training efforts

    Literally hundreds of training programs attempt to teach various aspects of consensus building, including negotiation, dispute resolution (i.e., mediation), and conflict prevention. There is growing pressure to add courses to public school curricula, college programs, professional degrees, and continuing education programs. We must determine which models of training and education are most effective under various circumstances.

    CBI designs and sponsors a limited number of training programs of its own, intended to test new approaches to the field. For example, through our Workable Peace Program we are offering courses and developing materials to help high school teachers teach conflict resolution in inner-city schools.

    For additional information, please direct your inquiries to

    The Consensus Building Institute
    131 Mt. Auburn Street
    Cambridge, MA 02138 USA
    tel: 617-492-1414
    fax: 617-492-1919
    e-mail: cconsensus@igc.org.
    http://www.cbi-web.org